Tomoyuki Nishita Qunsheng Peng
Hans-Peter Seidel (Eds.)

Advances in Computer Graphics

24th Computer Graphics International Conference, CGI 2006
Hangzhou, China, June 26-28, 2006
Proceedings

Springer

Volume Editors

Tomoyuki Nishita
University of Tokyo, Graduate School of Frontier Sciences
Department of Complexity Science and Engineering
Tokyo, Japan
E-mail: nis@is.s.u-tokyo.ac.jp

Qunsheng Peng
Zhejiang University, State Key Lab of CAD and CG
Hangzhou, China
E-mail: peng@cad.zju.edu.cn

Hans-Peter Seidel
Max-Planck Institute for Informatics
Stuhlsatzenhausweg 85, 66123 Saarbrücken, Germany
E-mail: hpseidel@mpi-sb.mpg.de

Library of Congress Control Number: 2006927817

CR Subject Classification (1998): I.3.5, I.4, I.5, I.2.10, H.5.1, F.2.2

LNCS Sublibrary: SL 6 – Image Processing, Computer Vision, Pattern Recognition, and Graphics

ISSN 0302-9743
ISBN-10 3-540-35638-X Springer Berlin Heidelberg New York
ISBN-13 978-3-540-35638-7 Springer Berlin Heidelberg New York

Springer is a part of Springer Science+Business Media

springer.com

Printed in Germany

Typesetting: Camera-ready by author, data conversion by Scientific Publishing Services, Chennai, India
Printed on acid-free paper SPIN: 11784203 06/3142 5 4 3 2 1 0

Lecture Notes in Computer Science 4035

Commenced Publication in 1973
Founding and Former Series Editors:
Gerhard Goos, Juris Hartmanis, and Jan van Leeuwen

Preface

The 24th Computer Graphics International Conference (CGI 2006) was held during June 26–28, 2006, in Hangzhou, China. This volume contains 39 full papers and 39 short papers accepted by CGI 2006. CGI conference was initially founded by the Computer Graphics Society in 1983 and has now become a widely recognized, high-quality academic conference in the field of computer graphics. Recent CGI conferences were held in New York (2005), Crete (2004), Tokyo (2003), Bradford (2002), Hong Kong (2001) and Geneva (2000).

The CGI 2006 Program Committee received an overwhelming 387 submissions from many countries worldwide. China and Korea contributed many enthusiastic submissions. Based on the strict review comments of international experts, we selected 38 full papers and 37 short papers for presentations.

The main topics covered by the papers in this volume include:

- Digital geometry processing and meshes
- Physically based animation
- Figure modeling and animation
- Geometric computing and processing
- Non-photorealistic rendering
- Image-based techniques
- Visualization

We are grateful to all the authors who submitted their papers to CGI 2006, to the international Program Committee members and external reviewers for their valuable time and effort spent in the review process, and members of the Organizing Committee for their hard work which made this conference successful. Finally, we would like to thank the National Natural Science Foundation of China and K. C. Wong Education Foundation, Hong Kong, for their financial support.

Hans-Peter Seidel, Tomoyuki Nishita, Qunsheng Peng
Program Co-chairs
Nadia Magnenat-Thalmann, Yunhe Pan, Heung-Yeung Shum
Conference Co-chairs

Committee List

Conference Co-chairs

Nadia Magnenat-Thalmann (University of Geneva, Switzerland)
Yunhe Pan (Zhejiang University, China)
Heung-Yeung Shum (Microsoft Research Asia)

Program Co-chairs

Hans Peter Seidel (MPI, Germany)
Tomoyuki Nishita (Tokyo University, Japan)
Qunsheng Peng (Zhejiang University, China)

Organizing Committee Co-chairs

Jiaoying Shi (Zhejiang University, China)
George Baciu (Hong Kong Polytechnic University, China)
Hanqiu Sun (The Chinese University of Hong Kong, China)

Organizing Committee

Xiaogang Jin, Wei Chen, Hongxin Zhang, Qi Shen, Jinhui Yu, Min Hu (Zhejiang University, China)

Publication Chair

Hongxin Zhang (Zhejiang University, China)

Treasurer Chair

Min Hu (Zhejiang University, China)

Program Committee

Ken Anjyo (OLM Digital, Inc., Japan)
George Baciu (Hong Kong Polytechnic University, China)
Norman Badler (University of Pennsylvania, USA)
Hujun Bao (Zhejiang University, China)
Dominique Bechmann (Louis Pasteur University Strasbourg, France)
Kadi Bouatouch (University of Rennes, France)

Pere Brunet (Technical University of Catalonia, Spain)
Wei Chen (Zhejiang University, China)
Fuhua (Frank) Cheng (University of Kentucky, USA)
Daniel Cohen-Or (Tel Aviv University, Israel)
Frederic Cordier (KAIST, Korea)
Guozhong Dai (The Chinese Academy of Sciences, China)
Oliver Deussen (University of Konstanz, Germany)
Yoshinori Dobashi (Hokkaido University, Japan)
Gershon Elber (Israel Institute of Technology, Israel)
Thomas Ertl (University of Stuttgart, Germany)
Shiaofen Fang (Indiana University-Purdue University Indianapolis, USA)
Dieter Fellner (Graz University of Technology, Austria)
Robin Forrest (University of East Anglia, UK)
Issei Fujishiro (Tohoku University, Japan)
Martin Goebel (GMD, Germany)
Michael Goesele (University of Washington, USA)
Mark Green (UOIT, Canada)
Xianfeng Gu (Stony Brook University, USA)
Baining Guo (Microsoft Research Asia)
Wolfgang Heidrich (University of British Columbia, Canada)
Shimin Hu (Tsinghua University, China)
Horace H.S. Ip (City University of Hong Kong, China)
Ioannis Ivrissimtzis (Coventry University, UK)
Xiaogang Jin (Zhejiang University, China)
Tao Ju (Washington University in St. Louis, USA)
Kazufumi Kaneda (Hiroshima University, Japan)
Sing Bing Kang (Microsoft Research Asia)
Hyung Woo Kang (University of Missouri, USA)
Jan Kautz (MIT, USA)
Deok-Soo Kim (Hanyang University, Korea)
Kujin Kim (Kyungpook National University, Korea)
Myoung Jun Kim (Ewha Womans University, Korea)
Myung-Soo Kim (Seoul National University, Korea)
Hyeong-Seok Ko (Seoul National University, Korea)
Leif P. Kobbelt (RWTH Aachen, Germany)
Rynson Lau (City University of Hong Kong, China)
Jehee Lee (Seoul National University, Korea)
Seungyong Lee (Pohang University of Science and Technology, Korea)
Hendrik Lensch (Stanford University, USA)
Zicheng Liu (Microsoft Research, USA)
Kwan-Liu Ma (University of California, USA)
Weiyin Ma (City University of Hong Kong, China)
Nadia Magnenat-Thalmann (University of Geneva, Switzerland)
Marcus Magnor (Technical University Braunschweig, Germany)
Xiaoyang Mao (Yamanashi University, Japan)
Ahmad Nasri (American University of Beirut, Lebanon)

Miguel Otaduy (ETH-Zurich, Switzerland)
Ming Ouhyoung (National Taiwan University, China)
Zhigeng Pan (Zhejiang University, China)
Jean-Claude Paul (CNRS, France)
Les Piegl (University of South Florida, USA)
Werner Purgathofer (Vienna University of Technology, Austria)
Dongxu Qi (Macao University of Science and Technology, China)
Hong Qin (State University of New York, USA)
Stephane Redon (INRIA, France)
Jon G. Rokne (University of Calgary, Canada)
Lawrence Rosenblum (Naval Research Laboratory, USA)
Bodo Rosenhahn (Max Planck Center, Germany)
Dimitris Samaras (State University of New York, USA)
Hyewon Seo (Computer Graphics and Applications Lab at CNU, Korea)
Jiaoying Shi (Zhejiang University, China)
Hyunjoon Shin (Ajou University, Korea)
Sung Yong Shin (KAIST, Korea)
Yeong-Gil Shin (Seoul National University, Korea)
Yoshihisa Shinagawa (University of Illinois, USA)
Harry Shum (Microsoft Research Asia)
Claudio Silva (University of Utah, USA)
Michela Spagnuolo (IMATI Genova, Italy)
Jos Stam (Alias Systems, USA)
Hanqiu Sun (The Chinese University of Hong Kong, China)
Chiew-Lan Tai (Hong Kong University of Science and Technology, China)
Kai Tang (Hong Kong University of Science and Technology, China)
Demetri Terzopoulos (University of Toronto, Canada)
Daniel Thalmann (Swiss Federal Institute of Technology, Switzerland)
Holger Theisel (MPI, Germany)
Xing Tong (Microsoft Research Asia)
George Turkiyyah (University of Washington, USA)
Amitabh Varshney (University of Maryland, USA)
Wenping Wang (University of Hong Kong, Hong Kong)
Joe Warren (Rice University, USA)
Tien Tsin Wong (The Chinese University of Hong Kong, China)
Enhua Wu (The Chinese Academy of Sciences, China)
Brian Wyvill (University of Calgary, Canada)
Geoff Wyvill (University of Otago, New Zealand)
Yingqing Xu (Microsoft Research Asia)
Ruigang Yang (University of Kentucky, USA)
Steve S.N. Yang (National Tsing Hua University, China)
Jingyi Yu (University of Delaware, USA)
Yizhou Yu (University of Illinois, USA)
Hongxin Zhang (Zhejiang University, China)

Additional Reviewer List

Yiyu Cai (Nanyang Technological University , Singapore)
Weiqun Cao (Beijing Forestry University, China)
Baoquan Chen (University of Minnesota at Twin Cities, USA)
Yanyun Chen (Microsoft Research Asia)
Falai Chen (University of Science and Technology of China, China)
Bingyu Chen (National Taiwan University, Taiwan)
Sung Woo Choi (Korea University, Korea)
Yung-Yu Chuang (University of Washington, USA)
Gordon Clapworthy (University of Luton, UK)
Shihai Dong (Peking University, China)
Jieqing Feng (Zhejiang University, China)
Shuming Gao (Zhejiang University, China)
Weidong Geng (Zhejiang University, China)
Craig Gotsman(Harvard University, USA)
Eran Guendelman (Stanford University, USA)
Yongjun Hai (Chongqing University of Posts and Telecommunications, China)
Xuli Han (Central South University, China)
Mark Harris (NVIDIA Corporation, USA)
Yuanjun He (Shanghai Jiaotong University, China)
Pheng-Ann Heng (The Chinese University of Hong Kong, China)
Wei Hua (Zhejiang University, China)
Zhiyong Huang (National University of Singapore, Singapore)
Zhongding Jiang (Fudan University, China)
Arie Kaufman (State University of New York at Stony Brook, USA)
Yingling Ke (Zhejiang University, China)
John Keyser (Texas A&M University, USA)
Yoshifumi Kitamura (Osaka University, Japan)
Shigeru Kuriyama (Toyohashi University of Technology, Japan)
Guiqing Li (South China University of Technology, China)
Sikun Li (National University of Defense Technology, China)
Hua Li (The Chinese Academy of Sciences, China)
Youdong Liang (Zhejiang University, China)
Xueyan Lin (Tsinghua University, China)
Hongwei Lin (Zhejiang University, China)
Xuehui Liu (The Chinese Academy of Sciences, China)
Yongkui Liu (Dalian Nationalities University, China)
Dingyuan Liu (Fudan University, China)
Xinguo Liu (Microsoft Research Asia)
Yanxi Liu (Carnegie Mellon University, USA)
Ligang Liu (Zhejiang University, China)
Yusheng Liu (Zhejiang University, China)
Hanqing Lu (The Chinese Academy of Sciences, China)
Lizhuang Ma (Shanghai Jiao Tong University, China)
Xiaohu Ma (Soochow University, China)

Huadong Ma (Beijing University of Posts and Telecommunications, China)
Ralph Martin (Cardiff University, UK)
Simon Masnou (Université Pierre-et-Marie-Curie, France)
Radomír Mech (University of Calgary, Canada)
Yutaka Ohtake (Max-Planck-Institut fur Informatik, Germany)
Rick Parent (Ohio State University, USA)
Kaihuai Qin (Tsinghua University, China)
Xueyin Qin (Zhejiang University, China)
Erik Reinhard (University of Bristol, UK)
Zen Chung Shih (National Chiao Tung University, China)
Huahao Shou (Zhejiang University of Technology, China)
Vaclav Skala (University of West Bohemia, Czech Republic)
Jizhou Sun (Tianjin University, China)
Zheng Tan (Xi'an Jiaotong University, China)
Zesheng Tang (Macao University of Science and Technology, China)
Chi-Keung Tang (The Hong Kong University of Science and Technology, China)
Frank Van Reeth (Limburgs Universitair Centrum, Belgium)
Justin W.L. Wan (University of Waterloo, Canada)
Huagen Wan (Zhejiang University, China)
Wencheng Wang (The Chinese Academy of Sciences, China)
Huamin Wang (Georgia Institute of Technology, USA)
Lifeng Wang (Microsoft Research Asia)
Jiaye Wang (Shandong University, China)
Zhaoqi Wang (The Chinese Academy of Sciences, China)
Niniane Wang (Google Inc., USA)
Guojin Wang (Zhejiang University, China)
Jin Wang (Zhejiang University, China)
Kelly Ward (The University of North Carolina at Chapel Hill, USA)
Liyi Wei (Microsoft Research Asia)
Xiaogang Xu (Dalian Naval Academy, China)
Guangyou Xu (Tsinghua University, China)
Guoliang Xu (The Chinese Academy of Sciences, China)
Dan Xu (Yunnan University, China)
Xunnian Yang (Zhejiang University, China)
Xiuzi Ye (Zhejiang University, China)
Junhai Yong (Tsinghua University, China)
Jinhui Yu (Zhejiang University, China)
Richard Zhang (Simon Fraser University, Canada)
Shusheng Zhang (Northwestern Polytechnic University, China)
Caiming Zhang (Shandong Economic University, China)
Jian J. Zhang (Bournemouth University, UK)
Jiwen Zhang (Zhejiang University, China)
Hongkai Zhao (University of California, USA)
Jianmin Zheng (Nanyang Technological University, Singapore)
Kun Zhou (Microsoft Research Asia)
Miaoliang Zhu (Zhejiang University, China)

Table of Contents

Regular Papers

Short Papers

Wang-Tiles for the Simulation and Visualization of Plant Competition

Monssef Alsweis and Oliver Deussen

Department of Computer and Information Science
University of Konstanz, Germany
{Alsweis, deussen}@inf.uni-konstanz.de
http://graphics.uni-konstanz.de

Abstract. The Wang Tiles method is a successful and effective technique for the representation of 2D-texture or 3D-geometry. In this paper we present a new method to fill Wang tiles with a 2D-FON distribution or a 3D-geometry in order to achieve a more efficient runtime. We extend the Wang Tiles method to include information about their position. We further demonstrate how the individual tiles are filled with different intensities by using the FON distribution. Additionally, we present several new methods to eliminate errors between the tile edges and the different resource areas applying FON and corners relaxation techniques.

1 Introduction

Modelling and visualization of large complex scenes of plants is a difficult and time consuming task. For example, the storing of plant compositions is extremely difficult because a square kilometer of forest consists of millions of plants, hundred of thousands of small trees, and numerous small scrubs. To model intricate natural scenes, several methods already exist in computer graphics. The primary method was introduced in [1]. A new stochastic algorithm was non-periodically presented to cover the area with a small set of Wang Tiles [2, 3]. This method provides Wang Tiles with the efficiency of being re-usable tiles, which in turn allows for rendering larger areas of complicated textures, patterns or prelighted geometry at more efficient runtime. Wang Tiles are a set of squares in which each edge of each tile is colored. Matching colored edges are aligned to tile an area. In [1] a set of eight tiles were used to cover an area, and a 2D Poisson Disk distribution was applied to fill the tiles. The aim is to render beautiful and realistic natural scenes. We use four sets or more of tiles instead of one set. Each set of tiles consists of eight tiles. All sets of tiles share the same color coding. However, they differentiate from each other through the intensity of the distributions on the tiles. In the final tiling and scene, rsp., the intensity of the distribution depends on the terrain or on the amount of the resources in which the tiles are positioned. For example, the intensity of the distribution of the plants in an area with poor resources differs from those in the area with rich resources. Applying this method enables to generate large differences in the intensity of the plants in

H.-P. Seidel, T. Nishita, and Q. Peng (Eds.): CGI 2006, LNCS 4035, pp. 1–11, 2006.

two areas. To eliminate this problem, we use several sets and apply some kind of super sampling (antialiasing) method for the selection of the matching sets.

Often plant positions form a 2D Poisson Disc Distribution: each object is presented by a circular area in which are no other objects and in which no other areas overlap. This is done due to what happens in nature when plants prevent other plants to grow in their vicinity. To model this behaviour, we applied the so-called FON (Field-Of-Neighbourhood) distribution model [4]. In the FON model each object is presented in a circular area. The size of this circle depends of the size of the object and of the terrain or the amount of resources.

2 Previous Works

There have been different approaches for accelerating of rendering for complex models. Many approaches aimed to avoid visual artifacts which have been repeatedly created using simple methods.

One of these approaches is the rendering of complicated natural scenes through the application of the **Wang Tiling Method** [1, 2, 3] in which a limited set of tiles is used to layout a possibly infinite plane. We combined this model with an ecosystem simulation model, the so-called **FON (Field Of Neighbourhood) Modell** by Berger und Hildenbrandt in [4] and [5]. This model is an individuum-based model and describes a circular zone of the area of influence around the plant. The radius of this area determines the distance in which the neighboring plants influence each other. In [6] the radius of this zone is specified by a non-linear function which depends from the basal radius of the plant, the size of the plant, the amount of resources needed by the plant, and the area necessary to provide the resources.

Modelling of Complex Ecosystems: In some earlier works [7, 8, 9] nature was rendered using artificial mechanisms. Other scientists [10, 11] tried to imitate the actual natural processes. Both approaches are still used and many natural and other complex phenomena were modelled in [12, 13, 14]. In [15, 16, 17] most important factors that influence the shape, the structure, and the development of a plant were modeled. The first work that simulated the competition and the development of the plants was published by [18]. Lane and Prusinkiewicz extended this work and developed a new method called Multiset L-Systems that was used for the description of the competition between plants. In [19] is described how plants grow in groups, and how the communities compete for resources. In [20], a new method was introduced for the visualization and simulation of the developments of a plant group. In this method, the plant competition for resources was presented as a symmetric and asymmetric competition. Asymmetric competition takes place when plants differ in size or in type.

3 Our Method

To tile an area, we apply the Wang Tiling Method. A Wang Tile set consists of square tiles with color-coded edges. The squares cannot be rotated. A valid

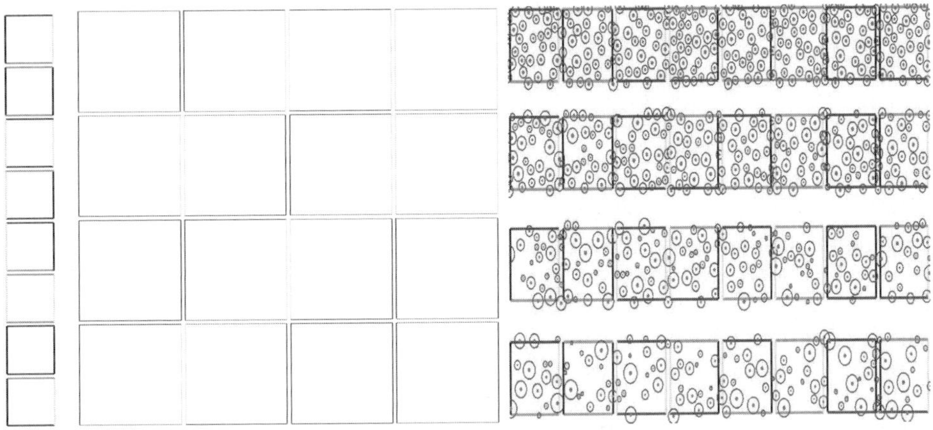

(a) (b) (c)

Fig. 1. a) Tile set; b) Valid tiling; c) four sets of Wang tiles with different distribution intensity

tiling of the infinite plane consists of any number of copies from the set laid down such that all continuous edges have matching colors. (s. Fig. 1).

3.1 Tiling

In this work we use four sets or more, each consisting of a set of eight tiles. Each set resembles the other in the color at the edge of the tiles, and differentiates itself from the others through the intensity of the distribution in the tiles. The reason for the use of of four or more sets of tiles with different intensity on the edges is as follows: From Fig. 2(a) it can be seen that the area as well as the different levels of resources differ for different terrains. Consequently, the in the white circles marked tiles from Fig. 2(b) contain different numbers of plants although all marked tiles have the same edge color. In order to receive a soft border between two different resource areas, and at the same time to position

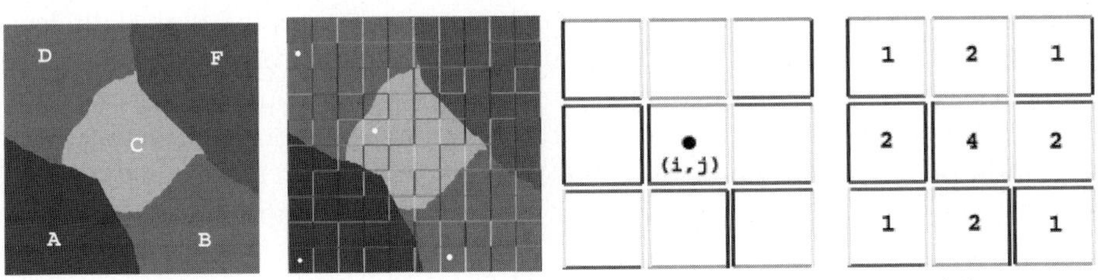

(a) (b) (c) (d)

Fig. 2. (a) area covered with five intensities of the resources; (b) the edges of the resulting tiling match, different intensities are applied; (c) a window is centered around the sampled value (i, j); (d) a filter kernel is multiplied with each respective sampled value the tiles matching the set of tile I' in the area, we apply an image operator for averaging. The intesnsity $I'(i,j)$ is computed as:

$$\frac{1}{M}\sum_{p=S_i-k}^{S_i+k}\sum_{q=S_j-k}^{S_j+k} I(p,q)h(S_i-p,S_j-q) \tag{1}$$

Whereby (i,j) indicates the tile in the position (i,j) (see Fig. 2(a)), S is a scaling factor, and h is a filter of the dimension k. The selection of the set order is easy to understand and to realize, however, it is computationally expensive. In Fig. 2(a)-(b) a window is centered over an sampled value and a weighted sum of products is achieved by means of multiplication of each sampled value with the respective weight in the filter. The weight can be adjusted in order to implement differing filter kernels. The digital filtering continues in that the window is moved through $n = k * k$ sampling value and the next weighted sum of products is computed.

The use of a 3×3 window indicates that nine sampled values are part of the final tile computation. On the other hand, the use of a 7×7 windows includes a computation of 49 integer multiplication. The result of this computational expense is obvious. For a virtual 3×3 window filter, a filter on tiles in the virtual image can be positioned, in that step-by-step three super-sampling tiles are used. M is computed by the following equation:

$$M = \sum_{p'=0}^{2k}\sum_{q'=0}^{2k} h(p',q') \tag{2}$$

Here, I is the sampling value of the level of the resources in a tile. In order to determine this value in a tile, the resources from different positions in certain tiles are sampled. The average of these sampled resources levels is designated to be the sampled value.

3.2 FON Distribution

In order to fill each individual tile with different intensity, we use the already mentioned FON Modell Distribution. In this model each individual plant has a circular zone of influence (ZOI), the radius of the zone determines the distance in which the individual plant influences the neighboring plant.

Each individual plant is identified in the tile through its position, size, and the age. Additionally, each plant has a FON influence zone. To determine the FON influence zone, a non-linear function of the basal radius is applied [4] (s. Fig. 3).

$$R_{FON} = a\,(R_{basal})^b \tag{3}$$

R_{FON} is the radius of the FON influence zone of the individual plant. R_{basal} is the radius of the individual plant (Fig. 3). a and b are constants and depend on the intensity of the resources in the ground and of the intensity of the light in above-ground. Typically a has the range of $[12, 133]$ and $b \in [1.2, 2.3]$.

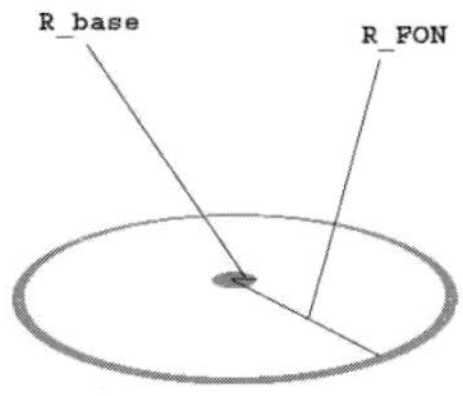

$$R_{FON} = a\,R_{basal}^{b}$$

Fig. 3. The FON model. The zone of influence (R_{FON}) depends on the diameter of the trunk.

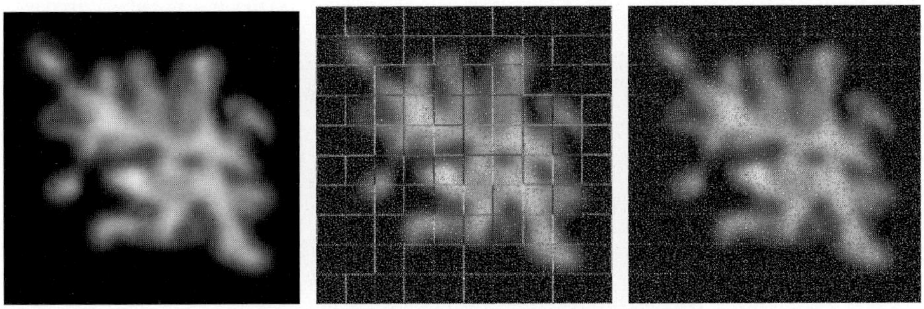

(a) (b) (c)

Fig. 4. In (a) represents the intensity of the resources. In (b) the FON-Tile Method is applied. In (c) shows the noice between the tiles.

Application of the tiles and the FON Distribution in Fig. 4 produces the result in subfigure (b). Subfigure (a) shows an image map of the intensity of the resources in the ground. In (b) is shown that the intensity of the plants in the resource-poor areas is less than in the resource-rich areas. As a result of implementing the averaging, we can derive a gradual change of that the intensity of the plants between two different regions.

3.3 FON Relaxation

In Fig. 4(c)we note that an uneven distribution at the tile borders is produced. In order to eliminate this error, we apply the FON relaxation method at the edge of the tiles.

The FON relaxation method is applied to test whether the FON-zone of plants positioned at the edge of one tile overlap with the FON-zone of the plants positioned at the edge of the neighboring tile, and whether the FON-zone of one plant is smaller or larger than that of the neighboring plant at a certain threshold. If the test is positive, the plant must be removed from the respective tile.

In Fig. 5 it is shown that plant number one passed the test and has to be removed from the tile. On the other side the test was not passed for plant number two, and therefore it can remain in the tile. If we compare Fig. 4(c) with

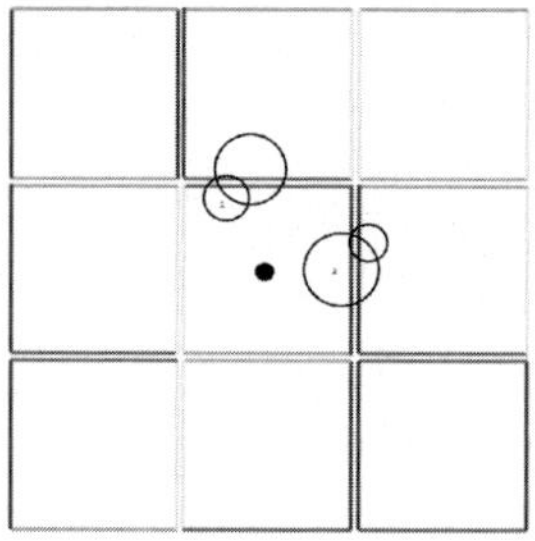

Fig. 5. The circles are presented in two conditions at the edge of the tiles. The first circles is smaller than the other one. The second circle is larger than the other one.

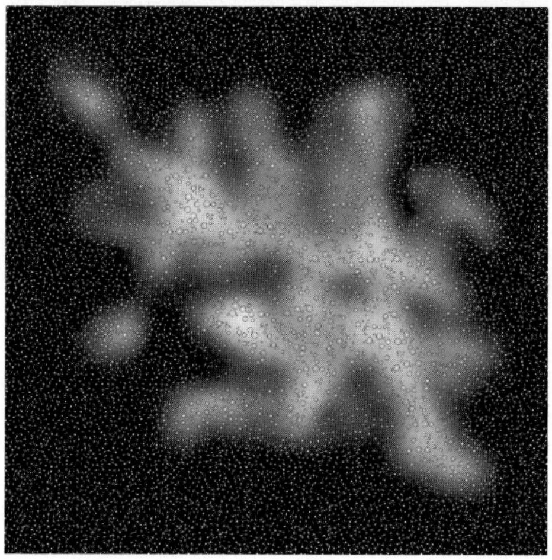

Fig. 6. As a result of implementing the FON relaxation in (*c*) (Fig. 4), the noise between the tiles was removed.

Fig. 6, we note, that the distribution of the plants is now more even. However, the price is that some small amount of computation has to be done during the tile-based layout.

3.4 Relaxation of Corners

From Fig. 7 we note that the difference of the plant intensity between the tile A and the tiles B, C und D creates corners. These corners produces a non-realistic appearance about the appearance of the plants in the scene. To eliminate this unwanted appearance, we apply the relaxation method to tile A. The implementation of the this relaxation method is divided into the following steps:

1. It is tested whether tile A produces corners This happens when the intensity in A differs from the intensity in B, C und D.

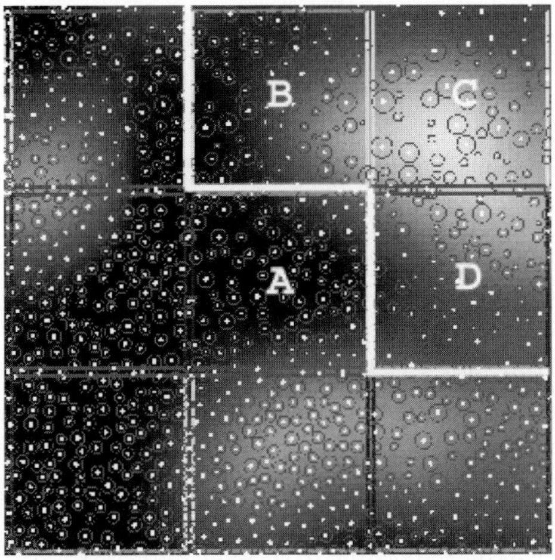

Fig. 7. The intensity corners between the tiles A and tiles B, C and D

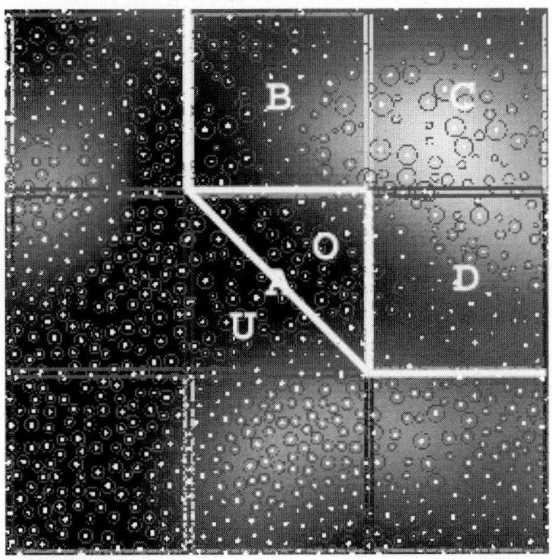

Fig. 8. Distribution of the tiles A into two parts U and O

2. The tile A is divided into two diagonal parts (lower part U and upper part O) in order to be filled with two different intensities. For example as in (Fig. 8).
3. The intensity in part U will not be changed. against it the intensity in part O depends on the intensities in tiles B, C und D. The arrangements of B, C und D control the definition in the set order in part U.
4. Fon-relaxation is applied between diagonal parts.

The application of the last four steps in Fig. 4(c) results in an evenly natural plant distribution without corners in Fig. 6.

4 Implementation

Implementation of this method results in a good quality of a natural scene, so that the noise between the tiles and the noise between the two different resource areas are improved. Additionally, this scene is rendered in real-time. To implement this method, we use a discrete system of several sets. The implementation of these systems can be divided into the following steps:

1. We produce different sets of tiles. Each set differs in plant intensity from the other.
2. each plant is presented in two circles. The first represents the size of the plants, and the second represents the FON-zone of the plant.
3. We apply the Wang-Tiling method for different sets in order to cover the area.
4. In order to eliminate the noise between the tiles, we apply the FON-relaxation method.
5. In order to remove the corners between the tiles, we apply the corner relaxation method.

The plants used in this approach were modelled with the Xfrog Software [21], and were then imported into our systems as POVRAY MESH2 in Fig. 9 and Fig. 10.

Fig. 9. This image shows the rendering of a scene of a meadow and flowers applying the tiling method with different intensities of resources

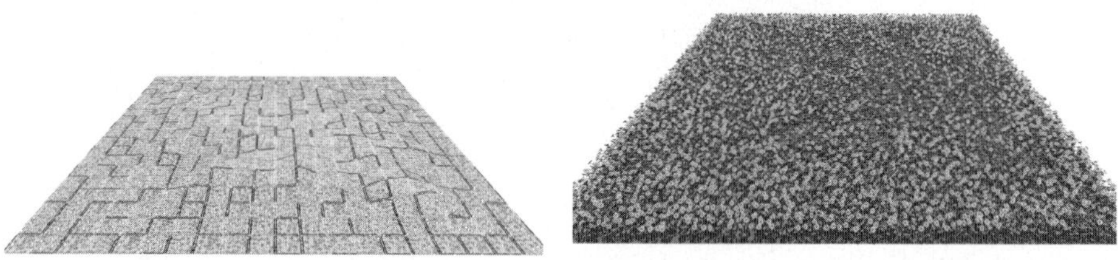

Fig. 10. In this image different resource intensities in a field of sunflowers are shown

5 Results

We introduced a fine efficient method to render natural scenes with a more realistic appearance. The use of more sets of tiles with different intensity produces

Fig. 11. In this image different resource intensities in African landscape are shown

Fig. 12. In this image different resource intensities in African landscape from other camera position are shown

Fig. 13. In this image different resource intensities in Amazon landscape are shown

scenes that have a more natural appearance (see Figs. 9 and 10). The implementation of the FON-relaxation and corner relaxation in one scene produces smooth edges between the tiles and a gradual transformation between two different resource intensities (Figs. 11, 12 and 13).

References

1. Michael F. Cohen, Jonathan Shade, Stefan Hiller, and Oliver Deussen. Wang tiles for image and texture generation. *Proceedings of ACM SIGGRAPH.*, pages 287–294, July 2003.
2. H. WANG. Proving theorems by pattern recognition ii. *Bell Systems Technical Journal.*, 40:142, 1961.
3. H. WANG. Games, logic, and computers. *Scientific American (November).*, page 98106, 1965.
4. Berger U. and Hildenbrandt H. A new appoarch to spatially explicit modelling of forest dynamics: Spacing, ageing and neighbourhood competition of mangrove trees. *Ecological Modelling*, 132:287302, 2000.
5. S. Bauer, U. Berger, H. Hildenbrandt, and V. Grimm. Cyclic dynamics in simulated plant populations. *Proc R Soc Lond B Biol Sci.*, 269(1508):2443–2450, 2002.
6. U. Berger, H. Hildenbrandt, and V. Grimm. Towards a standard for the individual-based modeling of plant opulations: self-thinning and the field of neighbourhood approach. *Nat. Ressource Model*, 15:3954, 2002.

7. Geoffrey Y.Gardner. Visual simulation of clouds. in proceedings of the 12th annual conference on computer graphics and interactive techniques. *ACM Press.*, page 297304, 1985.
8. Robert Marshall., Rodger Wilson., and Wayne Carlson. Procedure models for generating three-dimensional terrain, in proceedings of the 7th annual conference on computer graphics and interactive techniques. *ACM Press.*, page 154162, 1980.
9. Nelson L. Max. Vectorized procedural models for natural terrain: Waves and islands in the sunset, in proceedings of the 8th annual conference on computer graphics and interactive techniques. *ACM Press*, page 317324, 1981.
10. Alain Fournier and William T. Reeves. A simple model of ocean waves. in proceedings of the 13th annual conference on computer graphics and interactive techniques. *ACM Press*, page 7584, 1986.
11. Craig W., Reynolds., Flocks, herds, and schools. A distributed behavioral model, in proceedings of the 14th annual conference on computer graphics and interactive techniques,. *ACM Press*, page 2534, 1987.
12. Yoav I., H. Parish, and Pascal Muller. Procedural modeling of cities, in proceedings of the 28th annual conference on computer graphics and interactive techniques,. *ACM Press*, page 301308, 2001.
13. Yoshinori Dobashi., Kazufumi Kaneda., Hideo Yamashita., Tsuyoshi Okita., and Tomoyuki Nishita. A simple, efficient method for realistic animation of clouds,in proceedings of the 27th annual conference on computer graphics and interactive techniques. *ACM Press/Addison-Wesley Publishing Co*, page 1928, 2000.
14. Paul Fearing. Computer modelling of fallen snow. in proceedings of the 27th annual conference on computer graphics and interactive techniques. *ACM Press/Addison-Wesley Publishing Co*, page 3746, 2000.
15. J. Arvo and D. Kirk. Modeling plants with environment-sensitive automata. *In Proceedings of Ausgraph88*, I:2733, 1988.
16. R. Mech and P. Prusinkiewicz. Visual models of plants interacting with their environment. in proceedings of siggraph96. *ACM Press*, 30(4):397410, 1996.
17. P. Prusinkiewicz, J. Hanan, M. Hammel, , and R. Mech. Lsystems: from the theory to visual models of plants. *Machine Graphics and Vision*, 2(4)(1508):1222, 1993.
18. O. Deussen, P. Hanrahan, B. Lintermann, R. Mech, M. Pharr, and P. Prusinkiewicz. Realistic modeling and rendering of plant ecosystems. in proceedings of siggraph98, annual conference series 1998. *ACM Press*, page 275286, 1998.
19. Bedrich Benes. and Juan Miguel Soto Guerrero. Clustering in virtual plant ecosystems. *WSCG SHORT Communication papers proceedings.*, 2004.
20. M. Alsweis and O. Deussen. Modeling and visualisation of symmetric and asymmetric plant competition. *Eurographics Workshop on Natural Phenomena.*, 2005.
21. O. Deussen and B. Lintermann. A modelling method and user interface for creating plants. In *Proc. Graphics Interface 97*, pages 189–198. Morgan Kaufmann Publishers, May 1997.

Multi-layered Stack Mosaic with Rotatable Objects

Jin Wan Park[1], Kyung Hyun Yoon[2], and Seung Taek Ryoo[3]

[1] GSAIM Dep. Chung-Ang Univ.
221 Heukseok-dong, Dongjak-gu, Seoul, Korea
jinpark@cau.ac.kr
[2] CS Dep. Chung-Ang Univ.
221 Heukseok-dong, Dongjak-gu, Seoul, Korea
khyoon@cau.ac.kr
[3] Software Dep. Han-Shin Univ.
411 Yongsan-dong, Osan-si, Gyonggido, Korea
stryoo@hs.ac.kr

Abstract. We present a new type of mosaic, the multi-layered stack mosaic with photographs of rotated objects. Our algorithm uses multi-layered Photomosaics with database enrichment by element rotation. The benefit of this algorithm is that an artist can not only produce a digital mosaic with a relatively small database without degrading the quality of the mosaic, but that the Multi-layered Stack Mosaic also generates unique and strong artistic expressions which gives an illusion of piled stackable objects. Since the result has a unique visual style, we intend to exhibit our mosaic images at galleries such as the Epson Color Imaging Contest and the CAU Art Center[1].

1 Introduction

The mosaic is an intriguing subject in computer graphics because it involves scientific and artistic research simultaneously. The mechanism of traditional mosaic creation is based on the visual perception of artists. Although it is difficult to quantify, the process is systematic and methodical. In recent years, many mosaic schemes for generating free-form 2D images have been suggested in the area of non-photorealistic rendering. In 1996 Robert Silvers devised the concept of Photomosaics [1] in which one big picture is generated from thousands of smaller pictures. These pictures are then placed in patterns like traditional mosaics, and each cell is an actual photograph. Each tile of a Photomosaic contains a photographic image, causing perceptual confusion in the observer in a delightful way. The perceptual range changes from elements to the whole and vice versa. However, for producing quality Photomosaic artwork, an abundant image database must be prepared making this one of the most laborious aspects of Photomosaics. What makes this worse is that every picture may have its own copyright

[1] This work was supported by grant No. (R01-2005-000-10940-0) from the Basic Research Program of the Korea Science & Engineering Foundation.

H.-P. Seidel, T. Nishita, and Q. Peng (Eds.): CGI 2006, LNCS 4035, pp. 12–23, 2006.

license. We will present a new type of mosaic scheme which contains elements of stacked and rotated objects. Although our algorithm is an outcome of scientific research, we also focus on the artistic side of mosaics with regard to visual expression. In other words, our goal is not only producing quality mosaics with a limited picture database size, but also creating beautiful and impressive mosaics as art. This paper is organized as follows: related research of mosaics are presented in the next section; in section 3, we analyze and evaluate our algorithm; in section 4, resulting images will be presented.

2 Related Research and Issues

As we can judge from the thousands of years of history, the mosaic is one of the oldest methods of artistic expression. Various mosaics, in which a large image is formed by a collection of small images can be created depending on the type of tiles used and the restrictions in their placement [2][3][4]. In the case of each tile as meaningful subject, for example, Guiseppe Arcimboldo [5] in 16th century, and Chuck Close in 20th century [6] have the common feature of multi-range perceptive target sizes. This type of mosaic is revised again by Robert Silvers in his Photomosaics, a collection of small images that are arranged in a rectangular grid and form a larger image in the distance. This has strong expression because there is no photograph that is absolutely free from the photographer's opinion. When we use photographs as elements of mosaics, the mixed perceptual range provides pleasurable games and challenges for the observer. A rich photograph database is the essential condition to produce good Photomosaics. This huge database is not only hard to build, but also extremely expensive to use due to the fact that each picture may carry a copyright license. There are some well known tricks to reduce the number of pictures in the library, such as self duplication by flipping or resizing images, or by changing color value, but the damaged images can degrade the quality of Photomosaics because each element is as an important perceptual subject in relation to the whole image. We seek to prevent the loss of the each picture's significance.

3 Method Overview

The method we present in this paper is divided into two primary steps.

- Rotate the object to improve the possibility of a better match. The meaning of each photograph has to be preserved and garbage data due to rotation has to be minimized.
- Fill the empty space (hole) that is produced in the above step, with multiple layers.

Each step is important to visualize the unique style of the suggested mosaic. This also improves the likeness of two images, a source image and an output mosaic image, so we can get a better output result compared to the conventional Photomosaics algorithm under the same database conditions especially when the database size is small.

3.1 Objects Rotation

Image Selection Process. The Photomosaic algorithm is used for image selection and database management[10]. It does not attempt shape or edge analysis. Rather, it seeks to minimize a distance measure based purely on differences of pixel values that are its red, green, and blue components [12]. The original image is divided into rectangular blocks of the same dimensions as the tiles. The algorithm scans the blocks of the original images from left to right and top to bottom, replacing each block with a tile before considering the next. Thus, each pixel in each cell of the original image is compared with each pixel of every picture in the database. However, it takes a huge amount of time to search for the best image [10][11]. As suggested by Silver, to improve the speed we use an index system that reduces candidate images. With this Photomosaic algorithm, each block of the original image will be replaced with the best matching; in other words the most similar photograph in the database. There is no color correction in this process.

$A_{w\times h}$ is the image's rectangular blocks as a matrix while $T^k_{w\times h}$ is tile k as a matrix, and $A_r(i,j)$, $A_g(i,j)$, $A_b(i,j)$ are the red, green and blue components of a given pixel. The Photomosaic algorithm seeks to minimize the following distance over all tiles in the library.

$$d=min_k\left[\sum_{i=1}^{w}\sum_{j=1}^{h}\left|A_r(i,j)-T_r^k(i,j)\right|+\left|A_g(i,j)-T_g^k(i,j)\right|+\left|A_b(i,j)-T_b^k(i,j)\right|\right] \tag{1}$$

To increase the variety measure of the generated Photomosaics, two modifications are made to the basic algorithm. First, a limit is imposed on the number of times a tile can be selected. Second, a minimum distance is required between any two copies of a tile. To implement these changes, the count and last selected position is maintained for each tile [10].

Rotation Sampling Rate. The traditional Photomosaic algorithm does not alter the database so the quality of the output image depends on the number of collected images. We suggest that without collecting extra images we can improve the result by enriching the library; by rotating photographs in the library. Theoretically we could reproduce infinite copies of each image with this trick, but the fact is that rotated images are very similar with each other, so the rotation does not effectively enrich the library when the angle is close between images. Note that more pictures are not always better because this will slow down the database searching time. Therefore, it is important to find a balance between quality and price although the best case varies depending on a type of project. It is clear that a dense sampling rate will guarantee the best result, but the degree of improvement is not linear. We show the relation between sampling rate and similarity of two images in this section. As we can see the following test, the steep improvement becomes negligable with finer samples. To test under the harshest environment, we limit the picture database to one hundred

Fig. 1. Part of the coins that are used for artworks. The small coins and big coins are mixed to reduce patterns.

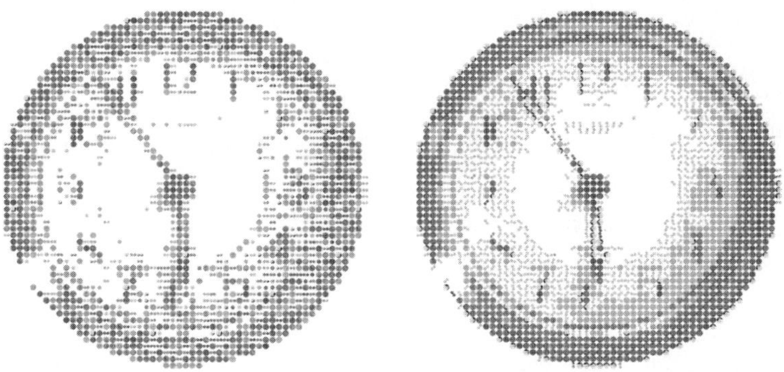

Fig. 2. $2PI/\text{N}$ Sampling (N=1 Left), (N=128 Right) the finer sampling, the better output

coins produced by the United States mint office. The pictures do not have to be circular in shape, but this shows the features of our algorithm more easily.

Depending on the type of images used in the test, the number in the table will be changed but the rate of increase remain constant. Average color distance means the average distance of each corresponding pixel between the original image and the output image in green, red and blue components

Suitable Object for Rotation. Rotating photographs generates problems. Traditional Photomosaics place a photograph in a rectangular cell. This naturally matches with rectangular shaped pictures in the database. When we rotated pictures, two main problems appear. First, as we can see from Figure 3, it spoils the contents of a photograph, and second, it generates unwanted data in the cell. The unwanted data has two types, first is garbage data or empty space (hole) which is the red part, 'A', and the other is the data loss part truncation which is the blue area, 'B', in the Figure 3.

Most pictures are intolerant to rotation because they have a definite orientation. When an image is rotated, it becomes an obstacle to perceive the picture as a meaningful object. The conditions for a safe image, when it is rotated, are as follows (Figure 4).

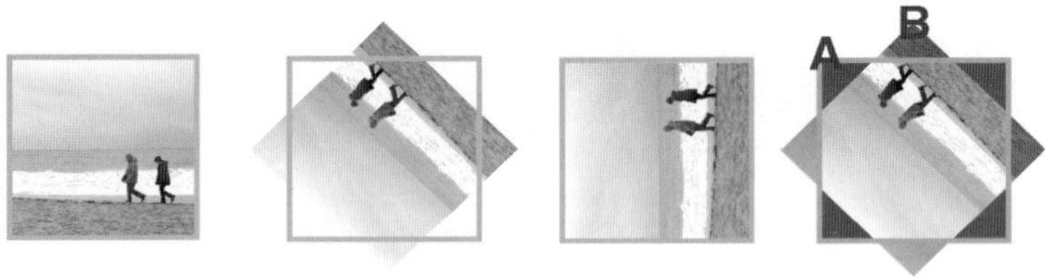

Fig. 3. Rotation of a picture destroys the meaning of the photograph. Image rotation generates unwanted data in the cell-'A' and data loss-'B'.

Fig. 4. Rotation of a coin image. Sampling rate is 30 degree. It produces 11 more images from the original image.

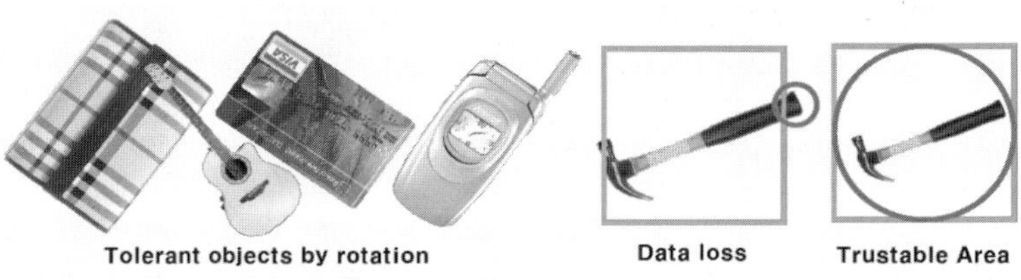

Fig. 5. Left images show examples of Tolerant Objects by rotation. Right image shows data loss by rotation. The object should be in the inscribed circle area in the cell to prevent any data loss by truncation.

The first type of images that are rotation invariant are of objects that are viewed from above. (Figure 5 Left). The second type are ones that have less data loss and produce less garbage data by rotation. Valid data is contained in a circle inscribed in the cell (Figure 5 Right). As we can see from Figure 4, the object 'Coin' satisfies these conditions.

When the cell is a square and an object in a photograph is a circular shape, this produces the least unwanted data because the two conditions maximize the trustable area; the inscribe circle area is the only trustable data.

3.2 Stacking Objects – Multilayering with Angled Grid System

Angled Grid System. The method in the previous section inevitably produces garbage data. The inscribed circular area is the region we may trust in a square

Fig. 6. Single layer. White area is the 'Empty space'(left). Double layers , less 'empty space' than the single layer(center). Multilayer eliminates the empty space from top to bottom, 1 layer, 2 layers, and 3 layers stacked (right).

cell. The other area in the cell, we define as empty space (hole), because that area has no information. Due to the law of simplicity in Gestalt theory [7] we can still recognize the larger image without trouble. However, there is a way to improve the quality of mosaic when we use the empty space aggressively by replacing the empty space with the information from other layers [8]. The angled grid system was designed for this process. The blocks in traditional Photomosaics are aligned along horizontal and vertical lines, and this is suitable because the photograph in each block is rectangular in shape and should be aligned upright to be recognized. This makes output images uniform (e.g Figure 6). The angled grid system has two advantages. First, it eliminates empty space efficiently when the layers are stacked. Second, it produces fewer patterns. The degree of grid rotation is free as long as it does not produce significant patterns while covering empty space well. As we can see from Figure 6, multi-layering in various angles not only covers the empty space but also produces a strong illusion of randomly stacked objects.

Multiple Layers. How Many? Using multiple layers has two important roles. First it improves the quality of the mosaic, and second, it gives the effect of piling objects. As we can see from the Figure 6, multilayering covers the empty space effectively. The question is, how much it will improve the quality when another layer is added?

The right of Table 1 shows a similar result to what we saw in the section 3.1. More layers produce better output, but too many layers cost too much rendering time while only improving output quality slightly. More than three layers do not help the quality much, so in general we use three layers to produce the artworks shown. When we define x as the similarity between the result and the original image, we can expect that single layer mosaics describe a similarity as $(PI/4 \times x)$ because the inscribe circle area is the trustable area. When we apply the multilayer mosaic method, the empty space of each cell is eliminated and we can expect a better result than the single layer. The multilayer mosaic without the empty space is $4/PI$ times better than the single layer mosaic. In other word, we can expect a similarity to traditional Photomosaics without using rectangular, uniformed tiles.

Table 1. Average color distance value of pixels with each rotation sampling rate(left). The more layers, the better quality(right).

Sampling Rate	Avg. distance	Number of layers	Avg. distance
$2PI/1$	34.994	1	29.673
$2PI/2$	32.466	2	27.318
$2PI/4$	31.659	3	26.066
$2PI/8$	31.018	4	25.535
...	...	5	25.206
$2PI/64$	30.105	...	...
$2PI/128$	30.103	...	...

3.3 Shadow

The multilayer mosaic generates the spatial order in elements. Applying a shadow effects to them creates a stronger illusion of depth. For shadow effects, we treat each layer as a two dimensional thin film rather than a three dimensional object. We simply spread out the edge of each object and darken the edge area. This simple process creates a very strong sense of depth.

Fig. 7. Before adding shadows to each layer vs. After adding shadows to each layer

4 Result

4.1 Circular Objects – e.g. Coins

Figure 9 and 10 are two artworks made using the suggested algorithm. Two hundred coin images are used, and the rotation sampling rates are ten degrees. We used three layers for these images. These artworks received an award from the Epson Color Imaging Contest, a competitive international contest in traditional photography. This suggests the judges were convinced that these images are real photographs. It was a unique experience because the output has both artistic and technical issues. To verify the quality of the algorithm and to prove the artistic value of the images, we showed the results to public to be judged by experts trained in the arts.

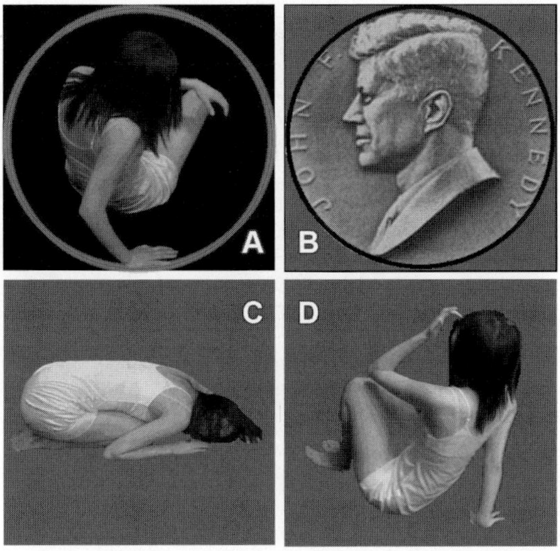

Fig. 8. B,C,D shows empty space as red color

4.2 Non-circular Objects – e.g. Human Body

As we mentioned in Section 3.1.3 the objects in our library do not have to be circular in shape as long as the valid data is inside of inscribed circle area (Figure 8-A). A circular object has the biggest valid data area, but it does not guarantee the minimum color difference between original source image and output mosaic image. The most important part of this algorithm is that we do not want to solve all the problems in a single layer because the other layers will help to complete the mosaic. The more layers, the less empty space that remains. Figure 8 shows a non-rectangular shaped object. In the case of coins, we defined the empty space as non-inscribed circle area (Figure 8-B), but for these pictures we define the empty space as the non-object area in red (Figure 8-C,D).

Figure 11 is an example mosaic produced by the suggested algorithm. We used three layers and a library with eighty pictures. None of them is a circular-type object, so we blue-screened the background when we shot the figure of a female dancer. This dancer mosaic was selected for the Shichon-Seoul Art Festival 2004 main poster.

5 Conclusion and Future Work

The Multi-layered stack mosaic algorithm with photograph rotation improves image quality, especially when the database is limited. We also tested this new mosaic style by opening it to the public with a gallery exhibition [9]. The exhibition was successful and the images were well received. However, some people complained that they are too mechanical. Therefore, in future work, we hope to

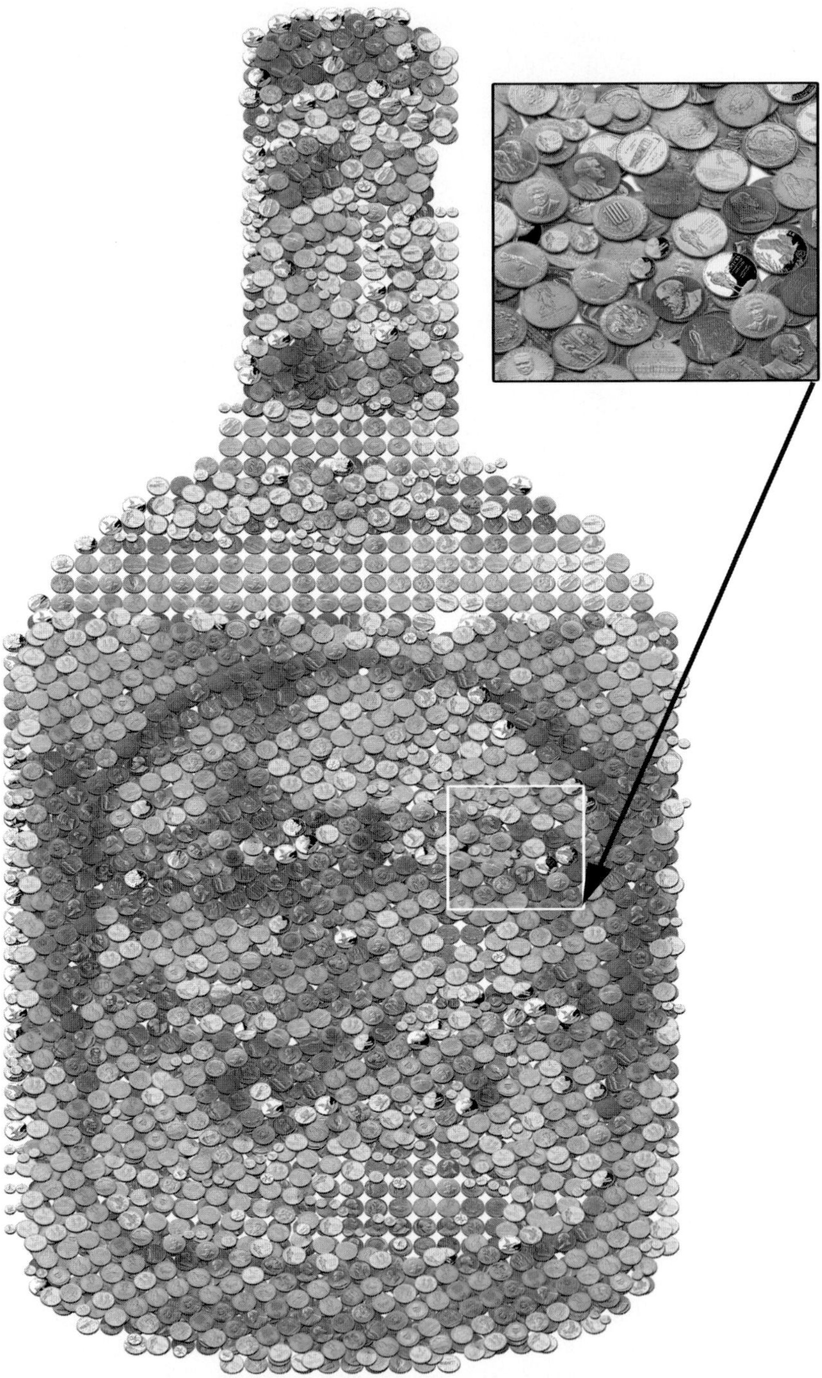

Fig. 9. Whisky. 200 coins of database.

Fig. 10. Mosaice of a girl with a bag. 200 coins of database.

Fig. 11. As we can see detailed 'A' area, pile of small pictures of a dancer makes smooth curve in bigger mosaic picture.

refine this algorithm with a flexible grid to create a more natural looking collage. This will be a challenge because the algorithm has to understand the substance of each object. The study of how artists select objects for painting is essential to move on to the next step of art in science.

References

1. Silver, R and Hawley, M.: Photomosaics. New York, Henry Holt (1997)
2. Hausner A, "Simulating decorative Mosaics", In: Proceedings of ACM SIGGRAPH 2001: 573-580
3. Kim J, Pellacini F, "Jigsaw Image Mosaics", In Proceedings of ACM SIGGRAPH 2002,: 657-664
4. Gershon Elber, George Wolberg, "Rendering traditional mosaics" The Visual Computer 2003: 67-78.
5. Strand, C. Hello, Fruit Face! The Paintings of Guiseppe Arcimboldo, Prestel (1999)
6. Thomas G. West, Artist discoveries and graphical histories, ACM SIGGRAPH Computer Graphics, Volume 33 , Issue 4 Nov.2000 12-13
7. Koffa, K. : Principles of Gestalt Psychology, London, Routledge and Kegan Paul (1935)
8. Rensink, R. A. : Seeing, Sensing, and Scrutinizing. Vision Research (2000) 40, 1469-1487
9. Park, Jin Wan : The Coinage Project No.1 "Time Is Money", Leonardo 38:2, MIT Press (2005)
10. Nicholas Tran: Generating Photomosaics: An Empirical Study. SAC1999:105-109
11. Tom McKenna and Gonzalo R. Arce. New Image Mosaic Structures. Technical report, De-partment of Electrical and Computer Engineering, University of Delaware, August 1999.
12. Adam Finkelstein and Marisa Range. Image Mosaics. Technical Report TR-574-98, Princeton University, Computer Science Department, March 1998.

Appearance and Geometry Completion with Constrained Texture Synthesis

Chunxia Xiao, Wenting Zheng, Yongwei Miao, Yong Zhao, and Qunsheng Peng

State Key Lab of CAD&CG, Zhejiang University, 310027, Hanghou, P.R. China

Abstract. A novel approach for appearance and geometry completion over point-sampled geometry is presented in this paper. Based on the result of surface clustering and the given texture sample, we define a global texture energy function on the point set surface for direct texture synthesis. The color texture completion is performed by minimizing a constrained global energy using the existing texture on the surface as the input texture sample. We convert the issue of context-based geometry completion into a task of texture completion on the surface. The geometric detail is then peeled and converted into a piece of signed gray-scale texture on the base surface of the point set surface. We fill the holes on the base surface by smoothed extrapolation and the geometric details over these patches are reconstructed by a process of gray-scale texture completion. Experiments show that our method is flexible, efficient and easy to implement. It provides a practical texture synthesis and geometry completion tool for 3D point set surfaces.

1 Introduction

As numerous 3D surface scanning devices are available in recent years, 3D scanning has become a major approach for acquiring the shape of complex 3D objects. However, obtaining a fine and usable 3D model from the acquired surface samples is still a difficult task. Due to occlusions, low reflectance, measure error in the scanning, the acquired geometry is frequently imperfect, that is, it contains holes. In addition, large holes may also be introduced by some surface editing operations. These holes have to be filled in a manner not only conforming to the global shape of the entire surface but also exhibiting its primary geometric detail. At the same time the color texture of the defective surface should also be repaired consistently.

Compared with the problem of inpainting and texture synthesis of 2D image, the geometry completion and texture synthesis on 3D point-sampled geometry is more challenging for many reasons. The point sampling is irregular and does not give rise to a regular parameter domain as the image. In addition, the similarity measurements between the point sets are difficult to define. In this paper, we propose a novel method for appearance and geometry completion on point-sampled surface, our major contributions are as follows:

Firstly, Based on global optimization we present a novel texture synthesis producing smooth texture synthesis effects while keeping the intrinsic structures

H.-P. Seidel, T. Nishita, and Q. Peng (Eds.): CGI 2006, LNCS 4035, pp. 24–35, 2006.

of the sample texture over the point-sampled geometry. By regarding the textures on the existing surface as the input texture sample, the texture completion can be accomplished by optimizing a constrained global texture energy function. Secondly, By performing a mean curvature flow we derive the base surface of the sampled geometry. We define the geometric details as the displacement between the surface and its base surface. The geometric details are then peeled and converted into a signed gray scale texture attached to the base surface for the downstream processing. Thirdly, our approach reconstructs the geometric details on the smooth patch by implementing texture completion in the gray scale texture space, therefore some troublesome operations such as similarity measurement, rigid transformation of the 3D points set are avoided.

By applying the above algorithms we can achieve consistent context-based completion and can deal with more complex boundary condition compared with the texture and geometry completion algorithms employing PDE. Furthermore, by converting the 3D geometry completion into the task of 3D texture completion, we are able to further utilize a wealth of currently available surface texture synthesis and completion technique to serve our purpose.

2 Related Works

There has been a number of works focused on Example-based texture synthesis for 3D surface. A comprehensive survey is outside the scope of this paper. It is found that most of existing texture synthesis algorithms on 3D surface are mesh oriented. Since texture synthesis algorithms on meshes normally make use of the topology information, they cannot be applied to the point set surface directly. By now, few works are focused on texture synthesis over point set surface. In our scope, Alexa et al. [1] and Clarenz et al. [2] showed some texture synthesis results on point set surface as the application of their algorithm. Recently, geometry completion focused on repairing the uncompleted meshes or point-sampled surface has received much attention in computer graphics. Lots of works have been presented, and these methods can be mainly divided into two categories according to the strategies they adopted.

One strategy is to create a smooth patch covering the hole-region and satisfying the boundary conditions. [3] used globally supported radial base functions (RBFs) to fit data points by solving a large dense linear system, [4] proposed a hierarchical approach to 3D scattered data interpolation with compact RBFs. Davis et al. [5] constructed a volumetric signed distance function around the surface samples, and then applied an iterative Gaussian convolution to propagate adjacent distance values to patch the holes. Liepa [6] proposed a hole filling technique to interpolate the shape and density of the surrounding mesh. Verdera et al. [7] extended a PDE-based image inpainting technique to 3D geometry meshes. Ju [8] constructed an inside/outside volume using octree grids for any model represented as a polygon soup, then the holes were repaired by contouring.

The other strategy is to repair the holes according to the context information so that the geometry detail can be reconstructed at the same time. Sharf et al. [9]

introduced a context-based method which extended the texture synthesis techniques from 2D image to 3D point-based models for completing the defective geometry models. Pauly [10] presented a method using a database of 3D shapes to provide geometric priors for regions of missing data. Lai et al. [11] proposed a method of geometric detail synthesis and transferring for meshes based on the concept of geometry images. Park et al. [12] restored both shape and appearance from the incomplete point surfaces by conducting a local parameterization to align patches and then solved a Poisson equations on 2D domain for warping the patch to cover the hole region. Minh et al. [13] transformed the 3D geometry synthesis problem into the 2D domain by parameterizing surfaces, and then solved the geometry completion problem with an interactive PDE solver.

3 Texture Synthesis

Recently, Kwatra et.al [14] presented an approach for 2D texture synthesis based on global optimization of texture quality with respect to a similarity metric based on Markov Random Field (MRF) similarity criterion. In this section, we extend this method to point-sampled surface. As the point surface is irregularly sampled in 3D, it is difficult to define such a kind of global texture energy on point-sampled geometry. Preprocessing of the point set surface is necessary as the preparation.

The point-sampled geometry $M = \{p_1, p_2, ...p_n\}$ is firstly clustered into uniform patches $\{C_{o,i}\}$ that are the units for further computing. The neighboring patches are overlapped to make it less computationally expensive for computing the energy, furthermore, avoid the synthesized texture getting blurred in regions where there is a mismatch between the overlapping clusters. We then set up a global continuous direction field on the point set surface to conduct local parameterization for each patch. By building up the correspondence between irregularly 3D sampling points and the regular 2D texture samples, the global texture energy can be defined directly on the surface and to be optimized.

3.1 Surface Clustering

We first utilize the hierarchical clustering algorithm [15] to split the point cloud. The point cloud M is then divided into a number of subsets $\{C_i'\}$. Nevertheless, these initial clusters contain sharp edges and corners, as shown in Fig.1(a). Let $y_i^{'}$ be the centroid of the cluster C_i'. To get a more even distribution of clusters, we find neighbor $N_i = \{j : 0 <= \|y_j^{'} - y_i^{'}\| < r\}$ for each point $y_i^{'}$. For each point sample $p_i \in C_i'$, we locate $y_j^{'} \in N_i$ that is the nearest to p_i, and then p_i is adjusted to the new cluster C_j. Therefore, the partitioning result of the entire point set is reformed to uniform clusters $\{C_i\}$, as illustrated in Fig 1(b).We then grow each $\{C_i\}$ and form the new generated clusters $\{C_{O,i}\}$, such that each $C_{O,i}$ overlaps with its neighboring cluster $C_{O,j}$. Within a band of width h. In our experimentation we set $h = 0.5 \cdot d$, where d is the average radius of the clusters $\{C_i\}$. In Fig1. (c), the green color indicates the overlapped area of adjacent clusters, in Fig1. (d), the parameter h takes a larger value.

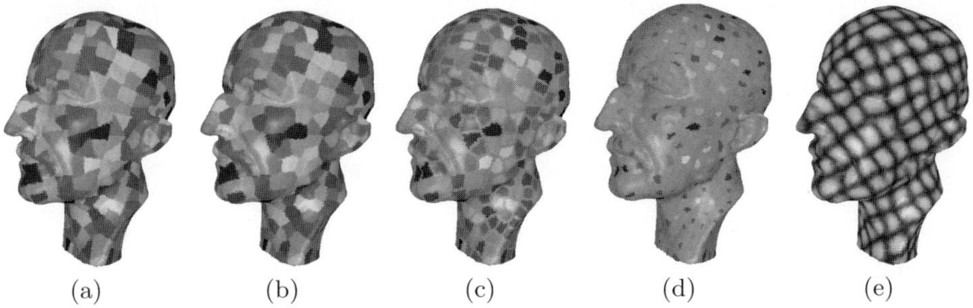

Fig. 1. Surface clustering of point-sampled geometry. (a) Initial clustering, (b) uniform clustering, (c) overlapped cluster with small overlapping parameter, (d) Larger overlapping area, (e) The texture synthesis result.

3.2 Global Optimized Surface Texture Synthesis

We establish the texture energy function directly on the point set surface in several steps. We first define the global energy on the point-sampled surface.

Let y_i be the centroid of the cluster $C_{O,i}$. By applying the method presented in [1], we can establish a global direction field on the point set surface $Y = \{y_1, ...y_m\}$. Based on the direction field and the tangent plane computed by covariance analysis, we set up a local frame for each cluster $C_{O,i}$ to facilitate the local parameterization.

Let ν_i be the direction of y_i, and n_i be the normal of y_i. We define ν_i the up direction and $\mu_i = \nu_i \times n_i$ the right direction for the texture, as shown in Fig. 2(a). A local frame $\{\mu_i, \nu_i, n_i\}$ is then established. We project the vectors from y_i to all surrounding points x_i in the cluster $\in C_{o,i}$ onto the tangent plane of y_i. The resulting vectors are normalized and multiplied by the distance between y_i and p_i(Fig. 2(a)). In this way we preserve the distance information between the points on the surface to some extent.

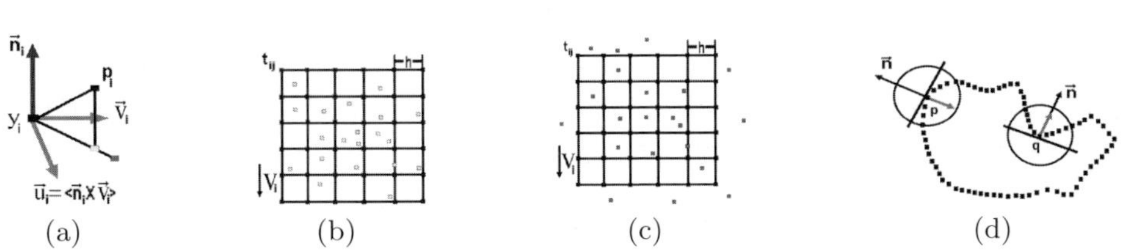

Fig. 2. the construction of the grid for each patch (cluster). (a) Local parameterization by projection, (b) regular grid G generated on the parameterization domain, (c) to generate the sample texture from user specified region. (d) mean curvature flow.

Now a regular parameterization grid G_i of $n \times n$ centered on y_i with the interval of h on the tangent plane is generated for each $C_{O,i}$, G_i aligns with the direction ν_i as up vector and the μ_i as right vector (Fig.2(b)). The parameter at each grid

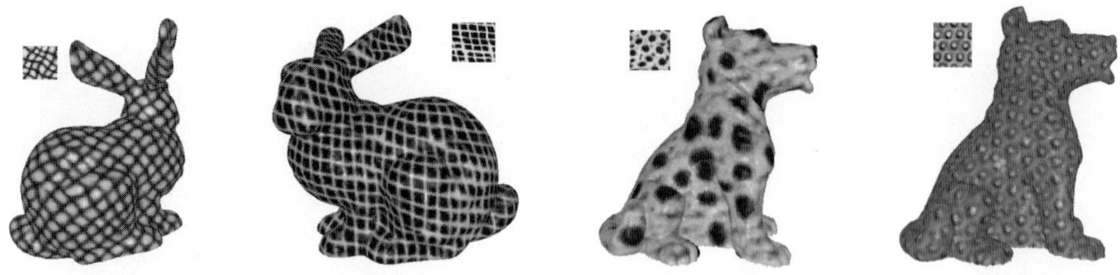

(a) (b) (c) (d)

Fig. 3. Some texture synthesis results based on the global optimization

point t_{ij} is obtained by interpolating the parameters of points in the surrounding cells. So with the regular grid G_i, the correspondence between irregularly 3D sampling points and the regular 2D texture samples can be built for defining the global texture energy. Let $X = \{G_i\}$ denote the surface parametric space over which we want to compute the texture energy and Z denote the input texture sample. Let Z_i be the vectorized pixel neighborhood in Z whose appearance is most similar to G_i under the Euclidean norm. Then, we define the texture energy over X to be

$$E_t(x; \{Z_i\}) = \sum_{p \in Y} \parallel G_i - Z_i \parallel^2 \tag{1}$$

Similar to the algorithm presented in [14], we use the EM-like algorithm to optimize the texture energy over X. We modify the E and M steps to account for the specific feature of the discrete point set.

The M-step of our algorithm minimizes (1) with respect to the set of input neighborhoods $\{Z_i\}$, keeping G_i fixed and for each G_i, we find its nearest neighbor Z_i from Z.

In the E-step, we need to minimize (1) w.r.t. G_i. We resolve it in a way different from [14]. Once we find the closest input neighborhood Z_i for each G_i, the texture intensity at point p_i enclosed in G_i can be obtained using bilinear interpolation. Suppose cluster $C_{O,i}$ and $C_{O,j}$ overlap with each other, some points will be contained in both $C_{O,i}$ and $C_{O,j}$. Each of the common points may take possibly different intensity values from G_i and G_j. The minimization procedure assigns each common point an intensity value that is equal to the average of the original values in $C_{O,i}$ and $C_{O,j}$. Since the intensity at the common point has changed, the intensity at t_{ij} in G_i is updated which is used for the next M-step.

The energy of the synthesized texture will converge after a number of iterations. Fig.1 (e) is the result using our method, and Fig.3 shows more results. Multi-scale synthesis can also be performed in our approach by adjusting the grid $G_i(n \times n)$.

4 Color Texture Completion

In this section, we complete the color texture of the point-sampled geometry with a constrained texture synthesis algorithm, and the completed color texture should be consistent with the surrounding existing texture. We select a user specified region D on the existing surface to serve as input sample texture. For each point p_i in D, similar to the method presented in section 3.3, we find its neighborhood N_i and build a colored regular Grid Z_i of $n \times n$, as shown in (Fig.2(c)). The set $\{Z_i\}$ is used as the input texture for color completion.

To make the boundary between the completed and original regions imperceptible, similar to the controllable image synthesis [14], we add a additional term to Eq.(1) to achieve a general constrained energy function for texture completion.

$$E_t(x; \{Z_i\}) = \sum_{p \in Y} \| G_i - Z_i \|^2 + \sum_{k \in \varphi} (x(k) - x^c(k))^2 \quad (2)$$

In our approach, φ is the set of boundary points, or the set of boundary clusters which contain some boundary points, x^c is a vector containing the current color values at the boundary points.

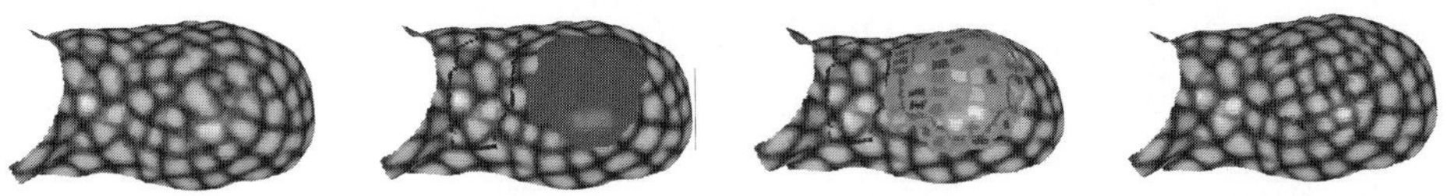

(a) (b) (c) (d)

Fig. 4. Texture completion. (a)Original point model,(b)defective texture model, (c)the defective regions is covered by the clusters,(d)completed texture point model.

Note that to generate a seamless boundary texture, the cluster set $\{C_{O,i}\}$ should be chosen to cover the color defective regions and contain the boundary points, as shown in Fig.4(c).As shown in Fig.4(b), the region enclosed by the blue curve is used for generating the sample texture, the red patch is the region to be completed, the result is shown in Fig.4(d). In Fig.5, we present the completion result with isolated islands left on the flawed region. With our constrained texture filling technique, the result is consistent with islands as well as the boundary of the existing surface color. This situation is difficult to handle if one applies the Poisson equation interpolation method [12].

5 Geometry Detail Encoding

The geometric detail is an important attribute of a surface. It is defined as the difference between the original point-sampled surface and its base surface. In our method, the base surface is built by smoothing the point set surface. Covariance analysis on local point cloud can be applied to estimate various local surface properties, for example, normal ν_0 and the curvature σ_n at each point p_i on the point set surface[15]. Based on the normal and curvature, we are able to define a curvature flow equation[16]. The basic idea of defining such a diffusion flow is to allow the point moving along the normal with a speed equal to the curvature σ_n

(a) (b) (c)

Fig. 5. (a) The original Chameleon model, (b) corrupted texture model with islands, (c) the completed texture

as shown in Fig.2 (d). Since the position of a point is adjusted along the normal direction, the proposed curvature flow will not introduce undesirable point drifting over the surface. The curvature flow equation is an isotropic smoother and a low frequency base surface can be received applying this filtering operator.

5.1 Encoding Geometric Details as Texture

Assume that the surface M is filtered, yielding a base surface M'. Let $p \in M$,$p' \in M'$ is its corresponding point, and n' is the normal at point p'. Let $\delta = \| p - p' \|$ be the geometric detail of point p. Let $dire = (p - p') \cdot n'$, if $Dire \geq 0$, then $sign = 1$, else $sign = -1$. We define $c' = sign \cdot \| p - p' \|$ as the the signed gray-scale of p'.

Once the normal n' and signed gray-scale c' of p' are obtained, its geometry information is approximately reconstructed as $\overline{p} = p' + c' \cdot n'$. Using this technique, a surface $\overline{M}$ is reconstructed by the base surface and the signed gray-scale C which approximates M. The normal information of the reconstructed points can be recomputed using the minimum spanning tree [17].With the mean curvature flow filter, the reconstructed surface from the signed geometric gray level is a good approximation to the original surface, as shown in Fig.7. With different iteration times for the mean curvature flow, various frequency band of geometric detail can be extracted effectively and efficiently.

6 Geometry Completion

Similar to the color texture completion, the completed geometry should keep consistent with the surrounding geometry and the boundary between the completed and existing regions should be continuous. Using a hierarchical compactly supported basis functions [4], we first complete the base surface by smoothed extrapolation, as shown in Fig.6(d). Further, the geometry detail on the base surface patch should be reconstructed.

6.1 Context-Based Geometry Completion

Using the method presented in previous sections we can complete the signed gray-scale texture on the patched smooth surface (Fig.6 (e)). The completed

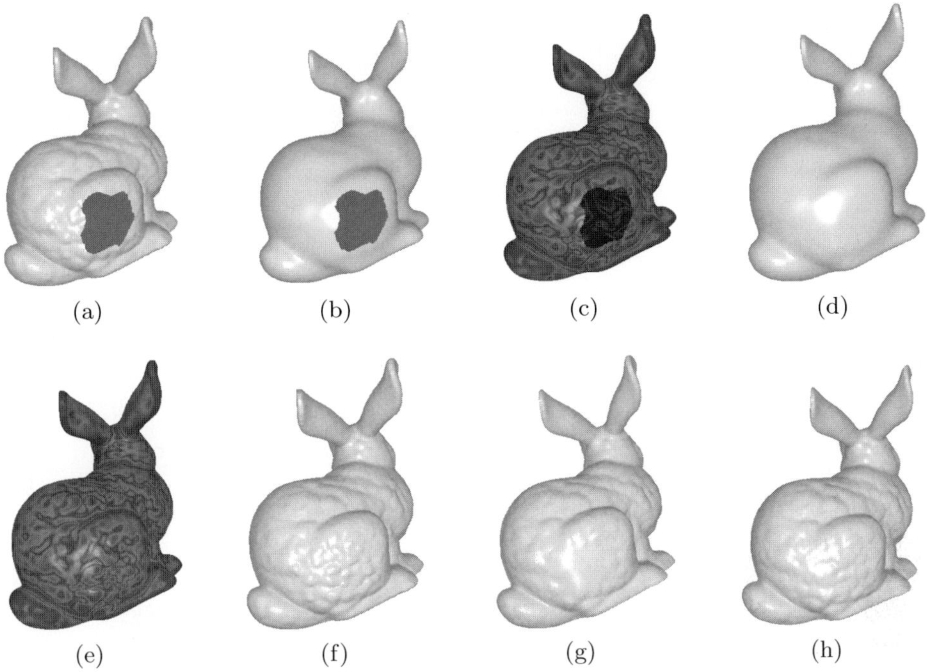

Fig. 6. Overview of our entire processing pipeline for geometry completion. (a) The defective bunny model, (b) the base surface of (a), (c) the signed gray-scale texture on the base surface. Pseudo color is used to illustrate the value clearly. Red color indicates the largest gray-scale value, while the blue indicate the least value, (d) completed base surface, (e) the completed signed gray-scale texture in pseudo color, (f) the final result of geometry completion, (g) RBF interpolation of (a), (h) the original bunny model.

signed gray-scale texture is then converted back to geometric details (Fig.6 (f)), and the context-based geometry completion is achieved. This procedure is regarded as a reverse procedure of the geometric detail encoding.

Let $p \in M$ with normal n, p' is its corresponding point on M' with normal n'. We interpolate the defective base surface M' to get the completed base surface N'. Suppose $\Omega' = N' - M'$ is the newly constructed patch which is consistent with the boundary of the M', we then complete the texture C' of Ω' based on the existing texture on M employing the technique presented in section 4. For each point $\nu' \in \Omega'$ with normal n', let c' be its synthesized signed gray-scale, the reconstructed location is defined as $\nu = \nu' + c' \cdot n'$, its normal can be recalculated using the technique described in [17]. Using this approach, the completed patch Ω captures the context information of the existing surface. Compared with other geometry completion approach [9] that added points by rotating, translating, and possible warped copies of points from another region, our approach is more efficient, controllable and easy to implement.

Assume N be the reconstructed surface based on N' and its signed gray-scale. Ω, M and N are all continuous inside their interior region. When we adopt the

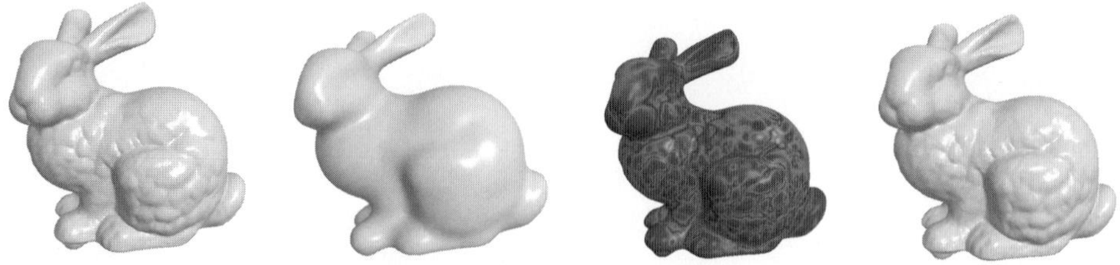

(a) (b) (c) (d)

Fig. 7. Surface reconstruction from the signed gray scale texture. (a) Original Bunny model M, (b) Smoothed Bunny model M', (c) Signed gray-scale texture in pseudo color C, (d) Reconstructed surface $\overline{M}$.

points from M and the other points from Ω in the final completion result, small crack may occur in the boundary region between Ω and M. To resolve this problem, we modify the normal of the boundary points in Ω'.

Suppose p is a boundary point on M, and p' is its corresponding point on base surface M' with normal $n' = (n_x^{p'}, n_y^{p'}, n_z^{p'})$. Let $\delta = (\delta_x, \delta_y, \delta_z)$ be the normalized vector of the difference vector $p - p'$. The vector difference $\Delta\mu_{p'}$ between δ and n' is defined as $\Delta\mu_{p'} \triangleq (\Delta_x^{p'}, \Delta_y^{p'}, \Delta_z^{p'}) \triangleq (\delta_x - n_x^{p'}, \delta_y - n_y^{p'}, \delta_z - n_z^{p'})$.

We define a band with radius d around the boundary of the smoothed surface patch Ω'. For each point $q' = (x_{q'}, y_{q'}, z_{q'})$ with normal $n_{q'} = (n_x^{q'}, n_y^{q'}, n_z^{q'})$ in the band, we find its nearest point p' on the boundary of M'. Let the distance between p' and q' be s, we set the weight $\omega = (d - s)/d$, then the normal $n_{q'}$ of q' is adjusted as $(\overline{n_x^{q'}}, \overline{n_y^{q'}}, \overline{n_z^{q'}}) \triangleq (n_x^{q'} + \omega \cdot \Delta\mu_x^{p'}, n_y^{q'} + \omega \cdot \Delta\mu_y^{p'}, n_z^{q'} + \omega \cdot \Delta\mu_z^{p'})$.

By normalizing above vector we get its modified normal $\overline{n}$, then the geometry position of q' can be reconstructed as $q = q' + c' \cdot \overline{n}$. As the completed base surface N' is continuous, its normal is also continuous. In addition, the completed texture C is continuous around the boundary region. By using this technique, we are able to produce a continuous surface around the boundary and the holes are filled consistent to the existing surface(Fig.6(f)).

6.2 Geometry Completion with Structure Propagation

The synthesis order of geometry completion is also important. By augmenting texture synthesis with some automatic guidance or interactive guidance, it can significantly improves the quality of completion by preserving some salient structures. Similar to Sun et. al. [18], we propose a geometry completion method based on structure guided synthesis. The missing structure information is specified by extending a few curves or line segments from the known regions to the unknown regions, then the patches along these user-specified curves in the unknown region is synthesized using patches selected around the curves in the known region by using a global optimization. After the salient structure is completed, the remaining regions can be completed. In our method both the salient structures and remaining missing regions are completed based on the constrained global

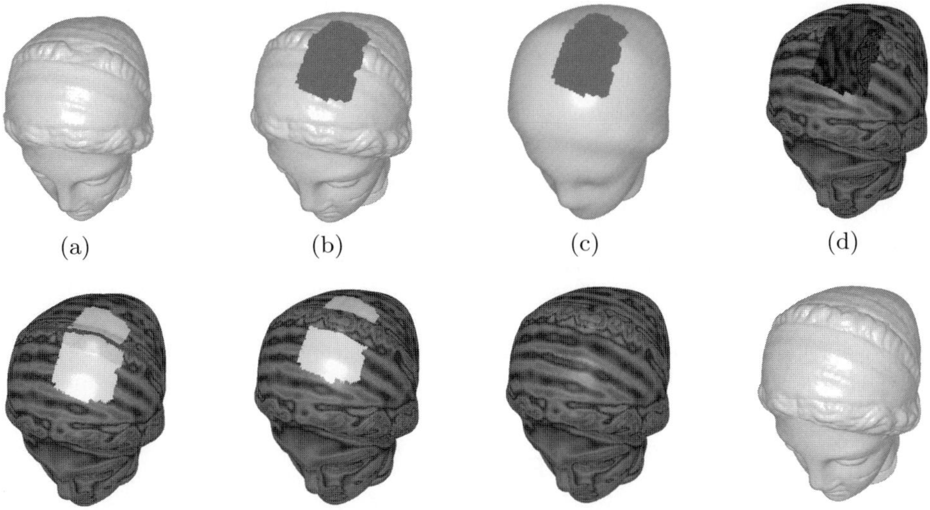

(a) (b) (c) (d)

(e) (f) (g) (h)

Fig. 8. Geometry completion with structure propagation. (a) Original Venus model, (b) uncompleted Venus M, (c) the base surface M' of M, (d) the geometry detail of M is converted to the signed gray-scale texture on M', (e) One red line specified by the user in completed base surface, the yellow region is the structure region needed be synthesized firstly. (f) intermediate result after synthesizing structure and texture information along the user-specified line, (g) final result after filling in the remaining unknown regions. (h) Result of geometry reconstruction.

optimization. As shown in Fig.8, we want to fill the missing geometry on the Venus. The user specifies the important missing texture structure by extending a few curves from the known to the unknown regions on the base surface, the signed gray-scale texture along the specified curves in the unknown region is first completed with structure guided synthesis and the other regions are then completed by texture optimization.

6.3 Geometry Completion with Detail Cloning

Our method also provides a seamless geometry cloning tool for surface based detail cloning. The missing region of one model can be completed with the geometry details of other models as the geometry texture. The user specifies a source region S in an arbitrary surface and the missing region D on target surface. By smoothing the source region S, we get its signed gray-scale texture. Using the constrained optimization texture completion technique described in above sections, the signed gray-scale texture is adopted as the input texture sample to complete the texture of the smooth patch filling hole D. After converting the gray-scale texture back to the geometric detail, we obtain the cloning result as shown in Fig.9. The defective region of model Lady is completed by transferring the geometric details of the bob region on model Venus.

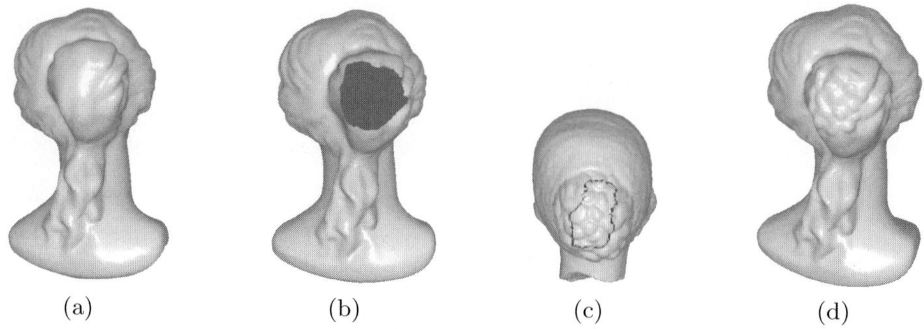

Fig. 9. Geometry completion based on geometry transfer. (a) Original lady model, (b), uncompleted lady model, (c) the sample model Venus, (d) the completion result.

7 Implementation and Results

The proposed algorithm was implemented on a Microsoft Windows XP PC with a Celeron 2.00GHz CPU and 1.00GB RAM. The computational complexity of our approach is dominated by the process of texture synthesis which is based on the nearest neighbor search. In the example shown in Fig.3, there are 240,000 points in the Stanford Bunny, the execution time per iteration takes 8-10 seconds, and the total execution time is 10-12 minutes for about 50 iterations. In the context-based geometry completion stage, the execution time is much less as the patched region is much smaller. In fig 6, there are 22,000 points in the patched regions, it takes less than one minute to accomplish the texture completion operation. In our experiments, there are usually about 300 points in each overlapped cluster, the scale of the synthesized texture can be controlled by adjusting size of the regular grid G.

8 Conclusion and Future Work

We have presented a novel approach for appearance and surface content completion for the acquired 3D data set based on global optimization. We transform the task of surface content completion into that of surface texture completion. The major benefit is that it is flexible and efficient to implement. Our system can be extended to the mesh models easily. Further research will be focused on performing a user controllable non-uniform clustering so that the scale of synthesized texture can vary progressively through the point cloud.

Acknowledgement

The work is supported by the National Grand Fundamental Research 973 Program of China (No.2002CB312101)and the National Natural Science Foundation of China under Grant Nos.60503056.

References

1. M. Alexa, T. Klug, and C. Stoll. Direction fields over point-sampled geometry. *Journal of WSCG*, 11(1):27–32, 2003.
2. U. Clarenz, M. Rumpf, and A. Telea. Finite elements on point based surfaces. In *Proc. EG Symposium of Point Based Graphics*, 2004.
3. J. C. Carr, R. K. Beatson, J. B. Cherrie, T. J. Mitchell, W. R. Fright, B. C. McCallum, and T. R. Evans. Reconstruction and representation of 3d objects with radial basis functions. In *ACM SIGGRAPH*, pages 67–76, 2001.
4. Y. Ohtake, A. Belyaev, and H-P Seidel. A multi-scale approach to 3d scattered data interpolation with compactly supported basis functions. In *Shape Modeling International*, pages 153–161, 2003.
5. J. Davis, Stephen, R. Marschner, M. Garr, and M. Levoy. Filling holes in complex surfaces using volumetric diffusion. In *First International Symposium on 3D Data Processing, Visualization, and Transmission*, pages 428–438, 2002.
6. P. Liepa. Filling holes in meshes. In *Proceedings of the Eurographics/ACM SIGGRAPH symposium on Geometry processing*, pages 200–205, 2003.
7. J. Verdera, V. Caselles, M. Bertalmio, and G. Sapiro. Inpainting surface holes. In *Proceedings of International Conference on Image Processing*, pages 903–906, 2003.
8. T. Ju. Robust repair of polygonal models. *ACM Trans.Graph*, 23(3):888–895, 2004.
9. A. Sharf, M. Alexa, and D. Cohen-Or. Context-based surface completion. *ACM Trans.Graph*, 23(3):878–887, 2004.
10. M. Pauly, N. Mitra, J. Giesen, M. Gross, and L. J. Guibas. Example-based 3d scan completion. In *Symposium on Geometry Processing*, pages 23–32, 2005.
11. Y.-K. Lai, S.-M. Hu, D. X. Gu, and R. Martin. Geometric texture synthesis and transfer via geometry images. In *Proceedings of the 2005 ACM symposium on Solid and physical modeling*, pages 15–26, 2005.
12. S. Park, X. Guo, H. Shin, and H. Qin. Shape and appearance repair for incomplete point surfaces. In *International conference on computer graphics*, pages 1260–1267, 2005.
13. M. X. Nguyen, X. Yuan, and B. Chen. Geometry completion and detail generation by texture synthesis. In *Proceeding of Pacific Graphics*, pages 23–32, 2005.
14. V. Kwatra, I. A. Essa, A. F. Bobick, and N. Kwatra. Texture optimization for example-based synthesis. *ACM Trans.Graph*, 24(3):795–802, 2005.
15. M. Pauly, M. Gross, and L. Kobbelt. Efficient simplification of point-sampled surfaces. In *IEEE Visualization*, pages 1260–1267, 2002.
16. C. Xiao, Y. Miao, S. Liu, and Q. Peng. A dynamic balanced flow for filtering point-sampled geometry. *The Visual Computer*, 2006. to appear.
17. H. Hoppe, T. DeRose, T. Duchamp, J. McDonald, and W. Stuetzle. Reconstruction from unorganized points. In *ACM SIGGRAPH*, pages 71–78, 1992.
18. J. Sun, L. Yuan, J. Jia, and H. Y. Shum. Image completion with structure propagation. *ACM Trans.Graph*, 24(3):861–868, 2005.

Highly Stylised Drawn Animation

Fabian Di Fiore[1], Frank Van Reeth[1], John Patterson[2], and Philip Willis[3]

[1] Hasselt University
Expertise Centre for Digital Media
transnationale Universiteit Limburg
Wetenschapspark, 2
BE-3590 Diepenbeek Belgium
{fabian.difiore, frank.vanreeth}@uhasselt.be
http://www.edm.uhasselt.be
[2] Dept. of Computing Science
Glasgow University 17 Lilybank Gardens
Glasgow G12 8QQ Scotland, UK
jwp@dcs.gla.ac.uk
http://www.dcs.gla.ac.uk
[3] Media Technology Research Centre
Dept. of Computer Science
University of Bath
Bath Avon BA2 7AY England, UK
P.J.Willis@bath.ac.uk
http://www.bath.ac.uk/media

Abstract. In this paper we argue for our NPAR system as an effective 2D alternative to most of NPR research which is focused on frame coherent stylised rendering of 3D models. Our approach gives a highly stylised look to images without the support of 3D models, and yet they still behave as though animated by drawing, which they are.

First, a stylised brush tool is used to freely draw extreme poses of characters. Each character is built up of 2D drawn brush strokes which are manually grouped into layers. Each layer is assigned its place in a drawing hierarchy called a Hierarchical Display Model (HDM). Next, multiple HDMs are created for the same character, each corresponding to a specific view. A collection of HDMs essentially reintroduces some correspondence information to the 2D drawings needed for in-betweening and, in effect, eliminates the need for a true 3D model.

Once the models are composed the animator starts by defining keyframes from extreme poses in time. Next, brush stroke trajectories defined by the keyframe HDMs are in-betweened automatically across intermediate frames. Finally, each HDM of each generated in-between frame is traversed and all elements are drawn one on another from back to front.

Our techniques support highly rendered styles which are particularly difficult to animate by traditional means including the 'airbrushed', scraperboard, watercolour, Gouache, 'ink-wash', and the 'crayon' styles.

We believe our system offers a new fresh perspective on computer aided animation production and associated tools.

Keywords: Artist driven, stylised modelling, stylised animation, computer animation, computer-assisted animation, NPR, NPAR.

H.-P. Seidel, T. Nishita, and Q. Peng (Eds.): CGI 2006, LNCS 4035, pp. 36–53, 2006.

1 Introduction

Motivation. Although 3D animation is a popular form, because of the indirect nature of the interaction model, many details are extremely hard to construct and animate, while it is much simpler to design very convincing lookalikes in 2D. For example, ask a modeler to make an animation of a walking dinosaur and watch another artist draw a much more fancy 2D version during the time needed to start up the designer's favourite 3D software.

The difference between 2D and 3D modelling is even more apparent when subtle animation effects (artistic expressions, caricatures, ...) are involved. The stylistic possibilities afforded by 2D animation mean that 2D animations can be rich in a way which is seldom achieved by 3D animations (even with significantly more effort).

It is our contention that this overhead is unnecessary. Figure 1(a) shows a 2D image rendered without the use of a 3D model; it is inexpensively animatable, open to visual modification to suit the animator's individual style, yet still 'highly rendered' in appearance.

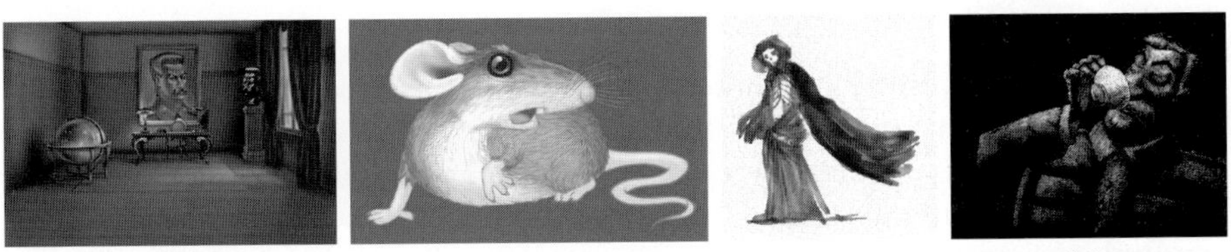

(a) (b) (c) (d)

Fig. 1. Snapshots of highly stylised animations. a) Highly rendered 2D image © Beb Deum/CALON. b) Mouse raising its head in an *airbrushed* style. c) Death in the guise of the 'Grim Reaper' in an *Oriental black ink* style. d) Stalin character drinking tea in a *scraperboard* style.

Contribution. We present here a system which is an effective 2D alternative to most of NPR research that is focused on frame coherent stylised rendering of 3D models. It supports 2D drawing instead of stylising strokes on 3D geometries. Furthermore, it relies on the simulation of natural materials and processes involved in making brush-strokes.

Our approach gives a highly stylised look to drawn animation but also allows an artist to give a 3D-like look to images yet they still behave as though animated by drawing, which they are. We believe our system offers a new fresh perspective on computer aided animation production and associated tools.

A series of examples are shown in Figure 1. We emphasise that at no time any 3D modelling is performed and in particular no 3D models are used to support the rendering of the images, scenes and animations we show.

Approach. Technically the challenge is to achieve stable rendering across frames. Artists find it difficult to achieve temporally coherent lighting and shading effects, potentially resulting in jittery, unpleasant imagery. To achieve such consistency the simulation is associated with the trajectory of the brush stroke itself and these brush trajectories are in-betweened across frames so the artist needs only to paint up a single frame. The brush trajectories are thus in-betweened and the simulation reproduced, possibly requiring some 'touching up' in more distant frames. While the method of managing consistency is essentially the same across all simulations, individual simulations may require different controls to manage different evolutions of effects like texture behaviour.

Paper Organisation. This paper is structured as follows. Section 2 surveys work we consider related to ours. Section 3 describes the data path to be followed to create highly stylised animations. In Section 4 we show some examples. Finally Section 5 is our conclusions section in which we also discuss our results and set the contexts for future work.

2 Related Work

In this section we elaborate on work we consider related to ours.

2.1 The Traditional Approach to Drawn Animation

Broadly speaking, traditional animation is defined as a technique in which the illusion of movement is created by depicting a series of individual drawings on successive frames. Unlike live action, where the camera is running continuously, each frame of an animation film is shot one by one. Moreover, as characters are separated into several layers, each single frame might consist of numerous layers stacked up together.

What we give here is an account as it might be in a large industrial studio. The overall work can be thought of as falling into two phases, that of *pre-production or design* (15% of the total effort) and *production* (about 85%). The stages are story development, Leica reel test, scene staging, exposure sheet preparation (which completes *preproduction*); then drawing, line test, ink-and-paint, rostrum camera stage (otherwise known as composition), and sound-track synchronisation or 'synch' (which completes *production*).

The drawing process itself is done in three phases: (i) lead animators draw the most significant images, which are referred to as extreme frames or poses, containing the major features of the action; (ii) assistant animators produce key frames between the extreme frames, hence detailing the desired animation action; while (iii) less experienced animators (in-betweeners) are responsible for creating all the remaining in-between frames of the animation, resulting in a smooth sequence of drawings. Drawing these frames is known as 'in-betweening' or 'tweening'.

We refer to Patterson & Willis [1] and Preston Blair [2] for readers interested in an in-depth explanation.

2.2 The Use of Computers in Drawn Animation

By far the most common use of computers in drawn animation is in the stage which in a feature film would be referred to as postproduction, namely the inking, painting and compositing of the artwork, as discussed in the previous section. Generally speaking they are not used earlier in the data path although there is a small proportion of studios whose style is well-suited to automatic in-betweening and use it. Software to support artists to produce in-between drawings are becoming more widely used but these just provide on-line support for making the drawings, checking and line testing on the assumption that a sequence of drawings is going to be produced by hand. On the whole, animators do not like automatic in-betweening precisely because they want to break the rules in some way on just about every frame.

In-Betweening. In-betweening is effected on the basis of one of two models: *shape-based* (e.g., Reeves [3], Sederberg & Greenwood [4], Ranjian [5] and Kort [6]) and *skeleton-based* methods (e.g. Burtnyk & Wein [7], Shapira & Rappoport [8] and Jinhui Yu [9]), which are often used in combination. The skeleton-based methods use an articulated skeletal structure which is normally layered to reflect the order in which the skeleton elements are encountered but may sometimes exceptionally be retained as a 3D entity, then layered on the basis of view-dependency. Each skeletal element in the view-dependent form will have a shape associated with it and this will follow the movements of the skeleton which is defined in terms of the movements of the skeletal joints. There is the issue of the control of the skeleton which can be determined by motion capture or manual posing.

The shapes associated with the skeletal elements can themselves be in-betweened using such techniques as Moving Reference Points (MRPs) [3]. A MRP reflects common animator's practice in selecting a point on the drawing and describing its trajectory in 2D with associated timing. A set of MRPs subdivides a line into segments which in its original formulation implicitly define a 3D patch of which the evolution of the segment is a 2D projection. The segment is initially oriented by the movement of the skeleton, then re-shaped according to the MRP trajectory as mapped into the 2D space defined by the skeleton element itself.

More recently, Kort presented a rule-based method for computer aided in-betweening [6]. The content of each key drawing is analysed and classified into strokes, chains of strokes and relations that hold among them. Rules decide what parts of different drawings may be matched. Finally, generated animation paths between corresponding strokes determine the resulting in-betweens.

Rotoscoping. When artwork is animated from film or video footage this is referred to as rotoscoping [10] and typically rotoscoped artwork differs significantly in timing and behaviour from drawn animation. Rotoscoped artwork, however, is 'trapped' by being too realistic: since the underlying outlines are rendered too accurately, a very realistic silhouette is generated which we especially want to avoid.

Non-photorealistic Animation and Rendering. It is fair to say that our work intrudes into the area generally known as Non-photorealistic Animation and Rendering (NPAR). We do not build 3D models so we do not render in the conventional sense, and the work of Hays and Essa [11] comes closest to what we do. However, Hays and Essa use photographic images as source material, analyse them down into brush-strokes decorated with parameters which may be interpreted in different ways to achieve different appearances, then use optical flow analysis to determine how to interpolate the brush-strokes. In our approach the artist applies the strokes to obtain the visual effect wanted — which requires a real-time simulation — then an in-betweener interpolates the stroke trajectories.

While the idea of simulating the physical effects of drawing tools has been presented before [12, 13] it is also the case that the stability of the renderings in animation has been identified as a continuing research problem. Existing methods of toon rendering [14, 15] and painterly rendering [16, 17, 18] have to build 3D models or infer them [19]. Such approaches swiftly run into being too '3D-ish': the enforcement of the geometric, illumination and shading rules of the model often give a salient sense of the 3D aspects of a scene inappropriate to the intended staging the animator seeks. Of course a view-dependent layered model [20] could be extracted from an underlying 3D model but that still doesn't help us when we want the idea of the 3D in an scene to be unobtrusive or even exaggerated. In the end, rendering directly from a drawing means that shading, texturing and lighting (e.g. highlights) are all mixed up together and so are wholly a product of the artist's vision with an appearance finally determined by the last brush stroke. In 3D they are all separate and for the most part independent, making reworking a technical guessing game. How, for example can one manage the behaviour of the textures if you want them to be part of the animation? With direct control this is possible but models and interpretations of models make the problem far more difficult.

2.3 The Limits of Traditional 2D Animation

Our work has been focused on topics which are very hard to impossible for animators to do by hand and are the sorts of things animators would like to have automated. These include highly-rendered strip cartoon (*bande dessinnée*) styles with *faux* lighting and shading effects, 'difficult' materials which are visually appealing, and some aspects which are currently impossible to handle in animation. These include: avoiding 'boiling' or instabilities on highly rendered images, (e.g. smooth airbrush style, *Carte à Gratter Noire*, childrens' book illustrations, watercolours etc.), and topics like very slow movements and varying perspectives on complex mechanisms which we are not tackling here. In fact these last are best handled using explicit modelling whether or not wholly 3D. Childrens' books in particular often contain beautiful, highly rendered images which give the story much of their charm but they are often made with materials which are impossible to manage in animation by manual means or are impracticably expensive to animate. The methods we describe here are aimed at making this potential business a practical proposition.

While abandoning 3D models seems a retrograde step [21] in view of the elaborate machinery which 3D graphics and animation provide, our argument is that it is that very machinery which gets in the way when an artist turns to achieve a given look or staging. So far we have focused on giving artists direct access to intuitive, even familiar, methods for deriving the finished look although the extended structures they have built need controls of their own to keep the creative process manageable and this is an on-going task. The examples we show here are all studies carried out for the express purpose of understanding how to provide convenient and productive interface to these techniques and the evaluations of the experiences of creating these examples are themselves data we are currently interpreting. For example, many of the rendering techniques impose secondary patterns in the form of textures and these, too, need to be the subject of animation management processes. For example the *Carte à Gratter Noire* style imposes a texture in the form of the prevailing directions of the scraper tool as it cuts the surface. On a static background they take up orientations which vary only as the notional camera position moves but on a foreground object they will reorient not only to match the virtual camera but also the movements of the foreground character as it is affected by plays of light and shadow. The problem here is not what the textures do in the foreground or the background but what happens where the textures join. One imagines an intermediate area in which the behaviour of the texture is the dominant character and it has to somehow integrate foreground and background. While an artist can decide what to do here no obvious 3D model, as is often invoked to deal with issues of varying lighting in NPAR, comes to mind.

3 Data Path of Highly Stylised Drawn Animation

In this section we describe the data path to be followed to create highly stylised animations.

3.1 Overview

Figure 2 depicts a schematic overview of the main parts of the data path.

Starting from a blank canvas, a stylised brush tool (simulating a particular style) is first used to freely draw extreme poses of characters. Each drawing of an extreme pose is built up of a collection of 2D drawn strokes which are manually grouped into layers. Each layer is assigned a place in the Hierarchical Display Model (HDM).

Next, multiple HDMs are created for the same character, each instance corresponding to a specific view (another extreme pose) of the character. A collection of HDMs essentially reintroduces some correspondence information to the 2D drawings needed later for in-betweening and, hence, substitutes for a true 3D model.

Once the extreme poses are properly composed, the animation phase can start. The animator first defines keyframes by specifying extreme poses/HDMs in time. Next, corresponding brush trajectories defined by the HDMs of the keyframes are then in-betweened automatically across intermediate frames. Finally, each HDM of each generated in-between frame is traversed and all elements are drawn one on another from back to front.

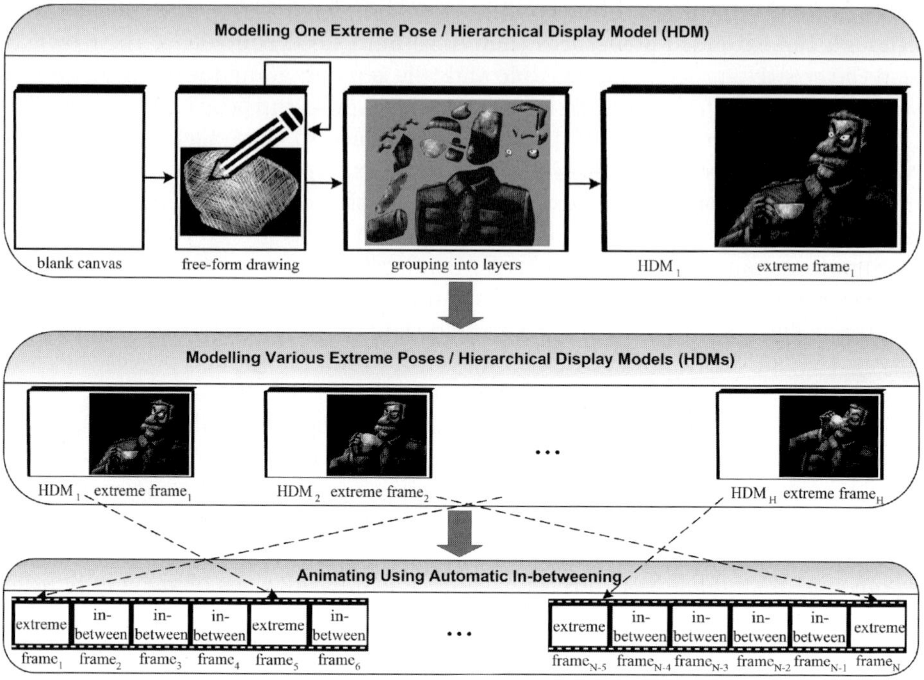

Fig. 2. Schematic overview of the main parts of the data path

The following subsections describe the data path in detail. We start with a description of how to simulate highly rendered styles which are particularly difficult (if not impossible) to animate by traditional means (being traditional 2D handcrafted techniques or traditional 3D animation techniques). Next, the different stages of the data path are elucidated: modelling, manipulating and animating stylised drawings.

3.2 Simulation of Highly Rendered Styles

As we are interested in creating stylised animations, all simulated styles will be based on drawing using a free-form sketching tool [22] which is similar to what is available in any professional-standard vector drawing program.

In our system the creation of a stroke is done interactively by sampling a stylus along the trail of the stroke. Our freeform curve model is that of a Bézier chain. However, instead of approximating the Bézier chain by polylines, purpose-made drawing primitives are employed including paint and air brushes, crayon textures, cross hatched strokes, and pigment particles. All these drawing primitives fully utilise graphics hardware including multi texturing and anti-aliased rendering. This way the artist gets visual feedback immediately. The following subsections give an overview of the realised highly rendered styles.

Airbrush. Figure 3 depicts the pipeline of the paintbrush tool [23]. The tool creates three objects: (i) a colour layer with (ii) a mask, and (iii) a temporary bitmap layer. Depending on the user input from the canvas, the tool renders the brush into the mask. Circular brushes have the following parameters: radius, opacity, and softness. The mask is a greyscale image used to mask painting. Using this mask, the colour layer is rendered into the working layer. Rendering the colour just copies the colour into the destination layer. Brushes can overlap each other and will create more opaque areas. An airbrush not only releases paint on movement, but at regular intervals while the stylus is down.

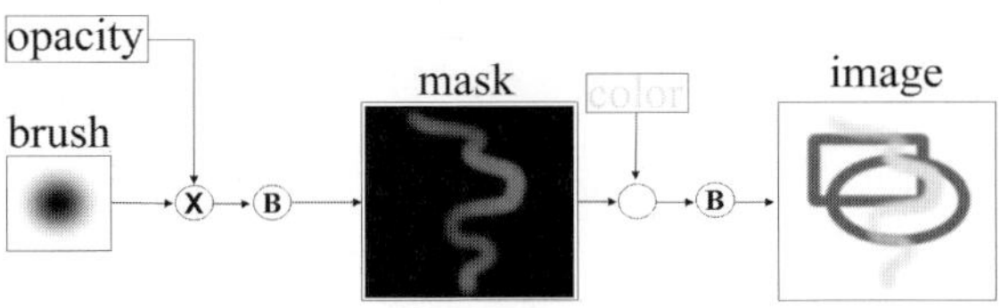

Fig. 3. Pipeline of the airbrush tool

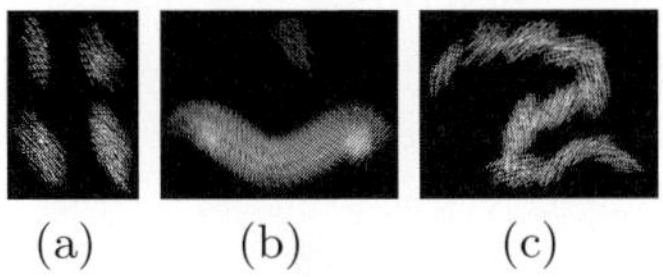

Fig. 4. a) Pressure sensitive scraperboard paintbrush. b–c) Cross hatched strokes.

Scraperboard (*Carte à Gratter Noire*). For the *Carte à Gratter Noire* style the airbrush tool is adapted. Instead of the circular brush that is procedurally created using the softness and radius parameters, the user is allowed to import a sequence of textured bitmaps which are used as one pressure sensitive *Carte à Gratter Noire* paintbrush (Figure 4(a)). Figure 4(b) illustrates the effect of a spline made out of cross hatched strokes while Figure 4(c) shows how the pressure controls which brush from the image is used. Furthermore, because the brushes are not circular anymore, an option is available, which links the orientation of the brush to the direction of the stroke.

Crayon. For the crayon style, a paper height map model [18] is used to represent the rough texture of the paper which is frequently used when drawing with chalk sticks. The chalk sticks themselves are simulated using an 1D alpha texture.

Using the points of the strokes, along with width and pressure values, a mesh is created representing the geometry of the strokes [24]. Using the paper height map and the stroke's pressure values, the mesh is coloured using the colour of the chalk stick. Furthermore, an additional 1D alpha texture is used representing the cross section of the chalk stick in order to simulate the soft edges some chalk sticks have (see Figure 5).

Watercolour/Gouache/Ink. The watercolour painting system employed [25] targets the real-time interactive creation of watercolour images. This is in contrast to most existing work on watercolour applications, which is mostly focused

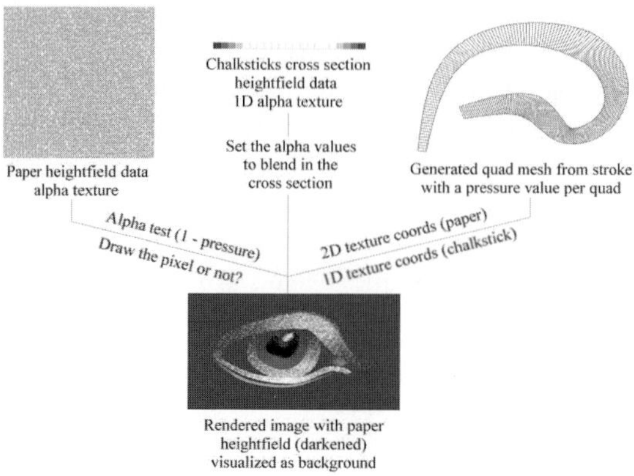

Fig. 5. Schematic overview of the crayon and chalk stick rendering algorithm

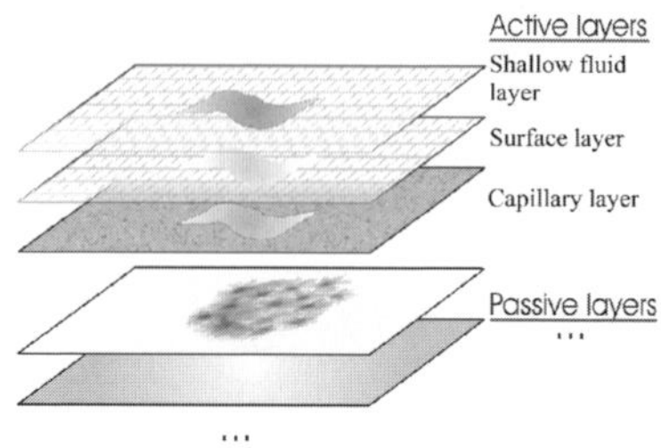

Fig. 6. The canvas model with a layered design

on automatic generation of painterly-style watercolour images from input images. The simulation adopts stable fluid dynamics algorithms to transfer pigment densities and water quantities on top of the canvas. Heuristic rules handle the deposition of pigment within the irregularities of the canvas surface, as well as the evaporation, absorption and capillary diffusion of water inside the canvas structure.

The canvas model has a layered design, consisting of three active layers (shallow, surface and capillary layer) and an unlimited number of passive layers, which are considered to contain previously drawn strokes that have dried and no longer participate in the simulation, except in the final step when the canvas is rendered (Figure 6).

First, some sort of brush puts a mixture of water and pigment onto a paper canvas. At this instant, the paint fluid acts like a flow of water, carrying pigment particles. This 'fluid body' is modelled using the *Navier-Stokes* equations. At some point, depending on the paper fabric, the water will be absorbed into the paper and spread throughout the paper structure. As the pigment particles are too large to be absorbed, they will be deposited on the surface and possibly picked up by the paint fluid later on.

Although the brushes and techniques used in Oriental paintings are very different from those in Western painting, the mechanics of pigment and water are quite similar. For Oriental paintings such as shown in Figure 1(c), the canvas is generally more textured and more absorbent, and the dense black carbon particles are smaller and able to diffuse into the paper. The former property is easily expressed in a watercolour simulation by generating a rougher canvas texture and using a higher absorption constant. Despite the fact that the canvas model does not simulate pigment particles inside the canvas structure, ink diffusion can still be handled by the top layer and produce the typical feathery pattern. The palette consists of very dark pigment with high density.

3.3 Modelling Stylised Drawings

Starting from a blank canvas, the artist starts by using one brush tool (corresponding to one of the styles described in Section 3.2) and freely drawing extreme poses of characters. This corresponds to the drawing of extreme frames by lead animators in traditional animation (see Section 2.1). Each character is built up of a collection of 2D drawn strokes which are imposed one on another. As is illustrated in Figure 7 this process of drawing characters and objects very much resembles traditional painting: first, a basic (rough) image is drawn, and this is followed by adding detail stroke-by-stroke.

Fig. 7. Overview of the drawing process

While each stroke could be placed on a single layer it is far more efficient to group these together into a few layers which would tend to be in-betweened together. In fact layers can be grouped together in the usual way in a drawing hierarchy known as an Hierarchical Display Model (HDM). Figure 8 shows a representation for an HDM for the 'Stalin' figure in *Carte à Gratter Noire.* If each drawing component is thought of as a leaf element the composition steps are shown on the left. Each node of the HDM is the potential recipient of a channel stream which redefines any parameter that might be there, for example an orientation transformation like rotate about an arbitrary axis or a parameterised warp. Typically an animator will make a series of reference drawings to define the action. An example is shown in Figure 9 below. Note that these are all breakdown poses, at least 4 frames apart so the action covers only 2 seconds. In some cases, particularly for figures and heads, it is desirable to make a series of view-dependent studies, for a standing human figure at 45° angles all round

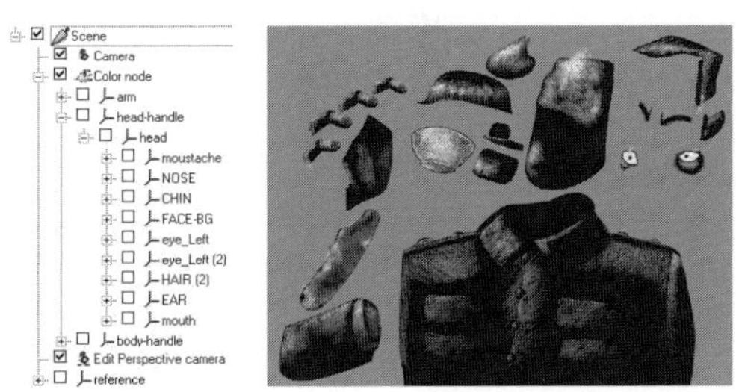

Fig. 8. Stalin drinking a cup of tea. a) Hierarchy Display Model (HDM). b) All separate elements.

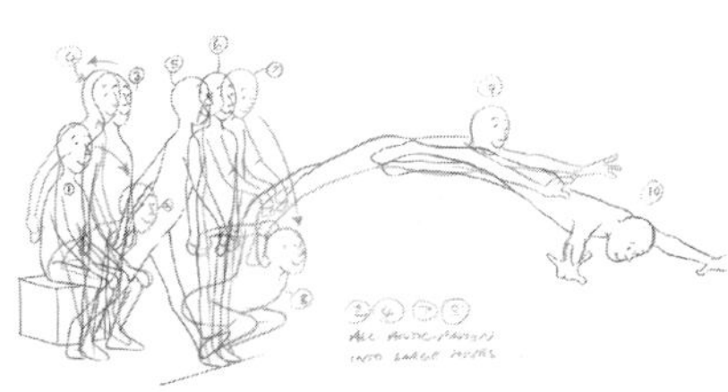

Fig. 9. Sequence showing a dive off the end of a pool from a sitting position © Les Orton 2005

and horizontally, $\pm 45^o$ vertically (and optionally views from above or below). Hierarchies for these are all constructed and these give the rendering order for the elements of the character.

In our system, multiple HDMs for the same character can easily be created by using techniques described in [26] and [6] or simply by altering a duplicate of the original HDM. Each HDM corresponds to a specific view of the character. Consequently, a collection of HDMs for the same character forms the main set of entries of an electronic model sheet for that character and, in effect, substitutes for a true 3D model. Using model sheets like this is usually referred to as 2++D modelling — not 2D but not really 3D either. A collection of HDMs essentially reintroduces some 3D information to the 2D drawings (see Figure 10). Besides brush strokes, other elements can be part of a HDM having its own place in the hierarchy. For example, if lighting and texturing needs to be altered systematically this can be done by adding another layer and managing that layer to provide the desired effect. This will be exemplified by a step by step overview of building up a *Carte à Gratter Noire* version making use of masks and lighting effects. To start the drawing, an area is filled with white strokes (Figure 11(a)). Next, invisibility masks (b) are added to ensure the correctness of the silhouettes. These masks are built up from vectors, without any texture association. Each of these masks will also have its own time line and its independent place in the hierarchy tree. Similar to traditional animation the animator does need to care herself/himself about lighting and shadowing effects by applying the correct densities to create the desired dark and light regions. In this case the animator added some extra layers (c) to obtain a hazy effect (d). These 'hazy layers' separate the different parts and give them a feeling of depth.

Fig. 10. Three HDMs each depicting a specific view of the same character

3.4 Manipulating Stylised Drawings

In this section, we will introduce some tools that enable the animator to manipulate the drawings on a higher level than altering single brush strokes.

We successively implemented a grouping tool, transformation tools, and deformation tools. Each of these tools can operate on both the whole drawing and on a user selected part of the drawing. Existing applications manipulate drawings on a per-pixel basis which results in artifacts because the manipulated parts are cut out and then pasted at a new position. In contrast, due to the use of curve

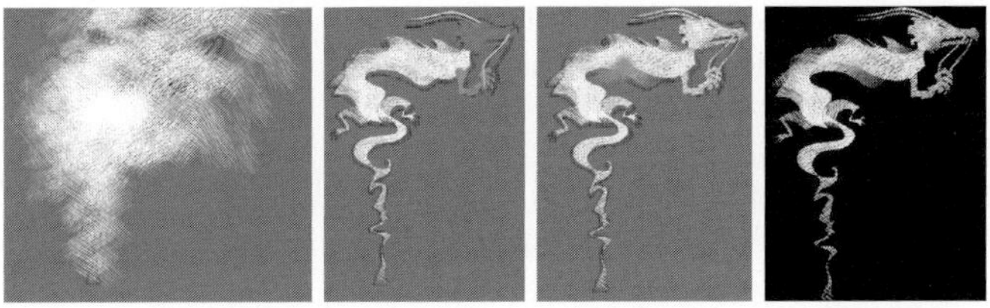

(a) (b) (c) (d)

Fig. 11. Example of applying masks and defining lighting effects

Fig. 12. Subsequent images of a deformation process

primitives, manipulations can also be performed on parts of the drawn character. In our case the manipulation tools (translate, rotate, scale, deform, ...) only affect the control points selected by the grouping tool and so the animator has local control over the drawing while preserving the continuity and connectivity of strokes. As most transformations are rather straightforward to implement, we only highlight the use of locally interpolating subdivision surfaces on model elements in order to realise deformations on the characters to be animated. The locally interpolating nature allows precise control over the shape of the surfaces: the surfaces are attached to specific parts of the hierarchical models, so the deformation realised only affects the control points of the brush strokes targeted. Figure 12 shows the deformation process in action on an airbrushed cat: (a) positioning of top level subdivision surface grid, (b) an additional subdivision step, (c) deformation of the surface and hence the underlying control points of the targeted brushes (in this case: those of the left hind leg), and (d) the final deformed result.

3.5 Animating Stylised Drawings

In the previous sections (Sections 3.3 and 3.4) we focused on the modelling and manipulation of highly stylised drawings. Once the models are properly composed, the animation phase can start:

(i) the animator has to define keyframes by specifying extreme poses in time;
(ii) all brush trajectories defined by the keyframes are then in-betweened automatically across intermediate frames, creating intermediate HDMs;

(iii) all HDMs (extreme as well as intermediate) are traversed and all strokes are drawn one on another from back to front.

Regarding the second step two issues need to be addressed: (i) the correspondence problem should be solved, and (ii) a suitable in-betweening algorithm should be employed. This will be explained in the following subsections.

Correspondence Problem. The use of Hierarchical Display Models (HDMs) to represent various instances (i.e. extreme poses) of a particular drawn image also lends itself to easily find a correspondence between them.

Drawing a collection of HDMs, each depicting a different view of the same character, is currently implemented by using similar techniques as described in [26] and [6] or simply by altering a duplicate of the original HDM (see Section 3.3). As a result, two subsequent HDMs share a large number of subparts and attributed elements (e.g., brush strokes), yet have a different drawing order, and so there is a 1-to-1 mapping between these elements. For the strokes which have no correspondences in the next or previous predefined view, fade-in and fade-out is used in a similar matter to Hays [11].

Furthermore, as our freeform curve model to represent brush strokes is that of a Bézier chain, the curve control points are what are interpolated when in-betweening different instances of the same brush stroke.

In-Betweening Algorithm. As we already have a correspondence between HDMs and a mapping of the shared accompanying elements (e.g., brush stroke parameters), any in-betweening algorithm found in the literature (Section 2.2) could be employed.

In the current system, we use a wholly 2D based 'Moving Reference Point'-inbetweener [26] (based on Reeves' MRP-inbetweener [3]) which, however, lacks the vices that Reeves reports. The Coons patch algorithm used by Reeves sometimes contorts when trying to obey cross-boundary constraints in the absence of twist vectors, producing 'clicks' in the behaviour. As a result, interpolated curves sometimes fold over in the interior of the patch. This contortion can only be controlled by specifying an additional straightforward keyframe constraint. However, Reeves pointed out that it was often necessary to specify many more static keyframes than were wanted when using their version of MRP.

In our implementation, the animator can control the interpolation between more than two keyframes with as many moving points as necessary — by default, each control point is treated as a MRP. This means we have a set of 2D patches, each defining the trajectory and timing between two extreme frames. At run-time, interpolated versions of the patches are created so the MRPs do not necessarily follow the exact paths defined by the patches but instead can follow an intermediate path. As a result, our MRPs do not necessarily pass through all defined keyframes and hence 'clicks' are eliminated in the animated sequence.

4 Examples

In the following subsections several ways to animate are discussed: pose-to-pose animation, step-ahead animation, and performance-driven animation.

4.1 Pose-to-Pose Animation

Drawing or setting up key poses followed by drawing or creating in-between images is referred to as pose-to-pose animation. This is the basic computer keyframe approach to animation and is excellent for fine-tuning, timing, and planning out the animation ahead of time. First, the animator starts with developing/planning the extreme poses of the characters in the modelling phase. Next, once the animator has created the extreme frames, s/he only has to specify keyframes. Finally, the automatic in-betweening method comes into play and generates the desired animation.

The pictures in Figure 13 display an airbrushed cat starting to run. For the animation of the cat the different extreme frames (about 30) were created using the subdivision free-form deformation tool. Afterwards, pose-to-pose animation was used to in-between these keyframes. The background is a 3D background. For the airbrushed mice flying on a paper airplane (Figure 14) about 15 extreme frames were used. 20 extreme frames were involved to create the Gouache simulation of waving flags as shown in Figure 16.

Note that the complexity of the animation involved determines how many extreme poses have to be provided by the animator and thus how much of the in-betweening is left to the system.

4.2 Step-Ahead Animation

In straight-ahead animation the animator draws or sets up objects one frame at a time in sequential order until the sequence is complete. In this way there is one drawing or image per frame that the animator has setup. This approach tends to yield a more creative and fresh look but can be difficult to time correctly, and tweak. Our system supports straight-ahead animation by making use of the subdivision freeform deformation tool (see Section 3.4) which permits the simultaneous control of many MRPs.

Figure 15 shows that it is possible to control the movement of scraperboard rendering both within a shape and around it in a coherent way. For this *Carte à Gratter Noire* animation only step-ahead animation was employed as complex movements are involved: rising smoke transforming itself into an evanescent creature.

4.3 Performance-Driven Animation

The example shown in Figure 17 depicts an animation of a human face which was integrally driven by externally gathered facial motion data. After processing the facial motion data and generating a HDM for each frame, the animation was rendered in a crayon style. Note that for this animation we deliberately

Fig. 13. Airbrush - animation of an airbrushed cat starting to run

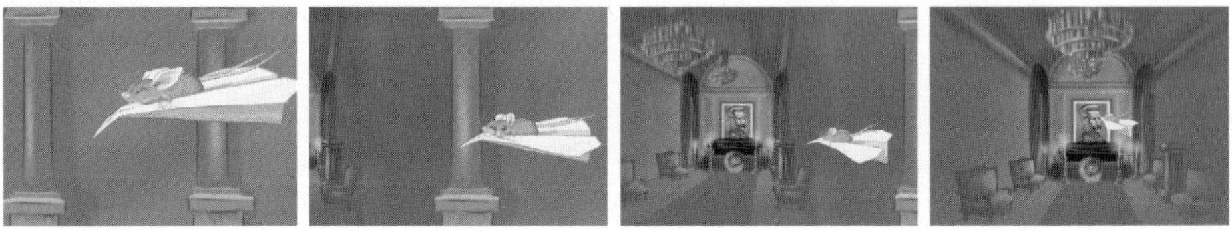

Fig. 14. Airbrush - excerpt of a stylised 2D movie

Fig. 15. Scraperboard - rising smoke transforming into an evanescent dragon

Fig. 16. Gouache - excerpt of a sequence depicting waving flags

Fig. 17. Crayon - some snapshots of an animated sequence of a human face

introduced a 'shower-door' effect by superimposing a paper-like structure on the canvas. We believe this 'shower-door' effect would be the case as well when creating a real physical chalk animation. In addition, the paper texture could be animated as well thereby mitigating the shower-door effect to some extent.

5 Conclusions

In this paper we introduced techniques and tools to draw, manipulate and animate new forms of stylised animation in computer assisted animation production. We focused on realising highly rendered styles which are particularly difficult (if not impossible) to animate by traditional means including the 'airbrushed' style, the scraperboard ('scratched card' or '*Carte à Gratter Noire*') style, the 'watercolour / gouache' style, and the 'crayon' (chalk) style.

The introduction of the physical simulation of materials without reference to 3D models has many implications for animation. It is apparent that the production values of 3D animation can be approached if desired or that styles utterly unlike 3D, yet relying and retaining complex textures and structures, can be handled quite stably. While this has a direct commercial value, making possible many projects which were not possible before, it has a wider value in not only allowing styles which artists have wanted to use in animation for a long time but also to allow effects deemed impossible before, acetates which 'take' watercolour or ink washes, etc. Many strip cartoon styles, which often have quite high-quality artwork in them, imaginatively if unrealistically staged, have been thought unanimatable precisely because of the problem of frame-to-frame stability. No longer.

Discussion. Traditional brush strokes are pixel based and so can be applied immediately which is a cheap operation in terms of processing power. Highly rendered strokes, on the other hand, are based upon curves which are fitted to user input in real-time. As a reference to the geometry of the strokes is stored, they can be animated easily and the brush properties can be changed after they are applied. One issue with highly rendered strokes, however, is the high fill rate which makes the real-time requirement for the drawing process difficult to achieve without graphics acceleration.

The tools and techniques described also create different ways of looking, at the digital tools (created by engineers, but destined to be used by animators, artists and illustrators), at the rigidity of configuration of certain digital 'traditions' inherited from 3D (the timeline, for example), as well as at the relevance of certain fundamental working practices that require a rather laborious apprenticeship. Moreover, these techniques also point to abundant and fruitful exchanges between software engineers and artists in an attempt to find solutions to these various problems.

Future Work. We have limited ourselves in this paper to the issue of character drawing and backgrounds only where it has been a matter of rendering style and supporting it. Composition is an equally important component of the model and we will be returning to this topic to do it proper justice in due course. The reader should be thinking about simulation of the acetate stack, the separation of colour and illumination, and all the many effects which a Rostrum camera is capable of with real physical materials.

Also to be fair to 3D NPR techniques, there are aspects of lighting and proportion that 3D models can give which are difficult to imagine for non-skilled artists. In the future we want to explore the suitability of a system that combines the 2D capabilities of our system with 3D shading results shown as a visual reference only.

Acknowledgements

We gratefully express our gratitude to the European Fund for Regional Development (ERDF), the Flemish Government and the Flemish Interdisciplinary institute for Broadband Technology (IBBT), which are kindly funding part of the research at the Expertise Centre for Digital Media. Part of the work is also funded by the European research project IST-2001-37116 'CUSTODIEV'. Many thanks go also to Xemi Morales for his artistic contribution.

References

1. Patterson, J.W., Willis, P.J.: Computer assisted animation: 2D or not 2D? The Computer Journal **37**(10) (1994) 829–839
2. Blair, P.: Cartoon Animation. Walter Foster Publishing Inc., ISBN: 1-56010-084-2 (1994)
3. Reeves, W.: Inbetweening for computer animation utilizing moving point constraints. Computer Graphics **15**(3) (1981) 263–269
4. Sederberg, T.W., Greenwood, E.: A physically based approach to 2D shape blending. Computer Graphics **26** (1992) 25–34
5. Ranjian, V., Fournier, A.: Matching and interpolation of shapes using unions of circles. Computer Graphics Forum **15** (1996) 129–142
6. Kort, A.: Computer aided inbetweening. NPAR2002: Symposium on Non-Photorealistic Animation and Rendering (2002) 125–132
7. Burtnyk, N., Wein, M.: Computer-generated key-frame animation. Journal of the Society Motion Picture and Television Engineers **8**(3) (1971) 149–153
8. Shapira, M., Rappoport, A.: Shape blending using a star-skeleton representation. IEEE Computer Graphics and Applications **15** (1995) 44–51
9. Yu, J., Patterson, J.W.: Object deformation using quaternions. In: Proceedings of Eurographics UK Chapter 14th Annual Conference. (1996) 75–88
10. Agarwala, A., Hertzmann, A., Salesin, D., Seitz, S.: Keyframe-based tracking for rotoscoping and animation. In: Proceedings of SIGGRAPH, ACM (2004) 584–591
11. Hays, J., Essa, I.: Image and video based painterly animation. NPAR2004: Symposium on Non-Photorealistic Animation and Rendering (2004) 113–120
12. Hertzmann, A.: Painterly rendering with curved brush strokes of multiple sizes. In: Proceedings of SIGGRAPH, ACM (1998) 453–460

13. Hertzmann, A., Perlin, K.: Painterly rendering for video and interaction. NPAR2000: Symposium on Non-Photorealistic Animation and Rendering (2000) 7–12
14. Decaudin, P.: Modélisation par Fusion de Formes 3D pour la Synthèse d'Images - Rendu de Scènes 3D Imitant le Style "Dessin Animé". PhD thesis, Université de Technologie de Compiegne (France) (1996)
15. Lake, A., Marshall, C., Harris, M., Blackstein, M.: Stylized rendering techniques for scalable real-time 3D animation. NPAR2000: Symposium on Non-Photorealistic Animation and Rendering (2000) 13–20
16. Meier, B.J.: Painterly rendering for animation. In: Proceedings of SIGGRAPH. Volume 25(4)., ACM (1996) 477–484
17. Daniels, E.: Deep canvas in Disney's Tarzan. In: Conference abstracts and applications of SIGGRAPH, New York, NY, USA, ACM Press (1999) 200
18. Kalnins, R.D., Markosian, L., Meier, B.J., Kowalski, M.A., Lee, J.C., Davidson, P.L., Webb, M., Hughes, J.F., Finkelstein, A.: WYSIWYG NPR: drawing strokes directly on 3D models. In: Proceedings of SIGGRAPH, ACM (2002) 755–762
19. Cohen, J.M., Hughes, J.F., Zeleznik, R.C.: Harold: A world made of drawings. NPAR2000: Symposium on Non-Photorealistic Animation and Rendering (2000) 83–90
20. Rademacher, P.: View-dependent geometry. In Rockwood, A., ed.: Proceedings of SIGGRAPH, Los Angeles, ACM, Addison Wesley Longman (1999) 439–446
21. Catmull, E.: The problems of computer-assisted animation. In: Proceedings of SIGGRAPH. Volume 12(3)., ACM (1978) 348–353
22. Vansichem, G., Wauters, E., Van Reeth, F.: Real-time modeled drawing and manipulation of stylized cartoon characters. In: Proceedings of the IASTED International Conference on Computer Graphics and Imaging, Honolulu, HI, USA, IASTED (2001) 44–49
23. Di Fiore, F., Van Reeth, F.: Modelling in 2D enabling fluid stylised animation. In: Proceedings of GraphiCon, International Conference on Computer Graphics & Vision. (2003) 124–130
24. Northrup, J.D., Markosian, L.: Artistic silhouettes: A hybrid approach. NPAR2000: Symposium on Non-Photorealistic Animation and Rendering (2000) 31–37
25. Van Laerhoven, T., Van Reeth, F.: Real-time simulation of watery paint. Computer Animation and Virtual Worlds (2005) 429–439
26. Flerackers, C.: New algorithms and techniques in 2.5d animation. Master's thesis, Transnationale Universiteit Limburg (2002)

Non-uniform Differential Mesh Deformation

Dong Xu, Hongxin Zhang, and Hujun Bao

State Key Laboratory of CAD&CG, Zhejiang University, P.R. China
{xudong, zhx, bao}@cad.zju.edu.cn

Abstract. In this paper, we propose a novel mesh deformation approach via manipulating differential properties non-uniformly. Guided by user-specified material properties, our method can deform the surface mesh in a non-uniform way while previous deformation techniques are mainly designed for uniform materials. The non-uniform deformation is achieved by material-dependent gradient field manipulation and Poisson-based reconstruction. Comparing with previous material-oblivious deformation techniques, our method supplies finer control of the deformation process and can generate more realistic results. We propose a novel detail representation that transforms geometric details between successive surface levels as a combination of dihedral angles and barycentric coordinates. This detail representation is similarity-invariant and fully compatible with material properties. Based on these two methods, we implement a multiresolution deformation tool, which allows the user to edit a mesh inside a hierarchy in a material-aware manner. We demonstrate the effectiveness and robustness of our methods by several examples with real-world data.

1 Introduction

Mesh deformation has been widely studied in computer graphics. Most existing techniques, such as freeform deformations, multiresolution techniques and recently introduced differential domain methods are mainly designed to propagate the deformation imposed by the user evenly into the influence region. However, real world object often contains parts with different materials. Given outside forces, for a certain part how it deforms is determined by its corresponding material properties. Using material-oblivious deformation techniques to edit objects with non-uniform material properties often produces implausible results with unnatural shape artifacts.

In this paper, we present a novel mesh deformation technique that allows the surface mesh to be deformed in a non-uniform way. It is based on material-dependent Poisson equations and supplies non-uniform controls in both the propagation process and the reconstruction process. The user is involved into the deformation process by setting material properties to indicate non-uniform regions while the rest takes the default value. These user-specified material properties guide the propagation of local transformations as well as the reconstruction to absolute coordinates. Our method inherits the advantages of differential domain methods and provides more flexible control of the deformation process. In particular, surface details can be well preserved during the deformation, and in a material-aware manner.

To facilitate the editing of large meshes, we further extend our non-uniform deformation technique into a multiresolution version. Multiresolution techniques have been

H.-P. Seidel, T. Nishita, and Q. Peng (Eds.): CGI 2006, LNCS 4035, pp. 54–65, 2006.

proved to be powerful to process gigantic models. However, lack of material-dependent mechanism prevents existing multiresolution deformation approaches to be adapted for our purpose. Instead we propose a novel detail representation that transforms geometric details between successive surface levels as a combination of dihedral angles and barycentric coordinates. This detail representation is similarity-invariant while existing representations, such as local frame displacements [1,2,3] and displacement volumes [4], are rigid-invariant. More importantly, the similarity-invariant detail representation is fully compatible with material properties. Based on it, the user can edit the simplified base mesh with our single-resolution non-uniform editor and obtain the detailed result automatically.

The rest of this paper is organized as follows. After briefly reviewing the prior arts with a focus on multiresolution techniques and differential domain methods in Section 2, we present the non-uniform deformation technique in Section 3. In Section 4 we elaborate how to perform non-uniform deformations in the multiresolution context. We demonstrate that more realistic results can be generated with the help of material properties in Section 5. Finally, we draw conclusions and point out possible future work in Section 6.

2 Related Work

Our approach builds on recently introduced differential domain methods [5] that represents surface details as differential properties. These approaches manipulate differential properties and reconstruct vertex coordinates via solving a sparse linear system. They have a valuable feature that geometric details can be well-preserved during the editing process. Since differential properties are only translation-invariant, they must be properly transformed according to user interactions. The determination of local transformations can be achieved by either explicit interpolation [6,7,8] or implicit fitting [9]. Zhou et al. [10] extend the Laplacian coordinates to the volumetric graph to address problems with large mesh deformations. However, all of these approaches regard the edited mesh to be made up of a uniform material, thus lacking of additional control of the

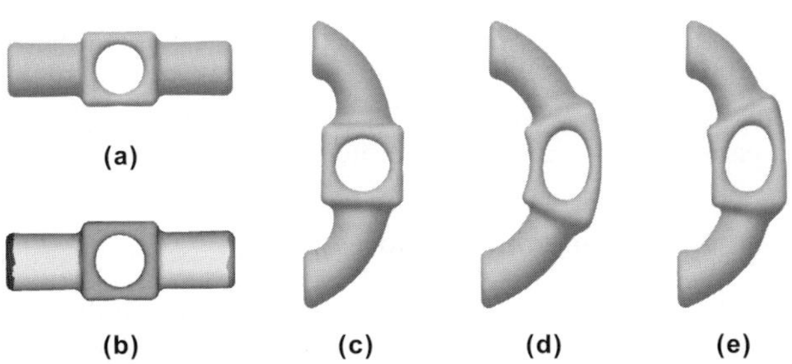

Fig. 1. Mesh deformation with non-uniform control. (a) is the original model; (b) is the color plot of user-specified materials, the green region is the handle and the blue region is the constraint; (c) and (d) are results generated with and without non-uniform control respectively; (e) is the result generated with the non-uniform propagation but with the uniform reconstruction.

deformation process. Based on this observation, we extend differential domain methods to supply position-dependent control by incorporating user-specified material properties.

In the context of boundary constraint modeling, Botsch and Kobbelt [11] propose a freeform modeling framework based on a family of linear differential equations. They point out that the deformation in certain direction can be enhanced by explicitly shrinking the underlying parameter domain in the same direction, which affects the discretization of Laplacian operator consequently. Our method achieves more general control of the deformation by allowing the user to specify per-face material properties, which implicitly modifying the domain mesh in a non-linear manner. Material properties have also been considered by Popa et al. [12] to control the propagation of local transformations. Our method differs in the way that we also consider material properties in the reconstruction process (See Figure 1).

Multiresolution technique has been introduced into computer graphics community for more than ten years [13]. Some approaches depend on semi-regular meshes [1] while others work on irregular meshes directly [2, 3, 11]. Most multiresolution editing techniques manipulate a static surface hierarchy, but vertex connectivity of the base surface [14] or the hierarchy itself [15] can also be dynamically rearranged during large deformations. These approaches share a common aspect that geometric details between successive levels are encoded as local frame displacements. These displacements can be scalars along the normal directions [16] or vectors [1, 2, 3]. Since local frame displacements are handled individually, the reconstructed detailed surface may have unnatural volume changes when the base surface endures large deformations. Consequently, Botsch and Kobbelt [4] propose to use displacement volumes instead. Displacement volumes are kept locally constant during the reconstruction process to preserve volume and avoid local self-intersections. However, both local frame displacements and local volumes do not support material-dependent reconstructions, making us exploring a new detail representation.

3 Mesh Editing with Non-uniform Control

Previous differential domain methods deform surfaces in a material-oblivious way. In this section, we present how to enhance these techniques by incorporating user-specified non-uniform materials. With the non-uniform control mechanism, the deformation process can be tuned in a finer granularity than previous differential domain methods. Therefore, more realistic results can be generated easily.

3.1 Material-Dependent Poisson Equation

A simple form of Poisson equation have been successfully applied to the context of mesh editing [6]. In physics a more general form of this elliptic equation is used to describe the phenomena of steady-state heat conduction in a 3D solid medium. Commonly, the exact form in 3D Euclidian space is

$$\Delta_{\kappa} T = \frac{\partial}{\partial x}\left(\kappa_x \frac{\partial T}{\partial x}\right) + \frac{\partial}{\partial y}\left(\kappa_y \frac{\partial T}{\partial y}\right) + \frac{\partial}{\partial z}\left(\kappa_z \frac{\partial T}{\partial z}\right) = -q_v. \quad (1)$$

Here T is a steady-state temperature field, q_v is the source term in the interior. And κ_x, κ_y and κ_z are speed functions, namely thermal conductivities along three axial directions. Therefore, different solid medium results different steady-state temperature field even under the same set of boundary conditions. This basic observation motivates us to use material-dependent control for differential mesh editing.

In this paper we only consider isotropic materials, i.e, $\kappa_x = \kappa_y = \kappa_z = \kappa$. When κ is constant, Eq. (1) describes a uniform material case which is applied in [6]. In the following we explore the Poisson equation defined on surfaces with non-uniform materials, and the thermal conductivity κ is a scalar field on manifold surface.

Since we adopt triangle meshes as the underlying surface representation, we have to discretize material-dependent differential operators on 2-manifold meshes. For this purpose, we first briefly review the uniform case, i.e., the standard differential operators used in [6]. Given a piecewise linear scalar field $f(\mathbf{v}) = f_i\phi_i(\mathbf{v})$ defined on a 3D mesh, the gradient operator is defined as $\nabla f(\mathbf{v}) = f_i\nabla\phi_i(\mathbf{v})$, where f_i is the scalar value on vertex $\mathbf{v}_i$, $\phi_i(\mathbf{v})$ is the piecewise linear basis and $\nabla\phi_i(\mathbf{v})$ is its gradient. Given a piecewise constant vector field $\mathbf{w}$, the divergence of the vector field $\mathbf{w}$ is defined as

$$\nabla\cdot\mathbf{w}(\mathbf{v}_i) = \sum_{T\in N_T(\mathbf{v}_i)} A_T\nabla\phi_i^T\cdot\mathbf{w}, \tag{2}$$

where $N_T(\mathbf{v}_i)$ is the adjacent triangle set of the vertex $\mathbf{v_i}$ and A_T is the area of the triangle T. Combining the gradient operator and the divergence operator, we get the Laplacian operator

$$\Delta f(\mathbf{v}_i) = \frac{1}{2}\sum_{j\in N_\mathbf{v}(\mathbf{v}_i)} (\cot\alpha_{ij} + \cot\beta_{ij})(f_i - f_j), \tag{3}$$

where $N_\mathbf{v}(\mathbf{v}_i)$ is the adjacent vertex set of the vertex $\mathbf{v}_i$, α_{ij} and β_{ij} are two opposite angles of the edge $(\mathbf{v}_i, \mathbf{v}_j)$.

Now we extend the above procedure to the material-dependent case. We assume that the material property κ is a piecewise constant function i.e., $\kappa \equiv \kappa_T$ in a triangle T. Note that the thermal conductivity terms are attached after first partial differential operator in Eq.1. We thus define material-dependent gradient of basis $\phi_i(\cdot)$ as $\kappa_T\nabla\phi_i^T$. In other words, the gradient of the pieces linear basis is resized according to its material property. Then we can represent the material-dependent divergence operator as

$$\nabla_\kappa\cdot\mathbf{w}(\mathbf{v}_i) = \sum_{T\in N_T(\mathbf{v}_i)} \kappa_T A_T\nabla\phi_i^T\cdot\mathbf{w}, \tag{4}$$

and the material-dependent Laplacian operator as

$$\Delta_\kappa f(\mathbf{v}_i) = \frac{1}{2}\sum_{j\in N_\mathbf{v}(\mathbf{v}_i)} (\kappa_{j-1}^2\cot\alpha_{ij} + \kappa_j^2\cot\beta_{ij})(f_i - f_j). \tag{5}$$

Given the guidance field $\mathbf{w}$ and boundary conditions $f_i = f_i^*, \mathbf{v}_i \in \partial\Omega$, we get the material-dependent Poisson equations:

$$\Delta_\kappa f = \nabla_\kappa\cdot\mathbf{w}. \tag{6}$$

3.2 Non-uniform Propagation

To ensure visually desirable deformation results, local transformations imposed by user interactions must be propagated (weighted with a fall-off function) into the region of interest (ROI) smoothly. Inspired by [7], we consider the material-dependent propagation as a analogy of the heat conduction in a non-uniform medium. Here, material properties are interpreted as their thermal conductivity. The scalar field function f guided the propagation process can be computed by the following material-dependent Laplace equation:

$$\Delta_{\kappa} f = 0, \tag{7}$$

where Δ_{κ} is material-dependent Laplacian operator (See Eq. 5).

Actually, the propagation field f is equivalent to the steady-state temperature field with boundary temperatures set to be 1 on handle vertices and 0 on constrained vertices. f is also the minimizer of the following energy function:

$$\min_{f} \int_{\Omega} \|\kappa(\omega)\nabla f\|^2 d\omega, \tag{8}$$

where $\kappa(\omega)$ is the user-specified material property as thermal conductivity. Intuitively, if the user wants to keep some regions as rigid as possible, he/she can set the material properties of these regions with a large value. On the contrary, if the user expects certain regions to be freely deformed, he/she can set them with a small value.

After the propagation field f is solved, we use it as the fall-off function to weight local transformations. For rotation transformation, we use f to multiply the rotation angle while for scaling transformation, we adopt f to linearly interpolate between the scaling ratio r and 1 (no scale). Then we combine these local transformations together according to the user-selected transformation option.

3.3 Non-uniform Reconstruction

The propagation process assigns a local transformation to each triangle and we obtain guidance vectors by applying it to original gradient vectors. Unlike [6], we consider material properties in the reconstruction process as well. The Poisson mesh solver used in [6] can be regarded as a special case of our material-dependent one. Our method is equivalent to the minimization of the following energy:

$$\min_{f} \int_{\Omega} \kappa^2(\omega) \|\nabla f - \mathbf{w}\|^2 d\omega. \tag{9}$$

Note that the material-dependent Laplacian operator (cf. Eq. 5) defined on a domain mesh M with a non-uniform material can be regarded as a standard one (cf. Eq. 3) defined on another domain mesh M' with a uniform material. The relationship between M and M' lies in for each edge $(\mathbf{v}_i, \mathbf{v}_j)$, the following equation is satisfied:

$$\kappa_{j-1}^2 \cot\alpha_{ij} + \kappa_j^2 \cot\beta_{ij} = \cot\alpha'_{ij} + \cot\beta'_{ij}. \tag{10}$$

From this aspect, we can think of that material properties act as the modifying factors of the original domain mesh M.

3.4 The User Interface

We adopt the handle-based editing metaphor. During editing, the user selects the region of interest (ROI) and deforms the mesh by manipulating a small region inside the ROI, called handle. The user manipulates the handle with a 9 degree-of-freedom manipulator. Besides this editing interface, we design a simple pick-and-drag interface that only takes the pure translation of the handle as the input. In addition, user can paint different parts of ROI with different colors that represent corresponding materials. After the user drags the handle, our method automatically induces the necessary rotation and scaling for the ROI as well as the handle itself.

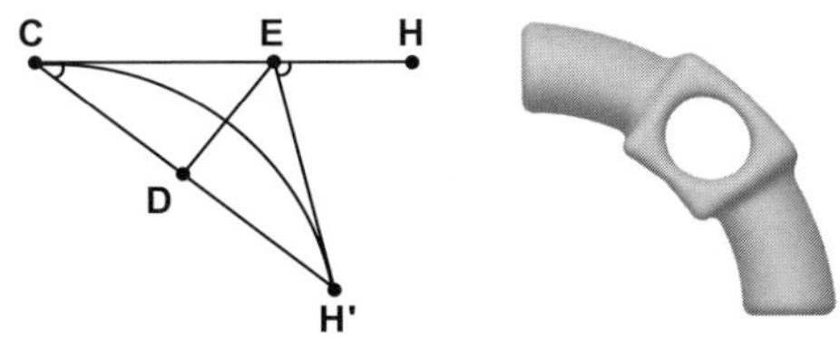

Fig. 2. Illustration of the determination of local transformations from the handle movement

The basic idea of determining the rotation and scaling from the handle movement comes from the Hermite interpolation, as shown in Figure 2. Let C denotes the center of the boundary connecting constrained vertices and free vertices, H denotes the center of handle vertices and $H^{'}$ denotes the new center of handle vertices after translation. Note that the three points C, H and $H^{'}$ can uniquely determine a plane provided they are not degenerate. The rotation axis $\mathbf{a}$ can be easily determined by the cross product of two vectors $\overrightarrow{HC}$ and $\overrightarrow{H^{'}C}$. The scaling factor s is defined to be the ratio between the length of $\overrightarrow{H^{'}C}$ and that of $\overrightarrow{HC}$. The left problem is to define the rotation angle. We consider the circle passing through two points C and $H^{'}$ and tangent to the vector $\overrightarrow{HC}$ at the point C. Then, we define the rotation angle θ to be $\angle(HEH^{'})$, where the point E is the intersection of the line $\overrightarrow{HC}$ and the perpendicular bisector of the line $\overrightarrow{H^{'}C}$. Actually, the angle θ is twice the angle $\angle(HCH^{'})$. Therefore, we do not need to construct the circle at all. Provided the three points C, H and $H^{'}$ are coplanar, we simply ignore the rotation transformation. We supply several options to support different combination of these local transformations. These estimated local transformations are propagated into the ROI (See Section 3.2) to generate guidance fields and the deformed surface mesh is reconstructed with Poisson equations (See Section 3.3).

4 Multiresolution Non-uniform Editing

The multiresolution paradigm is an efficient way to deforming large meshes with complex geometric details. Typically, a multiresolution editing framework consists of three major components - the decomposition component, the reconstruction component and the deformation component. Since the non-uniform control of mesh deformation is the focus of this paper, in this section we show how to achieve this goal in the multiresolution scenario. Note that the decomposition component is independent to material properties as a pre-processing step while the rest two are material-dependent.

4.1 Mesh Decomposition and Detail Encoding

Aiming at editing large meshes, we employ the Progressive Mesh (PM) [17] to represent the surface hierarchy. A PM is created by recursively applying edge-collapse operations to a detailed input mesh. In a PM representation, the edge-collapse and the vertex-split are atomic operations for the decomposition component and the reconstruction component respectively. Note that in both operations, only the central one or two vertices' coordinates are modified while all the rest do not change their position. This observation is particularly important since it allows us to localize the detail encoding and decoding procedures only with respect to the local stencil of a given edge.

After the surface hierarchy is created, geometric details between successive levels need to be encoded. Geometric details are typically defined as the difference between the original geometry and the approximated smoothed geometry. We consider the membrane surface as the smoothed approximation, which can be obtained by solving a Laplace equation defined on the local stencil of the given edge e, denoted as $L(e)$ with Dirichlet boundary conditions given by vertex coordinates on the boundary $\partial L(e)$. Since only two free vertices in the local stencil, the corresponding Laplace equation is a linear system with two equations:

$$\begin{bmatrix} a & b \\ b & c \end{bmatrix} \begin{bmatrix} \mathbf{v}_1 \\ \mathbf{v}_2 \end{bmatrix} = \begin{bmatrix} \mathbf{u}_1 \\ \mathbf{u}_2 \end{bmatrix}, \tag{11}$$

where a, b, c come from Eqn. 3 and $\mathbf{u}_1$ and $\mathbf{u}_2$ are boundary conditions.

We adopt the original geometry to define the Laplacian operator so that we can smooth the geometry without affecting the underlying parameterization [18]. The corresponding weights used to define the Laplacian operator can be stored or computed on the fly, trading off speed versus memory. After the smoothed approximation is solved, we define the detail coefficients between a pair of triangles coming from the original geometry and the smoothed approximation respectively (see Figure 3).

Generally speaking, locating one detail triangle $T_1 = (\mathbf{w}_1, \mathbf{w}_2, \mathbf{w}_3)$ with respect to the corresponding base triangle $T_2 = (\mathbf{v}_1, \mathbf{v}_2, \mathbf{v}_3)$ can be decomposed into two steps, which are summarized by nine independent parameters $(x, y, z, \theta_1, \theta_2, \alpha_1, \beta_1, \alpha_2, \beta_2)$ (See Figure 3). The first step aligns the vertex $\mathbf{w}_1$ to the vertex $\mathbf{v}_1$ and the offset vector is (x, y, z). The second step rotates the triangle T_1 along the axis *dir* defined by the cross product of the normal vector $\mathbf{n}_2$ and $\mathbf{n}_1$ so that both triangles are co-planar. The rotation angle θ_1 is equivalent to the dihedral angle between the two triangles. For the sake of the reconstruction process, we need to encode the axis *dir* with respect to the base triangle as well. Since the vector *dir* is co-planar with the base triangle T_2, it can be located by rotating the vector $\mathbf{v}_2 - \mathbf{v}_3$ around the axis $\mathbf{n}_2$ with a rotation angle θ_2. After the second step, we get the rotated detail triangle $T_1' = (\mathbf{w}_1', \mathbf{w}_2', \mathbf{w}_3')$ that lies in the same plane with triangle T_2. Now we can record the coordinates of vertices $\mathbf{w}_2'$ and $\mathbf{w}_3'$ with respect to the triangle $T_2 = (\mathbf{v}_1, \mathbf{v}_2, \mathbf{v}_3)$ and results in the rest four barycentric coordinates $(\alpha_1, \beta_1, \alpha_2, \beta_2)$.

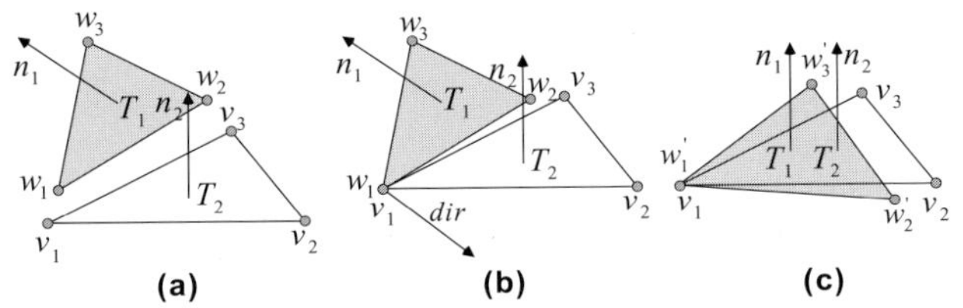

Fig. 3. Encoding a detail triangle T_1 w.r.t. a base triangle T_2

Actually, since our reconstruction method can automatically determine the position of the detailed triangle from the base one, we do not need to record the offset vector (x, y, z). Therefore, our similarity-invariant detail coefficients consist of the rest six parameters $(\theta_1, \theta_2, \alpha_1, \beta_1, \alpha_2, \beta_2)$.

4.2 Detail Reconstruction

After the user performs a material-dependent deformation on a base mesh, we need to reconstruct pre-recorded geometric details with respect to user-specified material properties. There are two issues concerning material-dependent detail reconstruction process. The first one is that material properties specified on the low-resolution mesh should be up-sampled. The second one is each refinement step should take the (up-sampled) material properties into account. We present our solutions in the following paragraphs in details.

Specifically, after a vertex-split operation is performed, we immediately up-sample the material properties. The material property of a newly-split triangle is set to be the weighted average of its adjacent triangles. We adopt the invert-distance as the weighting scheme. Then, a three-step reconstruction process is employed to reconstruct geometric details from previously encoded detail coefficients. The first step is to generate the approximated smoothed geometry by material-dependent Laplace equation(Eqn. 11) with new Dirichlet boundary conditions given by the deformed base surface. Now we can retrieve the detail triangles from the corresponding base triangles one-by-one. In fact, the second step is carried out in the reverse order of the encoding process. First, we determine the intermediate detail triangle $T_1' = (\mathbf{w}_1', \mathbf{w}_2', \mathbf{w}_3')$ using the barycentric coordinates $(\alpha_1, \beta_1, \alpha_2, \beta_2)$ with respect to the base triangle $T_2 = (\mathbf{v}_1, \mathbf{v}_2, \mathbf{v}_3)$. Note that the vertex $\mathbf{w}_1$ is superposed on the vertex $\mathbf{v}_1$. Then, the axis dir is obtained by rotating the vector $\mathbf{v}_2 - \mathbf{v}_3$ around the axis $\mathbf{n}_2$ with the rotation angle θ_2. Finally, the intermediate detail triangle T_1' is rotated around the axis dir with the rotation angle $-\theta_1$, resulting in the detail triangle T_1.

Since the detail triangles have been extracted from the corresponding base triangles independently, the third step is to glue them together and generate the consistent vertex position for the central two vertices come from the vertex-split operation. To serve for the purpose, a local material-dependent Poisson equation is employed. We gather gradient vectors from broken detail triangles as the guidance field, which determines the vertex position together with the new boundary conditions:

$$\begin{bmatrix} a_K & b_K \\ b_K & c_K \end{bmatrix} \begin{bmatrix} \mathbf{v}_1 \\ \mathbf{v}_2 \end{bmatrix} = \begin{bmatrix} \mathbf{u}_1' + \mathbf{w}_1 \\ \mathbf{u}_2' + \mathbf{w}_2 \end{bmatrix}, \tag{12}$$

where a_K, b_K and c_K come from Eqn. 5, $\mathbf{u}_1'$ and $\mathbf{u}_2'$ are new boundary conditions, $\mathbf{w}_1$ and $\mathbf{w}_2$ are the material-dependent divergence of vertex $\mathbf{v}_1$ and $\mathbf{v}_2$ respectively.

Although multiresolution techniques [3] have been employed in the Poisson-based mesh solver [6] for acceleration, our framework differs in the way that it can automatically adapt geometric details to a scaled base surface via incorporating similarity-invariant detail representation. Moreover, our detail reconstruction method is particularly suitable to material-dependent multiresolution editing while previous methods are generally difficult for this purpose.

5 Results and Discussions

Based on techniques presented in Section 3 and Section 4, we implement a multiresolution editing tool for surface meshes. It can work on the single-resolution mode as well as the multi-resolution mode. Our editing tool can run interactively for moderate models with around 20k vertices in the single-resolution mode. In the multi-resolution mode, comparing with local frame displacements, our material-aware detail-reconstruction runs about 10-20% slower.

When editing CAD models, material properties can help certain feature regions to be better preserved. Figure 1(c) demonstrates such a task. The central feature region of the Mechpart model need to be preserved during the resizing of the main body. We achieve this goal by painting these feature regions with a large material valued 5 and perform non-uniform deformation with our technique.

Changing the value of material properties can lead to different deformation effects under the same user interaction. Figure 4 demonstrates several results obtained with different material settings. The default value of material properties is set to 1 and we have found the range $[1,5]$ is enough to simulate most of real world material-dependent deformations. We incrementally paint material properties on the crus part and the foot part with the value 2, and on the thigh part with the value 5. At the same time, we get more and more realistic results as shown in Figure 4 (b), (c) and (d).

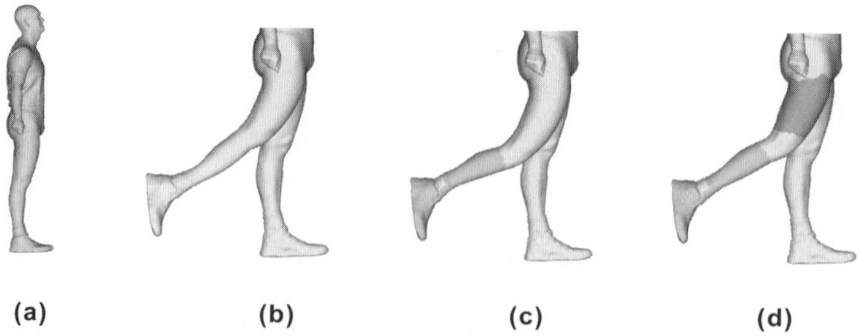

Fig. 4. Deforming the right leg of the Man model with different material settings

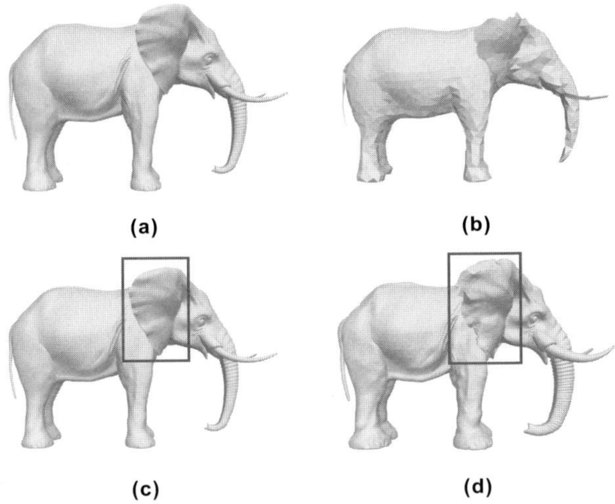

Fig. 5. The ability of similarity-invariance is over-looked in existing detail representations

Figure 5 illustrates and compares results obtained with different detail representations. We simplify the Elephant model (Figure 5 (a)) and reconstruct geometric details from a uniformly shrunken base mesh (Figure 5 (b)). This experiment is fairly simple, but we can clearly distinguish the difference between the result generated with our method (Figure 5 (c)) and that with local frame displacement (Figure 5 (d)). Note that fine details around the elephant's ear are not well-preserved in Figure 5(d) due to the lack of adaptation to arbitrary scaling. Figure 5 (c), (d) are zoomed in two times for better visualization.

Figure 6 shows the Armadillo model kicking a soccer, which is generated with the multiresolution editing mode. We decimate the original model (170k vertices) to a simplified version (15k vertices). We perform three non-uniform edits on the both hands and the right leg of the simplified model. The detailed edited version is automatically reconstructed by our tool with the help of similarity detail coefficients and material properties. See our video submission for the whole editing process.

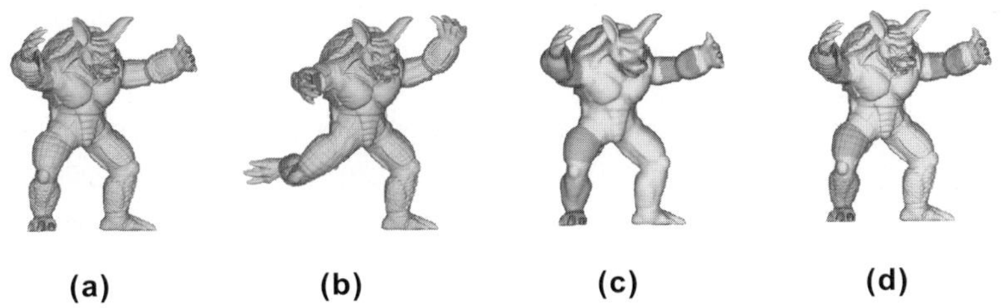

Fig. 6. After applying three non-uniform deformations, the Armadillo model (a) is now ready to kick a soccer (b). (d) is the visualization of material properties on the detailed mesh, which are automatically up-sampled from material properties specified by the user on the base mesh (c).

6 Conclusions and Future Work

In this paper, we propose a novel technique to deform the surface mesh non-uniformly by incorporating user-specified material properties. This goal is achieved by overloading previous material-independent discrete differential operators and Poisson equations. Moreover, we allow multiresolution mesh editing in a material-aware manner by incorporating a novel similarity-invariant detail representation. Several real world examples demonstrate that plausible material-dependent deformation results can be generated by our method easily. As pointed out in Section 3.3, designing a tailored domain mesh for a specific deformation task is a valuable research direction.

Acknowledgement

This work is supported in part by the National Basic 973 Program of China (Grant No. 2002CB312102) and the National Natural Science Foundation of China (Grant Nos. 60021201 and 60505001).

References

1. Zorin, D., Schröder, P., Sweldens, W.: Interactive multiresolution mesh editing. In: Proceedings of ACM SIGGRAPH 1997, ACM Press (1997) 259–268
2. Kobbelt, L., Campagna, S., Vorsatz, J., Seidel, H.P.: Interactive multi-resolution modeling on arbitrary meshes. In: Proceedings of ACM SIGGRAPH 1998, ACM Press (1998) 105–114
3. Guskov, I., Sweldens, W., Schröder, P.: Multiresolution signal processing for meshes. In: Proceedings of ACM SIGGRAPH 1999, ACM Press (1999) 325–334
4. Botsch, M., Kobbelt, L.: Multiresolution surface representation based on displacement volumes. Computer Graphics Forum (Eurographics 2003) **22**(3) (2003) 483–491
5. Sorkine, O.: Laplacian mesh processing. In: Eurographics 2005 STAR report. (2005)
6. Yu, Y., Zhou, K., Xu, D., Shi, X., Bao, H., Guo, B., Shum, H.Y.: Mesh editing with poisson-based gradient field manipulation. ACM Trans. Graph. **23**(3) (2004) 644–651
7. Zayer, R., Rössl, C., Karni, Z., Seidel, H.P.: Harmonic guidance for surface deformation. Comput. Graph. Forum **24**(3) (2005) 601–609
8. Lipman, Y., Sorkine, O., Levin, D., Cohen-Or, D.: Linear rotation-invariant coordinates for meshes. ACM Trans. Graph. **24**(3) (2005) 479–487
9. Sorkine, O., Cohen-Or, D., Lipman, Y., Alexa, M., Rössl, C., Seidel, H.P.: Laplacian surface editing. In: Symposium on Geometry Processing. (2004) 179–188
10. Zhou, K., Huang, J., Snyder, J., Liu, X., Bao, H., Guo, B., Shum, H.Y.: Large mesh deformation using the volumetric graph laplacian. ACM Trans. Graph. **24**(3) (2005) 496–503
11. Botsch, M., Kobbelt, L.: An intuitive framework for real-time freeform modeling. ACM Trans. Graph. **23**(3) (2004) 630–634
12. Popa, T., Julius, D., Sheffer, A.: Material aware mesh deformations. In: Proceedings of ACM SIGGRAPH 2005. (2005) Posters.
13. Eck, M., DeRose, T., Duchamp, T., Hoppe, H., Lounsbery, M., Stuetzle, W.: Multiresolution analysis of arbitrary meshes. In: Proceedings of ACM SIGGRAPH 1995. (1995) 173–182
14. Botsch, M., Kobbelt, L.: A remeshing approach to multiresolution modeling. In: Symposium on Geometry Processing. (2004) 189–196

15. Kobbelt, L., Bareuther, T., Seidel, H.P.: Multiresolution shape deformations for meshes with dynamic vertex connectivity. Comput. Graph. Forum **19**(3) (2000)
16. Guskov, I., Vidimce, K., Sweldens, W., Schröder, P.: Normal meshes. In: Proceedings of ACM SIGGRAPH 2000. (2000) 95–102
17. Hoppe, H.: Progressive meshes. In: Proceedings of ACM SIGGRAPH 1996. (1996) 99–108
18. Desbrun, M., Meyer, M., Schröder, P., Barr, A.H.: Implicit fairing of irregular meshes using diffusion and curvature flow. In: Proceedings of ACM SIGGRAPH 1999. (1999) 317–324

Skeleton-Based Shape Deformation Using Simplex Transformations

Han-Bing Yan[1], Shi-Min Hu[1], and Ralph Martin[2]

[1] Dept. of Computer Science and Technology, Tsinghua University, P.R. China
yanhb02@mails.tsinghua.edu.cn,
shimin@tsinghua.edu.cn
http://cg.cs.tsinghua.edu.cn
[2] School of Computer Science, Cardiff University, U.K.
Ralph.Martin@cs.cardiff.ac.uk
http://ralph.cs.cf.ac.uk

Abstract. This paper presents a novel skeleton-based method for deforming meshes, based on an approximate skeleton. The major difference from previous skeleton-based methods is that they used the skeleton to control movement of vertices, whereas we use it to control the simplices defining the model. This allows errors, that occur near joints in other methods, to be spread over the whole mesh, giving smooth transitions near joints. Our method also needs no vertex weights defined on the bones, which can be tedious to choose in previous methods.

1 Introduction

Mesh deformation is widely used in computer animation and computer modeling. Many techniques have been developed to help artists deform body shapes for 2D and 3D characters, such as free-form deformation (FFD), differential methods, simplex transformation methods, and skeleton-based methods.

The latter use a 'skeleton', in which two or more 'bones' meet at each joint, to control shape deformation. This allows intuitive control, naturally describing the way in which many objects, e.g. animals, deform: the muscles and other tissues follow motions of the underlying bones. Such methods are usually controlled by an user-specified skeleton, rather than the exact medial axis. However, traditional skeleton-based methods are widely criticised for requiring a tedious process of weight selection to obtain satisfactory results. Seemingly, there is no criterion for weight selection which is universally applicable to *all* cases.

This paper presents a novel mesh deformation method which combines the skeleton-based method and the simplex transformation method, with two main differences from traditional skeleton-based methods. Firstly, we use the skeleton to drive the transformation of *simplices*, rather than vertices as in previous methods. Secondly, we avoid the use of *any* weights, yet our approach still gives high quality results.

Our approach can be applied to 2D and 3D meshes. Our inputs are the initial mesh, the initial skeleton—a set of straight line segments connected together at joints, and the deformed skeleton. The output is the deformed mesh.

H.-P. Seidel, T. Nishita, and Q. Peng (Eds.): CGI 2006, LNCS 4035, pp. 66–77, 2006.

The main steps of our method are as follows:

- Decide which bone of the skeleton controls each simplex.
- Find the transformation relating the initial and final position of each bone, and apply it to the simplices under its control.
- Use optimisation to stitch the simplices together while keeping each simplex transformation as close as possible to the value calculated above.

Our main contribution is to provide a skeleton-based deformation method which does not require a tedious weight adjustment process, yet which gives very good results. Our key new idea is to use the bones to control mesh simplices instead of mesh vertices, and hence to take advantage of the connectivity information between vertices. To achieve this, we also present a segmentation approach to determine the correspondence between mesh simplices and the bones.

2 Related Work

One of the best known methods for carrying out deformation, widely used in commercial software, is *FFD*. The classic FFD method [1] encloses a shape in an elastic control lattice, such as a Bézier volume, or a more general lattice [2], then deforms the volume by moving the control vertices: as a result, the shape inside is deformed.

Differential deformation methods have recently become popular [3, 4, 5, 6]. Laplacian coordinates [3] are used to represent surface detail as differences from the local mean. Poisson mesh methods [6] manipulate gradients of the mesh's coordinate functions and then reconstruct the surface using the Poisson equation.

Simplex transformation is another approach to deformation and morphing. The use of global transformations combined with matrix decomposition was proposed in [7] as a means to carry out morphing. This method was extended to local transformations by [8], in which meshes are stitched using an optimization method. Simplex transformation has also been used with surface triangle meshes to perform deformation learnt from existing examples [9, 10].

None of the above methods take into account the way in which shapes' features are naturally controlled. However, the shape and movement of an animal is determined by its skeleton, so the latter provides an intuitive approach to control the deformation of animal-like shapes. Such concepts are also referred to as *skinning*, *envelopes* or *skeletal subspace deformation* [11].

Existing skeleton-based algorithms define the final position of a point as a weighted sum over its initial position projected into n moving coordinate frames, corresponding to the n bones. Its position $\mathbf{p}'$ after deformation is:

$$\mathbf{p}' = \sum_{k=1}^{n} w_k \mathbf{p} M_k, \tag{1}$$

where $\mathbf{p}$ is its initial position, M_k is a transformation matrix that transforms bone k from its initial position to its new position, and w_k is the weight of this point relative to bone k. Because each point is controlled by several bones, careful choice of weights w_k is needed to avoid self-intersections, especially near the joints, and to keep the surface smooth. Appropriate weight selection is an extremely tedious problem if done manually. Much research has focused on how to calculate appropriate weights [12, 13], or how to learn weights from examples [11, 14], but no single method works well in all cases [15]. As a result, [15] proposes that each component of the matrix M_k is given a *separate* weight to provide maximum flexibility, instead of a single weight for the whole matrix. Clearly, this means even more weights must be adjusted, To do so, this method calculates weights from a class of basic deformation shapes.

The underlying problem here is that each point is updated independently using Eqn. 1, which requires the w_i to be carefully chosen to avoid gaps and artifacts. However, the points are embedded in a shape, and are related; the *mesh* provides connectivity information, but it is not directly used. We do so, to our advantage. By retaining skeleton-based control, we still have a natural and easily-understood approach. By using the connectivity information, we avoid the above weight adjustment problem and instead solve a linear equation to perform a similar task. This simpler approach still gives high quality results.

There has been much work on skeleton construction and segmentation, either independently, or doing both at once [16, 17, 18, 19]. We focus on how to segment the model from a given skeleton, as often artists wish to create the skeleton themselves. [19] proposed creating the skeleton and segmentation iteratively, but this changes the skeleton during iteration. [17] showed how to derive a segmentation from a given skeleton using space-sweeping method, but this does not work well if the skeleton is coarse. We give a new effective method to segment the model which considers both spatial distance, and the shortest path distance in the mesh, between each simplex and the bones.

We provide basic concepts concerning simplex transformations and skeletons in Section 3. We first apply our method to 2D triangle meshes in Section 4, then 3D triangle meshes in Section 5. We give conclusions in Section 6.

3 Simplex Transformations and Skeletons

Simplices are triangles in 2D and tetrahedra in 3D. Given two simplices S_1 and S_2 in some space, there exists a unique transformation that changes S_1 into S_2. In 2D, this can be written as: $v_i = Ru_i + T$, where the matrix R represents rotation and shape change information, T is a translation vector, u_i are the vertices of S_1, and v_i are the corresponding vertices of S_2. R and T can be calculated from the vertex coordinates of S_1 and S_2, by first finding R using $R = VU^{-1}$, where in 2D, $V = \begin{bmatrix} v_1 - v_3 \; v_2 - v_3 \end{bmatrix}$, $U = \begin{bmatrix} u_1 - u_3 \; u_2 - u_3 \end{bmatrix}$, and in 3D, $V = \begin{bmatrix} v_1 - v_4 \; v_2 - v_4 \; v_3 - v_4 \end{bmatrix}$, $U = \begin{bmatrix} u_1 - u_4 \; u_2 - u_4 \; u_3 - u_4 \end{bmatrix}$. Having found R, T can now be calculated.

The mathematical skeleton, or *medial axis*, is generally quite complex even for simple 3D shapes, and is sensitive to small perturbations of the shape boundary. It can also contain sheets rather than lines. For simplicity, most skeleton-based deformation methods use an approximate skeleton to control deformation, consisting of articulated straight lines or *bones*. As noted, often, artists prefer to create the skeleton by hand since this is easy to do interactively, and allows appropriate control. The skeleton can also be generated automatically [16, 17].

4 2D Triangle Mesh Deformation

We first consider the case of deforming a 2D triangle mesh in the plane.

4.1 Correspondence Between 2D Triangles and Bones

In our approach, each simplex is controlled by *one* bone, so we need to segment the model according to the given skeleton: deciding which bone controls each 2D triangle is the first step of our algorithm. Only after doing this can we decide how each triangle should deform. We determine the controlling bone as follows:

1. Calculate the minimum *effective distance with penalty* from the simplex to those bones for which it is *within range*.
2. Decide if the minimum *effective distance with penalty* is less than a threshold.
   (a) If so: the bone with the minimum *effective distance with penalty* controls this simplex.
   (b) Otherwise: calculate the *shortest path distance* from the simplex to those bones for which it is within range. The bone with the *shortest path distance* is the control bone.

We now explain the details. Normally, a skeleton lies within the volume defined by the mesh. However, we require that *free* ends of bones (i.e. ends not connected to other bones) must lie just *outside* the mesh, to ensure that each bone properly controls all the triangles in its control domain, as explained later.

Consider Fig. 1. AB, AC, and AD are three bones connected at the articulating joint A. We use *range lines* to define the border of each bones' control domain. The control domain for each bone determines which simplices that bone *may* control. If the centroid of a simplex lies within a given bone's control domain, the bone is a *candidate* for the control bone for that simplex; note that the

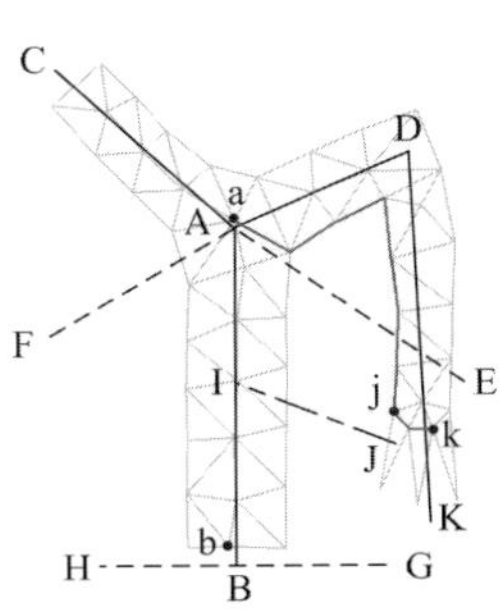

Fig. 1. Range lines

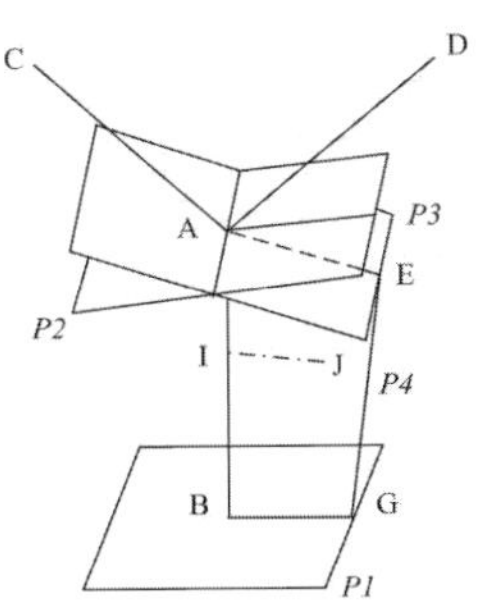

Fig. 2. Range planes

centroid of a given simplex may lie within the control domain of *several* bones. First, we construct *range lines* for each bone. For free ends of bones, like B, the range lines are *perpendicular rays*, like BG and BH. Where several bones meet, we determine the adjacent bones in both clockwise and anticlockwise directions, and draw *bisecting rays* between the current bone and the adjacent bones to give the range lines, like AE and AF. Each such range line divides the plane into 2 parts, one on the same side as the bone, and one on the opposite side. Given any point (or simplex), and a bone, if the point (or centroid of the simplex) lies on the same side as the bone for *all* of the bone's range lines, we say the point (or simplex) is within the *range* of this bone. We can now determine for which bones each simplex is within range.

If a given point J is within the range of some bone, we define its *effective distance* to the bone as follows (see Fig. 1). We find the corresponding point I on the bone AB as explained next; we call line IJ an *effective line* for bone AB. The direction of ray IJ is found by interpolating the normals of range lines AE and BG using Eqn. 2 where N denotes the normal to a line:

$$[(1-t_I)N_{AE}+t_I N_{BG}]\times[(1-t_I)v_A+t_I v_B-v_J]=0. \qquad (2)$$

Here, t parameterises the bone from 0 at A to 1 at B; t_I is its value at I. Solving Eqn. 2 for t_I gives the position of point I. We call the distance from J to I the *effective distance* from point J to bone AB, or from the corresponding simplex if J is its centroid.

Deciding which bone has minimum effective distance from a simplex is not by itself sufficient to decide which bone should control a simplex. For example, if a man stands with hands by his sides, a point on his waist may have a smaller effective distance to a hand bone than to any spine bone, but clearly waist points should be controlled by spine bones. We overcome this problem by using a penalty δ, equal to twice the overall mesh size. We determine how many outer edges of the triangulation the effective line IJ intersects, by constructing a binary tree for the whole mesh using ideas from [20]. We now define the *effective distance with penalty* d_{effpen} as $d_{\text{effpen}}=d_{\text{eff}}+n\delta$, where n is the number of intersections, and d_{eff} is the *effective distance*.

Suppose point J is within the range of several bones, each giving a value for d_{effpen}. If d_{effpen} from J to *some* bone is smaller than δ, i.e. IJ does not intersect the boundary of the mesh, we say point J can be *seen* from the bone. If J can be *seen* by at least one bone, we select the bone that has the minimum d_{effpen} as the controller of point J, and hence the corresponding simplex.

If the minimum d_{effpen} of J is larger than δ, this means IJ intersects the mesh boundary. To determine the controller of point J, we calculate the shortest path from J to each join, using Dijkstra's algorithm across the mesh, after first finding the nearest mesh vertex to J and to the end of each bone. (This distance is not sensitive to the exact connectivity of the mesh). We select the bone with the minimum shortest path distance, amongst the bones that the point is within the range of, as the controller of the point. The red lines in Fig. 1 show the shortest paths from J to bone AB and to bone DK. The controller of point J is bone DK, since the shortest path distance from J to bone DK is smaller.

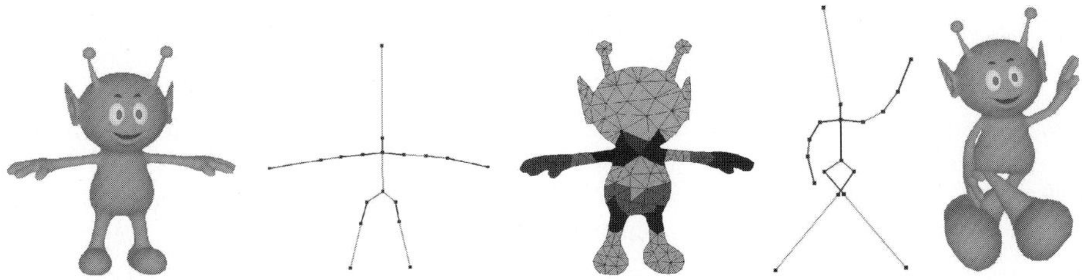

(a) (b) (c) (d) (e)

Fig. 3. (a) 2D Cartoon character (b) Skeleton (c) Skeleton control domain (d) Deformed 2D skeleton, (e) Deformed cartoon character

Fig. 3(a) shows a 2D cartoon character, Fig. 3(b) shows an appropriate 2D skeleton and Fig. 3(c) shows, using corresponding colors, which bone controls each triangle, as determined by the method above.

4.2 Transformation for 2D Bones

Given the initial skeleton, and user-determined deformed skeleton, the transformation matrix for each bone can be calculated. Fig. 4 shows a bone at A_1B_1 in the initial skeleton, and at A_2B_2 in the deformed skeleton. Normally the bone transformation matrix does not involve scaling, but later we show how to take it into account if required.

We translate A_1B_1 so that A_1 is at the origin, the translation vector being T_1. A_1B_1 is then rotated around the origin to lie in the same direction as A_2B_2, θ being the anticlockwise angle of rotation. We then translate A_1B_1 so that A_1 coincides with A_2, the translation vector being T_2. This transformation process can be expressed as $v' = R'(u' + T_1) + T_2$, where u' is a point on the bone before deformation, and v' is the corresponding point afterwards. The transformation matrix of this equation is R', given as usual by

$$R' = \begin{bmatrix} \cos\theta & -\sin\theta \\ \sin\theta & \cos\theta \end{bmatrix} . \tag{3}$$

If scaling is desired, we translate A_1 to the origin as before, then rotate A_1B_1 to lie along the x axis using a rotation R_1. we then scale A_1B_1 until it has the same length as A_2B_2, using a scaling matrix S:

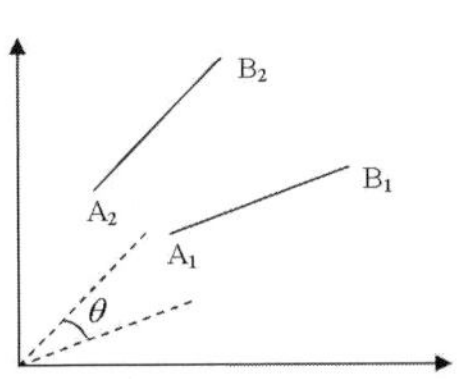

Fig. 4. 2D Bone transformation

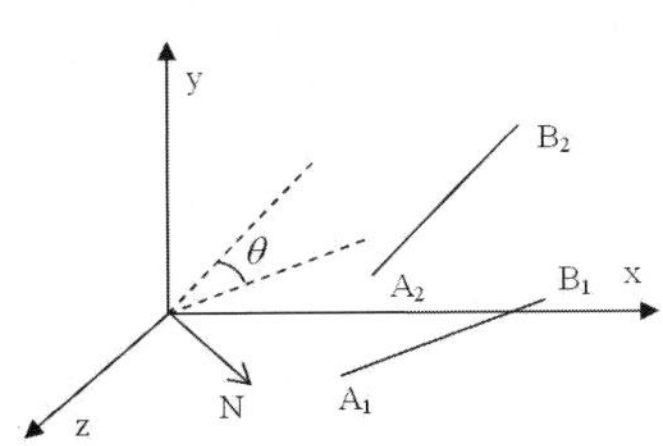

Fig. 5. 3D Bone transformation

$$S = \begin{bmatrix} \alpha & 0 \\ 0 & \beta \end{bmatrix}. \tag{4}$$

Here, α represents the scaling along the direction of the bone, determined by the relative lengths before and after deformation, whereas β represents scaling in the direction perpendicular to the bone. The animator will usually choose this to be 1.0, or the same as α, according to his needs. Finally we rotate A_1B_1 into the same orientation as A_2B_2, using a matrix R_2 and translate A_1B_1 until A_1 coincides with A_2 as before. Overall, we can write $v' = R_2SR_1(u' + T_1) + T_2$ where the transformation matrix in this step is given by $S' = R_2SR_1$.

We can write the overall transformation matrix between bone A_1B_1 and A_2B_2 as the combination of a rotation part and a scaling part:

$$M' = S'R'. \tag{5}$$

4.3 2D Triangle Mesh Deformation

If every triangle were to transform rigidly in the same way as its controlling bone, gaps would arise between the triangles controlled by adjacent bones, causing tears in the object. We must enforce vertex consistency requirements to prevent this. We do so using an optimization method, while trying to keep each simplex transformation as close as possible to that of its control bone. For simplicity, as in previous work on simplex transformations [8, 9], we only take into account the non-translation part of the transformation, and in practice, doing so provides good results for the deformed shape. An error function is used to represent the difference between the *actual* simplex deformation and the deformation determined by the control bone:

$$E = \sum_{i=1}^{n} A_i \|M_i - M_i'\|_F^2, \tag{6}$$

where F is the Frobenius norm, A_i is the area of the ith triangle, n is the number of simplices in the mesh, M_i is the *actual* transformation matrix for the ith triangle, given by Section 3 and M_i' is the ideal transformation matrix of this triangle, given in Section 4.2. We minimize E to get the best deformation results while ensuring mesh connectivity: the variables in the minimization problem are the vertex coordinates of the deformed mesh.

This classical quadratic optimization problem can be transformed into a linear equation by setting the gradient of E to zero, giving

$$K'X' = d'. \tag{7}$$

This set of equations can be separated into 2 independent groups corresponding to the x and y coordinates of the deformed mesh. Furthermore, the coefficient matrix for each group is the same, providing a more efficient solution than by treating them as a single system: $KX = d_x$, $KY = d_y$. Here X and Y are the x and y coordinate vectors of the deformed mesh, of size m, where m is the number of vertices in the mesh. K is a sparse $m \times m$ matrix, and d_x and d_y are vectors with dimension m. Generally, m is small enough that LU-decomposition provides an efficient solution method. In order to ensure a unique solution, at least one vertex position should be fixed in advance.

Fig. 3(d) shows a deformed skeleton and Fig. 3(e) the resulting deformed mesh for the cartoon character in Fig. 3(a). The character's legs are scaled using a factor of 2 both along and perpendicular to the the bone, while other parts are unscaled. The corresponding mesh has 251 vertices, and 0.12s were required to calculate the result on a 2.4Ghz Pentium 4 machine.

Local self-intersection seldom happens in our method, because the errors near the joints, which often arise in traditional skeleton-based methods, are spread from the joints to the neighboring domain by our optimization method.

5 3D Triangle Mesh Deformation

The method used for a 2D triangle mesh can also be extended to a 3D volume tetrahedron mesh, but in practice *surface* triangle mesh models are far more widely used. Furthermore, the latter have far fewer elements than tetrahedron models and thus require much lower processing times.

5.1 Correspondence Between 3D Triangles and Bones

As in 2D, we use the minimum *effective distance with penalty* and the minimum *shortest path distance* to decide the controlling bone for each triangle.

We now create range *planes* for bones in 3D, instead of range *lines* in 2D. In Fig. 2, AB, AC, AD are three bones connected at joint A. At free ends of bones, such as B, we create a range plane like $P1$, through B, and perpendicular to bone AB. At other ends of bones, such as A, we create a bisection range plane like planes $P2$ and $P3$ corresponding to each other bone meeting at this joint. Each bone may now have a varying number of range planes, unlike the 2D case where each bone has exactly 4 range lines.

Again we calculate the *effective line* from point J to bone AB. We create a plane $P4$ that passes both through bone AB and point J. This plane intersects the range planes in many rays. At each end of the bone, we select the nearest ray to point J as the *range line*: these are AE and BG in the example. Thus, at each joint of the bone we now have one range line. We now interpolate the *effective line* from the range lines as before.

Having found the effective line IJ, we can calculate the *effective distance with penalty* between the triangle S and the bone as in 2D. The intersection count n in 3D in computing the effective distance with penalty does not include the current triangle itself. If the minimum d_{effpen} of J is smaller than δ, we can decide the controlling bone for this triangle directly by selecting the bone with minimum d_{effpen}. If the minimum d_{effpen} of a triangle is larger than δ, we calculate the shortest path distance across the mesh from the triangle to those bones for which it is within range. The bone with minimum shortest path distance to the triangle is selected as its controller.

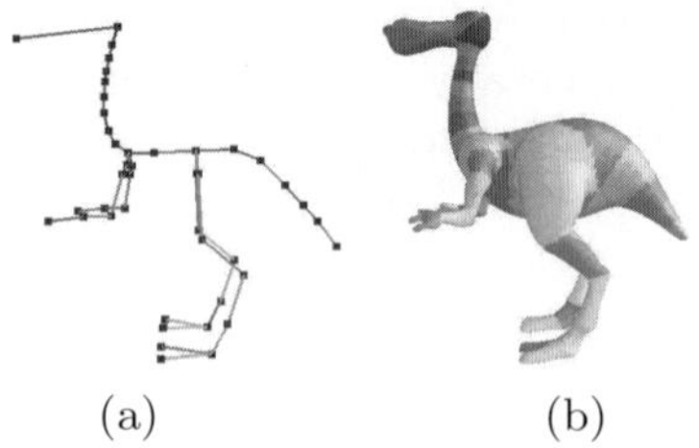

Fig. 6. Skeleton (a) and control domain (b) of Dinopet

Fig. 6(a) shows a skeleton for the Dinopet, and Fig. 6(b) shows the control domain of each bone.

5.2 Transformation for 3D Bones

We now consider how to calculate the transformation matrix for bones in 3D. In Fig. 5, suppose A_1B_1, A_2B_2 represent a bone in 3D before and after deformation. We translate A_1B_1 so that A_1 coincides with the origin. We then create a unit vector N based at the origin, perpendicular to A_1B_1 and A_2B_2 and rotate A_1B_1 around N until A_1B_1 is in the same direction as A_2B_2; let θ be the rotation angle. Finally we translate A_1B_1 until A_1 coincides with A_2. The transformation matrix R' (ignoring the translation) can be calculated in a similar way to the 2D case and is found to be:

$$R = \begin{bmatrix} a^2 + (b^2 + c^2)cos\theta & ab(1 - cos\theta) + csin\theta & ac(1 - cos\theta) - bsin\theta \\ ab(1 - cos\theta) - csin\theta & b^2 + (a^2 + c^2)cos\theta & bc(1 - cos\theta) + absin\theta \\ ac(1 - cos\theta) + bsin\theta & bc(1 - cos\theta) - absin\theta & c^2 + (a^2 + b^2)cos\theta \end{bmatrix} \quad (8)$$

where $N = (a, b, c)$. If scaling is also required, we can determine the scale matrix S as in Section 4.2; the transformation matrix has the same form as Eqn. 5.

5.3 3D Triangle Mesh Deformation

The 3D triangle mesh case is very different from the 2D triangle mesh case, because a triangle is not a simplex in 3D, nor is there a unique transformation matrix for changing one triangle into another. [9] gave a clever way of extending simplex transformation methods to a 3D triangle mesh by constructing a tetrahedron for each triangle. We follow these ideas, except that we put the new vertex above the centroid of the triangle rather than over one of its vertices.

We add a fourth vertex to each triangle of both the initial and deformed mesh to give a tetrahedron. For the initial mesh, the fourth vertex is added in the normal direction over the triangle's centroid. Let v_1, v_2, v_3 be the vertices of a triangle on the initial mesh. The fourth vertex is placed at

$$v_4 = \frac{(v_1 + v_2 + v_3)}{3} + \frac{(v_2 - v_1) \times (v_3 - v_2)}{\sqrt{(v_2 - v_1) \times (v_3 - v_2)}}.$$

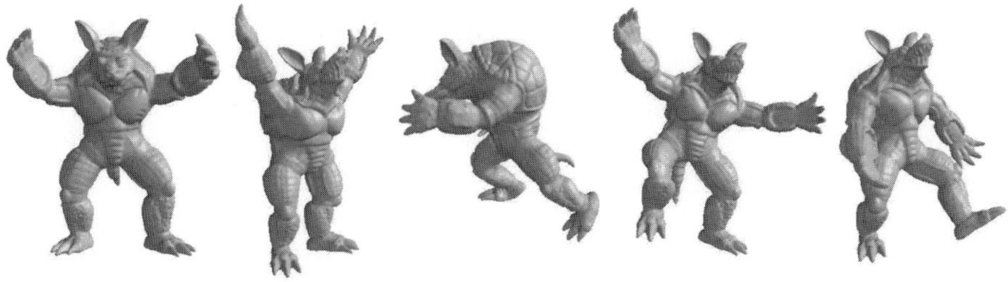

Fig. 7. Armadillo model

Fig. 8. Dinopet model

Table 1. Statics and timing

	Armadillo	Dinopet
Mesh Vertices	50852	13324
Segmentation time (seconds)	22.26	3.12
Deformation time (seconds)	68.63	7.83

Note that the above equation is only used to calculate v_4 in the initial mesh. v_4 in the deformed mesh are determined by the optimisation process.

The 3D triangle mesh is now deformed using the same process as for the 2D triangle mesh in Section 4.3; Eqn. 7 in 3D separates into 3 independent groups: $KX = d_x$, $KY = d_y$, $KZ = d_z$. The dimension of the vectors in Eqn. 7 is now $m + k$ for a mesh with m vertices and k faces. We use the conjugate gradient method to efficiently solve these large sparse linear equations.

Figures 7–8 illustrate 3D deformation results obtained using our technique. The first model in each Figure is the original model; others are deformed results by our method. All results were calculated on a 2.4Ghz Pentium 4 machine. Table 1 shows the timings of 3D models presented in this paper.

6 Conclusions

We have presented a novel mesh deformation method which combines the skeleton-based and simplex transformation approaches. We first determine the transformation for bones of the skeleton, and then transfer each bone's transformation matrix to those simplices it controls. The correspondence between simplices and bones is determined automatically. We use an optimization method to eliminate gaps between triangles controlled by different bones, while keeping the mesh deformation as close as possible to the deformation of the skeleton.

The main advantage over earlier skeleton-based methods is that we directly use the connectivity information in the mesh while they do not. As a result, our method is much simpler since no weight selection nor any arbitrary parameters are needed, yet we can achieve high quality results.

We currently only take into account the non-translation part of the transformation. Although this provides good shape results, we need to arbitrarily fix one vertex to decide the final position of the deformed model. It would be more useful to make the deformed mesh automatically follow the deformed skeleton, and we are investigating including the translation in the Equation system as a way of doing this.

Our method can be easily adapted to control deformation by moving a few chosen line segments or vertices embedded in the object, rather than a skeleton. It can also be extended to twist part of the mesh if required, by defining twist axes. Space precludes demonstration of these capabilities.

Acknowledgements

We would like to thank Gwenael Allard, Shuai Xin and Yu Zang for kind help, and C. Gotsman, T. Ju, R. Sumner and J. Popovic for helpful discussions. This work was partially supported by the Natural Science Foundation of China (Projects 60225016, 60333010, 60321002) and the National Basic Research Project of China (Project 2002CB312101).

References

1. Sederberg, T., Parry, S.: Free-from deformation of solid geometric models. Computer Graphics (Proc. SIGGRAPH1986) **20**(4) (1986) 151–160
2. Coquillart, S.: Extended free-form deformation: A sculpturing tool for 3d geometric modeling. Computer Graphics (Proc. SIGGRAPH1990) **24**(4) (1990) 187–196
3. Alexa, M.: Differential coordinates for local mesh morphing and deformation. The Visual Computer **19**(2) (2003) 105–114
4. Lipman, Y., Sorkine, O., Cohen-Or, D., Levin, D., Rössl, C., Seidel, H.P.: Differential coordinates for interactive mesh editing. In: Proceedings of Shape Modeling International, IEEE Computer Society Press (2004) 181–190
5. Sorkine, O., Lipman, Y., Cohen-Or, D., Alexa, M., Rössl, C., Seidel, H.P.: Laplacian surface editing. In: Proceedings of the Eurographics/ACM SIGGRAPH symposium on Geometry processing, Eurographics Association (2004) 179–188
6. Yu, Y., Zhou, K., Xu, D., Shi, X., Bao, H., GUO, B., Shum, H.Y.: Mesh editing with poisson-based gradient field manipulation. ACM Trans. Graphics (Proc. SIGGRAPH2004) **23**(3) (2004) 644–651

7. Shoemake, K., Duff, T.: Matrix animation and polar decomposition. In: Proc. Conference on Graphics Interface '92. (1992) 258–264
8. Alexa, M., Cohen-Or, D., Levin, D.: As-rigid-as-possible shape interpolation. In: Proc. SIGGRAPH2000. (2000) 157–165
9. Sumner, R.W., Popovic, J.: Deformation transfer for triangle meshes. ACM Trans. Graphics (Proc. SIGGRAPH2004) **23**(3) (2004) 399–405
10. Sumner, R.W., Zwicker, M., Gotsman, C., Popovic, J.: Mesh-based inverse kinematics. ACM Trans. Graphics (Proc. SIGGRAPH2005) **24**(3) (2005) 488–495
11. Lewis, J., Cordner, M., Fong, N.: Pose space deformation: a unified approach to shape interpolation and skeleton-driven deformation. In: Proc. SIGGRAPH2000. (2000) 165–172
12. Bloomenthal, J.: Medial-based vertex deformation. In: Proc. 2002 ACM SIGGRAPH/Eurographics Symp. Computer Animation. (2002) 147–151
13. Mohr, A., Tokheim, L., Gleicher, M.: Direct manipulation of interactive character skins. In: Proc. 2003 Symp. Interactive 3D Graphics. (2003) 27–30
14. Allen, B., Curless, B., Popovic, Z.: Articulated body deformation from range scan data. ACM Trans. Graphics (Proc. SIGGRAPH2002) **23**(3) (2002) 612–619
15. Wang, X.C., Phillips, C.: Multi-weight enveloping: least-squares approximation techniques for skin animation. In: Proc. 2002 ACM SIGGRAPH/Eurographics Symp. Computer Animation, New York, NY, USA, ACM Press (2002) 129–138
16. Verroust, A., Lazarus, F.: Extracting skeletal curves from 3D scattered data. The Visual Computer **16**(1) (2000) 15–25
17. Li, X., Woon, T.W., Tan, T.S., Huang, Z.: Decomposing polygon meshes for interactive applications. In: ACM Symposium on Interactive 3D Graphics 2001. (2005) 35–42
18. Katz, S., Tal, A.: Hierarchical mesh decomposition using fuzzy clustering and cuts. ACM Transactions on Graphics **22**(3) (2003) 954–961
19. Lien, J.M., Amato, N.M.: Simultaneous Shape Decomposition and Skeletonization. Technical Report, TR05-015, Parasol Laboratory, Department of Computer Science, Texas A&M University (2005)
20. de Berg, M., van Kreveld, M., Overmars, M., Schwarzkopf, O.: Computational geometry : algorithms and applications. Springer (1997)

Skeleton-Driven Animation Transfer Based on Consistent Volume Parameterization

Yen-Tuo Chang[1], Bing-Yu Chen[2], Wan-Chi Luo[1], and Jian-Bin Huang[1]

National Taiwan University, Taiwan
[1]{draphix, maggie, azar}@cmlab.csie.ntu.edu.tw,
[2]robin@ntu.edu.tw

Abstract. To edit or create the animation of a 3D character model has always been an important but time-consuming task, since the animator usually needs to set up the character's skeleton, paint its binding weights, and adjust its key-poses. Hence, we propose an animation transfer system in this paper to take a well-edited character animation as the input. Then, the system can transfer the skeleton, binding weights, and other attributes of the given character model to another static model with only few corresponding feature points specified. The transferring process is based on a mapping between the space around two character meshes. In this paper, the mapping is called consistent volume parameterization, which inherits consistent surface parameterization. Hence, the animator can start to create a skeleton-driven animation for the new character model without any prior setting. Moreover, our system is also capable of cloning a skeleton-driven animation to several other character models which can be used in a crowd animation.

1 Introduction

3D virtual characters are getting widely used in movies with special visual effects, computer generated animations, computer games, etc. Animator brings a 3D character model to life by making plausible and lifelike motions, and one of the common solutions is to set up the character's skeleton, paint its binding weights on the surface, and adjust its key-poses. The skeleton of a character model consists of a set of bones, which connect each other with a set of joints. Its binding weights define the binding relationship between its skin (surface of the model) and the skeleton. This relationship specifies the degree of dependencies of each vertex on the surface to a set of bones of the skeleton. After the skeleton and binding weights are well set up, the animator can edit the key-poses by adjusting the skeleton, then the mesh surface of the character model is deformed with the adjusted skeleton according to the binding weights. By interpolating the key-poses, a skeleton-driven animation is generated.

Besides creating an animation of one 3D character model, a crowd animation, which includes vast amount of 3D character models in a scene, is also widely used, such as hundreds of guests dancing simultaneously in a royal hall, or hundreds or thousands of soldiers fighting in a battle. As we mentioned above,

H.-P. Seidel, T. Nishita, and Q. Peng (Eds.): CGI 2006, LNCS 4035, pp. 78–89, 2006.

the process of creating or editing a character animation is a time-consuming task. To create a crowd animation including huge amount of different character models is thus extremely tedious. Although we can create only few character models and repeatedly put the same set of models everywhere in the scene to form the crowd animation, this method leads to low quality of visual feelings.

Therefore, in this paper we propose a system to transfer the skeleton of a given 3D character model to any other models which originally have only mesh data. Furthermore, the motion data well-edited previously for the given character model could also be transferred to the target models, such as binding weights, key-poses, and texture coordinates, as shown in Fig. 2. Hence, our system makes it much easier to create a huge amount of character models performing the same actions in a scene. Besides, the animators can also import the transferred skeleton, binding weights, and other data to an animating software for further editing. The whole system is fully automatic except few feature points are specified by the user to establish the correspondence between the source model and the target one at the beginning.

In order to transfer the skeleton from the source character model to the target one, a mapping between two mesh surfaces is first required. We use cross parameterization proposed by Kraevoy and Sheffer in [1] to construct this mapping relationship. Generally, parameterization refers to mapping a geometry to a domain of lower dimension, and makes it easier to be processed. We consistently parameterize two mesh surfaces to the same base domain, which is basically a simplicial complex consists of all the user-specified feature points. The system then automatically partitions and cross-parameterizes the surfaces of the two models. Right after the correspondence between the two surfaces is established, the consistent volume parameterization, which is a mapping from the space of the source model body to that of the target one, is generated by using the 3D mean value coordinates adapted from [2]. The space of a 3D model body is defined as the space around and inside the model body in this paper. For each joint of the source model skeleton, which usually lies inside the mesh surface, a corresponding 3D position is found for the target model by applying a smooth and continuous function. The skeleton of the source model is thus appropriately transferred to the target model. Then, the key-poses can be also transferred through the skeleton transferring. The binding weights and other attributes of the source model, such as texture coordinates, can be transferred through consistent surface parameterization which has already been established before generating consistent volume parameterization.

2 Related Work

In this paper, we take the advantages from several parameterization methods to develop a best way to construct the correspondence between two or more models. In order to parameterize a 3D mesh with or without holes to a 2D domain, most of the methods cuts the mesh surfaces into some patches which are homeomorphic to disks. Eck *et al.* [3] proposed a classic method to parameterize a model of any topology. The triangular mesh is partitioned using Voronoi diagram and Delaunay triangulation. However, this method is hard to adapt into consistent parameterization because the Voronoi sites are selected randomly. Zhou *et al.* [4] partitioned the mesh without any user specified features. Their system analyzes the spectrum information along the surface and automatically cut the mesh into some charts according to a stretch-minimizing criterion. Although this approach gained both the advantage on efficiency and the stretch-minimization of parameterization, it is still rather hard to be applied to make correspondence between two or more models.

Cross parameterization or inter-surface mapping refers to the mapping between two models. Lee *et al.* [5] used MAPS [6] to get the base domains of two models after some corresponding feature points and lines are specified by the user. They then created an inter-surface parameterization between the two models by mapping the two models to their base domains first, and constructing a correspondence between the two base domains with user assistance. Praun *et al.* [7] provided consistent mesh parameterization to get the inter-surface mapping. In their method, the user first specifies a common base domain and maps it to all models manually. Then, the consistent parameterization can be done by subdividing the base domain for each model. Schreiner *et al.* [8] established a common base domain of two models based on the corresponding feature points specified by the user. They created the common base domain by linking all common feature pairs together, then used progressive meshes [9] with constraints to create multiresolution meshes of the path networks and used a coarse-to-fine mapping optimization method to find a continuous mapping between the multiresolution meshes. Kraevoy and Sheffer [1] created the common base domain in a similar way as in [8]. They then used mean value parameterization to map the vertices of a model to their belonging triangle on the common base domain. The inter-surface mapping was finally constructed through mapping the base domains.

In the topic of representing a position in 3D space by other primitives, convex combination is usually used for parameterization in several different approaches. It means that every vertex can be represented as a convex combination of its neighboring vertices. Ju *et al.* [2] applied the mean value coordinate [10] into triangular mesh parameterization, and made it possible to represent a vertex in a closed 3D mean-value domain.

For transferring the animation to other static models, Sumner and Popović [11] proposed a method to transfer the deformation by first matching the features of the inputs and then transforming each triangle with this mapping. Bregler *et al.* [12] transferred the motion of a 2D character animation to other 3D models by analyzing its affine transformations and key-poses on the plane. Zhou *et al.* [13] turned a 3D static model into a solid wire-frame, then the deformation can be edited according to graphical Laplacian. Their system also accomplishes the transfer of planar deformation from 2D cartoons. However, all these animation transfer methods are not able to generate the skeleton or other animation data for the target static model, to use the transferred animation for further editing is not easy. Allen *et al.* [14] also presented a method which is able to transfer the skeleton of a 3D human model to other ones. Their method records the position of each joint with only two or three vertices around, thus it may introduce great distortion in most of our cases.

3 System Overview

As shown in Fig. 4, our system takes the animated source model and a static target one as the input (upper-left two squares in the figure), and requires the user to specify some corresponding feature points as the first step of the whole processes (upper-middle). The rest processes of our system are fully automatic. The common base domain derives from the corresponding feature points on the surface of each model (middle blue-shaded figure in upper-right rectangle). Then, the two input meshes are partitioned and mapped to the common base domain to construct the consistent surface parameterization (upper-right). We then apply the 3D mean value coordinates to achieve the consistent volume parameterization using the constructed consistent surface parameterization (middle-left). Due to the consistent volume parameterization, the skeleton of the source model can be transferred to the target one (middle-right), and the binding weights and other attributes are also copied according to the consistent surface parameterization to complete the animation transfer process (lower two figures).

4 Consistent Surface Parameterization

To construct the consistent surface parameterization of two meshes is to find a correspondence map $\mathbf{M}_{ts}$, so that for each vertex $v_i^t \in \mathbf{V}_t$, $i = 1, ..., N_t$ of a *target* mesh M_t with N_t vertices can have a meaningful position $\mathbf{M}_{ts}(v_i^t)$ on the surface of a *source* mesh M_s with N_s vertices, where $\mathbf{V}_t$ is a set of vertices of M_t. The correspondence position $\mathbf{M}_{ts}(v_i^t)$ may be a vertex $v_i^s \in \mathbf{V}_s$, $i = 1, ..., N_s$ of M_s or inside a triangle of M_s which consists of three vertices in $\mathbf{V}_s$. The quality of the consistent surface parameterization $\mathbf{M}_{ts}$ depends on how much the new position $\mathbf{M}_{ts}(v_i^t)$ of each vertex v_i^t signifies its original position.

The first step of our system is to specify the corresponding feature points of two models manually by the user through a typical user interface as shown in Fig. 3. The feature points should be the vertices of the two models. Hence, we can define a correspondence map of U pairs of the common feature points as $\mathbf{M}_{ts}(v_i^t) = v_i^s$ for $i = 1, ..., U$, where $U < N_t, N_s$, and vise versa, i.e., $\mathbf{M}_{st}(v_i^s) = v_i^t = \mathbf{M}_{ts}^{-1}(v_i^s)$. After specifying U pairs of the common feature points on the surfaces of the two models, we adapt Kraevoy and Sheffer's method [1] to create the cross parameterization $\mathbf{M}_{ts}$ of the two models for the rest vertices v_i^t, $i = U + 1, ..., N_t$ of M_t.

Fig. 1. The motion of the fat-man model (left) is transferred to the alien (middle) and Mario (right) models

Fig. 2. The transferred skeleton and binding weights

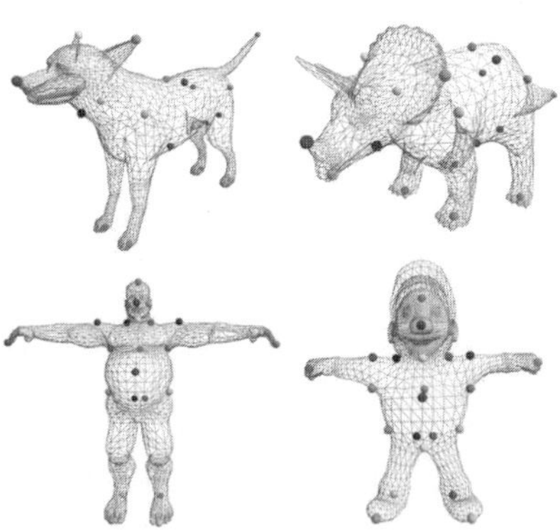

Fig. 3. Few pairs of feature points are specified on the surfaces of the dog (upper-left) and triceratops (upper-right) models, and also for the fat-man (lower-left) and Mario (lower-right) models

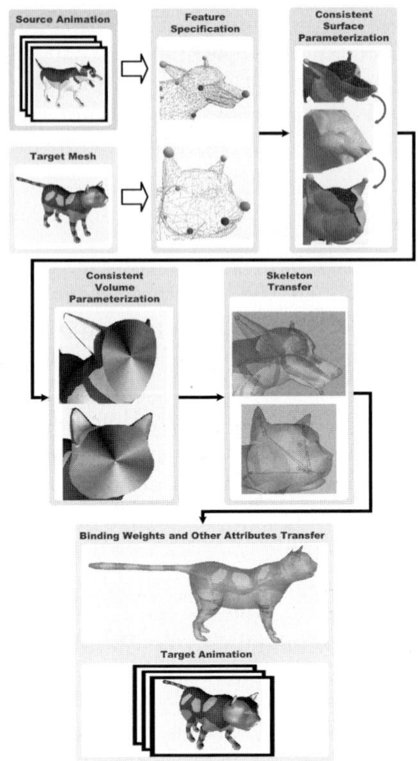

Fig. 4. System flowchart of our method

Fig. 5. The meshes are partitioned into some patches according to the paths of the base domain. This leads to a meaningful mapping between the segments of the dog (upper-left) and triceratops (upper-right) models, and also for the fat-man (lower-left) and Mario (lower-right) models.

Before constructing the cross parameterization of the two models, we first connect the feature points to establish the base domains B_s and B_t of the two models M_s and M_t, respectively. The base domains are required to be consistent, which means that there are one-to-one correspondences among the vertices and paths of the two base domains. To connect two feature points, we use the Dijkstra's algorithm to trace the shortest paths along the edges between two feature points on the surface of the mesh and add some Steiner points to subdivide the edges while tracing if necessary.

When connecting the feature points, we also keep the consistence of the corresponding paths on both meshes in each tracing step. Hence, when we connect two feature points v_i^t and v_j^t of M_t, we must connect their corresponding feature points v_i^s and v_j^s of M_s to check if the two paths are both valid to add to the base domains B_s and B_t, where $i, j = 1, ..., U$. To identify a path is valid or not, we test if it intersects any existing path. The cyclical order of the paths emitted from one feature point is also compared to those of its corresponding feature point on the other model to check if they are consistent. The same-sidedness of a vertex relative to a path is also examined on both models to ensure the correctness of the topology. If there is no valid path when connecting two feature points, we will try to add some Steiner points to the faces between the two feature points, so that a valid path can be found for the two feature points.

Finally, the base domains B_s and B_t of the two models M_s and M_t are constructed and guaranteed to be consistent. Then, the two models are partitioned to be some patches and the number of patches of the two models are the same as shown in Fig. 5. Moreover, every patch consists of three feature points and three paths connected the three feature points, so that when replacing the paths with straight lines, the base domains consist of some planar triangles as shown in Fig. 6.

The partitioned model is then parameterized to its base domain. Initially, a mean value parameterization approach in [10] is applied to every patch and put all triangles of the patch onto the corresponding planar triangle of the base domain. The corner vertices are fixed on the feature location of the base domain, while the interior vertices are placed with barycentric coordinates. The algorithm then applies a smoothing step to improve the distribution of the parameterization by refining the shapes of the patches. To avoid too sparse or too dense distribution on a parameterization which introduces large distortion, the vertices are shifted to its neighboring patches and thus relax the unbalancing on the surface.

Finally, we establish the mapping $\mathbf{M}_{ts}^B$ between the two consistent base domains B_t and B_s of the two models M_t and M_s by just mapping their patches one-by-one. Hence, the mapping $\mathbf{M}_{ts}$ between the target model M_t and the source one M_s can be constructed through the following equation:

$$\mathbf{M}_{ts} = \Pi_s^{-1} \cdot \mathbf{M}_{ts}^B \cdot \Pi_t,$$

where Π_t refers to the parameterization between model M_t and its base domain B_t, and so does Π_s.

5 Consistent Volume Parameterization

After the consistent surface parameterization between two models is established, in this section, a mapping called consistent volume parameterization is then constructed for the 3D space of two models. For representing the volumetric space around a surface model, we adapt the 3D mean value coordinates proposed by Ju *et al.* [2]. The original 2D mean value coordinates was proposed by Floater [10], which is used to construct a continuous distribution of an attribute value $f[x]$ of a weighting function f for all points x inside or outside a planar polygon. The value can be any kind of data such as color, heat, or texture coordinate. Ju *et al.* extended this approach to compute the 3D mean value coordinates inside a closed triangular mesh.

The mean value coordinates has the following general form:

$$f[x] = \frac{\sum_{i=1}^{n} w_i f_i}{\sum_{i=1}^{n} w_i},$$

where $f[x]$ is the interpolated value, w_i and f_i are the weight and attribute value of each vertex v_i of the closed triangular mesh M. By applying this algorithm, a set of weights w_i are determined to represent the relationship between a specific position x inside the mesh M and all the triangles that have a projection area on the unit sphere of x. The value f_i on the vertices v_i of all these triangles are interpolated according to the weights w_i, and then the value $f[x]$ for x can be obtained.

To construct the consistent volume parameterization is to define a correspondence map $\mathbf{M}_{ts}^V$, so that for each point x^t inside or closely outside the target closed triangular mesh M_t can have a meaningful position $x^s = \mathbf{M}_{ts}^V(x^t)$ inside or closely outside the source closed triangular mesh M_s. Hence, we define the weighting function f_i^s for each vertex v_i^s of the source model M_s as the mapping position of x^t, then we can obtain the mapping from x^t to x^s through f_i^s. According to the consistent surface parameterization,

$$f_i^s = \sum_{j=1}^{m} \alpha_j \mathbf{M}_{ts}(f_j^t),$$

where α_j is the weights for barycentric coordinate and $\sum_{j=1}^{m} \alpha_j = 1$, $m = 1$ or 3. If v_j^t is mapped to a vertex v_i^s, m is set to be 1, i.e., $v_i^s = \mathbf{M}_{ts}(v_j^t)$, otherwise m is set to be 3, since v_i^s is mapped by a triangle of M_t. Using the 3D mean value coordinates:

$$f[x^s] = \frac{\sum_{i=1}^{n} w_i f_i^s}{\sum_{i=1}^{n} w_i},$$

we define a mapping function $x^s = \Omega_s(f_i^s)$ from the vertices v_i^s on the surface of M_s to one of their interior points x^s through the 3D mean value coordinates.

Thus, the consistent volume parameterization is established by interpolating the mapping value generated by the consistent surface parameterization, and finding a corresponding position x^t around M_t for any specified position x^s around M_s by

$$x^s = \Omega_s\left(\sum_{j=1}^{m} \alpha_j \mathbf{M}_{ts}(f_j^t)\right),$$

and $f_j^t = \Omega_t^{-1}(x^t)$. Hence, the mapping $\mathbf{M}_{ts}^V$ between the space of the target model M_t and that of the source one M_s can be constructed through the following equation:

$$\mathbf{M}_{ts}^V = \Omega_s \cdot \mathbf{M}_{ts} \cdot \Omega_t^{-1}.$$

As shown in Fig. 7, the consistent volume parameterization is constructed between the two models. For each point of the source (fat man on left side) model, we can find its corresponding point around the target (Mario on right side) model. The points inside the models are corresponding joints. Other places inside the models are also mapped smoothly.

Although we call this method as consistent volume parameterization, it does not always find a mapping position inside the target mesh for a joint inside the source. The exception may happen when the source mesh is convex but the target is not. The mapped position may be closely outside the target surface, but it still belongs to the volumetric space of the character. Fortunately, the joints of a skeleton are not necessary to be all inside the mesh surface. The transferred animation still looks well under this circumstances.

6 Animation Transfer

To transfer the animation data from a skeleton-driven source animation model to a target static one, we first transfer the skeleton of the source animation model through the consistent volume parameterization of the two models. Then, the binding weights and other attributes of the source animation model can be transferred to the target static one through the consistent surface parameterization of the two models. Finally, the key-poses are transferred by applying the same animation data to the generated skeleton of the target model as that of the source animation model. If an animator wishes to modify the transferred animation, he or she can use model editing tools to edit the transferred skeleton, binding wights, key-poses, or other attributes of the target model.

6.1 Skeleton Transfer

The skeleton of a 3D character model is defined to be a set of "joint and bone" pairs. The definition basically imitates the skeleton structure of a vertebrate, in which bones are rigid sticks and connect each other by a set of joints. Each joint has a rotation vector representing the current direction which the bone connected to it points toward. Therefore, transferring a skeleton is identical to transferring the positions of all the joints of a given skeleton to their new positions, and connects them with bones according to the structure of the original one.

Our system automatically finds the corresponding position of each joint inside the target model through the consistent volume parameterization. After the skeleton is transferred from the source animation model to the target static one, the skeletons of the two models are consistent which means there are one-to-one correspondences among their joints and bones. Hence, the key-poses of the source animation model can easily be transferred by assigning the same motion

Fig. 6. The triangular patches are parameterized onto the base domain and form a pair of coarse meshes with the same topology of shape

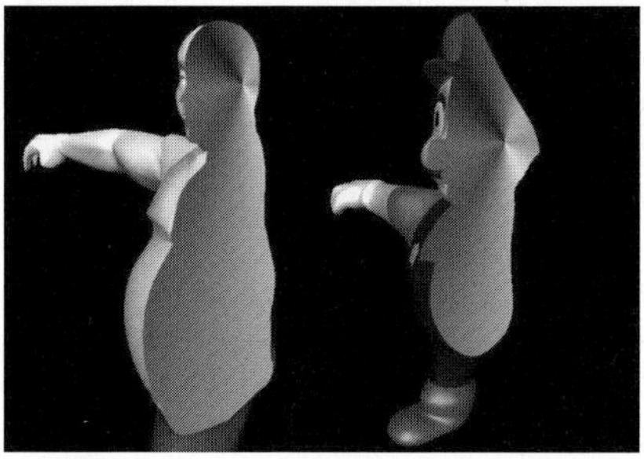

Fig. 7. The graphical representation of mapping a joint in the center of the head of the fat man model (left) to a corresponding position inside the Mario model (right) by applying the 3D mean value coordinates

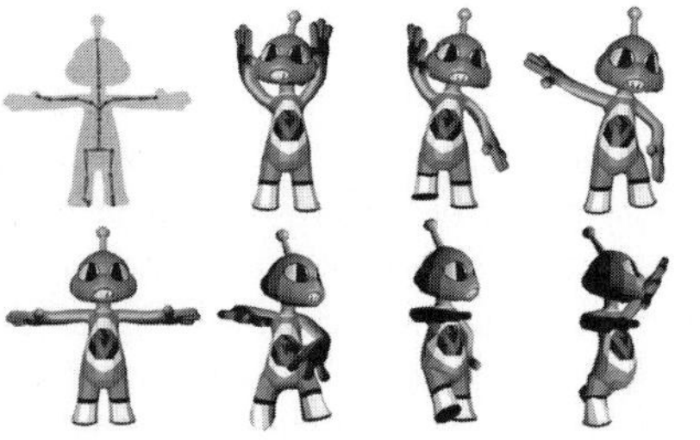

Fig. 8. A transferred skeleton-driven animation generated by our system. The skeleton is nicely shaped according to the character model (upper-left) and the motion can also be transferred from the fat man model shown in Fig. 1 (left).

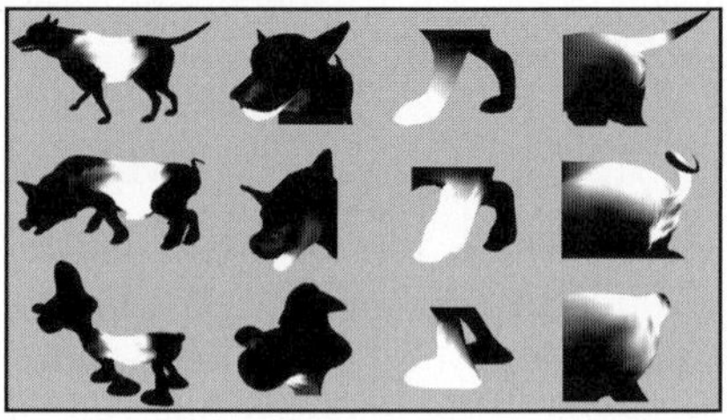

Fig. 9. The binding weights of the black dog model (upper) is transferred to the pig (middle) and brown dog (lower) models. The black dog model is shown in Fig. 10 (upper) and Fig. 11 (upper), the pig model is shown in Fig. 11 (middle), and the brown dog model is shown in Fig. 10 (lower).

Fig. 10. The motion of the black dog model (upper) is transferred to the cat (middle) and brown dog (lower) models

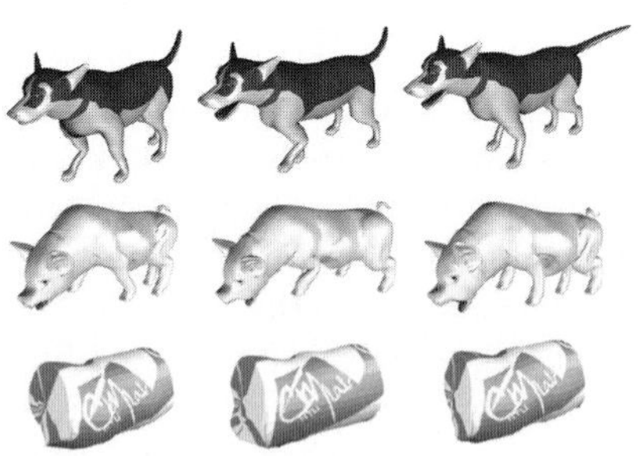

Fig. 11. The motion of the black dog model (upper) is transferred to the pig (middle) and can (lower) models

data, such as the rotation angle of a joint of the source model, to its corresponding joint of the target model as shown in Fig. 8.

6.2 Binding Weights Transfer

The binding weights, like other surface attributes such as texture coordinate, are assigned to the vertices on the surface of the model. Hence, we can transfer the binding weights from the source model to the target one through the consistent surface parameterization as shown in Fig. 9.

7 Results

Fig. 10 and Fig. 11 show the animation transfer results from a black dog model to a cat model, a brown dog model, a pig model, and a can model, which originally have only mesh data. Hence, our system works well when the target model has a shape similar to the source one, as was expected.

According to the experiments, our system processes with a desirable efficiency in all cases. For a novel user who can use a 3D model viewing system with a mouse, he or she can use our system with nearly no training in advance. As shown in Table 1, 15 $\sim$ 30 features are required to produce a good parameterization. This takes about 5 $\sim$ 10 minutes in specifying the corresponding feature points on the surface of the two models. After the feature specifying stage, our system is fully automatic. In all cases, the bottleneck of performance is the construction of the consistent surface parameterization. Besides this stage, the rest processes of our system is typically performed in real-time. As shown in Table 1, the construction of the consistent surface parameterization consists of partitioning two models consistently according to the corresponding feature points, and parameterizing the patches to the base domain. Although the processing time of the construction of the consistent surface parameterization requires from seconds to few minutes, this is still extremely tolerable to the user, since it may be an off-line process. The testing platform is a desktop PC with an Intel Pentium 4 3.4GHz CPU and 1.5GB memory.

Table 1. The performance testing of four pairs of animation transfer, including the time for partitioning and parameterization, which are the two main steps of constructing the consistent surface parameterization. The numbers of vertices and faces of the source and target models and the number of corresponding feature points specified on the two models are also listed. The dog and cat models are shown in Fig. 10 (upper and middle), the fat man and Mario models are shown in Fig. 1 (left and right), and the dog and pig models are shown in Fig. 11 (upper and middle).

Source	#vertex/#face of Source	Target	#vertex/#face of Target	#feature	time for partitioning (sec.)	time for parameterization (sec.)
dog	4070/8136	cat	2702/5400	17	50	67
fat man	3426/6848	Mario	2934/5864	25	107	17
dog	4070/8136	pig	5570/11136	22	276	23

8 Conclusions and Future Work

In this paper, we propose a system to transfer the skeleton and animation data from a source animation model to a target static one which has only mesh data. The system requires the user to mark few feature points, and then generates the output skeleton and animation data for the target model automatically. The skeleton has a nice shape and can be edited to produce other animation by the animator by importing the generated skeleton and animation data to a model editing tool. Our system runs in a range from 30 seconds to 5 minutes, thus enormously saves the time and work for the animators.

For our future work, there are some possible ways to improve the efficiency and quality of our system. Surazhsky *et al.* [15] proposed a robust algorithm to trace the geodesic directly on the mesh surface, regardless of the topology below. It is possible to modify our system to partition the meshes according to this method. From our experiments, the initial poses of the input models affect the quality of the transferred animation greatly. Inconsistency in initial poses may distort the distribution and default angles of each joint, and thus produce animation that is not concurrent to the source. We can add one more step to automatically adjust the pose of the target model to fit that of the source after transferring the skeleton. The adjusted model could be treated as a new input with the new initial pose, so the system may redo the consistent surface parameterization process again and find some more accurate position for all the joints, as long as the output animation. Although the feature specification is regarded necessary, it is still desirable to derive some methods to automatically detect and specify the common feature points.

Finally, the consistent volume parameterization may benefit a lot of areas in computer graphics. It is possible to transfer the inside structure of a model to another, thus may reduce many work in 3D modeling. It can also be used to transfer the internal texture, layered information, or the structure needed to shade with translucency.

Acknowledgements

This work was supported in part by the National Science Council of Taiwan under Grant No. NSC93-2213-E-002-084 and NSC94-2213-E-002-097.

References

1. Kraevoy, V., Sheffer, A.: Cross-parameterization and compatible remeshing of 3d models. ACM Transactions on Graphics (SIGGRAPH 2004 Conference Proceedings) **23**(3) (2004) 861–869
2. Ju, T., Schaefer, S., Warren, J.: Mean value coordinates for closed triangular meshes. ACM Transactions on Graphics (SIGGRAPH 2005 Conference Proceedings) **24**(3) (2005) 561–566

3. Eck, M., DeRose, T., Duchamp, T., Hoppe, H., Lounsbery, M., Stuetzle, W.: Multiresolution analysis of arbitrary meshes. In: ACM SIGGRAPH 1995 Conference Proceedings. (1995) 173–182
4. Zhou, K., Synder, J., Guo, B., Shum, H.Y.: Iso-charts: stretch-driven mesh parameterization using spectral analysis. In: Proceedings of the 2004 Eurographics Symposium on Geometry Processing. (2004) 45–54
5. Lee, A.W.F., Dobkin, D., Sweldens, W., Schröder, P.: Multiresolution mesh morphing. In: ACM SIGGRAPH 1999 Conference Proceedings. (1999) 343–350
6. Lee, A.W.F., Sweldens, W., Schröder, P., Cowsar, L., Dobkin, D.: Maps: multiresolution adaptive parameterization of surfaces. In: ACM SIGGRAPH 1998 Conference Proceedings. (1998) 95–104
7. Praun, E., Sweldens, W., Schröder, P.: Consistent mesh parameterizations. In: ACM SIGGRAPH 2001 Conference Proceedings. (2001) 179–184
8. Schreiner, J., Asirvatham, A., Praun, E., Hoppe, H.: Inter-surface mapping. ACM Transactions on Graphics (SIGGRAPH 2004 Conference Proceedings) **23**(3) (2004) 870–877
9. Hoppe, H.: Progressive meshes. In: ACM SIGGRAPH 1996 Conference Proceedings. (1996) 99–108
10. Floater, M.S.: Mean value coordinates. Computer Aided Geometric Design **20**(1) (2003) 19–27
11. Sumner, R.W., Popović, J.: Deformation transfer for triangle meshes. ACM Transactions on Graphics (SIGGRAPH 2004 Conference Proceedings) **23**(3) (2004) 399–405
12. Bregler, C., Loeb, L., Chuang, E., Deshpande, H.: Turning to the masters: motion capturing cartoons. In: ACM SIGGRAPH 2002 Conference Proceedings. (2002) 399–407
13. Zhou, K., Huang, J., Snyder, J., Liu, X., Bao, H., Guo, B., Shum, H.Y.: Large mesh deformation using the volumetric graph laplacian. ACM Transactions on Graphics (SIGGRAPH 2005 Conference Proceedings) **24**(3) (2005) 496–503
14. Allen, B., Curless, B., Popović, Z.: The space of human body shapes: reconstruction and parameterization from range scans. ACM Transactions on Graphics (SIGGRAPH 2003 Conference Proceedings) **22**(3) (2003) 587–594
15. Surazhsky, V., Surazhsky, T., Kirsanov, D., Gortler, S.J., Hoppe, H.: Fast exact and approximate geodesics on meshes. ACM Transactions on Graphics (SIGGRAPH 2005 Conference Proceedings) **24**(3) (2005) 553–560

Sketch Based Mesh Fusion

Juncong Lin[1], Xiaogang Jin[1], and Charlie C.L. Wang[2]

[1] State Key Lab of CAD & CG, Zhejiang University, Hangzhou 310027, P.R. China
[2] Department of Automation and Computer-Aided Engineering,
The Chinese University of Hong Kong
{linjuncong, jin}@cad.zju.edu.cn,
cwang@acae.cuhk.edu.hk

Abstract. In this paper, we develop a novel mesh fusion method controlled by sketches, which allows users to construct complex 3D polygon models fast and easily. The user first cuts needed parts from some existing objects and puts them in right pose. Then, a radial basis function (RBF) based implicit surface is adopted to smoothly fuse the parts. To achieve better shape control for the transition part in fusion, our method let users using sketches to specify the expected silhouette. After that, the implicit surface is sampled by particles and meshed into a polygonal surface joining the separated parts into one single model. Compared with other previous methods, our mesh fusion approach overcomes the topological limitations and can merge multiple parts together at once.

1 Introduction

Researches for providing a user-friendly modelling system to create complex 3D models quickly have been with a long history in computer graphics. A lot of works have been conducted in this area. However, it is still a tedious job even for those well-trained experts to construct desired models by using current commercial modelling system, not to say for novices. This paper aims at providing a simple and intuitive modelling approach for creating a complex 3D mesh model from the existing 3D polygonal objects.

From investigation (ref. [1]), we know that the sketching interface is still the most welcome manner for designers to model their creation in a computer system. Based on this reason, several sketching interfaces have been developed for modelling 3D objects (see [1, 2, 3]). The authors in [1] presented a system using intuitive guesses to govern the construction of geometric objects. Igarashi et al. in [2] extended the idea of [1] to develop a system for modelling 3D freeform objects in the representation of polygon mesh, while the approach in [3] implemented a similar sketching interface using variational implicit surfaces. However, the geometry of objects created in these systems is relatively simple.

For geometry modelling, the Constructive Solid Geometry (CSG) provides an efficient way to construct complex geometric shapes by applying operations on primitive objects in a top-down manner. A wide variety of researches have been conducted in the CSG operations on the models represented in numerous methods. Unfortunately, it seems hard to directly apply the Boolean operations of

H.-P. Seidel, T. Nishita, and Q. Peng (Eds.): CGI 2006, LNCS 4035, pp. 90–101, 2006.

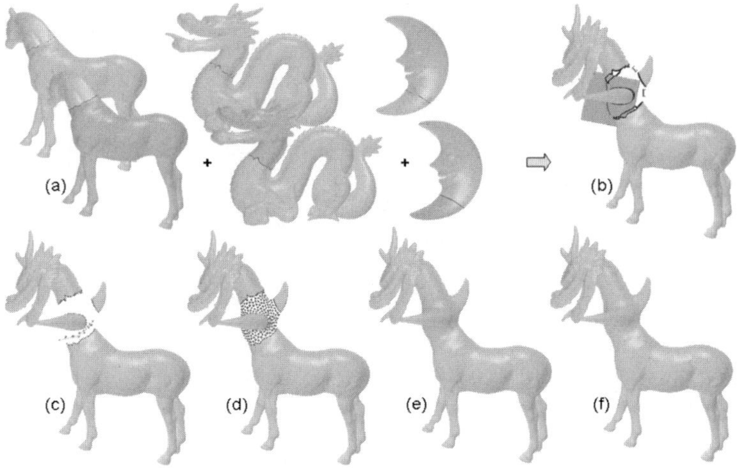

Fig. 1. Screenshots of sketch based mesh fusion: (a) scissoring existing models, (b) placing the constructive parts together and sketching the silhouette of fusion, (c) specifying the part of transient surface to be remained, (d) sampling the transient surface by particles, (e) tessellating the particles into a mesh surface patch joining the separated parts, and (f) the final result of mesh fusion

CSG in mesh fusion, especially when there is a large hole between the separated parts to be fused - for instance, the model created in Figure 1. Furthermore, the robust implementation of Boolean operations on complex polygonal models is by no means an easy job.

Recently, several approaches [4, 5, 6, 7, 8, 9, 10, 11] in literature took a *design by example* way to construct complex 3D models from existing ones. The methods presented in [4, 5, 6, 7] focused on the cut-and-paste operation on meshes. They could produce seamless composed models. However, in [4, 5, 6], the joined objects were required to be topologically equivalent to a disk for the necessary mapping between source and target models. [7]required the boundary openings of a model lying on a plane and [8, 9]required the boundary openings had similar topological structures. In [10], input models were cut using intelligent scissors. Then those cut portions were stitched to form a composition result by using the method of [5] - so that the boundaries with similar topology are required. The method presented in [11] was devoted to finding the best place to clip on two well aligned models then clipping and stitching those retained model parts. In summary, there are various topological limitations in all above methods.

In this paper, we present a sketch-based modelling method by a modelling framework of mesh fusion, where the selected parts from complex models are merged through a transient implicit surface. The topological limitation in previous work is overcome in our mesh fusion approach. More specifically, the major contributions of this paper are as follows.

- A topology-free mesh fusion scheme is introduced, where a variational implicit surface based on RBFs is conducted as the transient surface to interpolate the position and normal constraints on the boundaries of given models. The transient surface overcomes the topological limitation on the openings of given models, so that a topology-free mesh fusion result can be achieved after tessellating the transient surface.
- As only part of the implicit surface belongs to the region to be fused, a new tessellation method is developed in this paper to triangulate the transient implicit surface so that the separated polygonal parts are joined smoothly with triangles with good shapes.
- A novel sketching interface is provided to control the silhouette of the transient surface through strokes. The shape of the transient surface will follow the specified silhouette.

In the following, the modelling framework of mesh fusion is first described. After that, the sketching interface for scissoring parts and specifying profiles is introduced. To finally join the constructive parts, the particle-based tessellation scheme is presented in section 4. After showing the results in section 5, our paper ends with the conclusion section.

2 Framework of Mesh Fusion

The basic idea of the mesh fusion framework is to construct a transient surface interpolating the position and the normal constraints on the boundaries of the scissored models to be fused. To overcome the topological limitation on the openings, implicit surface is the best candidate for the transient surface. Here, we use one particular type of variatonal implicit surfaces - the RBF-based implicit surface to represent the transition surface.

Following [12], the RBF-based implicit surface can be expressed by a weighted sum of appropriate *radial basis functions* plus an affine term as

$$\Gamma(\mathbf{x}) = p(\mathbf{x}) + \sum_{i=1}^{N} \lambda_i \phi(\|\mathbf{x} - \mathbf{x}_i\|) \tag{1}$$

where λ_is are weights, and $\{\mathbf{x}_i = \{x_i, y_i, z_i\}\}_{i=1}^{N}$ are the location constraints, and $p(\cdots)$ is a linear affine function of position in the form of

$$p(\mathbf{x}) = p_0 + p_1 x + p_2 y + p_3 z.$$

For the radial basis functions, we commonly use $\phi(\mathbf{x}) = \|\mathbf{x}\|^3$. For N position constraints, they can be rewritten as N linear equations as

$$\Gamma(\mathbf{x}_i) = p(\mathbf{x}_i) + \delta_i + \sum_{i=1}^{N} \lambda_i \phi(\|\mathbf{x} - \mathbf{x}_i\|) = f_i \tag{2}$$

with $i = 1, \ldots, N$ and f_i is the function value shown on the location $\mathbf{x}_i$. The unknown λ_is in above linear equation system can be solved by adding the following compatible conditions

$$\sum_{i=1}^{N} \lambda_i = \sum_{i=1}^{N} \lambda_i x_i = \sum_{i=1}^{N} \lambda_i y_i = \sum_{i=1}^{N} \lambda_i z_i = 0.$$

It is not difficult to find that in Eq.(2) we add some new scalars, δ_i. These parameters are conducted to control the property of the implicit surface defined by Eq.(2) (ref. [13]). When $\delta_i \neq 0$, the variational implicit function will approximate the corresponding constraint points rather than interpolate them. Every position constraint then becomes a weighted average of the interpolating position and the regularization position (which is actually a low-pass filtering), so that the results are smoothed.

Equipped by the above RBF-based implicit surface modelling method, the framework of topology-free mesh fusion can be elegantly constructed. Taking the models shown in Figure 1 as an example, we want to fuse the scissored models in Figure 1(a) into a single object. The mesh fusion result is determined in three phases.

In the first phase, an initial RBF-based implicit surface Γ is constructed to smoothly interpolate the boundary openings on the given separated models. To achieve the position interpolation, every vertex on the openings leads to a linear equation as shown in Eq.(2), where $\mathbf{x}_i$ is the Euclidean coordinate of the vertex. Since the transient surface should exactly pass all the vertices on openings, the function values of Γ shown on the vertices are zero (i.e.,$f_i = 0$). However, simply setting these position constraints leads to vanishing side conditions, so that the surface Γ cannot be determined by Eq.(2). So we also define normal constraints in the same manner as [14].

In the second phase, the transient implicit surface Γ is adjusted by the user specified sketches. Our approach allows users to specify the shape of Γ through strokes (e.g, the strokes given in Figure 1(b)). To embed these inputs into our mesh fusion framework, the input strokes are first discreted into sampling points (in the screen plane) and then projected into the 3D space. The transient implicit surface is asked to approximately pass these sampling points. This can be achieved by adding the projected points into the RBF-based linear equation system (i.e., Eq.(2)) as position constraints. Note that in order to remove the dithering which is usually given on the user inputs, we only request the surface Γ to approximate but not to interpolate the sampling point by using $\delta_i \neq 0$.

The transient surface constructed so far is represented implicitly in a scalar function. Therefore, the last phase of our approach is to tessellate the transient surface into meshes so that the fused polygonal object is finally determined. However, as mentioned above, only one part of the implicit surface belongs to the transient region. The transient region and the non-transient region on the implicit surface Γ are separated by the openings on the given models. A user stroke is employed to specify the transient region (Figure 1(c)). By this specification, the tessellation scheme is able to avoid tessellating the non-transient region. Besides, for preventing the artificial results, the tessellation scheme is desired to generate well-shaped triangles that are adaptive to the mesh densities on the models to be fused. Here, we develop a particle sampling based tessellation method to generate the mesh surface smoothly joining the given models. Figure 1(d-e) show the particles sampled and the tessellation result. Details about tessellation will be presented in section 4 after introducing the sketching interface in the following section.

3 Sketching Interface

This section addresses the sketching interface implemented for letting users easily scissor and fuse the given polygonal models. The illustration for all these sketching tools is given in Figure 2.

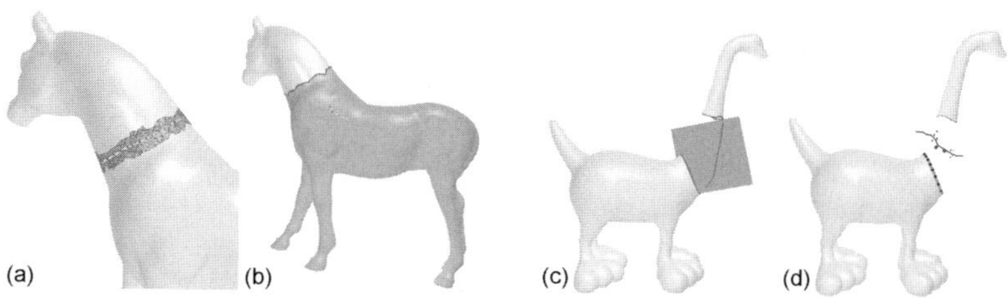

Fig. 2. Different sketches in our system: (a) *scissoring sketch* used for cutting input models, (b) *selecting sketch I* for the selection of the remained part, (c) *silhouette sketch* specifying the profile of the transition surface, and (d) *selecting sketch II* used to select the sampling region of tessellation

3.1 Scissoring Sketching

The scissoring of existing models is governed by user's strokes. Each stroke is projected onto the surface of the given model with a user-specified width (r in pixels) along the current viewing direction. The strokes actually specify an uncertain region where the cut following the nature seams of the mesh will be computed. Our implementation follows the intelligent scissoring method presented in [10] - computing a shorted path on the edges weighted with their dihedral-angle by using the Dijkstra's algorithm. The same as [10], the cutting path passes along the polygonal edges.

3.2 Sketching for Selection

Two types of sketches are implemented in our system for selection. The first one is adopted to specify the part to be cut off after the cutting path is determined. The user input stroke is projected onto the model along the viewing direction, then the selected faces will serve as seeds in a flooding algorithm to determine the region. When the cutting edges are met, the flooding algorithm stops. The second type of selecting sketches is for the tessellation of the transient implicit surface, Γ. As mentioned above, since only part of Γ needs to be tessellated to fuse the existing models, we should prevent sampling the undesired regions. Therefore, the selecting stroke is first discreted into several points, and then the points are projected onto the implicit surface Γ along the viewing direction. The projected points then serve as seeds in the particle-based tessellation scheme.

3.3 Silhouette Sketching

This sketching method is employed to control the silhouette of the transient surface. The user input is gathered as a collection of screen-space points, where the 2D points arrive at a rate that we cannot control. We resample these points following the algorithm of [2] so that they are not bunched up too closely.

The planar coordinates of the sampling points are easily determined by the coordinate transformation between the screen space and the object space. The same as all other sketching interfaces, the most difficult task is to determine the depth coordinates. Our solution is as illustrated in Figure 3. The silhouette sketching is assumed to specify the profile of the transient surface between two openings. First of all, we find the two openings A and B by the closest boundary points to the starting and ending points of P_{list} in the screen plane. The two ending points $\mathbf{P}_A$ and $\mathbf{P}_B$ on the silhouette of these two openings are then searched. After that, a plane Ω passing $\mathbf{P}_A$ and $\mathbf{P}_B$ whose normal vector is closest to the viewing vector is determined. The depth coordinates of all points in P_{list} are finally computed by projecting them onto the plane Ω. The projected points are then added into the RBF-based linear equation system (i.e., Eq.(2)) to control the shape of the transient implicit surface, Γ.

However, only adding the project points of P_{list} is not enough. We cannot ensure that the points falling on the silhouette of Γ. From the definition of silhouette in computer vision, we know that for a point on a silhouette, the surface normal on this point is perpendicular to viewing direction. Therefore, the normal constraints on the points in P_{list} also need to be added. With the tangent vector $\mathbf{t}_p$ at $\mathbf{p}$ in the plane Ω and the viewing vector $\mathbf{n}_v$, the normal on a point $\mathbf{p}$ is defined by $\mathbf{n}_p = \mathbf{t}_p \times \mathbf{n}_v$. The constraint of $\mathbf{n}_p$ is then added following the manner of the normal constrain on openings in the framework of mesh fusion - converted into a set of position constraints with a small offset.

4 Transient Surface Tessellation

After the RBF-based implicit surface Γ has been generated, we need to tessellate the transient region of the surface to construct the final model of mesh fusion. Based on the requirements of mesh fusion, the tessellation scheme should provide the following abilities:

- Be able to distinguish the transient and the non-transient regions so that only the transient part is tessellated.

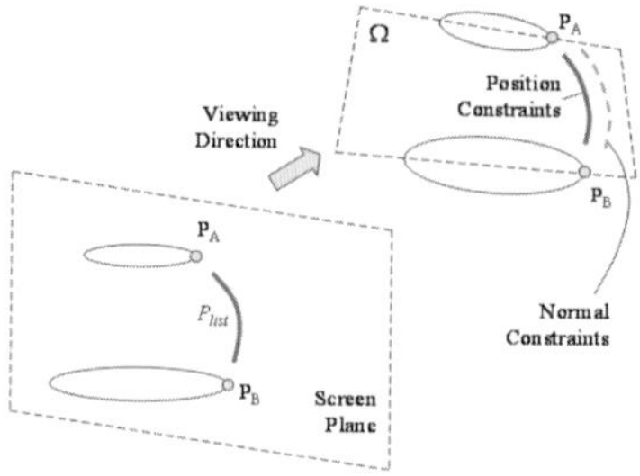

Fig. 3. Illustration for determine the depth coordinate for silhouette sketching

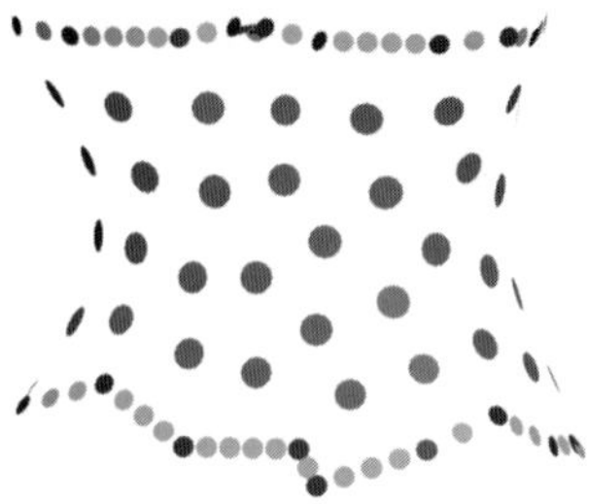

Fig. 4. Our compound particle system: red points represent *dynamic particles*, blue ones are *boundary particles*, and green ones are *virtual particles*

- Be able to construct the mesh compatible to the connectivity of openings on the scissored models.
- Be able to generate well-shaped triangles adaptive to the meshes on the models to be fused.

However, previous works rarely satisfy these requirements. Thus, a new tessellation scheme is developed. Our method first samples the implicit surface using a particle system, and then a triangular mesh surface is reconstructed by these sampling particles. The methodology of this scheme gives the potential for providing the above abilities. More specifically, the first one is satisfied as long as we only sample the transient region, the second ability could be provided by a constrained triangulation, and the last one is satisfied if we adaptively sample the transient surface and conduct an element-shape preserved triangulation method.

4.1 Compound Particle Sampling

First of all, we need to sample the transient region on Γ. Our particle sampling method borrows some idea from the method of Witkin and Heckbert [15], but with several necessary modifications and extensions. The same, we also diffuse particles on the implicit surfaces using the repulsion energy defined between the particles lying on Γ. For particle i, the energy due to another particle j is defined as:

$$E^{ij} = \alpha exp(-\frac{\|\mathbf{r}^{ij}\|^2}{2(\sigma^i)^2}), \tag{3}$$

where $\mathbf{r}^{ij} = \mathbf{p}^i - \mathbf{p}^j$ is the vector between the positions of particles, σ^i is the particle repulsion radius, and α is a global repulsion amplitude parameter (we choose $\alpha = 6$ in all our examples). The totally energy at particle i is defined as $E^i = \sum_{j=1}^{n}(E^{ij} + E^{ji})$, which leads the repulsion force be proportional to the gradient of energy with respect to position p^i:

$$F^i = (\sigma^i)^2 \sum_{j=1}^{N} (\frac{\mathbf{r}^{ij}}{(\sigma^i)^2} E^{ij} + \frac{\mathbf{r}^{ij}}{(\sigma^j)^2} E^{ji}) \tag{4}$$

By this repulsion force, the velocity of particle i in the diffusion on Γ is computed by

$$\mathbf{v}^i = F^i - \frac{\Gamma_x(\mathbf{p}^i) \cdot F^i}{\Gamma_x(\mathbf{p}^i) \cdot \Gamma_x(\mathbf{p}^i)} \Gamma_x(\mathbf{p}^i) \tag{5}$$

which is just the orthogonal projection of F^i onto the surface's tangent plane at $\mathbf{p}^i$.

Different from [15], three types of particles are defined in our compound particle sampling scheme:

1. **Boundary Particles** (e.g., the blue ones in Figure 4)**:** The particles coincide with the boundary vertices on given models - these particles will keep static during the particle diffusion.
2. **Dynamic Particles** (e.g., the ones in red color in Figure 4)**:** The particles that are dynamically moved on Γ driven by the repulsion forces. The particles are also adaptively re-sampled through a fission-death procedure.
3. **Virtual Particles** (coloured green in Figure 4)**:** They will be inserted on the edge between two neighbouring boundary particles. The virtual particles also keep static. These particles and the boundary particles will prevent the dynamic particles from running out the bounded area.

The repulsion energy defined among different types of particles follows the same formula as in Eq.(3).

The boundary and the virtual particles are first generated on the openings of given models. Their repulsion radius are assigned as 0.8 times of the average edge length $\bar{L}_k$ on the corresponding boundary k - so that they can provide enough repulsion forces to prevent the dynamic particles moving outwards the bounded region. The number of virtual particles defined on a boundary edge with length L is computed by $\lceil L/(\varepsilon \bar{L}_k) \rceil$, where ε is a small number usually chosen between 0.05 and 0.1. For better illustration, we adopt $\varepsilon = 0.3$ in Figure 4.

As discussed in section 2, the seed particles generated from user strokes are then defined as dynamic particles. The initial repulsion radius of each particle is defined as the average edge length of all the boundary edges. The dynamic particles are moved on the implicit surface by a diffusion process with the velocity defined in Eq.(5). At the same time, the dynamic particles are processed by the following fission-death process when they reach the equilibrium (e.g.,$\|\mathbf{v}^i\| < 4\sigma^i$):

- **Fission:** A dynamic particle is fission if its repulsion radius is greater than the desired one (i.e.,$\hat{\sigma}^i$). However, to ensure particles not been moved beyond the region bounded by boundary/virtual particles, the fission is prevented when a particle is near boundary or virtual particles.
- **Death:** A dynamic particle dies if its repulsion radius is too small (e.g., $\sigma^i < 0.5\hat{\sigma}^i$) and $R = 1$, where R is a uniform random number between 0 and 1 to prevent mass suicide in overcrowded regions.

In order to let the sampling adaptive to the mesh densities shown on the boundary of given models, we modify the sampling scheme to be resolution-dependent. For a dynamic particle i, a different desired radius is defined by

$$\hat{\sigma}_i = \hat{\sigma} M \sum_{k=1}^{M} (d_k^{-2} \bar{L}_k) / (\sum_{k=1}^{M} \bar{L}_k \cdot \sum_{k=1}^{M} d_k^{-2}) \tag{6}$$

where $\bar{L}_k$ is the average edge length of boundary k, d_k is the distance between particle i and the centroid of boundary k, and $\hat{\sigma}$ is the generally desired radius (we choose $\hat{\sigma}$ as the average edge length of all the boundary edges).

4.2 Triangulation

After sampling the transient surface, we reconstruct the mesh surface by the sampled particles so that the fused model is obtained. The intrinsic-property preserved method in [16] is adopted and modified to generate boundary compatible triangulations.

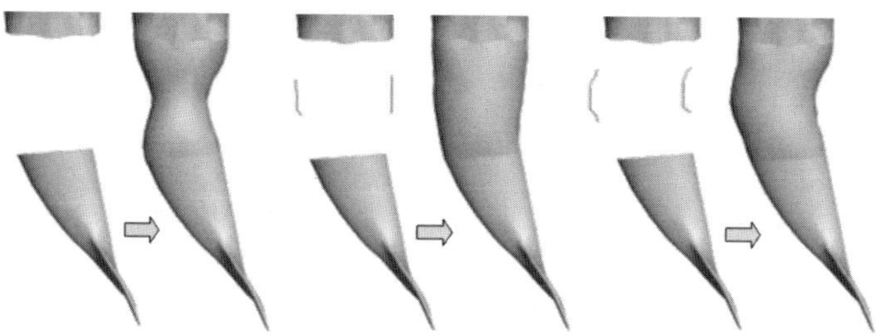

Fig. 5. Comparison of fusion with and without silhouette sketching: left column, no silhouette is defined; middle column, the generated transient surface by silhouette sketching is good; right column, more adjustment can be given

5 Results and Discussion

Our first example shown in this section (Figure 5) is employed to compare the results generated with vs. without silhouette sketching. In the left column of Figure 5, the transient surface tends to shrink due to the reason that the distance between two models to be fused is too far. To improve the shape of the fused object, two strokes are specified in the middle column of Figure 5 to specify the silhouette of the transient surface so that a much better result is obtained. Furthermore, we can even go on modifying the shape by sketching some new profiles (see the right column of Figure 5 - a mermaid with bended tail is produced).

The second test (see Figure 6) is to show the effect of the parameter δ conducted in specifying the silhouettes. As mentioned above, letting $\delta = 0$ will generate a surface interpolating the projected silhouette strokes which usually include dithering; when using $\delta \neq 0$, smoother results are obtained. Figure 7

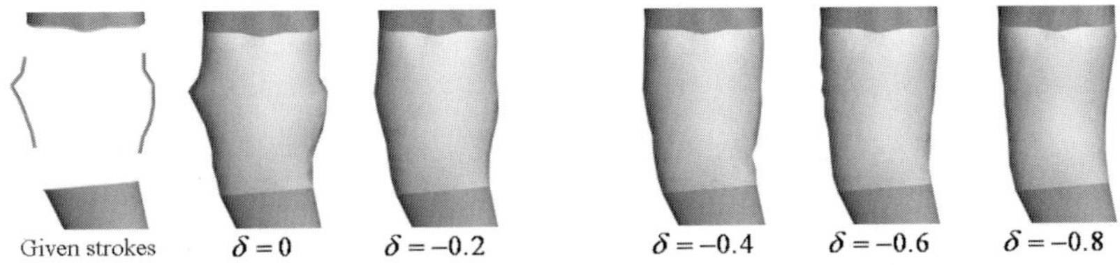

Fig. 6. A comparison of approximation and interpolation schemes with different δ

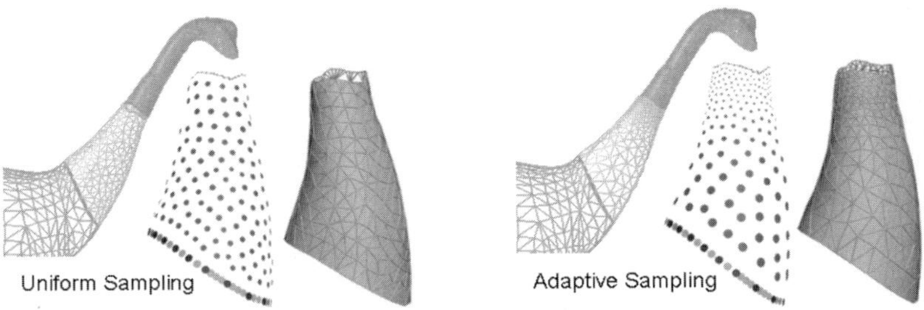

Fig. 7. Tessellation results from the uniform sampling vs. the adaptive sampling

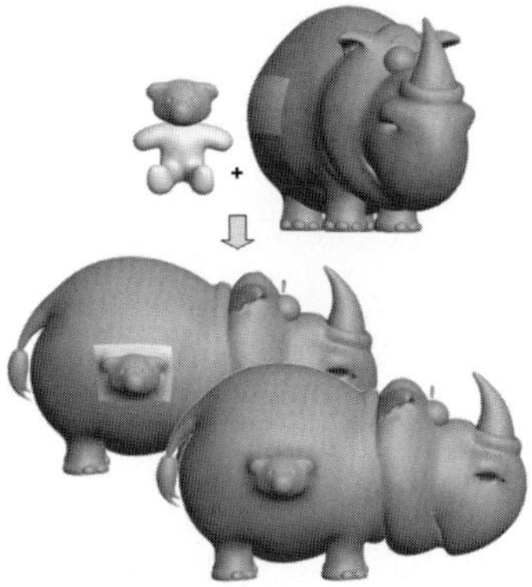

Fig. 8. The head of bear is cut and fused onto the rhinoceros

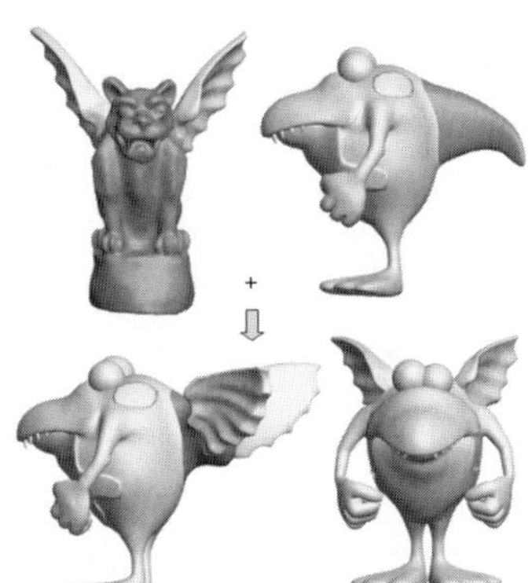

Fig. 9. Two wings cut from the gargoyle are fused onto the kill-whale

shows the comparison between the result generated by the uniform particle sampling (letting $\hat{\sigma}_i = \hat{\sigma}$) and the result from the adaptive sampling (using Eq.(6)). It is easy to find that the tessellating result with adaptive sampling gives better triangle-shape near the upper boundary of the fused region (see the part circled in dash lines in Figure 7). More examples can be found in Figure 8 and 9, where in Figure 8 the bear head is fused onto the body of a rhinoceros and the two wings of the gargoyle are cut and fused onto the kill-whale in Figure 9.

Table 1. Computing time taken in examples

Figure	RBF Fitting		Tessellation	
	Constraint Number	Time (sec)	Particle Number	Time (sec)
Fig. 1	574	0.592	578	4.522
Fig. 8	486	0.409	301	3.810
Fig. 9	330	0.207	250	3.924

We test our examples on a PC with Inter Pentium IV 2.4GHz CPU + 512M RAM. Table 1 summarizes the timing statistics for these examples. We use the matcom math library [17] to solve the linear system of RBF fitting (Eq. (2)).

Limitations: The current implementation of our approach presented in this paper has the following limitations.

- Firstly, seed particles in the tessellation scheme are specified by the region selecting strokes. In some extreme cases, it could be possible that no point from the strokes can be projected onto the transient implicit surface. An automatic method to generate seeding particles is expected.
- The second limitation comes from the assumption in the silhouette sketching. Our current method assumes that every stroke generates a curve linking to the endpoints of two openings in the screen plane. This is relative simple. In a more complex interface, one silhouette can be specified by several strokes as what is used in charcoal drawings.
- The third limitation of our sketch-based mesh fusion is that it always generate smooth transient surfaces lacking complex details. It is caused by the nature of RBF-based implicit surfaces.

6 Conclusions

In this paper, we developed a novel sketch-based mesh fusion interface for creating 3D models from existing ones. The mesh fusion is controlled by sketches which are intuitive and are easy to use even for novices. Complex 3D models can be constructed in a very short time. The developed sketching interface is based on a modelling framework of mesh fusion, where the transient surface interpolating the boundary openings on the given models is first modelled by a RBF-based implicit function and then meshed into a polygonal surface by an adaptive tessellation scheme. Compared to other previous methods, our method overcomes the topological limitation and multiple parts can be merged together at once.The limitations listed in Section 5 will be further investigated in our future research.

Acknowledgements. This project is supported by the National Natural Science Foundation of China (Grant No. 60573153), Natural Science Foundation of Zhejiang Province (Grant No. R105431), Huo Ying-Dong Education Foundation

(Grant No. 91069) and Program for New Century Excellent Talents in University(Grant No. NCET-05-0519). The author from the Chinese University of Hong Kong would like to thank the support from the projects CUHK/2050341.

References

1. R. Zeleznik, K. Herndon, and J. Hughes. Sketch: an interface for sketching 3d scenes. In *Proceedings of SIGGRAPH*, pages 163–170. 1996.
2. T. Igarashi, S. Matsuoka, and H. Tanaka. Teddy: a sketching interface for 3d freeform design. In *Proceedings of SIGGRAPH*, pages 409–416. 1999.
3. O. Karpenko, J. Hughes, and R. Raskar. Free form sketching with variational implicit surfaces. *Computer Graphics Forum*, 21(3):585–594, 2002.
4. H. Biermann, I. Martin, F. Bernardini, and D. Zorin. Cut-and-paste editing of multiresolution subdivision surfaces. *ACM Transactions on Graphics*, 21(3):312–321, 2002.
5. T. Kanai, H. Suzuki, J. Mitani, and F. Kimura. Interactive mesh fusion based on local 3d metamorphosis. In *Graphics Interface*, pages 148–156. 1999.
6. H. Fu, C.L. Tai, and H. Zhang. Topology-free cut-and-paste editing over meshes. In *Geometric Modeling and Processing*, pages 173–184. IEEE Computer Society Press, 2004.
7. J. Lin, X. Jin, C.C.L. Wang, J. Feng, and H. Sun. Topology free mesh fusion. In *Pacific Graphics*, pages 38–40. 2005.
8. Y. Yu, K. Zhou, D. Xu, X. Shi, H. Bao, B. Guo, and H.Y. Shum. Mesh editing with poisson-based gradient field manipulation. *ACM Transactions on Graphics*, 23(3):664–651, 2004.
9. O. Sorkine, Y. Lipman, D. Cohen-Or, M. Alexa, C. Rossl, and H.P. Seidel. Laplacian surface editing. In *Proceedings of the Eurographics/ACM SIGGRAPH Symposium on Geometry processing*, pages 179–188. 2004.
10. T. Funkhouser, M. Kazhdan, P. Shilane, P. Min, W. Kiefer, A. Tal, S. Rusinkiewicz, and D. Dobkin. Modelling by example. *ACM Transactions on Graphics*, 23(3): 652–663, 2004.
11. T. Hassner, L. Zelnik-Manor, G. Leifman, and R. Basri. Minimal-cut model composition. In *Proceedings of the International Conference on Shape Modelling and Applications*, pages 72–81. 2005.
12. M. Botsch and L. Kobbelt. Real-time shape editing using radial basis functions. *Computer Graphics Forum*, 24(3):611–621, 2005.
13. G. Yngve and G. Turk. Robust creation of implicit surfaces from polygonal meshes. *IEEE Transactions on Visualization and Computer Graphics*, 8(4):346–359, 2002.
14. G. Turk and J. O'Brien. Shape transformation using variational implicit functions. In *Proceedings of SIGGRAPH*, pages 335–342. 1999.
15. A.P. Witkin and P.S. Heckbert. Using particles to sample and control implicit surfaces. *Computer Graphics*, 28(2):269–277, 1994.
16. H.W. Lin, C.L. Tai, and G.J. Wang. A mesh reconstruction algorithm driven by an intrinsic property of a point cloud. *Computer-Aided Design*, 36(1):1–9, 2004.
17. The MathWorks. http://www. mathworks. com.

Real-Time Rendering of Point Based Water Surfaces

Kei Iwasaki[1], Yoshinori Dobashi[2], Fujiichi Yoshimoto[1], and Tomoyuki Nishita[3]

[1] Wakayama University
[2] Hokkaido University
[3] The University of Tokyo

Abstract. In recent years, attention has been paid to particle-based fluid simulation, with several methods being developed to incorporate particle-based simulation into CG animations. These methods reconstruct water surfaces that are usually represented by polygons. However, the computational cost of the surface reconstruction is quite high. Therefore, it is difficult to render the result of the particle-based simulation at interactive frame rates. To address this, we present a real-time method for rendering water surfaces resulting from particle-based simulation. We present an efficient GPU accelerated surface reconstruction method from particles, sampling the water surface point by point. In addition to rendering the point based water surfaces, the use of the GPU permits efficient simulation of optical effects such as refraction, reflection, and caustics.

1 Introduction

The research into fluid simulation is one of the most important research topics in computer graphics. Many methods have been developed for the simulation of fluids such as water, smoke, and fire [1, 2, 3, 4]. Most of these methods subdivide the simulation space into grids and solve the Navier-Stokes equations by discretizing the equations, using the grids to simulate the fluid dynamics. These methods are based on the Eulerian method. On the other hand, particle-based fluid simulations have been developed that represent the fluid as particles and calculate the fluid dynamics by solving the particles dynamics [5]. Particle-based fluid simulation has received attention since this simulation method is free from the numerical diffusions in the convection terms, suffered by the Eulerian method, and the surface transformation is easy to handle.

One of the methods of visualizing particle-based simulation is to reconstruct the water surface by polygons and to render these polygons. The water surface is reconstructed as follows. Initially, a density function, (or smoothing kernel), is defined with the distance from the center of the particle as parameter. The simulation space is subdivided into a grid and the summation of the densities of the particles is calculated at each grid point. Then the water surface is extracted as an iso-surface by using either the marching cube [6] or the level set method [3, 7]. To render high quality images of the water surfaces, the simulation space must be subdivided into numerous small cells. This indicates that the computational cost of the density calculation at each cell also increases and thus the cost of the reconstruction of the water surface becomes quite high. Moreover, many small polygons are generated from a fully subdivided grid. For the animation of the particle-based fluid simulation, the processing of enormous numbers of small polygons

H.-P. Seidel, T. Nishita, and Q. Peng (Eds.): CGI 2006, LNCS 4035, pp. 102–114, 2006.

compared to the number of screen pixels in each frame results in bandwidth bottlenecks. Therefore, these problems prevent the particle-based fluid simulation from being applied to interactive applications such as the preview of the simulation, video games and virtual reality.

In recent years, point based rendering methods have been developed, using the points as primitives instead of the polygons [8, 9]. Several methods that are accelerated by the GPU have been presented [10, 11]. Moreover, a point based method has been developed for visualizing iso-surfaces [12]. This method demonstrates that the point based visualization method for iso-surfaces can obtain storage and rendering efficiency compared with standard polygon-based methods.

Particle-based fluid simulation represents the fluid as particles and calculates the dynamics. Therefore, visualizing the particle-based fluid simulation by using point primitives is straightforward, since both of the result data of the simulation and the data from the rendering are unified into points.

This paper presents a fast rendering method, resulting in the particle-based fluid simulation without explicitly constructing polygons. In this paper, we deal with the water as a fluid and describe a rendering method for the water, represented by point primitives. To render the water surface, we have to take into account optical effects due to water surfaces such as reflection, refraction, and caustics. Rendering these optical effects is essential to increase realism. We present a fast rendering method for these effects from water surfaces, represented by points.

The contributions of our method are as follows.

- Fast generation of point primitives, representing water surfaces by using the GPU
- Fast rendering of the water surface, represented by points to obtain optical effects such as refraction, reflection, and caustics

The rest of our paper is organized as follows. Section 2 describes the related work. In Section 3, the overview of our method is presented. Section 4 describes the calculation of the density at each grid point by using the GPU. The method of rendering water surfaces, represented by points, is described in Section 5. The rendering results of point based fluid simulation are shown in Section 6. Finally, conclusions and future work are summarized in Section 7.

2 Previous Work

There have been many methods for visualizing the results of the fluid simulation. These are categorized into two types. One is to polygonize the iso-surfaces, represented by implicit functions, and then to render the polygons. Another is to directly render the implicit surface, without creating polygons. One of the methods to create the implicit surface using polygons is the marching cube method [6]. Many methods have employed this marching cube approach to render the water surface [13, 14, 4]. Moreover, a GPU accelerated iso-surface polygonization method has been proposed in recent years. Matsumura et al. proposed a fast method of iso-surface polygonization using programmable graphics hardware [15]. Reck et al. developed a hardware accelerated method to extract iso-surfaces from unstructured tetrahedral grids [16]. Although the marching cube method is efficient, representing iso-surfaces by creating polygons requires the memory for the connectivity information and two different data structures are required for points and polygons.

Another visualization method for fluid simulation of water involves the rendering of the iso-surface directly. Enright et al. [3] and Premoze et al. [7] employed a level set method to represent the water surface. Their methods render the water surface by using Monte Carlo path tracing methods. Whilst these methods can render realistic images, the computational cost for the rendering is high.

Although not for the rendering of the results of the fluid simulation, a visualization method has been developed for iso-surfaces using point primitives. Co et al. proposed a new algorithm called iso-splatting for rendering iso-surfaces using point primitives [12]. This method shows that the point based rendering of iso-surfaces can exceed the traditional polygon based approach such as a marching cube method in time and space efficiency. This method, however, does not describe the calculation method of the scalar(density) field, whose computational cost is high.

To solve these issues, we present a novel approach to render the water surface in a particle-based fluid simulation. In our method, the iso-surface, representing the water surface, is calculated efficiently by using fluid particles. Then the water surface is sampled, point by point, and rendered by surfels [8]. This makes it possible to unify the data structure into points in the simulation and then rendering, without the construction of polygons. Moreover, our method presents a fast rendering method for reflection, refraction, and caustics by use of the point sampled water surface.

3 Overview

Fig. 1 shows the overview of our method. This method deals with the results of the particle-based fluid simulation (Fig. 1(a)), calculated by particle-based simulation methods such as Moving Particle Semi-Implicit(MPS) and Smoothed Particle Hydrodynamics(SPH). Then the water surfaces, including caustics, are rendered as shown in Fig. 1(d). To render the water surfaces including caustics, particles that represent the surfaces must be extracted. Directly rendering the particles representing surfaces is one solution to visualize the result of the particle-based fluid simulation. However, the number of particles used in the simulation is usually between about $1,000$ and $100,000$ so that the number of particles representing a surface is, at most, several ten thousands. As Muller pointed out, this is not sufficient number to render high quality images [14]. On the other hand, point based rendering methods [8, 9, 10, 11] are designed to render huge number of points measured by range scanners. Thus, it is difficult to create high quality images of water surfaces by rendering only the particles used in the simulation.

Therefore, our method generates dense sampled surfels (Fig. 1(c)), representing water surfaces from all the particles used in the simulation (Fig. 1(a)). We create a temporary grid in the simulation space, where the densities of the particles are accumulated in each grid point (Fig. 1(b)). The density at each grid point is calculated as a density function.

The cost of the density computation at each grid point is quite high, since it depends on the number of grid points and the number of particles. We present a fast method for

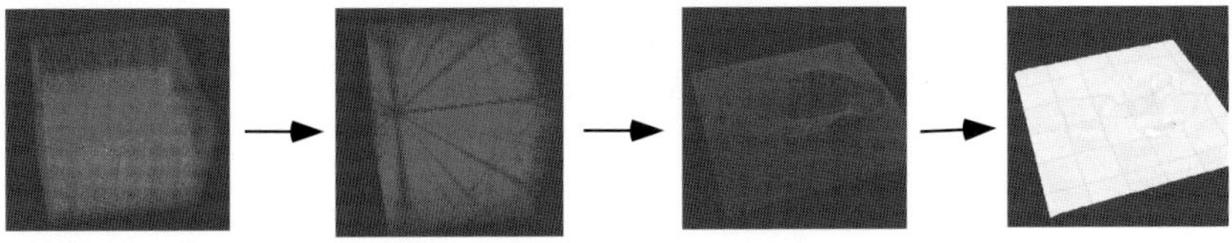

(a) result of particle based simulation (b) calculate density (c) extract surfels (d) render water surface and caustics

Fig. 1. Overview of our method

accumulating densities of particles by using the GPU. Our density calculation method can be applied not only to the particle-based simulation, but also to the grid based simulation, since the marching cube method requires the density at each grid. The points (surfels) on the iso-surface representing the water surface are then extracted. The calculation of surfels on the water surface is explained in Section 4.

The water surfaces are rendered by splatting surfels (Fig. 1(d)). Refraction and reflection of light is calculated by using refraction and reflection mapping of surfels. The rendering method of caustics from water surfaces represented by surfels is described in Section 5.

4 Generation of Surfels of the Water Surface Using a GPU

This section describes the method for generating dense surfels representing the water surface by using the particles. We create a grid in the simulation space and calculate the densities at each grid point by using particles. The simulation space is subdivided into $n_x \times n_y \times n_z$ grid points.

The density function $F(r, h)$ in this paper is calculated from the following equation [17].

$$F(r,h) = \begin{cases} \frac{405}{748\pi h}(-\frac{4}{9}a^6 + \frac{17}{9}a^4 - \frac{22}{9}a^2 + 1) & (0 \leq r \leq h), \\ 0 & (r > h), \end{cases} \tag{1}$$

where $a = r/h$, and where r is the distance from the center of particle to a calculation point, and h the effective radius of the particle. Although we have used this smoothing function as a density function for the prototype, other smoothing functions such as the smoothing kernel of the SPH could also be used as the density function.

The simulation space is located as shown in Fig. 2 and the z-axis is set to be the vertical direction. A virtual camera is set along the z-axis and the reference point of the virtual camera is set to be the center of the simulation space. A virtual screen is then set to be perpendicular to the z axis. The virtual screen consists of $n_x \times n_y$ pixels. Each pixel corresponds to a grid point on the grid planes perpendicular to the z axis, as shown in Fig. 2. The pixels in the screen frame buffer consist of R, G, B, and α components. To calculate the density of each grid point influenced by a particle, we use a metaball whose center is the position of the particle. The circle of intersection between the grid plane and the metaball, of effective radius is h, is calculated. The densities of pixels

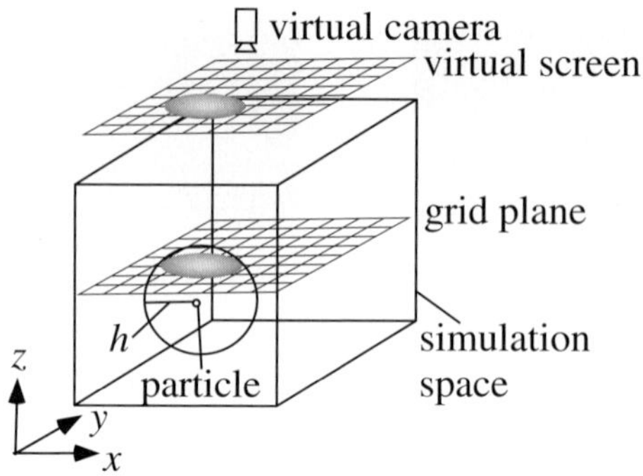

Fig. 2. Calculation of densities at each grid point by using splatting

within the circle of intersection are calculated. By drawing the circles of intersection with the densities and accumulating the densities in the frame buffer, the density of each pixel, corresponding to each grid point of the grid plane, is calculated by using the GPU.

The surfels on the water surface are generated using the following steps.

step1. Cluster the metaballs according to the z coordinate of the particle position.
step2. Project the metaballs in each cluster onto the screen and calculate the densities at each grid point.
step3. Generate the surfels on the iso-surface (water surface).

4.1 Clustering Particles

As shown in Eq.(1), the density contribution from the particle at the grid point is zero, when the distance between the particle and the grid point is larger than the effective radius h. To reduce the computational time of the density calculation, the particles whose density contributions are zero are eliminated. The particles are classified into N_c clusters by using the z coordinates of the particles. Cluster C_k (k is the cluster number) includes the particles p^k whose z coordinate p^k_z satisfies $z_k \leq p^k_z < z_{k+1}$. Then the particles belonging to the cluster C_k are taken into consideration only for the calculation of the grid points of the grid planes whose z coordinate z_i satisfies $z_k - h \leq z_i < z_{k+1} + h$.

4.2 Density Calculation and Generating Surfels

To calculate the density at each grid point, texture-mapped disks are projected onto the screen corresponding to the grid planes (see Fig. 2). The disk corresponds to the circle of intersection between the grid plane and the metaball whose center is the particle and the effective radius of h. The texture mapped onto the disk represents the density function F on the disk. The densities on the disk are calculated from the distance from the center of the particle to the grid point using Eq. (1). By projecting the disks of the particles, intersecting the grid plane, onto the screen, and accumulating the densities, the densities of the grid points on each grid plane are calculated by using the GPU. In this calculation, the quantization error problem can occur since the density is quantized

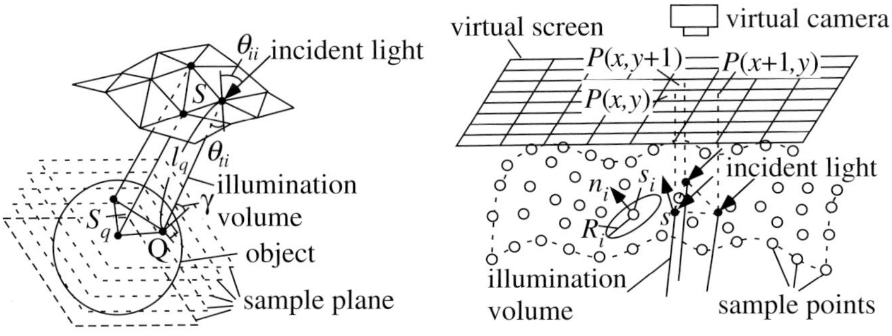

(a) illumination volume (b) virtual screen and camera

Fig. 3. Creation of illumination volume

with 8bit precision in most graphics hardware. This problem causes the error of the accumulated densities by using the GPU. To reduce the error, we use a floating point buffer for the precise calculation of accumulation of densities.

The disks are rendered by using point sprites. This makes it possible to accelerate the rendering process by the GPU. The point sprites are hardware functions that render a point by drawing a square, consisting of four vertices, instead of drawing a single vertex. The point sprites are automatically assigned texture coordinates for each vertex corner of the square. This indicates that each pixel inside the point sprite is automatically parameterized in the square. Therefore, the distance, d, from the center of the particle to each pixel of the point sprites can be calculated by using the fragment program. By comparing the distance, d, with the effective radius h, we can determine whether the pixel is within the circle of intersection or not. The density of the grid point corresponding to the pixel is calculated by inserting the distance, d, into the density function F. For the density calculation, we prepare a texture whose parameter is the distance from the calculation point to the center of the particle. The density of the pixel corresponding to the grid point is efficiently calculated by mapping this texture.

The density is scalar and the pixel of the frame buffer consists of four components. Therefore, our method calculates circles of intersection between the particle and four grid planes at once, and renders four disks by storing four densities in the RGB and α components. After drawing all the disks intersecting the four grid planes, the RGBα components are read from the frame buffer into the main memory. Then the points on the iso-surfaces for the four grid planes, corresponding to the RGBα components, are extracted. The density of the surface is specified by the user. We clear the frame buffer and draw all the disks intersecting the next four grid planes in the frame buffer. We repeat this for all grid planes that intersect the metaballs. Therefore, our method consumes texture memories only for the four grid planes.

The positions of the surfels, s_i, are set to the positions of these extracted points. The radius, R_i, of the surfel, s_i, is assigned and is determined so that there are no gaps between the surfels. Normal vector, n_i, of surfel s_i is calculated by using the gradient of the densities. If the distance between the extracted point and neighbor point is larger than a threshold, we add points on the iso-surface to fill gaps between the surfels.

5 Rendering Point Based Water Surface

This section describes the rendering method for water surfaces represented by surfels. To render the water surfaces, a disk is assigned to surfel s_i. The radius of the disk is R_i and the disk is perpendicular to normal n_i of the surfel. In this section, we first explain the rendering method of caustics due to water surfaces represented by surfels. Then the rendering method of water surfaces is described.

5.1 Rendering Caustics for Point Based Water Surface

Our rendering method for caustics is based on Nishita's and Iwasaki's methods [18, 19]. In these methods, the water surface is represented by a triangular mesh. At each vertex, the refracted direction of the incident light is calculated. Then the volumes are created by sweeping the vectors refracted from the triangle mesh. These volumes are called illumination volumes [18] (see Fig. 3). Caustics are rendered by accumulating the intensities of the areas of intersection between the object surface and the illumination volumes. The intensity, L_q, at point Q of the intersection area is calculated from the following equation,

$$L_q(\lambda) = L_i(\lambda)\cos\theta_{ii} T(\theta_{ii}, \theta_{ti}) \exp(-c(\lambda) l_q) F_q K(\lambda) + L_a(\lambda) \tag{2}$$

where λ is the wavelength, which is sampled for RGB components, $L_i(\lambda)\cos\theta_{ii}$ is the intensity of the incident light onto the water surface, $T(\theta_{ii}, \theta_{ti})$ is the Fresnel transmittance, $\exp(-c(\lambda) l_q)$ is the extinction of light from the water surface to point Q. F_q is the flux ratio and is calculated from the equation $F_q = S/S_q$, where S is the area of the triangle mesh of the water surface and S_q is the area of the intersection area between the illumination volume and the object (see Fig. 3). $K(\lambda)$ is the reflectance of the object surface and L_a is the intensity of the ambient light.

Our method is based on Iwasaki's method [19] that sets virtual planes (called sample planes) around the object and calculates the intensities of caustics on the object surface by using the intensities incident onto the sample planes. The intensities of the sample planes are calculated by accumulating the intersection triangles between the illumination volumes and the sample planes.

However, illumination volumes cannot be created, since the surfels representing water surfaces have no connectivity. To address this problem, we propose a method for creating illumination volumes from surfels.

5.2 Creation of Illumination Volumes

To create illumination volumes from the surfels, a virtual screen is set horizontally as shown in Fig. 3(b).The normal vector and the depth of a point that corresponds to each pixel, $P(x, y)$, of the frame buffer of the virtual screen are calculated by interpolating the normal and the depth values of the surfels representing the water surface.

The basic idea to create the illumination volumes is as follows. First, the depth of the water surface, $d_{(x,y)}$, from the virtual screen is calculated for each pixel, $P(x, y)$. Using the depth, points $s_{(x,y)}$ on the water surface are obtained. The normal vector, $n_{(x,y)}$,

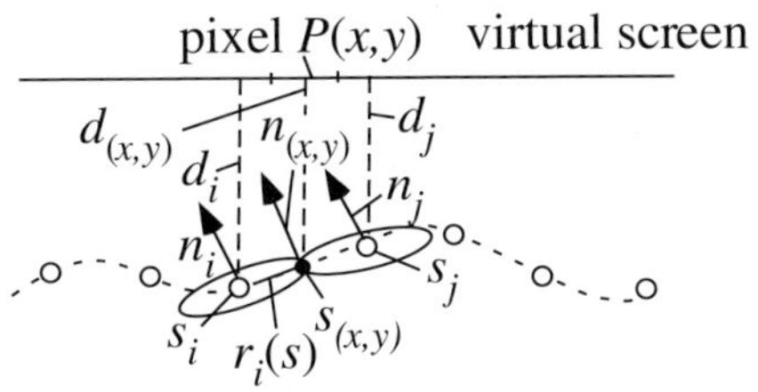

Fig. 4. Calculation of normal $n_{(x,y)}$ at point $s_{(x,y)}$ on the water surface, and depth $d_{(x,y)}$ from point $s_{(x,y)}$ to the virtual screen

of $s_{(x,y)}$ is also calculated by interpolating the normals of the nearby surfels. Then a refraction vector at $s_{(x,y)}$ is computed. An illumination volume is created by sweeping the refracted vectors from points $s_{(x,y)}$, $s_{(x+1,y)}$, and $s_{(x,y+1)}$ (or $s_{(x+1,y+1)}$, $s_{(x+1,y)}$, and $s_{(x,y+1)}$) that correspond to neighboring pixels. In the following, the calculation method for the normal and the depth from the virtual camera is explained.

Normal, $n_{(x,y)}$, and depth, $d_{(x,y)}$, at point $s_{(x,y)}$ on the water surface are calculated from the following equations (see Fig. 4),

$$n_{(x,y)} = \frac{\sum_i g(\frac{r_i(s)}{R_i})n_i}{\sum_i g(\frac{r_i(s)}{R_i})}, d_{(x,y)} = \frac{\sum_i g(\frac{r_i(s)}{R_i})d_i}{\sum_i g(\frac{r_i(s)}{R_i})}, \tag{3}$$

where g is a Gaussian function whose parameter is distance, $r_i(s)$, between each surfel, s_i and $s_{(x,y)}$, and returns 0 if $r_i(s)$ is larger than radius R_i.

The calculation of the normal, $n_{(x,y)}$, and depth, $d_{(x,y)}$, is accelerated by using the GPU. We create the normal map that stores the normal information at each point, $s_{(x,y)}$, corresponding to each pixel of the virtual screen. The normal map of the water surface is calculated by splatting the surfels. To create the normal map, calculated from Eq.(3), the xyz components of normal vector, n_i, of surfel, s_i, are encoded as RGB component of the color of surfel. Then the surfels are projected onto the screen with a radially decreasing Gaussian weight function $g(\frac{r_i(s)}{R_i})$. The value of Gaussian weight function $g(\frac{r_i(s)}{R_i})$ is stored in the α component of pixel, $P(x, y)$, and is used as a blending factor to calculate Eq.(3). We prepare a 1D texture for the Gaussian weight function. This texture is mapped onto each surfel and is multiplied by the RGB components of the surfel, corresponding to the normal vector of that surfel. The texture-mapped surfels are rendered and the resulting colors are accumulated in the frame buffer by using additive color blending functions. The resulting image is stored as a texture. Normal, $n_{(x,y)}$, at surface point, $s_{(x,y)}$, corresponding to pixel, $P(x, y)$, is calculated by dividing the RGB components of each pixel that store the summation of weighted color ($\sum_i g(\frac{r_i(s)}{R_i})n_i$), by the α component that stores the summation of weight ($\sum_i g(\frac{r_i(s))}{R_i})$). This per-pixel normalization is accelerated by using the fragment program of the GPU. The depth, $d_{(x,y)}$, is calculated in the same manner. The normal and depth information are read back to the main memory and the point, $s_{(x,y)}$, and refracted direction of the incident light onto $s_{(x,y)}$ are calculated. Illumination volumes are created by sweeping the refracted direction from each point, $s_{(x,y)}$.

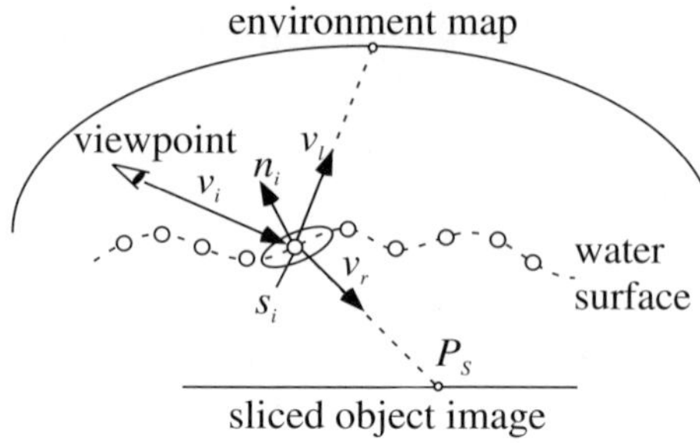

Fig. 5. Rendering water surfaces by surfels

When the illumination volumes are created, caustics are rendered, using Iwasaki's method [19]. To render caustics due to water surfaces, sample planes are set around the objects within the water, and the intensities of caustics on the surface of the object are calculated by using the illumination distribution on the sample planes. In Iwasaki's method, an object is represented by a set of images of the object surface, that are created by rendering the object between two adjacent sample planes (see Fig. 3). These images are called the sliced object images [19]. The refracted object with caustics is rendered by refraction mapping of the sliced object images.

5.3 Rendering Water Surfaces Represented by Surfels

Water surfaces are rendered through the use of a splatting technique. Our rendering method extends the method proposed by Bostch et al. [10] to take into account refraction, reflection and caustics. The refraction of an object, with caustics through the water surface is rendered through the use of refraction mapping of sliced object images. The reflection of the environment is rendered through the use of reflection mapping. We use a three-pass rendering approach. Before rendering, we eliminate invisible surfels by using a backface-culling method. In a first pass, the surfels are rendered only to the z buffer with all z values having an ϵ offset added. ϵ is specified by the user.

In the second pass, the z-buffer update is turned off so that the overlapping surfels are blended if and only if the difference of their depth values is less than ϵ. For each visible surfel, the reflection vector v_l and the refraction vector v_r of the viewing ray are calculated (see Fig. 5). We calculate the intersection point P_S between the sliced object image and the refracted viewing ray from the surfel, and the texture coordinate of P_S for the sliced object image. The texture coordinate for the environment map of the surfel is also calculated. The surfel is rendered by mapping the sliced object image and the environment map texture onto the point sprite. At each pixel corresponding to the disk of the surfel, the Gaussian weight function is associated to blend the overlapping surfels. The RGB components of the pixel are multiplied by the Gaussian weight function by mapping the texture of the Gaussian weight onto the surfel.

In the third pass, the values of RGB components of each pixel, storing the accumulated weighted color must be normalized by dividing by the value of the alpha component that stores the accumulated Gaussian weights. The per-pixel normalization is performed by the method described in Section 5.2. This per-pixel normalization results in high quality images.

6 Results

Figs. 6 and 7 show the result of the MPS simulation rendered by our method. These figures are stills from an animation of dropping a parallelepiped into the water pool. The numbers of the points representing the water surface are from 61,500 to 77,000 in this animation. The average rendering time of these figures is about 0.039 sec (25.5fps). Our method can render the water surfaces, represented by points, including caustics, refraction, and reflection in real-time. These images are created on a desktop PC (CPU: Pentium4 3.4GHz, 2GB memory) with a nVidia GeForce6800 GT. The image size of these figures is 512×512. The size of the virtual screen for creating illumination volumes is 128×128.

The number of particles used for the simulation is about 210,000. The temporary grid is subdivided into 256^3. The computational time of density calculation from the particles using the GPU is 0.91 sec. The memory for calculating the density in the GPU is only 1MB. For the software calculation, the computational time is about 80 sec. That is, our method using the GPU can calculate the densities about 88 times faster than the method using the software. The computational time for extracting the surfels on the iso-surface is about 0.16 sec. Our GPU based method extremely reduces the time of reconstructing the water surface from the particles compared to the software based method. The relative difference between the densities calculated by the GPU and those by the software is about 1.9%. To verify the quantization error due to the GPU based density calculation, Fig. 8 shows the comparisons of the water surface that is extracted from the densities calculated by the GPU and that by the software. The image quality of

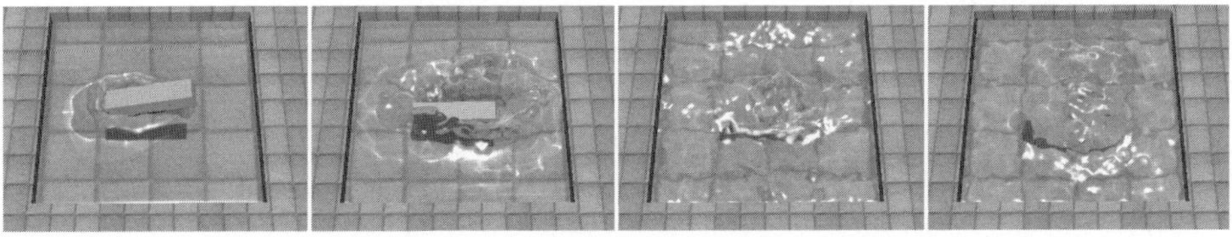

Fig. 6. Rendering the result of the MPS simulation

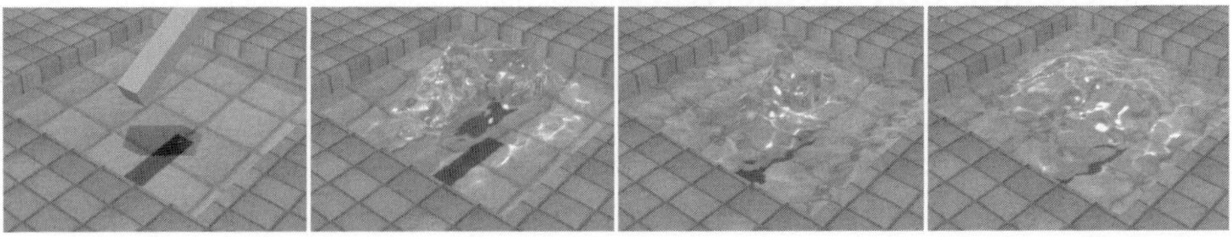

Fig. 7. Rendering the result of the MPS simulation viewed from another viewpoint

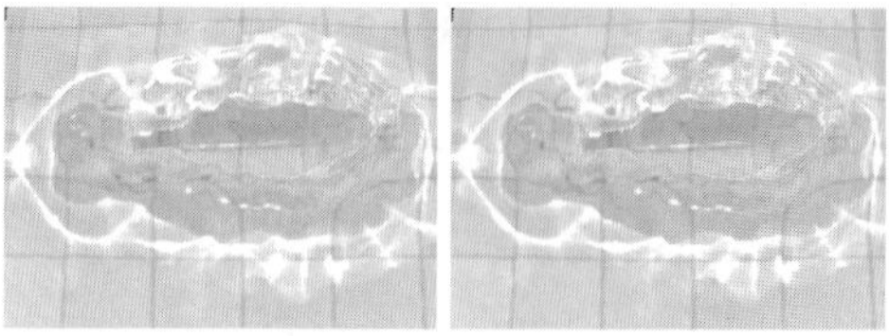

(a) (b)

Fig. 8. Comparisons of the water surface generated by using the GPU based density calculation (a) and the water surface calculated by the software (b)

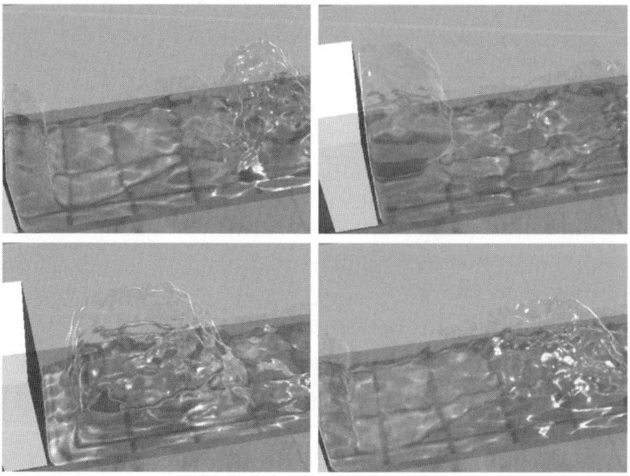

Fig. 9. Rendering the result of the MPS simulation of making waves

the water surface (Fig. 8(a)) calculated by using the GPU based density calculation is indistinguishable from that by using the software based density calculation (Fig. 8(b)).

Fig. 9 shows the result of MPS simulation of making waves. These figures show that our method can extract complex shape of water surfaces. The average rendering frame rate of these figures is about 21.7fps. The numbers of the points representing the water surface are from 55,000 to 120,000 in this animation.

7 Conclusions and Future Work

In this paper, we have presented a fast rendering method for the particle-based simulation. To calculate the water surface from the result of the particle-based simulation, a temporary grid is created and the densities at each grid point by using the particles are calculated. We accelerate this density calculation by using a GPU based splatting method. Then the iso-surface is extracted and represented by surfels. The rendering method has been developed for a water surface, which is represented by the surfels. Moreover, our method can render the reflection, refraction, and caustics due to the point based water surface in real-time. Our method drastically reduces the time of the surface reconstruction and rendering. This makes it possible to easily preview the result of the particle-based simulation.

In future work, we plan to develop a method for improving the quality of images of the water surface by adaptively adding surfels, i.e., we need to add the surfels adaptively according to the intensity distribution at the water surface since the number of the surfels is sometimes insufficient when the light intensities drastically change at the water surface. Moreover, we would like to develop a method for rendering splashes and foams using surfels.

Acknowledgements

We thank Prometech Software Inc. for providing MPS simulation data and thank Kaori Ono and Yoshitaka Moro for their help.

References

[1] Stam, J.: Stable fluids. In: Proc. SIGGRAPH'99. (1999) 121–128
[2] Foster, N., Fedkiw, R.: Practical animation of liquids. In: Proc. SIGGRAPH 2001. (2001) 23–30
[3] Enright, D., Marschner, S., Fedkiw, R.: Animation and rendering of complex water surfaces. In: Proc. SIGGRAPH 2002. (2002) 736–744
[4] Takahashi, T., Fujii, H., Kunimatsu, A., Hiwada, K., Saito, T., Tanaka, K., Ueki, H.: Realistic animation of fluid with splash and foam. Computer Graphics Forum **22**(3) (2003) 391–400
[5] Koshizuka, S., Tamako, H., Oka, Y.: A particle method for incompressible viscous flow with fluid fragmentation. Computational Fluid Dynamics Journal **29**(4) (1995) 29–46
[6] Lorensen, W., Cline, H.: Marching cubes: A high resolution 3D surface construction algorithm. In: Proc. SIGGRAPH'87. (1987) 163–169
[7] Premoze, S., Tasdizen, T., Bigler, J., Lefohn, A., Whitaker, R.: Particle based simulation of fluids. Computer Graphics Forum **22**(3) (2003) 335–343
[8] Pfister, H., Zwicker, M., Baar, J., Gross, M.: Surfels: Surface elements as rendering primitives. In: Proc.SIGGRAPH 2000. (2000) 335–342
[9] Zwicker, M., Pfister, H., Baar, J., Gross, M.: Surface splatting. In: Proc. SIGGRAPH 2001. (2001) 371–378
[10] Bostch, M., Kobbelt, L.: High-quality point-based rendering on modern GPUs. In: Proc. Pacific Graphics 2003. (2003) 335–343
[11] Guennebaud, G., L.Barthe, M.Paulin: Deferred splatting. Computer Graphics Forum **23**(3) (2004)
[12] Co, C., Hamann, B., Joy, K.: Iso-splatting: A point-based alternative isosurface visualization. In: Proc. Pacific Graphics 2003. (2003) 325–334
[13] Kunimatsu, A., Watanabe, Y., Fujii, H., Saito, T., Hiwada, K., Takahashi, T., Ueki, H.: Fast simulation and rendering techniques for fluid objects. Computer Graphics Forum **20**(3) (2001) 57–66
[14] Muller, M., Charypar, D., Gross, M.: Particle-based fluid simulation for interactive applications. In: Proc. Symposium on Computer Animation 2003. (2003) 154–159

[15] Matsumura, M., Anjo, K.: Accelerated isosurface polygonization for dynamic volume data using programmable graphics hardware. In: Proc. Electronic Imaging2003. (2003) 145–152
[16] Reck, F., Dachsbacher, C., Grosso, R., Greiner, G., Stamminger, M.: Realtime isosurface extraction with graphics hardware. In: Proc. Eurographics 2004 Short Presentation. (2004)
[17] Wyvill, G., Trotman, A.: Ray-tracing soft objects. In: Proc. Computer Graphics International. (1990) 439–475
[18] Nishita, T., Nakamae, E.: Method of displaying optical effects within water using accumulation-buffer. In: Proc. SIGGRAPH'94. (1994) 373–380
[19] Iwasaki, K., Dobashi, Y., Nishita, T.: A fast rendering method for refractive and reflective caustics due to water surfaces. Computer Graphics Forum **22**(3) (2003) 601–609

Controllable Multi-phase Smoke with Lagrangian Particles

Byung-Seok Roh and Chang-Hun Kim

Dept. of Computer Science & Engineering, Korea University,
Asan Science Building 249, Anamdong, Seongbuk-ku, Seoul, Korea
{prayforher, chkim}@korea.ac.kr

Abstract. This paper describes a method for controlling the multi-phase smoke animation that uses Lagrangian particles. Previous methods need several density fields to simulate different types of smoke. We use a single field, which is more like a natural phenomenon to obtain the interactive motions of fluid. Also, whereas existing methods which apply control forces to cells only, we define particle forces which enable each particle to move independently towards to target shape. Additionally, we set up internal target forces which distribute the particles uniformly within the target shape, no that it is represented more precisely.

1 Introduction

The simulation of natural phenomena is now sufficiently realistic to be included in digital animations and virtual environments. It is essential that computer animators are able to control fluid simulations without having to subordinate their creative inspiration to technical barriers. Recently introduced for controlling fluids [2], [9], [11] are efficient and easy to implement. Recent simulations based on three-dimensional Navier-stokes equation are not only realistic but also allow control of the fluid, so that it moves toward a target shape.

Existing methods for controlling a fluid which is moving towards a target shape focuses on controlling the shape of the target feature. These methods use a distance field to create an additional force which propels the fluid towards the target shape. This leads to limitations in achieving various effects, because the direct route to the target shape is not always the one that the animator wants the fluid to follow.

We have therefore chosen a different strategy. Instead of exerting external control forces on the fluid at each frame, we adjust the physical properties of the simulation space, so that the fluids in this space to follow the required trajectory. We can, for instance, simulate smoke which follows the required path towards a target shape, while still exhibiting behavior that is interesting and looks natural. This is made possible by three new terms which we add to the standard flow equations: (i) the control forces on a cell that cause the fluid to carry the smoke towards a target shape, (ii) particle forces enable each particle to move independently and allow some particles to move against the control forces, (iii) internal forces make the particles diffuse uniformly within the target shape.

Our main contributions are, because our method use Lagrangian particle, simulation of different types of smoke and their interactions.

H.-P. Seidel, T. Nishita, and Q. Peng (Eds.): CGI 2006, LNCS 4035, pp. 115 – 123, 2006.

The remainder of this paper is structured as follows. In the next section we briefly introduce the relevant previous work. In Section 3 we review the standard equations commonly used for simulating fluid flow, and Section 4 describes the three new terms that we propose. We present a selection of the results we have achieved with our technique in Section 5. Section 6 concludes the paper.

2 Related Work

Many researchers in the field of computer graphics have used physical-based models and computational fluid dynamics (CFD) to simulate fluid flows. We will not attempt to provide a complete survey of such methods; the interested reader can find good surveys elsewhere [3], [8], [18]. Instead, we focus on the different mechanisms for controlling fluid flows.

Foster and Metaxas [7] allowed animators to control a fluid without knowing all about the underlying physics of the simulation, because the low-level details were concealed. However, animators using this technique still need some knowledge of fluid dynamics, and it does not allow them to manipulate the target shape.

Treuille et al. [17] proposed a new method to control smoke, using efficient optimization of control forces. This is based on earlier work on controlling rigid bodies [16]. Unfortunately, the number of degrees of freedom in fluids is much larger, and so this method needs hours of computing time, even for simple two-dimensional target shapes such as letters of the alphabet.

Fattal et al. [2] introduced a new and efficient method to match smoke density against user-specified distributions, which involved a model with a driving force term and a smoke-gathering term. It achieves much shorter computing times than nonlinear optimization. They mentioned about multiphase smoke, but their treatment is simple and their technique does not allow different phase to interact each other.

Following Fattal et al. [2], Hong and Kim [9] proposed another efficient, simple method to control a fluid animation, in which a potential field is based on the shape of the target. An external force obtained from the negative gradient of the potential field enable the smoke to move towards the target shape.

Shi and Yu. [11] introduced a method based on the level-sets of the smoke, which uses velocity constraints on the smoke boundary to match the shape of the target. It controls the shape of the more efficiently and effectively the forcing and gathering terms required by Fattal et al. [2].

All of the methods reviewed above simulated a single phase of smoke. We propose a method that matches smoke density against user-specified distributions accurately and rapidly. Furthermore, our technique can simulate the interaction of different types of smoke by using Lagrangian particles.

3 Overview

To simulate smoke motion realistically, we need to use either the Navier-Stokes or the Euler equation. We will briefly explain the Euler equation that we use. Let $\mathbf{u}=\mathbf{u}(x, t)$ denote the time-dependent vector field that specifies the velocity of location x on a cell at time t and its temporal derivative by $\mathbf{u}_t$. The Euler equation that satisfies the incompressibility condition can then be written as:

$$\mathbf{u}_t = -\mathbf{u} \cdot \nabla \mathbf{u} - \nabla p + \mathbf{f} \tag{1}$$

$$\nabla \cdot \mathbf{u} = 0 \ , \tag{2}$$

where $p=p(x, t)$ is the hydrostatic pressure and **f** accounts for the external forces that affect fluid flow, such as gravity and buoyancy. This external force **f** is important in controlling the fluid, and follows Fattal et al. [2] and Hong and Kim [9]. However, we extend the score of there authors' work by considering multiple target shapes.

We will describe in detail now **f** can be used to achieve multiple target shapes, and we will propose internal target forces which enable the particles to be distributed uniformly within the target shape.

4 Modified Equations of Flow

Our approach entails three modifications to Equation 1. Firstly, we add control forces acting on each which cell move the fluid that the cell controlling toward target shape; secondly, we add particle forces which apply to each particle individually, and may appose the control forces; and finally, we add internal target forces to increase the accuracy with which the target shapes are achieved.

These three new terms are controlled by the non-negative parameters v_c, v_p, and v_I, whose effect is discussed in Section 4.4.

$$\mathbf{u}_t = -\mathbf{u} \cdot \nabla \mathbf{u} - \nabla p + v_c \mathbf{F}_T(\rho, \rho^T) + v_p \mathbf{F}_{T_i}(\rho, \rho^{T_i}) + v_I \mathbf{F}_I \tag{3}$$

4.1 Control Forces Acting on a Cell

We will now describe the control force $\mathbf{F}_T$ that influences a cell. To determine the control force $\mathbf{F}_{T,}$ we need to create a distance field D_i ($1 \le i \le P_n$, where P_n is the number of target shape). Each cell in the distance field is associated with a value which represents the closest distance value to target shape, and the value of cell in the target is zero. Figure 1 shows an example of a two-dimensional field. We need to make separate distance fields for each target.

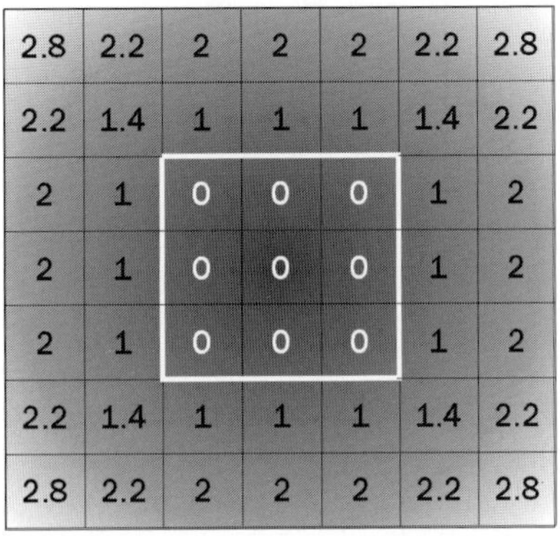

Fig. 1. An example of two-dimensional distance field. (The white square is the target shape).

After creating the distance fields, we need to calculate the control force $\mathbf{F}_T$ that will make the smoke move toward the target shape. The control force $\mathbf{F}_{T_i}$ for a target i is obtained by calculating the negative gradient of the distance field D_i:

$$\mathbf{F}_{T_i} = -\nabla D_i \tag{4}$$

Let us denote by the time-dependent scalar field that specifies the smoke density of grid at location x and time t as $\rho(x, t)$, and the final smoke density that we require at the target shape finally by $\rho^T(x)$. The control force $\mathbf{F}_T(x)$ that acts on the particles in cell x at time t is written as $\mathbf{F}_T(x, \rho, \rho^T)$ and is formulated as follows:.

$$\mathbf{F}_T(x,\rho,\rho^T) = \frac{\sum_{i=1}^{P_n}\left(p_i \mathbf{F}_{T_i}(x,\rho,\rho^T)\right)}{\sum_{i=1}^{P_n} p_i} \tag{5}$$

where p_i is the number of particles in cell x that are moving towards the ith target.

Consider cell x is Figure 2. If $\mathbf{F}_{T_1}$ points towards the target of the blue particles, and $\mathbf{F}_{T_2}$ points towards the target of the red particles, then the control force on a cell x is

$$\mathbf{F}_T(x,\rho,\rho^T) = 0.3\mathbf{F}_{T_1}(x,\rho,\rho^{T_1}) + 0.7\mathbf{F}_{T_2}(x,\rho,\rho^{T_2}).$$

The weights 0.3 and 0.7 represent the proportion of blue and red particles in cell x.

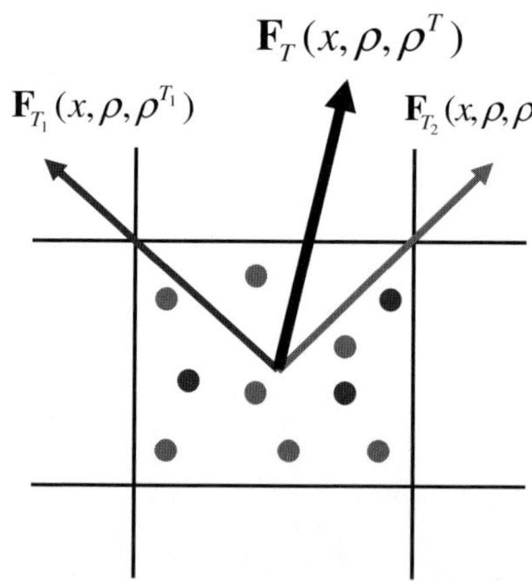

Fig. 2. The control forces on a cell

4.2 Particle Forces

When there are few particles of a certain type in a cell, they will tend not to follow the desired path if they are only subject to the control forces on cell. Therefore we give each particle its own force, directed towards its target.

We discovered by experiment that the magnitudes of the particle forces should be less than that of the control force, to achieve a natural-looking result. The possibility remains that a particle while move against the control forces on its cell to the extent that it crosses to a neighboring cell (Figure 3).

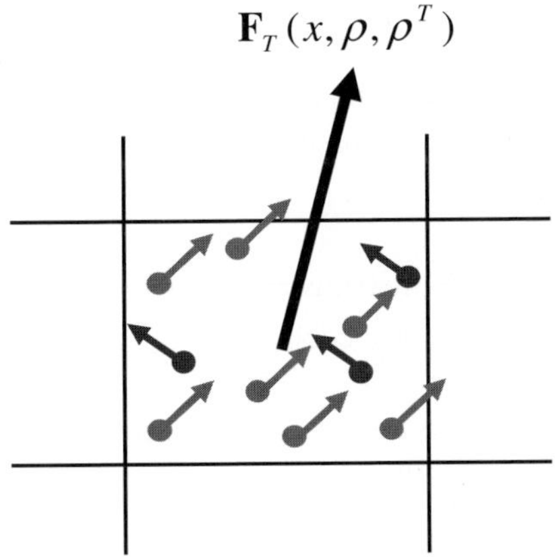

Fig. 3. Each particle has its own force

4.3 Internal Target Forces

Previous methods of controlling fluids [2], [9] are only concerned with propelling the fluid towards the target shape. No control forces are defined inside the target. This limits the complexity of the target that can be achieved. We overcome the problem by means of additional control forces that act on particles inside the target.

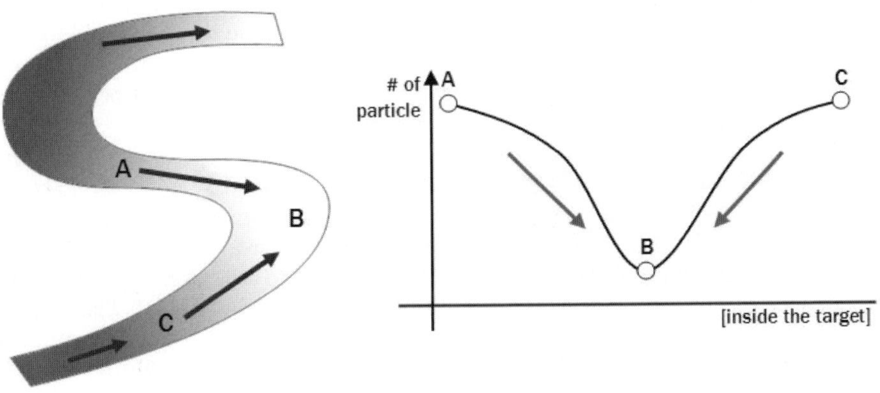

Fig. 4. Internal target forces that act inside the target. (Red region is denser than white region).

The internal target force $\mathbf{F}_I$ is defined as:

$$\begin{cases} \mathbf{F}_I = -\nabla\rho & \text{inside the target} \\ \mathbf{F}_I = 0 & \text{outside the target.} \end{cases} \tag{6}$$

$\mathbf{F}_I$ is directed towards regions of low particle density inside the target. Its purpose is to redistribute particles uniformly within the target shape, so as to achieve detailed features of the target shape.

In Figure 4, the internal target forces act in directions from A and C and toward B, because the density at A and C is greater than that at B.

4.4 Control Parameters

The simulations produced by our methods are controlled via three parameters: the control force coefficient ν_c, particle force coefficient ν_p, and internal force coefficient ν_I:

- ν_c This parameter allows the animator to boost or weaken the control force, thus affecting the speed at which the simulation progresses towards the current target state.
- ν_p This parameter determines the rate of particle force. Increasing it results show that different types of smoke move independently. If ν_p is bigger than ν_c, it is less likely for interactive smoke.
- ν_I This parameter determines the rate of internal force. Increasing it oscillates results.

5 Results and Discussion

We implemented our method in both 2D and 3D using C++ and tested it on a Windows PC with an Intel Pentium IV processor running at 3.0GHz and 1GB of RAM. 2D simulations were performed a 300^2 grid, and each a single time step took 0.5 seconds. 3D simulations were performed a 100^3 grid and each time step took about 11 seconds. The forces $\mathbf{F}_T$ and $\mathbf{F}_I$ that we have introduced add about 20 percent to the computation time.

Figure 5-7 show the control of smoke in two-dimensional environment. The input was standard bitmap images which were converted to a distance field during preprocessing. Figure 5 shows two regions of different-colored smoke moving diagonally across each other and ending up in two circular target regions.

In Figure 6, four types of smoke moves consecutively to two targets. Figure 7 compares images of our technique with image follow from Fattal et al. [2]. The eight images on the left are close-ups of each of the center of the density field, and the two images on the right are the results of each method. In our results, a swirling effect can be seen at the center of density field because our method uses a single density field which enables each particle to move interactively.

Finally, Figure 8 shows a three-dimensional animation, using three-dimensional polygon models as input data.

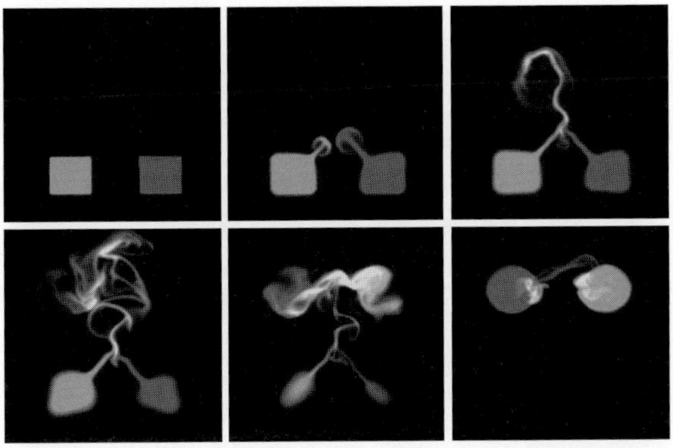

Fig. 5. Interaction of two types of smoke

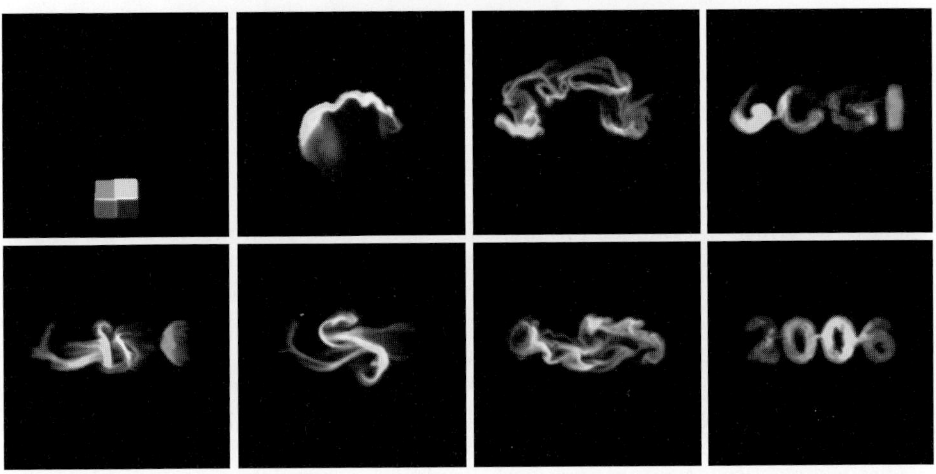

Fig. 6. Four types of smoke move towards the 'CGI' target and are then modified towards '2006'

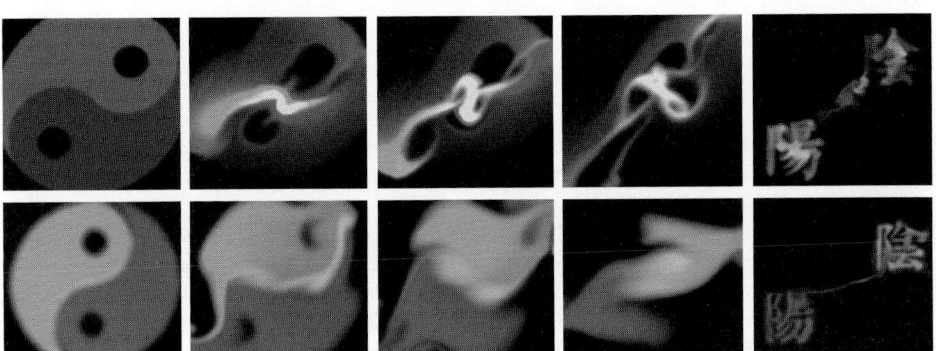

Fig. 7. Two types of smoke move from a 'yin-yang' shape to targets which are the corresponding Chinese characters. The top row of images shows the motion achieved by our method, and the bottom row shows that achieved by the method of Fattal et al. [2].

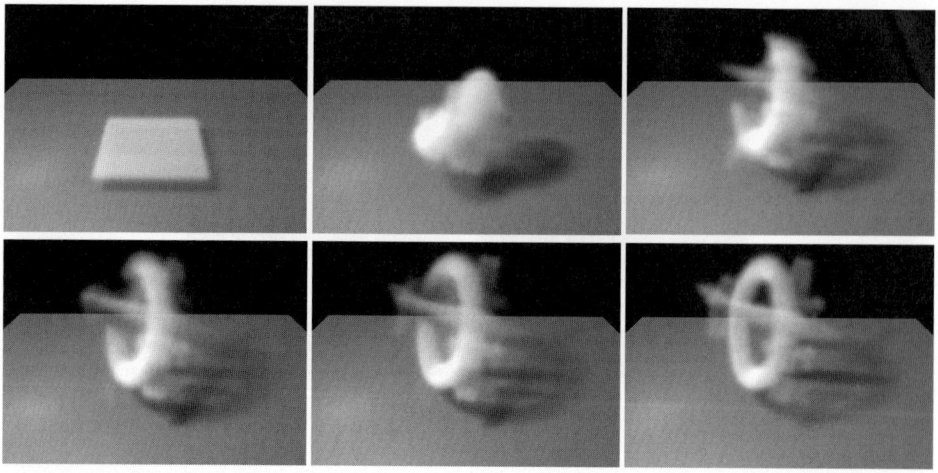

Fig. 8. Frames from a three-dimensional simulation; the target of the white smoke is a thin torus, while the yellow smoke moves to essence the airplane shape

6 Conclusion

We have described a technique for animating multi-phase controllable smoke. This is a significant improvement on an earlier method that is realized to a single phase. Our method allows the animator to specify the desired path. The particles follow it, but are also able to move independently.

Like previous techniques for simulating smoke at [3], [18], our method is easily extended to support additional external forces, such as gravity and buoyancy, in addition to the driving force. It is also possible to add obstacles represented by internal boundary conditions.

One technical extension of this work would be to simulate a controllable multi-phase liquid such as water and oil using ghost-fluid method such as that described by Hong and Kim [10].

References

1. Enright, D., Marschner, S. and Fedkiw, R. Animation and rendering of complex water surfaces. ACM Transactions on Graphics (Proceedings of ACM SIGGRAPH 2002) 21, 3, 736-744, 2002
2. Fattal, R. and Lischinski, D. Target-driven smoke animation. ACM Transactions on Graphics (Proceedings of ACM SIGGRAPH 2004) 23, 3, 439-446, 2004.
3. Fedkiw, R., Stam, J. and Jensen, H. W. Visual simulation of smoke. ACM Transactions on Graphics (Proceedings of ACM SIGGRAPH 2001) 20, 3, 15-22, 2001.
4. Feldman, B. E., O'Brien, J. F. and Arikan, O. Animating suspended particle explosions. ACM Transactions on Graphics (Proceedings of ACM SIGGRAPH 2003), 22, 3, 708-715, 2003.

5. Feldman, B. E., O'Brien, J. F. and Klingner, B. M. Animating gases with hybrid meshes. ACM Transactions on Graphics (Proceedings of ACM SIGGRAPH 2005) 24, 3, 904-909, 2005.
6. Feldman, B. E., O'Brien, J. F., Klingner, B. M. and Goktekin, T. G. Fluids in deforming meshes. ACM SIGGRAPH/Eurographics Symposium on Computer Animation, 255-259, 2005.
7. Foster, N. and Metaxas, D. Controlling fluid animation. Proceedings of Computer Graphics International '97, 178-188, 1997.
8. Foster, N. and Fedkiw, R. Practical animations of liquids. ACM Transactions on Graphics (Proceedings of ACM SIGGRAPH 2001) 20, 3, 23-30, 2001.
9. Hong, J.-M. and Kim, C.-H. Controlling fluid animation with geometric potential. Computer Animation and Virtual Worlds 15, 3-4(2004), 147-157, 2004.
10. Hong, J.-M. and Kim, C.-H. Discontinuous fluids. ACM Transactions on Graphics (Proceedings of ACM SIGGRAPH 2005) 24, 3, 915-920, 2005.
11. Shi, L. and Yu, Y. Controllable smoke animation with guiding objects. ACM Transactions on Graphics 24, 1, 140-164, 2005.
12. Shi, L. and Yu, Y. Taming liquids for rapidly changing targets. ACM SIGGRAPH/Eurographics Symposium on Computer Animation, 229-236, 2005.
13. Lossao, F., Gibou, F. and Fedkiw, R. Simulating water and smoke with an octree data structure. ACM Transactions on Graphics (Proceedings of ACM SIGGRAPH 2004) 23, 3, 455-460, 2004.
14. Nguyen, D. Q., Fedkiw, R. and Jensen, H. W. Physically based modeling and animation of fire. ACM Transactions on Graphics (Proceedings of ACM SIGGRAPH 2002) 21, 3, 721-728, 2002.
15. Osher, S. and Fedkiw, R. Level set methods: an overview and some recent results. Computational Physics 169, 2, 2001.
16. Popovic, J., Seitz, S. M., Erdmann, M., Popovic, Z. and Witkin, A. Interactive manipulation of rigid body simulations. ACM Transactions on Graphics (Proceedings of ACM SIGGRAPH 2000) 19, 3, 209-218, 2000.
17. Treuille, A., Mcnamara, A., Popovic, Z. and Stam, J. Keyframe control of smoke simulations. ACM Transactions on Graphics (Proceedings of ACM SIGGRAPH 2003) 22, 3, 716-723, 2003.
18. Stam, J. Stable fluids. ACM Transactions on Graphics (Proceedings of ACM SIGGRAPH 1999) 18, 3, 121-128, 1999.

An Approximate Image-Space Approach for Real-Time Rendering of Deformable Translucent Objects

Yi Gong, Wei Chen*, Long Zhang, Yun Zeng, and Qunsheng Peng

State Key Lab of CAD&CG, Zhejiang University, 310027, Hangzhou, China
{ygong, chenwei, lzhang, yzeng, peng}@cad.zju.edu.cn

Abstract. Although lots of works have been engaged in interactive and realistic rendering of translucent materials, efficient processing for deformable models remains a challenging problem. In this paper we introduce an approximate image-space approach for real-time rendering of deformable translucent models by taking account of diffuse multiple subsurface scattering. We decompose the process into two stages, called the *Gathering* and *Scattering* corresponding to the computations for incident and exiting irradiance respectively. We derive a simplified all-frequency illumination model for the *gathering* of the incident irradiance, which is amenable for deformable models using two auxiliary textures. We introduce two modes for efficient accomplishment of the view-dependent *scattering*. We implement our approach by fully exploiting the capabilities of graphics processing units (GPUs). Our implementation achieves visually plausible results and real-time frame rates for deformable models on commodity desktop PCs.

1 Motivation

Nowadays, photo-realistic modeling and rendering have proven to be capable of simulating the appearances of almost all types of objects, especially those with ideal diffuse, specular or gloomy materials. Even for the objects with complex materials like skin, jade, marble and milk, there have been well-established techniques in the computer graphics community. Among them, one challenging task is the simulation of translucent materials. Translucent objects are not fully transparent and allow light to transport and diffuse through their interiors, making their appearances somewhat mellow and quite different from other materials.

1.1 Previous Works

Translucency can not be simulated by simply using reflection or transparent illumination models because it is formed by single and multiple scattering of the light. As a consequence, to accurately mimic a light transport in a translucent object, time-consuming path sampling and a lot of multi-integral computations

* Corresponding author.

H.-P. Seidel, T. Nishita, and Q. Peng (Eds.): CGI 2006, LNCS 4035, pp. 124–135, 2006.

are required. Traditional solutions include the finite element methods [1][2][3], diffusion approximation [4], path tracing [5], bidirectional path tracing [6] and photon mapping [7].

To make it amenable for real-time processing, sample based rendering techniques are adopted. Hanrahan and his colleagues [5] used *Bidirectional Reflectance Distribution Function (BRDF)* for subsurface scattering, with which the existing light is assumed to be emitted at the same point as the incident light on the surface of the object. Later, Jensen and his colleagues [8] introduced the dipole source method based on a more accurate *Bidirectional Subsurface Reflectance Distribution Function (BSSRDF)* model, which consists of two parts, namely the exact single scattering and the multiple scattering. Although the dipole source method is only suitable for the case where the incident point and the existing point of the light are on a plane, applying it to an arbitrary surface can still generate appealing results with appropriate restrictions on the discretization of the underlying surface [8]. Jensen and his colleagues [9] further proposed an acceleration technique by employing a hierarchical structure. Thereafter, many approaches have been introduced for improving the performance by either pre-computing and reusing the radiance or simplifying the illumination model.

Lensch and his colleagues proposed a texture atlas aided algorithm [10] which preprocesses the handled geometry to collect the impulse response of each surface point under subsurface scattering. It separates the response into local and global parts. The local response is modeled as a filter kernel stored in the textures and the global response is calculated and stored in the vertices. It is apparent that the requirement of costly preprocessing limits its application for deformable models. Recently, Hao and his colleagues [11] implemented a spherical harmonics based real-time rendering approach. Although visually plausible results are achieved, it is likely to be fit for undeformable models. The similar situations happen with the pre-computed radiance transfer (PRT) techniques [12, 13], as they follow the same pre-computation mechanism which demands too many memory consumptions. More recent work by Sloan and his colleagues [14] allows for local deformations, while is not sufficient for large and deformable models.

By simplifying the illumination computation, interactive rendering of deformable models is made possible at the expense of the loss of image quality. Mertens and his colleagues [15] proposed a clustering based algorithm which achieves interactive frame rates even for deformable models. They also proposed an importance sampling based method, which only consider the local scattering [16]. Dachsbacher and Stamminger [17] introduced an efficient two-phase image-space technique by using the shadow map to store the irradiance from the light sources for latter scattering computation. Due to the limited accuracy of the sampling and filtering provided by the graphics hardware, the results are a little bit far from perfect. In addition, the algorithm can not simulate all-frequency lighting [13] because shadow map is only feasible for point lights and directional lights.

There are also some works on the simulation of inhomogeneous materials. For instance, Goesele and his colleagues [18] proposed a so-called DISCO algorithm based on the measured sub-scattering data. Later, Xin Tong and his colleagues [19] put forward a quasi-homogeneous material modeling and rendering method with a special-purposed sampling device.

1.2 Our Contributions

Based on the investigations on the related literature, we understand that there are still challenges for real-time rendering of deformable translucent objects. Most of existing approaches suffer from either efficiency issue such as [14, 13], or lacking photo-realistic effects like [10, 17], in terms of deformable models.

This paper describes our efforts on boosting the performance and quality with a new approximate image-space approach. Our method adopts also BSSRDF model, and mimics most kinds of light sources by integrating the contributions from point lights, directional lights and the ambient lights. Conceptually, we decompose the computation of translucency into two stages. In the first stage, the radiances from all types of lights are collected over the surfaces. We call this procedure the *gathering* of irradiance. To facilitate its efficient computation at runtime, we derive a simplified computational model that is especially adoptable for the ambient lights. In addition, we employ an intermediate data sheet to store the gathered incident irradiance.

On the other hand, in our approach the computation of outgoing irradiance under a given viewpoint is a simplified imitation of the light transport inside the objects. We denote it as the *scattering* operation, where the color of each visible surface point depends on a variable number of lightened source points. This makes the implementation with current graphics hardware nontrivial because the rendering pipeline is designed as amenable for *gathering* operations, where the destination of each pixel is defined before rasterization. With an attempt to convert the *scattering* operations into a *gathering* procedure in GPUs, one may implement it at the fragment level. This scheme requires lots of texture lookups at the complexity of the image resolution. We overcome this inefficiency with hierarchical sampling scheme.

In the rest of this paper, we first introduce a simplified translucent illumination model based on a brief overview of the BSSRDF model. We then present the gathering of irradiance in Section 3. Section 4 describes how to implement the scattering process in programmable graphics hardware. The experimental results are presented in Section 5. Finally, we conclude the whole paper and highlight the future work in Section 6.

2 A Simplified Illumination Model

BSSRDF is a more accurate lighting model than BRDF. While BRDF only considers the link between the incoming light and the outgoing light at the same point of the surface, BSSRDF can depict the light transport between two different points, x_i and x_o, on a surface. The relationship between the illumination at one surface point x_i with light distribution at another surface points x_o is expressed as follows [8]:

$$dL_o(x_o, \overrightarrow{\omega}_o) = S(x_i, \overrightarrow{\omega}_i; x_o, \overrightarrow{\omega}_o) d\Phi_i(x_i, \overrightarrow{\omega}_i) \quad (1)$$

where $L_o(x_o, \overrightarrow{\omega}_o)$ is the outgoing radiance at x_o along the direction $\overrightarrow{\omega}_o$. $\Phi_i(x_i, \overrightarrow{\omega}_i)$ is the incident flux at x_i along the direction $\overrightarrow{\omega}_i$, and $S(x_i, \overrightarrow{\omega}_i; x_o, \overrightarrow{\omega}_o)$ denotes the value of BSSRDF. By integrating over all incoming directions and areas, the total outgoing radiance is computed.

Typically, BSSRDF model considers the effects of two terms, single scattering and multiple scattering:

$$S(x_i, \overrightarrow{\omega}_i; x_o, \overrightarrow{\omega}_o) = S_d(x_i, \overrightarrow{\omega}_i; x_o, w_o) + S^{(1)}(x_i, \overrightarrow{\omega}_i; x_o, \overrightarrow{\omega}_o) \quad (2)$$

where $S^{(1)}$ and S_d stand for the single and multiple scattering terms respectively. In fact, a simplification can be made by skipping the single scattering term alone to simulate the effect of highly scattering materials [9]. Moreover, as multiple scattering smoothes the incident light from different directions, S_d can be further approximated by a low-dimensional function, R_d, which depends only on the incident angle and outgoing position [8], yielding simplified BSSRDF model:

$$\begin{aligned} S(x_i, \overrightarrow{\omega}_i; x_o, \overrightarrow{\omega}_o) &\approx S_d(x_i, \overrightarrow{\omega}_i; x_o, \overrightarrow{\omega}_o) \\ &= \frac{1}{\pi} F_t(\eta, \overrightarrow{\omega}_o) R_d(x_i; x_o) F_t(\eta, \overrightarrow{\omega}_i) \end{aligned} \quad (3)$$

where $F_t(\eta, \overrightarrow{\omega}_i)$ and $F_t(\eta, \overrightarrow{\omega}_o)$ denote the fresnel transmission terms. R_d is the dipole approximation for multiple scattering, indicating how much proportion of light will be transported from x_i to x_o on a plane. That is, the dipole source method converts the part of incoming light at x_i, which will transport to x_o, to a couple sources above and over x_i (at z_v and z_r) as Figure 1 depicts.

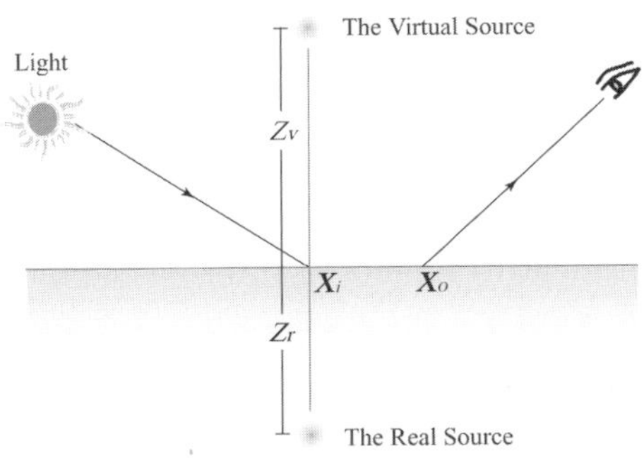

Fig. 1. The dipole approximation of multiple scattering

The single dipole approximation for multiple scattering is formulated as

$$R_d(x_i; x_o) = \frac{\alpha'}{4\pi}[z_r(1 + \sigma_{tr} d_r)\frac{e^{(-\sigma_{tr} d_r)}}{d_r^3} + z_v(1 + \sigma_{tr} d_v)\frac{e^{(-\sigma_{tr} d_v)}}{d_v^3}] \quad (4)$$

Here, α' is the reduced albedo, σ_{tr} is the effective transport coefficient, z_r and z_v are the distances from the dipole lights to the surface, d_r is the distance from x to the real source, and d_v is the distance from x to the virtual source.

We make two assumptions here to simplify the translucent simulation process. Firstly, we assume the light transfers uniformly in all directions on its surface. Thus, together with Equation 1 and 3, we obtain:

$$L_o(x_o, w_o) = \frac{1}{\pi} F_t(\eta, \overrightarrow{\omega}_o) B(x_o) \tag{5}$$

$$B(x_o) = \int_s E(x_i) R_d(x_i; x_o) dx_i \tag{6}$$

$$E(x_i) = \int L(x_i, \overrightarrow{\omega}_i) F_t(\eta, \overrightarrow{\omega}_i)(\overrightarrow{n}_i \cdot \overrightarrow{\omega}_i) d\overrightarrow{\omega}_i \tag{7}$$

Secondly, as the light transmission in translucent objects decays exponentially with the distance, the far points on the surface make very little contribution to the current shading pixel and thus can be neglected. Namely, samplings are only necessary in a small near region of current pixel. Moreover, S varies smoothly except in the very local region near x_o. Consequently, we can discretize the surface near x_o into hierarchical pieces–small in near region, and large in far region. Thus the $E(x_i)$ and $R_d(x_i; x_o)$ can be treated as constant in each piece. Equation (6) can be further reformulated as:

$$B(x_o) \approx \sum_i E(x_i) R_d(x_i; x_o) A(x_i) \tag{8}$$

where the $A(x_i)$ is the area of the region surrounding x_i, after our surface discretization.

Finally, suppose that the light varies not very frequently, Equation 7 can be simplified by discretizing the incident light direction into several basis:

$$E(x_i) = \sum_j E_j(x_i) F_t(\eta, \overrightarrow{\omega}_j) \psi_j(x_i) \tag{9}$$

where $E_j(x_i)$ is the incident irradiance of x_i projected on the basis ψ_j.

3 The Gathering of Irradiance

With the simplified illumination model, we classify the light sources into two categories, namely the point or directional lights and the ambient lights. We employ an intermediate sheet buffer to keep the diffused incident irradiance from all light sources, called *Diffusion Source Map* (DSM). Ideally, it should collect all possible $E(x_i)$ for each surface point. Although the representation of DSM is flexible, one fundamental requirement is that it should facilitate fast neighbor searching for subsequent scattering operations. Accordingly, we propose to generate a multi-chart paramerization of the handled surface and keep multiple textures as DSMs. Depending on the parameriztion manner, the textures can be represented as plane maps, spherical maps or cubemaps. As a consequence, the searching of the neighboring regions can be accomplished by the texture look-up operations in GPUs.

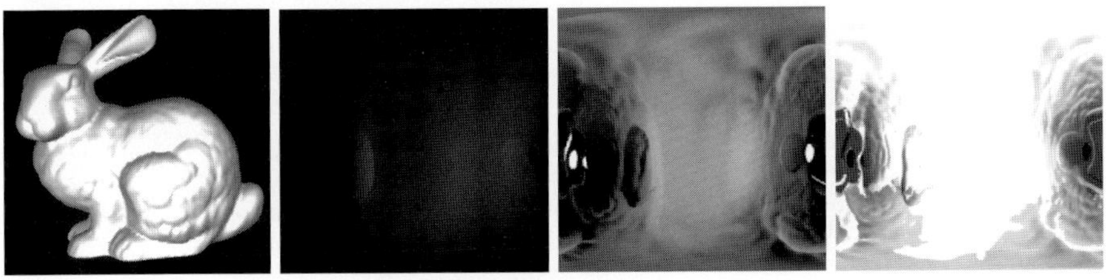

(a) (b) (c) (d)

Fig. 2. Illustration of the DSM for the Bunny model. (a) The Bunny model; (b) The component for the surface location; (c) The component for the surface orientation; (d) The component for the incident irradiance

For each element of DSM, we record the surface location, the surface orientation and the sum of the incident irradiance (Figure 2). These attributes are to be used in the scattering stage. To accumulate the contributions from the point or directional lights and the ambient lights, we use two auxiliary textures as described below. With hardware-accelerated texture mapping technique, the irradiance from the shadow map and the cube map can be accumulated in the DSM in one rendering pass.

3.1 The Point and Directional Lights

To determine the contributions from each point or directional light to the handled surface, we employ a shadow map for the storage of the irradiance in the visible surface at the viewpoint of the light source. The shadow map [20] is a commonly used technique in real-time rendering. Because we do not consider the decay of the light, this scheme amounts to add a constant value to the irradiance map a constant value for each light source. Figure 3 illustrates the usage of the shadow map in the accumulation of the irradiance from the point and directional lights.

3.2 The Ambient Lights

The second auxiliary texture is a spherical or cubical environment map for storing the irradiance caused by the ambient lights. We utilize the simplified Equation (9) to calculate the environmental irradiance at each surface location x_i from multiple lighting directions. The irradiance from ambient lights are determined by using sphere harmonic method adopted in the PRT (Pre-computed Radiance Transfer) algorithm [12]. In the preprocessing stage, we compute the

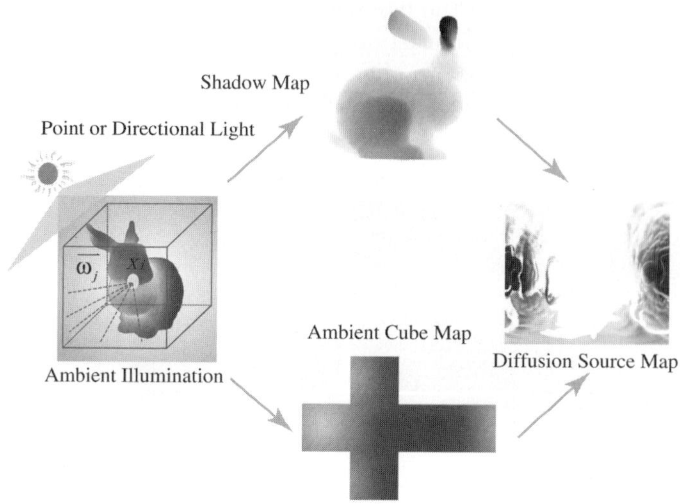

Fig. 3. The DSM is determined by accumulating the contributions from the point or directional lights and the ambient lights at each surface location

(a) (b)

Fig. 4. (a) The original environment cube map; (b) Ambient cube map computed by using spherical harmonic function

basis and coefficients of the sphere harmonic functions and record them as a cube map. To simulate the ambient light affecting, the cube map is represented as a texture and kept in the local video memory for efficient processing, as depicted in Figure 4.

4 The Scattering of Irradiance

After gathering the irradiance from each light source into the DSM, the outgoing irradiance is to be evaluated at runtime with the derived Equation 8. It requires lots of texture look-up operations which are a little bit costly in programmable

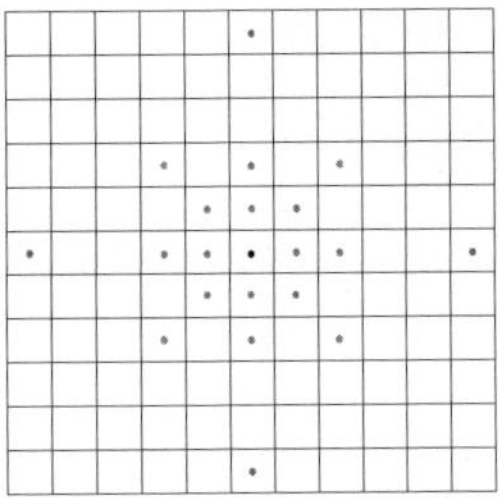

Fig. 5. Hierarchical sampling in DSM. The black point denotes the handled surface location. Other points with different colors show the sampling locations for the irradiance computation of the black point.

graphics hardware. For deformable models, this computation has to be performed at each frame. In practice, there are two ways to implement the scattering processing in GPUs. The first one fulfills the irradiance computation in a per-vertex basis. We call it the VTF mode, which makes use of the newly introduced *vertex texture fetch* feature for accessing the DSM in the vertex processing stage. One of its disadvantages is that it requires the model to be well-shaped and uniformly sampled. In addition, it is quite expensive for large-sized model because the vertex texture accesses are not efficient yet with current graphics hardware [21]. Therefore, VTF mode is suitable only for small models. The other mode, called FTF mode, performs the irradiance computation in the fragment processing stage, yielding more accurate results than that of the VTF mode. Although it has image-space complexity, the *early-z-culling* feature of graphics hardware favors efficient culling of hidden surface parts. Our experiments show that the FTF mode leads to higher performance for large-sized models than the VTF mode.

Note that, uniformly sampling a large neighborhood of each vertex in the texture space is probably expensive and unnecessary. Thus, we make use of an hierarchial irradiance accumulation algorithm to efficiently sample the DSM for the computation of Equation 8. The light scattering of highly scattering translucent objects attenuate exponentially with the distance. Therefore, we do not need to consider the contributions from very far surface locations. Even for the moderately far surface locations, the irradiance computation can be hierarchically simplified. Inspired by this investigation, for each handled surface location, we sample twelve points (shown with red color) on its near neighborhood uniformly, and eight points (shown with green and blue colors) for moderately far regions. Figure 5 illustrates this hierarchical scheme, where the black point denotes the underlying surface location.

5 Experimental Results

We have implemented our algorithms with DirectX 9.0c SDK. Performance has been measured on a 2.4 GHz P4 system with 2 GB memory and an NVidia 6800 GT video card with 256 MB video memory.

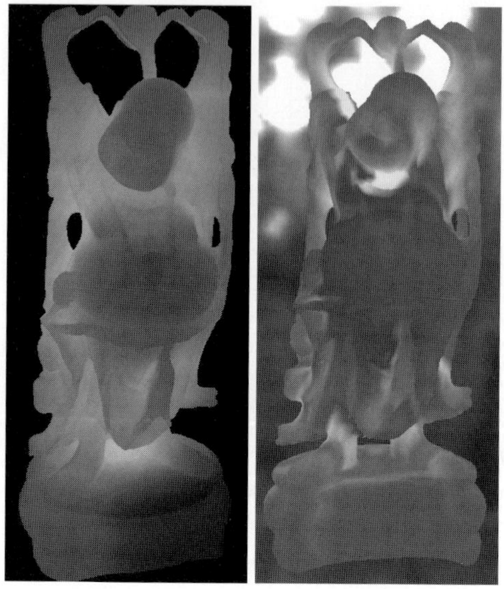

(a) (b)

Fig. 6. Our results for the buddha model: (a) with one point light; (b) with the point light and ambient lights

Table 1. Performance statistics for various data sets

Data	#T	#V	FTF	VTF
Teapot	2256	1177	48.34	90.72
Buddha	50000	24974	24.59	22.47
Max Planck	50801	25445	32.92	25.68
Bunny	69451	34834	26.15	19.98

We adopted the BSSRDF coefficients presented in [8] for the experiments. Our hardware implementation integrates several commonly used hardware optimization techniques such as deferred shading and dynamic branching.

We first compared two implementations with and without the ambient lighting effects. Figure 6 demonstrates the results of both schemes. Although we only employ a simple cube map for simulating the ambient lighting effects, it still adds lots of visual realism.

Table 1 lists the performance for various data sets with the FTF and VTF modes. #T and #V denote the triangle and vertex numbers of the models. Apparently, VTF mode is suitable for small-sized models only. Figures 7 illustrates the rendering results for these models.

We also tested our approach with a set of morphable models. Note that, our approach can be applied to deformable models directly without special cares. Table 2 collects the performance for several morphable models, which are shown in Figure 8.

Table 2. Performance statistics for deformable models

Data	#T	#V	FTF	VTF
Cube/Machine	13162	6583	41.97	37.18
Rabbit/Bunny	15720	7862	38.13	31.60
Bunny/Egg	50236	25120	25.21	20.54

Fig. 7. Translucent rendering for Teapot (2256 triangles, 1177 vertices, 90fps), Bunny (69451 triangles, 34834 vertices, 20fps), Buddha (50000 triangles, 24974 vertices, 22fps) and Max Planck (50801 triangles, 25445 vertices, 25fps) data sets at the image resolutions of 512×512

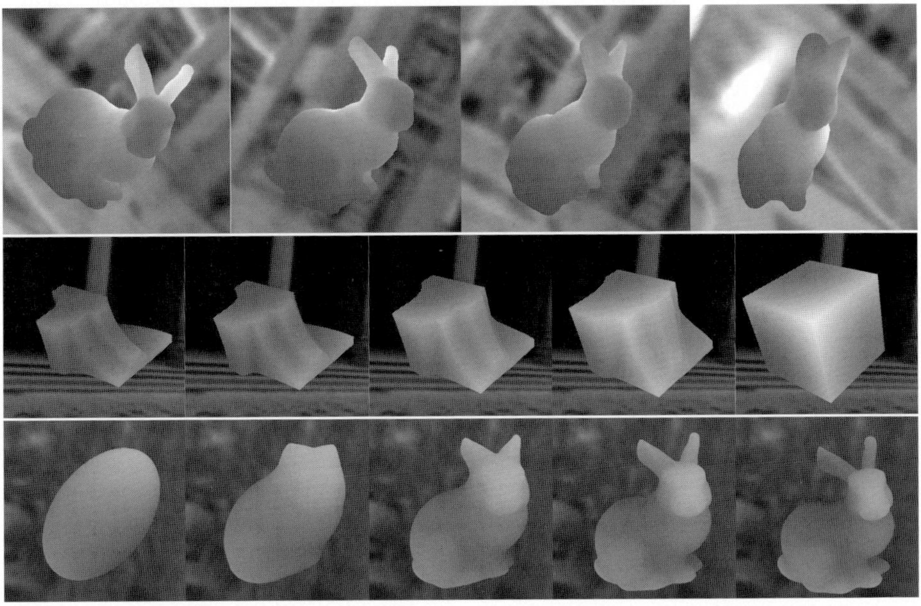

Fig. 8. The selected frames from a set of morphing models

6 Conclusions and Future Work

This paper presents an efficient image-space rendering approach for highly scattering translucent materials. We divide the simulation procedure into two stages, each of which can be efficiently accelerated with GPUs. Because no precomputation is involved, our approach is inherently feasible for deformable models. Despite the simplification of the translucent lighting model, our experimental results demonstrate desirable translucency effects. With all the proposed acceleration techniques, it achieves real-time frame rates for large-sized and deformable models.

In our implementations, the ambient lights are approximated with a spherical harmonic functions evaluated from environmental map. It neglects the scene occlusions or self-occlusions which lose visual reality in some cases. We would like to exploit efficient solution to take the ambient occlusion and more general light sources into account. In addition, we have great interests on the modeling and rendering of inhomogeneous translucent objects as they are quite common in real world. Accelerating the rendering with newest hardware features is also in our near schedule.

Acknowledgments

This work is partially supported by 973 program of China (No.2002CB312100), NSF of China for Innovative Research Groups (No.60021201), National Natural Science Fund of China (No.60303028), Zhejiang Provincial Natural Science Fund (No.Y105269) and Zhejiang Provincial Natural Science Special Fund for Youth Scientists' Cultivation (No.R603046).

References

1. Philippe Blasi, Bertrand Le Saëc, and Christophe Schlick. A rendering algorithm for discrete volume density objects. *Computer Graphics Forum*, 12(3):201–210, 1993.
2. Holly E. Rushmeier and Kenneth E. Torrance. Extending the radiosity method to include specularly reflecting and translucent materials. *ACM Transactions on Graphics*, 9(1):1–27, 1990.
3. François X. Sillion. A unified hierarchical algorithm for global illumination with scattering volumes and object clusters. *IEEE Transactions on Visualization and Computer Graphics*, 1(3):240–254, 1995.
4. Jos Stam. Multiple scattering as a diffusion process. In *Proceedings of Eurographics Rendering Workshop 1995*, pages 41–50, 1995.
5. Pat Hanrahan and Wolfgang Krueger. Reflection from layered surfaces due to subsurface scattering. In *Proceedings of ACM SIGGRAPH 1993*, pages 165–174, 1993.
6. Eric P. Lafortune and Yves D. Willems. Rendering participating media with bidirectional path tracing. In *Proceedings of Eurographics Rendering Workshop 1996*, pages 91–100, 1996.
7. Henrik Wann Jensen and Per Christensen. Efficient simulation of light transport in scenes with participating media using photon maps. In *Proceedings of ACM SIGGRAPH 1998*, pages 311–320, 1998.

8. Henrik Wann Jensen, Stephen Marschner, Marc Levoy, and Pat Hanrahan. A practical model for subsurface light transport. In *Proceedings of ACM SIGGRAPH 2001*, pages 511–518, 2001.
9. Henrik Wann Jensen and Juan Buhler. A rapid hierarchical rendering technique for translucent materials. *ACM Transactions on Graphics*, 21(3):576–581, July 2002.
10. Hendrik Lensch, Michael Goesele, Philippe Bekaert, and Jan Kautz. Interactive rendering of translucent objects. In *Proceedings of Pacific Graphics 2002*, pages 214–224, October 2002.
11. Xuejun Hao and Amitabh Varshney. Real-time rendering of translucent meshes. *ACM Transactions on Graphics*, 23(2):120–142, April 2004.
12. Peter-Pike Sloan, Jan Kautz, and John Snyder. Precomputed radiance transfer for real-time rendering in dynamic, low-frequency lighting environments. In *Proceedings of ACM SIGGRAPH 2002*, pages 527–536, July 2002.
13. Rui Wang, John Tran, and David Luebke. All-frequency interactive relighting of translucent objects with single and multiple scattering. *ACM Transactions on Graphics*, 24(3):1202–1207, August 2005.
14. Peter-Pike Sloan, Ben Luna, and John Snyder. Local, deformable precomputed radiance transfer. *ACM Transactions on Graphics*, 24(3):1216–1224, 2005.
15. Tom Mertens, Jan Kautz, Philippe Bekaert, Hans-Peter Seidel, and Frank Van Reeth. Interactive rendering of translucent deformable objects. In *Proceedings of Eurographics Rendering Workshop 2003*, pages 130–140, Aire-la-Ville, Switzerland, Switzerland, 2003. Eurographics Association.
16. Tom Mertens, Jan Kautz, Philippe Bekaert, Frank Van Reeth, and Hans-Peter Seidel. Efficient rendering of local subsurface scattering. In *Pacific Graphics 2003*, pages 51–58, 2003.
17. Carsten Dachsbacher and Marc Stamminger. Translucent shadow map. In *Proceedings of Eurographics Symposium on Rendering 2003*, pages 197–201, 2003.
18. Michael Goesele, Hendrik Lensch, Jochen Lang, Christian Fuchs, and Hans-Peter Seidel. Disco: acquisition of translucent objects. *ACM Transactions on Graphics*, 23(3):835–844, 2004.
19. Xin Tong, Jiaping Wang, Stephen Lin, Baining Guo, and Heung-Yeung Shum. Modeling and rendering of quasi-homogeneous materials. In *Proceedings of ACM SIGGRAPH 2005*, pages 1054–1061, 2005.
20. Lance Williams. Casting curved shadows on curved surfaces. In *Proceedings of ACM SIGGRAPH 1978*, pages 270–274, 1978.
21. NVIDIA. GPU programming guide. 2005.

Interactively Rendering Dynamic Caustics on GPU

Baoquan Liu[1,3], Enhua Wu[1,2], and Xuehui Liu[1]

[1] State Key Lab. of Computer Science, Institute of Software,
Chinese Academy of Sciences, Beijing
{lbq, lxh}@ios.ac.cn
http://lcs.ios.ac.cn/~lbq/

[2] Department of Computer and Information Science, University of Macau, Macao
ehwu@umac.mo
http://www.fst.umac.mo/en/staff/fstehw.html

[3] Graduate University of Chinese Academy of Sciences

Abstract. In this paper, a new technique is presented for interactive rendering of caustics fully processed on GPU. Without any pre-computation required, the algorithm can directly render refractive caustics from complex deformable transparent objects onto an opaque receiver surface. By the technique we accurately trace the path of the photons and calculate the energy carried by the photons emitted from the light source, and distribute the energy onto the receiver surface according to Gauss basis function. As a result, photorealistic caustic image is calculated without post-processing and temporal filtering over recent frames. We demonstrate that the interactive caustics can be rendered by our method in real-time for non-uniform deformation of both refractive object and receiver surface, and at the same time, interactive change of light and camera in terms of position and direction could be made.

1 Introduction

Transparent materials like glass, ice and water exist widely in our real life. It is a ubiquitous physical phenomenon that when transparent objects are illuminated by light source such as the sun, caustics will appear on the surface of receiver. The caustics are formed by light rays refracted through the refractive object and converged on a small region of the receiver surface. This small region appears very bright in comparison with other dark region in shadow, so the caustic region produces highly immersive visual appeal. Using brute-force ray tracing and photon mapping method is easy to perform caustics rendering, however, the computational cost of these offline rendering systems is very high due to the intensive calculations required for path tracing and intersection testing in the scene geometry space.

Until recently techniques for applying GPU to interactively rendering refractive effects come to emerge. However, almost all these works need pre-computations prior to the rendering process, and as a consequence, it was hard to deform the objects dynamically through the interaction of users during the rendering phase. Such pre-computation steps restrict their applications from the domain such as games.

In this paper, we present a new technique for caustics rendering entirely on GPU without any pre-computation performed on CPU. The algorithm allows refraction

H.-P. Seidel, T. Nishita, and Q. Peng (Eds.): CGI 2006, LNCS 4035, pp. 136 – 147, 2006.

through double interfaces of a transparent object, and traces the accurate path of the rays, which intersect with the front and back face of the transparent object, and further intersect with the receiver surface by an efficient ray-surface intersection algorithm. In our method, both the refractive object and the receiver surface expressed by polygonal meshes can be dynamically deformed at runtime. The calculation of the intensity of caustics is physically based on energy transportation and distribution of photons. So the caustic image produced by our algorithm is highly smooth without any post-processing required such as low pass filtering, or temporal filtering over recent frames previously rendered. We support fully dynamic deformation (especially non-uniform deformation) of refractive object's geometry, since no pre-computation is involved. This is very important for certain applications, such as games where the models need deformation for animation.

In the remainder of this paper, Section 2 will give a short survey of the related work, and Section 3 will present our double surface refraction algorithm in more detail. Section 4 describes the caustics rendering algorithm. Rendering results will be demonstrated in Section 5. We conclude with a summary of the ideas presented in the paper in Section 6.

2 Related Work

In this section, we will review some of the earlier work in offline caustics rendering and the recent attempts for achieving interactive rendering on GPU.

Photon mapping, introduced by Jensen[1][2], is a standard technique for rendering beautiful caustics. By the method, a photon map is constructed to store the results of the photon tracing. The intensity of caustics at a point of the receiver surface is computed by estimating the surface area covered by its k nearest neighbors. Variants and optimized versions of path tracing algorithms were presented by utilizing CPU clusters [3], but the expensive computational costs limit these techniques from real-time applications. Beam tracing [4] is an important technique to produce physically accurate optical caustic effects. Watt [5] applied backward beam tracing to generate caustic polygons. Ernst et al. [6] followed this scenario and presented a caustic intensity interpolation scheme to reduce aliasing effect for generating smoother caustics. Nishita[7] proposed a model based on beam tracing for underwater caustics rendering, and the idea was implemented on GPU by Iwasaki et. al. in [8].

Concurrently and independently of our work, Shah and Pattanik[9] developed a similar method for interactive caustics rendering. By their technique, light is emitted using a vertex-tracing approach, and the computation of the intensity and energy of caustics was conducted by using the method similar to beam tracing. However, their method requires pre-computing the projected area of all triangles, so it does not allow non-uniform deformation of the transparent object, although they present a way by using key frame configuration for subtle deformations. The method also needs some form of filtering to improve the aliasing appearance.

Recently Wyman[10] offered a new technique for rendering transparent geometry supporting double-sided refraction, but his technique requires pre-computing the distance along normal for each vertex. As an extension to [10], [11] approximates caustics rendering by employing another new computing method for caustic intensity, but we may find that the computation in the method is not very accurate, which will be pointed out in the following content. The method also needs low pass filtering to improve their aliasing appearance, and a temporal filtering over recent frames has also been used to reduce the frame-to-frame popping artifacts. [12] offers an approximate ray-tracing technique on GPU with distance impostors, but the impostor had to be pre-computed too.

3 Computation of Ray-Surface Intersection

Our double-sided refraction algorithm is an extension to the technique by Wyman[10]. The key improvement in our technique lies on the more accurate computation for the second intersection point of the ray with refractive object, and moreover it does not require any pre-computation.

3.1 Review of the Previous Techniques

The technique in [10] approximates the second intersection *P2* by an interpolation between $d_{\vec{V}}$ and $d_{\vec{N}}$ based on incident angle and refracted angle. One limitation of the approach is that when the refractive object has high surface curvature or high refraction index, the approximation of the second intersection will become less accurate. The interpolation just give a coarsely approximate value P_2', which may be located in the interior or exterior of the refractive object instead of on the boundary of the object.

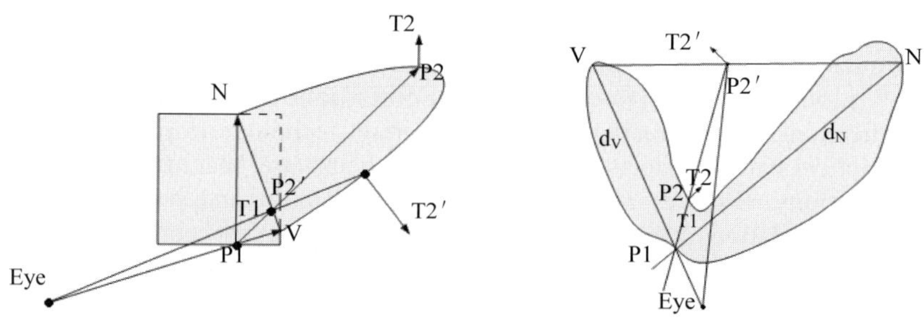

Fig. 1. Two erroneous cases of the approximation method in [10]

As shown in the left of Fig. 1, when the surface curvature is high, the approximated value P_2' would be far away from *P2*, and the approximated refracted vector $\vec{T}_2$ would be almost opposite to the true vector $\vec{T}_2$. And also as shown in the right of Fig. 1, to the V-shape object, the approximated value P_2' is entirely outside of the object, and the approximated refracted vector $\vec{T}_2'$ is also far away from the true vector $\vec{T}_2$ .Pre-computation of $d_{\vec{N}}$ is another limitation of the approach.

3.2 A More Accurate Ray-Surface Intersection Testing on GPU

Instead of approximating *P2* by interpolation as in [10], we propose to accurately compute the ray-surface intersection on GPU by a binary search process. Then the pre-computation of $d_{\vec{N}}$ in [10] is no longer necessary. We propose to represent the refractive object as two depth images corresponding to the back-facing surface and the front-facing surface respectively, and then we compute *P2* by ray-intersection with these two depth images.

Our approach needs three passes to compute *P2*. In the first two passes, we set the projection to parallel mode to get the two z-buffers corresponding to the object's backward surface and forward surface, as marked by red and green colors in Fig.2, by rendering the refractive object with the depth test set as GL_GREAT and GL_LESS respectively. We also output a normal vector texture for each pass. The two z-buffer textures will be used as an orthogonally projected depth images to calculate the accurate position of *P2* by ray-intersection in the third pass. The reason that we use orthogonal projection instead of perspective projection during the first two rendering passes is that the z-buffer generated from perspective projection is distributed nonlinear, and suffers from perspective distortion. Besides, because the backward surface is farther from the center of projection than the forward surface is, the sampling rate for the backward surface is somewhat low and not enough to represent the highly detailed model. Therefore we adopt orthogonal projected depth image to compute the ray-surface intersection, which is more accurate than using perspective projected depth image.

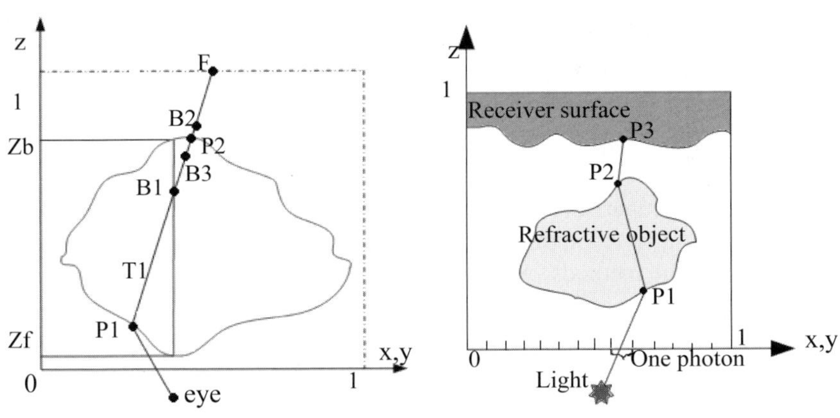

Fig. 2. (a) Ray-intersection computation via binary search, (b) The path of the photon

In the third rendering pass, we set the projection mode to perspective and render the object with standard depth test. The pixel shader of this pass will transform all the vectors(*T1*, *V*,and *N1*) and point *P1* to orthogonal projection space by a matrix to make the ray-intersection computation in one space. The pixel shader uses a binary search to calculate the accurate intersection *P2*. As illuminated in Fig. 2(a), *F* is the intersection point of *T1* with plane z=1, the far clipping plane in the projection space. So given *T1*, we can loop for a fixed number of steps, and at each step we will get closer to the true intersection position *P2* and converge quickly to the exact solution. In Fig. 2(a), the first iteration result is *B1*, the midpoint of *P1* and *F*. The blue line shows the two z-buffer values(*Zf* and *Zb*), which are indexed by texture coordinates *B1.xy*. If $Zf \leqslant B1.z \leqslant Zb$, *B1* is still inside the refractive object, otherwise it is outside. Because *F* is outside and *P1* is inside, there must be a solution between them. The second iteration result is *B2*, and the third *B3* is close enough to the true solution *P2*. Finally we use (*P2.x, P2.y*) as texture coordinates to index into the corresponding normal texture to find *P2*'s normal *N2* to be used to calculate the intersection *P3* of the ray with the receiver surface.

The Cg code of the binary search function BS() for calculating *P2* is shown below.

```
float3 BS(float3 P1, float3 F )
{
      float3 P_inside  = P1;
      float3 P_outside = F;
      int binary_search_steps = 8;
      float3 P2= (P_inside + P_outside) *0.5;
      for( int i=0; i<binary_search_steps; i++)
      {
            Zf=tex2D(FrontDepthTexture, P2.xy); //The Z value in the front surface
            Zb=tex2D(BackDepthTexture, P2.xy); //The Z value in the back surface
            if (P2.z ⩽Zb&&P2.z⩾Zf)  // P2 is inside the object
                  P_inside =P2;
            else              // P2 is outside the object
                  P_outside =P2;
            P2= (P_inside + P_outside) *0.5;
      }
      return P2;
}
```

Fig. 3 shows a comparison of the rendering quality of double-sided refraction by different methods. The resolution of the output image and all the texture buffers is 512 by 512 for all the methods. And the transparent sphere, whose index of refraction is 1.5, is rendered in an environment map. We can see that the rendering quality of our method is more accurate and closer to ray-tracing approach than [10], especially in the region of silhouette.

4 Caustics Rendering Algorithm

Our approach to rendering caustics is a procedure of three-steps: (1). emitting photons from the light and tracing photons' path to obtain a photon buffer; (2). calculating all the photons' contributions into a buffer, called caustic map; (3). projecting this caustic map to the final rendering result.

(a) 55.33 fps (b) 3.03 fps (c) 61.28 fps

Fig. 3. Comparison of rendering quality of double-sided refraction by different methods: (a) method of [10], (b) ray-tracing, (c) our method

4.1 Emitting Photons to Obtain "Photon Buffer"

We emit photons by rendering the refractive object from the light's view. Through each pixel in this light buffer, the light source will emit one photon. This photon will transmit through point *P1* and *P2* on the refractive object, and finally hit the receiver surface at P3. The path of the photon is shown in Fig 2(b).

To trace photon's path, our approach utilizes the same ray-surface intersection approach as described in Section 3.2 to computing the intersection point *P1* and *P2*, with one additional pass to render the receiver surface in orthogonal projecting space to obtain *P3*. After *P2* and *N2* are obtained, we need to use binary search again to find *P3* in the depth image of the receiver surface. Finally in the pixel shader, we output *P3*'s *xy* coordinates to a buffer, photon buffer, which records the position where the photon hits the receiver surface.

4.2 Computation of Caustics Intensity

In order to render caustics, the intensity of caustics must be calculated by all the rendering approach. Let's first review the intensity computation method in [11], as shown in Fig. 4(a). At first, it calculates the energy E_{α_j} carried by photon αj, and the energy E_{p3} arriving at *P3* in absence of the refractive object. And then it sets the intensity of the caustics as E_{α_j} / E_{p3} .We may find that the computation here is inaccurate, even erroneous in some cases. The reason is that the energy E_{p3} arriving at P3 in absence of the refractive object has no relationship with the energy of E_{α_j} carried by photon αj . So the ratio is in fact meaningless. Even worse, when the point light is inside the same plane as the receiver surface, as shown in Fig. 4(b), the solid angle $\vec{\omega}_{p3}$ subtended from the light will be zero, so E_{p3} will be zero too, then the ratio of the two energies would become infinite. While we think that the intensity of *P3* is related to the focal point (shown as a green point in Fig. 4) of the refractive object, and the solid angle $\vec{\omega}_{P3}$ should subtend from this focal point instead of from the light source as in [11]. So the correct solid angle $\vec{\omega}_{P3}$ should be calculated by subtending it from the focal point, instead of from the light as in [11], and also the correct intensity I_{p3} should be calculated based on this correct solid angle.

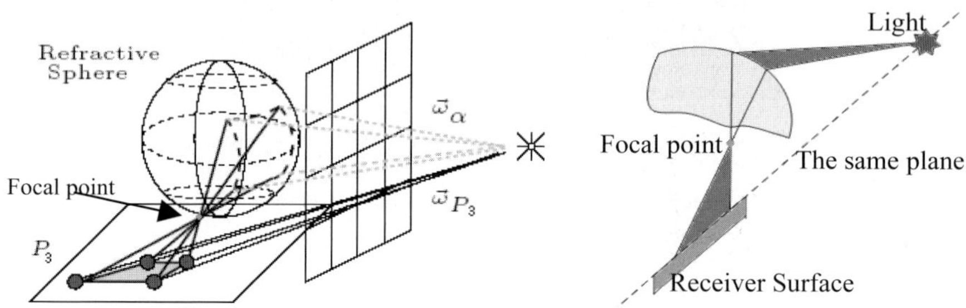

Fig. 4. (a). The intensity computation method of [11] (courtesy of Chris Wyman & Scott Davis, authors of [11]). (b). When the light and the receiver surface share a same plane, $\vec{\omega}_{P3}$ will be zero

In this paper, we choose to just compute the energy E_{α_j} carried by photon αj, but not the solid angle directly, because it is hard to find the exact focal point of a complex refractive object. To obtain the intensity on the caustic receiving surface at *P3*, we make calculation physically through energy transportation and distribution inspired by [13]. Assume that each photon in the light buffer carries an initial energy, $E = I_L * Parea(pixel\ i)$ where I_L is the intensity of the light source, and *Parea(pixel i)* is *pixel i*'s projected area in the direction of the light source. If the refractive object absorbs no energy, *E* will thus be the energy incident on the receiving surface due to this photon hitting, and eventually gets deposited on the diffuse receiver surface. And instead of focusing on and burning out one single point at *P3*, it will spread around *P3* and extend to the surrounding region. This energy splatting procedure corresponds to a physical model that can be represented by a Gauss basis function G(u) with local support. So based on the law of energy conservation, we distribute the energy *E* over the surrounding region of *P3* according to Gauss basis function. We assign the intensity I_{u_i} at each point u_i in the surrounding region of *P3* as $E * G(u_i - P3)$.

Finally we accumulate the contributions of all the photons into a buffer, called caustic map, in a 2D rendering pass by rendering a 2D regular triangle for each photon. This triangle behaves as a photon, and has a Gauss texture. We originally put this triangle centered at the left-bottom corner(*x= 0, y=0*), and then we design a vertex shader program to offset the 2D vertex of the triangle, so that the triangle will be translated to P3's orthogonal projection space position(*x=P3.x, y=P3.y*), which can be retrieved in the "photon buffer" by access to the vertex texture in the vertex shader. The radius *R* of the surrounding region extended by the Gauss basis function can be interactively adjusted by users at runtime to make the caustics look sharp or soft. The smaller R is, the sharper the caustic will be. Finally graphics hardware will additively blend all these 2D triangles, so the intensity contribution from all the photons will be accumulated into the rendering buffer, called caustic map, which records the caustic intensity, as shown in Fig. 5.

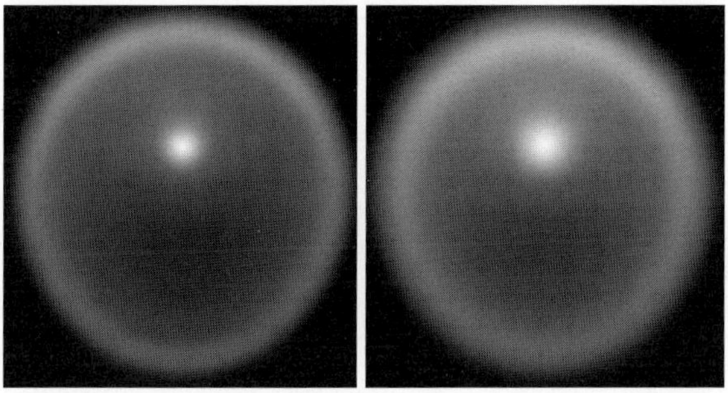

Fig. 5. Two caustic maps of a sphere with different refraction index

4.3 Projection of Caustic Map to Final Rendering Result

Finally, we render the 3D scene(both the refractive object and the receiver surface) to the frame buffer from the camera's viewpoint. In the pixel shader, we project each pixel of the receiver surface into the caustic map to retrieve an intensity value, which is used to modulate the color of the pixel. In this last rendering pass from the camera's viewpoint, the projection is in perspective mode. Therefore, all the images in the rendering results of this paper and the attached video were generated by perspective projection.

5 Results

Our implementation used OpenGL version 1.5 and Cg version 1.4 on a platform with an nVidia GeForce 6600 and a CPU of 2.8GHz Pentium IV. Comparison has been made on rendering quality of our method with the offline rendering method, photon mapping by POV-Ray, as shown in Fig. 6. We can see that the rendering quality of our method is very close to the photon mapping, but the rendering speed(53.24fps, or 0.01878 second per frame) of our method is more than 400 times faster than photon mapping (7.82 seconds per frame). Table 1 gives the statistics of rendering speed for the scene used in the paper and the attached video. The resolution of all the buffers used is 512×512. Fig. 7 shows some dynamic rendering results by our technique on a variety of geometries. In Fig 7, (a) and (b) show the change of lighting direction; (c) and (d) show the dynamic non-uniform deformation of a sphere; (e) and (f) show the change of refraction index of a teapot, and (g) shows the non-uniform deformation of the teapot: scaling along x direction only. More demo videos can be downloaded from http://lcs.ios.ac.cn/~lbq/Publications.htm.

Fig. 6. Comparison of rendering quality: left column is by photon mapping of POV-Ray, while right column by our method

Table 1. Frame rates of our method

Scene	Number of triangles	Static light (fps)	Dynamic light (fps)
Teapot & Dragon	185,208	54.58	22.47
Dolphin & Dragon	191,240	57.88	23.76
Sphere & Dragon	188,824	48.63	21.15
Sphere & Buddha	70,000	83.98	31.74
Beethoven & Dragon	173,852	49.90	21.91
Beethoven & Buddha	5,5028	84.98	33.59
Bunny & Buddha	119,474	49.60	22.38
Bunny & Dragon	238,298	28.73	13.83
Dragon & Dragon	337,648	18.41	9.86

6 Conclusions and Future Work

This paper presented a practical interactive algorithm for caustic rendering that runs entirely on GPU without any pre-computation. It calculates the ray-surface intersection more accurately, and calculates the caustic energy distributed on the receiver surface according to Gauss basis function. Our method can achieve photorealistic caustic image requiring no post-processing or temporal filtering. In addition, the rendering allows change of lighting and viewing direction, as well as deformation of the scene at runtime in an interactive rendering speed.

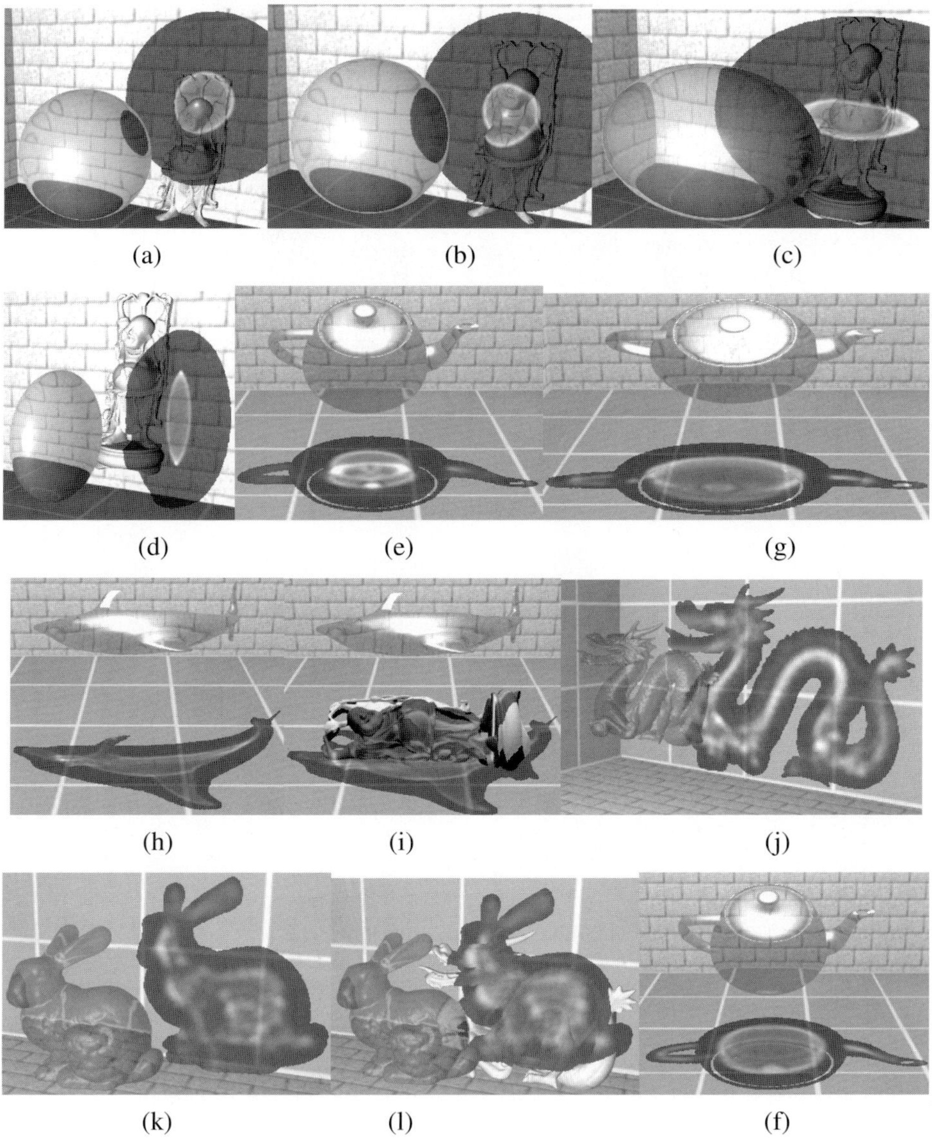

Fig. 7. Rendering dynamic caustics (The blue transparent objects cast shadow and caustics on the background geometry)

Fig. 8. Interactively changing refraction index from low to high

Fig. 9. Top: interactively increasing the index of refraction step by step; bottom: interactively rotating the blue transparent object

One limitation of our method is that refractions are limited to two interfaces. For refractive objects with higher depth complexity, the rendering results may be not very accurate. Another limitation is the under-sampling problem. Since we chose a sampling approach to render caustics, the aliasing problem inherited from shadow mapping technique can occur under certain configuration. We plan to solve these problems in future works and extending our technique to reflective caustics.

Acknowledgements

We would like to thank the anonymous reviewers for their helpful remarks and suggestions. This work is supported by National Key Fundamental Research and Development Project (973) with Grant No. 2002CB312102, NSFC (60473105) and Research Grant of University of Macau.

References

1. Jensen, H.W: Global Illumination using Photon Maps. In Rendering Techniques '96, Springer (1996) 21-30
2. Jensen, H.W: Rendering Caustics on Non-Lambertian Surfaces. In Proceedings of Graphics Interface '96 (1996) 116-121
3. Johannes Guenther, Ingo Wald, and Philipp Slusallek: Realtime caustics using distributed photon mapping. In Eurographics Symposium on Rendering (2004) 111–122
4. Heckbert, P. S., and Hanrahan, P: Beam tracing polygonal objects. In Proceedings of SIGGRAPH (1984) 119–127
5. Watt, M: Light-water interaction using backward beam tracing. In Proceedings of SIGGRAPH (1990) 377–385
6. Manfred Ernst, Tomas Akenine-Moller, and Henrik Wann Jensen: Interactive rendering of caustics using interpolated warped volumes. In Proceedings of Graphics Interface (2005)
7. Tomoyuki Nishita and Eihachiro Nakamae: Method of displaying optical effects within water using accumulation buffer. In Proceedings of 21st annual conference on computer graphics and interactive techniques, New York, NY, USA (1994) 373–379
8. Kei Iwasaki, F. Yoshimoto, Yoshinori Dobashi, Tomoyuki Nishita.: A Fast Rendering Technique of Transparent Objects and Caustics. In Proceedings of CASA, HongKong (2005) 165-170
9. Shah, M., and Pattanaik, S.: Caustics mapping: An image-space technique for real-time caustics. Tech. Rep. CS-TR-50-07, University of Central Florida (2005)
10. Chris Wyman: An approximate image-space approach for interactive refraction. In SIGGRAPH 2005. ACM Transactions on Graphics 24 (3) (July 2005) 1050–1053
11. Chris Wyman and Scott Davis: Interactive Image-Space Techniques for Approximating Caustics. To appear in Proceedings of 2006 ACM Symposium on Interactive 3D Graphics and Games 2006, March 14-17, Redwood Shore, CA, USA (2006)
12. L Szirmay-Kalos, B Aszodi, I Lazanyi, and M Premecz: Approximate Ray-Tracing on the GPU with Distance Impostors. Proceeding of Eurographics2005 Computer graphics forum 24(3), Dublin (2005) 171-176
13. W. Stürzlinger, R. Bastos: Interactive Rendering of Globally Illuminated Glossy Scenes, Rendering Techniques '97, Eds. Dorsey, Slusallek, Springer, ISSN 0946-2767 (June 1997) 93-102

Fuzziness Driven Adaptive Sampling for Monte Carlo Global Illuminated Rendering

Qing Xu[1], Mateu Sbert[2], Zhigeng Pan[3], Wei Wang[1], and Lianping Xing[1]

[1] Tianjin University, Tianjin 300072, China
qingxu@tju.edu.cn
[2] University of Girona, Girona 17003, Spain
mateu@ima.udg.es
[3] Zhejiang University, Hangzhou 310027, China
zgpan@cad.zju.edu.cn

Abstract. Monte Carlo is the only choice for a physically correct method to compute the problem of global illumination in the field of realistic image synthesis. Adaptive sampling is an interesting means to reduce noise, which is one of the major problems of general Monte Carlo global illumination algorithms. In this paper, we make use of the fuzzy uncertainty existing in image synthesis and exploit the formal concept of fuzziness in fuzzy set theory to evaluate pixel quality to run adaptive sampling efficiently. Experimental results demonstrate that our novel method can perform significantly better than classic ones. To our knowledge, this is the first application of the fuzzy technique to global illumination image synthesis problems.

1 Introduction

Global illumination plays an important role in realistic image synthesis, and Monte Carlo based algorithms are the unique choice of physically correct methods to compute the problem of global illumination [1]. The general Monte Carlo global illumination methods, including both the view dependent solutions and the final gathering schemes involved in radiosity, usually employ the baseline Monte Carlo path tracing (MCPT) [2] to produce the synthetic images pixel by pixel. MCPT uses sample paths through a pixel to calculate the pixel value by averaging the sample values, namely the light transport contributions of sample paths. Figure. 1 illustrates a sample path $\overline{x}$ for a pixel. The path is constructed by random sampling a point y_0 on the area of the pixel, and tracing a ray through y_0 into the scene and finding the closest hit point y_1. The path is continued by stochastically choosing a direction according to the surface scattering properties at y_1 and identify the next intersection y_2, and so successively. The path can be stopped with an arbitrarily chosen termination probability t_i at any intersection. The radiance contribution $L(\overline{x})$ gathered by the path $\overline{x}$ is calculated with the Monte Carlo estimator $< L(y_0 \leftarrow y_1) >$ of the light transported from y_1 to y_0: $< L(y_0 \leftarrow y_1) > = < L_{dir}(y_0 \leftarrow y_1) > + \frac{1}{1-t_1} < L(y_1 \leftarrow y_2) >$. $< L_{dir}(y_0 \leftarrow y_1) >$ is the estimator of the radiance from the light source that arrives at y_0 after

H.-P. Seidel, T. Nishita, and Q. Peng (Eds.): CGI 2006, LNCS 4035, pp. 148–159, 2006.

scattering at y_1. The estimator $< L(y_1 \leftarrow y_2) >$ can be solved in the same way as $< L(y_0 \leftarrow y_1) >$. Usually, MCPT gives very noisy images when inadequate samples are used because of the slow convergence of the Monte Carlo techniques. Taking a large enough number of samples for each pixel can render images without noise, but it is too time consuming.

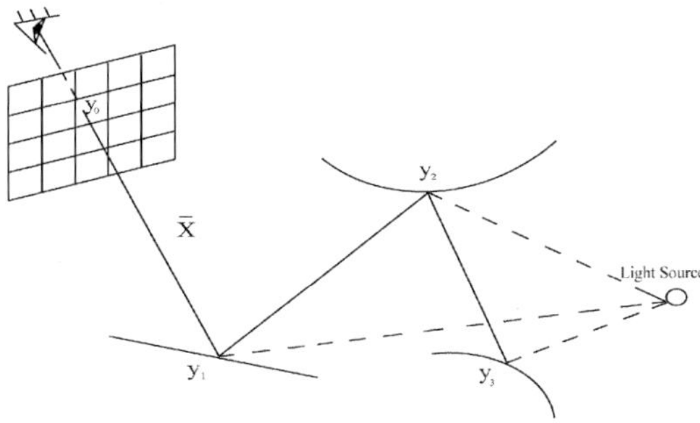

Fig. 1. Monte Carlo Path Tracing

Adaptive sampling, which is an interesting tool to lower the global noise level of the synthesized image without using a fixed number of samples per pixel, is to try to use more samples for the high noisy pixels discovered by some criterion. That is, a few samples are taken at first for a pixel, and then the dedicated criterion or the pixel quality is derived from these samples to determine whether super sampling is needed or not. The pixel quality estimated from the pixel's sample values is the point to do adaptive sampling. Actually, homogeneity of the pixel's sample values is the key to feature the pixel quality, due to the stochastic nature of the Monte Carlo estimation of sample values.

In fact, the difficulty with adaptive sampling is how to locate all of the pixels where more samples are needed because the variation found by the pixel's sample values could not tell us the exact situation with certainty. We furthermore emphasize the high-level ambiguousness resulted from the human perception of incompleteness. In this paper, we introduce fuzzy set theory, which is a powerful tool to handle fuzzy uncertainty [3], into the context of adaptive sampling for Monte Carlo global illumination. We make full use of the fuzziness inherent in image synthesis, and employ sample values within a pixel to define a fuzzy set. Fuzziness of the fuzzy set is calculated and considered as the pixel quality. Experimental results show that our new method can achieve much larger improvements than previously typical approaches. To our knowledge, this is the first application of the fuzzy technique to global illumination image synthesis problems.

The remainder of this paper is organized as follows. In section 2, previous work on adaptive sampling is described. In section 3, a novel adaptive sampling method driven by fuzziness is developed and detailed. Implementation and some results are demonstrated in section 4. Finally, conclusion and some future work are presented.

2 Related Work

Adaptive sampling can be traced back to the research on anti-aliasing in ray tracing [4], for example, Painter and Sloan [5] presented adaptively progressive refinement on the entire image plane to locate image features and place more samples along edges. Here we are going to focus on the pixel based approach in the context of Monte Carlo global illumination.

Based on the root mean square signal to noise ratio (RMS SNR), Dippe and Wold [6] proposed an error estimate of the mean to do adaptive sampling. Lee et al. [7] sampled pixel adaptively based on the variance of sample values. Purgathofer [8] used the confidence interval for instructing adaptive sampling. Kirk and Arvo [9] demonstrated a correction scheme to avoid the bias of variance based approaches. Rigau, Feixas and Sbert [10] [11] introduced the Shannon entropy and also the f-divergences as the measure to conduct adaptive sampling.

Mitchell [12], and later Simmons and Sequin [13] utilized the contrast to do adaptive sampling. Tamstorf and Jensen [14] refined Purgathofer's approach to propose the tone operated confidence interval. Bolin and Meyer [15] developed a perceptually based approach by using a vision model.

All these methods have both merits and limitations. The methods based on absolutely stochastic estimate neglect the fact that the image or pixel quality usually depends on the appearance human eyes can observe. Traditionally we can only get one dimensional vision functions that are often experimentally measured under reductionistic conditions inside the laboratory, but the practical models with significant interactions between different dimensions of visual mechanism are really useful [16]. We can get and use the complex vision model, but the computational cost is probably a problem with the complex vision model based adaptive sampling algorithm [17].

Castro, Feixas and Sbert [18] used the word "fuzzy" in their Monte Carlo radiosity work, but the exact meaning of this word is the probabilistic uncertainty that is far from the fuzzy uncertainty [19].

3 Fuzziness Driven Adaptive Sampling

The image or pixel quality evaluation is of inherent fuzzy uncertainty, which can be well managed by the fuzzy set theory. Our motivation is to incorporate the fuzzy set theory to characterize the refinement metric to do adaptive sampling.

3.1 Intrinsic Fuzziness in Image Synthesis

Perceptually based techniques, a hot field of current computer graphics [20], maybe a good choice for adaptive sampling, because the images produced by graphics algorithms are often observed by human eyes. Actually, image or pixel quality evaluation considering human factors can conveniently act very close to the human way in higher-levels. Humans often use imprecise but integrated descriptors when they describe objects [21]. Due to the fuzziness or fuzzy uncertainty of the human senses, image or pixel quality evaluation is of inherent vagueness from the view of a human observer [22]. For example, when the image created by a Monte Carlo global illumination algorithm is placed in front of a human being, maybe the one and only possibility of the visual response is given by words like "too noisy" or "high quality". Obviously, this is the appearance of fuzzy uncertainty [23].

The fuzziness management in fuzzy set theory can be used to do a variety of actions without any crisp measurements and any crisp computations [24] [25]. We are going to incorporate fuzzy set theory to handle the intrinsic fuzziness existing in the adaptive sampling for Monte Carlo global illumination to do adaptive sampling efficiently.

3.2 Brief Introduction to Fuzzy Set and Fuzziness

We just review several basic concepts in fuzzy set theory here, in order to explain our practice in this paper. Please refer to some typical textbooks, such as [3], for details.

Let U be the universe of discourse. A fuzzy set A is a subset of U, and it is characterized by a membership function $\mu_A(\bullet)$. The membership function $\mu_A(\bullet)$ associates to each $x \in U$ a membership value from [0, 1], and represents the grade of membership of x in A. The value of the fuzzy set originates from the fact that it can deal with imprecise, inexact and uncertain information, which is always used by a human being when describing objects. The so-called fuzziness is a measure of uncertainty, and it is the amount of average ambiguity presented by a fuzzy set. There exist a large number of uncertainty measures for fuzzy sets, and each is with its own objectives, advantages and disadvantages [23].

3.3 Fuzziness Based Pixel Quality

Pixel value is the average of sample values. So the high or low quality of a pixel depends on the small or large deviations between sample values and their average, respectively.

Apparently, "high" or "low", and "small" or "large" indicate the concept of fuzziness. We can measure pixel quality by the formal concept of fuzziness in the fuzzy domain. A fuzzy set X, corresponding to a pixel, is defined as such that the membership of a sample denotes the big and small degree of the absolute difference between its value and the pixel value. The smaller the absolute difference is, the larger the membership value becomes. The fuzzy information associated with X expresses the average amount of the grade of the small or large deviations between sample values and the pixel value. As a result, the fuzziness with X characterizes the pixel quality. The bigger the fuzziness is, the lower the pixel quality is.

Assume that we have N sample values $L_i (1 \leq i \leq N)$ for a pixel. The membership function for the fuzzy set X is formulated as follows:

$$\mu_i = \mu(L_i) = e^{-\frac{\Delta_i^2}{2\beta^2}} \tag{1}$$

$$\Delta_i = \|L_i - \overline{L}\| \tag{2}$$

$$\overline{L} = \frac{1}{N}\sum_{i=1}^{N} L_i \tag{3}$$

Here Δ_i is the color difference between sample value L_i and pixel value $\overline{L}$. We adopt the CIELAB color to calculate difference because CIELAB is a perceptually uniform color space [26]. The formula 1 manifests a gradual increase in the deviation, which is described by the common Gaussian function. Since each sample should belong to the pixel to some possibility degree, the parameter β is automatically selected to ensure that the membership of any sample is in the range [0.5, 1]. The β is chosen as such that it can be used to restrict the membership of a sample to be 0.5, if the color difference between sample value and pixel value is maximal. We choose Deluca-Termini fuzziness [23], in the normalized form, as our pixel quality measure because it is popularly used in many engineering fields:

$$Q = \frac{\sum_{i=1}^{N} [\mu_i \log \mu_i + (1 - \mu_i) \log(1 - \mu_i)]}{N \log 0.5} \tag{4}$$

Figure. 2 shows the effectiveness of the fuzziness based measure of pixel quality. The generated image for a complex scene is produced by MCPT with 400 samples per pixel. The temperature map is the color visualization of pixel fuzziness in which red color corresponds to high fuzziness (low quality) and blue to low fuzziness (high quality). Here the pixel fuzziness is calculated by using 200 sample values. Our metric is sensitive to different levels of pixel quality and behaves well in difficult areas, for example, the area A shows the detailed color changes which exhibit varied pixel qualities in this softly shadowed region. Due to the application of fuzziness measure, our pixel quality metric can take human factors, or exactly speaking, the high-level human factors, into account, rather

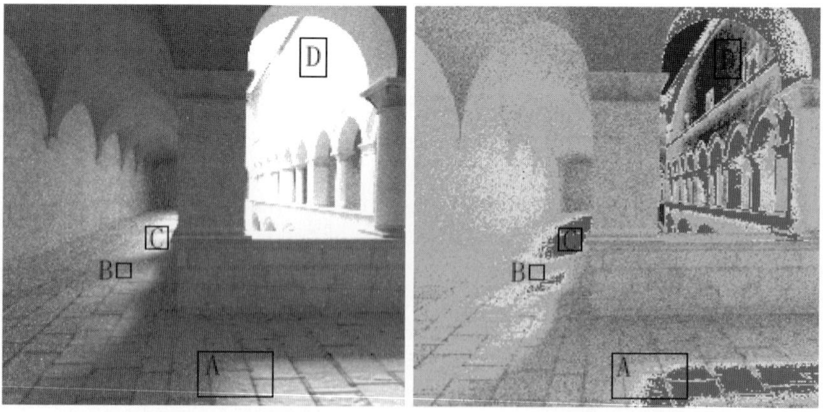

(a) Generated image (b) Temperature map

Fig. 2. Fuzziness visualization

than only considering the quantified variations between the sample values. For instance, the pixels in the area B are indirectly illuminated and their pixel variances would be larger than those of the pixels in the area C that is directly illuminated. But the area C attracts more from human eyes and behaves itself in the low level of quality, and this is the situation of our metric. Similarly, the area D is regarded as a high quality region because the pixel values here are outside the perceivable range.

3.4 Fuzzy Uncertainty Driven Adaptive Sampling

As the pixel quality measure, the fuzziness defined in Section 3.3 is incorporated into the Monte Carlo Global Illumination based adaptive sampling. That is to say, a first batch of pilot samples is used for each pixel to compute the fuzziness of pixel. Then more batches are employed if the fuzziness is not smaller than the predefined threshold, and these successive batches will improve the fuzziness or the pixel quality.

The applied adaptive super sampling procedure is as follows:

STEP 1. An initial batch of N_{Init} stochastically distributed samples at a pixel is taken and the corresponding color values $L_i(1 \leq i \leq N_{Init})$ are estimated to compute the fuzziness, namely the pixel quality Q (see the formula 4, here the number of pixel's samples $N = N_{Init}$).
STEP 2. The conditional test

$$Q < Threshold \tag{5}$$

is operated. Where $Threshold$ is the predefined threshold, which is used to control whether the super sampling is terminated or not.
STEP 3. Consecutive batches of N_{Add} additional samples are introduced until the conditional test is valid. The number of samples is changed by

$$N = N + N_{Add} \tag{6}$$

whenever a batch of N_{Add} additional samples is used.

4 Implementation and Results

We have implemented the new adaptive sampling scheme for MCPT. We use the tabulated Gaussian function values and the tabulated power function values in the calculation of fuzziness, and accordingly our algorithm does not increase the running time when compared with other methods. Furthermore, the computational cost of our method is even smaller than that of the entropy based scheme [10]. The parameter $Threshold$, which is used in the procedure of adaptive super sampling, is tuned so that all the result images for each test scene are obtained with a very similar average samples per pixel. All the synthetic images are generated without filtering.

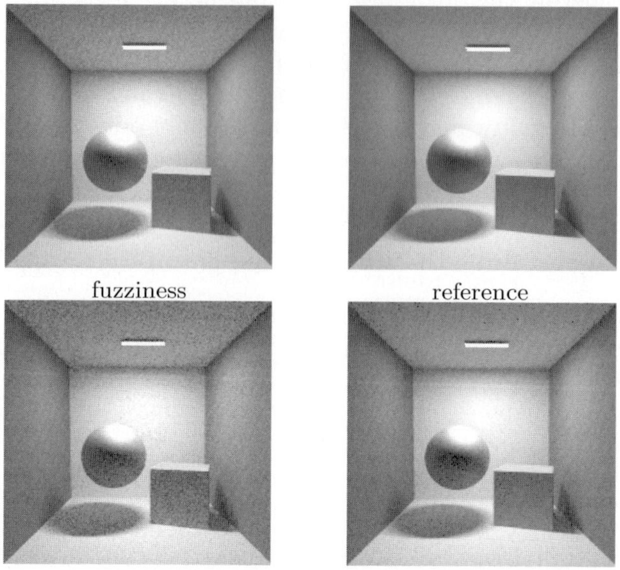

fuzziness reference

contrast variance

Fig. 3. Result images for the test scene 1

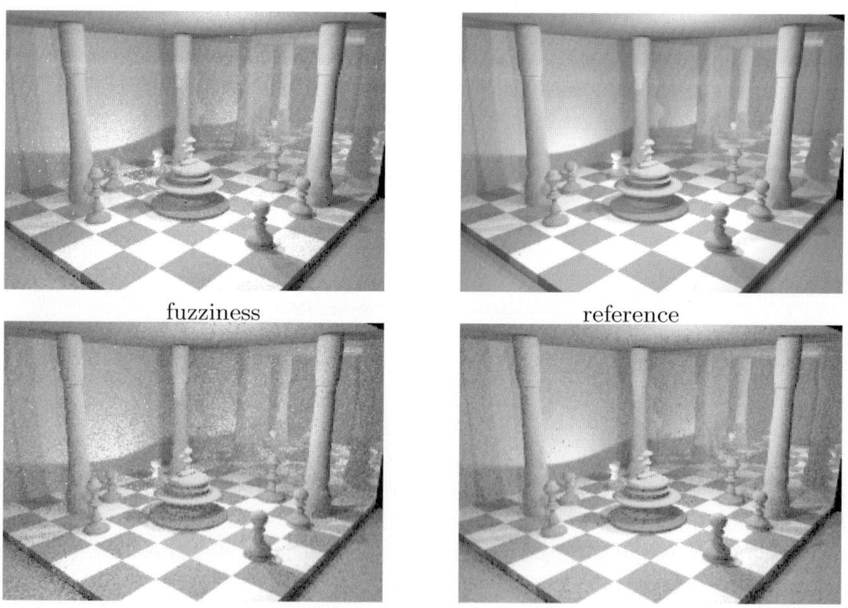

fuzziness reference

contrast variance

Fig. 4. Result images for the test scene 2

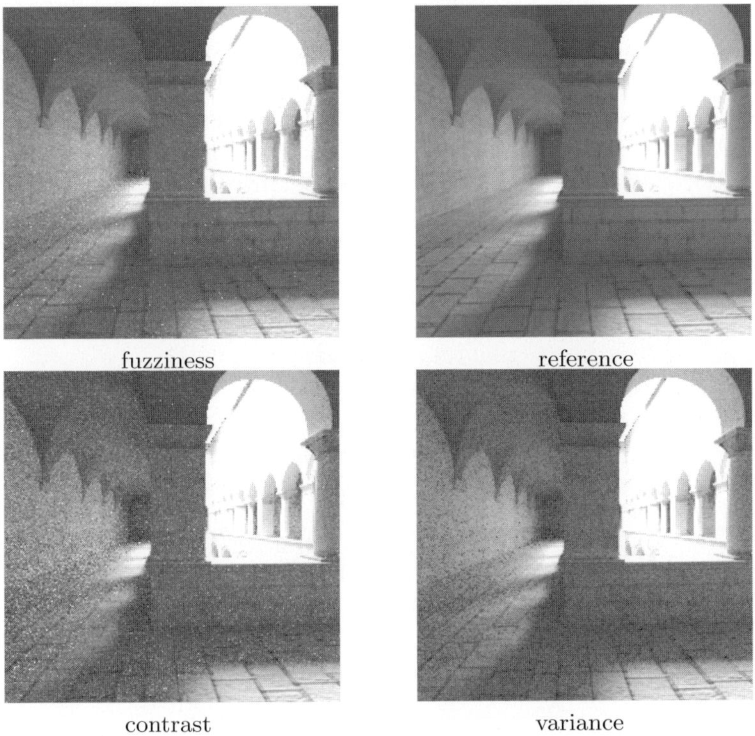

Fig. 5. Result images for the test scene 3

We compare our method with the two classic ones, the contrast [13] and the variance [8] [14] based methods. Three test scenes are used for the comparisons. The test scene 1 is similar to the famous Cornell box. The complex test scene 2 and 3 include 24500 and 60000 textured triangles respectively, in diffuse and glossy scattering attributes. Especially, the test scene 3 is indirect lighting dominated, and it is very complex from the viewpoint of global illumination computation. For each of the three test scenes, all the approaches use the same number of initial samples (8 for the first two scene, 50 for the third scene) and the same number of additional samples (8 for the first two scene, 15 for the third scene) to do adaptive sampling to produce the result images.

The reference images of the three test scenes, which are generated by MCPT using 10000, 40000 and 40000 samples per pixel, are used to judge the quantitative magnitude of errors for the images created by different algorithms. The three reference images are placed in the following Figure. 3, Figure. 4 and Figure. 5 respectively to assist the visual comparisons of the different produced images.

The images with 200 × 200 pixels for the test scene 1 synthesized by 3 approaches with average 90 samples per pixel are shown in Figure 3. The highest global image quality resulted from our method is evident from the observation of the blue sphere, the shadow regions and the flat red and green walls. For instance, the most noise reduction can be easily found at the center part of the sphere.

The images with 256×192 pixels for the test scene 2 produced by 3 methods with average 80 samples per pixel are presented in Figure. 4. Our algorithm achieves the best results, for example, this can be observed from the mirrored areas, the shadow zones and the green grounds. In particular, we can observe the big differences from the rightest mirrored pillar.

The images with 250×250 pixels for the test scene 3 created by 3 algorithms with average 400 samples per pixel are demonstrated in Figure. 5. The new scheme outperforms the others, and this is presented from all the parts of the generated images. For example, the noise reductions arrived at the roof, the indirect lighting areas and the texture details are very apparent.

Table 1. RMS comparisons for the new method and the contrast based method

RMS	Scene 1	Scene 2	Scene 3
Fuzziness	3.84	4.63	4.18
Contrast	7.36	7.47	8.18
RMS-reduce	47.83%	38.02%	48.90%

Table 2. RMS comparisons for the new method and the variance based method

RMS	Scene 1	Scene 2	Scene 3
Fuzziness	3.84	4.63	4.18
Variance	4.31	5.34	6.17
RMS-reduce	10.90%	13.30%	32.25%

Table. 1 and Table. 2 show the RMS errors of the above images generated by different methods respective to the reference images for the three test scenes. The quantified RMS reductions by the novel method over the two other methods are also listed in the two tables. The RMS analysis justifies the largest noise reduction of our method. The RMS reduction of our scheme is from about 11 % to 49 %. Moreover, we can find that the proposed method can attain more noise reductions for the more complex scenes. Thus, it is highly promising to use the novel scheme to render the complex scenes.

In addition, we compare our algorithm with the the entropy based approach [10]. Two test scenes are used for this time. The test scene 4 is a simple box with a spot light, and with diffuse and glossy surfaces accounting for different global illuminated effects. The test scene 5, with multiple and a variety of indirect illuminated light sources, includes 870000 textured triangles, in both diffuse and glossy scattering attributes. For each of the two test scenes, all the approaches use the same number of initial samples (8) and the same number of additional samples (8) to generate the result images.

The images with 200 × 200 pixels for the test scene 4 by 2 techniques with average 100 samples per pixel are given in Figure. 6. The best image quality resulted from the new method is apparently presented in the indirect lighting zones, such as the mirror, the shadows, and the upper red and green walls.

The images with 256 × 192 pixels for the test scene 5 by 2 approaches with average 200 samples per pixel are shown in Figure. 7. The new method performs better in the complex parts, such as the three pictures hung on the walls, the floor, the upper walls and the roof.

Table. 3 presents the RMS reductions by the new scheme over the entropy based method.

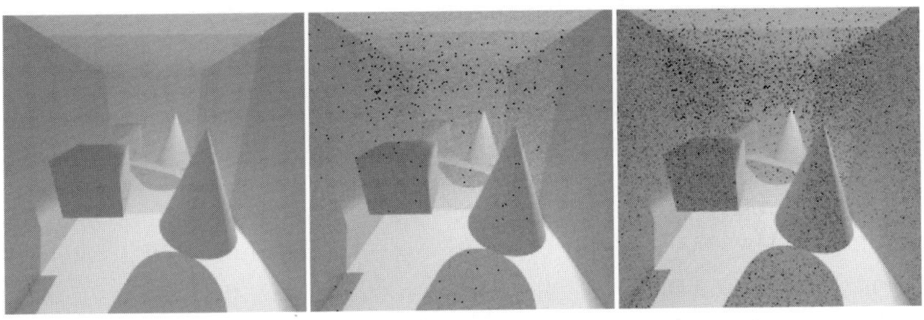

reference fuzziness entropy

Fig. 6. Result images for the test scene 4

reference fuzziness entropy

Fig. 7. Result images for the test scene 5

Table 3. RMS comparisons for the new method and the entropy based method

RMS	Scene 4	Scene 5
Fuzziness	3.71	9.40
Entropy	8.12	10.59
RMS-reduce	54.31%	11.31%

5 Conclusion and Future Work

We have presented a new adaptive sampling scheme. The pixel quality measured by fuzziness is sensitive and discriminating. Implementation results demonstrate quite better advantages of the novel approach. With the help of fuzzy set theory, it becomes promising to do adaptive sampling more effectively. To our knowledge, this is the first try to use the fuzzy technique for global illuminated image synthesis problems. Just as almost all the existing adaptive sampling approaches, our method is biased. In the near future, the bias embedded in adaptive sampling would be investigated in a fuzzy way.

Acknowledgements

This work is sponsored by the Scientific Research Foundation for the Returned Overseas Chinese Scholars, State Education Ministry of China (No. D4200407), and also is sponsored by the National Natural Science Foundation of China (No. 60572169). Mateu Sbert is partially supported by grant number TIN2004-07451-C03-01 from the Spanish Government. The authors are grateful to the anonymous reviewers for their helpful suggestions and comments.

References

1. Greenberg, D.P.: A framework for realistic image synthesis. In Communications of the ACM, 42(8),Aug (1999)
2. Kajiya, J.T.: The rendering equation. In Computer Graphics, 20(4): 143-150, (1986)
3. Wang, L.X.: A Course in Fuzzy Systems and Control. Prentice-Hall Inc, (1997)
4. Whitted, T.: An Improved Illumination Model for Shaded Display. In Communications of the ACM, 32(6): 343-349, (1980)
5. Painter, J., Sloan, K.: Antialiased Ray Tracing by Adaptive Progressive Refinement. In SIGGRAPH '89 23(3): 281-288, (1989)
6. Dippe, M.A.Z., Wold, E.H.: Antialiasing through Stochastic Sampling. In SIGGRAPH '85 19(3): 69-78, July (1985)
7. Lee, M.E., Redner, R.A., Uselton, S.P.: Statistically optimized sampling for distributed ray tracing. In SIGGRAPH '85: Proceedings of the 12th annual conference on Computer graphics and interactive techniques, pages 61-68, (1985)
8. Purgathofer, W.: A Statistical Method for Adaptive Stochastic Sampling. In SIGGRAPH '87 11(2): 157-162, (1987)
9. Kirk, D., Arvo, J.: Unbiased variance reduction for global illumination. In Proceedings of the 2nd Eurographics Workshop on Rendering, May (1991)
10. Rigau, J., Feixas, M., Sbert, M.: New Contrast Measures for Pixel Supersampling. In Proceedings of CGI'02, pages 439-451, July (2002)
11. Rigau, J., Feixas, M., Sbert, M.: Refinement Criteria Based on f-Divergences. In Proceedings of Eurographics Symposium on Rendering 2003, June (2003)
12. Mitchell, D.P.: Generating Antialiased Images at Low Sampling Densities. In SIGGRAPH '87 21(4): 65-72, (1987)

13. Simmons, M., Sequin, C.: Tapestry: A Dynamic Mesh Based Display Representation for Interactive Rendering. In Proceedings of the 11th Eurographics Workshop on Rendering. (2000)
14. Tamstorf, R., Jensen, H.W.: Adaptive Sampling and Bias Estimation in Path Tracing. In Proc. of Eurographics Workshop on Rendering '97, pages 285-295, (1997)
15. Bolin, M.R., Meyer, G.W.: A perceptually based adaptive sampling algorithm. In Proceedings of SIGGRAPH'98, pages 299-309, July (1998)
16. Greenberg, D.P., Torrance, K., Shirley, P., Arvo, J., Ferwerda, J.A., Pattanaik, S., Lafortune, E., Walter, B., Foo, S., Trumbore, B.: A framework for realistic image synthesis. In Proceedings of SIGGRAPH'97, pages 477-494, (1997)
17. Farrugia, J.P., Peroche, B.: A Progressive Rendering Algorithm Using an Adaptive Perceptually Based Image Metric. In Proceedings of Eurographics'2004, (2004)
18. Castro, F., Feixas, M., Sbert, M.: Fuzzy Random Walk. In Computer Graphics International 2002, (2002)
19. Liang K.H., Mao J.J.W.: Image Thresholding By Minimizing the Measures of Fuzziness. In Pattern Recognition, 28(1): 41-51, Jan (1995)
20. O'Sullivan, C., Howlett, S., McDonnell, R., Morvan, Y., O'Conor, K.: Perceptually Adaptive Graphics. State of The Art Report. In EUROGRAPHICS 2004, (2004)
21. Sonka, M., Hlavac, V., Boyle, R.: Image Processing, Analysis, and Machine Vision (2nd edition). Thomson Learning Vocational, (1998)
22. Pal, S.K.: Fuzzy Sets in Image processing and Recognition. In Proceedings of the 1992 IEEE International Conference on Fuzzy Systems, (1992)
23. Pal, N.R., Bezdek, J.C.: Measuring Fuzzy Uncertainty. In IEEE Transactions on Fuzzy Systems, 2(2): 107-118, May (1994)
24. Zadeh, L.A.: From computing with numbers to computing with words - From manipulation of measurements to manipulation of perceptions. In IEEE Transactions on Circuits and Systems I: Fundamental Theory and Applications, 46(1): 105-119, Jan (1999)
25. Zadeh, L.A.: Fuzzy logic = computing with words. In IEEE Transactions on Fuzzy Systems, 4(2): 103-111, May (1996)
26. Sharma, G., Trussell, H.J.: Digital Color Imaging. In IEEE Transactions on Image Processing, 6(7): 901-932, Jul (1997)

Manifold Parameterization

Lei Zhang[1,2], Ligang Liu[1,2,⋆], Zhongping Ji[1,2], and Guojin Wang[1,2]

[1] Department of Mathematics, Zhejiang University, Hangzhou 310027, China
[2] State Key Lab of CAD&CG, Zhejiang University, Hangzhou 310027, China
ligangliu@zju.edu.cn

Abstract. Manifold parameterization considers the problem of parameterizing a given triangular mesh onto another mesh surface, which could be particularly plane or sphere surfaces. In this paper we propose a unified framework for manifold parameterization between arbitrary meshes with identical genus. Our approach does this task by directly mapping the connectivity of the source mesh onto the target mesh surface without any intermediate domain and partition of the meshes. The connectivity graph of source mesh is used to approximate the geometry of target mesh using least squares meshes. A subset of user specified vertices are constrained to have the geometry information of the target mesh. The geometry of the mesh vertices is reconstructed while approximating the known geometry of the subset by positioning each vertex approximately at the center of its immediate neighbors. This leads to a sparse linear system which can be effectively solved. Our approach is simple and fast with less user interactions. Many experimental results and applications are presented to show the applicability and flexibility of the approach.

Keywords: Surface parameterization, compatible meshes, least squares mesh, morphing.

1 Introduction

Surface parameterization can be viewed as a one-to-one mapping from a mesh surface onto a suitable domain. There are lots of work on surface parameterizations in the literature [1]. Typically, surfaces that are homeomorphic to a disk are mapped onto the plane. For closed genus-zero models, the unit sphere is a natural parameterization domain. More complicated mesh can be mapped to a coarse simplicial domain such as a cube or its simplified mesh.

In general, the parameter domain itself will be a surface and so constructing a parameterization means mapping one surface onto another. This is widely used in applications such as shape morphing that require *compatible* meshes or *consistent/cross* parameterization [2, 3, 4], i.e., meshes with identical connectivity.

In previous approaches, consistent parameterizations are generally constructed by partitioning the meshes using a set of consistent cuts and creating an intermediate common domain [2, 3, 4, 5, 6]. There are many drawbacks for these approaches. It may require extra user input such as specifying the cut connectivity to partition two meshes

⋆ Corresponding author.

H.-P. Seidel, T. Nishita, and Q. Peng (Eds.): CGI 2006, LNCS 4035, pp. 160–171, 2006.

into a set of consistent patches. This is difficult for many models with dissimilar geometry. Furthermore, the mutual tessellation during optimization process is rather time-consuming which makes it take a couple of hours to create inter-surface maps between two meshes.

Unlike previous approaches we try to *directly* create a one-to-one map between topologically equivalent models. Our approach thinks of consistent parameterization as embedding its connectivity graph onto another surface directly. We call it *manifold parameterization* for the reason that manifold could refer to plane, sphere, and any other manifold surface.

Our approach does this task by directly mapping the connectivity of one mesh onto another mesh surface without any intermediate domain and partition of the meshes. Considering Fig. 1 for an illustration example, in (c), the connectivity graph of the mannequin head mesh (a) have been embedded on the surface of the Max-Planck head mesh (b). Mesh (c) looks the same with mesh (b) in shape but has the same connectivity with (a).

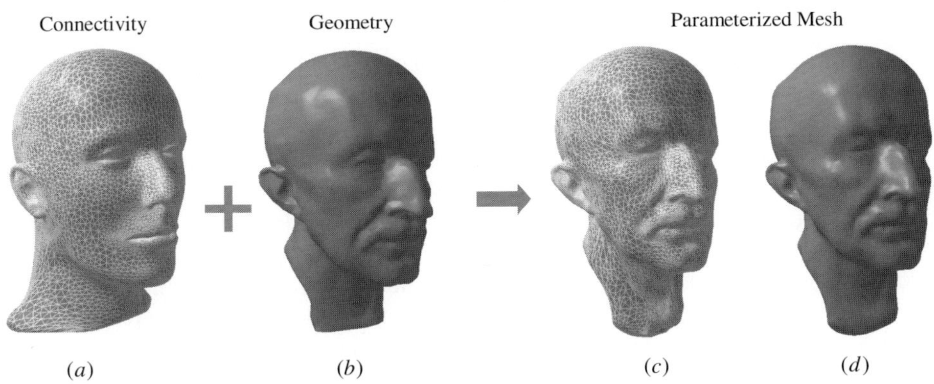

Fig. 1. Manifold parameterization: mapping the connectivity of a mesh (a) onto another mesh (b) directly to obtain a new mesh (c). The new mesh (c) has almost the same geometry with mesh (b) and has identical connectivity with mesh (a). (d) is the smooth shading of (c).

Our approach is rather intuitive and simple based on least squares meshes [7]. Using the same notations above, we use the connectivity of M_s by discarding its geometry information. A subset of the vertices are then constrained to have the geometry information of M_t. The geometry of the mesh vertices is reconstructed in a least-square sense while approximating the known geometry of the subset by positioning each vertex approximately at the center of its immediate neighbors [7]. This leads to a sparse linear system which can be effectively solved. The location of each vertex in the subset is carefully chosen to be the features and saliency points of mesh M_t so that the reconstructed surface captures the overall geometric shape of M_t. In this process, no any geometry information of M_s is used. Since the reconstruction system accounts for both the given connectivity of mesh M_s and the given geometry of mesh M_t, it yields a shape which is a consistent parameterization between M_s and M_t.

To our knowledge, our approach is the first approach to directly generate the consistent parameterization between two manifold meshes without partitioning the meshes using a set of consistent cuts and creating an intermediate common domain.

2 Related Work

2.1 Mesh Parameterizations

Planar parameterization methods established mappings between non-closed mesh and planar domains. There have been many methods developed to date, see [1] for a recent survey. An important limitation of planar parameterization techniques is that it generally requires that an entire surface be cut into one or more disk-like charts, where each chart is parameterized independently[8, 9].

A closed genus-zero surface can be parameterized into the unit sphere without any cuts. Examples of spherical parameterization approaches include [10, 11, 12].

2.2 Consistent Parameterizations

Consistent parameterizations have been done for morphing application in much of the previous work, see a recent review on consistent parameterizations developed for morphing [13].

The typical approaches for consistent parameterization first parameterize the meshes on a common base domain and then compute the overlapped triangulations on the based domain. Sphere is chosen as a base domain for consistent parameterization in [14]. An inherent limitation is that it can only be applied to closed, genus zero surfaces.

A more general approach is to parameterize the models over a common intermediate simplicial mesh [5, 2, 3, 4]. The meshes are partitioned into matching patches with an identical inter-patch connectivity using a set of consistent cuts. Then each patch is parameterized onto the corresponding face in the based domain.

The work of [5] first constructs simplicial parametrizations from two meshes to their respective base domains. User assistance is required to form a good map between the different domain meshes, and this map construction is not robust. The common metamesh is typically a reported 10 times more complex than either original mesh. A set of genus-zero models is parameterized onto a simplicial complex in [2]. They create consistent parameterizations by partitioning the mesh based on the connectivity of the simplicial complex and parameterizing each patch onto the respective simplical complex face. The work of [3] improves the technique of [2] by not requiring the simplicial complex to be specified a priori. However, their algorithm does not scale well with regard to the number of models to be consistently parameterized. In more recent work [4] they construct consistent parameterizations between two models without going through an intermediate domain. To generate a smooth consistent parameterization, they use a symmetric, stretch based relaxation procedure, which trades high computational complexity for quality of the mapping. However the method is limited to dealing with only two models and is very slow.

In this paper, we directly map the connectivity of one mesh onto another mesh without any intermediate domain. Our approach needs not partition the meshes so that no extra user inputs are required to specify the set of consistent cuts. Our system can easily construct the consistent parameterization among multiple meshes as shown in Section 5.1. Moreover, our approach is fast and efficient as it only needs to solve a sparse linear system.

3 Least Squares Mesh

Least squares meshes (LS meshes) are meshes with a prescribed connectivity that approximate a set of control points in a least-squares sense [7]. For a given mesh connectivity, LS mesh allows that only a sparse subset of the mesh vertices contains geometric information. The geometry of the mesh is reconstructed in a least squares sense by approximating the known geometry of the subset and positioning each vertex in the center of gravity of its immediate neighbors. It can be obtained by solving a sparse linear system. The linear system not only defines a surface that approximates the given control points, but it also distributes the vertices over the surface in a fair way.

We now go through the contexts of LS mesh quickly. For a vertex $\mathbf{v}_i$ of mesh M, the following equation defines its smoothness condition:

$$\mathbf{v}_i - \sum_{j \in i^*} \frac{1}{d_i} \mathbf{v}_j = \mathbf{0}, \tag{1}$$

where i^* is the vertex index set of neighborhood vertices to the vertex $\mathbf{v}_i$ and d_i is the valence of $\mathbf{v}_i$.

It can be seen that the equations in Eq. 1 of all the vertices form a sparse linear system. The linear system can be written in matrix form:

$$\mathbf{LX} = \mathbf{0}, \tag{2}$$

where $\mathbf{L}$ is an $n \times n$ matrix, known as the Laplacian of the mesh, with elements as:

$$L_{ij} = \begin{cases} 1, & i = j, \\ -\frac{1}{d_i}, & (i,j) \in E, \\ 0, & \text{otherwise}, \end{cases}$$

$\mathbf{X}$ is the $n \times 1$ column vector of the corresponding vertices. The above system had been used in the planar graph drawing [15] and planar parameterization [16].

If the geometry of a subset of the vertices are provided, we can reconstruct the geometry of the rest of the mesh vertices by solving the sparse linear system in Eq. 2 in a least square sense [7]. If we carefully select the provided vertices as feature points of the surface, the reconstructed mesh can effectively approximate the original mesh.

Providing the 3D location for some s control vertices $\{\mathbf{v}_k = (x_k, y_k, z_k) | k \in C\}$, where $C = \{i_1, i_2, \ldots, i_s\}$ is the set of indices. The system reconstructs the positions of all the vertices $\mathbf{v}'$ of mesh M to minimize the following error functional:

$$\min_{\mathbf{X}'} \|\mathbf{LX}'\|^2 + \sum_{k \in C} \|\mathbf{v}'_k - \mathbf{v}_k\|^2. \tag{3}$$

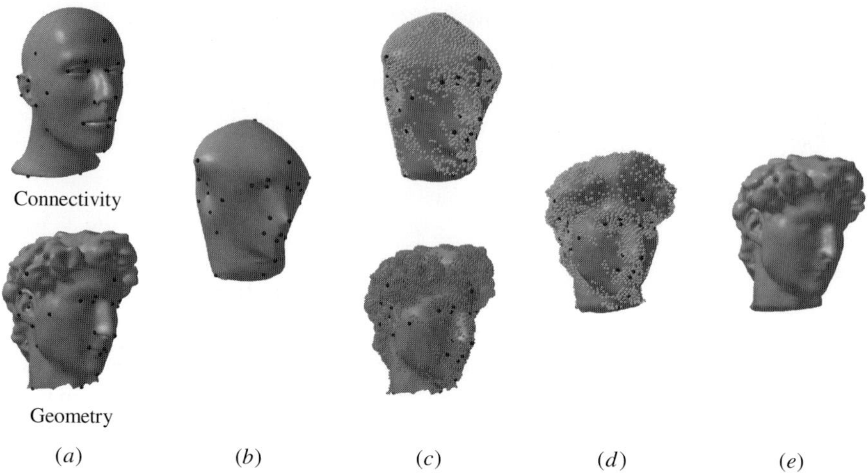

Fig. 2. Manifold parameterization pipeline: mapping the connectivity of mannequin head model (M_s) onto David head model (M_t). (a) Two head models (Upper: mannequin head; Lower: David head) with user markers in blue; (b) LS mesh using the connectivity graph of mannequin head mesh and user specified control points on the David head mesh; (c) Lower: the feature points detected by mesh saliency approach [17] shown in pink; Upper: the detected feature points are mapped onto (b) shown in green; (d) LS mesh using the connectivity graph of mannequin head mesh and control points including user markers and mapped feature points on the upper mesh of (c); (e) smooth shading of (d). The mesh (e) has the same geometry with David head model and has the same connectivity with mannequin head model.

The above functional is quadratic in every vertex and hence its partial derivatives are linear expressions. The unique minimum is found if all partial derivatives with respect to the vertices vanish, which results in a sparse linear system as the following:

$$\mathbf{AX}' = \begin{pmatrix} \mathbf{L} \\ \mathbf{F} \end{pmatrix} \mathbf{X}' = \begin{pmatrix} \mathbf{0} \\ \mathbf{b}^F \end{pmatrix} = \mathbf{b}, \tag{4}$$

where $\mathbf{F}$ is an $s \times n$ matrix in which each row contains only one non-zero element used to constrain the position of the control vertices with the element:

$$f_{kj} = \begin{cases} 1, & j = i_k \in C, \\ 0, & \text{otherwise}, \end{cases} \quad 1 \leq k \leq s,\ 1 \leq j \leq n;$$

and $\mathbf{b}^F$ is an $s \times 1$ column vector:

$$b_k^F = g_{i_k},\ \ 1 \leq k \leq s,\ \ g = x, y, \text{or } z.$$

Note that the linear system is defined for each component of the coordinates x, y, and z. The positions of the vertices can be found by solving the sparse linear system in Eq. 4 in a least square sense as:

$$\mathbf{X}' = (\mathbf{A}^T\mathbf{A})^{-1}\mathbf{A}^T\mathbf{b}.$$

4 Our Approach for Manifold Parameterization

4.1 Our Approach

Inspired by LS meshes, we develop a new technique for manifold parameterization, i.e., mapping the connectivity graph of one mesh onto another mesh. Given two manifold meshes M_s and M_t, our goal is to generate a new mesh M_r which has the same connectivity with M_s and the same geometry with M_t, as shown in Fig. 3.

Our strategy is to use the connectivity graph of M_s and use the constraints of control points from M_t in the linear system Eq. 4. We need to carefully choose a set of control points on M_t in order to bring the surface of M_r close to M_t.

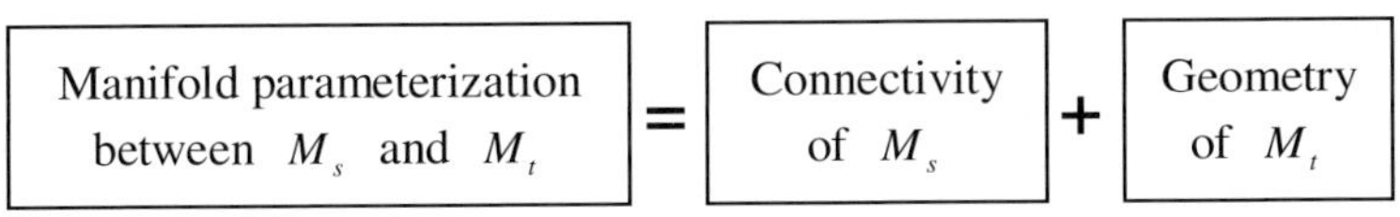

Fig. 3. Manifold parameterization: mapping the connectivity of M_s onto surface M_t

4.2 User Markers

Usually the consistent parameterization must respect the similar features between the models. For example, when mapping between two human head models, the mouth must map to the mouth, the nose to the nose, and so on. This is typically achieved by specifying the correspondence for a small set of feature vertices by the user, called user markers, and using a consistent parameterization that preserves the user-defined feature vertex correspondence.

In our system, the user can easily specify the corresponding marker points on two given mesh shown side by side. Fig. 2(a) shows two mesh models, the mannequin head mesh in the upper as M_s and the David head mesh in the lower as M_t, with user specified corresponding feature points shown in blue.

4.3 Feature Detection

The LS mesh $\bar{M}_t$ constructed by the connectivity of M_s and the control points from the user markers on M_t is shown in Fig. 2(b). It is seen in the figure that the LS mesh is distorted and bears almost no similarities to the original shape of M_t due to the small amount of control points.

Usually only a small number of marker paris is specified by the user. Thus we need find more control points automatically to make the reconstructed $\bar{M}_t$ get closer to the shape of M_t.

Intuitively, the control points should be places in important locations where geometric detail is present on the surface, such as high curvature points, ridges and valleys, and the tips of extruding parts.

In [17], the idea of mesh saliency is introduced as a measure of regional importance for meshes, which is inspired by low-level human visual system cues. Mesh saliency is defined in a scale-dependent manner using a center-surround operator on Gaussian-weighted mean curvatures.

The pink points on David head mesh shown in lower row of Fig. 2(c) are the detected feature points by approach of mesh saliency.

4.4 Mapping Feature Points

The feature points detected on mesh M_t should be mapped to the constructed mesh $\bar{M}_t$ so that $\bar{M}_t$ can be reconstructed using these control points to get closer to the shape of M_t.

We adopt an intuitive and simple method. Each vertex of the feature points on M_t is mapped to the closet vertex on $\bar{M}_t$. Note that these closest points are required to be the vertices $\bar{M}_t$.

It is required that the normals of the feature point on M_t and the corresponding mapped point on $\bar{M}_t$ should have compatible directions in the meaning of that their inner product is larger than 0. This is to avoid mismatching so that front-facing surfaces will not be matched to back-facing surfaces. The distance between the mapped pair points is within a threshold and we use a distance threshold of 10% (measured as a percentage of the bounding box diagonal) in our experiments.

There might be cases that multiple feature points on M_t are mapped onto one vertex on $\bar{M}_t$. In these cases, we simply keep the closest pair and discard the other pairs.

It is also noted that simply mapping each feature point on M_t to its closest point on $\bar{M}_t$ will not always result in a very good matching as neighboring parts of M_t could get mapped to disparate parts of $\bar{M}_t$. To constrain this problem, we use a heuristic criteria by checking the normal changes in triangles related to mapped points over $\bar{M}_t$. Large normal variation will penalize the point mapping. In our experimentation this method can efficiently prevent adjacent parts of M_t from being mapped to disparate parts of $\bar{M}_t$. As we will see in the following sections, the mismatching cases would seldom occur for all testing examples after couples of iteration of LS mesh reconstruction as M_t and $\bar{M}_t$ are very close to each other.

To accelerate the minimum-distance matching, we use the ANN library [18] of approximating nearest neighbor searching, which performs quite efficiently in a linear time.

The upper figure of Fig. 2(c) shows an example of this mapping. The feature points (in pink color) on David head mesh shown in the lower figure of Fig. 2(c) are mapped onto $\bar{M}_t$ shown in Fig. 2(b). The mapped points on $\bar{M}_t$ are shown in green in the upper figure of Fig. 2(c). The mapped points are added into control points in LS mesh construction and obtain the mesh $\bar{M}_t$ shown in Fig. 2(d). It is seen that the reconstructed mesh $\bar{M}_t$ quickly gets closer to mesh M_t as the number of control points increases.

4.5 Algorithm Steps

We summarize the steps of our approach as following:

Input: Two manifold triangular meshes M_s and M_t.
output: A consistent parameterization M_r between M_s and M_t.
Step 1. Specify some corresponding marker pairs on M_s and M_t manually.
Step 2. Detect the feature points with importance values on M_t by the approach of mesh saliency.

Step 3. Construct $\bar{M}_t$ by LS mesh using connectivity of M_s and markers' geometry on M_t as control points.
Step 4. Map the feature points of M_t onto $\bar{M}_t$.
Step 5. Construct $\bar{M}_t$ by LS mesh approach using markers' geometry and mapped points' geometry on M_t as control points.
Step 6. Perform adaptive refinements on $\bar{M}_t$ and M_s simultaneously.
Step 7. Repeat Step 4 to Step 6 until the approximation error between $\bar{M}_t$ and M_t is within a prior tolerance. Then we get $M_r = \bar{M}_t$.

4.6 Discussion

At the first iteration, as $\bar{M}_t$ is generated using only the user markers, the shape is much different from M_t as shown in Fig. 2(b). Practically we do not use distance threshold in the process of mapping feature points at the first iteration.

It can be seen that the connectivity of M_s should be dense enough to represent the geometric details of M_t. Or else large distortion will occur. Although the adaptive refinement can alleviate this occasion, we usually subdivide/refine the mesh M_s at the beginning to guarantee that there are enough triangles in its connectivity for some examples.

We would like to stress that the quality of the parameterization $\bar{M}_t$ strongly depends on the shape of M_s and M_t and the specified marker pairs. In some cases the connectivity of M_s is not dense enough to represent the geometry details of M_t globally or locally. In other case there will be skinny triangles on $\bar{M}_t$ which cause numerical problems in many applications. To account for this, we use two adaptive refinement operators, i.e., edge split and edge flip, to yield the parameterization $\bar{M}_t$ representing the geometry details of M_t with a better triangle shape.

A small quantity of feature points may be detected in some relatively smooth region of M_t using the computed scale by mesh saliency approach. Then this region can not be well approximated by LS mesh processing. Thus we select some random vertices in this region and add these selected random vertices to the set of feature points generated by mesh saliency.

Furthermore, our algorithm can be easily applied locally. Our system also allows to consistently parameterized a part of a mesh less than another one, which happens to be useful in practice.

5 Experimental Results and Applications

We will show some examples illustrating the applicability and flexibility of our manifold parameterization approach in a few exemplary applications. All the examples presented in this paper were made on a 2.8GHz Pentium IV computer with 1G memory.

5.1 Consistent Parameterizations Between Multiple Meshes

Our approach can be easily used to establishes parameterizations for a set of models. In Fig. 4, the mannequin head model is parameterized on the other head models. After the parameterizations, all the head models have identical connectivity with the mannequin head model.

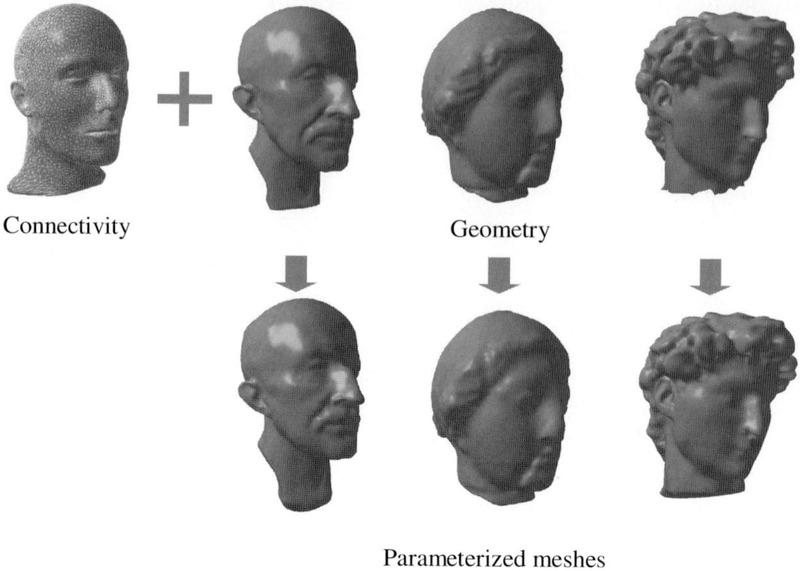

Fig. 4. Consistent parameterizations between multiple meshes: all the other head model are parameterized using the connectivity of the mannequin head model

5.2 Spherical Parameterization

As we have mentioned in previous sections, if the target mesh M_t has the geometry of a plane, our approach can be regarded as an approach of planar parameterization; if the target mesh M_t has the geometry of a sphere, our approach can be regarded as an approach of spherical parameterization. Fig. 5 shows a spherical parameterization of Venus head model by setting M_t as a sphere surface.

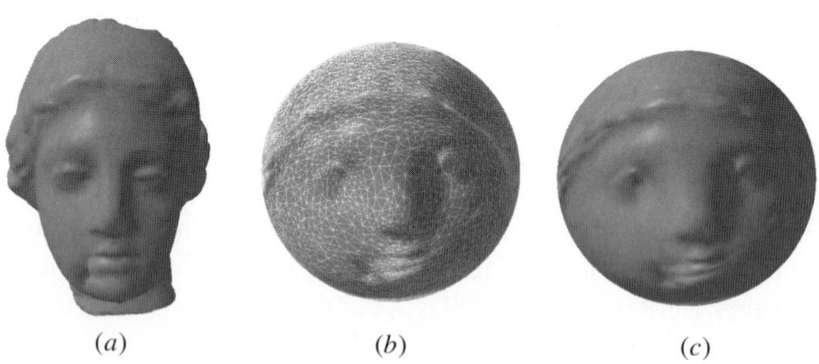

Fig. 5. Spherical paramterization of Venus head model. (a) Venus head mesh model; (b) the spherical parameterization of Venus head model; (c) smooth rendering the spherical parameterization using the normal from original Venus head model.

5.3 Mesh Morphing

Establishing a one-to-one mapping between different shapes is the first step in morphing application. Fig. 6 shows the use of the computed compatible meshes for morphing between dinosaur and horse models. The morphing examples shown in Fig. 7 between torus and mug demonstrates our approach's ability to handle high genus models. Linear interpolation is used in the above morphing examples. The accompany live video shows the animation sequence of these morphing.

Fig. 6. Morphing sequence between dinosaur and horse models

Fig. 7. Morphing sequence between torus and mug models

5.4 Texture Transfer

Attributes from different models can be easily transferred through direct parametric mapping if these models have the consistent parameterizations. Fig. 8 shows a simple example of transferring texture. The texture of the tiger model is applied to the cheetah model.

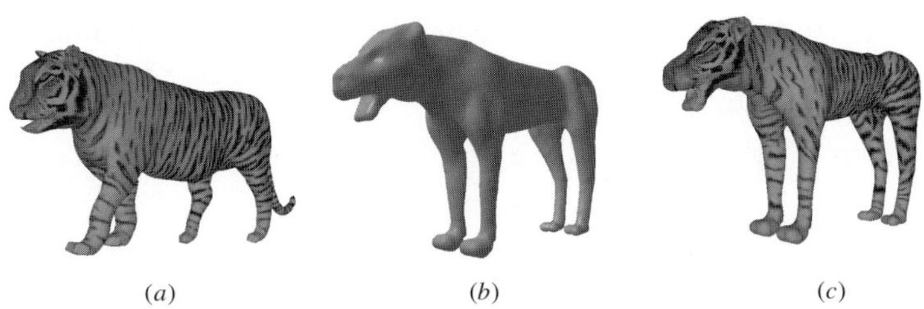

Fig. 8. Example of texture transfer. (a) A tiger model with textures; (b) a cheetah model; (c) transferring texture of (a) onto (b).

Table 1 shows the statistics for the examples shown in the paper, including the vertex number, the running time, and the Hausdorff distance [19] (with respect to the size of bounding box). As we can see, our approach achieves a good combination of speed, mesh quality, and shape preservation.

Table 1. Statistics including the vertex number, the running time, and the Hausdorff distance [19] for the examples shown in the paper

Model	Vertex#	Running Time(s)	Distance
Planck (Fig. 4)	10,139	91.5	0.0303
Venus (Fig. 4)	10,139	108.1	0.0051
David (Fig. 4)	10,139	133.3	0.057
Sphere (Fig. 5)	8,628	12.8	0.0063
Horse (Fig. 6)	10,189	10.8	0.0091
Mug (Fig. 7)	38,400	82.5	0.0314
Cheetah (Fig. 8)	22,192	172.4	0.0105

6 Conclusion

A unified manifold parameterization approach is presented in this paper. The connectivity of the source mesh is mapped onto another mesh surface directly without the intermediate domain and specifying the consistent cuts. Our approach is based on the least squares mesh. The geometry of the mesh vertices is reconstructed in a least-square sense while approximating the known geometry of the subset by placing each vertex approximately at the center of its 1-ring neighbors. Our approach provides a unified framework for creating consistent parameterization between two manifold meshes with higher (but same) genus if only a sufficient number of feature points are specified to define a correspondence between the handles. Many experimental results have been presented to show the applicability and flexibility of the approach.

The presented approach still has much to do for improvements and extensions. First, our approach can not guarantee that all the vertices of parameterized mesh $\bar{M}_t$ lie on the surface of the target mesh M_t. A possible way to solve it might be combining with Turk's retiling approach [20]. Second, multiresolution solution could be integrated into the framework to generate higher quality compatible triangulations between two much dissimilar meshes. Last, it is also much worthwhile to extend our approach to generate consistent parameterization between manifold surfaces with different topologically genus. We believe that this extension is feasible but not straightforward.

Acknowledgements. We would like to thank Zhonggui Chen for his help in video production. The textured tiger model used in Fig. 8 is courtesy of Dr. Kun Zhou from Microsoft Research Asia. This work is supported by the National Natural Science Foundation of China (No. 60503067, 60333010), Zhejiang Provincial Natural Science Foundation of China (No. Y105159) and the National Grand Fundamental Research 973 Program of China (No. 2002CB312101).

References

1. Floater, M.S., Hormann, K.: Surface parameterization: a tutorial and survey. In Dodgson, N.A., Floater, M.S., Sabin, M.A., eds.: Advances in Multiresolution for Geometric Modelling. Springer-Verlag, Heidelberg (2005) 157–186
2. Praun, E., Sweldens, W., Schroder, P.: Consistent mesh parameterizations. In: Proceedings of SIGGRAPH. (2001)
3. Kraevoy, V., Sheffer, A.: Cross-parameterization and compatible remeshing of 3d models. In: Proceedings of SIGGRAPH. (2004)
4. Schreiner, J., Asirvatham, A., Praun, E., Hoppe, H.: Inter-surface mapping. In: Proceedings of SIGGRAPH. (2004)
5. Lee, A., Dobkin, D., Sweldens, W., Schrder, P.: Multiresolution mesh morphing. In: Proceedings of SIGGRAPH. (1999) 343–350
6. Lee, A., Sweldens, W., Schroder, P., Cowsar, L., Dobkin, D.: Maps: Multiresolution adaptive parametrization of surfaces. In: Proceedings of SIGGRAPH. (1998) 95–104
7. Sorkine, O., Cohen-Or, D.: Least-squares meshes. In: Proceedings of Shape Modeling International. (2004) 191–199
8. Gu, X., Gortler, S., Hoppe, H.: Geometry images. In: Proceedings of SIGGRAPH. (2002) 356–361
9. Sheffer, A.: Spanning tree seams for reducing parameterization distortion of triangulated surfaces. In: Proceedings of Shape Modeling International. (2002) 61–66
10. Praun, E., Hoppe, H.: Spherical parameterization and remeshing. In: Proceedings of SIGGRAPH. (2003) 340–350
11. Gotsman, C., Gu, X., , Sheffer, A.: Fundamentals of spherical parameterization for 3d meshes. In: Proceedings of SIGGRAPH. (2003) 358–364
12. Gu, X., Wang, Y., Chan, T.F., Thompson, P.M., Yau, S.T.: Genus zero surface conformal mapping and its application to brain surface mapping. IEEE Transaction on Medical Imaging **23**(7) (2004) 119–127
13. Alexa, M.: Recent advances in mesh morphing. Computer Graphics Forum **21**(2) (2002) 173–196
14. Alexa, M.: Merging polyhedral shapes with scattered features. The Visual Computer **16**(1) (2000) 26–37
15. Tutte, W.T.: How to draw a graph. In: Proceedings of London Mathematical Society. (1963) 743–768
16. Floater, M.S.: Parameterization and smooth approximation of surface triangulations. Computer Aided Geometric Design **14**(3) (1997) 231–250
17. Lee, C.H., Varshney, A., Jacobs, D.: Mesh saliency. In: Proceedings of SIGGRAPH. (2005)
18. Mount, D., Arya, S.: Ann: A library for approximate nearest neighbor searching (version 1.1). In: http://www.cs.umd.edu/ mount/ANN/. (2005)
19. Cignoni, P., Rocchini, C., Scopigno, R.: Metro: measuring error on simplified surfaces. Computer Graphics Forum **17**(2) (1998) 167–174
20. Turk, G.: Re-tiling polygonal surface. In: Proceedings of SIGGRAPH. (1992) 55–64

Sub-sampling for Efficient Spectral Mesh Processing

Rong Liu, Varun Jain, and Hao Zhang

GrUVi Lab, School of Computing Sciences, SFU, BC, Canada
{lrong, vjain, haoz}@cs.sfu.ca

Abstract. In this paper, we apply Nyström method, a sub-sampling and reconstruction technique, to speed up spectral mesh processing. We first relate this method to Kernel Principal Component Analysis (KPCA). This enables us to derive a novel measure in the form of a matrix trace, based soly on sampled data, to quantify the quality of Nyström approximation. The measure is efficient to compute, well-grounded in the context of KPCA, and leads directly to a greedy sampling scheme via trace maximization. On the other hand, analyses show that it also motivates the use of the max-min farthest point sampling, which is a more efficient alternative. We demonstrate the effectiveness of Nyström method with farthest point sampling, compared with random sampling, using two applications: mesh segmentation and mesh correspondence.

1 Introduction

Spectral methods for data modeling and processing have been well studied in machine learning and pattern recognition, e.g., for clustering [1, 2] and correspondence analysis [3, 4]. The idea is to derive, from relational data given as a matrix and typically of high dimensionality, a low-dimensional and information-preserving spatial embedding based on the eigenvectors of the matrix, to facilitate the processing or analysis task at hand. Recently, spectral techniques have been applied successfully to several mesh processing problems, including spectral decomposition for mesh compression [5], spectral clustering for mesh segmentation [6], 3D shape correspondence in the spectral domain [7], spectral sequencing for mesh streaming [8], segmentation [9], and as an aid to surface reconstruction [10], as well as surface flattening via multidimensional scaling [11].

One of the main drawbacks of spectral methods is that they can be computationally expensive for large data sets since they rely on eigenvector computation and at times also require a non-sparse matrix, whose construction involves determining pairwise affinities between a large number of points. Nyström approximation [12], a sub-sampling and reconstruction technique originated from integral calculus, has been proposed as a remedy, e.g., for image segmentation [13], but there lacks a formal analysis of its quality and the influence of the sampling procedure. So far, random sampling [13, 14] has been used predominantly.

In this paper, we cast Nystöm approximation in the context of kernel PCA (KPCA), where the samples are treated as training data. The ability of the

H.-P. Seidel, T. Nishita, and Q. Peng (Eds.): CGI 2006, LNCS 4035, pp. 172–184, 2006.

training set to capture the probabilistic distribution of the whole data set in the feature space induces a way to measure the quality of the Nyström method. The resulting measure can be derived as a matrix trace, which depends only on sampled data. This measure is more desirable than the Schur complement [13], the only known quality measure for Nyström so far. Empirically, we show that both measures produce consistent evaluation results. Furthermore, our novel quality measure is more efficient to compute and leads directly to a greedy sampling scheme via trace maximization. On the other hand, analyses of the measure show that it motivates the use of a more efficient heuristic sampling scheme, which turns out to be the *max-min farthest point sampling*.

The rest of the paper is organized as follows. After discussing previous work, we describe Nyström approximation and spectral embedding in Section 3. KPCA is briefly reviewed in Section 4. Relating Nyström to KPCA, we propose our quality measure for Nyström in Section 5. We then discuss the relevance of our quality measure to sampling and motivate the use of the farthest point scheme. In Section 7, we demonstrate experimentally the effectiveness of the Nyström method and farthest point sampling, compared to random sampling, using two applications. Finally, we conclude and comment on possible future work.

2 Previous Work

The graph Laplacian operator has been well studied in geometry processing, e.g., see the recent survey [15]. In particular, the Fiedler vector, eigenvector of the graph Laplacian corresponding to the second smallest eigenvalue, has been used in graph partitioning [16] and mesh sequencing [8]. For the planar mesh graph, the Laplacian is sparse, for which fast multilevel methods, e.g., ACE [17], can compute the leading eigenvectors efficiently. However, when many eigenvectors are needed, e.g., for spectral mesh compression [5], the cost would be too high for large data sets. In this case, the mesh is often partitioned into smaller pieces and the operation proceeds in a piecewise manner [5].

Problems such as surface flattening [11], mesh segmentation [6, 9], shape correspondence [7], and most instances of clustering and dimensionality reduction considered in the machine learning and pattern recognition literature, e.g., [1, 2], rely on more global relational information. In these cases, an affinity matrix is defined by applying a Gaussian-like filter to a distance matrix H, where H_{ij} is a suitably defined distance, e.g., Euclidean [1], geodesic [7, 11], graph distance, or a combination of them [6, 9], between points i and j in a data set. Computing the full affinity matrix takes quadratic time and since it is generally non-sparse, it is computationally expensive to obtain its eigenvectors. Nyström approximation has been proposed recently to speed up spectral methods in this case [13, 18].

The Nyström method only requires a small number of sampled rows of the affinity matrix. It solves a small-scale eigenvalue problem and then computes approximated eigenvectors via extrapolation. One of the main questions is how to design appropriate sampling schemes to obtain more accurate approximations of the ground-truth eigenvectors. To the best of our knowledge, this problem has not been studied before. So far, random sampling predominates [13, 14] and other simple schemes, e.g., max-min farthest point sampling [14], have been mentioned in passing, but with no analysis given.

3 Nyström Approximation and Spectral Embeddings

Applications [16, 7, 2] utilizing spectral embeddings start by building a matrix which encodes certain relationship, called affinities, between each pair of elements in a data set. Depending on the application (see Section 7), this matrix may be transformed and then its eigenvectors and possibly eigenvalues are used to obtain a spatial embedding of the original data points in the spectral domain. Computing spectral embeddings is time-consuming due to the quadratic complexity, in terms of the data size, of affinity computation and up to cubic-time complexity for eigenvalue decomposition. Nyström method [13, 18] is therefore proposed to overcome this problem via sub-sampling and reconstruction.

Consider a set of n points $\mathcal{Z} = \mathcal{X} \bigcup \mathcal{Y}$, where $\mathcal{X}$ and $\mathcal{Y}$, $\mathcal{X} \bigcap \mathcal{Y} = \varnothing$, are two subsets of size l and m. Write the symmetric affinity matrix $W \in \mathbb{R}^{n \times n}$ in block form $W = [A \;\; B; B^T \;\; C]$, where $A \in \mathbb{R}^{l \times l}$ and $C \in \mathbb{R}^{m \times m}$ are affinity matrices for points in $\mathcal{X}$ and $\mathcal{Y}$, respectively; $B \in \mathbb{R}^{l \times m}$ contains the *cross-affinities* between points in $\mathcal{X}$ and $\mathcal{Y}$. Without loss of generality, we designate the points in $\mathcal{X}$ as *sample points*. Let $A = U \Lambda U^T$ be the eigenvalue decomposition of A, then the eigenvectors of W can be approximated, using the Nyström method [13], as

$$\bar{U} = \begin{bmatrix} U \\ B^T U \Lambda^{-1} \end{bmatrix}. \tag{1}$$

This allows us to approximate the eigenvectors of W by only knowing the sampled sub-block $[A \;\; B]$. The overall complexity is thus reduced from $O(n^3)$, without sub-sampling, down to $O(ml^2) + O(l^3)$, where $l \ll n$, in practice.

The rows of $\bar{U}$ define the spectral embeddings of the original data points from $\mathcal{Z}$. From (1), we see that the ith row of U, which is completely determined by A, gives the embedding $\bar{x}_i$ of point x_i in $\mathcal{X}$ and the jth row of $B^T U \Lambda^{-1}$ is the embedding $\bar{y}_j$ of point y_j in $\mathcal{Y}$. If we let $\lambda_1 \geq \lambda_2 \geq \ldots \geq \lambda_l$ be the eigenvalues of A, and $\bar{y}_j^d$ denote the dth component of $\bar{y}_j$, then equation (1) can be rewritten as

$$\bar{y}_j^d = \frac{1}{\lambda_d} \sum_{i=1}^{l} \bar{x}_i^d B(i,j) = \frac{1}{\lambda_d} \sum_{i=1}^{l} \bar{x}_i^d W(i, j+l), \qquad 1 \leq d \leq l. \tag{2}$$

Namely, the embedding $\bar{y}_j$ is extrapolated using the coordinates of the $\bar{x}_i$'s, weighted by the corresponding cross-affinities in B.

With $\bar{U}$, we obtain an approximation $\bar{W}$ of the original affinity matrix W,

$$\bar{W} = \bar{U} \Lambda \bar{U}^T = \begin{bmatrix} A & B \\ B^T & B^T A^{-1} B \end{bmatrix}.$$

Clearly, $\bar{W}$ replaces block C of W with $B^T A^{-1} B$. Hence it is suggested to quantify the approximation quality using the norm of the *Schur complement*,

$C - B^T A^{-1} B$. The smaller the norm, the better the approximation. Schur complement has been used as the *de facto* quality measure for Nyström method [13].

4 Review of Kernel PCA

Suppose that the points in set $\mathcal{Z}$ lie in the Euclidean space $\mathbb{R}^g$. Kernel PCA (KPCA) [19], an extension to the standard PCA, first applies to $\mathcal{Z}$ a generally non-linear mapping $\phi : \mathbb{R}^g \rightarrow \mathcal{F}$, where $\mathcal{F}$ is referred to as the *feature space*. Then the standard PCA is carried out in $\mathcal{F}$ on the point set $\phi(\mathcal{Z}) = \{\phi(z_i)|z_i \in \mathcal{Z}\}$. Since $\mathcal{F}$ may have a very high, possibly infinite, dimensionality, the non-linear properties of the data $\mathcal{Z}$ can be "unfolded" into linear ones. Thus algorithms that work on linear structures, e.g., PCA, can be effectively applied in $\mathcal{F}$.

The mapping ϕ is never explicitly given, but implicitly specified by the inner products between the data and encoded in a *kernel matrix* $K \in \mathbb{R}^{n \times n}$, where $K_{ij} = k(z_i, z_j) = \phi(z_i) \cdot \phi(z_j)$. Algorithms running in the feature space based only on inner products can be efficiently executed in the original space by replacing inner products with the kernel function k. Gaussian radial basis function [19]

$$k(z_i, z_j) = e^{-\frac{d_{ij}^2}{2\sigma^2}}, \quad d_{ij} = ||z_i - z_j||^2. \tag{3}$$

is one of the most commonly used kernels. Note that in our applications, we set σ to the average of all distances computed. Assume that $\mathcal{Z}$ obeys a certain probability distribution and $\mathcal{X} \subseteq \mathcal{Z}$ is chosen as a *training set* and centered. Although ϕ is not known explicitly, it is still possible to compute the projections $\tilde{x}_i$, the *features*, of $\phi(x_i)$ into the space where the basis are the principal components of the point set $\phi(\mathcal{X}) = \{\phi(x_i)|x_i \in \mathcal{X}\}$, as follows. Let $L \in \mathbb{R}^{l \times l}$ be the upper-left block of K and $L = E \Lambda E^T$ the eigenvalue decomposition of L, where eigenvectors, the columns of E, are in descending eigenvalue order. Let e_r denote the rth row of E, then the dth coordinate of $\tilde{x}_i$ is given by $\tilde{x}_i^d = \frac{1}{\sqrt{\lambda_d}} \sum_{r=1}^{l} e_r^d k(x_r, x_i)$. This can be seen as a "black box", which returns the feature $\tilde{x}_i$ for any given point x_i. If the training set $\mathcal{X}$ characterizes the distribution well, it is then reasonable to apply it to $y_j \in \mathcal{Y}$ similarly,

$$\tilde{y}_j^d = \frac{1}{\sqrt{\lambda_d}} \sum_{r=1}^{l} e_r^d k(x_r, y_j) = \frac{1}{\sqrt{\lambda_d}} \sum_{r=1}^{l} e_r^d K(r, j+l). \tag{4}$$

It can be seen that the embedding of $\tilde{y}_j$ in the feature space can be constructed using the eigenvector entries of the sub-kernel L, weighted by the kernel entries defined between the x_i's and the y_j's. Here it is worth noting that a resemblance between KPCA and Nyström approximation (2) is emerging.

5 Quality Measure for Nyström Approximation

While the affinity matrix W defines spectral embeddings and the kernel K is used in KPCA, both matrices can be seen as an implicit definition of relations between data points. Equating W with K and comparing equation (2) with (4), we see that $\bar{y}_j^d$ and $\tilde{y}_j^d$ have essentially identical expressions up to a scaling factor $\lambda_d^{-1/2}$; this fact has been previously noted in [18] as well. Therefore, Nyström approximation can be considered as a process of running KPCA on new patterns through a training set. In this section, we investigate the approximation quality of Nyström method in the context of KPCA.

5.1 Quality Measure as a Matrix Trace

Considering the Nyström method in the context of KPCA, we treat the sample set $\mathcal{X}$ as the training set. Thus points in $\mathcal{X}$ are first mapped into the feature space $\mathcal{F}$ and then the features corresponding to points in $\mathcal{Y}$ are approximated. In this setting, a good training set $\mathcal{X}$ for accurate Nyström approximation should be a set that, as stated in Section 4, reflects the same probability distribution function as $\mathcal{Y}$. This implies that $\phi(\mathcal{Z})$ and $\phi(\mathcal{X})$ should roughly lie in the same space. To this end, we stipulate that an accurate Nyström approximation necessitates that the sum of squared distances from all the $\phi(z_i)$'s to the space spanned by the $\phi(x_i)$'s be small. Now we derive our quality measure.

Denote by Σ the covariance matrix of the point set $\phi(\mathcal{X})$. Note that although the $\phi(x_i)$'s can be high-dimensional, the rank of Σ can be no larger than $l = |\phi(\mathcal{X})|$ and Σ has at most l eigenvectors $(\xi_1, \xi_2, \dots \xi_l)$, corresponding to non-zero eigenvalues. Let $P = [\xi_1|...|\xi_l]$, then the squared distance from $\phi(z_i)$ to the space spanned by the $\phi(x_i)$'s (equivalently, the column space of P) is

$$\rho_i = ||\phi(z_i) - PP^T\phi(z_i)||^2 = ||\phi(z_i)||^2 - ||PP^T\phi(z_i)||^2,$$

where PP^T is the *orthogonal projection operator* which projects any vector into the column space of P. Hence we wish to minimize the objective function

$$\begin{aligned}\sum_{i=1}^{n} \rho_i &= \sum_{z_i \in \mathcal{X}} \rho_i + \sum_{z_j \in \mathcal{Y}} \rho_j \\ &= \left(\sum_{i=1}^{l} ||\phi(x_i)||^2 - \sum_{i=1}^{l} ||PP^T\phi(x_i)||^2\right) + \left(\sum_{j=1}^{m} ||\phi(y_j)||^2 - \sum_{j=1}^{m} ||PP^T\phi(y_j)||^2\right).\end{aligned}$$

Note that $\sum_{i=1}^{l} ||\phi(x_i)||^2 + \sum_{j=1}^{m} ||\phi(y_j)||^2 = \sum_{i=1}^{n} ||\phi(z_i)||^2 = \sum_{i=1}^{n} K_{ii}$. Also, $\sum_{i=1}^{l} ||PP^T\phi(x_i)||^2 = \sum_{i=1}^{l} ||\phi(x_i)||^2 = \sum_{i=1}^{l} K_{ii}$. For our purpose, K is derived using the Gaussian kernel (3), thus the diagonals of K are constant 1. As a result, the first three terms of the objective function are constant, given that the size of $\mathcal{X}$ is fixed. Our goal is then reduced to *maximizing* the quantity

$$\Gamma = \sum_{j=1}^{m} ||PP^T\phi(y_j)||^2 = \sum_{j=1}^{m} (P^T\phi(y_j))^T(P^T\phi(y_j)). \tag{5}$$

Denote by $U_1, U_2, \dots, U_l$ the eigenvectors of A, as first defined in Section 3. Note that since we now make no difference between K and W, A is also the upper-left block of K. It is known [19] the principal component ξ_i of $\phi(\mathcal{X})$ can be written as a linear combination of the $\phi(x_i)$'s, i.e. $\xi_i = \sum_{d=1}^{l} \lambda_i^{-\frac{1}{2}} U_i^d \phi(x_d)$. We then have $\xi_i^T \phi(y_j) = \sum_{d=1}^{l} \lambda_i^{-\frac{1}{2}} U_i^d [\phi(x_d) \cdot \phi(y_j)] = \sum_{d=1}^{l} \lambda_i^{-\frac{1}{2}} U_i^d k(x_d, y_j)$. Therefore

$$P^T \phi(y_j) = [\xi_1 | \ldots | \xi_l]^T \phi(y_j) = [\xi_1^T \phi(y_j) | \ldots | \xi_l^T \phi(y_j)]^T = (U \Lambda^{-\frac{1}{2}})^T B_j,$$

where B_j is the j-th column of B. Thus (5) is simplified to

$$\Gamma = \sum_{j=1}^{m} B_j^T U \Lambda^{-1} U^T B_j = \mathrm{tr}(B^T A^{-1} B), \tag{6}$$

where $\mathrm{tr}(\cdot)$ denotes the matrix trace. When Γ attains a larger value, in the feature space, points in $\mathcal{Z}$ lie closer to the space spanned by $\mathcal{X}$. Consequently, Nyström method achieves a better approximation. Thus Γ provides a quality measure for Nyström method. The time complexity for computing Γ is $O(ml^2) + O(l^3)$. In practice, $l \ll n$ and can be regarded as a constant. Throughout our experiments (Section 7), we set $l = 10$. Next, we empirically verify the accuracy of Γ against Schur complement and then use it to derive a heuristic sampling scheme.

5.2 Comparison with Schur Complement

Typically, the norm of the Schur complement $C - B^T A^{-1} B$, defined in Section 3, is used to measure the approximation quality of Nyström. But the time complexity involved would be $O(n^2)$, since C is required. For efficiency, C should never be computed fully; this excludes the possibility of using the Schur complement on the fly as a measure to supervise the sampling process. On the other hand, Γ does not suffer from this problem and is much more efficient to compute.

Quality-wise, let us use the Schur complement as the ground truth to evaluate the accuracy of Γ, empirically. In each run of our experiment, a set of points is generated using a Gaussian distribution. From these points, two sample sets S_1 and S_2 of equal size are randomly chosen. We check whether the two measures would rank the two sample sets consistently. Denote by $\eta(S_i)$ and $\gamma(S_i)$ the approximation error values resulting from using the norm of the Schur complement and Γ, respectively, on sample set S_i. We plot, as a red marker, the position of the 2D point $(\eta(S_1) - \eta(S_2), \gamma(S_2) - \gamma(S_1))$. Obviously, the marker would appear in the

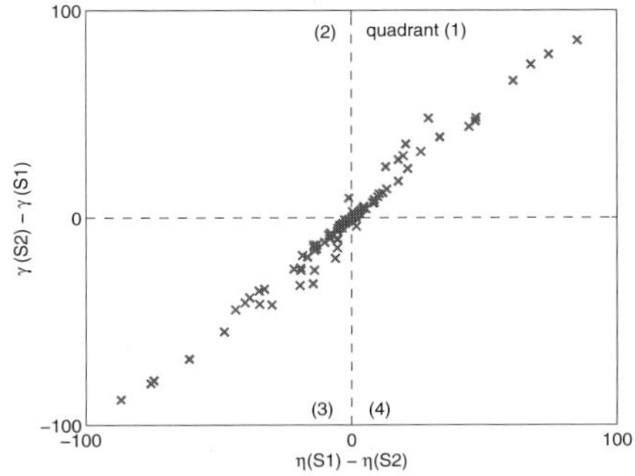

Fig. 1. Only 4% of the red markers lie in the second and fourth quadrants. This shows the consistence between Γ and the norm of the Schur complement, in evaluating sampling schemes for Nyström approximation.

first or third quadrant if and only if the two approaches had produced the same ranking of the sample sets. In Fig. 1, results from 100 test runs are shown. Evidently, almost all points lie in the first and third quadrants. This verifies, experimentally, the robustness of Γ as a quality measure for Nyström approximation.

6 Sampling Scheme

Depending on the application, different sampling strategies for Nyström method may be considered. But so far random sampling [13, 14] has been the norm. Random sampling may work well when the sample size is sufficiently large. But large sample size will increase the workload. In the applications we discuss in Section 7, we wish to take few samples while still achieving good performance.

6.1 Greedy Sampling Based on Γ

As verified in Section 5.2, Γ provides a good quality measure for Nyström method. Furthermore, due to its simplicity, it can also be used *on the fly* to guide a *greedy sampling procedure*. Specifically, each time a new sample is added, its affinities to the remaining points are maintained. This way we always know the current A and B, the within-sample and cross-sample affinities. To select the next sample, we consider all the un-sampled points. For each point, the current B and A are updated accordingly and the new Γ is computed. The new sample is the one which maximizes Γ. Our experiments show that this greedy scheme works quite well and fast since a very low sampling rate can be used. However, it can be made more efficient without computing Γ explicitly, as we show below.

6.2 The Max-Min Farthest Point Sampling Scheme

To further speed up the greedy sampling scheme without sacrificing much of its quality, we propose to use a heuristic which would not require explicit computation of Γ. This is made possible by examining the mathematical properties of Γ. Based on the cyclic property of matrix trace operation, we know that

$$\Gamma = \mathrm{tr}(B^T A^{-1} B) = \mathrm{tr}(A^{-1} B B^T) = \mathrm{tr}(A^{-1} \sum_{j=1}^{m} B_j B_j^T).$$

When m is large, entries of $M = \sum_{j=1}^{m} B_j B_j^T$ are close to each other. If we rewrite $M \approx \tau \mathbf{1}\mathbf{1}^\mathbf{T}$, with $\tau \in (0, m)$ a fixed value, then $\Gamma \approx \tau \mathrm{tr}(A^{-1}\mathbf{1}\mathbf{1}^\mathbf{T}) = \tau \mathbf{1}^\mathbf{T}(\mathbf{A}^{-1}\mathbf{1})$. Observe that there are two conditions for Γ to attain a relatively large value. The first is to have a large $\mathbf{1}^T(A^{-1}\mathbf{1})$. Note that $A^{-1}\mathbf{1}$ gives the coefficients of the expansion of $\mathbf{1}$ in the space whose basis are the columns of A. Moreover, the diagonals of A are 1 and its other entries lie in $(0, 1)$. It is easy to show, in 2D, that the sum of these coefficients, $\mathbf{1}^T(A^{-1}\mathbf{1})$, is no larger than l. The maximal l is obtained when A's columns are the canonical basis of the Euclidean space. This is generalizable to arbitrary dimensions. In order for A's columns to be close to the canonical basis, the off-diagonal entries should be close to zero. Thus samples should be taken *mutually far away* from each other.

The second condition is to have a larger τ. To this end, entries of B should be large, meaning that the distances from the samples to the remaining points should be small on average. When a sufficient number of sample points are distributed mutually far away, the average distances from the remaining points to the sample points tend to converge, making this condition much less influential. Our experiments also verify that the first condition plays a dominant role.

Stimulated by the first condition, we propose to use the more efficient max-min farthest point sampling scheme for Nyström method, which works as follows:

1. Randomly pick a point q and find p which is farthest away. Switch p and q and repeat. After several iterations, p is chosen as the first sample s_1. This procedure will most likely place s_1 close to an extremity of the point set.
2. At step i, a new sample s_i is chosen as the one which maximizes the minimum distance (hence "max-min") to the previous samples $s_1, s_2, \ldots, s_{i-1}$.

The significance of having the quality measure Γ is that it induces a greedy sampling scheme, which dramatically speeds up the spectral embedding as a very low sampling rate can be used. Moreover, it provides an underlying motivation for using farthest point sampling at an even lower computational cost.

7 Applications

Now we apply Nyström method with max-min farthest point sampling to two applications and evaluate the results both numerically and visually.

7.1 Mesh Correspondence

A recent variant to the classical mesh parameterization problem is to compute a *cross parameterization* [20] between two meshes directly, where mesh correspondence, computed over sets of selected features on the two meshes, is often the first step. Currently, most methods [20] rely on manual feature selection and correspondence. Spectral techniques have been proposed in the past to compute correspondence between feature points on two 2D images [4, 21] and they can be applied to find the much needed initial mapping between mesh features as well [7]. In this section, we apply Nyström method to a simple 3D extension of one such spectral correspondence algorithm by Shapiro and Brady [21]. Specifically, pairwise similarities between data points are given by the L_2 distances between their spectral embeddings and best matching is used to recover correspondence.

Instead of using Euclidean distances [21] to define the affinities, we use geodesic point-to-point distances on the meshes to better handle articulated shapes. We also make two modifications to the original algorithm as follows. First we use only the leading k eigenvectors of the affinity matrix to compute the spectral embeddings and secondly, we scale the eigenvectors with the square root of the corresponding eigenvalues. Both modifications have been shown to improve the correspondence in the case of 3D meshes [7].

In Fig. 2(a) we show the effect of applying Nyström method to the above algorithm. In these experiments, we fix $k = 6$ and choose only 10 samples on meshes of 500 triangles. To visualize the correspondence, we use color coding of vertices. If X and Y are the two meshes to be matched, we first assign colors to every vertex in Y; we carefully assign colors so that different parts of the mesh are colored differently. Then, we set the color of every vertex of X to be the color of the matching vertex in Y. Thus a good correspondence induces similar coloring in the two shapes. Also shown is a comparison between random and farthest point sampling. Clearly, the matching obtained using Nyström approximation with farthest point sampling is comparable to the ground truth, which is the matching computed via eigen-decomposition of the full affinity matrix. Fig. 2(b) shows more correspondence results obtained using Nyström approximation on larger meshes (4000 triangles), with the same k and sample size.

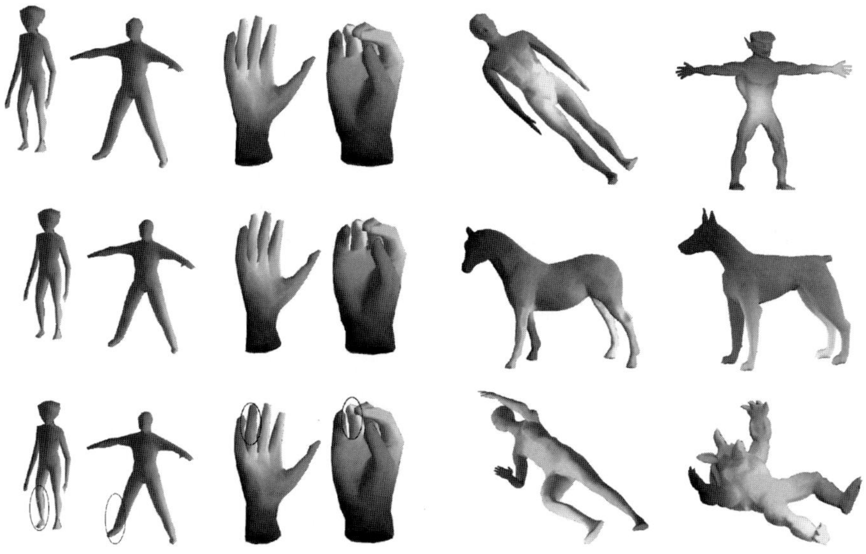

(a) (b)

Fig. 2. Results from spectral mesh correspondence. (a) Top row: ground truth, without sampling. The next two rows show results using Nyström, with farthest-point and random sampling, respectively. Inconsistent coloring at badly matched points for the latter are highlighted by circles. (b) Results for larger meshes (4000 faces) using Nyström and farthest point sampling. Shapes on the left are matched with those on the right. As we can see, with only 10 samples, we already obtain excellent correspondence results.

Note that results shown in Fig. 2(a) and 2(b) are subjective. Evaluating a dense correspondence objectively is non-trivial since the ground-truth correspondence is not known and is impractical to establish manually for large data sets. To present a more objective evaluation, we use the following trick. We first construct a series of decimated meshes using QSLIM [22]. Then we find the correspondence between the original mesh and a decimated version. Since QSLIM does not alter the position of undecimated vertices, the ground-truth correspondence can be trivially computed from a decimated mesh. The correspondence error at a vertex is defined as the geodesic distance between the found matching point for the vertex and its ground-truth matching point. In Fig. 3, the total error is plotted for all vertices against the size of the mesh. This plot is averaged over several meshes. Again, it can be seen that Nyström method, when combined with farthest sampling, has comparable performance to its much more costly counterpart, where the full affinity matrices are used and the eigenvectors are accurately computed.

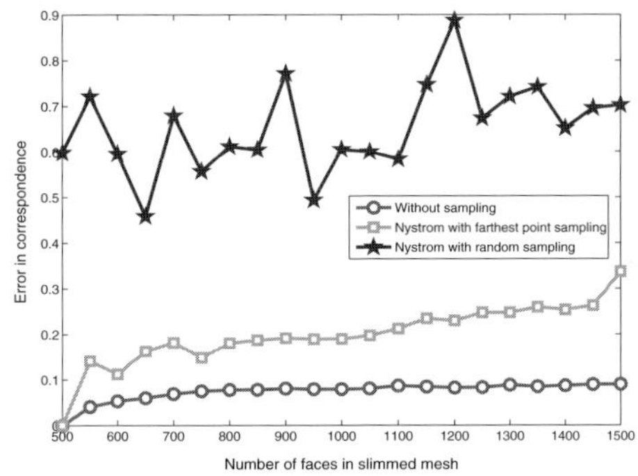

Fig. 3. Plot of correspondence error against mesh size. Nyström with farthest point sampling has comparable performance to the un-sampled case.

7.2 Mesh Segmentation

In part-type mesh segmentation [23], the goal is to decompose a mesh shape into its constituent components according to human intuition. Since mesh segmentation can be considered as a problem of clustering mesh faces, spectral clustering becomes applicable. In the work of [6], spectral embeddings of faces are first derived from the intrinsic geometric property of the shape, followed by a K-means clustering in the spectral embedding space. The rationale behind this approach is that face clusters in the embedding space correspond to parts of the shape. In [6], sub-sampling is not conducted and all pairwise distances have to be computed and converted into affinities. Subsequently, the eigenvectors of the affinity matrix are computed to find the face embeddings. Although it is possible to lower the workload by computing only the leading eigenvectors, it is still prohibitive for large meshes, since computing pairwise distances alone would take $O(n^2 \log n)$ time for an n-face mesh.

Alternatively, we can apply max-min farthest point sampling and Nyström method to approximate the spectral embeddings of faces. Supposing that the sample size is l, we only need to compute the distances from the l sample faces to the remaining faces since only the sub-block $[A \;\; B]$ of W is needed. The whole process for computing the embeddings then takes $O(ln \log n)$ time. Since $l \ll n$, the computational overhead is dramatically reduced.

Fig. 4 presents several segmentation results using Nyström method with farthest point sampling, where parts are indicated by different colors. As we can see, the segmentation results are quite intuitive even at a very low sample rate of 10. Table 1 reports the timing. Compared with the results in [6], which only handles meshes of size up to 4000 faces, in about 30 seconds, the improvement is quite evident.

Table 1. Statistics of segmentation experiments on a 2.2 GHz Pentium machine with 1.0 GB RAM. Note that since iterative 2-means, instead of a single K-means, is used on the horse and hand bone models, their running time is relatively higher.

Model	Heart	Igea	Headless	Smile	Horse	Hand bone
Face #	1619	2000	32,574	34,712	39,698	65,001
Part #	4	3	7	5	8	7
Time (s)	0.03	0.07	2.23	3.32	6.86	9.67

(a) Headless (b) Smile (c) Horse (d) Hand bone

Fig. 4. Segmentation results. We test the effectiveness of Nyström method for both K-means (a, b) and iterative 2-means (c, d). Farthest point sampling is used.

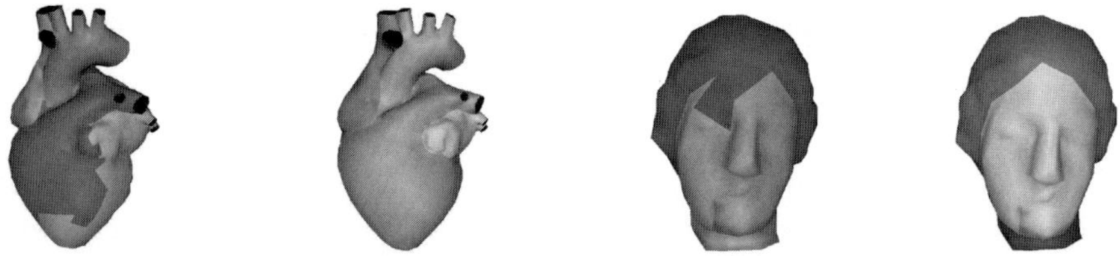

(a) Heart [0.75] (b) Heart [1.06] (c) Igea [0.636] (d) Igea [0.99]

Fig. 5. Comparison of segmentation results under different sampling schemes. (a, c) are results when random sampling is taken; (b, d) are obtained using farthest point sampling. The numbers in brackets are the Γ values divided by the number of faces.

In Fig. 5, we compare the performance of Nyström method under random and farthest point sampling. It is easy to see that Nyström method works much better with farthest point sampling. Also shown in this figure is that a better sampling (indicated by a larger Γ value) leads to a more meaningful segmentation. For the two pictures, (b) and (d), produced using Nyström and farthest point sampling, no visually differences from those obtained in [6] can be observed.

8 Conclusion and Future Work

In this work, we study the approximation quality of Nyström approximation, an important approach for speeding up kernel based algorithms. To overcome the difficulty of investigating the method directly, we cast it in the context of KPCA. With the help of the geometric intuition offered by the KPCA framework, a simple yet accurate quality measure for the Nyström method is derived. This quality measure can be used on the fly to guide a greedy sampling process for better approximation. To improve efficiency, we analyze its mathematical properties and motivate the use of the max-min farthest point sampling scheme. We apply Nyström method and farthest point sampling to two mesh processing algorithms, correspondence and segmentation, to demonstrate their effectiveness. At the same time, we also experiment with applying the same framework to spectral sequencing with positive results achieved. But due to limited space, we shall report those results elsewhere.

One possible future work is to consider in more detail the relationship between KPCA and Nyström method when various preprocessing procedures are applied to the affinity matrix. Another improvement is to study how different kernels, such as Gaussian, exponential kernel and polynomial kernels, would influence the behaviors of the Nyström method. It is also interesting to come up with application-based evaluation for the effectiveness of Γ. With mesh segmentation as an example, it is desirable to be able to measure the segmentation quality quantitatively so that the approximation performance of Nyström method can be evaluated based on the final result directly.

References

1. Ng, A.Y., Jordan, M.I., Weiss, Y.: On spectral clustering: analysis and an algorithm. In: NIPS. (2002) 857–864
2. Weiss, Y.: Segmentation using eigenvectors: a unifying view. In: ICCV. (1999) 975–982
3. Caelli, T., Kosinov, S.: An eigenspace projection clustering method for inexact graph matching. IEEE Trans. on PAMI **26**(4) (2004) 515–519
4. Carcassoni, M., Hancock, E.R.: Spectral correspondence for point pattern matching. Pattern Recognition **36** (2003) 193–204
5. Karni, Z., Gotsman, C.: Spectral compression of mesh geometry. In: SIGGRAPH 2000. (2000) 279–286
6. Liu, R., Zhang, H.: Segmentation of 3d meshes through spectral clustering. In: Proc. Pacific Graphics. (2004) 298–305
7. Jain, V., Zhang, H.: Robust 3d shape correspondence in the spectral domain. In: Shape Modeling International. (2006) to appear
8. Isenburg, M., Lindstrom, P.: Streaming meshes. In: IEEE Visualization. (2005) 231–238
9. Zhang, H., Liu, R.: Mesh segmentation via recursive and visually salient spectral cuts. In: Vision, Modeling, and Visualization. (2005)
10. Kolluri, R., Shewchuk, J.R., O'Brien, J.F.: Spectral surface reconstruction from noisy point clouds. In: Eurographics SGP. (2004) 11–21

11. Zigelman, G., Kimmel, R., Kiryati, N.: Texture mapping using surface flattening via multidimensional scaling. IEEE TVCG **8**(2) (2002) 198–207
12. Press, W., Tekolsky, S., Vetterling, W., Flannery, B.: Numerical Recipies in C. Cambridge Univ. Press (1992)
13. Fowlkes, C., Belongie, S., Chung, F., Malik, J.: Spectral grouping using the nyström method. IEEE Trans. PAMI **26** (2004) 214–225
14. de Silva, V., Tenenbaum, B.: Sparse multidimensional scaling using landmark points. Technical report, Stanford University (2004)
15. Sorkine, O.: Laplacian mesh processing. In: Eurographics State-of-the-Art Report. (2005)
16. Shi, J., Malik, J.: Normalized cuts and image segmentation. In: CVPR. (1997) 731–737
17. Harel, D., Koren, Y.: A fast multi-scale method for drawing large graphs. In: Graph Drawing. (2000) 183–196
18. Williams, C., Seeger, M.: Using the nyström method to speed up kernel machines. In: Advances in Neural Information Processing Systems. (2001) 682–688
19. Scholkopf, B., Smola, A., Muller, K.R.: Nonlinear component analysis as a kernel eigenvalue problem. Neural Computation **10** (1998) 1299–1319
20. Kraevoy, V., Sheffer, A.: Cross-parameterization and compatible remeshing of 3d models. In: ACM SIGGRAPH. (2004)
21. Shapiro, L.S., M., B.J.: Feature based correspondence: An eigenvector approach. Image and Vision Computing **10**(5) (1992) 283–288
22. Garland, M.: (Qslim simplification software — qslim 2.1)
23. Shamir, A.: A formalization of boundary mesh segmentation. In: Proc. 2nd Int'l Symposium on 3D Data Processing, Visualization, and Transmission. (2004) 82–89

Active Contours with Level-Set for Extracting Feature Curves from Triangular Meshes

Kyungha Min[1,⋆], Dimitris N. Metaxas[1], and Moon-Ryul Jung[2,⋆⋆]

[1] CBIM, Rutgers Univ., USA
[2] Dept of Media Technology, Sogang Univ., Korea

Abstract. In this paper, we present a novel algorithm that extracts feature curves from triangular mesh domains. It is an extension of the level-set formulation of active contour model in image space to triangular mesh domains. We assume that meshes handled by our method are smooth overall, and feature curves of meshes are thin regions rather than mathematical curves such as found in mechanical parts. We use a simple and robust scheme that assigns feature weights to the vertices of a mesh. We define the energy functional of the active contour over the domain of triangular mesh and derive a level-set evolution equation that finds feature regions. The feature regions are skeletonized and smoothed to form a set of smooth feature curves on the mesh.

1 Introduction

Triangular meshes are one of the most widely-used representation schemes in computer graphics for the shape of 3D objects. For applications of triangular meshes such as simplification, deformation, remeshing, fairing and morphing, features on triangular meshes provide very important information in manipulating the meshes. In other applications such as NPR (Non-Photorealistic Rendering), mesh features such as a silhouette or a contour, play an important role. Consequently, there have been increased research efforts towards the development of methods for feature extraction in triangular mesh domains.

It is the research of computer vision and image processing that has developed various methods that extract features and detect edges in image space. The active contour model, also known as Snake [8], is one of the most widely and frequently used methods. In early research, the active contour models were designed using explicit curves such as B-spline curve. One of their critical problems is that the results heavily depend on the user-created initial curves. In order to remedy this problem, many researchers [2, 3, 11] have extended the active contour models using implicit curves such as level-sets [14]. In computer graphics, several researchers [13, 10, 6, 1] presented feature extraction methods

⋆ This research has been supported by the foreign postdoctoral research program from KRF (Korea Research Foundation).

⋆⋆ This research has been supported by the fund (R01-2002-000-00311-01) from KOSEF (Korea Science and Engineering Foundation).

H.-P. Seidel, T. Nishita, and Q. Peng (Eds.): CGI 2006, LNCS 4035, pp. 185–196, 2006.

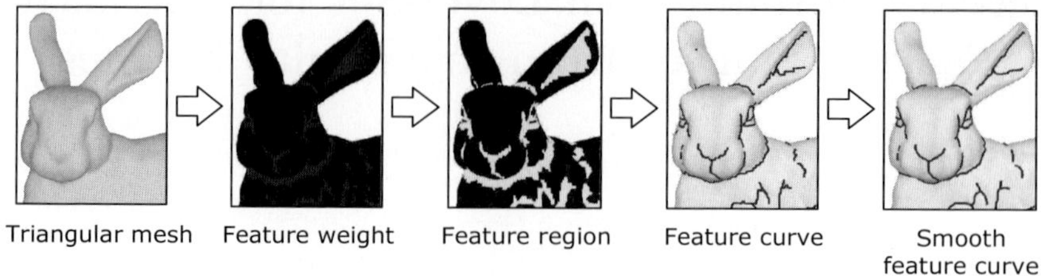

Fig. 1. Outline and dataflow of our algorithm. The model in the example is the Stanford Bunny model, and the target feature is valley curve. The feature weights are colored in blue, and the feature regions in yellow.

in triangular mesh domains by extending the active contour models for image space to mesh space. They used explicit curves such as B-spline curves [10] or line segments [1, 13, 6].

For the first time in computer graphics, we formulate a level-set formulation of active contour over triangular meshes, in order to devise novel a feature curve extraction algorithm on triangular meshes. We assume that meshes handled by our method are smooth overall, and feature curves of meshes are thin regions rather than mathematical curves such as found in mechanical parts. Hence our formulation is "region-oriented" in that the features are not represented by the curves defined by the zero-level sets but by the regions inside those curves. So, we develop efficient algorithms that skeletonize the feature regions into a set of line segments and smooth them. We extract three kinds of feature curves from meshes, that is, "ridge curves", "valley curves", and silhouettes. The algorithm for extracting feature curves in this paper is composed of the following steps (See Figure 1):

1. **Estimating feature weights:** For each vertex of the mesh, assign weights or likelihoods that the vertex belongs to ridge, valley, or silhouette.
2. **Evaluating feature regions:** Find the vertices that belong to the feature regions by executing the active contour model. .
3. **Extracting feature curves:** Extract a set of linear curves from the feature regions by computing skeletons from them. The piecewise linear curves are called *feature curves.*
4. **Smoothing feature curves:** Smooth feature curves.

This paper is organized as follows. In Section 2, we review related research. In Section 3, we describe a scheme that assigns feature weights at each vertex. In Section 4, we describe how the problem of finding feature regions in 3D meshes can be formulated as the "minimum partition problem" and develop methods to extract feature curves from feature regions in Section 5. In Section 6, we present the implementation results of our proposed algorithm. Finally, we draw conclusions and suggest the directions of future work in Section 7.

2 Related Work

2.1 Active Contours in Triangular Mesh

Milroy et al. [13] suggested a method of moving a snake directly on 3D meshes. It was devised to perform an edge-based segmentation over a 3D mesh. Surface differential properties are estimated at each vertex, and curvature extrema are identified as possible edge points. Small closed contours are defined within the regions to be segmented, and the contour is inflated until it is trapped by edge points. Lee and Lee [10] proposed a method which projects a region surrounding a snake on the 3D mesh on to the rectangular 2D domain, moves the 2D snake using one of the methods developed for image snakes, and then maps the 2D snake back on to the 3D mesh. Jung and Kim [6] have also proposed a snake-based feature extraction scheme for triangular meshes. Jung and Kim [6] have also proposed a snake-based feature extraction scheme for triangular meshes. Unlike Lee and Lee, they move the snake directly on the surface of the 3D mesh, until the snake stops at the feature curves which are defined in terms of curvature. This method automatically modifies the topology of the feature curve to suit the geometry of the object. Bischoff et. al. [1] proposed a snake on triangular meshes by representing snakes as a piecewise linear curve whose vertices lie on the edges of the mesh.

2.2 Threshold-Based Methods

Watanabe and Belyaev [19] proposed a stable feature detection scheme for triangular meshes. They use a new approximation algorithm for the mean and Gaussian curvature of a mesh, which are combined in a nonlinear way. They extract feature regions by applying a threshold-based filtering scheme to extremes of curvature. Then they skeletonize the resulting feature region to discriminate narrow feature regions including valley, ridges, and creases. Pauly et al. [15] have put forward a multi-scale feature extraction scheme for point-sampled surfaces. These authors select feature candidates through principal component analysis, and build initial feature curves by using hysteresis threshold to compute a minimum-cost spanning tree. The initial feature curves are subsequently smoothed by active contour models.

3 Assigning Feature Weights

We derive formulae that assign feature weights at each vertex. Instead of previous schemes [9, 12, 18] that require intensive computation and produce unstable results, we approximate curvatures of each vertex by the hinge angles of that vertex. The hinge angles of a vertex are the hinge angles of the edges incident to the vertex. The hinge angle of an edge is the angle between the normal vectors from the two faces adjacent to the edge. The angle of an edge is positive when the edge is convex, negative when the edge is concave. The *ridge* feature weight of a vertex $\mathbf{v}$, that is, the likelihood that the vertex belongs to a ridge is represented by the maximum hinge angle of the vertex. Similarly, the *valley* feature weight of a vertex is represented by the minimum hinge angle of the vertex. The silhouette weight for a vertex is represented by the angle between the view vector and the normal vector at the vertex. Figure 2 shows a mesh colored by ridge, valley, and silhouette feature weights.

(a) **(b)** **(c)**

Fig. 2. Mesh colored by feature weights: (a) valleys (blue); (b) ridges (red); (c) silhouettes (greed)

We denote the feature weight of a vertex $\mathbf{v}$ as $u(\mathbf{v})$. The hinge angle of an incident edge e is denoted by $d(e)$. Let the set of edges incident to $\mathbf{v}$ be $\{e_1^{\mathbf{v}}, ..., e_n^{\mathbf{v}}\}$. We define the feature weights differently depending on on the kinds of features to detect, as follows:

$$u(\mathbf{v}) = \begin{cases} \max\limits_{1 \le i \le n} \{\ d(e_i^{\mathbf{v}})\ \}, \text{for extracting ridges,} \\ \min\limits_{1 \le i \le n} \{\ d(e_i^{\mathbf{v}})\ \}, \text{for extracting valleys,} \\ \max\limits_{1 \le i \le n} \{1 - |\mathbf{n}(e_i^{\mathbf{v}}) \cdot \mathbf{V}|\}, \text{for extracting silhouettes,} \end{cases}$$

where $\mathbf{V}$ is the view vector, and $\mathbf{n}(e)$ is a normal vector associated with edge e, which is the average of the normals to the adjacent faces of the edge. The operator $\cdot$ in $\mathbf{v} \cdot \mathbf{w}$ denotes an inner product between $\mathbf{v}$ and $\mathbf{w}$.

4 Active Contours on Triangular Meshes

We formulate the problem of extracting feature curves from meshes as the "minimum partition problem" [3]. This problem was formulated as a particular case of the image segmentation problem. Given an image, the minimum partition problem comes down to finding a curve C such that the region inside C and the region outside C are each homogeneous as far as possible and thereby the curve C forms a sharp boundary. This problem is formulated as an energy minimization problem. We can formulate the same problem over a 3D mesh once we have assigned weights to each vertex of the mesh.

Suppose e_1^+ is surrounded by two vectors $(\mathbf{v}_i^p - \mathbf{v})$ and $(\mathbf{v}_{i+1}^p - \mathbf{v})$ (See Figure 3 (b)). The value of $\phi_+^{e_1}$ is obtained by interpolating $\phi(\mathbf{v}_i)$ and $\phi(\mathbf{v}_{i+1})$, and the value of $h_+^{e_1}$ by interpolating $(|\mathbf{v}_i^p - \mathbf{v}|)$ and $(|\mathbf{v}_{i+1}^p - \mathbf{v}|)$, according to the following Equations (See Figure 3 (c)):

$$\phi_+^{e_1} = \frac{\theta_b \phi(\mathbf{v}_{i+1}) + \theta_a \phi(\mathbf{v}_i)}{\theta_a + \theta_b}$$

$$h_+^{e_1} = \frac{\theta_b h_{i+1} + \theta_a h_i}{\theta_a + \theta_b} = \frac{\theta_b |\mathbf{v}_{i+1}^p - \mathbf{v}| + \theta_a |\mathbf{v}_i^p - \mathbf{v}|}{\theta_a + \theta_b}$$

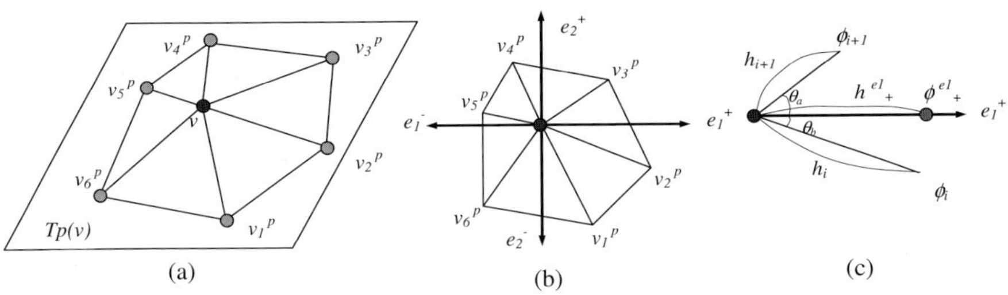

Fig. 3. (a) v_i^p is the projection of vertex v_i on to the tangent plane $Tp(v)$ at the vertex v. (b) The coordinate system (e_1, e_2) defined on the tangent plane $Tp(v)$. (c) The interpolation of $\phi_+^{e_1}$ and $h_+^{e_1}$ by using the values associated with the neighbor vertices v_{i+1}, v_i.

4.4 Implementation of the Active Contours

We use a signed distance function to initialize the level set function. Of course, the level set function is initialized differently depending on whether ridge, valley, or silhouette is looked for. The initial level set function ϕ^0 is initialized in two steps. In the first step, $\phi^0(\mathbf{v})$ is assigned 1.0 at each vertex $\mathbf{v}$ whose feature value is greater than a seed threshold. Then, $\phi^0(\mathbf{v})$ is assigned $\max(L, -dist(\mathbf{v}))$ at the remaining vertices $\mathbf{v}$. Here L is the lower bound for ϕ^0, and the $dist(\mathbf{v})$ is the distance of $\mathbf{v}$ from the nearest vertex whose ϕ^0 value is positive. We use -10.0 for L.

5 Extracting Feature Curves

5.1 Skeletonization

We extract feature curves from the smoothed feature regions by exploiting a peeling-based skeletonization algorithm [7, 16], which removes a vertex in a region repeatedly until the remaining vertices form a set of skeleton curves of the region. In such skeletonization strategies, the results of the algorithm depend on the order of vertex removal. In our method, vertices with lower feature weight values are removed first. The remaining vertices are those with highest feature weights, that is, highest curvatures in our case. The resulting skeleton curves are smoothed by applying the minimization algorithm suggested in Section 5.2.

5.2 Smoothing

The extracted feature curve is a piecewise linear curve that connects the vertices on triangular mesh, and it may not be smooth. We call the non-smooth feature curve as a *raw feature curve.* We smooth a raw feature curve by finding the smooth feature curve so that it is sufficiently smooth and deviates from the raw feature curve as little as possible. In other words, we define the internal and "external" energy to the potential smooth curve and minimize them to find the smooth feature curve.

Internal energy. Let $\mathcal{C} = (\ q_0,\ ...,\ q_{n-1}\ )$ denote the potential smooth feature curve, where q_i lies within or at the end of edges of the mesh. The internal energy I of the curve is defined as follows:

$$I \ = \ \sum_{i=0}^{n-2} |q_i - q_{i+1}|^2.$$

External energy. Let the distance between a point q_i on the potential feature curve and the corresponding raw feature curve $\mathcal{R} = (r_0,\ ...,\ r_{m-1})$ is defined as follows:

$$d(q_i, \mathcal{R}) \ \equiv \ \min_j \{d(q_i,\ r_j) \mid r_j \ \in \ \mathcal{R}\},$$

where $d(q_i, r_j)$ is a mesh-dependent distance between q_i and r_j.

The external energy E of the potential feature curve is defined as follows:

$$E \ = \ \sum_{i=0}^{n-1} d^2(q_i, \mathcal{R}).$$

A point q_i on the potential feature curve lies within or at the end of an edge in the mesh, and the candidate edges are extremely limited. So we can find easily q_i's that minimizes $I + E$, and hence determine the smooth feature curve.

6 Implementation and Results

We implemented the proposed algorithm on an IBM PC computer with Pentium IV 2.0 GHz CPU and 512 MB main memory. We tested five models: A Bunny, a Buddha, a Dragon, a Horse, and a Venus from Stanford University's Computer Graphics Laboratory 3D scanning repository. We measured the computation time as the sum of three three parts: a) time for initialization, b) time for executing the active contours, and c) time for skeletonization and smoothing. Table 1 illustrates the complexity of the models and the required computational time.

Figure 4 illustrates the feature-curves extracted from the models. An important fact that affects the performance of the model is the seed threshold that determines the initialization of the level set function. To determine a proper seed threshold, we apply histogram analysis of the feature values and select a feature value in the highest 5 % as the seed threshold.

Table 1. The time complexities for the tested models

Model	# of Vertices	Estimating Feature Weights	Computing Feature Regions	Extracting Feature Curves	Smoothing	Total
Bunny	35,952	6.8	4.9	13.6	8.3	33.6
Buddha	32,331	13.8	4.2	27.3	12.7	58.0
Dragon	22,998	8.5	3.7	18.4	6.7	37.3
Horse	48,485	19.3	6.5	37.4	15.2	78.4
Venus	67,173	25.9	8.3	49.8	21.1	105.1

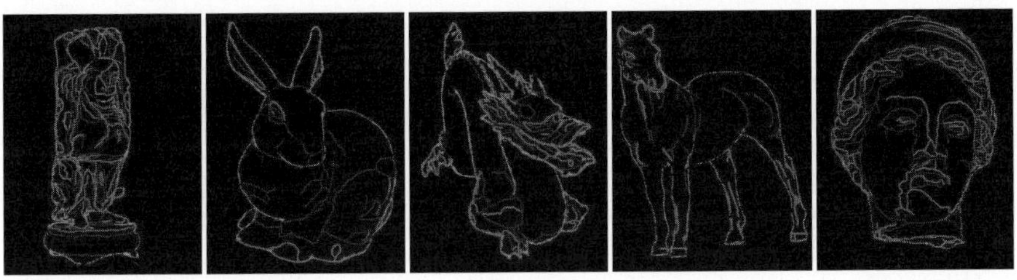

Buddha Bunny Dragon Horse Venus

Fig. 4. Smooth feature curves on five models. Note that red curve denotes a ridge, blue curve denotes a valley, and green curve denotes a silhouette.

7 Conclusions and Future Work

In this paper, we presented a novel algorithm that extracts features on triangular mesh domains by extending the level-set active contour model devised for image to mesh. The proposed algorithm provides a generalized framework for extracting various feature curves such as ridges, valleys and silhouettes from triangular meshes without user's initialization.

Possible future work is as follows. This algorithm can extract features that have semantic meaning defined by shape information or prior knowledge. If we can combine a particular knowledge base and the proposed algorithm, we can provide more intelligent feature extraction algorithm. The another extension is to provide more opportunities to users in controlling the feature extraction process.

References

[1] Bischoff, S., Weyand, T., Kobbelt, L.: Snakes on triangular meshes. Bildverarbeitung fur die Medizin. (2005) 208–212.

[2] Caselles, V., Kimmel, R., Sapiro, G.: On geodesic active contours. International Journal of Computer Vision. **22(1)** (1997) 61–79.

[3] Chan, T., Vese, L.: An active contour model without edges. IEEE Transactions on Image Processing. **10(2)** (2001) 266–277.

[4] Gumhold, S. and Wang, X. and McLeod, R.: Feature extraction from point clouds. Proceedings of 10th International Meshing Roundtable (2001) 293–305.
[5] Jones, T., Durand, F., Desbrun, M: Non-iterative, feature-preserving mesh smoothing. ACM Transcations on Graphics. **22(3)** (2003) 943–949.
[6] Jung, M., Kim, H.: Snaking across 3D meshes. Proceedings of Pacific Graphics. (2004) 415–420.
[7] Kalles, D., Morris, D.: A novel fast and reliable thinning algorithm. Imaging and Vision Computing. **11(9)** (1993) 588–603.
[8] Kass, M., Witkin, A., Terzopoulos, D.: Snakes: Active contour models. International Journal of Computer Vision. **1(4)** (1987) 321–331.
[9] Kobbelt, L.: Discrete fairing. Proceedings of 7th IMA Conference on the Mathematics of Surfaces. (1997) 101–131.
[10] Lee, Y., Lee, S.: Geometric snakes for triangular meshes. Computer Graphics Forum. **21(3)** (2002) 229–238.
[11] Malladi, R., Sethian, J., Vemuri, B.: Shape modeling with front propagation: A level set approach. IEEE Transactions on Pattern Analysis and Machine Intelligence. **17(2)** (1995) 158–175.
[12] Meyer, M., Desbrun, M., Schroder, P., Barr, A.: Discrete differential-geometry operators for triangulated 2-manifolds. Proceedings of International Workshop on Visualization and Mathematics. (2002) 35–58.
[13] Milroy, M., Bradley, C., Vickers, G.: Segmentation of a wrap-around model using an active contour. Computer-Aided Design. **29(4)** (1997) 299-320.
[14] Osher, S., Sethian, J.: Fronts propagating with curvature-dependent speed: Algorithms based on Hamilton-Jacobi formulation. Journal of Computational Physics. **79(1)** (1988) 12–49.
[15] Pauly, M., Keiser, R., Gross, M.: Multi-scale extraction on point-sampled surfaces. Computer Graphics Forum. **22(3)** (2003) 281–289.
[16] Pavlidis, T.: A thinning algorithm for discrete binary images. Computer Vision, Graphics and Image Processing. **13** (1980) 142–157.
[17] Rudin, L., Osher, S., Fatemi, E.: Nonlinear total variation based noise removal algorithms, Physica D. **60** (1992) 259–268.
[18] Taubin, G.: Estimating the tensor of curvature of a surface from a polyhedral approximation. Proceedings of International Conference on Computer Vision (ICCV). (1995) 902–907.
[19] Watanabe, K., Belyaev, A.: Detection of salient curvature features on polygonal surfaces. Computer Graphics Forum. **20(3)** (2001) 385–392.
[20] Zhao, H., Chan, T., Merriman, B., Osher, S.: A variational level set approach to multiphase motion. Journal of Computational Physics. **127(1)** (1996) 197–195.

A Feature-Preserving and Volume-Constrained Flow for Fairing Irregular Meshes

Chunxia Xiao[1], Shu Liu[1], Qunsheng Peng[1], and A.R. Forrest[2]

[1] State Key Lab of CAD&CG, Zhejiang University, 310027, Zhejiang , P.R. China
[2] School of Computing Sciences, University of East Anglia, Norwich, England

Abstract. In this paper, we introduce a novel approach to denoise meshes taking the balanced flow equation as the theoretical foundation.The underlying model consists of an anisotropic diffusion term and a forcing term. The balance between these two terms is made in a selective way allowing prominent surface features and other details of the meshes to be treated in different ways. The forcing term keeps smoothed surface close to the initial surface.Thus the volume is preserved, and most important, the shape distortion is prevented. Applying a dynamic balance technique, the equation converges to the solution quickly meanwhile generating a more faithful approximation to the original noisy mesh. Our smoothing method maintains simplicity in implementation and numerical results show its high performance.

1 Introduction

Mesh de-noising is an active research area in digital geometry processing. Acquired 3D models are often noisy no matter if they are generated with high-fidelity scanners or are extracted from volume data. To facilitate a robust and efficient geometry process, these acquired models need first to be de-noised. Many authors have focused on mesh de-noising. However, it still remains a challenge to remove the noise while preserving the geometric features of the underlying sampled surface, such as edges and corners. Besides the elementary function of noise removal, a good mesh-filtering algorithm should have the following properties. (1) feature preservation; significant sharp feature such as edges and corners of a surface should not be blurred after being smoothed. (2) volume-preservation; the denoised shape should maintain the shape volume without manifest change. In addition, the smoothed model should be faithful to original model without distortion. (3) anti-vertex drifting; vertices should keep close to their original position without noticeable drift,otherwise,the regularity of the mesh will decreases.

The focus of our work is aimed at the above three problems. There are two terms in our model: the diffusion and the forcing term. The diffusion term simulates a well-posed anisotropic flow. A curvature operator for feature detection is embedded in this term, the curvature operator is calculated on the Gaussian-filtered mesh which makes the anisotropic flow mathematically well posed. Therefore, the undesired deformation or degeneration of the mesh, that

H.-P. Seidel, T. Nishita, and Q. Peng (Eds.): CGI 2006, LNCS 4035, pp. 197–208, 2006.

usually happened during anisotropic filtering,is avoided. With the forcing term, the algorithm converges to a solution that is very close to initial mesh, thus the volume is preserved. The balance between these two terms is made in a selective way, in which prominent surface features and other finer details of the mesh are treated differently. Our algorithm moves vertices along the normal direction, thus, limiting the effects of vertex-drift. Compared with other smoothing techniques [5, 7, 8], Our model defines the shape operator and balanced flow operator for 3D surfaces explicitly in terms of a discrete surface, thus eliminates the need of complex computation. Consequently, the side effects introduced by using higher order approximations are avoided in our small stencil of operators.

1.1 Related Works

Many papers on mesh smoothing have been presented in recent years. Mesh-denoising methods are mostly inspired by image denoising approaches. Peng et al. [10] applied locally adaptive Wiener filtering to meshes. Both Fleishman et al. [2] and Jones et al. [1]used bilateral filtering for smoothing surfaces based on the idea of bilateral filtering for gray and color images [9]. The main difference between these two methods is in the surface predictor. More specifically, Jones et al. [1] took the distance between the point and its projection onto the plane of a neighboring triangle, whereas Fleishman et al. [2] took the distance between a neighboring point and the tangent plane. To smooth a mesh, Fleishman et al.[2] performed several filtering iterations, while Jones et al.[1]smoothed a surface in a single pass.

One of the most common techniques for mesh filtering is the diffusion-based algorithm. Most of these methods also obtain their ideas from image denoising approaches. Based on the definition of the Laplacian operator on images, Taubin [3] introduced signal processing on surfaces. Desbrun et al. [4] extended this method to irregular meshes by improving the constancy of the discrete operator on arbitrary meshes, to acquire stable numerical smoothing schemes, they introduced an implicit discretization of geometric diffusion, the vertex-drifting problem is prevented as the position of vertices are adjusted in the normal direction. Ohtake et al. [12] extended the Laplace geometry smoothing by combining it with mesh regularization. While all these methods are isotropic, that is, smooth noise and salient features are treated without discrimination, some important features are blurred.

By modifying the diffusion coefficient at the edges, Perona et al. [13] proposed an anisotropic diffusion method to obtain an efficient edge detector for image processing. Based on this pioneered work, many feature-preserving smoothing method have been presented recently. Desbrun et al. [5] introduced Anisotropic diffusion for height fields, Clarenz et al. [7] extended the Anisotropic diffusion for meshes by formulating and discretizing the anisotropic diffusion. Taubin [14] and Tasdizen et al.[15] apply anisotropic diffusion to smooth the normal field of the mesh surfaces. By combining the limit representation of Loop's subdivision for triangular surface meshes and vector functions on the surface mesh, Bajaj et al.[8] arrived at a discretized version for the established anisotropic diffusion problem in the spatial direction and achieved impressive results. Recently, Hildebrandt et al. [16] presented an anisotropic meshes filtering approach based on prescribed mean curvature flow (PMC). Other mesh-denoising methods have also been presented to improve the performance of the traditional approaches[17, 18, 19].

2 Well-Posed Anisotropic Flow

As an isotropic shape smoothing technique similar to Laplacian filtering, Desbrun et al. [4] proposed a mean curvature flow that dispersed the noise of a smooth mesh appropriately by minimizing the surface area. Assume that $N_1(i)$ is the 1-ring neighbors of v_i, their approach adopts the following mean curvature flow equation:

$$\frac{\partial v_i}{\partial t} = -\bar{\kappa_i} n_i \tag{1}$$

where $\bar{\kappa_i} n_i$ is the curvature normal. A normalized version can be used in an explicit integration for quick smoothing:

$$(\bar{\kappa_i} n_i)_{normalized} = \frac{1}{\sum_j (\cot\alpha_j + \cot\beta_j)} \cdot \sum_{j \in N_1(i)} (\cot\alpha_j + \cot\beta_j)(v_j - v_i) \tag{2}$$

where α_j and β_j are the two angles opposite to the edge e_{ij} in the two triangles having the edge in common. Unlike the Laplacian of the surface at a vertex, which has both normal and tangential components, mean curvature flow is a noise removal procedure that does not depend on the parameterization. Curvature flow smoothes the surface by moving vertices along the surface normal with a speed equals to the mean curvature $\bar{\kappa}$. So the unpleasing side effects such as vertex drifting are avoided.

This approach provides a good result for mesh smoothing. However, most meshes acquired from 3D scanning tools contain prominent features such as corners and ridges, which will be blurred using this isotropic denoising approach. Therefore, a preferred filtering algorithm should get rid of the noise, meanwhile preserving prominent edges. For this reason, we would like to resort to the idea of the anisotropic image smoothing methods [13]that have been studied extensively in image restoration.

If $\bar{\kappa_i}$, i.e. local curvature of vertex v_i has a large value, then this vertex is considered as an features vertex. Anisotropic mesh smoothing should slow down the smoothing process in regions with prominent features, while other regions with low curvature are smoothed out quickly. Therefore, one natural idea is to present the following anisotropic curvature flow:

$$\frac{\partial v_i}{\partial t} = -g(|\bar{\kappa_i} n_i|)\bar{\kappa_i} n_i \tag{3}$$

where $g(s) \geq 0$ is a non-increasing function, satisfying $g(0) = 1$ and $g(s) \to 0$ when $s \to \infty$. Here we set $g(x) = 1/(1 + K * x^2)$, where K is a parameter that can be tuned by the user to control the diffusion speed.

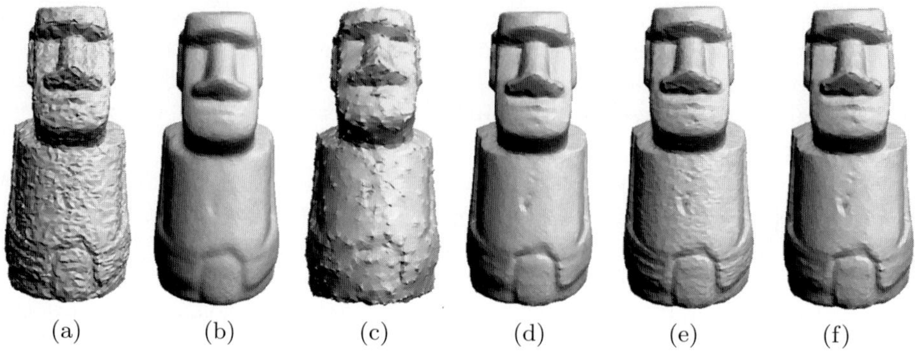

Fig. 1. (a) Noisy model, (b) Mean curvature flow, (c) Naive anisotropic flow, (d) Well-posed anisotropic flow, (e) Volume-preserving flow, (f) Well-balanced flow

Fig. 2. (a) Original noisy curve, (b) smoothed curve. It can be seen from the illustrations that shape operator defined on the smoothed surface is more accurate.

Unfortunately, this anisotropic curvature flow equation (3) is not an most appropriate equation for meshes smoothing, since undesired results such as degeneration of the mesh will be produced when dealing with seriously noisy meshes using this method, as illustrated in Figure.1(c).

What causes this problem? Evaluating geometric features directly based on the original noisy surface is inappropriate, Since it is difficult to discriminate the noise vertex and the feature vertex on the noisy surface,as illustrated in figure 2,the vertex k_i and vertex k_j. we would like to define the diffusivity coefficient g on an alternative filtered surface as shown in figure 2(b). In this paper, we adopt the Gaussian filter to pre-filter the current surface M, although many other filters can be employed. Then, we employ curvature κ_H evaluated on the filtered mesh $M_\sigma^{'}$ used for feature detection, where σ is Gaussian filter width. By substituting $|\bar{\kappa_i} n_i|$ with $|\kappa_H(G_\sigma * u)|$,where κ_H is computed using the formulation (2), we present the following well-posed Anisotropic flow equation.

$$u_t = g(|\kappa_H(G_\sigma * u)|)(-\bar{\kappa} n) \tag{4}$$

where G_σ is a convolution kernel(here, a Gaussian function),$G_\sigma(x) = e^{-\frac{x^2}{2\sigma^2}}$, σ is the noise standard deviation, which is also called the scale . We call model (4) the

"Well posed anisotropic model". The term $|\kappa_H(G_\sigma * u)|$ is the local estimate of $|\kappa_H(u)|$ used for more accurate curvature estimate. The term $g = g(|\kappa_H(G_\sigma * u)|)$ is used for geometric feature detection and controls the diffusion speed. Using this model, undesired deformation is avoided, as shown in Figure 1(d), and prominent features like boundaries are kept, while noisy and are smoothed.Similar technique capturing shape to obtain more reliable detection of features based on a smoothed shape is also used in meshes smoothing. For example, to make a robust estimator, Jones et al.[1] modified the estimators by smoothing the normal which also corresponds to a simple Gaussian smoothing.

3 Volume-Preserving Flow

Both Laplacian smoothing and mean curvature flow tend to minimize surface area. Although well-posed anisotropic flow can be used for selective smoothing,in essence,it is a flow equation that is not energy preserving. Therefore, this method will also introduce shrinkage when it is used as mesh smoother. As anisotropic diffusion method does not seek an optimal solution of any kind, hence, we would like to find a flow model that has an optimal and stable solution, and converges to the solution quickly. Many techniques have been applied to eliminate the shrinkage. These methods whether heavily require fine-tuning [3] or is global re-scale operation[4],whereas de-noising is a local operation.Therefore these algorithm are not optimal approaches for volume preservation.

Motivated by the Nordstrom [21],we modify the equation (4) by introducing the forcing term $(I-u)$, where I is the original mesh surface. The term $(I-u)$ has the property of preserving $u(x, y, z, t)$ close to the initial mesh $I(x, y, z)$: we add the term $(I-u)$ to the well-posed equation(4) and propose the following equation:

$$u_t = g(|\kappa_H(G_\sigma * u)|)(-\bar{\kappa}n) + (I - u) \tag{5a}$$

Since our interest is in the steady state solution, the initial condition of above equation can also be replaced by an arbitrary initial condition.

$$u(x, y, z, 0) = \chi(x, y, z) \tag{5b}$$

In all our experiments , we set the initial condition $u(x, y, z, 0) = I(x, y, z)$.The steady state of this initial value problem (5a,5b)is a solution of following equation:

$$u = I + g(|\kappa_H(G_\sigma * u)|)(-\bar{\kappa}n) \tag{6}$$

The continuity control function g plays the role of the diffusivity.

We call the system (5a), (5b)the "Volume-preserving flow" model. The solutions of this model are well behaved, in that they do not stray too far away from the original mesh surface I , unless forced to by the initial condition χ; even if so, they eventually approach the range of I as $t \to \infty$.

Intuitively, the forcing term $I-u$ has the effect of locally moderating the diffusion as the diffused surface u diffuses further away from the original mesh I. The following physical representation of this initial value problem further confirms this belief: Let Ω be a thin anisotropic annular solid of some material resting on top of another solid Ω_0 of some (other) material as in figure 3(a). Suppose that the space and time varying thermal conductivity of Ω is given by ag,where the constant a is the coefficient of heat transfer between Ω and Ω_0. If the initial temperature at each point p of Ω is given by $\chi(x, y, z)$, and the temperature distribution of Ω_0 is fixed with the value I, then u represents the space-and time-varying temperature of Ω . By introducing the forcing term $(I - u)$, the estimated image function u is guaranteed to be a faithful approximation of the original surface function I. The forcing term $I - u$ performs the role of drawing the anisotropic diffused u back to I .

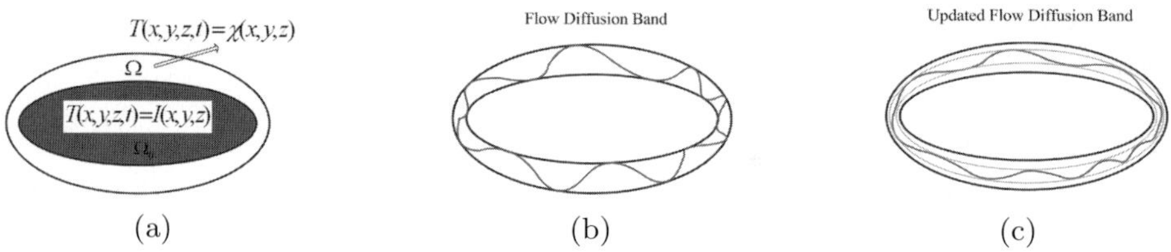

Fig. 3. (a) Physical models of volume-preserving flow, (b) The flow diffusion band of the original surface. (c) Dynamically updated flow diffusion band.

From the volume-preserving flow, we can draw the conclusion that the solution u will converge, and is restricted within the flow diffusion band B of the original surface I, as illustrated in figure 3(b). Therefore,the volume-preserving model produces an estimated surface function, whose range is contained inside that of the original function. The performance of the anisotropic diffusion is confined to the flow diffusion band B of the original surface I:

$$\inf_{\xi \in B} I(\xi) \leq u(x,t) \leq \sup_{\xi \in B} I(\xi) \quad \forall x \in B \;\; for\ any \;\; t < \infty$$

Therefore the resulted model's volume is well preserved, as shown in Figure 1(e).

In particular, Let $M^{'}$ be the corrupted models of the original smooth meshes M_0 formed by adding random noise. The initial value χ in formulation (5b) is replaced by $M^{'}$, I is substituted by M_0 , then the solution u will converge to M_0 .

We present one special example to substantiate the idea, which is showed in Figure 4. Let p be a vertex on the original surface M_0 (Figure 4(b)) , and $p^{'}$ be its corresponding vertex on the solution u (Figure 4(f)) . Let $dist(p_i, p_i^{'})$ be the distance error between p_i and $p_i^{'}$ and $E_v = \sum_{i=0}^{N} dist(p_i, p_i^{'})/N$ is the average distance error. The radius of the bounding box of model Octa-flower is 16.17, the volume of the original mesh is 1565.16. The volume of the solution u is 1567.21 and the average distance error E_v is 0.12. The numerical results suggest that the solution u converge to the original surface M_0 ,which further confirms the results achieved in Volume-preserving flow.

Note that here we only take a special example to confirm the belief that the solution u of Eq.(5) converges to a faithful approximation of the original surface I.

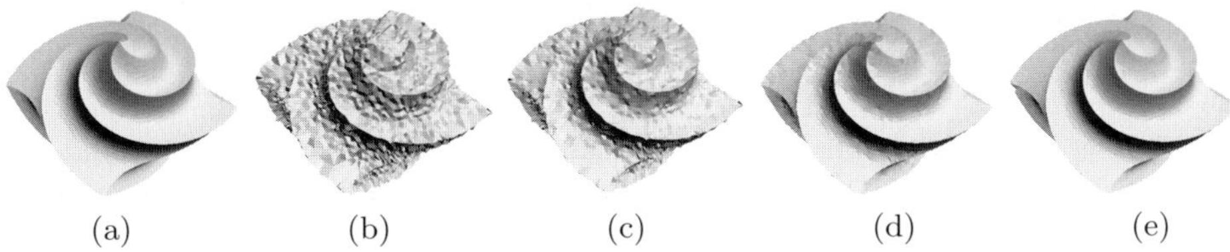

Fig. 4. Volume-preserving flow. (a) Original model Octa-flower M_0 , (b) Corrupted ModelM'. The solution converge to M_0 as shown in the sequence (c), (d), (e), (f).

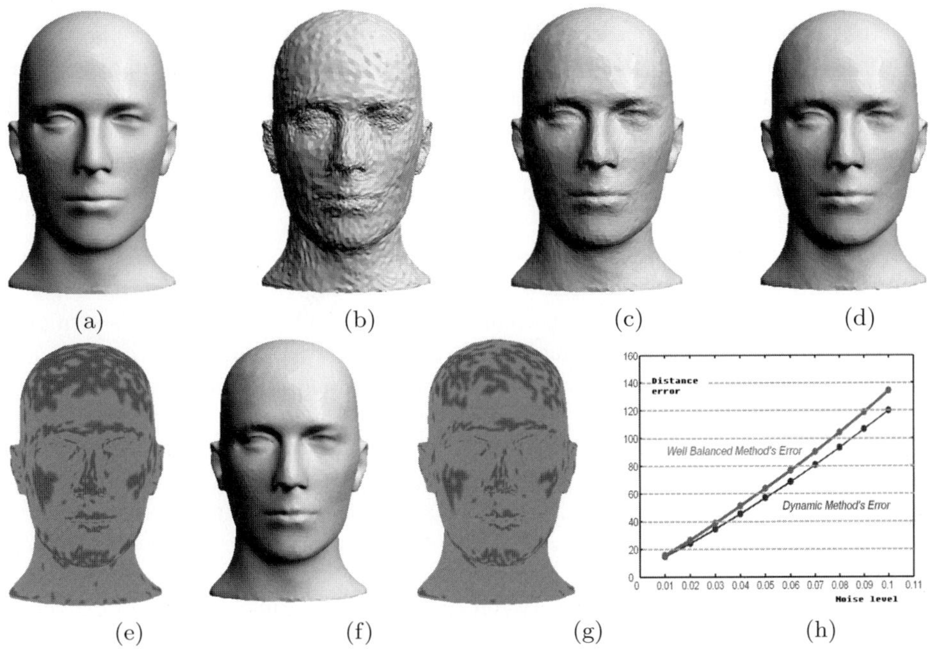

Fig. 5. Dynamic volume preserved flow, (a) original model, (b) Corrupted model, (c) Volume-preserved flow, (d) Well-balanced flow, (e) Error visualization of Well-balanced flow, (f) Dynamic balanced flow, (g) Error visualization of Dynamic balanced flow, (h) Error visualization of different noise level

Of course,in all the other examples, we take I as the original noised meshes. By adding the forcing term $I - u$ to formulation (5), we bring the well-posed diffusion method to an appealing sense of optimality, therefore intuitively explains its excellent properties such as volume preserving ,as illustrated in Fig.1(e) and Fig.5(c).

4 Well-Balanced Flow

To denoise models with relative low noise, we can receive satisfactory results with several iterations meanwhile preserving the volume. Whilst to deal with corrupted model with heavy noise, desirable smoothed result cannot be obtained, as shown in Figure1 (e), Figure 5(c), the noise has not been smoothed completely. As all the vertices are drawn back to its original position without distinction, the anisotropic curvature flow cannot work very well in the error diffusion band B .

Motivated by the idea based on well-balanced flow equation [20], we improve the equation (5) further by the following balanced flow equation.

$$u_t = g(|\kappa_H(G_\sigma * u)|)(-\bar{\kappa}n) + (1 - g(|\kappa_H(G_\sigma * u)|))(I - u)$$
$$u(x, y, z, 0) = I(x, y, z) \tag{7}$$

where $I(x, y, z)$is the original mesh surface, and $(1 - g)$works as a moderated selector of the diffusion process. We call the above equation "well-balanced flow equation ". Thus, the proposed model is capable of selectively applying the Well-posed model in the areas of the mesh where feature preservation is required. This model is also capable of forcing the smoothed mesh to remain close to the initial mesh surface I in the features areas where $g \to 0$. On the other hand, in homogenous areas $g \to 1$, the forcing term will have weak effect, which allows for a better finer detail smoothing of the meshes.

This simple change of the Volume-preserving flow model generates high performance filtering results, as shown in Fig1 (f), Fig 5(d), where the noise is removed and the prominent features are preserved well. The concept is straightforward and the model has appealing physical interpretations. Much more, the computational scheme is simple and is efficient for the implementation.

In the proposed model, the users can tune two parameters to control the performance: The first one is the Gaussian filter width σ, which plays dual roles. One is to pre-filter the surface to obtain more accurate mean curvatures evaluation used for feature detection, the other role is to make our proposed method mathematically well-posed and more robust. The second one is the constant K, which also carries dual roles : one is to allow the function $g(s)$ to carry out a moderated selection to balance between the diffusion term and the forcing term, the other is to allow the anisotropic diffusion.

5 Dynamic Balanced Flow

Although well-balanced flow is an optimal process, the flow diffusion band B of initial surface is broadened as the noise is increased, leading to increasing inaccuracy of the solution. We introduce a dynamic flow algorithm to address this problem. The key ingredient of the techniques is that instead of setting I the fixed original noisy surface M , we would like to dynamically update I with the immediate generated solution u , which can be described in brief as following. After every L iterations we achieve the immediate fairing surface u_L , then the original I is replaced with u_L , the iteration process goes on. With several such repetitions, satisfactory results are received. The motivation for applying this technique is that when dealing with severely corrupted models, the original I should be dynamically updated with the newly generated u_L surface after several iterations. The anisotropic flow equation will be performed in a thinner flow diffusion band B' , as illustrated in Figure 3(b)that is, flow diffusion band $B$is also updated dynamically according to the dynamically updated I. As the updated flow diffusion band B' is contained in the original flow diffusion band B, the accuracy of solution is increased and the volume is naturally conserved. This computational mechanic provides another important advantage: the balanced state is dynamically broken, the original I is dynamically updated, and the flow equation converges to the solution quickly. Dynamic balanced flow is especially suitable for denoising severely noisy surface.

As show in Figure 5, it takes 7 iterations for both well-balance flow and dynamic balanced flow to smooth the corrupted Mannequin(Figure 5(b))(I is of course set as the noisy model Figure 5(b)). As for dynamic balanced flow we set L = 3. Figure 5(e) is the distance error visualization between the corresponding vertices of the smoothed model(Figure (d))performed by Well-balanced flow and original smooth model (Figure (a)). Figure 5(g) is the distance error visualization between the corresponding vertices of the smoothed model(Figure (f))performed by Dynamic balanced flow and original smooth model (Figure (a)). These results show that the result from dynamic flow is more faithful approximation. Figure 5(h) illustrates the average error comparison of all vertices performed using well-balanced flow and dynamic balanced flow for various noise levels, which shows that dynamic balanced flow always generates more faithful results with different level of noise. The experimental results also show that dynamic balanced flow converges to the solution faster than well-balanced flow.

6 Implementations

We have demonstrated the results of the balanced flow diffusion algorithm and compared them with several other smoothing algorithms.

As have pointed out in previous section, there are two parameters at the disposal of the users to tune the performance. The Gaussian filter width σ is also called the standard deviation. In this paper, the Gsussian filter performs based on the 1-ring of the vertices. Let L be the arithmetic mean of the edge lengths of the neighboring vertices of vertex v , then we set $\sigma = \varepsilon L$, where$\varepsilon$is a user-selected value. To process seriously noisy model, the parameter σ is usually set to a relatively large value to capture the accurate features of the models. Similarly, to preserve or enhance the prominent features such as shape edges of Cube model, we would assign a relatively large value for the parameter K .

One benefit of anisotropic diffusion is the ability to iteratively enhance edges and corners whilst prevented shape distortion. In Figure 6, we can observe that the edges of the cube with 11k triangles are preserved and sharpened. The noise is smoothed out and the face is smoothed into a flat plane. At the same time, the volume is also preserved. The original volume is 7.730, while the resulting volume is 7.695. Both mean curvature method [4]and the bilateral method [2]will cause obvious shrinkage whilst the non-iterative method [1]is also not necessarily volume-preserving. In this example it takes 6 iterations using the dynamic balanced flow while the iterations also depend on the step length.

(a) (b) (c) (d) (e)

Fig. 6. (a) original model, (b) Mean curvature flow [Desbrun99], (c) Bilateral method [Fleishman03], (d) Non-iterative method [Jones03]. (e) Dynamic balanced flow.

(a) (b) (c) (d)

Fig. 7. (a) Original model, (b) Corrupted model, (c) Dynamic balanced flow, (d) Non-iterative method [Jones03]

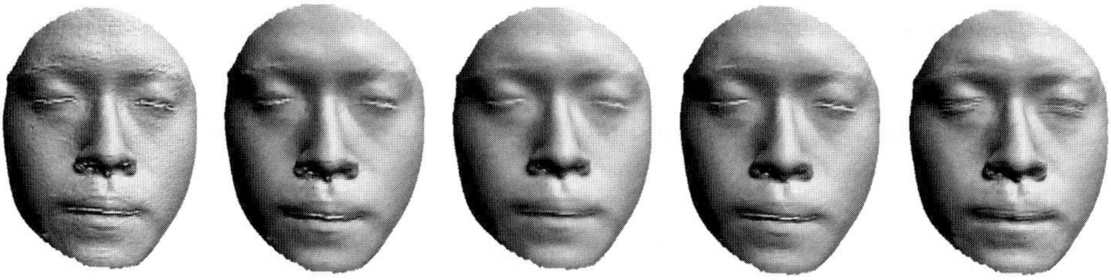

(a) (b) (c) (d) (e)

Fig. 8. (a) original mesh, (b) Dynamic balanced flow, (c) mean curvature flow [Desbrun99]. (d) Bilateral method [Fleishman03], (e) Non-iterative method [Jones03]. Data courtesy of Alexander Belyaev.

Figure 8 shows the results of applying the proposed method to a scanned model. We also show a comparison with above-mentioned three methods. The model has 17,000 vertices, and it was smoothed in 7 iterations using our method. In figure 8(b), compared with others methods, observe that the features, for example , the features around the mouth, are well preserved. The vertices with large error are treated as outliers and thus are not smoothed out in our method, while the noise is smoothed out.

The non-iterative method is not able to perform iterative enhancement in a single pass, resulting in a slightly different overall appearance, figure 8(e).

Moreover, the property of the non-iterative method makes it highly dependent on the choice the neighborhood while our methods traditionally uses only the 1-ring neighborhood. Their method estimates the new position of each vertex based on the predictions from its spatially nearby triangles, and in particular, when dealing with such meshes as Figure 7(b), the smoothed mesh will change shape (Figure 7(d)). Since our method allows the anisotropic diffusion flow to be restricted to the flow diffusion band of the original surface, the result is faithful to original model as shown in Fig 7(c).

Our method also has some disadvantages compared with [2] and [1]. Since balanced flow diffusion seeks an optimal solution, compared with these two methods, relatively more iterations are required, while the iterations also depend on the step length. In addition, the only property of the mesh that these two methods use is the topological information, and therefore, the algorithms can be adapted to point based geometry. Specifically, the non-iterative techniques can be performed on arbitrary "triangle soups", while our method is difficult to smooth "triangle soups" due to the curvature normal calculation (2).

7 Conclusions and Future Work

We have presented a novel approach to mesh filtering taking the well-balanced flow equation as the theoretical foundation. The algorithm converges to the solution of interest and seeks to find an optimal solution. The proposed model is mathematically well posed and robust. Our approach has such desirable properties as noise removal, features preservation, and automatic volume-preservation, as well as anti-vertex drifting. Balanced flow diffusion is simple, practical as well as having intuitive physical interpretations. In the future work we will extend our approach to the filtering of the point-sampled geometry.

Acknowledgements

We would thank Alexander Belyaev for his Model data. The work is supported by the National Grand Fundamental Research 973 Program of China (No.2002CB312101).

References

1. T.R. Jones and F. Durand and M. Desbrun, Non-iterative, feature-preserving mesh smoothing, *Proc. of ACM SIGGRAPH, 2003*
2. S. Fleishman and I. Drori and D. Cohen-Or, Bilateral mesh denoising, *Proc. of ACM SIGGRAPH, 2003,950-953*
3. G. Taubin, A signal processing approach to fair surface design, *Proc. SIGGRAPH, 1995,351-358*
4. M. Desbrun and M. Meyer and P. Schroer and A. Barr, *Implicit fairing of irregular meshes using diffusion and curvature flow,Proc. SIGGRAPH, 1999,317-324*

5. M. Desbrun and M. Meyer and P. Schroer and A. Barr, Anisotropic feature-preserving denoising of height fields and bivariate data, *Graphics Interface, 2000,145-152*
6. M. Meyer and M. Desbrun and P. Schroder and A.H. Barr, Discrete differential-geometry operators for triangulated 2-manifolds, *In Visualization and Mathematics III, 2003,35-57*
7. U. Clarenz and U. Diewald and M. Rumpf, Anisotropic geometric diffusion in surface processing, *Proc. IEEE Visualization, 2000,397-405*
8. C. Bajaj and G. Xu, Anisotropic diffusion on surfaces and functions on surfaces, *ACM Transactions on Graphics, 2003,22,4-32*
9. C. Tomasi and R. Manduchi, Bilateral filtering for gray and color images, *ICCV, 1998,839-846*
10. J. Peng and V. Strela and D. Zorin, A simple algorithm for surface denoising, *Proc. IEEE Visualization, 2001*
11. M. Black and G. Sapiro and D. Marimont and D. Heeger, Robust anisotropic diffusion, *IEEE Trans. Image Processing, 1998, 7, 3,421-432*
12. Y. Ohtake and A. Belyaev and I. Bogaevski, Mesh regularization and adaptive smoothing, *Computer Aided Design, 2001,33,11,789-800*
13. P. Perona and J. Malik, Scale-Space and Edge Detection Using Anisotropic Diffusion, *IEEE Transactions on Pattern Analysis and Machine Intelligence, 1990,12,7,629-639*
14. G. Taubin, Linear anisotropic mesh filtering, *IBM Research Report RC2213, 2001*
15. T. Tasdizen and R. Whitaker and P.Burchard and S. Osher, Geometric surface smoothing via anisotropic diffusion of normals, *Proc. of IEEE Visualization , 2002,125-132*
16. K. Hildebrandt and K. Polthier, Anisotropic Filtering of Non-Linear Surface Features, *Computer Graphics Forum (Eurographics2004) , 2004,23,3,391-400*
17. X. Liu and H. Bao and H.-Y. Shum and Q. Peng, A novel volume constrained smoothing method for meshes, *Graphical Models , 2002,64,169-182*
18. J. Vollmer and R. Mencl and H. Muller, Improved Laplacian smoothing of noisy surface meshes, *Proc. of Eurographics , 1999,131-138*
19. I. Guskov and W. Sweldens and P. Schroder, Multiresolution signal processing for meshes, *In Proceedings of SIGGRAPH, 1999,325-334*
20. Caz. Barcelos and M. Boaventura and Ec. Silva, A well-balanced flow equation for noise removal and edge detection, *IEEE Trans. on Image Processing, 2003,14,751-763*
21. K.N. Nordstrom, Biased anisotropic diffusion: a unified regularization and diffusion approach to edge detection, *Image Vis. Comput, 1990,8,318-327*

Matching 2D Shapes Using U Descriptors

Zhanchuan Cai[1], Wei Sun[1], and Dongxu Qi[1,2]

[1] School of Information Science and Technology,
Sun Yat-sen University, Guangzhou, 510275, P.R. China
[2] Faculty of Information Technology,
Macao University of Science and Technology, Macao
zhchcai@126.com, sunwei@mail.sysu.edu.cn, dxqi@must.edu.mo

Abstract. In this paper, we propose a novel U-System-based approach for representing and matching similar shapes. U-system is a complete orthogonal piecewise k-degree polynomials in $L^2[0,1]$and it has some good properties,such as regeneration,convergence by group. Using U-system with finite items, it can be realized to accurate representation of shapes. This paper make shapes analysis in theory. We experimentally demonstrate that U descriptors are more suitable for representing and matching 2D shapes than Fourier descriptors.

1 Introduction

Large image databases are more and more used in many application areas, such as advertising, architectural and engineering design, fashion, medical diagnosis, journalism, crime prevention, and land analysis. This has motivated growing research interest on efficient and effective methods enabling the matching of images on the basis of their content from large databases. With respect to other features, like color and texture, shape is much more effective in semantically characterizing the content of an image [1] [2] [3] [4]. However, properly representing and matching shape information are still challenging tasks. The problem of representing them so as to allow the implementation of efficient and effective matching and retrieval methods is still not solved in a satisfactory way. The scenario is further complicated when invariance, with respect to a number of possible transformations, such as scaling, shifting, and rotation, is required [5].

Among the different approaches that are available for the representation of shape information, those based on the Discrete Fourier Transform (DFT) describe the outside contour by means of a limited number of coefficients in the frequency domain. It has to be observed that, since DFT derive from Fourier system [6][7], they cannot accurate represent commonly shapes information by using finite items.such as the phenomena of Gibbs(see Fig.1) [15][16].So Fourier system are not suitable for shapes analysis for images [15][17].

In 1980s, Qi and Feng created a class of complete orthogonal functions. It is composed of a series of k-degree piecewise polynomials and called k-degree U-system[8]. It includes not only smooth functions but also discontinuous ones. In fact, Walsh-system is the special case of U-system, i.e. 0-degree U-system.

H.-P. Seidel, T. Nishita, and Q. Peng (Eds.): CGI 2006, LNCS 4035, pp. 209–220, 2006.

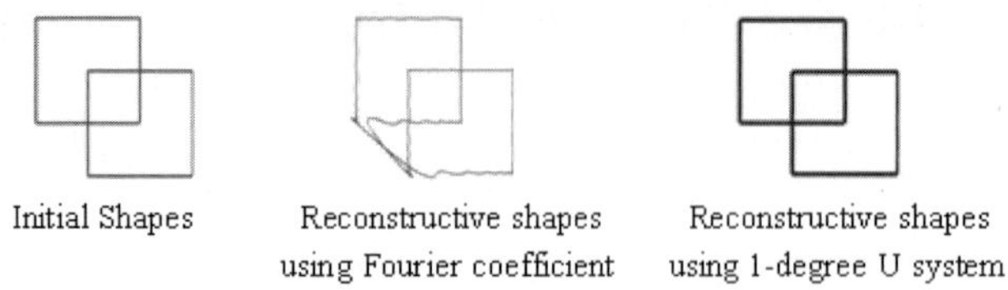

Fig. 1. Comparing Fourier transform with U system

Slant transformation, which is commonly used in the digital image processing, is the 1-degree discrete U-system. Based on the special properties of the structure, after many complex signals are decomposed by U-system, they are exactly regenerated with finite items in U-system. This is the most important properties of U-system.It means that U-system are conducive to express shapes information.

In addition, in [19], Qi and Feng study a similar idea on the triangle. Using these theories, in [9], motivated by in the work in [8], Micchelli and Xu had done some interesting work. This indicates the application foreground of U-system [9-13].

In this paper, we propose a novel U-system-based approach for shape analysis. U system can accurate represent shapes by using finite items. So U system are suitable for shapes analysis. Moreover, we analyze frequency and normalized frequency properties of shapes in theory.In the end, some experimental results are given.

2 The k-Degree U-System

k-degree U-system is the class of complete orthogonal functions in $L^2[0,1]$.where $k = 0, 1, 2, 3, ...$

$U^1_{k,k}(x), U^2_{k,k}(x), ..., U^{k+1}_{k,k}(x), U^1_{k,k+1}(x), U^2_{k,k+1}(x), ..., U^{k+1}_{k,k+1}(x),$
$U^1_{k,k+2}(x), U^2_{k,k+2}(x), ...$

$$U^{2j-1}_{k,n+1}(x) = \begin{cases} U^j_{k,n}(2x), & 0 \le x < \frac{1}{2} \\ U^j_{k,n}(2-2x), & \frac{1}{2} < x \le 1 \end{cases}$$

$$U^{2j}_{k,n+1}(x) = \begin{cases} U^j_{k,n}(2x), & 0 \le x < \frac{1}{2} \\ -U^j_{k,n}(2-2x), & \frac{1}{2} < x \le 1 \end{cases}$$

$j = 1, 2, ..., (k+1)2^{n-k}, n = k+1, k+2, ...$ where $U^1_{k,k}(x), U^2_{k,k}(x), ..., U^{k+1}_{k,k}(x)$ are the front $k+1$ items of Legendre polynomials. $U^1_{k,k+1}(x), U^2_{k,k+1}(x), ..., U^{k+1}_{k,k+1}(x)$ are the piecewise polynomials,and orthogonal with each other and $U^1_{k,k}(x)$, $U^2_{k,k}(x)$, ..., $U^{k+1}_{k,k}(x)$. The value, at the discontinuous point, is the arithmetic average value of two sides limit.

In $k-$degree U-system, the $n+1^{th}$ group includes $(k+1)2^{n-k}$ functions. In turn, we take 2^{n-k} as a "class", The result includes $k+1$ "classes".The ith is gotten with some items of "squish-repeat" of $U^i_{k,k+1}$. $U^{i,j}_{k,n+1}$ is the jth function of ith "class" of $n+1^{th}$ group in U-system, where $i = 1, 2, ..., k+1$; $j = 1, 2, ..., 2^{n-k}$; $n = k+1, k+2, ...$ In order with "group-class", k-degree U-system is:

$$U^1_{k,k}(x), U^2_{k,k}(x), ..., U^{k+1}_{k,k}(x), U^1_{k,k+1}(x), U^2_{k,k+1}(x), ..., U^{k+1}_{k,k+1}(x),$$
$$U^{1,1}_{k,k+2}(x), U^{1,2}_{k,k+2}(x), ..., U^{1,2^{n-1}}_{k,k+2}(x), U^{2,1}_{k,k+2}(x), U^{2,2}_{k,k+2}(x), ..., U^{2,2^{n-1}}_{k,k+2}(x),$$
$$\dots \dots U^{k+1,1}_{k,k+2}(x), U^{k+1,2}_{k,k+2}(x), ..., U^{k+1,2^{n-1}}_{k,k+2}(x),$$
$$U^{1,1}_{k,k+3}(x), U^{1,2}_{k,k+3}(x), ..., U^{1,2^{n-1}}_{k,k+3}(x), U^{2,1}_{k,k+3}(x), U^{2,2}_{k,k+3}(x), ..., U^{2,2^{n-1}}_{k,k+3}(x), ...$$

......

When $k = 0, 1, 2, 3$, the partial figure of U-system are shown in Fig. 2. It is obvious that Walsh-system is the 0-degree U-system.

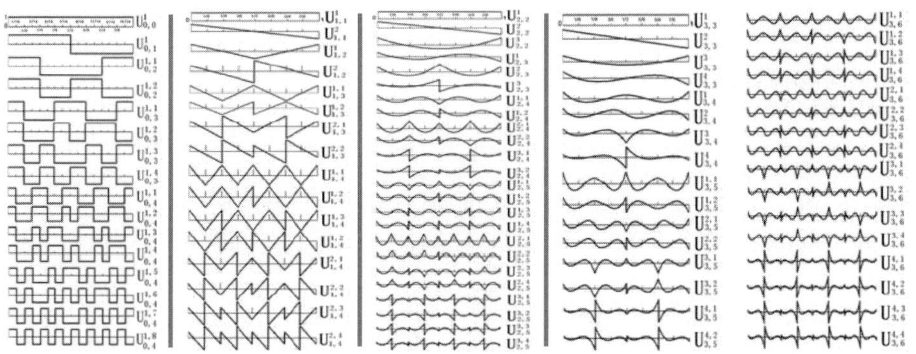

k=0 k=1 k=2 k=3

Fig. 2. $k-$degree U-system (when k=0,1,2,3)

It is noticeable that, for a given function F, let

$$P_{n+1}F = \sum_{i=0}^{n} a_i U_{k,i}$$

let $P_{n+1}F$ is the best L_2-approximation to F from the space $span(U_{k,j})_0^n$. Thus we have

$$\lim_{n \longrightarrow \infty} ||F - P_nF||_2 = 0, F \in L_2[0,1]$$

$$\lim_{n \longrightarrow \infty} ||F - P_nF||_\infty = 0, F \in C[0,1]$$

These denote that Fourier-U series have the properties of L_2-convergence, completeness and convergence uniform by group.

If F is a piecewise k-degree polynomial, which has some discontinuous points on $x = \frac{q}{2^r}$ (q and r are integers), it can be exactly represented with finite items of Fourier-U series.This important property is called "Fourier-U series regeneration".

3 U Transform and Its Properties for Shapes

3.1 Orthogonal Representation of Parametric Shapes

Let $t \in [0,1]$,for simplicity, we take one degree U-system as an example. Assuming that the interval [0,1] is divided into 2^n sub-intervals. Then, approximation function is represented: $F_f(t) = f_i(t)$. Where $t \in [\frac{i}{2^n}, \frac{i+1}{2^n}), i = 0, 1, ..., 2^n$. Let

$$P(t) = \begin{pmatrix} x(t) \\ y(t) \end{pmatrix} = \sum_{i=0}^{2^{n+1}-1} \lambda_i U_{2^{n+1}-1}(t)$$

The shapes are represented parametric polynomials:

$$\begin{cases} x(t) = F_x(t) \\ y(t) = F_y(t) \end{cases}$$

Where $\lambda_j = \int_0^1 P(t)U_j dt$, for $j = 0, 1, 2, ..., 2^{n+1} - 1$.$P(t)$ can be exactly represented by the given $F_f(t)$ with finite items. So we call λ_j as U-transform coefficient,also call as frequency spectrum of $P(t)$. Especially, when $j = 0$, we call λ_0 as "DC" term. The "energy" of $P(t)$ is defined as following:

$$E = (\sum_{j=0}^{n} \lambda_j^2)^{\frac{1}{2}}$$

3.2 The Properties of Frequency Spectrum

According to the above defined $\lambda_j = \int_0^1 P(t)U_j dt$, for $j = 0, 1, 2, ..., 2^{n+1} - 1$. have the following properties.

Theorem 1. *The above defined $\lambda_j$have the basic properties in geometric transformation.*

(i)Translation transformation

if $P^{'}(t) = P(t) + P_0$ *then* $\lambda_j^{'} = \lambda_j + P_0\delta_k$, *where* $\delta_k = \begin{cases} 0, \ k \neq 0 \\ 1, \ k = 0 \end{cases}$

(ii)Scale transformation

if $P^{'}(t) = \alpha P(t)$ *then* $\lambda_j^{'} = \alpha\lambda_j$. *where α is the scale factor.*

(iii)Rotation transformation

if $[P^{'}(t)^T, 1] = [P(t)^T, 1]A$ *then* $[\lambda_j^{'}, 1] = A[\lambda_j, 1]$. *where T demotes transpose of a matrix, A is rotation matrix.*

Theorem 2. *Energy is invariant in rotation for the same shapes.*

In order to make the frequency satisfy the invariance in rotation, translation, scale transforms, it can be defined normalized frequency as following:

$NF_j = \frac{||\lambda_j||}{||\lambda_1||}, j = 1, 2, ..., n$

Theorem 3. *Normalized frequency is invariant in rotation, translation, scale transforms for the same shapes.*

3.3 U Descriptors

In this section,we will give the discrete case for U-transformation.so it can be defined U descriptors and discussed some relative properties.

Polygonal curve, which is gotten by sampling, is commonly expressed as following: $z(n) = x(n)+iy(n), n = 0, 1, ..., N-1$. Where $i^2 = -1$. For convenience, we take the 1-degree U-system as example to introduce U descriptors and their properties. For simplification, U_k is the kth base in 1-degree U-system. The coefficients $\lambda(k)$ of U transformation are called U descriptors trough formula as following:

$$\lambda(k) = \sum_{n=0}^{N-1} z(n)U_k(\frac{n}{N-1}), 0 \le n \le N-1 \quad (1)$$

$$z(k) = \frac{1}{N}\sum_{k=0}^{N-1} \lambda(k)U_k(\frac{n}{N-1})^{-1}, 0 \le k \le N-1 \quad (2)$$

Theorem 4. *The defined U descriptors above have the basic properties in geometric transformation.*

(i)Translation transformation
if $z_1(n) = z(n) + z_0$ *then* $\lambda_1(k) = \lambda(k) + Nz_0\delta(k)$, *where*
$\delta(k) = \begin{cases} 0, \ k \ne 0 \\ 1, \ k = 0 \end{cases}$
(ii)Scale transformation
if $z_1(n) = \alpha z(n)$ *then* $\lambda_1(k) = \alpha\lambda(k)$ *where* α *is the scale factor.*
(iii)Rotation transformation
if $z_1(n) = z(n)e^{i\theta}$ *then* $\lambda_1(k) = \lambda(k)e^{i\theta}$ *where* θ *is the rotation angle.*

Similarly, it can be defined normalized U descriptors in order to make the U descriptors satisfy the invariance in rotation, translation, scale transform.

$$du(k) = \frac{||\lambda(k)||}{||\lambda(1)||}, k = 1, 2, ..., N-1.$$

Theorem 5. *Normalized U descriptors are invariant in rotation, translation, scale transform.*

Theorem 5 indicates that normalized U descriptors can have some applications in shapes analysis.

3.4 Comparing Shapes Descriptors

The standard approach [3][20] to compare signals $\overrightarrow{z}$ and$\overrightarrow{z'}$ makes use of the Euclidean distance, i.e.

$$L_2(\overrightarrow{z}, \overrightarrow{z'}) = \sqrt{\sum_{k=0}^{N-1} |\overrightarrow{z_k} - \overrightarrow{z'_k}|^2}$$

Accordingly, we may define measurement method of shapes similarity.

Let $du_{S_1}(k)$ and $du_{S_2}(k)$ denote the normalized U descriptors of the two shapes S_1 and S_2, respectively, and the similarity of the two shapes S_1 and S_2 defined as follows:

$$Dis = ||du_{S_1}(k) - du_{S_2}(k)||_2 = \sqrt{\sum_{k=1}^{N-1} |du_{S_1}(k) - du_{S_2}(k)|^2}$$

It is easy to see that the smaller the Dis-value is, the more similar the shape is. vice versa. Especially, when $Dis = 0$, it shows that S_1 and S_2 are same.

4 The Method of Matching Shapes

Fig.3 presents a general step of our methods.Starting from a boundary description obtained through a shape extraction algorithm, we first parameterize the boundary to obtain a discrete complex signal.Then, and the U descriptors of the signal are computed. Finally, these coefficients are normalized so as to achieve the invariance we are interested in and are then stored in the database. At query time, the shape descriptor of the query object is obtained in the same way. The two descriptors are then compared using the Euclidean distance.

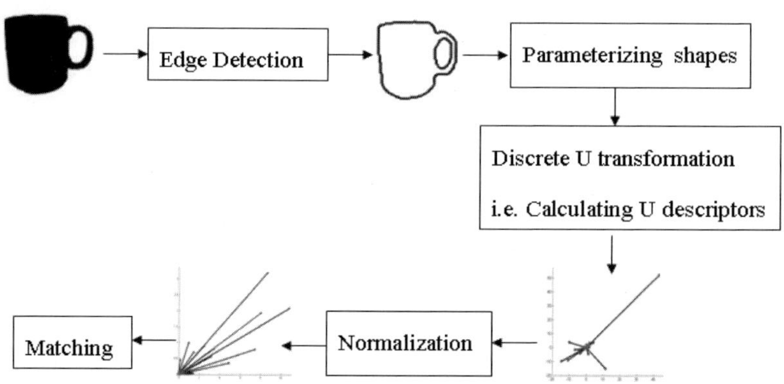

Fig. 3. Basic step for matching shapes

5 Experimental Results

In this section, we will give some experimental results.

Experiment 1. In this experiment, we used images from an existing data base [22][23]. These images are the boundary of 128×128 pixel sized black and white images, The Spectrum and normalized spectrum are shown in below fig.4 for different 10 fish shapes. The Euclidean distance of 10 shapes in the U-system are shown in table 1.

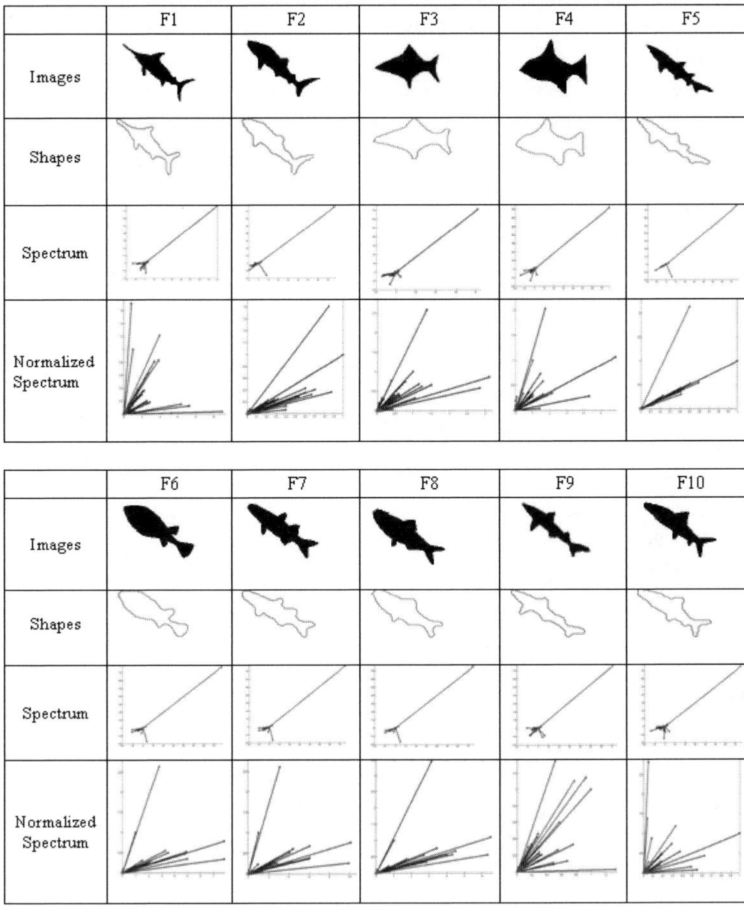

Fig. 4. Shapes analysis for 10 fishes

Table 1. The Euclidean distance of 10 shapes in the U-system

dis	F1	F2	F3	F4	F5	F6	F7	F8	F9	F10
F1	0	15.574	13.5	12.655	16.169	8.9393	10.062	7.9639	15.691	16.239
F2	15.574	0	2.4586	6.3221	0.20227	13.703	17.859	10.362	0.66006	0.72838
F3	13.5	2.4586	0	2.8324	3.2713	10.765	14.838	8.3386	1.8579	3.5179
F4	12.655	6.3221	2.8324	0	6.9038	7.2808	11.228	4.5853	5.7705	6.8536
F5	16.169	0.20227	3.2713	6.9038	0	14.691	18.815	11.361	0.38495	0.90847
F6	8.9393	13.703	10.765	7.2828	14.691	0	4.1531	1.8295	12.566	14.268
F7	10.062	17.859	14.838	11.228	18.815	4.1531	0	5.6437	16.692	18.362
F8	7.9639	10.362	8.3386	4.5853	11.361	1.8295	5.6437	0	9.6048	12.077
F9	15.695	0.660066	1.8597	5.7705	0.38495	12.566	16.692	9.6048	0	0.24734
F10	16.239	0.72838	3.5197	6.8536	0.90847	14.268	18.362	12.077	0.24734	0

Experiment 2. In this experiment, the group of images consists of 7 tools. Their normalized spectrum results are shown in Fig.5. The Euclidean distance of 7 shapes in the U-system are shown in table 2.According to their the Euclidean distance, matching of tools are shown in Fig.6.The first column shows the best match, second column the second-best match and so on. As the matching of any shape with itself matches 0, the fist column also represents the shapes to be matched.

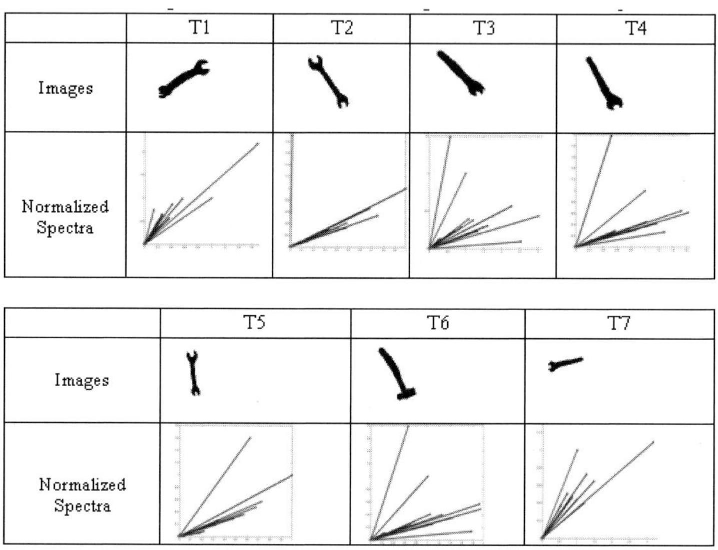

Fig. 5. Shapes analysis for 7 tools

Table 2. The Euclidean distance of 7 shapes in the U-system

dis	T1	T2	T3	T4	T5	T6	T7
T1	0	0.76836	3.7036	2.2414	0.019327	2.7259	1.4794
T2	0.76836	0	3.965	2.1644	0.33331	3.0702	2.7543
T3	3.7032	3.965	0	1.6308	4.0936	1.1396	3.1096
T4	2.2414	2.1644	1.6308	0	1.6477	0.61201	1.8556
T5	0.019327	0.33331	4.0936	1.6477	0	2.7848	2.2994
T6	8.9393	13.703	10.765	7.2828	14.691	0	4.1531
T7	1.4794	2.7543	3.1096	1.8556	2.2994	2.1324	0

6 Conclusions and Future Work

We introduced a new way to represent and compare shapes based on U-system. Using U-system with finite items, it can be realized exactly representation of shapes. So U-system is suitable for shapes analysis. In theory, we have proved that normalized frequency and normalized energy for the same shapes are

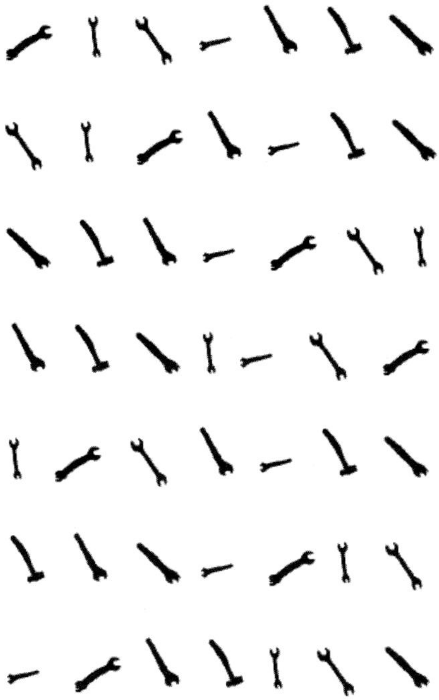

Fig. 6. Matching of tools

invariant in geometric transforms, such as rotation, translation, scale transforms. Examples show the usability of the proposed method.

In the theories and applications of communication and signal processing, U-system is the basic and important math tool. So, Future work will focus on improvement of our algorithm and on the influence of alternative difference measures besides the Euclidean distance.

Acknowledgments

We thank anonymous reviewers for their suggestions and comments. This work is supported by "Mathematics mechanization method and its application on Information Technology" (the National Grand Fundamental Research 973 Program of China under Grant No.2004CB3180000) , the National Natural Science Foundation of China (No.60133020) and Guangdong Provincial Science and Technology Foundation (No.2004A10302005, No.051Z205005).

References

1. T. Pavlidis,*A Review of Algorithms for Shape Analysis.* Computer Vision, Graphics, and Image Processing.**7** (1978), 243-258.
2. Y. Rui, A.C. She, and T.S. Huang,*Modified Fourier Descriptors for Shape Representation-A Practical Approach.* Proc. First Int'l Workshop Image Databases and Multi Media Search. Aug.1996, 22-23.

3. W.-Y. Ma and B.S. Manjunath, *NeTra:A Toolbox for Navigating Large Image Databases.* Multimedia Systems. **7(3)** (1999), 184-198.
4. S. Berretti, A. Del Bimbo, and P. Pala,*Retrieval by Shape Similarity with Perceptual Distance and Effective Indexing.*IEEE Trans. Multimedia.**2(4)** (2000),225-239.
5. Ilaria Bartolini, Paolo Ciaccia and Marco Patella, *WARP: Accurate Retrieval of Shapes Using Phase of Fourier Descriptors and Time Warping Distance.*IEEE Transactions on Pattern Analysis And Machine Intelligence.**27(1)** (2005),142-147.
6. Chong Zhongkan,*Orthogonal functions and its applications.*1982.
7. Henning F. Harmuth, *Sequency Theory Foundations and Applications.*1977.
8. Yuyu Feng , Dongxu Qi, *A Sequence of Piecewise Orthogonal Polynomials.* J. of SIAM J. Math. Anal. **15(4)** (1984), 834–844.
9. Charles A. Micchelli and Yuesheng Xu, *Using the Matrix Refinement Equation for the Construction of Wavelets on Invariant Sets.* Applied and Computational Harmonic Analysis. **1** (1994), 391–401.
10. G. Battle, *Wavelets of Federbush-Lemarie type.* preprint, 1993
11. P. Federbush, *A mass zero cluster expansion.* Part 1, The expansion, Comm.Math.Phys. **81** (1981), 327–340.
12. Qi Dongxu, Feng Yuyu, *On the Convergence of Fourier-U Series.* J. of University of Science and Technology of China,Issue of Math.... **5** (1983), 7–17.
13. Qi Dongxu, Feng Yuyu, *On the Orthogonal Complete system U.* Acta.Scientiarum Naturalium Universitatis Jilinensis **2** (1984), 21–31.
14. Zhang Qishan, Zhang Youguang, *The Theory of Bridge Function and Its Application.*Beijing: National Defence Industry Press, 1992 (in Chinese).
15. Dongxu Qi,*Frequency Spectrum Analysis in Digital Geometry (Special report).*Hefei City,2005.
16. Dongxu Qi,Chenjun Tao,Ruixia Song, Hui Ma, Wei Sun, Zhanchuan Cai, *Representation for a Group of Parametric Cures Based on the Orthogomal Complete U-system.*J. of Computer,2005(accepted).
17. Hui Ma, Ruixia Song, Chenjun Tao, Dongxu Qi,*Orthogonal Complete U-system and Its Application in CAGD.*the first Korea-Chin Joint Conference on Geometric and Visual Computing,2005(accepted).
18. Ruixia Song, Hui Ma, Dongxu Qi, *A New Class of Complete Orthogonal Functions and Its Applications Based on U-system.*The 4th International Conference on Wavelet Analysis and Its Applications2005(accepted).
19. Y.Y.Feng and D.X.Qi,*On the Harr and Walsh Systems on a Triangle.*MRC Technical Summary Report No.2235, University of Wisconsin-Madison, 1981.
20. H. Kauppinen, T. Seppanen, and M. Pietikainen, *An Experimental Comparison of Autoregressive and Fourier-Based Descriptors in 2D Shape Classification.*IEEE Trans. Pattern Analysis and Machine Intelligence.**17(2)** (1997), 201-207.
21. D. Zhang and G. Lu,*A Comparative Study of Fourier Descriptors for Shape Representation and Retrieval.*Proc. Fifth Asian Conf. Computer Vision(ACCV'02). Jan.2002, 646-651.
22. M. Pelillo, K. Siddiqi, and S. Zucker,*Matching hierarchical structures using association graphs.*IEEE Transactions on Pattern Analysis and Machine Intelligence. **21(11)** (1999),1105-1120.
23. T.B. Sebastian, P.N. Klein, and B. B. Kimia,*Recognition of shapes by editing shock graphs.*In Proceedings of the 8th International Conference on Computer Vision (2001).2001,755-762.

Appendix

(1) The proof of theorem 1

Proof. Here, we only give the proof of translation transform. The others are similar. if $P^{'}(t) = P(t) + P_0$ then

$$\begin{aligned}\lambda_j^{'} &= \int_0^1 (P(t) + P_0)U_j dt \\ &= \int_0^1 P(t)U_j dt + \int_0^1 P_0 U_j dt \\ &= \lambda_j + P_0\delta_k\end{aligned}$$

where $\delta_k = \begin{cases} 0, \, k \neq 0 \\ 1, \, k = 0 \end{cases}$

(2) The proof of theorem 2

Proof. Supposed shapes rotated by θ circled coordinates axes x, then $x^{'} = x\cos\theta - y\sin\theta, y^{'} = y\cos\theta + x\sin\theta$,

So $(\lambda_j)_x^{'} = \int_0^1 (x(t)\cos\theta - y(t)\sin\theta)U_j dt$
$= \cos\theta \int_0^1 x(t)U_j dt \; - \; \sin\theta \int_0^1 y(t)U_j dt$
$= (\cos\theta)(\lambda_j)_x - (\sin\theta)(\lambda_j)_y$.

The same as, $(\lambda_j^{'})_y = (\cos\theta)(\lambda_j)_y - (\sin\theta)(\lambda_j)_x$.

So $((\lambda_j^{'})_x)^2 + ((\lambda_j^{'})_y)^2 = ((\lambda_j)_x)^2 + ((\lambda_j)_y)^2$.

That is , $E^{'} = E$.

(3) The proof of theorem 3

Proof.

Let $\lambda_j^{'}$ be obtained fromλ_j , $\lambda_j$translated byP_0 and scaled by γ. The corresponding $\lambda_j^{'}$ is

$\lambda_j^{'} = \int_0^1 \gamma(P(t) + P_0)U_j dt$
$= \gamma[\int_0^1 (P(t)U_j dt + \int_0^1 P_0 U_j dt]$
$= \gamma(\lambda_j + P_0\delta_k)$, where $\delta_k = \begin{cases} 0, \, k \neq 0 \\ 1, \, k = 0 \end{cases}$

So $NF_j^{'} = \frac{||\lambda_j^{'}||}{||\lambda_1^{'}||} = \frac{||\lambda_j||}{||\lambda_1||} = NF_j$.

that is, normalized frequency is invariant in translation, scale transform.

Similarly, it is easily proved that normalized frequency is invariant in rotation transform.

(4) The proof of theorem 4

Proof. Here, we only give the proof of translation transform. The others are similar.

if $z_1(n) = z(n) + z_0$ then

$$\begin{aligned}\lambda_1(k) &= \sum_{n=0}^{N-1} z(n)U_k(\frac{n}{N-1}) + \sum_{n=0}^{N-1} z_0 U_k(\frac{n}{N-1}) \\ &= \lambda(k) + z_0 \sum_{n=0}^{N-1} U_k(\frac{n}{N-1}) \\ &= \lambda(k) + N z_0 \delta(k)\end{aligned}$$

So, $\lambda_1(k) = \lambda(k) + N z_0 \delta(k)$, $\delta(k) = \begin{cases} 0, \, k \neq 0 \\ 1, \, k = 0 \end{cases}$

(5) The proof of theorem 5

Proof. Let $z^{'}(n)$ be a shape obtained from $z(n)$: $z^{'}(n)$ translated by z_0 , rotated by θ, and scaled by γ . The corresponding normalized U descriptors of $z^{'}(n)$ is

$$\begin{aligned}\lambda^{'}(k) &= \sum_{n=0}^{N-1} (z(n) + z_0)\gamma e^{i\theta} U_k(\frac{n}{N-1}) \\ &= (\sum_{n=0}^{N-1} (z(n) + z_0) U_k(\frac{n}{N-1}))\gamma e^{i\theta} \\ &= (\sum_{n=0}^{N-1} z(n)U_k(\frac{n}{N-1}) + \sum_{n=0}^{N-1} z_0 U_k(\frac{n}{N-1}))\gamma e^{i\theta} \\ &= (\lambda(k) + N z_0 \delta(k))\gamma e^{i\theta}, \quad \delta(k) = \begin{cases} 0, \, k \neq 0 \\ 1, \, k = 0 \end{cases}\end{aligned}$$

So $du^{'}(k) = \frac{||\lambda^{'}(k)||}{||\lambda^{'}(1)||} = \frac{||\lambda(k)||}{||\lambda(1)||} = du(k)$, that is, normalized U descriptors are invariant in rotation, translation, scale transform.

Electric Field Force Features-Harmonic Representation for 3D Shape Similarity

Yujie Liu[1,2,3], Zongmin Li[1], and Hua Li[2]

[1] School Of Computer Science And Communication Engineering, China University Of Pe-troleum, Dongying 257062, P.R. China
[2] Institute of Computing Technology Chinese Academy of Science, Beijing 100080, P.R. China
[3] Graduate School of Chinese Academy of Science, Beijing 100039, P.R. China
{yjliu, zmli, lihua}@ict.ac.cn

Abstract. This paper proposes a novel shape representation "electric force features", which is based on electric field theory. This representation has several benefits. First, it is invariant to scale and rigid transform. Second, it can represent complex and ill-defined models because of its physical background. 3D model supposed as charged body, we get the electric field force distribution by placing some testing charges around the 3D model. The force distribution is the feature of the 3D model. Orientation invariance is achieved by calculating the spherical harmonic transform of this distribution. The experiments illuminate that this representation has high discriminating power.

1 Introduction

With the development of advanced 3D hardware and software, such as laser range finder and stereo, 3Dmax, AUTOCAD, and the rise in computational processing power, the types of 3D models are increasing fast. So it leads us to the need to compare and recognize 3-D models. Object comparison is the key technique in applications such as shape similarity based 3-D objects matching, recognition and categorization [FM][OO][SM][TV].

The difficulty of automatic annotation[MK] demonstrates the advantage of using shape-based matching methods over text-based methods for retrieval of 3D models.

Many features are characteristic of 3D models, such as shape, color and texture. As the color and texture information tend to be affected by the environment, the shape of 3D models carries the basic information of 3D models. Geometric models include boundary and voxel representation, CSG trees, point clouds, range images and implicit functions, among which polygonal mesh is the most common way of representing 3D models.

The shape descriptors are usually extracted from the geometric models to be used directly for comparison. Ideally, these descriptors should be scale and rigid transform invariant, capable of good discriminability, robust to noise, and

H.-P. Seidel, T. Nishita, and Q. Peng (Eds.): CGI 2006, LNCS 4035, pp. 221–230, 2006.

independent of specific geometric representations. Not many current descriptors fit all these criteria.

In this paper, electric field theory is used to define a kind of electric force features. 3D models being assumed as charged object, we get the electric force distribution by setting many fixed testing electric charges around the 3D model. According to the uniqueness principle, the electric force distribution is the feature of the 3D model. In order to achieve oriented invariance, we translate the electric features to spherical harmonic representation, and then construct matrix descriptor. Examples are included.

The rest of this paper is organized as follows. After summarizing related approaches in Section 2, we describe the electric principal theory in Section 3. Section 4 illustrates the electric force features vector and spherical harmonic representation. In Section 5, we present some object comparison and retrieval results. We provide concluding remarks in Section 6.

2 Relative Work

Some most related shape matching methods will be discussed briefly In the following.

Osada et al. [OF] introduce and compare shape distributions. The main idea is to randomly select points on the surface of a 3D model, compute certain geometric proper-ties including distance, angle, area, volume, and create a histogram of obtained values. They evaluate the similarity between the models using a pseudo-metric which measures distances between distributions. The authors suggest that the best choice of the geometric function is D2 (the distance between two random points on the surface). In their experiments the D2 shape distribution measuring distances between random surface points is most effective.

The skeletons of 3D models are extracted using the topology-based approach in [HS][SS]. And then some graph matching algorithms are used for shape comparison. Al-though these approaches are flexible and can be used for matching deformable models, the time-consuming nature prevents the methods from real time applications. And, the topology matching process is difficult to accelerate, which will be problematic for large databases.

Vranić et al. [VS] propose the use of feature vectors based on spherical harmonic analysis. They uses ray casting from the centroid of a model in the directions per latitude and longitude to estimate 3D shape. Then distances from the centroid to the intersection points in each concentric shell are used to define the spherical functions. The methods employed by articles [LS][LP] improve this kind of feature.

In [QH], Quan et al resolve image identify from the electric field position. Detection techniques and the corner points achieve the edge of binary image by polygonal ap-proximation, and then the electric field characters are derivate. By normalizing observation points, they get the feature vector.Effective is confirmed through deduction and experiments.

3 Electric Field Theory

Each electrically charged object generates an electric field, which permeates the space around it, and exerts pushes or pulls whenever it comes in contact with other charged objects. The electric field around an object with electric charge is unique. The electric field is related to the object's size, the density of electric charge and the shape of the object. And this electric field is responsive for the object. So, if there is any difference between the objects, the electric field around the objects varies correspondingly. We can differentiate the object according to the electric field.

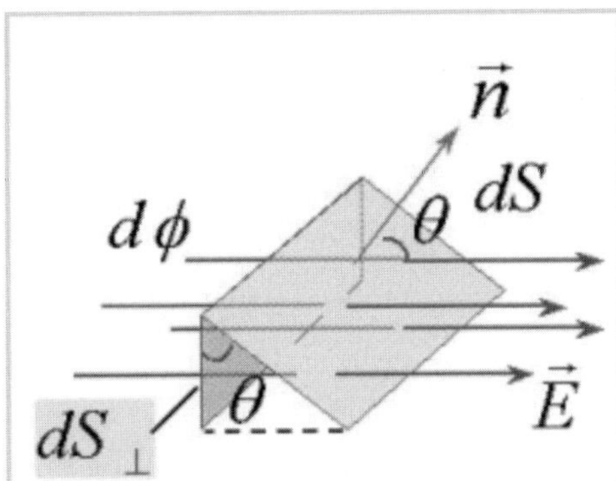

Fig. 1. Intensity of electric field

Intensity of electric field created by the object with continue charges is:

$$\mathbf{E} = \int_{\mathbf{S}} \mathbf{dE} = \int_{\mathbf{S}} \frac{\mathbf{dq}}{4\pi\varepsilon_0 \mathbf{r}^2}\mathbf{r} \tag{1}$$

where $dq = \sigma ds$,σ is the density of electric charge, ε_0 is coulomb's constant. r is the distance between the position and the integral cell, $\mathbf{r}$ is the direction vector.

And multiple charge particles is:

$$\mathbf{E} = \sum_{\mathbf{i}} \mathbf{E_i} = \sum_{\mathbf{i}}^{\mathbf{n}} \frac{\mathbf{dq}}{4\pi\varepsilon_0 \mathbf{r_i^2}}\mathbf{r_i} \tag{2}$$

The Coulomb's law describes the force exerted by electric field. The force of charge q in the electric field is:

$$\mathbf{F} = \mathbf{E} \cdot \mathbf{q} \tag{3}$$

4 Electric Force Features

In this section, we introduce the Electric field force features-harmonic representation for 3-D shapes. The electric force features have the invariant properties and can sufficiently testify 3-D shape similarity estimation.

4.1 Electric Field Around the 3D Model

In this section, the electric field simulated by the 3D model is illustrated.

The polygonal meshes are used to represent 3D models. And we can iterate through all polygons splitting them into triangle. In what follows, we illustrate the problem by using triangle mesh representation.

We regard a given triangle mesh as consisting of a set of triangles $T = \{T_0, T_1, T_2, \cdots, T_{m-1}\}$,$T_i \in R^3$,where m is the number of triangles.

Given by a set of vertices $P = \{\mathbf{p_i} | \mathbf{p_i} = (x_i, y_i, z_i) \in R^3, 0 \leq i < n\}$,where n is the number of vertices.

And a list of indices of three vertices for each triangle $L = \{(A_i, B_i, C_i) | A_i, B_i, C_i \in \{0, 1, 2, \cdots, n-1\}, 0 \leq i < m\}$.

Calculate the triangle mesh area:$area = \{tri\_area_0, tri\_area_1, \cdots, tri\_area_m\}$.

The total area of the model mesh is:

$$Area = \sum_{i=0}^{m-1} tri\_area_i \tag{4}$$

Every triangle mesh area is normalized using the total area,

$$no\_tri\_area_i = \frac{tri\_area_i}{Area} \tag{5}$$

Let $tri\_cen_i = (cx_i, cy_i, cz_i)$,$i = 0, 1, \cdots, m-1$ be the centroid of the ith triangle mesh.

The electric field of 3D model is made up of a set of electric particles, which are located at the centroid of triangle mesh, and the charge of each particle is proportionate to the area of the triangle mesh.

$\{ele\_par_i | Loc(ele\_par_i) = tri\_cen_i, Cha(ele\_par_i) = \varepsilon_0 \times no\_tri\_area_i, 0 \leq i < m\}$, $Loc(\cdot)$ represents the location of the particle, and $Cha(\cdot)$ is the charge of the particle.

The intensity of point $p(x, y, z)$ in the electric field can be obtained from Coulomb's law:

$$E_x = \sum_{i=0}^{m} \frac{\varepsilon_0 \times no\_tri\_area_i \times (x - x_i)}{((x - x_i)^2 + (y - y_i)^2 + (y - y_i)^2)^{\frac{3}{2}}} \tag{6}$$

$$E_y = \sum_{i=0}^{m} \frac{\varepsilon_0 \times no\_tri\_area_i \times (y - y_i)}{((x - x_i)^2 + (y - y_i)^2 + (y - y_i)^2)^{\frac{3}{2}}} \tag{7}$$

$$E_z = \sum_{i=0}^{m} \frac{\varepsilon_0 \times no\_tri\_area_i \times (z - z_i)}{((x - x_i)^2 + (y - y_i)^2 + (y - y_i)^2)^{\frac{3}{2}}} \tag{8}$$

where ε_0 is coulomb's constant,$i = 0, 1, 2, \cdots, m-1$.

4.2 Setting the Testing Charge

In order to get the electric field features, we set some testing electric charge around the 3D model.

First, calculate the centroid of the model,

$$\mathbf{X} = \{(\mathbf{x}, \mathbf{y}, \mathbf{z}) | \mathbf{x} = \frac{\mathbf{M_{100}}}{\mathbf{M_{000}}}, \mathbf{y} = \frac{\mathbf{M_{010}}}{\mathbf{M_{000}}}, \mathbf{z} = \frac{\mathbf{M_{001}}}{\mathbf{M_{000}}}\} \tag{9}$$

Where, $M_{lpq} = \sum_{i=0}^{L} \sum_{j=0}^{P} \sum_{k=0}^{Q} x_i^l \times y_j^p \times z_k^q$.

Second move the center of mass of mesh models to the origin of the coordinate system,Scaled by the max radius, the model is translated into the unit sphere.

$$\mathbf{p_i} = \frac{\mathbf{1}}{\delta} \times (\mathbf{p_i} - \mathbf{X}) \tag{10}$$

where,δ is the radius of the farthest vertice.

Fig. 2. Testing electric charge positioning

Then define the sampling points,$\{(r, \theta_i, \phi_j) | \theta_i = (i+0.5) \times \frac{\pi}{N_s}, \phi_j = (j+0.5) \times \frac{2\pi}{N_s}, 1 \leq i, j \leq N_s\}$,where,$N_s \in Z^+$ is called sampling rate.
Which is illustrated in fig. 2.

4.3 Calculation of the Electric Field Force

We set testing charges on the testing point. The charge of testing charge is $tc_0 = tc_1 = \cdots = tc_{n-1} = q_0, n = N_s \times N_s$.

Then the force of testing charge in the electric field is calculated as follow, $X = r \times \cos\phi \times \sin\theta, Y = r \times \cos\phi \times \cos\theta, Z = r \times \sin\phi$.

Then,

$$F^x(\theta, \phi) = \sum_{i=0}^{m} \frac{\varepsilon_0 \times no\_tri\_area_i \times q \times (x - x_i)}{((x - x_i)^2 + (y - y_i)^2 + (y - y_i)^2)^{\frac{3}{2}}} \tag{11}$$

$$F^y(\theta,\phi)=\sum_{i=0}^{m}\frac{\varepsilon_0\times no\_tri\_area_i\times q\times(y-y_i)}{((x-x_i)^2+(y-y_i)^2+(y-y_i)^2)^{\frac{3}{2}}} \tag{12}$$

$$F^z(\theta,\phi)=\sum_{i=0}^{m}\frac{\varepsilon_0\times no\_tri\_area_i\times q\times(z-z_i)}{((x-x_i)^2+(y-y_i)^2+(y-y_i)^2)^{\frac{3}{2}}} \tag{13}$$

$$F^r(\theta,\phi)=((F^x)^2+(F^y)^2+(F^z)^2)^{\frac{1}{2}} \tag{14}$$

then we get four feature vectors: $\{F^x(\theta_i,\phi_j)\}$,$\{F^y(\theta_i,\phi_j)\}$,$\{F^z(\theta_i,\phi_j)\}$, $\{F^r(\theta_i,\phi_j)\}$,$i=1,2,\cdots,N_s-1, j=1,2,\cdots,N_s-1$.

4.4 Spherical Harmonic Transform

Spherical harmonic decomposition is used to translate directional shape features to rotation invariant forms.

We give two main mathematical properties of spherical harmonic in the following. You can find more detailed descriptions in [PH][HR].

Property 1: A spherical function $f(\theta,\phi)$ could be decomposed as a series of spherical harmonic functions $Y_l^m(\theta,\phi)$

$$f(\theta,\phi)=\sum_{l=0}^{\infty}\sum_{m=-l}^{l}a_{l,m}Y_l^m(\theta,\phi) \tag{15}$$

Property 2: The harmonics with a fixed l constitute a subspace under rotation transforms:

$$R(Y_l^m(\theta,\phi))=\sum_{l=0}^{\infty}a_{l,t}Y_l^t(\theta,\phi),\ \sum_{t=-l}^{l}|a_{l,t}^2|=1 \tag{16}$$

Here, R is an arbitrary rotation.[LS][LP]

Now, the component of electric field force and the resultant force can be regarded as spherical function defined on the unit sphere respectively.

Using spherical harmonic analysis, the electric field force can be expressed:

$$F(\theta,\phi)=\sum_{l=0}^{\infty}\sum_{m=-l}^{l}f_{l,m}Y_l^m(\theta,\phi) \tag{17}$$

where $Y_l^m(\theta,\phi)$ is spherical harmonic,$f_{l,m}=<F(\theta,\phi),Y_l^m(\theta,\phi)>$.

We suppose that $F(\theta,\phi)$ is limited frequency, and first N frequency is used. We get formula (18)

$$F(\theta,\phi)=\sum_{l=0}^{N}\sum_{m=-l}^{l}f_{l,m}Y_l^m(\theta,\phi) \tag{18}$$

The electric field force harmonic representation is defined on the base of spherical harmonic coefficients. It is a matrix descriptor E.

$$E = \{a_l^i\}_{4 \times N} \tag{19}$$

Where,$a_l^i = \sqrt{\sum_{m=-l}^{l} f_{lm}^i(\theta, \phi)}$.

By the above definition, a_l^i is the energy sum of the $F^i(\theta, \phi), i \in \{x, y, z, r\}$ in the frequency l . It is proved that the descriptor is invariant to rotation, translation and scaling.

The L2-norm is used to measure the dissimilarity between two different feature matrices. That is:

$$Dissimilarity = \sqrt{\sum_{i=1}^{4} \sum_{l=0}^{N_s} (a_l^i - \widehat{a}_l^i)^2} \tag{20}$$

The calculating electric field force time is proportional to the number of the testing charge, $t_e = O(N_s^2 \times M)$, while the time needed for spherical harmonics transform can be expressed as $t_{sh} = O(N_s^3)$. We can write the total time complexity as $t_{total} = O(N_s^2 \times M) + O(N_s^3)$, where N_s is the sampling rate, and M is the number of the triangle mesh of the model.

5 Experiments

In this section, we illuminate the retrieval results of our method (EFSH), which is implemented on our prototype 3D retrieval system. The 113 models, which we use, come from Princeton shape benchmark.

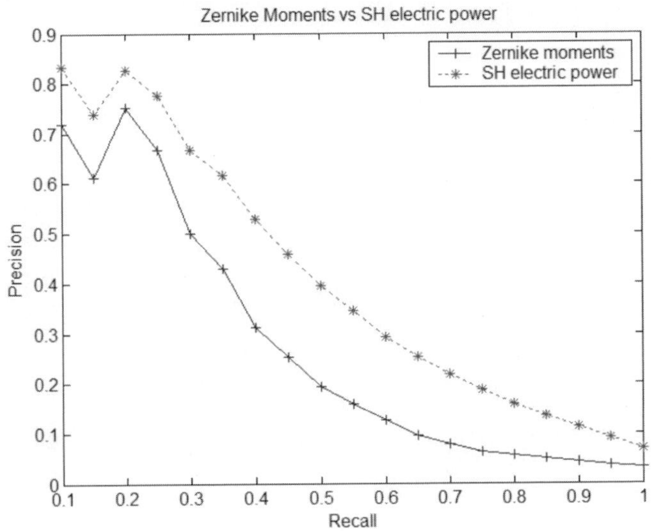

Fig. 3. Precision-recall curve. The blue curve is the result of Zernike moments, and the red is the result in this paper.

Fig. 4. Examples of 3-D object retrieval. In each row, the first model is the input sample object, the others is the most similar object retrieved on order. The word under the picture is the name of the model.

The features of the models in the database are precomputed and stored. In the experiment, the sampling rate is 256. The average time spent is computing descriptor is about 168.448 second for each model. This performance is tested on P4 2.0GHZ PC with 256 MB memory.

Because spherical harmonic transform is also used in Zernike moments, we compare our method with Zernike moments. The average precision-recall curves over all classes are shown in fig. 3. Including Zernike moments (blue curve) and EFSH (red curve). We can see that EFSH has much better performance than Zernike moments descriptors.

And some of the retrieval results are demonstrated in fig. 4.

6 Conclusions and Future Work

In this paper, we study the 3D model retrieval from the point of view of physics, present the electric field force-based descriptor of 3D model, and construct rotated invariant using spherical harmonic transform.

The major advantage of our method is that it avoids the instability and ambiguity in specifying the intersections of rays. Because the shape descriptor proposed in this paper is from physical point, it gets a spherical function on the basis of electric theory, and apples spherical harmonics to achieve invariant,it suits complex, ill-defined polygon-soup models, and then suitable for many special applications of 3D shape retrieval.

There are two major shortcomings: (1) it only captures the global shape, and (2) it is dependent on the shape and distribution of the meshes of the models.

In the future, we would like to test the performance of our shape descriptor on large available 3D shape repositories, which contains more general 3D models than our experiment database.

Acknowledgment

This work was supported by National Key Basic Research Plan (grant No: 2004CB318000).

References

[FM] T. Funkhouser, P. Min, M. Kazhdan, J. Chen, A. Halderman, D. Dobkin, and D. Jacobs.: A search engine for 3D models.ACM Transactions on Graphics, 22(1),2003:83-105

[OO] R. Ohbuchi, T. Otagiri, M. Ibato, and T. Takei.:Shape Similarity search of three-dimensional models using parameterized statistics. In Pacific Conference on Computer Graphics and Application(PG'02), 2002:265-274.

[SM] P. Shilane, K. Michael, M. Patrick, and T. Funkhouser:The Princeton Shape Benchmark. International Conference on Shape Modeling(SMI'04), IEEE Computer Society Washing-ton,2004:167-178

[TV] J. Tangelder and R. Veltkamp:A Survey of Content Based 3D Shape Retrieval Methods, International Conference on Shape Modeling(SMI'04), IEEE Computer Society Washing-ton,2004:145-156

[MK] Patrick Min, Michael Kazhdan, and Thomas Funkhouser:A Comparison of Text and Shape Matching for Retrieval of Online 3D Models, In Proc. European Conference on Digital Li-braries, Bath, Springer Berlin,2004:209-220

[OF] R. Osada, T. Funkhouser, B. Chazelle and D. Dobkin.: Shape distribution [J], ACM Transac-tions on Graphics, 21(4) ,2002:807-832

[HS] M. Hilaga, Y. Shinagawa, T. Kohmura and T. L. Kunii:Topology matching for fully auto-matic similarity estimation of 3D shapes, in Proceedings of ACM SIGGRPAH 2001, New York,2001: 203-212

[SS] H. Sundar, D. Silver, Gagvani and S. Dickinson:Skeleton based shape matching and re-trieval, International Conference on Shape Modeling (SMI'03), 2003:130-143.

[VS] D.V. Vranić, D. Saupe, and J. Richter.: Tools for 3D-object retrieval: Karhunen-loeve trans-form and spherical harmonics. In IEEE 2001 Workshop Multimedia Signal Processing, 2001:293-298

[LS] Xinguo Liu, Robin Sun. Sing Bing Kang Heung-Yeung Shum.: Directional Histogram Model for Three-Dimensional Shape Similarity, Proceedings of the 2003 IEEE Computer Society Conference on Computer Vision and Pattern Recognition (CVPR'03)[C],2003:813-820

[LP] Yi Liu, Jiantao Pu, Guyu Xin, Hongbin Zha.: A Robust Method for Shape-based 3D Model Retrieval, IEEE Proceedings of the 12th Pacific Conference on Computer Graphics and Ap-plications (PG'04)[C], 2004:3-9

[QH] Quan Quan, Zhang Hong, Xie Feng-ying.: Educing a new shape identify method form posi-tion of electric field, Journal of image and graphics, 9(7), 2004:798-803(in chinese)

[PH] E. Praun, H. Hoppe.: Spherical parametrization and Remeshing, ACM. Transaction on Graphics, 22(3), 2003:340-349

[HR] D. Healy Jr., D. Rockmore, P. Kostelec and S. Moore.: FFTs for the 2-sphere - improve-ments and variations,The Journal of Fourier Analysis and Applications, 9(4), 2003:341 - 385

A Novel Data Hiding Algorithm Using Normal Vectors of 3D Model

Chung-Hsien Chang, Chung-Ming Wang, Yuan-Yu Tsai, and Yu-Ming Cheng

Institute of Computer Science, National Chung Hsing University, Taichung, Taiwan
{cschang, cmwang, cuckoo, s9156048}@cs.nchu.edu.tw

Abstract. This paper presents a novel data hiding algorithm for 3D polygonal models whose vertices have given normal vectors. The key idea of our algorithm is to embed messages by adjusting the normal vector of a vertex according to the pivot vector. All vertices in a 3D model can be embedded with multiple-bit payloads by using multiple pivot vectors. The distortion is measured by the angle between the adjusted normal vector and the original normal vector to distortion. A distortion coefficient is also introduced to control the distortion rate during the embedding process. Experimental results demonstrate that our algorithm can achieve high data capacity (up to 12 bits per normal vector), and is robust against rotation, translation, and uniform scaling attacks.

1 Introduction

Data hiding is embedding data in other harmless messages and does not allow anyone, except those with the secret key, to detect the secret message. Data hiding [5, 8] usually uses digital multimedia data, such as movies, music, and images, as cover media to embed hidden information. Preferred data hiding algorithms embed as much data as possible and form the stego model with as little distortion as possible. There are different representations used for three-dimensional (3D) models. A 3D model can be described as a set of parametric curves or a collection of defining functions. For example, the equation $x^2+y^2+z^2=1$ describes a sphere with a unit radius in 3D space. More commonly, polygonal meshes are used to represent a 3D model. The normal vector assigned at a vertex is generated automatically in the shading process. Sometimes, to describe the curvature of a surface more precisely, given normal vectors will be associated with vertices. Thus, a vertex in 3D model can be defined as a set of six floating point numbers. For example, $P_x\ P_y\ P_z\ N_x\ N_y\ N_z$ where $(P_x\ P_y\ P_z)$ is the position of the vertex and $(N_x\ N_y\ N_z)$ is the normal of the vertex. Recently, many data hiding and watermarking algorithms have been presented for 3D models. Most of them support polygonal models [1, 2, 3, 6, 7, 11] while a few of them are for point-sampled geometries [4, 10]. Although embedding data into the topology and geometry of models has been explored extensively, its counterpart for normal vectors has not been explored as much as it deserves.

In this paper, we propose a new data hiding technique for 3D models whose vertices have given normal vectors. For each vertex, we embed a payload by adjusting the direction of its normal vector. We use one or multiple pivot vectors as keys for

H.-P. Seidel, T. Nishita, and Q. Peng (Eds.): CGI 2006, LNCS 4035, pp. 231 – 241, 2006.

embedding and extracting data. The angle between a pivot vector and normal vector is used to determine embedded information. The more pivot vectors are involved, the more payloads we can embed. This scheme allows our method to achieve a huge capacity for data hiding. In our algorithm, we leave the position information untainted. Therefore, our method is robust against rotation, uniform scaling, and translation attack.

This paper is organized as follows: section 2 discusses related works. The proposed algorithm including the information embedding process and extracting process is presented in section 3. Section 4 shows experimental results using several models. Conclusions and future work are described in the final section.

2 Related Work

Many watermarking and data hiding techniques have been proposed on 3D models. Aspert et al.[1] proposed an approach which transformed Wagner's watermarking technique[11] into a data hiding algorithm for 3D polygonal meshes. They use small displacements of the vertices in the model to embed the information. Recently, Maret and Ebrahimi[6] made some improvements to [1, 11] by increasing the embedding capacity and reducing the complexity of data extraction. They increased the capacity by adapting the embedding process to the sample distribution in the similarity-transform invariant space. They reduced the complexity of message extraction by making use of a similarity invariant space.

Cayre and Macq[3] described an algorithm for 3D polygonal models in the spatial domain. The message was embedded within the model topology and the key idea was to consider a triangle as a two–state geometrical object. They established a list of admissible triangles from the cover model. The position of a vertex in each admissible triangle was changed or not, according to the embedding bits. Wang and Cheng[9] presented a more efficient approach. They considered every vertex of a triangle as a message vertex and adopted a triangle neighbor table and an advanced jump strategy to assign embedding order to the message vertex quickly. They also defined a metric of distortion evaluation which helped them forecast and control the distortion rate.

Cotting et al.[4] presented a watermarking approach for point-sampled geometry. They embedded watermarks into the low frequency components, and employed statistical methods based on correlation to analyze the extracted watermarks. Wang and Wang[10] proposed two data hiding approaches for point-sampled models. They established a list of intervals for each axis according to the secret key, and embedded a bit into each interval by changing the points' position. They also used a list of macro embedding primitives to achieve higher data capacity.

Most of the abovementioned works presented for data hiding or watermarking are based on the topology and geometry of models. We propose a novel data hiding algorithm that exploits the feature of those 3D models which have given normal vectors. This algorithm provides a huge capacity and resists rotation, translation, and uniform scaling attacks.

3 The Proposed Algorithm

3.1 Basic Idea

There are two vectors $\vec{N}$ and $\vec{V}$ in 3D space and $\vec{V}$ is denoted as a pivot vector. When we want to embed a one bit payload "0", we modify $\vec{N}$ as $\vec{N}'$ where $\lfloor \cos^{-1}(\vec{N}' \cdot \vec{V}) \rfloor \bmod 2 = 0$. The arccosine function returns an angle, denoted as α, in degree where $0° \le \alpha \le 180°$. If $\vec{N}'$ meets the condition $\lfloor \cos^{-1}(\vec{N}' \cdot \vec{V}) \rfloor \bmod 2 = 1$, a one bit payload "1" is hidden in $\vec{N}'$. Geometrically speaking, we categorize the integer part of the angle between a pivot vector and a normal vector into odd and even regions. The odd region indicates that "1" is hidden, and the even region indicates "0". Figure 1 shows the embedding space formed by a pivot vector, $\vec{V}_p$. The embedding criterion subdivides the spherical embedding space into several regions. $\vec{A}$ is in the blue embedding region whose embedding pattern is "1". $\vec{B}$ is in the yellow embedding region whose embedding pattern is "0". That means "1" and "0" are hidden in $\vec{A}$ and $\vec{B}$ respectively. To simplify the illustration, we only show the hemi-spherical embedding space and magnify the scale of one degree. Each region has a corresponding embedding pattern. In figure 1, the blue region has embedding pattern "0" and the yellow region has embedding pattern "1". If $\vec{V}$ is the same in the cover model and the stego model, it is easy to extract the hidden message by testing whether the angle between $\vec{N}$ and $\vec{N}'$ is even or odd. When we use multiple pivot vectors, we can embed a multiple-bit payload by modifying $\vec{N}$ to meet the same criterion for various pivot vectors simultaneously and sequentially.

3.2 Embedding Process

First, we construct a unique coordinate for a model. P_{gc} is the geometric center of all vertices in the model. The closest vertex to P_{gc} is P_{c1}. P_{c2} is the second closest. P_{c3} is the third closest, and so on until $\overline{P_{c1}P_{c2}}$ and $\overline{P_{c1}P_{c3}}$ are not parallel. Then we use $\overline{P_{c1}P_{c2}}$ as X-axis and $\overrightarrow{P_{c1}P_{c2}} \times \overrightarrow{P_{c1}P_{c3}}$ as Z-axis to construct a right-handed coordinate system for this model. Once this unique local coordinate system, denoted the pivot coordinate system, for our model is constructed, we set up the number of pivot vector n_{pv} depending on how many bits we want to hide in a normal vector. The pivot vectors are chosen in respect to the pivot coordinate system. We denote all pivot vectors as $\overrightarrow{V_{pi}}$ *where* $i = 0 \cdots n_{pv} - 1$. The embedded payload is represented as a bitstream given by $(b_i)^N$, where $b_{n_{pv}} b_{n_{pv}-1} b_{n_{pv}-2} \cdots b_1 b_0$ are N binary words of n_{pv} bits each. The embedding procedure modifies the cover normal vector $\vec{N}$ to $\vec{N}'$ so that $\vec{N}'$ must match

$$b_i = \lfloor \cos^{-1}(\overrightarrow{N}' \cdot \overrightarrow{V_{pi}}) \rfloor \bmod 2 \quad where\ i = 0\ to\ n_{pv} - 1 \tag{1}$$

Figure 2 shows the embedding space formed by two pivot vectors. The embedding pattern "00" is hidden in the green region, "01" in the yellow region, "10" in the pink region, and "11" in the orange region. In our algorithm, every vertex in the model can be used to hide data. If a model has n_{vertex}, we can hide at most $n_{pv} * n_{vertex}$ bits in it. The embedding order is simply assigned by the loading order. Consequently, we only use the required number of vertices to hide the data, and leave the others unchanged.

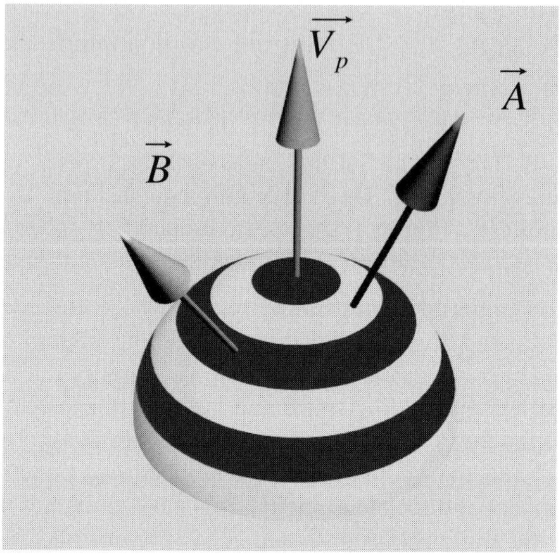

Fig. 1. The embedding space formed by a pivot vector

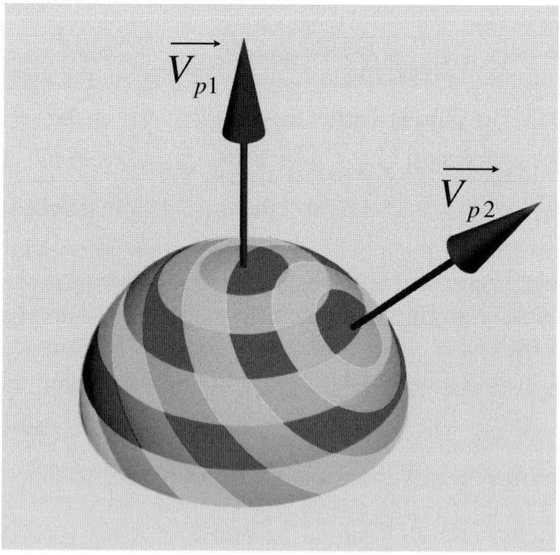

Fig. 2. The embedding space formed by two pivot vectors

Fig. 3. The unbalanced embedding space formed by two pivot vectors that are too close

Fig. 4. Three pivot vectors form the balanced embedding space

Any modification causes distortions and distortions grow with n_{pv} during the embedding process. To control the distortion rate, we introduce a coefficient, denoted as distortion coefficient β and $\beta \in N$. We modify (1) to

$$b_i = \lfloor \beta \cos^{-1}(\overrightarrow{N'} \cdot \overrightarrow{V_{pi}}) \rfloor \bmod 2 \quad where\ i = 0\ to\ n_{pv} - 1 \tag{2}$$

The distortion coefficient subdivides one degree into β parts. Thus, it is easy to control distortions by employing a larger β. Since each adjustment to the normal vector depends on the pivot vectors, each pivot vector must be chosen carefully. If two pivot vectors are too close, they will form an unbalanced embedding space. That means the area of each embedding region will vary widely, which may cause serious distortion. Figure 3 shows an unbalanced embedding space formed by two pivot vectors that are too close. In such cases, the cover normal vector will be over modified. To avoid this, any pair of pivot vectors will be restricted by

$$\left|\cos^{-1}(\vec{V_1}\cdot\vec{V_2})\right| > \cos^{-1}(\frac{1}{\beta}) \tag{3}$$

Figure 4 illustrates three pivot vectors, *(1,0,0)*, *(0,1,0)*, and *(0,0,1)*, forming a balanced embedding space. Since it is difficult to find $\vec{N}'$ analytically, we use a brute-force method. $\vec{N}$ is treated as the pole of a spherical coordinate. $1/\beta$ is the increment for both the azimuthal angle and polar angle. The Following is the pseudo-code of our algorithm:

```
BuildPivotCoordinate( );
for(i=0; i<NUM_VERTEX_USED; i++)
{
     BuildLocalCoordinate( N⃗ );
     for(j=0; j<NUM_PIVOT_VECTOR; j++)
            Pivot2Local( V⃗_pi );
     found= false;
     theta = 1/β;
     do
     {
            for( phi = 0; phi < 360 && !found; phi += 1/β)
            {
                   N⃗_tmp =Spherical2Cartesian(theta, phi);
                   Code = 0;
                   for(k = 0; k < NUM_PIVOT_VECTORS; k++)
                   {
                          angle[k] = ⌊cos^-1(N⃗_tmp · V⃗_pk)*β⌋ );
                          code += (angle[k] mod 2)* 2^k;
                   }
                   if(target == code)
                          found = True;
            }
            theta += 1/β;
```

```
    } while ( !found && theta <= 90);
    Local2Pivot( N_tmp );
    AdjustNormal( N , N_tmp );
}
```

3.3 Extracting Process

Since the positions of vertices are not changed during the embedding process, the pivot coordinate system remains the same for the cover model and the stego model. To be able to extract the payload from a model, the payload extractor will need to know the number of embedded vectors and all pivot vectors. In addition, the distortion coefficient β used during the embedding process is also needed. It is easy to reconstruct the pivot coordinate system used in the embedding process. Thus, the embedded message in each normal vector is extracted by

$$b_i = \lfloor \beta \cos^{-1}(\overrightarrow{N'} \cdot \overrightarrow{V_{pi}}) \rfloor \bmod 2 \quad where\ i = 0\ to\ n_{pv} - 1 \tag{4}$$

The extracting process consists of some simple calculations whose processing time is negligible.

4 Experimental Results

We implemented the proposed algorithm using Microsoft Visual C++ programming language, and collected the experimental results on a personal computer with Pentium IV 3GHz processor and 512 MB RAM. Figure 6 shows the models used in this paper. Bunny, figure 6(a), has 35947 vertices and 69451 faces. Hand, figure 6(b), has 327323 vertices and 654666 faces. Dragon, figure 6(c), has 437645 vertices and 871414 faces. Happy-Buddha, figure 6(d), has 543652 vertices and 1087716 faces.

Table 1 is the result of embedding data in four different models. Each vertex is embedded with a 1 bit payload. It shows that even with a 30,000 bit payload, it only takes 0.8 second to hide the payload in the Bunny model. The processing time is proportional to the length of the payload. Embedding data in other models provides similar results. It takes 0.13, 0.17, and 0.23 second to hide the payload in the Hand, Dragon, and Happy-Buddha models.

For data hiding applications, one of the most important criteria is the embedding capacity. In our algorithm, the normal vector of each vertex in 3D model can be embedded with multiple-bit information depending on the number of pivot vectors. In table 2, Bunny is used as a cover model where 1,000 vertices are used to hide data and the distortion coefficient is set to 1. If we hide 1 bit payload in each vertex, 1,000 bits of payload are embedded. The processing time is 0.03 second. The distortion is 0.951 degree. When we increase the number of bits embedded in each vertex, the processing time and distortion will also increase. However, embedding even up to 12 bits per vertex can still be done under a reasonable processing time. As a result, our method significantly increases the embedding capacity.

Table 1. Embedding data on 3D models. Each vertex is embedded with 1 bit. The distortion coefficient is 1.

Payload (bits)	Processing time (sec.)			
	Bunny	Hand	Dragon	Happy-Buddha
5000	0.11	0.13	0.17	0.23
10000	0.22	0.25	0.33	0.44
15000	0.39	0.44	0.48	0.65
20000	0.48	0.52	0.63	0.84
25000	0.62	0.66	0.78	1.02
30000	0.80	0.89	0.97	1.20

Table 2. Embedding data on Bunny. 1,000 vertices are used. The distortion coefficient is 1.

Bit(s) per vertex	Payload (bits)	Processing time (Sec.)	Average distortion(deg.)
1	1000	0.03	0.951
2	2000	0.13	0.975
3	3000	0.26	1.097
4	4000	0.58	1.367
5	5000	1.11	1.755
6	6000	2.00	2.432
7	7000	3.42	3.580
8	8000	5.68	4.916
12	12000	40.15	23.237

Table 3. Embedding data on Bunny. 1,000 vertices are used. Each vertex is embedded with 8 bits. There are 8,000 bits embedded in the Bunny model.

Distortion coefficient	Processing time (Sec.)	Average distortion (deg.)
1	5.68	4.916
2	10.25	2.411
3	14.98	1.518
4	20.80	1.247
5	25.06	0.985
10	49.05	0.469

The other important criterion is the imperceptibility. When we embed payloads in most data hiding algorithms, we change the cover model and cause distortion. In our algorithm, we use the average of those angles between normal vectors of the cover model and those of the stego model to estimate the distortion caused by the embedding process. The distortion rate rises as embedded payload per vertex increases but we can use the distortion coefficient to control it. In table 3, we embed 8 bits in each vertex, and the distortion coefficient is 1. It causes 4.916 degrees of average distortion. Setting the distortion coefficient to 10, it takes 49.05 seconds and causes only 0.469 degrees of average distortion.

In figure 5, we use the Bunny model which contains 35,947 vertices. Figure 5(a) is the cover model. Figure 5(b) which embedded 3 bits per vertex looks slightly different from 5(a) and its distortion is 0.84 degree where the distortion coefficient is 1.

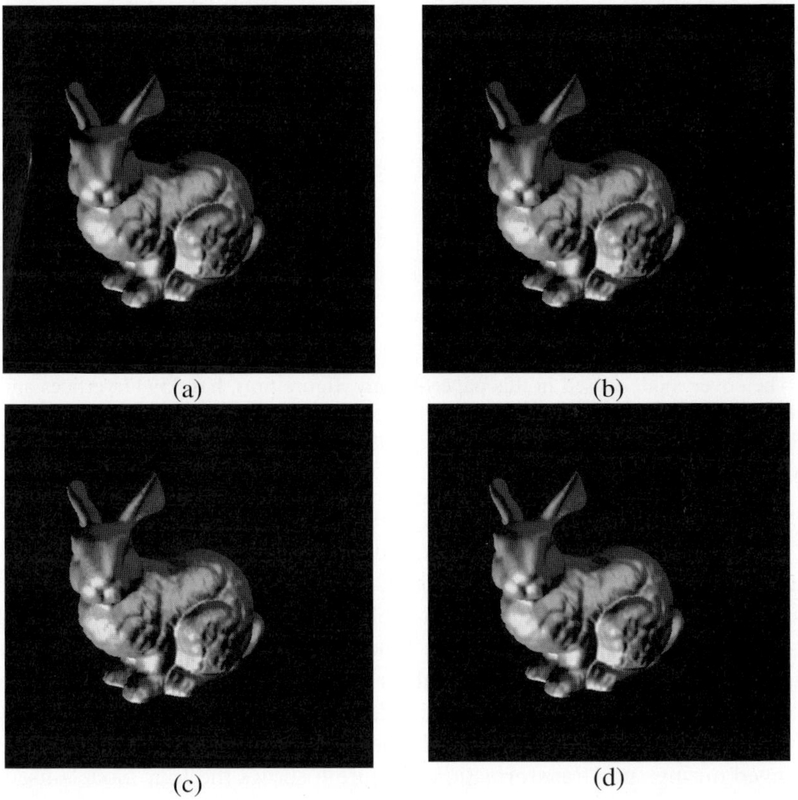

Fig. 5. (a) Bunny has 35,947 vertices and 69,451 faces. (b) There are 3 bits of data hidden in each vertex. The distortion coefficient is 1 and the distortion is 0.84 degree. (c) There are 6 bits of data hidden in each vertex. The distortion coefficient is 1 and the distortion is 2.58 degree. (d) There are 6 bits of data hidden in each vertex. The distortion coefficient is 5 and the distortion is 0.28 degree.

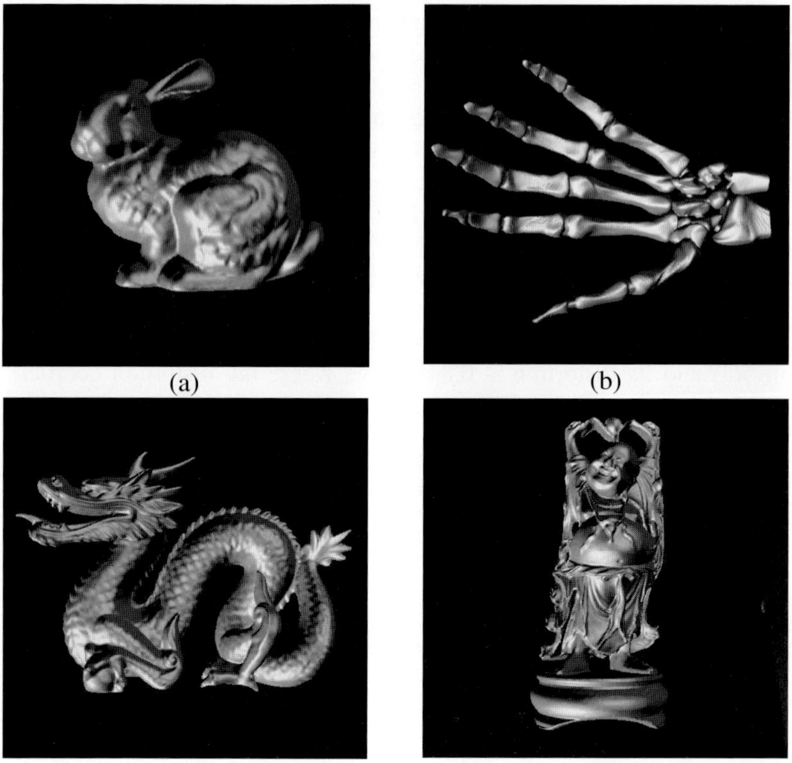

(a) (b) (c) (d)

Fig. 6. The cover models used in this paper. Bunny, figure 6(a), has 35947 vertices and 69451 faces. Hand, figure 6(b), has 327323 vertices and 654666 faces. Dragon, figure 6(c), has 437645 vertices and 871414 faces. Happy-Buddha, figure 6(d), has 543652 vertices and 1087716 faces.

When 6 bits are embedded in one vertex, the distortion is 2.58 degrees and it is obviously distinguishable from the cover model. However, figure 5(d) shows imperceptible distortion by using 5 as the distortion coefficient. Its distortion is only 0.28 degree. Larger distortion coefficients take more time but it reduces more distortion as well. Furthermore, when we apply transformations such as rotations, translations, and uniform scalings, to our stego models, the hidden payload can still be extracted with no error because the relationship between the normal vectors and the pivot coordinate is not changed during such transformations. Figure 6 shows the four models used in our algorithm.

5 Conclusion and Future Work

This paper presents a data hiding algorithm to embed messages on 3D-models whose vertices have given normal vectors. The main feature of our algorithm is huge embedding capacity. Every vertex in a 3D model can be used to hide a multiple-bit payload. According to our experimental results, it can hide 12 bits of payload per vertex. The extracting process is very simple. In our experiments, the extracting process always takes less than 0.1 second. Therefore, the processing time is almost negligible. We also introduce the distortion coefficient to control the distortion rate during the embedding process. Our algorithm resists basic geometric transformations such as translation, uniform scaling, and rotation.

We use a brute-force method to locate the embedding region. Although it can get the resolution in a couple of seconds, it is hard to perform further analysis such as distortion rate forecasting. Future work will focus on finding the embedding region analytically and increasing robustness to resist other attacks.

References

1. Aspert, N., Drelie, E., Maret, Y., Ebrahimi T.: Steganography for Three- Dimensional Polygonal Meshes. In SPIE 47th Annual Meeting (2002) 705-708
2. Benedens, O.: Geometry-Based Watermarking of 3D Models. IEEE Computer Graphics and Applications, Vol. 19, No. 1. (1999) 46-55
3. Cayre, F., Macq, B.: Data Hiding on 3D Triangle Meshes. In IEEE Trans. on Signal Processing, Vol. 51. (2003) 939-949
4. Cotting, D., Weyrich, T., Payly, M., Gross, M.: Robust Watermarking of Point-Sampled Geometry. In Proc. of International Conference on Shape Modeling and Applications 2004 (2004) 233-242
5. Katzenbeisser , S., Petitcolas, F. A. P.: Information Hiding Techniques for Steganography and Digital Watermarking, Artech House London (2000)
6. Maret, Y., Ebrahimi, T.: Data Hiding on 3D Polygonal Meshes. In Proc. of the Multimedia and Security Workshop 2004 (2004) 68-74
7. Ohbuchi, R., Mukaiyama, A., Takahashi, S.: A Frequency-Domain Approach to Watermarking 3D Shapes. Computer Graphics Forum, Vol. 1, No. 3 (2002) 373-382
8. Petitcolas, F. A. P., Anderson, R. J., Kuhn, M. G.: Information Hiding - A Survey. In Proc. of the IEEE, Special Issue on Protection of Multimedia Content, Vol. 87, No. 7. (1999) 1062-1078
9. Wang, C. M., Cheng, Y. M.: An Efficient Information Hiding Algorithm for Polygon Models. Computer Graphics Forum, Vol. 24, No. 3. (2005) 591-600
10. Wang, C. M., Wang, P. C.: Steganography on Point-Sampled Geometry. To Appear in Computers & Graphics (2006)
11. Wagner, M.: Robust Watermarking of Polygonal Meshes. In Proc. of Geometric Modeling and Processing 2000 (2000) 201-208

Shape Matching Based on Fully Automatic Face Detection on Triangular Meshes

Wolfram von Funck, Holger Theisel, and Hans-Peter Seidel

MPI Informatik, 66123 Saarbruecken, Germany
{wfunck, theisel, hpseidel}@mpi-inf.mpg.de

Abstract. This paper tackles a particular shape matching problem: given a data base of shapes (described as triangular meshes), we search for all shapes which describe a human. We do so by applying a 3D face detection approach on the mesh which consists of three steps: first, a local symmetry value is computed for each vertex. Then, the symmetry values in a certain neighborhood of each vertex are analyzed for building sharp symmetry lines. Finally, the geometry around each vertex is analyzed to get further facial features like nose and forehead. We tested our approach with several shape data bases (e.g. the Princeton Shape Benchmark) and achieved high rates of correct face detection.

1 Introduction

Due to the fast development of new 3D scanning and modelling techniques, the number and complexity of surfaces which Computer Graphics deals with is currently dramatically increasing. Because of this, the retrieval and search of shapes in the internet becomes an important and challenging issue. Shape matching aims in choosing shapes of certain characteristics out of a shape data base. These characteristics are usually the similarity to a given shape which is described either as a particular surface, a sketching, or a rather abstract description [1]. Recently, a number of shape matching approaches have been developed which are based on shape histograms [2], extended Gaussian images [3], spherical extend functions [4, 5], shape distributions [6], spherical harmonics [7], light fields [8], 3D Fourier transforms [9], the topology of Reeb graphs [10], or anisotropy [11]. A part-in-whole approach was introduced by [12] which allows searching 3D models with parts matching a query.

The problem we want to tackle in this paper is a particular shape matching problem which can be formulated as follows:

Problem 1. Given a data base of shapes, get all which describe a human.

The main application of this problem relates to the applications of shape matching in general: imagine a user who wants to build up a virtual 3D scene of many different humans in different positions. Instead of modelling them, he or she may search the internet for appropriate shapes.

Figure 1 shows a number of shapes which obviously describe humans in different positions and states of completeness. Contrary, figure 3 shows a number of shapes which do not describe humans. Note that the above-mentioned shape matching approaches detect significantly different shapes in the examples of figure 1. This is due to the fact that we did not make any assumption about the position of the human body. Arms and

H.-P. Seidel, T. Nishita, and Q. Peng (Eds.): CGI 2006, LNCS 4035, pp. 242–253, 2006.

legs may be outstretched (figure 1 (a)) or bent (figure 1 (b)), merged with the rest of the body (figure 1 (c)) or even non-existing at all (figure 1 (d), (e)). Since shape matching algorithms are sensitive against these features, they tend to give a higher similarity for instance between the shapes in figures 1 (a) and 3 (c) than between the shapes 1 (a) and 1 (c). Hence, the above-mentioned shape matching approaches are not suitable for problem 1.

Our starting point for a solution of problem 1 lies in the assumption that a shape describing a human should contain the human's face. (In fact, this seems to be the only property which all examples of figure 1 have in common.) Hence we can reformulate problem 1 to

Problem 2. Given a data base of shapes, find all shapes which contain a human's face.

Note that problem 2 does not make any assumption about size and location of the face. Neither it does about size and resolution of the model. The only assumption we use is that – if the shape describes a human – only one human (and nothing more) is contained in the shape. We also assume that the shapes are described as triangular meshes, and – if a face is present – the part of the mesh representing the face has a disc-like topology, i.e., it is a manifold without holes. Then problem 2 appears to be a *face detection problem* for triangular meshes.

A variety of algorithms for detecting faces in images has been developed which roughly can be classified into knowledge base methods [13, 14], feature based methods [15, 16], template matching [17], and appearance based methods. Having these algorithms available, a straightforward approach to detect faces on meshes is to render the meshes from different view points and then apply 2D face detection methods on the resulting images. However, this approach appears to be not reliable because of two reasons: First, there is no control about how many and which view points to choose for rendering. Second, there is no texture information in the mesh which gives for instance different colors for a face and the surrounding hair. Because of this, we have to apply face detection approaches which work directly on the meshes.

A well-researched problem on triangular meshes is the problem of face recognition [18, 19, 20, 21]. For this class of problems an a-priory knowledge about the location of a face is assumed. In this sense, our problem 2 can be considered as a preceding step of 3D face recognition.

The face of a human is approximately mirror-symmetric. This fact – already used for face detection in 2D images [22] – gives the key of our approach: we search for face symmetry lines as shown in figure 2 (a).

The paper is organized as follows: Section 2 describes our detector for the case that the size (given by a radius) of the face is known. Section 3 extends this to the case of an unknown radius of influence. In section 4 we apply our algorithm to several representative data sets. Section 5 draws conclusions and mentions issues in future research.

2 Our Approach – Single Search Radius

Symmetry is a feature which is well-researched in Computer Vision both for images and for 3D objects. Generally, two kinds of symmetry can be distinguished: rotation and mirror symmetry where for our purposes we are interested in the last-named.

Fig. 1. A collection of human shapes

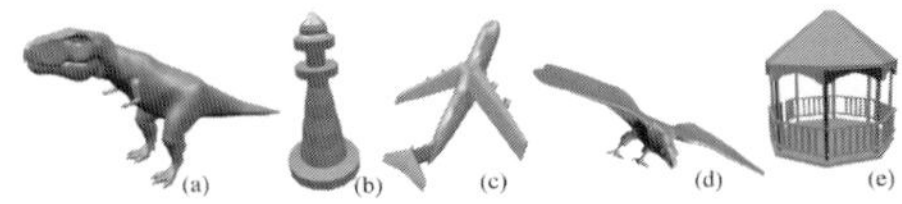

Fig. 3. Non-human shapes

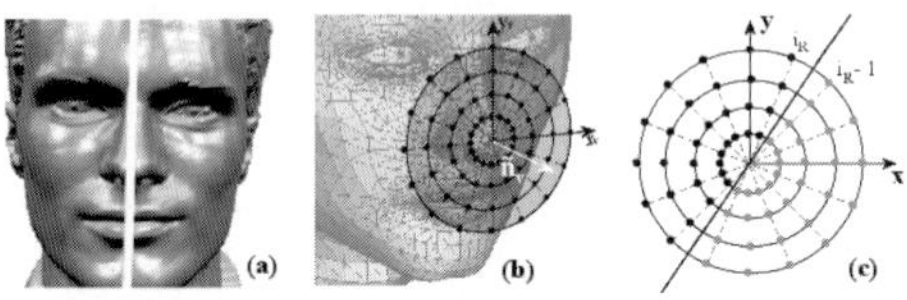

Fig. 2. (a) A face with a symmetry axis. (b) Sampling the surface around vertex v. (c) The mirror axis corresponding to rotation index i_R.

Fig. 4. Some meshes and their symmetry fields

For 2D images, most of the existing work considers symmetry as a binary feature (i.e., and object is symmetric or not [23, 24]). In addition, [25, 26, 22, 27] compute symmetry as a local feature and apply it to detect faces in 2D images. For 3D objects, mirror symmetry is usually considered as a global feature. This means that a main symmetry plane is searched [28], or all symmetry planes through the center of gravity are evaluated [29]. What we need for our purpose is a local symmetry detection on a surface. This means that we need two pieces of information for each surface point: the strength of local symmetry ("how symmetric is the surface at a certain point?"), and the best symmetry axis. These values depend on the choice of a search radius r: only the parts of the surface with a distance smaller than r are incorporated in the local symmetry analysis. Thus, the evaluation of local symmetry is always connected to a particular choice of r. The best detection of a symmetry line in a face can be expected if r is approximately half the diameter of the face. If r is larger, other parts of the human body influence the analysis while a smaller r detects too many symmetry lines on a face.

In this section we describe our symmetry-based face detection approach for the case of a particular given symmetry radius r. This means that we decide whether or not the mesh contains a face of approximately the diameter $2r$. For doing so, we start to compute symmetry values for each vertex.

2.1 Computing the Symmetry Field

Let M be a triangle mesh with vertices $V(M)$. For each vertex $v \in V(M)$, $\mathbf{p}_v$ denotes the vertex position, while $\mathbf{n}_v$ is the (exact or estimated) normal in v. Then let $\text{dist}(\mathbf{p}, \mathbf{d})$ denote the minimum (signed) distance of point $\mathbf{p}$ along direction vector $\mathbf{d}$ to the surface defined by M, where $\text{dist}(\mathbf{p}, \mathbf{d}) = \infty$ if there is no intersection. We compute $\text{dist}(\mathbf{p}, \mathbf{d})$ by a raytracing approach using a kd-tree.

For each vertex v of the mesh, we sample a height field on a circle in the tangent plane through $\mathbf{p}_v$ by measuring the distance in normal direction to the mesh at a number of sample points (figure 2 (b)). In order to discard small-scale variations of the normals, we use an average surface normal $\tilde{\mathbf{n}}_v$ of all vertices which have an Euclidian distance smaller than r:

$$\tilde{\mathbf{n}}_v = \frac{\sum_{u\in N_v} w_u \mathbf{n}_u}{\|\sum_{u\in N_v} w_u \mathbf{n}_u\|} \text{ with } N_v = \{u \in V(M) : \|\mathbf{p}_v - \mathbf{p}_u\| \leq r\}, \tag{1}$$

where w_u is the total area of the triangle fan surrounding vertex u. $\tilde{\mathbf{n}}_v$ can be considered as a strong smoothing at v. Now, we choose two orthogonal normal vectors $\mathbf{x}_v$ and $\mathbf{y}_v$ which are perpendicular to $\tilde{\mathbf{n}}_v$. We sample the height field in this plane on n_C concentric circles where n_R sample points are placed equidistantly on each circle (we used are $n_C = 8$ and $n_R = 64$). This way we get all sample points as

$$\mathbf{s}_v(i_C, i_R) = \mathbf{p}_v + \frac{i_C + 1}{n_C} \cdot r \cdot \cos\left(\frac{i_R}{n_R} \cdot 2\pi\right) \cdot \mathbf{x}_v + \frac{i_C + 1}{n_C} \cdot r \cdot \sin\left(\frac{i_R}{n_R} \cdot 2\pi\right) \cdot \mathbf{y}_v \tag{2}$$

for $i_C = 0, ..., n_C - 1$ and $i_R = 0, ..., n_R - 1$. We can compute the height map h_v at each sample point as

$$h_v(i_C, i_R) = \text{dist}(\mathbf{s}_v(i_C, i_R), -\tilde{\mathbf{n}}_v). \tag{3}$$

Using this, measuring the symmetry of the surface surrounding v is quite straightforward. As illustrated in figure 2 (c), each rotation index corresponds to a mirror axis that can be used for symmetry analysis. Basically, we simply have to compare the sample values on the one side of the mirror axis with the values on the other side. Since we want to constrain the analysis to the surface close to v, we limit the valid height map values to the range $[-r, r]$. Hence for each mirror axis, defined by rotation index i_R, we define a set of valid mirror pairs $M_v(i_R) = \{(i_C, i_{R1}, i_{R2}) : h_v(i_C, i_{R1}) \in [-r, r] \wedge h_v(i_C, i_{R2}) \in [-r, r] \wedge i_{R2} = 2i_R - i_{R1} - 1\}$. Now we can measure the error between both sides of the mirror axis by computing the mean difference between the sample values of all mirror pairs:

$$e_v(i_R) = \frac{1}{|M_v(i_R)|} \sum_{(i_C, i_{R1}, i_{R2}) \in M_v(i_R)} \|h_v(i_C, i_{R1}) - h_v(i_C, i_{R2})\| \tag{4}$$

To get a meaningful symmetry measure from this value, we normalise it by dividing it by the maximum difference of valid height map values. We define the symmetry measure of v as:

$$s_v = 1 - \frac{\min\limits_{i_R \in \{0,...,n_R - 1\}} e_v(i_R)}{\max\limits_{(i_C, i_R) \in D_v} h_v(i_C, i_R) - \min\limits_{(i_C, i_R) \in D_v} h_v(i_C, i_R)} \tag{5}$$

where $D_v = \{(i_C, i_R) \in \{0, \ldots, n_C - 1\} \times \{0, \ldots, n_R - 1\} : h(i_C, i_R) \in [-r, r]\}$ is the set of valid samples. Furthermore, we can compute the normal of the corresponding mirror plane as follows: First, we get the rotation index $i_v = \text{argmin}_{i_R \in \{0,...,n_R-1\}} e_v(i_R)$ and the corresponding rotation angle $\alpha_v = (i_v - \frac{1}{2}) \cdot \frac{2\pi}{n_R} + \frac{\pi}{2}$. Finally, we get the symmetry plane normal:

$$\mathbf{m}_v = \cos(\alpha_v) \cdot \mathbf{x}_v + sin(\alpha_v) \cdot \mathbf{y}_v. \tag{6}$$

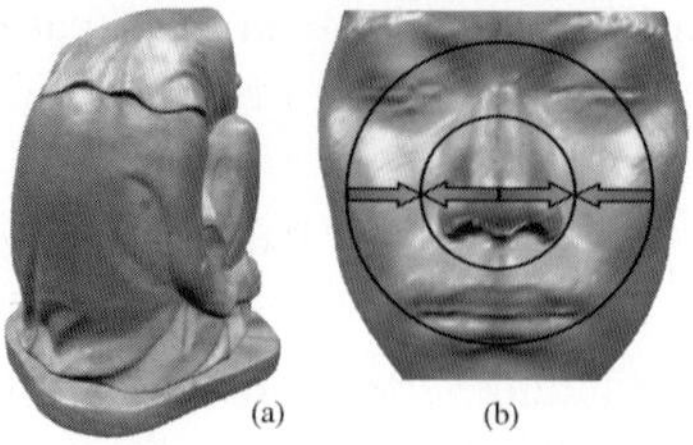

Fig. 5. (a) Smooth surfaces are highly symmetric. (b) Symmetry decrease in human faces.

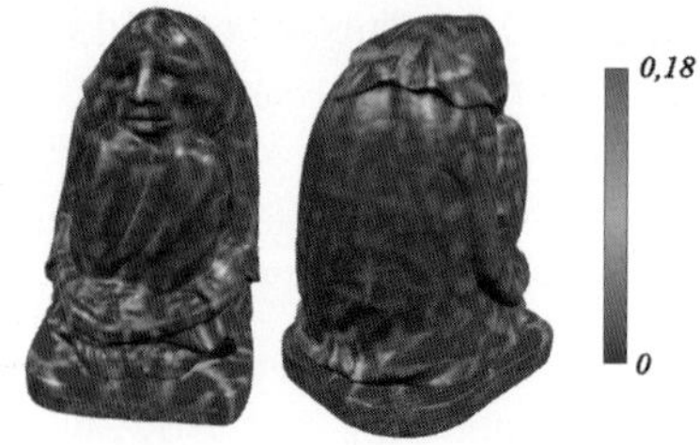

Fig. 6. The extracted symmetry lines

2.2 Analysis of the Symmetry Field

As expected, the symmetry values are high for vertices located close to the horizontal center of a human face (see figure 4). Furthermore, the symmetry values are very low for most of the other vertices on the face. This results in a sharp line of high-symmetry vertices running from the forehead over the nasal bone to the mouth. Figure 5 (a) shows that other areas are detected to have a high symmetry as well. In the following section, we provide an algorithm that can be used to extract those significant areas.

2.3 Extracting Symmetry Features

Let $\mathrm{sym}(\mathbf{p},\mathbf{d})$ denote the linearly interpolated symmetry value at the intersection point between the mesh surface and the ray from $\mathbf{p}$ along $\mathbf{d}$. Analogically to the height map h_v, we can sample the symmetry values around a vertex v:

$$\sigma_v(i_C,i_R) = \mathrm{sym}(\mathbf{s}_v(i_C,i_R), -\tilde{\mathbf{n}}_v) \tag{7}$$

This function uses the same sample distribution as h_v. We want to extract those parts of the symmetry field that form narrow areas of high symmetry, bordered by areas of low symmetry. More precisely, we want to measure how much the symmetry values decrease in both directions orthogonal to the symmetry plane at vertex v. We can project every sample point into the symmetry plane normal $\mathbf{m}_v$ (i.e. compute its signed distance to the symmetry plane) and normalise it with respect to the symmetry radius r, obtaining a scalar value:

$$d_v(i_C,i_R) = \frac{(\mathbf{s}_v(i_C,i_R) - \mathbf{p}_v)\cdot \mathbf{m}_v}{r} \tag{8}$$

For each side of the mirror plane, we can define a set of two-dimensional points:

$$\begin{aligned} R_v &= \{(d_v(i_C,i_R), s_v - \sigma_v(i_C,i_R)) : (i_C,i_R) \in D_v \wedge i_C < \frac{n_C}{2} \wedge d_v(i_C,i_R) > 0\} \\ L_v &= \{(d_v(i_C,i_R), \sigma_v(i_C,i_R) - s_v) : (i_C,i_R) \in D_v \wedge i_C < \frac{n_C}{2} \wedge d_v(i_C,i_R) < 0\} \end{aligned} \tag{9}$$

The first coordinate of each point corresponds to the normalised distance of sample (i_C,i_R) to the symmetry plane. The second coordinate is the difference between the symmetry value of v and the symmetry value of sample (i_C,i_R), where this difference is negated in R_v. The reason for this negation will become clear in the next step. Note that only samples whose circle index i_C is smaller than $\frac{n_C}{2}$ are considered because it has turned out that the decrease of symmetry in human faces ranges from the face center approximately to half of the symmetry radius (see figure 5 (b)). In the next step, we fit a line through origin to the points in $R_v \cup L_v$. Since we negated the symmetry coordinates of the points in R_v, the gradient of the line will be positive if the symmetry decreases in both directions. The value of the gradient is computed as follows:

$$g_v = \frac{\sum_{(d,s) \in R_v \cup L_v} d \cdot s}{\sum_{(d,s) \in R_v \cup L_v} d^2} \tag{10}$$

The complete extraction process is depicted in figure 7. Expressed graphically, g_v weakens the large high-symmetry areas of the symmetry field mentioned above and intensifies the narrow lines of high symmetry as found in human faces (figure 6)). Interestingly, a common threshold seems to exist for all human faces that can be used to classify a vertex (more precisely its surrounding surface) as symmetric or non-symmetric. Provided that the symmetry radius r matches approximately the size of the face, by marking only those vertices whose gradient value g_v exceeds the threshold, a complete line of vertices running from the root of the nose to the nose tip is marked for all kinds of human faces (see figure 11). In our implementation, we used the threshold $t_{Sym} = 0.06$. This way, the number of potential face vertices has been decimated by a large amount and we even have an indication for the orientation of the face (symmetry plane direction m_v) as well as for the size of the face (radius r).

2.4 Analysis of the Face Geometry

In the following section, we examine the surrounding surfaces of all vertices that have been classified symmetric. More precisely, we try to find out if these vertices are located on the nose tip of a human face. Given a potential "nose tip vertex" v, we know that the corresponding face has two possible up-directions:

$$\mathbf{u}_v^1 = \tilde{\mathbf{n}}_v \times \mathbf{m}_v \text{ and } \mathbf{u}_v^2 = -\tilde{\mathbf{n}}_v \times \mathbf{m}_v \tag{11}$$

From now on, the up-vector is simply referred to as $\mathbf{u}_v^a$ since the algorithm works analogically for $\mathbf{u}_v^1$ and $\mathbf{u}_v^2$.

First we analyse the curves running horizontally from the nose over the cheeks as illustrated in figure 8 (a). Since the curves may run both over the left and the right side, we define a direction vector $\mathbf{d}_v^b$ with $\mathbf{d}_v^1 = \mathbf{m}_v$ and $\mathbf{d}_v^2 = -\mathbf{m}_v$. Given the number of curves n_Y, the i_Y-th curve is defined by

$$c_v^{a,b}(i_Y, x) = \frac{1}{r} \mathrm{dist}(\mathbf{p}_v + \frac{i_Y}{n_Y - 1} \cdot \frac{r}{2} \cdot \mathbf{u}_v^a + x \cdot \mathbf{d}_v^b, -\tilde{\mathbf{n}}_v). \tag{12}$$

First of all, we measure how far the potential nose sticks out of the face with respect to the cheeks (figure 8 (b)):

$$noseheight_v^{a,b} = \frac{1}{n_Y} \sum_{i_Y=0}^{n_Y-1} (c_v^{a,b}(i_Y, \frac{r}{2}) - c_v^{a,b}(i_Y, 0)) \tag{13}$$

Next, we measure the mean nose width. For each curve, we define the width as the position within the range $[0, \frac{3}{4}r]$ where the curve gradient is maximal (figure 8 (c)). Given n_X samples per curve, we get the mean nose width

$$nosewidth_v^{a,b} = \frac{1}{n_Y} \sum_{i_Y=0}^{n_Y-1} w_{i_Y} \tag{14}$$

with $w_{i_Y} = \frac{3}{4n_X} \operatorname{argmax}_{i_X \in \{1,\ldots,n_X\}} (c_v^{a,b}(i_Y, \frac{i_X}{n_X} \cdot \frac{3}{4}r) - c_v^{a,b}(i_Y, \frac{i_X-1}{n_X} \cdot \frac{3}{4}r))$.

All curves should begin with a bulge and end with a relatively flat region. Figure 10 (a) shows how we can measure two heights on the curve whose difference gives us a meaningful value. By computing the mean value of all curves we get

$$\begin{aligned} nosecurve_v^{a,b} = \frac{1}{n_Y} \sum_{i_Y=0}^{n_Y-1} & (c_v^{a,b}(i_Y, w_{i_Y} + \frac{r}{4}) - c_v^{a,b}(i_Y, 0) \\ & -|c_v^{a,b}(i_Y, w_{i_Y} + \frac{r}{2}) - c_v^{a,b}(i_Y, w_{i_Y} + \frac{r}{4})|). \end{aligned} \tag{15}$$

The nose and the cheeks are quite smooth and contain no cracks. We cope with this fact by fitting a quadratic B-spline to each curve and measuring the error, as illustrated in figure 10 (b). Let $\text{splinedist}_v^{a,b}(i_Y)$ denote the maximum height difference between curve i_Y and its corresponding B-spline. Then the mean smoothness error is defined as:

$$facesmoothness_v^{a,b} = \frac{1}{n_Y} \sum_{i_Y=0}^{n_Y-1} \text{splinedist}_v^{a,b}(i_Y) \tag{16}$$

The nose bridge is relatively smooth and contains no cracks. Hence we measure the maximum distance between the nose profile and the straight line from the nose tip to the root (figure 10 (c)). Given the nose profile as height function $\text{nose}_v^a(y) = \frac{1}{r}\text{dist}(p_v + y \cdot \mathbf{u}_v^a, -\tilde{\mathbf{n}}_v)$, we can define the line as

$$noseline_v^a(y) = y \cdot \frac{\text{nose}_v^a(\frac{3}{4}r)}{\frac{3}{4}r} \tag{17}$$

We suspect the nose root of being located at a distance of $\frac{3}{4}r$ upwards the nose tip. Then we can measure the error with

$$nosesmoothness_v^a = \text{maxdist}(\text{nose}_v^a, \text{noseline}_v^a) \tag{18}$$

Noses stick out of the face, especially with respect to the region directly below the nose tip (figure 10 (d)). Thus, we measure the minimum distance to this spot.

$$nosebottom_v^a = \frac{1}{r} \min_{i_X \in \{-n_X,\ldots,n_X\}} \text{dist}(\mathbf{p}_v - 0.2 \cdot r \cdot \mathbf{u}_v^a + \frac{i_X}{2n_X} r \cdot \mathbf{m}_v, -\tilde{\mathbf{n}}_v) \tag{19}$$

Next, we measure the smoothness of the forehead by sampling the heights of a rectangular region on the forehead (figure 9 (a)):

$$headsmoothness_v^a = \frac{\max H - \min H}{r} \tag{20}$$

with $H = \text{dist}(\mathbf{p}_v + (1.3 + 0.2\frac{i_Y}{n_Y-1}r)\mathbf{u}_v^a + 0.5\frac{i_X}{n_X}\mathbf{m}_v, \tilde{\mathbf{n}}_v) : (i_X, i_Y) \in \{-n_X, ..., n_X\} \times \{0, ..., n_Y - 1\}\}$.

Another feature of human faces is the convexity of the forehead (figure 9 (b)). Hence we compute the difference between the central and outer height of the forehead:

$$headconvexity_v^{a,b} = \frac{1}{r}(\text{dist}(\mathbf{p}_v + 1.3 \cdot \mathbf{u}_v^a + 0.8 \cdot \mathbf{d}_v^b, -\tilde{\mathbf{n}}_v) - \text{dist}(\mathbf{p}_v + 1.3 \cdot \mathbf{u}_v^a, -\tilde{\mathbf{n}}_v)) \quad (21)$$

The last property we examine are the eyes. Depending on the mesh resolution the eyes are described more or less detailed, but the eye-sockets should always be present. As figure 9 (c) shows, the eye-sockets are located deeper in the head than the forehead. We scan the region where the eye is assumed and compute the difference between the largest height value and the height of the forehead center:

$$\begin{aligned} eyedepth_v^{a,b} = \frac{1}{r}(\max\{\text{dist}(\mathbf{p}_v + (0.5 + 0.4\frac{i_Y}{n_Y - 1}r)\mathbf{u}_v^a + (0.2 + 0.3\frac{i_X}{n_X - 1})\mathbf{d}_v^b, -\tilde{\mathbf{n}}_v) : \\ (i_X, i_Y) \in \{0, ..., n_X - 1\} \times \{0, ..., n_Y - 1\}\} \\ -\text{dist}(\mathbf{p}_v + \mathbf{u}_v^a, -\tilde{\mathbf{n}}_v)) \end{aligned} \quad (22)$$

Using all the measures defined above, we impose the following set of constraints that need to be fulfilled if a vertex v is located on the nose tip of a human face:

$$\begin{aligned} noseheight_v^{a,1} > c_{NH} \wedge noseheight_v^{a,2} > c_{NH} \wedge \\ nosewidth_v^{a,1} < c_{NW} \wedge nosewidth_v^{a,2} < c_{NW} \wedge \\ nosecurve_v^{a,1} > c_{NC} \wedge nosecurve_v^{a,2} > c_{NC} \wedge \\ facesmoothness_v^{a,1} < c_{FS} \wedge facesmoothness_v^{a,2} < c_{FS} \wedge \\ eyedepth_v^{a,1} > c_{ED} \wedge eyedepth_v^{a,2} > c_{ED} \wedge \\ headconvexity_v^{a,1} > c_{HC} \wedge headconvexity_v^{a,2} > c_{HC} \wedge \\ nosesmoothness_v^a < c_{NS} \wedge nosebottom_v^a > c_{NB} \wedge headsmoothness_v^a < c_{HS} \end{aligned} \quad (23)$$

The parameters c_{NH}–c_{HC} are supposed to be constant for all meshes and can be trained (manually) with a database of human and non-human meshes (see section 4).

3 Our Approach – All Radii

Up to now our face detection approach was based on a particular choice of the search radius r: this way faces of the approximate diameter $2r$ are detected (or excluded) on a mesh. In fact, all thresholds and parameters of the approach are tuned to depend exclusively on r. For the complete solution of problem 2, we would have to apply the algorithm for all r. However, the following observations lead to the results that only a certain number of search radii have to be checked: First, the face detection algorithm appears to be rather stable against small variations of r. In fact, a face with a diameter fd is generally detected for any choice of r between $0.7\frac{fd}{2}$ and $1.2\frac{fd}{2}$. Second, giben the size d of the whole mesh (which we estimate by the length of the diagonal of the minimal enclosing bounding box), the diameter fd of the face is limited to a certain interval. If the mesh describes a complete stretched-out human, we can estimate the size of the face to be not smaller than 5% of the size of the mesh ($fd \geq 0.05d$). On the other hand, if the mesh describes only a face, then the size of the mesh and the face coincide ($fd \leq d$). Because of this, for each mesh we check 32 different search radii $r_0,...,r_{31}$ which are chosen as $r_0 = 0.05\frac{d}{2}$, $r_{31} = 0.7\frac{d}{2}$, and the remaining r_i are placed in a quadratic distribution between r_0 and r_{31} allowing a higher density for smaller radii. This way our algorithm becomes independent of any parameter.

4 Applications and Results

We trained the parameters c_{NH}–c_{HC} of the geometry constraints manually using the Princeton Shape Benchmark and found the following configuration: $c_{NH} = 0.2$, $c_{NW} = 0.4$, $c_{NC} = 0.2$, $c_{FS} = 0.2$, $c_{NS} = 0.1$, $c_{NB} = 0.1$, $c_{ED} = 0.1$, $c_{HS} = 0.2$, $c_{HC} = 0.01$. In order to test our approach, we applied it to several shape databases: The Princeton Shape Benchmark [30] (our training database), the CCCC database [5], the Utrecht database [31] and the aim@shape database [32]. Altogether, we tested 4429 meshes. Most of the databases provide shape classifications like "human", "human_arms_out", "head", "face". However, these classifications are inappropriate for our purpose due to the following reasons: many of the shapes classified as human have holes (figure 14 (b)) or don't contain human faces (figure 14 (c)). Therefore, we identified the human faces in each database manually in order to evaluate the algorithm.

The Princeton Shape Benchmark consists of 1814 meshes. We identified 141 human faces without holes. Many of these faces are very coarse and have non-human features (figure 14 (a)). For this database, the algorithm detected 51 meshes to be human. All detected shapes are indeed human, i.e. no non-human mesh was found. The CCCC database contains 1841 meshes. We identified 49 valid faces, our algorithm detected 20. Again, no "wrong" face was detected. The Utrecht database consists of 684 meshes and contains no human face. The algorithm correctly detected no face in this database. Finally, we applied the algorithm to 90 high-resolution meshes of the aim@shape repository. 16 meshes have human faces, where 6 faces contain holes or are incomplete. The algorithm detected 12 faces (figure 13) – although two detected faces contain holes – and there was no incorrect detection.

The evaluation shows that the algorithm is able to detect humans in different states of completeness: complete bodies (figure 12 left), incomplete bodies, heads and single faces (figure 12 right). For a better visualisation, the application automatically displays "glasses" on each detected face and marks the nose tip red. Furthermore, there was no incorrect detection in all tested meshes. However, the algorithm cannot detect faces with non-human features like non-convex foreheads, or faces hidden by masks, glasses or hair. There were totally 11 non-detected meshes with one of these properties. The remaining meshes that have not been detected are very coarse (figure 14 (a) shows some examples): the number of face triangles lies between 50 and 400 and averages to 150. In contrast, the average triangle number of the detected faces amounts approximately to 4000, i.e. the algorithm requires a certain resolution of the face meshes in order to work reliably. The computing time for our approach is approximately linear to the number of

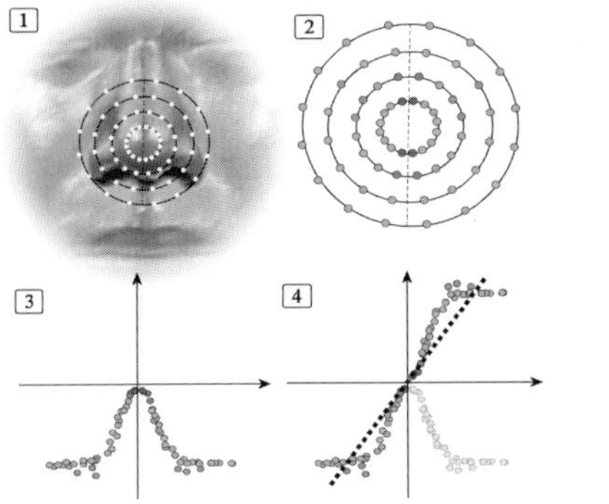

Fig. 7. 1.+2. Sampling of symmetry values. 3. Each sample is transformed to a 2D point (x = distance to symmetry plane, y = symmetry difference). 4. Fitting a line.

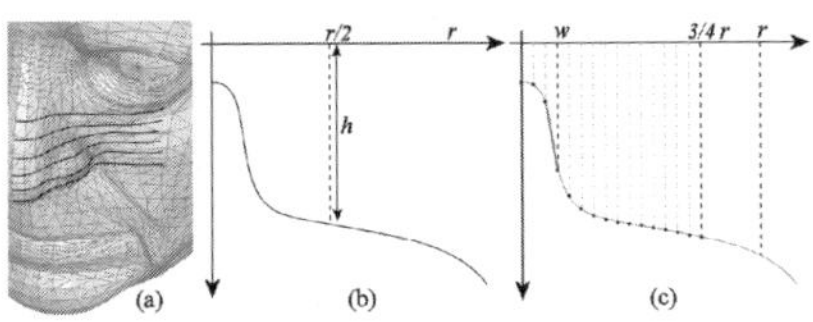

Fig. 8. (a) The curves that are analysed. (b) Computing the nose height. (c) The nose width w.

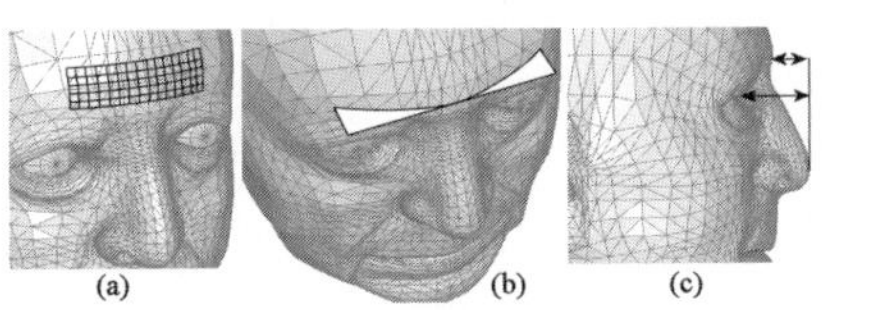

Fig. 9. (a) Measuring the forehead smoothness. (b) The human forehead is convex. (c) The eyes are located deeper in the head than the forehead.

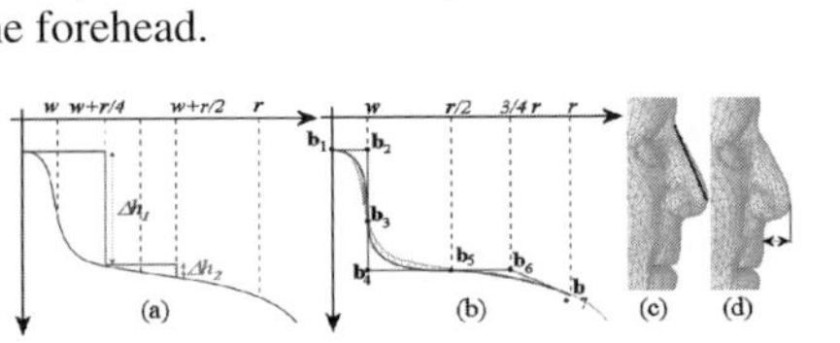

Fig. 10. (a) $\Delta h_1 - \Delta h_2$ is used to compute $nosecurve_v^{a,b}$. (b) We fit a quadratic B-spline to the curve. (c) The deviation between the nose profile and the straight line is very low. (d) The nose tip sticks out.

Fig. 11. Marked vertices

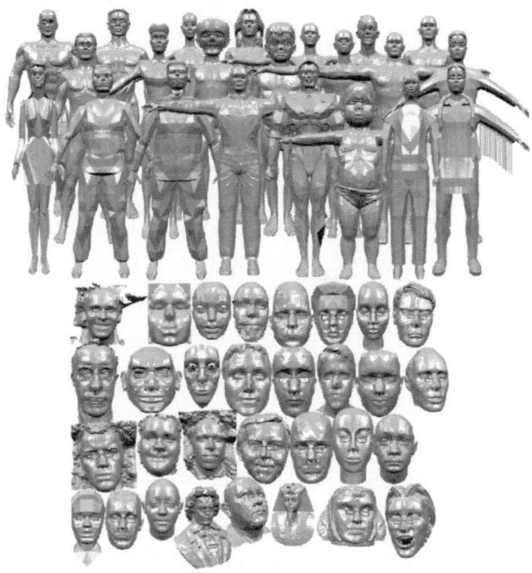

Fig. 12. Faces detected in complete bodies (top) and incomplete bodies (bottom)

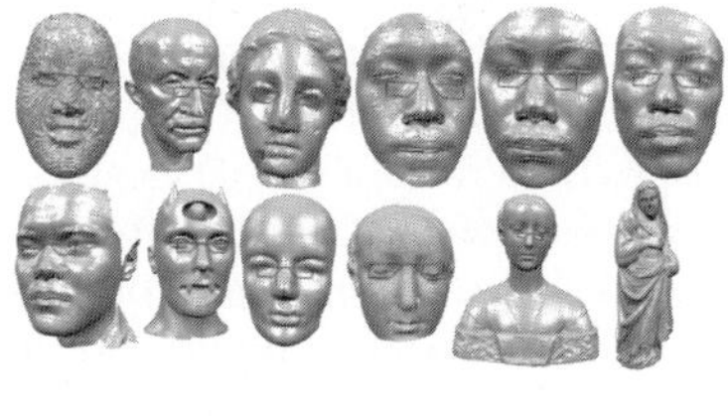

Fig. 13. Faces in the aim@shape database

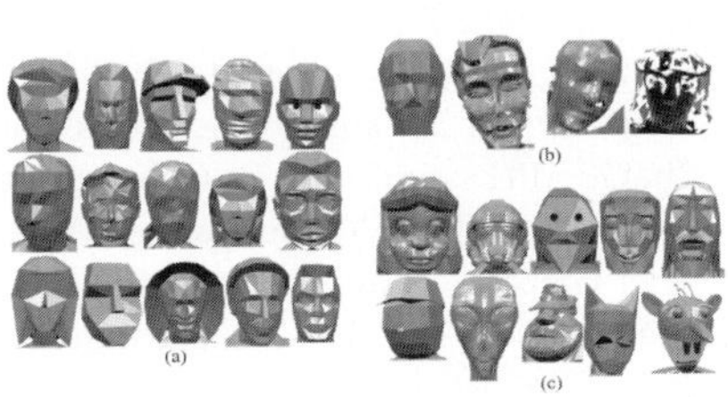

Fig. 14. Faces that could not be detected

vertices in the mesh: an AthlonXP 2400+ processor with 512 MB RAM took approx. 15 minutes for a mesh with 20000 triangles, 40 minutes for 60000 triangles, and 70 minutes for 100000 triangles. Since in our application scenario each mesh of a data base has to be checked only once and the result can be stored with the mesh, our algorithm can be considered as a preprocess of a web-search for meshes describing humans.

5 Conclusions

In this paper we made the following contributions: We introduced a domain-specific shape matching approach which is based on a fully-automatic face detection on triangular meshes. To decide whether a mesh contains a human face, each vertex undergoes a three-step test for being part of a face. This test is repeated for different radii of influence to ensure that faces of arbitrary scaling are detected. We trained the parameters of our algorithm and applied it to a number of different shape databases. No wrong face was detected. In general, we detected most faces as long as they did not contain holes and had a sufficently high triangular resolution. We conclude that, given that the meshes describe human faces in enough detail, the algorithm is able to differentiate between human and non-human meshes very reliably. For future research we intend to make the algorithm more robust against holes in the meshes, since a number of meshes comes with holes in the eye and mouth regions.

References

1. Funkhouser, T., Min, P., Kazhdan, M., Chen, J., Halderman, A., Dobkin, S.: A search engine for 3D models. ACM Transactiond on Graphics **22**(1) (2003) 83–105
2. Ankerst, M., Kastenmüller, G., Kriegel, H.P., Seidl, T.: Nearest neighbor classification in 3D protein data bases. In: Proc. 7th International Conference on Intelligent Systems for Molecular Biology. (1999) 34–43
3. Kang, S., Ikeuchi, K.: Determining 3-D object pose using the complex extended gaussian image. In: IEEE Conf. on Comp. Vision and Patt. Recog. (1991) 580–585
4. Saupe, D., Vranic, D.: 3D model retrieval with spherical harmonics and moments. In: Proceedings of the 23rd DAGM-Symposium on Pattern Recognition. (2001) 392–397
5. Vranic, D.: An improvement of rotation invariant 3D shape descriptor based on functions on concentric spheres. In: Proc. IEEE International Conference on Image Processing (ICIP 2003),. (2003) 757–760
6. R.Osada, T.Funkhouser, B.Chazelle, D.Dobkin: Shape distributions. ACM Trans. Graph. **21**(4) (2002) 807–832
7. Kazhdan, M., Funkhouser, T., Rusinkiewicz, S.: Rotation invariant spherical harmonic representation of 3D shape descriptors. In: SGP '03: Proceedings of the Eurographics/ACM SIGGRAPH symposium on Geometry processing. (2003) 156–164
8. Chen, D., X. Tian, Y., Ouhyoung, M.: On visual similarity based 3d model retrieval. Computer Graphics Forum **23**(3) (2003) 223–232 (Proceedings Eurographics 2003).
9. Vranic, D., Saupe, D.: 3D shape descriptor based on 3D fourier transform. In: Proc. ECMCS 2001. (2001) 271–274
10. Hilaga, M., Shinagawa, Y., Kohmura, T., Kunii, T.: Topology matching for fully automatic similarity estimation of 3D shapes. In: Proc. SIGGRAPH. (2001) 203–212

11. Kazhdan, M., Funkhouser, T., Rusinkiewicz, S.: Shape matching and anisotropy. In: Proc. SIGGRAPH. (2004) 623–629
12. Funkhouser, T., Kazhdan, M., Shilane, P., Min, P., Kiefer, W., Tal, A., Rusinkiewicz, S., Dobkin, D.: Modeling by example. ACM Transactions on Graphics (SIGGRAPH 2004) (2004)
13. Yang, G., Huang, T.: Human face detection in a complex background. Pattern Recognition **27**(1) (1994) 53Ű–63
14. Kotropoulos, C., Pitas, I.: Rule-based face detection in frontal views. In: ICASSP '97: Proceedings of the 1997 IEEE International Conference on Acoustics, Speech, and Signal Processing (ICASSP '97) -Volume 4, IEEE Computer Society (1997) 2537
15. Leung, T., Burl, M., Perona, P.: Finding faces in cluttered scenes using random labeled graph matching. In: Proc. Fifth International Conference on Computer Vision. (1995) 637–Ű644
16. Yow, K., Cipolla, R.: Feature-based human face detection. Technical report, Department of Engineering, University of Cambridge, England (1996)
17. Sinha, P., Torralba, A.: Detecting faces in impoverished images. Journal of Vision **2**(7) (2002) 601a
18. Gordon, G.: Face recognition based on depth and curvature features. In: Proc. IEEE Conference on Computer Vision and Pattern Recognition. (1992) 108–110
19. Hallinan, P., et al.: Two- and Three-Dimensional Patterns on the Face. AK Peters, Natick (1999)
20. Huang, J., Heisele, B., Blanz, V.: Component-based face recognition with 3D morphable models. In: Proc. of the 4th Int. Conf. on Audio- and Video-Based Biometric Person Authenticitation. (2003) 27–34
21. Blanz, V., Vetter, T.: Face recognition based on fitting a 3D morphable model. IEEE Trans. Pattern Anal. Mach. Intell. **25**(9) (2003) 1063–1074
22. Zabrodsky, H., Peleg, S., Avnir, D.: Symmetry as a continuous feature. IEEE Transactions on Pattern Analysis and Machine Intelligence **17**(12) (1995) 1154–1166
23. Marola, G.: On the detection of the axes of symmetry of symmetric and almost symmetric planar images. IEEE Trans. Pattern Anal. Mach. Intell. **11**(1) (1989) 104–108
24. Shen, D., Ip, H., Cheung, K., Teoh, E.: Symmetry detection by generalized complex (gc) moments: A close-form solution. IEEE Transactions on Pattern Analysis and Machine Intelligence **21**(5) (1999) 466–476
25. Reisfeld, D., Wolfson, H., Yeshurun, Y.: Detection of interest points using symmetry. In: ICCV90. (1990) 62–65
26. Reisfeld, D., Wolfson, H., Yeshurun, Y.: Robust facial feature detection using local symmetry. In: Proc. International Conference on Pattern Recognition. (1990) 117–120
27. Kovesi, P.: Symmetry and asymmetry from local phase. In: AI'97. (1997) 185–190
28. Sun, C., Sherrah, J.: 3D symmetry detection using the extended gaussian image. IEEE Trans. Pattern Anal. Mach. Intell. **19**(2) (1997) 164–168
29. M.Kazhdan, Chazelle, B., Dobkin, D., Finkelstein, A., Funkhouser, T.: A reflective symmetry descriptor. In: ECCV '02: Proceedings of the 7th European Conference on Computer Vision-Part II. (2002) 642–656
30. Shilane, P., Min, P., Kazhdan, M., Funkhouser, T.: The princeton shape benchmark. In: Proc. Shape Modeling International. (2004) 167–178
31. Tangelder, J., Veltkamp, R.: Polyhedral model retrieval using weighted point sets (2003)
32. aim@shape: (2004) http://www.aimatshape.net.

Skin Color Analysis in HSV Color Space and Rendering with Fine Scale Skin Structure

Dae Hyun Kim[1] and Myoung-Jun Kim[2,⋆]

[1] Institute for Graphic Interfaces, South Korea
cregeo@fxcode.com
[2] Ewha Womans University, South Korea
mjkim@ewha.ac.kr

Abstract. Among many skin color sources, hemoglobin and melanin components are regarded most significant in determining the final color of human skin. In extracting the two components, this paper proposes to use a more intuitive color model, HSV, than the RGB color space. For 3D rendering, we propose a novel method to reconstruct the fine-scale structure (normal map) of the human skin from a single highly specular image, or from a pair of highly specular and diffusive images. In the *shape-from-shading* algorithm, several photos varying light positions should have been taken to compute the normal of diffusive surfaces; which, however, was hardly the case for capturing fine skin structure since the human subjects cannot keep still while taking many photos. Therefore, our approach rids us of the difficult task to register several images.

1 Introduction

We often see digital actors replacing human actors in recent movies. To make them look more realistic, more cares have to be taken to reproduce human skin color and texture. So far, the easiest way was to map a skin image onto the 3D mesh of face. However, since the source image already contains a certain illumination (i.e., the illumination present at the capture) applying additional lighting model, such as *Phong* shading [3], tends to be unrealistic. Texturing human faces through matching between 2D textures and the target face mesh can be found in [9].

Therefore, we could easily get down to a conclusion that the digital camera images for the texture map first have to be decomposed into more primitive components for the later synthesis. One interpretation to this decomposition can be found in [10]. In that paper, Tsumura et al. take two photos: 'surface plus body reflection' and 'body reflection' as [1] also did using linear polarization filters. The body reflection part is then separated into three: melanin, hemoglobin, and shading [10]. They then obtained surface reflection from the two photos. However, their final goal was to synthesize the image again in 2D space (i.e., no need for 3D mesh of a face), there was no need to further analyze the surface reflection; rather, they added the surface reflection part to the final image synthesized from the two body reflected images.

Their approach to separate skin color is based on RGB color model; first they seek a plane in the RGB cube closest to the colors sampled from a user selected skin region in a single skin image; subsequently, we call the plane sought above color plane.

⋆ Corresponding author.

H.-P. Seidel, T. Nishita, and Q. Peng (Eds.): CGI 2006, LNCS 4035, pp. 254–264, 2006.

Within this plane two vectors regarded most independent for the samples are found, through independent component analysis (ICA). All the colors in the image are then projected onto the color plane along the direction vector, (1, 1, 1), implying illumination effect from a white light source, and projected again to the two vectors from ICA; those are considered imitating hemoglobin and melanin respectively. One crucial problem of using RGB color model is that the direction of the color plane changes as the sample region changes. When the normal of the color plane is tilted largely from the illumination direction, projected color values can be out of the color cube; in this case the user has to give different region for the sampling. Therefore, their approach cannot produce absolute quantity of the pigments for the different human subjects; rather, it produces relative quantities varying from one subject to the other. Moreover, the RGB color model does not properly represent continuous hue and saturation value, the two independent axes sought could not properly represent saturation change of the two skin components.

[6] have done work on capturing BRDFs from the images coming from a calibrated digital camera with subjects wearing a pattern. [1] measures skin reflectance properties using video cameras. To extract the surface normal they applied color space analysis technique to row resolution images (i.e. 720x480 pixels) taken with light sources located in different positions. Their concern was not in extracting fine-scale structure like wrinkles of the skin as the image resolution implied; image registration in pixel-by-pixel level was not necessary. Since very high resolution images (e.g. 3000x2000 pixels) are required to capture the fine-scale skin structure, their method can be hardly used.

There has been much work in the area of realistic facial rendering. However, only a few results have been published on capturing or synthesizing fine-scale skin structure. [4] used silicone mold employed in cosmetology to capture fine-scale skin structure. Using the shape-from-shading algorithm (for a survey on this, see [13]), they could recover the normals from the images taken after the silicone mold with varying light sources. Since the samples taken from a mold are small, a texture synthesis algorithm (i.e. [11, 2]) is performed for whole area of the face. [5] use Voronoi diagram to represent the different skin cells; geometric diversity is obtained using pseudo-fractal subdivision in the Voronoi procedure. Meanwhile, [12] use Delaunay triangulation in texture space. The edges of the triangles are raised or lowered to create hight field which is then used as a bump map.

Contributions: This paper contributes in two parts: pigment separation and normal extraction from skin images. For the former, we propose a novel method for separating pigments in the HSV color model, which results in two pigment maps: hemoglobin and melanin map. The color plane perpendicular to the *value* axis contains all hue and saturation values; color planes from different human subjects or from varying sampling regions are different only in their brightness. Since HSV color wheel (i.e. the circular cross section of the HSV color cone, the color plane) well sorts out its hue values radially around the center of the wheel, the way human perceives color object can be directly applied to find out the two independent color vectors to separate the skin pigment, without counting on a statistical method such as ICA. Moreover, a consistent color separation across different human subjects can be made on the HSV color wheel because of its capability to contain most hue and saturation values and its inherent sorting function.

For the latter, we developed a novel method to recover fine-scale skin structure (normal map), which requires one only one image; thereby, the seemingly impossible or very time consuming task to register the facial images can be avoided. Moreover, using additional materials such as silicone mold as [4], which is not as welcome by the human subjects as just photographing, can be avoided too. Our approach reads in only one image for the normal map computation: the image after high-pass filtering the 'surface plus body reflection', or the image with only surface reflection. The normal at each pixel of the image is then decided by the inverse of a specular illumination model.

Paper Organizations: In Section 2, we discuss the the photographing environments for the experiments we have carried out and describes overall pipeline of our approach. Next, we describe our algorithm to separate the diffuse map using HSV color model in Section 3. In section 4, our method to extract fine-scale normal map from a single image is detailed; the results from this paper are shown in Section 5.

2 Overview

We take the first photo in the environment as illustrated in Fig.1; polarization filters are positioned in front of both the camera and the light sources. For the second photo, we rotated the polarization filter of the camera 90 degrees. If we take only two photos, it is highly probable that the two images are not properly registered. Therefore, we take more than ten photos in short time by rotating the filter in front of camera and choose a pair of photos best registered.

The two photos represent, respectively, body plus surface reflection and body reflection. We separate the body reflection image into hemoglobin map, melanin map using HSV color model. Using the images taken, we compute the surface reflection by subtracting the body reflection from the body plus surface reflection. We apply a high-pass filter to the body plus surface reflection to separate the a detailed map. We then try to compute the normal map from the surface reflection and from the detailed map. This process is shown in Fig.2.

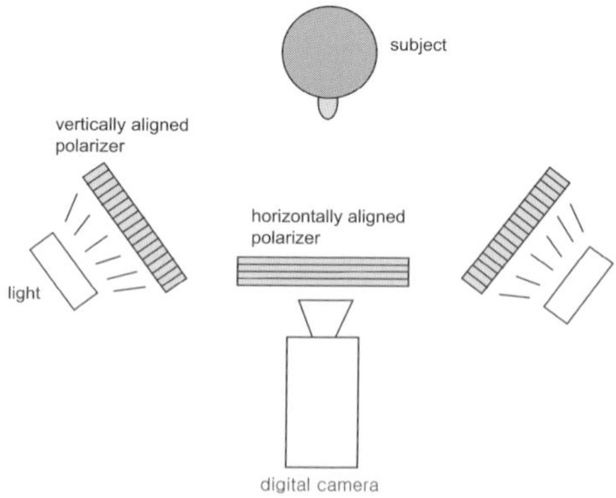

Fig. 1. Photographing environment

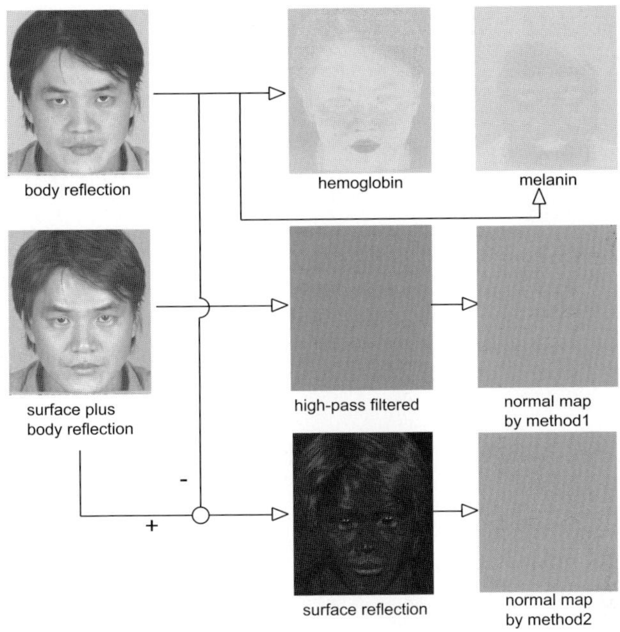

Fig. 2. Overview

3 Skin Color Decomposition Using HSV

We now explain how to separate the body reflection image using the HSV color model. The HSV color model is commonly used in computer graphics applications because of its similarities to the way humans tend to perceive color. HSV color consists of three components: hue, saturation, and value. One visualization method of the HSV model is the cone. In this representation, the hue is depicted as the color wheel of a 3D cone. The saturation is represented by the distance from the center of a circular cross-section of the cone as shown in Fig.3 (2), and the value is the distance from the apex of the cone representing the brightness. HSV color space can also be modeled as cylinder, which is mathematically accurate; however, this is not practical because the number of visually distinct saturation levels and hues decreases as the value approaches black.

The user selects a sampling region, R, within the body reflection image, as shown in Fig.3 (1). RGB color values, (r_i, g_i, b_i), of the pixels, $p_i \in R$, are mapped to HSV color space: (h_i, s_i, v_i). Since v, the third component of the HSV color, indicates the luminance we average them: $v_a = \sum v_i / n$, where n is the number of the samples. The circular cross section (h, s, v_a) can then be used as a color plane onto which the sample colors are projected along (h_i, s_i, v_i) vector, as shown in Fig.3. This projection is the big difference from that of [10], who used $(1,1,1)$ vector in RGB cube, which is assumed to be the color of the light source; ours always map a valid color value in the hue/saturation plane, but theirs not always, in particular when the projection plane is tilted largely from the direction, $(1,1,1)$, implying illumination effect from the light source.

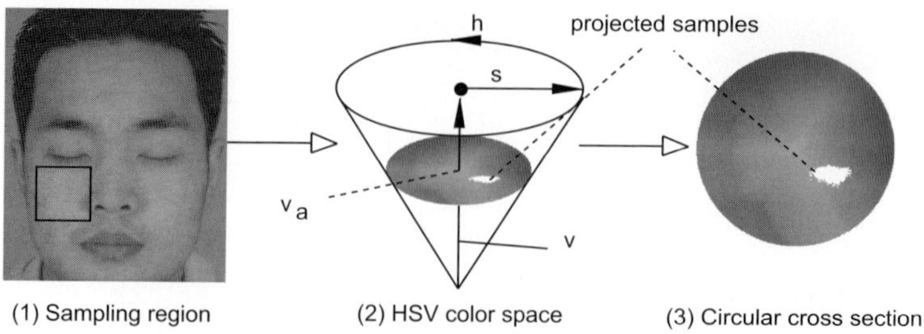

Fig. 3. (1) The user draws the sampling region. (2) The circular cross section, (h, s, v_a), is computed by averaging the brightness values of the samples. (3) The sample colors are projected along the direction, (h_i, s_i, v_i) onto the circular cross section.

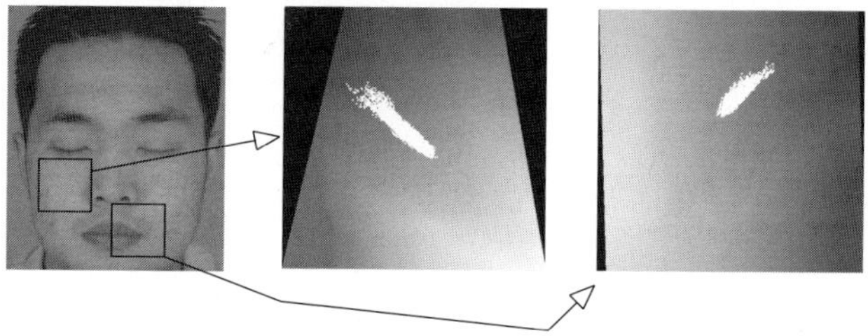

Fig. 4. Two different planes in RGB cube corresponding to each sampling region

Fig.4 shows two color planes computed by using principal component analysis (PCA) as in [10], corresponding to the different sampling regions. Unlike the cross sectional planes located in the RGB color cube, in HSV we could simply choose a circular cross section orthogonal to the v axis. It was acceptable because most perceptible colors can be represented within this. It is notable that, in RGB color model, the two color planes produce different shape of data distribution from one sampling region to the other as shown in Fig.4. Meanwhile, in HSV, the cross sections have almost the same data distribution across different sampling regions.

Hemoglobin and melanin pigments are separated by projecting the colors onto the color plane to two independent axes. To do this, first we need to infer the two independent vectors from Fig.3 (3).

In HSV, the sample colors are distributed nearly in the same area of green to red hues and the color wheel well sorts out hue radially around the center of the wheel. Therefore, it becomes easy for the user to perceive where the independent color vectors are; this can be procedurally done simply by radially searching the hue values, that encompass the samples, on the cross section around the center point, as shown in Fig.5. Unless the user specifies non-skin area (e.g. hair) for sampling, this does not fail the job. In [10], the two independent vectors have been found via a statistical method, independent component analysis (ICA). ICA was somewhat necessary for the blind source separation; in the RGB cross sections unlike the HSV cross sections the independent vectors are not salient. However, the outcome from the ICA does not necessarily

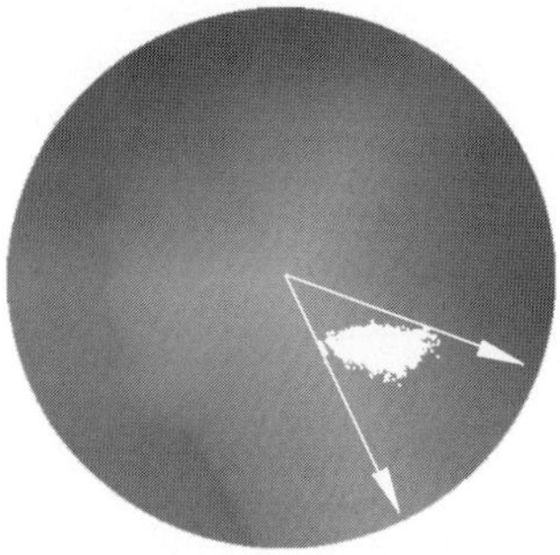

Fig. 5. Color samples on a HSV color wheel and two independent vectors found by searching the hue values encompassing the samples

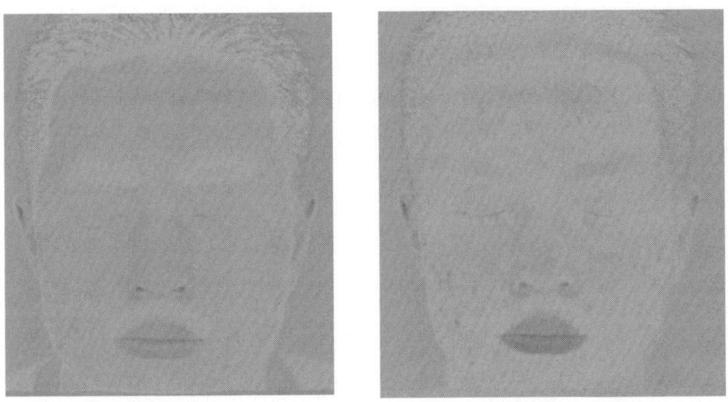

Fig. 6. Hemoglobin map from ICA in RGB space (left), and from radial searching (right) for the same samples

correctly represent varying saturation, which corresponds to the quantity change of each pigment. As noted above, this is why HSV color model invented. Fig.6 compares the two methods; it can be noticed that our method yields the hemoglobin map closer to real hemoglobin distribution of the human subject.

4 Fine-Scale Normal Map

We now explain our method to extract the fine-scale normal map from the input images mentioned in Section 1: high-pass filtered image or surface reflection image. Our basic idea can be explained with the aid of Fig.7 and Fig.8. Geometry of the final model in Fig.7 can be interpreted as the result of adding the fine-scale geometry to the underlying geometry. Interestingly, this fine-to-coarse change in geometry can also be found within the images with different lighting setup as in Fig.8: the top left image (body reflection) does not show the fine-scale geometry, but the top right image (surface plus body

Fig. 7. Fine-scale skin structure versus underlying global geometry

reflection) shows both the underlying geometry and the fine-scale geometry together. It can be presumed that the fine-scale geometry can be better seen after subtracting the first image from the second, or, after just removing the image portion of low frequency (i.e. smooth tone of the top right figure). The resulting images after these operations are shown in the bottom of Fig.8.

For the surface reflection image or the high-pass filtered image, our illumination model is defined for each pixel as follows:

$$\alpha(H \cdot N)^{1/\rho} = I, \tag{1}$$

where each variable is defined as following: N is the unknown surface normal, L is the light vector, and H is the half vector between L and the camera vector E such that $H = \widehat{E+L}$. I is the intensity value of the pixel. This can be depicted by Fig.9. Here we pose two assumptions that the camera vector, the light vector, and z axis are the same and the image gradient never vanishes (i.e., $\nabla I \neq 0$). The former assumption is especially plausible since we are extracting the normals from a single image.

After rewriting Eq.1 as

$$(H \cdot N)^{1/\rho} = I/\alpha, \tag{2}$$

we know that the left term is no larger than one because H and N are unit vector. Therefore, the right term of Eq.2 can be restated as I/M, where M is the local maximum of I. Since H is in the same direction with z axis, the left term can be written as $(N_z)^{1/\rho}$, where N_z indicates the z component of the unknown normal. Now, N_z is given by

$$N_z = (I/M)^{\rho}. \tag{3}$$

For the remaining part of the unknown normal vector, we use the image gradient, ∇I. This can be justified simply by differentiate Eq.2:

$$1/\rho (N_z)^{1/\rho - 1} \nabla N_z = \nabla I/M. \tag{4}$$

From the above equation, we could notice that ∇N_z has the same direction as ∇I. We assume that ∇N_z has the same horizontal direction with the unknown normal N. That

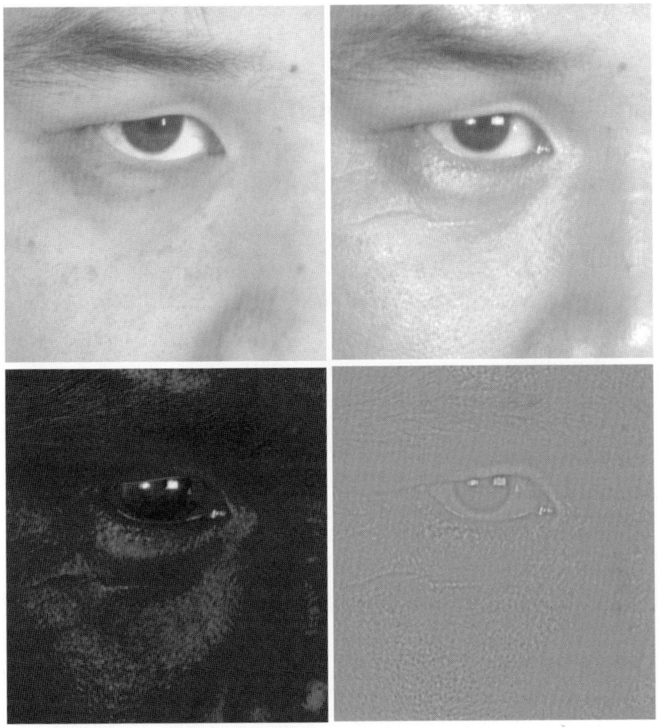

Fig. 8. Top Left: body reflection image. Top Right: body + surface reflection. Bottom Left: Image computed by subtracting the body reflection from the body plus surface reflection. Bottom Right: Image after high-pass filtering the the body plus surface reflection.

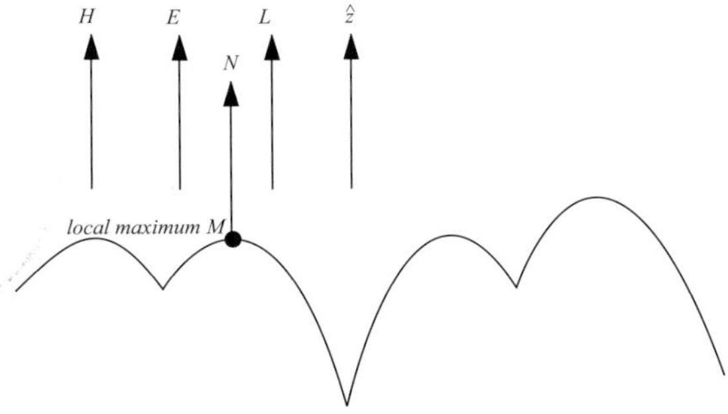

Fig. 9. Assumption on the light vector, camera vector, and local geometry of the surface. Note that the normal at peak is in z direction.

is, we use ∇I for the horizontal component of the normal. Although this assumption is not generally true, it is valid for the local geometries we have assumed in Fig.9, such as sphere, ellipsoids. The normal vector can then be computed as follows:

$$N = -\sqrt{1 - {N_z}^2} \cdot \widehat{\nabla I} + N_z \cdot \hat{z}.$$

5 Results

Fig.10 is the result of the normal map computation of Sect.4 for the two images shown in Fig.8. It is notable that sharp features are better preserved in the normal map obtained from the surface reflection image, but some higher frequency fine-scale structures such as pores are somehow exaggerated. Meanwhile, high-pass filtered image can better be used to extract high frequency features such as pores.

Fig.11(a) shows the results after composing the hemoglobin map and the melanin map, which are shown in Fig.2. Completely removing shading effect from the image (i.e., by projecting the color values onto the color plane) does not produce realistic image to be used as a diffuse color texture, therefore, we added a slight amount of shading effect by remembering each projection path.

Fig.11(b) has been used for the later 3D image rendering as a color texture. Fig.11(c) could not be used because it contains too much dark shades already, e.g., near nose;

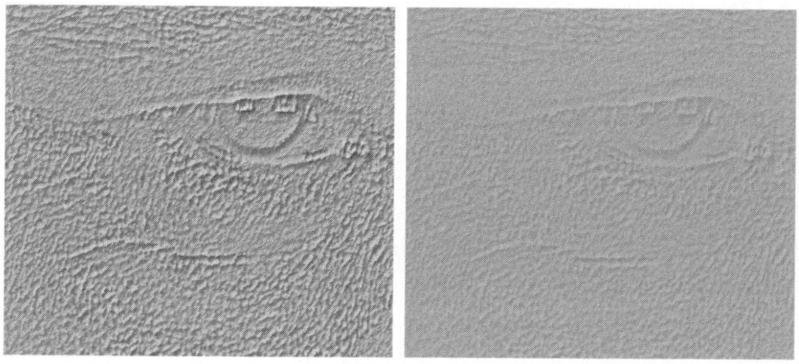

(a) (b)

Fig. 10. (a) Normal map with the surface reflection in Fig.8: it reveals sharp features such as crease better. (b) Normal map with the high-pass filtered image in Fig.8: it yields a smoother normal map.

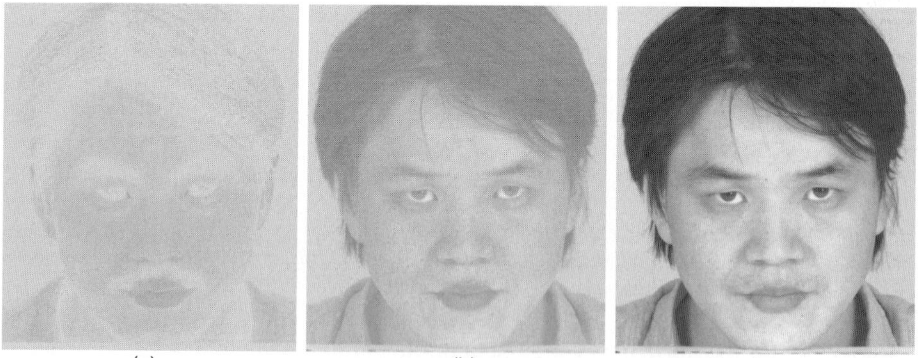

(a) (b) (c)

Fig. 11. (a) Result adding hemoglobin map and melanin map virtually with no shades. (b) After adding a slight amount of shading; compare this with the body reflection (c).

Fig. 12. Left: Normal map from the high-pass filtered image. Right: Normal map from the surface reflection.

this could result in redundant shading from 3D lighting. Fig.12 shows the result after rendering a 3D model with the normal map from the surface reflection and the high-pass filtered image, respectively, left to right in Fig.8.

6 Conclusion and Future Work

We have presented techniques to model and render realistic human facial image: in extracting the two skin pigment maps, hemoglobin and melanin, this paper proposes to use a more intuitive color model, HSV. We also developed a method to recover fine scale skin structure, which requires only one image; this tackles the problem of using shape-from-shading algorithm, which needs many registered photos. To obtain fine-scale geometry from one image, we formulated an inverse specular illumination model.

For the future work, we are considering developing more accurate illumination model for the normal extraction; in fact, we have used some assumptions which could have been quite unrealistic for coarse-scale geometry. However, as the realism of skin structure can be somewhat mimicked by, for example, using voronoi diagram, these assumptions could be applied without losing realism.

References

[1] Debevec, P., Hawkins, T., Tchou, C., Duiker, H.-P., and Sarokin, W. 2000. Acquiring the reflectance field of a human face. In *SIGGRAPH 2000*, ACM, 145–156.

[2] Efros, A., and Leung, T. 1999. Texture synthesis by non-parametric sampling. In *IEEE International Conference on Computer Vision*, IEEE, 1033–1038.

[3] Foley, J. D., van Dam, A., Feiner, S. K., and Hughes, J. F. 1996. *Computer Graphics: Principles and Practice*. Addison-Wesley.

[4] Haro, A., Guenter, B., and Essa, I. 2001. Real-time, photo-realistic, physically based rendering of fine scale human skin structure. In *12th Eurographics Workshop on Rendering*.

[5] Ishii, T., Yasuda, T., and Toriwaki, J. 1993. A generation model for human skin texture. In *Proc. CG International 1993*, 139–150.

[6] Marschner, S. R., Westin, S. H., Lafortune, E. P., Torrance, K. E., and Greenberg, D. P. 1999. Image-based brdf measurement including human skin. In *Proceedings of 10th Eurographics Workshop on Rendering*, 139–152.

[7] , 2005. www.microchip.com.

[8] Poirier, G. 2003. *Human Skin Modelling and Rendering*. Master's thesis, University of Waterloo, Waterloo, Ontario, Canada.

[9] Tarini, M., Yamauchi, H., Haber, J., and Seidel, H.-P. 2002. Texturing faces. In *Graphics Interface 2002*, 89–98.

[10] Tsumura, N., Ojima, N., Sato, K., Shiraishi, M., and Shimizu, H. 2003. Image-based skin color and texture analysis/synthesis by extracting hemoglobin and melanin information in the skin. In *SIGGRAPH 2003*, ACM, 770–779.

[11] Wei, L.-Y., and Levoy, M. 2000. Fast texture synthesis using tree-structured vector quantization. In *SIGGRAPH 2000*, ACM, 479–488.

[12] Wu, Y., Kalra, P., and Magnenat-Thalmann, N. 1997. Physically-based wrinkle simulation and skin rendering. In *Eurographics Workshop on Computer Animation and Simulation*.

[13] Zhang, R., Tsai, P.-S., Cryer, J. E., and Shah, M. 1999. Shape from shading: A survey. *IEEE Transactions on Pattern Analysis and Machine Intelligence 21*, 690–706.

Comprehending and Transferring Facial Expressions Based on Statistical Shape and Texture Models

Pengcheng Xi[1], Won-Sook Lee[1], Gustavo Frederico[1], Chris Joslin[2], and Lihong Zhou[3]

[1] School of Information Technology and Engineering, University of Ottawa, ON., Canada
{pxi086, wslee, gfred006}@uottawa.ca
http://www.site.uottawa.ca/~wslee

[2] School of Information Technology, Carleton University, Ottawa, ON., Canada
Chris_joslin@carleton.ca

[3] Information Security Center, Southeast University, Nanjing, China
lihzhou@gmail.com

Abstract. We introduce an efficient approach for representing a human face using a limited number of images. This compact representation allows for meaningful manipulation of the face. Principal Components Analysis (PCA) utilized in our research makes possible the separation of facial features so as to build statistical shape and texture models. Thus changing the model parameters can create images with different expressions and poses. By presenting newly created faces for reviewers' marking in terms of intensities on masculinity, friendliness and attractiveness, we analyze relations between the parameters and intensities. With feature selections, we sort those parameters by their importance in deciding the three aforesaid aspects. Thus we are able to control the models and transform a new face image to be a naturally masculine, friendly or attractive one. In the PCA-based feature space, we can successfully transfer expressions from one subject onto a novel person's face.

1 Introduction

There have been many techniques developed for image compression by catching statistical information with encoders. Representative methods are fractal, wavelet, Differential Pulse Code Modulation and the most recent version of JPEG for still imagery [1]. However, almost all conventional methods captured the information in only one particular image. When we have a set of similar images, PCA should be an excellent technique in dimension reduction as well as in novel-image creation [2] [3]. After conducting a statistical analysis on the image dataset, the dimensions of the images are greatly reduced by mapping each image onto particular eigen-vectors with eigen-decomposition. Thus shape and texture models can be represented as a sum of average vectors and weighted variances along eigen-vectors. The weights, i.e., the parameters of the models, are normally referred to as "modes". Modifications on these modes help learn relations between the variances of parameter values and changes in facial image expressions.

It is of great interest to find the reason for those preferable faces. Do viewers' physical conditions affect their judgment? What kind of features can be observed from one's face, hatred, love, or happiness? Are there any relations between these

H.-P. Seidel, T. Nishita, and Q. Peng (Eds.): CGI 2006, LNCS 4035, pp. 265 – 276, 2006.

features and facial attributes? Current solutions to these questions can be divided into two categories: geometry-based and psychology-based approaches.

The geometry-based methods are mainly concerned with geometric measurements, such as the distance between the eyes, the eye width and the context location of the nose. In the representative literature of [4], fractal geometry analysis is conducted on facial images and a female "attractive" face is created according to fractal rules. Artists such as Leonardo and Dürer also provide some criteria in this field [4]. Moreover, expression ratio images were proposed to map one person's expression details to a different subject's face. Given the feature point motions of an expression, this method requires an additional input of a different person's image with the same expression [5]. For situations where expression ratio images are unavailable, a geometry-driven facial expression synthesis approach based on feature point positions of an expression is more applicable [6].

Psychology-based approaches mainly argue the relations between attractiveness and symmetry, averageness as well as nonaverage sexually dimorphic features, i.e., the hormone markers [7]. They also analyze the relationship between female viewers' menstrual shift and their choice of male faces for dominance and short-term mates [8]. And certain researchers find that "shape normalized faces" and "texture normalized faces" are more attractive and younger than original faces [9].

In [10], a technique for defining facial prototypes supports transformations along quantifiable dimensions in "face space". Shape and color information are used to perform predictive gender and age transformations. Flexible models are also introduced for identification and coding of facial images [11]. In [12], linear object classes are learnt from a basis of 2D prototypical views and then used for 2D image synthesis.

Based on the above literatures, we try to combine geometry-based and psychology-based approaches as well as to imbibe ideas from [11] and [12] for our research. The basic idea is to utilize PCA as applied in [13] for building statistical shape and texture models with a facial image database. Utilizing these models, we can thus create more novel images with different expressions and poses. After some reviewers mark these images in terms of masculinity, friendliness and attractiveness, we can thus analyze the relations between parameter values and the facial expressions with certain feature selection scheme. This knowledge can thus help us transform a new face image to be more masculine, friendly or attractive. We can also introduce a neutral face image into the eigen-space and transfer different expressions among faces.

We organize our paper as follows. Section 2 is for building parameterized shape and texture models, where section 2.1 is to introduce the image database, section 2.2 for triangulation of facial images, 2.3 to present the PCA, 2.4 to build the models, and 2.5 is to interpret the effects on facial expressions after changing parameter values. In section 3.1, we present the survey results as well as feature selection scheme. In 3.2, we utilize the feature space to transfer expressions from one subject onto a novel face image. And we conclude our paper and mention some future work in section 4.

2 Parameterized Facial Models

In this section, we will introduce how to build statistical shape and texture models. We will also interpret the changes on facial expressions with parameter adjustments.

2.1 Database of Facial Images

We need parameterized facial models which can represent great differences in shape and texture vectors among images; therefore in our experiment, we take facial photos from 8 males of different ethnicities as shown in first row of Fig. 1. For each person, we take his photos with different expressions and poses. From all these images, we select 112 ones into our final database which can represent the maximum variances in facial expressions and poses.

All the face images are taken at the same lighting condition. Since the facial parts in the originally taken images are different in their scale, poses and locations, firstly we need to perform similarity transformation so as to get normalized images [14].

Fig. 1. Our database: different subjects with different expressions

2.2 Triangulation of Facial Images

To get texture vectors of faces, the first step is to get feature points of face contours. We define 44 control points for the human face, such as nose tip, eye and lip contours, middle chin, and so on. These points are the solid dots in Fig. 2. Besides these control points, we also define another 70 points among the solid dots to describe the detailed contours. These points well represent the main action units of expressions and are marked as hollow dots in Fig. 2 [15] [16].

Based on similarity transformations, we acquire the transformed coordinates of these 70 points in all the images of the database to reduce manual work of registering points. Therefore, for each image in the database, only 44 control points are located manually but locations of other 70 points can be decided automatically [17] [18].

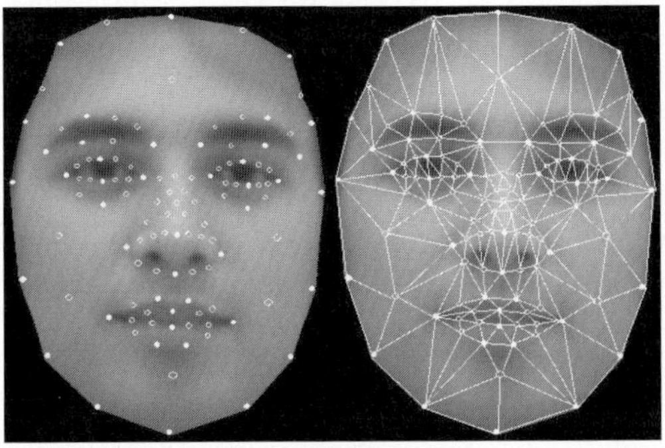

Fig. 2. Feature points on the average face as well as the triangulations

With the 114 control points, we triangulate the average human face into 209 small triangles, as can be found out in Figure 2. In the eye, nose, and mouth portions, we create more triangles than we make in other parts so as to represent facial appearances in greater detail. The point selection is better than MPEG-4 in creating new faces from our experiments [19].

2.3 Principal Components Analysis

Principal components define a projection that catches the maximum amount of variation in a dataset and is orthogonal to the previous principle component [2].

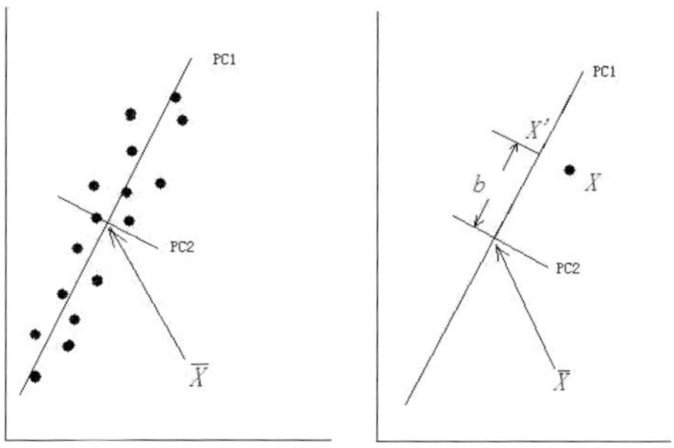

Fig. 3. Principal components analysis

After conducting eigen-decomposition in Fig. 3, we find two orthogonal vectors, i.e. principal component I (PC1) and principal component II (PC2). We observe that the main difference in the dataset is distributed along PC1, while less obvious differences lie on PC2. Therefore, data X can be approximated by $X' = \overline{X} + b \cdot PC_1$.

2.4 Parameterized Shape and Texture Models

After we get the shape and texture vectors for each training image, we build the parameterized shape and texture models in equation 1:

$$S = \overline{S} + \Phi_s b_s, \quad T = \overline{T} + \Phi_t b_t \tag{1}$$

where $\overline{S}$ and $\overline{T}$ is the average shape and texture vectors, Φ_s and Φ_t are eigenvectors for shape and texture models respectively. And b_s and b_t are shape and texture parameters [19]. 31 out of 228 principal components selected represent 99.23% variances in the original dataset. And we keep 93.95 of texture variance with the PCA.

Here we separately adjust shape and texture parameters to create new shapes and textures. Then we morph the new textures into new shapes with thin-plate splines [19].

2.5 Interpretation of Parameter Values

In this session, we interpret the effects of adjustments in shape and texture parameters. This analysis helps create images of different appearances for psychological analysis.

We increase the first element value in the b_s from equation (1) and keep other elements to be zero. Then we warp the average texture T to the new shape contour and acquire the smoothly transformed image sequence in first row of Fig. 4.

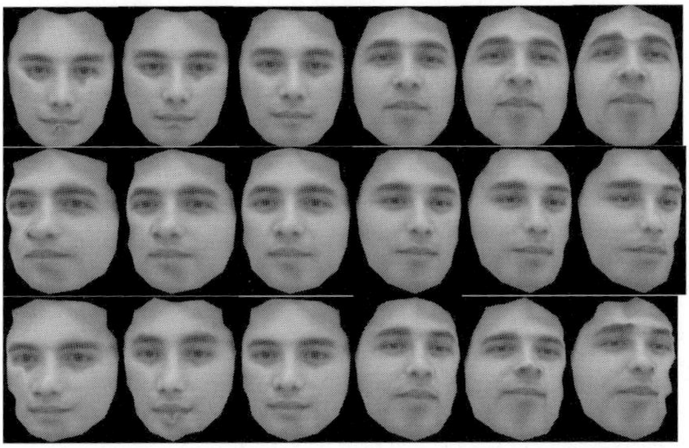

Fig. 4. Changes in expression and pose by changing parameters

The most obvious difference among images of first row in Fig. 4 is in the pose. With the changes of head pose, the proportion of upper face size to the lower size also differs. Another less significant change in this sequence is the mouth shape.

Second row of Fig. 4 shows the transformation of facial shapes by changing the second element in b_s. Though the viewing direction changes, the proportion in these faces keeps the same.

Changing $b_s(1)$ and $b_s(2)$ simultaneously can lead to transformations in third-row images of Fig. 4, where face poses and proportions are simultaneously modified because of the alternation in coordinates of both the outer and inner control points.

Therefore we find that pose transformations with changes in different modes equal to the sum of transformations in each mode transformation. Therefore, after we learn more relationships, we can combine them together so as to perform more complicated transformations on faces.

Now another series of experiments is to increase the value of elements in the texture parameter vector b_t from equation (1).

In first row of Fig. 5, the main shift lies in the facial hair, the cheek, the beard as well as the mouth. Basically the general change is from a bonny boy with dark eyelid, thick eyebrow, black beard and small nose to a fleshy man with light eyelid, thin eyebrow, no beard and big nose. And a light smile keeps on every face in this sequence.

In second row of Fig. 5, generally the face becomes more Asian alike during the process. Also the mouth opens gradually during the changes of the parameter, which leaves an impression of light smiling.

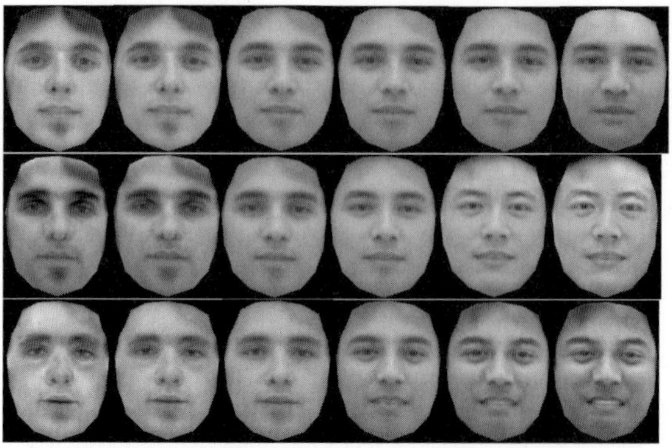

Fig. 5. Expression changes with the variance on first three texture parameters

In the third row of Fig. 5, main difference lies in the mouth area besides changes in eyebrow, skin color and extent of flesh cheeks.

Then how about changing the elements in shape and texture parameter vectors at the same time? Fig. 6 shows the effect of facial expression changes after we increase values of $b_s(1)$ and $b_t(1)$ simultaneously.

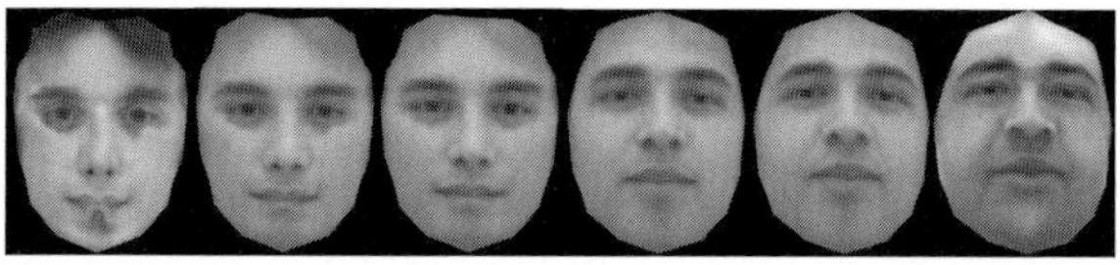

Fig. 6. Changes with the increment of first texture parameter

The alteration in Fig. 6 represents the combinatorial effects, i.e. the pose change and cheek variance.

These analyses can thus direct the creation of novel faces we need if only faces in our dataset are as different as possible. This is due to the fact that our models can represent most of the differences in shape and texture and can produce novel images which are outside of our dataset.

3 Manipulation on Novel Faces

In this part, we are addressing applications based on the information we learnt from the previous reconstructions and analysis.

3.1 Making Chubby and Skinny Faces

Manipulating faces to be chubby or skinny ones is widely applied in facial image processing as well as in face recognition.

Suppose our datasets are in a Gaussian distribution, then adding a new data into the space will not change the distribution. Thus we can replace the mean shape and texture vectors in equations (1) by those from a novel image. Then we perform transformations on our new facial images by changing the model parameters.

According to previous analysis, the 1st and 3rd texture parameters represent an effect of changing chubby faces. We also learn that modifications of the 14th and 17th shape modes play a significant role in getting skinny faces. By increasing these parameter values for a novel face, we achieve the transformed images as in Fig. 7.

As observed from Fig. 7, the transformed face (g) looks skinnier than (d), which is chubbier than (a), the previously neutral face.

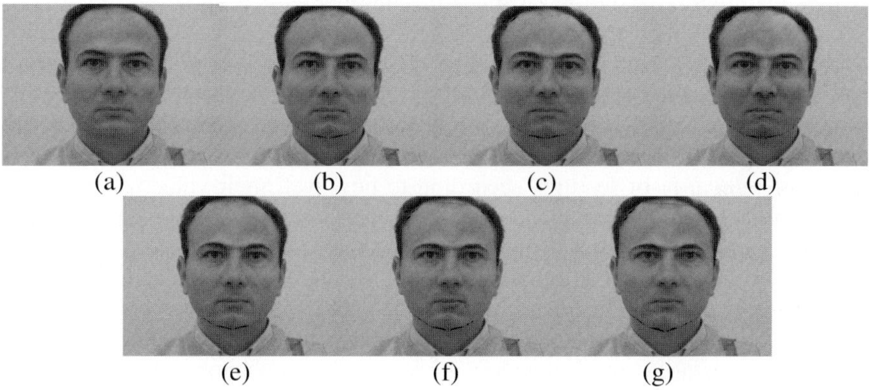

Fig. 7. (a) Neutral face, (b ~ d) chubby and (e ~ g) skinny faces

3.2 Comprehension on Expression

The parameterized model introduced above brings us a good approach for creating facial images with different contours as well as expressions. These images are also a good source for image understanding. We discuss the relations between parameters and viewers' understanding on masculinity, friendliness and attractiveness.

3.2.1 Collection of Survey Results

We applied the parameterized shape and texture model to create 58 images in different expressions. Then we presented these pictures to 59 volunteers from 8 different ethnicities, half of which are females. They were asked to mark each image on masculinity, friendliness and attractiveness. After deleting those obviously improper results, finally we get 1004 data on each aspect.

The first step in processing these datasets is to standardize them so as to reduce personal differences in scales of scoring.

The next step, also the key process, is to find the sequence of those parameters' importance in deciding the created images on masculinity, friendliness and attractiveness. Here we use feature selection to solve this problem.

3.2.2 Feature Selection

Feature selection aims at picking out some original input features (i) for performance issues by facilitating data collection as well as compressing storage space and processing time, (ii) to perform semantics analysis for understanding the problem, and (iii) to improve prediction accuracy [20].

According to [21], [22], and [23], feature selection approaches can be divided into three categories: filters, wrappers and embedded approaches. The filter model relies on general characteristics of the training dataset to select some features without involving any learning algorithm [24]. The wrapper model requires one predetermined learning algorithm in feature selection and uses its performance to evaluate and determine which features are selected [24]. The embedded approaches simultaneously determine features and classifier during the training process [20].

Wrapper models tend to find features better suited to the predetermined learning algorithm resulting in superior learning performance, but it is also computationally expensive compared to the filter model [25].

Concerning the above analysis, we apply ReliefF, a filter model, to be the attribute evaluation approach for our dataset. ReliefF is an extension to Relief, which is to estimate the relevance of features according to how well their values distinguish between the instances of the same and different classes that are close to each other [24]. It randomly samples a number of instances from the training set and updates the relevance estimation of each feature based on the differences between the selected instance and the two nearest instances of the same and opposite classes [24].

For search method, we utilize Ranker to discover the final sequence of model parameters. Ranker, used in conjunction with attribute evaluators, attributes by their individual evaluations [26].

In our experiments, we use the WEKA software for feature selection [26]. This free software is a collection of machine learning algorithms for data mining tasks: data-processing, classification, clustering, association and data visualization. It provides us a complete scheme: ReliefF for attribute selection, and Ranker for searching. After processing our datasets with WEKA, we achieve the ranking sequence of model parameters in determining masculinity, friendliness and attractiveness as in Table 1, where s_i represents the ith shape parameter, while t_i denotes the ith texture parameter.

Table 1. Ranking sequences of model parameters in determining the three aspects

Mascu.	s_2	t_2	s_3	s_1	t_1	t_5	s_6	t_3	s_5	s_4	t_6	s_8	s_7	t_7	t_4
Friend.	t_3	s_1	s_2	t_5	t_6	s_4	t_2	s_3	t_1	s_6	t_4	s_5	t_7	s_8	s_7
Attrac.	s_2	t_3	s_4	s_6	t_2	t_5	s_5	t_6	s_1	s_7	t_1	s_8	t_7	t_4	s_3

3.2.3 Face Transformation Results

By changing the first 15 shape (s_i in Table 1) and texture parameter values (t_i in Table 1) according to the feature selection result in Table 1, we create the transformed images based on a neutral boy's face shown in Fig. 8.

After presenting these four images to our volunteers again, 92.1% of them agreed on masculinity in the second face, 89.3% volunteers believed the third image is friendlier than the first one, and 83.6% viewers considered the last one to be more attractive.

Fig. 8. Neutral, masculine, friendly and attractive faces

3.2.4 Transferring Facial Expressions

We notice that a feature space has been constructed after we perform PCA on our dataset. To make use of this space, we also attempt to transfer expression changes from one person's faces onto another subject. This can be explained by Fig. 9.

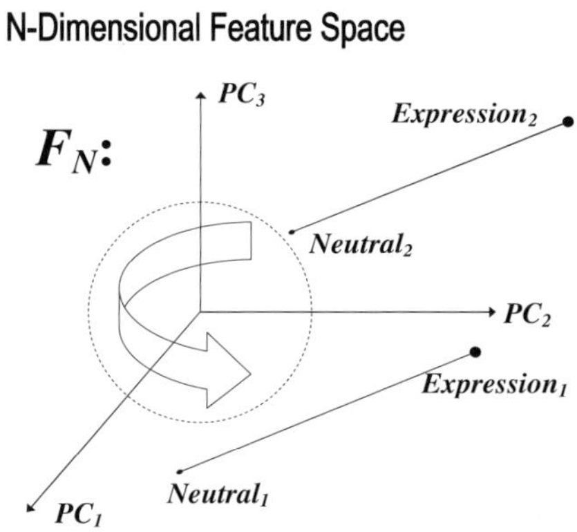

Fig. 9. Illustration of expression transfers in feature space

In Fig. 9, we simplify the explanation on N-Dimensional feature space into that in a 3-D space, where PC_1, PC_2 and PC_3 denote the first three eigen-vectors of our dataset. "Neutral$_1$" represents the reference person's neutral face, and the "Expression$_1$" denotes the person's face with certain expression. Then the directed vector from "Neutral$_1$" to "Expression$_1$" can denote the facial expression changes.

Mappings from the directed difference vector onto each eigen-vector correspond to various weights on each feature vector. Then we can contribute these weights to "Neutral$_2$", which denotes a target neutral face. The contribution creates the final "Expression$_2$" as shown in Fig. 9.

Figure 10 provides one good example for this expression transfer. Besides our previously collected facial image database, we asked another volunteer to make up angry, disgust, feared, surprised and sad faces. Then we perform the calculation on contour vectors in the feature space. The novel neutral face in Figure 10 is out of our database. After performing the contribution, we reconstruct the transformed faces by warping previous face patch to the transformed shape contours.

The whole procedure is automatic except for the manual work on locating contour points. We find that better expressions can be captured by controlling the transformations on different facial parts. For example, we can increase the weights on mouth area to make the transformed face in a more surprised way.

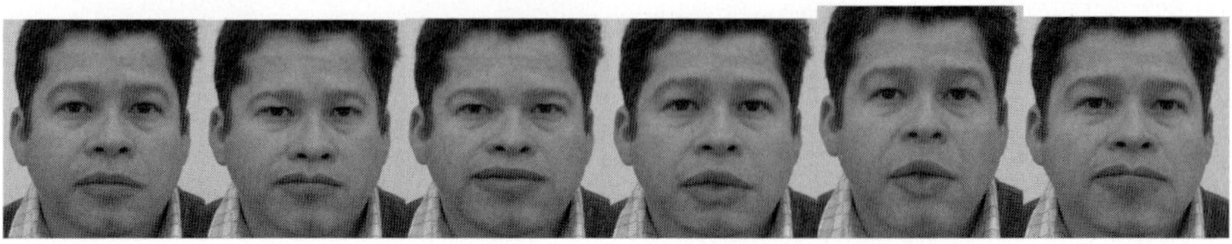

Fig. 10. Neutral, angry, disgust, feared, surprised and sad faces

4 Conclusions and Future Work

The main role of this paper is to disclose the relations between model parameters and subjective understanding on facial images concerning masculinity, friendliness and attractiveness. Applications include transforming a novel face image to be more masculine, friendly or attractive as well as transferring expressions from one subject's face onto another one's.

To avoid the disadvantages of conventional approaches, we do not rely on the geometric measurements but conduct much analysis on the shape and texture models' parameters. Specifically, we apply the face-space to leap over the complicated and normally inaccurate geometric measurements of distances and ratios on human faces.

The PCA-based model is an excellent source for creating images of many differences in their contour and texture vectors. It is also robust in image compression.

We separate shape and texture models so that the two models can create more faces. This should be an important improvement to previous approaches [14].

We received a large dataset from a survey and well analyzed the relations between parameter values and subjective understanding on the created faces. This knowledge helps us create a masculine face from the original neutral face image. Similar approaches also work for creating friendly and attractive faces out of a neutral one.

Based on the feature space, we also successfully transfer facial expressions from one subject's face onto another face. This is not a simple adding or subtraction as it seems to be, but an important manipulation in feature space.

Although Table1 provides the ranking of model parameters, it is not easy to decide the exact values for them. We are going to try another approach called expressional image synthesis controlled by emotional parameters [28]. Borrowing the idea from expression transfer, we can also perform transfer on masculinity, friendliness and attractiveness if we can have such reference faces. Moreover, since mouth in the neutral face is always closed, we need to add teeth to transformed faces when the transformation leads the mouth to be widely opened.

Acknowledgement

Many thanks to colleagues at the DISCOVER laboratory of University of Ottawa for their devotion of facial images to our research. And we would like to express our gratitude to those volunteers in University of Ottawa (Canada) and Southeast University (China) who helped us to finish the survey. Also we would like to thank anonymous reviewers for their invaluable comments.

References

1. Marvel, L. M., Hartwig Jr, G. W.: A Survey of Image Compression Techniques and their Performance in Noisy Environments. Final report number: A409623, (May 1996–Jan. 1997) pages: 98
2. Smith, L. I.: A tutorial on Principal Components Analysis, maintained by Cornell Unviersity, U.S.A. (Feb. 26, 2002)
3. Yeung, K. Y., Ruzzo, W.: Principal Component Analysis for Clustering Gene Expression Data. Bioinformatics 17(9): (2001)763-774
4. Schmidhuber, J.: Facial Beauty and Fractal Geometry, Technical report. IDSIA-28-98, IDSIA, Corso Elvezia 36, 6900 Lugano, Switzerland, 1998
5. Liu, Z., Shan, Y., and Zhang, Z.: Expressive Expression Mapping with Ratio Images. Computer Graphics, Siggraph, (August 2001) 271-276
6. Zhang, Q., Liu, Z., Guo, B., Terzopoulos, D., Shum, H.: Geometry-Driven Photorealistic Facial Expression Synthesis. IEEE Trans. on Visual. and Comp. Graph., Volume 12, Issue 1, (2006) 48-60
7. Fink, B., Penton-Voak, I.: Evolutionary Psychology of Facial Attractiveness, Current directions in psychological sciences, Vol. 11, Num. 5, Blackwell Publishing, (2002) 154-158
8. Johnston, V. S., Hagel, R., Franklin, M., Fink, B., Grammer, K.: Male Facial Attractiveness Evidence for Hormone-Meditated Adaptive Design, Evolution and human behavior 22, Elsevier, (2001) 251-267
9. O'Toole, A. J., Price, T., Vetter, T., Bartlett, J. C., Blanz, V.: Three-Dimensional Shape and Two-Dimensional Surface Textures of Human Faces: The Role of "Averages" in Attractiveness and Age, Im. and Vis. Comput. Journ. 18 (1999) 9-19
10. Rowland, D., Perrett, A. D. I.: Manipulating Facial Appearance through Shape and Color, IEEE Computer Graphics and Applications, 15(5), (1995) 70-76
11. Lanitis, A., Taylor, C. J., Cootes, T. F.: Automatic Interpretation and Coding of Face Images Using Flexible Models, IEEE Trans. on PAMI, Vol. 19, No. 7, (1997) 743-756
12. Vetter, T., Poggio, T.: Linear Object Classes and Image Synthesis from a Single Example Image, IEEE Trans. on PAMI, Vol. 19, No. 7, (1997) 733-742
13. Cootes, T. F., Edwards, G. J., Taylor, C. J.: Active Appearance Models, IEEE Trans. on PAMI, Vol. 23, No. 6, (2001) 681-685
14. Cootes, T. F., Taylor, C. J.: Statistical Models of Appearance for Computer Vision, Technical report, University of Manchester, UK, (1999)
15. Tian, Y.L., Kanade, T., Cohn, J. F.: Recognizing Action Units for Facial Expression Analysis, IEEE Trans. on PAMI, Vol. 23, No. 2, (2001) 97-115
16. Ekman, P., Friesen, W. V.: Facial Action Coding System: A Technique for the Measurement of Facial Movement. Consulting Psychologists Press, Palo Alto, CA, (1978)

17. Lee, W., Magnenat-Thalmann, N.: Head Modeling from Pictures and Morphing in 3D with Image Metamorphosis Based on Triangulation, Proc. Captech98, Geneva, (1998) 254-267
18. Goto, T., Lee, W., Magnenat-Thalmann, N.: Facial Feature Extraction for Quick 3D Face Modeling, Signal processing: Image communication, Elsevier Science, Vol. 17, Issue 3, (2002) 243-259
19. Xi, P., Xu, T., Zhao, Zh.: Knowledge-Based Active Appearance Model Applied in Medical Image Localization, Proc. of IEEE International conference on Mechatronics and automation (ICMA'05), Niagara Fall, Canada, (2005) 637-642
20. Neumann, J., Schnorr, C., Steidl, G.: Combined SVM-Based Feature Selection and Classification, Machine Learning, 61, (2005) 129-150
21. Guyon, I., Elisseeff, A.: An Introduction to Variable and Feature Selection, Journal of Machine Learning Research, (2003) 1157-1182
22. John, G., Kohavi, R., Pfleger, K.: Irrelevant Features and the Subset Selection Problem, Proc. of the 11th International Conference on Machine Learning, (1994) 121-129
23. Bradley, P. S., Mangasarian, O. L.: Feature Selection via Concave Minimization and Support Vector Machines, Proc. of the 15th International Conference on Machine Learning, San Francisco, CA, USA, (1998) 82-90
24. Yu, L., Liu, H.: Feature Selection for High-Dimensional Data: A Fast Correlation-Based Filter Solution. In Proceedings of the Twentieth International Conference on Machine Leaning (ICML-03), (2003) 856-863
25. Langley, P.: Selection of Relevant Features in Machine Learning, Proc. of the AAAI Fall Symposium on Relevance, AAAI press, (1994)
26. Witten, H.I., Frank, E.: Data Mining: Practical Machine Learning Tools and Techniques, 2nd edition, Morgan Kaufmann, San Francisco
27. Penrose, R., A Generalized Inverse for Matrices, Proc. Cambridge Phil. Soc. 51, (1955) 406-413
28. Zhou, C., Lin, X.: Facial Expressional Image Synthesis Controlled by Emotional Parameters. Pattern Recognition Letters 26, (2005) 2611-2627

Real-Time Facial Expression Mapping for High Resolution 3D Meshes

Mingli Song[1], Zicheng Liu[2], and Baining Guo[3]

[1] College of Computer Science, Zhejiang University
brooksong@cs.zju.edu.cn
[2] Microsoft Research, Redmond
zliu@microsoft.com
[3] Microsoft Research, Asia
bainguo@microsoft.com

Abstract. We present a learning-based 3D facial expression mapping technique that preserves facial expression details and works in real time for even high resolution meshes. Our approach is inspired by a previously developed technique called deformation transfer [1]. The deformation transfer technique preserves facial expression details but its computational overhead makes it not suitable for real time applications. To accelerate computation, we use a piecewise linear function to represent the mapping from the *direct motion* (the difference between the expression face and the neutral face) to the motion obtained by the deformation transfer method. This piecewise linear function is learned offline from a small set of training data. The online computation is thus reduced to the evaluation of the piecewise linear functions which is significantly faster. As a result, we are able to perform real time expression mapping for even high resolution 3D meshes.

1 Introduction

How to synthesize convincing 3D facial expressions has been an interesting yet challenging problem in computer graphics. Facial expressions exhibit not only feature point motions, but also subtle changes in illumination and appearance due to skin deformation (e.g., facial creases and wrinkles). These details are important visual cues, but they are difficult to synthesize.

Recently, Sumner and Popović[1] developed a technique named *deformation transfer* that is capable of transferring 3D facial expression details from a performer to a target face model. One drawback of this technique is that its computation overhead makes it difficult to be used in real time applications. Given the rapid development of real time high resolution 3D scanning technology [2, 3, 4], people will soon be able to capture a performer's dense 3D facial expressions and animate a virtual face model in real time. To this end, it is necessary to be able to transfer 3D facial expressions in real time while preserving expression details.

To accelerate computation, we propose to use a piecewise linear function to approximate the mapping from the *direct motion*, which is the difference between an expression face and the neutral face, to the motion obtained by the

H.-P. Seidel, T. Nishita, and Q. Peng (Eds.): CGI 2006, LNCS 4035, pp. 277–287, 2006.

deformation transfer technique. The advantage of the piecewise linear function is that its evaluation is very fast. Thus we are able to perform real time expression mapping for even high resolution 3D meshes.

2 Related Work

There has been a lot of research in facial animation. It is virtually impossible to enumerate all of them. The book by Parke and Waters [5] provides an excellent survey.

Expression mapping (also called performance-driven animation) has been a popular method for generating facial animations [5, 6, 7, 8]. In addition to the deformation transfer work, there has been a lot of research done in the last a few years to improve the basic expression mapping technique.

Liu et al. [9] proposed a 2D technique, called the expression ratio image (ERI), that is able to map one person's expression details to a different person's face image.

Pighin et al. [10] parameterized each person's expression space as a convex combination of some basis expressions and proposed mapping one person's expression coefficients to those of another person. This technique was later on extended by Pyun et al. [11] who used radial basis functions to parameterize the expression space.

Noh and Neumann [12] developed a technique to automatically find a correspondence between two faces based on small number of user-specified correspondences. They also developed a new motion mapping technique that adjusts the direction and magnitude of the motion vector based on the local geometries of the source and target model. So far, we have not seen any work that applies this technique to transferring 3D expression details for high resolution meshes.

Zhang et al. [13, 14] proposed a technique to synthesize facial expression details of the target face model (2D or 3D) based on the feature point motions of a performer. It requires example expressions of the target face model.

3 Basic Facial Expression Mapping

The basic facial expression mapping method is very simple and has been a popular method for generating facial animations. For example, this technique was used to produce some of the facial animations in the renowned film "Tony de Peltrie".

Let $G_{s,n}$ denote a source subject's neutral face mesh and assume it has N vertices. We use the same notation $G_{s,n}$ to denote the $3N$ dimensional vector consisting of all the vertex coordinates. Let $G_{s,e}$ denote an expression mesh of this person. Let $G_{t,n}$ denote a target person's face mesh. Assuming there is a vertex correspondence between $G_{s,n}$, $G_{s,e}$, and $G_{t,n}$, the basic facial expression mapping works simply by computing the difference vector of $G_{s,e}$ and $G_{s,n}$, and adding it to ${}_{t,n}$. That is, the expression mesh for the target model is obtained by

$$G_{t,e} = G_{t,n} + G_{s,e} - G_{s,n} \tag{1}$$

This method is simple to implement and is fast. One drawback is that it creates artifacts when applied to high resolution meshes. Fig. 5 shows the results obtained by the basic expression mapping. In the first and second expressions, we can see the artifacts around cheekbone area. In the third and fourth expressions, the mesh is not smooth on the regions near the external eye corners.

4 Deformation Transfer

Deformation transfer technique, which was proposed by Sumner and Popović [1], provides a solution to this problem. It estimates the target vertex motion $(G_{t,e} - G_{t,n})$ by optimizing a global objective function. Fig. 6 shows the results generated by the deformation transfer technique. There are almost no visible artifacts while the facial expression wrinkles are transferred nicely.

One drawback with the deformation transfer technique is that it is computationally expensive. Even though LU-decomposition can be done just once, for each frame it needs to evaluate the fourth vertex for each triangle and perform back substitution (the user is referred to [1] for details). According our measurement, it takes more than one second per frame on a mesh with 19142 vertices and 37551 triangles on a 3.0GHz processor. How to accelerate the computation while preserving the motion quality is the focus of this work.

5 Learning-Based Expression Mapping

To accelerate computation, we propose to use a piecewise linear function to approximate the mapping from the difference vector to the motion obtained by the deformation transfer technique.

Let Ω_s denote the space of difference vectors of the source person's facial expressions. That is

$$\Omega_s = \cup_e \{\Delta G_{s,e}\} \tag{2}$$

where $\Delta G_{s,e} = G_{s,e} - G_{s,n}$, and e ranges over all possible expressions of the source person.

Let Π denote the deformation transfer function. That is, for any given expression e, $\Pi(\Delta G_{s,e})$ is the motion obtained from the deformation transfer algorithm.

Let $v_{s,n,j}$ and $v_{s,e,j}$ denote the coordinates of vertex j in $G_{s,n}$ and $G_{s,e}$, respectively, where $j = 1, \cdots, N$. Denote $\Delta v_{s,e,j} = v_{s,e,j} - v_{s,n,j}$. Let $Pi_j(\Delta v_{s,e,j})$ denote the deformation transfer result for vertex j.We wish to approximate Π_j with a linear transformation. In other words, we'd like to find a 3×3 matrix A_j such that

$$\Pi_j(\Delta v_{s,e,j}) = A_j \Delta v_{s,e,j} \tag{3}$$

for all expression e. In practice, it is impossible to find a single matrix A_j that works for all expressions. Therefore, we classify the expression space into multiple classes, and estimate a 3×3 matrix for each class. The 3×3 matrix is the linear approximation of the deformation transfer function for the expressions in that class. In this way, we obtain a piecewise linear approximation of the deformation transfer function.

5.1 Training

Given a set of training data of the source object's expressions, let Ω_s^T denote the set of difference vectors corresponding to the training expressions. We use the K-Nearest-Neighbor (KNN) classifier [15] to classify Ω_s^T into K classes where K is specified by the user. Therefore,

$$\Omega_s^T = \cup_{k=1}^{K} \Omega_{s,k}^T \tag{4}$$

where $\Omega_{s,k}^T$ is the kth class.

Suppose there are I_K expressions in $\Omega_{s,k}^T$ and $\Omega_{s,k}^T = \{\Delta G_i : i = 1, \cdots, I_k\}$. For each ΔG_i in $\Omega_{s,k}^T$, let Δv_j^i denote its component corresponding to vertex j, that is,

$$\Delta G_i = (\Delta v_1^i, \Delta v_2^i, \cdots, \Delta v_N^i)^T \tag{5}$$

Let $\Delta^* G_i$ be the resulting motion vector of deformation transfer, and

$$\Delta^* G_i = (\Delta^* v_1^i, \Delta^* v_2^i, \cdots, \Delta^* v_N^i)^T \tag{6}$$

For each vertex j, we would like to find a 3×3 matrix A_j^k, such that

$$\Delta^* v_j^i = A_j^k \Delta v_j^i, i = 1, \cdots, I_K \tag{7}$$

We use a linear least square method to solve equation (7) and obtain A_j^k. Thus we obtain a piecewise linear approximation of Π.

5.2 Data Interpolation

After training is done, for each new expression, we could simply compute its class index, and for each vertex, apply the corresponding linear transformation in that class to obtain the vertex motion for the target mesh. One drawback with this nearest-neighbor approach is that when a source expression, which is at the border of two classes, slowly changes to the other group, there will be a sudden jump on the target expression. The sudden jump is due to the fact that the linear transformation matrix suddenly changes from the first class to the second class.

One remedy to this problem is to use data interpolation, that is, a weighted sum of the results from multiple classes.

For each class $\Omega_{s,k}^T$, let $\Delta \overline{G}_k$ denote its mean vector, where

$$\Delta \overline{G}_k = (\Delta \overline{v}_{1,k}, \Delta \overline{v}_{2,k}, \cdots, \Delta \overline{v}_{N,k})^T \tag{8}$$

Let ΔG denote any given new expression where

$$\Delta G = (\Delta v_1, \Delta v_2, \cdots, \Delta v_N)^T \tag{9}$$

For each vertex j, the weight for class $\Omega_{s,k}^T$ is defined as

$$c_{j,k} = \frac{\Delta v_j \cdot \Delta \overline{v}_{j,k}}{|\Delta v_j||\Delta \overline{v}_{j,k}|} \tag{10}$$

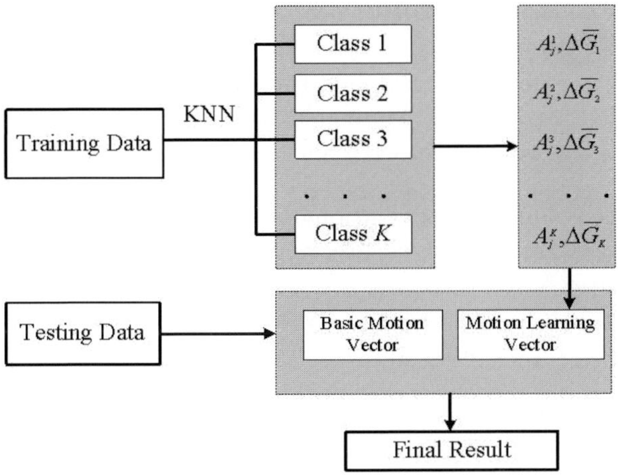

Fig. 1. Overview of learning based method

The interpolated motion for the target model is

$$\Delta v_{t,j}^{L} = \sum_{k=1}^{K} \frac{c_{j,k} A_j^k \Delta v_j}{\sum_{k=1}^{K} c_{j,k}}, j = 1, \cdots, N \tag{11}$$

Note that in equation (10), we use the angle between two vectors to measure the similarity instead of using the Euclidean distance. The reason is that matrix Aj^k is much more sensitive to direction changes than magnitude changes. From our experiments, we observe that in general if matrix A_j^k works well for one motion vector, it also works well for the scaled version of this vector.

Finally, to handle the case when a test expression is far away from all of the class centers, we use a weighted sum of $\Delta v_{t,j}^{L}$ (equation (11)) and the direct motion, that is, the final motion for the target model is

$$\Delta v_{t,j} = w_s \Delta v_j + (1 - w_s) \Delta v_{t,j}^{L} \tag{12}$$

where w_s is a function of the distance between ΔG and the class center $\Delta \overline{G}_k$, $k = 1, \cdots, K$, and is defined as follows. Denote

$$Dist(\Delta G) = \frac{\sum_{k=1}^{K} (\Delta G - \Delta \overline{G}_k)(\Delta G - \Delta \overline{G}_k)^T}{K} \tag{13}$$

w_s is set to be

$$w_s = \frac{\delta(\Delta G)(\Delta G)^T}{Dist(\Delta G) + (\Delta G)(\Delta G)^T} \tag{14}$$

where δ is a predefined constant between 0 and 1.

Fig. 1 is a summary of the learning based method.

6 Vertex Correspondence

Before we perform expression mapping, the source mesh and target mesh needs to have vertex correspondence. Sumner and Popović [1] proposed a method to compute vertex correspondence between two meshes of arbitrary objects (not necessarily face meshes). Due to the fact that they have to handle general meshes, their method needs human interventions and is quite tedious. Since face model has a much more constrained structure, we use a GPU-accelerated [16] face mesh re-sampling approach.

First, a set of face feature points are marked manually on both the source and target meshes. Fig. 2 shows the feature points that we use. Second, a global transformation (scale, rotation, and translation) [17] is computed to globally align the marked source and target mesh. Third, for each mesh, we create a 2D image called *mesh image*. The mesh image is created by projecting each vertex on a cylinder (i.e. cylindrical projection) while the (x, y, z) coordinate is encoded in the (r, g, b) color channels. Fig. 3 shows an example of a mesh image. The two mesh images are then pixel-aligned by a triangulation-based image warping [9]. This step is done by GPU. To re-sample the source mesh so that its topology is the same as the target mesh, for each vertex on the target mesh, we find its pixel location on its mesh image. At the same location in the source's mesh image, we obtain its (x, y, z) coordinates from the color channel.

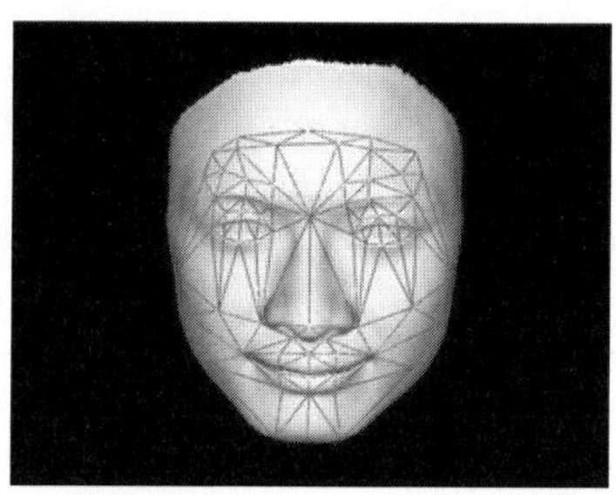

Fig. 2. Feature points

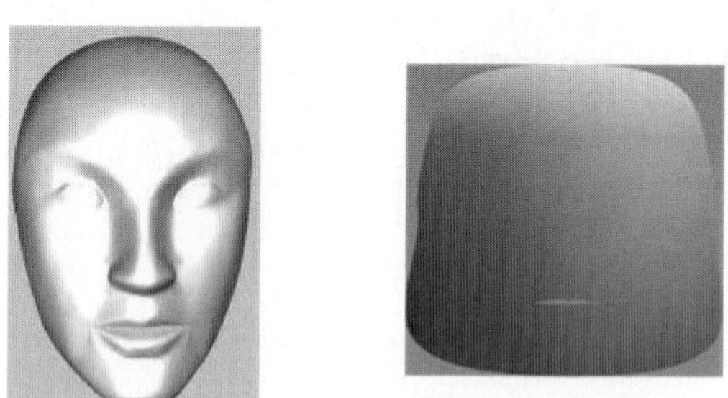

Fig. 3. A 3D mesh and its mesh image

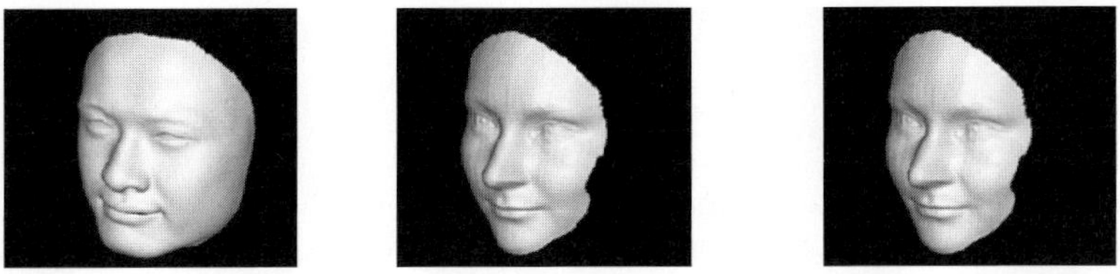

(a) Source mesh (b) Target mesh (c) Re-sampled mesh of the target

Fig. 4. Face correspondence

Fig. 4 shows a result of the vertex correspondence. The source mesh (a) and target mesh (b) have different topology. (c) is the re-sampled mesh of the target mesh. The re-sampled mesh (c) looks the same as the original target mesh. But its topology is the source mesh's topology. The entire process of vertex correspondence computation including mesh image generation, image warping, and mesh re-sampling, takes less than 2 seconds on a pair of meshes each with approximately 20000 vertices and 40000 triangles.

7 Experiment Results

To validate our approach, we have implemented the basic expression mapping, deformation transfer, and the learning-based technique. We performed experiments on the 3D facial expression sequence captured by a structure-light based 3D capturing system which was developed by Zhang et al. [4]. There are about 300 frames in total. We select 30 frames as the training data and use the rest of the frames as the test data. The training expressions are classified into 6 classes, that is, $K = 6$. We find that $\delta = 0.6$ works well in general. We first empirically select 6 representative expressions from the training images as shown in Fig. 8. The rest of the training images are classified into these 6 classes through a K-nearest-neighbor technique.

Source

Target

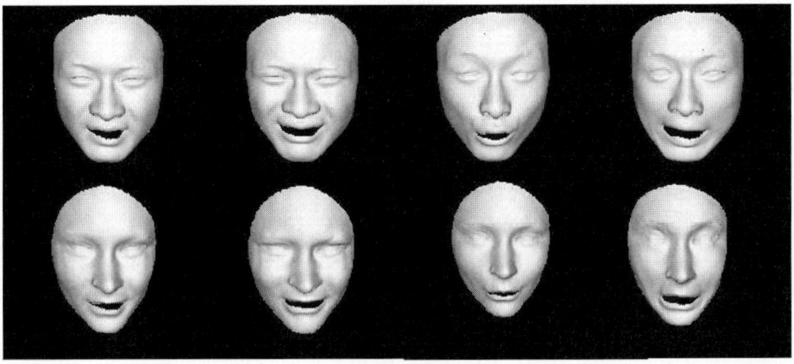

Fig. 5. Basic expression mapping

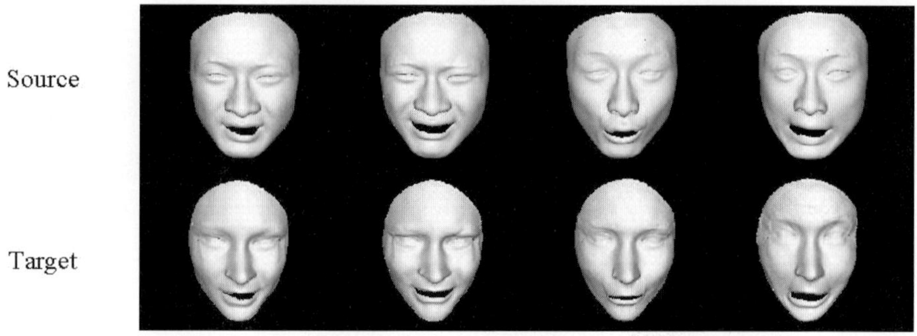

Fig. 6. Deformation transfer based expression mapping

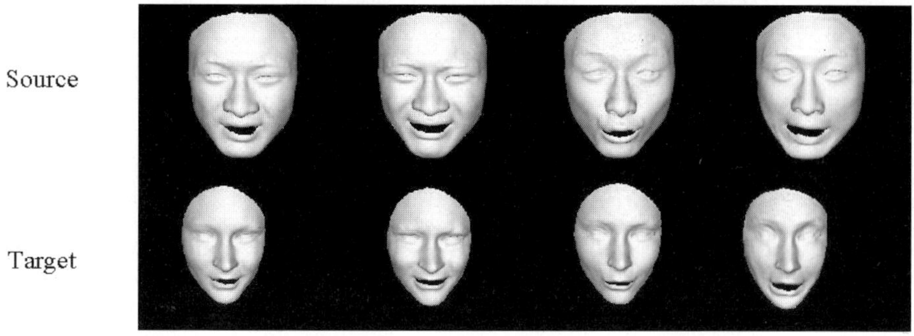

Fig. 7. Learning based expression mapping

Fig. 7 shows the experiment results of the learning based expression mapping method which is compared with the basic expression mapping results in Fig. 5 and the deformation transfer results in Fig. 6. We can see that the results from the learning-based method are much better than that of the basic expression mapping. Its quality is very close to the deformation transfer algorithm.

Fig. 9 shows experiment results on another target mesh. Again, the quality of the results from learning based method is close to the quality of the results obtained by deformation transfer method.

We have applied the three techniques on a video sequence with 120 frames. The accompanying video material contains 3 video clips each corresponding to a different method.

We have also measured average CPU time for a total of 120 frames on a machine with Pentium IV 3.0 GHz with 512MB memory. There are 19142 vertices and 37551 triangles. For the deformation transfer, we perform LU decomposition [1, 18] as a pre-processing step, and its computation time is not included. For each frame, we only include the time for evaluating the right hand side and performing back substitution. The average CPU time per frame for basic expression mapping, deformation transfer, and learning based method are 0.0152

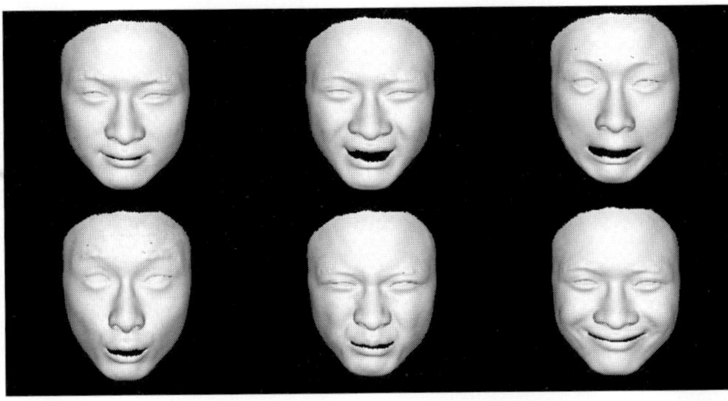

Fig. 8. Samples of the training set

Fig. 9. Results comparison among the three methods. (From top to bottom: Basic expression mapping, deformation transfer based expression mapping and learning based expression mapping).

seconds, 1.3253 seconds, and 0.1074 seconds, respectively. We obtain more than one magnitude of speed up over the deformation transfer method.

Furthermore, we have measured the difference between learning based expression mapping results and deformation transfer results. The average difference between the results of learning based method and those of deformation transfer is $(0.054460, 0.021996, 0.418960)$ (corresponding to (x, y, z) components). In comparison, the average difference between the results of the basic method and deformation transfer is $(0.605108, 0.244402, 4.655119)$.

8 Conclusion and Future Direction

We have developed a novel learning-based facial expression mapping technique. It is significantly faster than the deformation transfer algorithm while the resulting facial expression quality is close to the results obtained from deformation transfer. We have shown experiments on high resolution 3D expression sequences.

In the future, we would like to integrate our technique with a real time 3D facial expression capturing system so that we can perform live demonstrations of high resolution real time 3D expression mapping.

We are planning on further reducing computation by using a locally weighted sum to reduce the number of the summation terms in equation 12.

It is quite tedious to manually mark the feature points on the meshes. We would like develop an automatic feature point detection system on 3D meshes.

Acknowledgements

We would like to thank Li Zhang and David Xianfeng Gu for kindly providing their 3D face data.

References

1. Sumner R. W., Popović J. : Deformation Transfer for Triangle Meshes. in ACM Siggraph. (2004) 399-405
2. Kähler K., Haber J., Seidel H.-P.: Geometry-based Muscle Modeling for Facial Animation. in Graphics Interface. (2001) 37-46
3. Lee Y. and Terzopoulos D. and Waters K.: Realistic Modelling for Facial Animation. in ACM Siggraph. (1995) 55-62
4. Zhang L., Snavely N., Curless B., Seitz S. M.: Spacetime faces: high resolution capture for modeling and animation. ACM Transaction on Graphics, **23(3)** (2004) 548-558
5. Parke F. I. and Waters K.: Computer Facial Animation. Wellesley, Mass: AK Peters (1996)
6. Brennan S. E.: Caricature Generator, MS Visual Studies, Dept. of Architecture, Massachusettes Inst. Of Technology, Cambridge, Mass. (1982)
7. Litwinowcz P. and Williams L.: Animating Images with Drawings, In ACM Siggraph, (1994) 409-412
8. Williams L.: Performance-Driven Facial Animation. Computer Graphics, (1990) 235-242
9. Liu Z., Shan Y., and Zhang Z.: Expressive expression mapping with ratio images. In ACM Siggraph, (2001) 271-276
10. Pighin F., Hecker J., Lischinski D., Szeliski R., and Salesin D. H.: Synthesizing realistic facial expressions from photographs. In ACM Siggraph, (1998) 75-84
11. Pyun P., Kim Y., Chae W.: An Example-based Approach for Facial Expression Cloning. In ACM Siggraph/EuroGraphics Symposium on Computer Animation, (2003) 277-288
12. Noh J.-Y, Neumann U.: Expression Cloning. In ACM Siggraph, (2001) 277-288

13. Zhang Q., Liu Z., Guo B., and Shum H.: Geometry-Driven Photorealistic Facial Expression Synthesis. In Eurography/Siggraph Symposium on Computer Animation, (2003) 177 - 187
14. Zhang Q., Liu Z., Guo B., Terzopoulos D., and Shum H.: Geometry-Driven Photorealistic Facial Expression Synthesis. In IEEE Transaction on Visualization and Computer Graphics, **12(1)** (2006) 48-60
15. Duda R. O., Hart P. E. and Stork D. G.: Pattern Classification, Wiley Interscience, (2000)
16. Krüger J. and Westermann R.: Linear Algebra Operators for GPU Implementation of Numerical Algorithms. In ACM Siggraph. (2003) 908-916
17. Challis J. H.: A procedure for determining rigid body transformation parameters. In Journal of Biomechanics, **28(6)** (1995) 733-737
18. Davis T. A.: Umfpack version 4.1 user guide, In Technical report, University of Florida. TR-03-008. (2003)

A Comparison of Three Techniques to Interact in Large Virtual Environments Using Haptic Devices with Limited Workspace

Lionel Dominjon[1], Anatole Lécuyer[2], Jean-Marie Burkhardt[3], and Simon Richir[1]

[1] P & I Laboratory, ENSAM Angers, France
dominjon@ingenierium.com, simon.richir@angers.ensam.fr
[2] SIAMES Project, INRIA/IRISA, France
anatole.lecuyer@irisa.fr
[3] EIFFEL Project, University of Paris 5/INRIA, France
jean-marie.burkhardt@inria.fr

Abstract. This paper describes an experiment that was conducted to evaluate three interaction techniques aiming at interacting with large virtual environments using haptic devices with limited workspace: the Scaling technique, the Clutching technique, and the Bubble technique. Participants were asked to paint a virtual model as fast and as precisely as possible inside a CAVE, using a "desktop" haptic device. The results showed that the Bubble technique enabled both the quickest and the most precise paintings. It was also the most appreciated technique.

1 Introduction

Haptic interfaces were shown to greatly enhance interaction with Virtual Environments (VE) [1, 2]. Most of the current haptic interfaces are well suited for "desktop" applications, in which the dimensions of the *visual display* of the virtual environment do not exceed the size of the *haptic workspace* of the manipulated device. However, with large immersive systems – such as CAVE [3], RealityCenter or Holobench – becoming more common, the potential haptic interaction becomes limited to a small portion of the VE.

To overcome the mismatch between the haptic and the visual workspaces, several software interaction techniques have been developed. In the present paper, we compare the uses of three of these interaction techniques: the Clutching technique [4], the Scaling technique [5], and the Bubble technique [6]. The proposed experiment is based on a task of 3D painting in which participants were asked to paint a virtual model in a large VE as fast and as precisely as possible, using a desktop haptic device.

Therefore, this paper starts with an overview of related work in the field of 3D interaction techniques designed for haptic interaction with a VE that is larger than the workspace of the haptic device. Then we report on the experiment conducted to compare the uses of the three aforementioned techniques. The paper ends with a general discussion, a conclusion and a description of future work.

H.-P. Seidel, T. Nishita, and Q. Peng (Eds.): CGI 2006, LNCS 4035, pp. 288 – 299, 2006.

2 Related Work

Several software solutions were proposed as interaction techniques to overcome the limitations of current haptic devices when interacting with large VEs [4-6].

A first interaction technique is based on the concept of clutching [4]. It is inspired by the use of a classical 2D mouse. When reaching the limits of the mouse's workspace, the user may lift (declutch) the mouse, in order to put it down on a new location (clutch). This technique was implemented in haptic APIs (Application Programming Interface) such as in the VIRTUOSE API from Haption [7]. When the user reaches an uncomfortable posture with the force-feedback interface, he/she may declutch and freeze the virtual cursor in the VE by pressing a button. Then he/she can move the haptic device, reach a more comfortable position, and then clutch again by releasing the button to unfreeze the virtual cursor.

A second interaction technique is the scaling technique, introduced by Fischer and Vance [5] who integrated a PHANToM 1.5 haptic interface in the C6 (a CAVE-like system). They used an amplification of the user's motion, i.e. a motion scaling between the haptic workspace and the VE [8]. The link between the two spaces is defined by a scaling factor equal to the ratio: 'largest dimension of the workspace of the haptic device' to 'largest dimension of the virtual environment'.

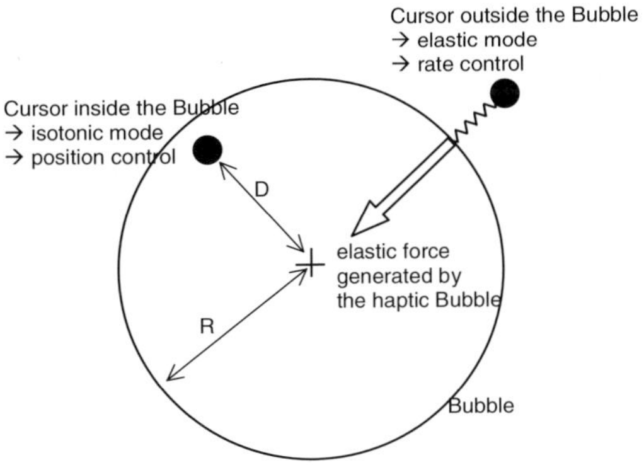

Fig. 1. Control modes according to cursor position

A third interaction technique is the Bubble technique developed by Dominjon et al. [6]. The Bubble technique is based on a hybrid position/rate control [9, 10]. Position control is used around the central position of the haptic device, for fine positioning, while rate control is used at the boundaries of the device, for coarse positioning. The boundary between the position-control zone and the rate-control zone is visually displayed as a semi-transparent sphere, looking like a soap bubble (see Fig. 1). The boundary is also haptically displayed by applying a radial force when crossing the surface of the bubble. The user may thus "feel" the inner surface of the bubble and slide on it. Furthermore, thanks to force-feedback of the device, the Bubble technique simulates the use of an elastic device when the cursor is rate-controlled (i.e. outside the bubble) [6].

3 Comparison of the Clutching, the Scaling and the Bubble Techniques in a Large Virtual Environment

To compare the uses of the three aforementioned techniques, we have conducted an experiment based on a task of 3D painting. In this task, participants were asked to paint a 3D virtual model as fast and as precisely as possible. The performance of participants was recorded in terms of task completion time and quality of the final painting. At the end of the experiment, a preference test was also proposed, in which participants had to choose their favourite technique according to several subjective criteria.

3.1 Participants

15 participants aged from 22 to 46 (mean=28, sd=6) took part in this experiment. Six of them were females. All of them, except one, were right-handed. None of them had known perception disorders, and all participants were naïve to the purpose of the present experiment.

3.2 Experimental Apparatus

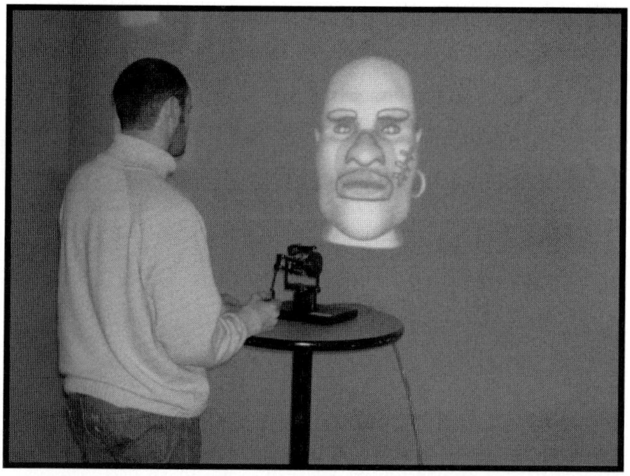

Fig. 2. Experimental set-up

3.2.1 Haptic and Visual Displays

We used a generic "desktop" haptic device: the PHANToM Premium 1.0 (see Fig. 2) from SensAble Technologies [11]. A small spherical cursor was manipulated in the VE via the PHANToM (see Fig. 3). It was used to apply paint directly on the virtual model, as if a brush was embedded at the tip of the PHANToM. Thanks to the force-feedback of the device, participants were also able to feel the contact between the cursor and the virtual model.

The PHANToM was placed inside a 4-screen CAVE-like display (see Fig. 2). For simplicity reasons, only one screen was used to display the virtual environment. This screen was a 3x3m rear-projected screen. The visual feedback was displayed at a frequency of 120 Hz, in monoscopic conditions. The visual display of the virtual environment consisted in a 3D model of a face to be painted (see Fig. 4), and a button bar which was used to change the paint colour. Six colours were available: yellow, blue, green, pink, red, and brown. The face model was displayed in the centre of the screen, in front of the participant. The button bar was located on the left-side, near the border of the screen.

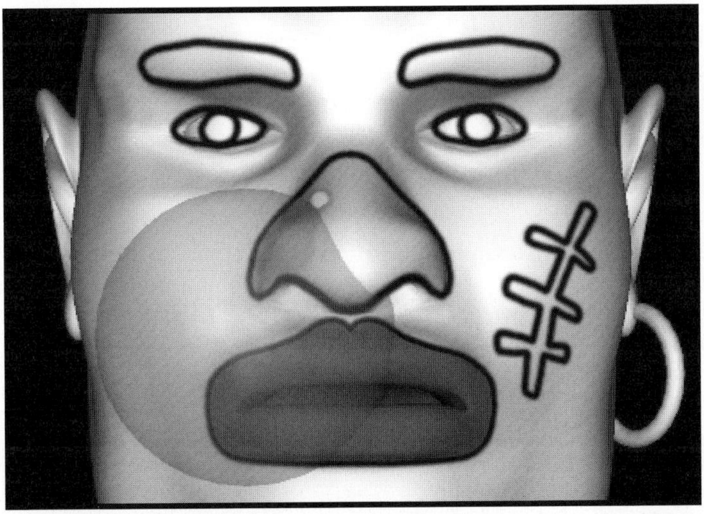

Fig. 3. Close-up view of the Bubble in case of contact and painting of the virtual model

3.2.2 Interaction Techniques Compared

Four interaction techniques were implemented for the purpose of the experimental evaluation.

(a) Motion Amplification

The motion amplification technique (**Scaling**) is described by Fischer and Vance in [5]. It is based on a reduced Control/Display ratio, i.e. a *scaling* between the user's motion (Control) and the motion of the virtual cursor (Display).

The scaling factor, *world_haptic_scale*, is defined in [5] as: the largest dimension of the workspace of the haptic device (*max_workspace_size*) divided by the largest dimension of the virtual environment (*max_virtual_size*), as in Equation (3).

$$world\_haptic\_scale = \frac{\max\_workspace\_size}{\max\_virtual\_size} \quad (3)$$

In our experimental conditions, max_workspace_size was equal to 10cm (which prevents the PHANToM endpoint from colliding with its base) and max_virtual_size was equal to 3.5m. This resulted in a world_haptic_scale equal to 1/35.

(b) Clutching Technique

The clutching technique (**Clutching**) was designed as in [7]. Participants had to press the space bar of a keyboard – placed on the table in front of them – to declutch the virtual cursor from the PHANToM. As the space bar remained pressed, the cursor remained declutched and the participant could freely move the PHANToM, without any consequence on the cursor. Then, once the PHANToM extremity was positioned at a comfortable position (e.g. near the centre of its workspace), the participant could release the space bar and then re-clutch the cursor and the PHANToM.

(c) Bubble Technique

The Bubble technique (**Bubble**) was implemented as described in [6] (see related work). The radius of the bubble was set to 5cm, and the velocity vector applied to the cursor when in rate control was calculated as in Equation (2), with K set to 0.03 $N^{-3}.s^{-1}$ (see Fig. 1).

$$\vec{V}=K(D-R)^3.\vec{r} \tag{2}$$

(d) Bubble Technique with Camera Motion

In this second implementation (**BubbleCam**), the Bubble technique was implemented with a camera motion (see Fig. 4), as described in [6]. The camera is thus linked to the bubble, which allows to keep the main zone of interaction (i.e. inside the bubble) in front of the participant.

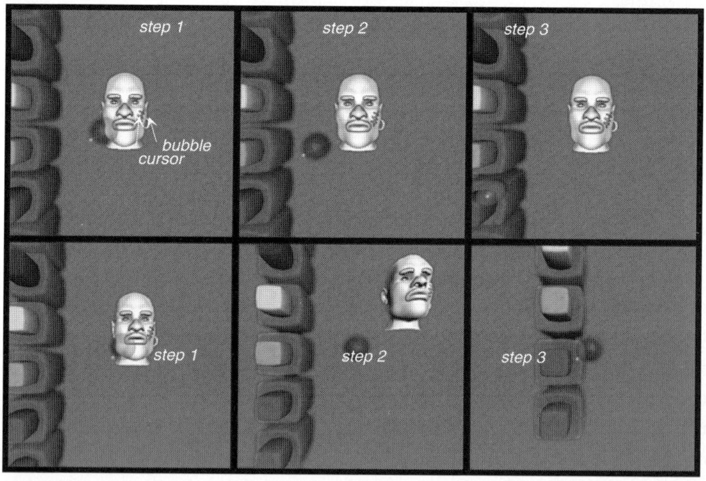

Fig. 4. Reaching the button bar using the Bubble technique without (top) and with (bottom) the camera metaphor

We intentionally did not mix several of these basic techniques. For example, using a Clutching technique with a Scaling factor (C/D ratio smaller than 1) could have reduced the need for clutching by increasing the cursor travel distances when clutched. This consequently, could have increased the global performance in terms of task completion time. In the same way, using a C/D ratio smaller than 1 with the Bubble technique would probably result in the similar increase of the global performance. Our intention was here to test and compare the possibilities of each "raw" technique (the technique as described in the literature) separately, in order to find out their main advantages and drawbacks distinctly.

3.3 Method

We selected a painting task which requires both to reach distant regions and to move to accurate positions in the 3D space. The painting task was to be performed in a large environment, as fast as possible and with a maximum precision. Such a task seems close to the current perspectives and developments in the artistic domain, concerning either painting or sculpture applications.

Participants were standing in front of the large screen. The PHANToM force-feedback device was placed on a table in front of them at a 110 cm height. They placed the index finger of their dominant hand inside the extremity (tip) of the PHANToM.

A learning phase was proposed, in which they were invited to read a set of instructions about the experiment and the apparatus. They were then demonstrated how to use the PHANToM and how to apply painting on the model. They had an unlimited period of time to get used to the technique and to the task before they began their final painting.

The experiment was then divided into 2 separate parts: one painting task, and one preference test.

In the **painting task**, participants had to paint selected parts of the virtual model. Three techniques were possibly used: the motion amplification technique (Scaling), the clutching technique (Clutching), and the Bubble technique without camera motion (Bubble). (The BubbleCam technique was eliminated here in order to limit the number of factors in the experimental plan). The 15 participants were divided into 3 groups. Each group used only 1 technique among the 3 possibilities. In other words, each interaction technique was used for painting by 5 participants.

Participants were then instructed to paint selected parts of the model with given colours as fast and as precisely as possible. They were asked to entirely paint each zone, without crossing their borders. The order and colours were the same for each participant. They first had to paint the mouth in red, then the nose in green, the eyebrows in blue, the eye in brown, the scar in pink and finally the ear-ring in yellow.

The **preference test** was passed immediately after the painting task. It consisted in a free evaluation of the 4 possible interaction techniques, i.e. the 3 techniques mentioned above plus the BubbleCam technique. Participants tested the 4 techniques in an arbitrary order for 2 minutes each. They were then allowed to re-test the 4 techniques at their will.

The experiment ended with a subjective questionnaire in which participants had to rank the 4 techniques according to 4 criteria: (1) *global appreciation*, (2) *cognitive load*, (3) *physical tiredness*, and (4) *precision for painting*.

The global experiment lasted about 40 minutes including the learning phase and breaks.

3.4 Collected Data

Three data were collected for each participant after the painting task:

1. the *total time* needed to perform the painting (in seconds);
2. the *painting time* (in seconds), i.e. the time when the participant was actually painting the model;
3. the resulting painted model (the 2D texture of the painted surface of the 3D model).

After the preference test, the *rankings* of the 4 interaction techniques, according to the subjective criteria were also collected in the questionnaire.

3.5 Results

3.5.1 How Did the Interaction Technique Affect Performance of Participants?

The performance of participants was analysed in terms of *time* (i.e. duration to perform the task) and *precision* (i.e. quality of the resulting painting, as compared to the original model).

Total task completion time and painting time

We computed a Multivariate Analysis of Variance (MANOVA) on two performance indicators: the *total time* (time to complete the whole task), and *relative painting time* (proportion of time devoted to the painting, i.e. painting time divided by total time). The between participants factor was the interaction technique used during the painting test (Scaling vs. Bubble vs. Clutching). There was a significant main effect of the interaction technique (Lambda Wilks=0.316; $F(4,22)=4.283$, $p<0.01$). The quickest completion of the task was achieved first with the Bubble technique (mBubble=810.9 sec., sd=137) and then with the Scaling technique (mScaling=830.3 sec., sd=164) whereas 1.5 more time was necessary with the Clutching technique (mClutch=1209.3, sd=410).

Due to the relatively small number of participants and to the similar duration for the Bubble and Scaling techniques, the subsequent ANOVA (analysis of variance) test on the *total time* showed a not significant trend ($F(2,12)=3.547$, $p<0.06$). However, post-hoc test indicated a significant difference between Clutching and the other two techniques for the total time to complete the task (corresponding Fischer PLSD comparisons at $p<0.05$).

We observed a different schema concerning the proportion of time devoted to painting. With the Bubble technique, participants painted during 90.6% of the time (sd=14%), whereas they only spent nearly half of the total time in painting with the other two techniques (mClutch=63.0%, sd=30; mScaling=61.1%, sd=31%) (see Fig. 5). The ANOVA test was highly significant ($F(2,12)=5.884$, $p<0.02$). Post-hoc tests indicated a significant difference between Bubble and Scaling for the *relative painting time* (Fisher PLSD comparison at $p<0.05$).

Quality of painting

The 15 resulting paintings were analysed and ranked according to the following three indicators:

1. the quantity of white space remaining unpainted inside the areas to be painted;
2. the quantity of paint overlapping the edges of the areas to be painted;
3. the quantity of paint outside the area to be painted.

The three rankings corresponding to the three indicators were summed for each painting. This provided a unique grade for each painting. A final grade was then computed for each technique, by averaging the five grades of the five paintings made with the same technique (i.e. for one group of participants). A small final grade meant precise and high quality of painting, whereas a high final grade meant a poor quality of painting (see Fig. 6).

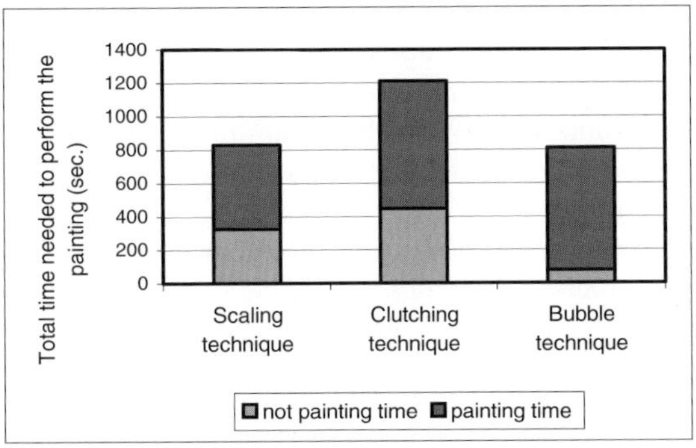

Fig. 5. Time needed to perform the painting

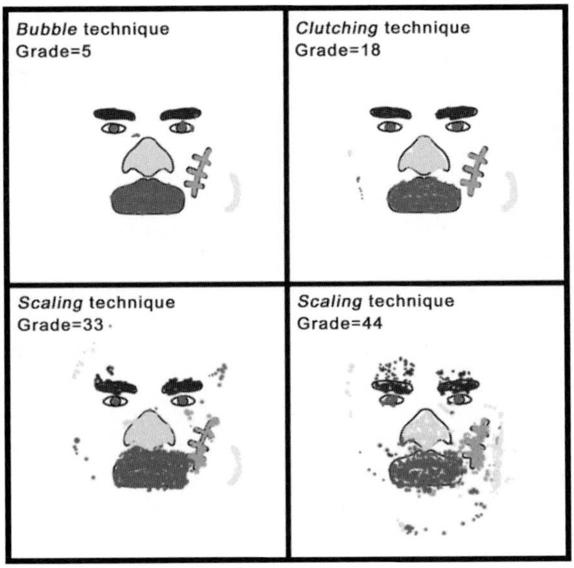

Fig. 6. Examples of paintings made by participants

We performed an ANOVA using the interaction technique as a between-participants factor. We found a significant main effect of the interaction technique on the quality (i.e. grade) of the painting ($F(2,12)=14.270$, $p<0.0007$). Participants obtained the poorest quality of painting with the Scaling technique (mean grade for Scaling: mScaling=39, sd=4.3). The best performances were found with the Bubble technique (mBubble=15, sd=10). A slightly lower quality of painting was observed with the Clutching technique (mClutching=18, sd=8). A posteriori test shows that Scaling differs significantly from the other two techniques (Fisher PLSD tests significant at $p<0.002$).

3.5.2 How Did Participants Subjectively Evaluate the Different Techniques?

We performed a mixed-design MANOVA on the four subjective dimensions used to rank the four proposed techniques: *global appreciation* of the techniques, *cognitive load*, *physical tiredness,* and *precision for painting*.

The between participants factor was the technique tested during the painting task. The within participants factors were the four techniques evaluated: *Scaling*, *Bubble*, *Clutching* and *BubbleCam*.

We found that subjective evaluations of participants differed significantly depending on the interaction technique (Lambda Wilks=0.302; $F(12,119)=5.697$, $p<0.0001$). However, no significant effect of the first phase of the experiment (painting task) was found on the second phase (subjective evaluation). Thus, the technique the participants used during the painting task had no impact on the technique they preferred during the preference test (Lambda Wilks=0.982; $F(8,90)$ n.s.).

Subsequent ANOVA demonstrated significant differences between interaction techniques for every criterion: *global appreciation* ($F(3,48)=16.382$, $p<0.0001$), *cognitive load* ($F(3,48)=11.454$, $p<0.0001$), *physical tiredness* ($F(3,48)=13.645$, $p<0.0001$), and *precision for painting* ($F(3,48)=15.902$, $p<0.0001$).

Post-hoc tests showed that the Bubble and BubbleCam techniques were significantly better appreciated than the other two techniques (Scaling and Clutching) for the *global appreciation* dimension (mBubble=1.8, sd=0.77; mBubbleCam=1.8, sd=0.94; mClutch=3.0, sd=0.93; mScaling=3.6, sd=0.63; corresponding Fisher PLSD comparisons significant at $p <0.0004$), as well as for the level of *cognitive load* (mBubble=1.7, sd=0.59; mBubbleCam=1.9, sd=1.0; mClutch=3.1, sd=1.0; mScaling=3.3, sd=0.9; corresponding Fisher PLSD comparisons significant at $p <0.001$). The Bubble and BubbleCam techniques were also significantly more appreciated concerning *physical tiredness* (mBubble=1.9, sd=0.64; mBubbleCam=1.7, sd=1.0; mClutch=2.9, sd=0.88; mScaling=3.5, sd=0.64; corresponding Fisher PLSD comparisons significant at $p <0.004$). Quite the same schema was found for the last criterion, i.e. the *precision* of the interaction technique, for which Bubble and BubbleCam were again the best rated techniques (mBubble=mBubbleCam=1.9, sd=0.80). The Clutching technique was less appreciated than the two previous ones (mClutch=2.4, sd=1.1) although post-hoc tests did not show any significant difference between the techniques. Finally, the rankings of the Scaling technique were significantly worse than the three other techniques (mScaling=3.7, sd=0.80; corresponding Fisher PLSD comparisons at $p<0.0001$).

To summarize (see Fig. 7), the Scaling technique was systematically rated as the worst technique. The Clutching technique was also poorly evaluated except for precision for which it was estimated as efficient as both Bubble and BubbleCam. The two implementations of the Bubble technique were systematically rated as the best techniques, and it seemed difficult to distinguish between them.

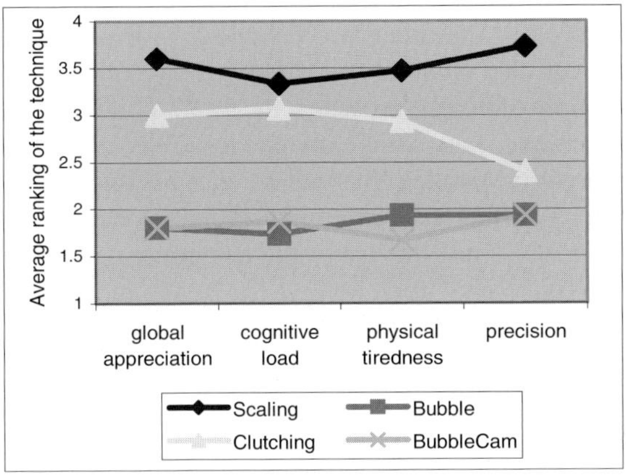

Fig. 7. Average ranking of every technique according to the 4 subjective criteria

3.6 Discussion

The performance data of the painting task illustrate an interesting property of the Bubble technique as compared with the Scaling and the Clutching techniques. Indeed, this technique seems to be optimally designed for tasks requiring both precise activity and large gestures in VEs.

On the one hand, with our technique, participants used more than 90% of their time for performing the painting, while with the other two techniques they were painting for only 60% of the total time. Thus, our technique provided the best ratio between navigation and fine operations in large virtual environments. On the other hand, the participants needed less time to complete the task with the Bubble technique than with the Clutching technique, and they needed about the same time as the Scaling technique. But even if the Bubble and the Scaling techniques required the same completion time, the resulting painting performance was drastically different: the Bubble technique was associated with the best results, and the Scaling technique was associated with the poorest ones. Furthermore, the quality of painting obtained with the Bubble was still equivalent (and even slightly better) than the one obtained with the Clutching.

This suggests that the technique used may affect the strategy adopted by the participants. The Scaling technique resulted in short completion time but in poor quality of painting, whereas the Clutching technique resulted in a great quality of painting but in a long completion time. In the case of the Scaling technique, speed was favoured against precision maybe because precision generated a high cognitive load for the participants. In the case of the Clutching technique, the opposite effect was observed: the precision was favoured versus speed, maybe because the speed constraint would also be highly overloading.

With the Bubble technique, none of these strategies seemed to be privileged. This resulted in the ability to achieve a precision similar to the Clutching technique while spending the same amount of time than with the Scaling technique.

The Bubble and BubbleCam techniques were substantially preferred by the participants as compared to the other two techniques for all subjective criteria. The global appreciations of the Bubble and BubbleCam techniques were equivalent, indicating that they both globally provided the same comfort of use. Nevertheless, the BubbleCam technique has some advantages. We indeed noticed that most participants spontaneously painted the whole ear of the model when using the BubbleCam technique, during the preference test. The ear was actually hidden in the main view (see Fig. 3). Thus, the use of the camera metaphor made it possible for the participants to navigate and reach some parts of the model in a more convenient view. This suggests that the use of the BubbleCam technique has a direct impact on the tasks the participants can potentially perform. For instance, we used a virtual scene which was as large as the virtual display (here a CAVE like system). Unlike the other techniques, BubbleCam could also be used in other conditions, i.e. with a visual display smaller than the virtual scene (e.g. displaying a whole town at scale 1 in a CAVE). Indeed, the camera motion could be used to navigate inside the VE and reach any part of it, keeping the visual focus on the zone of interest (zone of haptic interaction). Moreover, since the camera is attached to the bubble when using the BubbleCam technique, a higher co-location of haptic and visual spaces is possible, which could be interesting to use in immersive systems such as a Workbench or a CAVE.

4 Conclusion

We have conducted an experiment to compare the uses of three techniques to interact with large virtual environments using haptic devices with a limited workspace: the Scaling, the Clutching and the Bubble technique. Our results showed that the Bubble technique could be successfully used to perform 3D painting tasks involving simultaneously large movements and precise positioning. The 3D painting task enabled us to observe the users' performance in terms of both the time needed to achieve the task and the quality of the resulting painting. The Bubble technique was found to lead to both a greater accuracy in the painting and a lower completion time. Furthermore, users reported a higher level of satisfaction with the Bubble technique than with the two other interaction techniques.

Acknowledgements. The authors would like to thank Mrs. Valérie Moreau for her valuable help. They would also like to thank all the participants who took part in this experiment for their kindness and their patience.

References

[1] S. Volkov and J. Vance, "Effectiveness Of Haptic Sensation For the Evaluation of Virtual Prototypes", *ASME Journal of Computing and Information Science in Engineering*, 2001.

[2] S. Wall and W. Harwin, "Quantification of the effects of haptic feedback during motor skills tasks in a simulated environment", presented at 2nd PHANToM Users Research Symposium, Zurich, Switzerland, 2000.

[3] C. Cruz-Neira, D. Sandin, and T. Defanti, "Surround-Screen Projection-Based Virtual Reality: The Design and Implementation of the CAVE", presented at SIGGRAPH, 1993.

[4] E. Johnsen and W. Corliss, *Human Factors Applications in Teleoperator Design and Operation*, John Wiley & Sons ed, 1971.

[5] A. Fischer and J. Vance, "PHANToM Haptic Device Implemented in a Projection Screen Virtual Environment", presented at 7th International Immersive Projection Technologies Workshop and 9th Eurographics Workshop on Virtual Environments, Zurich, Switzerland, 2003.

[6] L. Dominjon, A. Lécuyer, J.-M. Burkhardt, G. Andrade-Barroso, and S. Richir, "The "Bubble" Technique: Interacting with Large Virtual Environments Using Haptic Devices with Limited Workspace", presented at World Haptics Conference (joint Eurohaptics Conference and Haptics Symposium), Pisa, Italy, 2005.

[7] HAPTION, "VIRTUOSE API V2.0 Programming Manual", 2004.

[8] C. Preusche and G. Hirzinger, "Scaling issues for Teleoperation", presented at Fifth PHANToM Users Group Workshop, Aspen, Colorado, US, 2000.

[9] R. L. Hollis and S. E. Salcudean, "Lorentz Levitation Technology: a New Approach to Fine Motion Robotics, Teleoperation, Haptic Interfaces, and Vibration Isolation", presented at International Symposium for Robotics Research, 1993.

[10] G. Casiez, "Contribution à l'étude des interfaces haptiques - le DigiHaptic : un périphérique haptique de bureau à degrés de liberté séparés." *PhD Thesis*. Lille, University of Lille, 2004.

[11] SensAble Technologies Incorporated, http://www.sensable.com

Trajectory-Based Grasp Interaction for Virtual Environments

Zhenhua Zhu, Shuming Gao, Huagen Wan, and Wenzhen Yang

State Key Lab of CAD&CG, Zhejiang University
Hangzhou 310027, P.R. China
{cocoon, smgao, hgwan, ywenz}@cad.zju.edu.cn

Abstract. Natural grasp interaction plays an important role in enhancing users' immersion experience in virtual environments. However, visually distracting artifacts such as the interpenetration of the hand and the grasped objects are always accompanied during grasp interaction due to a simplified whole-hand collision model, discrete control data used for detecting collisions and the interference of device noises. In addition, complicated distribution of forces from multi-finger contacts makes the natural grasp and manipulation of a virtual object difficult. In order to solve these problems, this paper presents a novel approach for grasp interaction in virtual environments. Based on the research in Neurophysiology, we first construct finger's grasp trajectories and detect collisions between the objects and the trajectories instead of the whole-hand collision model, then deduce the grasp configuration using collision detection results, and finally compute feedback forces according to grasp identification conditions. Our approach has been verified in a CAVE-based virtual environment.

1 Introduction

Virtual environments (VE) provide a platform for users to experience and work with three-dimensional computer generated scenes just like in real environments. Yet, after many years of research and development virtual environments are still used mainly as a visualization tool with some simple or specialized interaction techniques. Although some finger tracking devices such as instrumented gloves have made natural grasp interaction possible at least at hardware level, the interaction using a virtual hand as an avatar has come true only to a very limited extent. It is probably because the use of multi-finger grasp interaction with a haptic device presents a number of new challenges over that of single point interaction.

These challenges include: 1) how to simplify collision models in order to get high update rate for haptic rendering; 2) how to control visually distracting artifacts, such as interpenetration of a hand and grasped objects, mainly aroused by the interference of device noise and the discrete control data used for collision detection acquired from interaction devices; 3) how to model friction and resolve the distribution of finger force from multiple finger contact points.

Aiming to solve these problems, this paper proposes a simple and novel approach for users to naturally grasp and manipulate objects via a dexterous hand as an avatar in a virtual environment.

H.-P. Seidel, T. Nishita, and Q. Peng (Eds.): CGI 2006, LNCS 4035, pp. 300 – 311, 2006.

The rest of the paper is organized as follows. Related works are briefly reviewed in the next section. Section 3 overviews the approach. In Section 4, the construction of grasp trajectories is presented, while issues related to multi-finger grasp interaction using grasp trajectories is described in Section 5. Experiment results are shown in Section 6. Some conclusions and future works are discussed in Section 7.

2 Related Works

In virtual environments, real-time collision detection between a dexterous hand and objects is premier. Although the technology of continuous collision detection ([1] and [2]) has improved greatly, the requirement of high update rate makes it still expensive in virtual environments with haptic rendering. So, some discrete collision detection methods, such as VOXMAP-PONTSHELL [3], Bounding Sphere Tree [4], Axis Aligned Bounding Box Tree [5], Oriented Bounding Box Tree [6] and Convex Hull Tree [7] are still preferred. But those discrete methods inevitably arouse interpenetration.

In order to alleviate the unrealistic vision of interpenetration, Rezzonico et al. correct hand posture by unfolding the closet proximal joint (wrist side) until the corresponding sensor is tangent to the object or the joint reaches its limit [8]. Zachmann et al. convert the problem of natural grasping into a minimization problem for a joint vector under the constraint that finger-joints (and palm) must not penetrate the object [9].But their iterative adjustment is time-consuming.

Recently, physical-based dynamic simulation is employed for multi-finger grasp and manipulation of a virtual object. Based on point collision response forces, Hirota et al develop a manipulation system [10]. Melder et al. present an approach to allow users to manipulate a virtual object through multiple PHANToM devices by using friction cone ([11], [12] and [13]). Borst et al. develop a system to support natural whole-hand interactions in a desktop-sized workspace [14]. Yet, all of these methods are not very stable and sometimes face difficulties when grasping or manipulating objects. Therefore, approaches dependent on heuristic analysis of grasp stability or user intent are still applicable. Iwata et al. consider whether an object is captured by testing 16 points on a hand model [15]. Maekawa et al provide two finger grasp conditions to manipulate objects in virtual environments [16]. Piater et al. determine grasp configurations by using visual features [17]. Tzafestas et al. take into account the unilateral nature of the contacts and the limitations due to static friction to identify whether grasp is still maintained [18].

3 Overview of the Approach

Before outlining our approach, we narrow down the discussion scope of this paper within pinch, based on users' common operations performed in virtual environments and at the same time for the sake of reducing interaction complexities between a hand and virtual objects. Therefore, consistent and independent fingertip motion for reach-to-grasp movements is fully utilized here. According to the research result of Neurophysiology "For reach-to-grasp movements to a variety of objects, fingertip motion was quite similar. The movement tended to follow a particular curved path." [19], our approach first constructs each fingertip's grasp trajectory and then detects collisions between objects and trajectories. Subsequently, the fingers' automatic contact conditions are estimated and the grasp configurations of the relevant fingers are deduced according to the collision detection results. Finally the finger feedback forces when grasping or manipulating an object is computed based on grasp identification conditions. Overall, the approach is composed of the pre-processing stage and the running stage, whose schematic overview is shown in Fig.1.

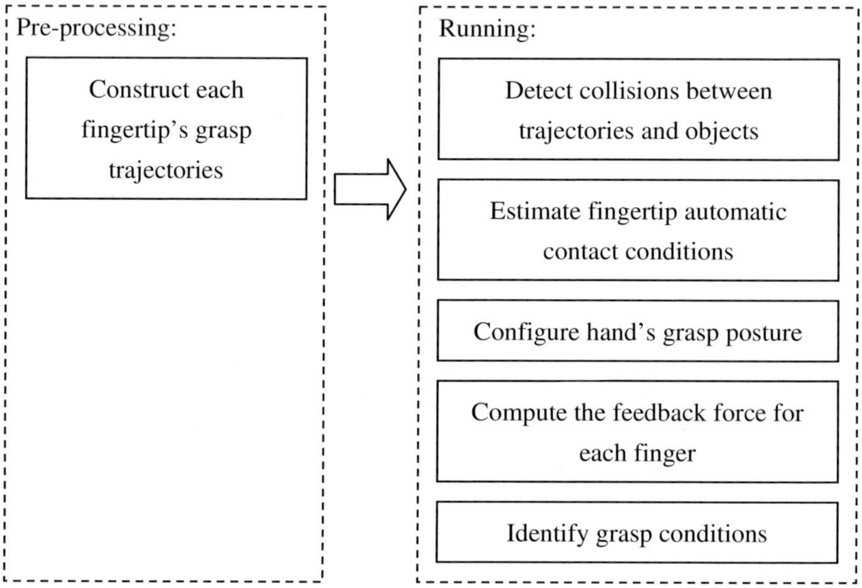

Fig. 1. Schematic overview of the approach

4 Construction of Grasp Trajectories

To gain real-time performance in virtual environments, most traditional methods have to maintain two kinds of hand models, one for display and the other, much simpler, for detecting collisions. Although two kinds of hand models could speed up collision detection, the simplified collision model, discrete control data used for collision detection and the interference of device noise will more or less lead to interpenetration of the hand into grasped objects.

The research result of Neurophysiology mentioned in Section 3 provides us a new promising way to solve this problem. In this section, we will put our emphasis on the construction of a fingertip's grasp trajectory, while leave the issue of how to use trajectories to control the visually distracting artifacts to the next section.

Similar to the method presented in [19], the construction of finger's grasp trajectories is described as follows:

1) Manually select a point in each fingertip surface as a seed point for that finger. The point should be located in the center of the fingertip's surface, where we think the first contact generally happens when pinching an object (Fig.2).

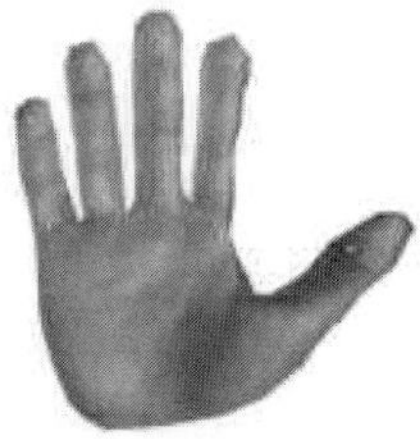

Fig. 2. Seed points on five fingertip

2) Ask a user to participate in a grasping task and his finger joint angles acquired from CyberGlove® are recorded at approximately 50 Hz. The process is repeated several times to eliminate the side effect of some accidental factors such as device noises as far as possible.
3) Simulate the user's grasping process and generate the motion of the seed point for each finger with those recorded joint angles. The seed point's motion trajectory is regarded as a grasp trajectory for that finger.
4) Approximate the grasp trajectory of each finger with a series of line segments. We pick up a number of recorded finger's joint angles as critical joint angles and the positions of seed point corresponding to those joint angles are computed to form critical points on the grasp trajectory. All of these critical points form a series of line segments to approximate the grasp trajectory tightly (Fig.3).

We have to admit that the approximation will result in some inaccuracies both in detecting collision and determining the grasp configuration of the finger. Fortunately, we can control these inaccuracies by determining the number of these critical points on the trajectory. Moreover the speed of collision detection between an object and a series of line segments is obviously far faster than that of collision detection between an object and a curve.

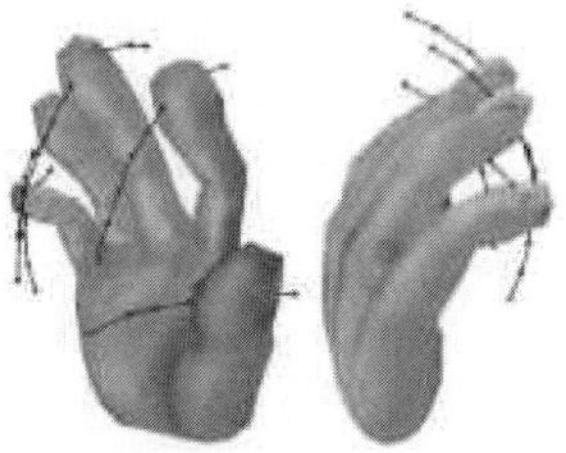

Fig. 3. Line segments to approximate grasp trajectories

5 Grasp Interaction

Fig.4 presents the process of a dexterous hand interacting with an object we are conceiving, and more details will be described below.

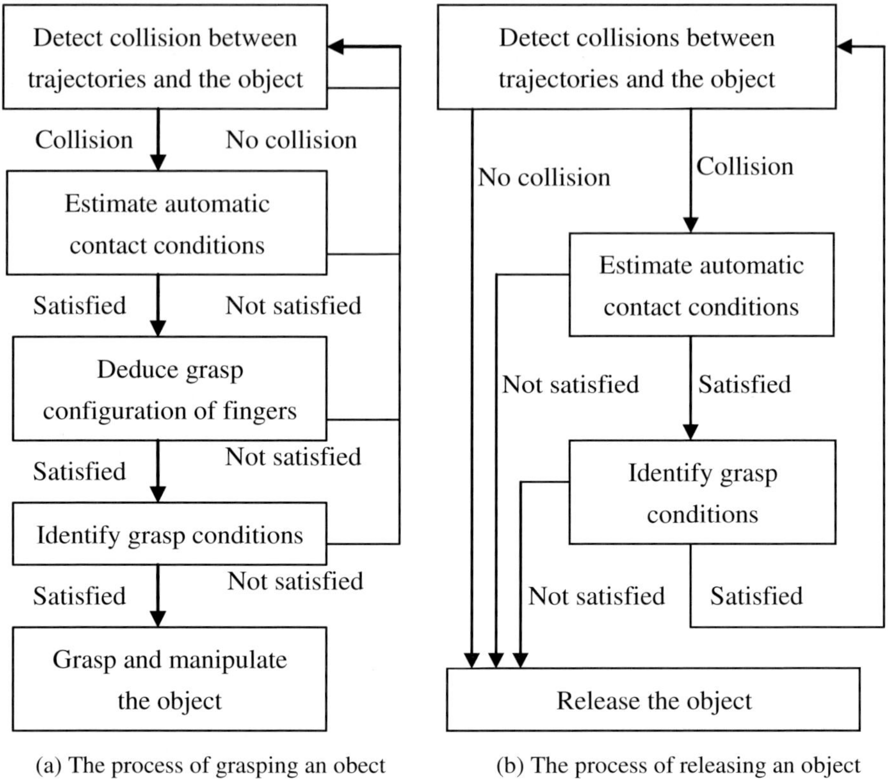

Fig. 4. Grasp Interaction between a hand and an object

5.1 Collision Detection Between Trajectories and Objects

The collision detection is performed between objects and the grasp trajectories instead of the virtual hand. As the grasp trajectory of each fingertip is approximated by a series of line segments, the problem of collision detection can be therefore converted to perform an intersection test between the objects and the line segments.

An intersection test between a line segment and an object could be implemented by a general ray-tracing algorithm [20]. But to accelerate the intersection computation, an OBB-tree for each object is created. Ray-Box intersections are firstly tested and if a line passes through all Ray-Box intersection tests, a Ray-Triangle intersection is performed (An object is represented by mesh in this work). For Ray-Triangle intersection, the algorithm presented by Möller [21] is applied, while for Ray-Box intersection, the Mahovsky's algorithm [22] is employed. The algorithm makes use of Plücker coordinates and tests the ray against the edges comprising the silhouette of the box instead of testing against individual faces so that the technique's performance is up to 93% faster.

5.2 Automatic Contact Estimation

When pinching, an automatic contact condition is provided to estimate whether fingers contact an object, since it is difficult to predicate when the fingers will contact the object. At first, the line segment intersecting with an object is found during collision detection and then an auxiliary plane passing the start point of the intersecting line segment and perpendicular to the line segment is created to divide the space into the positive and negative subspaces respectively. If the seed point on the fingertip resides in the positive subspace, an automatic contact condition is thought to be satisfied and the corresponding finger will be automatically moved to contact the object. Otherwise, the corresponding finger is still allowed to move along its trajectory. The condition is illustrated in Fig.5.

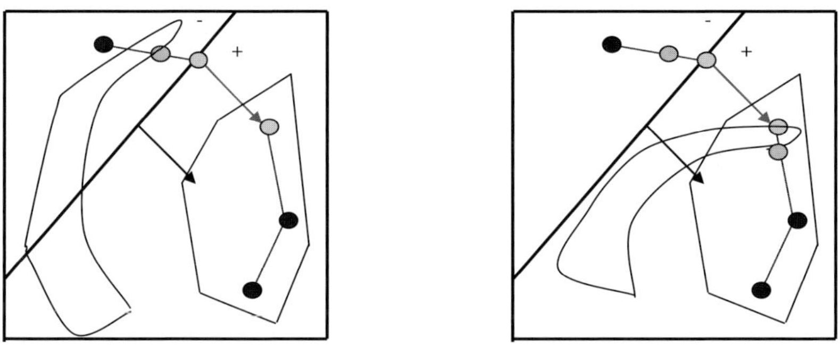

(a) Seed point in negative sub-space (b) Seed point in positive sub-space

Fig. 5. Illustration of automatic contact estimation

5.3 Grasp Configuration Deduction

After it has been estimated that one finger should be automatically moved to contact a virtual object, it is necessary to determine the grasp configuration of that finger. Without iteratively adjusting finger's posture, our method is able to deduce the grasp configuration of the finger immediately. During our construction of finger's trajectory, the flexion/extension of the distal inter-phalangeal (DIP), proximal inter-phalangeal (PIP), and metacarpal-phalangeal (MCP) joints as well as its corresponding abduction, such as Ring-Middle abduction, are recorded and represented as a set of angles (θ_{n1}, θ_{n2}, θ_{n3}, θ_{n4}) for each critical point P_n. As illustrated in Fig.6, the grasp configuration of the finger could be deduced based on these data as follows:

1) For the finger whose grasp trajectory intersects with an object on the point C_n, determine a variable t that makes

$$C_n = P_{n-1} + t \times (P_n - P_{n-1}) \qquad (1)$$

2) Get corresponding joint angles (θ_{n-11}, θ_{n-12}, θ_{n-13}, θ_{n-14}) about P_{n-1} and (θ_{n1}, θ_{n2}, θ_{n3}, θ_{n4}) about P_n;

3) Compute approximate joint angles (θ_{c1}, θ_{c2}, θ_{c3}, θc_4) about C_n by using linear interpolation:

$$\theta_{cx} = \theta_{n\text{-}1x} + t\times(\theta_{nx} - \theta_{n\text{-}1x}) \ (x = 1,2,3,4) \tag{2}$$

4) Apply (θ_{c1}, θ_{c2}, θ_{c3}, $\theta_{c4)}$ to formulate the grasp configuration of the finger, i.e. the flexion or extension of DIP, PIP and MCP and the abduction.

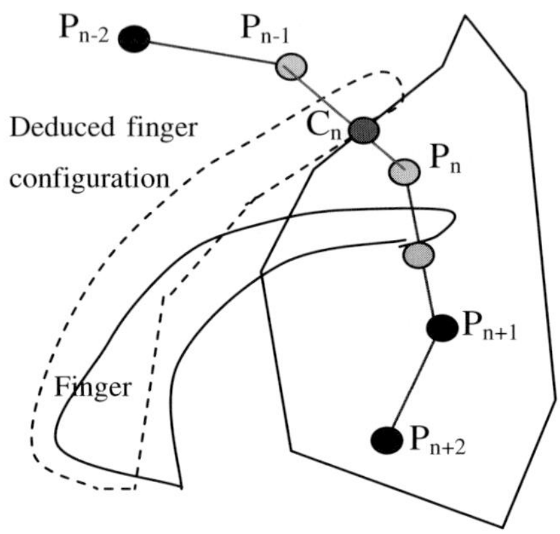

Fig. 6. Illustration of deducing finger's grasp configuration

5.4 Finger Force Computation and Feedback

The finger force responding to collision and being fed back to a user is generated, when collision happens. Realistic finger feedback forces are very important to enhance users' immersion experience in virtual environments. In this paper, the feedback force for each finger is computed according to the relationship between the dexterous hand and the object collided with and two kinds of computation models are presented. One is grasping force computation model, which is utilized when the dexterous hand contacts the object but does not grasp and manipulate it. The other is manipulating force computation model, which is used when the dexterous hand grasps and manipulates the object. No matter which one is used, the feedback forces will finally be mapped to the user's fingertips through CyberGrasp, a haptic feedback device developed by Immersion Corp using its application programmer interface (API): vhtCyberGrasp->setforce() [23].

5.4.1 Grasping Force Computation

For force calculation at a single finger, we refer to the penalty-based force computation model. The force generated on each finger is calculated by utilizing the Hooke's law:

$$\vec{F} = (K_f \times d)\vec{N} \tag{3}$$

Where d is the penalty depth, namely the distance from the collision point to the seed point on finger's surface along the vector $\vec{N}$, and K_f is the stiffness coefficient of the object collided with.

5.4.2 Manipulation Force Computation

Most often, besides the grasping force, object's gravity also has an effect on finger force distribution when an object is manipulated. Considering force effects alone, we observe that the effect of the object's gravity on a finger is relevant to the angle between the grasping force of the finger and the gravity of the grasped object. The bigger the angle, the larger the force received by the finger. So, we allocate the gravity of the object to fingers using dynamic weights, described as follows, and then feed them back to the user plus the grasping forces calculated before.

1) For the i-th contact finger, the angle α_i between the grasping force $\vec{F}$ and the gravity force $\vec{G}$ is calculated.
2) For the i-th contact finger, its new feedback force, $\vec{F}'$, is calculated as:

$$\vec{F}' = \vec{F} + (\alpha_i/\Sigma\alpha_i)\ \vec{G} \tag{4}$$

5.5 Multi-finger Grasp Identification

In order to judge which finger force computation model should be used, some conditions must be provided. Here, both elementary and advanced grasp identification conditions are given. Actually, these conditions could also be used to identify the state of the hand. More details refer to [24].

5.5.1 Elementary Grasp Identification

Elementary grasp identification condition is employed to preliminarily determine whether the hand is able to grasp an object, when collision occurs between them. The condition is that object must be contacted by the thumb and any other finger of the hand. Obviously, if a user wants to grasp an object later, the elementary grasp identification condition must be first satisfied.

5.5.2 Advanced Grasp Identification

Elementary grasp identification condition only preliminary differentiate whether the hand is able to grasp an object. It is advanced grasp identification conditions that determine whether the user could manipulate an object via the dexterous virtual hand from physical aspects.

Considering that the forces exerted on the grasped object include not only press but also friction, which is variable, before describing the advanced conditions, the following two suppositions are introduced:

1) If the forces exerted by the dexterous hand on the object can counteract its gravity force in Z-Axis and the forces' directions can balance in X or Y axis, then the object can be manipulated.
2) The direction of the i-th finger's friction is identical with the negative direction of the projection of the gravity vector of the object on the contact plane (For each contact point, we define a plane passing the point and perpendicular to the direction of the grasping force as the contact plane) and its magnitude ranges from 0 to f_{imax} ($f_{imax} = \mu F_i$, where F_i is the grasping force of the i-th finger to the object, μ is the static friction coefficient, and f_{imax} means the i-th finger's maximum static friction.).

According to the above suppositions, the advanced conditions are given as follows:

1) The inequation below should be satisfied.

$$\sum_{i=1}^{k}(F_{iz}+f_{imaxz})+G_z \geq 0 \tag{5}$$

Where k is the number of contact fingers, F_{iz} (f_{imaxz}) is the z-component of F_i (f_{imax}). The physical meaning behind this condition is that the forces the virtual hand exerts on the virtual object could counteract its gravity.

2) If one finger has a force component along the positive direction of X-axis (or Y-axis), there must be another finger which has a force component along the negative direction of X-axis (or Y-axis) and vice versa. The physical meaning behind this condition is that the virtual object could resist any impulse from X (or Y) direction.

6 Experiment Results

We have implemented the approach in a CAVE-based virtual environment using the CAVELib™. The CAVELib™ is a powerful API that provides the cornerstone for creating robust interactive three-dimensional (i3D) environments [25]. An Ascension 6 degrees of freedom (DOF) tracking sensor is used for tracking user's hand motion. The CyberGlove® and the CyberGrasp® [23] are used to capture finger motions and

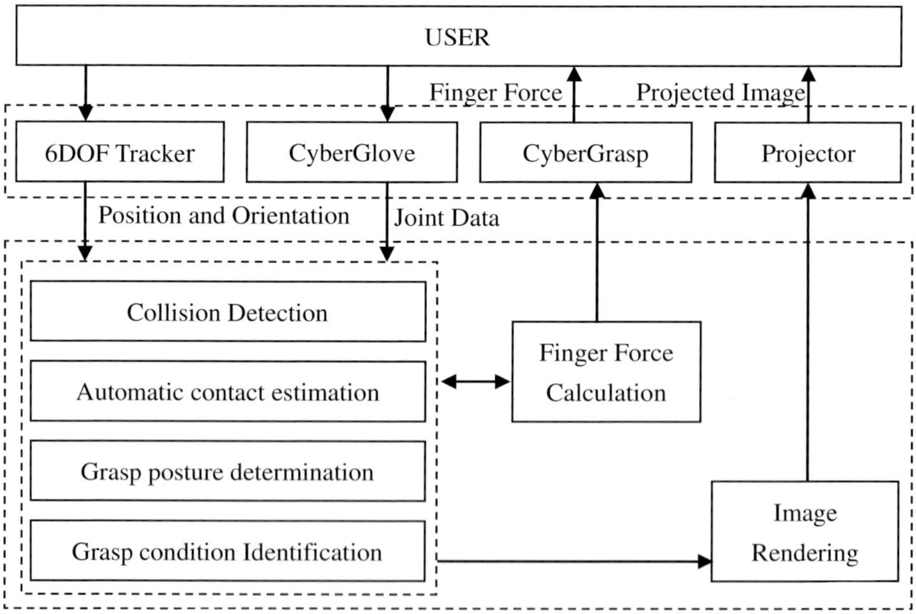

Fig. 7. Architecture of implementation

provide force feedback respectively. The program runs on an SGI Onxy2 (with 4 CPUs and 2 IR4 graphic pipelines). High-resolution stereo images are projected onto four imaging surfaces of the CAVE by four projectors. The overall architecture of the implementation is illustrated in Fig.7.

Fig.8 shows a virtual one-cylinder motor assembly scene we created to test the presented method. The virtual assembly scene is comprised of some common mechanical components such as nuts, bolts. A dexterous virtual hand as well as the proposed grasp interaction is used to perform assembly tasks, and four grasp actions are displayed in Fig.9. Fig.10 gives a snapshot of a user's hand when performing virtual assembly tasks with the CyberGrasp® in our CAVE-based environment.

Fig. 8. One-cylinder motor assembly scene

(a) (b) (c) (d)

Fig. 9. Grasp interaction with different mechanical components: *(a)* a nut; *(b)* a crank; *(c)* a gasket and *(d)* a piston

Fig. 10. A snapshot of performing a virtual assembly task using CyberGrasp®

7 Conclusion and Future Work

Natural grasp interaction and its realistic vision play important roles in enhancing users' immersion experience in virtual environments.

In this paper, a trajectory-based approach to grasp interaction is presented. The approach is based on the research result of Neurophysiology and enables a user to grasp and manipulate an object naturally with a dexterous virtual hand. Unlike some traditional methods which totally rely on computer performance to alleviate visually distracting artifacts, our approach can control artifacts by determining the proper number of sampling points on the grasp trajectories. Moreover, automatic contact estimation conditions, grasp identification conditions, and the grasp configuration of the virtual hand can be determined rapidly utilizing the grasp trajectories, which will inevitably save time for more realistic finger feedback force computation, given that the requirement of update rate in haptic rendering is up to 1 KHz.

Future works will include: 1) to propose more reasonable conditions for grasp identification and 2) to provide more realistic force computation model.

References

1. S. Redon, A. Kheddar and S. Coquillart. CONTACT: arbitrary in-between motions for continuous collision detection. In Proceedings of IEEE ROMAN'2001, Sep. 2001.
2. S. Redon, A. Kheddar and S. Coquillart. Fast Continuous Collision Detection between Rigid Bodies. In proceedings of Eurographics 2002. September 2002
3. McNeely W, Puterbaugh K, Troy J. Six Degree-of-freedom Haptic Rendering Using Voxel Sampling. In Proceedings of Siggraph 1999, LosAngeles, CA
4. Palmer I, Grimsdale R. Real-time collision detection for animation using Sphere-Trees. Computer Graphics Forum 1995, 14(2):105-116
5. Zachmann G. Optimizing the Collision Detection Pipeline, In Proceedings of the First International Game Technology Conference(GTEC), Hong Kong, 18-21 January 2001
6. Gottschalk S, Lin M, Manocha D. OBB-Tree: A Hierarchical Structure for Rapid Interference Detection, the Proceedings of ACM SIGGRAPH'96, 1996:171-180
7. Ehmann S, Lin MC. Accurate and Fast Proximity Queries between Polyhedra using Convex Surface Decomposition. In Proceedings of the Eurographics Conference, Manchester, 2001:500-510
8. S. Rezzonico, Z. Huang, R. Boulic, N. Magnenat Thalmann, D. Thalmann, Consistent Grasping Interactions with Virtual Actors Based on the Multi-sensor Hand Model, Proc. 2nd Eurographics workshop on Virtual Environments, Monte Carlo.
9. G.Zachmann and A. Rettig, "Natural and Robust Interaction in Virtual Assembly Simulation," presented at Eighth ISPE International Conference on Concurrent Engineering: Research and Application, Anaheim, 2001
10. K. Hirota and M. Hirose, Dexterous Object Manipulation Based On Collision Response. Presented at IEEE Virtual Reality, Los Angeles, 2003
11. W.S.Harwin and N. Melder. Improved Haptic Rendering for Mult-Finger Manipulation Using Friction Cone based God-Objects. Proceedings of Eurohaptics Conference, 2002.
12. N.Melder, W.S.Harwin, P.M.Sharkey. Translation and Rotation of Multi-Point Contacted Virtual Objects. Proceedings of Eurohaptics 2003 pp 218-227
13. N.Melder and W.S.Harwin. Extending the Friction Cone Algorithm for Arbitrary Polygon Based Haptic Objects. Proceedings of the 12th International Symposium on Haptic Interfaces for Virtual Environments and Teleoperator Systems, Chicago, 2004.
14. Christoph W. Borst and Arun P. Indugula. Realistic Virtual Grasping. Presened at IEEE Virtual Reality 2005 pp. 91-98.

15. H. Iwata. Artificial Reality with Force-Feedback: Development of Desktop Virtual Space with Compact Master Manipulator. Computer Graphics, vol. 24, pp. 165-170, 1990.
16. Maekawa, H. and JM Hollerbach. Haptic Display for Object Grasping and Manipulating in Virtual Environment. Proc. of Int. Conf. on Robotics and Automation, pp. 2566-2573, 1998
17. Justus H. Piater. Learning Visual Features to Recommend Grasp Configurations. CMPSCI Technical Report 2000-40. July 2000
18. Costas S. Tzafestas. Whole-Hand Kinesthetic Feedback and Haptic Perception in Dexterous Virtual Manipulation. IEEE Trans. on Sys. Man and Cybernatics, 33(1):100-113, January 2003
19. D. G. Kamper, E. G. Cruz and M. P. Siegel. Stereotypical Fingertip Trajectories During Grasp. Journal of Neurophysiology 90: 3702-3710, 2003
20. T.Whitted, An improved Illumination Model for Shaded Display, Comm ACM Vol.32, No. 6, 1980
21. Möller T. Trumbore B. Fast, Minumum Storage Ray-Triangle Intersection Journal of Graphics Tools, 1997, 2(1):21-28
22. Jeffrey Mahovsky, Brian Wyvill, Fast ray-axis aligned bounding box overlap tests with Plücker coordinates. Jour-nal of Graphics Tools: JGT, 2004, 9(1):35-46
23. Hand SDK, last visit: Aug 20, 2005, http://www.immersion.com
24. Z. Zhu, S. Gao, H. Wan, Y. Luo and W. Yang. Grasp Identification and Multi-Finger Haptic Feedback for Virtual Assembly. In Proc. Of DETC'04 Salt Lake City, Utah USA, 2004
25. CAVELib Manual, last visit: Aug 20, 2005, http://www.vrco.com/CAVE_USER

Research on User-Centered Design and Recognition Pen Gestures

Feng Tian, Tiegang Cheng, Hongan Wang, and Guozhong Dai

Intelligence Engineering Laboratory, Institute of Software, Chinese Academy of Sciences
{tf, ctg, wha, dgz}@iel.iscas.ac.cn
http://iel.iscas.ac.cn

Abstract. Pen-based user interface has become a hot research field in recent years. Pen gesture plays an important role in Pen-based user interfaces. But it's difficult for UI designers to design, and for users to learn and use. In this purpose, we performed a research on user-centered design and recognition pen gestures. We performed a survey of 100 pen gestures in twelve famous pen-bases systems to find problems of pen gestures currently used. And we conducted a questionnaire to evaluate the matching degree between commands and pen gestures to discover the characteristics that a good pen gestures should have. Then cognition theories were applied to analyze the advantages of those characteristics in helping improving the learnability of pen gestures. From these, we analyzed the pen gesture recognition effect and presented some improvements on features selection in recognition algorithm of pen gestures. Finally we used a couple of psychology experiments to evaluate twelve pen gestures designed based on the research. It shows those gestures is better for user to learn and use. Research results of this paper can be used for designer as a primary principle to design pen gestures in pen-based systems.

1 Introduction

Pen-based user interface is one of the main styles in Post-WIMP user interface. It has become a hot research field in recent years. It is designed on the Pen-Paper metaphor which is a universal and fundamental way for capturing daily experiences, communicating ideas, recording important events, conducting deep thinking and visual descriptions. Researches on pen-based user interface intend to make these traditional activities computable while retaining the flexibility and fluidity of normal pen and paper. Consequently, with the assistance of computing resources, people can achieve easier manipulations to information, such as maintenance, modification, retrieval, transferring, further processing and analysis. Many famous systems have built in this field, such as Tivoli [1], LiveBoard [2], SILK [3], DENIM [4], Cocktail Napkin [5], Flatland [6], Classroom 2000 [7], ASSIST [8], Teddy [9]. Currently, some corporations like Microsoft and Apple, have push pen-based interaction techniques in their operating system, such as Windows XP Tablet PC Edition [10] and Mac OS X Tiger [11]. In these systems, Pen Gesture plays a very important role. Pen Gesture is a hand make mark used to give a command to a computer. It is a single stroke indicates the operation, the operand, and additional parameters [12] [13]. In pen-based user interface, user uses pen gesture to perform various tasks, such as text editing, sketch

H.-P. Seidel, T. Nishita, and Q. Peng (Eds.): CGI 2006, LNCS 4035, pp. 312 – 323, 2006.

modeling, UI design, 3D manipulation and navigation, etc. Long has performed a survey of gesture usage from PDA users. It showed that users think gestures are powerful, efficient, and convenient. And users want more gestures in applications [14].

Unfortunately, there are little pen gesture design guidelines or theories currently existing. So it's hard for designers to design pen gestures in systems. Consequently, gestures used in systems are hard for user to learn and remember. From Tivoli, we can see that the problem with gestures is that "novice users may not remember them [1]". Long's survey also revealed that users often find gestures difficult to remember, and they become frustrated when the computer misrecognizes gestures [14]. In the purpose of helping designing gestures with good learnability, and high recognition accuracy, we performed a serial of research work.

First, we conduct a survey of single-stroke gestures currently used in systems. The survey is based on observation and usage of twelve famous pen-based systems. From the survey, we divided pen gestures into three categories: pen gestures with "iconicness" property [15] (A pen gesture with iconicness property can be considered as that the shape of the gesture is dependent in part on the meaning of the command which the gesture represent.). Pen gestures represented by the first character of command name, and pen gestures with no obvious relation with command it represented. A questionnaire is conducted to evaluate the matching degree between commands and different categories of gesture. It can be used to discover the characteristics that "good" gestures should have, and to find characteristics as the foundation of pen gesture classification. Then double-code theory [16] and other cognition theories are applied to analyze the advantages of those characteristics in helping improving the learnability of pen gestures. From these, we analyze the pen gesture recognition effect from user-centered viewpoint, and present some improvements on features selection in recognition algorithm of pen gestures. Finally we use a couple of psychology experiments to evaluate twelve pen gestures designed based on the research. Comparing with other pen gestures that perform same tasks currently used in pen-based systems, it shows those gestures is better for user to learn and use.

The rest of this paper is organized as follows. After discussing related work, we describe the survey and questionnaire we conducted. After them, we analyze how to improve the learnability and recognition accuracy of pen gestures. And we depict the two experiments on pen gestures we designed. Finally, the conclusion is concluded.

2 Related Work

Some existing tools and recognition methods can support creating pen gestures. Rubin presented GRANDMA [12], a tool that dramatically reduces the effort involved in creating a gesture-based interface to an application. Starting with an application with a traditional direct manipulation interface, GRANDMA lets the designer specify gestures by example, associate those gestures with views in the interface, and specify the effete each gesture has on its associated views through a simple programming interface. Zhao Rui presented concepts and techniques about incremental recognition to support gesture recognition in gesture-based and syntax directed editors [17]. The essential idea of his concept is the tight integration between on-line pattern recognition and diagram parsing. The incremental recognition strategy improves not only the recognition performance, but also the directness of gestural interfaces.

Peter Tandler proposed to give incremental gesture recognition to provide immediate feedback while drawing pen gestures [18], giving feedback continuously while users draw, as this allows immediate correction of minor mistakes.

Allan Chris Long developed gdt [19], a prototype gesture design tool that is loosely based on Agate. gdt are visualizations intended to help designers discover and fix recognition problems. It allows designers to enter and edit training examples, train the recognizer, and recognize individual examples.

Tools and recognition methods build the basis on how to create and training pen gestures. But it can not help designers on how to design pen gestures with good learnability and memorability. Currently, there are some researches in this field.

Allan Chris Long performed a survey of PDA users [14]. It intended to illuminate the problems users have and benefits users enjoy with gesture-based user interfaces. From the results of the survey, he concluded that: users value gestures yet problems with gestures remain; users demand more gestures; and Newtons are used largely as notebooks whereas Pilots are used mostly has personal datebooks and addressbooks. The results of the survey provide insight for designers of pen-based user interfaces and related tools.

Axel Kramer described an initial classification of interactive characteristics of two dimensional gestures in interactive systems [20]. Such a classification describes one design space for the usage of two-dimensional gestures in interactive systems and thus presents possible choices to system designers. Empirical researchers can make use of such a classification to make systematic choices about aspects of gesture based systems that are worth studying. Finally, it can serve as a starting point for drawing parallels and exploring differences to gestures used in three-dimensional interfaces.

Allan Chris Long performed a pair of experiments to determine why users find gestures similar [21]. From these experiments, he has derived a computational model for predicting perceived gesture similarity that correlates 0.56 with observation. He incorporated the results of these experiments into Quill [15]. Quill can help designers create and improve gestures. It is designed to allow designers with no expertise in gesture recognition or in psychology to create gestures that are easy for the computer to recognize and that people will not easily confuse with one another.

Allan Chris Long also performed an experiment to determine what factors affect gesture memorability [15]. This experiment showed iconicness to be the single most important factor for gesture memorability, which is consistent with memorability of other objects. Based on the partial success of prediction based on geometry, he believes it may be possible with more data to partially predict memorability.

3 Survey on Pen Gestures

The survey is based on observation and usage of twelve famous pen-based systems, including Windows XP Tablet Edition[10], Mac OS X Tiger[11], Newton[22], Palm OS[23], Cinema Listing Application [24], Tivoli[1], Quickset[25], Teddy[9], SILK[26], Air Traffic Control[27], CADesk [28], MindManager [29]. These systems can be divided into five fields: Text Editing, Ink Editing, sketch modeling & 3D manipulation, UI designs and Air Control. We have investigated 100 pen gestures in these systems. These gestures can be divided into three categories. First category is pen gestures with "iconicness" property. Second category is pen gestures represented by the first character of command name. Third category is pen gestures with no obvious relation with command it represent. For example, 'Delete' command is used in lots of pen-based system. It can be represented by three pen gestures: , , . First gesture simulates scissors. Second gesture is the first character of 'Delete'. And we can not find any relation between the 'Delete' command and the third gesture. In 100 gestures, we found 64 gestures have iconicness property. 12 gestures are represented by the first character of command name. 24 gestures have no obvious relation with command they represented. We also found two main problems of pen gestures from these systems. First, one gesture is applied in different systems in same field to do different commands. For example, and are used as "Scroll up" command and "Scroll down" command in Tivoli. These two gestures are also used in Mindmanger as "Zoom in" command and "Zoom out" command. is used as "Undo" command in Air Traffic Control, and used as "Delete" command in Quickset. Once user needs to use both systems, he will easily do wrong operations in each system. And it will make him confused with the relation between pen gesture and command. Second, different gesture categories are designed in one system. For example, gesture and are used in SILK [26]. Gesture used to perform "Delete" command. is used to perform "Copy" command. is in first gesture category which simulate scissors. is in second gesture category which is the first character of the word "Copy". Pen gestures in different gesture categories applied in one system make user confused and influenced his learning and memorizing ability.

From the survey, we consider that there should be a uniform gesture design principle for designers. And gestures in different gesture categories shouldn't be designed in one system.

4 Questionnaire

In order to validate whether pen gestures with "iconicness" property help to improve their learnablity, we conducted a questionnaire to evaluate the matching degree between commands and pen gestures, to discover the characteristics that user-centered pen gestures should have.

We chose 20 text editing commands and pen gesture candidates to each command. These pen gestures came from two sources, one source is from pen-based systems currently used, the other is from our own design through group discussion. Based on these commands and corresponding gesture candidates, we designed a questionnaire to evaluate the matching degree between commands and gestures, and to discover the characteristics that "good" gestures should have and to set up the foundation for the gestures' classification by characteristics.

In our questionnaire, participants were assumed editing an electronic document with a pen and performing editing tasks with pen gestures. One document contains 20 items. Each item has an editing task. And each task has 4 pen gesture candidates listed which are related to the task. Participants were asked to sort the pen gestures by the rule that the most matching pen gesture should be arranged to the first, the second most matching gesture to the second, and so on. Simultaneously, participants were also asked to give the reasons why the first gesture is the best one.

Our participants were selected from postgraduates. They are all skilled in using computer and Microsoft Office. And they are familiar with editing tasks listed in our questionnaire. We had totally sent out 60 questionnaire forms and received 58. From received questionnaires, we made a statistic analysis with SPSS. Then, we analyzed the reasons participants expressed, and classified these reasons. These classifications can indicate the characteristics which they think good gestures should have.

Iconicness. 90% and more participants held that pen gestures with visual meaningful related to commands are easy to be remembered and learned.

Operating easily. Over 50% participants considered that easy operating gestures should have some characteristics. First, it should be operated conveniently. Second, it's better to draw one pen gesture in one stroke. Third, pen gestures should be designed as a curve.

Good-looking on figures. About 10% participants like gestures of close curve. Some participants like comfortable and good-looking gestures.

From results, we can see that over 90% participants consider iconic is an important characteristic for good pen gestures. In next chapter, we will conduct a survey on single-stroke gestures currently used in pen-based systems, to investigate the current using status of pen gestures with this characteristic.

5 Pen Gesture Learnability Analysis

According to the results, "iconic" pen gestures are more learnable by participants. It is probably because these gestures are visual and meaningful, and are easier to connect the meanings of commands. Dual Coding Theory [16] can give a good explanation.

The point of the fact that participants learn the pen gestures is that they need to form gestures' representation of imagery in their minds at first, and then store them into long-term memory by rehearsal. At the same time, participants need not only to remember the gestures, but also to connect the gestures, which can cause participants to form representation of imagery in their minds, and the matching commands, which can cause participants to form prepositional representation in their minds. The dual coding theory proposed by Paivio assumes that there are two cognitive subsystems, one specialized for the representation and processing of nonverbal objects/events (i.e. imagery), and the other specialized for dealing with language.

Paivio also postulates two different types of representational units: "imagens" for mental images and "logogens" for verbal entities. Logogens are organized in terms of associations and hierarchies while imagens are organized in terms of part-whole relationships. Dual Coding theory identified three types of processing how two systems can been connected: (1) representational, the direct activation of verbal or non-verbal representations, (2) referential, the activation of the verbal system by the nonverbal system or vice-versa, and (3) associative processing, the activation of representations within the same verbal or nonverbal system. A given task in our experiment may require all of the three kinds of processing. As we can see, verbal system and nonverbal system can be associated together in terms of referential connections between logogens and imagens. If stimulus such as pen gestures and commands can improve the connections, these two systems will also have cumulate improve effect for the users' remember to the stimulus. For our design, the gestures directed clearly, object-metaphor and established by usage, can not only benefit users' representation of imagery, but also benefit referential connections between two systems. So they are easy to remember.

From the viewpoint of Norman [30], when a user performs a task, his processing ability is limited by two factors: the processing resources available and the quality of data available. There is a trade-off between resources and data quality. Because lots of resources required in a task will cause heavy cognitive load. A primary design objective should be to minimize resource consumption by improving data quality. But the data quality improvement relies on training for the task. So lots of time will be spent. How to get high data quality without spending lots of time in training? Pen gesture with "iconicness" property gives us a good solution. The information presentation style in those gestures is analogous to natural working style in paper. It makes use of human's knowledge about the natural working environment which exists in human's mind for many years. So when a user interacts with those pen gestures, he will feel familiar with such interaction context. And the interaction efficiency will be increased.

6 Pen Gesture Recognition Effect Analysis

Besides learnability, recognition effect is another important factor that influences the usability of pen gesture. It is typical perceptual process for people to recognize gestures. This process of recognition is to compare the sensory information in a gesture sample with the relative information stored in people's long-term memory, and to determine the best match between items in long-term memory and the sensory information. In this paper, we do not design a new recognition algorithm for pen gesture. Instead, we applied a widely used algorithm from Rubine [12] as our recognition algorithm for pen gestures. And based on it, we will analyze Rubine's feature set, and improve the feature set to gain higher recognition accuracy.

Rubine's algorithm takes a statistical approach to recognition, based on a set of measurable geometric features about the pen gesture, including features about initial angle, length of bounding box diagonal, angle of bounding box diagonal, distance between first and last points, angle between first and last points, length, total angle traversed, sum of absolute value of angle at each point, sum of squared angle at each point (sharpness), square of maximum speed, duration etc. Rubine chose these features because they relate to observable geometric properties, which is helpful for people understand the recognition [15].

We built a tool for designing and recognizing pen gestures based on Rubine's algorithm. It is used to collecting samples, recognizing samples and evaluation. The algorithm is nearly ideal if the set of samples and the Mahalanobis distance [33] is small. But after lots of testing, we found some problems about the algorithm. And we add some improvements on it.

The Feature of Point of Intersection

When we designed two kinds of pen gesture shown in figure 1, we found that the last kind is used to being recognized as first kind. Though the set of sample has been adjusted several times, the problem still exists. Figure 2 is two strokes input by user that has wrong recognition result. And we found that the Mahalanobis distance of two strokes is between 20 and 30. It is far smaller than 150: the normal value of rejecting recognition.

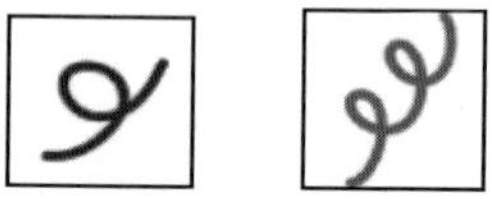

Fig. 1. Two kinds of pen gesture

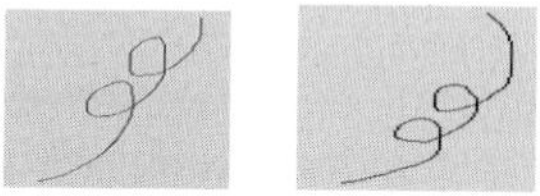

Fig. 2. Two samples with wrong recognition result

It makes us know that the features between samples and the average value of recognition result are very close. And after carefully check of our set of sample, the possibility of the problem caused by the wrong or tousy samples are excluded. It is confusing because user considers these two kinds of pen gesture is dissimilarity. The most obvious feature is that the first kind of pen gesture has one close circle, the second kind has two.

After we analyze Rubine's algorithm, we found that f9, f10, f11 in Rubine's feature set are related to curvature property of pen gesture. From figure 2, we can see that in two samples, the closed circles in pen gestures sketched are all not roundness. It can be considered as composed of a part of arc and a section of curve with low curvature. It is possible that the feature about f9, f10, f11 in the second kind of pen gesture is same as the first kind. That's the reason why high wrong recognition rate exist between these two kinds of pen gestures.

In order to solve the problem, we added a new feature to Rubine's feature set. We select the property: num of point of intersection in the stroke to judge the num of close curve in a pen gesture. There are some reasons for us to select the feature. First, it's a nature feature for human to judge the num of close curve in a stroke. Second, it can completely solve this kind of problem we discussed. Third, it can be calculated easily. After adding the feature, we still use the same set of samples to build new classifier. We found that the problem is disappeared. At the same time, the recognition accuracy of other pen gestures is not influenced obviously.

The Size of Samples

Rubine's algorithm does not use stroke normalization. The algorithm uses the weight of different features to embody the influence of difference between sample sizes. If the difference is obvious, the weight of angle of bounding box diagonal, length, and distance between first and last points will be small. If the training environment and application environment is different. It's possible that the value of specific feature can not embody the right weight. Then the recognition accuracy will be influenced. We found this problem when we use hand-hold devices to test pen gestures that were trained on pc. The rejected recognition rate of some pen gestures is over 20% on hand-hold devices. However, those gestures can be nearly 100% recognized correctly on desktop pc. The reason is that the point num in one kinds of pen gesture in different environment is very different. The input area and display resolution on desktop pc is far higher than on hand-hold devices. Therefore, the point num of same kind of pen gesture input on desktop pc is far more than on hand-hold devices. And it result in the bounding box diagonal, length, distance between first and last points is very different.

There are two methods to solve the problem. The first method is to training pen gestures on hand-hold devices to build new classifier. The second method is to do stroke normalization before building classifier. The first method isn't a good choice because every new application environment will cause additional work to training and building new classifier. The second is good that it can eliminate the influence of difference between sample sizes on Rubine's feature set. Therefore, the user did not care what size of the pen gesture he should input, he just focus on the inner geometric features of the pen gesture.

7 Evaluation

In these experiments, we compared the pen gestures with "iconicness" property related to commands designed by us, the gestures designed by A Chris Long [15], and gestures used in pen-based systems, to see which kinds of gestures is benefit to users on learnability. Correspondingly, we built three groups: visual-gestures group, criterion-gestures group and general-gestures group. We selected 12 editing commands from foregoing questionnaire investigation. Commands and related pen gestures in three groups are listed in Table 1.

Table 1. The experimental materials

Commands	undo	redo	rotate	select all	align left	align right
visual-gestures group	撤销	重做	旋转	全选	齐左	齐右
criterion-gestures group	撤销	重做	旋转	全选	齐左	齐右
general-gestures group	撤销	重做	旋转	全选	齐左	齐右
Commands	**cut**	**zoom in**	**zoom out**	**scroll up**	**scroll down**	**delete**
visual-gestures group	剪切	缩小	放大	下翻	上翻	删除
criterion-gestures group	剪切	缩小	放大	下翻	上翻	删除
general-gestures group	剪切	缩小	放大	下翻	上翻	删除

Fifty one sophomore and junior volunteers were recruited from a university. All participants took part in the first experiment, and forty seven participants took part in the second experiment. Experimental procedure in practice was as follows.

The first experiment was to ask participants to remember the matching experimental materials, which was used the anticipation method in memory research. When participants were coming into the experimental room, the experimental experimenter distributed them into three different process levels by the way of randomizing entirely. Before the experiment was beginning, the experimenter presented experimental instruction. Then, participants did exercises. When the experiment was beginning, the experimental software presented the matching materials of commands and gestures by 2 seconds per matching material, which was the stage of presentation. Each participant should learn twelve matching materials in one process level and try their best to remember these materials. Afterwards, the stage of test started. In this stage, the software only presented commands' name, and asked participants to recall the gestures, then drew them onto the screen with the stylus. After four seconds, the software gave a right feedback to participants. At the same time, the experimenter had the task to check participants' responses. If their responses were right, the experimenter wrote "√"; else, wrote "×". If participants couldn't recall all gestures right in one serial, experimenter should asked them to do another serial, until they can recall all gestures right in two continuous serials.

The second experiment was to measure participants' retention of memories. Participants came into the experimental room again at intervals of 48 hours since the first experiment ended. This procedure was similar to the first one. However it directed into the stage of test, without the stage of presentation.

The data was imported into SPSS and MS Excel for analysis. Times of learning experimental materials are the main index of gesture's learnability. We first compared the different among times of learning three materials in the first experiment. We then analyzed the data by Nonparametric Tests for 2 Independent Samples.

According to the results, we can see that there are no statistically significant differences between the learning times of visual-gestures group and of criterion-gestures group in first experiment, which indicates that there are no significant differences between the learning effect of visual-gestures group and of criterion-gestures group in first experiment. However, the learning times of visual-gestures group are significantly less than of general-gestures group, which indicates that the first learning effect of visual-gestures group is better than of general-gestures group.

We analyzed participants' mean percent rates of right response for their every learning time in the first experiment. The results are shown in figure 3.

Then we analyze times of learning three materials in the relearning experiment. According to the results, we can see that the learning times of visual-gestures group are higher significantly than those of criterion-gestures group and those of general-gestures group, which indicates that the relearning effect of visual-gestures group is better than those of criterion-gestures group and those of general-gestures group. According to the results, it also indicates that the relearning effect of criterion-gestures group is better than those of general-gestures group. The results are shown in figure 4.

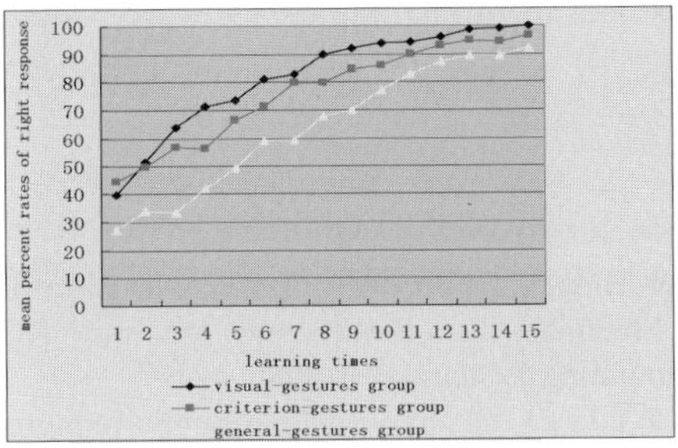

Fig. 3. Result in the first experiment

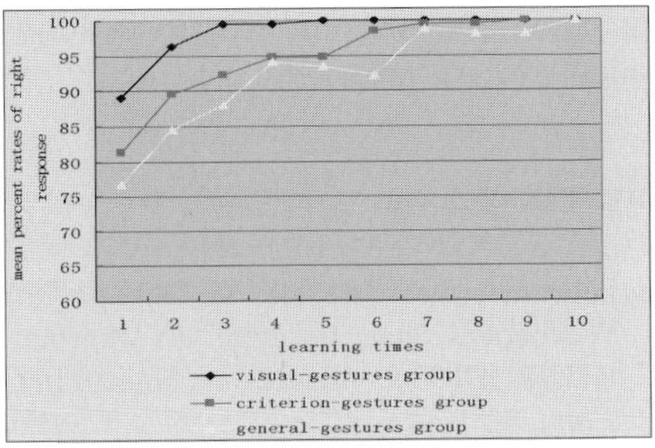

Fig. 4. Result in the second experiment

Cooper considered that good habitual usages can be learned only one time [34]. We measured the gestures which 95% percent and more participants could response rightly and could be right continuously. We named these gestures as one-time-learned gestures. The formula for the memorial retains is as follows.

*Percent of the memorial retains = 100% * (times of the first learning – times of re-learning)/times of the first learning.*

According to this formula, we calculated memorial retains at intervals of forty-eight hours between two experiments, then, compared whether there are significantly different among these three gestures' groups. We can see that the memorial retains of visual-gestures group are higher significantly than those of criterion-gestures group. And they are also higher than those of general-gestures group, but it doesn't access to the significant levels. There are no significant differences of memorial retains between criterion-gestures group and general-gestures group.

8 Conclusion

In this paper, we performed a research on user-centered design and recognition to improve the learnability and recognition accuracy of pen gestures. Firstly we performed a survey of 100 pen gestures in twelve famous pen-bases systems to find problems of pen gestures currently used. And we conducted a questionnaire to evaluate the matching degree between commands and pen gestures to discover the characteristics that a good pen gestures should have. Then cognition theories are applied to analyze the advantages of those characteristics in helping improving the learnability of pen gestures. From these, we analyze the pen gesture recognition effect and present some improvements on features selection in recognition algorithm of pen gestures. Finally we use a couple of psychology experiments to evaluate twelve pen gestures designed based on the research. It shows those gestures is better for user to learn and use. Research results of this paper can be used for designer as a primary principle to design pen gestures in pen-based user interfaces.

Acknowledgements

This research is supported by No. 2002CB312103 from the National Grand Fundamental Research 973 Program of China, No. 60503054 from National Natural Science

Foundation of China, and Key Innovation Project from Institute of Software, Chinese Academy of Sciences.

References

1. Pedersen, E.R., McCall, K., Moran, T.P. & Halasz, F.G. (1993). Tivoli: An Electronic Whiteboard for Informal Workgroup Meetings. In Proceedings of the ACM INTERCHI'93 Conference on Human in Computing Systems, 391-398.
2. Elrod, S., Bruce, R., et al. (1992). Liveboard: a large interactive display supporting group meetings, presentations, and remote collaboration. In Proceedings of the ACM Conference on Human Factors in Computing Systems: CHI'92, Monterey, CA, May 3 - 7, 1992, pp.599-607
3. Landay, J.A., and Myers, B.A. Interactive Sketching for the Early Stages of User Interface Design. Proceeding of CHI'95, 45-50
4. Lin, J., Newman, M., Hong, J., & Landay, J. (2000). DENIM: Finding a Tighter Fit Between Tools and Practice for Web Site Design. CHI Letters: Human Factors in Computing Systems, CHI '2000, 2(1): p. 510-517
5. Gross, M. D., The Electronic Cocktail Napkin. A computational environment for working with design diagrams. Design Studies, 17(1):53--69, 1996
6. Mynatt, E.D., Igarashi, T., Edwards, W.K. & LaMarca, A. (1999). Flatland: new dimensions in office whiteboards. In Proceedings of CHI'99 Human Factors in Computing Systems (May 15-20, Pittsburgh, PA), ACM, 1999, pp.346-353.
7. Abowd, G.D. et al.. Teaching and learning as multimedia authoring: the classroom 2000 project, Proceedings of the fourth ACM international conference on Multimedia, p.187-198, November 18-22, 1996, Boston, Massachusetts, United States.
8. Alvarado, C. & Davis, R. Resolving ambiguities to create a natural sketch based interface. Proceedings of IJCAI-2001, August 2001.
9. Igarashi, T., Matsuoka, S. and Tanaka, H. (1999) Teddy: a sketching interface for 3D freeform design. Computer Graphics Proceedings, Annual Conference Series, 1999, ACM SIGGRAPH: 409-416.
10. Windows XP Tablet PC Edition, http://www.microsoft.com/windowsxp/tabletpc/default.mspx
11. MAC OS X Tiger, http://www.apple.com/macosx/overview/
12. Rubine, D. Specifying gestures by example. In Computer Graphics. ACM SIGGRAPH, Addison Wesley, Jul. 1991 329-337.
13. Rubine, D. Combining gestures and direct manipulation, Proceedings of the SIGCHI conference on Human factors in computing systems, 1992 659 - 660
14. Long, Jr., A.C., Landay, J.A., and Rowe, L. A. PDA and gesture use in practice: Insights for designers of pen-based user interfaces. Tech. Rep. UCB//CSD-97-976, U.C. Berkeley, 1997. Available at http://bmrc.berkeley.edu/papers/1997/142/142.html.
15. Long, Jr., A.C. Quill: A gesture design tool for pen-based user interfaces [Ph.D. Thesis]. Berkeley: University of California, 2001.
16. Paivio, A., Mental representations: A dual coding approach, Oxford University Press, 1986
17. Zhao, R., Kaufmann, H.-J., Kern, T., and Miiller, W. Pen-based interfaces in engineering environments. In International Conference on Human-Computer Interaction (Anzai, Y., Ogawa, K., and Mori, H., eds.), vol. 20B of Advances in Human Factors/Ergonomics. Information Processing Society of Japan and others, Elsevier Science, Jul. 1995 531-536.

18. Tandler, P., Thorsten Prante. Using Incremental Gesture Recognition to Provide Immediate Feedback while Drawing Pen Gestures. UIST 2001. 18--25.
19. Long, Jr., A.C., Landay JA, Rowe LA. Implications for a gesture design tool. In: Human Factors in Computing Systems (SIGCHI Proc.). ACM Press, 1999. 40.47.
20. Kramer, A, Classifying Two Dimensional Gestures in Interactive Systems, Lecture Notes In Computer Science, Vol. 1371 Proceedings of the International Gesture Workshop on Gesture and Sign Language in Human-Computer Interaction, P37 - 48 1997.
21. Long, Jr., A.C., Landay JA, Rowe LA, Michiels J. Visual similarity of pen Gestures. In: Proc. of the Human Factors in Computing Systems SIGCHI 2000. 2000,2(1):360.367.
22. Newton, Apple Computer, Inc., http://www.apple.com
23. Palm Computing. http://www.palm.com
24. Nicholson, M., Vickers, P., Pen-Based Gestures: An Approach to Reducing Screen Clutter in Mobile Computing, S. Brewster and M. Dunlop (Eds.): MobileHCI 2004, LNCS 3160, pp. 320–324, 2004.
25. Cohen,P. R., Michael Johnston, David McGee, Sharon L. Oviatt, Jay Pittman, Ira A. Smith, Liang Chen, Josh Clow: QuickSet: Multimodal Interaction for Distributed Applications. ACM Multimedia 1997: 31-40
26. Landay, J.A. and Myers, B.A. 2001. "Sketching Interfaces: Toward More Human Interface Design." IEEE Computer, vol. 34, no.3, March, 56-64.
27. Chatty, S. and Lecoanet, P. Pen computing for air traffic control. In Human Factors in Computing Systems (SIGCHI Proceedings) . ACM, Addison-Wesley, Apr. 1996 87-94.
28. Bimber, O., Miguel Encarnac, L., Stork, A., A multi-layered architecture for sketch-based interaction within virtual environments, Computers & Graphics 24 (2000) 851-867.
29. MindManager, http://www.mindjet.com
30. Norman, D., and Bobrow, D. On Data-Limited and Resource-Limited Processes, Cognitive Psychology 7, 1975, 44-64.
31. Michael Eysenck, Mark T. Keane, Cognition Psychology: A Student's Handbook, Fourth Edition, Psychology Press, 2000
32. Sergios Theodoridis, Konstantinos Koutroumbas, Pattern Recognition, Second Edition, , Elsevier Science, 2004
33. DIJDA, R., AND HART, P. Pattern Classification and Scene Analysis. Wiley Interscience, 1973.
34. Cooper, A., About Face 2.0: The Essentials of Interaction Design, John Wiley & Sons Inc, 2003.

Simulating Pedestrian Behavior with Potential Fields

Fábio Dapper[1], Edson Prestes[1], Marco A.P. Idiart[2], and Luciana P. Nedel[1]

[1] Instituto de Informática, Universidade Federal do Rio Grande do Sul
[2] Instituto de Física, Universidade Federal do Rio Grande do Sul,
Porto Alegre – RS – Brazil
{fdapper, prestes, nedel}@inf.ufrgs.br, idiart@if.ufrgs.br

Abstract. The main challenges of realistically simulating the displacement of humanoid pedestrians are twofold: they need to behave realistically and they should accomplish their tasks. Here we present a field potential formalism, based upon boundary value problems, that allows a group of synthetic actors to move negotiating space, avoiding collisions, attaining goals in prescribed sequences while at same time producing very individual paths. The individuality of each pedestrian can be set by changing its inner field parameters. This leads to a broad range of possible behaviors without jeopardizing its task performance. Simulate situations as behavior in corridors, collision avoidance and competition for a goal are presented and discussed.

1 Introduction

The use of synthetic actors able of acting as autonomous agents in applications involving virtual environments is becoming more and more common [1]. Suitable skills for those actors (often simulating human beings) include: a realistic appearance, the ability to produce natural movements, and the aptitude to reasoning and act in an unforeseeable way.

To simulate the behavior of human beings, it is usual to consider system architectures implemented in layers. The lowest one deals with the rotation of each body joint. The intermediary level is responsible for encapsulating composed movements that bring together a set of single joint motions. These movements can represent simple tasks (e.g. stand-up, sit-down, take something, give a step) that used together can provide a higher abstraction level, so called behaviors (e.g. open the door, walk from one position to another one, etc). Finally, the higher abstraction motion layer (cognitive) involves a reasoning mechanism that makes decisions and commands actions in view of the context information (e.g. position, orientation, and distance to target) and humanoids intentions, beliefs and desires.

In a previous work [2] we presented a well succeeded proposal for the implementation of the cognitive level using the BDI (beliefs, desires and intentions) architecture to simulate autonomous agents reasoning. However, good solutions for lower level behaviors may also be investigated. Such solutions should preview

H.-P. Seidel, T. Nishita, and Q. Peng (Eds.): CGI 2006, LNCS 4035, pp. 324–335, 2006.

not just a handy manner to specify complex tasks based on simple ones, but also to consider the addition of expressiveness on those tasks.

The simulation of virtual humans moving into a synthetic world involves mainly the environment specification, the definition of the agent initial position as well as its target position in the world (also called *goal*). By setting those parameters, a path-planning algorithm can be used to find a trajectory to be followed. However, in a real world, if we consider several persons (all in the same initial position) looking for achieving the same target position, each individual path followed will be different. Even if we have the same task, the strategy used for each one to reach his/her goal will depend on his/her physical constitution, personality, mood and reasoning.

In this paper we propose a path-planning approach based on boundary value problems to find paths between an initial and a target position in a dynamic environment. The paths found by our algorithm are smooth and variable, depending on the individual characteristics of each agent, which can be dynamically changed.

The paper is organized as follows. In Section 2 we presented some related work on path-planning techniques for virtual humans. Section 3 describes our path planner based on harmonic functions and Section 4 presents our main contribution, involving the extensions for the basic method. In Section 5 we deeply explain the way we implemented the method and in Section 6 we present our results. Finally, in Section 7 we present the conclusions and point out some future work.

2 Related Work

Motion planning methods have been largely studied by the robotics community. As in this paper our focus is on its use for simulating human beings behaviors while walking, we limit this Section scope for the works involving humanoids animation.

Lengyel *et al.* [3] have published one of the first articles on the subject of motion planning as a computer graphics problem. Their work presented a solution for the classical *Piano Movers* problem based on the use of standard graphics hardware to rasterize obstacles and generates the configuration space. The motion path produced by the planner is minimal with respect to the Manhattan distance metric and includes rotations and translations.

In order to generate more realistic results and allows its use in real-time applications, several authors proposed motion planning solutions based on two steps. In general, the first step is dedicated to define a valid path, while the second adapts this path in order to generate a more realistic movement. Kuffner [4] proposed a technique with the first step dedicated to the path-planning and the second to the path-following. The 3D scenario is projected in 2D and the humanoid treated as a disc, reducing the planning problem to a 2D problem.

Metoyer and Hodgings [5] proposed a similar technique also based on two steps. In their method, the characters have a pre-defined path to follows and this path is smoothed and slightly changed to avoid collisions by using force fields.

The development of randomized path-finding algorithms, specially the PRM (Probabilistic Roadmaps) [6] and RTT (Rapidly-exploring Random Tree) [7], allow the use of large and most complexes configuration spaces, generating paths most efficiently. In this way, the challenge becomes more the generation of realistic movements than finding a valid path. Choi *et al.* [8] proposed the use of a captured movements library associated to the PRM to generate realistic movements in a static environment. Despite the fact the path maps should be generated in a pre-processing phase, the results are very realistic.

Thanks to the researches in robotics, the path-planning problem is almost solved. However, in the computer graphics domain, to find a natural and realistic way to move a character is as important as to find a path between two points. The most part of the works developed since now propose methods based on two separate phases. In the next sections we present our own proposal for generating realistic paths based on a single phase.

3 Harmonic Functions Path Planner

Whether it is a human being, a robot or a synthetic actor the action of moving from an initial position to a goal position in space consists of at least two stages: a planning stage when a path is devised; and an implementation stage when the path is followed by the moving agent. The first stage deals with a combination of concepts like efficiency, risk avoidance, computability, etc. To the second stage belongs the series of routines or corrections that the agent has to perform to adapt its motion when the predefined path cannot be followed due to unpredictable changes in the agent's surrounds, or in case of robotics, due to machine limitations.

In a seminal work in the field of robotics, Khatib [9] proposed a method that fuses these two stages in a very elegant way. He considered that instead of looking for a good path and trying to control the agent's movement around it a good planner should provide a potential field, or a force field (its gradient), that expanded the whole region of manoeuvre, producing a continuum of alternative paths. The potential field is devised to incorporate obstacles and goals, and should guide agent at all times indicating the best direction to follow. Its most straightforward implementation is a simple superposition of fictitious forces: obstacles forces that repel the agent to prevent collisions; and target forces that attract the agent. Such superposition is not always successful since for some environment configuration the agent can end up trapped in local minima before reaching the target.

Up to this date, the best way to produce a potential field that is free from local minima is through the numerical solution of a convenient partial differential equation with boundary conditions - a boundary value problem (BVP). The boundary conditions are central to the method indicating which regions in the environment are obstacles and which are targets.

The first proposal in this direction was made by Connolly and Grupen [10] and it is called the method of the harmonic functions. In their method the potential fields are the solutions of the Laplace's equation - whose solutions are called harmonic functions

$$\nabla^2 p(\mathbf{r}) = \sum_i \frac{\partial^2 p(\mathbf{r})}{\partial x_i^2} = 0 \quad (1)$$

where $\mathbf{r}$ is the environment coordinates. The Laplace's equation does not present local minima, and that is why it was chosen. They also proposed boundary conditions such that the potential should be one in the contours of the obstacles and zero in the region of the target. Setting up the value of the function in the boundaries is called a Dirichlet boundary condition in the language of a BVP.

The agent uses the gradient descent of this potential to determine the path that connects its current position to the target. As there is only a minimum defined in target position, it exists exactly one path from any point to the potential to the target. This method is formally complete, i.e., if there is a path that connects the agent position to the target it will be found. The resulting path is smooth and safe and it minimizes the collision probability with the obstacles.

4 Beyond Path Planner Based on Harmonic Functions

Laplace's equation is not the only partial differential equation that generates functions without local minima. In [11], Trevisan *et al.* came up with a framework for exploratory navigation based on a family of potential field functions that does not possess local minima. The authors suggest the following equation

$$\nabla^2 p(\mathbf{r}) + \epsilon \mathbf{v}.\nabla p(\mathbf{r}) = 0 \quad (2)$$

for handling sparse environments, where $\mathbf{v}$ is a bias vector and ϵ is a scalar. The addition of the term $\epsilon \mathbf{v} \nabla p$ breaks the symmetry of vector field generated by Laplace's equation increasing the system performance in sparse environments during the exploration process.

The central contribution of this paper is to use the Equation 2 for generating different behaviors (illustrated in this work through the path followed by each agent) for several agents in a known environment. As discussed before, if the agent is controlled by a vector field produced by harmonic functions, it will always tend to follow a path that minimize the collision probability with the obstacles, i.e., in an indoor environment the agent will tend to follow a path equidistant to the walls, as shown in Figure 1(a). This behavior is not always adequate to simulate humanoid motion since it looks very stereotyped.

The adjustment of the vector $\mathbf{v}$ can produce a path close to the walls, as shown in Figures 1(b) and (c). The vector $\mathbf{v}$, also called *behavior vector*, can be seen as an external force field that counteract the natural tendency of agent moving away from the obstacles. The parameter ϵ can be understood as the *strength* or *influence* in following the direction defined by vector $\mathbf{v}$ instead of the direction produced by harmonic functions.

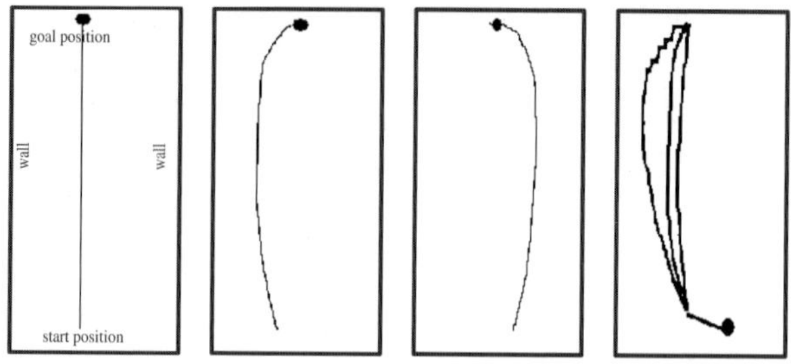

(a) (b) (c) (d)

Fig. 1. Different paths followed by agents using Equation 2: (a) path produced by harmonic potential, i.e., with $\epsilon = 0$; (b) with $\epsilon = 0.8$ and $\mathbf{v} = (1, 0)$; (c) with $\epsilon = 0.8$ and $\mathbf{v} = (-1, 0)$; and using the same vector $\mathbf{v} = (1, 1)$ and different values to the parameter ϵ (0.4, 0.8, 1.2, 1.6, 2.0, 2.4 and 7.2)

Figure 1(d) shows the results obtained in several experiments that use different ϵ and the same vector $\mathbf{v} = (1, 1)$. This flexibility allows to develop different and interesting behaviors to generate realistic humanoid motion during the navigation process. In our case, we simulated several agents with different v and ϵ and put them into a known environment to perform a couple of navigation tasks.

5 Implementation

In this section, we present the global environment representation, the structure of the agents that act on the environment, as well as the mechanisms used to control each agent behavior.

5.1 Environment Global Map

The environment is represented by a *set* of homogenous meshes $\{m_k\}$, where each mesh m_k is associated to a target o_k and has $L_x \times L_y$ cells, denoted by $\{c^k_{i,j}\}$. Each cell $c^k_{i,j}$ corresponds to a squared region centered in environment coordinates $r = (r_i, r_j)$ and stores a particular potential value $p^k_{i,j}$. These maps are used by the harmonic path planner (see Section 3) to assist the agent to reach a specific target.

Each mesh m_k has the potential values of its cells relaxed independently using the Equation 1. After the convergence, the map m_k stores a potential field that is used to reach the target o_k. This procedure is performed before the simulation starts and we consider that the environment is surrounded by obstacles in order to delimit the agent navigation space.

5.2 Agent Local Map

Each agent a_k has one map am_k that stores the current local information about the environment obtained by its sensors. This map is centered in the current agent position and represents a small fraction of the global map, nearly 10% of the total area covered by the global map.

The map am_k has $l_x^k \times l_y^k$ cells, denoted by $\{ac_{i,j}^k\}$ and can be divided in three regions: the update zone (*u-zone*); the free zone (*f-zone*) and the border zone (*b-zone*), as shown in Figure 2(a). In a similar way, each cell corresponds to a squared region centered in environment coordinates $r = (r_i, r_j)$ and stores a particular potential value $ap_{i,j}^k$.

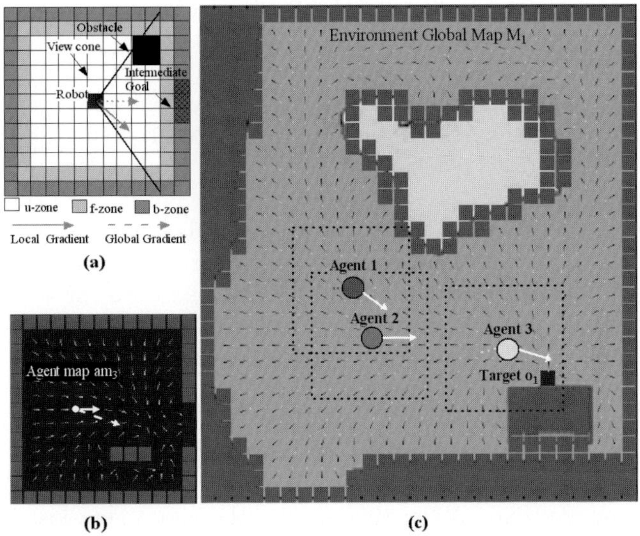

Fig. 2. (a)Agent Local Map. The white, light gray and dark gray cells comprise the update, free and border zones, respectively. (b,c)Agents acting in the real environment. Each agent senses the environment, updates its local map (b) and navigates towards the target o_1 (c).

The area associated to each agent map cell is smaller than the area associated to the global map cell. The main reason is that the agent map is used to produce a refined motion, hence, the smaller cell size the better the quality of motion; while the global map is used only to assist the long-term agent navigation.

5.3 Updating Local Maps Using Global Maps

Each agent a_k has a well determined goal $o_{goal(k)}$ (the function *goal* maps the agent number k into its current target number. In this description, we will consider that each agent must reach only one target. The extension to multiple targets is straightforward and will be commented in Section 5.5), a particular vector $\mathbf{v}_k$, that controls its behavior, and a ϵ_k that determines the influence of $\mathbf{v}_k$. The same goal, $\mathbf{v}$ and ϵ can be designated to several agents.

When the agent a_k navigates the environment, it uses its sensors to perceive the environment and to update its local map with the information about the obstacles and other agents. The agent sensors set a view cone with aperture α.

Figure 2(b) sketches a particular instance of the agent local map. The *u-zone* cells $\{ac^k_{i,j}\}$, inside the view cone, with obstacles or agents have their potential value set to 1. Obstacles are not considered in the *u-zone* out of the view cone. This procedure assures that dynamic or static obstacles behind the agent do not interfere in its future motion.

The agent a_k calculates the global descent gradient on the cell in the global map $m_{goal(k)}$ containing its current position. The gradient direction is used to generate an intermediate goal in the border of the local map setting the potential values to 0 of a couple of *b-zone* cells. While the other *b-zone* cells are considered as obstacles having their potential values set to 1. In Figure 2(c), each agent calculates the global gradient in order to project an intermediate goal in its local map. As the agent local map is delimited by obstacles, the agent is pulled towards the intermediate goal using the direction of its local gradient. The intermediate goal helps the agent a_k to reach its target $o_{goal(k)}$ while allowing it to produce its particular motion.

In some cases, the target $o_{goal(k)}$ is inside both the view cone and the *u-zone*, and consequently, the local map cells associated are set to 0. The intermediate goal is always projected even if the target is mapped onto the *u-zone* otherwise the robot can easily get trapped because the robot would be taking into consideration only the local information about the environment, in a same way as traditional potential fields [9].

The *f-zone* cells are always considered free of obstacles, even when there are obstacles there. The absence of this zone may close the connexion between the current agent cell and the intermediate goal due to the mapping of obstacles in front of intermediate goal. When this occurs, the robot gets lost because there is no information coming from the intermediate goal to produce a path to reach it. The *f-zone* cells handle the situation permitting always that the information about the goal is propagated to the cells associated to the agent position.

After the sensing and mapping steps, the agent updates the potential value of its map cell using a discrete version of Equation 2,

$$
\begin{aligned}
ap^k_{i,j} &= \frac{1}{4}(ap^k_{i-1,j} + ap^k_{i+1,j} + ap^k_{i,j-1} + ap^k_{i,j+1}) + \\
&\frac{\epsilon^k}{8}((ap^k_{i+1,j} - ap^k_{i-1,j})v^k_x + (ap^k_{i,j+1} - ap^k_{i,j-1})v^k_y)
\end{aligned}
\tag{3}
$$

where $\mathbf{v}^k = (v^k_x, v^k_y)$ is the vector that controls the behavior of agent a_k and $\epsilon^k \in [-2, +2]$ and represents the *influence* of vector $\mathbf{v}^k$. The local potential is partially relaxed [12] and the agent calculates the gradient descent of its position in the local map am_k by

$$
\mathbf{dgrad}^k = \Big((ac^k_{p_x+1,p_y} - ac^k_{p_x-1,p_y})/2, (ac^k_{p_x,p_y+1} - ac^k_{p_x,p_y-1})/2\Big)
$$

where $p_x = \lceil l^k_x/2 \rceil$ and $p_y = \lceil l^k_y/2 \rceil$, and it follows the direction θ^k calculated by $\theta^k = \arctan(dgrad^k_x, dgrad^k_y)$ where $\arctan(.,.)$ is the inverse tangent taken in the interval $[-\pi, +\pi]$.

5.4 Characterizing the Agent Behavior

In the real world, even if several people have the same goal, the strategy used for each one to reach it will depend on different factors as: physical constitution, personality, mood, and reasoning. In Figure 1 we shown we can simulate different behaviors by setting both the behavior vector v and ϵ differently for each agent. In this first example we kept the variables constant during the animation, however we can produce more interesting behaviors dynamically changing vector $\mathbf{v}$ and ϵ. For instance, the vector $\mathbf{v}$ can be controlled by a function defined by the user, as in Figure 3. Even with this new complex behavior, which simulates a *drunk* agent, the resulting potential guarantees that the robot reaches safely the target.

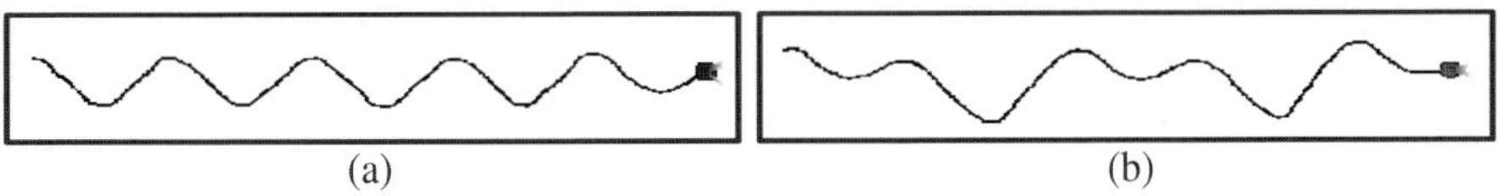

Fig. 3. Paths followed by agents using different equations that control the behavior vector $\mathbf{v}$: (a) $\mathbf{v} = (1, \sin(\omega * t))$; (b) $\mathbf{v} = (1, \sin(\omega * t) + \sin(\omega/2 * t))$, with $\omega = \pi/18$ and t the current simulation step

We can change $\mathbf{v}$ in a regular periodic fashion, as shown above, but it does not need always to be the case. We can consider an agent that randomly changes its behavior vector. Each new value of $\mathbf{v}$ is kept constant during an also random time interval.

5.5 Algorithm

In this section we present the algorithm that implements the concepts shown before and produce the humanoids simulation.

1. computes all the environment global maps (one for each possible goal o_k)
2. for each agent a_k, defines the behavior vector $\mathbf{v}_k$ and ϵ_k. Each variable can be either static or dynamic. If a variable is chosen to be dynamic then the function that controls it must be specified.
3. for each agent a_k do (asynchronously)
   (a) reads its sensors in order to detect static and dynamic obstacles
   (b) updates its map with local information about the obstacles and other agents
   (c) computes the global gradient descent and generates the intermediate goal
   (d) updates the potential field
   (e) computes the local gradient descent and follows the gradient direction
   (f) while not reaching the target $o_{goal(k)}$ repeat the steps from (a) to (f), otherwise stops moving

The first two steps are performed in a pre-process phase. In relation to the step 3, each agent executes independent and asynchronously the actions from (a) to (f). This algorithm considers each agent must reach only one target. However, the agent can be in charge of reaching several targets orderly. In this case, the step (f) must be changed to

(f) while not reaching the target $o_{goal^i(k)}$ repeat the steps from (a) to (f), otherwise if $goal^i(k) = goal^{last}(k)$ then stops moving. Else repeats the process with the next target $o_{goal^{i+1}(k)}$.

6 Results

In order to illustrate the potentialities of our path-planning approach we made some experiments considering a realistic situation. Taking into account the scenario described bellow, we have induced some agents' behaviors to verify some considerations made before, as: how to accomplish the same task in different ways; or how different agents avoid collisions, for example. In another set of tests we have ran the algorithm considering a variable number of agents with random objectives, behaviors and velocities. Our goal with these experiments was to verify the motion diversity. Finally, we made some considerations about performance.

We consider a small park in a town (see Figure 4). It has five accesses, a lake in the middle and a popcorn-cart in the south. Characters in the simulation can simply cross the park or stop to buy a popcorn bag and continue their walking. It is a quite familiar real scenario; the large open area makes easy and clear the simulation of different agents behaviors that will not be constrained by an excessive amount of obstacles; by simulating a group of agents walking in the park it is easy to verify the collision avoidance with dynamic obstacles (here represented as other agents).

The set up for this scenario involves the statement of six possible goals, one for each park access and another in front of the popcorn-cart. We will need to compute 6 environment global maps. In our tests, we used a matrix with 60x60 cells to represent global maps and a matrix with 11x11 cells for the agent local maps.

The first situation induced by us consists in simulating the behavior of 4 agents while accomplishing the same task. The agents are initially disposed somewhere in the park access west and their task consists on go to the popcorn-cart and after, to quit the park by the access north. Figure 4 illustrates the results of animation. Each agent accomplishes its task individually without the intervention of the others. The small square specifies the moment where the agent 3 changes its behavior vector $\mathbf{v}$.

Figure 4(b) shows the same task of Figure 4(a), but in this case all the agents are moving at the same time, therefore they compete for the targets. The paths drawn in these two figures are slightly different and these differences are duo the collision detection and avoidance between the agents.

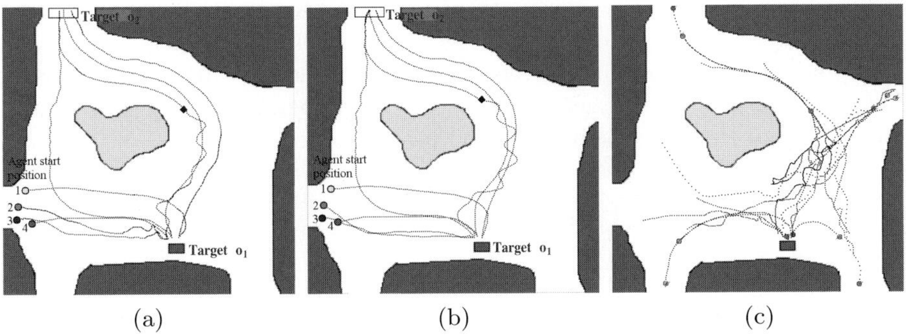

Fig. 4. Four agents individually accomplishing the same task (a) and accomplishing the same task concurrently (b). Agent 1: $\mathbf{v} = (-0.707, -0.707)$, $\epsilon = 0.8$ and $step = 0.6$ cells per frame; agent 2: $\mathbf{v} = (0.707, 0.707)$, $\epsilon = 0.8$ and $step = 0.5$ cells per frame; agent 3: initially $\mathbf{v} = (\sin(\omega * t), 1)$, changing to $\mathbf{v} = (0.707, 0.707)$ after some time, $\epsilon = 0.8$ and $step = 0.35$ cells per frame; agent 4: $\epsilon = 0$, and $step = 0.46$ cells per frame.(c) Simulation of a set of 12 agents walking around the park with random behaviors.

Figure 5 shows two frames of the animation of two agents. One agent walks from the north to the south while the other one walks from the south to the north. Using our algorithm we automatically avoid the collision between the two agents, since each agent is considered as a dynamic obstacle by the other. However, the final path definition can be more or less natural, depending on the parameters definition. In the sequence presented on Figure 5(a), we set ϵ as 0. In this way, the behavior vector $\mathbf{v}$ is not considered. For the animation shown in Figure 5(b), both agents begins the animation with $\epsilon = 0.0$. When the proximity is detected, the behavior vector $\mathbf{v}$ of each agent is oriented orthogonally to the collision direction, forcing the movement to its right direction. At the same time, the ϵ becomes equal to 0.6.

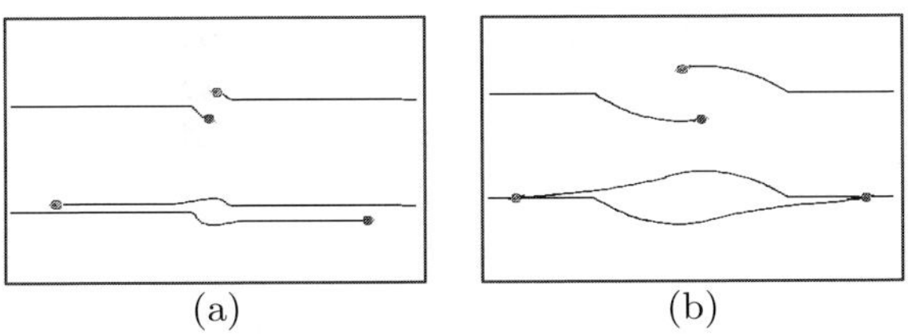

Fig. 5. Two collision avoidance animation sequences produced with different values for the behavior vector and ϵ

Finally, we generated some animation sequences without searching to reproduce any specific behavior. In those sequences we used 12 agents, $\epsilon = 0.8$ for all agents and the components of $\mathbf{v}$ randomly varying between -1 and 1. The agents step size are also randomly defined between 0.3 and 1.0 cells per frame. The initial and final positions for the agents are arbitrarily chosen. The agents can begin its movement from any valid position in the environment and its goal is one of the 6 possible target positions described before. Figure 4(c) shows a frame of one of the animation generated by us.

7 Conclusions and Future Work

This article presents a new approach for generating pedestrian behavior using path planning based on numerical solution of boundary value problems. We demonstrate that the correct adjustment of behavior vector and the parameter ϵ, that determines the vector influence, can produce interesting behaviors, as illustrated in Figures 1 and 3. These behaviors can be interchanged to produce complex motions, as shown in Figure 4, oriented to the agent personality. In this work, we do not implement the agent personality. This step is actually in progress and will be shown in our future submissions.

The guiding potential of Equation 2 is free of local minima what constitutes a great advantage when compared to the traditional potential fields. Furthermore, the method proposed is formally complete and generates smooth and safe paths that can be directly used in mobile robots. The local information gathered by agent sensors allows treating the dynamic obstacles, as other agents navigating in the environment.

We handle the usual costs associated to BVP calculations by using small local maps, instead of a large map that cover all the environment, for each agent. This permits to have several agents acting in the environments while keeping an acceptable running time. Even with only local information about the environment, the intermediate goals computed from the environment maps add global information about the agent target in order to treat conveniently local minima and to allow the agent to reach its target.

Another drawback is that the potential gets flat far from the target position due to numerical precision. In these regions, the gradient is very small to provide useful information to guide the robot. In this case, the robot can easily get lost. We have successfully overcome this problem by using intermediate goals in the flat region.

In the future, we intend: to test different path planners to minimize the computational cost associated to the environment global map; to develop an architecture to be implemented into the GPU to reduce the potential time computation; and to develop an efficient data structure to compact the environment information, such as quadtree, and an efficient algorithm to access this information in real-time.

Acknowledgments

We would like to thank FAPERGS and CNPq for financial support and Renato Oliveira for helping with the figures.

full awareness are on one hand that it limits the number of neighbors that a given avatar can see. When avatars move following a non-uniform movement pattern, some regions of the virtual world can be crowded. In this case this scheme cannot guarantee awareness. On the other hand, in this proposal the awareness of a given avatar i depends on the spatial location of the neighbors of avatar i. If the location of these neighbors is not uniform around avatar i, some other avatars could approach i without being detected by the neighbors of i. This case is particularly frequent when avatars follow non-uniform movement patterns. Something similar could happen if the method proposed in [12] is used, as described in [10].

A different approach uses Frontier Sets to provide awareness in DVE systems simulating a structured virtual world [34]. Nevertheless, in this approach awareness is based on exchanging information between each pair of avatars. Those avatars not having any frontier between them must exchange information about their location and actions 10 times per second, while those avatars having a frontier between them must check this frontier every 5-10 seconds. This massive exchange of information is very costly in terms of scalability. As a result, this proposal does not show that full awareness is guaranteed while maintaining scalability.

Finally, the method proposed in [10] is based on the use of Voronoi diagrams, and it seems to provide full awareness. However, the use of Voronoi diagrams makes this method require each avatar i to communicate with a high number of avatars, even though they are located far away from i and they have a small Area Of Interest (AOI) [30]. This feature suggests that this method is not able to provide full awareness in a scalable way. In fact, this proposal lacks a performance evaluation (either on a real system or with a simulation tool) that shows an actual scalability of the method while providing a 100% of awareness. Therefore, the efficiency and scalability of this proposal cannot be stated.

3 A New Awareness Method: COVER

In order to provide awareness to a given avatar i, the propose method (called COVER) involves all the avatars surrounding i up to the second level of neighborhood, like the method proposed in [10]. The first-level neighbors of an avatar i are those avatars in the DVE system in whose AOI avatar i appears. The second-level neighbors of i are all the neighbor avatars of the first-level neighbors of i. In order to avoid cyclic relationships (redundant messages), if a second-level neighbor is also a first-level neighbor, then it is not considered as a second-level neighbor. Each time an avatar i moves, it sends an updating message to each of its first-level neighbors. These neighbors in turn propagate the updating message of i to the second-level neighbors of i.

Unlike the methods proposed in the previous section [11, 10], COVER classifies avatars in two categories: covered or uncovered. Each avatar checks its classification each time it moves and each time that any of its neighboring avatars moves. We denote an avatar i as *covered* if its first or second-level neighbors are located in such a way that the intersections of their AOIs totally cover the

AOI of i. Otherwise, it is considered as an *uncovered* avatar. COVER method offers auto-awareness to covered avatars, because no avatar can approach them without being detected by their neighbor avatars.

Unlike the method proposed in [11], our approach provides awareness also for uncovered avatars, by means of using *supernode* avatars. These avatars play multiple roles, acting not only as simple avatars but also as pseudo-servers [30]. Supernodes represent an upper layer in the awareness scheme, and they provide the required scalability while ensuring a awareness rate of 100%. Supernodes are responsible of providing awareness to the uncovered avatars in their surroundings, and they are initially designated by the entity in charge of the initialization of new avatars (denoted as *Loader* [26] or Bootstrap server [11]) when they join the DVE system. At boot time, the loader divides the 3-D virtual scene into square sections called *regions*. For each region, the closest avatar to the geometric center of each region is selected by the loader as the supernode for that region. From that instant, supernodes are responsible of providing awareness to those uncovered avatars that are located within their regions. Uncovered avatars must send their updating messages not only to their neighbors, but also to the corresponding supernode of the region where they are located. In this way, supernodes can notice uncovered avatars when another uncovered avatar(s) cross their AOI. The auto-awareness of covered avatars ensures that before a covered avatar k can enter the AOI of an uncovered avatar i, another uncovered avatar j will cross the AOI of i. Therefore, this scheme does not require supernodes to notice uncovered avatars about the movement of covered avatars, significantly reducing the communications required for providing awareness.

As an example, figure 1-left shows a 2-D region containing five avatars, represented as dots, and their respective AOIs, represented as circumferences around the dots. In this region avatars B, C, D and E are uncovered avatars. Since the circumference around avatar A is totally covered by the AOIs of avatars D, C and E, avatar A is classified as a covered avatar. Also, in this case avatar A has been chosen as supernode of the region (we have represented supernodes by depicting their AOI with a thicker circumference), and therefore this avatar will receive updating messages from all the uncovered avatars in this region (the rest of the avatars).

COVER limits the maximum number of uncovered avatars which are simultaneously connected to the same supernode. This parameter is called *MNUA*, (for Maximum Number or Uncovered Avatars). Whenever MNUA is exceeded, the supernode divides that region in four different subregions and computes a new supernode for each subregion, based on the criterion of geometric distance to the center of the subregion. Once the division has been performed and a new supernode is selected for each subregion, the uncovered avatars in each subregion are re-assigned to the new supernodes. It is worth mention that the criterion used for selecting new supernodes does not distinguishes between covered or uncovered avatars. When the system is running, this mechanism defines a dynamic quad-tree structure where each supernode has four sons. Two or more supernodes are *brothers* if they have been generated in the same division operation. Brother

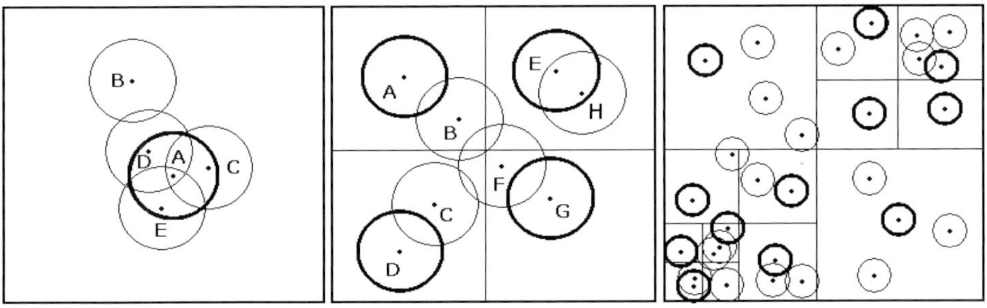

Fig. 1. An example of a virtual scene composed of a single region where a covered avatar is the supernode at the same time (left). As more avatars come into the scene a division into four (center) or more regions (right) can be performed.

nodes are constantly monitoring each other to detect if the total number of uncovered avatars located in the four regions is under MNUA. In this case, a fusion operation is performed. In this operation the four brother subregions are joined to become a unique, larger region, and a new supernode for the new region is computed based on the same criterion of distance to the geometric center of the resulting region.

As an example, figure 1-center shows the evolution of figure 1-left when the proposed scheme is applied and the MNUA parameter has value of six avatars. Since three more avatars have joined the system and the MNUA value has been exceeded, the supernode has divided the region in four subregions. In this case, the resulting supernodes are now avatars A, D, E, and G. These brother supernodes monitor the total number of uncovered avatars in the zones that they control. COVER method does not require that supernodes exchange the position of the avatars in their respective regions, like networked-server architectures do [30, 3]. This key issue allows COVER method to limit the amount of messages generated to provide awareness.

In order to offer full awareness to those avatars located at the borders of different regions (denoted as *critical* avatars), *secondary* supernodes are used. Critical avatars are defined as those uncovered avatars whose AOIs intersect with more than a single region. Critical avatars should send updating messages not only to the supernode managing the region where they are located, but also to the supernodes managing the adjacent regions. These supernodes show uncovered avatars located in different regions, and they are considered as secondary supernodes for critical avatars. Figure 1-center shows that avatar B and F must be considered as critical avatars, because the area of their AOI exceed the limits of the subregion where they are located. The solution for this situation is to force B to send the updating messages not only to supernode A, but also to supernodes D and E, as discussed below. In the same way, avatar F must send updating messages to the four supernodes.

Following with the same situation, figure 1-right shows the result of the proposed awareness scheme when it is a applied to a larger DVE system composed of thirty avatars. It shows the behavior of the proposed technique and how the different levels of the quad-tree structure are dynamically generated. In this figure, there are several avatars whose AOI intersect with different regions or subregions. These are critical avatars.

4 Performance Evaluation

We propose the evaluation of generic DVE systems by simulation. Concretely, (as we did for the case of DVE systems based on networked-server architectures [25]) we have developed a standalone simulation tool, denoted as SimPeerDve (SPD), that models the behavior of a generic DVE system based on a P2P architecture as a set of independent avatars. These avatars are located within a seamless 3D virtual world [1] following three different and well-known initial distributions: uniform, skewed and clustered [15, 25]. Starting from these initial locations, in each simulation avatars perform 100 iterations. Each iteration consists of each avatar independently moving into the scene. Iterations are performed at the typical rate of 1 avatar movement every 2 seconds [15, 24, 23]). We have considered three different movement patterns: Changing Circular Pattern (CCP) [3], HP-All (HPA) [9] and HP-Near (HPN) [19]. CCP considers that all avatars in the virtual world move randomly around the virtual scene following circular trajectories. HPA considers that there exists certain "hot points" where all avatars approach sooner or later. This movement pattern is typical of multiuser games, where users must get resources (as weapons, energy, vehicles, bonus points, etc,) that are located at certain locations in the virtual world. Finally, HPN also considers these hot-points, but only avatars located within a given radius of the hot-points approach these locations. We have chosen the number of 100 iterations (movements) for a simulation because it is the number of movements that the most distant avatar needs to reach the center of the square virtual world. For evaluation purposes, we have considered the nine possible combinations of the three initial distributions of avatars in the virtual world and the three movement patterns.

Using SimPeerDve, we have performed experimental studies to evaluate the performance of the proposed technique. For comparison purposes, we have simulated the awareness method proposed in the previous section and also the awareness method proposed in [11], since this method currently provides the best awareness results for DVE systems based on P2P architectures (as stated above, the method proposed in [10] has not been evaluated). In order to ensure that the evaluation is performed under the worst case, SimPeerDve allows the overlapping of different avatars at the same location of the virtual environment. Although this situation would be erroneous in a real environment, it allows us to increase the number of avatars located in a given region of the virtual world beyond the limits of a real environment. If awareness is provided under such circumstances, then awareness is guaranteed under real conditions.

Figure 2-left shows the evaluation results for the awareness method proposed in this paper (labeled as COVER) as well as for the awareness method described in [11] (labeled as K(x-x)), under all the possible combinations of initial distributions and movement patterns of avatars. This figure shows a representative example of the experiments performed with a DVE system composed of 1000 avatars. On the X-axis this figure shows the iteration number of the simulation performed, and on the Y-axis it shows the percentage of awareness. This figure shows that for a large scale DVE configuration the method described in [11] only is able to provide a high percentage of awareness (around a 85%) under the uniform movement pattern. For the rest of combinations of initial distributions and movement patterns of avatars, the method proposed in [11] provides a awareness rate below 50%. The worst results of this method are provided for the combination of a clustered initial distribution of avatars and HPA movement pattern, being lower than 10% at the end of the simulation. The reason for this behavior is that for non uniform movement patterns, avatars are unevenly distributed in the virtual world most of the simulation time. Under this situation, the probability that a given avatar i has one or more unknown neighbors crossing its AOI increases, since its known neighbors of i also tend to be unevenly distributed around the AOI of i. The use of supernodes avoids inconsistencies under such situations when using COVER method.

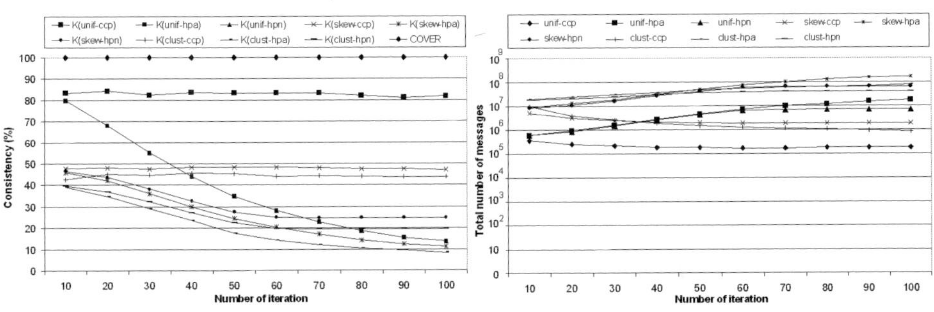

Fig. 2. Left: Percentage of awareness provided for all combinations of initial distributions of avatars and movement patterns. Right: Total number of messages exchanged by avatars during the simulations when using COVER method.

In order to show that COVER method provides total awareness without increasing the number of messages exchanged by avatars, figure 2-right shows the number of messages sent during the simulations whose awareness rates are summarized in figure 2-left. The plots in this figure show the number of messages exchanged when using COVER method for the different combinations of initial distributions and movement patterns of avatars. Since the method proposed in [11] limits the number of neighbors that a given avatar can communicate with, the number of messages sent when using this method is not comparable with the number of messages sent when using COVER method. All the simulations whose results are shown in this figure have been performed in a DVE system composed of 1000 avatars. Each point in the plots represents the average value of messages sent by all the avatars in the DVE system during the last 10 iterations.

In order to show the scalability of COVER method, we have also studied the number of messages sent and received by supernodes under different movement patterns and for simulations performed with different numbers of avatars. For the sake of shortness, we present here the results for those combinations of initial distributions and movement patterns of avatars that show the largest (skewed-HPA) and the smallest (unif-CCP) number of messages exchanged among avatars in figure 2-right. Concretely, figure 3-left shows the average number of messages handled (sent or received) by each supernode in the system during the simulations performed under the combination of a uniform initial distribution of avatars and CCP movement pattern. Each point in these plots is computed as follows: after each iteration in a simulation, the number of supernodes in the system as well as the number of messages sent and received by supernodes are counted, and the *average number of messages per supernode* (ANMS) is computed. Since the number of supernodes dynamically varies, when the simulation finishes, the average value of the 100 ANMS values (each simulation is composed of 100 iterations) is computed. This is the value represented in each point in the plots.

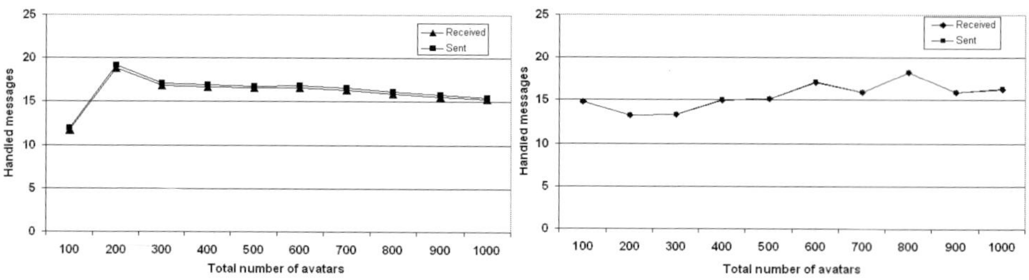

Fig. 3. Number of messages handled by supernodes for the uniform-CCP (left) and skewed-HPA (right) combinations

Figure 3-right shows the average number of messages handled by each supernode in the system during the simulations performed under the skewed-HPA combination, the one requiring the largest number of messages exchanged among avatars. The shape of the two plots in this figure is similar to those in figure 3-left, showing a flat slope. The average number of messages handled by each supernode remains within a range of values between 13 and 19, showing that the proposed method scales well with the number of avatars in the system. Moreover, when comparing this figure with figure 3-left, we can see that this range of values is approximately the same for both figures. That is, the behavior of the proposed method does not depend on the movement pattern nor on the initial distribution of avatars in the virtual world. This feature is a key issue to provide an actually scalable awareness method, but it has not been shown in any of the currently proposed methods.

5 Conclusions and Future Work

In this paper, we have proposed a new awareness method for large-scale DVE systems based on P2P architectures, denoted as COVER. Unlike the currently proposed methods, COVER uses two kind of neighbors to provide awareness, normal neighbors and supernodes. While the former ones provide awareness to avatars in the same way other methods do, the latter ones allow to provide awareness to those avatars that are isolated or not completely surrounded by other avatars. This key feature allow to provide full awareness (awareness to 100% of avatars), regardless of the distribution of avatars in the virtual world.

Performance evaluation results show that the proposed method is able to provide full awareness to large scale DVE systems composed of up to 1000 avatars, regardless of both the movement pattern and the initial distribution of avatars in the virtual world. This results have not been shown by any of the currently proposed methods. Due to the quad-tree segmentation algorithm used to select new supernodes, neither the movement pattern of avatars nor the initial distribution of avatars have a significant effect on the number of messages sent by avatars as simulations proceed. Evaluation results also show that this number remains with a flat slope, even for those movement patterns that in the last iterations tend to group avatars in certain points of the virtual world. This result indicates that the proposed method properly balances the workload generated to provide awareness to all avatars. Also, performance evaluation results show that the number of messages handled by supernodes does not increase as new avatars are added to the DVE system. This scalability is achieved by selecting new supernodes when MNUA parameter is exceeded and merging several supernodes into a single supernode when adjacent supernodes manage less than MNUA avatars.

As a result, we can conclude that COVER method provides full awareness to large-scale DVE systems based on P2P architectures in a scalable and efficient way.

References

1. T. Alexander. *Massively Multiplayer Game Development II.* Charles River Media, 2005.
2. Anarchy Online: : http://www.anarchy-online.com.
3. N. Beatrice, S. Antonio, L. Rynson, and L. Frederick. A multiserver architecture for distributed virtual walkthrough. In *ACM VRST'02*, pages 163–170, 2002.
4. C. Bouras, D. Fotakis, and A. Philopoulos. A distributed virtual learning centre in cyberspace. In *Proc. of Int. Conf. on Virtual Systems and Multimedia (VSMM'98)*, November 1998.
5. Everquest: http://everquest.station.sony.com/.
6. E. Frecon and M. Stenius. Dive: A scalable network architecture for distributed virtual environments. *Distributed Systems Engineering Journal*, 5(3):91–100, September 1998.
7. R. M. Fujimoto and R.M. Weatherly. Time management in the dod high level architecture. In *Proceedings tenth Workshop on Parallel and Distributed Simulation*, pages 60–67, 1996.
8. L. Gautier and C. Diot. Design and evaluation of mimaze, a multi-player game on the internet. In *Proceedings of IEEE Multimedia Systems Conference*, 1998.

9. C. Greenhalgh, Adrian Bullock, Emmanuel Frïon, David Llyod, and Anthony Steed. Making networked virtual environments work. *Presence: Teleoperators and Virtual Environments*, 10(2):142–159, 2001.
10. S. Y. Hu and G. M. Liao. Scalable peer-to-peer networked virtual environment. In *ACM SIGCOMM 2004 workshops on NetGames '04*, pages 129–133, 2004.
11. Y. Kawahara, T. Aoyama, and H. Morikawa. A peer-to-peer message exchange scheme for large scale networked virtual environments. *Telecommunication Systems*, 25(3):353–370, 2004.
12. J. Keller and G. Simon. Solipsis: A massively multi-participant virtual world. In *Proceedings of Parallel and Distributed Processing Techniques and Applications (PDPTA)*, pages 262–268, Las Vegas, USA, 2003.
13. B. Knutsson, H. Lu, W. Xu, and B. Hopkins. Peer-to-peer support for massively multiplayer games. In *Proceedings of IEEE InfoCom'04*, 2004.
14. Lineage: http://www.lineage.com.
15. John C.S. Lui and M.F. Chan. An efficient partitioning algorithm for distributed virtual environment systems. *IEEE TPDS*, 13, 2002.
16. John C.S. Lui, M.F. Chan, and K.Y. Oldfield. Dynamic partitioning for a distributed virtual environment. Technical report, Department of Computer Science. Chinese University of Hong Kong, 1998.
17. Michael R. Macedonia. A taxonomy for networked virtual environments. *IEEE Multimedia*, 4(1):48–56, 1997.
18. Michael R. Macedonia, M. Zyda, David R. Pratt, Donald P. Brutzman, and Paul T. Barham. Exploiting reality with multicast groups: A network architecture for large-scale virtual environments. In *Proceedings of the 1995 IEEE Virtual Reality Annual Symposium*, pages 2–10, 1995.
19. M. Matijasevic, K. P. Valavanis, D. Gracanin, and I. Lovrek. Application of a multi-user distributed virtual environment framework to mobile robot teleoperation over the internet. *Machine Intelligence & Robotic Control*, 1(1):11–26, 1999.
20. D.C. Miller and J.A. Thorpe. Simnet: The advent of simulator networking. *IEEE TPDS*, 13, 2002.
21. D. Milojicic, V. Kalogeraki, R. Lukose, K. Nagaraja, J. Pruyne, B. Richard, S. Rollins, and Z. Xu. Peer-to-peer computing. Technical report, Technical Report HPL-2002-57, HP Laboratories, Palo Alto, 2002.
22. S. Mooney and B. Games. *Battlezone: Official Strategy Guide.* BradyGame Publisher, 1998.
23. P. Morillo, J. M. Orduña, M. Fernández, and J. Duato. An adaptive load balancing technique for distributed virtual environment systems. In *Proc. of Intl. Conf. on Parallel and Distributed Computing and Systems (PDCS'03)*, pages 256–261. IASTED, ACTA Press, 2003.
24. P. Morillo, J. M. Orduña, M. Fernández, and J. Duato. A fine-grain method for solving the partitioning problem in distributed virtual environment systems. In *Proc. of Intl. Conf. on Parallel and Distributed Computing and Systems (PDCS'04)*, pages 292–297. IASTED, ACTA Press, 2004. Best paper award in the area of load balancing.
25. P. Morillo, J. M. Orduña, M. Fernández, and J. Duato. Improving the performance of distributed virtual environment systems. *IEEE Transactions on Parallel and Distributed Systems*, 16(7):637–649, 2005.
26. M. Oliveira, J. Crowcroft, and M. Slater. Components for distributed virtual environments. *PRESENCE, The MIT Press*, 10(1):56–61, 2001.
27. Quake: http://www.idsoftware.com/games/quake.

28. D. Roberts and R. Wolff. Controlling consistency within collaborative virtual environments. In *Proceedings of IEEE Symposium on Distributed Simulation and Real-Time Applications (DSRT'04)*, pages 46–52, 2004.
29. J.M. Salles, Ricardo Galli, and A. C. Almeida et al. mworld: A multiuser 3d virtual environment. *IEEE Computer Graphics*, 17(2), 1997.
30. S. Singhal and M. Zyda. *Networked Virtual Environments.* ACM Press, 1999.
31. J. Smed, T. Kaukoranta, and H. Hakonen. A review on networking and multiplayer computer games. Technical report, Turku Centre for Computer Science. Tech Report 454., 2002.
32. Randall B. Smith, R. Hixon, and B. Horan. *Collaborative Virtual Environments*, chapter Supporting Flexible Roles in a Shared Space. Springer-Verlag, 2001.
33. Startcraft: http://www.blizzard.com/starcraft.
34. A. Steed and C. Angus. Supporting scalable peer to peer virtual environments using frontier sets. In *IEEE Virtual Reality-2005.* IEEE Computer Society, 2005.
35. P.T. Tam. Communication cost optimization and analysis in distributed virtual environment. Technical report, Department of Computer Science. Chinese University of Hong Kong, 1998.
36. S. Zhou, W. Cai, B. Lee, and S. J. Turner. Time-space consistency in large-scale distributed virtual environments. *ACM Transactions on Modeling and Computer Simulation*, 14(1):31–47, 2004.

Motion Editing with the State Feedback Dynamic Model

Dengming Zhu[1,2], Zhaoqi Wang[1], and Shihong Xia[1]

[1] Institute of Computing Technology, Chinese Academy of Sciences
[2] Graduate School of the Chinese Academy of Sciences P.O. Box 2704, Beijing 100080, China
{mdzhu, zqwang, xsh}@ict.ac.cn

Abstract. In this paper, a novel motion editing tool, called the state feedback dynamic model, is proposed and demonstrated for the animators to edit the pre-existing motion capture data. The state feedback dynamic model is based on the linear time-invariant system (LTI). Compared with previous works, by this model, the animators need only modify a few keyframes manually, and the other frames can be adjusted automatically while preserving as much of the original quality as possible. It is a global modification on motion sequence. More important, the LTI model derives an explicit mapping between the high-dimensional motion capture data and low-dimensional hidden state variables. It transforms a number of possibly correlated joint angle variables into a smaller number of uncorrelated state variables. Then, the motion sequence is edited in state space, and which considers that the motion among joints is correlated. It is different from traditional methods which consider each joint as independent of each other. Finally, an effective algorithm is also developed to calculate the model parameters. Experimental results show that the generated animations through this method are natural and smooth.

1 Introduction

High-quality articulated figure animations are widely used in the movie and video games. Due to the complexity of the human configurations, generating new motions from the existing data is still one of the most challenging tasks in the computer animation. In the past years, the motion may be created by the skilled animators with the aid of the software tools. The motion capture data used for computer animation is relatively new and now is beginning to become widespread. Motion capture is the recording of the human body movement. The recorded performance can be applied to a computer-generated character to make the character move in the same way as the performer moved. Its main advantage is that it allows the production of both complex and realistic motions. Its disadvantage is the visibility, and the recorded data lack of flexibility.

In order to achieve the desirable animation, usually, the animators have to modify some keyframes manually in original motion sequence. But it is still a difficult problem to naturally generate intermediate frames between keyframes.

H.-P. Seidel, T. Nishita, and Q. Peng (Eds.): CGI 2006, LNCS 4035, pp. 348–359, 2006.

Traditional methods, such as keyframe interpolation and motion displacement mapping [1, 2], can generate the intermediate frames automatically. However, these methods consider each joint as independent of each other. It is not reasonable for real human motion. For example, the ankle angle and the hip ankle are usually correlated when human walking.

Recently, Y.Li et al. [3] employ the linear dynamic system to model a motion sequence, which is called motion texton. They draw samples from the white noise to change the details of a specific motion texton. Their algorithm also allows animators to edit motion texton while preserving same dynamic property. But one may not obtain the desirable poses through it.

In this paper, we propose a novel technology, called state feedback dynamic model, to edit the motion sequence. By our model, the animators need only modify a few keyframes manually, and the other frames can be adjusted automatically while preserving as much of the original quality as possible. The LTI model derives an explicit mapping between the high-dimensional motion capture data and low-dimensional state variables. Then, the motion sequence is edited in state space, which considers that the motion among joints is correlated. It is also a global modification on motion sequence. This work is different from the former one by Y.Li et al. [3]. Our model can naturally change the dynamic property of the original system to satisfy the practical demands through controlling the input signal of system. Our work extends previous investigations in the area about using LTI to synthesize complex human animation.

The remainder of this paper is organized as follows. In the next section, we review the related works. In section 3, we introduce the linear time-invariant system and use it to construct the motion model. In section 4, we introduce the state feedback dynamic system to edit motion sequence, and provide an effective solution to solve the optimization problem. In section 5, we show the experimental results. Finally, we discuss the results in section 6.

2 Related Work

Motion editing is to alter the raw motion capture data to satisfy the geometry or spatial constraints. Recently, the focus is on editing and reusing existing motion data. Many techniques have been developed to tackle it. An excellent review and comparison of such methods is provided by Gleicher [4]. But these methods may not be distinguished each other clearly.

2.1 Linear Time-Invariant System

Linear time-invariant system is the most important dynamic systems in reality. It is true because it represents the idealization of the processes encountered in real life. Y.Li et al. [3] use the linear time-invariant system to model the motion texton. This technique is also used to capture the dynamic textures [13]. Eugene Hsu et al. [14] employ the method to represent stylistic differences. The relationship between the input style and output style are described by the linear time-invariant system.

2.2 Motion Displacement Mapping

Displacement mapping [1, 2] provides a method to change the shape of a signal locally through a displacement mapping, while maintaining the continuity and preserving the global shape of the signal. It is widely used by the animators to alter the motion sequence. Its basic advantage is that the animators need only modify a few keyframes. A spline curve is fitted through these displacements for each degree of freedom involved. A new motion can be created by adding a special motion into the original motion. Lee and Shin [12] employed the displacement mapping in the interactive motion editing. Their approach combined a hierarchical curve fitting technique with a new inverse kinematics solver. Through this, one could obtain the new motion with the desired features from the pre-existing motion capture data. But the displacement mapping assumes that each joint is independent, which is not reasonable for real human motion.

2.3 Motion Signal Processing

Motion signal processing [1, 2, 5, 6] is to investigate the motion data in the frequency domain. Bruderlin and Williams [1] treated data as a sampled signal. They presented a number of different signal processing techniques to synthesize the human animation. Unuma et al. [5] proposed using the Fourier analysis to model the human figure animation with emotion. Fourier expansions of the experimental motion data are a basis, and based on this, the method can be used to interpolate or extrapolate the human locomotion. Pullen and Bregler [6] also use frequency analysis to divide the data into different bands. Furthermore, the high pass-band of motion sequences is used to enhance the details of animation in the missing information in the partial key-frame data. Signal processing method provides a global animation control. It is an important method to edit motion capture data.

2.4 Spacetime Constraints

There are continuing interests in the studies of human motion by the spacetime constraints, which is firstly introduced by Witkin and Kass [7]. The solution for creating animation is a physically valid motion satisfying the "what" constraints and optimizing the "how" criteria. It has been proved to be a valuable approach for creating lifelike animation. Cohen [8] showed that the spacetime constraints are a useful technique for creating physically based and goal directed motion of linked figures. Liu et al. [9] made use of it to investigate the motion of a linked figure to achieve the given tasks. Gleicher and co-workers employed this method to solve the problem of the constraint-based motion editing [10, 11]. But the spacetime constraints method requires great mathematical complexity and computational cost.

Our intention is similar to the work by Y.Li et al. [3]. But we extend their work on using LTI model for motion editing. Animations can be easily created from pre-existing motion capture data by modifying a few important keyframes. Moreover, we provide a novel technology to editing motion sequence while considering the correlation between joint angles. It is different from the above approaches.

3 Motion Dynamic Model

3.1 Motion Data Representation

Motion data are sampled at a sequence of discrete time instances with a uniform interval. These data consist of a sequence of frames denoted by $m(t) = (p(t), q_1(t), q_2(t), ..., q_N(t))$, where $p(t) \in R^3$ and $q_1 \in S^3$ respectively describe the position and orientation of the root segment. $q_n \in S^3$ denotes the orientation of joint n with respect to its parent at frame t, and N is the number of joint. The joint rotation angles are presented by quaternions and parameterized with exponential map [16, 17]. Then we define as follows:

$$y_t = (p(t), \log(q_1(t)), \log(q_2(t)), ..., \log(q_N(t)))) \tag{1}$$

Where are the angles of all the joints including the root orientation and root position.

3.2 Linear Time-Invariable System(LTI)

LTI model has a wide application area in our environment. It can model a complex physical system based on observable signal. In this paper, we used it for motion editing. Linear dynamic system is also called the state-space models. The state space representation of a system with m inputs, p outputs, and k hidden state variables is written as,

$$\begin{cases} x_{t+1} = Ax_t + B\mu_t + \omega_t \\ y_t = Cx_t + D\mu_t + v_t \end{cases} \tag{2}$$

Where

$$\omega_t \sim N(0, Q), v_t \sim N(0, R), dim(A) = k \times k$$
$$dim(B) = k \times m, dim(C) = p \times k, dim(D) = p \times m$$

In general, $k \ll p$. Equation (2) drives an explicit mapping between the high-dimensional motion data and low-dimensional state variables. It transforms a number of possibly correlated joint angle variables into a smaller number of uncorrelated state variables. In Equation (2), the first equation is called the state equation and the second equation is called the observation equation. In this model, x_t is the hidden state variable, μ_t is the input vector, and y_t is the output observation represented by Equation (1). A is the state transition matrix, B is the input matrix, C is the output matrix, and D is the feedforward matrix. The k-vector and p-vector are the random variables representing the state evolution and observation noises, respectively, which are temporally uncorrelated and independent Gaussian noise, with a mean of zero and covariance matrices denoted by Q and R .

3.3 Learning Model Parameters

Equation (2) describes the relationship between the input μ_t and output y_t . For an pre-existing motion sequence, it can be regarded as an independent dynamic system only excited by the initial state x_0 with a zero-input, i.e. $\mu_t = 0$. Then Equation (2) can be simplified as,

$$\begin{cases} x_{t+1} = Ax_t + \omega_t \\ y_t = Cx_t + \upsilon_t \end{cases} \tag{3}$$

The unknown parameters in Equation (3) are A, C, R, Q, and x_0 , where x_0 denotes the initial state. Only y_t is the known parameter. The model parameters $\{A, C, x_0\}$ can be obtained by EM algorithm [15].

4 Algorithm for Motion Editing Based on LTI

Our purpose is to take a motion that has the basic form as we want. It should be adjustable to satisfy some specific or unsatisfied need. Some keyframes may also be modified by animators. Traditional methods, such as keyframe interpolation or motion displacement mapping, provide a solution to solve the problem. But in these methods each joint is considered to be independent. Therefore, the animation created by these approaches may lose some correlation among the joints. In our editing of the motion sequence, we consider the joints correlation to preserve the content of the original motion. Our approach is an improvement, rather than a replacement of above mentioned techniques.

When a motion sequence is edited, the original dynamic system can be affected by the external stimulus. The problem of motion editing can be regarded as designing suitable input signal to achieve desired output . In other words, the original motion sequence can be edited through controlling the input of the dynamic system. From a viewpoint of control theory, it is to design the controller to accomplish a desired task. Usually, the state feedback dynamic system is used to finish it [19]. Finally, an effective algorithm for designing state feedback dynamic system is illustrated as follows.

4.1 State Feedback Dynamic Model

In the following, we use the state feedback dynamic model [19] for motion editing. Then, the input μ_t in Equation (2) is given by

$$\mu_t = Kx_t \tag{4}$$

K is the feedback matrix which is $m \times k$. Then, Equation (2) can be rewritten as,

$$\begin{cases} x_{t+1} = Ax_t + BKx_t + \omega_t \\ y_t = Cx_t + DKx_t + \upsilon_t \end{cases} \tag{5}$$

For a pre-existing motion capture data, the model parameters in Equation (5) can be easily obtained from Equation (3). Unfortunately, the parameters can not be acquired at the same time. In the practical application, it is very difficult to solve the Equation (5). In order to simplify computation, we take an approximation of Equation (5),

$$\begin{cases} x_{t+1} = Ax_t + p_t + \omega_t \\ y_t = Cx_t + Gx_t + \upsilon_t \end{cases} \tag{6}$$

Where

$$p_t = BKx_t, G = DK$$
$$dim(p_t) = k \times 1, dim(G) = p \times k$$

The main difference between Equation (5) and Equation (6) is that the state equation is generalized. This generalization is not strict for Equation (5).

But it simplifies the computation, and it transforms the original complex optimization problem into two quadratic optimization problems while preserving good animation results. The detail of algorithm is illustrated in section 4.2.

4.2 Algorithm for Motion Editing

We consider the problem of motion editing as the design of a controller. In the following, we will introduce an effective algorithm to solve the unknown model parameters $\{p_t, G, x_t\}$ in Equation (6).

Suppose that some keyframes in the original motion sequence are modified by the animator. Step 1 is to choose the bound in the original motion sequence to be adjusted. In step 2, we divide the area into several segments at keyframes. Then every segment is denoted by a state feedback dynamic system, which has the same parameters $\{A, C\}$ but different parameters $\{p_t, G, x_t\}$. In order to ensure the frame coherence and avoid glitches in the animation, every keyframe modified by animator is used as the last frame of front segment and the first frame of next segment as constraints.

For each segment, we use $(\overline{y}_m, \overline{y}_n)$ to denote the first frame and the last frame and substitute it to the original (y_m, y_n) . There are three kinds of possible cases between them:

Case 1 when $(y_m = \overline{y}_m, y_n \neq \overline{y}_n)$, only the last frame is modified.

Case 2 when $(y_m \neq \overline{y}_m, y_n \neq \overline{y}_n)$, the first frame and the last frame are modified simultaneously.

Case 3 when $(y_m \neq \overline{y}_m, y_n = \overline{y}_n)$, only the first frame is modified.

In order to obtain the model parameters $\{p_t, G, x_t\}$, we transform the difficult problem into two quadratic optimization problems. One is the optimal state estimation model to compute the parameters $\{p_t, x_t\}$, and the other optimal objective is measuring the kinematic smoothness for solving the parameter G. Then, the whole process of solving is decomposed into two sub-processes.

In the following, we will introduce the detail of the algorithm to calculate the parameters of the state feedback dynamic model, including x_m, p_m , p_{m+1} ,..., p_{n-1} and G in Equation (6).

Optimal State Estimation Model. For one segment, computing the unknown parameters p_m , p_{m+1} ,..., p_{n-1} from the given parameters $\{A, x_m, x_n\}$, $m < n$ is a numerical problem of constrained optimization. An optimal state estimation objective function is defined as,

$$h(p_t) = \sum_{t=m}^{n-1} \|p_t\|^2 \qquad (7)$$

$$Subject \quad to \quad c(p_t) = 0$$

Where

$$c(p_t) = \|x_n - (A^{n-m}x_m + A^{n-m-1}(p_m + \omega_m) + \cdots + A(p_{n-2} + \omega_{n-2}) + (p_{n-1} + \omega_{n-1}))\|^2 \qquad (8)$$

The Levenberg-Marquart optimization and quadratic penalty methods [18] can be combined to solve the Equation (7). Then the original constraint optimization problem can be converted into unconstraint one by introducing penalty into objective function. We define

$$H_M(P_t) = h(p_t) + M \cdot c(p_t) \qquad (9)$$

Where M is a positive penalty parameter. Now we describe the algorithm to minimize the Equation (9).

Function: StateEstimate(x_m, x_n, A)
Initialize: $p^0_m, p^0_{m+1}, \ \ldots, \ p^0_{n-1}, \omega_m, \omega_{m+1}, \ \ldots, \ \omega_{n-1};$
$\varepsilon > 0, \ M_0 > 0, \ e > 1;$
$k \leftarrow 0;$
Repeat:
$Min \ H_{M_k}(p^k_t);$
(Using Levenberg-Marquart Method and quadratic penalty methods):
Then find optimal parameters:
$p^{k+1}_m, \ p^{k+1}_{m+1} \ldots, \ p^{k+1}_{n-1};$
if$(M_k \cdot c(p^{k+1}_t) < \varepsilon)$
{
Refer Equation (6), calculate:
$x_{m+1}, x_{m+2}, \ \ldots, \ x_{n-1};$
Return : $x_{m+1}, \ x_{m+2}, \ldots, \ x_{n-1};$
Stop;
}
else

```
    {
      M_{k+1} ← e · M_k;
      k ← k + 1;
    }
    end(if)
End (repeat)
```

Kinematic Smoothness. From the above statement, the parameters $p_m, p_{m+1}, \ldots, p_{n-1}$ in Equation (6) can been solved if we gave the parameters $\{A, x_m, x_n\}$. But the parameter G is still unknown. A measurement of the kinematic smoothness is essential in the animation synthesis algorithm. It can ensure the frame coherence and avoid glitches in the animation. We measure smoothness with the magnitude of the second-order derivative of:

$$f(G) = \sum_{t=m}^{n} \|\ddot{y}_t(G)\|^2 \tag{10}$$

$$Subject \quad to \quad g_1(G) = 0, \quad g_2(G) = 0$$

Based on Equation (6), where

$$g_1(G) = \|\overline{y}_m - (C+G)x_m - \nu_m\|^2 \tag{11}$$

$$g_2(G) = \|\overline{y}_n - (C+G)x_n - \nu_n\|^2 \tag{12}$$

To approximate the time derivatives of y_t , we use the finite difference formulas,

$$\ddot{y}_t = \frac{y_{t+1} + y_{t-1} - 2y_t}{h^2} \tag{13}$$

with h the time interval between the samples. Combining Equation (6) and Equation (13), we obtain:

$$\ddot{y}_t = \frac{(C+G)(x_{t+1} + v_{t+1} + x_{t-1} + v_{t-1} - 2(x_t + v_t))}{h^2} \tag{14}$$

Then the objective function $f(G)$ can also be written as,

$$f(G) = \frac{\sum_{t=m}^{n} \|(C+G)(x_{t+1} + v_{t+1} + x_{t-1} + v_{t-1} - 2(x_t + v_t))\|^2}{h^4} \tag{15}$$

We introduce the penalty function into Equation (15). The objective function $f(G)$ can also be written as,

$$F(G) = f(G) + M \cdot \sum_{i=1}^{2} g_i(G) \tag{16}$$

The Equation (16) is a quadratic function which is similar to the Equation (9). The Levenberg-Marquart optimization and quadratic penalty methods can also be used to minimize the Equation (16). Then, the algorithm for motion editing is illustrated as follows.

LTIModelParameter($\overline{y}_m, \overline{y}_n, A, C$)
Initialize: $G^0,\ \varepsilon > 0,\ \nu_m,\ \nu_{m+1},\ \ldots,\ \nu_n;$
$k \leftarrow 0;$
Repeat:
Refer Equation (6), Calculate;
$x_m^{k+1} = (C + G^k)^+(\overline{y}_m - \nu_m);$
$x_n^{k+1} = (C + G^k)^+(\overline{y}_n - \nu_n);$
($(C + G^k)^+$ is pseudo-inverse matrix)
StateEstimate(x_m^{k+1}, x_n^{k+1}, A);
(Return $x_{m+1}^{k+1}, x_{m+2}^{k+1}, \ldots, x_{n-1}^{k+1}$)
$G^{k+1} = argminF(G);$
(Using Levenberg-Marquart Method and quadratic penalty methods):
$f_2 = F(G^{k+1});$
if($k = 0$)
{
$f_1 = f_2;$
$k \leftarrow k + 1;$
}
else if ($f_1 - f_2 > \varepsilon$)
{
$f_1 = f_2;$
$k \leftarrow k + 1;$
}
else
{
return: $x_m, x_{m+1}, \ldots, x_{n-1}, x_n, G;$
Stop;
}
end(if)
End (repeat)

From above algorithm, we can easily obtain the rotation angle of each joint through exponential map. But the generated motion sequence may have foot skating. We use Kovar's algorithm [20] as our footskate cleanup algorithm.

5 Results

Our approach in this paper is general and can be used in various motion analysis and motion editing. In our 3D examples, the motion data is captured at a high frequency of 60 Hz. The human model is composed of 17 joints, a total of 54 DOFs, including 3 DOFs for the root global position located at the pelvis. The root orientation and joint angles are all represented by quaternion. We perform experiments on an Intel Pentium PC (P4 2.6GHz processor and 512 MB memory).

Walking to Running. In this experiment, the original walking motion in Fig.1 has 63 frames. The frame 42 is modified to bow-walking posture and, simultaneously, the last frame is modified to running. A total of 41 frames, which are from 23th frame to 63th frame, are chosen to be adjusted. We divide it into two segments which are presented by two state feedback dynamic systems. It totally takes approximately 5.2 minutes to get the model parameters, and the hidden state variable is presented by a 13-dimension vector. The editing result is illustrated on the bottom of Fig.1.

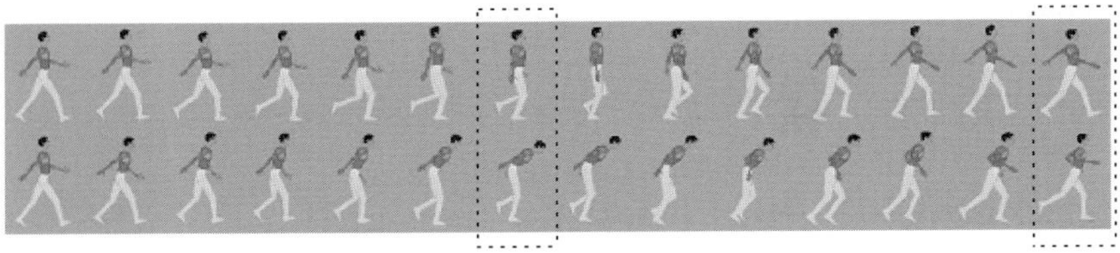

Fig. 1. The top and bottom rows are respectively the original and generated motion. Two original keyframes in the rectangles are modified manually to desired poses (from top to bottom). The remaining frames of the original motion sequence are then adjusted to bottom ones through our method automatically. The generated motion is natural and smooth.

Kicking Ball. In Fig.2, the motion of the kick soccer has 45 frames. Only the amplitude of the last frame is modified to be larger. We choose 20 frames (26th frame to 45th frame) to be adjusted and one state feedback dynamic system is used. In the example, the dimension of parameter is 11, and the computation cost is 2.3 minutes. The editing result is showed in Fig.2.

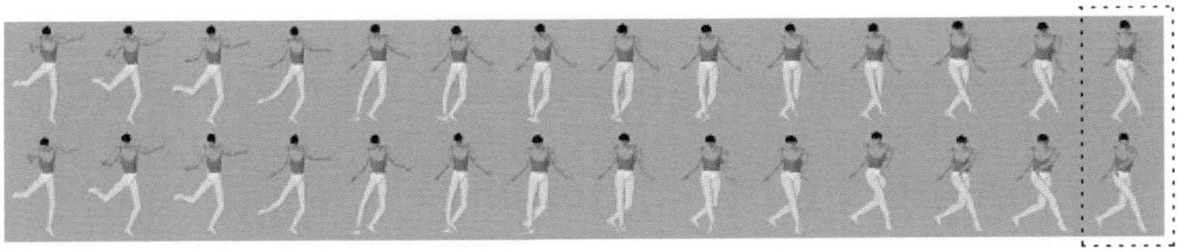

Fig. 2. The top row is the original motion of kicking ball, and the last frame in rectangle is modified manually to desired poses (bottom row). Then large amplitude kicking ball motion (bottom row) can be created naturally.

Picking Up. This experiment shows that our motion editing method adjusts the picking up motion in animation (Fig.3). The top row is the original motion. It has 38 frames. The first frame, 21th frame, and the last frame are modified to the desired poses manually. Then, the original motion sequence is divided into two segments, and two state feedback dynamic systems are used to model them. The generated animations in bottom row illustrate that the whole motion

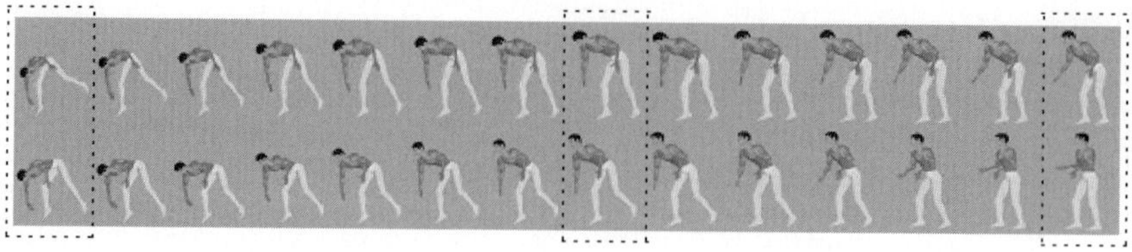

Fig. 3. The top row is the original motion of picking up something, and three keyframes in rectangles are modified manually to the desired poses (bottom row). Then the whole motion sequence (bottom row) can be adjusted automatically.

sequence is adjusted naturally. In this example, it costs 4.5 minutes to obtain the model parameters, and the dimension of parameter is 8.

6 Discussion

In this paper, we have proposed a novel technique, i.e. the state feedback dynamic model, to create animations from the input motion sequence. Animators need only modify a few keyframes, and the remaining motion sequence can be adjusted automatically. The shortcoming of our approach is that the position constraints can not be directly incorporated into our model. It would be a key problem to be solved in the future.

Compared with previous works, our method has following advantages: **Firstly**, the motion sequence is edited in low-dimensional state space, and it considers the correlation of the motion among joints. **Secondly**, it can naturally and smoothly change the dynamic property of original motion, through controlling the input signal, to achieve desire animation. This is a global modification on motion sequence. **Thirdly**, the animators need only modify a few important keyframes. Intermediate frames can be generated automatically while preserving original motion quality. This will largely reduce the work of animator.

Our work take a step forward to reuse existing motion capture data. Experimental results also demonstrate that it can create natural and smooth animations according to the desire of the user.

Acknowledgements

We would like to thank our colleagues in virtual human group for the fruitful discussion on animation synthesis. This research is supported by National 973 project (2002CB312104); Key project of international technology cooperation (2005DFA11060); Key Project of NSF (60533070); NSF of China (60573162, 60403042, 60473002); 863 Plan of China (2005AA114010); National Special Item for Olympics (Z0004024040231, Z0004027040331); Beijing Natural Science Foundation (4051004,4062032); and Knowledge Innovation Project (20056380) of Institute of Computing Technology, Chinese Academy of Sciences.

References

1. A. Bruderlin and L. Williams.: Motion signal processing. In Proceedings of ACM SIGGRAPH 95. 1995, 97-104
2. Witkin, A, Popovic, Z.: Motion Warping. Computer Graphics(SIGGRAPH 95). Vol. 29, No. 4, August 1995, 105-108
3. Yan Li, Tianshu Wang, Heung-Yeung Shum.: Motion Texture: A Two-Level Statistical Model for Character Motion Synthesis. ACM Transactions on Graphics. **21(3)**(2002):465-472
4. Gleicher M.: Comparing constraint-based motion editing methods. Graph Models **63**(2001):107-134
5. M. Unuma, K. Anjyo, and R. Takeuchi.: Fourier principles for emotion-based human figure animation. In Proceedings of ACM SIGGRAPH 95, 91-96
6. K. Pullen,C. Bregler.: Motion Capture Assisted Animation: Texturing and Synthesis. Proc SIGGRAPH 2002, 501-508
7. Andrew Witkin and Michael Kass.: Spacetime constraints. Computer Graphics (SIGGRAPH 88). **22**(1988):159-168
8. Michael F. Cohen.: Interactive spacetime control for animation. SIGGRAPH 1992, 293-302
9. Zicheng Liu, Steven J. Gortler, and Michael F. Cohen.: Hierarchical Spacetime Control. SIGGRAPH 1993, 35-42
10. Gleicher, M.: Retargetting motion to new characters. SIGGRAPH 1998, vol. 32, 33-42
11. Michael Gleicher.: Motion Editing with Spacetime Constraints. Proceedings of the 1997 Symposium on Interactive 3D Graphics. 1997, 139-148
12. Lee, J., Shin, S. Y.: A hierarchical approach to interactive motion editing for human-like figures. SIGGRAPH 1999, 39-48.
13. S. Soatto, G. Doretto, and Y. N. Wu.: Dynamic textures. In IEEE International Conference on Computer Vision. 2001, 439-446
14. Eugene Hsu, Kari Pulli, Jovan Popovi.: Style translation for human motion. ACM Transactions on Graphics (TOG). Volume 24, Issue 3, 2005, 1082 - 1089
15. Ghahramani, Z. and Hinton, G.E.: Parameter estimation for linear dynamical systems. University of Toronto Technical Report CRG-TR-96-2, 6 pages, 1996
16. Jehee Lee, Jinxiang Chai, Paul Reitsma, Jessica Hodgins, and Nancy Pollard: Interactive Control of Avatars Animated with Human Motion Data. ACM Transactions on Graphicsvolume 21, number 3, 2002, 491-500
17. F. S. Grassia.: Practical parameterization of rotations using the exponential map. Journal of Graphics Tools, **3(3)**(1998):29-48
18. J. Nocedal and S. Wright.: Numerical Optimization. Springer Verlag 1999
19. Gene. F. Franklin, J.David.Powell, Abbas. Emami-Naeini.: Feedback Control of Dynamic Systems (4th Edition). Prentice Hall, 2002.
20. Lucas Kovar, John Schreiner, Michael Gleicher.: Footskate cleanup for motion capture editing. In Proceedings of ACM SIGGRAPH Symposium on Computer Animation. 2002, 97-104

Content-Based Human Motion Retrieval with Automatic Transition

Yan Gao[1], Lizhuang Ma[1], Yiqiang Chen[2], and Junfa Liu[2]

[1] Department of Computer Science & Engineering
Shanghai Jiao Tong University
No. 1954, HuaShan Rd., Shanghai, P.R.C(200030)
gaoyan73@hotmail.com
ma-lz@cs.sjtu.edu.cn

[2] Institute of Computing Technology, Chinese Academy of Sciences
Beijing, China
yqchen@ict.ac.cn
jfliu@jdl.ac.cn

Abstract. This paper presents a framework for efficient content-based motion retrieval. To bridge the gap between user's vague perception and explicit motion scene description, we propose a *Scene Description Language* that can translate user's input into a series of set operations between *inverted lists*. Our *Scene Description Language* has three-layer structures, each describing scenes at different levels of granularity. By introducing automatic transition strategy into our retrieval process, our system can search motions that do not exist in a motion database. This property makes our system have potentials to serve as motion synthesis purpose. Moreover, by using various kinds of qualitative features and adaptive segments of motion capture data stream, we obtain a robust clustering that is flexible and efficient for constructing *motion graph*. Some experimental examples are given to demonstrate the effectiveness and efficiency of proposed algorithms.

1 Introduction

Motion capture is an increasingly popular approach for synthesizing human motion. As rich repertoires have become available in motion database, example-based approaches have been explored to synthesize novel motions either by blending similar motions [1] or by rearranging unlabelled motion clips [2,3]. Only recently, motion capture data have become publicly available on a larger scale [e.g. 4], driving the need for efficient indexing and retrieving methods.

The objective of motion retrieval is to identify and extract those motion clips from a large motion database that are in some sense similar to a query motion. The query motions are usually short clips, which represent specific actions. If the query motions include too many sequences of actions, retrieval results are likely to be no hits. Usually, a long motion is comprised of a sequence of short motion clips that have specific semantics. It is desirable to automatically construct transitions during motion retrieval. In this paper, we present a framework for content-based motion retrieval, which incorporates motion transition scheme into retrieval process. Our methods

H.-P. Seidel, T. Nishita, and Q. Peng (Eds.): CGI 2006, LNCS 4035, pp. 360 – 371, 2006.

combine advantages of motion rearrangement and motion retrieval so that can search motions inexisted in a database according to user's high-level control.

Some *motion graph*-liked systems [2,3,5] can synthesize new and realistic motions from example motions through reordering motion clips. The key of such systems is how to automatically construct a graph that encapsulates connections among different pieces of motions. The construction of such graph needs compare every pair of F frames in the database to locate candidate transitions, which involves $O(F^2)$ operations. The bad scalability makes it infeasible for large data sets even though precomputing strategy is adopted. Moreover, as Kovar etc. [2] pointed out, it remains a problem that how to automatically set appropriate transition thresholds for different motion types in an unlabelled database.

Suppose there are F frames in a motion database. Then the total operations for comparing every pair of the F frames are about $F^2/2$. If we have a way to divide all frames in the database into different categories, e.g. 1000 categories each with same frames, the total operations will be about $1000*(F/1000)*(F/1000)/2=F^2/1000/2$, which is just 1/1000 of the original computation amounts. That is, clustering gives us an efficient way to reduce computation costs for constructing a transition graph. Moreover, by dividing the motion database into different categories, we can set each category with different thresholds according to its motion numbers automatically. However, it is also a challenging problem for finding an effective clustering algorithm to handle the high dimensions of human motions.

Our work involves three main contributions. First, we propose a robust clustering algorithm to divide the unlabelled motion database into different classes. By constructing transitions in each class separately, we can reduce most operations of comparing the similarity between different frames in *motion graph*-liked systems. Second, we introduce a transition strategy into motion retrieval process so that we can retrieve motions inexisted in the database. For example, suppose we want to retrieve a walking motion with 10 steps but no such motions exist in the database. By constructing transitions at one walking step, we can find desired motions. The third main contribution of our work is to present a *Scene Description Language*, which can describe user's sketchy idea about desired motions effectively.

2 Related Work

Data-driven motion synthesis. A number of graph-based approaches to motion synthesis have recently been developed that can piece together example motions from a database. Kovar and his colleagues [2] generated a graph structure from motion data and used branch and bound search for path synthesis. Arikan and Forsyth [5] used a hierarchy of graphs to represent connectivity of a motion database and perform randomized search strategy for synthesizing a new motion subject to temporal and position constraints. Lee et al. [3] represented captured motion data with a two-layer structure, and provided effective user interfaces for interactive character control. All these approaches allow transitions between individual motion frames rather than clusters of motions, which are computationally infeasible for large data sets.

Recently, many researchers try to combine the idea of motion blending and posture rearrangement. Kim et al. [8] identified and clustered the elemental movements of the example motions based on their rhythmic pattern. Unfortunately, this method is not applicable to non-rhythmic motions. Park et al. [1] modelled labelled motion clips as a motion transition graph of which every node represents a set of parameterized example motions of the same type and each directed edge represents the transition from a motion to a motion. However, the authors did not address how to obtain the labeled motion clips to construct the motion transition graph. Kwon and Shin [9] decomposed the example motions into groups of motion segments to construct a hierarchical motion transition graph by footstep patterns. Their method used only footstep pattern to classify motion segments, making it not suitable for motion types other than locomotion. Instead, our qualitative geometric features are related to a broad spectrum of motion types, making our method applicable to general motion types.

Content-based motion retrieval. So far, there are few literatures on content-based motion retrieval. Liu et al. [11] partitioned the motion library and constructed a motion index tree based on a hierarchical motion description that uses joint angles as feature vectors. Chiu et al. [10] constructed an index map for each skeletal segment according to its segment-posture distribution through SOM clustering. Keogh et al. [12] described the first technique for indexing time series with invariance to uniform scaling. Motion data are regarded as multi-dimensional time series that are indexed by bounding envelopes. However, all these techniques relied on numerical local cost-measures to compare motions, making them not meet the demand of searching logically similar motions.

To the best of our knowledge, Kovar and Gleicher [6] first proposed a way for identifying logically similar motions in a database through multi-step search process. Such DTW based technique is infeasible for large data sets due to its $O(n^2)$ complexity. Muller et al. [7] grasped spatio-temporal invariance in geometric features and induced segments, allowing for exact matchings at the segment level. The time and space required to build and store their index structure are *linear*, opposed to DTW-based strategies, which are *quadratic*. In this paper, we adopt their index structure but introduce a pre-computation scheme to speed up motion retrieval process.

3 Geometric Features and Adaptive Segmentation

In siggrapgh 05, Müller et al. [7] introduce a class of qualitative boolean features expressing geometric relations between body points of a pose. These geometric features are designed to characterize a broad spectrum of motion types. We used the same features as them except "right/left foot fast" features. According to the author's opinion, threshold of such features is set relatively low to robustly discriminate standing still from the feet moving at all. We use "right/left foot plant" features instead, for which are richer semantics-related than the old ones. We adopt both velocity and duration time thresholds to identify footplants semi-automatically. All features that we used are listed in table 1 as follows:

Table 1. The four sets of features

F_1	left/right knee bent(F_1^1/F_1^2), legs crossed (F_1^3), left/right foot plant(F_1^4/F_1^5), left/ right foot front(F_1^6/F_1^7)
F_2	left/right foot raised(F_2^1/F_2^2), left/right leg sideways(F_2^3/F_2^4), left/right elbow bent (F_2^5/F_2^6), left/right hand fast (F_2^7/F_2^8)
F_3	arms crossed(F_3^1), hands touching(F_3^2), left/right hand in front(F_3^3/F_3^4), left/ right hand raised (F_3^5/F_3^6), left/right arm sideways(F_3^7/F_3^8)
F_4	torso bent(F_4^1), root fast (F_4^2), left/right hand touching any leg (F_4^3/F_4^4), left/right hand touching head or neck (F_4^5/ F_4^6), left/right hand touching hip area (F_4^7/ F_4^8)

Geometric features can be referred to as a *feature function* F: $P \rightarrow (0,1)^f$, where P $\in\xi$is a pose,ξdenotes the set of poses, and f is the total feature numbers. We say that two poses P_1, $P_2\in\xi$are *F-equivalent* if the corresponding *feature vectors* $F(P_1)$ and $F(P_2)$ coincide, i.e. $F(P_1)=F(P_2)$. Denote a motion capture data stream by D. Then, an *F-run* of *D* is defined to be a subsequence of *D* consisting of consecutive *F-equivalent* poses, and the *F-segments* of *D* are defined to be the *F*-runs of maximal length. The sequence of *F-segments* of *D* induces a sequence of feature vectors, which we refer to as *F-feature sequence* of D and denote F(D). About this section, more details are discussed in [7].

4 Transitions Construction

We assume the user has a database of unlabelled motion capture data in a standard skeletal format. We introduce a transition scheme to enhance motion retrieval ability so that resulting hits may include concatenated novel motions inexisted in the database. For example, consider a query consisting of three segments A, B and C. However, there are only examples, including (A, B) or (B, C) sub-sequences respectively, in the database. Obviously we cannot retrieve any hits if we do not introduce transition strategy at B.

4.1 Pruning the Segments

Kovar et al. [2] pruned their motion graph by computing the strongly connected components (SCCs) of every subgraph in order to generate arbitrarily long streams of motion of the same type. In their approach, every frame of original data has to be associated with a set of labels. In contrast, we regard each *inverted list* as a subgraph and use the following rules to prune these segments with bad transition potentials in it. As a result, the construction of motion transitions graph can be greatly speeded up.

1. The motion segments with too few frames (less than a threshold T) should be deleted because they are hard to find suitable transition points.
2. The *inverted list* with few segments in it should be emptied for its bad connectivity.
3. The first and last few motion segments of the original motions should be deleted because they are *dead ends*.
4. The motion segments with feet on the fly (both F_1^4 and F_1^5 are false) should be deleted because such motions have to preserve their own dynamics features.

4.2 Detecting Candidate Transitions

If we classify a database into small sets and locate candidate transitions in it separately, we can reduce large numbers of comparison operations. However, the curse of dimensions in motion capture data hampers the effectiveness of current clustering algorithms.

Recall that our geometric features are semantically rich, which give a rough outline to characterize a broad spectrum of different motion types. In consequence, they provide an intuitive metric for clustering motion frames. Each boolean features bisection the space of possible end-effector locations into two pose-dependent sub-space so that the whole database is divided into 2^{31} categories, each corresponding to an *inverted list*. Though not all segments in a category are definitely similar, similar segments ought to be in the same category. Note here we ignore the case that postures lie at the boundary of neighboring sub-spaces. Now we only need compare the similarity between each pair of frames in a same category without introducing any extra data structure.

4.3 Selecting Transition Points

After computing the distance between each pair of frames, local minima below a user-defined threshold are considered as potential transition points. Usually, the threshold is picked as an acceptable tradeoff between having good transitions (low threshold) and having high connectivity (high threshold). However, as Kovar et al. [2] pointed out, different kinds of motions should have different fidelity requirements. It remains a problem for the unlabelled motion data that how to set different motion types with different thresholds.

By dividing the database into a set of small categories, we can select suitable threshold for each category respectively. The numbers of motion segments in every category indicates the frequency of such kind of motion appeared in the database. This also provides a natural way to weigh the degree of people's familiarity with this motion type. In general, people have a keener sense of what motions in a bigger category should look like than these motions in a smaller category. We use a piecewise linear function to model the relation between the threshold and the segment numbers of a category, seeing figure 1.

Note we select a bit high thresholds to ensure good connectivity. We also maintain a flag for each transition node to indicate whether it is used. When user selects lower thresholds for some categories through interaction, we do not need compute transitions again but set the nodes whose distances less than thresholds unused.

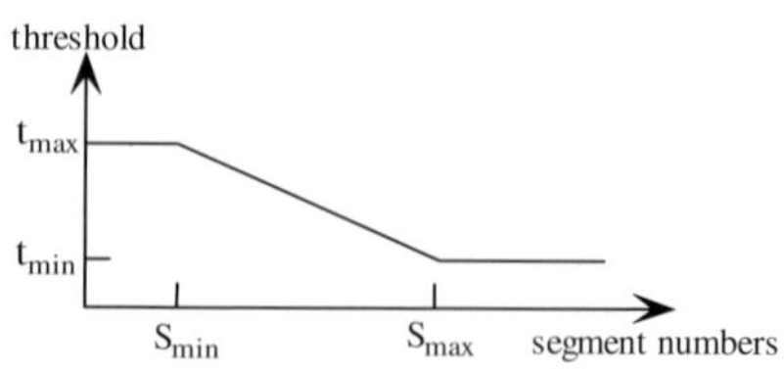

Fig. 1. Relation between threshold and segment numbers of a category. We set S_{min}=30 and S_{max}=2000, t_{min}=3*D_{min} and t_{max} =10*D_{min}, where D_{min} is the minimum distance between all pairs of consecutive frames in the database.

5 Indexing and Retrieval

5.1 Indexing and Searching

In general situations, user would like to mask out certain aspects of irrelevant body areas to avoid a large number of *false negatives* due to over-specification. Muller et al. [7] proposed the concepts of *fuzzy query* and *fuzzy hit* to deal with such situations. However, a specific movement usually involves only a few geometric features. It means that many union operations of the *inverted lists* are needed to constitute *fuzzy sets*. To avoid these operations, we add a value 2, which means *don't care*, to each geometric feature. This also provides an intuitive way to describe a query motion for user.

Now *Feature function* becomes F: P->$(0,1,2)^f$ and accordingly we have 3^{31} *inverted lists* totally. It is infeasible for both time and storage requirement to compute and store 3^{31} *inverted lists* in advance. Here we adopt divide-and-conquer scheme to reduce the overall numbers of *inverted lists* just as [7]. The process is as follows: we divide the set of 31 boolean features into the four sets F_1 (7 features), F_2 (8 features), F_3 (8 features), and F_4 (8 features) as indicated by Table 1. We then construct separate indexes I_1, I_2, I_3, and I_4. Now the amount of *inverted lists* is reduced to $(3^7+3^8+3^8+3^8)$. The trick is that we only store $(2^7+2^8+2^8+2^8)$ basic *inverted lists* on disk and merge the additional $(3^7+3^8+3^8+3^8)$ - $(2^7+2^8+ 2^8+2^8)$ *inverted lists* from them at initialization time. Here we give a comparison to the performance between our indexes with these of [7]. The storage required for our indexes is about 1/6 of [7] ($2^7+2^8+2^8+2^8$ *inverted lists* to $2^{11}+2^{12}+2^8$ *inverted lists*). In addition, our method reduces $(2^{11}+2^{12}+2^8)$-$(2^7+2^8+2^8+2^8)$=5504 times of disk I/O operations instead of $(3^7+3^8+3^8+3^8)$ - $(2^7+ 2^8+2^8+2^8)$=20974 times of merging operations between the basic *inverted lists*. The overall time for building our indexes is also reduced relative to [7] because the time for reduced I/O operations outweighs that for the additional merging operations.

Our indexes also improve the performance of retrieval in comparison with [7]. This can be seen from the amount of reduced union operation of the *inverted lists*. As Müller et al. [13] mentioned, in view of efficiency, it is important to have both few lists (leading to few merging and intersecting operations) and short lists (leading to fast merging and intersecting operations), which are mutually exclusive demands. They gave their conclusion that a choice of $f \in [8: 12]$ results in a good tradeoff between these two requirements.

However, in general, fine features, i.e., feature functions with many components, induce segmentations with many short segments, whereas coarse features lead to a smaller number of long segments. For example, suppose we have induced 2^m *inverted lists* from m boolean features. After introducing a new feature f_{m+1}, each of 2^m *inverted lists* will derive two children lists by setting f_{m+1} to 0 or 1 respectively. By l_f we denote the father list's length and by l_{c1}, l_{c2} the two children lists, respectively. Obviously, we have $l_f \leq l_{c1} + l_{c2}$, i.e. more features lead to longer lists on average. Recall that user usually selects a few features to look for a specific motion class and leaves the others unspecific. In such situations, the indexes in [7], which divide the set of all 31 boolean features into the three sets F_{lower}(11 features), F_{upper}(12 features), and $F_{interaction}$(12 features), also involve too many union operations. For example, it is easy to prove by induction that if one wants to obtain an *inverted list* with m unspecific features, 2^m-1 union operations between 2^{31} *inverted lists* are needed. Now suppose user only selects 2 features in F_{upper} and leaves the others unspecific. Then $2^{11}+2^{12-2}+2^8-3=3325$ union operations and 2 intersection operations are needed at each step of retrieval opposite to our 3 intersection operations. That is, Müller et al.'s indexing method does not fulfill the pre-computing capability fully.

5.2 Scene Description Language

Often, the user will only have a sketchy idea of which kind of motion to look for in the motion database, for example "a walking step followed by right hand punch". As Müller et al. [7] pointed out, vaguely specified motions such as kicking, punching, or clapping can often be specified by a very small set of basic geometric constellations. They gave an experiment to characterize sketchy query such as "right foot kick followed by a left hand punch", as shown in Figure 2. Müller et al. [7] process such kinds of geometric scene descriptions by first querying for each progression separately and then suitably intersecting the retrieved hits to account for cooccurrence conditions.

Instead, we present a *Scene Description Language* to handle scene definition problem more effectively. Our *Scene Description Language* includes three-level structures, which are *word*, *movement* and *scene*. The basic unit *word* has 31 bits, each corresponding to one geometric feature. Given a query as a sequence (V_1, V_2, …, V_N) of *fuzzy sets*, each *fuzzy set* V_l, $1 \leq l \leq N$ can be represented by a *word*. The definition formula of a *word* is as: *name* =(***…***), where *name* is the alias, = means *denote by*, and $* \in (0,1,2)$. A *movement*, comprising of a series of words, is used to represent a specific motion such as kick, punch, a walking step and so on. The keywords of *movement* include *start*, *next*, *step*, *fuzzy*, *null,* and *end*. Among them, *start* and *end* represent the first and last *fuzzy set* V_1 and V_N, respectively. *Next* indicates the next *fuzzy set*. *Null* is used to assign a null *word*. *Step* indicates the query content at current step in *multi-step querying*. *Fuzzy* means that *one-mismatch* is allowed between two consecutive *words*, which handles the overlapping *fuzzy sets*. The definition formula of a *movement* is as: *name*=({*step* 1=} *start*: $word_1$, {*fuzzy,*} {*next*=$word_2$, {*fuzzy,*}… {*fuzzy,*}, *next*= $word_{n-1}$,} {*fuzzy,*} *end*= $word_n$ | {*step* 2 =}…), where *name* is alias, the items in { } is choice items. We maintain a *movement* library so that the basic *movements* can be reused.

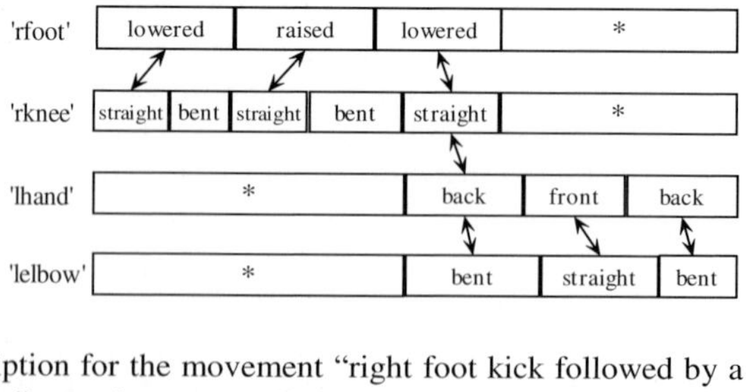

Fig. 2. Scene description for the movement "right foot kick followed by a left hand punch" in [7]. The symbol * indicates that a constellation is unspecified. Arrows indicate which constellations are to occur simultaneously.

A sequence of *movements* can generate complicate scenes. The keywords of *scene* include *start*, *next*, *cycle*, *concatenate*, *transition*, *null*, and *end*. Among them, *start* and *end* represent the first and last *movements*, respectively. *Next* indicates the next *movement*. *Null* is used to assign a null *movement*. *Cycle* represents the repetition times of a *movement* for cyclic motions such as the step numbers in a walking motion. *Concatenate* is used to concatenate the consecutive *movements*. *Transition* represents that transitions occur at current *movement*. The definition formula of a *scene* is as: (*start*: $movement_1$, {*cycle*(m): $movement_2$,} {*next*: $movement_3$, …, *next*: $movement_{n-3}$,} { *concatenate*: $movement_{n-2}$,} {*transition:* $movement_{n-1}$,} *end*: $movement_n$), where the items in { } is choice items and m is the repetition times.

In figure 3, we explain the scene of figure 2 using a *Scene Relation Graph* so that it can be translated into our *Scene Description Language* efficiently. From figure 3, we can see that the overlapping between "rknee bent" and "rfoot raised" of the scene in figure 2 is conducted effectively by adding a possible node "rknee straight & rfoot raised". This corresponds to *one-mismatch* case in [7] and we use *fuzzy* keyword to express it. We use the keyword *concatenate* to specify the relation "kick followed by punch", which means that the frame intervals between two consecutive *movements* are no more than a threshold L. We depict the same scene using our *Scene Description Language* in figure 4.

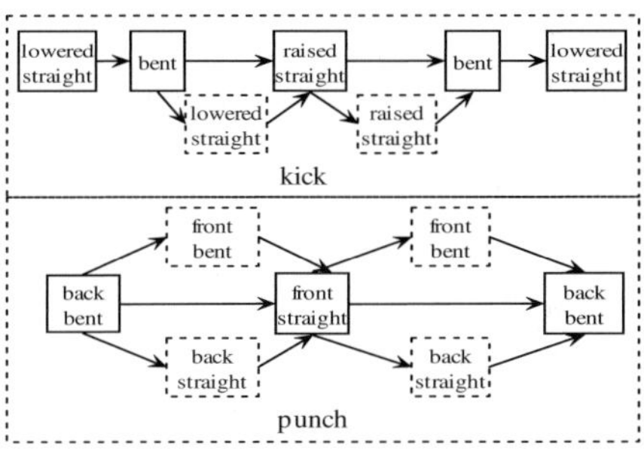

Fig. 3. Scene explanation for the movement "right foot kick followed by a left hand punch" in figure 2. The dot line rectangle represents uncertainty.

```
K_Straight & F_Lower: word1=(2022222202222222222222222222222)
K_Straight & F_Raise:  word2=(2022222212222222222222222222222)
H_Back & E_Bent:       word3=(2222222222221222220222222222222)
H_Front & E_Straight:  word4=(2222222222220222221222222222222)
rknee bent:            word5=(2122222222222222222222222222222)
kick=(start: word1, next:word5, fuzzy, next:word2, next:word5, \
        fuzzy, end: word1)
punch=(start: word3, fuzzy, next:word4, fuzzy, end: word3)
scene1=(start: kick, concatenate: punch,end: null)
```

Fig. 4. Our scene definition for "right foot kick followed by a left hand punch". Denote "rknee straight" by K_Straight, "rknee bent" by K_Bent, "rfoot raised" by F_Raise, "rfoot lowered" by F_Lower, "lhand front" by H_Front, "lhand back" by H_Back, "lelbow bent" by E_Bent, and "lelbow straight" by E_Straight.

6 Experiments and Results

We tested our algorithm on a database D from CMU [4] containing roughly 2,556,000 frames of motion capture data (sampled at 120 Hz). The experiments are performed on a Pentium PC (Pentium 4 1.8GHz processor and 768MB memory).

6.1 Indexing

The total size of represented in the text-based AMC motion capture file format was 2.01 GB. Assistant storage for files recording footplant information is 1.22 MB. Index sizes are linear in the number of segments extracted from the database, which are drastic reduced relative to the database size. For example, the whole F-index contained 186237 segments, requiring 1.6 MB of storage. Among them, F_1-index, F_2-index, F_3-index and F_4-index required 695 KB, 287 KB, 468 KB, and 186 KB of storage, respectively. The total indexing time is linear in the number of frames. To create an index file, the running time spent on reading motion files is 1353s, the feature extraction time is 180s, and the inverted list build-up time is 71s. However, such time is needed only at the database build-up time. At system initialization time, it takes 55s to build up indexes by reading data from the index file.

6.2 Retrieval

The running time to process a query depends heavily on the query length and the number of the resulting hits. In an experiment, we posed 10000 random queries for each of 3 query scenarios to our indexes in comparison with the performance in [7], see table 2.

Table 2. The average query time of ours in comparison with that in [7]

	query	1-9 hits	10-99 hits	>=100hits
Ours	$\|Q\|=5$	25	37	95
	$\|Q\|=10$	27	49	108
	$\|Q\|=20$	36	57	121
[9]	$\|Q\|=5$	23	29	291
	$\|Q\|=10$	28	35	281
	$\|Q\|=20$	42	35	294

From table 2, we can find that improvement of retrieval performance for our algorithm is more notable in case many hits exist in results. This is because in general the more hits in results mean that the fewer features are selected for query. Therefore, our pre-computing strategy can reduce more union operations during retrieval process.

Figure 5 shows 8 hits out of resulting 23 hits for a "kicking" motion (retrieval time: 19 ms) in a query-by-example mode, where only the four features F_1^1/F_1^2 and F_2^1/F_2^2 have been selected, see table 1. Out of these, 7 hits are actual kicking motions. The remaining 16 hits are dancing moves containing kick-like component. A manual investigation of the motion database showed that there are 17 reported kicks in the database as well as other kick-like motions. The missing motions are caused by the over-exactness of motion description in query-by-example mode. Further reducing the number of features by selecting only F_1^2 and F_2^2 induces 3-segment query sequence and results in 700 hits, comprising various kinds of kick-like motions. Using the motion description in figure 4 instead, all "kicking" motions are included in the resulting 138 hits, opposite to 700 hits in the query-by-example mode. This shows that our *Scene Description Language* benefits to overcome the shortage in query-by-example mode that is apt to induce *fuzzy sets* of either over-coarseness (too few selected features) or over-exactness (too many selected features).

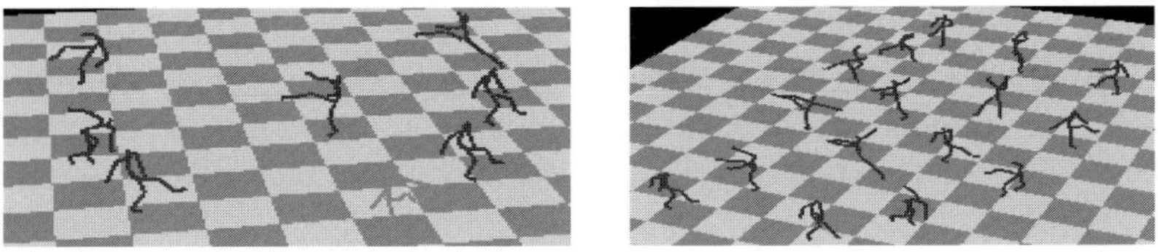

(a) (b)

Fig. 5. (a) Selected frames from the 8 query-by-example hits for a squatting motion. Query motion is green. (b) Selected frames from the 16 hits using the scene description in figure 4.

We regard each *inverted list* as a category and construct a motion transition graph among the frames of it, respectively. To maintain the size of the transition graph at an acceptable level, we remain only N nearest neighboring transition points for each frame and prune the others. We select N=20 and T (in rule 1)=10 as our configurations for constructing transition graphs. The running time for loading transition graphs from a transition file is about 230s at system's initialization and 29828s for building. Comparing with Kovar's method [2] (a running time of roughly 25 minutes to locate all candidate transition points for a subgraph containing only 6000 frames), our algorithm shows good scalability for much larger database.

We test the transition ability of our system. We using (F_1^6=1&F_1^7=1), (F_1^6=1&F_1^7=0), (F_1^6= 1&F_1^7=1), (F_1^6=0&F_1^7=1) as our queries and set the cycle times to 30 and 50 to retrieve walking motions with 30 and 50 steps, respectively. There are 9 resulting hits for 30-steps walking motions but no hits for 50-steps. After introducing transition at the 20th step, we obtain 135 30-setps walking (retrieved time: 6s) and 7 50-steps (retrieved time: 8s) walking motions in results. The results are shown in figure 6.

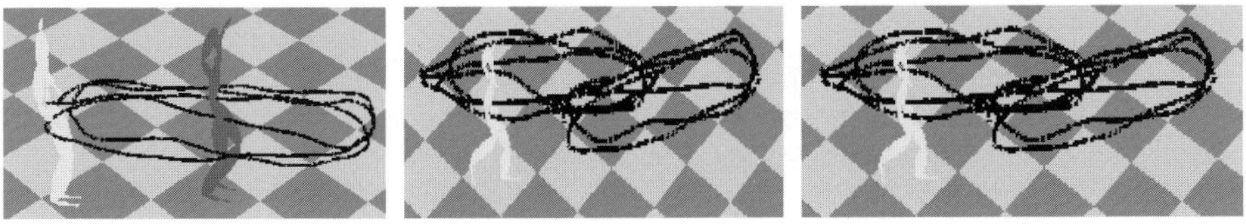

(a) (b) (c)

Fig. 6. (a) The source walking motions 1. The yellow skeleton shows the beginning frame and the red one is the transition point. (b) The source walking motions 2. (c) The resulting walking motions that transit from 1 to 2 automatically. The black line is root trajectory.

7 Discussion

In this study, we propose a novel framework for constructing a content-based human motion retrieval system. Our main contribution of this work is that we combine the framework of motion retrieval with motion graph, making our retrieval system with the potentials for motion synthesis purpose. By using geometric features as clustering metric, we reduce the computation costs of transition construction greatly, making it applicable to a database even more than 10^6 frames. Another contribution is the introduction of *Scene Description Language*, which bridges the gap between user's vague perception and explicit motion scene description.

For future work, we will incorporate motion-blending scheme in our transition construction. We also plan to employ statistical methods to automatically identify expressive geometric features from typical example motions. Moreover, we want to design an expendable structure so that user can expend the feature set efficiently.

Acknowledgements

We would like to thank Meinard Müller and Tido Röder for their helpful discussions. The motion data used in this project were obtained from mocap.cs.cmu.edu. This work was supported by National Natural Science Foundation of China (grant No.60573147, No. 60373070, and No. 60303018), and Microsoft Research Asia (Project-2004-Image-01).

References

1. Park S.I., Shin H.J., Kim T., Shin S.Y.: On-line motion blending for real-time locomotion generation. Computer Animation and Virtual Worlds, Vol. 15, No. 3 (2004) 125-138.
2. Kovar L, Gleicher M, Pighin F.: Motion graphs. ACM Transactions on Graphics, Vol. 21, No. 3 (2002) 473-482.
3. Lee J., Chai J., Reitsma P., Hodgins J., Pollard N.: Interactive control of avatars animated with human motion data. ACM Transactions on Graphics, Vol. 21, No. 3 (2002) 491-500.
4. CMU. Carnegie-Mellon Mocap Database. (2003) http://mocap.cs.cmu.edu.
5. Arikan O., Forsyth D.A.: Interactive Motion Generation from Examples. ACM Transactions on Graphics, Vol. 21, No. 3 (2002) 483-490.
6. Kovar L., Gleicher M.: Automated extraction and parameterization of motions in large data sets. ACM Transactions on Graphics, Vol. 23, No. 3 (2004) 559-568.
7. Müller M., Röder T., M. Clausen.: Efficient content-based retrieval of motion capture data. ACM Transactions on Graphics, Vol. 24, No. 3 (2005) 677-685.
8. Kim T.H., Park S.I., Shin S.Y.: Rhythmic-motion synthesis based on motion-beat analysis. ACM Transactions on Graphics, Vol. 22, No. 3 (2003) 392-401.
9. Kwon T., Shin S.Y., Motion modeling for on-line locomotion synthesis. Proc. ACM SIGGRAPH/ Eurographics Symposium on Computer Animation (2005) 29-38.
10. Chiu C., Chao S., Wu M., Yang S., Lin H.: Content-based retrieval for human motion data. Journal of Visual Communication and Image Representation, Special Issue on Multimedia Database Management Systems, Vol. 15, No. 3 (2004) 446-466.

11. Liu F., Zhuang Y., Wu F., Pan Y.: 3D motion retrieval with motion index tree. Computer Vision and Image Understanding, Vol. 92 (2003) 265-284.
12. Keogh E.J., Palpanas T., Zordan V.B., Gunopulos D., Cardle M.: Indexing large human-motion databases. Proc. 30th VLDB Conf (2004) 780-791.
13. Müller M., Röder T., Clausen M.: Efficient Indexing And Retrieval of Motion Capture Data Based on Adaptive Segmentation. Proceedings of the 4th Intl. Workshop on Content-Based Multimedia Indexing, Riga, Latvia (2005).

MIP-Guided Vascular Image Visualization with Multi-Dimensional Transfer Function

Ming-Yuen Chan[1], Yingcai Wu[1], Huamin Qu[1], Albert C.S. Chung[1,2], and Wilbur C.K. Wong[1,2]

[1] Department of Computer Science, and
[2] Lo Kwee-Seong Medical Image Analysis Laboratory,
The Hong Kong University of Science and Technology,
Clear Water Bay, Hong Kong
{pazuchan, wuyc, huamin, achung, cswilbur}@cs.ust.hk

Abstract. Direct volume rendering (DVR) is an effective way to visualize 3D vascular images for diagnosis of different vascular pathologies and planning of surgical treatments. Angiograms are typically noisy, fuzzy, and contain thin vessel structures. Therefore, some kinds of enhancements are usually needed before direct volume rendering can start. However, without visualizing the 3D structures in angiograms, users may find it difficult to select appropriate parameters and assess the effectiveness of the enhancement results. In addition, traditional enhancement techniques cannot easily separate the vessel voxels from other contextual structures with the same or very similar intensity. In this paper, we propose a framework to integrate enhancement and direct volume rendering into one visualization pipeline using multi-dimensional transfer function tailored for visualizing the curvilinear and line structures in angiograms. Furthermore, we present a feature preserving interpolation method to render very thin vessels which are usually missed using traditional approaches. To ease the difficulty in vessel selection, a MIP-guided method is suggested to assist the process.

1 Introduction

Prevention and treatment of vascular diseases can be improved if prompt and precise diagnosis can be performed with the aid of sophisticated vascular image visualization techniques. In practice, clinicians visualize the vascular images slice by slice or using the MIP. However, it is time consuming and difficult to realize the 3D structures. Less obvious structures may not be revealed because of other bright objects in the MIP. It cannot give the perception of depth and thus physical reality is lost as a result. Several recently published clinician studies [3] comparing DVR with surface rendering and MIP confirm that it is a more effective technique for angiography. Unlike other images, angiograms have several characteristics which make them difficult to visualize using traditional methods. First, the vessel intensity value is not fixed and is different in different types of images. The contextual objects may appear as bright structures and the intensity of vessels is suppressed after rescaling. Even the same vessel may have different intensity values in different parts. This makes it difficult to classify the vessels by mere intensity for visualization. Another challenge is the small vessels which are dim and obscure. They can be barely recognized even with the help of MIP. As the contrast

H.-P. Seidel, T. Nishita, and Q. Peng (Eds.): CGI 2006, LNCS 4035, pp. 372–384, 2006.

of the vessels is small, it is difficult to separate simply by thresholding. Thinning or over-segmentation of vessels are common and noise is introduced into the final result. Furthermore, the vessels are usually accompanied by background structures which are not relevant but present an obstacle to classification. Removal of these contextual structures is difficult due to the potential overlapping between the intensity value intervals of different objects and vessels.

In this paper, we integrate filtering techniques into the visualization process under the framework of multi-dimensional transfer function. Segmentation and rendering processes are combined so that various visualization goals can be achieved by users with a higher flexibility. Besides, as we found that rendering of small vessels is problematic using conventional approaches, we proposed a new interpolation method to preserve the thin features. A MIP-guided selection method is suggested for vessel selection.

This paper is organized as follows: We introduce the previous work related to vascular image visualization in Section 2 and describe our framework which integrates both enhancement and visualization processes using multi-dimensional transfer function in Section 3. MIP-guided vessel selection method is explained in Section 4. A new feature preserving rendering approach is covered in Section 5. We demonstrate some experimental results in Section 6 and conclude our work in Section 7.

2 Previous Works

2.1 Extraction and Enhancement

Segmentation of vessels in medical images is important for diagnosis of the pathology of vessels. There are many promising segmentation methods developed, although none of them can outperform the others in every medical image modality. Recently, Kirbas and Quek [9] have done a survey on vessel extraction techniques. However, most of them are not fully automatic and require a certain degree of human interaction. For better visualization and diagnosis, vessel enhancement is another important issue. Different techniques for enhancement are reviewed in [18].

2.2 Visualization

Traditional approaches only show the planar cross-sections through the data volume. However, it is inefficient as only a small portion of the vessels is revealed in each slice. Curved Planar Reformation [7] tried to generate a cross-section through the centerline of the vessels. The correctness of the plane depends on the accuracy of the estimation of centerlines. Techniques based on the fusion of different rendering methods have been proposed. They use adaptive methods on the vascular image according to certain predefined criteria. In the two level volume rendering approach of Hauser et al. [4], different rendering techniques are selectively used for different parts of a 3D image. All the results of subsequent object renderings are then combined. Zhou et al. [19] developed a system to realistically render the region of focus, while data outside the region are rendered by NPR approaches. VesselGlyph [15], on the other hand, fused DVR and CPR in their solution according to the distance to the centerlines.

2.3 Multi-Dimensional Transfer Function

Multi-dimensional transfer function (MDTF) was first proposed by Levoy [11] who added the gradient as the second dimension to the transfer function in order to classify the boundaries of different classes of objects. Various approaches focusing on the use of the first and second derivatives in the design of the transfer function, such as semi-automatic transfer function generation [8] and manipulation widget design [10] have been investigated. Sato et al. [13] used more complicated classification rules to identify different structures and incorporated them into the feature space design of transfer function. Huang et al. [6] recently proposed a shaped-based approach for the segmentation of thin structures. Other related works like [5] tried to classify features using different types of parameter.

2.4 Thin Structure Rendering

The width of the vessels from different image modalities and resolutions can be quite different. Some of the small vessels can be as small as one voxel wide. In this case, displayed image is not satisfactory using the typical rendering approach. Aliasing effect and poor re-sampling results of the small vessels have to be handled. Dong et al. [1] proposed to find the presence of fine structures in a preprocessing stage by gradient estimation and render them with normal reconstruction. Their focus is on depiction of fine details and texture on a surface. The work of Sen et al. [14], although not directly related to fine structure rendering, tackled the aliasing problem of texture magnification using some sophisticated interpolation method. It is similar to the aliasing problem of small vessels.

3 Multi-Dimensional Transfer Function Design

Owing to the complexity of angiograms, they cannot be effectively visualized using 1D transfer function. It is hard to determine the nature of the voxel by considering only the intensity. Vessels and other contextual structures may be misinterpreted in this mapping. Several ambiguous cases are summarized as follows.

First, two voxels with the same intensity are considered as the same class of objects in 1D mapping. However, it is possible that voxels with the same intensity represent different objects at different locations because of the overlapping of intensity interval of different object classes. Second, even if the voxels with the same intensity are proximate to each other, they may be of different classes. Due to the partial volume effect, a voxel may consist of different classes of structures(vessel and context). The voxels with the same intensity should not always be mapped to the same class. Lastly, in most cases, the intensity range of vessels is very small and overlaps with other classes. It is very difficult to distinguish the vessels in the intensity profile.

Therefore, we choose to extend the transfer function to higher dimension in order to resolve the uncertainty and limitations in the 1D approach. Previous work of Kniss et al. [10] indicated the importance of multi-dimensional transfer function in extracting materials and boundaries. Simply using derivatives as the second dimension of feature space [8] is not effective in our case. The gradient map of the angiogram can only show the boundary of different structures. The vessel response is relatively weak and cannot be distinguished from other contextual structures. This indicates that we should not only consider the boundaries of objects but also the contextual information or other higher level details of the objects in order to reveal the object of interest. In this paper, we focus on the problems arising from angiograms of different modalities and design a proper feature space for effective visualization of the vascular structures.

3.1 Filtering Techniques

As mentioned in Section 2.1, various kinds of vessel filtering techniques have been proposed mainly based on the characteristics of vascular structures. In this paper, we use a curvilinear structure filter and a line filter to assist the process of visualization.

Filter for Curvilinear Structure. Vessels are considered as curvilinear structures by the filter and strong responses are generated at locations where similar structures are likely to be present. Among those filters in this category, vesselness measurement based on Hessian is adopted as it is widely used [12][13] and we found that it can reveal the tabular structures of vessels more precisely. The eigenvalues of the Hessian matrix are used to determine locally the likelihood of the presence of vessels. This helps discriminate the vessels from other contextual structures and recover those corrupted vessels. The Hessian matrix is given by

$$H = \begin{pmatrix} I_{xx} & I_{xy} & I_{xz} \\ I_{yx} & I_{yy} & I_{yz} \\ I_{zx} & I_{zy} & I_{zz} \end{pmatrix} \tag{1}$$

where partial second derivative of image I(x) is represented by I_{xx}, I_{xy}, etc. For each point of the image, the second order structure of intensity variation is captured by the matrix and the corresponding eigenvalues and vectors which are represented by $\lambda_1, \lambda_2, \lambda_3$ and e_1, e_2, e_3 (where$\lambda_1 \geq \lambda_2 \geq \lambda_3$), can be computed. By analyzing the eigenvalues, different local structures can be predicted. The thin line structure of vessels results in a small λ_1 and large negative λ_2 and λ_3. To signify the line-like structure of vessels in the filter response, we use the line structure similarity measure suggested by Sato et al. [12] which is given by $L = f(\lambda_1, \lambda_c) \times \lambda_c$, where $\lambda_c = min(-\lambda_2, \lambda_3)$ and

$$f(\lambda_1, \lambda_c) = \begin{cases} exp(-\frac{\lambda_1^2}{2(\alpha_1 \lambda_c)^2}) & \text{if } \lambda_1 \leq 0, \lambda_c \neq 0 \\ exp(-\frac{\lambda_1^2}{2(\alpha_2 \lambda_c)^2}) & \text{if } \lambda_1 > 0, \lambda_c \neq 0 \\ 0 & \text{if } \lambda_c = 0 \end{cases} \tag{2}$$

By applying the filter, unrelated contextual structures can be removed. However, the performance depends on whether the filter scale is proper or not. It turns out that only vessels of a similar size can give a significantly high response. As we are dealing with the problem of small vessels, the smallest filter size is chosen. Users can selectively choose different filter sizes in their preferences for different visualization goals.

Filter for Line Structure. Although the result of structural filter is pretty good, there are artifacts due to imperfect values of filter parameters or the variation of background tissue of the original image. These factors reduce the detectability of the small vessels. Uneven or unclear response and fragmentation can be found along the vessel. Refinements should be done on the response to connect those disconnected vessels and suppress those single bright voxels of noise. There are many line filters proposed which are quite similar in nature. The enhancement method proposed by Sun and Parker [16] is a simpler one and therefore can ease the burden of computation for real-time visualization. The idea is to find out the local mean of every line segment passing through the voxel of interest, while all the line segments are within a cubic kernel centered at the voxel. The local maximum mean (LMM) is defined as the maximum of the local means. By assigning the LMM to the previous response, the overall response is strengthened, especially for the vessel voxels.

$$LMM(\text{vec}x) = max_{j=1,\ldots,13}\{L_d(\text{vec}x, j)\} \tag{3}$$

where

$$L_d(\text{vec}x, j) = \frac{1}{k}\sum_{l=-k/2}^{k/2} S(\text{vec}x, j, l)$$

However, the simplicity of the method comes with drawbacks. Bright vessels are widened and small vessels at bifurcation are blurred. Besides, the improvement is less significant for the dim vessels, therefore, an amendment is made to the original method.

To avoid the thickening of bright vessels, voxel intensity should not be raised significantly by a nearby single bright voxel. This can be done by lowering the intensity of other context voxels during the mean calculation. The context voxel can be identified by a threshold which is sufficiently lower than the intensity of the vessel. This can balance and suppress the increase of the final result due to the bright voxel. The original vessel is not affected as the highest mean does not change if it is connected with other bright voxels along the vessel. To suppress the context intensity, we can use a simple formula

$$I'(x) = \begin{cases} I(x) \times (\frac{T-I(x)}{T})^c & \text{if } I(x) < T \\ I(x) & \text{if } I(x) \geq T \end{cases} \tag{4}$$

where T is the threshold value and c is the constant for the power function used in the intensity transformation. After applying the filtering methods described in the last two sections, we can get a clear filter response image which highlights and reveals the structure of the vessels in the original image. It can be added to the feature space of the vessel and participate in the transfer function and rendering process.

3.2 Interface

Recall that it is difficult to use a 1D transfer function to classify the vessels from the context due to the overlapping of intensity interval. As the intensity interval of vessels is small and not obvious compared with other background structures, it brings about difficulties in finding an optimal transfer function for visualization. Therefore, we use the multi-dimensional transfer function approach to ease the difficulties. Instead of using gradients [17] or derivatives [10], the aforementioned filtering response is treated as the second feature. To allow easy manipulation, we provide a 2D transfer function interface in which a user can define a transfer function by creating a polygonal region on the plane (Fig. 1(a)).

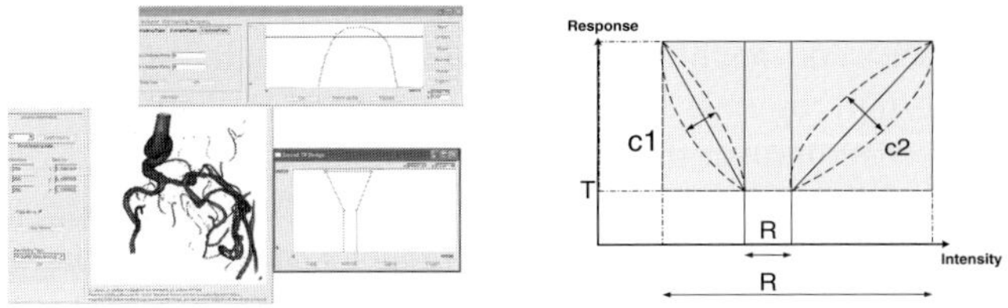

(a) (b)

Fig. 1. (a) Interfaces of our system; (b) 2D transfer function Interface

We can simplify the searching process by starting with a set of parameters. First, we define an approximate intensity range R of the vessels. The semi-automatic transfer function generation approach [8] can be a good initial guess which usually covers a larger interval than we need. Another range R', which is a smaller interval within R and can be more confidently classified as vessels, is defined. As a vessel would give a reasonably high response value, we can classify those voxels in the range R but not in range R' with a threshold defined by a curve or line. The transfer function is shown in Fig. 1(b). The curve is controlled by a threshold value T and a constant c. Users can manually change these parameters or directly manipulate the shape of the function in order to get a better visualization result.

3.3 Framework

In a typical medical imaging system, the dataset is first preprocessed with different image processing tools and is subsequently put into the pipeline of visualization. This separated architecture reduces the users' interactivity in the course of finding a proper view for their visualization goals. Besides, the result of image processing cannot be

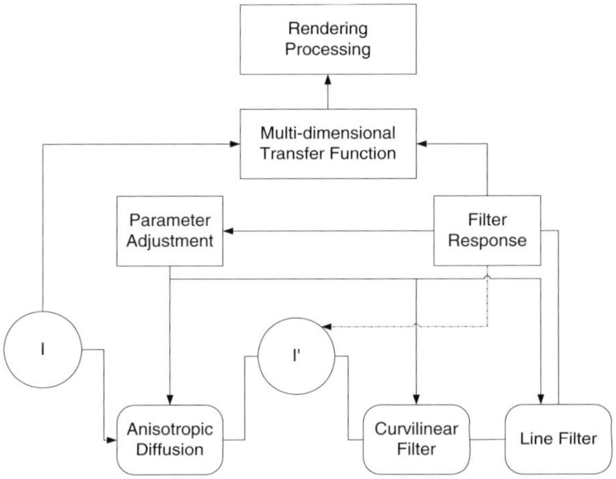

Fig. 2. A diagram of the visualization framework

accurate or proper for visualization without the interactive adjustments from users. For example, the preprocessed image may be suitable for visualizing large structures but not tiny vessels in certain regions. This indicates the need for better integration of both processes in order to accomplish the visualization goals of different users. Fang et al. [2] suggested a transfer function model in this spirit to fuse the processes. We adapt their hybrid approach for our purpose (Fig. 2). Instead of applying the filtering operations directly to the displayed image, the operations are performed on the responses. We consider the responses as the output of the image-based transfer function which is defined by F:I→I' where $F = f_n \otimes f_{n-1} \otimes \cdots \otimes f_1$.

As users can interactively change the parameters of the filter, it provides higher flexibility. Without this, the result would be affected by poor preprocessed results. To avoid deterioration of performance due to filtering processes, the original method tries to relieve the computational cost by restricting the processes only on visible regions and voxels used for rendering. In our case, we restrict them by the first dimension of the transfer function. As vessels occupy only a small intensity interval and region, which are much less than 10% of the total number of voxels, this allows the process to be done more efficiently in real-time.

4 MIP-Guided Selection

The visualization result depends on viewers' concerns and therefore a proper user selection is a critical starting point for conveying results in an expected way. However, it is difficult to specify a region of interest in a volume data using a 2D interface. Instead of performing the selection on each slice, we use the MIP to assist the process as it can provide useful information about the location of vessels. The idea is that the small vessels are usually projected on the MIP due to the relatively high intensity, but not on the direct volume rendered images. By choosing pixels belonging to vessels on the MIP, the corresponding voxels in the volume can be selected. Conventional region growing techniques can be applied to the selected voxels and a proper region which can capture the vessels is defined.

4.1 Depth Encoding

Vessels which are spatially close and have similar intensity values can lead to ambiguity. Without the depth information, it is difficult to identify the vessels individually and they are perceived as a clutter of connected vessels (Fig. 3(a)). To solve this problem, we encode the depth information using a spectrum of colors. First, we generate a depth map according to the distance of the voxels from the viewing plane. The depth map is encoded with colors and then composited with the mono-color MIP. This allows users to identify different vessels which overlap in the MIP. In our experiment, we use a color spectrum between red and blue to deliver depth cues (Fig. 3(b)). The twisted vessels in the MIP can be identified clearly. Without the aid of depth encoding, it is difficult to classify a vessel in the fuzzy context. By considering the color difference, users can select a vessel at different depth levels and understand the connectivity between vessels.

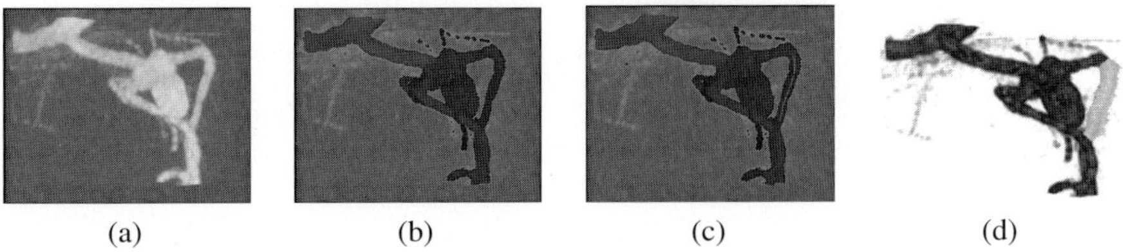

Fig. 3. MIP images: (a) Original; (b) Color encoded; (c) User selection; (d) Region growing

4.2 Modification on MDTF

In addition to the scalar intensity and vesselness measure, the distance to the selected voxels should be considered. We add this as another parameter to the MDTF. The opacity is adjusted accordingly and is increase near the selected regions. This opacity modulation can reflect the selection of users by highlighting the region of interest. The structure of the selected vessel (Fig. 4) which is otherwise occluded by other vessels can be shown clearly in the result. Actually, colors can also be adjusted based on the same principle. This method is also very useful for rendering those thin vessels of interest.

Fig. 4. Results of DVR: (a) Original; (b) Result of opacity modulation based on user selection

5 Feature Preserving Interpolation

The intensity along the narrow and weakly connected part of the vessel is uneven and it is rendered in a ripple shape. Thin vessels may become invisible at certain viewing angles although they actually exist in the image. The reason for this artifact is that we cannot guarantee that a good sampling point can always be found along the rays from all angles. Although a ray passes through the vessel, the distance of the sampling point to the vessel varies from different viewing angles. We cannot guarantee that the sampling value is always close to the vessel's intensity. Therefore, part of a small vessel occasionally darkens or even becomes invisible from certain viewing angles. The artifacts can be attributed to the interpolation method used in the rendering process and can be reduced by increasing the sampling rate so that the chance of getting a representative sample point is increased. However, this is expensive and still cannot solve the problem of uneven density distribution. The basic problem is that the trilinear interpolation method in a typical rendering process has no idea of the existence of vessels (or more precisely, it does not know whether the voxels are connected within a cell). For example, the two diagonal voxels are weakly connected in the cell in Fig 5. The sampling value cannot truly reflect the situation if they are actually connected. This is a serious problem for small vessels. Inspired by Sen [14], we use a new interpolation method to preserve the connectivity of thin vessels.

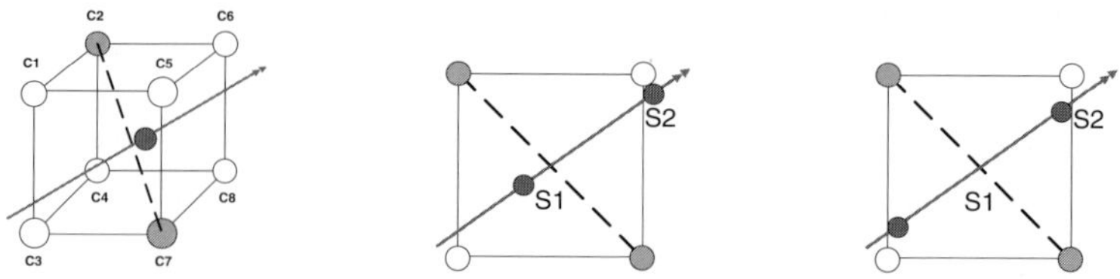

(a) (b) (c)

Fig. 5. Shaded voxels are the diagonal vessel voxels in a cell. The arrows are the rays passing through the cell and the circles on the rays are the sample points. A representative sample point S1 is found in (b) but not in (c). However, intensity of S1 in (b) still falls out of the intensity range of vessel after interpolation.

5.1 Interpolation Method

Our proposed rendering method takes weak connectivity into consideration. For the weakly connected vessels, we render them using a special interpolation method. Our objective is to ensure that the sampled intensity does not drop to a value lower than those of the connected voxels. A simple solution is to perform a linear interpolation between the two connected voxels for every connectivity. The intensity along the line changes smoothly from one voxel to another. Then, the intensity of the sampling point is the value of the projected point of the sampling point on the line.

$$I(P_s) = \begin{cases} \frac{I(c_i)\times dist(P_s',c_i)+I(c_j)\times dist(P_s',c_j)}{dist(P_s',c_i)+dist(P_s',c_j)} & \text{if } dist(P_s',P_s) \le R_0 \\ I_{Trilinear}(c_1,\ldots,c_8) & \text{if } dist(P_s',P_s) > R_0 \end{cases} \quad (5)$$

where $c_1,\ldots,c_8$ are the voxels of the cell, P_s is the sampling point and P_s' is the projected point of P_s on line c_ic_j of the vessel. R_0 is the radius parameter used to control the width of the vessel. It should be a value large enough to ensure that at least one sampling point can be found in this cell when a ray passes through this vessel volume from any angles. For the volume outside the defined region, we can use the trilinear interpolation method.

5.2 Connectivity

We have to define the connectivity between voxels such that the vessels can be rendered accurately. If we only consider the intensity of the voxels, ambiguity may arise. For example, two voxels may be from two separate vessels or the same vessel. Therefore, we try to use the filter responses to predict the existence of connectivity. First, we identify the vessel voxels according to their response values. Then, we check the likelihood of connectivity by measuring the similarity of their structures. If these voxels have similar response value, we treat them as connected vessels. This criterion can be written like this:

Definition 1. *Cell* $C = [c_1, \ldots, c_8]$*, where* c_i *is a corner of C. For every pair of* c_i *and* c_j*, find* $R_{diff}(i,j) = \frac{|R(c_i)-R(c_j)|}{min(R(c_i),R(c,j))}$ *where* c_i *and* c_j*, are in diagonal. If* $R_{diff}(i,j) < Threshold$*, connectivity exists between i and j.*

As the diagonal voxels may be connected indirectly with a voxel which is on the same edge with each connected voxel, the connectivity is preserved in the original interpolation method. Therefore, we can ignore these connectivity cases. There may be more than one connectivity in a cell. Performing interpolation for all the lines of connectivity is expensive and unnecessary. We only perform interpolation on the nearest edge to the sample point. For example, if the number of vessel voxels in a cell is quite a few (say, more than 4), we can assume that the vessels dominate the cell and the original interpolation can reveal the connectivity among them. In practice, we can get an improved result by considering only the case of 2-3 voxels.

6 Experimental Results

In order to demonstrate that our approach can reveal the thin vessel structures and discard the unrelated structures and noises, two medical datasets are tested in our experiment. The first medical dataset is a 3D rotational X-ray angiographic image (3DRA) of size $256 \times 256 \times 256$. It shows the abdominal region of a patient. In the MIP (Fig. 6(a)), we find many thin vessels which are obscured by the other tissues. Fig. 6(b) and 6(c) show the results of applying 1D TF and no suitable transfer function can be found after many trials. In Fig. 6(b) we adjust the transfer function to a higher intensity range so that noise is minimized. It can clearly show the large vessels but thin vessels are

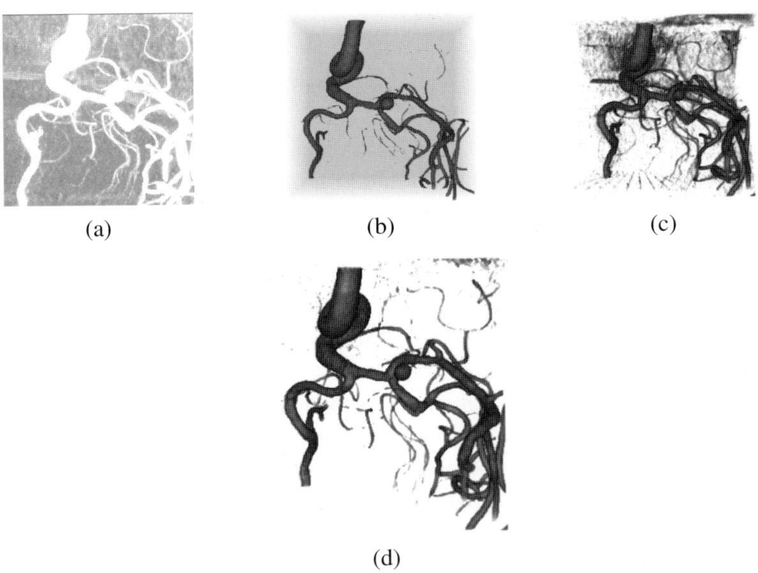

Fig. 6. 3DRA images: (a) MIP image; (b)(c) Results using 1D TF; (d) Result using MDTF

missed. In the right image, all the missing thin structures are revealed by broadening the intensity range. However, it is accompanied with noise and other tissues. This is due to the overlapping of the intensity intervals between vessels and soft tissues, which make it difficult to classify the vessels using 1D TF. We apply the MDTF with enhanced features to visualize the data (Fig. 6(d)). The feature response allows us to classify ambiguous voxels with similar intensity. By choosing a proper transfer function using the 2D interface, the result is better than the previous images. The noise, which has low response value, is greatly suppressed. Most of the small vessels are revealed clearly in the image.

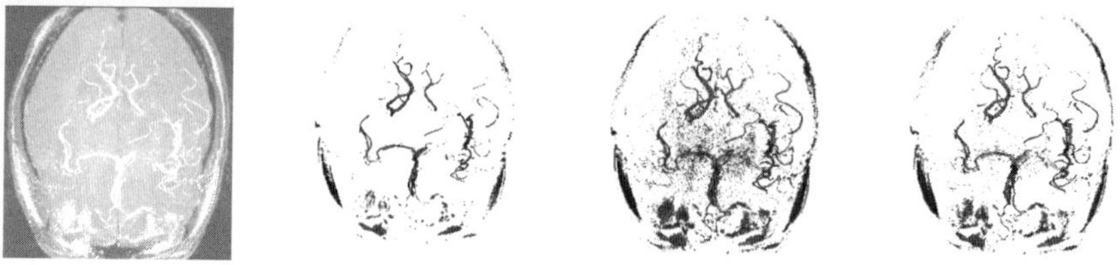

(a) (b) (c) (d)

Fig. 7. Brain MRA: (a) MIP image; (b)(c) Results of using 1D TF; (d) Result using MDTF

(a) (b) (c) (d) (e)

Fig. 8. Results using conventional approach (a) (b) (d) and feature preserving approach (c)(e)

In addition, a more complicated TOF MRA image is tested (Fig. 7). It is a $512 \times 512 \times 52$ brain image consisting of skull and brain matters. The vessels are small and dim and are embedded in different locations of the brain. Similar to the previous case, 1D TF cannot give a good result (Fig. 7(b) and 7(c)). Our result preserves more details of the vessels while keeping the noise at minimum. As the brain image is noisy and fuzzy (Fig. 7(a)), some regions of the brain with similar structures may be misinterpreted as vessels and introduce noise. It is impossible to remove them completely. However, the improvement is obvious in the comparison of our result with the original one.

Finally, we show the result of our feature preserving rendering method. Fig. 8(a) shows a small vessel extracted from the 3DRA data. The width of the vessel is about 1-4 voxels. In the conventional approach, vessels which are actually connected become broken or even invisible at certain viewing angles due to a poor sampling value being retrieved with the interpolation scheme (Fig. 8(b) and 8(d)). By using our method, the thin and weakly connected vessels can be seen clearly at any angle (Fig. 8(c) and 8(e)). As a representative sampling point is guaranteed to be found within a pre-defined radius, a strong connectivity is established without thickening the vessel.

7 Conclusion

This work presents a framework for visualization of vascular images. We integrate the enhancement process and visualization pipeline using multi-dimensional transfer function. Segmentation of small vessels is difficult and cannot be easily achieved by using 1D transfer function. The enhancement techniques help classify the curvilinear and line structures of vessels during the interactive visualization process. Thin vessels are highlighted and visualized. Also, we use a new feature preserving interpolation method to render the thin vessels. This ensures that the thin vessels can be seen clearly at any viewing angle and are not affected by poor sampling results of conventional interpolation methods. Moreover, we suggest a MIP-guided selection of vessel which helps users specify the structure of interest and deliver a better result based on the selection.

Acknowledgments

We would like to thank Dr. Simon C. H. Yu from Prince of Wales Hospital, Hong Kong for providing the medical data. This work is partially supported by RGC grant CERG 618705 and HKUST grant DAG 04/05 EG02.

References

1. F. Dong, G. J. Clapworthy, and M. Krokos. Volume rendering of fine details within medical data. In *the proceedings of IEEE Visualization 2001*, pages 387–394, 2001.
2. S. Fang, T. Biddlecome, and M. Tuceryan. Image-based transfer function design for data exploration in volume visualization. In *the proceedings of IEEE Visualization 1998*, pages 319–326, 1998.
3. E. K. Fishman. CT angiography and MDCT: Detection, characterization and staging of abdominal disease. *RSNA*, 2000.
4. H. Hauser, L. Mroz, Bischi, and E. Groller. Two-level rendering. pages 242–252, 2001.
5. J. Hladuvka, A. Konig, and E. Groller. Curvature-based tranfer functions for direct volume rendering. In *Proceeding of Spring Conference Computer Graphics*, pages 58–65, May 2000.
6. A. Huang, G. M. Nielson, A. Razdan, G. E. Farin, D. P. Baluch, and D. G. Capco. Thin structure segmentation and visualization in three-dimensional biomedical images: A shape-based approach. In *IEEE Trans. on Visualization and Computer Graphics*, volume 12, pages 93–102, 2006.
7. A. Kanitsar, D. Fleischmann, R. Wegenkittl, P. Felkel, and E. GrSller. CPR - curved planar reformation. In *the proceedings of IEEE Visualization 2002*, pages 37–44, 2002.
8. G. Kindlmann and J. W. Durkin. Semi-automatic generation of transfer functions for direct volume rendering. *In IEEE Symposium On Volume Visualization*, pages 79–86, 1998.
9. C. Kirbas and F. Quek. A review of vessel extraction techniques and algorithms. *ACM Computing Surveys*, 36(2):81–121, June 2004.
10. J. Kniss, G. Kindlmann, and C. Hansen. Multidimensional transfer functions for interactive volume rendering. *IEEE Trans. on Visualization and Computer Graphics*, 8(3), 2002.
11. M. Levory. Display of surfaces from volume data. *IEEE Computer Graphics and Applications*, 8(5):29–37, 1988.
12. Y. Sato, S. Nakajima, H. Atsumi, T. Koller, G. Gerig, S. Yoshida, and R. Kikinis1. 3D multi-scale line filter for segmentation and visualization of curvilinear structures in medical images. In *IEEE Medical Image Analysis*, pages 143–168, June 1998.

13. Y. Sato, C.-F. Westin, A. Bhalerao, S. Nakajima, N. Shiraga, S. Tamura, and R. Kikinis. Tissue classification based on 3d local intensity structures for volume rendering. *IEEE Trans. on Visualization and Computer Graphics*, 6(2):160–180, 2000.
14. P. Sen. Silhouette maps for improved texture magnification. In *Eurographics Graphics Hardware*, 2004.
15. M. Straka, M. C. A. L. Cruz, A. Kochl, M. Sramek, E. Groller, and D. Fleischmann. The vesselglyph: Focus and context visualization in CT-Angiography. In *the proceedings of IEEE Visualization 2004*, 2004.
16. Y. Sun and D. Parker. Small vessel enhancement in MRA images using local maximum mean processing. *IEEE Trans. on Image Processing*, 10(11), Nov. 2001.
17. F. Vega, P. Hastreiter, B. Tomandl, C. Nimsky, and G. Greiner. 3D visualization of intracranial aneurysms with multidimensional transfer functions. *Bildverarbeitung fur die Medizin*, pages 46–50, 2003.
18. W. C. S. Wong and A. C. S. Chung. A review on enhancement techniques in 2D and 3D vascular images. *Technical Report(HKUST-CS06-02), The Hong Kong University of Science and Technology*, 2002.
19. J. Zhou, M. Hinz, and K. D. Tonnies. Hybrid-focal region based rendering of medical data. *Bildverarbeitung fur die Medizin*, pages 113–116, 2002.

Automatic Foreground Extraction of Head Shoulder Images

Jin Wang[1], Yiting Ying[2], Yanwen Guo[2,3], and Qunsheng Peng[2]

[1] Xuzhou Normal University, Xuzhou, China
[2] State Key Lab of CAD&CG, Zhejiang University, Hangzhou 310027, China
[3] School of Computer Science and Technology, Shandong University, Jinan 250100, China

Abstract. Most existing techniques of foreground extracting work only in interactive mode. This paper introduces a novel algorithm of automatic foreground extraction for special object, and verifies its effectiveness with head shoulder images. The main contribution of our idea is to make the most use of the prior knowledge to constrain the processing of foreground extraction. For human head shoulder images, we first detect face and a few facial features, which helps to estimate an approximate mask covering the interesting region. The algorithm then extracts the hard edge of foreground from the specified area using an iterative graph cut method incorporated with an improved Gaussian Mixture Model. To generate accurate soft edges, a Bayes matting is applied. The whole process is fully automatic. Experimental results demonstrate that our algorithm is both robust and efficient.

1 Introduction

Foreground extraction is a long lasting topic in computer vision and graphics. Early research focused on fast and precise interactive segmentation tools. Intelligent Scissors [6], Snakes [4] and Level sets [5] are several typical methods, which present hard edges. Then, matting techniques were developed to get soft edges with a transparent alpha mask. Poission [9] and Bayes [8] matting are the two representative algorithms. Recently, researchers attempt to enhance the automatization [1], [2], [3]. In [3], an intuitive user interface is suggested, but is still complex for some images. [2] present the up-to-date technique on image cutout, which only requires the user to draw a rectangle surrounding the desired object. Fully automatic foreground extraction is still a big challenge today. It seems impossible to develop a universal algorithm to recognize the shape of interested object out of complex background, because objects in the world vary greatly. We must take the knowledge of the foreground objects into account. Fortunately, many objects have their certain characteristics which help to locate those objects' outline. Many detection techniques for special objects, such as car, face, text, etc., have been proposed. Those detection results will facilitate automatic image segmentation. Based on above analysis, we present a novel framework for fully automatic foreground extraction of special objects.

H.-P. Seidel, T. Nishita, and Q. Peng (Eds.): CGI 2006, LNCS 4035, pp. 385–396, 2006.

Our paper focuses on making the most use of prior knowledge to select more precise sample set of the background and foreground, remove unwanted pieces and retrieve lost patches.

Our algorithm has three stages. First, we locate some obvious features on the object and get its probable outline by the prior knowledge of the object. With these information, we secondly apply an iterative Graph cut algorithm based on improved Gauss Mixture Model (GMM) to estimate the foreground over the mask and generate the hard edges. Thirdly, along a narrow strip around the hard edges, Bayesian matting is used to refine the cutout boundary and generate the final soft edges.

Human face and body are the most familiar things in our life, whose extraction is significant and meaningful. So we choose the head shoulder images as examples to validate our algorithm. Its prior knowledge can be represented as facial organ, which can be obtained with face detection and features locating.

The main contribution of this paper is that we introduce a novel, robust algorithm to extract foreground automatically for special objects, in which we make full use of the prior knowledge as strong constraint. This work is of great significance for those embedding devices without interactive tools, such as digital cameras and mobile phones.

2 Related Work

For automatic image cutout, there are few achievements up to now. We will describe briefly and compare several representative interactive image cutout techniques, which focus on presenting convenient interactions. In addition, GMM will be addressed briefly which will be improved in the next section.

Image Cutout. Several early image segmentation methods have been applied in commercial products, such as Snakes [4], Level sets [5] and Intelligent Scissors [6], all of which are interactive tools. Users first define an initial contour. Then driven by different forms of energy minimization, these contours can be refined and snapped to the image edges iteratively. The main disadvantage of above methods is that the final segmentation result depends on the initialization heavily, especially in camouflage. Excessive interaction also limits their application.

Recently, a powerful image segmentation technique Graph cut [1] is presented. Graph cut poses image cutout as a binary labelling problem, which means that each pixel p belongs to either foreground or background. Define L_p as the transparency of p. If p belongs to foreground, denote it as $L_p = 1$; otherwise $L_p = 0$. Guided by the observed foreground and background greylevel histograms, the solution L, i.e. a segmentation, can be obtained by minimizing a Gibbs energy $E(L)$ with the form:

$$E(L) = U(p, L_p) + V(p, L_p) \tag{1}$$

where the first term represents penalty energy for pixel labelling and the latter term is the smoothing term indicating the interaction between neighboring pixels. Usually $U(p, L_p)$ and $V(p, L_p)$ can be defined as follows:

$$U(p, L_p) = \lambda \cdot \sum_{p \in P} -lnh(p; L_p), \tag{2}$$

$$V(p, L_p) = \sum_{(p,q) \in N} \frac{e^{-\frac{(I_p - I_q)^2}{2\sigma^2}} \cdot |L_p - L_q|}{dist(p, q)} \tag{3}$$

in which λ is a weight between the penalty energy and the smoothing term, $(p, q) \in N$ means p, q are neighboring pixels, h is the color distribution, I_p is the grey value of pixel p, σ is a constant and $dist(p, q)$ is the Euclidean distance between p and q. Minimization of $E(L)$ is done by using a standard minimum cut algorithm. More details about the Graph cut algorithm can be found in [1].

GrabCut [2] extended Boykov's algorithm on several aspects to improve the efficiency and reduce user interaction. Firstly, it replaces color histograms with GMM to achieve more accurate color sampling. Secondly, it adopts an iterative Graph cut procedure to substitute for the one-shot minimum cut estimation. It requires only a rectangle surrounding the desired object for foreground extraction, which is the most automatic algorithm for foreground extraction up to now. However, the algorithm is not robust enough since it samples background and foreground in a imprecise region, so further interactions are still needed in many cases.

Lazy Snapping [3] is another fine Graph cut based cutout algorithm. It separates coarse and fine scale processing, making object specification and detailed adjustment easy. In the coarse process, the image is clustered adaptively and Graph cut is applied to these clusters to generate an initial segmentation fast. While in the fine process, a set of user interface tools is designed to provide flexible control and editing. To obtain satisfactory results, usually the exigent interaction is also unavoidable.

Above approaches mainly focus on the hard segmentation, which can not get smooth edge information, whose results can not be composed with another image smoothly. Some work has been addressed in the soft segmentation [7], [8], [9], which endows the pixel around the boundary with continuous alpha values. Usually, for these approaches, a user-supplied trimap $T = \{T_F; T_U; T_B\}$ is needed, where T_F is the user specified foreground, T_B is background and T_U is the the unknown region whose alpha values are to be solved. Bayes matting [8] models the color distributions with oriented Gaussian covariance, and relies on a Bayesian approach to solve the matting problem. Poisson matting [9] formulates the problem as solving Poisson equations with the matte gradient field.

Gaussian Mixture Model (GMM). GMM is a type of probability density composing of a set of Gaussian models. The GMM with K Gaussian models is:

$$p(\omega|x) = \sum_{k=1}^{K} \alpha_k G(x; \mu_k, \sigma_k) \tag{4}$$

where $\alpha_1, ..., \alpha_k$ is the mixing proportions satisfying $\Sigma_{k=1}^{K} \alpha_k = 1$, μ_k, σ_k is the mean value and covariance of kth Gaussian model. A commonly used approach for determining the parameters of GMM is the Expectation-Maximization(EM) algorithm [10].

3 Head Shoulder Cutout Algorithm

The process of automatically extracting foreground of head shoulder pictures is divided into three steps: make a rough mask with the face detection and feature location techniques; extract the hard edges of the foreground with the constraints of the mask by Graph cut; refine the result and generate soft edges with matting.

3.1 Face and Feature Detection

Face and facial feature detection have been studied for many years, with many techniques proposed [15], [16], [18]. A detailed comparison and survey on face detection algorithms can be found in [15]. Among the face detection methods, learning-based algorithms have demonstrated excellent results. Recently, P. Viola [18] presented an efficient and robust method with AdaBoost and integral image. We adopt an improved Adaboost algorithm to search the face candidate in head shoulder image.

In order to enhance the detection ratio and performance of Adaboost algorithm, we make two improvements. First, an adaptive Gauss mixture skin color model is employed to ignore those non-skin regions, and canny filter is used to reduce those chaos regions. Second, in Adaboost algorithm, when the number of features exceeds 200, the distribution of face and non face classes in Harr-like features space almost completely overlap in later stages of the cascade training. In order to solve this problem, PCA feature is introduced in the later stages of cascaded training. Adaboost with PCA can get much higher detection ratio than that without PCA at the same false alarm ratio.

Further, we also employ Adaboost algorithm to locate eye corners and mouth corners based on the detected face, and apply VPF [13] algorithm to locate jaw and jowl feature points. The whole process abides to the idea of LFA [14], which enhances the efficiency and increases detection ratio. In general, we detect 9 feature points: eye corners, mouth corners, left/right jowl and jaw.

3.2 Face Mask

With the help of the the detected face and features, we create a mask to define the region of interest in the image, which indicates the approximate position of the head and shoulder. This mask will strongly constrain the whole Graph cut process to emphasize foreground, remove fractional pieces and unwanted patches, and retrieve the lost foreground.

Candide is a wire-frame face model to define a basic facial structure, which has been popular in video coding research for many years [19]. The new variant of this model is also compliant to MPEG-4 Face Animation. We adopt the frontal projection of Candide to assist in constructing the face mask, as shown in Fig.1. The green points denote the detected features and the blue ones are estimated with Candide. The region surrounded by the pink polygon demonstrates the approximate face area and the half ellipse adhering to the face mask denotes the shoulder position. Besides, the proportions of all parts are also fixed.

In Fig.1, the area covered by face mask and the half ellipse is deemed as the estimated initial foreground served for the further Graph cut, while the rest region is the background. Obviously, this initial samples selection of background/foreground is more accurate than previous semi-automatic approaches.

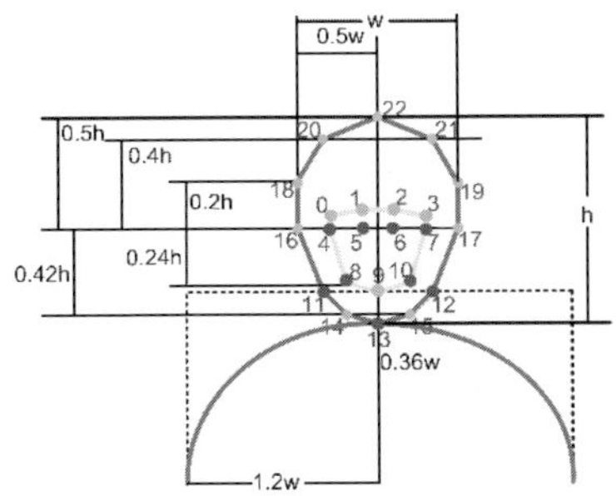

Fig. 1. The head and shoulder mask. The green points are automatically detected and the blue ones are estimated with Candide model; Some length proportions are also labeled, wherein h, w represent the length and width of the face respectively.

3.3 Color Distribution

GMM is a widely used model for the description of color distribution. Based on that, we propose a new model, named multi-GMM, to achieve more robust effect.

When colors in an image are complicated, a single GMM doesn't fit well. As is shown in Fig. 2(b), if we model all the colors with a single GMM, it is significantly inaccurate in the pink region. This would further lead to a poor cut between the foreground and background. In such case, we split the model into 4 separate GMMs, as show in Fig. 2 (c), according to the distances between each Gaussians. In our algorithm, we use this multi-GMM to model the foreground and background color distributions. We firstly employ the algorithm in [17] to determine the proper number of color clusters. Secondly, we group the clusters into multi-GMM. For the initialization of each GMM, we use LBG [22] algorithm, which generates more precise initial value compared to the splitter [20] and k-means [21] methods. Then we apply EM algorithm [11] to get our GMMs.

Sampling all pixels within the mask to construct the multi-GMM is not necessary and results in great mistake since the mask is just a rough estimation of the head shoulder position. To reduce the affection of above problem and decrease the computational complexity for constructing multi-GMM, we adopt the sampling principles as follows. First, in general cases, the central area of the mask and half ellipse should belong to foreground doubtlessly, which is deemed as foreground without sampling (Φ in Fig. 3 (a)). This area is almost worthless for the segmentation. On the contrary, it may bring some false cut patches. Moreover, sampling this region costs a lot to construct the color model. Second, the region near the boundary of the mask and half ellipse is the unknown area (Ω in Fig. 3 (a)). The narrow strip near the boundary will be sampled sparsely while gradually becoming dense away from the boundary; the sampling ratio is lowest on boundary. Third, similar to the central region, the region (Ψ in Fig. 3(a)) near the image border is certainly the background, so its sampling ratio should be low or zero.

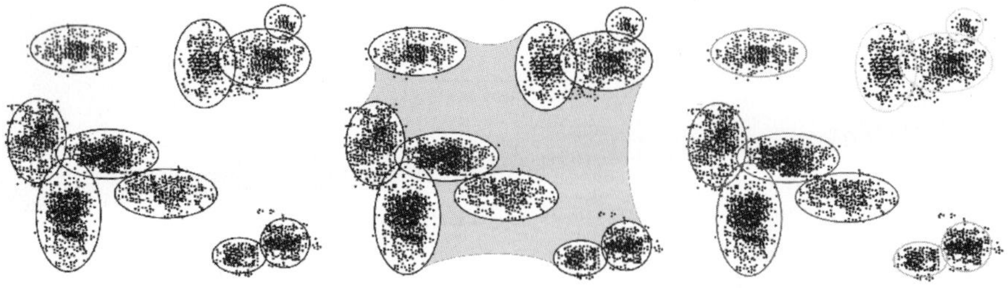

Fig. 2. Multi-GMM. (a) Color clustering; (b) Colors modeled with a single GMM; (c) Colors modeled with multi-GMM, each of which represents a different color.

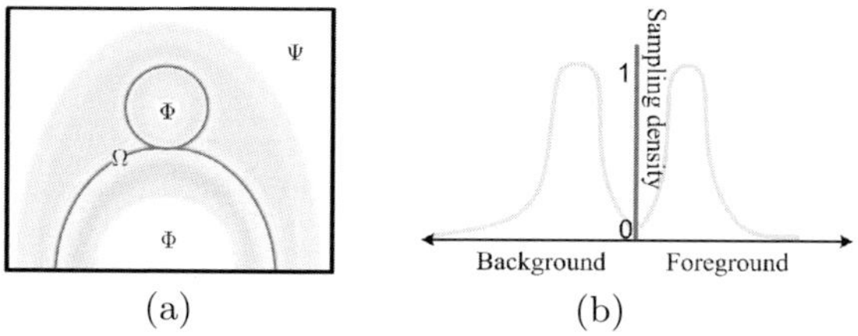

Fig. 3. Pixel sampling principles. (a) The thick yellow and light yellow area represent the high and low sampling area separately, while the blank means non-sampling; (b) visualizes the sample function.

We adopt the probability density function of F-distribution to guide us sampling the foreground/background:

$$P_F = \frac{\Gamma(\frac{m+n}{2})}{\Gamma(\frac{n}{2})\Gamma(\frac{m}{2})} n^{\frac{n}{2}} m^{\frac{m}{2}} \frac{x^{\frac{n}{2}-1}}{(nx+m)^{\frac{m+n}{2}}} \quad (5)$$

where Γ is the Gamma distribution, the parameters m, n determine the sample principle (we set m, n to 10 in our experiment). The gradual changing of sampling ratio is visualized as Fig 3. In (a) the thick yellow area represents a high sampling ratio and the light yellow region is lower, whereas the blank means non-sampling; (b) visualizes the sampling function, reflecting the relation between the sample ratio and the distance of a certain area to the pink boundary.

In addition, we divide the whole interested object into multiple sub-regions, so that we can reduce color cluster number, generate more fitting color model and speed up as well. For head shoulder photos, we divide them into two sub-regions of head and shoulder, in which shoulder mask can be adaptively created based on the head clustered result. While for other special objects, we can divide different number of sub-regions according to its physical structure.

3.4 Image Cutout

With the multi-GMM obtained, an improved Graph cut algorithm is employed to cut out the head and shoulder from the pictures.

For a clear description, we define the pink curve C in Fig. 3 (a) as the contour consisting of the outer edge of the face mask and its adhering half ellipse. We represent the sampled pixel set out of C as P_b, the interior set as P_f. Obviously, for the pixel belonging to P_b , the farther from C, the more probable it is background. The same for the sampled pixel of P_f . This fact is imposed in Graph cut by appending prior weight function to the penalty energy term of the Graph cut objective function.

For a pixel p, $dis(p)$ denotes the Euclidean distance from p to C. If p belongs to P_f, define $D(p) = dis(p)$ as the distance from p to the contour; otherwise, define a negative $D(p) = -dis(p)$ as its oriented distance to C. We adopt a normalized function $W(p, L_p)$ as the prior coefficient with the form:

$$W(p, L_p) = \begin{cases} \frac{1}{\sqrt{2\pi}} \int_{-\infty}^{p} e^{-\frac{x^2}{2}} dx + \frac{1}{2} & , \quad L_p = 0 \\ 1 & , \quad L_p = 1. \end{cases}$$

The Gibbs energy of (1) is modified as:

$$E(L) = W(p, L_p) U(p, L_p, G_p) + V(p, L_p) \tag{6}$$

where $W(p, L_p)$ acts as the intensity to emphasize the constraint of prior knowledge and is valued as the displacement of the distribution function of the standard normal distribution for $L_p = 0$. It takes effect on the background energy or foreground energy. For background energy, if p belongs to P_f, its background energy is reduced, otherwise increased.

$U(p, L_p, G_p)$ derived from $U(p, L_p)$ of (1) is the new penalty energy incorporated with GMM by substituting the pixel's weighted Gaussian distributions: G_p for the color distribution in monochrome image. It can be formulated as:

$$U(p, L_p, G_p) = \lambda \cdot \sum_{p \in P} [-ln(\bigodot_{i=1}^{n} \alpha_i(p) \sum_{j=1}^{l_i} \beta_{ij} G(p, \mu_{ij}, \sigma_{ij}))] \tag{7}$$

in which λ inherited from (1). n represents the number of GMM and l_i means the number of Gaussians contained in ith GMM. The symbol $\bigodot$ represents whether p belongs to ith GMM. In our color multi-GMM distribution, each pixel p only belongs to a GMM in general, assumed as kth ($k \in [1, n]$), then $\alpha_k(p)$ is set to 1, others set to zero. β_j is the coefficient of jth Gaussian's probability weight among ith GMM and is computed by dividing the sample number in jth Gaussian by the pixel number contained in ith GMM.

We adopt an iterative method to solve $E(L)$. It starts with minimizing $E(L)$ with the standard minimal cut algorithm, and regards the cutout result as the initial estimation of the foreground/background for the next iteration. After every iteration, the multi-GMM is applied again to model the color data of the new estimated foreground/background. Since after every iteration the estimated foreground/background becomes more accurate, the iteration is convergent.

For each iteration with our new form of Gibbs energy, the pixels on estimated foreground/background is resampled and clustered by LBG algorithm, then EM optimization is performed. The rules for computing $W(p, L_p)$ holds unchanged, so the distance $D(p)$ for every sample is computed only once.

3.5 Matting

Image matting used to generate soft edges, and is especially useful for transparent objects, such as hair and feathers. We perform Bayesian matting along the hard edges generated with above Graph cut. The unknown area of trimap is generated by dilating along the hard edges with a constant width (we set 12 pixels in our experiments), while interior and exterior strip regions are labeled as foreground and background separately.

Note that, to enhance the efficiency of our algorithm, Graph cut can be implemented on the down-sampled image, whereas the matting algorithm is performed on the original image, which doesn't basically affect the last results in principle.

4 Experimental Results

We have tested our algorithm with 263 normal upright head shoulder pictures with over 70% success ratio on an Intel Pentium IV 2.4GHz PC with 512MB main memory under the Windows XP operating system. The detection costs 1-2 seconds, cutout stage costs 1-3 seconds and matting takes 1-3 seconds.

Fig. 4(b), (e) show the poor cutout results without the constraint of prior weight function $W(p, L_p)$ while solving the objective function $E(L)$. The reason lies in that the color distribution of foreground is similar to its nearby background. (c), (f) are the right cutout results by taking the constraint of prior knowledge into account.

Fig. 5 demonstrates the iterative process of solving $E(L)$. Here we give the cutout result of the head part step by step as (b), (c) and (d). On the other hand, although the facial detection result (a) is not fully exact inducing inaccurate mask, our algorithm can generate proper cutout (e) as well.

Fig. 6 shows the matting effect of the hair. Fig. 7 presents some other examples. Fig. 8 composes a cutout result with a different background smoothly.

A few of the above pictures are fetched from the papers: [2] and [23]. We also selected a few samples from our test library, and submitted them with our prototype system to the online submission web page, the user can implement it and test the pictures according to the user instruction.

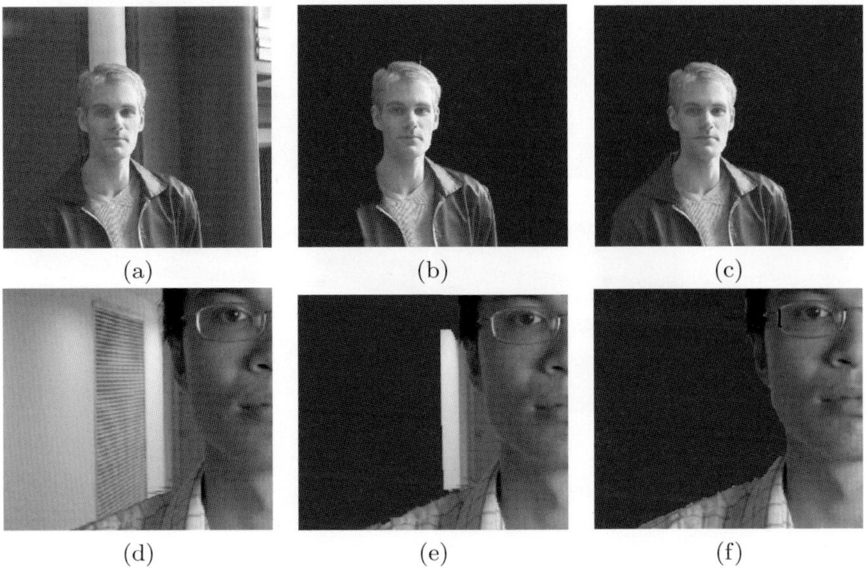

Fig. 4. The constraint of prior knowledge. (a), (d) are the original images; (b), (e) are the cutout results without the constraint of $W(p, L_p)$, (b) loses a few pieces and (e) generates some unwanted patches; (c) (f) are the results taking account of $W(p, L_p)$.

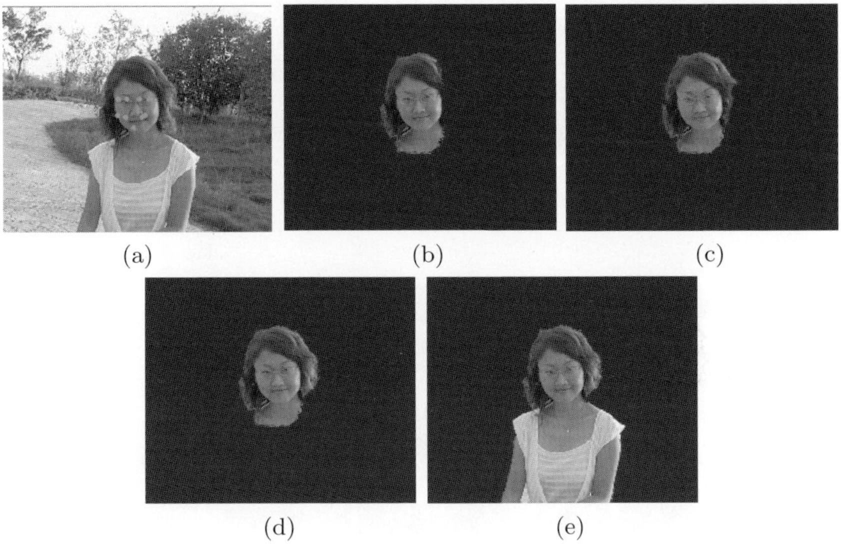

Fig. 5. The process of iteration. (a) The original image with detected feature points; (b), (c) and (d) show the iterative results of head; (e) The last cutout result.

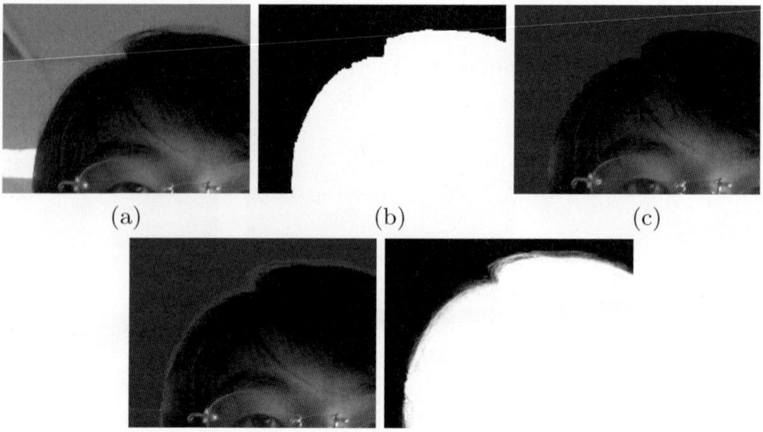

(a) (b) (c) (d) (e)

Fig. 6. Bayes matting. (a) The original image; (b)(c) The cutout matte and result with hard edge; (d)(e) The matting result corresponding to (d).

Fig. 7. Some other results of our algorithm. The upper row shows four original head shoulder pictures and the lower row presents the corresponding cutout results.

(a) (b) (c)

Fig. 8. One cutout and composite example. (a) The original picture; (b) The cutout result; (c) The composite result.

5 Conclusions and Future Work

We have presented a novel approach to automatically extract special object and verified it with head shoulder images. The key point is how to make full use of prior knowledge of the object to estimate the region of interest, model the foreground and background color distributions and implement a robust and rapid Graph cut algorithm. The main advantage of this approach is that it requires no user interactions.

Although initial experiments generated some encouraging results, our approach is not yet robust enough to handle all cases. One main problem is that our face detection algorithm has not considered the cases of rotation and varying of lights, which affects the results sometimes. To resolve this problem and abide this tolerance is a future work. Besides, the speed is not fast enough yet. The extraction process costs 2 to 5 seconds in general. Our future works include the following aspects. The processing, with the GMM construction and Graph cut can be optimized to a real-time speed. We are also doing some research on extraction of the full body. In addition, similar to the head shoulder images, the automatic extraction of other special objects, such as cars, trees, animals, can be applied.

Acknowledgements

This research work is supported by The National Basic Research Program of China (973 Program) under Grant No. 2002CB312101, NSFC under Grant No. 60403038 and Direct Research Grant (No. 2050349).

References

1. Boykov, Y., Jolly, MP. Interactive Graph cuts for Optimal Boundary and Region Segmentation of Objects in N-D Images. In: IEEE International Conference on Computer Vision, pp 105-112 (2001)
2. Rother, C., Kolmogorov, V., Blake, A. Grabcut - Interactive Foreground Extraction Using Iterated Graph cuts. In: ACM SIGGRAPH 2004, pp 309-314 (2004)
3. Li, Y., Sun, J., Tang C., Shum, H. Lazy Snapping. In: ACM SIGGRAPH 2004, pp 303-308 (2004)
4. Kass, M., Witkin, A., Terzolpoulos, D. Snakes: Active Contour Models. International Journal of Computer Vision, Vol. 2, pp 321-331 (1988)
5. Caselles, V., Kimmel, R., Sapiro, G. Geodesic Active Contours. In: IEEE International Conference on Computer Vision, pp 694-699 (1995)
6. Mortensen, EN., and Barrett, WA. Intelligent Scissors for Image Composition. In: ACM SIGGRAPH 95, pp 191-198 (1995)
7. COREL Corporation. *Knockout user guide.* (2002)
8. Chuang, YY., Curless, B., Salesin, D., Szeliski, R. A Bayesian Approach to Digital Matting. In: IEEE Conference on Computer Vision and Pattern Recognition, pp 264-271 (2001)
9. Sun, J., Jia, J., Tang, C., Shum, H. Poisson Matting In: ACM SIGGRAPH 2004, pp 315-321 (2004)

10. Vasconcelos, N., Lippman, A. Embedded Mixture Modeling for Efficient Probabilistic Content-Based Indexing and Retrieval. In: Proc. of SPIE Conf. on Multimedia Storage and Archiving Systems III, Boston, (1998)
11. McLachlan, G., Krishnan, T. The EM Algorithm and Extensions. Wiley Series in Probability and Statisticcs, John Weley & Sons.
12. Lai, ZB., Gao, P., Wang T., et al., Comparison on Bayesian YING-YANG Theory Based Clustering Number Selection Criterion with Information Theoretical Criteria. In: IEEE International Joint Conference on Neural Networks, Anchorage, USA, Vol. 1, pp 725-729 (1985)
13. Geng, X., Zhong, XP., Zhou, XM., Sun, SP., Zhou, ZH. Refining Eye Location Using VPF for Face Detection. In: Proc. of the 3rd Conference of Sinobiometrics, Xi'an China, pp 25-28 (2002)
14. Mandel, ED., Penev, PS., Facial Feature Tracking and Pose Estimation in Video Sequences by Factorial Coding of the Low-Dimensional Entropy Manifolds due to the Partial Symmetrie s of Faces. In: Proc. 25th IEEE Int'l Conf. Acoustics, Speech and Signal Processing (ICASSP 2000), Vol. 4, pp 2345-2348 (2000)
15. Yang, MH., Kriegman, DJ., Ahuja, N. Detecting Faces in Images: A Survey. IEEE Transactions on Pattern Analysis and Machine Intelligence, Vol. 24(1), pp 34-58 (2002)
16. Chua, TS., Zhao, YL., Kankanhalli, MS. Detection of human faces in a compressed domain for video stratification. The Visual Computer, Vol. 18, pp 121-133 (2002)
17. Gao, P., Lyu, MR. A Study on Color Space Selection for Determining Image Segmentation Region Number. In: Proc. of the 2000 International Conference on Artificail Intelligence, Monte Carlo Resort, Las Vegas, Nevada, USA, June 26-29, Vol 3, pp 1127-1132 (2000)
18. Viola, P., Jones, M. Rapid Object Detection using a Boosted Cascade of Simple Features. In: IEEE Conf. on Computer Vision and Pattern Recognition, Kauai, Hawaii, USA, Vol 1, pp 511-518 (2001)
19. Ahlberg, J., Candide-3 – an Updated Parameterized Face. Technical Report LiTH-ISY-R-2326, Linkping University, Sweden, (2001)
20. Senior, A., Hsu, RL., Mottaleb, MA., Jain AK. Face Detection in Color Images. IEEE Computer Society, Vol. 24(5), ISSN:0162-8828, pp 696-706 (2002)
21. MacQueen, JB. Some Methods for classification and Analysis of Multivariate Observations. In: Proc. of 5-th Berkeley Symposium on Mathematical Statistics and Probability, Berkeley, University of California Press, Vol. 1, pp 281-297 (1967)
22. Orchard, MT., Bouman, CA. Color Quantization of Images. IEEE Transactions on Signal Processing, Vol. 39(12), pp 2677-2690 (1991)
23. Chuang, YY., Agarwala, A., Curless, B., Salesin, D., Szeliski, R. Video Matting of Complex Scenes. In: ACM SIGGRAPH 2004, Vol. 21(3), pp 243-248 (2002)

Direct Volume Rendering of Volumetric Protein Data

Min Hu, Wei Chen*, Tao Zhang, and Qunsheng Peng

State Key Lab of CAD & CG, Zhejiang University,
Hangzhou, 310058, China
{humin, chenwei, zhangtao, peng}@cad.zju.edu.cn

Abstract. The visualization of 3D volume data of proteins synthesized by quantum mechanics is a new topic and is of great importance in modern bio-computing. In this paper, we introduce our primary attempts on the volume visualization of the 3D macro-molecular scalar field. Firstly, we transform one protein molecular structure into a regularly sampled 3D scalar field according to the theories in quantum chemistry, in which each node records the combined effect of different actions in protease. We then exploit volume rendering techniques to find the macro-structure inside the data field based on a convenient mapping mechanism. We also propose an improved transfer function mode, facilitating the flexible visualization of the 3D protein data sets. Finally, combined with the iso-surface extraction technique, our approach allows for interactive exploration of the potential "tunnel" region which exhibits biological sense. With our approach, we show the escape route of water molecules hidden in the HIV-1 protease, which conforms to the experimental results.

1 Motivation

One challenging problem in life science is to understand the functions of proteins. Based on the hypothesis that the 3D protein structure uniquely determines its function, researchers try to explore the protein structure for the prediction of its functions. The difficulty in predicting the structure and function of proteins has led to the emergence of numerous approaches. Generally speaking, these methods can be divided into two classes. On one hand, the real structure can be measured by techniques of X-ray crystallography and NMR[9]. 3D structural prediction is accomplished by similarity comparison[4]. However, it can not provide a long dynamic sequence of the underlying proteins due to the limited image resolution. On the other hand, the protein structure can be simulated by many computing techniques[1]. Although the size of protein is within several tens of nanometers, many interesting properties can be faithfully analyzed by quantum mechanics. This scheme can provide dynamic simulation of proteins.

In the last decade, many synthesized protein data became available with the boost of the computing ability. And lots of methods have been developed to achieve the overall electron density distribution of bio-molecules. Visualizing this type of data set is quite helpful for exploring the underlying mechanism of proteins. Note that the

* Corresponding author.

H.-P. Seidel, T. Nishita, and Q. Peng (Eds.): CGI 2006, LNCS 4035, pp. 397 – 403, 2006.

simulation data are usually scalars in 3D space, which can be regarded as a 3D volume data. Although there are several well-established volume visualization approaches for visualizing scalar data, there still exist some practical problems in terms of the domain knowledge of the molecular graphics.

In this paper, we introduce our efforts on visualizing the quantum mechanics simulation data of proteins by direct volume rendering techniques. The main challenges lie in:

1) The data are usually of very small values with dynamic range, such as $[0,10^{-10}]$. Typically, the handling data value in volume rendering should be within the interval of [0,255]. How to automatically adjust the small floating values to be in an appropriate range is an interesting problem.
2) The 3D volumetric data have both negative and positive values, which has special physical significance. Scientists would like to see different parts of them and the crossing region. Thus we need a method to distinguish the different parts automatically.
3) When some portion of the whole data is difficult to be investigated, we need a user-friendly interface to allow the users adjust the parameters for different region of interest (ROI).

The rest of this paper is organized as follows. We will briefly review the related work in Section 2. Our approach and the experimental results are introduced in Section 3. We conclude the whole paper in Section 4.

2 Related Work

With the attempt to explore the complex structures of proteins, researchers have developed several molecular visualization software packages. Graphics visualization tools, such as RasMol[26], VMD[23], PE[25], can interactively display the molecule in a variety of representations. Existing geometric representations include wire-frame bonds, cylinder stick bonds, alpha-carbon trace, space-filling spheres, macromolecular ribbons (either smoothly shaded solid ribbons or parallel strands), hydrogen bonding and point surface representations. These representations provide geometrical and topological information according to the types of atoms and corresponding distance. And they offer biologists a quite good means to intuitively describe the overall shape of molecule, backbone of protein and secondary structures. However, they are not able to provide the whole-scale volume rendering capabilities for synthesized protein data set.

The synthesized protein data by quantum mechanics are inherently a kind of volumetric data set. To efficiently process and visualize these data sets, volume visualization is highly required. There are a number of publications on volume visualization[3][8][21]. Sine 1980s, volume visualization has experienced a development from simple rendering techniques to advanced processing, analysis and data mining. To achieve high quality of direct volume rendering, researchers keep exploring effective transfer functions, especially for semi-automatic and automatic algorithms. Extracting effective volumetric features, such as geometrical and topological properties is one commonly used technique[2][5][6][7][10][12][13][15][17][20]. However, most of them work on medical images directly.

On the contrary, there are much less works dedicated to the visualization of synthesized molecular data. Shigeo *et al*[19] proposed an automatic transfer function in volume visualization by extracting volume skeleton tree, which consists of volumetric critical points and their connectivity. Recently, Qiao *et al*[22] presented a hardware-accelerated direct volume rendering system for visualizing multivariate wave functions in semi-conducting quantum point simulations. Sameep *et al*[18] explored features from electron density data from molecular dynamic simulation by statistical iso-value analysis and designed an effective transfer function to visualize the anomalous structures from regular Si system.

3 Our Approach

Following the quantum chemical theory[11], we transform one protein molecular structure into a regularly sampled 3D scalar field, in which each node records the combined effect of different actions in proteins. The scalar values are usually separated into two parts: positive and negative ones, each possessing special physical meaning. The so-called "nodal surfaces" refers to the region where the wave function crosses zero. Scientists would like sometimes to see the positive region, the negative region, as well as the "nodal surfaces". Thus we need to calculate the two ranges of scalar data falling into the negative and positive number sets respectively. The location of zero is the watershed for the "nodal surfaces". The synthesized data calculated by the wave function for protein molecule are very small and highly dynamic. For instance, the electron density data of HIHIP (High Potential Iron Protein)[20] may fall into the range of $[0,10^{-10}]$. Thus, the first step for viewing the data is to transform the raw data to an appropriate range to color index.

Let V_s denote the whole data set. We adopt the logarithmic function to represent it. As the domain of the logarithmic function should be greater than zero, the mapping should be considered separately as follows:

$$V_S^{'} = f(V_S) = \begin{cases} \log(s) & ; s > 0 \\ 0 & ; s = 0 \\ \log(-s) & ; s < 0 \end{cases}$$

The range of the new volume data $V_s^{'}$ is then mapped into the color range of [0,255]. We assign the red and blue color to positive and negative values respectively which ensures that the two parts besides the "nodal surfaces" is distinguished. We experiment with the HIHIP HOMO orbital data and charge density data from a part of the active site of HIV protease 1A30 in water solution[24]. The size of the former data set is 64×64×64, and the latter is 28×20×20. Fig.1 shows the results of direct volume rendering by ray casting algorithm. The red and blue colors represent positive and negative data respectively, where different distribution of the correspondence physical quantities can be easily watched.

We observed that when rendering the whole data sets, the resulting images become rather confused if there is no appropriate transfer function. It does not work well when we intend to view some important information hidden inside a cluster of data but we

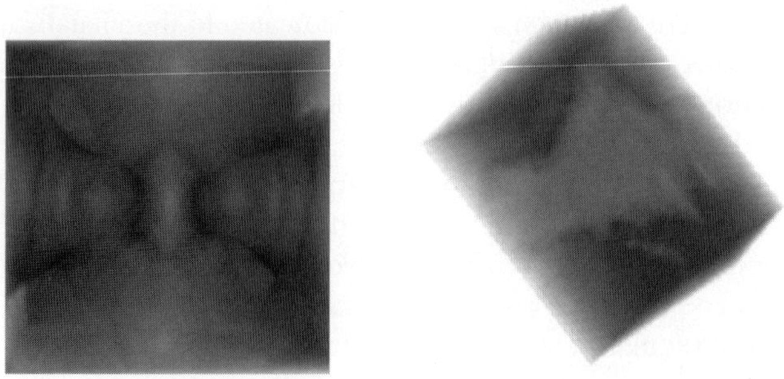

Fig. 1. (left)The rendering result for HIHIP volume data; (right) The rendering result for HIV-1 volume data

do not know where they are, in this case, trial and error will be done. It usually needs to manually adjust opacity transfer function by interactive editing tools painstakingly and inevitably. We simplify this operation when viewing the whole volume as well as a focused region. We design a composite transfer function by combining a global function with a local function. The global transfer function is responsible for viewing the whole range of the data set and the local transfer function makes the salient regions distinct.

Let f_g and f_l denote the global function and local one respectively, then the model of composite function f can be described as:

$$f = \begin{cases} \max(f_g, f_l) & ; \quad if\,(x \in [Sp - w, Sp + w]) \\ f_g & ; \quad otherwise \end{cases}$$

where *Sp* is the location we are interested in and *w* is the local dynamic range. Local information around *Sp* thus can be accentuated without modifying the original global one. The composite transfer function is modified by just moving the slider of *Sp*, which simplifies the interactive operation on transfer function modification.

For the sake of simplicity, we assume that the global function is $f_g = ax + b$; $x \in [0, S_{max}]$, and the local function is a piecewise widget shape function, where $S_{max} = 0.2$, as shown in Fig.2.

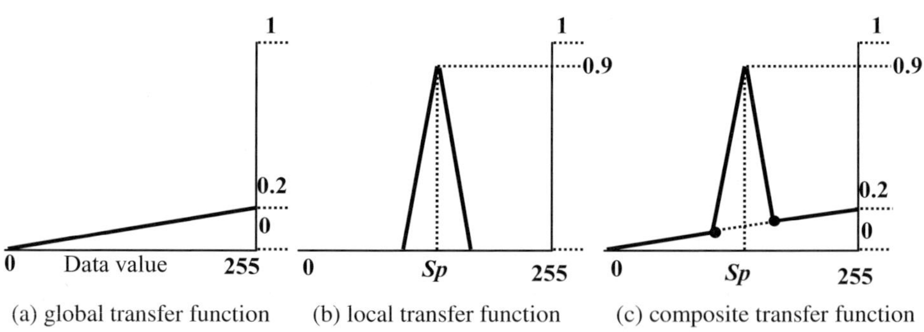

Fig. 2. The combining process of the composite transfer function

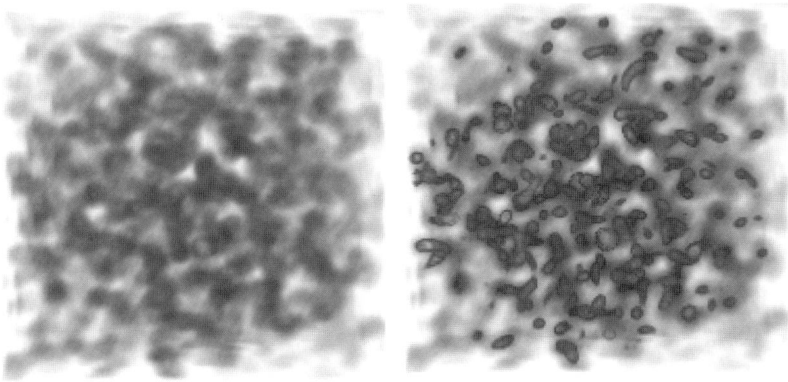

Fig. 3. (left) when applying the global transfer function; (right) when applying the composite transfer function

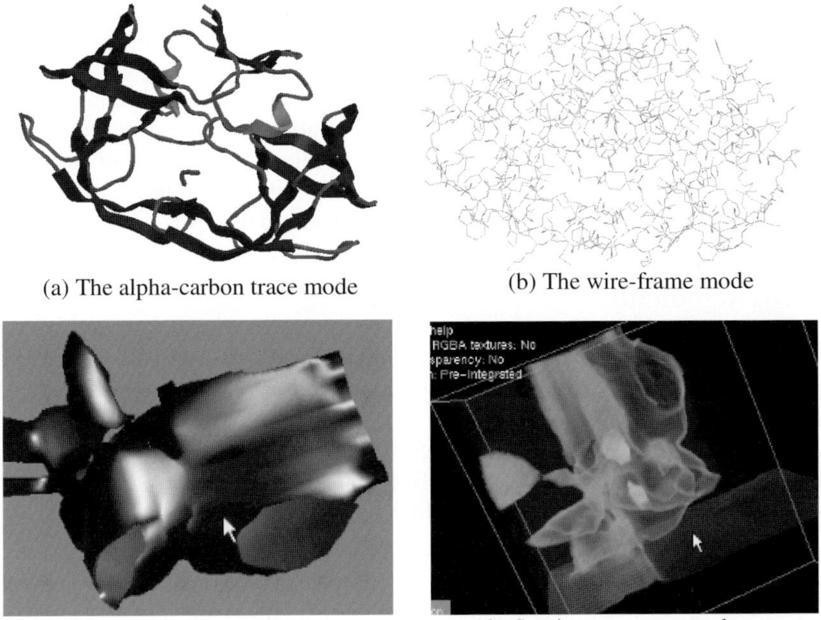

(a) The alpha-carbon trace mode

(b) The wire-frame mode

(c) Iso-surface mode

(d) Semi-transparent mode

Fig. 4. (a-b) Traditional illustrations of the structure data of the HIV-1 protein (drawn by Chem3D); (c-d) The 3D volume rendering results of a part of the active site of HIV-1 protein in water solution

When *Sp* moves within the range of the whole scalar values, we can easily obtain the new opacity transfer function and see the scalar values near Sp. We experiment with the data set of SOD, which is an electron density map of active site of superoxide dismutase enzyme[20], as illustrated in Fig.3. The right picture is rendered by combining the global transfer function used in Fig.3 (left) with a local one, in which teardrop shapes and clumps of atomic density are seen.

We also examined the HIV-1 protease data with the ray casting[16] and 3D texture slicing approach[14] respectively. The first algorithm is used to accomplish the isosurface like volume rendering (Fig.4(c)). We employed the 3D texture slicing approach in a semi-transparent mode (Fig.4(d)). Compared to traditional illustration methods (Fig.4 (a-b)), the visualization results are very useful for the exploration of the spatial energy distribution of the proteins. Specifically, we show the escape route of water molecules hidden in the HIV-1 protease, which conforms to the experimental results[24].

4 Conclusions and Future Work

The 3D volume data of proteins synthesized by quantum mechanics is highly dynamic and contains negative and positive values. Their visualization is of great importance in modern bio-computing. In this paper, we introduce a convenient mapping mechanism to support efficient direct volume rendering of these data sets. We propose an improved transfer function mode, resulting in flexible visualization of the 3D protein data sets.

There are higher requirements on exploring the underlying relationship between protein structure and function. Detection and visualization of useful features hidden behind the synthesized data is one challenging problem. As a result of our initial effort, we envision to research on the domain associated visualization techniques and to develop new data mining methods for protein simulation data.

Acknowledgements

We would like to express our best acknowledgements to Dr.Tao Wu and Prof.Qi Wang for their cooperation on the molecular simulation. We also thank to the anonymous reviewers for their helpful comments. This paper is supported by National Science Fund Key Project of China under grant No. 60533050, National Science Fund Project of China under grant No. 60503056 and National Natural Science Funds of China for Innovative Research Groups under grant No.60021201.

References

[1] A.R.Leach, Molecular Modelling Principles and Applications, Prentice Hall, 2001.

[2] C. Bajaj, V.Pascucci, D.Schikore, The Contour Spectrum, Proceedings of the 1997 IEEE Visualization Conference, 167-173.

[3] Chris Johnson, Top Scientific Visualization Research Problems, IEEE Computer Graphics and Applications, 24(4), 13-17, 2004.

[4] C.Stan, Tsai, An introduction to computational biochemistry, Wiley-Liss, Inc. New York, 2002.

[5] Dieter Hoenigmann, Johannes Ruisz, Christoph Haider, Adaptive Design of a Global Opacity Transfer Function for Direct Volume Rendering of Ultrasound Data, 489-496, IEEE Visualization 2003, Seattle, Washington, USA.

[6] Gordon Kindlmann, Ross Whitaker, Tolga Tasdizen , Torsten Moeller, Curvature-Based Transfer Functions for Direct Volume Rendering: Methods and Applications, IEEE Visualization 2003, 513-520, Seattle, Washington, USA.

[7] Gordon Kindlmann and J. W. Durkin, Semi-Automatic Generation of Transfer Functions for Direct Volume Rendering, Proceedings of the 1998 Symposium on Volume visualization, 79-86.

[8] Guido Gerig, Gordon Kindlemann, *et al*, Image Processing for Volume Graphics, A Course for SIGGRAPH 2002.

[9] H.M. Berman, J. Westbrook, Z. Feng, G. Gilliland, T.N. Bhat, H. Weissig, I.N. Shindyalov, P.E. Bourne: The Protein Data Bank. Nucleic Acids Research, 28 pp. 235-242, 2000.

[10] Hanspeter Pfister, Bill Lorensen, Chandrajit Bajaj, Gordon Kindlmann, The Transfer Function Bake-Off, IEEE Computer Graphics and Applications, 21(3), 16-22, 2001.

[11] IRA N.LEVINE, Quantum Chemistry, PRENTICE HALL, 2004.

[12] Joe Kniss, Gordon Kindlmann,Charles Hansen, Multidimensional Transfer Functions for Interactive Volume Rendering, IEEE TRANSACTIONS ON VISUALIZATION AND COMPUTER GRAPHICS, 8(3), 270-285, JULY-SEPTEMBER 2002.

[13] Joe Kniss, Simon Premoˇze, Milan Ikits, Aaron Lefohn, etc. , Gaussian Transfer Functions for Multi-Field Volume Visualization, IEEE Visualization 2003, 497-504, Seattle, Washington, USA.

[14] K.Engel, M.Kraus, T.Ertl High-Quality Pre-Integrated Volume Rendering Using Hardware-Accelerated Pixel Shading. Eurographics/SIGGRAPH Workshop on Graphics Hardware 2001.

[15] Kniss, J.M.; Van Uitert, R.; Stephens, A.; Guo-Shi Li; Tasdizen, T., Statistically Quantitative Volume Visualization, 287- 294, IEEE Visualization 2005, Minneapolis, USA.

[16] M.Levoy. Display of Surfaces from Volume Data. IEEE CG & A, 8(5), 29-37,. May 1988.

[17] Nicoletti, G.M., Volume visualization: advances in transfer and opacity function generation for interactive direct volume rendering, Proceedings of the Thirty-Sixth Southeastern Symposium on System Theory, 1 – 5, 2004

[18] Sameep Mehta, Kaden Hazzard, Raghu Machiraju, Detection and Visualization of Anomalous Structures in Molecular Dynamics Simulation Data, IEEE Visualization 2004, 465-472, Texas, USA.

[19] Shigeo Takahashi, Yuriko Takeshima and Issei Fujishiro, Topological volume skeletonization and its application to transfer function design, Graphical Models , 66 , 24–49, 2004.

[20] Simeon Potts, Torsten Möller, Transfer Functions on a Logarithmic Scale for Volume Rendering, Proceedings of Graphics Interfaces 2004, 57-63, May, London, Ontario.

[21] T. Todd Elvins, A Survey of Algorithms for Volume Visualization, Computer Graphics , 26(3), 194-201, August 1992.

[22] Wei Qiao; Ebert, D.S.; Entezari, A.; Korkusinski, M.; Klimeck, G. , VolQD: Direct Volume Rendering of Multi-million Atom Quantum Dot Simulations, IEEE Visualization 2005, 319- 326, October, inneapolis, MN, USA.

[23] William Humphrey, Andrew Dalke and Klaus Schulten , VMD - Visual Molecular Dynamics. Journal of Molecular Graphics, 14(1):33-38, 1996.

[24] Wu Tao, Personal Communication.

[25] Weblink:http://molvis.sdsc.edu/protexpl/frntdoor.htm. Last visiting data: 2006-1-12.

[26] Weblink:http://www.rasmol.org/. Last visiting data: 2006-1-12.

Subdivision Depth Computation for Extra-Ordinary Catmull-Clark Subdivision Surface Patches

Fuhua (Frank) Cheng[1], Gang Chen[1], and Jun-Hai Yong[2]

[1] University of Kentucky, Lexington, KY, USA
[2] Tsinghua University, Beijing, China

Abstract. A second order forward differences based subdivision depth computation technique for extra-ordinary Catmull-Clark subdivision surface (CCSS) patches is presented. The new technique improves a previous technique in that the computation of the subdivision depth is based on the patch's curvature distribution, instead of its dimension. Hence, with the new technique, no excessive subdivision is needed for extra-ordinary CCSS patches to meet the precision requirement and, consequently, one can make trimming, finite element mesh generation, boolean operations, and tessellation of CCSSs more efficient.

1 Introduction

Research work for subdivision surfaces has been done in several important areas, such as surface parametrization [6][10][11][14], surface trimming [7], boolean operations [1], mesh editing [13], and *error estimate/control* [3][12]. For instance, given an error tolerance, [3] shows how many times the control mesh of a Catmull-Clark subdivision surface (CCSS) patch should be recursively subdivided so that the distance between the resulting control mesh and the *limit surface patch* would be less than the error tolerance. This error control technique, called *subdivision depth computation*, is required in all tessellation based applications of CCSSs. [3]'s subdivision depth computation technique for regular CCSS patches is optimum. However, for an extra-ordinary CCSS patch (a patch with an extra-ordinary vertex), since the subdivision depth computed by [3] depends on first order forward differences of the control points, its value could be bigger than what it actually should be and, consequently, generates excessive mesh elements for regions that are already flat enough.

In this paper we will present a new subdivision depth computation technique for extra-ordinary CCSS patches. The new technique is based on the second order forward differences of an extra-ordinary patch's control points.. The computed subdivision depth reflects the patch's curvature distribution, not its dimension. Hence, with the new technique, no excessive subdivision is needed for regions that are already flat enough and, consequently, trimming, finite element mesh generation, boolean operations, and tessellation of CCSSs can be made more efficient.

H.-P. Seidel, T. Nishita, and Q. Peng (Eds.): CGI 2006, LNCS 4035, pp. 404–416, 2006.

2 Problem Formulation and Background

Given the control mesh of an extra-ordinary CCSS patch and an error tolerance ϵ, the goal here is to compute an integer d so that if the control mesh is iteratively refined (subdivided) d times, then the distance between the resulting mesh and the surface patch is smaller than ϵ. d is called the *subdivision depth* of the surface patch with respect to ϵ. Before we show the computation technique, we need to define related terms and review related techniques for regular CCSS patches.

2.1 Catmull-Clark Subdivision Surfaces

Given a control mesh, a CCSS is generated by iteratively refining (subdividing) the control mesh to form new control meshes [2]. The refining process consists of defining new vertices (*face points*, *edge points* and *vertex points*) and connecting the new vertices to form new edges and faces of a new control mesh. The limit surface of the iteratively refined control meshes is called a *subdivision surface* because the mesh refining (subdivision) process is a generalization of the uniform bicubic B-spline surface subdivision technique. Therefore, CCSSs include uniform B-spline surfaces and piecewise Bézier surfaces as special cases. Actually CCSSs include non-uniform B-spline surfaces and NURBS surfaces as special cases as well [9]. The control mesh of a CCSS patch and the new control mesh after a refining (subdivision) process are shown in Figures 1(a) and (b), respectively. This is a conceptual drawing, the location shown for a new vertex might not be its exact physical location.

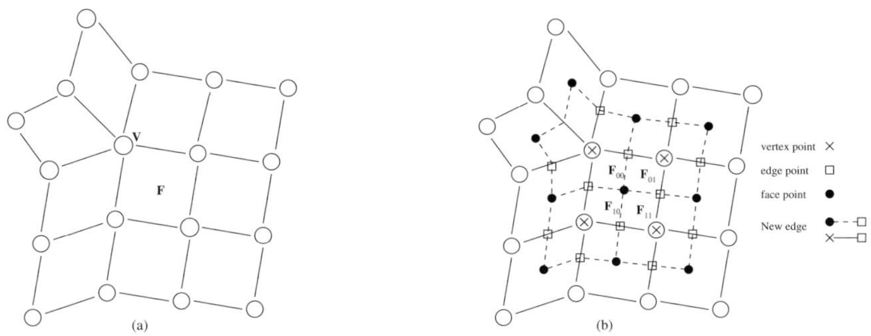

Fig. 1. (a) Control mesh of an extra-ordinary patch; (b) new vertices and edges generated after a Catmull-Clark subdivision

The given control mesh will be referred to as $\mathbf{M}_0$ and the limit surface will be referred to as $\bar{\mathbf{S}}$. For each positive integer k, $\mathbf{M}_k$ refers to the control mesh obtained after applying the Catmull-Clark subdivision k times to $\mathbf{M}_0$.

The power of CCSSs comes from the way mesh vertices are connected. If the number of edges connected to a mesh vertex is called its *valence*, then the valence of an interior mesh vertex can be anything ≥ 3, instead of just four. Those mesh vertices whose valences are different from four are called *extra-ordinary vertices* to distinguish them from the *standard* or *regular mesh vertices*. Vertex **V** in Figure 1(a) is an extra-ordinary vertex of valence five. An interior mesh face is called an *extra-ordinary mesh face* if it has an extra-ordinary vertex. Otherwise, a *standard* or *regular mesh face*. Mesh face **F** in Figure 1(a) is an extra-ordinary mesh face. we assume all the mesh faces in $\mathbf{M}_0$ are quadrilaterals and each mesh face of $\mathbf{M}_0$ has at most one extra-ordinary vertex. Otherwise, simply perform the subdivision step twice on the given control mesh.

For each interior face **F** of $\mathbf{M}_k$, $k \geq 0$, there is a corresponding patch **S** in the limit surface $\bar{\mathbf{S}}$. **F** and **S** can be parametrized on the same parameter space $\Omega = [0,\ 1] \times [0,\ 1]$ [10]. **F** is a bilinear *rule surface*. **S** is a uniform bicubic B-spline surface patch if **F** is a regular face. However, if **F** is an extra-ordinary face then **S**, defined by $2n + 8$ control points where n is the valence of **F**'s extra-ordinary vertex, can not be parametrized as a uniform B-spline patch. In such a case, **S** is called an *extra-ordinary patch*. Otherwise, a *regular patch* or *standard patch*. The control mesh shown in Figure 1(a) is the control mesh of an extra-ordinary patch whose extra-ordinary vertex is of valence five.

2.2 Distance and Subdivision Depth

For a given interior mesh face **F**, let **S** be the corresponding patch in the limit surface $\bar{\mathbf{S}}$. The control mesh of **S** contains **F** as the center face. If we perform a subdivision step on the control mesh, we get four new mesh faces in the place of **F**. This is the case no matter **F** is a regular face or an extra-ordinary face (see Figure 1(b) for the four new faces $\mathbf{F}_{00}$, $\mathbf{F}_{10}$, $\mathbf{F}_{01}$ and $\mathbf{F}_{11}$ obtained in the place of the extra-ordinary face **F** shown in Figure 1(a)). Since each of these new faces corresponds to a quarter subpatch of **S**, we shall call these new faces *subfaces* of **F** even though they are not pyhsically subsets of **F**. Therefore, each subdivision step generates four new subfaces for the center face **F** of the control mesh. Because the correspondence between **F** and **S** is one-to-one, sometime, instead of saying performing a subdivision step on **S**, we shall simply say performing a subdivision step on **F**.

The *distance* between an interior mesh face **F** and the corresponding patch **S** is defined as the maximum of $\|\mathbf{F}(u,v) - \mathbf{S}(u,v)\|$:

$$D_{\mathbf{F}} = max_{(u,v)\in\Omega} \|\mathbf{F}(u,v) - \mathbf{S}(u,v)\| \tag{1}$$

where Ω is the unit square parameter space of **F** and **S**. $D_{\mathbf{F}}$ is also called the distance between **S** and its control mesh. For a given $\epsilon > 0$, the *subdivision depth* of **F** with respect to ϵ is a positive integer d such that if **F** is recursively subdivided d times, the distance between each of the resulting subfaces and the corresponding subpatch is smaller than zero.

2.3 Subdivision Depth Computation for Regular Patches

A regular patch is a standard uniform bicubic B-spline surface patch. Therefore, the computation process for a regular patch is the same as the computation process for a standard uniform B-spline surface patch. We review the evaluation of the distance between a B-spline patch and its control mesh first.

Distance Evaluation. Let $\mathbf{S}(u,v)$ be a uniform bicubic B-spline surface patch defined on the unit square $\Omega = [0,1] \times [0,1]$ with control points $\mathbf{V}_{i,j}$, $0 \leq i,j \leq 3$, and let $\mathbf{L}(u,v)$ be the bilinear parametrization of the center mesh face $\{\mathbf{V}_{1,1}, \mathbf{V}_{2,1}, \mathbf{V}_{2,2}, \mathbf{V}_{1,2}\}$ (see Figure 2):

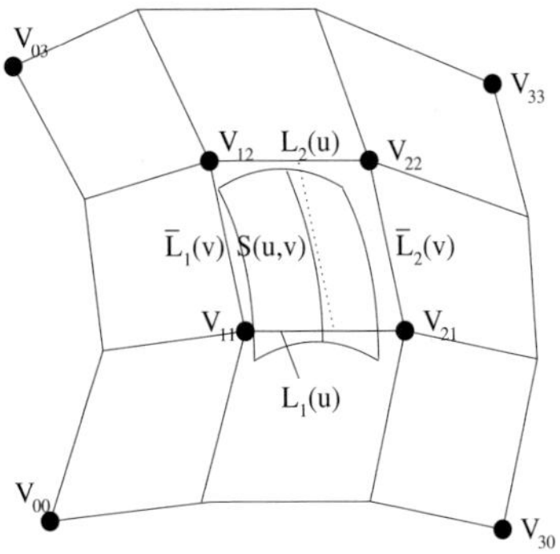

Fig. 2. Definition of $\mathbf{L}(u,v) = (1-v)\mathbf{L}_1(u) + v\mathbf{L}_2(u) = (1-u)\bar{\mathbf{L}}_1(v) + u\bar{\mathbf{L}}_2(v)$

$$\mathbf{L}(u,v) = (1-v)[(1-u)\mathbf{V}_{1,1} + u\mathbf{V}_{2,1}] + v[(1-u)\mathbf{V}_{1,2} + u\mathbf{V}_{2,2}], \quad 0 \leq u,v \leq 1.$$

The distance between $\mathbf{S}(u,v)$ and $\mathbf{L}(u,v)$ satisfies the following lemma [3].

Lemma 1. The distance between $\mathbf{L}(u,v)$ and $\mathbf{S}(u,v)$ satisfies the following inequality

$$\max_{0 \leq u,v \leq 1} \|\mathbf{L}(u,v) - \mathbf{S}(u,v)\| \leq \frac{1}{3}M$$

where M is the second order norm of $\mathbf{S}(u,v)$ defined as follows

$$M = \max_{i,j}\{\ \|2\mathbf{V}_{i,j} - \mathbf{V}_{i-1,j} - \mathbf{V}_{i+1,j}\|,\ \|2\mathbf{V}_{i,j} - \mathbf{V}_{i,j-1} - \mathbf{V}_{i,j+1}\|\ \} \tag{2}$$

Recurrence Formula for Second Order Norm. Let $\mathbf{V}_{i,j}$, $0 \leq i,j \leq 3$, be the control points of a uniform bicubic B-spline surface patch $\mathbf{S}(u,v)$. We use $\mathbf{V}^k_{i,j}$ to represent the new control points of the surface patch after k levels of recursive subdivision. The indexing of the new control points follows the convention that $\mathbf{V}^k_{0,0}$ is always the *face point* of the mesh face $\{\mathbf{V}^{k-1}_{0,0}, \mathbf{V}^{k-1}_{1,0}, \mathbf{V}^{k-1}_{1,1}, \mathbf{V}^{k-1}_{0,1}\}$. The new control points $\mathbf{V}^k_{ij}$ are called the *level-k control points* of $\mathbf{S}(u,v)$ and the new control mesh will be called the *level-k control mesh* of $\mathbf{S}(u,v)$.

If we divide the parameter space of the surface patch, Ω, into 4^k regions as follows:

$$\Omega^k_{mn} = [\frac{m}{2^k}, \frac{m+1}{2^k}] \times [\frac{n}{2^k}, \frac{n+1}{2^k}], \qquad 0 \leq m,n \leq 2^k - 1$$

and denote the corresponding subpatches $\mathbf{S}^k_{mn}(u,v)$, then each $\mathbf{S}^k_{mn}(u,v)$ is a uniform bicubic B-spline surface patch defined by the level-k control point set

$\{\mathbf{V}_{pq}^k \mid m \leq p \leq m+3, n \leq q \leq n+3\}$. $\mathbf{S}_{mn}^k(u,v)$ is called a *level-k subpatch* of $\mathbf{S}(u,v)$. Let $\mathbf{L}_{mn}^k(u,v)$ be the bilinear parametrization of the center face of $\mathbf{S}_{mn}^k$'s control mesh, $\{\mathbf{V}_{pq}^k \mid p = m+1, m+2; q = n+1, n+2\}$. We say the *distance between* $\mathbf{S}(u,v)$ *and the level-k control mesh is smaller than* ϵ if the distance between each level-k subpatch $\mathbf{S}_{mn}^k(u,v)$ and the corresponding level-k bilinear plane $\mathbf{L}_{mn}^k(u,v)$, $0 \leq m, n \leq 2^k - 1$, is smaller than ϵ. A technique to compute a subdivision depth k for a given ϵ so that the distance between $\mathbf{S}(u,v)$ and the level-k control mesh is smaller than ϵ is presented in [3]. The following lemma is needed in the derivation of the computation process. If we use M_{mn}^k to represent the second order norm of $\mathbf{S}_{mn}^k(u,v)$, i.e., the maximum norm of the second order forward differences of the control points of $\mathbf{S}_{mn}^k(u,v)$, then the lemma shows the second order norm of $\mathbf{S}_{mn}^k(u,v)$ converges at a rate of $1/4$ of the level-$(k-1)$ second order norm [3].

Lemma 2. If M_{mn}^k is the second order norm of $\mathbf{S}_{mn}^k(u,v)$ then we have

$$M_{mn}^k \leq \left(\frac{1}{4}\right)^k M \tag{3}$$

where M is the second order norm of $\mathbf{S}(u,v)$ defined in (2).

Subdivision Depth Computation. With Lemmas 1 and 2, it is easy to see that, for any $0 \leq m, n \leq 2^{k-1}$, we have

$$\max_{0 \leq u,v \leq 1} \|\mathbf{L}_{mn}^k(u,v) - \mathbf{S}_{mn}^k(u,v)\| \leq \frac{1}{3} M_{mn}^k \leq \frac{1}{3}\left(\frac{1}{4}\right)^k M \tag{4}$$

where M_{mn}^k and M are the second order norms of $\mathbf{S}_{mn}^k(u,v)$ and $\mathbf{S}(u,v)$, respectively. Hence, if k is large enough to make the right side of the above inequality smaller than ϵ, we have

$$\max_{0 \leq u,v \leq 1} \|\mathbf{L}_{mn}^k(u,v) - \mathbf{S}_{mn}^k(u,v)\| \leq \epsilon$$

for every $0 \leq m, n \leq 2^{k-1}$. This leads to the following subdivision depth computation process for a regular CCSS patch [3].

Theorem 3. Let $\mathbf{V}_{ij}$, $0 \leq i, j \leq 3$, be the control points of a uniform bicubic B-spline surface patch $\mathbf{S}(u,v)$. For any given $\epsilon > 0$, if

$$k \geq \lceil \log_4\left(\frac{M}{3\epsilon}\right) \rceil$$

levels of recursive subdivision are performed on the control points of $\mathbf{S}(u,v)$ then the distance between $\mathbf{S}(u,v)$ and the level-k control mesh is smaller than ϵ where M is the second order norm of $\mathbf{S}(u,v)$ defined in (2).

3 Subdivision Depth Computation for Extra-Ordinary Patches

In the following, we will define second order forward difference patterns to be used for an extra-ordinary patch and derive a recurrence formula for the corresponding second order norm, like the one used for a regular patch in Section 2.

3.1 Second Order Norm and Recurrence Formula

Let $\mathbf{V}_i$, $i = 1, 2, ..., 2n + 8$, be the control points of an extra-ordinary patch $\mathbf{S}(u, v) = \mathbf{S}_0^0(u, v)$, with $\mathbf{V}_1$ being an extra-ordinary vertex of valence n. The control points are ordered following J. Stam's fashion [10] (Figure 3(a)). For convenience of subsequent reference, we shall call the control mesh of $\mathbf{S}(u, v)$ $\Pi = \Pi_0^0$. By performing a subdividion step on Π, one gets $2n + 17$ new vertices $\mathbf{V}_i^1$, $i = 1, ..., 2n + 17$ (see Figure 3(b)). These control points form four control point sets Π_0^1, Π_1^1, Π_2^1 and Π_3^1, representing control meshes of the subpatches $\mathbf{S}_0^1(u, v)$, $\mathbf{S}_1^1(u, v)$, $\mathbf{S}_2^1(u, v)$ and $\mathbf{S}_3^1(u, v)$, respectively (see Figure 3(b)) where $\Pi_0^1 = \{\mathbf{V}_i^1 \mid 1 \le i \le 2n + 8\ \}$, and the other three control point sets Π_1^1, Π_2^1 and Π_3^1 are shown in Figure 4. $\mathbf{S}_0^1(u, v)$ is an extra-ordinary patch but $\mathbf{S}_1^1(u, v)$, $\mathbf{S}_2^1(u, v)$ and $\mathbf{S}_3^1(u, v)$ are regular patches. Therefore, second order norm similar to (2) can be defined for $\mathbf{S}_1^1$, $\mathbf{S}_2^1$ and $\mathbf{S}_3^1$.

To define a second order norm for $\mathbf{S}$, one needs to choose appropriate second order forward differences from Π. For the second order norm to be recursively defined, second order forward differences that are required in the child control meshes should also appear in the parent control mesh. For instance, $2\mathbf{V}_1 - \mathbf{V}_4 - \mathbf{V}_8$ and $2\mathbf{V}_1 - \mathbf{V}_2 - \mathbf{V}_6$ should be chosen for Π because these patterns are required for Π_1^1 and Π_3^1, respectively. On the other hand, for a recurrence formula to hold effectively, second order forward differences that are not required in the child control meshes should not be used in the parent control mesh either.. For instance, one should not choose $2\mathbf{V}_1 - \mathbf{V}_2 - \mathbf{V}_8$ for Π because this pattern is not required in any of Π_1^1, Π_2^1 or Π_3^1. Therefore, for those cases that involves the extra-ordinary point $\mathbf{V}_1$ as the center point, one should only consider

$$2\mathbf{V}_1 - \mathbf{V}_{2i} - \mathbf{V}_{2(i\%n+2)}, \qquad 1 \le i \le n. \tag{5}$$

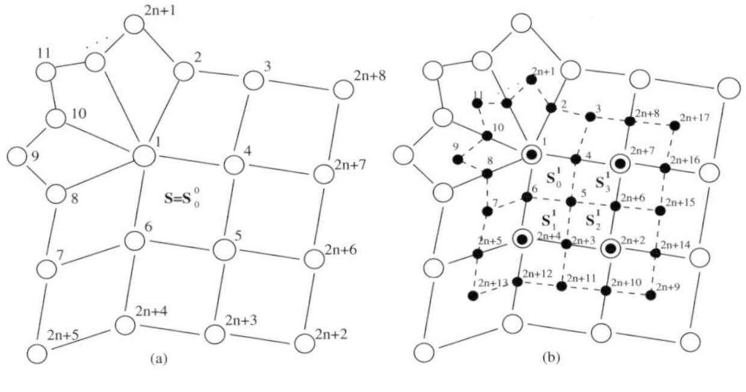

Fig. 3. (a) Ordering of control points of an extra-ordinary patch. (b) Ordering of new control points (solid dots) after a Catmull-Clark subdivision.

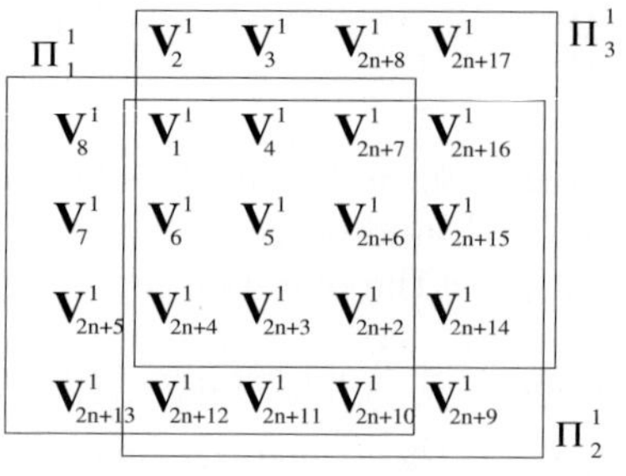

Fig. 4. Control vertices of subpatches $\mathbf{S}_1^1$, $\mathbf{S}_2^1$ and $\mathbf{S}_3^1$

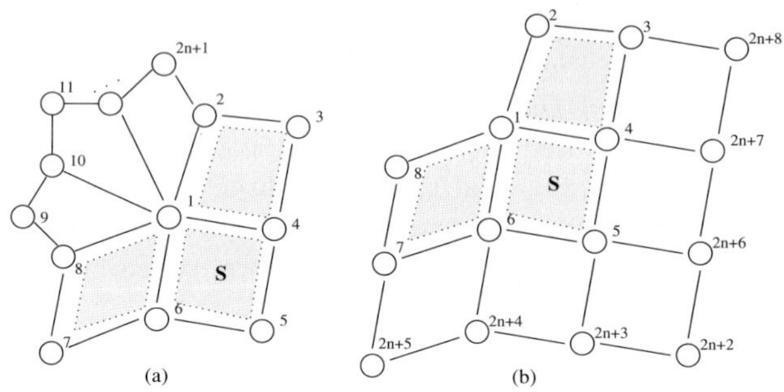

Fig. 5. (a) Vicinity of the extra-ordinary point. (b) The extended remaining part.

To ensure the boundary of the vicinity of the extra-ordinary point is covered (Figure 5(a)), one should consider

$$2\mathbf{V}_{2(i\%n+1)} - \mathbf{V}_{2i+1} - \mathbf{V}_{2(i\%n+1)+1}, \qquad 1 \le i \le n. \tag{6}$$

One also has to consider second order forward differences that cover the extended remaining part (Figure 5(b)). There are ten of them (actually twelve, but two of them have been used in (6)). So, totally, $2n + 10$ ($n + 10$ when $n = 3$) second order forward differences should be considered for Π and the *second order norm* of $\mathbf{S}$, $M = M_0$, is defined as the maximum norm of these $2n + 10$ second order forward differences:

$$\begin{aligned}
M = max\{ &\{ \|2\mathbf{V}_1 - \mathbf{V}_{2i} - \mathbf{V}_{2(i\%n+2)}\| \mid 1 \le i \le n \} \cup \\
&\{ \|2\mathbf{V}_{2(i\%n+1)} - \mathbf{V}_{2i+1} - \mathbf{V}_{2(i\%n+1)+1}\| \mid 1 \le i \le n \} \cup \\
&\{ \| 2V_3 - V_2 - V_{2n+8} \|, \| 2V_4 - V_1 - V_{2n+7} \|, \| 2V_5 - V_6 - V_{2n+6} \|, \\
&\| 2V_5 - V_4 - V_{2n+3} \|, \| 2V_6 - V_1 - V_{2n+4} \|, \| 2V_7 - V_8 - V_{2n+5} \|, \\
&\| 2V_{2n+7} - V_{2n+6} - V_{2n+8} \|, \| 2V_{2n+6} - V_{2n+2} - V_{2n+7} \|, \\
&\| 2V_{2n+3} - V_{2n+2} - V_{2n+4} \|, \| 2V_{2n+4} - V_{2n+3} - V_{2n+5} \| \} \}
\end{aligned} \tag{7}$$

Following this definition, one can define a similar second order norm, M_1, for the control mesh of $\mathbf{S}_0^1$. In general, for any $k \geq 0$, we can define second order norm similar to (7) for $\mathbf{S}_0^k$ and $\mathbf{S}_0^{k+1}$. The second order norms of $\mathbf{S}_0^k$ and $\mathbf{S}_0^{k+1}$ are denoted M_k and M_{k+1}, respectively. We have the following lemma for M_k and M_{k+1}. The proof is shown in the complete version of the paper [4].

Lemma 4. For any $k \geq 0$, if M_k represents the second order norm of the extra-ordinary sub-patch $\mathbf{S}_0^k$ after k Catmull-Clark subdivision steps, then M_k satisfies the following inequality

$$M_{k+1} \leq \begin{cases} \frac{2}{3} M_k, & n = 3 \\ 0.72 M_k, & n = 5 \\ (\frac{3}{4} + \frac{8n-46}{4n^2}) M_k, & n > 5 \end{cases}$$

Actually, the lemma works in a more general sense, i.e., if M_k stands for the second order norm of the control mesh $\mathbf{M}_k$, instead of Π_0^k, the lemma still works. The second order norm of $\mathbf{M}_k$ is defined as follows: for regions not involving the extra-ordinary point, use standard second order forward differences; for the vicinity of the extra-ordinary point, use second order forward differences defined in (7). The proof is essentially the same.

3.2 Distance Evaluation

To compute the distance between the extra-ordinary patch $\mathbf{S}(u, v)$ and the center face of its control mesh, $\mathbf{L}(u, v)$, we need to parameterize the patch $\mathbf{S}(u, v)$ first.

Note that by iteratively performing Catmull-Clark subdivision on $\mathbf{S}(u, v)$, we get a sequence of regular patches $\{ \mathbf{S}_b^m \}$, $m \geq 1$, $b = 1, 2, 3$, and a sequence of extra-ordinary patches $\{ \mathbf{S}_0^m \}$, $m \geq 1$. The extra-ordinary patches converge to a limit point which is the value of $\mathbf{S}$ at $(0, 0)$ [5]. This limit point and the regular patches $\{ \mathbf{S}_b^m \}$, $m \geq 1$, $b = 1, 2, 3$, form a partition of $\mathbf{S}$. If we use Ω_b^m to represent the parameter space corresponding to $\mathbf{S}_b^m$ then $\{ \Omega_b^m \}$, $m \geq 1$, $b = 1, 2, 3$, form a partition of the unit square $\Omega = [0, 1] \times [0, 1]$ (see Figure 6) with

$$\begin{aligned} &\Omega_1^m = [\tfrac{1}{2^m}, \tfrac{1}{2^{m-1}}] \times [0, \tfrac{1}{2^m}], \qquad \Omega_2^m = [\tfrac{1}{2^m}, \tfrac{1}{2^{m-1}}] \times [\tfrac{1}{2^m}, \tfrac{1}{2^{m-1}}], \\ &\Omega_3^m = [0, \tfrac{1}{2^m}] \times [\tfrac{1}{2^m}, \tfrac{1}{2^{m-1}}]. \end{aligned} \tag{8}$$

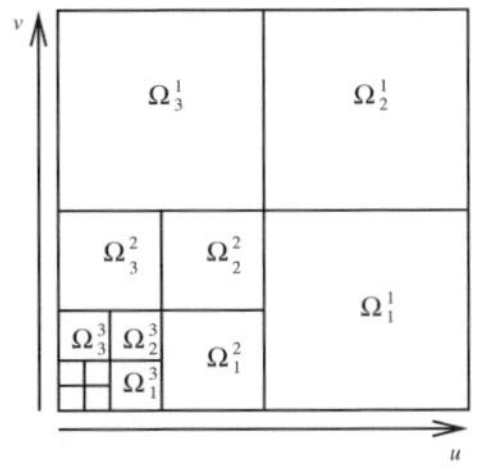

Fig. 6. Ω-partition of the unit square

The parametrization of $\mathbf{S}(u,v)$ is done as follows. For any $(u,v) \in \Omega$ but $(u,v) \neq (0,0)$, first find the Ω_b^m that contains (u,v). m and b can be computed as follows.

$$m(u,v) = \min\{\lceil log_{\frac{1}{2}} u\rceil,\ \lceil log_{\frac{1}{2}} v\rceil\}$$
$$b(u,v) = \begin{cases} 1, & if\ 2^m u \geq 1\ and\ 2^m v \leq 1 \\ 2, & if\ 2^m u \geq 1\ and\ 2^m v \geq 1 \\ 3, & if\ 2^m u \leq 1\ and\ 2^m v \geq 1 \end{cases} \tag{9}$$

Then map this Ω_b^m to the unit square with the mapping: $(u,v) \rightarrow (u_m, v_m)$ where

$$t_m = (2^m t)\%1 = \begin{cases} 2^m t, & if\ \ 2^m t \leq 1 \\ 2^m t - 1, & if\ \ 2^m t > 1 \end{cases}. \tag{10}$$

The value of $\mathbf{S}(u,v)$ is equal to the value of $\mathbf{S}_b^m$ at (u_m, v_m), i.e., $\mathbf{S}(u,v) = \mathbf{S}_b^m(u_m, v_m)$. Let $\mathbf{L}_b^m(u,v)$ be the bilinear parametrization of the center face of $\mathbf{S}_b^m$'s control mesh. Since $\mathbf{S}_b^m$ is a regular patch, following Lemma 1, we have

$$\|\mathbf{L}_b^m(u,v) - \mathbf{S}_b^m(u,v)\| \leq \frac{1}{3} M_b^m$$

where M_b^m is the second order norm of the contol mesh of $\mathbf{S}_b^m$. But the second order norm of $\mathbf{S}_b^m$ is smaller than the second order norm of $\mathbf{M}_m$, M_m. Hence, the above inequality can be written as

$$\|\mathbf{L}_b^m(u,v) - \mathbf{S}_b^m(u,v)\| \leq \frac{1}{3} M_m. \tag{11}$$

So the maximum distance between the original extra-ordinary mesh $\mathbf{L}(u,v)$ and the patch $\mathbf{S}(u,v)$ can be written as

$$\begin{aligned} \parallel \mathbf{L}(u,v) - \mathbf{S}(u,v) \parallel &= \parallel \mathbf{L}(u,v) - \mathbf{L}_b^m(u_m,v_m) + \mathbf{L}_b^m(u_m,v_m) - \mathbf{S}(u,v) \parallel \\ &\leq \parallel \mathbf{L}(u,v) - \mathbf{L}_b^m(u_m,v_m) \parallel + \parallel \mathbf{L}_b^m(u_m,v_m) - \mathbf{S}_b^m(u_m,v_m) \parallel \end{aligned} \tag{12}$$

where $0 \leq u, v \leq 1$ and u_m and v_m are defined in (10). Since the second term on the right hand side can be estimated using (11), the only thing we need to work with is $\|\mathbf{L}(u,v) - \mathbf{L}_b^m(u_m,v_m)\|$.

It is easy to see that if $(u,v) \in \Omega_b^m$ then $(u,v) \in \Omega_0^k$ for any $0 \leq k < m$ where $\Omega_0^k = [0,\ \frac{1}{2^k}] \times [0,\ \frac{1}{2^k}]$. Ω_0^k corresponds to the subpatch $\mathbf{S}_0^k$. This means that $(2^k u, 2^k v)$ is within the parameter space of $\mathbf{S}_0^k$ for $0 \leq k < m$, i.e., $(2^k u, 2^k v) = (u_k, v_k)$ where u_k and v_k are defined in (10). Consequently, we can consider $\mathbf{L}_0^k(u_k, v_k)$ for $0 \leq k < m$ where $\mathbf{L}_0^k$ is the bilinear parametrization of the center face of the control mesh of $\mathbf{S}_0^k$ (with the understanding that $\mathbf{L}_0^0 = \mathbf{L}$). What we want to do here is to write the first term on the right hand side of (12) as

$$\begin{aligned} \mathbf{L}(u,v) - \mathbf{L}_b^m(u_m,v_m) &= \mathbf{L}_0^0(u,v) - \mathbf{L}_0^1(u_1,v_1) + \mathbf{L}_0^1(u_1,v_1) - \mathbf{L}_0^2(u_2,v_2) \\ &\quad + \mathbf{L}_0^2(u_2,v_2) - \mathbf{L}_0^3(u_3,v_3) + \mathbf{L}_0^3(u_3,v_3) - \mathbf{L}_0^4(u_4,v_4) \\ &\quad + \cdots + \mathbf{L}_0^{m-1}(u_{m-1},v_{m-1}) - \mathbf{L}_b^m(u_m,v_m) \end{aligned} \tag{13}$$

and get an estimate for its norm by estimating the norm of each consecutive pair on the right hand side. We have the following two lemmas. The proofs of these lemmas are shown in the complete version of the paper [4].

Lemma 5. If $(u, v) \in \Omega_b^m$ where b and m are defined in (9) then for any $0 \leq k < m - 1$ we have

$$\| \mathbf{L}_0^k(u_k, v_k) - \mathbf{L}_0^{k+1}(u_{k+1}, v_{k+1}) \| \leq \frac{1}{\min\{ n, 8 \}} M_k$$

where M_k is the second order norm of $\mathbf{M}_k$ and $\mathbf{L}_0^0 = \mathbf{L}$.

Lemma 6. If $(u, v) \in \Omega_b^m$ where b and m are defined in (9) then we have

$$\| \mathbf{L}_0^{m-1}(u_{m-1}, v_{m-1}) - \mathbf{L}_b^m(u_m, v_m) \| \leq \begin{cases} \frac{1}{4} M_{m-1}, & if \;\; b = 2 \\ \frac{1}{8} M_{m-1}, & if \;\; b = 1 \; or \; 3 \end{cases}$$

where M_{m-1} is the second order norm of $\mathbf{M}_{m-1}$.

By applying Lemmas 5 and 6 on (13) and then using (11) on (12), we have the following lemma. Proof of this lemma is shown in [4].

Lemma 7. The maximum of $\| \mathbf{L}(u, v) - \mathbf{S}(u, v) \|$ satisfies the following inequality

$$\| \mathbf{L}(u, v) - \mathbf{S}(u, v) \| \leq \begin{cases} M_0, & n = 3 \\ \frac{5}{7} M_0, & n = 5 \\ \frac{4n}{n^2 - 8n + 46} M_0, & 5 < n \leq 8 \\ \frac{n^2}{4(n^2 - 8n + 46)} M_0, & n > 8 \end{cases} \tag{14}$$

where $M = M_0$ is the second order norm of the extra-ordinary patch $\mathbf{S}(u, v)$.

Since the coefficient in the third case $(4n/(n^2 - 8n + 46))$ is smaller than the coefficient in the second case $(5/7)$, we can combine these two cases into one case $(5 \leq n \leq 8)$ to make the above expression (14) simpler.

3.3 Subdivision Depth Computation

Lemma 7 is important because it not only provides us with a second order norm based simple mechanism to estimate the distance between an extra-ordinary surface patch and its control mesh, it also allows us to estimate the distance between a level-k control mesh and the surface patch for any $k > 0$. This is because the distance between a level-k control mesh and the surface patch is dominated by the distance between the level-k extra-ordinary subpatch and the corresponding control mesh which, accoriding to Lemma 7, is

$$\| \mathbf{L}_k(u,v) - \mathbf{S}(u,v) \| \leq \begin{cases} M_k, & n = 3 \\ 0.72 M_k, & 5 \leq n \leq 8 \\ \frac{n^2}{4(n^2-8n+46)} M_k, & n > 8 \end{cases}$$

where M_k is the second order norm of $\mathbf{S}(u,v)$'s level-k control mesh, $\mathbf{M}_k$ (see the remark at the end of Section 3.1 for the definition of M_k). By combining the above result with Lemma 4, we have the following subdivision depth computation theorem for extra-ordinary surface patches.

Theorem 8. Given an extra-ordinary surface patch $\mathbf{S}(u,v)$ and an error tolerance ϵ, if k levels of subdivisions are iteratively performed on the control mesh of $\mathbf{S}(u,v)$, where

$$k = \left\lceil log_w \frac{M}{z\epsilon} \right\rceil$$

with M being the second order norm of $\mathbf{S}(u,v)$ defined in (7),

$$w = \begin{cases} \frac{3}{2}, & n = 3 \\ \frac{25}{18}, & n = 5 \\ \frac{4n^2}{3n^2+8n-46}, & n > 5 \end{cases} \quad and \quad z = \begin{cases} 1, & n = 3 \\ \frac{25}{18}, & 5 \leq n \leq 8 \\ \frac{2(n^2-8n+46)}{n^2}, & n > 8 \end{cases}$$

then the distance between $\mathbf{S}(u,v)$ and level-k control mesh is smaller than ϵ.

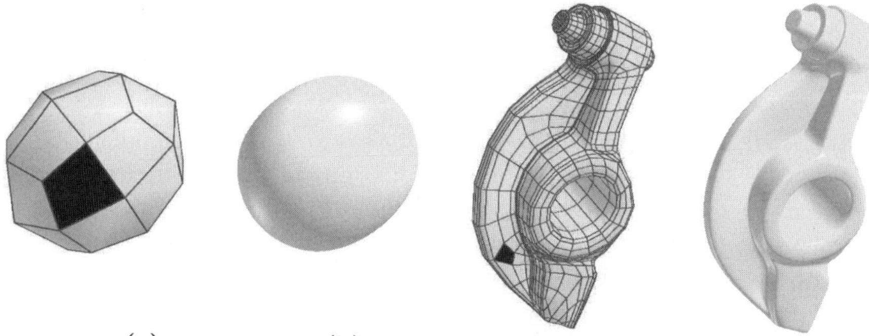

(a) (b) (c) (d)

Fig. 7. Examples: **(a)** an extra-ordinary CCSS mesh face of valence 3, **(b)** limit surface of the control mesh shown in (a), **(c)** an extra-ordinary CCSS mesh face of valence 5, **(d)** limit surface of the control mesh shown in (c)

4 Examples

Some examples of the presented distance evaluation and subdivision depth computation techniques are given in this section. In Figures 7(a) and 7(c), the distances between the blue mesh faces of the control meshes and the corresponding limit surface patches are 0.16 and 0.81, respectively. For the blue mesh face shown in Figure 7(a), the subdivision depths for the error tolerances 0.1, 0..01, 0.001, and 0.0001 are 2, 7, 13, and 19, respectively.. For the blue mesh face shown in Figure 7(c), the subdivision depths for the error tolerances 0.1, 0.01, 0.001, and 0.0001 are 7, 14, 21, and 28, respectively. Note that in the previous approach [3], the subdivision depths for these error tolerances are 9, 24, 40, and 56, respectively. Hence, the new approach presented in this paper indeed improves the previous, first order norm based approach.

5 Conclusions

A new subdivision depth computation technique for extra-ordinary CCSS patches is presented. The new technique computes the subdivision depth based on norms of the second order forward differences, not the first order forward differences, of the patch's control points. Hence, the computed subdivision depth reflects the curvature distribution of the extra-ordinary patch, not its dimension. Our result also points out that as long as the design objective can be achieved, one should try to use extra-ordinary vertices with smaller valence because, according to Theorem 8, smaller valence gives higher convergence rate and, consequently, smaller subdivision depth for the same precision.

Although the new technique improves the previous approach [3], it is not clear if the new approach is optimum for extra-ordinary CCSS patches. This will be a study direction in the future.

Acknowledgements. Work of the first two authors is supported by NSF under grants DMS-0310645 and DMI-0422126. Work of the third author is supported by NSF of China (60533070), NCET(NCET-04-0088) and FANEDD (200342).

References

1. Biermann H, Kristjansson D, Zorin D, Approximate Boolean Operations on Free-Form Solids, *Proceedings of SIGGRAPH 2001*, 185-194.
2. Catmull E, Clark J, Recursively Generated B-spline Surfaces on Arbitrary Topological Meshes, *Computer-Aided Design 10*, 6, 350-355, 1978.
3. Cheng F, Yong J, Subdivision Depth Computation for Catmull-Clark Subdivision Surfaces, *Computer Aided Design & Applications 3*, 1-4, 2006.
4. Cheng F, Chen G, Yong J, Subdivision Depth Computation for Extra-Ordinary Catmull-Clark Subdivision Surface Patches (complete version), www.cs.uky.edu/~cheng/PUBL/sub_depth_2.pdf
5. Halstead M, Kass M, DeRose T, Efficient, Fair Interpolation Using Catmull-Clark Surfaces, *Proceedings of SIGGRAPH 1993*, 35-44.

6. Lai S, Cheng F, Parametrization of General Catmull-Clark Subdivision Surfaces and its Applications, *Computer Aided Design & Applications 3*, 1-4, 2006.
7. Litke N, Levin A, Schröder P, Trimming for Subdivision Surfaces, *Computer Aided Geometric Design 18*, 5, 463-481, 2001.
8. Peters J, Patching Catmull-Clark Meshes, *Proceedings of SIGGRAPH 2000*, 255-258.
9. Sederberg T W, Zheng J, Sewell D, Sabin M, Non-Uniform Recursive Subdivision Surfaces, *Proceedings of SIGGRAPH 1998*, 387-394.
10. Stam J, Exact Evaluation of Catmull-Clark Subdivision Surfaces at Arbitrary Parameter Values, *Proceedings of SIGGRAPH 1998*, 395-404.
11. Stam J, Evaluation of Loop Subdivision Surfaces, *SIGGRAPH'99 Course Notes*, 1999.
12. Wu X, Peters J, An Accurate Error Measure for Adaptive Subdivision Surfaces, *Proc. Shape Modeling International 2005*, 1-6.
13. Zorin, D., Schröder, P., and Sweldens, W. Interactive Multiresolution Mesh Editing. *Proceedings of SIGGRAPH 1997*, 259-268.
14. Zorin D, Kristjansson D, Evaluation of Piecewise Smooth Subdivision Surfaces, *The Visual Computer*, 18(5/6):299-315, 2002.

An Approach for Embedding Regular Analytic Shapes with Subdivision Surfaces

Abdulwahed Abbas[1], Ahmad Nasri[2,*], and Weiyin Ma[3]

[1] Department of Computer Science, The University of Balamand
abbas@balamand.edu.lb

[2] Department of Computer Science, American University of Beirut
anasri@aub.edu.lb

[3] Dept. of Manufacturing Engr. & Engr. Management, City University of Hong Kong
mewma@cityu.edu.hk

Abstract. This paper presents an approach for embedding regular analytic shapes within subdivision surfaces. The approach is illustrated through the construction of compound Spherical-Catmull-Clark subdivision surfaces. It starts with a subdivision mechanism that can generate a perfect sphere. This mechanism stems from the geometric definition of the sphere shape. Thus, it comes with a trivial proof that the target of the construction is what it is. Furthermore, the similarity of this mechanism to the Catmull-Clark subdivision scheme is exploited to embed spherical surfaces within Catmull-Clark Surfaces, which holds a great potential for many practical applications.

1 Introduction

This paper presents an approach for embedding regular geometries within free-form features. As an illustration, Catmull-Clark subdivision surfaces [3] are considered for representing free-form features and circles and spheres represent regular analytical shapes. The technique easily covers other conical shapes as well.

A first exposure to subdivision techniques raises several obvious concerns (also see [15]):

1) The limit curve (or surface) is usually stored as a huge set of vertices and faces, as opposed to a clean mathematical function. This raises an obvious concern for space limitation.
2) Continuity at various regions of the curve (or surface), especially at irregular spots or junctions, cannot be improved beyond a certain limit.
3) The limit curve (or surface) is tied up very tightly to (in fact, it is a function of) the initial control polyhedron as well as the rules and coefficients of the corresponding subdivision scheme.

For item 1), research is already published on exact evaluations of subdivision surfaces at arbitrary parameters and, in theory; one can obtain limit positions analytically in a single step. The technique is applicable to all stationary subdivision schemes. While for item 2), research is still continuing on establishing subdivision schemes with higher order continuity for control meshes with arbitrary topology.

* Correspondence author.

H.-P. Seidel, T. Nishita, and Q. Peng (Eds.): CGI 2006, LNCS 4035, pp. 417 – 429, 2006.

Item 3) is also of particularly concern. In fact, obtaining a particular surface that the designer has in mind, from a particular control polyhedron, could be quite difficult with a given subdivision scheme. This might be the reason why, there has been plenty of research targeting well-known subdivision schemes in an attempt to modify or adapt its subdivision coefficients in order to meet user design constraints that would be difficult or impossible to satisfy without special treatments [8].

Other attempts have also been going on for the development of unified subdivision schemes and combined subdivision schemes with added capacity in modeling various engineering objects [14, 17, 21].

In summary, the general tendency seems to be leaning toward gaining more flexibility. The desired degree of flexibility exists, for example, in domains such as sculpture, where one is able to come up with more than one statue from a given raw stone. The circle and the sphere design problems are just two cases in prospect. In the context of subdivision, the following are two possible scenarios for added flexibility:

1) Trace the reverse process, starting from the desirable surface hoping to reach an initial control polyhedron whose subdivision will lead there.
2) Manipulate the subdivision coefficients hoping for a positive outcome, which leads to the development of improved subdivision schemes, new subdivision schemes, and unified and combined subdivision schemes.

Active research in both areas may be found in the literature. Some of that is reviewed in the subsection below in connection with the reported work of this paper,

2 Related Literature

Many recent recursive subdivision schemes associate the success of their formulation; automatically it seems, with the ability to generate a perfect circle (or a perfect sphere) as the limit of subdivision of a control polygon (or of a control polyhedron). The monotony with which this association is repeated gives the impression that generating a perfect circle or a perfect sphere is a goal that is worth pursuing in its own right.

Beets et al. [2] introduce, in a quite readable presentation, a novel subdivision scheme that locally tends to minimize variation of curvature. This scheme is able to produce a circle, and a generalization of that is able to generate spherical regions. Chalmovianský and Jüttler [5] describe an interpolating refinement procedure which, through approximation of adjacent points and the corresponding normals and by iterated application, is able to reproduce a circle. Morin et al. [11] make their starting point higher-order differential equation which results in corresponding subdivision masks. This way, they were able to come up with a subdivision scheme unifying known subdivision rules for cubic B-splines and splines-in-tension and a certain class of trigonometric functions. This scheme is able to reproduce circles. A generalization of that is able to produce surfaces of revolution.

Nasri et al. [12] present an algorithm that is able to generate a piecewise circular spline curve from an arbitrary control polygon. This is used in conjunction with the Doo-Sabin subdivision scheme [6] to blend subdivision surfaces with other surfaces having circular boundaries. This is about the closest work in this brief review in line with the research we are pursuing in this paper. Nasri and Farin [13] describe a modification of Chaikin's algorithm able to produce rational piecewise curves. Their modification is able to produce a circle from a give square. They cite the inability of Chaikin's algorithm to do that as a disadvantage.

Sabin [15], in a general argument regarding the shortcoming of present-day subdivision schemes, cites their inability to produce a perfect circle as a target for criticism. This argument agrees with our point of view presented above. Sabin and Dodgson [16] describe a geometry-sensitive variant of the 4-point subdivision scheme that can generate a circle regardless of the spacing of the initial data.

Warren and Weimer [20] provide an excellent introduction to subdivision techniques, including subdivision-based approaches for defining regular features. Warren and Schaefer [19] also describe a general framework for defining surfaces of revolution using subdivision techniques (also see [18]).

In subdivision-based modeling, special rules can also define creases and sharp features. Combined subdivision schemes may also connect subdivision surfaces with other analytical features. This paper presents another approach for blending subdivision surfaces with regular features.

2.1 An Alternative Approach

We designate as type T_0 shapes that are regular. These are shapes that have precise analytic expressions (e.g. circles and spheres). By contrast, we designate as type T_1 other freeform surfaces that can be generated by a subdivision scheme, for example.

In this context, it is not at all clear why one should go to extremes in trying to generate T_0 surfaces as T_1 surfaces, except to be able to embed them seamlessly within the latter ones. To this end, pretending that the analytic expression of T_0 surfaces is not there, whenever it actually is, always seems like throwing away valuable resources, while exploiting the analytic expression of the surface always seems to be the more natural approach. In other words, one should try to make the best use of any available information that can help in achieving the computational goals.

Along these lines, regardless of the type subdivision scheme being used, we seem to need to flag the current patch being subdivided to distinguish the type of surface being targeted (T_0 or T_1), in order to apply the appropriate subdivision rules. For patches of free-form features T_1, we apply the respective subdivision rules. For patches with regular features T_0, we develop a simple mechanism to construct them.

As one might expect, this mechanism stems from the geometric definition of the shape. This also comes with a simple mathematical proof that the target of the construction is what it is. The mechanism can easily be generalized to other analytic and regular shapes. Furthermore, the mechanism mimics some well-known subdivision schemes. This makes it straightforward to embed those regular shapes with free-form shapes at the limit of subdivision of those schemes.

This paper is structured as follows. Section 3 presents a corner-cutting scheme that can easily generate a circle. However, since generalizing this scheme to the sphere case does not seem to be straightforward, section 3 also presents a corner-creation scheme that can generate a circle and a sphere. Section 4 discusses the similarity of this latter scheme with some of the better know subdivision schemes and provides further illustrations. Section 5 demonstrates how these similarities help in embedding regular shapes with free-form shapes, by intersection, blending and interpolation. Finally, section 6 provides conclusions and other useful suggestions for further work.

3 An Interpolatory Subdivision for Regular Shape Construction

In this section, we present a subdivision mechanism that can minimize the effort that goes into constructing regular analytic shapes. This uses the geometric information available in those shapes. The method resembles those used for direct grid generation of analytic objects. The literature covering spherical grid generation is vast and those methods can produce grids of very high quality.

3.1 The Corner Cutting Scheme

Given are a square (S) with centre O (see Fig. 1) and a circle (C) centered at O and embedded in (S). Since (C) is tangent to the edges of (S), start by cutting the corners of (S) so that the newly arising edges are constantly tangent to (C) at their midpoints.

This process parallels the Chaikin's algorithm [4] for curves and Doo-Sabin's for surfaces. The success of this scheme rests on how efficiently it can be applied and on whether it is applicable in all stages of the process down to the limit curve or surface.

In Fig. 2, A is the centre of the sphere whose radius is **R** and B is a selected corner of the engulfing polyhedron and BC is an edge incident on that corner. The point D is on AB such that |AD| = **R**. Parametrically, D = (1-u)A + uB, where u = **R** / |AB|.

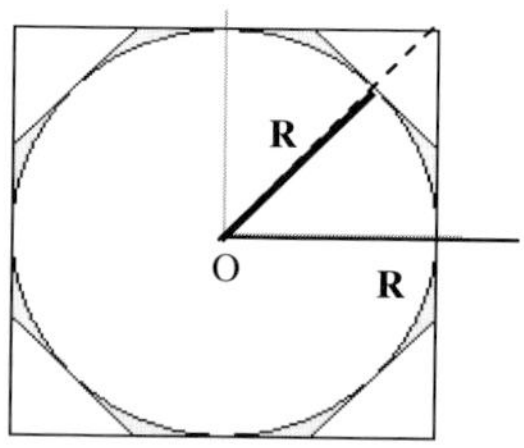

Fig. 1. The Corner-Cutting Process

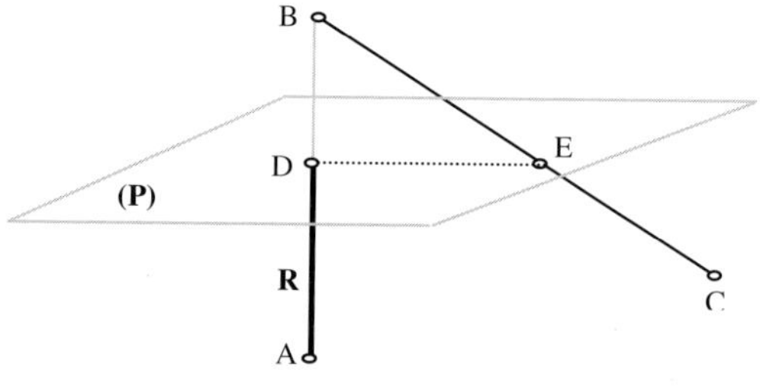

Fig. 2. Subdividing for a Circle

The plane **(P)** orthogonal to AB and cutting AB in D also cuts BC in E, which is determined by the following expression: E = (1-v)C + vB, where v = AB·CD/AB·CB, where "·" is the vector scalar product. Accordingly, v does not exist when BC is parallel to (P). Moreover, E lies outside the segment [B..C], when v is outside the range [0..1]. Thus, for the corner-cutting scheme to work in practice, it is important to make sure that the above two situations do not take place at any stage during the application of this process.

The Circle Case. Fig. 1 illustrates that the maintaining distance R from O to each of the resulting edges will be sufficient to ensure that the limit curve is a circle of radius R centered at O. An alternative starting control polygon could be an equilateral triangle (see Fig. 3). In both cases, the initial control polygons will gradually and consistently converge to a limit circle.

Note however that reaching a circle at the limit of the corner cutting process depends on a uniform way of cutting these corners. The same is probably true for the sphere and for other analytic objects.

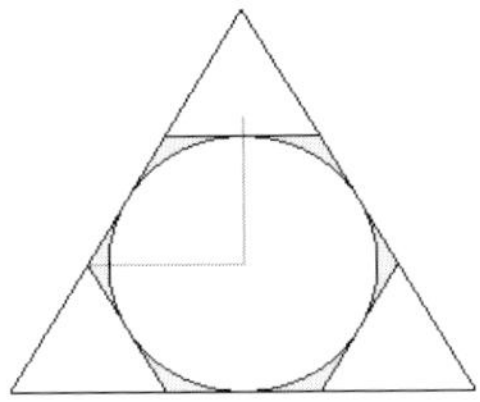

Fig. 3. An Alternative Starting Polygon

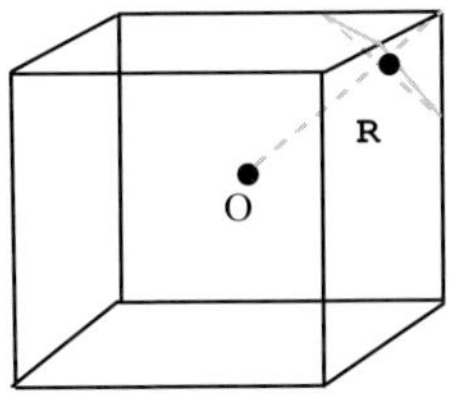

Fig. 4. Subdividing for a Sphere

The Sphere Case. The initial control polyhedron (see Fig. 4) is a cube, where the distance from the centre O to each of the faces is a constant R.This is projected to be the radius of the sphere, limit of the subdivision. The same can perhaps be said when the starting polyhedron has fewer number of vertices and faces than a cube; e.g., a regular prism (see Fig. 5).

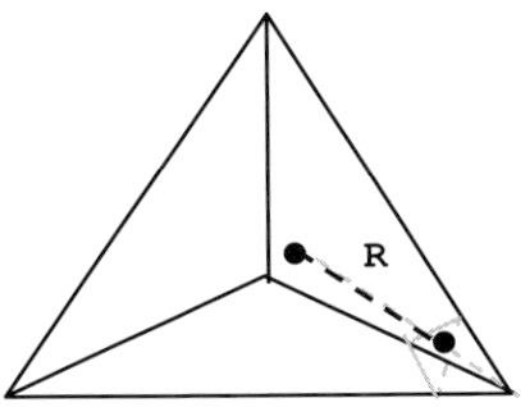

Fig. 5. The Regular Prism Alternative

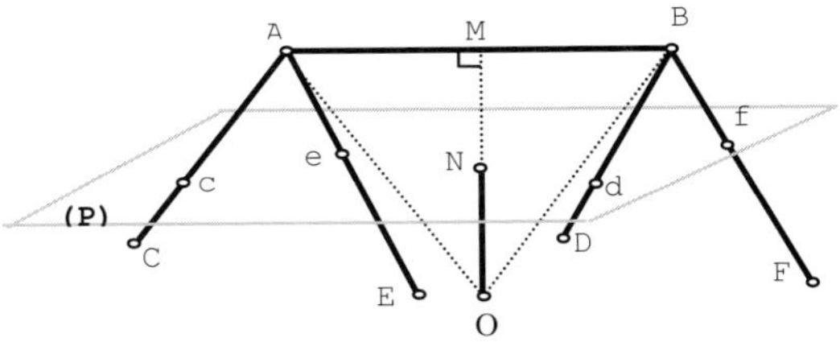

Fig. 6. The Edge-Cutting Process

In both cases, the scheme makes necessary the repeated use of an edge-cutting procedure (see Fig. 6). The formula here is identical in format to the one used in the corner-cutting scheme. For example, the intersection point c of the plane (P) with the edge AC is given by c = (1-w)C + wA, where w = OM·CA/ OM·CN.

When the cube is subdivided this way, it will be sufficient to maintain R as the distance from O to each of the resulting faces. If this relation is maintained at every subdivision step all the way to the limit surface, then surely the limit surface will be a sphere of radius R centered at O.

The method presented in this subsection forms a corner-cutting scheme similar to the topological rule of the Doo-Sabin scheme [6]. It is workable and in fact produces good results for circles. However, it is difficult to manage for the case of surfaces.

3.2 The Corner-Creation Scheme

An alternative approach is to start from a square or a cube and proceed by shifting the midpoint of every edge out toward the target point on the limit circle, which is now

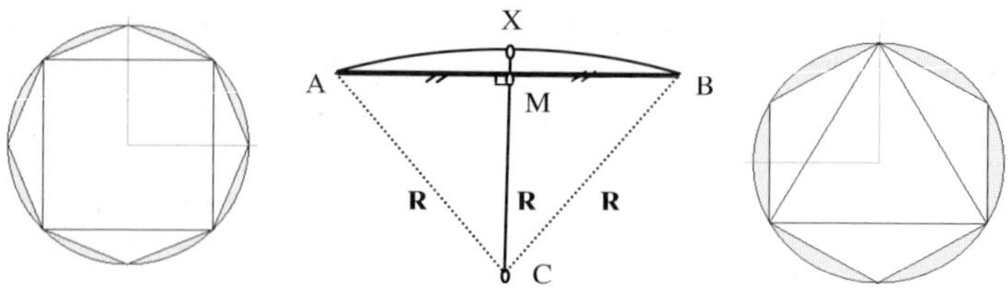

Fig. 7. The Circle Case

engulfing the initial polygon (see Fig. 7). This subdivision method is interpolatory, as opposed to the previous one, which is approximatory.

This is somewhat reminiscent of the Catmull-Clark [3] (and also perhaps of the Butterfly [7], or maybe $\sqrt{2}$ [9]) subdivision scheme. It is the first similarity that we are particularly targeting for the benefit of the embedding techniques discussed below. Note here that the starting control polygon in this case can be any control polygon on condition that its vertices are interpolated by the target circle.

With the existence of the centre of the circle (or the sphere), storing the radius is not necessary, as it is the distance from the centre to any of the vertices of the polygon (or polyhedron). This technique can easily be extended to apply as well to other type T_0 curves or surfaces such as ellipses, cones, cylinders, torii, etc.

The Circle Case. Given the distance R from C to A and from C to B (see Fig. 7), the midpoint M of AB is stretched so that R = |CX|. Repeating the process on AXB leads to an arc of a circle centered at C and passing by A and B. With C being the centre of the triangle (T) and R the distance from C to any of the corners of (T), performing the process on each edge of (T) results in a circle centered at C and engulfing (T). The same can be said about the square in the same figure.

The Sphere Case. In Fig. 8, given that R is the distance from C to A, from C to B and from C to D, the centre G of the triangle ABD is stretched so that the distance from C to Y is also R. Repeating the process on the resulting polyhedron leads to a section of a sphere centered at C and passing by the points A, B and D (also see Fig. 9).

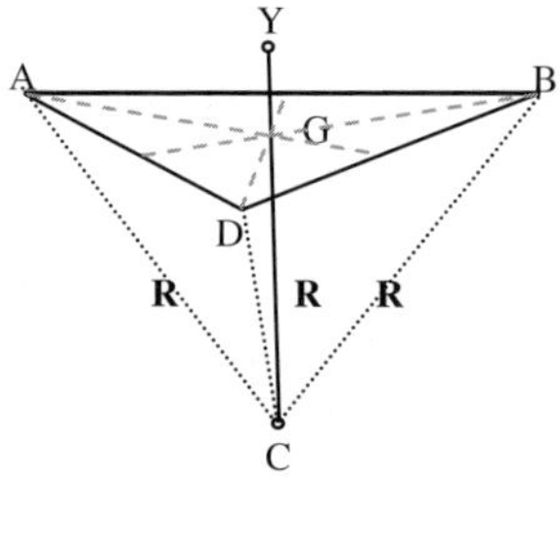

Fig. 8. The Sphere Case (1)

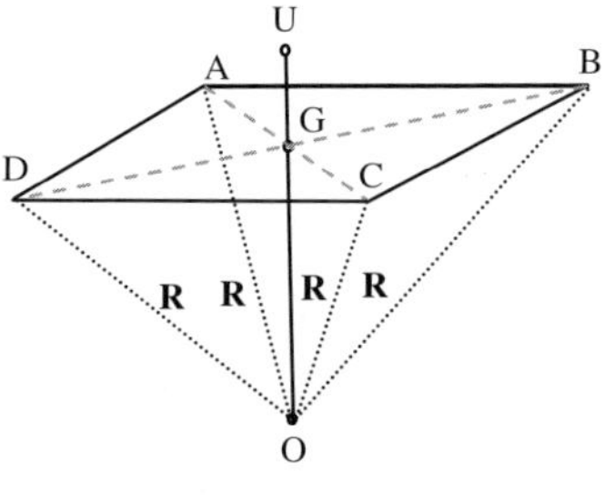

Fig. 9. The Sphere Case (2)

It is worthy to mention that one may also use a non-uniform polygon in case of curves and a polyhedron with arbitrary topology for the subdivision shown in Figs. 7-9, and not just be limited to triangular faces or quadrilateral faces.

Further Discussion. The geometrical approach pursued in this paper has the advantage that it comes together with a trivial mathematical proof that the resulting limit curve is exactly that of a perfect circle. Moreover, the sphere generalization problem is just a generalization of the above approach to the 3-dimensional space, which is another assurance of its validity.

Additionally, it has a simple and, hopefully, efficient implementation that closely resembles some of the well-known subdivision schemes. This approach works in a sense that it will generate a subdivision surface that will converge on a perfect sphere, circle, ellipsoid, torus, etc. It can also reach the desired shape from a variety of initial control polyhedrons, using a variety of subdivision rules.

However, some work remains to be done regarding the corresponding subdivision coefficients of the scheme, in order to break away from the geometric intuition of this solution. However, seeing relevant work in this area, such coefficients are more likely to be non-linear.

The approach discussed in this section (3.2) is interpolating. The topological subdivision rules that might be followed can come from various possible directions:

- The topological rule is similar to that of Catmull-Clark [3], if both face points and edge points are inserted.
- The topological rule is a $\sqrt{2}$ [9] subdivision, if only a face point is inserted.
- The topological rule can also be based on Loop [10] or butterfly [7] subdivisions, if only edge vertices are created and triangle meshes are involved.

We can be certain now that the existence of the extraordinary points on the surface will not affect continuity, as this will be counterweighted by the existence of the tension parameter; which is R in this case. In fact, we are going to get a perfect sphere at the end, no matter which choice we may follow.

Reflecting a little bit on the last point, one can see that the subdivision coefficients need not be analyzed for verifying continuity, because the method comes ready with a mathematical proof that the limit surface is what it is. As such, this will be sufficient to assure the continuity of the resulting surface. Extraordinary corners might arise in all cases of the topological rules mentioned above, but there will be a unified formula for computing the newly inserted points (that would only be depending on the topology).

The method presented in this subsection forms an interpolating scheme relying on an edge splitting and a face splitting procedures, but the topological rule is similar to that of Catmull-Clark subdivision. Fig. 8 and Fig. 9 produce perfect spheres using this method. In addition, here are some other ideas and a summary for spherical surface subdivision (also good for circles). All approaches discussed here should be simple to implement:

- There are various topological rules that we can use. One topological rule is similar to that of Catmull-Clark subdivision and another one is a 1-4 splitting for triangular meshes similar to that of Loop subdivision [10]. One may also apply other topological rules, such as $\sqrt{2}$ [9].

- There are two geometric rules are involved. One is the production of an edge point similar to that shown in Fig. 7, and the other one is for the production of a face point as shown in Figs. 8-9 (but need to know the centre of the sphere).
- The starting control mesh can be any mesh with two or more faces whose vertices are on the sphere (may start from a cube for a complete sphere).

4 Embedding Regular Shapes with Catmull-Clark Surfaces

While one may use various topological rules as indicated earlier, this section focuses on Catmull-Clark subdivision and its subdivision and blending with spheres. Embedding regular shapes within freeform surfaces is more interesting than just constructing isolated regular shape modeling, even more so when the subdivision rules are not so complicated and are easy to use!

This situation is commonly found in engineering objects, such as the definition of a piecewise surface with regular shape and free-form shape as a single subdivision surface. Embedding the first within the second may occur as a crease feature or as a radius blending.

The general idea is that subdivision is performed using different rules for different parts of the mesh, which heads towards subdivision-based modeling of compound shape with regular geometry spherical and/or others) and free-form geometry as a single subdivision surface.

According to our approach, constructing a hybrid regular-freeform surface starts from a control mesh where faces are designated as contributing to a regular or a free-form surface from the start. The construction of the hybrid surface will have plenty to gain from the similarities between both schemes.

In fact, the F-vertex of a face will be determined according to CC-subdivision rules if the face is labeled as a CC-face, and the F-vertex will be determined according to the S-Subdivision if the face is labeled as an S-face. On the other hand, determining which subdivision rules to apply when calculating the E-vertex of an edge and the V-vertex of a vertex will depend on the type of faces connected to the edge or to the vertex, because this is where the two types of surfaces may meet.

Obviously, when all the faces connected to an edge (or to a vertex) are of the same type, the resulting E-vertex (or V-vertex) is calculated according to rules corresponding to this type. However, the decision about how to subdivide when the types of meeting faces differ will determine how the regular surfaces are embedded within free-form faces.

Finally, what remains to be decided is how to label the faces of the next subdivided mesh. In fact, remembering that the corner-creation scheme is interpolatory, a face is labeled as an S-face if all its vertices belong to the same sphere, otherwise it is a CC-face. We distinguish two kinds of situations that are commonly encountered in practice:

- when the CC-surface intersect with an S-surface;
- when the CC-surface blends with an adequate degree of continuity with the S-surface.

4.1 Regular and Freeform Intersection

This can be seen as intersecting a circular shape with a normal uniform cubic spline, or as intersecting Catmull-Clark surfaces with spherical and other regular shapes. This should be of interest for engineering applications.

It is important to keep in mind here that the intersection problem is addressed in this subsection and it leads to crease features at the intersection of the free-form feature and the regular feature. However for blending, a smooth connection is expected between the two features.

S-Faces Intersection. Keeping in mind that the intersection of two different spheres is a perfect circle, and since the corner-creation scheme is interpolatory, the only thing that remains to be determined is how to calculate the E-vertex of the edge corresponding to such spheres is calculated.

In Figs. 10, 11 and 12, H is the midpoint of the edge common to the two faces corresponding to the spheres centered at C1 and C2 respectively. The E-Vertex in this situation is a point I whose position is calculated as follows (see Figs. 10, 11):

$$\Delta = |C_1C_2| < R_1+R_2,\ \Delta_1+\Delta_2 = \Delta,\ \ \Delta_1^2 + \delta^2 = R_1^2,\ \Delta_2^2 + \delta^2 = R_2^2,\ \ \Delta_1^2 - \Delta_2^2 = R_1^2 - R_2^2$$

$$(\Delta_1 - \Delta_2)(\Delta_1 + \Delta_2) = R_1^2 - R_2^2,\quad (\Delta_1 - \Delta_2) = (R_1^2 - R_2^2)/\Delta,\ \ 2\Delta_1 = \Delta + (R_1^2 - R_2^2)/\Delta$$

$$\Delta_1 = (\Delta^2 + R_1^2 - R_2^2)/2\Delta,\qquad \delta^2 = R_1^2 - \Delta_1^2,\ \delta = \sqrt{R_1^2 - \Delta_1^2}$$

$$I = (1 - \delta/|HM|)*H + (\delta/|HM|)*M,\quad H = (1 - \Delta_1/\Delta)*C_1 + (\Delta_1/\Delta)*C_2$$

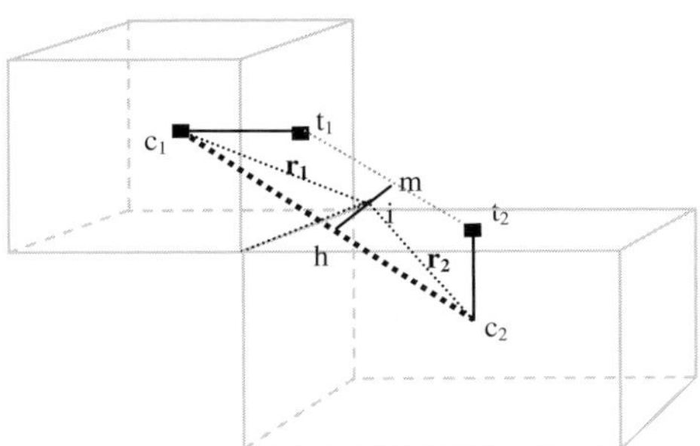

Fig. 10. Two S-Faces Intersection (1)

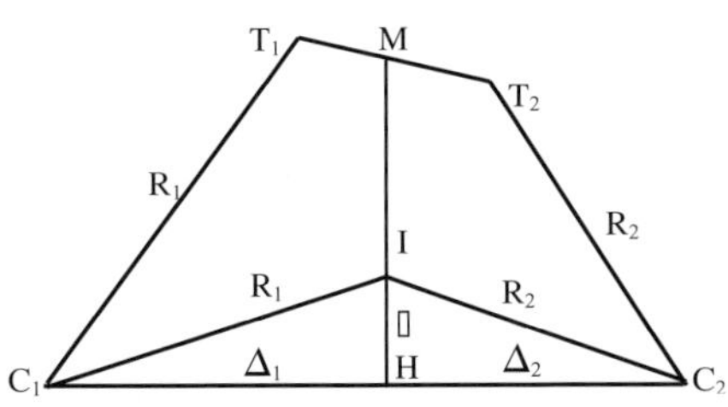

Fig. 11. S-Faces Intersection (2)

Fig. 12. S-Faces Intersection (3)

Intersecting an S-Face with a CC-Face. Keeping in mind that the intersection of a sphere with a CC-surface is a curve on the spherical surface, and since the corner-creation scheme is interpolatory, the only thing that remains to be determined is how to calculate the E-vertex of the edge corresponding to such situation is calculated.

In Figs. 13, 14, 15 and 16, the E-Vertex D need to be located to intersect the CC-face on the side of A with the S-face corresponding to the sphere centered at C and of radius R. The position of D is calculated as follows (see Fig. 13 and Fig. 14):

$$D = (1-t)A + tB,\ D = A + (B-A)t,\ |CD| = R,$$
$$(x_A + (x_B - x_A)t - x_C)^2 + (y_A + (y_B - y_A)t - y_C)^2 = R^2$$
$$(x_A - x_C)^2 + (y_A - y_C)^2 + ((x_B - x_A)^2 + (y_B - y_A)^2)\,t^2$$
$$+ 2\,((x_A - x_C)(x_B - x_A) + (y_A - y_C)(y_B - y_A))t = R^2$$
$$|AB|^2 t^2 + 2(\overrightarrow{AB}.\overrightarrow{AC})t + |AC|^2 - R^2 = 0$$

$$t = \frac{\sqrt{(\overrightarrow{AB}.\overrightarrow{AC})^2 - |AB|^2.(|AC|^2 - R^2)} - (\overrightarrow{AB}.\overrightarrow{AC})}{|AB|^2}$$

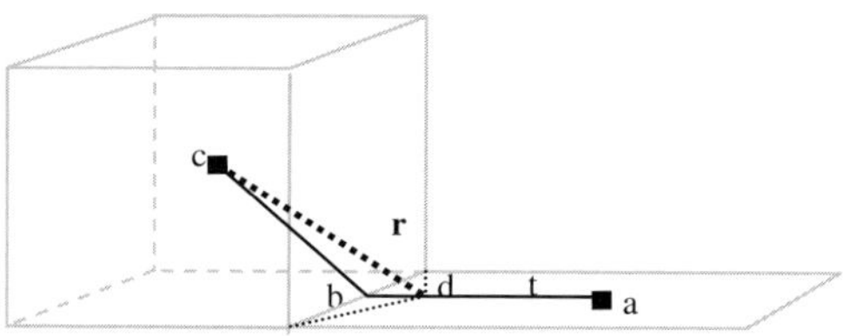

Fig. 13. S-Face - CC-face Intersection (1)

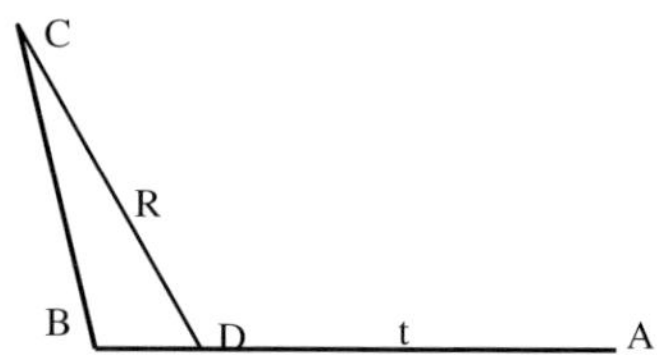

Fig. 14. S-Face - CC-face Intersection (2)

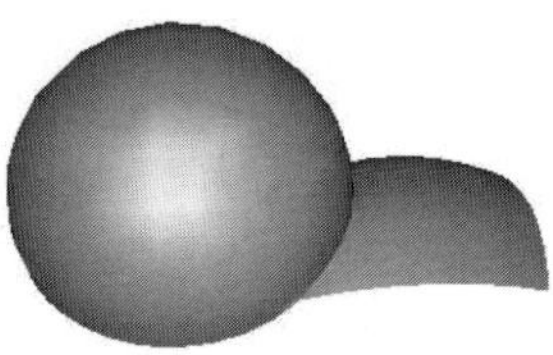

Fig. 15. S-Face – CC-face Intersection (3)

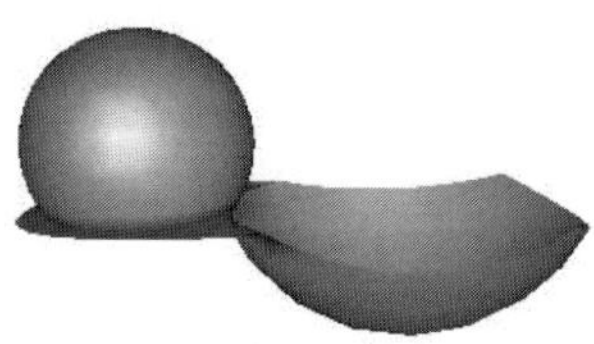

Fig. 16. S-Face - CC-face Intersection (4)

4.2 Regular and Free-Form Blending

This can be seen as blending a circular shape with a normal uniform cubic spline, or as blending Catmull-Clark surfaces with spherical and other regular shapes. This should be of interest for many applications (see Figs. 17, 18 and 19).

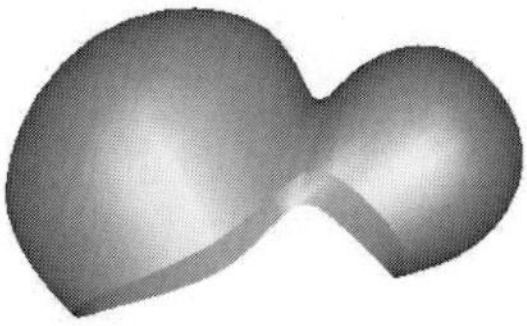

Fig. 17. S-Faces Blending

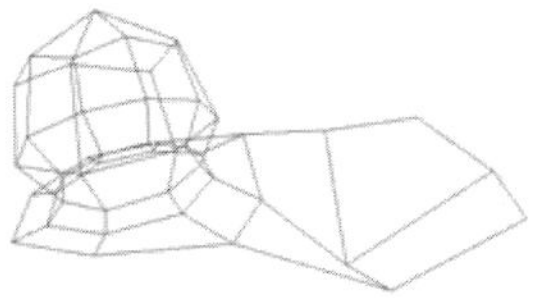

Fig. 18. S-CC-faces Blending (1)

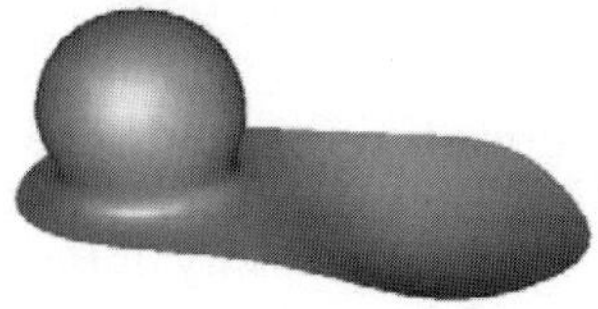

Fig. 19. S-CC-face Blending (2)

It is important to keep in mind here that smoothness should be guaranteed when a spherical surface blends with another surface of the same type or of another type.

It is in the case of blending where the interplay between subdivision rules of the CC-scheme and the S-scheme has its maximum advantage. This provides a clue for performing Boolean-like operations on any surfaces.

In fact, in the case of blending, both the V-vertex at a mixed edge and the V-Vertex at a mixed vertex have to be determined. To insure smoothness in this region, we simply adopt the CC-rules in both situations.

4.3 Curves on Composite Subdivision Surfaces

With the subdivision scheme we are suggesting, the interpolation of points and curves on a spherical surface is pretty straightforward [1]. Moreover, blending such curves with adjacent curves on the Catmull-Clark Surface comes with little or no effort (se illustration in Fig. 20).

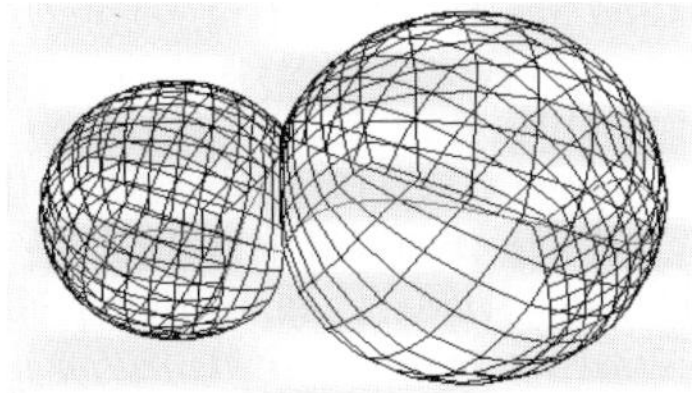

Fig. 20. Curves on Composite Subdivision Surfaces

5 Conclusions and Further Work

This paper presents an interpolatory corner-creation scheme which may be used to generate circular and spherical surfaces with ease. The scheme resembles the subdivision rules of the Catmull-Clark subdivision scheme. This resemblance is exploited to generate compound surfaces of both kinds.

The approach being suggested in this paper can also be extended to other subdivision surfaces, such as Loop[10] and $\sqrt{2}$ [9], and other regular analytic curves and surfaces such as ellipsoids and torii.

Acknowledgements

The work presented in this paper is supported by the Research Grants Council of Hong Kong through a CERG grant (CityU 1131/03E) and a research grant from the American University of Beirut, URB DDF111130-688129.

References

1. Abbas, A. and Nasri, A., *A Generalized Scheme for the Interpolation Of Arbitrarily Intersecting Curves by Subdivision Surfaces,* IJCC Journal, Japan, 2005.
2. Beets, K., Claes, J. and Van Reeth, F., *A Subdivision Scheme to Model Surfaces with Spherelike Features*, WSCG, 2005: 103-108.
3. Catmull, E. and J. Clark, *Recursively generated B-spline surfaces on arbitrary topological meshes,* Computer-Aided Design, Vol. 10, 1978, pp. 350-355.
4. Chaikin, G., *An algorithm for high-speed curve generation,* Computer Graphics and Image Processing, Vol. 3, 1974, pp. 346-349.
5. Chalmovianský, P., Jüttler, B.: *A Circle-preserving Subdivision Scheme Based on Local Algebraic Fits*, A. Neubauer, J. Schicho (Eds), November, 2003
6. Doo, D. and M. Sabin, *Behaviors of recursive division surfaces near extraordinary points,* Computer-Aided Design, Vol. 10, 1978, pp. 356-360.
7. Dyn, N., D. Levin and J. A. Gregory, *A butterfly subdivision scheme for surface interpolation with tension control,* ACM Trans. Graph., Vol. 9, No. 2, 1990, pp. 160-169.
8. Levin, A., *Combined Subdivision Schemes,* Ph.D. Thesis, Tel Aviv University, 2000.
9. Li, G., W. Ma and H. Bao, $\sqrt{2}$ *subdivision for quadrilateral meshes,* The Visual Computer, Vol. 20, Nos. 2-3, 2004, pp. 180-198.
10. Loop, C., *Smooth Subdivision Surfaces Based on Triangles,* Master Thesis, University of Utah, 1987.
11. Morin, G., Warren, J., D., and Weimer, H., *A subdivision scheme for surfaces of revolution,* Computer Aided Geometric Design 18(5): 483-502 (2001).
12. Nasri, A. H., Cornelius WAM van Overveld, and Brian Wyvill., *A Recursive Subdivision Algorithm for Piecewise Circular Spline*, Computer Graphics Forum 20(1): 35-45 (2001).
13. Nasri, A., and G. Farin, 2001, *A subdivision algorithm for generating rational curves*, Journal of Graphical Tools (AK Peters, USA) 3(1): 00–12.
14. Oswald, P. and P. Schröder, *Composite primal/dual sqrt3-subdivision scheme,* Computer Aided Geometric Design, Vol. 20, No. 2, 2003, pp. 135-164.
15. Sabin, M. A., *What is wrong with subdivision surfaces?* Workshop on Industry Challenges in Geometric Modeling in CAD, Darmstadt University of Technology, March 17 - 18, 2004.
16. Sabin M. A. and N.A. Dodgson, *A Circle Preserving Variant of the Four-Point Subdivision Scheme*, In M. Daelen, K. Morken and L.L. Schumaker (eds.), Mathematical Methods for Curves and Surfaces, Nashboro Press, Brentwood, TN, 2005, pp. 275-286.
17. Stam, J., *On subdivision schemes generalizing uniform B-spline surfaces of arbitrary degree,* Computer Aided Geometric Design, Vol. 18, No. 5, 2001, pp. 383-396.
18. Stam, J. and C. Loop, *Quad/triangle subdivision,* Computer Graphics Forum, Vol. 22, No. 1, 2003, pp. 1-7.
19. Warren, J., and S. Schaefer, *A Factored Approach to Subdivision Surfaces*, Computer Graphics & Applications, 24 (2004): 74-81.

20. Warren, J., and H. Weimer, *Subdivision Methods for Geometric Design – a Constructive Approach*, Morgan Kaufmann Publishers, San Francisco, 2002.
21. Zorin, D. and P. Schröder, *A unified framework for primal/dual quadrilateral subdivision scheme,* Computer Aided Geometric Design, 2001, Vol. 18, No. 5, pp. 429-454.

Adaptive Point-Cloud Surface Interpretation

Q. Meng[1], B. Li[2], and H. Holstein[1]

[1] Dept. of Computer Science, University of Wales,
Aberystwyth, SY23 3DB, U.K
qqm@aber.ac.uk

[2] Dept. of Computing and Mathematics,
Manchester Metropolitan University, M1 5GD, U.K
b.li@mmu.ac.uk

Abstract. We present a novel adaptive radial basis function network to reconstruct smooth closed surfaces and complete meshes from non-uniformly sampled noisy range data. The network is established using a heuristic learning strategy. Neurons can be inserted, removed or updated iteratively, adapting to the complexity and distribution of the underlying data. This flexibility is particularly suited to highly variable spatial frequencies, and is conducive to data compression with network representations. In addition, a greedy *neighbourhood* Extended Kalman Filter learning method is investigated, leading to a significant reduction of computational cost in the training process with desired prediction accuracy. Experimental results demonstrate the performance advantages of compact network representation for surface reconstruction from large amount of non-uniformly sampled incomplete point-clouds.

1 Introduction

Nowadays, digitisation techniques such as range scanning devices are widely used for model acquisition in the domains of sculptures, archaeological artifacts, engineering CAD-CAM prototyping, medical and geophysical imaging, and scientific visualisation. However, sampling complex real-world geometry from a particular viewpoint almost always yields surface reconstruction imperfections, in particular "holes". Faithful reproduction of incomplete meshes in the presence of holes and data noise is a ubiquitous problem for scientific visualisation and engineering modelling.

Efficient and reliable surface reconstruction requires a functional representation residing in a low dimensional and, therefore, computationally manageable feature space. Inspired by advances in radial basis functions (RBFs) for solving function approximation and pattern classification problems [1, 2], in this paper, we present a new approach that adapts the advantages of the RBFs to the framework of neural networks. The proposed hybrid RBF-network aims to satisfy the desirable criteria of speed, functional representation compactness, robustness to data noise, and adaptivity to highly variable spatial densities and data complexity.

H.-P. Seidel, T. Nishita, and Q. Peng (Eds.): CGI 2006, LNCS 4035, pp. 430–441, 2006.

2 Geometric Modelling from Point Clouds

Most implicit shape reconstructions from point clouds are based on Blinn's idea of blending local implicit primitives [3] by using Gaussian blobs, signed distance functions, union of spheres or patches to meet the boundary conditions [4, 5, 6]. Such approaches could work well for holes that are small compared to the geometric variation in the surface.

The RBFs allow another approach due to their good global generalisation abilities in function approximation and simple topological structure [7, 8]. These properties make RBFs well suited for accommodating irregular scattered data distributed across large, irregular holes, requiring neither object topology constraints nor *a priori* shape knowledge. However, problems of computational cost in high dimensional parameter space and approximation accuracy remain, particularly for locally sharp features, since RBF solutions are global in nature. Consequently, fitting and evaluating RBFs by means of nonlinear least squares optimisation for large data sets is challenging for most present PCs.

The multi-scale RBF [9] employs locally supported basis functions within coarse-to-fine hierarchy in order to achieve efficient adaptivity to underline geometric variation. In [10], the authors utilise error controlled octree subdivision as partition strategy to adapt to the local complexity of shape. It allows selection of piecewise quadratic functions to capture local variation. Smooth blending and weighting between subdivisions are then applied for surface reconstruction. In [11], an objects surface is defined implicitly as set of zero-valued RBF thin-plate splines fitted to the given surface data. Greedy methods for fitting and evaluating RBFs are explored to reduce the number of RBF centres required to represent a surface. A hierarchical network reconstruction [12] attempted to use multi-scale coarse-to-fine RBF subnetworks to achieve desirable accuracy. However, neurons in the network were located evenly on pre-defined regular grids for each layer, allowing predetermined increasing resolution scales at higher layers. The network structure was fixed *a priori*, based on pre-knowledge of the training data. The lack of adaptivity to the underlying data could necessitate large numbers of neurons to meet a desired accuracy [13].

We concentrate in this paper on a hybrid adaptive RBF network algorithm. The employed topological model of the network has benefitted from concepts found in the self-organising sequential learning of the *resource-allocating network* (RAN) [14, 15, 16]. The novelty of the proposed RBF network is that neurons can be located and adjusted iteratively in full dimension according to the distribution and complexity of the underlying data. This adaptivity is particularly suited to cases of highly varying spatial density and provides the possibility of compact representations using networks. Furthermore, we report a greedy learning algorithm that uses a local-based *neighbourhood extended Kalman filter* (NEKF), leading to significant computation reduction in the training process.

3 An Adaptive RBF Network

3.1 The RBF Network Topology and Adaptivity

A typical feed-forward RBF network is shown in Fig. 1. It has a simple structure composed of an input layer of i independent inputs $\mathbf{x}(x_1, ..., x_i)$, a hidden layer with K radial basis functions $\phi_k(\mathbf{x})$. The network output $f(\mathbf{x})$ is a linear combination of RBFs and takes the form

$$f(\mathbf{x}) = a_0 + \sum_{k=1}^{K} a_k \phi_k(\mathbf{x}) \quad (1)$$

where a_k is the real-valued *weight* of kth RBF connecting to the output, and a_0 is the bias term. Gaussian radial functions, acting as nonlinear kernels of the hidden layer, monotonically decrease with the distance from their centre, and they are local and finite, giving a significant response only in a central neighbourhood. Therefore, Gaussian RBFs of the form

$$\phi_k(\mathbf{x}) = \exp\left(-\frac{1}{\sigma_k^2} \|\mathbf{x} - \mu_k\|^2\right) \quad (2)$$

are used in our study to interpolate irregularly distributed noisy data on restricted surfaces. In Eq. (2), $\|.\|$ denotes the Euclidean norm, μ_k locates the *centre* of the kth neuron, and σ_k (standard deviation) denotes its *width* (coverage).

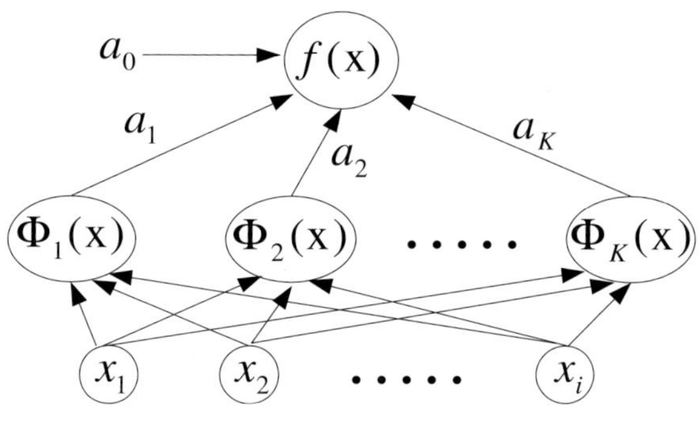

Fig. 1. The RBF network topology

The adaptivity of the network derives from the flexibility of structure construction and parameter evaluation. The network starts with no hidden units. At each learning step: 1) the network grows one neuron, where necessary, based on the "novelty" of the input observation; 2) if the "novelty" criteria are unsatisfied, resulting in no newly added neuron at this instance, a subset of neuron parameters are adjusted in full dimension in accordance with a neighbourhood extended Kalman filter (NEKF) algorithm; 3) network compaction is obtained by *pruning* "pseudo" neurons that consistently make little contribution to the network output. The remainder of this section describes the learning process in these three stages.

3.2 Network Growth

In the case of surface reconstruction from 3D point clouds, the training set $\mathcal{T} = \{\mathbf{x}_n, z_n\}_{n=1}^N$ consists of normalised and randomised 3D point data. The N pairs of 2D points $\mathbf{x}_n = [x_n, y_n]^T$ are network inputs having associated z_n as outputs. The distribution of the N points $\mathbf{x}_n$ is irregular.

The network starts with no hidden unit. It grows by inserting a new hidden unit if the current observation $\{\mathbf{x}_n, z_n\}$ satisfies the following three novelty conditions:

Condition 1: the input of the observation is far away from all existing neurons:

$$d_n = \|\mathbf{x}_n - \mu_{nr}\| > \eta_n \tag{3}$$

where μ_{nr} is the neuron centre nearest to the current input $\mathbf{x}_n$, and η_n indicates the scale of neuron resolution in network space.
Condition 2: the network prediction error for the current learning observation is significant:

$$|e_n| = |z_n - f(\mathbf{x}_n)| > E \tag{4}$$

where E denotes the *desired accuracy* of the network approximation.
Condition 3: the prediction error within a sliding window W is significant:

$$\sqrt{\frac{\sum_{i=n-(W-1)}^{n} e_i^2}{W}} > E_{rms} \tag{5}$$

where E_{rms} is the threshold to ensure smooth network growth.

The algorithm begins with $\eta_n = \eta_{max}$, η_{max} being chosen as the largest scale of interest in the input space. It decays exponentially according to

$$\eta_n = \max\{\eta_{\max}\gamma^n, \eta_{\min}\}, \; 0 < \gamma < 1, \tag{6}$$

until it reaches $\eta_{\min}$. The *decay constant* γ indicates the speed of the process, and $\eta_{\min}$ represents the desired *neuron resolution* of the network. The exponential decay of the distance criterion allows fewer neurons with large widths (smoother basis functions) initially. With increasing number of observations, more functions with smaller widths are recruited to refine the approximation.

When the three conditions are met, a new neuron is inserted into the current network of K units, with the following parameters at the position coincident at input $\mathbf{x}_n$:

$$\begin{aligned} \mu_{K+1} &= \mathbf{x}_n \\ a_{K+1} &= e_n \\ \sigma_{K+1} &= \psi \|\mathbf{x}_n - \mu_{nr}\| \end{aligned} \tag{7}$$

where ψ is an *overlap factor* between hidden units, and the number of units $K+1$ is renamed as K.

If an observation does not satisfy the novelty criteria Eq. (3) $\sim$ Eq. (5), no new hidden unit is added. Instead, an EKF-based learning method, described below, is utilised to adjust the network parameters to best fit the current observation.

3.3 Sequential Learning by Neighbourhood EKF

Classical methods for updating network parameters in nonlinear networks use *least mean squares* (LMS) or gradient descent (GD) [14, 17]. To avoid expensive nonlinear optimisation and achieve a global minimum, we employed the Extended Kalaman filters (EKF) that have a more compact structure and better accuracy [15, 16, 18, 19, 20]. The EKF usually updates all network parameters for all neurons $\mathbf{w} = [a_0, a_1, \mu_1^T, \sigma_1, ..., a_K, \mu_K^T, \sigma_K]$ at each learning step; we therefore refer to it as *global EKF* (GEKF). The computational complexity of the GEKF is $O(A^2)$ per learning step, where A denotes the number of parameters [18]. In our case, each neuron has four network parameters, represented by two scalars a_k and σ_k, and one neuron centre μ_k in 2D, as $\mathbf{w}_k = (a_k, \mu_k^T, \sigma_k)$. Therefore, the computational cost of global EKF is $O((4K)^2)$ per learning step for updating all K hidden units.

To avoid the high computational cost of the global EKF, we utilise a local approach, called *neighbourhood EKF* (NEKF). At each learning step, only a subset of network parameters $\mathbf{w}_n = \left\{a_0, \mathbf{w}_{n_i} \middle| \mathbf{w}_{n_i} = (a_{n_i}, \mu_{n_i}^T, \sigma_{n_i}),\ i = 1..B_n\right\}$ of B_n neighbour neuron(s) around the nth observation are updated. A neighbour neuron is selected, if it is 1) the nearest neighbour to the current observation; or 2) within a distance threshold $\mathcal{D}$ from the current observation. The computational cost of neighbourhood EKF is reduced to $O\left((4B_n)^2\right)$. The minimum cost can be O (constant) in the extreme case when only the first criterion is applied ($B_n = 1$) to update the nearest neighbour at each learning step. Experimental results show this improvement leads to considerable reduction of the computation load in network training compared to the GEKF or GD. It also obtains good accuracy, competitive with the GEKF and the GD, by consistently employing further-to-nearer refinement towards local fidelity (Ref. Section 4.4).

Using the neighbourhood EKF, we update the selected network parameters $\mathbf{w}_n = \{a_0, \mathbf{w}_{n_i}\}_{i=1}^{B}$ at the nth instance by

$$\mathbf{w}_n = \mathbf{w}_{n-1} + \mathbf{K}_n e_n \tag{8}$$

where $e_n = z_n - f(\mathbf{x}_n)$ is the prediction error at the nth observation $(\mathbf{x}_n, z_n)$, and $\mathbf{K}_n$ is the Kalman gain matrix calculated by

$$\mathbf{K}_n = \mathbf{P}_{n-1}\mathbf{B}_n \left[\mathbf{R}_n + \mathbf{B}_n^T \mathbf{P}_{n-1}\mathbf{B}_n\right]^{-1} \tag{9}$$

in which $\mathbf{R}_n$ is the variance of the measurement noise, $\mathbf{B}_n = \nabla_{\mathbf{w}_n} f(\mathbf{x}_n)$ is the gradient matrix of the function $f(\mathbf{x}_n)$ with respect to the parameter vector $\mathbf{w}_n$, and $\mathbf{P}_n$ is an error covariance matrix, which is updated by

$$\mathbf{P}_n = \left[\mathbf{I} - \mathbf{K}_n \mathbf{B}_n^T\right] \mathbf{P}_{n-1} + q\mathbf{I} \tag{10}$$

where scalar q determines the allowed random step in the direction of the gradient vector.

3.4 Network Pruning

The network size can become large when using only the above growth strategy, possibly leading to network overfit. To avoid this and obtain a compact network, a pruning strategy is applied [16]. Pruning removes those hidden units that make an insignificant contribution to the network output over a number of consecutive training observations. The pruning strategy is defined as follows:

For the current observation $(\mathbf{x}_n, z_n)$, compute the outputs of each hidden unit $o_k^n,\ k = 1..K$:

$$o_k^n = a_k \exp\left(-\frac{\|x_n - \mu_k\|^2}{\delta_k^2}\right) . \tag{11}$$

Calculate the normalised output values r_k^n over the largest absolute hidden unit output:

$$r_k^n = \frac{o_k^n}{\max(o_1^n, o_2^n, ..., o_K^n)} . \tag{12}$$

If $r_k^n < \rho$ for W consecutive observations, then the kth node is removed, where ρ is the *pruning threshold.*

4 Experimental Results

We have implemented the proposed adaptive RBF network algorithm in C++. We tested the algorithm on 3D surface reconstruction from the range images obtained from the Signal Analysis and Machine Perception Laboratory (SAMPL) of Ohio State University [21]. The range images were acquired by a Minolta scanner at image pixel resolution of 200 × 200. The scattered data are typically irregularly sampled with varying spatial densities. They contain measurement noise and holes.

In order to apply the RBF network, actual surface data stored in a 200 × 200 matrix associated to their locations were normalised and re-sampled in a random order. Such a normalised random sequence was used as a training set $\mathcal{T} = \{(x_n, y_n, z_n)\,|x_n, y_n, z_n \in [0,1], n = 1..N\}$ of N 2D observation inputs $\mathbf{x}_n = [x_n, y_n]^T$ and outputs z_n.

4.1 Mesh Repair and Surface Reconstruction

Figure 2 shows examples of surface reconstruction. Typical network parameters used in the experiments were: desired accuracy $E = 0.01$ (Eq. 4); $E_{rms} = 0.01$ in a sliding window $W = 1000$ (Eq. 5); largest scale of interest $\eta_{\max} = 0.4$ in the normalised space; neuron resolution $\eta_{\min} = 0.01$ for an average distribution density 1/200 of the range data. The decay constant was set as $\gamma = 0.999$ (Eq. 6) for an even sparse-to-dense spread of neurons in network space. The overlap factor ψ (Eq. 7) was chosen to reflect the spatial correlation and frequency varying

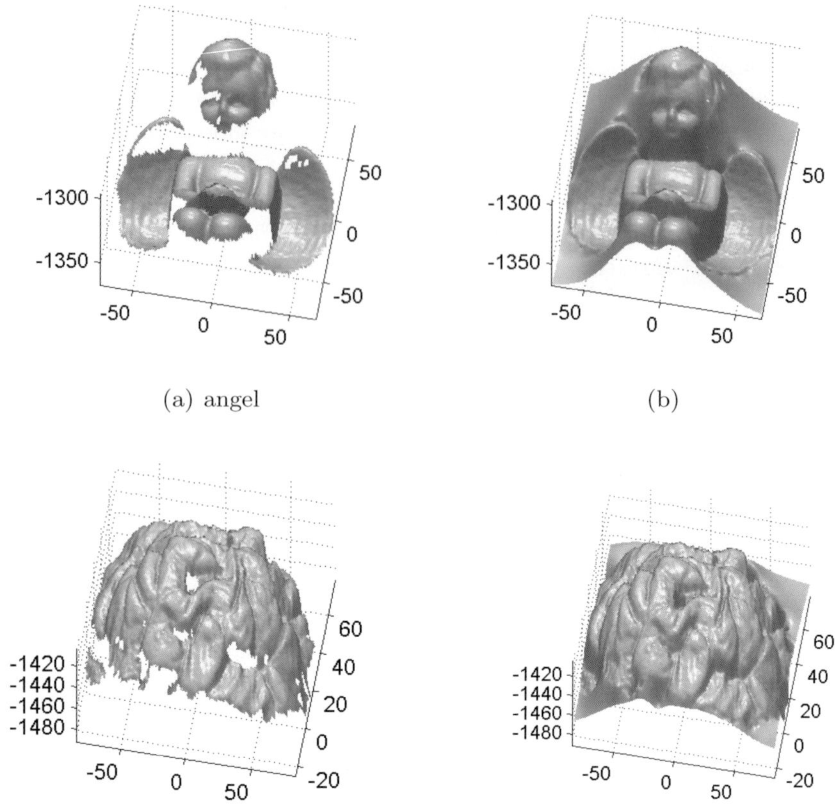

(a) angel (b)

(c) brain (d)

Fig. 2. Surface reconstruction: incomplete rendered meshes in the left column, repaired meshes in the right column

complexity in an image. For the examples in Fig. 2, we set $\psi = 0.7$ for the brain and valve images which contain high spatial frequency, while $\psi = 0.9$ was chosen for the angel and teletubby with relatively small geometric variation in the surface. The pruning threshold was set to $\rho = 0.001$ for 1000 consecutive observations (Eq. 12). From Fig. 2, we observe that Gaussian RBF networks provide extraordinary inter/extrapolation capabilities to: 1) smoothly reconstruct surfaces from non-uniformly sampled data with highly variable spatial frequencies; 2) smoothly blend and repair between raw noisy data to fill irregular holes that are large compared to the geometric variation in surfaces; 3) smoothly extend surfaces where there is no data by extrapolation.

Figure 3 illustrates the effectiveness of adaptive network learning using the example of angel reconstruction in Fig. 2(b). Figure 3(a) shows that at the start of training, neurons were steadily added to the network, and prediction error reduced rapidly as shown in Fig. 3(b). When the network tended to a desired accuracy after 5000 learning steps with about 800 units, the pruning strategy worked effectively to control network growth. "Pseudo" neurons, wrongly added due to noise points or exhibiting insignificant action were detected and removed based on observations over a period of learning instances.

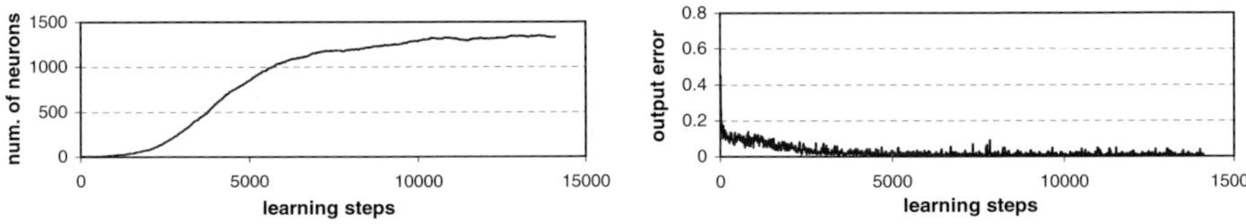

(a) neuron adding and pruning (b) prediction error

Fig. 3. Learning process of the angel reconstruction in Fig. 2(b)

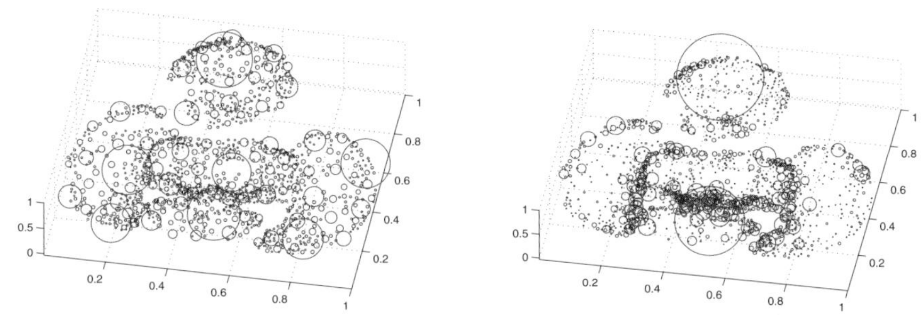

(a) width (b) weight

Fig. 4. Structure of output neurons for the reconstructed angel in Fig. 2(b) at display ratio 3:1

Figure 4 shows the distribution, width and weight of neurons in the resulting network representation. Neurons are represented by circles in normalised space at display ratio 3:1. For intuitive visualisation of neurons distributed in 2D network space associated with 3D geometry of the underlying data, we display the neurons in 3D space with their corresponding vertical z values estimated from the network. In Fig. 4(a), we used the radius of a circle to indicate neuron width. The maximum width is 0.33 for the angle example. In Fig. 4(b), we used the diameter of a circle to represent the absolute value of a neuron weight, with the maximum weight 0.92. We observe that distribution and density of neurons are highly adaptive to the complexity of the underlying data. Some neurons with large widths or high weights could often be generated initially for smooth bases within specified data ranges. Although there is an inherent tendency by the greedy algorithm to favour absorption of lower frequencies before higher ones, smaller neurons consistently refine the smoothness against fidelity to the local data so as to guarantee a coarse-to-fine optimality.

4.2 Data Compression

Data compression is achieved during adaptive learning. Table 1 presents network compression results from the reconstructions in Fig. 2, in which N stands for the number of 3D points in each range image of Fig. 2 left, and K denotes the number of neurons in the generated network representation. Storage compression rate is calculated by $3N : 4K$, since each neuron has 4 parameters. The prediction error $\bar{e}$ of the network is the average of absolute errors on all training points $\frac{1}{N}\sum_{n=1}^{N}|e_n|$.

Table 1. Data compression and accuracy

range image	number of points N	number of neurons K	compression rate	prediction error $\bar{e}$
angel	14,089	1345	7.9	.0059
brain	20,634	1964	7.9	.0043

4.3 Smooth Approximation

An exact surface reconstruction from scattered data is usually, but not always, desirable. A smooth approximation may be useful when the data are corrupted with noise, or contain excessive details that would require sub-sampling. The proposed network provides a capability of reconstructing surfaces at different resolution levels. This can be achieved by appropriately choosing the neuron resolution $\eta_{\min}$. Figure 5 demonstrates surface reconstruction at varying resolution and detail. Water-tight meshes with desired accuracy in Fig. 5(d) are smoothly completed at $\eta_{\min} = 0.01$ with $K = 1345$ neurons.

4.4 Comparison of Learning Algorithms

The computational cost of network training is mainly determined by the learning algorithm used for updating network parameters. We tested and compared the proposed neighbourhood EKF (NEKF) algorithm with two common learning methods, the gradient descent (GD) [17] and the global extended Kalman filter (GEKF). The comparison was executed on a Pentium 4 PC with 3GHz CPU and 512MB of RAM.

We used randomly sampled subsets from the angel data in Fig. 2(a) as training sets. Each trial had 4500 points. From the results, we found prediction errors of the three learning methods were very similar in terms of decreasing speed and accuracy achieved. However, the training time used at each learning step with increasing number of neurons, shown in Fig. 6 obtained on average from 10 randomly sampled trials, varies largely. To demonstrate the nature of the NEKF, the result presented for NEKF in Fig. 6(c) was obtained for the extreme case of updating only the nearest neighbour at each learning step, with very small increase of prediction error. We observed for GEKF the very high cost of 8.5 seconds for updating about 590 units towards the end of network training

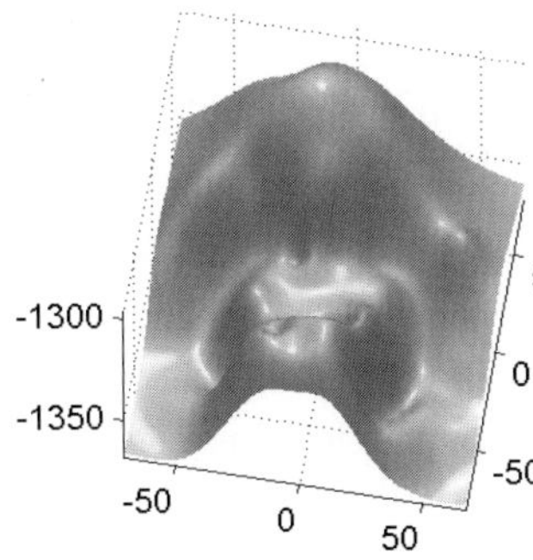

(a) $\eta_{\min} = 0.1$, $K = 62$

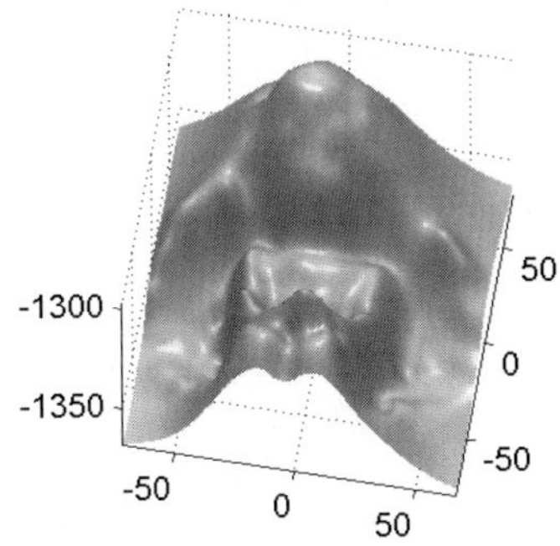

(b) $\eta_{\min} = 0.05$, $K = 182$

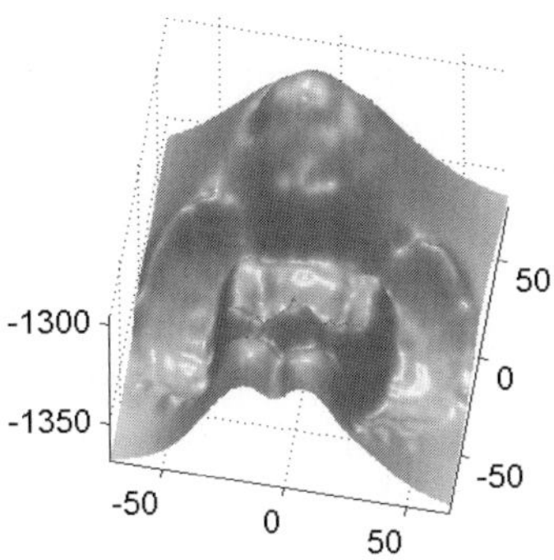

(c) $\eta_{\min} = 0.03$, $K = 408$

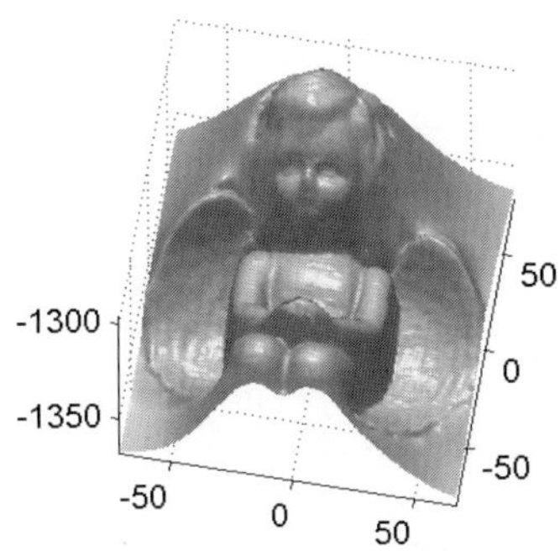

(d) $\eta_{\min} = 0.01$, $K = 1345$

Fig. 5. Surface reconstruction of the angel data in Fig. 2(a) at varying resolutions

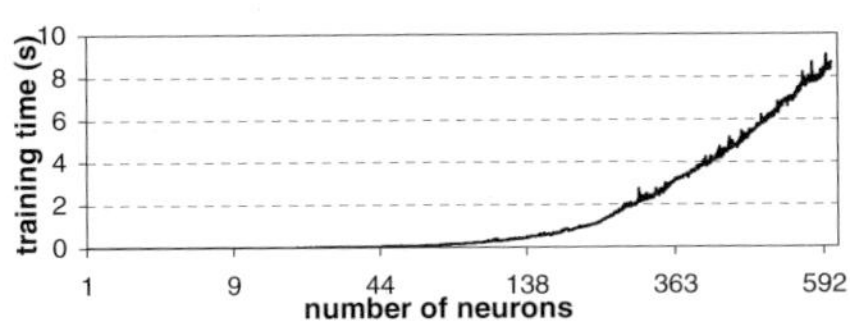

(a) GEKF

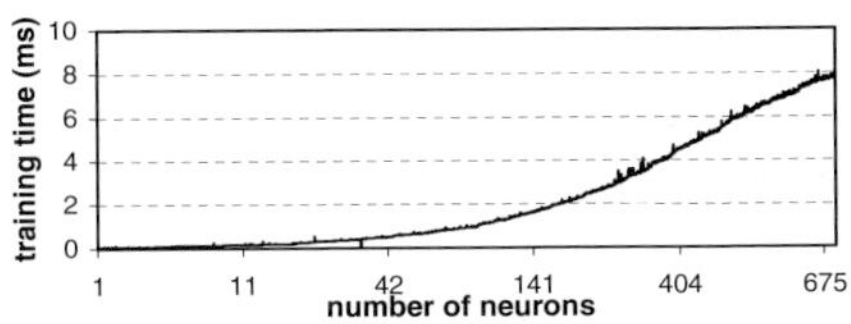

(b) GD

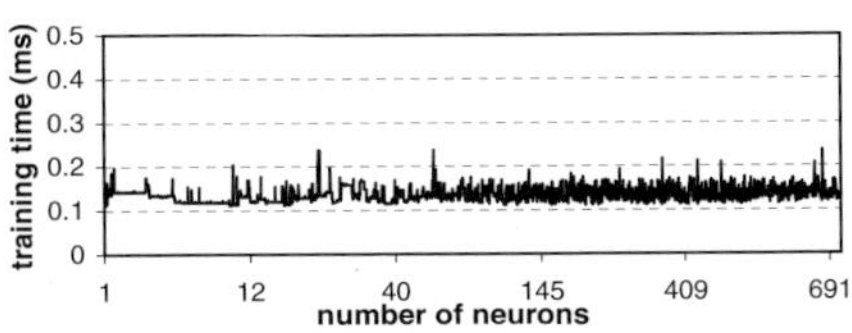

(c) NEKF

Fig. 6. Training time comparison executed on a Pentium 4 PC in C++

(Fig. 6(a)), with GD using around 8 milliseconds (ms) for 670 units (Fig. 6(b)), while NEKF spent an average of 0.14ms throughout the training process until 690 units were involved (Fig. 6(c)). Compared to GEKF, the computational load of NEKF was dramatically reduced by a factor 10^5.

5 Conclusion

We presented an adaptive RBF network using a heuristic learning strategy to interpret non-uniformly sampled scattered data and to complete surfaces from noisy range images. The network is established by adaptively locating neurons accompanied by a pruning strategy, reflecting the fidelity of underlying data. The full dimensionality of network parameters, corresponding to location, weight and width for each neuron, is refined iteratively. Compared to approaches using pre-defined fixed network structures, the greedy learning strategy provides a significant flexibility that is particularly suitable for highly variable spatial frequencies. It consequently guarantees the possibility of data reduction derived from only a subset of novelty points. Additionally, instead of using global EFK or GD to update network parameters at each learning step, we developed a neighbourhood EKF learning algorithm. This improvement led to a remarkable reduction on computation load and achieved desired global accuracy by providing local fidelity. Experimental results demonstrate that the network approach proves fruitful line of surface reconstruction with repaired incomplete meshes, geometric formulation and compression with potential applications in scientific visualisation and engineering modelling.

References

1. M. Musavi, W. Ahmed, K. Chan, K. Faris, and D. Hummels. On the training of radial basis function classifiers. *Neural Networks*, 5(4):595–603, 1992.
2. S. Chen, S. Billings, and P. Grant. Recursive hybrid algorithm for non-linear system identification using radial basis function networks. *Int. J. Control*, 55:1051–1070, 1992.
3. J. Blinn. A generalization of algebraic surface drawing. *ACM Trans. Graph.*, 1(3):235–256, 1982.
4. S. Muraki. Volumetric shape description of range data using blobby model. In *Proc. ACM SIGGRAPH*, 1991.
5. C. Lim, G. Turkiyyah, M. Ganter, and D. Storti. Implicit reconstruction of solids from cloud point sets. In *Proc. of the third ACM symposium on Solid modeling and applications*, pages 393–402, 1995.
6. A. Sharf, M. Alexa, and D. Cohen-Or. Context-based surface completion. *ACM Trans. Graph.*, 23(3):878–887, 2004.
7. N. Kojekine, I. Hagiwara, and V. Savchenko. Software tools using csrbf for processing scattered data. *Computer & Graphics*, 27(2):463–470, 2003.
8. G. Turk and J. O'Brien. Modelling with implicit surfaces that interpolate. *ACM Trans. on Graphics*, 21(4):855– 873, 2002.

9. Y. Ohtake, A. Belyaev, and H. Seidel. A multi-scale approach to 3D scattered data interpolation with compactly supported basis functions. In *SMI '03: Proc. Shape Modeling International*, pages 153–164, Washington, DC, USA, 2003. IEEE Computer Society.
10. Y. Ohtake, A. Belyaev, M. Alexa, G. Turk, and H. Seidel. Multi-level partition of unity implicits. *ACM Trans. Graph.*, 22(3):463–470, 2003.
11. J. Carr, R. Beatson, J. Cherrie, T. Mitchell, W. Fright, B. McCallum, and T. Evans. Reconstruction and representation of 3D objects with radial basis functions. In *ACM SIGGRAPH*, pages 67–76, 2001.
12. S. Ferrari, M. Maggioni, and N. A. Borghese. Multiscale approximation with hierarchical radial basis functions networks,. *IEEE Trans. on Neural Networks*, 15(1):178–188, 2004.
13. A. Bors and M. Gabbouj. Minimal topology for a radial basis functions neural network for pattern classification. *Digital Signal Processing*, 4(3):173–188, 1994.
14. J. Platt. A resource-allocating network for function interpolation. *Neural Comput.*, 3(2):213–225, 1991.
15. V. Kadirkamanathan and M. Niranjan. A function estimation approach to sequential learning with neural networks. *Neural Computation*, 5(6):954 – 975, 1993.
16. Y. Lu, N. Sundararajan, and P. Saratchandran. A sequential learning scheme for function approximation using minimal radial basis function neural networks. *Neural Comput.*, 9(2):461–478, 1997.
17. N. Karayiannis. Reformulated radial basis neural networks trained by gradient descent. *IEEE Trans. on Neural Networks*, 10(3):657–671, 1999.
18. D. Simon. Training radial basis neural networks with the extended Kalman filter. *Neurocomputing*, 48:455–475, 2002.
19. Y. Lu, N. Sundararajan, and P. Saratchandran. Performance evaluation of a sequential minimal radial basis function (rbf) neural network learning algorithm. *IEEE Trans. Neural Networks*, 9(2):308–318, 1998.
20. S. Haykin. *Kalman filtering and neural networks.* Wiley Intercience, 2001.
21. Range image database at Ohio SAMPL. http://sampl.ece.ohio-state.edu/data/3DDB/RID/minolta.

An Accurate Vertex Normal Computation Scheme*

Huanxi Zhao[1] and Ping Xiao[2]

[1] School of Information Science and Engineering,
Central South University, 410083, Changsha, China
[2] School of mathematical science and computing technology,
Central South University, 410083, Changsha, China
{hxzhao, xiaoping}@csu.edu.cn

Abstract. There are a number of applications in computer graphics and computer vision that require the accurate estimation of normal vectors at arbitrary vertices on a mesh surface. One common way to obtain a vertex normal over such models is to compute it as a weighted sum of the normals of facets sharing that vertex. But numerical tests and asymptotic analysis indicate that these proposed weighted average algorithms for vertex normal computation are all linear approximations. An open question proposed in [*CAGD,17:521-543, 2000*] is to find a linear combination scheme of the normals of the triangular faces, based on geometric considerations, that is quadratic convergence in the general mesh case. In this paper, we answer this question in general triangular mesh case. When tested on a few random mesh with valence 4, the scheme proposed by this paper is of second order accuracy, while the existing schemes only provide first order accuracy.

1 Introduction

Many algorithms in image processing, computer vision and computer graphics rely on the computation of surface normals. For example ([4, 11, 12]), shading an object is to simulate the behavior of light incident on its surfaces, and it is necessary to calculate normal vectors on the surfaces of the object for shading it. Since objects do not contain surface inclination in vertex-based representation, a normal vector for each vertex must be estimated from the relative position of its neighboring vertexes. Since the early 1970s, graphics researchers have produced several algorithms to compute vertex normals. These algorithms differ substantially from each other, but they all have in common the notion of weighting adjacent face normals in some fashion, that is, the formula of the vertex normal computation is of the following form:

$$\mathbf{n} = \frac{\sum_{i=1}^{n} \omega_i \mathbf{n}_i}{\| \sum_{i=1}^{n} \omega_i \mathbf{n}_i \|} \tag{1}$$

* Partially supported by Natural Science Foundation of China (10371130) and Youth Research Foundation of Central South University.

H.-P. Seidel, T. Nishita, and Q. Peng (Eds.): CGI 2006, LNCS 4035, pp. 442–451, 2006.

where the weight ω_i for normal $\mathbf{n}_i$ depends only on edge lengths and enclosed angles, and $\mathbf{n}_i$ is the face normal of the ith face (see fig.1). Various weights have been proposed for that purpose. Here, we decide to take a closer look at some of them that are widely used. The first vertex normal algorithm, which we will refer

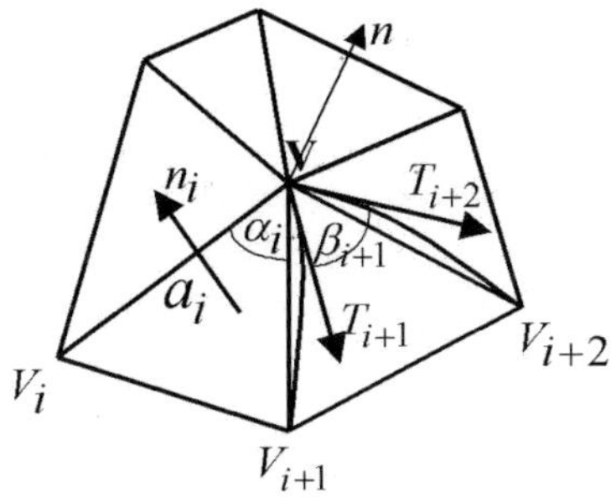

Fig. 1. One-ring of a vertex, edge, tangent vector, angle, vertex normal and facet normal

to as the mean weighted equally (MWE) algorithm, was introduced by Henri Gouraud [6] in 1971. In his algorithm, $\omega_i = 1$, that is, the normal of each adjacent facet contributes equally to the vertex normal. In 1998, however, Thurmer and Wuthrich [10]found that the results of the Gouraud's method strongly depend on the topology of the mesh around the vertex being processed. To improve the accuracy of the vertex normal computation method suggested by Gouraud, they proposed a new method for computing vertex normals which is mathematically more accurate and is referred to as "Mean Weighted by Angle" (MWA). In their algorithms, $\omega_i = \alpha_i$, where α_i is the angle between the two edge vectors $\mathbf{a}_i = \mathbf{VV}_i$ and $\mathbf{a}_{i+1} = \mathbf{VV}_{i+1}$ of the ith facet sharing the vertex. Unlike MWE, MWA suggested that facets which are "attached" to a vertex normal should have their contribution to the vertex normal weighted by the angle of the triangle that the vertex is part of. Not long after Thurmer & Wuthrich proposed their new vertex normal algorithm, in 1999, Max [8] suggested assigning non-equal weights deriving from the geometry. In his non-equal weighted vertex normal algorithm, which is referred to as the mean weighted by sine and edge length reciprocals (MWSELR), the weight $\omega_i = \frac{\sin \alpha_i}{a_i a_{i+1}}, a_i = ||\mathbf{a}_i||$, and the weight proposed in his paper give the correct normals for a polyhedron inscribed in a sphere. His formulation accounts for the differences in size of the facets surrounding the vertex by assigning larger weights for smaller facets, which he found helped handle the cases when the facets surrounding a vertex differ greatly in length. In addition, Max also presented several other vertex normal algorithms besides MWSELR, and we will list these here for brevity. The weights are $\omega_i = a_i a_{i+1}$, $\omega_i = \frac{1}{a_i a_{i+1}}$, and $\omega_i = \frac{1}{\sqrt{a_i a_{i+1}}}$. Recently, Chen and Wu [3] found from the theory of curvatures of regular surfaces, two triangles with equal area may have different effect on normal vectors computation, which indicates that the area-weights need to reflect this observation. Therefore, they proposed a so-called centroid-weight algorithm (CW), in which $w_i = ||g_i - P||^{-2}$ where g_i is the center of mass of the triangle $\triangle \mathbf{V}_i \mathbf{V} \mathbf{V}_{i+1}$. They claimed that the centroid-weights reflect its mathematical or physical meaning.

Jin et al in [7] investigate the above-mentioned vertex normal computation algorithms except for CW algorithm. They found that the most accurate algorithm depends on the class and that for some classes, in absolute sense, none of the available algorithms is particularly good. All that they can recommend is to increase the spatial sampling frequency when possible. In fact, numerical tests and asymptotic analysis indicate that the existing weighting schemes for mesh normals behave asymptotically similar, converging linearly in general and quadratically for a wide class of regular vertices (see [2]).

An open question raised by Meek and Walton [9] is to find a linear combination of the normals of the triangular faces, based on geometric considerations, that approximates the normal of the general surface mesh to second order accuracy. In this paper, we will answer this question. To obtain more accurate normal calculation, we should considers the more geometric contribution of each facet beside the edges and angles of adjacent triangles. In this paper, we will construct a second order approximation scheme for normal computation by adding a geometric contribution. Numerical results are given to support the theoretical results.

2 The New Weights

Since MWSELR accounts for the difference in size of these facets by assigning larger weights for smaller facets, and Max claimed that this algorithm is superior to other popular weighting methods by testing the algorithm on random cubic polynomial surfaces, so the weight that we shall present will be based on MWSELR. Furthermore, We will consider another geometric contribution due to the following observation. As we know, if the rate of change of the tangent vector is more fast, then the change of the normal vector along this tangent direction is more sensitivity. This seems to indicate that the weights need to reflect this observation, that is, in the non-equal weighted vertex normal algorithm, we should also consider the $||\mathbf{T}'||$ as a new geometric contribution of each facet. See Fig. 2, given a dense mesh M interpolating a smooth surface S and a mesh vertex V, let $\mathbf{V}_1, \mathbf{V}_2, ..., \mathbf{V}_n$ be the immediate neighbors of $\mathbf{V}$, ordered counterclockwise with respect to the chosen normal. In the MWSELR, if two triangles $\triangle \mathbf{V}_i \mathbf{V} \mathbf{V}_{i+1}$ and $\triangle \mathbf{V}'_i \mathbf{V} \mathbf{V}'_{i+1}$ have the same normal vector and are congruent, then they will have equal contributions to the resulting normal vector. However, from the above analysis, $\triangle \mathbf{V}_i \mathbf{V} \mathbf{V}_{i+1}$ and $\triangle \mathbf{V}'_i \mathbf{V} \mathbf{V}'_{i+1}$ should have different effect on estimation of the normal vector at point $\mathbf{V}$. Because of $||\mathbf{T}'|| = k(s)$, where $k(s)$ is the normal curvature of the geodesic $g_i(s)$ connecting $\mathbf{V}$ and $\mathbf{V}_i$, this suggests that we should chose the weights:

$$w_i = \frac{\sin \alpha_i}{a_i a_{i+1} k_i k_{i+1}} \tag{2}$$

in equation (1), and so we may obtain a more accurate algorithm for the vertex normal vector.

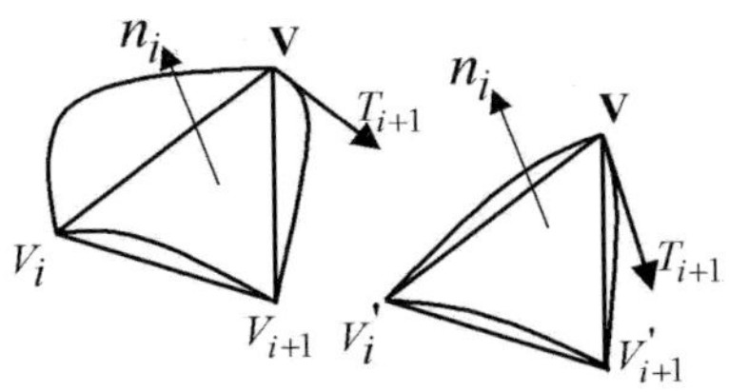

Fig. 2. They have the same effects under MWSELR, but they have different effect on vector normal vector under our weight

3 The Estimation of Normal Curvature

In the above defined weights, however, we don't know the value of the normal curvature k_i, hence, at present, we can not compute the normal vector by means of (1) and (2) without the estimation value of k_i. In this section, we will give a first order approximation value of normal curvature k_i.

See Figure 2, for each edge $\mathbf{VV}_i$, consider the geodesic curve $g_i(s)$ parameterized by arc length s, connecting $\mathbf{V}$ and $\mathbf{V}_i$, $g_i(0) = \mathbf{V}, g_i(s_i) = \mathbf{V}_i$, where $s_i = \widehat{\mathbf{VV}}_i$ is arc length. For each geodesic $g_i(s)$, consider its Darboux frame $\{\mathbf{T}_i, \mathbf{B}_i, \mathbf{N}\}$, where $\mathbf{N}$ and $\mathbf{T}_i$ is the unit surface normal and the unit tangent vector at $\mathbf{V}$, respectively, and $\mathbf{B}_i = \mathbf{N} \times \mathbf{T}_i$. Given the above curve $g_i(s)$, we have the well known Frenet equations

$$\frac{d\mathbf{T}_i}{ds} = k_i\mathbf{N}, \frac{d\mathbf{B}_i}{ds} = \tau_i\mathbf{N}, \frac{d\mathbf{N}_i}{ds} = -k_i\mathbf{T} - \tau_i\mathbf{B}.$$

where τ_i is geodesic torsion of $g_i(s)$. Differentiating the curve $g_i(s)$ with respect to its arc length s, then yields

$$g_i' = \frac{dg_i}{ds} = \mathbf{T}_i; g_i'' = k_i\mathbf{N}; g_i''' = k_i'\mathbf{N} - k_i^2\mathbf{T} - k_i\tau_i\mathbf{B}$$

and so on. Now we can use Taylor expansion to express

$$\begin{aligned}\mathbf{a}_i = \mathbf{g}(s_i) - \mathbf{g}(0) = s_i g_i' + \frac{s_i^2}{2}g_i'' + \frac{s_i^3}{6}g_i''' = \mathbf{T}_i(s_i - \frac{s_i^3}{6}k_i^2 + O(s_i^4)) \\ + \mathbf{N}(\frac{1}{2}s_i^2k_i + \frac{1}{6}s_i^3k_i' + O(s_i^4)) + \mathbf{B}_i(-\frac{1}{6}s_i^3k_i\tau_i + O(s_i^4)).\end{aligned} \quad (3)$$

Since $(\mathbf{N}, \mathbf{T}_i, \mathbf{B}_i)$ is an orthogonal basis, we can compute the length a_i of $\mathbf{a}_i$ in terms of s_i by

$$a_i = ||\mathbf{a}_i|| = s_i - \frac{s_i^3}{24}k_i^2 + O(s_i^4).$$

Substituting the expansion of s_i into the formula (3) for $\mathbf{a}_i$ and dividing by a_i yields (see also [1])

$$\frac{\mathbf{a}_i}{a_i} = \mathbf{T}_i(1 - \frac{a_i^2}{8}k_i^2 + O(a_i^3)) + \mathbf{N}(\frac{1}{2}a_ik_i + \frac{1}{6}a_i^2k_i' + O(a_i^3)) + \mathbf{B}_i(-\frac{1}{6}a_i^2k_i\tau + O(a_i^3)).$$

Let β_i be the angle between $\mathbf{T}_i$ and $\mathbf{T}_{i+1}$ (indices taken modulo n), see Figure 1. Now we can compute the normal of an incident triangle at $\mathbf{V}$ as (see also [1])

$$\begin{aligned}\frac{\mathbf{a}_i}{a_i} \times \frac{\mathbf{a}_{i+1}}{a_{i+1}} &= \mathbf{N}(1 + O(a_i^2, a_{i+1}^2)) \\ &+ \mathbf{B}_i(-\frac{a_{i+1}}{2\sin\beta_i}k_{i+1} + O(a_i^2, a_{i+1}^2)) \\ &+ \mathbf{B}_{i+1}(\frac{a_i}{2\sin\beta_i}k_i + O(a_i^2, a_{i+1}^2)) \\ &+ (\mathbf{T}_i + \mathbf{T}_{i+1})O(a_i^2, a_{i+1}^2).\end{aligned}$$

Since $\alpha_i = \beta_i + O(a_i^2)$, the above equation can be written as

$$\begin{aligned}\frac{\mathbf{a}_i}{a_i} \times \frac{\mathbf{a}_{i+1}}{a_{i+1}} &= \mathbf{N}(1 + O(a_i^2, a_{i+1}^2)) \\ &+ \mathbf{B}_i(-\frac{a_{i+1}}{2\sin\alpha_i}k_{i+1} + O(a_i^2, a_{i+1}^2)) \\ &+ \mathbf{B}_{i+1}(\frac{a_i}{2\sin\alpha_i}k_i + O(a_i^2, a_{i+1}^2)) \\ &+ (\mathbf{T}_i + \mathbf{T}_{i+1})O(a_i^2, a_{i+1}^2).\end{aligned} \tag{4}$$

By simple computation, we obtained

$$\begin{aligned}< \frac{\mathbf{a}_{i-1}}{a_{i-1}}, \frac{\mathbf{a}_i \times \mathbf{a}_{i+1}}{\|\mathbf{a}_i \times \mathbf{a}_{i+1}\|} >&= \frac{1}{2}a_{i+1}k_{i+1}\frac{\sin\alpha_{i-1}}{\sin\alpha_i} - \frac{1}{2}a_i k_i \frac{\sin(\alpha_{i-1}+\alpha_i)}{\sin\alpha_i} \\ &+ \frac{1}{2}a_{i-1}k_{i-1} + O(a_{i-1}, a_i, a_{i+1}).\end{aligned} \tag{5}$$

Hence, if we remove the last term from the right hand side of equation (5), we obtain the n equations with n knowns k_i^* $(i = 1, 2, ..., n; n > 3)$, which are first order approximations of k_i, that is,

$$\begin{aligned}< \frac{\mathbf{a}_{i-1}}{a_i}, \frac{\mathbf{a}_i \times \mathbf{a}_{i+1}}{\|\mathbf{a}_i \times \mathbf{a}_{i+1}\|} >&= \frac{1}{2}a_{i+1}k_{i+1}^*\frac{\sin\alpha_{i-1}}{\sin\alpha_i} \\ &- \frac{1}{2}a_i k_i^* \frac{\sin(\alpha_{i-1,i})}{\sin\alpha_i} + \frac{1}{2}a_{i-1}k_{i-1}^*.\end{aligned} \tag{6}$$

where $\alpha_{i-1,i} = \alpha_{i-1} + \alpha_i$ and the lower indices are taken modulo n. The above linear systems (6) can be represented in matrix form as the following matrix equation

$$A\mathbf{x} = \mathbf{b}, \tag{7}$$

where

$$\mathbf{x} = \begin{pmatrix} a_1k_1^* \\ a_2k_2^* \\ \vdots \\ a_nk_n^* \end{pmatrix} := \begin{pmatrix} x_1 \\ x_2 \\ \vdots \\ x_n \end{pmatrix}, \mathbf{b} = \begin{pmatrix} < \frac{\mathbf{a}_1}{a_1}, \frac{\mathbf{a}_2 \times \mathbf{a}_3}{\|\mathbf{a}_2 \times \mathbf{a}_3\|} > \\ < \frac{\mathbf{a}_2}{a_2}, \frac{\mathbf{a}_3 \times \mathbf{a}_4}{\|\mathbf{a}_3 \times \mathbf{a}_4\|} > \\ \vdots \\ < \frac{\mathbf{a}_n}{a_n}, \frac{\mathbf{a}_1 \times \mathbf{a}_2}{\|\mathbf{a}_1 \times \mathbf{a}_2\|} > \end{pmatrix},$$

and

$$A = \frac{1}{2}\begin{pmatrix} 1 & -\frac{\sin\alpha_{1,2}}{\sin\alpha_2} & \frac{\sin\alpha_1}{\sin\alpha_2} & 0 & \cdots & 0 & 0 \\ 0 & 1 & -\frac{\sin\alpha_{2,3}}{\sin\alpha_3} & \frac{\sin\alpha_2}{\sin\alpha_3} & \cdots & 0 & 0 \\ \vdots & \vdots & \ddots & \ddots & \ddots & \vdots & \vdots \\ 0 & 0 & 0 & 0 & \cdots & -\frac{\sin\alpha_{n-2,n-1}}{\sin\alpha_{n-1}} & \frac{\sin\alpha_{n-2}}{\sin\alpha_{n-1}} \\ \frac{\sin\alpha_{n-1}}{\sin\alpha_n} & 0 & 0 & 0 & \cdots & 1 & -\frac{\sin\alpha_{n-1,n}}{\sin\alpha_n} \\ -\frac{\sin\alpha_{n,1}}{\sin\alpha_1} & \frac{\sin\alpha_n}{\sin\alpha_1} & 0 & 0 & \cdots & 0 & 1 \end{pmatrix}.$$

Hence, the weights w_i can be written as

$$w_i = \frac{\sin\alpha_i}{x_i x_{i+1}}$$

As we known, if the matrix A is nonsingular, then the above equation (7) has a nonzero solution, and we get the first order approximation value $(k_1^*, k_2^*, ..., k_n^*)$ of $(k_1, k_2, ..., k_n)$. But, at the same time, from equation (7), we can also obtain an important information, that the stability of algorithm (1) depends on the vertex angle of the mesh, that is, the condition number of matrix A depends on the vertex angle α_i. If the distribution of the vertex angles makes the matrix A ill-conditioned, then the accuracy may be only first order, and in this case, this algorithm is degenerative.

4 Quadratic Convergence and Numerical Experiments

It is easy to prove that algorithm (1) with (2) and $\mathbf{n}_i = \frac{\mathbf{a}_i}{a_i} \times \frac{\mathbf{a}_{i+1}}{a_{i+1}}$ defined in (4) is a second order approximation of the real normal $\mathbf{N}$. In fact, substituting the expansion (4) of $\frac{\mathbf{a}_i}{a_i} \times \frac{\mathbf{a}_{i+1}}{a_{i+1}}$ and (2) into $\sum_{i=1}^{n} \omega_i \mathbf{n}_i$, we have

$$\sum_{i=1}^{n} \omega_i \mathbf{n}_i = \sum_{i=1}^{n} (\mathbf{N}\omega_i - \mathbf{B}_i \frac{1}{2a_i k_i} + \mathbf{B}_{i+1} \frac{1}{2a_{i+1}k_{i+1}} + \omega_i(\mathbf{N} + \mathbf{B}_i + \mathbf{B}_{i+1} + \mathbf{T}_i + \mathbf{T}_{i+1}) O(a_i, a_{i+1})^2) \tag{8}$$

Since the lower indices are taken modulo n, that $n_{n+1} = n_1$, (8) can be written as

$$\sum_{i=1}^{n} \omega_i \mathbf{n}_i = \sum_{i=1}^{n} (\mathbf{N}\omega_i + \omega_i(\mathbf{N} + \mathbf{B}_i + \mathbf{B}_{i+1} + \mathbf{T}_i + \mathbf{T}_{i+1}) O(a_i, a_{i+1})^2)$$

where $\mathbf{W}_i$ is a linear combination of vectors $\mathbf{N}, \mathbf{B}_i, \mathbf{B}_{i+1}, \mathbf{T}_i, \mathbf{T}_{i+1}$. If $w_1 + w_2 + ... + w_n \neq 0$, a good approximation for the vertex normal $\mathbf{N}$ defined in (1) would look like this:

$$\mathbf{n} = \frac{\sum_{i=1}^{n} \omega_i \mathbf{n}_i}{\| \sum_{i=1}^{n} \omega_i \mathbf{n}_i \|} = \mathbf{N} + \mathbf{W} O((a_1, a_2, ..., a_n)^2),$$

where $\mathbf{W} = \sum_{i=1}^{n} c_i \mathbf{W}_i (c_i$ are constants), and this is second order accuracy scheme.

The second aim of this section is to exhibit the numerical behaviors of the vertex normal calculation scheme proposed by this paper, and determine whether it quadratic converges numerically to the exact normal vector. In our numerical examples, the approximation are found using heightfield data, which are two-dimensional arrays of height values, and are commonly used to store terrain or water surface data, and are also commonly used for calculating bump maps. In this case, the vertex valence n are taken to be 4, and the equations can be written as

$$AK = \mathbf{b}$$

where the matrix

$$A = \frac{1}{2}\begin{pmatrix} 1 & \frac{\sin\alpha_{1,2}}{-\sin\alpha_2} & \frac{\sin\alpha_1}{\sin\alpha_2} & 0 \\ 0 & 1 & \frac{\sin\alpha_{2,3}}{-\sin\alpha_3} & \frac{\sin\alpha_2}{\sin\alpha_3} \\ \frac{\sin\alpha_3}{\sin\alpha_4} & 0 & 1 & -\frac{\sin\alpha_{3,4}}{\sin\alpha_4} \\ \frac{\sin\alpha_{4,1}}{-\sin\alpha_1} & \frac{\sin\alpha_4}{\sin\alpha_1} & 0 & 1 \end{pmatrix},$$

the vector

$$\mathbf{K} = \begin{pmatrix} a_1 k_1^* \\ a_2 k_2^* \\ a_3 k_3^* \\ a_4 k_4^* \end{pmatrix}, \quad \mathbf{b} = \begin{pmatrix} < \frac{\mathbf{a}_1}{a_1}, \frac{\mathbf{a}_2 \times \mathbf{a}_3}{\|\mathbf{a}_2 \times \mathbf{a}_3\|} > \\ < \frac{\mathbf{a}_2}{a_2}, \frac{\mathbf{a}_3 \times \mathbf{a}_4}{\|\mathbf{a}_3 \times \mathbf{a}_4\|} > \\ < \frac{\mathbf{a}_3}{a_3}, \frac{\mathbf{a}_4 \times \mathbf{a}_1}{\|\mathbf{a}_4 \times \mathbf{a}_1\|} > \\ < \frac{\mathbf{a}_4}{a_4}, \frac{\mathbf{a}_1 \times \mathbf{a}_2}{\|\mathbf{a}_1 \times \mathbf{a}_2\|} > \end{pmatrix}.$$

To show the numerical convergence, we take several two variable functions as artificial heightfield data over xy-plane as surfaces in $\mathbf{R}^3$ so that the exact normal vector can be easily computed. Both the exact and approximated normal vectors are computed at some selected domain points $q_{ij} = (x_i, y_j) \in [0,1]\times[0,1]$. These points are chosen as $(x_i, y_j) = (\frac{i}{20}, \frac{j}{20})$ for $i = 1, \cdots, 19,\ j = 1, \cdots, 19$. The domain around q_{ij} is triangulated locally by choosing 4 distributed points:

$$q_k = q_{ij} + r_k(\cos\theta_k, \sin\theta_k), \tag{9}$$

where $r_k = r(1 + 0.0001 * k)$, $\theta_k = (k - 1 + 0.0001 * k)2\pi/4, k = 1, \cdots, 4$, then we map the plane triangulation onto the surfaces by the selected bivariate functions. The convergence property and the convergence rate are checked by taking $r = 1/8, 1/16, 1/32, \cdots$. The functions we use are the following

$$
\begin{aligned}
F_1(x,y) &= 0.75\exp\{\frac{-(9x-2)^2-(9y-2)^2}{4}\\
&+0.75\exp\{-[\frac{(9x+1)^2}{49}+\frac{(9y+1)}{10}]\}\\
&+0.5\exp\{\frac{-(9x-7)^2-(9y-3)^2}{4}\}\\
&-0.2\exp\{-[(9x-4)^2+(9y-7)^2]\},\\
F_2(x,y) &= \frac{1.25+\cos(5.4y)}{6+6(3x-1)^2},\\
F_3(x,y) &= \frac{\exp\left\{-\frac{81}{16}\left[(x-0.5)^2+(y-0.5)^2\right]\right\}}{3},\\
F_4(x,y) &= ((\frac{8}{9})^2-(x-\frac{1}{2})^2-(y-\frac{1}{2})^2)^{\frac{1}{2}}-\frac{1}{2},
\end{aligned}
$$

The numerical experiments show that as $r \to 0$, the maximal error of the approximated vertex normal computed by our algorithm over the above mentioned local triangulations and the exact vertex normal computed from the continuous surfaces defined by F_j tend asymptotically to the form $e_k(F_j, r) := C_{kj}r^k$ for a constant C_{kj} and an integer k. Table 1-4 show the asymptotic maximal error $e_0(F_j)$, $e_1(F_j)$ and $e_2(F_j)(j = 1, 2, 3, 4)$.

Table 1. The Asymptotic Maximal Errors $e_i(F_1, n)(i = 0, 1, 2)$

$1/r$	$e_0(F_1)$	$e_1(F_1)/r$	$e_2(F_1)/r^2$
8	2.434794e+000	1.947835e+001	1.558268e+002
16	2.743809e-001	4.390095e+000	7.024152e+001
32	7.004962e-002	2.241588e+000	7.173081e+001
64	1.357551e-002	8.688325e-001	5.560528e+001
128	3.372997e-003	4.317436e-001	5.526318e+001
256	8.461392e-004	2.166116e-001	5.545258e+001
512	2.118293e-004	1.084566e-001	5.552977e+001
1024	5.303229e-005	5.430507e-002	5.560839e+001
2048	1.329102e-005	2.722001e-002	5.574658e+001
4096	5.423823e-006	2.221598e-002	9.099664e+001
8192	2.716222e-006	2.225129e-002	1.822826e+002

Table 2. The Asymptotic Maximal Errors $e_i(F_2, n)(i = 0, 1, 2)$

$1/r$	$e_0(F_1)$	$e_1(F_1)/r$	$e_2(F_1)/r^2$
8	9.321696e-002	7.457357e-001	5.965886e+000
16	2.648828e-002	4.238126e-001	6.781001e+000
32	6.827666e-003	2.184853e-001	6.991530e+000
64	1.719685e-003	1.100598e-001	7.043828e+000
128	4.306928e-004	5.512868e-002	7.056471e+000
256	1.077086e-004	2.757340e-002	7.058792e+000
512	2.692294e-005	1.378455e-002	7.057687e+000
1024	1.031466e-005	1.056221e-002	1.081570e+001
2048	5.265508e-006	1.078376e-002	2.208514e+001
4096	2.777209e-006	1.137545e-002	4.659384e+001
8192	2.247672e-006	1.841293e-002	1.508387e+002

Table 3. The Asymptotic Maximal Errors $e_i(F_3, n)(i = 0, 1, 2)$

$1/r$	$e_0(F_1)$	$e_1(F_1)/r$	$e_2(F_1)/r^2$
8	2.452809e-002	1.962247e-001	1.569798e+000
16	6.101349e-003	9.762158e-002	1.561945e+000
32	1.527159e-003	4.886909e-002	1.563811e+000
64	3.833783e-004	2.453621e-002	1.570317e+000
128	9.669281e-005	1.237668e-002	1.584215e+000
256	2.460076e-005	6.297794e-003	1.612235e+000
512	6.364165e-006	3.258453e-003	1.668328e+000
1024	1.702576e-006	1.743437e-003	1.785280e+000
2048	6.361572e-007	1.302850e-003	2.668237e+000
4096	2.730245e-007	1.118309e-003	4.580592e+000
8192	1.868947e-007	1.531041e-003	1.254229e+001

Table 4. The Asymptotic Maximal Errors $e_i(F_4, n)(i = 0, 1, 2)$

$1/r$	$e_0(F_1)$	$e_1(F_1)/r$	$e_2(F_1)/r^2$
8	1.575054e-001	1.260044e+000	1.008035e+001
16	5.278866e-002	8.446185e-001	1.351390e+001
32	1.381857e-002	4.421942e-001	1.415022e+001
64	3.479125e-003	2.226640e-001	1.425050e+001
128	8.726080e-004	1.116938e-001	1.429681e+001
256	2.191618e-004	5.610541e-002	1.436299e+001
512	5.527276e-005	2.829965e-002	1.448942e+001
1024	1.405792e-005	1.439531e-002	1.474080e+001
2048	3.634249e-006	7.442941e-003	1.524314e+001
4096	9.684482e-007	3.966764e-003	1.624787e+001
8192	3.971585e-007	3.253523e-003	2.665286e+001

From these numerical results (see the above tables, $e_0(F_j, r)/e_0(F_j, 2r) \simeq 4 = 2^2, r = \frac{1}{8}, \frac{1}{16}, ..., \frac{1}{4096}; j = 1, 2, 3, 4.$), we can draw the following conclusion for the irregularly distributed domain vertices: the approximate normal converges in the rate $O(r^2)$.

5 Conclusions and Further Work

By intuitive differential geometry observation and asymptotic analysis, we present a quadratic approximation scheme for vertex (its valence $n > 3$) normal over general triangular mesh, and find that the stability of second order scheme depends on the vertex angles. If the vertex angles are not well-posed, then this kind of second order algorithm is not appropriate for noisy data (but least squares methods are appropriate in this case.). Because, in this case, the second order scheme may be degenerative, and may be only of first order accuracy. In addition, since our approach need to solve a linear system, compared to the explicit scheme, our algorithm is more time-consuming. So, we will look for more concision and more robust second order approximation schemes for the vertex normal vector.

References

1. T.Langer, A.G. Belyaev, and H.P. Seidel, Asymptotic Analysis of Discrete Normals and Curvatures of Polylines , In: Spring Conference on Computer Graphics SCCG 2005 Juttler, Bert (Eds.)(2005)229-232.

2. T. Langer, A. G. Belyaev, and H.-P. Seidel. Analysis and design of discrete normals and curvatures. Research Report MPI-I-2005-4-003, Max-Planck Institut für Informatik, 2005.
3. S.G. Chen , J.Y. Wu, Estimating normal vectors and curvatures by centroid weights, Computer Aided Geometric Design, v.21(5), (2004)447-458.
4. D.Cohen, A.Kaufman, R.Bakalash and S.Bergman, Real-Time Discret hading, The Visual Computer, 6(1),(1990)16-27.
5. A. S. Glassner, Computing surface normals for 3D models. In A. S. Glassner, editor, Graphics Gems, pages 562-566. Academic Press, 1990.
6. H.Gouraud, Continuous shading of curved surfaces. IEEE Transactions on Computers C-20(6),(1971)623-29.
7. S.S Jin, R.R. Lewis and D.West,A comparison of algorithms for vertex normal computation. The Visual Computer 21:(2005)71-82.
8. N.Max, Weights for computing vertex normals from facet normals. J Graph Tools 4(2):(1999)1-6.
9. D. Meek and D. Walton, On surface normal and Gaussian curvature approximation given data sampled from a smooth surface, Computer-Aided Geometric Design 17,(2000)521-543.
10. G.Thurmer,C. Wuthrich, Computing vertex normals from polygonal facets. J Graph Tools 3(1),(1998)43-46.
11. R.E. Webber, Ray Tracing Voxel Based Data via Biquadratic Local Surfac nterpolation, The Visual Computer, 6(1),(1990) 8-15.
12. R.Yagel, D.Cohen and A. Kaufman, Discrete Ray Tracing, IEE omputer Graphics & Applications, 12(5),(1992)19-28.

A Visibility-Based Automatic Path Generation Method for Virtual Colonoscopy

Jeongjin Lee, Moon Koo Kang*, and Yeong Gil Shin

School of Electrical Engineering and Computer Science, Seoul National University, San 56-1 Shinlim 9-dong Kwanak-gu, Seoul 151-742, Korea
jjlee@cglab.snu.ac.kr, moonkang@ee.snu.ac.kr, yshin@cglab.snu.ac.kr

Abstract. In virtual colonoscopy, it is crucial to generate the camera path rapidly and accurately. Most of the existing path generation methods are computationally expensive since they require a lengthy preprocessing step and the 3D positions of all path points should be generated. In this paper, we propose a visibility-based automatic path generation method by emulating the ray propagation through the conduit of the colon. The proposed method does not require any preliminary data preprocessing steps, and it also dramatically reduces the number of points needed to represent the camera path using control points. The result is a perceivable increase in computational efficiency and easier colon navigation with the same level of accuracy.

1 Introduction

Colon cancer is among the leading causes of cancer deaths, yet it can be cured by proper treatment and early detection. The colon examination usually resorts to the invasive methods such as optical endoscopy and barium enema. In optical endoscopy, the inspector examines the inner surface of the colon by manipulating a small camera at the tip of an optical probe. Controlling the camera requires great skill and precision, and the examination of the entire colon takes a long time. Also, the invasion of a probe is uncomfortable, as well as demanding a lengthy preparation step and causing contagion and bleeding [1-2]. In barium enema, the inspector examines the contrast material adhering to the colon wall using X-ray radiographs. In this examination, the patient needs to go through a serious discomfort and the polyp detection sensitivity is not as good as that of optical endoscopy.

Virtual colonoscopy as an alternative can ease a lot of difficulties in the conventional methods. Also, this method enables higher sensitivity and specificity of the examination as well as reducing the discomfort that the patient should bear [3-6]. With the recent introduction of multi-detector CT, the CT processing has become remarkably fast and the polyp detection sensitivity is enhanced [7]. In contrast to optical endoscopy, a virtual camera can move in any direction to thoroughly examine the colon improving the efficiency of diagnosis [8].

In current virtual colonoscopy, the camera path should be determined in prior to the examination process. The center position of the colonic section is to be

* Corresponding author.

H.-P. Seidel, T. Nishita, and Q. Peng (Eds.): CGI 2006, LNCS 4035, pp. 452–459, 2006.

determined on each 2D image by a skilled physician, and these positions are to be interpolated for virtual navigation. It takes a long time to determine all the center positions for the entire colon sections, necessitating an automated path finding scheme since the average colon length usually measures over 1.5m and the conduit of colon is tortuous. A topological thinning algorithm can be used to eliminate the outermost layer of the segmented colon images reconstructed in 3D, until the centerline voxels are finally left over [3][9]. While the path defined by this method is accurate in the geometric sense, the path finding time could be excessively long to carry out all the necessary processing of the entire segmented voxels. The navigation path calculation can be done by using the shortest-path algorithm suggested by Dijkstra with a lengthy preprocessing step. However, the preprocessing and searching for all the points on the path takes a long time [10-12].

In this paper, we propose an efficient path generation method by emulating the propagation of rays through the conduit of colon. The proposed method can be executed in runtime without any preliminary data processing steps. Instead of generating all points of the path, it generates only a small number of control points to represent the camera path to increase computational efficiency. Experiments were performed to illustrate the effectiveness of the proposed scheme. Since the path is determined based on the visibility, the virtual camera moves along a path on which the navigator can inspect the colon with the least eye-strain.

2 A Visibility-Based Automatic Path Generation Method

The path generation scheme proposed in this paper is to be carried out in the following steps. First, the seed point is provided by the physician on a 3D volume rendered image of a colon and the starting position and direction of the initial reference ray is determined. Next, control points of the optimal path are to be found by using the algorithm of simulating ray propagation. Finally, the camera path is generated by interpolating these control points in both forward and backward directions and will be merged together to make the final navigation path.

2.1 Initializing the Reference Ray

The path generation algorithm begins by determining the starting position and direction of the reference ray. First, the physician defines the seed point on the 2D projection image. A 2D image coordinate should be transformed into a 3D object coordinate by propagating a ray along the direction perpendicular to the image plane. Two intersection points between the ray and the colon walls are found. The center point between two intersection points is the optimal starting position of the reference ray. Rays are progressed in all visible directions from the starting position and the intersection points between the ray and the colon wall are found. The direction in which the ray can reach the farthest from the starting point is regarded as the direction having the highest visibility from the starting point. This direction will be taken as the direction of the initial reference ray, $\vec{R}_{d0}(\theta_0, \phi_0)$.

2.2 Making the Look-up Table for Expanding a Virtual Sphere

The procedure for a path generation can be accelerated by employing a look-up table. In our method, a virtual sphere will be located on the newly generated control point, $P_{candidate}$, and the radius of the sphere will be expanded by 1 voxel at a time. The contact point between the expanding sphere and the colon wall will be found as shown in Fig. 3(c). A pre-calculated look-up table can aid in this procedure. The pre-calculated look-up table contains relative coordinates from the center of the sphere in the order of increasing distance from the center point. The surface point, P_{sphere} can be obtained by adding the relative coordinates in the offset table(OT) to the coordinate of $P_{candidate}$ as shown in Eq. (1).

$$P_{sphere} = P_{candidate} + (OT\_x(i), OT\_y(i),\ OT\_z(i))\,. \tag{1}$$

In Fig. 1, the distance between each integer vertex (i, j) and the origin (0, 0) can be calculated and round off, and the vertices having the same D value are to be lined up in the 2-D space. An offset table is then constructed by storing the vertices in order, as shown in Fig. 2. This table can be used to accelerate the expansion of the disk on the x-y plane, and the same thing applies for the sphere in the 3-D space.

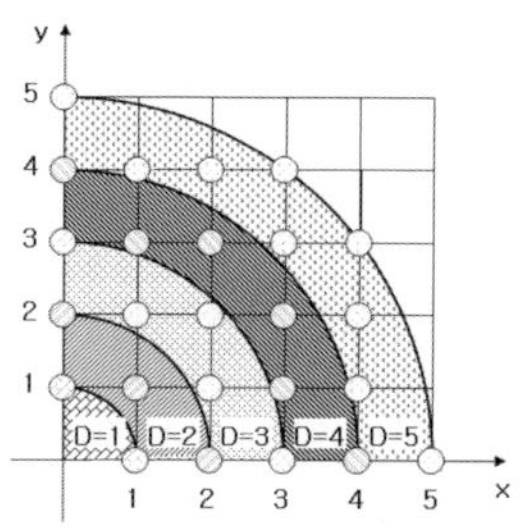

	(x,y)								
D=1	(1,0)	(0,1)							
D=2	(2,0)	(1,1)	(0,2)						
D=3	(3,0)	(2,1)	(2,2)	(1,2)	(0,3)				
D=4	(4,0)	(3,1)	(3,2)	(2,3)	(1,3)	(0,4)			
D=5	(5,0)	(4,1)	(4,2)	(4,3)	(3,3)	(3,4)	(2,4)	(1,4)	(5,0)

Fig. 1. Listing the points having the same D value (illustration for the first quadrant only)

index	0	1	2	3	4	5	6	7	8	9	10	11	···
OffsetTable_x	1	-1	0	0	2	-2	1	1	-1	-1	0	0	···
OffsetTable_y	0	0	1	-1	0	0	1	-1	1	-1	2	-2	···

Fig. 2. An example of 2D offset table

2.3 The Path Generation Procedure

Control points representing the path are successively calculated by applying following procedures shown in Fig. 3. The preliminary preparation of this procedure is to generate the starting position and direction of the reference ray as described in Section 2.1. In the first step, the direction having the maximum visibility with respect to the starting point, P_0, along the ray, R is found. The mathematical representation of the ray can be given as follows.

$$R = P_0 + l \cdot \vec{R}_d(\theta, \phi), \tag{2}$$

where $\vec{R}_d$ is the direction of a ray, and l is the propagated length of a ray. We progress a ray, R around the reference ray, $\vec{R}_{d0}(\theta_0, \phi_0)$ in the following range.

$$\theta_0 - k_1 \le \theta \le \theta_0 + k_1,\ \phi_0 - k_1 \le \phi \le \phi_0 + k_1, \tag{3}$$

where the parameter, $\boldsymbol{k_1}$ represents the field of view. As the ray is progressed around the reference ray, the intersection point between the ray and the colon wall is determined. The intersection point having the maximum distance from the starting point is regarded as the point having the maximum visibility. In other words, this position is where the viewer can see the farthest from the viewpoint without being blocked by the colon wall. In Fig. 3(a), $P_{\max}$ is calculated as the maximum visibility position with respect to P_0 and $\vec{R}_{d0}(\theta_0, \phi_0)$. As previously stated, the parameter $\boldsymbol{k_1}$ from Eq. (3) represents the field of view. When $\boldsymbol{k_1}$ is large, the field of view becomes broader since visibility is determined with a larger range of view directions. However, the path generation time is prolonged. When $\boldsymbol{k_1}$ is small, the opposite case happens. The optimal value of $\boldsymbol{k_1}$ needs to be determined empirically.

In the next step, $P_{candidate}$ is selected on the line between P_0 and $P_{\max}$ using Eq. (4) as shown in Fig. 3(b). The parameter, $\boldsymbol{k_2}$ controls the distance between control points in the neighborhood. When $\boldsymbol{k_2}$ is large, a smaller number of control points will be needed to represent the whole colon and the path generation becomes faster. However, the path accuracy could be poor with large values of $\boldsymbol{k_2}$ especially in the narrow regions of the colon, since a single control point represents a larger range of the colon. When $\boldsymbol{k_2}$ is small, the opposite case happens. The optimal value of $\boldsymbol{k_2}$ needs to be determined empirically.

$$P_{candidate} = P_0 + k_2 \cdot (P_{\max} - P_0). \tag{4}$$

The accuracy of the point determined by the visibility criterion, $P_{candidate}$, can be further enhanced in the procedure. First, a virtual sphere is expanded around $P_{candidate}$ to find the intersection points between the expanding sphere and the colon wall, as shown in Fig. 3(c). For expanding the sphere, we add a displacement vector to the point, $P_{candidate}$ and generate surface points using the offset table described in Section 2.2. When the expanding sphere encounters the colon wall, the intersection point is labeled as $P_{contact}$. $P_{contact}$ must satisfy the angle criteria in Eq. (5). α is the angle between the lines $\overrightarrow{P_{contact} - P_{candidate}}$ and $\overrightarrow{P_{candidate} - P_0}$ in Fig. 3(c). In Eq. (5), the parameter, $\boldsymbol{k_3}$ sets the range of α in the vicinity of 90 degree. This condition prevents

$P_{contact}$ from being located in front of the path, especially for complicated colon sections. The optimal value of $\boldsymbol{k_3}$ should also be determined empirically.

$$\left|\alpha - 90°\right| < k_3, \ \alpha = \cos^{-1}\frac{(P_{contact} - P_{candidate}) \cdot (P_{candidate} - P_0)}{\left|P_{contact} - P_{candidate}\right|\left|P_{candidate} - P_0\right|}. \tag{5}$$

After finding a set of contact points by expanding a sphere, we progress a ray from each contact point in the set, $P_{contact}$, through $P_{candidate}$ to the colon wall on the opposite side. This is done to find a new intersection point, $P_{contact2}$, between this ray and the colon wall as shown in Fig. 3(d). A set of midpoints can be determined using each set of $P_{contact}$ and $P_{contact2}$. Finally, the control point for the navigation path, P_{final}, is determined by finding the average of these middle points. The next control point is generated with the new starting position, P_{final}, and new reference ray direction $P_{final} - P_0$ by applying the steps illustrated in Fig. 3. The cubic spline method is used to interpolate the control points to have the final navigation path.

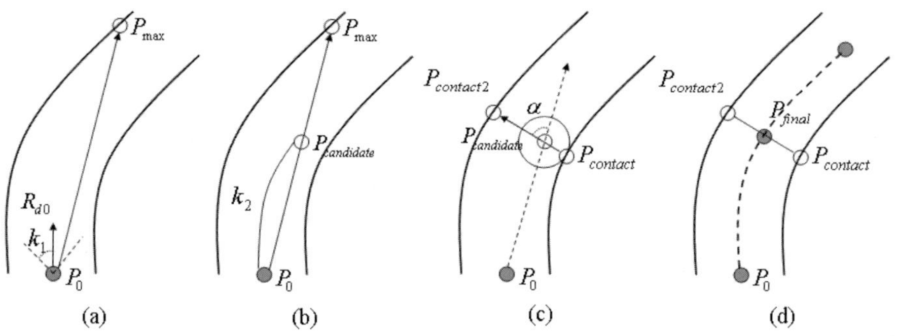

Fig. 3. The procedure for a path-generation

3 Experimental Results

The proposed method was tested on an Intel Pentium IV PC with a 2.4 GHz CPU and 1.0 GB of main memory. Four sets of CT scans were examined using the image data, which has 512x512 pixels in x, y dimension and 213 ~ 579 slices.

The proposed path generation scheme does not require segmenting the colon from other organs, and the segmentation is only for the visual display. The initial seed point is to be set on the volume rendered image in Fig. 4(a). Fig. 4 is shown to represent the starting point that is located at the center of the colonic section.

To find optimal parameters for the proposed method, we considered the path generation ratio in Eq. (6). A reference path was chosen manually by an expert for comparison. The path generation ratio is defined as the ratio of the total number of

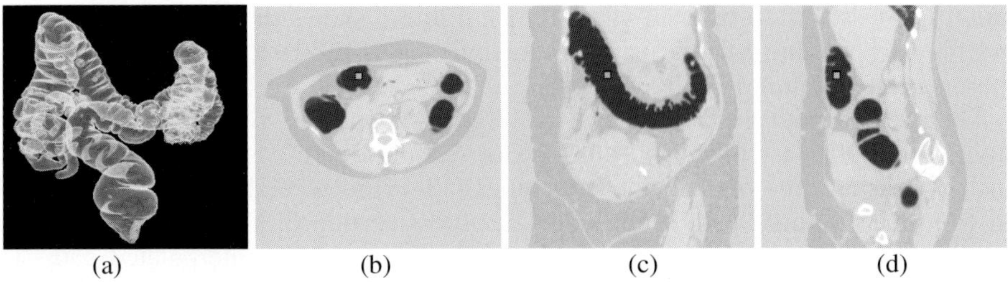

Fig. 4. The starting point (a) on the 3D volume rendered image (b) on the axial image (c) on the coronal image (d) on the sagittal image

points on *our interpolated path* intersecting each slice, to the total number of points on the *reference path* intersecting each slice within the error bound, 3mm.

$$\text{Path generation ratio}[\%] = \frac{\sum \begin{array}{l}\text{number of points on our interolated path}\\ \text{intersecting each slice within the error bound}\\ \text{from corresponding points on the reference path}\end{array}}{\sum \begin{array}{l}\text{number of points on the reference path}\\ \text{intersecting each slice}\end{array}} \times 100\,. \tag{6}$$

Table 1 summarizes the path generation time and ratio by varying $\boldsymbol{k_1}$ with fixed other values. Large values of $\boldsymbol{k_1}$ yield high path generation ratio. However, the increase of the path generation ratio becomes insignificant when $\boldsymbol{k_1}$ is raised over 30°, and we suggest 30° for an optimal value of $\boldsymbol{k_1}$. Table 2 shows the path generation time and ratio by varying $\boldsymbol{k_2}$ with fixed other values. While small $\boldsymbol{k_2}$ yields a better path generation ratio, the improvement becomes marginal for the values of $\boldsymbol{k_2}$ below 0.5,

Table 1. The path generation time and ratio by varying $\boldsymbol{k_1}$ ($\boldsymbol{k_2}$ = 0.5, $\boldsymbol{k_3}$ = 30°)

	The path generation time					The path generation ratio				
k_1	20°	25°	30°	35°	40°	20°	25°	30°	35°	40°
Average	14	20	25	29	32	68.31	70.01	72.96	73.33	74.05

Table 2. The path generation time and ratio by varying $\boldsymbol{k_2}$ ($\boldsymbol{k_1}$ = 30°, $\boldsymbol{k_3}$ = 45°)

	The path generation time					The path generation ratio				
k_2	0.3	0.4	0.5	0.6	0.7	0.3	0.4	0.5	0.6	0.7
Average	32	28	25	19	15	97.92	97.24	96.90	77.34	66.50

Table 3. The path generation time and ratio by varying $\boldsymbol{k_3}$ ($\boldsymbol{k_1}$ = 30°, $\boldsymbol{k_2}$ = 0.5)

	The path generation time					The path generation ratio				
k_3	30°	40°	45°	50°	60°	30°	40°	45°	50°	60°
Average	25	23	25	26	16	72.96	91.61	96.90	92.44	70.37

which is chosen as an optimal value for k_2. Table 3 shows the path generation time and ratio by varying k_3. The path generation ratio is the best around 45°, which is chosen as an optimum for k_3.

The average path generation time is 25 seconds and the average path generation ratio was 96.90% as shown in Table 3. Our fast algorithm has dramatically reduced total processing time from about 10 minutes [13-14] to seconds. The path is slightly off from the reference path in the large-area cross section of a colon but well within an allowable range. Fig. 5 shows the control points and the interpolated path. The control points are uniformly distributed along the colon centerline to model the shape of the colon efficiently and accurately. The generated path is located around the center region of the colon.

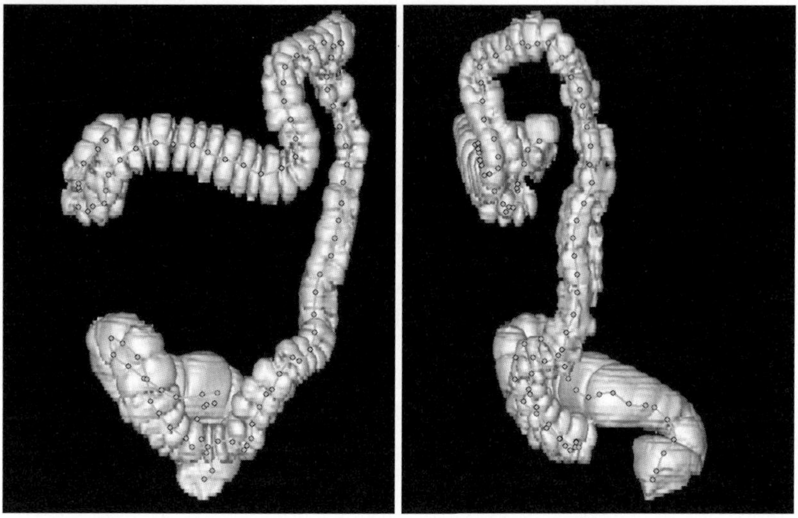

(a) (b)

Fig. 5. Generated control points and the interpolated path of subject 1 (a) in the anterior view (b) in the left view

4 Conclusion

In this paper, we proposed an automated path finding algorithm to be used in virtual colonoscopy. The proposed method uses a fast algorithm to emulate the propagation of ray, eliminating the time-consuming preliminary procedure. The proposed method requires a small number of control points to represent the whole navigation path that is properly aligned along the centerline of the colon. The experimental results on four clinical datasets show that the navigation path is generated rapidly and that the path is located in the center of the colonic section for an effective clinical examination. The computational efficiency was enhanced without sacrificing the accuracy using the proposed algorithm. Also, the proposed method is able to smooth out the camera path so that the eyestrain on the inspector can be minimized. Our method can be successfully applied to a wide range of applications that require path generation for virtual navigation.

References

1. Dogramadzi, S., Allen, C. R., Bell G. D., Computer Controlled Colonoscopy, Proceedings of IEEE Instrumentation and Measurement Technology Conference Vol. 1 (1998) 210-213
2. Phee, S. J., Ng, W. S., Chen, I. M., Seow-Choen, F., Davies, B. L., Automation of Colonoscopy. II. Visual control aspects, IEEE Engineering in Medicine and Biology Magazine Vol. 17, No. 3 (1998) 81-88
3. Hong, L., Kaufman, A., Wei, Y., Viswambharan, A., Wax, M., Liang, Z., 3D Virtual Colonoscopy, Proceedings of IEEE Biomedical Visualization (1995) 26-32
4. Lee, T. Y., Lin, P. H., Lin, C. H., Sun, Y. N., Lin, X. Z., Interactive 3-D Virtual Colonoscopy System, IEEE Transactions on Information Technology in Biomedicine Vol. 3, No. 2 (1999) 139-150
5. Hong, L., Muraki, S., Kaufman, A. E., Bartz, D., He, T., Virtual Voyage: Interactive Navigation in the Human Colon, Proceedings of ACM SIGGRAPH (1997) 27-34
6. Rubin, G., Beaulieu, C., Argiro, V., Ringl, H., Norbash, A., Feller, J., Dake, M., Jeffey, R., Napel, S., Perspective Volume Rendering of CT and MR Images: Applications for Endoscopic Imaging, Radiology Vol. 199, No. 2 (1996) 321-330
7. Pickhardt, P. J., Choi, J. R., Hwang, I., Butler, J. A., Puckett, M. L., Hildebrandt, H. A., Wong, R. K., Nugent, P. A., Mysliwiec, P. A., Schindler, W. R., Computed Tomographic Virtual Colonoscopy to Screen for Colorectal Neoplasia in Asymptomatic Adults," The New England Journal of Medicine Vol. 349 (2003) 2191-2200
8. Vining, D., Gelfand, D., Bechtold, R., Scharling, E., Grishaw, E., Shifrin, R., Technical Feasibility of Colon Imaging with Helical CT and Virtual Reality, Annual Meeting of American Roentgen Ray Society (1994) 104
9. Paik, D. S., Beaulieu, C. F., Jeffery, R. B., Rubin, G. D., Napel, S., Automated Flight Path Planning for Virtual Endoscopy, Medical Physics Vol. 25, No. 5 (1998) 629-637
10. He, T., Hong, L., Reliable Navigation for Virtual Endoscopy, IEEE Nuclear Science Symposium Vol. 3 (1999) 1339-1343
11. Zhou, Y., Kaufman, A. E., Toga, A. W., Three-dimensional Skeleton and Centerline Generation Based on an Approximate Minimum Distance Field, The Visual Computer Vol. 14 (1998) 303-314
12. Bitter, I., Kaufman, A. E., Sato, M., Penalized-distance Volumetric Skeleton Algorithm, IEEE Transactions on Visualization and Computer Graphics Vol. 7, No. 3 (2001) 195-206
13. Bitter, I., Sato, M., Bender, M. McDonnel, K., Kaufman, A., Wan, M., CEASAR: A Smooth, Accurate and Robust Centerline Extraction Algorithm, Proceedings IEEE Visualization (2000) 45-52
14. Wan, M, Dachille, F., Kaufman, A., Distance-field Based Skeletons for Virtual Navigation, Proceedings of IEEE Visualization (2001) 239-246

Dynamic Medial Axes of Planar Shapes

Kai Tang[1] and Yongjin Liu[2]

[1] The Hong Kong University of Science and Technology
[2] Tsinghua University, Beijing, P.R. China

Abstract. In this paper a computational model called *dynamic medial axis* ($\mathcal{DMA}$) is proposed to describe the internal evolution of planar shapes. To define the $\mathcal{DMA}$, a symbolic representation called *matching list* is proposed to depict the topological structure of the medial axis. As shown in this paper with provable properties, the $\mathcal{DMA}$ exhibits an interesting dynamic skeleton structure for planar shapes. Finally an important application of the proposed $\mathcal{DMA}$ — computing the medial axis of multiply-connected planar shapes with curved boundaries — is presented.

1 Introduction

The medial axis of a planar shape $\Omega \subset \mathbb{R}^2$ is the closure of the set of points in Ω that have more than one closest point among the boundary points $\partial\Omega$ of Ω. The medial axis was first introduced by Blum [2] to capture biological forms of shape. It provides an important skeleton structure of the shape that has found rich applications; See [7] for an overview.

In this paper a computational model called *dynamic medial axis* ($\mathcal{DMA}$) is proposed for planar shapes. The depiction of $\mathcal{DMA}$ is symbolic in nature. Experimental results are presented, showing that the $\mathcal{DMA}$ offers an interesting dynamic skeleton structure inside the planar shapes. An important application of $\mathcal{DMA}$ is also studied.

2 Preliminaries

Let Ω be a connected and bounded domain in $\mathbb{R}^2$ and $\partial\Omega$ be its boundary. The simple closed curve that bounds the unbounded connected component in $\mathbb{R}^2 \setminus \Omega$ is called the *outer loop* of Ω. The rest curves in $\partial\Omega$ are called the *inner loops*. The number h of the inner loops is called the *genus* of Ω. A domain Ω is *simply connected* if it has no inner loops, i.e., $h = 0$; otherwise, it is *multiply connected*.

Each loop in $\partial\Omega$ is composed of a finite number of real analytic curve segments. The curve segments are *oriented* such that when one walks from their starting points to end points, the interior of Ω always lies to the left side. For each loop, its constituting curve segments are separated by *vertices*. A vertex is called *convex* if its interior angle is less than π; otherwise it is *concave*. The set of *boundary entities* of $\partial\Omega$ is defined as a union of all curve segments together with all concave vertices. Each boundary entity is parameterized in a one dimensional interval.

H.-P. Seidel, T. Nishita, and Q. Peng (Eds.): CGI 2006, LNCS 4035, pp. 460–468, 2006.

Let $D_r(p)$ denote the closed disk of radius r centered at p. A disk $D_r(p) \in \Omega$ is called a *maximal disk* if $\exists D_s(p) \in \Omega$ containing $D_r(p)$, then $D_s(p) = D_r(p)$. Let $\mathcal{D}(\Omega)$ be the set of all maximal disks in Ω. The medial axis of a planar shape Ω is defined as

$$\mathcal{MA}(\Omega) = \{p \in \Omega \mid \exists D_r(p) \in \mathcal{D}(\Omega)\},$$

and the medial axis transform of Ω is defined as

$$\mathcal{MAT}(\Omega) = \{(p, r) \in \Omega \times (\mathbb{R}^+ \cup \{0\}) \mid \exists D_r(p) \in \mathcal{D}(\Omega)\}.$$

Both $\mathcal{MA}(\Omega)$ and $\mathcal{MAT}(\Omega)$ have the structure of geometric graphs [3]. The edges in the graph of $\mathcal{MA}(\Omega)$ are trimmed bisectors of two boundary entities [4, 5]. The *contact set* $C(p)$ of $p \in \mathcal{MA}(\Omega)$ is defined to be the set of $\partial D_r(p) \cap \partial \Omega$. Each element in $C(p)$ is called a *contact point* of p. The medial axis points $p \in \mathcal{MA}(\Omega)$ can be characterized by the number n of the elements in $C(p)$: a point p is called a *terminal point* if $n = 1$, or a *branch* (or *bifurcation*) *point* if $n \geq 3$. A branch point is *regular* if $n = 3$; otherwise it is *irregular*.

3 Dynamic Medial Axis

Consider a planar shape Ω. Let Ω be partitioned into two sub-shapes Ω_1 and Ω_2 by introducing a straight line $\mathcal{L}$ in Ω. Refer to Fig. 1. Without loss of generality, assume $\mathcal{L}$ to be horizontal with range $[0, 1]$ and its left endpoint to coincide with the origin. Denote the right endpoint of $\mathcal{L}$ by $\nu_{\mathcal{L}}$. To recover the original shape Ω evolutively from Ω_1 and Ω_2, the line $\mathcal{L}$ is shrunk by moving the vertex $\nu_{\mathcal{L}}$ from initial position $x = 1$ to the origin $x = 0$. Let $\Omega(x)$ symbolize this dynamically changed domain Ω when the abscissa of $\nu_{\mathcal{L}}$ is $x, 0 < x \leq 1$. To ensure that the domain $\Omega(x)$ is topologically correct, $\mathcal{L}$ is deemed to be special as compared to other entities in $\partial\Omega$ due to its orientation: it is a double-sided edge with both sides facing the interior of $\Omega(x)$. We can interpret $\mathcal{L}$ as a wedge in $\partial\Omega(x)$ with a zero width, as illustrated in Fig. 1. In the following, we denote the upper and lower edges of $\mathcal{L}$ as $\mathcal{L}^+$ and $\mathcal{L}^-$, respectively.

Let $\mathcal{L} = \{\mathcal{L}^+, \mathcal{L}^-\}$ and $\mathcal{L}_\nu = \{\mathcal{L}^+, \mathcal{L}^-, \nu_{\mathcal{L}}\}$. Conceivably when the x-coordinate of $\nu_{\mathcal{L}}$ continuously changes, so does the associated medial axis $\mathcal{MA}(\Omega(x))$. We call this continuously deformed $\mathcal{MA}(\Omega(x))$ the *dynamic medial axis* ($\mathcal{DMA}$). An example of $\mathcal{DMA}$ is shown in Fig. 2.

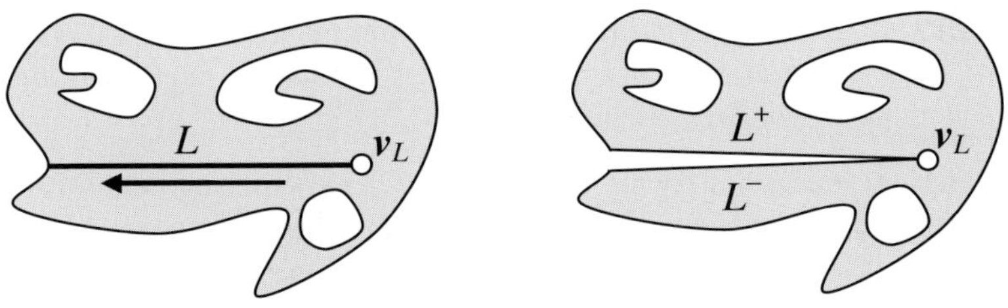

Fig. 1. The separator $\mathcal{L}$ as a special combinatory boundary entity

The first observation on $\mathcal{DMA}$ is that the difference between $\mathcal{MA}(\Omega_1) \cup \mathcal{MA}(\Omega_2)$ and $\mathcal{MA}(\Omega)$ is obviously localized in those medial axis points (shown in red color in Fig. 2) related to the separator $\mathcal{L}_\nu$. It is readily seen that these medial axis points constitute the boundary of the Voronoi cell $\mathcal{VC}(\mathcal{L}_\nu)$ of $\mathcal{L}_\nu$ (shown shaded in Fig. 2). To analyze the combinatorial and topological structures of $\mathcal{DMA}$, we first establish a symbolic representation of the medial axis.

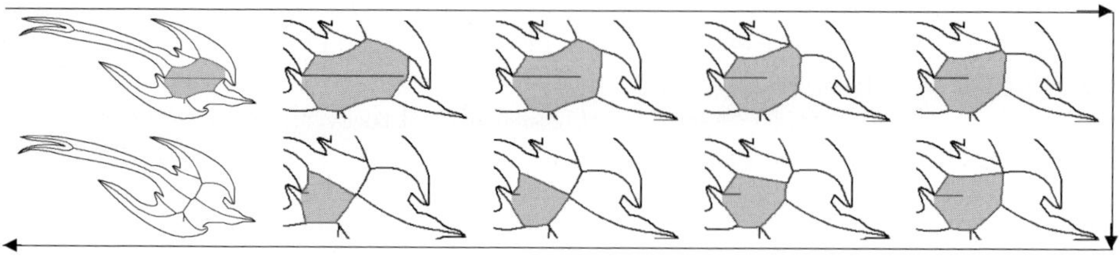

Fig. 2. The dynamic medial axis $\Omega(x)$

3.1 Symbolic Representation Using Matching Lists

Definition 1. *$\forall p \in \mathcal{MA}(\Omega)$, the contact points in the contact set $C(p)$ of p are called matching points to each other; p is called the $\mathcal{MA}$-center of its contact points.*

We use *match*() to denote this matching relation, i.e., given a contact point $c \in C(p)$, $match(c) = C(p) \setminus c$ (ref. Fig. 3). Let $\pi(\Omega)$ represent the union of all matching relations on $\partial\Omega$.

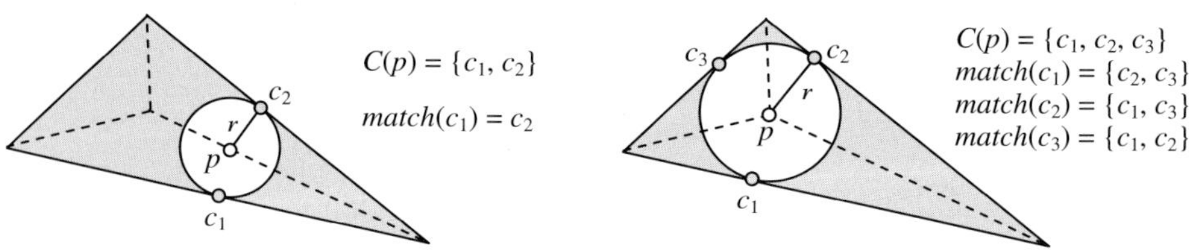

Fig. 3. The matching relationship

Definition 2. *A twice-differentiable curve segment $e(u), u \in (0, 1)$, is said to be singular if it contains at least one point having a positive curvature maximum; otherwise it is non-singular.*

Given a singular curve entity in a loop of $\partial\Omega$, we can segment it into non-singular entities by introducing vertices at points of positive maximal curvature. Hereafter domain Ω will be assumed to consist of non-singular curve segments. By Corollary 1 in [6], matching points in non-singular $\partial\Omega$ always belong to different boundary entities.

Definition 3. *Let $E(u), u \in (0,1)$, be a parameterized boundary entity in $\partial\Omega$. A consecutive portion α defined by $[u_1, u_2] \subset (0,1)$ on E is called a maximum matching interval (MMI) on E, if (1) all matching points $match(E(u)) : u \in [u_1, u_2]$ belong to another same boundary entity, say E', and (2) for an arbitrarily small value $\epsilon > 0$, the matching points $match(E(u))$ of either $u \in [u_1 - \epsilon, u_2]$ or $u \in [u_1, u_2 + \epsilon]$, fall into at least two different boundary entities.*

Let $match(\alpha)$ designate the set of matching points of an MMI $\alpha \subset E_i$. A simple argument can show that $match(\alpha)$ must also be an MMI itself, say $\beta \subset E_j, i \neq j$. The two MMIs α and β form a *matching pair.* Let $\{E_i, E_j\}$ denote a pair of matching entities.

Lemma 1. *If Ω is simply connected, then between any pair $\{E_i, E_j\}$ of matching entities, there exists one and only one matching pair $\{\alpha, \beta\}$ of MMIs.*

Proof. Due to limited pages, we omit the simple proof here. □

By Lemma 1 there is a unique pair of MMIs $\{\alpha, \beta\}$ in any matching entities $\{E_i, E_j\}$. The medial axis points contributed by $\{\alpha, \beta\}$ constitute a continuous trimmed bisector which we denote as $\chi = \tau(E_i, E_j) \subset \mathcal{MA}(\Omega)$. E_i and E_j are called the *source entities* of χ.

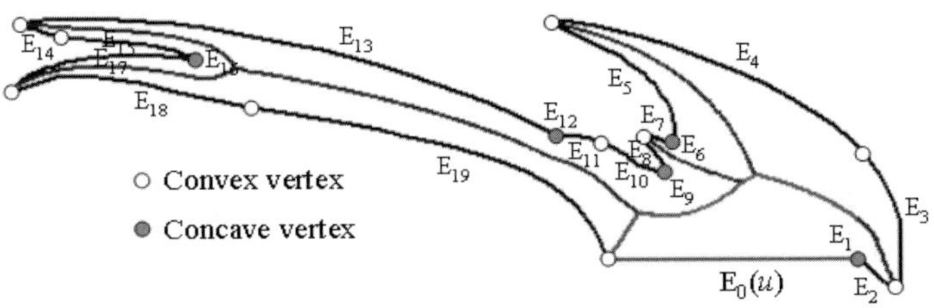

Fig. 4. Matching list: $\partial\Omega = \{E_0, E_1, \cdots, E_{19}\}$ and $\Phi(E_0) = \{E_{19}, E_{10}, E_9, E_6, E_4, E_3\}$. The medial axis points contributed by $\Phi(E_0)$ and E_0 is shown in red.

Definition 4. *Let a, b, c be three distinct points on a same loop in $\partial\Omega$ with a consistent orientation. Point b is said to be in front of c with respect to a, denoted as $b \prec_a c$, if when one staring at a walks along the loop with the predefined orientation, point b is encountered before c. Furthermore, if points a, b, c lie on three distinct entities E_a, E_b, E_c, then E_b is said to be in front of E_c with respect to E_a, denoted as $E_b \prec_{E_a} E_c$.*

The above defined "*in front*" relationship induces an ordering on the boundary entities of any loops in $\partial\Omega$. Let $\{\alpha_1, \alpha_2, \cdots, \alpha_m\}$ be the set of sorted MMIs of $(0,1)$ on an entity $E_0(u)$, $u \in (0,1)$, and $\{E_{01}, E_{02}, \cdots, E_{0m}\}$ be the matching entities contributing to $\{\alpha_1, \alpha_2, \cdots, \alpha_m\}$. Induced from the ordering of $\{\alpha_1, \alpha_2, \cdots, \alpha_m\}$, the list $\Phi(E_0) = \{E_{01}, E_{02}, \cdots, E_{0m}\}$ is also ordered (in the second subscript) with respect to E_0 (the first subscript); we call $\Phi(E_0)$ the *matching list* of E_0. See Fig. 4 for an illustration.

3.2 Topological Structure of $\mathcal{DMA}$

Definition 5. *Given a continuously changed domain $\Omega(x)$, two dynamic medial axes $\mathcal{DMA}(x_i)$ and $\mathcal{DMA}(x_j)$ are said to be topologically equivalent to each other if the separator $\mathcal{L}_\nu$ has the same matching list $\Phi(\mathcal{L}_\nu)$ in $\Omega(x_i)$ and $\Omega(x_j)$. In such a case, x_i and x_j are also said to be topologically equivalent to each other, denoted by $x_i \sim x_j$.*

The equivalent relation $\sim$ induces a topological partitioning in the linear space $\mathcal{L}_\nu(x), x \in (0,1)$, i.e., X is partitioned into a set of equivalent classes $[x]_\sim = \{x' \in X : x' \sim x\}$ which form a quotient space $X/\sim = \{[x]_\sim : x \in X\}$. The transition between equivalent classes $[x]_\sim$ can be geometrically characterized by critical points in X, i.e., when $\nu_\mathcal{L}$ moves towards the origin, $\mathcal{DMA}(x)$ remains topological equivalent until the matching list $\Phi(\mathcal{L}_\nu)$ undergoes a change.

3.3 Computing/Updating $\mathcal{DMA}$

First, consider the case with $\mathcal{L}^+$. The case with $\mathcal{L}^-$ can be analyzed similarly. Let $S_{\mathcal{L}^+} = \{x_1, x_2, \cdots, x_m\}$ be the set of sorted delimiting points of the MMIs in $\mathcal{L}^+$. When $\nu_\mathcal{L}$ crosses a delimiting point x_i, the change in $\Phi(\mathcal{L}_\nu)$ is easily seen to be limited to the boundary entities other than $\mathcal{L}^+$ that offers matching points to x_i. Let E and E' be such two boundary entities. Generally there exists an arbitrarily small value $\epsilon > 0$ such that the interval $(x_i - \epsilon, x_i) \cup (x_i, x_i + \epsilon)$ contains no delimiting points. When x_i is crossed, only four matching lists, $\Phi(E)$, $\Phi(E')$, $\Phi(\nu_\mathcal{L})$ and $\Phi(\mathcal{L}^+)$, are altered.

Let $S_{\mathcal{L}^+}$ be implemented by a stack whose top element always has the largest abscissa and **POP**$(S_{\mathcal{L}^+})$ symbolize the stack operation that pops out the top element. The following codes, taking constant time, carries out these changes:

```
Procedure Update_delimiting(S_L+)
Begin
    x_s ← POP(S_L+));
    If x_s ≠ nil then begin
        E, E' ← the two entities offering mating points to x_s;
        Delete L+ from Φ(E');
        Delete E' from Φ(L+);
        Add ν_L into Φ(E) at the position before L+;
        Add E as the first element into Φ(ν_L);
    End
End
```

Now consider the case with $\nu_\mathcal{L}$. Suppose at $x = x_0$, an MMI disappears in $\nu_\mathcal{L}$; that implies for an arbitrarily small positive ϵ, in the interval $x \in (x_0, x_0 + \epsilon)$, , $\nu_\mathcal{L}$ contributes a trimmed bisector χ of nonzero length which shrinks to a point at $x = x_0$. Refer to Fig. 5a. Let c_1 and c_2 be the branch points delimiting χ. Let χ_1 and μ_1 be another two bisectors meeting χ at c_1, χ_2 and μ_2 meeting χ at c_2. Since χ reaches zero length, at $x = x_0$, the four bisectors χ_1, χ_2, μ_1, and μ_2 meet at a common irregular branch point c^* as shown in Fig. 5b. x_0 is referred to as a *vanishing point*. Let $\{E, E_1\}$ and $\{E, E_2\}$ be the source entities contributing μ_1 and μ_2, respectively. If the intersection of untrimmed μ_1 and

μ_2 exists, it must be the irregular branch point c^*. Let C^* be the contact circle $\partial D_r(c^*), (c^*, r) \in \mathcal{MAT}(\Omega)$. Among the two intersection points of x-axis and C^*, the one with smaller abscissa is the vanishing point x_0.

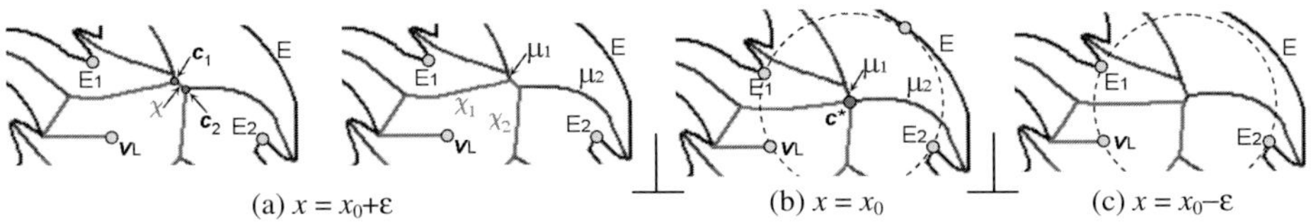

Fig. 5. Vanishing point identification

In addition to matching lists, the remaining vanishing points may also undergo changes after crossing a vanishing point. Let $\Phi(\nu_{\mathcal{L}}) = \{E_1, E_2, \cdots, E_k\}$ when $\nu_{\mathcal{L}} = x$. Let $\Psi(\nu_{\mathcal{L}}) = \{\chi_1, \chi_2, \cdots, \chi_k\}$ be the corresponding bisectors associated to $\nu_{\mathcal{L}}$, $\chi_i = \tau(E_i, \nu_{\mathcal{L}}), 1 \le i \le k$. Suppose x_0 of χ_i is the first vanishing point in $S_{\nu_{\mathcal{L}}}(x)$ to be crossed. When x_0 is crossed, E_i is removed from $\Phi(\nu_{\mathcal{L}})$, so is χ_i from $\Psi(\nu_{\mathcal{L}})$. In $S_{\nu_{\mathcal{L}}}(x)$ two bisectors adjacent to χ_i, i.e., χ_{i-1} and χ_{i+1}, if they exist, need to be examined for updating their vanishing points. For χ_{i-1}, the updated vanishing point is the intersection of $\tau(E_{i-1}, E_{i-2})$ and $\tau(E_{i-1}, E_{i+1})$. For χ_{i+1}, the two contributing bisectors are $\tau(E_{i+1}, E_{i-1})$ and $\tau(E_{i+1}, E_{i+2})$.

Let **INSERT**$(p, S_{\nu_{\mathcal{L}}})$ symbolize the operation that inserts a new vanishing point into $S_{\nu_{\mathcal{L}}}$. The procedure **Update_vanishing**$(S_{\nu_{\mathcal{L}}})$ summarized below carries out the vanishing point update of $\mathcal{DMA}$:

```
Procedure Update_vanishing(S_νL)
Begin
    x0 ← POP(S_νL));
    If x0 ≠ nil then begin
        χ0 ← the bisector in Ψ(νL) that contributes x0;
        χ1, χ2 ←the preceding and succeeding bisectors of χ0 in Ψ(νL);
        E ← the source entity (other than νL) of χ0;
        E0, E1 ← the two preceding entities of E in Φ(νL);
        E2, E3 ← the two succeeding entities of E in Φ(νL);
        Delete E from Φ(νL);
        Delete νL from Φ(E);
        Insert E2 into Φ(E1) between E and νL;
        Insert E1 into Φ(E2) between νL and E;
        If any of the vanishing points of χ1 and χ2 exists then begin
            Delete them from S_νL(x);
        End
        p ← τ(E1, E0) ∩ τ(E1, E2);
        If p ≠ nil then begin
            INSERT(p, S_νL);
        End
        p ← τ(E2, E1) ∩ τ(E2, E3);
        If p ≠ nil then begin
            INSERT(p, S_νL);
        End
    End
End
```

By implementing $S_{\nu_{\mathcal{L}}}$ as a stack, the above codes take $O(\log k_\nu)$ time, where $k_\nu \le n'$ is the maximum number of elements in $S_{\nu_{\mathcal{L}}}(x)$ and n' is the number of elements in $\partial\Omega_1 \cup \partial\Omega_2$. By combining the updating on both delimiting and vanishing points, the computation of $\mathcal{DMA}$ is summarized with the following pseudo-codes, which take $O(n' \log k_\nu)$ time:

```
Procedure DMA(Ω1, Ω2, L_ν)
Begin
    Do begin
        x_L+ ← POP(S_L+));
        x_L- ← POP(S_L-));
        x_S_νL ← POP(S_νL));
        If (x_L+ = ∅ and x_L- = ∅ and x_S_νL = ∅) then Exit
        Else begin
            If (x_L+ ≥ x_L- and x_L+ ≥ x_S_νL) then
                Update_delimiting(S_L+);
            Else If (x_L- > x_L+ and x_L- ≥ x_S_νL) then
                Update_delimiting(S_L-);
            Else
                Update_vanishing(S_νL);
        End
    End
    For every entity E in ∂Ω Do begin
        If any L+, L- or ν_L exists in Φ(E) then
            delete it from Φ(E);
    End
End
```

4 Applications

An important application of the proposed $\mathcal{DMA}$ is to compute the medial axes of a non-simple planar shapes with curved boundaries [1]. Referring to Fig. 6, two ideas are involved. First, given a multiply connected shape Ω^m, it can be cut into a simply connected shape Ω^s by introducing artificial separators. After computing the medial axis of Ω^s, applying the proposed $\mathcal{DMA}$ technique removes

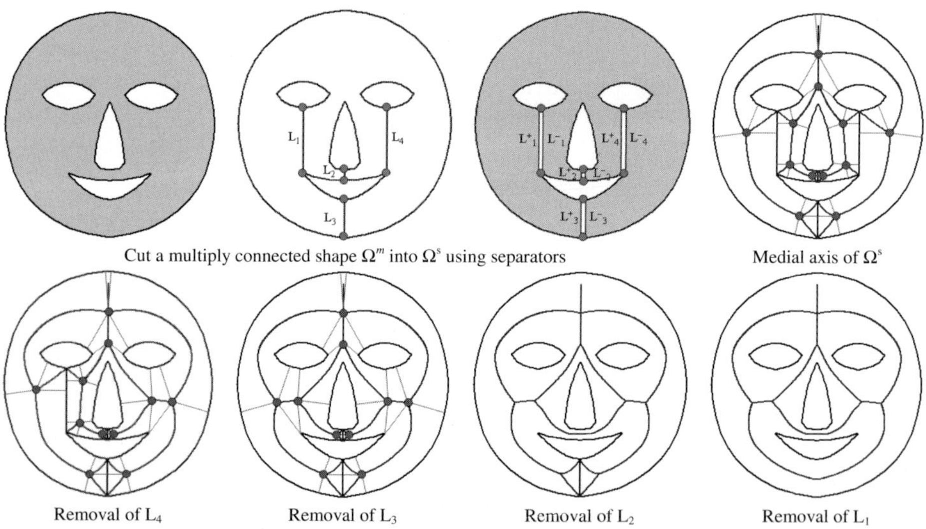

Fig. 6. Compute the medial axis of a multiply connected curved shape

the separators from Ω^s and thus offers the medial axis of Ω^m. Secondly, given a simply connected shape Ω^s, let Ω^s be recursively cut into two halves Ω_1^s and Ω_2^s until reaching a *fundamental shape* which contains only two non-singular boundary entities in addition to a separator. The following codes are readily seen:

```
Procedure MA_simple_domain(Ω^s)
Begin
    If shape Ω^s is not fundamental
        (Ω_1^s, Ω_2^s, L_ν) ← PARTITION(Ω^s);
        MA_simple_domain(Ω_1^s);
        MA_simple_domain(Ω_2^s);
        DMA(Ω_1^s, Ω_2^s, L_ν);
    Else
        Compute MA(Ω^s);
End
```

Theorem 1. *Given a multiply connected planar shape Ω^m with genus h and n curved boundary entities, its medial axis can be constructed in $O(Kn\log k_\nu + hn\log k_\nu)$ time, where K is the depth of recursion in the execution of $\mathcal{MA}$_simple_domain(Ω^s) and k_ν is the maximum number of vanishing points incurred in the procedure* **Update_vanishing**$(S_{\nu_\mathcal{L}})$.

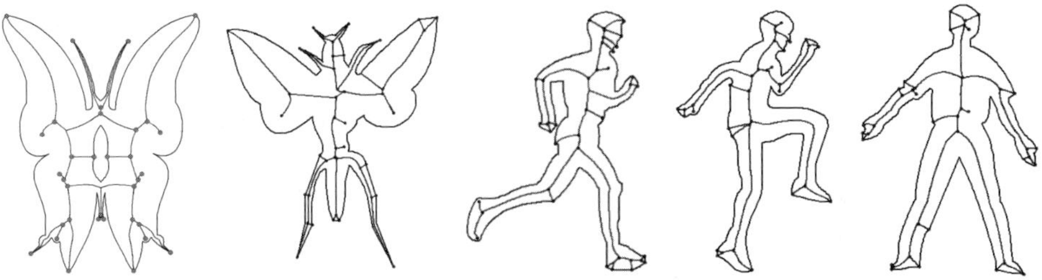

Fig. 7. More experimental results

5 Conclusions

In this paper a dynamic skeleton structure called $\mathcal{DMA}$ is proposed to describe the internal evolution of planar shapes. Detailed combinatorial and topological structures of $\mathcal{DMA}$ are analyzed. An important application of $\mathcal{DMA}$ on computing medial axes of multiply-connected curved planar shapes are also presented. Future work includes exploiting the full potential of the proposed $\mathcal{DMA}$ in the applications of biological shape analysis (ref. Fig. 7).

References

1. H. Alt, O. Cheong and A. Vigneron: The Voronoi diagram of curved objects. Discrete & Computational Geometry, **34(3)** (2005) 439–453
2. H. Blum: Biological shape and visual science. Journal of Theoretical Biology, **38** (1973) 205–287

3. H.I. Choi, S.W. Choi, and H.P. Moon: Mathematical theory of medial axis transform, Pacific Journal of Mathematics, **181(1)** (1997) 57–88
4. R.T. Farouki and J.K. Johnstone: The bisector of a point and a plane parametric curve, Computer Aided Geometric Design, **11(2)** (1994) 117–151
5. R.T. Farouki and R. Ramamurthy: Specified-precision computation of curve/curve bisectors, Internat. J. Comput. Geom. Appl. **8(5-6)** (1998) 599-617.
6. R. Kimmel, D. Shaked and N. Kiryati: Skeletonization via diatance maps and level sets. Computer Vision and Image Understanding **62(3)** (1995) 382–391
7. A. Okabe, B. Boots, K. Sugihara and S.N. Chiu: Spatial Tessellations: Concepts and Applications of Voronoi Diagram. 2^{nd}ed., John Wieley, 2000.

Steganography on 3D Models Using a Spatial Subdivision Technique

Yuan-Yu Tsai[1], Chung-Ming Wang[1], Yu-Ming Cheng[1], Chung-Hsien Chang[1], and Peng-Cheng Wang[1,2]

[1] Institute of Computer Science, National Chung-Hsing University, Taiwan, China
{cuckoo, cmwang, s9156048, cschang}@cs.nchu.edu.tw
[2] Department of Information Management, Hsiuping Institute of Technology, Taichung, 412, Taiwan, China
pcwang@mail.hit.edu.tw

Abstract. This paper proposes a new steganography algorithm for 3D models using a spatial subdivision technique. Our algorithm first decomposes the bounding volume of the cover model into voxels based on a Binary Space Partitioning (BSP) tree. The voxels are then further categorized into eight subspaces, each of which is numbered and represented as three-digit binary characters. In the embedding process, we first traverse the BSP tree, locating a leaf voxel; then we embed every three bits of the payload message into the vertex inside the leaf voxel. This is realized by translating a vertex's current position to the corresponding numbered subspace. This technique is a substitutive blind extraction scheme, where messages embedded can be extracted without the aid of the original cover model. This technique achieves high data capacity, equivalent to at least three times the number of the embedded vertices in the cover model. In addition, the stego model has insignificant visual distortion. Finally, this scheme is robust against similarity transformation attacks.

1 Introduction

Steganography is the art of communicating in a way which hides the existence of the communication. Compared with watermarking, which is a process for protecting copyright ownership, steganography is a technique that hides messages inside a host media in a way that does not allow any one, except those with the secret key, to even detect that there is a second secret message present. Therefore, the main application for steganography is the covert communication and digital multimedia data, such as movies, music, and images, which are often used as host media to embed information, usually denoted as the payload [7, 12]. Obviously, steganography algorithms tend to require higher data capacity but they can lead to relatively poor robustness.

With the development of various 3D applications and computer animation, many steganography and watermarking schemes have been presented for 3D models. Most of them support polygonal models [1, 2, 3, 6, 8, 9, 10, 13, 14, 16, 17] while a few of them are for point-sampled geometries [5, 15]. However, unlike the large data hiding capacity in a 2D image, the data hiding capacity for 3D models remains bottlenecked at a smaller capacity.

H.-P. Seidel, T. Nishita, and Q. Peng (Eds.): CGI 2006, LNCS 4035, pp. 469 – 476, 2006.

In this paper, we propose a new steganography technique for 3D models using a spatial subdivision technique. Our scheme supports both polygonal models and point-sampled geometries. Specifically, we decompose the bounding volume of the cover model into voxels based on a BSP tree data structure. The leaf node of the tree data structure corresponds to a 3D space, known as a voxel. The tree data structure is traversed in search of leaf nodes, where a payload can be embedded by changing the positions of vertices. Since the edge information for the polygonal model is not used in the proposed scheme, it can be extended to point-sampled geometries. Our scheme is simple and can achieve high data capacity with little visual distortion. Similarly to previous 3D data hiding algorithms [3, 14, 15], our scheme is robust against similarity transformation attacks, including rotation, translation, and uniform scaling.

This paper is organized as follows. Section 2 illustrates the process for the BSP tree construction, and section 3 presents the proposed data hiding technique. Section 4 shows the experimental result, followed by the conclusion and future work in section 5.

2 The Binary Space Partitioning Tree Construction

The first step before both the data embedding and data extracting procedures is to construct a BSP tree to decompose the bounding volume of the model into voxels. First, we describe an overview of the BSP tree construction. Second, we present the approach to ensure that the bounding volume of the stego model have the same orientation and similarity with that of the cover model. This can also ensure that the identical BSP tree will be produced in the embedding and the extracting processes. Finally, the BSP tree construction is illustrated in our implementation.

A BSP tree represents a recursive, hierarchical partitioning, or subdivision, of *n*-dimensional space into convex subspaces. The BSP tree construction process takes a universal space and partitions it by any hyperplane that intersects the interior of that space. In a three-dimensional space, the universal space is normally a bounding volume of a 3D model, and the hyper-plane is normally a three-dimensional plane which normal is parallel to one of axes. The result of the partition is two new subspaces that can be further partitioned by a recursive application of the method.

The BSP tree construction strongly depends on a model's initial bounding volume since different bounding volumes will result in different BSP trees. In addition, a stego model may be under similarity transformation attacks, including rotation, translation, and uniform scaling. These attacks may produce different bounding volumes between a cover and a stego model, resulting in different BSP tree structures. Therefore, we need to ensure that the bounding volume of the stego model has the same orientation and similarity as that of the cover model. As a result, the BSP tree data structure constructed by the stego model will be the same as that of the cover model.

To ensure the same orientation of the bounding volume, we adopt principal component analysis [11] to produce a coordinates system of the 3D cover model. Thus, when the coordinates system of the stego model are calculated in the extracting process, we can operate the alignment, together with the coordinates system of the 3D cover model, to obtain a bounding volume oriented to that of the cover model. After the coordinates system of the 3D model is available, we then transform all vertices of the 3D cover model to the new coordinates system. Obviously, the new coordinates system has a new origin, PCA_O, which is a gravity center of the 3D model; it also has three basis vectors, which are the three principal axes, called PCA_X, PCA_Y, and PCA_Z.

However, for the similarity of the bounding volume, all the vertices will be searched with the maximum and minimum values on each principal axis. Then these vertices NV_{BV}, at least two and at most six in 3D models, are used to construct the initial bounding volume, and the payload message is ***not*** embedded. Thus, even after uniform scaling attack, the bounding volume will be scaling proportionally.

For example, in Figure 1a the model consists of nine vertices, which are on the new coordinates, PCA_X and PCA_Y. From the above description, $\mathbf{P_1}$, $\mathbf{P_2}$, $\mathbf{P_3}$, and $\mathbf{P_4}$ will be used to construct the bounding volume. The reason is that they have the minimum and maximum X and Y values separately. These vertices will produce two boundary points, $\mathbf{BV_M}$ and $\mathbf{BV_m}$. In this instance, the diagonal length of the bounding volume, V_{BV}, can be derived by calculating the distance between them.

Next, we begin the recursive partition step. In this step, we first select a partition plane, say PL_1, parallel to the PCA_X-axis. This plane subdivides the bounding volume in half, producing two new subspaces, $+PCA_Y$ and $-PCA_Y$. The sign "+" represents the positive side of the partition plane, while the sign "−" indicates the negative side. To choose the next partition plane PL_2, we apply a rule that it must be perpendicular to the previous partition plane. Thus, the second partition plane subdivides each of the subspaces in the PCA_X direction. As a result, four subspaces are generated after the second partition, each of which may have a different volume because of the position of the partitioning plane. To simplify the situation, we divide the bounding volume at each node equally in our implementation. This process continues recursively until we reach the pre-defined termination criteria, which ends the partition of the subspaces. In the example, the termination criteria is that the maximum diagonal length of subspaces in the leaf node must be less than 2^{-4} times the diagonal length of the original bounding volume. Note that a voxel will be not divided into sub-voxels when no vertices are within the voxel. As a result, each vertex is inside an individual subspace as shown in Figure 1a. In addition, each vertex always belongs to one leaf node in the BSP tree as shown in Figure 1b. The point **C**, which is located at the center of the bounding volume, is the initial node of the BSP tree. Note that the leaf nodes that have no vertices are discarded in the Figure 1b, such as the subspace **S**.

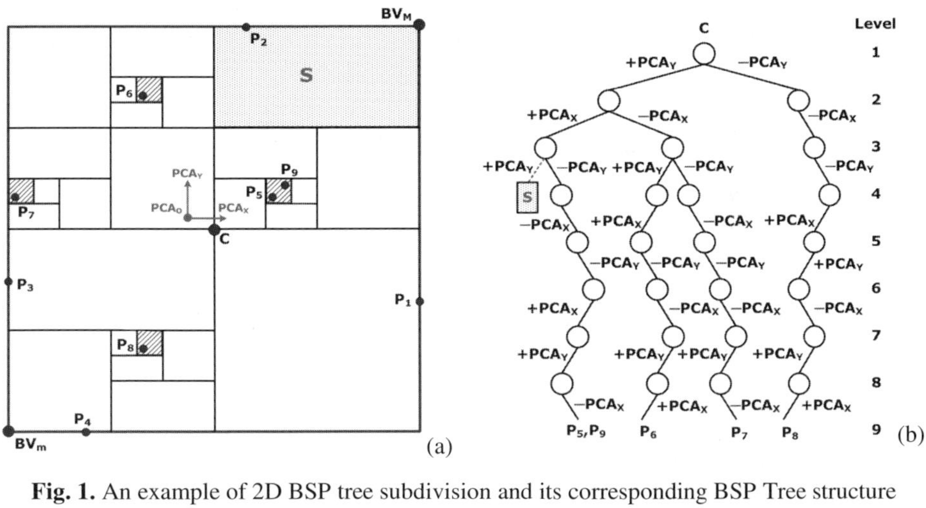

Fig. 1. An example of 2D BSP tree subdivision and its corresponding BSP Tree structure

There are many termination criteria that can be used to construct the BSP tree, such as the maximum diagonal length of the subspace in the leaf node, the maximum level of the leaf node, and the maximum number of vertices allowed in the leaf node.

3 The Proposed Technique

This section describes a new steganography technique for 3D models. The embedding data process takes as inputs a 3D cover model, the payload, and the secret key. This process produces a stego model. In contrast, the extracting data process takes the stego model and secret key as inputs to extract the payloads.

3.1 The Embedding Data Process

Once the BSP tree is constructed, we traverse the BSP tree to its leaf nodes to locate a voxel in which only a vertex of the cover model is located. For the leaf node with more than one vertex, no modification is employed for all vertices in that voxel. Thereafter, we subdivide the space of the voxel into smaller subspaces according to the magnitude of C_{max}, which represents the maximum bits that can be embedded into each vertex of the cover model. Let $m = 2^{C_{max}}$ be the number of subspaces that are subdivided. Figure 2 demonstrates a situation where four subspaces can be generated when C_{max} is set to two. Each subspace is numbered using a two-bit string, namely, 00, 01, 10, and 11. We acquire every two-bit string from the payload message and embed them into the vertex of the cover model. For example, in Figure 2, the vertex **A** currently is inside the 00-subspace, where we intend to embed the two-bit payload message "00." We let the vertex stay where it is, since the numbered subspace is coincident with the payload message. However, if we want to embed the two-bit payload message "10," then we must translate the position of the vertex from its current 01-subspace to the new 10-subspace, the vertex **A'**. This translation represents a status change for this vertex, and thus a message is embedded. The translation is based on a symmetric reflection with respect to the X-axis, Y-axis, or their combinations. Obviously, when we extend the method to 3D space, every vertex is able to have three bits of payload message embedded, since we can set C_{max} with a magnitude of three.

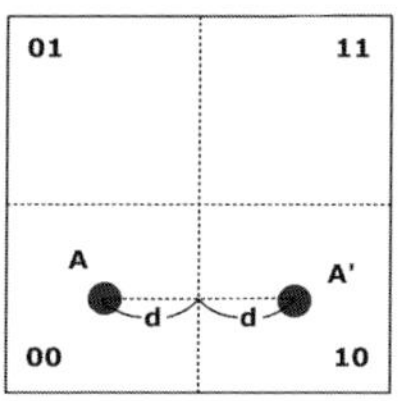

Fig. 2. Embedding two bits of data into the active vertex **A** by translating to the appropriate numbered positions

3.2 The Extracting Data Process

The purpose of the extracting data process is to recover the payload properly, given the stego model. This process is similar to the embedding process except that the input model is the stego model rather than the cover model. First, the BSP tree construction process illustrated in Section 2 is employed. Recall that the stego model will be aligned in that process using the PCA coordinates system of the stego model together with that of the cover model. Then we also transform all vertices of the stego model to the PCA coordinates system of the cover model and the bounding volume can be also derived from the boundary vertices. Next, the BSP tree can be reconstructed by the termination criteria. We then traverse the BSP tree to its leaf nodes to locate a voxel in which only a vertex of the stego model is located. Finally, the payload message can be extracted by checking the status of the vertex within that voxel.

4 Experimental Results

We implemented our technique using Microsoft Visual C++ programming language. We also performed experiments to validate the feasibility of our algorithms. Results were collected on a personal computer with a Pentium IV 2.4 GHz processor and 256 MB memory.

For our test, we took five polygonal models as the cover model. The results for all models are shown in Table I. *MV* means the number of the vertices which are within the same voxel. The payload message consists of a "random" 01 bit stream. In our implementation, L_{max} was no restriction, V_{max} was set to 0.05% to avoid visual distortion, and C_{max} was set to three. Therefore, the capacity is three times the number of embedded vertices, which is derived by subtracting the number of the vertices that are within the same voxel and the number of boundary vertices from the number of vertices in the 3D model. The embedding order for the vertices is decided by the in-order traversal order for the BSP tree; while the distortion between the cover and stego models is measured by using Hausdorff distance (HD) [4].

To test the robustness of our scheme, we randomly rotate, translate, and uniform scale each 3D model. The experimental results show that no error is in the extracted secret payload. One thing that deserves mention is the number precision of the model which is under the shrink attack; this is a kind of uniform scaling attack. Errors will be produced because some information about the model is missing without enough number precision.

Figure 3 shows the relationship between V_{max} and the BSP tree construction time, data embedding time, model distortion, and the ratio of the vertices within the same voxel for some models. In Figure 3a the BSP tree construction is terminated when the ratio of a voxel's diagonal length in a leaf node over V_{BV} is less than V_{max}. Obviously,

Table 1. The results for our test models

Model	$N_{vertices}$	N_{faces}	V_{BV}	HD	$Time_{BSP}$	$Time_{Emb}$	NV_{BV}	MV	Capacity
Venus-Body	19847	43357	50.2959	0.008208	0.781	0.063	6	223	58854
Bunny	35947	69451	2.6634	0.000461	1.860	0.110	6	2	107817
Horse	48485	96966	0.2722	0.000046	2.312	0.156	6	10	145407
Rabbit	67038	134074	84.0099	0.014208	3.532	0.203	6	4	201084
Venus-Head	134345	268686	0.1558	0.000027	7.609	0.391	6	0	403017

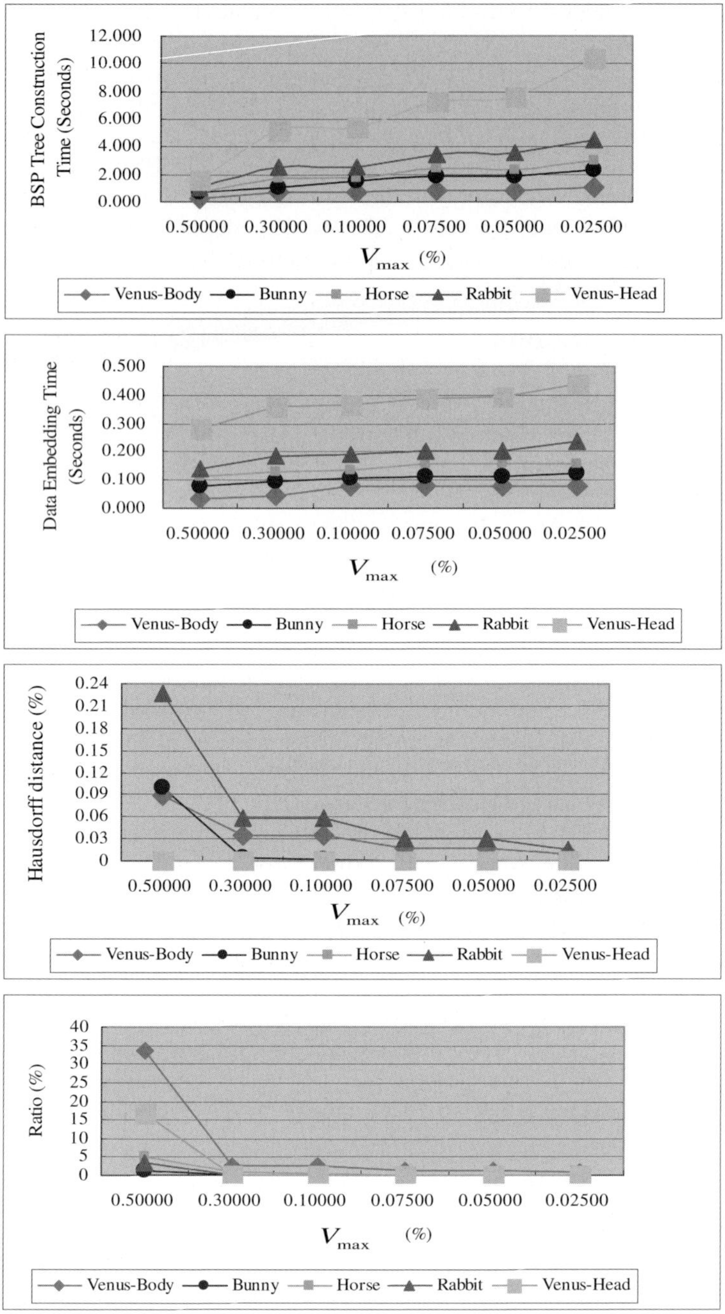

Fig. 3. The relationship between V_{max} and the BSP tree construction time, data embedding time, model distortion, and the ratio of *MV* for all test models

the BSP tree construction time is inverse proportional to V_{max}. A large V_{max} means the voxel in the leaf node can have a larger size and BSP tree construction can achieve the termination criteria earlier. In Figure 3b the data embedding time includes the tree traversal time and the time for changing the status. A large V_{max} makes the BSP tree smaller and tree traversal time is also less. However, the time required for constructing the BSP tree and for data embedding is less than four seconds and 0.5 seconds respectively for models with fewer than 70,000 vertices. This demonstrates the efficiency of the proposed method. In Figure 3c, the model distortion is relative to the diagonal length of the bounding volume. To avoid severe distortion, the value of V_{max} is usually small and the size of the leaf node will be also small. This reflects the fact that the maximal distortion is less than the value of V_{max}. The small values in the model distortion indicate that the stego models have insignificant visual difference in quantity. In Figure 3d, these vertices MV that are within the same voxel cannot embed any message since their extracting orders are unknown. To avoid prominent visual distortion, V_{max} has to be small, and we set it at 0.05% in our test models. As a result, the ratio corresponding to such V_{max} is less than 5%. This indicates that we can make use of a total of 95% of the vertices in our test models for data hiding.

5 Conclusion and Future Work

In this paper, we proposed a new steganography algorithm for 3D models using a spatial subdivision technique based on a Binary Space Partitioning (BSP) tree. Our scheme is a substitutive blind approach in the spatial domain; it is simple to implement. The data capacity in bits achieved is at least three times the number of the embedded vertices in the cover models. The capacity can be higher by carefully selecting the parameter representing the maximum bits that each embedded vertex of the 3D model can embed. In addition, we estimated the complexity of our scheme where it only requires several seconds to construct a BSP tree for a complex model. Our scheme can also be adapted to point-sampled geometries.

We use V_{max} as the termination criterion in our technique. However, this will result in multiple vertices within one voxel. In future, it would be wise to use several techniques to decide the data embedding/extracting order for these vertices to increase the data capacity. Furthermore, extending our technique to a fragile watermarking scheme based on the unique tree properties is also a research problem that deserves to be investigated.

Acknowledgements

This research was supported by the National Science Council (NSC) Taiwan under the grant numbers NSC 94-2213-E-005-022, NSC 94-2218-E-164-001, NSC 93-2213-E-005-018, NSC 93-2815-C-005-019-E, and NSC 92-2213-E-005-021.

References

1. Aspert, N., Drelic, E., Maret, Y., and Ebrahimi, T.: Steganography for Three-Dimensional Polygonal Meshes. Proc. of the SPIE 47th Annual Meeting (2002) 705–708
2. Benedens, O.: Geometry-Based Watermarking of 3D Models. IEEE Trans. Comput. Graph. Appl. 19(1) (1999) 46–55
3. Cayre, F., and Macq, B.: Data Hiding on 3-D Triangle Meshes. IEEE Trans. on Signal Process. 51(4) (2003) 939–949
4. Cignoni, P., Rocchini, C., and Scopigno, R.: Metro: measuring error on simplified surfaces. Comput. Graph. Forum 17(2) (1998) 167–174
5. Cotting, D., Weyrich, T., Pauly, M., and Gross, M.: Robust Watermarking of Point-Sampled Geometry. Proc. of International Conference on Shape Modeling and Applications (2004) 233–242
6. Kanai, S., Date, H., and Kishinami, T.: Digital Watermarking for 3D Polygons using Multiresolution Wavelet Decomposition. Proc. of Sixth IFIP WG 5.2 International Workshop on Geometric Modeling: Fundamentals and Applications (1998) 296–307
7. Katzenbeisser, S. and Petitcolas, F.A.P.: Information Hiding Techniques for Steganography and Digital Watermarking, Artech House, London (2000)
8. Maret, Y. and Ebrahimi, T.: Data Hiding on 3D Polygonal Meshes. Proc. of ACM Workshop on Multimedia and Security (2004) 68–74
9. Ohbuchi, R., Masuda, H., and Aono, M.: Watermarking Three-Dimensional Polygonal Models. Proc. of ACM Multimedia (1997) 261–272
10. Ohbuchi, R., Takahashi, S., Miyazawa, T., and Mukaiyama, A.: Watermarking 3D Polygonal Meshes in the Mesh Spectral Domain. Proc. of Graphics Interface (2001) 9–17
11. Rencher, A.C.: Methods of Multivariate Analysis, Second Edition, Wiley, New York (2002)
12. Petitcolas, F.A.P., Anderson, R.J., and Kuhn, M.G.: Information Hiding - A Survey. Proceedings of IEEE 87(7) (1999) 1062–1078
13. Wagner, M.G.: Robust Watermarking of Polygonal Meshes. Proc. of Geometric Modeling and Processing (2000) 201–208
14. Wang, C.-M. and Cheng, Y.-M.: An Efficient Information Hiding Algorithm for Polygonal Models. Comput. Graph. Forum 24(3) (2005) 591–600
15. Wang, C.-M. and Wang, P.-C.: Data Hiding Approach of Point-sampled Geometry. IEICE Trans. Comm. E88-B(1) (2005) 190–194
16. Zafeiriou, S., Tefas, A., and Pitas, I.: Blind Robust Watermarking Schemes for Copyright Protection of 3D Mesh Objects. IEEE Trans. Visual. Comput. Graph. 11(5) (2005) 596–607
17. Yu, Zhiqiang, Ip, Horace H.S., Kwok, L.F.: A robust watermarking scheme for 3D triangular mesh models. Pattern Recognition 36 (11) (2003) 2603–2614

Addressing Scalability Issues in Large-Scale Collaborative Virtual Environment

Qingping Lin, Liang Zhang, Norman Neo, and Irma Kusuma

Information Communication Institute of Singapore,
School of Electrical and Electronic Engineering,
Naynang Technological University, Singapore 639798
Tel.: (+65) 67904688; Fax: (+65) 67922971
iqplin@ntu.edu.sg

Abstract. The existing Collaborative Virtual Environment (CVE) systems have limited scalability due to the constraints in computer processing power and network bandwidth of participating hosts. In this paper, we propose a new approach for heterogeneous internet based users to construct large-scale CVE (LCVE) system: Mobile Agent Based Framework for LCVE (MACVE). In MACVE, the system workloads are decomposed into independent and fine grained tasks. The tasks are modelled as mobile agents which are not bound to any fixed nodes as the traditional CVE architectures do. As the mobile agents can migrate or clone dynamically at any suitable participating host include traditional servers and qualified user hosts, the system workloads can be distributed more pervasively to avoid potential bottleneck. This improves the scalability of LCVE. Experiments results have demonstrated the scalability of our proposed approach.

Keywords: CVE, scalability, mobile agent, network architecture.

1 Introduction

Collaborative Virtual Environment (CVE) is a shared 3D virtual world for the geographically dispersed people to interact with each others. In a CVE, participants are provided with graphical embodiments called avatars that convey their identity, presence, location, and activities to others. They are able to use these avatars to interact with the contents of the world and to communicate with one another using different media including audio, video, graphical gestures, and text in real-time[1]. CVE has many promising applications, such as military war simulation, medical or industrial team training, collaborative design and engineering, virtual shopping malls, virtual libraries, distance learning and Internet-based multi-user VR game.

Constructing a large-scale CVE (LCVE) system, which contains a large number of virtual entities and supports large number of concurrent users, is challenging because of the heterogeneous computing and network capability of each participating host. One of the key research issues in CVE is scalability. To solve the scalability issue in CVE, two types of communication architecture are adopted in the existing systems: peer-to-peer (P2P) model and multi-server model.

H.-P. Seidel, T. Nishita, and Q. Peng (Eds.): CGI 2006, LNCS 4035, pp. 477 – 485, 2006.

In the P2P architecture, there is no central server to manage the whole CVE. Each individual peer program exchanges data directly with other peer programs and maintains its own copy the VE state. By adopting IP-Multicast, this type of system can be scalable, such as NPSNET[2], DIVE[3], SPLINE[4], SCORE[5], etc. However, CVE systems with peer-to-peer architecture may not be suitable for supporting heterogeneous peers, such as the Internet users, since their network connection speed and computing power may vary greatly which will lead to difficulty in maintaining the consistency of the virtual world; the stability of peer computer hosts and their network connections also make persistency maintenance difficult.

In the multi-server architecture, the CVE is managed by multiple servers. Each participant exchange data with one or more servers, which can effectively manage the consistency and persistency of the CVE and the servers also can function as proxies to do the computation intensive jobs for the participants[6]. The workload on the servers may include: (1) delivering the static scene data to each participant; (2) processing and routing the participant's messages to maintain a consistency CVE state and delivering this consistent CVE state to newly arriving participants; (3) recording the state changes happening in the CVE to maintain its persistency. We defined these workloads on all the servers as system workloads/tasks. The successful multi-server CVE systems include RING[7], NetEffect[8], Community Place[9], CyberWalk [10,13], and some commercial multiplyer network games, such as EverQest[11], Ultima Online[12], etc. However, the scalability is not easy to realize for CVE systems with multi-server architecture, because certain servers may become bottleneck due to the unpredictable workloads on them, even through dynamic load distribution or balance are adopt in some systems.

In this paper, we proposed a new approach to construct LCVE: Mobile Agent Based Framework for LCVE (MACVE).

2 Design of MACVE

To effectively distribute the system workloads, firstly, the expected system tasks of a LCVE should be independent and fine grained. In MACVE, we model a LCVE as a group of collaborative agents. Each agent is a software component to assume an independent task to provide a certain service for the system. Agents collaborate with each other to maintain the entire LCVE system.

To improve the system scalability, MACVE allows all agents to be mobile without bonding to any fixed host. As the system scales up, agents will be able to clone or migrate to any suitable participating host (include Trusted User Nodes) to provide more services. The mutual independence of services and hosts provide large flexibility to utilize the computing and network resource of the system efficiently. Our proposed framework fully takes advantages of such flexibility via Agent Resource Management, Computing Resource Management, Database Resource Management, VE Content Management and VE Directory Management, which will be discussed in the following paragraphs.

Our framework is divided into three Layers: Resource Layer for System Resource Management, Content Layer for VE Content Management and Gateway Layer for VE Directory Management as illustrated in Figure 1. Each layer is composed of multiple collaborative mobile agents to achieve the management tasks. To ensure the system reliability, the critical system agents would migrate and reside in grid nodes.

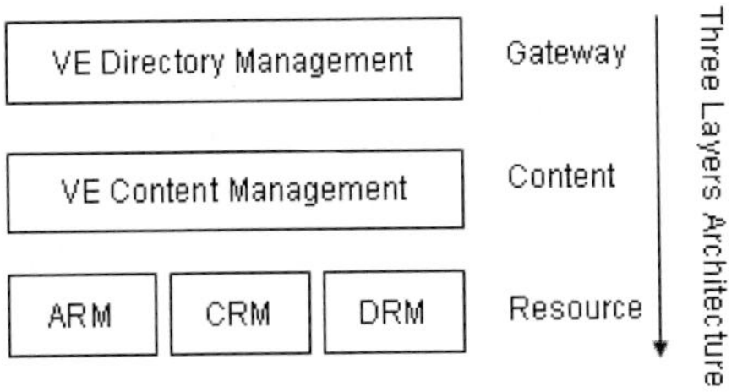

Fig. 1. Overall Architecture

2.1 System Resource Management

The bottom layer is Resource Layer which manages the distribution of Mobile Agents, System Computing Nodes and the Database in the system. This layer is further subdivided into three parts: ARM (Agent Resource Management), CRM (Computing Resource Management), and DRM (Database Resource Management).

2.1.1 Agent Resource Management

In a LCVE system, there are many agents running at different hosts. To manage all these agents effectively to achieve pervasive workload distribution, we use Agent Resource Management (ARM).

ARM is realized by an ARM Agent which functions as an Agent Code Repository, Agent Monitor Center, and Agent Command Center. Each kind of agent code should register at ARM Agent who manages these codes and guarantee the consistency and integrity of the agent code running in the whole system. When agents begin to run, they register their network locations and running states at ARM Agent. So the ARM Agent provides a directory for all running agents. When Agents execute some operations, such as cloning or migration, ARM Agent will record the Agent Operation Event log. As an Agent Command Center, ARM Agent can also send commands dynamically to launch agents, transfer agents and clone agents, update agents to new versions, kill agents etc. to manage the LCVE system at runtime.

Since ARM Agent only deal with the messages related to agent command information, which is small size and not frequent traffic, there is little chance for an ARM Agent to become a bottleneck. Even the remote chance happens; ARM Agent can clone and migrate to redistribute its load.

2.1.2 Computing Resource Management

To effectively manage all the participating hosts to share the system load on demand, we propose Computing Resource Management (CRM).

A typical LCVE system consists of a large number of computer hosts connected through networks. Each host is called a participating node. Based on the functional roles of each participating node, we classify them into two main categories: User Nodes and Service Provider Nodes. User Nodes refer to any user host participating in the LCVE. Service Provider Nodes refer to the nodes belonging to the LCVE system owner.

User Nodes are further classified into Normal User Nodes and Trusted User Nodes.

- Normal User Node is a host that only allows a user to navigate and interact with virtual entities or other users in the CVE.
- Trusted User Node is a host that not only functions as a Normal User Node, but also has spare capacity in terms of computing power, memory and network bandwidth to host mobile agents to run on it. It should at least meet the minimum capability and security requirements set by the LCVE system.

Service Provider Nodes are further classified into Controlling Nodes and DB Nodes.

- Controlling Node is a host provided by the system owner, which assumes multiple system computing tasks to manage a LCVE system and maintain the multiuser collaborative interactions in a consistent, persistent, and evolving LCVE.
- DB Node is a host provided by the system owner, which provides the database support for the LCVE system.

Since Controlling Nodes and Trusted User Nodes are used to share the workload of the LCVE system, we classify both of them as System Computing Nodes (SC Nodes).

In MACVE, the system computing tasks are shared not only by the Service Provider Nodes as most conventional LCVE systems do, but also by Trusted User Nodes. When a Trusted User Node log off, it transfer all the agents running on it to other SC Nodes. However, because it is less stable, a Trusted User Node may crush before it successfully transfers all the agents on it. MACVE has an agent recovery mechanism to restart the losing agent from the state before it crushes which will be discussed in Section 2.4. Thus, system computing tasks can be pervasive to more participating nodes. We define the computing resource in a LCVE system as the computing and network capability of all the joining SC nodes in the system.

CRM is responsible for managing the system computing resource so that each system task will receive enough computing resources. There maybe thousands of SC Nodes in a LCVE system. To improve the efficiency of data communication between the SC Nodes, the nodes are grouped according to their IP addresses. The nodes near to each other are allocated to the same group. Each group will have a Group Manager Node to reasonably distribute system workloads among the nodes in this group.

CRM is achieved by multiple Node Agents, Group Manager Agents, and a CRM Agent whose relationships can be illustrated as Figure 2.

A Node Agent runs in each SC Node which monitors computing load and network traffic of that node. When this node's workload reaches its threshold, Node Agent will decide whether to transfer certain mobile agents in this node to other node or to clone certain mobile agents to other node to alleviate this node's workloads. A Group Manager Agent runs at the Group Manager Node which is a SC Node designated by the CRM Agent. It will search for suitable nodes in the group. If it can not find a suitable node within its own group, the Group Manager Agent will negotiate CRM Agent to find a suitable node in other groups. The CRM Agent manages all the Group Manager Agents. When joining the LCVE system, every SC Node will register with the CRM Agent. CRM Agent allocates the SC Node to a group.

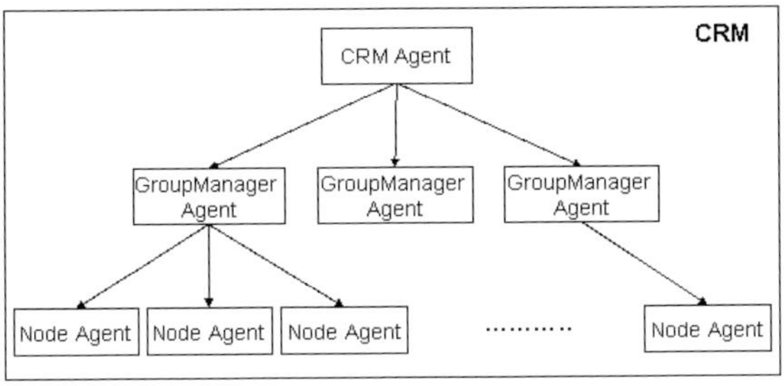

Fig. 2. Relationships of Agents for CRM

2.1.3 Database Resource Management

In order to support large VE content, the database is distributed to different DB Nodes. As the system evolves, new DB Nodes can be added into the system at any time. DRM is achieved by multiple DB Agents and a DRM Agent, which is responsible for managing the distributed DB. It provides a uniform interface for agents at content layer and gateway layer to access the system database.

2.2 VE Content Management

In MACVE, The VE is spatially divided into several manageable continuous regions. Each region maybe further divided into cells depending on the requirement of the VE contents. Each cell is a basic unit for VE content downloading, communication, consistency and persistency. And a set of multicast groups are assigned to a cell to achieve the communication in the cell.

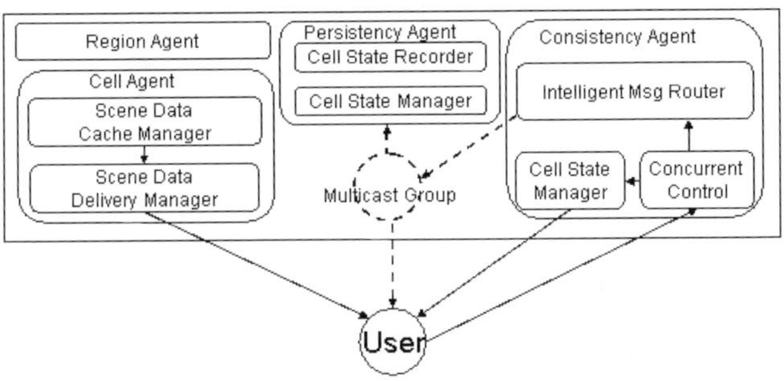

Fig. 3. VE Management

The management of the VE is in correspondent with the above Region-Cell hierarchy, which is achieved by Region Agents, Cell Agents, Consistency Agents and Persistency Agents as illustrated in Figure 3.

Region Agent only maintains the hierarchical relationship between itself and its Cell Agents. It does not maintain the VE contents.

A Cell Agent has two basic components: Scene Data Cache Manager and Scene Data Delivery Manager. Scene Data Cache Manager loads the scene data of a cell from the DB Agent and maintains local cache for them. Scene Data Delivery Manager delivers the scene data to users when the users need it. Because the scene data always has large volume, this kind of data is bandwidth and time consuming. Scene Delivery Manager implements the algorithm to delivery the most needed data with its appropriate level of detail timely, such as predictive pre-fetching or multi-resolution caching mechanism, etc.

A Consistency Agent has three basic components: Concurrency Control, Cell State Manager, and Intelligent Message Router. Concurrency Control guarantees there is no conflicts when multi-user access a same virtual entity concurrently. Cell State Manager maintains the real-time VE state of the cell and delivers the state to newly arriving users. Intelligent Message Router implements different interaction management strategies and route the message to different multicast groups.

A Persistency Agent has two basic components: Cell State Manager, Cell State Recorder. Cell State Manager maintains the real-time VE state of the cell. In a LCVE, the Persistency Agent and Consistency Agent usually run at different SC Node, so the Cell State Manager of Persistency Agent is also a real-time backup of the cell state for the Consistency Agent. If Consistency crushes, new Consistency Agent can get the latest cell state from its Persistency Agent. Because Consistency Agent and Persistency Agent subscribe to the same multicast group, the duplicated Cell State Manager at both agents will not create the any extra traffic to compromise the system scalability. Cell State Recorder sends the cell states data to DB Agent to save them periodically to maintain the persistency of the cell.

2.3 VE Directory Management

Since the management of VE is decentralized, it needs a directory service to locate a place in VE, search a Virtual Entity or a user in VE, etc. VE Directory Management provides such services. VE Directory Management is achieved by a group of Gateway Agents, which pervasive on different well-known Controlling Nodes on the Internet. When a user wants to enter the VE, the user node agent connects to a nearest Gateway Agent which directs the user to its intended destination in the VE. Gateway agent also provides user registration, authentication and user log record service.

2.4 Agent Recovery Mechanism in MACVE

In MACVE, the system workloads can be shared by the Trusted User Nodes. However, User Nodes tend to have less stability compared with Service Provider Nodes. So MACVE provides a mechanism for the agent recovery.

In MACVE, the management of all agents is organized by a tree-structure, such as Group Manager Agent manages the Node Agents which belong to the same group; or Region Agent manages its Cell Agents. The agent at the parent position is called the Parent Agent and the agent at the child position is called Child Agent. The Parent Agent is responsible for monitoring the proper execution of its Child Agents. Every Child Agent sends a "heartbeat" message (a living message) periodically to its Parent Agent. If the Parent Agent receives no heartbeat from the Child Agent within a timeout, it detects the crush of the Child Agent. The Parent Agent will ask the ARM Agent to send a new Child Agent to other available nodes to resume the system tasks.

For system stability reason, Persistency Agent of a cell is not allowed to be transferred to Trusted User Node, because it maintains the backup of the snapshot of the current cell state. When a Trusted User Node crushes and result in a Consistency Agent lost, the newly launched Consistency Agent will get the latest cell state from the corresponding Persistency Agent at the System Controlling Node. Thus, it will remove the impact of the crushes of Trusted User Node to allow effective recovery of the lost Consistency Agent.

3 System Prototype and Experimental Results

We have developed a prototype system to conduct experimental studies and evaluate MACVE. The prototype includes three parts: 11 types of Mobile Agents for different system workloads; a Mobile Agent Environment (MAE) for supporting agent migration and clone; and a web based client user interface for user navigation and interaction.

Our experimental CVE consists of 12 cells. Each cell is populated with interactive entities and concurrent users. Users in the CVE can add or remove or interact with entities and chat with each other. We have developed a RobotGroup to simulate a certain number of concurrent users, which send out messages for each simulated users at a constant rate. In the whole CVE, we collect experimental data for various number of concurrent users and virtual entities. Figure 4 is the screenshot of user interface during our experiment with 1000 concurrent users and 5000 virtual entities.

To study the agent migration impacts on CVE users, we do experiments to study the effect of number of concurrent users and the number of entities in a cell on the migration time spans of a Consistency Agent. The reason we choose to study Consistency Agent migration is that its migration is most complex among all types of agents and it has most impacts to users.

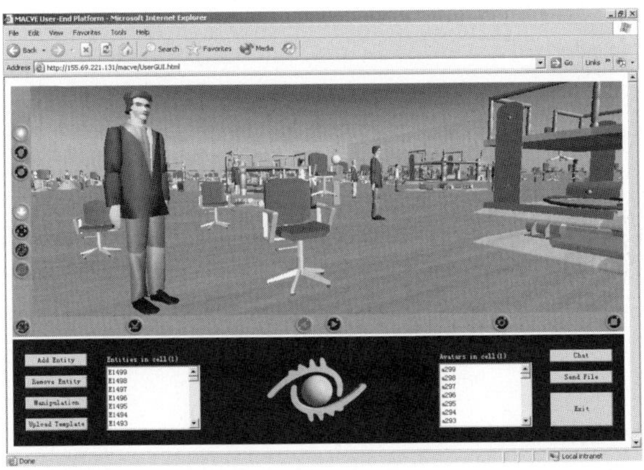

Fig. 4. Screenshot of MACVE User Interface

The migration of a Consistency Agent includes 3 steps: (1) transferring the agent code to the destination; (2) synchronizing the agent state; (3) shifting the agent control. Transfer & Synchronization Time measures the time required to transfer the agent code and synchronize the agent state. The Transfer & Synchronization process will not directly affect users' collaborative interaction in the CVE as it can be done in a separate thread while the CVE system tasks are performed by the current mobile agents. Handover Time measures the time required to shift agent control which will affect users' collaborative interaction in the CVE. Thus it is particularly important to evaluate the delay caused by the Handover Time.

As shown in Figure 5, we observe from our experiment that the Transfer & Synchronization Time increases with the increase of the number of current users, whereas the Handover Time is relatively stable which is 425.0 ms when the concurrent user number reaches 1000 in a cell. In Figure 6, we observe that the Transfer & Synchronization Time increases with the increase of the number of entities, whereas the Handover Time is relatively stable which is 344.4 ms when the number of entities in the cell reaches 3000. A temporary short delay of less than half a second in updating scene state caused by the Handover Time will have little impact on the performance of a CVE with a large number of concurrent users and virtual entities. We found from the experiment that the users would not feel the migration of the

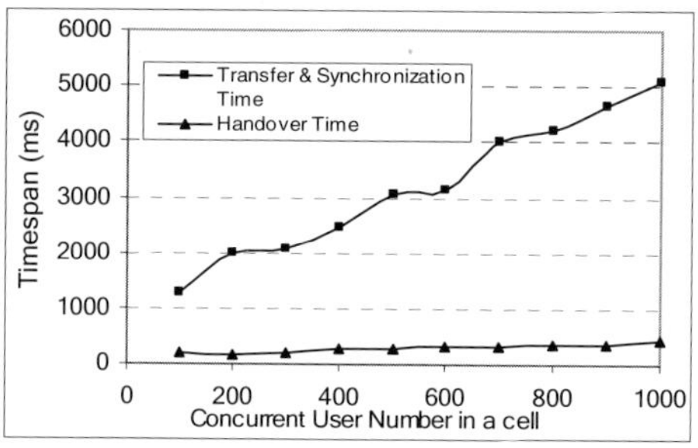

Fig. 5. Consistency Agent Migration Time on Concurrent User Number

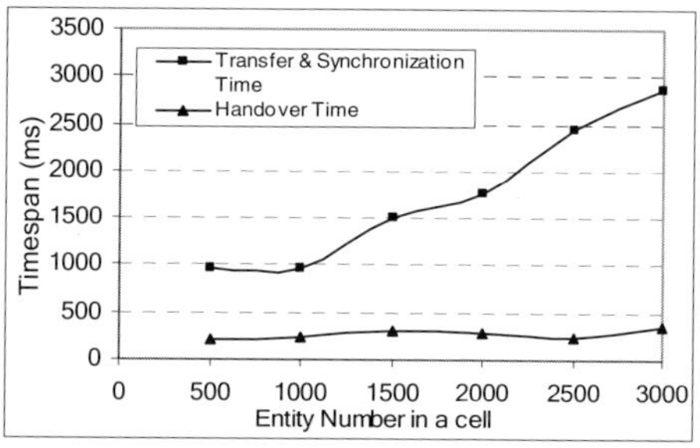

Fig. 6. Consistency Agent Migration Time on Entity Number

Consistency Agent as the user interaction with the LCVE will not be affected during the agent transfer and synchronization period while the agent control handover time is short enough to avoid apparent interruption.

Our experiments show that Consistency Agent migration does not affect the real-time interaction of the CVE users, and so do other types of agents. Therefore, our proposed MACVE will improve the scalability of LCVE without compromising its performance.

4 Conclusions and Future Work

In this paper, we have proposed a fully distributed mobile agent framework -- MACVE as a new approach to construct LCVE. In MACVE, the system tasks are decomposed into a group of collaborative mobile agents. By migrating and cloning these agents at System Controlling Node and Trusted User Node, the system workloads are distributed pervasively. Our experiments have demonstrated its effectiveness in supporting large number of concurrent users with real-time interaction in LCVE. In our future work, we will develop real-time self-learning intelligent decision making methods for different mobile agents to optimize the scalability and extensibility of LCVEs.

References

[1] C. G. Steve Benford, Tom Rodden, James Pycock, "Collaborative Virtual Environments," Communications of the ACM, vol. 44, pp. 79 - 85, 2001

[2] M. Macedonia, M. Zyda, D. Pratt, P. Barham, and S. Zestwitz, "NPSNET: A Network Software Architecture for Large-Scale Virtual Environments," Presence, vol. 3, pp. 265--287, 1994.

[3] O. Stahl and M. Andersson, "DIVE - a Toolkit for Distributed R Applications," presented at the 6th ERCIM workshop, Stockholm, 1994.

[4] J. W. Barrus, R. C. Waters, and D. B. Anderson, "Locales: Supporting Lange Multiuser Virtual Environments," IEEE Computer Graphics and Applications, vol. 16 (6), pp. 50-57., 1996.

[5] E. lety, T. Turletti, and F. Baccelli, "SCORE: A Scalable Communication Protocol for Large-Scale Virtual Environment," IEEE/ACM Transactions on Networking, vol. 12, pp. 247-260, 2004.

[6] C.-L. W. Tianqi Wang, Francis Lau, "A Grid-enabled Multi-server Network Game Architecture," presented at 3rd International Conference on Application and Development of Computer Games, 2004.

[7] T. A. Funkhouser, "RING: a client-server system for multi-user virtual environments " in Proceedings of the 1995 symposium on Interactive 3D graphics Monterey, California, United States ACM Press, 1995 pp. 85-ff. .

[8] T. K. Das, G. Singh, A. Mitchell, P. S. Kumar, and K. McGee, "NetEffect: A Network Architecture for Large-scale Multi-user Virtual Wrold," presented at the ACM symposium on Virtual reality software and technology, 1997.

[9] R. Lea, Y. Honda, K. Matsuda, and S. Matsuda, "Community Place: Architecture and Performance," presented at the second symposium on Virtual reality modeling language, 1997.

[10] R. W. H. Lau. Jimmy Chim, Va Leong, Antonio Si, "CyberWalk: A Web-Based Distributed Virtual Walkthrough Environment," IEEE Transactions on Multimedia, vol. 5, pp. 503-515, 2003.

[11] EverQest. Available at http://everquest.station.sony.com/.

[12] Ultima Online. Available at http://www.uo.com/.

[13] B. Ng, A. Si, R. W. H. Lau, and F. W. B. Li, "A Multi-Server Architecture for Distributed Virtual Walkthrough," presented at ACM VRST'02, Hong Kong, 2002.

Symmetric Tiling Patterns with the Extended Picard Group in Three-Dimensional Space*

Rui-song Ye, Jian Ma, and Hui-liang Li

Department of Mathematics, Shantou University
Shantou, Guangdong, 515063, P.R. China
rsye@stu.edu.cn

Abstract. Automatic generation of tiling patterns with the symmetry of the extended Picard group in three-dimensional hyperbolic space is considered. We generate the patterns by repeating the fundamental patterns created in the fundamental region to all other equivalent regions. We also produce such a kind of tiling patterns in the unit sphere by conformal mappings. The method provides a novel approach for devising exotic symmetric tiling patterns from a dynamical system's point of view.

1 Introduction

People have long been fascinated with symmetric patterns arising in nature, and artists have been creating intriguing works associated with variant kinds of symmetries [1], [2]. The Dutch artist, M. C. Escher, popularized the perception of symmetry in art. Escher was good at creating symmetric artistic works by taking advantage of the simultaneous sense of symmetry and the bizarre. He often considered planar crystallographic symmetries and hyperbolic symmetries in his works, for example, see his Circle Limit I-IV series of works [3], [4].

Symmetries are expressed by relationships between the points in the considered geometrical object, but symmetries can be understood more precisely by means of group theory [5], [6]. Actually a symmetric tiling is related to a particular group. For instance, a repeated pattern in the Euclidean plane is related to one of the seventeen wallpaper or crystallographic groups [6], [7], whereas a repeated pattern in the hyperbolic plane is related to one particular hyperbolic group [8], [9]. As a matter of fact, Escher had significant interaction with mathematicians who studied group theory, for example, he kept contacting with Coxeter, a famous mathematician in the same age. As a result, he made many valuable artistic works. Modern considerations with the aid of computers have become prolific, see for example [7], [8], [9], [10], [11]. In recent years, automatic generation of symmetric tiling patterns by means of computers attracts many mathematicians' interest. Wallpaper repeating patterns [7] and hyperbolic repeating patterns [9] are generated by visualizing dynamical systems' chaotic

* Supported by Tianyuan Foundation, National Nature Science Foundation of China (No. A0324649) and Guangdong Nature Science Foundation (No. 032035).

H.-P. Seidel, T. Nishita, and Q. Peng (Eds.): CGI 2006, LNCS 4035, pp. 486–493, 2006.

attractors and by making use of the properties of the considered dynamical systems respectively.

The automatic generation of symmetric patterns associated with the modular group in two-dimensional plane and the Picard group in three-dimensional hyperbolic space were considered in Chung et al [12] and [13] respectively. The Picard group contains the well-known modular group as its subgroup. The modular group is the most widely studied of all discrete groups due to its many connections with other branches of mathematics, especially with number theory. Chung et al generated many symmetric patterns with the modular group and the Picard group in their series papers. They proposed algorithms to generate tiling patterns from a dynamical system's point of view. By constructing some particular dynamical systems which satisfy the symmetries of the considered groups elaborately, the authors created many exotic patterns. But the construction of dynamical systems seems rather complicated and tedious. As a result, the proposed method is not easy to manipulate and generalize.

Ye et al [14] considered the extended modular group first to construct tiling patterns in two-dimensional space. It is well-known that the extended modular group consists the modular group as its subgroup with index 2. The symmetries appearing in the tiling patterns derived from the dynamical systems equivariant with the extended modular group are more than those with the modular group. It was also demonstrated that the construction of tiling patterns with the symmetries of the extended modular group is easier compared with the modular group. Furthermore the created tiling patterns are more beautiful usually. The reason lies in the fact that the extended modular group's fundamental region is only one half of the modular group's, as a result, it is easier to make the patterns' color vary continuously at the boundaries of the fundamental region.

In this paper, we extended the approach presented in [14]. We propose a fast algorithm for the generation of tiling patterns with the symmetry of the extended Picard group $\mathbb{P}_1$, which contains the Picard group $\mathbb{P}$ as a subgroup of index 2. It is easy and convenient to obtain unlimited varieties of tiling patterns. In section 2, we introduce some preliminaries about quaternion representation and the extended Picard group. Mappings equivariant with the extended Picard group are constructed in section 3. In section 4, we present a coloring scheme to generate tiling patterns with the symmetries of the extended Picard group.

2 Quaternion Representation and the Extended Picard Group

Quaternions were first presented by Hamilton in 1843. Much attention has been paid to quaternions since the mid 20th century. Let Z, R, C and H be the sets of integers, real numbers, complex numbers and quaternions, respectively. A quaternion z is expressed as the form $z = x + yi + rj + sk$, or equivalently, $z = (x, y, r, s)$, where $x, y, r, s \in R$; i, j and k are square roots of -1 such that the following equalities [15]

$$ii = jj = kk = -1, ij = -ji = k, jk = -kj = i, ki = -ik = j.$$

It is easy to show then that the multiplication of the quaternions satisfies the associative law but not the commutative law. Quaternions also satisfy $\overline{z} = x - yi - rj - sk$, $|z|^2 = z\overline{z} = x^2 + y^2 + r^2 + s^2$, and $z^{-1} = \frac{\overline{z}}{|z|^2} = \frac{(x-yi-rj-sk)}{|z|^2}$.

We can denote the upper half-space H^3 as $H^3 = \{(x, y, r)|(x, y, r) \in R^3,\ r > 0\}$. It is convenient to use H^3 in the form of quaternions with the k-part being 0: $H^3 = \{x + yi + rj|\ x, y, r \in R,\ r > 0\}$.

The Picard group $\mathbb{P}$ is the set of all fractional linear substitution transformations on H^3 [15]

$$w = \gamma z = (az + b)(cz + d)^{-1}, \tag{1}$$

where $\gamma \in \mathbb{P}$, $w, z \in H^3$, $a, b, c, d \in Z + Zi = Z^2, ad - bc = 1$. The elements of $\mathbb{P}$ are generated by the following four generators [13]

$$\alpha z = z + 1 = (x + 1) + yi + rj,\ \beta z = -z^{-1} = \frac{1}{|z|^2}(-x + yi + rj),$$

$$\xi z = z + i = x + (y + 1)i + rj,\ \eta z = izi = -x - yi + rj.$$

If the transformation κ ($\kappa z = -\overline{z} = -x + yi + rj$) is added into the Picard group, we will get the extended Picard group $\mathbb{P}_1$, which is generated by the five generators α, β, ξ, η and κ. It is obvious that $\mathbb{P}$ is a subgroup of $\mathbb{P}_1$.

Chung et al [13] had shown in the generated colored patterns that the generators α, ξ and η of the Picard group make the periodicity in x direction, the periodicity in y direction and two-fold symmetry in the cross section parallel to $x - y$ plane. More exactly, the cross section parallel to $x - y$ plane will own $c2$ symmetry in the unit region $I = \{(x, y, r)|(x, y) \in [-1, 1] \times [-1, 1],\ r = r_0\}$, and consequently the whole cross section $I_1 = \{(x, y, r)|r = r_0\}$ will have the symmetry of the wallpaper group $p2$. In this paper, we extend one generator κ into the Picard group. The generated patterns will then exhibit reflectional symmetry with respect to y axis, and therefore in the unit region I, the symmetry of the patterns changes from $c2$ to $d2$, while in the whole plane I_1, the patterns will have the symmetry of the wallpaper group pmm. We refer to [5], [6], [7] for more details about the wallpaper groups.

The extended Picard group acts on the upper half hyperbolic space H^3 onto itself. We next consider the fundamental region of the extended Picard group. A fundamental region is a connected set whose transformed copies under $\mathbb{P}_1$ cover the entire space without overlapping except at the boundaries.

Let $U = \{z = (x, y, r)|0 \leq x \leq \frac{1}{2}, 0 \leq y \leq \frac{1}{2}, |z| \geq 1\}$, then one can show that U is a fundamental region of the extended Picard group $\mathbb{P}_1$.

Automatic generation of symmetric patterns of the extended modular group was proposed in Ye at al [14]. As the group action of (1) is an extension of the extended modular group on the upper half-plane, the tessellation in the $x - r$ plane of H^3 exhibits the symmetry of the extended modular group. Fig. 1(a), (b) show the tessellations at different cross sections of H^3.

Tessellation in the hyperbolic three-dimensional space can also be expressed elegantly in the Poincaré model that contains all the points of the open unit sphere

$$S = \{z \in R^3 | z = (x, y, r)^T, |z| < 1\}.$$

The upper half-space is related to the Poincaré model by the conformal mapping Π as

$$v = \Pi(z) = \frac{(z - j)}{(1 - jz)},$$

where $z \in H^3$ and $v \in S^2$. One tessellation in the Poincaré model is shown in Fig. 1(c).

(a) (b) (c)

Fig. 1. (a) Tessellation in the upper half-space: $|x| \leq 1, |y| \leq 0.8$, $0.0001 < r \leq 1$; (b) Tessellation in the upper half-space: $|x| \leq 1, |y| \leq 0.8$, $0.0001 < r \leq 0.25$; (c) Tessellation in the Poincaré model: $x^2 + y^2 + r^2 < 1$

3 Mappings Equivariant with the Extended Picard Group

3.1 Equivariant Mappings

Let Γ be a group. We consider $\widehat{F}(z)$ which maps H^3 onto H^3

$$z_{i+1} = \widehat{F}(z_i), \qquad z_i \in H^3, i = 0, 1, 2...$$

$\widehat{F}(z)$ is called a Γ-equivariant mapping if

$$\widehat{F}(\gamma z) = \gamma \widehat{F}(z), \forall z \in H^3 \text{ and } \gamma \in \Gamma.$$

In the process of constructing equivariant mappings $\widehat{F}$, we first restrict our consideration to iterative mappings F in H^3, i.e.

$$F(z) = F_1(z) + F_2(z)i + F_3(z)j,$$

where$F_1(z), F_2(z), F_3(z) \in R$. In order to avoid the orbit of F falling into $R^3 \backslash H^3$, we then define the following mapping

$$\widehat{F}(z) = \begin{cases} F(z), & \text{if } F_3(z) \geq 0, \\ F_1(z) + F_2(z)i - F_3(z)j, & \text{if } F_3(z) < 0. \end{cases}$$

It is easy to show the following theorem.

Theorem 1. If $F(z)$ is a mapping equivariant with $\mathbb{P}_1$, then $\widehat{F}(z)$ is also a mapping equivariant with $\mathbb{P}_1$.

3.2 Construction of $\mathbb{P}_1$-Equivariant Mappings $F(z)$

We now turn to consider the construction of $\mathbb{P}_1$-equivariant mappings $F(z)$. We first construct $F(z)$ in the fundamental region.

Theorem 2. Suppose $F(z)$ is a $\mathbb{P}_1$-equivariant mapping in U. Let $z \in A$, where A is one of the four planes $x = 0, x = \frac{1}{2}, y = 0, y = \frac{1}{2}$ in U, then we have

(a) $F(z) \in A$. (b) $F(z) = 1$, if $|z| = 1$.

Proof. (a) Firstly, we show the case $x = 0$. In this case, $z = \kappa z$, and therefore

$$F(z) = F(\kappa z) = \kappa F(z)$$

which implies $F_1(z) = 0$, i.e., $F(z) \in A$. As for the other cases, it is also easy to prove by the facts $z = \alpha\kappa z$ for $z = \frac{1}{2} + yi + rj$, $z = \kappa\eta z$ for $z = x + 0i + rj$, and $z = \xi\kappa\eta z$ for $z = x + \frac{1}{2}i + rj$.

(b) If $|z| = 1$, then $z = \kappa\beta z$,

$$F(z) = F(\kappa\beta z) = \kappa\beta F(z), \ \kappa F(z) = \beta F(z).$$

As a result, we have $|F(z)| = 1$. □

We rewrite $F(z)$ as the form $F(z) = z + f(z)$. By theorem 2, we obtain

$$f_1(0 + yi + rj) = f_1(\frac{1}{2} + yi + rj) = 0, \ f_2(x + 0i + rj) = f_2(x + \frac{1}{2}i + rj) = 0.$$

Consequently we may express f_1, f_2 as the following forms

$$f_1(x, y, r) = g_1(x)h_1(x, y, r), \ f_2(x, y, r) = g_2(y)h_2(x, y, r),$$

where $g_i(0) = g_i(\frac{1}{2}) = 0$, and $h_i(x, y, r)$ $(i = 1, 2)$ are arbitrary.

It is free to construct f_3. We can choose

$$g(x, y, r) = |F(z)|^2 = (x + f_1)^2 + (y + f_2)^2 + (r + f_3)^2.$$

It follows from the fact $g(x, y, r) = 1$ if $|z| = 1$ that we may write $g(x, y, r)$ to be the form, for instance,

$$g(x, y, r) = |z|^2$$

which implies f_3 can be written as

$$f_3 = \sqrt{g(x, y, r) - (x + f_1)^2 - (y + f_2)^2} - r.$$

Finally, we extend $F(z)$ from the fundamental region U to the entire space H^3

$$F(z) = \gamma^{-1}F(\gamma z), \ z \notin U,$$

where $\gamma \in \mathbb{P}_1$ is such that $\gamma z \in U$, that is,

$$F(z) = \begin{cases} F(z), & \text{if } z \in U, \\ \gamma^{-1}F(\gamma z), & \text{if } z \notin U, \gamma z \in U. \end{cases}$$

(a) (b) (c)

Fig. 2. Three tiling patterns in the upper half-space: (a) $|x| \leq 1, |y| \leq 0.8$, $0.0001 \leq r \leq 1$; (b) $|x| \leq 1, |y| \leq 0.8$, $0.0001 \leq r \leq 0.25$; (c) Circular truncated cone in the upper half-space with top radius 0.6, bottom radius 1.0 and $0.0001 \leq r \leq 1$

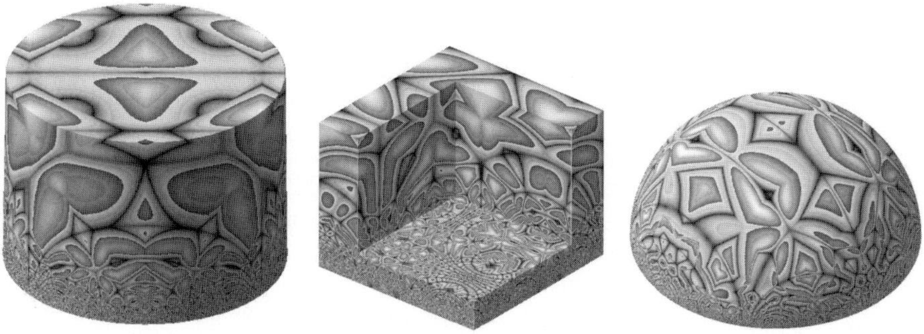

(a) (b) (c)

Fig. 3. (a) Cylindrical body in the upper half-space with radius 0.6 and $0.0001 \leq r \leq 1$; (b) Cut Cube in the upper half-space with cut point $(0.3, 0.3, 0.2)$.; (c) Half unit sphere in upper half-space: $x^2 + y^2 + r^2 < 1$

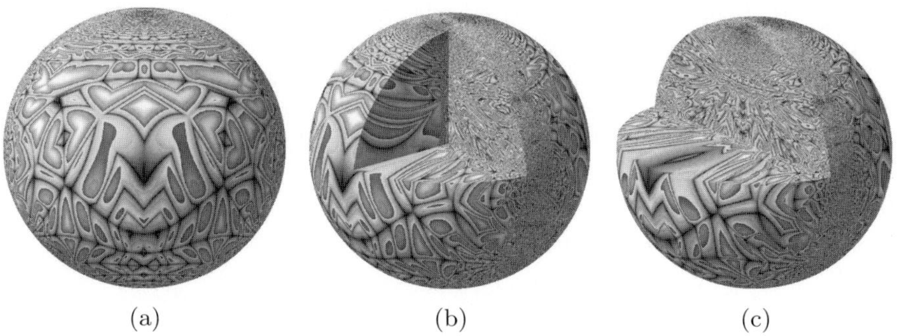

(a) (b) (c)

Fig. 4. Three tiling patterns in the Poincaré model: (a) $x^2 + y^2 + r^2 < 1$; (b) an one-eighth cut; (c) an one-fourth cut

4 Coloring Scheme

Motivated by the coloring scheme presented in [13], we make some modifications in the experimental. The orbit of $F(z)$ is defined as the iterated sequence of points $\{z_0, z_1, z_2, ...\}$. Fixing one integer k, we compute the distance $\mathbb{D}$ between z_k and z_{k-1}. $\mathbb{D}$ is define as

$$\mathbb{D}(z_1, z_2) = \frac{(x_1 - x_2)^2 + (y_1 - y_2)^2 + r_1^2 + r_2^2}{2r_1r_2}.$$

Then $\mathbb{D}$ is invariant under $\mathbb{P}_1$, i.e., for all $\gamma \in \mathbb{P}_1, z_1, z_2 \in H^3$, $\mathbb{D}(\gamma z_1, \gamma z_2) = \mathbb{D}(z_1, z_2)$. Since the distance $\mathbb{D}$ is invariant under $\mathbb{P}_1$, the symmetric points z and γz will have the same color. It follows that the generated tiling patterns also exhibit the symmetry of $\mathbb{P}_1$. In the experiment, we choose the following mappings

$$\begin{aligned} g_1(x) &= a_1 x(x - 0.5),\ g_2(y) = a_2 \sin(2\pi y), \\ h_i(x, y, r) &= b_i \sin(2\pi(x + y + r)), \quad i = 1, 2, \\ f_1(x, y, r) &= g_1(x)h_1(x, y, r),\ f_2(x, y, r) = g_2(y)h_2(x, y, r),\ g(x, y, r) = |z|^2, \\ f_3(x, y, r) &= \sqrt{g - (x + f_1)^2 - (y + f_2)^2)} - r,\ F(z) = z + f_1 + f_2 i + f_3 j. \end{aligned} \tag{2}$$

The corresponding tiling patterns with the extended Picard group in three-dimensional hyperbolic space are shown in Figs. 2-3. The tiling patterns in the Poincare model are demonstrated in Fig. 4. We note that all the figures are depicted by the $\mathbb{P}_1$-equivariant mapping $\widehat{F}(z)$ with $F(z)$ defined as (2). The parameters are $a_1 = a_2 = b_1 = b_2 = 0.2$.

5 Conclusion

Thanks to the advancement of computer graphic techniques, one can easily create fascinating and beautiful tiling patterns by iterating some simple mappings equivariant with the extended Picard group. A fast and new algorithm is proposed to automatically generate colored tiling patterns with the symmetry of the extended Picard group. Compared with the algorithm proposed in [13] for producing tessellation associated with the Picard group, the algorithm presented here is more easy and convenient to manipulate without requiring to construct complicated dynamical systems which satisfy the symmetry of the extended Picard group. We could produce unlimited variety of symmetric tiling patterns by just changing the mappings easily and could also produce different kinds of tiling patterns both in three-dimensional hyperbolic space and the unit sphere by conformal mappings. The fractal tiling patterns reveal more artistic appearance.

References

1. Zhu, M., Murray, J.D.: Parameter domains for spots and stripes in mechanical models for biological pattern formation. Journal of Nonlinear Science, **5** (1995) 317–336
2. Weyl, H.: Symmetry. Princeton University Press, Princeton (1952)

3. Escher, M.C.: Escher on Escher–Exploring the Infinity. Harry N. Abrams, New York (1989)
4. Schattschneider, D.: Visions of Symmetry: Notebooks, Periodic Drawings and Related Works of M.C. Escher. Freeman, New York (1990)
5. Coxeter, H.S.M., Moser, W.O.J.: Generators and Relations for Discrete Groups. 4th edition, Springer-Verlag, New York (1980)
6. Armstrong, M.A.: Groups and Symmetry. Springer-Verlag, New York (1988)
7. Carter, N., Eagles, R., Grimes, S., Hahn, A., Reiter, C.: Chaotic attractors with discrete planar symmetries. Chaos, Solitons and Fractals, **9** (1998) 2031–2054
8. Dunham, D.: Hyperbolic symmetry. Computers & Mathematics with Applications, **12B** (1986) 139–153
9. Chung, K.W., Chan, H.S.Y., Wang, B.N.: Hyperbolic symmetries from dynamics. Computers & Mathematics with Applications, **31** (1996) 33–47
10. Pickover, C.A.: Computers, Pattern, Chaos and Beauty. Alan Sutton Publishing, Stroud Glouscestershire (1990)
11. Field, M., Golubistky, M.: Symmetry in Chaos. Oxford University Press, New York (1992)
12. Chung, K.W., Chan, H.S.Y., Wang, B.N.: Tessellations with the modular group from dynamics. Computers & Graphics, **21** (1997) 523–534
13. Chung, K.W., Chan, H.S.Y., Wang, B.N.: Tessellations in three-dimensional hyperbolic space from dynamics and the quaternions. Chaos, Solitons and Fractals, **25** (2001) 1181–1197
14. Ye, R., Zou, Y., Lu, J.: Fractal tiling with the extended modular group. Lecture Notes in Computer Science Vol.3314, 286–291, Springer (2004)
15. Elstrodt, J., Grunewald, F., Mennicke, J.: Groups on hyperbolic space. Heidelberg, Springer (1998)

An Efficient Keyframe Extraction from Motion Capture Data

Jun Xiao, Yueting Zhuang, Tao Yang, and Fei Wu

Institute of Artificial Intelligence, Zhejiang University, 310027 Hangzhou, P.R. China
{junx, yzhuang, susanyang, wufei}@cs.zju.edu.cn
http://www.dcd.zju.edu.cn

Abstract. This paper proposes a keyframe extraction method based on a novel layered curve simplification algorithm for motion capture data. Bone angles are employed as motion features and keyframe candidates can be selected based on them. After that, the layered curve simplification algorithm will be used to refine those candidates and the keyframe collection can be gained. To meet different requirements for compression and level of detail of motion abstraction, adaptive extraction parameters are also applied. The experiments demonstrate that our method can not only compress and summarize the motion capture data efficiently, but also keep the consistency of keyframe collection between similar human motion sequences, which is of great benefit to further motion data retrieval or editing.

1 Introduction

Both in traditional hand-drawn [1][2] and computer animation [3], keyframes play a central role and can be used to produce final animation sequence. The keyframes contain the most meaningful information, which is the abstract representation of the whole animation sequence and is very useful for compression, browse (summarization) and reuse.

In recent years, Mocap system results in amount of realistic human motion data and is widely used in various applications. However, Mocap data are captured in a high frame rate and require huge storage space. So keyframe extraction technique is important for storage (compression), retrieval, browse (summarization) and reuse for human Mocap data. This paper focuses on keyframe extraction technique for human motion capture data. Keyframe collection should meet the following requirements:

- Keyframe collection should be able to summarize original motion efficiently while satisfying certain compression ratio.
- Keyframe collection can be used to reconstruct the original motion sequence as precisely as possible.
- Keyframe collection should keep the consistency between similar motions, which is convenient for following retrieval and editing operation.

Furthermore, two aspects should be considered besides keyframe extraction method itself. The first one is how to represent human motion and the second one is how to evaluate results of extraction. An effective motion feature representation is a key to extract satisfied keyframes, which has effect not only on results of extraction but also

H.-P. Seidel, T. Nishita, and Q. Peng (Eds.): CGI 2006, LNCS 4035, pp. 494 – 501, 2006.

on the algorithm's efficiency in running time. There are two evaluation criteria for keyframe extraction: error requirement and compression ratio. Almost all of available keyframe extraction methods extract keyframes by specifying error requirements [4][5][6]. Different error requirement results in different compression ratio.

Here we propose an efficient keyframe extraction method by which keyframe collections extracted are able to not only summarize and compress original human motion effectively, but also guarantee consistency between similar motions.

2 Related Work

Keyframe extraction techniques have been extensively explored in the research field of computer vision in which keyframes are used for video browsing and content-based video retrieval applications [7][8][9]. Similarly in recent years motion segmentation techniques are developed to extract distinctive motion clips from very long Mocap sequences and videos [10][11].

Besides the summarization ability, keyframes extracted from motion sequence should be used to reconstruct the original motion data as precisely as possible. But this reconstruction ability can not be achieved by the techniques mentioned above. To our knowledge, there are very few methods have been explored to extract keyframes from Mocap data sequence.

The simplest idea for keyframe extraction from Mocap data sequence is uniform sampling, but this method suffered from the over-sampling or under-sampling. Adaptive sampling methods extract keyframes according to performer's pose changes rather than motion time, which result in less keyframes in motion segments with less pose changes and more keyframes in motion segments with great pose changes. Lim et al. [6] treated Mocap data as high-dimensional curves and then applied a simple curve simplification algorithm to extract keyframes. But this method extracts keyframes regardless of human motion's geometric meaning so that extracted keyframe collection cannot guarantee the consistency between similar motions. In addition, error parameter should be specified manually before using those methods to extract keyframes.

Liu et al. [4] proposed a clustering-based method to extract keyframes adaptively. They assigned each frame to a corresponding cluster by the similarity. Then all of the first frames in those clusters compose keyframe collection. Park and Shin [12] chose quaternion as their representation for motion data and utilized PCA and k-means clustering to linearize quaternions and cluster them. Then they used scattered data interpolation to extract keyframes from clustered motion data. Huang et al. [13] proposed a constrained matrix factorization method for animation keyframe extraction, which result in a compact version of the original data.

In order to deal with Mocap data, several motion feature representations have been proposed. Liu et al. [4] applied a hierarchical motion representation. Lee et al. [14] described a two-layer structure for representing human Mocap data. These two representations generalize motion data, but motion physical features cannot be represented clearly. Chui et al. [15] proposed local spherical coordinates relative to the root orientation as the segments posture of each skeletal segment. But the skeletal segment is represented by two parameters which cannot benefit to observe posture of each skeletal segment. Mueller et al. [16] introduced 31 Boolean features expressing geometric relations between certain body points of a pose. This method can represent well motion's physical feature, but the number of features is too large.

Comparing with most previous methods of keyframe extraction and motion feature representation, there are four important features in our proposed approach: (1) We represent motion sequence by bone angles which are effective features for keyframe extraction operation; (2) A novel layered curve simplification algorithm is developed for keyframe extraction which is very simple and can generate keyframes collection more quickly; (3) The keyframes extracted by our method can be used to reconstruct original motion sequence precisely; (4) Our keyframe extraction method guarantees the consistency between similar motions, which is very useful for keyframe based motion retrieval applications.

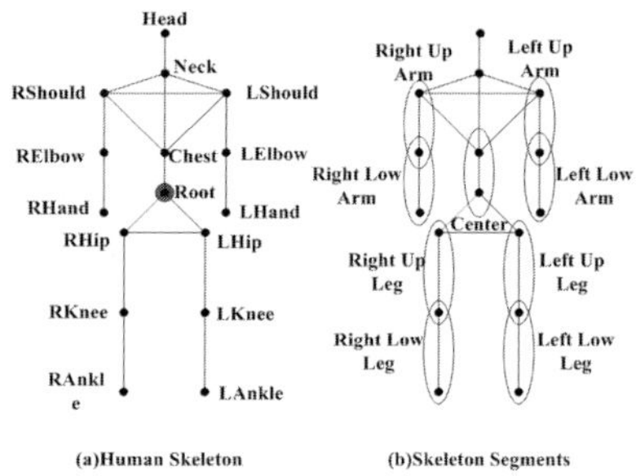

Fig. 1. Human skeleton and segments

3 Motion Feature Representation

A simplified human skeleton model is defined as Figure 1(a), which contains 16 joints that are constructed in the form of tree. 9 bones are extracted as the objects to represent motion feature, including 8 bones in human limbs and a central bone that is connected by *root* and *chest* joints as a reference bone (see Figure 1(b)). Each bone is defined as a vector from the upper joint to the lower joint in human skeleton. For every limb bone, bone angle is defined as the angle between the limb bone and the central bone. Given a limb bone $\vec{B}^{(k)}$, its bone angle at the *i*th frame is defined as follow:

$$\theta_i^{(k)} = \cos^{-1}\left(\frac{\vec{B}_i^{(k)} \cdot \vec{B}_i^{(center)}}{\left|\vec{B}_i^{(k)}\right|\left|\vec{B}_i^{(center)}\right|}\right), \ k = 1,..,8 \tag{1}$$

where $\vec{B}_i^{(center)}$ represents the central bone at the *i*th frame and θ is in the interval $[0,\pi]$. Consequently, by calculating 8 bone angles, the *i*th frame of human motion is represented by an 8-dimension angle vector: $F_i = (\theta_i^{(1)},...,\theta_i^{(8)})$.

4 Kyeframe Extraction

The human motion data represented by bone angle vectors can be treaded as trajectory curve in 8D bone angle space, and then keyframes can be extracted by approximating this high dimension motion curve. Figure 2 illustrates the trajectories of bone angles of right leg that is composed of right upper leg and right lower leg in a walk motion with 20 frames. We can see that the changes of bone angles of right leg describe well the movement of right leg in motion sequence. The postures at those extreme points can be selected as candidate keyframes because they are the most informative representatives of right leg's movement. According to all bone angles' changes, candidate keyframes can be obtained through collecting those frames at which local extreme points occur.

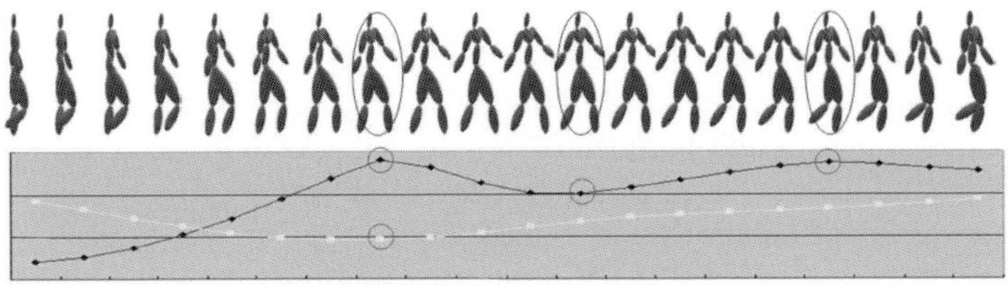

Fig. 2. Trajectories of bone angles of right leg in a walk motion with 20 frames. Yellow and blue curves show changes of the upper leg and the lower leg respectively. The extreme points on curves which correspond the extreme postures are marked by red circles and their corresponding postures are marked by blue circles.

In the process of human's movement, there are two phenomena: (1) The extreme points of different bone angles may not occur at the same time, but in a certain time interval; (2) There is some noise when human motion is being captured, which leads to some posture's distortions.

These phenomena result in that there are some candidates so near to each other and those candidates should be merged. On the other hand, due to existence of some motion clip with less bone angles' change, there are some adjacent candidates that are distant. For higher error requirement or stronger ability to summarize human motion, one or more frames should be selected as keyframes between those candidates.

Inspired by the simple curve simplification (SCS) algorithm [6][17], we propose a layered curve simplification (LCS) method to refine our candidate keyframes. The LCS algorithm statement is as follow: Given two sequence data sets M and C: $M = \{F_i \mid i = 1,...,N\}$, $F_i = (x_i^{(1)},...,x_i^{(m)})$, $C \subset M$, $F_1, F_N \in C$, try to find a sequence data set K which approximates curve of M under curtain error requirement, where $K \subset M$ and elements in K should be in C as more as possible. To solve this problem, M and C can be treated as curves in m-dimension space and they can be combined and constructed into a two-layer structure. The higher layer is C and the lower layer is M. In the beginning, we run SCS on the upper layer to find K. If the resulting approximation cannot satisfy the error requirement, then SCS runs on the lower layer. Those newly gained points at which curve is sub-divided would be inserted into the upper layer. After then, SCS runs to the upper layer again. This procedure is recursively repeated until the resulting approximation satisfies the error requirement specified for the given distance criterion. By running the SCS method to each layer alternately, the data set K would be gained finally.

5 Adaptive Extraction Parameters

In most applications users only have idea about the number of keyframes they do not care the value of extraction parameter which result in the actual number of keyframes. Here we employ adaptive extraction parameters to solve this problem.

Given the desired keyframe number which is set by user, if actual keyframe nuber is more than desired value, δ increases and the increase rate is $\delta\_inc(\delta\_inc \in (0,1))$. Otherwise, δ decreases and the decrease rate is $\delta\_dec(\delta\_dec \in (0,1))$. There are several factors that affect the convergence of the number of keyframes: (1) Greater initial value of δ and smaller change rate of δ lead to slow convergence of desired keyframe number; (2) Greater change rate of δ lead to the oscillation of actual value around desired value of the number of keyframes severely; (3) The actual value is oscillating around desired value of the number of keyframes in a small neighborhood, but the actual value cannot converge completely.

So if the changes of $d\delta$ are in the same direction in two consecutive loop, $d\delta$ increases to speed the change of $d\delta$. And when the actual value is oscillating around the desired value, $d\delta$ decreases to relieve the oscillation. The new $d\delta$ can be calculated as follows:

$$f_{inc}(d\delta) = \sqrt{1-(d\delta-1)^2}, f_{dec}(d\delta) = 1-\sqrt{1-d\delta^2} \quad (2)$$

A maximum oscillation number will be defined as a condition to jump out from the infinite oscillation.

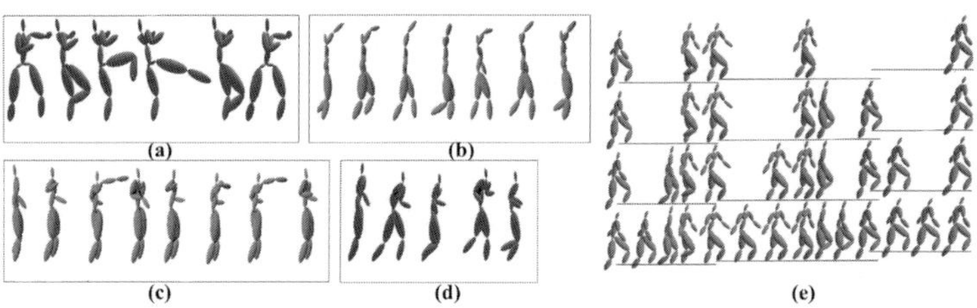

Fig. 3. Keyframe sequences extracted from human motions: (a) kick; (b) wave and walk; (c) punch twice; (d) run; (e) Keyframe collections for step-up motion with different number of keyframes. From bottom to top, the number of keyframes is 14, 10, 7 and 5 respectively.

6 Experiment Results

We captured more than 100 real human motion sequences with different motion types at 60Hz frame rate as our testing collection and implement our method by Matlab® which runs on an Intel Pentium 4 2.6GHz computer with 512 MB memory.

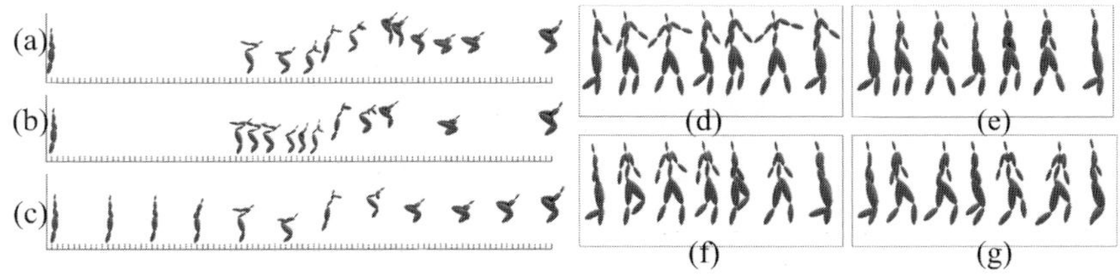

Fig. 4. (a) layered curve simplification based method (LCS); (b) simple curve simplification based method (SCS); (c) uniform sampling method (US); (d) walk with excessive arm swing; (e) normal walk; (f) walk with body leaning towards back; (g) shambling walk

As shown in Figure 3, our method can select extreme and important transitional postures from motion sequences with different motion types and different keyframe numbers precisely.

In Figure4(a)-(c), one non-periodical motion, *jump-up*, is demonstrated to make a comparison among different methods. We can see that under the same compression ratio, LCS achieves the best result, and the result of SCS is better than that of US.

In Figure 4(d)-(g), keyframe sequences of four similar motions correspond to each other basically. And comparing Figure 3(b) with Figure 4(d)-(g), we found that LCS also can get corresponding keyframes in those conditions that some motions are dissimilar in motion style but similar in the movements of parts of human body.

Table 1. Initial parameters and results of extraction. *Actual value of δ_inc approaches 1 but is not equal to 1.

ID	**1**	**2**	**3**	**4**	**5**
Motion (frames)	M1 (33)	M1 (33)	M2 (80)	M3 (209)	M3(209)
#Keyframes (desired/actual)	5/5	5/5	7 / 7	8/8	20 / 19
δ **(initial/actual)**	100/0.497	0.01/0.485	1/0.4149	1/0.274	0.5/0.165
δ_inc **(initial/actual)**	0.01/1*	0.9/1*	0.9/0.9	0.01/0.992	0.01/0.141
δ_dec **(initial/actual)**	0.01/0.141	0.9/0.564	0.01/0.873	0.9/0.564	0.9/0.174
# Loops	28	11	4	16	197
Time (s)	0.172	0.062	0.015	0.359	3.547
# Oscillation	8	2	0	6	100

Table 1 gives the initial parameters and results of extraction in the experiments. M1, M2 and M3 correspond to the (d), (b), (c) motions in Figure 3, and the maximum of the oscillation number is 100. We can see that the convergence of keyframe number is independent of initial parameters. Even for those that have too many frames and reaches the maximum of oscillation number (Experiment 5), our algorithm's running time is acceptable. Consequently, initial values of the algorithm's parameters can be defined at random in their range of value. It is noticed that δ is often in the interval (0,1) when the algorithm terminates, so initial value of δ is usually defined at random in the interval (0,1).

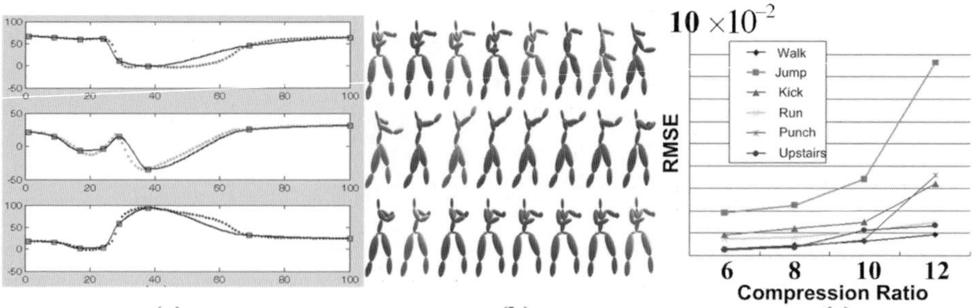

(a) (b) (c)

Fig. 5. (a) Motion reconstruction. The red, green and blue dot lines represent the original X, Y, and Z rotation values of RightShoulder joint in a punch motion. Green block is keyframe and solid line is reconstructed motion data. Here we use the piecewise cubic Hermite interpolation polynomial algorithm for reconstruction [18]; (b) Reconstructed sequence of punch motion. Greens represent the keyframes. Reds represent the postures which are reconstructed from keyframes; (c) Reconstructed error at different compression ratios.

Figure 5(a) compares the original motion data with reconstruction data which are generated from keyframes extracted by our method. Figure 5(b) shows the reconstructed sequence of this *punch* motion. Figure 5(c) shows the curve of reconstructed error at different compression ratios. Here we use the root mean square distance between the original and reconstructed motions to present the reconstructed error.

7 Conclusions and Future Work

The main contributions of this paper are: (1) bone angles as human motion feature representation, by which human motion's extreme postures are searched regardless of the motion type and style; (2) layered curve simplification method to refine candidate keyframe collection that comprises of extreme postures, which benefits comparison among the similar motions and can be used for multiple applications; (3) adaptive extraction parameters method by which keyframes can be extracted by specifying desired keyframe number instead of any other abstract extraction parameter.

Our keyframe extraction method can be used for multiple applications including motion ummarization for browsing, keyframe based motion retrieval, motion compression and reconstruction and keyframe based motion synthesis.

Currently by all of existing methods (including ours), users are required to specify the desired keyframe number and then system return the results, which requires that the users should have sufficient experiences and related knowledge to get a satisfied keyframe collection. So in future work we will try to find an extraction method and an evaluation mechanism to get keyframe collection with proper keyframe number automatically.

Acknowledgement

This work is supported by National Science Fund for Distinguished Young Scholars (No.60525108), the Key Program of National Natural Science Foundation of China (No.60533090), 973 Program (No.2002CB312101), Science and Technology Project of Zhejiang Province (2005C13032, 2005C11001-05).

References

1. S.C.L. Terra, R.A.Metoyer. Performance Timing for Keyframe Animation. Proceedings of Eurographics/ACM SIGGRAPH Symposium on Computer Animation, 2004: 253-258
2. Whitaker, H., Halas, J. Timing for Animation. Focal Press, Burlington, MA (1981)
3. Parent, R. Computer Animation: Algorithms and Techniques. Morgan Kaufmann, San Francisco (2001)
4. Liu F., Zhuang, Y., Wu F., and Pan, Y. 2003. 3d Motion Retrieval with Motion Index Tree[J]. Computer Vision and Image Understanding, 2003, 92(2-3): 265-284.
5. Shen Junxing, Sun Shouqian, Pan Yunhe. Key-Frame Extraction from Motion Capture Data. Journal of Computer-aided Design & Computer Graphics, China, 2004, 16(5): 719-723.
6. I. S. Lim, D. Thalmann, Key-Posture Extraction Out of Human Motion Data by Curve Simplification[C], Proc. EMBC2001, 23rd Annual International Conference of the IEEE Engineering in Medicine and Biology Society, 2001: 1167-1169.
7. Pickering, M.J., Ruger, S. Evaluation of key frame-based retrieval techniques for video. Comput. Vis. Image Understand. 92(2), 217-235 (2003)
8. Yueting Zhuang, Yong Rui, Thomas S.Huang. Adaptive Key Frame Extraction Using Unsupervised Clustering[A]. IEEE ICIP'98, Chicago, USA Oct.1998.
9. Yueting Zhuang, Yunhe Pan, Fei Wu. Web-based Multimedia Information Analysis and Retrieval. Tsinghua University Press (2002)
10. Jernej Barbic, Alla Safonova, Jia-Yu Pan, Christos Faloutsos, Jessica K. Hodgins, Nancy S. Pollard. Segmenting Motion Capture Data into Distinct Behaviors. Proceedings of Graphics Interface 2004: 185-194
11. M. E. Brand and V. Kettnaker. Discovery and segmentation of activities in video. IEEE Trans. on Pattern Analysis and Machine Intelligence (TPAMI), 22(8):844–851, 2000.
12. Park, M.J., Shin, S.Y. Example-based motion cloning. Comput. Animat. Virtual Worlds. 15(3-4), 245-257 (2004)
13. Ke-Sen Huang, Chun-Fa Chang, Yu-Yao Hsu, Shi-Nine Yang. Key Probe: a technique for animation keyframe extraction. The Visual Computer. 21(8-10), 532-541 (2005)
14. Jehee Lee, Jinxiang Chai, Paul S. A. Reitsma, Jessica K. Hodgins and Nancy S. Pollard. Interactive Control of Avatars Animated with Human Motion Data[A]. In proceedings: SIGGRAPH 2002[C], San Antonio, Texas, 2002: 491-500.
15. C. Y. Chui, S. P. Chao, M. Y. Wu, S. N. Yang, and H. C. Lin. Content-based Retrieval for Human Motion Data[J]. Journal of Visual Communication and Image Representation, 2004,16(3): 446-466.
16. Meinard Mueller, Tido Roeder, Michael Clausen. Efficient Content-Based Retrieval of Motion Capture Data[A]. Proceedings of ACM SIGGRAPH 2005[C], 2005, 24(3): 677-685.
17. P. L. Rosin. Techniques for Assessing Polygonal Approximations of Curve[J]. IEEE Transactions on Pattern Recognition and Machine Intelligence, 1997,19(6):659 – 666.
18. Fritsch, F. N. and R. E. Carlson, "Monotone Piecewise Cubic Interpolation," SIAM J. Numerical Analysis, Vol. 17, 1980, pp.238-246.

Visualization of Whole Genome Alignment with LOD Representation

Hee-Jeong Jin[1] and Hwan-Gue Cho[1,2]

[1] Dept.of Computer Science and Engineering, Pusan National University
[2] Research Institute of Computer Information and Communication, Pusan, South Korea
{hjjin, hgcho}@pusan.ac.kr

Abstract. The genome is the gene complement of an organism and it comprises the information of the entire genetic material of an organism. Many researchers use the *whole genome alignment* method to detect a genomic meaning between genomes. In this paper, we introduce a new method for whole genome alignment with LOD(Level-of-Detail) representation. It helps us to understand a relationship between two genomes and determine candidate sets from the whole genome alignment result.

1 Introduction

Alignment is the procedure of comparing two or more genome sequences by searching for a series of individual characters or character patterns that are in the same order in the sequences. The alignment method is especially important in bioinformatics. The ultimate goal of bioinformatics is to enable the discovery of new biological insights. Biological information can be discovered in biological sequences with the alignment method.

It helps us to assign functions to unknown proteins, determine the relationship of organisms, identify structurally and functionally important elements, and aid in the development of other insights [1, 2]. Similarities between large similar regions are determined by the whole genome alignment, and many researchers use this method to discover genomic information. An important thing is a detection of gene cluster or gene team identified as a result of the whole genome alignment. The gene cluster is a set of genes which tends to represent groups of gene with a functional relationship even if they are not contiguous. There are several methods for detecting gene clusters. However, currently the algorithms for finding gene clusters require strong and artificial constraints.

These analyses are difficult due to the huge size of genomes and alignment result. Figure 1 clearly illustrates this problem. The resolution of the snapshot in Figure 1 is 800 by 600 pixels, so one pixel corresponds to about 6000 bases of a given genome sequence. Figure 1 (a) shows the visualization of the whole genome alignment between two genomes, *B. subtilis(4.2Mbp)* and *B. halodurans(4.2Mbp)*, and (b) shows the local visualization of (a). In Figure 1 (b), the 259 alignment pairs in a local region of *B. subtilis* are visible, and the similar

H.-P. Seidel, T. Nishita, and Q. Peng (Eds.): CGI 2006, LNCS 4035, pp. 502–509, 2006.

sequences are spread all in the area(the entire region) of *B. halodurans*. However, this feature cannot be seen in (a) due to the large size of genomes and alignment pairs. So, we use filtering methods to determine the important sets of similar subsequences out of the subsequences being compared. Since the amount of an input alignment result can be decreased by filtering, the analysis of the genome alignment can be accomplished more easily.

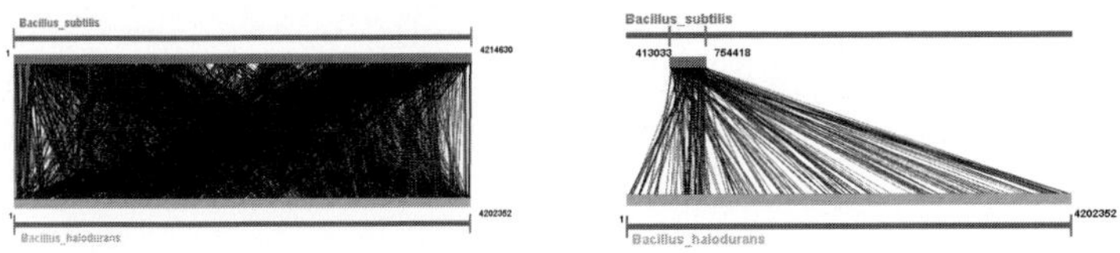

(a) alignment result between *B. subtilis* and *B. halodurans*. (b) local visualization of alignment pairs on 413,033 ∼ 754,418 of *B. subtilis*.

Fig. 1. Snapshot of the whole genome alignment at AlignScope

In this paper, we introduce a new method for the whole genome alignment with LOD(Level-of-Detail) representation to get candidate sets from the whole alignment result. We developed the system *AlignScope* to provide for this [3].

2 LOD(Level-of-Detail) Representation

2.1 Preliminary

A set of alignment pairs can be determined through the alignment process and these pairs are ordered according to their physical positions in each of the input sequences. Figure 2 shows the structure of alignment pairs between two sequences U and L. Each alignment pair consists of two aligned subsequences on two sequences. Let an alignment pair be $a_i = (u_p, l_q)$, and u_p and l_q be sequences aligned with each other on U and L, respectively. u_p is the $p-th$ gene on U and l_q is the $q-th$ gene on L in keeping with physical position of each sequence.

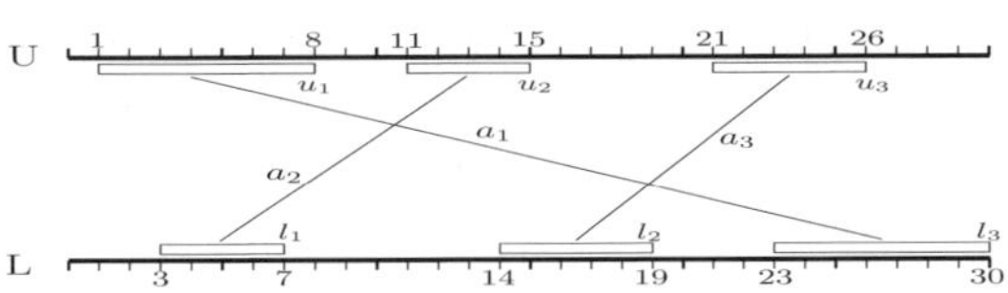

Fig. 2. Example of alignment pairs between two sequences U and L

In order to represent alignment pairs, we use the ordered bipartite graph structure. A graph is a mathematical structure that is widely used to describe the relationships among different objects.

Definition 1. A simple graph or multigraph G is **bipartite graph**, if its vertices can be partitioned into two sets(called partite sets) U and L in such a way, that no edge joins two vertices in the same set [5]. □

Definition 2. An **ordered bipartite graph** is a bipartite graph (U, L, E) with some linear orderings on U and L [6]. □

Each alignment pair a_i in Figure 2 is represented by an edge, and the aligned subsequences of each alignment pair are represented by two nodes. Therefore, alignment pairs can be converted into a graph and graph algorithms, which are well defined, can be used to analyze the whole genome alignment.

2.2 Construction of the LOD Structure

Clustering can be considered the most important unsupervised learning problem. In this paper, we use a hierarchical clustering method to represent a whole genome alignment with LOD structure. The crucial step of hierarchical clustering is selecting the next cluster(s) in order to split or merge. It starts with each case in a separate cluster and then combines the clusters sequentially, reducing the number of clusters at each step until only one cluster is left. When there are N input data, this involves $N - 1$ clustering steps, or fusions. The our clustering algorithm consists of the following steps;

1. Construct an ordered bipartite graph G_{order} using input alignment pairs. The two node groups are divided by two input genomes.
2. Assign each edge in a G_{order} to a base cluster. If there are n edges initially, there will be n clusters at the start.
3. For finding the nearest pair, we construct the Delaunay graph based on edges using a G_{order}, and then make a Minimum Spanning Tree T_{mst} using the constructed Delaunay graph. (This procedure will be explained later.)
4. Sort the edges in a T_{mst} using the weight of each edge.
5. Merge the two nodes based on an edge according to the weight of each edge of T_{mst}. In the merging step, the two nearest nodes are merged. This is the basic procedure of hierarchical clustering and this produces a clustering tree.

In our method, we construct the Delaunay graph using an ordered bipartite graph to find the nearest two alignment pairs. The Delaunay graph is a special type of triangulation. Its main characteristic is that for each circumscribing circle of a triangle formed by three nodes, no other nodes of the graph can be contained in the interior of the circle. The adjacent nodes of a node can be determined using Delaunay graph and the Delaunay graph is the base for constructing a Minimum Spanning Tree. A Minimum Spanning Tree is a spanning tree with the weight which is less than or equal to the weight of every other spanning tree. Consequently, the nearest node of each node can be derived using Minimum Spanning Tree. The method of constructing the Delaunay graph and Minimum Spanning Tree is as follows:

1. Let an edge in a G_{order} be a node for constructing Delaunay graph. The position of each node is a coordinate with the locations of two aligned sequences of an alignment pair.
2. Construct the Delaunay graph from generated nodes of step 1.
3. Construct the Minimum Spanning Tree of a generated Delaunay.

3 Complexity of an Alignment Cluster

Generally, the character of a graph can be expressed by the "number of edge crossings". In graph drawing, the number of edge crossings is minimized, because crossings significantly decrease the readability of a drawing. And we can know whether a cluster is a parallel or reverse using the number of edge crossing.

Figure 3 shows examples of the number of edge crossings of each cluster. In Figure 3 (a), the cluster is parallel, so, the number of edge crossings is 0. Therefore, the cluster in Figure 3 (a) is better than (b) in terms of a graph drawing. However, biologically, the information in the cluster in Figure 3 (b) can be detected. Since the order is completely reversed to the order of (a), the order of genes between the two genomes is highly conserved. It provides strong evidence of a close evolutionary relationship between the two input genomes.

Figure 4 shows a real gene team between *B. subtilis* and *B. halodurans*. We can see that the order of genes in *B. subtilis* is the reverse of the order of genes in *B. halodurans* [3]. In this case, the number of crossings is large but it is very important feature biologically, since the gene team seems to evolute inversely between *B. subtilis* and *B. halodurans*. Therefore, each cluster needs to be visualized with the measure for this concept.

A measure, "alignment complexity", $comp(a_i)$ and $comp(c_j)$, can be defined for each alignment pair, a_i and cluster c_j. The alignment complexity of a cluster is the average of all of the $comp(a_i)$'s in the cluster. This figure represents the

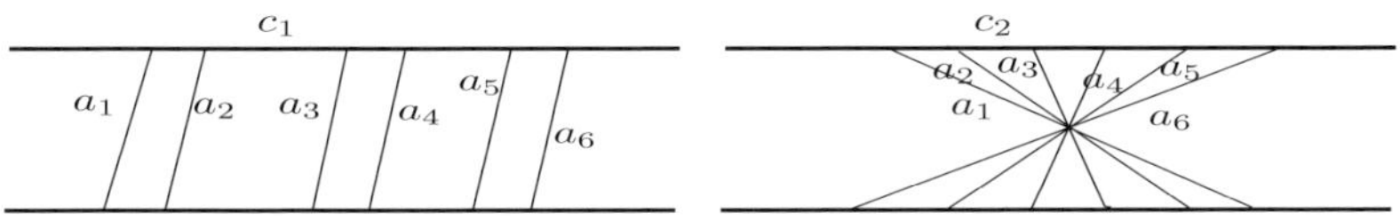

(a) a parallel cluster (b) a reversed cluster

Fig. 3. Example of the number of edge crossings in a cluster

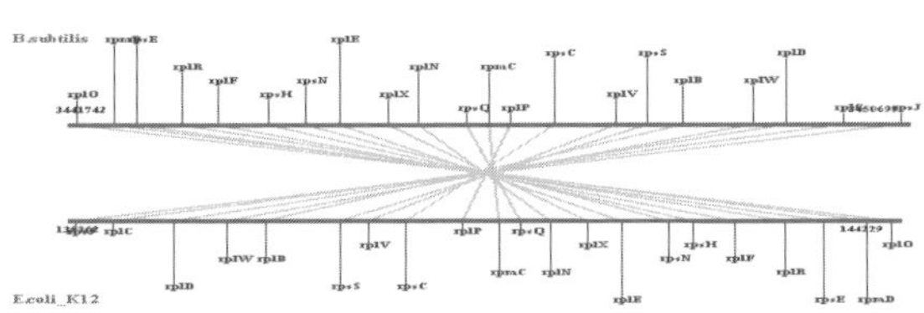

Fig. 4. Example of a gene team between *B. subtilis* and *B. halodurans*

degree that the order of genes between the two genomes is conserved or random. An order of genes in a cluster is highly conserved, when the order of genes on one genome is the inverse or equal to the other genome. Otherwise, if there is no continuous order between two or more genes in a cluster, the order of genesis highly random.

An alignment complexity of an alignment pair a_i between two genomes U and L is defined by three alignment pairs a_{i-1}, a_i and a_{i+1} which are sorted by physical positions on U. Let the three alignment pairs be $a_{i-1} = (u_{i-1}, l_p)$, $a_i = (u_i, l_q)$, and $a_{i+1} = (u_{i+1}, l_r)$. The alignment complexity may be different when we sort alignment pairs by genome L and then consider the order of aligned sequences on a genome U. The formal definition of the alignment complexity for a_i as follow: Let two variables, s and t, be defined as 2 or 1 to divide an order of alignment pairs in a cluster that is parallel or reversed (Equations (1) and (2)). If a $comp(a_i) > 0$, the alignment pair is parallel according to equation (3).

$$s = 2,\ (\text{if } (q-p) \geq 0) \text{ or } 1,\ (\text{if otherwise}) \tag{1}$$
$$t = 2,\ (\text{if } (r-q) \geq 0) \text{ or } 1,\ (\text{if otherwise}) \tag{2}$$
$$comp(a_i) = (-1)^s \cdot 1/2^{|q-p|} + (-1)^t \cdot 1/2^{|r-q|} \tag{3}$$

The range of the alignment complexity is $[-1, 1]$. If an order of genes in a cluster is highly conserved, the absolute value of alignment complexity of the cluster is 1. When the alignment complexity of a cluster is 0, the order of genes in the cluster is highly random. Figure 5 shows an example of an alignment complexity for the alignment pair. The alignment complexity for two alignment pairs, a_2 and a_8, will be calculated. In $comp(a_2)$, the two alignment pairs a_1 and a_3 will be considered. Similarly, in $comp(a_8)$, two alignment pairs a_7 and a_9 will be considered. So, $comp(a_2)$ is a 1 and $comp(a_8)$ is a 3/8.

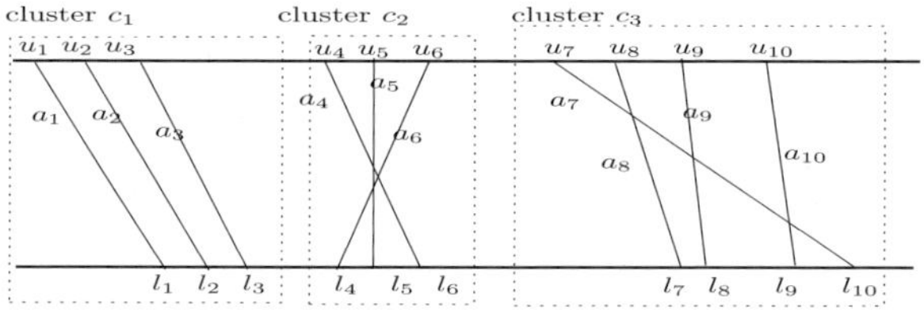

Fig. 5. Example of alignment complexity for an alignment pair

If there are just two alignment pairs a_i and a_{i+1}, let the alignment complexity of each alignment pair be a double value of the complexity of a neighboring alignment pair. So, $comp(a_{10}) = 2 \cdot (-1)^2 \cdot 1/2^1 = 1$.

Now the alignment complexity of three clusters, c_1, c_2, and c_3, will be calculated and compared with the number of edge crossing. Considering the number of edge crossings, the number of edge crossings in a cluster c_1 is the smallest and that of c_2 is the largest. Biologically, c_1 and c_2 are more conserved than c_3. However, the clusters cannot be divided according to the degree of conservation.

Otherwise, the alignment complexity of a cluster is useful for recognizing the degree of conservation. The alignment complexity of each cluster is computed as follows:

- $comp(c_1) = \frac{1}{3} \cdot \sum_{i=1}^{3} comp(a_i) = 1$. The number of edge crossings is 0.
- $comp(c_2) = \frac{1}{3} \cdot \sum_{i=4}^{6} comp(a_i) = -1$. The number of edge crossings is 3.
- $comp(c_3) = \frac{1}{4} \cdot \sum_{i=7}^{10} comp(a_i) = 0.53125$. The number of edge crossing is 2.

The absolute value of the alignment complexity is used for this. The absolute value of $comp(c_1)$ and $comp(c_2)$ is 1, and the value of $comp(c_3)$ is 0.53125. As can be seen the closer the absolute value of the alignment complexity is to 1, the more conserved the cluster is. So, two values can be determined by using the alignment complexity. One is the complexity of a cluster and the other is whether the cluster is parallel or reversed.

4 Experiments

Our algorithm has been tested on several genomes. The first data set is a group of three prokaryote genomes, *A.fulgidus* and *M.thermautotrophicus*. Figure 6 shows the LOD representation of the clusters at several LOD levels between these two genomes using AlignScope. The LOD levels range from 0.0 to 1.0. If the level is 0, clusters which contain one alignment pair will be seen, and they are input alignment pairs. Otherwise, a cluster which contains the whole input alignment pairs at level=1 will be seen. It is worth noting that the global structure of clusters becomes clear and vivid. Figure 7 shows other examples of LOD representation between *B. subtilis* and *E. coli K12* using AlignScope.

AlignScope provides the filtering method with the alignment complexity of each cluster. Figure 8 shows examples for detecting the conserved clusters between *B. subtilis* and *B. halodurans* using AlignScope. The several conserved

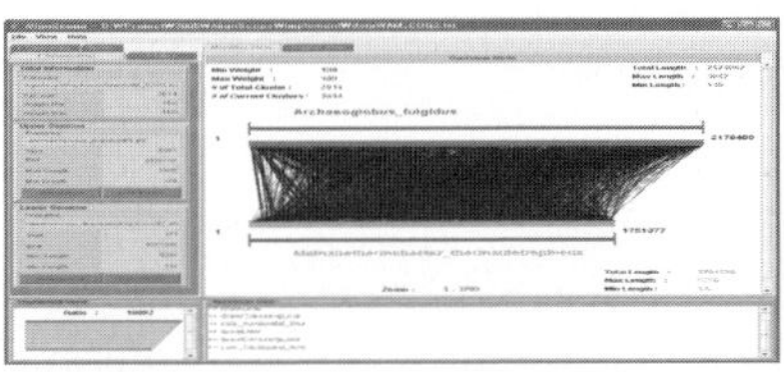

(a) level = 0.0

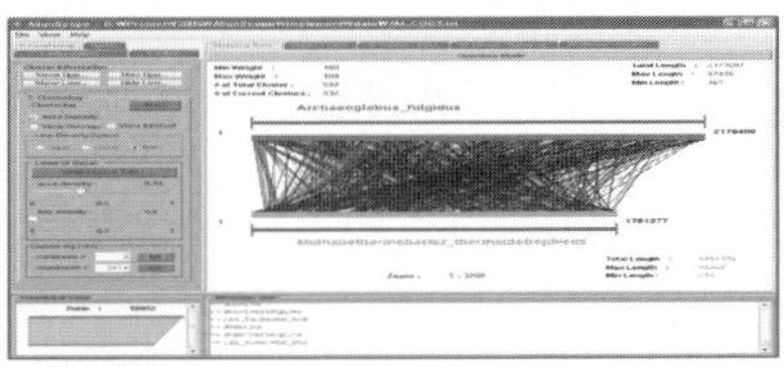

(b) level = 0.3

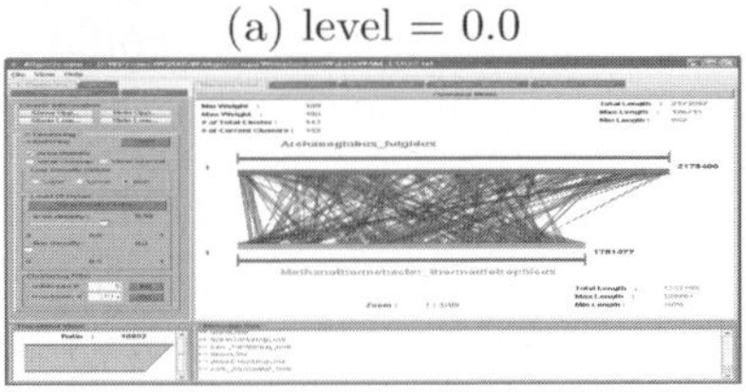

(c) level = 0.5

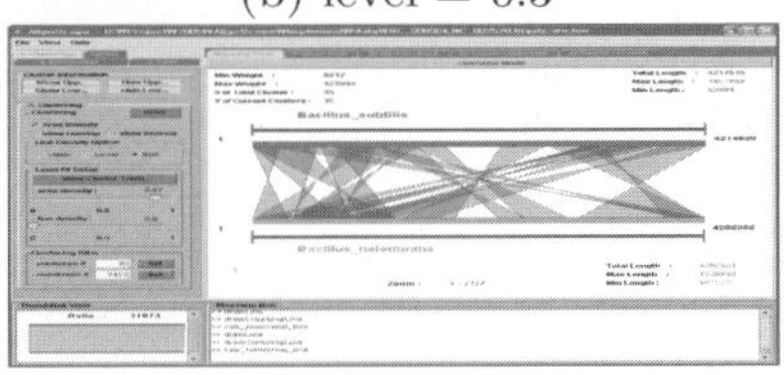

(d) level = 0.8

Fig. 6. Example of LOD representation between *A.fulgidus* and *M.thermautotrophicus*

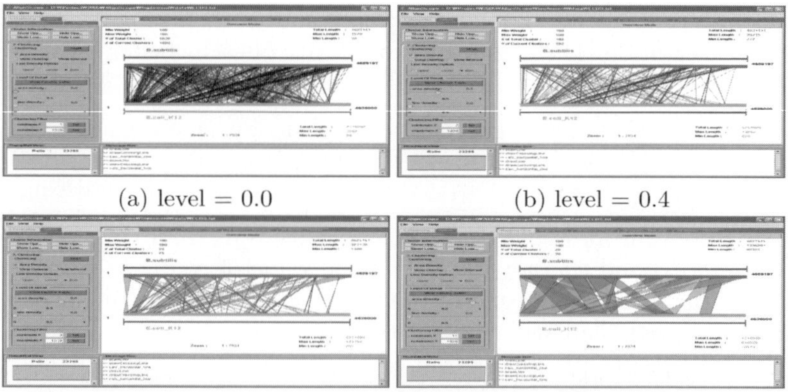

(a) level = 0.0 (b) level = 0.4

(c) level = 0.6 (d) level = 0.9

Fig. 7. Example of LOD representation between *B. subtilis* and *E. coli K12*

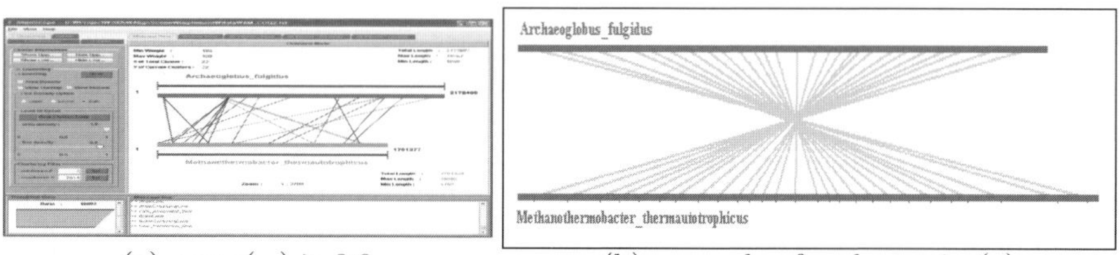

(a) $comp(c_i) \geq 0.9$ (b) example of a cluster in (a)

Fig. 8. Examples for detecting conserved clusters using AlignScope

regions according to the alignment complexity can be seen. Figures 8 (b) shows the detected clusters when the absolution of alignment complexity was larger than 0.9. It is highly conserved and the order of genes between the two genomes is reverse and the number of alignment pairs is 27.

5 Conclusion

In this paper, we proposed a new method for visualizing the whole genome alignment. A novel visualization tool for the whole genome alignment would be very useful for understanding genome organization and the detecting candidate sets from all of the data so that it can be easily analyzed by using various methods, such as detecting gene teams and regions with conserved orders of genes between the two genomes. AlignScope is easy to use in a computer environment and helps with understanding the relationship and conserved regions between two genomes. Our system is freely available on http://jade.cs.pusan.ac.kr/ alignscope. The main features of AlignScope are as follows:

– AlignScope provides intuitive controls for the visualization of the whole genome alignment at any simplified level.

- AlignScope is fast since we construct Delaunay graph and minimum spanning tree when computing hierarchical clustering. This improves the intractability between biologist and bioinformatics software.
- By using AlignScope, the candidate sets of conserved regions such as gene teams in the whole genome can be easily found.

References

1. Needleman S.B. and C.D. Wunsch : A general method applicable to the search for similarities in the amino acid sequences of two proteins. Journal of Moleculer Biology. **48** (1970)
2. Smith T.F and Waterman M.S : Identification of common molecular subsequences. Journal of Moleculer Biology. **147** (1981)
3. Hee-Jeong Jin and Hye-Jung Kim and Jung-Hyun Choi and Hwan-Gue Cho : AlignScope : A Visual Mining Tool for Gene Team Finding with Whole Genome Alignment 4th Asia Pacic Bioinformatics Conference. (2006)
4. Jacob, F. : Evolution and tinkering. Science. **196** (1977) 1161-1166
5. Jonathan L. Gross and Jay Yellen.: Handbook of graph theory. CRC Press. 24–25
6. Wasserman, S. and Faust, K. Social network analysis: methods and applications. Cambridge University Press. (1994)

Steganography for Three-Dimensional Models

Yu-Ming Cheng[1], Chung-Ming Wang[1], Yuan-Yu Tsai[1],
Chung-Hsien Chang[1], and Peng-Cheng Wang[1,2]

[1] Institute of Computer Science, National Chung Hsing University, Taichung, Taiwan
[2] Department of Information Management, Hsiuping Institute of Technology, Taichung, Taiwan
{s9156048, cmwang, cuckoo, cschang}@cs.nchu.edu.tw,
pcwang@mail.hit.edu.tw

Abstract. We present a data hiding algorithm for 3D models. It is based on a substitutive procedure in the spatial domain. We propose a Virtual Multi-Level Embed Procedure to embed information based on shifting the message point by its virtual geometrical property, the order of which is assigned by principal component analysis. We have defined and validated an effective metric of distortion anticipation, which can help us easily anticipate and control the distortion rate. Experimental results show that the proposed technique is efficient and secure, has high capacity and low distortion, and is robust against affine transformations. It provides a reversible method and has proven to be feasible in data hiding.

1 Introduction

Whereas classical cryptography is about protecting the content of messages, data hiding, or steganography, is about concealing their very existence [1].

With the development of various 3D applications and computer animation, many data hiding and watermarking schemes have been presented for 3D models [2], [3], [4], [5], [6], [7], [8]. However, research in data hiding has not kept pace with the advances of point-sampled geometries, even though some data hiding and watermarking schemes have been presented for conventional 3D polygonal models.

This paper presents an efficient, secure, high capacity, low distortion, and robust against affine transformations data hiding algorithm for 3D Models. Because we only consider point information of 3D models, our approach is well suited to point-sampled geometries and 3D polygonal models, for which type we discard topological information. We propose a Virtual Multi-Level Embed Procedure (VMLEP) that can embed at least three bits per point. In addition, we define a specific metric for distortion anticipation. Experimental results show that the proposed technique is feasible in data hiding.

In section 2, related work is described. In section 3, we present our algorithm. Experimental results are shown in section 4, followed by a brief conclusion in section 5.

2 Related Work

Several information hiding schemes for 3D models have been proposed. However, only a few watermarking approaches [7], [8] consider point-sampled geometry.

H.-P. Seidel, T. Nishita, and Q. Peng (Eds.): CGI 2006, LNCS 4035, pp. 510 – 517, 2006.

Unfortunately, only one data hiding approach [6] for point-sampled geometry has been proposed.

Wang and Cheng [5] proposed an efficient data hiding scheme for 3D triangle meshes. Their scheme, which is a blind scheme in the spatial domain, extends significantly the stego-system proposed by Cayre *et al.* [3], [4]. However, their scheme requires information of edge connection. As a result, the scheme is suitable to 3D triangle meshes, but is not appropriate to point-sampled geometry. Our method, on the other hand, works in both cases. Without the help of mesh connectivity, we would need a more sophisticated method to decide the embedding sequence list. Furthermore, the embedding method must not distort the list. Consequently, we use principal component analysis (PCA) [9] to decide the list, and we add a little advanced random noise to achieve higher capacity. Finally, embedding that relies on the angle between triangle planes is not still appropriate to point-sampled geometry, because such embedding can cause larger distortion for a larger radius. To solve this, we embed messages based on the arc length, which can efficiently avoid apparent distortion and yet still be useful for distortion control.

Research presented by Wang and Wang [6] seems to be the only source for data hiding on point-sampled geometries. Their scheme uses a PCA and symmetrical swap procedure. This algorithm suffers two drawbacks in the areas of capacity and processing time. As to the first, the data capacity in bits generally achieves only about half of the number of points in the models. Second, their scheme is inefficient; for example, for a model with around 35,947 points, the time required to embed data is approximately one minute. In contrast to this approach, our scheme can hide three bits per point. For a model with around 35,947 points, the time required to embed data is less than 0.7 second.

3 The Proposed Technique

This section describes the proposed algorithm for data hiding for 3D models (see Fig. 1).

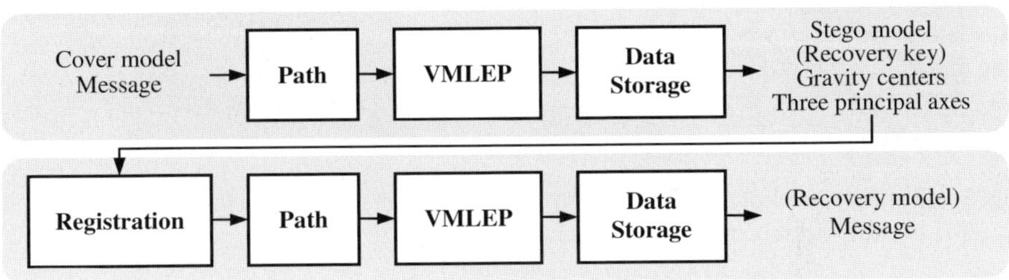

Fig. 1. An overview of the embedding and extraction procedures

3.1 Information Embedding

Path. To embed information, we must choose a sequence list (called a *path* in the following). We adopt PCA to produce three principal axes of the 3D model. We then translate the original points' coordinate system to a new coordinate system. Obviously, the new coordinate system has a new origin, which is a gravity center of the 3D model; it also has three basis vectors, which are the three principal axes. The first principal axis is the C_{p1}-axis, the second principal axis is the C_{p2}-axis, and so on. Next, we sort points according to coordinate values of the C_{p1}-axis. For security reasons, we employ a secret key to generate random sequence numbers for the embedding path.

However, the problem arises when two or more points have almost the same abscissa on the C_{p1}-axis. To solve this problem, we add advanced random noise (ARN) to these points to achieve higher capacity. We shift these points which have almost the same abscissa on the C_{p1}-axis parallel to the direction of C_{p1}-axis depending on the ARN, which makes these points have different abscissas on the C_{p1}-axis. Finally, since the VMLEP is robust against affine transformations and it is impossible to distort the sequence list resolved by PCA, we easily maintain this path at the extracting procedure when we keep the secret key, three principal axes, and the gravity center of the cover model.

Virtual Multi-Level Embedding Procedure (VMLEP). We consider every point of a model as a message point. To embed information in every point, we propose a VMLEP, which includes *Sliding*, *Extending*, and *Arching*. In VMLEP, we embed the information by modifying the message point based on virtual geometrical properties; it guides the change of the position of the orthogonal projection of the message point on the virtual base, height of the virtual triangle, and arc length of the virtual circle.

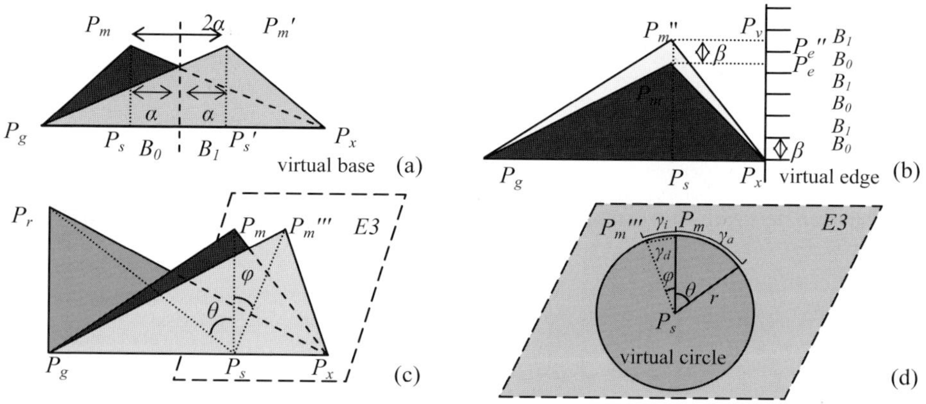

Fig. 2. (a) Sliding level of the VMLEP. (b) Extending level of the VMLEP. (c) Arching level of the VMLEP. (d) Virtual circle used on arching level.

First, we treat the gravity center of the cover model as a base point P_g and assume a base point P_x was extended from it; see equation 1.

$$P_x = P_g + p \times m \times \left(\frac{\overrightarrow{C_{p1}}}{\left| \overrightarrow{C_{p1}} \right|} \right), \tag{1}$$

where $p \in \{-1, 1\}$ is the pseudo random number sequence (PRNS) generated from a secret key. The m is the multiple of the unit vector of the C_{p1}-axis, which can resolve a virtual base. For simplicity, we chose 0.001 as the m in the following experiments.

In the sliding level, we let every point of a model be a message point P_m, and assume a virtual triangle $\Delta P_gP_xP_m$. Each virtual triangle is treated as a two-state geometrical object. The position of the orthogonal projection of the virtual triangle summit P_m on the virtual edge P_gP_x is denoted as P_s. Extending the QIM concept to triangles, the P_gP_x interval is divided into two sets, and both sets have α_s subsets. If $P_s \in B_0$, then we consider the triangle is in a '0' state; otherwise, $P_s \in B_1$, and the triangle is in a '1' state (see Fig. 2(a)).

The $P_m \rightarrow P_m'$ mapping is a symmetry across the closest axis orthogonal to P_gP_x that intersects the border of the closest subinterval belonging to B_i; the shifted distance between P_m and the closest axis is denoted as α, which α conforms to equation 2:

$$\alpha \leq \frac{\left|\overrightarrow{P_g P_x}\right|}{4 \times \alpha_s}. \tag{2}$$

Since we must keep the sequence list resolved by PCA after embedding procedure exactly the same as before, in the worst case two points may be shifted toward each other, which makes it possible for both points to change their order after their shift. To avoid this problem, we define the minimum distance of abscissa on the C_{p1}-axis between any two points as d and let the α_s conform to equation 3:

$$\alpha_s > \frac{\left|\overrightarrow{P_g P_x}\right|}{2 \times d}. \tag{3}$$

If we prefer to recover the original state of a message point, it is necessary to store an extra bit for every bit of the message, which is called the recovery key. The recovery key is set to 1 if the state of the interval is changed and 0 otherwise.

Similarly, we apply the same basic idea to the extending level and embed messages in the height of the virtual triangle. First, let a point P_v and the line defined by P_v and P_x be orthogonal to line P_gP_x; we define the state of the virtual triangle by the position of the orthogonal projection of the virtual triangle summit P_m on the virtual edge P_vP_x, which position is denoted as P_e. In addition, we define β_r as the interval distance ratio and β as the interval distance. We also divide the P_vP_x interval into two sets (see Fig. 2(b)). We prefer to use the ratio of P_gP_x to control movement of the message point (see equation 4).

$$\beta = \beta_r \times \left|\overrightarrow{P_g P_x}\right| \tag{4}$$

We can achieve this procedure by the following system of equations:

$$\begin{cases} \text{if } \left\lfloor \left(\dfrac{\left|\overrightarrow{P_s P_m}\right|}{\beta} \right) \right\rfloor \bmod 2 \in B_i : \text{ No modifications are needed.} \\ \text{if } \left\lfloor \left(\dfrac{\left|\overrightarrow{P_s P_m}\right|}{\beta} \right) \right\rfloor \bmod 2 \notin B_i : \overrightarrow{P_s P_m}'' = \overrightarrow{P_s P_m} + p \times \beta \times \left(\dfrac{\overrightarrow{P_s P_m}}{\left|\overrightarrow{P_s P_m}\right|} \right). \end{cases} \tag{5}$$

The shift of this level is perpendicular to the C_{p1}-axis, which should not change the abscissa on the C_{p1}-axis. It is impossible to distort the sequence list resolved by PCA.

Finally, we apply the same concept to the arching level and embed messages in the arc length of the virtual circle. First, we assume a reference point P_r by equation 6.

$$P_r = P_g + \left(\frac{\overrightarrow{C_{p2}}}{\left|\overrightarrow{C_{p2}}\right|} \right) \tag{6}$$

Both virtual triangles $\Delta P_gP_xP_m$ and $\Delta P_gP_xP_r$ form two individual planes. We define the degree of the angle between the two planes as θ. Let E3 be a plane with the normal vector $\overrightarrow{P_gP_x}$ and P_m, P_s, P_m''' be the points on the same E3 plane (equation 7).

$$\overrightarrow{P_gP_x} \cdot (x - x_{P_m}, y - y_{P_m}, z - z_{P_m}) = 0 \tag{7}$$

Next, we assume that the point P_s is the center of a virtual sphere and the radius of it is $|\overrightarrow{P_gP_x}|$ (replaced by r in the following explanation). Based on the virtual sphere, we can obtain a virtual circle on the E3 plane, then an arc length resolved by the radius r and angle θ denoted as γ_a (see equation 8). In addition, we define γ_r as the arc interval length ratio, and γ_i as the arc interval length (see equation 9). We also prefer to use the ratio of P_gP_x to control the γ_i here. In this level, we can simply embed or extract our secret messages based on the γ_a. We can obtain the real shift distance γ_d on this level by equation 10, where φ is the variation of angle introduced by the change of the arc length.

$$\gamma_a = 2 \times \pi \times r \times \frac{\theta}{360^\circ} \tag{8}$$

$$\gamma_i = \gamma_r \times \left|\overrightarrow{P_gP_x}\right| \tag{9}$$

$$\gamma_d = 2 \times r \times \cos\left(\frac{\pi - \varphi}{2}\right) \tag{10}$$

Similarly, we treat the γ_i as the interval length in this level and divide the arc length into two sets. As a result, we can fine tune the γ_a by adding or subtracting the γ_i, which leads to the change of angle φ based on equations 7, 8, 9 and 11 (see Fig. 2(c) and 2(d)).

$$\overrightarrow{P_sP_m} \cdot \overrightarrow{P_sP_m'''} = \left|\overrightarrow{P_sP_m}\right| \cdot \left|\overrightarrow{P_sP_m'''}\right| \cos\varphi = r^2 \cos\varphi, \textit{ where } r = \left|\overrightarrow{P_sP_m}\right| = \left|\overrightarrow{P_sP_m'''}\right| \tag{11}$$

To embed messages i (i=0 or 1) in the virtual circle, two cases occur:

$$\begin{cases} \textit{if } \left\lfloor \left(\frac{\gamma_a}{\gamma_i}\right) \right\rfloor \bmod 2 \in B_i: \text{ No modifications are needed.} \\ \textit{if } \left\lfloor \left(\frac{\gamma_a}{\gamma_i}\right) \right\rfloor \bmod 2 \notin B_i: \varphi = \left(\frac{360^\circ \times (\gamma_a + p \times \gamma_i)}{2 \times \pi \times r}\right) - \theta \end{cases} \tag{12}$$

The shift is a circle round the C_{p1}-axis, which should not change the abscissa on the C_{p1}-axis. Consequently, it is impossible to distort the sequence list resolved by PCA.

In fact, every method of these levels is not limited to embedding one bit per point. Te real limitation is data representation precision. For instance, in the sliding level, when we divide the P_gP_x interval into 2^s ($s \geq 1$) sets, we can embed s bits into each set. Let B_{max} be the maximal number of bits actually embedded and N_{point} be the number of points in the model. We can then state the following equation on our scheme:

$$B_{max} = 3 \times s \times N_{point} \tag{13}$$

Data Storage. In this step, the stego model and the recovery key are created. In addition, we keep three principal axes and the gravity center of the cover model to establish the same path during the extraction procedure. Furthermore, three principal axes and the gravity center of the stego model are retained to align the potentially attacked stego model during the registration process. Our approach achieves reversibility based on a recovery key which is constructed during embedding and kept private for retrieving the perfect original 3D model. Since the VMLEPs shift every message point symmetrically, if we prefer to recover the original state of a message point, it is necessary to store an extra bit for every bit of the message, and its size is exactly the same as the message size. Certainly, it should be compress using some lossless compression algorithms. In this way, reversibility is only granted to the holder of the recovery key and the secret key.

The VMLEP algorithm was developed to decrease distortion and increase capacity with respect to the human visual system (HVS). Recall that the sliding level embeds messages by shifting the message point P_m toward P_m'; the maximal distance of the shift is denoted as $2\alpha_{max}$. The maximal distance of the shift of the extending level and arching level is β and γ_{dmax}. As a result, the message point will be shifted toward the diagonal point in a box in the worst case. Here S_{dist} denotes the maximal distance of the shift:

$$\begin{aligned} S_{dist} &= \sqrt{(2 \times \alpha_{\max})^2 + \beta^2 + (\gamma_{d_{\max}})^2} \\ &\approx \sqrt{\left(\frac{\left|\overline{P_g P_x}\right|}{2 \times \alpha_s}\right)^2 + \left(\beta_r \times \left|\overline{P_g P_x}\right|\right)^2 + \left(\gamma_r \times \left|\overline{P_g P_x}\right|\right)^2} \;. \end{aligned} \tag{14}$$

Fortunately, the S_{dist} is always much smaller than the real distortion (see Table 1), since the probability of the three worst cases happening at the same point is rare and never happens in every point. In fact, the S_{dist} is somewhat similar to the Hausdorff distance, but always larger, and it is useful for anticipating and controlling the distortion rate.

3.2 Information Extracting

First, the new three principal axes and the gravity center of the potentially attacked stego model and the three principal axes and the gravity center of the original stego model have to be aligned using PCA, which leads to some affine transformations. After that, it produces the un-attacked stego model, which is the same as the original.

Since the remaining procedures of the algorithm are symmetrical, we easily extract the message using the method mentioned above if we have the help of the secret key, three principal axes, and the gravity center of the cover model.

4 Experimental Results

We implemented the proposed technique using C++ programming language. Results were collected on a computer with a Pentium IV 2GHz processor and 512 MB memory.

Table 1. For point-sampled geometries, we chose 32 as the α_s, 0.01 as the β_r, and 0.02 as the γ_r

cover model	points	embedded messages (bits)	distortion: S_{dist} / bounding diagonal	distortion: RMS / bounding diagonal	time cost (sec): embed	time cost (sec): extract
turbine blade	882,954	2,648,862	1.082×10^{-4}	6.690×10^{-6}	17.001	10.562
rabbit	67,038	201,114	5.408×10^{-4}	5.902×10^{-5}	1.296	0.812
horse	48,485	145,455	3.954×10^{-5}	1.957×10^{-5}	0.937	0.578

Table 2. For 3D polygonal models, we chose 32 as the α_s, 0.01 as the β_r, and 0.02 as the γ_r

cover model	vertices	faces	embedded messages (bits)	distortion		time cost (sec)	
				S_{dist} / bounding diagonal	RMS / bounding diagonal	embed	extract
happy buddha	543,652	1,087,716	1,630,956	2.327×10^{-5}	2.200×10^{-6}	10.344	6.484
dinosaur	56,194	112,384	168,582	8.311×10^{-4}	3.200×10^{-5}	1.079	0.672
venus body	19,847	43,357	59,541	3.580×10^{-6}	1.020×10^{-6}	0.375	0.235

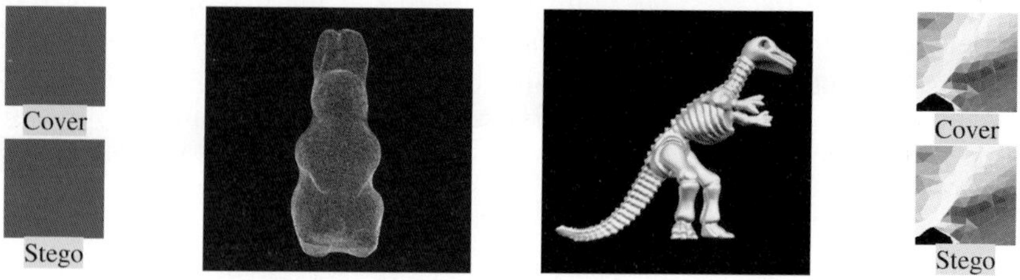

Fig. 3. From left to right, stego models are listed in the following order: rabbit and dinosaur

Model details, distortion, and processing time are detailed in Tables 1 and 2. As expected, no errors are found in the recovered messages. As a result, we exploit the feature of 3D more: every point can be represented by at least three bits in the three dimension space. Visual results of the stego models are shown in Fig. 3. The RMS values and visual appearance of images showed insignificant distortion for the models.

From the security point of view, finding the three principal axes and the gravity center of the cover model, getting the path over the model with secret key, and obtaining the p value of PRNS, m, α_s, β_r and γ_r are the challenges for an attacker. Just by looking at these issues, it is clear that our scheme is secure in the cryptographic sense.

Finally, we estimate the complexity by giving execution times, as shown in Tables 1 and 2. The time cost is very low, despite the embedding and extracting processes.

5 Conclusion

In this paper we have presented a data hiding algorithm for 3D models. Our technique provides data hiding with efficiency, security, high capacity, low distortion, reversibility, and robustness against affine transformations. Because we just consider the point information of 3D models, our approach is well suited to point-sampled geometries and 3D polygonal models, for which type we discard topological information.

Our scheme is fast; for a model with around 48,485 points, the time required to embed data is less than one second, and it takes about seventeen seconds even if the model has around 882,954 points. Extracting the messages without assistance of the key is virtually impossible. This problem is NP-hard in the cryptographic sense. Since our VMLEP shifts message points with respect to the HVS, we can easily anticipate and control the distortion rate. This process naturally leads to higher capacity and lower distortion. In addition, it recovers the perfect original model with the exact information that has been stored. We have demonstrated the feasibility of our technique for steganographic applications.

Acknowledgements

This research was supported by the National Science Council (NSC) Taiwan under the grant numbers NSC 94-2213-E-005-022, NSC 94-2218-E-164-001, NSC 93-2213-E-005-018, NSC 93-2815-C-005-019-E, and NSC 92-2213-E-005-021.

References

1. F. A. P. Petitcolas, R. J. Anderson and M. G. Kuhn. Information Hiding - A Survey. in Proc. IEEE Special Issue on Protection of Multimedia Content, 87: 7, pp. 1062-1078, 1999.
2. R. Ohbuchi, A. Mukaiyama and S. Takahashi. A Frequency-Domain Approach to Watermarking 3D Shapes. Computer Graphics Forum, 21: 3, pp. 373-382, 2002.
3. F. Cayre and B. Macq. Data Hiding on 3-D Triangle Meshes. IEEE Trans. Signal Processing, 51: 4, pp. 939-949, 2003.
4. F. Cayre, O. Devillers, F. Schmitt and H. Maitre. Watermarking 3D Triangle Meshes for Authentication and Integrity. Rapport de recherche 5223, INRIA, 2004.
5. C. M. Wang and Y. M. Cheng. An Efficient Information Hiding Algorithm for Polygon Models. Computer Graphics Forum, 24: 3, pp. 591-600, 2005.
6. C. M. Wang and P. C. Wang. Data Hiding Approach for Point-Sampled Geometry. IEICE Transactions on Communications E88-B, 1, pp. 190-194, 2005.
7. D. Cotting, T. Weyrich, M. Pauly and M. Gross. Robust Watermarking of Point-Sampled Geometry. in Proc. International Conference on Shape Modeling and Applications, pp. 233-242, 2004.
8. R. Ohbuchi, A. Mukaiyama and S. Takahashi. Watermarking a 3D Shape Model Defined as a Point Set. In Proc. of International Conference on Cyberwords, pp. 392-399, 2004.
9. A.C. Rencher, *Methods of Multivariate Analysis*. 2nd ed. New York: Wiley, 2002.

Feature Sensitive Out-of-Core Chartification of Large Polygonal Meshes

Sungyul Choe, Minsu Ahn, and Seungyong Lee

Dept. of Computer Science and Engineering
Pohang University of Science and Technology (POSTECH)
San 31, Hyoja-dong, Pohang, 790-784, Korea
{ggalssam, atom, leesy}@postech.ac.kr

Abstract. Mesh chartification is an important tool for processing meshes in various applications. In this paper, we present a novel feature sensitive mesh chartification technique that can handle huge meshes with limited main memory. Our technique adapts the mesh chartification approach using Lloyd-Max quantization to out-of-core processing. While the previous approach updates chartification globally at each iteration of Lloyd-Max quantization, we propose a local update algorithm where only a part of the chartification is processed at a time. By repeating the local updates, we can obtain a chartification of a huge mesh that cannot fit into the main memory. We verify the accuracy of the serialized local updates by comparing the results with the global update approach. We demonstrate that our technique can successfully process huge meshes for applications, such as mesh compression, shape approximation, and remeshing.

1 Introduction

Recently large polygonal meshes acquired by 3D scanning devices have become widely available. Processing these large meshes may be difficult or even impossible with existing mesh processing tools running on a fixed-size main memory. To handle large meshes, out-of-core algorithms have been introduced, where the whole mesh is not loaded into the main memory at the same time.

A simple but effective approach for out-of-core processing is to divide a huge mesh into several small pieces that can fit into the main memory. Then a mesh processing tool can be applied to each piece with a small memory footprint. Out-of-core algorithms based on mesh cutting or clustering have been proposed for mesh simplification [1, 2, 3] and mesh compression [4, 5].

Mesh partitioning for out-of-core processing can be obtained by dividing a large polygonal mesh into small pieces using the coordinate axes or voxel grids. However, in this case, the partitioning result does not reflect mesh features, which may degrade the performance of the processing. Hence, a feature-sensitive out-of-core mesh chartification technique will be a useful tool to improve the results of out-of-core processing.

Mesh chartification has been an active research area and used for numerous applications, such as texture atlas generation [6, 7], shape simplification [8], and shape decomposition [9]. Mesh chartification decomposes a mesh into charts,

H.-P. Seidel, T. Nishita, and Q. Peng (Eds.): CGI 2006, LNCS 4035, pp. 518–529, 2006.

where each chart consists of faces with similar properties. Excellent chartification techniques have been proposed, most of which try to generate flat and compact charts with features aligned at the chart boundaries. Unfortunately, these techniques assume the whole mesh can be accessed for processing at the same time and are not directly applicable to large meshes that cannot fit into the main memory.

In this paper, we propose a feature sensitive out-of-core chartification technique. Our technique adapts previous mesh chartification methods [7, 8] based on Lloyd-Max quantization to partition large meshes with limited main memory. The previous methods globally update chartification at each iteration of the Lloyd-Max quantization. In contrast, our technique locally updates the current chartification by considering only one chart and its neighborhood at a time. The chartification of the whole mesh is gradually updated by repeating the local update. We verify with experiments that the results of our technique are as good as those of the previous global update. As application examples, we show that the chartification results can be effectively used for mesh compression, shape approximation, and remeshing.

2 Related Work

2.1 Mesh Chartification

Mesh chartification techniques can be roughly classified into cluster merging and region growing algorithms. However, all the algorithms assume that the whole mesh resides in the main memory and cannot be used for out-of-core processing of large meshes.

A cluster merging algorithm consists of two steps: pair selection and merging [10, 11]. After evaluating the merging cost of each cluster pair, the algorithm selects and merges the pair having the minimum cost. After merging, the cost for the new cluster is updated and the process is repeated.

Lloyd-Max quantization, which is a well-known partitioning algorithm, has been widely used for data clustering and quantization [12, 13]. Sander et al. [7] introduced the Lloyd-Max quantization algorithm to mesh chartification, and Cohen-Steiner et al. [8] applied Lloyd-Max quantization for shape approximation.

2.2 Out-of-Core Algorithms

Several out-of-core techniques have been developed for simplification of huge meshes. Hoppe [1] segments a given mesh into charts and simplifies each chart independently while preserving the boundary edges. After independent simplification of charts, charts are merged and boundaries are simplified. Lindstrom [2] simplifies large meshes by vertex clustering. This algorithm can simplify large meshes with small overhead, but the connectivity and topology information are not utilized and removed. Isenburg et al. [3] proposed a local simplification technique. At each step, a small part of the mesh is partially loaded and simplified.

To compress large scanned meshes, Ho et al. [4] introduced an out-of-core compression technique. The technique partitions an input mesh into several exclusive charts and compresses charts independently with the Touma-Gotsman's algorithm [14]. The technique also maintains the gluing information to attach neighbor charts during decompression. Isenburg et al. [5] proposed an out-of-core data structure which is composed of small clusters. During compression, only necessary clusters are loaded into main memory and unnecessary clusters are released.

3 Out-of-Core Chartification

3.1 Overall Process

In this paper, we propose an out-of-core algorithm for feature sensitive chartification of large meshes. Our algorithm is based on Lloyd-Max quantization for meshes [7], which consists of two steps: region growing and seed recomputation. The region growing step creates a set of charts from given seeds. The seed recomputation step computes a new seed for each chart. The two steps are repeated in tandem until the terminal conditions are satisfied. However, for the region growing, we have to maintain the merging costs of all faces to neighbor regions. Thus, if an input mesh is too large to fit into the main memory, we cannot execute chartification with such a global approach. To enable chartification of large meshes, we propose a local update scheme for Lloyd-Max quantization. The basic idea is to keep a partial mesh in the main memory for processing which contains a subset of charts.

The overall process of the proposed out-of-core chartification algorithm is illustrated in Fig. 1. At the beginning, each chart is stored independently in a file. At the iterative optimization stage, we read and keep a few charts in the main memory, which are the selected chart and its neighborhood. We then update the charts in main memory by region growing similar to the original Lloyd-Max quantization. After updating the charts, we write and remove them from the main memory. By repeating this local update with varying selected charts, we can simulate the global update of chartification with limited main memory.

To bootstrap such repeating updates, we need an initial chartification. Previous methods [7, 8] randomly generate initial chartifications. In this paper, to

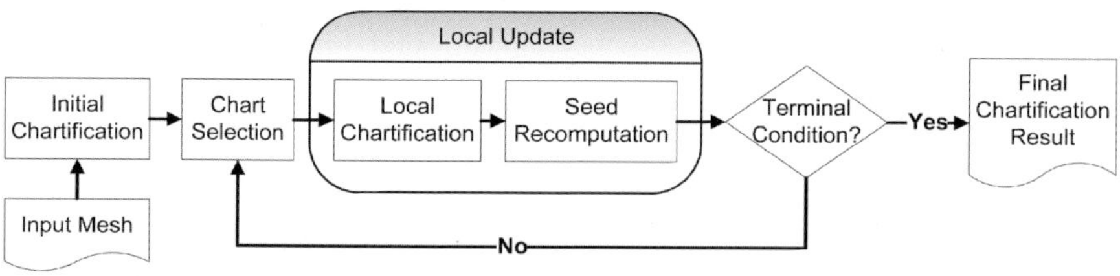

Fig. 1. Overall chartification process with local updates

achieve better results, we adopt the previous out-of-core chartification based on spatial subdivision [4, 5]. In addition, we execute post-processing to remove annuli charts along with charts that are too small or too big.

During the region growing step, a cost function is used to determine the conquered order of faces, and the shapes of charts are determined by the cost function. In this paper, we use cost functions proposed in [7] and [8]. To reflect mesh features in chartification, the cost functions incorporate the normal variations among faces. If we want other properties of charts, other cost functions can be used without changing the framework of the proposed algorithm.

4 Local Update Algorithm

4.1 Local Update

To update a chartification with Lloyd-Max quantization, the seeds are repositioned to the centroids of the current charts and the charts are recomputed with new seeds. In our out-of-core chartification method, the seed repositioning and chart recomputation are locally performed on a chart and its neighborhoods (see Fig. 2). With a local update, the boundary of the center chart is aligned with the features and the boundaries of neighbor charts are partially updated. In this paper, we call the previous algorithms [7, 8] the global update whereas our method is called the local update.

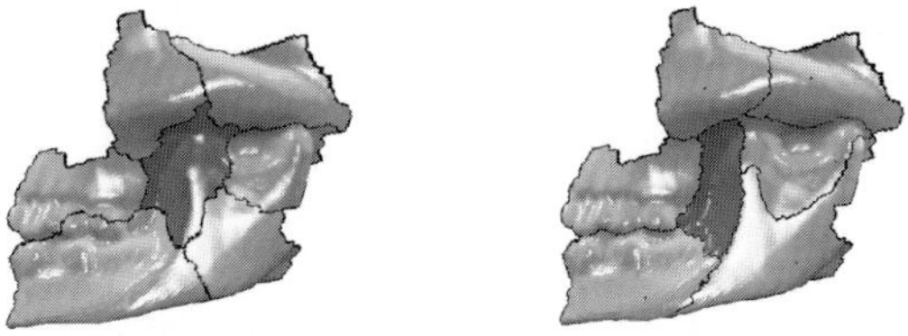

(a) before (b) after

Fig. 2. Local update of chartification: In (b), tiny black triangles are recomputed seeds

4.2 Update Ratio

In practice, for the global update scheme, a few iterations are sufficient for the convergence to optimal results [8]. Similarly, we use the number of iterations as the stopping condition for the local update scheme. However, it is difficult to count the number of updates in our framework. The boundaries of neighbor charts are partially updated in a local update and thus keeping track of update counts is not simple.

To resolve the problem, we define the *update ratio* of a chart. For a chart C, the update ratio is initially zero and increased by V_C with a local update, where

$$V_C = N_{pn}/N_n.$$

N_{pn} is the number of neighbor charts of C which has been involved in the local update. N_n is the total number of neighbor charts of C. For example, in Fig. 2, the update ratio of the center chart is increased by one and the update ratios of the neighbor charts are increased by the amounts less than one. If we want to obtain a result similar to that by n iterations of the global update, we repeat the local update until all charts have update ratios larger than n.

4.3 Chart Selection

In the iteration of local updates, the order of charts to be selected as the center chart influences the final result. A straightforward way is to select a chart whose update ratio is the minimum. However, such approach does not consider the effect of a local update on the neighbor charts and may cause over-updating of a neighbor chart if the chart already has a large update ratio. In this paper, we define the priority to determine the order of local updates as the average of update ratios of a chart and its neighbors. This priority considers the overall update ratio of a partial mesh that will be involved in a local update.

4.4 Local Update with the k-Ring Neighborhood

In Fig. 2, we only consider the center chart and its 1-ring charts for a local update. However, when the sizes of charts are relatively small, we can store a larger number of charts in the main memory. That is, we can process a center chart and its k-ring neighbor charts simultaneously. In this case, the priority to select the next chart to be processed can be computed as the average of the update ratios of the center and its k-ring neighbor charts, which constitute the region to be affected by a local update.

When we update a chart with its k-ring neighbor charts, the chart and its $(k-1)$-ring neighbor charts are fully updated and their update ratios are increased by one. That is, a larger number of charts are fully updated with this approach than with the local update of 1-ring neighborhood. Consequently, we can reduce the required number of iterations for local updates, which alleviates the overhead by file I/O and decreases the processing time.

4.5 Boundary Straightening

Some applications of mesh chartification need smooth and compact chart boundaries. To provide such results, we straighten chart boundaries after chartification. For each boundary shared by two adjacent charts, We find the shortest path from a corner vertex to the opposite one. To enhance the performance and maintain the shape features captured in the chartification process, a banded region is designated along the current boundary and the shortest path is calculated within the region. The banded region is defined by the k neighborhoods of the current boundary vertices.

Fig. 3 shows the effect of boundary straightening. Boundaries in Fig. 3(a) are created by chartification. Fig. 3(b) is the result of straightening, which shows smoothed boundaries.

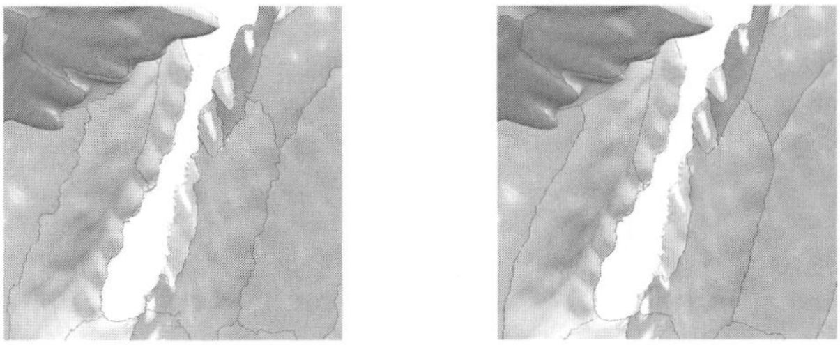

(a) before (b) after

Fig. 3. Chart boundary straightening

4.6 Local Minimum

Usually chartification algorithms based on region growing suffer from local minima. During a chart update, a growing chart region cannot jump through high curvature features. Suppose several seeds reside in the same region which is surrounded by features in the chartification process. Then, the charts from the seeds cannot escape the region and we are left with unnecessary charts which could have merged into one chart. Similarly chartification cannot capture a feature if no seed is placed in a region surrounded by the feature. To avoid such local minima, Cohen-Steiner et al. [8] insert or delete charts incrementally and introduce region teleportation, which is similar to vector splitting for scattered data [15].

In this paper, we adapt the solutions in an out-of-core way. In the local update step, we simulate chart deletion by comparing the local chartification quality before and after deleting a chart. The quality of a chartification can be measured by the sum of face distances from the seeds, which will be discussed in Sec. 5.1. If the distance sum after chart deletion is less than before, we perform the incremental chart deletion. In that case, we also perform the incremental chart insertion, constituting a region teleportation. To insert a chart, we place a new seed on the face with the maximum region conquering cost.

5 Experimental Results and Applications

5.1 Chartification Comparison

Fig. 4 shows the comparison of the chartification results from global and local update schemes. For the global scheme, we globally update all charts five times from the initial chartification. For the local scheme, we apply the local update to all charts one by one and repeat this process five times. Note that in the local scheme, each chart is updated more than five times because a chart is changed when the chart itself or its neighbor is selected as the center chart of a local update. The cost function used for region growing is the one proposed in [7]. In Fig. 4, we can see that the chartification results of the local scheme are as good as the global scheme even though only local information is used for chart update.

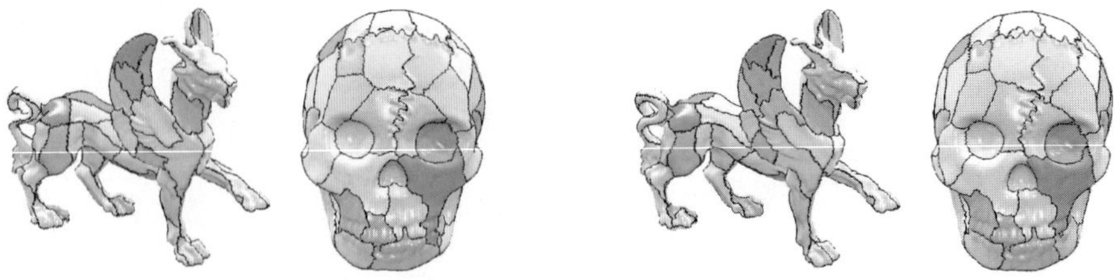

(a) global update (b) local update

Fig. 4. Comparison of global and local update schemes

Table 1. Comparison of chartification quality: The quality was measured by the average of the face cost sums of charts

# iterations	global update scheme					local update scheme				
	1	2	3	4	5	1	2	3	4	5
feline	8.09	5.90	5.47	5.35	5.39	5.48	5.47	5.46	5.32	5.27
skull	73.34	63.91	61.24	59.39	59.06	58.18	57.49	57.35	57.28	57.34

Table 2. Statistics of local updates with different k-ring neighborhoods

model	# faces	# charts	k-ring	# local updates	max # vertices in memory	total # loaded faces	processing time
dragon	800,000	300	1-ring	524	44,508	9,058,446	11m 36s
			2-ring	151	139,234	7,262,000	9m 54s
happy Buddha	1,082,760	600	1-ring	976	17,324	11,534,091	14m 3s
			2-ring	277	42,834	9,387,228	12m 27s
xyzrgb dragon	7,218,906	600	1-ring	949	109,125	76,532,952	2h 12m 13s
			2-ring	273	201,488	60,236,558	2h 2m 31s

Table 1 numerically compares the chartification quality between the global and local update schemes. The chartification quality is measured by the average of the face cost sums of charts. Once the chartification has been finished, each face has the cost (distance) from the seed of the chart it belongs to. The sum of the face costs of all charts is minimized when Lloyd-Max quantization is converged [16]. Hence, we can consider the average of the face cost sums of charts as the measure of the convergence for the iterative chart updates. Table 1 shows that the local updates result in smaller values of the measure, which is natural when we recall that a chart is updated more often with local updates than with global updates for the same number of iterations.

In Table 2, we also compare the chartification results of the 1-ring and 2-ring update strategies. In the experiment, the local update process was continued until the update ratios of all charts were larger than five. Table 2 shows that the 2-ring update strategy utilizes the main memory more efficiently and as a result, the file I/O overhead and processing time are decreased. The computation time was measured on a Windows PC with a Pentium D 3GHz CPU and 1GB memory.

5.2 Mesh Compression

Our out-of-core chartification technique can be used for effectively compressing large polygonal meshes. Choe et al. [17] proposed a framework for random accessible mesh compression, where a necessary mesh part can be decompressed without decoding other parts. By combining our out-of-core chartification technique with the framework, we can apply random accessible compression to large meshes that cannot fit into main memory.

To achieve a good compression ratio in the random accessible mesh compression framework, two properties of charts are important: planarity and compactness. Planar charts enable effective prediction in geometry encoding and shorter chart boundaries help achieve a better compression ratio. Hence, for the chartification for random accessible mesh compression, we use the cost function proposed in [7]. In Fig. 5, the first column shows the chartification results for the compression framework. In the experiments, local updates were performed until the update ratios of all charts were larger than five.

Table 3. Statistics of compression examples: The compression ratios were obtained with the random accessible mesh compression framework [17]

model	# vertices	# charts	compression ratio (bit/v)					
			with spatial subdivision			with our approach		
			connect.	geometry	total	connect.	geometry	total
dragon	400,000	271	2.04	16.71	18.75	1.99	16.58	18.57
happy Buddha	541,366	581	2.57	20.99	23.56	2.55	20.73	23.28
xyzrgb dragon	2,933,046	578	0.99	5.86	6.85	0.93	5.71	6.64
lucy	14,027,868	1,184	2.07	16.06	18.13	2.05	15.67	17.72

Table 4. Timing data of mesh compression examples: The chartification was obtained with the cost function proposed in [7]

model	# vertices	# charts	initial chartification	iterative local update	compression
dragon	400,000	271	5m 9s	10m 43s	1m 20s
happy Buddha	541,366	581	6m 50s	13m 12s	1m 40s
xyz rgb dragon	2,933,046	578	1h 55m	2h 30m	7m 45s
lucy	14,027,868	1,184	3h 15m	8h 55m	32m 30s

The compression results for several models are summarized in Table 3. To show the effect of chartification on the compression framework, we compare the compression results from the chartification obtained by spatial subdivision and the chartification obtained by our technique. We can see that the compression ratio is improved for every example because our chartification is better in terms of planarity and compactness of charts. Table 4 shows the timing data for mesh chartification and compression, which were measured on a Windows PC with a Pentium D 3GHz CPU and 1GB memory.

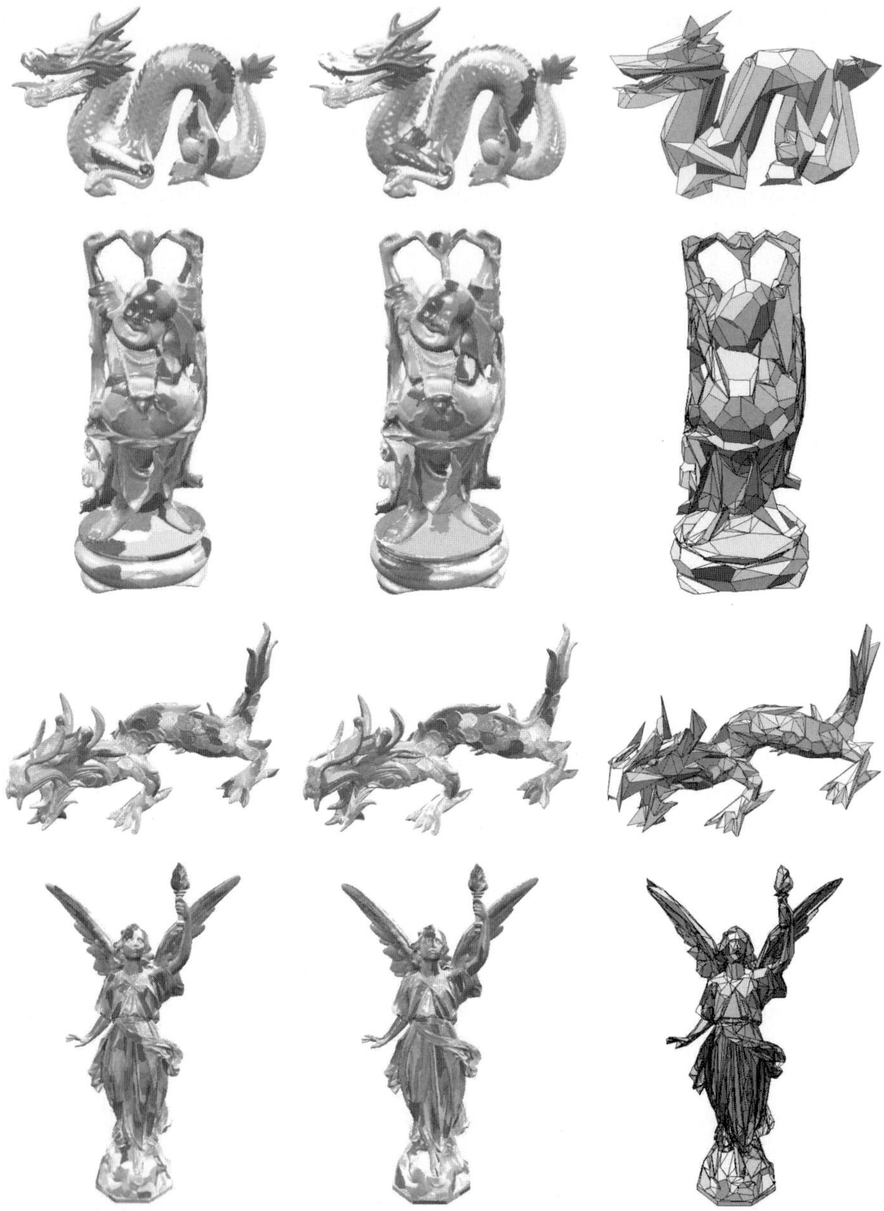

Fig. 5. Chartification and shape approximation results: The first column shows the chartification results for compression, the second column shows the chartification results for shape approximation, and the third column shows approximation meshes

5.3 Shape Approximation

Cohen-Steiner et al. [8] proposed an excellent shape approximation technique which obtains an approximation mesh from the original mesh using mesh

Table 5. Timing data of shape approximation examples: The chartification was obtained with the cost function proposed in [8]

model	# vertices	# charts	initial chartification	iterative local update	approximation mesh generation
dragon	400,000	789	5m 9s	10m 50s	2m 5s
happy Buddha	541,366	1,472	6m 50s	15m 30s	2m 54s
xyz rgb dragon	2,933,046	709	1h 55 m	3h 35 m	16m 31s
lucy	14,027,868	1,615	3h 15 m	31h 30 m	1h 56m

chartification. In this technique, the vertices, edges, and faces of an approximation mesh correspond to the corner vertices, chart boundaries, and chart interiors, respectively. Our out-of-core chartification method can be used to extend the shape approximation technique to process huge meshes. The resulting approximation mesh will nicely reflect the features of the original mesh. Note that the previous out-of-core mesh partitioning based on spatial subdivision [4] is not proper for this purpose because it does not generate feature-sensitive chartification.

In [8], to approximate a chart with a plane, the normals of faces in a chart should be similar to each other. Hence, the cost function used for region growing in [8] measures the variation of a face normal from the representative normal of a chart. In Fig. 5, the second column shows the chartification results with this cost function and the third column shows the shape approximation results. Table 5 shows the timing data of the shape approximation examples. Again, in the experiments, the local update process was continued until the update ratios of all charts were larger than five.

5.4 Remeshing

Our feature sensitive out-of-core chartification technique can be used to preform effective remeshing of very large meshes with limited memory. Once chartification has been obtained for a given mesh, we keep the chart boundaries and just modify the sampling and connectivity of inner vertices of each chart

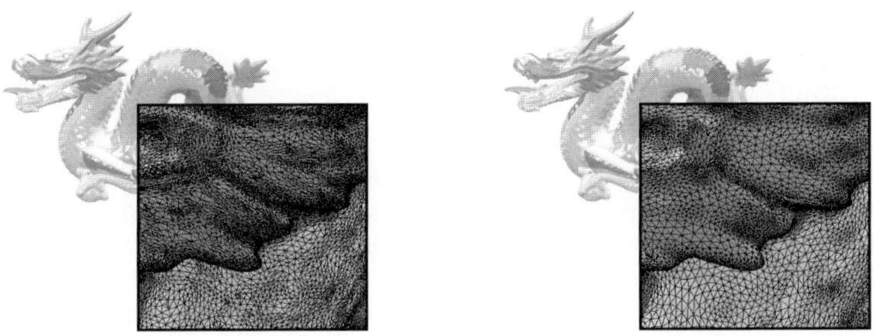

(a) before (b) after

Fig. 6. Remeshing example

during the remeshing process. With this approach, we can expect to obtain a remeshing result that nicely preserves the features of the original mesh because the chart boundaries are aligned with high-curvature features. For remeshing of chart interiors, we adopt the explicit surface remeshing technique [18], which can separately remesh chart interiors while keeping the chart boundaries.

Fig. 6 shows an example. In Fig. 6(b), the mesh generated by the remeshing has a simple and regular structure. Although we have reduced the size of the given mesh by a half, the new mesh still contains the original shape features. In addition, no artifacts are visible around the boundaries between charts even though each chart has been remeshed independently.

6 Conclusion and Future Work

In this paper, we introduced a feature sensitive out-of-core chartification technique for large polygonal meshes. To process huge meshes, our out-of-core algorithm keeps only a partial mesh in the main memory at a time and locally updates chartification. To verify the validity of our approach, we showed that the results of our local update scheme are as good as the previous global update scheme.

In the current implementation, after each local update, updated charts are written to the hard disk and released from the main memory although some of them can be used for successive chart updates. If we maintain a cache of charts in the main memory, we will be able to reduce the overhead by unnecessary file I/O. The design of a cache structure for the charts which improves the performance of out-of-core chartification is an interesting future work.

Acknowledgements

The authors would like to thank Junho Kim for helpful discussion. The dragon, happy Buddha, xyz rgb dragon, and lucy models are courtesy of Stanford Graphics Lab. The skull model is courtesy of Headus and Phil Dench. The dinosaur and feline models are courtesy of Cyberware and Multi-Res Modeling Group at Caltech, respectively. This research was supported in part by the BK21 program, the ITRC support program, and KOSEF (F01-2005-000-10377-0).

References

1. Hoppe, H.: Smooth view-dependent level-of-detail control and its application to terrain rendering. In: Proc. IEEE Visualization 1998. (1998) 35–42
2. Lindstrom, P.: Out-of-core simplification of large polygonal models. In Proc. ACM SIGGRAPH 2000 (2000) 259–262
3. Isenburg, M., Lindstrom, P., Gumhold, S., Snoeyink, J.: Large mesh simplification using processing sequences. In: Proc. IEEE Visualization 2003. (2003) 465–472
4. Ho, J., Lee, K.C., Kriegman, D.: Compressing large polygonal models. In: Proc. IEEE Visualization 2001. (2001) 357–362

5. Isenburg, M., Gumhold, S.: Out-of-core compression for gigantic polygon meshes. ACM Transaction on Graphics **22**(3) (2003) 935–942
6. Lévy, B., Petitjean, S., Ray, N., Maillot, J.: Least squares conformal maps for automatic texture atlas generation. ACM Transaction on Graphics **21**(3) (2002) 362–371
7. Sander, P.V., Wood, Z.J., Gortler, S.J., Snyder, J., Hoppe, H.: Multi-chart geometry images. In: Proc. Eurographics Symposium on Geometry Processing 2003. (2003) 146–155
8. D. Cohen-Steiner, P. Alliez, M.D.: Variational shape approximation. ACM Transaction on Graphics **23**(3) (2004) 905–914
9. Katz, S., Tal, A.: Hierarchical mesh decomposition using fuzzy clustering and cuts. ACM Transaction on Graphics **22**(3) (2003) 954–961
10. Sander, P.V., Snyder, J., Gortler, S.J., Hoppe, H.: Texture mapping progressive meshes. In Proc. ACM SIGGRAPH 2001 (2001) 409–416
11. Garland, M., Willmott, A., Heckbert, P.S.: Hierarchical face clustering on polygonal surfaces. In: Proc. 2001 ACM Symposium on Interactive 3D Graphics. (2001) 49–58
12. Lloyd, S.: Least square quantization in PCM. IEEE Transaction on Information Theory **28** (1982) 129–137
13. Max, J.: Quantizing for minimum distortion. IEEE Transaction on Information Theory **6** (1960) 7–12
14. Touma, C., Gotsman, C.: Triangle mesh compression. In: Proc. Graphics Interface 1998. (1998) 26–34
15. A.Gersho, R.M.Gray: Vector Quantization and Signal Compression. Kluwer Academic Publishers (1991)
16. Surazhsky, V., Alliez, P., Gotsman, C.: Isotropic remeshing of surfaces: A local parametrization approach. In: Proc. 12th International Meshing Roundtable. (2003)
17. Choe, S., Kim, J., Lee, H., Lee, S., Seidel, H.P.: Mesh compression with random accessibility. The 5th Korea-Israel Bi-National Conference on Geometric Modeling and Computer Graphics 2004 (2004) 81–86
18. Surazhsky, V., Gotsman, C.: Explicit surface remeshing. In: Proc. Eurographics Symposium on Geometry Processing 2003. (2003) 20–30

Simulating Reactive Motions for Motion Capture Animation

Bing Tang, Zhigeng Pan, Le Zheng, and Mingmin Zhang

State Key Lab of CAD&CG, Zhejiang University,
Hang Zhou, China, 310027
{btang, zgpan, zhengle, zmm}@cad.zju.edu.cn

Abstract. In this paper, we propose a new method for simulating reactive motions for motion capture animation. The goal is to generate realistic behaviors under unexpected external forces. A set of techniques are introduced to select a motion capture sequence which follows an impact, and then synthesize a believable transition to this found clip for character interaction. Utilizing a parallel simulation, our method is able to predict a character's motion trajectory under dynamics, which ensures that the character moves towards the target sequence and makes the character's behavior more life-like. In addition, the mechanism of parallel simulation with different time steps is flexible for simulation of multiple contacts in a series when multiple searches are necessary. Our controller is designed to generate physically plausible motion following an upcoming motion with adjustment from biomechanics rules, which is a key to avoid an unconscious look for a character during the transition.

1 Introduction

Reproducing human motion with realistic responses to unexpected impacts in a controllable way is challenging work in motion synthesis. Data-driven character animation, such as those based on motion capture or keyframed data can produce very natural-looking animation. Although there are some available techniques for editing and modifying existing data, data-driven techniques are not suitable for modeling the complex interactions between dynamically interacting characters. Under certain circumstances, for example, creating a believable response following an unexpected impact, modifications are particularly difficult. In our paper, we present a novel method for incorporating unexpected impacts into a motion capture animation through physical simulation. This process determines the best plausible time to return the character to an available motion from the motion library for the remainder of the dynamic response to the interaction.

2 Previous Work

Previous work on synthesizing complex animation has concentrated on either reproducing animation from motion data by kinematics, or by physically modeling the interacting characters using dynamics. A number of researchers focused on techniques that synthesize new motion by processing and editing existing motion. Motion

H.-P. Seidel, T. Nishita, and Q. Peng (Eds.): CGI 2006, LNCS 4035, pp. 530 – 537, 2006.

blending is the simplest motion editing technique, and it is widely used to perform transitions between motion segments [1, 2]. Some later researchers explored more complicated blending weights to produce better transitions and create parameterized motions by interpolating between the example motions [3, 4]. Kovar et al. [5] presented an approach for generating controllable motion by constructing a motion graph. Our motion search method is similar to these efforts; however, we compare the initial simulated trajectory with motion capture sequences from motion library, based on a simplified distance metric by decreasing the numbers of joints in frame-to-frame comparison.

A number of researchers have used physical simulation to generate motion for a wide variety of human behavior. Physical controllers have been successfully designed for specific human motions such as walking, running, vaulting, cycling, etc [6, 7]. Faloutsos et al. [8] introduced a composition framework to create many basic behaviors, such as balancing, falling, standing, sitting and these work in conjunction with a virtual stunt person. However, because of the complexity of dynamic controller design, and the lack of rules for human motion, it is difficult to achieve robust results by using only physics without the guide of motion data.

A small number of researchers presented an approach that combined physics and motion capture data with goals similar to ours'. Oshita and Makinouchi [9] used a tracking controller on inputting motion data to simulate the motion of a human when heavy luggage was suddenly attached to the back of the body. Similar work presented by Shapiro et al. [10] and Mandel [11] introduced hybrid methods, which allowed a character to be controlled to switch between physical simulation and kinematic motion data whenever necessary. The most closely related work was presented by Zordan et al. [12]. Zordan and his colleagues utilized a passive and active simulation to generate physical plausible motion, which depended upon a rewinding mechanism and then blended with the final motion. In their work, the results reported focused on heavy contact with burst impact and showing limited contacts of interactions. Conversely, we use a parallel simulation process to allow the simulated character to receive multiple contacts in series, providing more flexible opportunities for characters to be actively controlled between simulation and motion capture data.

3 Dynamics Model

To create believable responses and generate realistic motion conform to laws of physics, we first have to set up a dynamics model according to motion capture data. We map the recorded data to the character with an articulated model. The virtual character is presented as an articulated figure of a series of body parts connected by joints. The character we choose includes 15 joints; the same number of joints is used in our kinematic model. Each joint is specified as either a revolute or a spherical joint, with one or three degrees of freedom respectively . The size of each part of the character's body is determined by its skeleton from motion capture data. Stretchy tissues such as tendons and ligaments, which cause passive spring and damper forces around joints, are accounted in our dynamics model. Tendons and ligaments act as spring-like elements that dampen motion. It is worth noting that these passive generalized forces are used extensively in natural locomotion to reduce energy consumption, increase stability and simplify the control [13]. Each joint is attached with a linear spring and damper. We use the freely available NovodeX physics SDK to simulate rigid body dynamics and resolve collisions between the simulated characters and the environments.

Under normal conditions, the character animates according to the motion capture data, such as walking and running. At the same time, our system detects and reports contacts between the characters and environments. Physical simulation is required when the effects of a collision or impulse change the character's state. The momentum of the character is preserved when it switches from motion data to physical simulation, so that the motion can be exchanged smoothly.

4 Motion Search

Once a response is generated and the motion is to switch into physical simulation, we have to search for a transition-to motion capture sequence from our motion library, which can be used both as the target motion for our physical simulation and the sequence to play following the impact as soon as possible. Our motion search depends on the following two processes: simulated trajectory prediction and motion selection.

4.1 Simulated Trajectory Prediction

In the first step of motion search, a simulated trajectory should be obtained for motion comparison. Unfortunately, it can not be achieved until the simulation is finished. To solve this conflict, a parallel simulation mechanism is used with one special simulation process to forecast the simulation results and obtain the simulated trajectory. This prediction simulation, which starts at the same time as normal simulation, has a relative small time step compared to normal simulation (a 0.0016 seconds time step in most of our examples). We use multithread in implementation. Two identical scenes are created, so that they do not interact with each other. Therefore, we do not need to rewind back and conduct a secondary simulation, and our approach is feasible to simulate multiple contacts in series. After obtaining the simulated trajectory, we compare the simulated data with the sequences in our motion library to find the desired sequence, as well as the precise time and root transformation which aligns the found sequence with the simulated trajectory.

4.2 Motion Selection

Our search algorithm is similar to those suggested previously for reordering motion capture data in the motion comparison. As motion comparison is the most time- consuming part of this kind of system, we ignore some of the joints (such as wrists and ankles) in our calculation comparison, which have less influence in frame-to-frame motion, to reduce the time consumption. In our motion search, the distance metric is modeled most closely to the one introduced by Kovar et al. [5]. The distance metric, $D(f_s, f_m)$ is computed between the simulation and test motion capture sequences using joint positions of the poses in a small transition time window starting at f_{s0} and f_{m0}. The purpose of computing the metric over a window of frames is to ensure that velocity mismatches between the two frames are penalized in the calculated metric. The size of the window is chosen as the amount of time of a typical transition. Within windows, the distance function for pairs of frames f_{si} and f_{mi} is computed as the weighted sum of distances between the positions and orientations of matching body parts. The distance between two windows is found as the sum of distance between the corresponding frame pairs. The metric is shown as following equation:

$$D(f_s, f_m) = \sum_{i=0}^{ws} \sum_{J=0}^{J-5} \begin{pmatrix} w_{pj} \| p_j(f_{si}) - T(f_{s0}, f_{m0}) p_j(f_{mi}) \| \\ + w_{\theta j} \| \theta_j(f_{si}) - T(f_{s0}, f_{m0}) \theta_j(f_{mi}) \| \end{pmatrix} \tag{1}$$

Where *ws* is the size of the transition window, *J* is the number of joints in the character (Because ankle, wrist and neck joints have been ignored, only *J*-5 joints are used for distance calculation), $P_j(f_{si})$ is the global position of joint *j* at frame f_{si} and $\theta_j(f_{si})$ is the orientation. The weights w_{pj} and $w_{\theta j}$ scale the linear and angular distance for each body. As differences in the positions of the limbs can be more easily modified when computing the transition motion, we assign high weights to the trunk parts and use lower ones for limbs. And $T(f_{s0}, f_{m0})$ is the coordinate transformation that aligns the roots in the first frames of each window. To increase the efficiency of the search function, we simplified the distance metric calculation by decreasing the numbers of joints in frame comparison. In addition, the metric is computed as a weighted sum of distances between the positions and orientations of each joint rather than sum of squared differences.

5 Reactive Human Motion Simulation

While searching the desired next-play motion capture sequence, it is necessary to generate reactive motion to fill in the gap between the two motion capture sequences before and after the transition. This transition motion should be computed in a physically plausible manner which is consistent with the found motion and meet the desired state as closely as possible.

5.1 Physical Simulation of Human Motion

We use a parallel simulation mechanism, as previously described, to predict the simulated trajectory as well as generate the final simulated motion. The predicted trajectory is used to find the target motion capture sequence. At the same time, we create a normal simulated motion by using a joint-torque controller, which is informed the target motion sequence. Most of the time in physical simulation, the torque controller follows a blended sequence of joint angles, θ_{blend}, from the previous motion capture segment to the next. The controller uses a typical PD-servo at each joint to compute torques as

$$\tau = k_s(\theta_{blend}(t) - \theta_{cur}) - k_d(-\dot{\theta}_{cur}) \tag{2}$$

Where k_s and k_d are stiffness and damping gains respectively. The stiffness gain controls the strength of the spring while the damper gain adjusts how smoothly the joint arrives at the desired value. To fit different state requirements, these gains are not set fixed values any more in the transition, for example, falling sideways has lower gains for shoulder joints than falling forward does. θ_{cur} and $\dot{\theta}_{cur}$ correspond to current joint angles and velocities. The desired sequence to be tracked by the controller, $\theta_{blend}(t)$, is generated on the fly by blending the intermediate postures from the two motion capture sequences before and after the transition. By using this dynamic controller, the simulated motion follows the blending trajectory, moving toward the desired body posture over the course of the transition gap. However, human body usually displays a remarkable ability to quickly respond to unexpected impacts and generates protective behaviors to avoid injury when a loss of balance occurs, such as corrective steps to keep balance. It would behave unrealistically to let the character just follow the blending trajectory.

5.2 Biomechanics Inspired Adjustment

In order to make the character behave more lifelike, we add some active control for generating physically plausible recovery responses and protective behaviors inspired from biomechanics lecture. The main action is to absorb the shock of the impact by using arms. Researchers in the biomechanics community have looked at unexpected and trained responses to slips induced by various perturbations[14, 15].

In our design, we focus our active control on upper limbs. Because the aim of this work is not to respond to small impacts that could be resolved with a corrective step or other reactive responses, we make no attempt to use the ankle and hip strategies commonly used by humans to maintain balance under small perturbations. Additionally, we do not expect the simulation to return to a balanced posture but try to switch back to appropriate motion sequence. So, the control problem is simplified. We generate reactive responses and protective behaviors consistent with the upcoming motion in three phases: reactive recovery, protective response and posture settling.

After an unexpected impact, arms are actively controlled to track the predicted landing location of the body and generated protective behaviors to avoid injury. The control strategy is similar to those generated protective behaviors by using continuous pose controller [11]. Controlling the arms actively is to intersect the wrists with the line between the shoulder and its predicted landing position. Therefore, the accuracy of predicted falling direction of the character and the corresponding shoulder landing position is very important to produce natural behaviors. Benefited from our parallel simulation, the predicted trajectory of a character could be obtained accurately. The relative angels of the shoulder joint are determined by the vector $\vec{V}_{1humerus}$ and $\vec{V}_{2humerus}$ as illustrated in Figure 1.

Lastly, the controller tries to drive and settle the character to the desired posture of the found motion capture sequence following the intermediate blended sequence. From the physics-based simulation we generate a believable response motion, and then smoothly transfer this motion into the target sequence. We blend this motion with the found motion sequence by using interpolation to remove remaining discontinuities.

Fig. 1. An illustration of how the target joint angles of the shoulder are determined during a fall

6 Experimental Results

By using the system described, we implement a number of experiments to evaluate the feasibility of our system under a variety of initial conditions. Figure 2 shows a set of reactive responses when a character falls down after encountering an unexpected obstacle. During the falling process, arms of the character are controlled to generate convincing human behaviors: arms are rapidly elevated backward and outward in an attempt to stabilize the forward displaced COM after collision, and then adjust to track the predicted landing location of the body and generate protective behaviors to avoid injury. Figure 2 also shows a side-by-side comparison of the biomechanical inspired controller with the ordinary PD controller. The controller, with biomechanical adjustment, generates more realistic behaviors during impacts.

(a) Biomechanical inspired controller driven behaviours

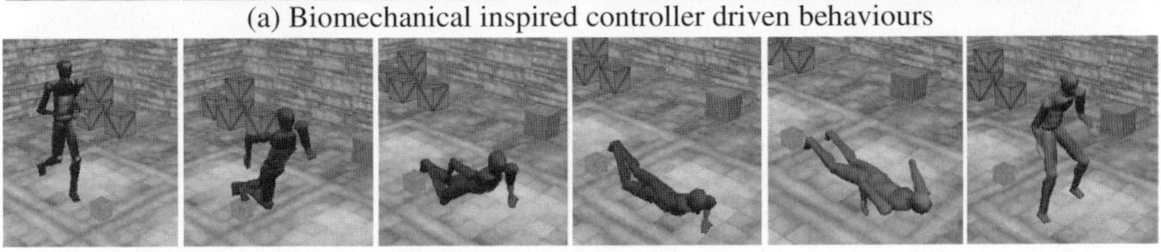

(b) Ordinary PD controller driven behaviours

Fig. 2. A side-by-side comparison of the biomechanical inspired controller driven behaviors with ordinary PD controller

7 Discussion and Conclusions

In this paper, we present a method to select a motion capture sequence designed to follow an impact and synthesize a believable transition to this found clip for interacting characters. The prediction of initial simulated trajectory is vital to smoothly perform a transition from physical simulation to motion capture data. The posture of the simulated character after an impact can not be easily predicted, because interactions and external forces with the environment are different in every impact. One of the contributions of our work is the adoption of parallel physical simulation, which helps to find the target motion capture sequences and generate simulated motion to fill the gap between the beginning of an interaction and the time before transition-to clip is played. The search for target motion sequences is critical to ensure our simulated motion in a conscious way.

Although our approach has been effective on generating realistic and dynamic motion, there still remain several areas for improvement. First, our controller was designed to generate physically plausible motion following an upcoming motion with adjustment from biomechanics rules, which is a key to avoid an unconscious look for a character during the transition. These biomechanical-based characteristics can adjust the simulated motion in a physical manner consistent with the upcoming motion. However, they are limited when the simulated character is actively controlled to respond to external perturbations inconsistent with the motion moving towards the desired posture. Additionally, our controller is able to generate protective behaviors when a complete loss of balance occurs in simulation. However, it can not account for taking corrective steps that could keep balance. Nevertheless, we provide a good initialization of generating physical and reactive response for interacting characters, which can be further improved by other animation approaches.

Acknowledgements

Many thanks to all reviewers for helping us improve this work and its presentation, to Dr. Rynson W.H. Lau and Dr. Weidong Geng for their helpful discussion and remarks. This research work is co-founded under Project 973 (grant NO: 2002CB312100), NSFC (grant NO: 60533080) and Microsoft Research Asia (MSRA) Regional Theme Project 2005.

References

1. Lee, J.,Shin, S.Y.: A hierarchical approach to interactive motion editing for humanlike figures. the 26th Annual Conference on Computer Graphics and Interactive Techniques, (1999) 39-48
2. Witkin, A.,Popovic, Z.: Motion warping. the 22nd Annual Conference on Computer Graphics and Interactive Techniques, (1995) 105-108
3. Gleicher, M.: Comparing constraint-based motion editing methods. Graphical models, Vol.63 (2001) 107-134
4. Park, S.I., Shin, H.J.,Shin, S.Y.: On-line locomotion generation based on motion blending. the 2002 ACM SIGGRAPH/Eurographics symposium on Computer animation. ACM Press, (2002) 105-111

5. Kovar, L., Gleicher, M.,Pighin, F.e.e.: Motion graphs. ACM Transactions on Graphics, Vol.21 (2002) 473-482
6. Hodgins, J.K., et al.: Animating human athletics. ACM Computer Graphics,(1995) 71-78
7. Wooten, W.L.: Simulation of Leaping, Tumbling, Landing, and Balancing Humans. Doctoral thesis. Georgia Institute of Technology (1998)
8. Faloutsos, P., Panne, M.v.d.,Terzopoulos, D.: Composable controllers for physics-based character animation. ACM SIGGRAPH 2001. ACM Press, (2001) 251-260
9. Oshita, M.,Makinouchi, A.: A dynamic motion control technique for human-like articulated figures. Eurographics 2001, (2001) 192-202
10. Shapiro, A.,Pighin, F.: Hybrid control for interactive character animation. the 11th Pacific Conference on Computer Graphics and Applications, (2003) 455-461
11. Mandel, M.: Versatile and interactive virtual humans: Hybrid use of data-driven and dynamics-based motion synthesis. Master's thesis. Carnegie Mellon University (2004)
12. Zordan, V.B., et al.: Dynamic response for motion capture animation. ACM SIGGRAPH 2005. ACM Press, (2005) 697-701
13. Liu, C.K., Hertzmann, A.,Popovi´c, Z.: Learning Physics-Based Motion Style with Nonlinear Inverse Optimization. ACM Transactions on Graphics, Vol.24 (2005) 1071-1081
14. Hsiao, E.T.,Robinovitch, S.N.: Biomechanical influences on balance recovery by stepping. Journal of Biomechanics, Vol.32 (1999) 1099-1106
15. Rogers, M.W., et al.: Triggering of protective stepping for the control of human balance: age and contextual dependence. Congitive Brain Research, Vol.16 (2003) 192-198

Real-Time Shadow Volume Algorithm for Subdivision Surface Based Models

Min Tang[1], Jin-Xiang Dong[1], and Shang-Ching Chou[2]

[1] College of Computer Science, Zhejiang University,
310027, Hangzhou, China
{tang_m, djx} @zju.edu

[2] Computer Science Department, Wichita State University,
67260-0083, Wichita, KS, USA
chou@cs.wichita.edu

Abstract. This paper presents a purely hardware-accelerated shadow volume algorithm for subdivision surface based models. By introducing SP (subdivision patterns), all procedures, including subdivision evaluation, silhouette extraction, shadow volume generation, and shadow rendering are executed on GPU (Graphics Process Units) efficiently. This not only alleviates the burden of CPU, but also guarantees the consistency of data among different processing stages. This also makes it possible to integrate some special effects imposed by other shaders, e.g., displacement mapping or vertex texturing, with the shadow volume algorithm. Experiments show that the algorithm is efficient, robust, and can be easily extended to other subdivision schemes and parametric surfaces.

1 Introduction

Shadows emphasize the direction of light source, make the related position of objects obvious, and enhance the reality of scenes. The shadow algorithms can be categorized mainly into two groups: shadow mapping and the shadow volume techniques. The shadow mapping method [1] is an image space algorithm. Its accuracy/resolution is limited by the size of the shadow map. The shadow volume algorithm was first proposed by Crow [2] and is an object space algorithm. For its high accuracy, it has become the de factor standard of shadow generation algorithms. With the gradual evolution of graphics hardware, many researchers have made improvements on the shadow volumes algorithm to boost its efficiency and to enhance its robustness. The shadow volumes algorithm is composed by following stages: silhouette extraction, shadow volume generation, stencil buffer updating, and shadow rendering based on the stencil buffer. In [3], the Z-Fail algorithm is used to overcome the disturbance caused by the font clipping plane which occurs frequently in the Z-Pass algorithm, and a two-sided stencil test is taken to improve the efficiency of stencil buffer updating.

Currently, all the extensions of the original shadow volume algorithm are mainly focus on dealing with polygonal models, the curved models defined by parametric surfaces or subdivision surfaces have to be converted to facet models before being processed.

H.-P. Seidel, T. Nishita, and Q. Peng (Eds.): CGI 2006, LNCS 4035, pp. 538 – 545, 2006.

Our contribution: We use Subdivision Pattern (SP) as a tool to build a purely hardware-accelerated shadow volume algorithm for subdivision surface based models. By using SPs, the whole pipeline, including subdivision surface evaluation, silhouette extraction, shadow volume generation, and shadowed scene rendering, are fulfilled on GPU. The only data needs transferred from CPU to GPU are the control meshes. No read-back is needed. All the data used in the difference stages are stored on GPU. This not only ensures the data consistency, but also avoids the communication latency between CPU and GPU. Another benefit of our method is that other special effects imposed by GPU shaders, e.g., displacement mapping or vertex texturing, can be integrated naturally and efficiently. This is hard for previous methods.

Organization: We first review the related work in Section 2. Then we present an overview of our shadow algorithm (Section 3). As an important component of our algorithm, the silhouette extraction method on GPU is discussed in Section 4. A comparison with previous GPU based silhouette extraction methods will also be made in this Section. Then the shadow volume generation method is presented in Section 5. The implementation details and some experiment results will be presented in Section 6. Conclusions are drawn in Sections 7.

2 Related Work

With the maturation of modern GPU, especially its programmability, researchers are striving to implement the whole lifecycle of the shadow volume algorithm on graphics hardware. In [4], the stages including silhouette extraction and shadow volume generation, which are formally implemented on CPU, have been integrated into a purely hardware-accelerated algorithm. But for lacking a fast data read-back mechanism from GPU to CPU, its efficiency is limited. Paper [5] presents an implementation of the shadow volume algorithm on GPU using Cg. All the edges are drawn as degenerated quadrangles. In a vertex shader, silhouette edges are identified, and the corresponding quadrangles are extended to shadow volumes. It can render shadowed scenes at an interactive speed. [6] presents a good survey about shadow volume algorithms, and also discusses some implementation details with OpenGL and DirectX. All the above methods focus on polygonal models. For curved models, they must be facetted before being processed.

Subdivision surfaces are widely used in Computer Graphics and Computer Animation fields. Subdivision surfaces have been used as a primitive in many graphics applications. So it makes sense to study the real-time shadow volume algorithm for subdivision surface based models.

Recently many works are focus on subdivision on GPU. Then the resultant can be directly used for rendering [7, 8, 9]. In [10], a mesh refinement method using vertex shaders is proposed. By using the local information on vertices, the PN surfaces can be implemented on various graphics hardware. But it is hard to further processing on the refined data.

3 Overview

Modern GPU is fast at processing stream data, i.e. at executing the same function on every element of the input data set and produce an output data set. On a stream processor, the function is called "Kernel", and the data set is called "stream". For our application and many other GPGPU applications, it is beneficial to make abstractions on the concepts likes vertices, pixels or fragments. It will simplify our design; make the design comprehensible and easy for implementation and extension. Fig. 1 shows the Kernels we have used:

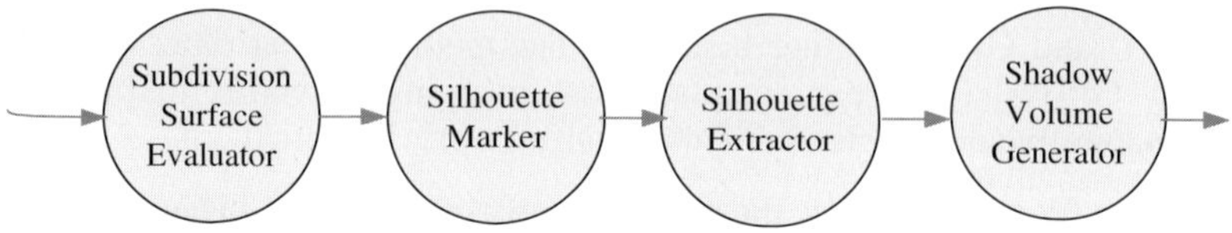

Fig. 1. The Kernel chain involved

1. **Subdivision surface evaluator** evaluates the input subdivision surfaces based on Subdivision Patterns and produces a vertex texture containing limit positions.
2. **Silhouette marker** determines the silhouettes and marks them into a flag texture.
3. **Silhouette extractor** extracts the silhouettes from the vertex texture and the flag texture. Result is stored into a silhouette texture.
4. **Shadow volume generator** generates shadow volumes from the silhouette texture.

3.1 Algorithm Flowchart

Our shadow algorithm has following steps:

1. The control mesh of the subdivision surface based model is broken into patches. The data of each patch will be sent to Kernel "Subdivision Surface Evaluator".
2. Kernel "Subdivision Surface Evaluator" will use SP (Subdivision Pattern) as a tool to generate a vertex texture containing the refined model.
3. Kernel "Silhouette Marker" and "Silhouette Extractor" take the vertex texture as input and produce a silhouette texture containing silhouette information.
4. Kernel "Shadow Volume Generator" will extrude the silhouettes to shadow volumes.
5. Then the shadow volumes will be used for shadow rendering.

3.2 Patching the Control Mesh

The control mesh is broken up into many patches on CPU. Each patch will be processed independently. If irregular vertices exist, we need to apply at most two subdivision operations on the initial control mesh to isolate the irregular vertices. By doing so, there is at most one irregular vertex in each patch. A patch consists of a quadrangle or a triangle and their surrounding vertices. For Catmull-Clark subdivision, if all vertices are regular (i.e., their valences equal to 4), we need to store 16 control points for a patch. For Loop subdivision, a regular patch (all vertices with valence equal to 3) consists of 12 control points. We generate one patch for each facet of the control mesh.

3.3 Subdivision Pattern (SP)

For a particular subdivision scheme, a specified subdivision level, and the valence of the irregular vertex (if any), we construct a corresponding SP. A SP is a mesh defined in unit space. It contains topological information and parametric information. Vertices of a SP store parametric information and combination coefficients calculated from the parameters. For the Loop subdivision, the vertices of SP contain the barycentric coordinates (u, v, w), where 0 <= u <= 1.0, 0 <= v <= 1.0, 0 <= w <= 1.0, and u+v+w = 1.0, and also coefficients calculated from the coordinates. For Catmull-Clark subdivision, data on SP are similar: parameters (u, v), where 0 <= u <= 1.0, 0 <= v <= 1.0, and coefficients calculated from the parameters.

We pack the parameters and coefficients into textures, and make them accessible for the Kernels running on GPU. In our application, Kernel "Subdivision Surface Evaluator" will use the coefficients.

3.4 Kernel: Subdivision Surface Evaluator

For a Catmull-Clark subdivision surface, we use the analytic evaluation method in [11]. By projecting the control points into the eigenspace, the limit position can be calculated as the weighted combination of the projected control points:

$$S_{k,n}(u,v) = (X^{-1}C_0)^T \Lambda^{n-1} (P_k \overline{A} X)^T b(u,v) \tag{1}$$

where A is the subdivision matrix, X is the matrix of eigenvector of A, and Λ is the diagonal matrix of eigenvalues. To accelerate the computation, we packed the terms which are independent of the control points into $Weight(u,v)$. We have:

$$\begin{aligned} &Weight(u,v) = (X^{-1})^T \Lambda^{n-1} (P_k \overline{A} X)^T b(u,v) \\ &S_{k,n}(u,v) = C_0^T Weight(u,v) \end{aligned} \tag{2}$$

All the $Weight(u,v)$ are pre-calculated according to the parameters (u, v) stored on SP. The combination of control points and the weights will be performed in the kernel.

4 Silhouette Extraction on GPU

Silhouettes are critical for shadow volume generation. What we need are silhouettes linked correctly in 3D space. We designed two Kernels "Silhouette Marker" and "Silhouette Extractor" to fulfill the task. Kernel "Silhouette Marker" finds out silhouettes and uses flags to mark correct link direction. Kernel "Silhouette Extractor" links the silhouettes correctly based on the flags.

The limit vertex attributes of the subdivision surfaces produced by Kernel "Subdivision Surface Evaluator" are organized in regular girds – limit vertex textures. They are the input of Kernel "Silhouette Marker" and Kernel "Silhouette Extractor".

4.1 Kernel: Silhouette Marker

For a vertex A in the vertex texture, by symmetry, we only need to consider its connections with the adjacent vertices B, C and D (Fig. 2). We draw a rectangle of the vertex texture size on the screen, and the Kernel works on each fragments of it. We

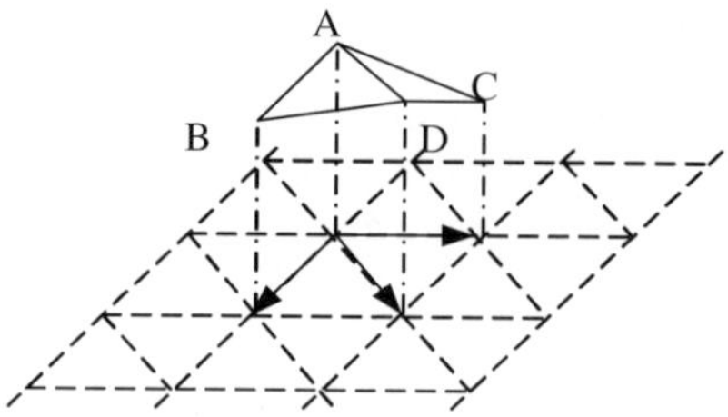

Fig. 2. Connections between vertex A and its adjacent vertices in the vertex texture

use visibility rules to test whether an edge is a silhouette, we also take its orientation into consideration. All the information will be save in a flag texture. We use the RGB three channels to save the flags for AB, AC, and AD respectively.

4.2 Kernel: Silhouette Extractor

After we have identified all the silhouettes and also their connection information, we have to link them correctly. To do this efficiently on GPU, we developed a method similar to image scaling. Our approach is to scale the vertex image by a factor of 2 in each dimension. We will generate a silhouette texture based on the vertex texture and the flag texture.

Four new vertices A', B', C' and D' are generated for a vertex A in the vertex image as shown in Fig. 3. A' is set to A. If AB is marked as a silhouette, then B' is set to B. Otherwise B' is set to A, so A'B' shirks to a degenerated edge (AA). Similarly, if AC is marked as a silhouette, C' is set to C, otherwise C' is set to A. if AD is marked as a silhouette, D' is set to D, otherwise D' is set to A.

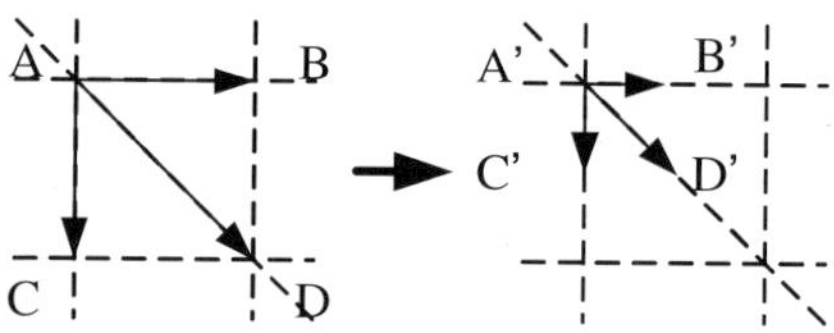

Fig. 3. New vertices generated by scaling

Since we marked reverse flags in the flag texture, the situations become more complex. First we exclude the situation where AB, AC and AD all are silhouettes. It is incorrect in topology. So there are at most two silhouettes at the same time. Then we have enough space to store all the silhouettes, as shown in Fig. 4.

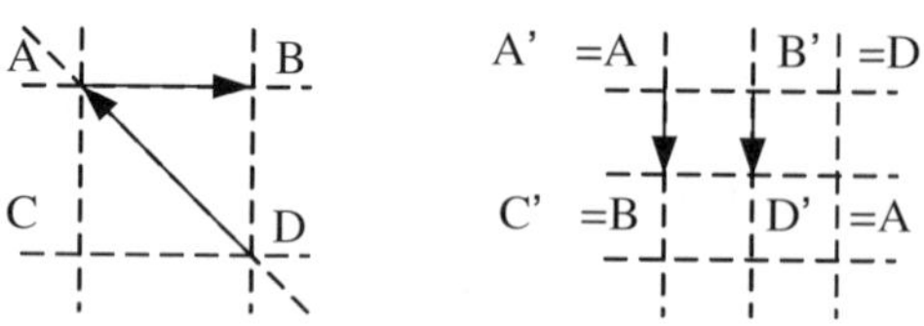

Fig. 4. An example of silhouette extraction (left: input in the vertex texture and the flag texture, right: Output in the silhouette texture)

5 Shadow Volume Generation

After we got the silhouettes, it is easy to construct shadow volumes from them. The extrusion operation for generating new vertices is shown in following equation:

$$Y = X + (X - O) * \infty \tag{3}$$

Here X is vertices on silhouettes, O is the light position.

5.1 Kernel: Shadow Volume Generator

Kernel "Shadow Volume Generator" is designed to do the extrusion on GPU. The procedure is similar to scaling the silhouette textures to size 2x1. All the information about shadow volumes is stored in shadow volume textures. The data on a shadow volume texture can be classified as two parts: the left are vertices on silhouette lines and the right are vertices extruded from them. The data layout is shown in Fig. 5.

For valid silhouettes, edge AB holds $A \neq B$, so the quadrangle AA'B'B is part of a shadow volume. For a degenerated edge AB, where $A = B$, a quadrangle AA'A'A degenerated to a line will be extruded. All degenerated quadrangles will be filtered out when rendering in fill mode.

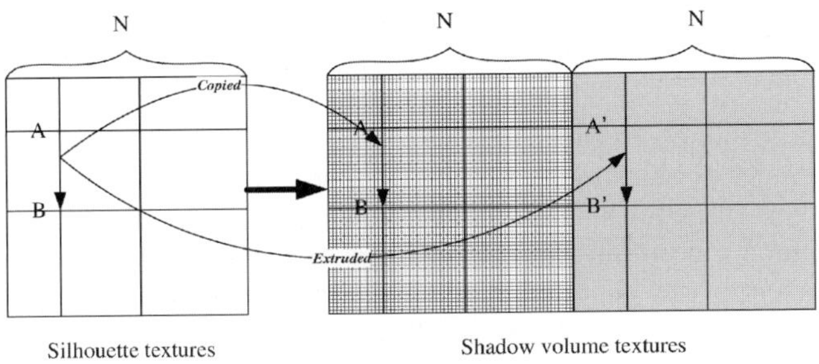

Fig. 5. Data layout on a shadow volume texture

6 Implementation and Results

We have implemented our algorithm using a NVIDIA GeForce 6800LE GPU (AGP 8x, 128 MB) on Windows XP/VC++/OpenGL platform. We use Cg to write shaders. We use OpenGL extension, FBO (Framebuffer Objects), to render data to textures.

The left part of Fig. 6 demonstrates the process procedures for models with irregular vertices. The model has many irregular vertices (valences equal to 3). Two initial subdivision operators are needed to isolate the irregular vertices. Here some new irregular vertices are generated. The valence of the central vertex is 12. The right part of Fig. 6 shows the integration with displacement mapping. A star is stored in the displacement map. Its FPS is about 20. The shadow volumes are displayed in transparent mode.

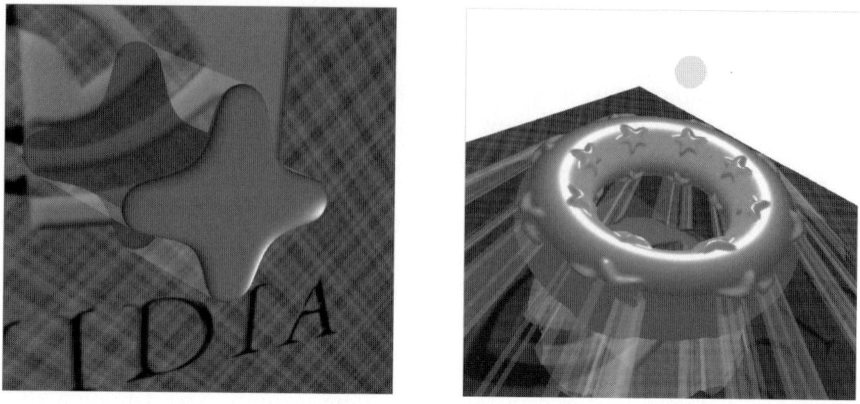

Fig. 6. Results of our implementation

One thing to note is our implementation is far from optimal. There are still spaces for improvement. So the results are provided only for reference. More pictures, AVI files, source code of shaders, and executable demo program are downloadable from this link: http://www.cs.wichita.edu/~tang/RTShadow/rtshadow.htm.

7 Conclusions

We propose a serial of Kernels to make the tasks including subdivision surface evaluation, silhouettes marking and extraction, shadow volumes generation and rendering are implemented fully on graphics hardware. By implement the whole pipeline of shadow volume algorithm for subdivision surface based models, the data can be processed efficiently and accurately. It has been proved that our algorithm can be easily incorporate with other GPU based effects, i.e. displacement mapping.

With the rapid evolution of graphics hardware, we can expect the efficiency of our method can be further prompted, and can be used for real-time graphics applications such as computer game, computer animation, etc.

References

1. Williams, L.: Casting curved shadows on curved surfaces. In Computer Graphics (SIGGRAPH '78 Proceedings), 270-274
2. Crow, F.C.: Shadow algorithms for computer graphics. In Computer Graphics (SIGGRAPH '77 Proceedings), (1977) 242-248
3. Brabec, S., Seidel, H.: Shadow Volumes on Programmable Graphics Hardware. In Proceedings of Eurographics, Vol. 22, (2003) 433-440
4. Everitt, C., Kilgard, M. J.: Practical and Robust Stencil Shadow Volumes for Hardware Accelerated Rendering. Austin, Texas. NVIDIA. Referenced: 5.4.2002. http://developer.nvidia.com/view.asp?IO=robust_shadow_volumes, 2002.
5. Surdulescu R.: Cg Shadow Volumes, http://www.gamedev.net/reference/articles/ article1990.asp, 2003.

6. Kainulainen, J.: An Introduction to Stencil Shadow Volumes. http://www.devmaster.net/articles/shadow_volumes/, 2004
7. Bolz, J., Schröder, P.: Evaluation of Subdivision Surfaces on Programmable Graphics Hardware, http://www.multires.caltech.edu/pubs/GPUSubD.pdf, 2003.
8. Bunnell, M.: GPU Gems 2: Programming Techniques for High-Performance Graphics and General-Purpose Computation. Addison-Wesley, Reading, MA. ch. Adaptive Tessellation of Subdivision Surfaces with Displacement Mapping, 2005.
9. Shiue, L-J, Peters, J.: A Realtime GPU Subdivision Kernel. In Proceedings of SIGGRPAH Computer Graphics Proceedings, http://www.cise.ufl.edu/research/SurfLab/papers/05hwSub.pdf, 2005
10. Boubekeur, T., Schlick, C.: Generic Mesh Refinement On GPU, In Proceedings of ACM SIGGRAPH/Eurographics Graphics Hardware, http://www.labri.fr/Perso/~boubek/ pub/GenericMeshRefinementOnGPU.pdf, 2005.
11. Stam, J.: Exact Evaluation of Catmull-Clark Subdivision Surfaces at Arbitrary Parameter Values. In Computer Graphics Proceedings, Annual Conference Series, 1998, 395-404
12. McGuire, M., Hughes, J.F.: Hardware-Determined Feature Edges. In Proceedings of Third International Symposium on Non Photorealistic Animation and Rendering (NPAR 2004), Annecy, France, June 7-9, pages 35-44, New York, 2004. ACM Press.

Human Animation from 2D Correspondence Based on Motion Trend Prediction

Li Zhang and Ling Li

Department of Computing, Curtin University of Technology,
WA 6845, GPO Box U1987, Perth, Australia
{zhangl, ling}@cs.curtin.edu.au

Abstract. A model-based method is proposed in this paper for 3-dimensional human motion recovery, taking un-calibrated monocular data as input. This method is designed to recover smooth human motions with high efficiency, while its outputs are guaranteed to resemble the original motion not only from the same viewpoint the sequence was taken, but also look natural and reasonable from any other viewpoint. The proposed method is called "Motion trend prediction (MTP)". To evaluate the accuracy of the MTP, it is first tested on some "synthesized" input. After that experiments are conducted on real video data, which demonstrate that the proposed method is able to recover smooth human motions from their 2D image features with high accuracy.

1 Introduction

Animation is the production of consecutive images, which, when displayed, conveys a feeling of motion [1]. In the past decade, with the rapid development of computer technology, computer animation, especially the representation of human body and its motion have received great attention, since human animation is quite popular and widely employed in many areas, such as games, movies, surveillance, scientific visualization, etc. As monocular images and video sequences are easily available, many great efforts have been made to reconstruct 3D human motion from them.

Taylor and Remondina et al. suggested adjusting the posture of a human model according to camera calibration information and biomechanical constraints applied on the model [2] & [3]. Only orthographic projection is discussed in their approaches. Liu et al. and Park et al. made use of the motion library [4] & [5]. In both attempts, a large motion library needs to be maintained and updated consistently. In [6] David et al. introduced an interactive system which combines biomechanical constraints on 3D motion with user interferences to reconstruct motion sequences in 3D. Similarly three possibilities for solving inverse kinematics problem during human animation are discussed where direct user interferences are involved [7]. Zhao et al. proposed a Global Adjustment (GA) system for posture reconstruction [8], where the accuracy and the consistency of the recovered postures are only guaranteed in the same viewing direction as the original.

Most existing methods introduce simplifications on human motion or require assistance such as user interference, motion library, or multiple cameras are requested to gather sufficient information about the original motion. This paper aims to propose a novel model-based human motion reconstruction method from un-calibrated 2D

H.-P. Seidel, T. Nishita, and Q. Peng (Eds.): CGI 2006, LNCS 4035, pp. 546 – 553, 2006.

monocular data with very little user interferences (only required for the 1st frame) and the human motion to be reconstructed is truly unrestricted.

The key component of our proposed system is a Motion Trend Prediction (MTP) method which aims to recover human posture at every single frame based on 3D human body information gathered through posture reconstruction in previous frames, except for the 1st frame. Unlike the proposed method for estimating 3D motion of an articulated object in [9], in our algorithm the whole skeletal model is always treated as a single object to ensure the consistency and smoothness of motions of different body parts. Further more, compared to the Kalman or the particle filtering prediction tracking algorithm [10], calculations of partial derivatives or an even more complicated infrastructure are unnecessary in our algorithm. Through a very small set of simple Approach Function (*AF*) formulas, continuous 3D human postures in a motion sequence can be tracked and recovered. The weighting parameter (*WP*), which plays an important role in determining the MTP's accuracy, can be derived through a low-pass filtering process. The proposed MTP method is simple to understand and implement, but it can efficiently generate smooth human animation.

The rest of this paper is organized as follows: the camera model and the 3D skeletal model used for motion reconstruction are described in the next section; section 3 discussed the key component of our work: the MTP method; experimental results are presented and analyzed in section 4; finally a conclusion is drawn in section 5.

2 Models

A camera model and a human model need to be set up beforehand in the proposed system. The camera is assumed to be located at a fixed position in virtual space with pre-defined focal length, and it does not require knowledge of the actual cameras from which the video sequence is taken since such information is unavailable most of the time in reality. This virtual camera is used to calculate the projections of the recovered postures, and to enable the comparison with the input 2D correspondences for reconstruction refinement. As this project focuses on recovering the whole body motion from monocular data, an articulated 3D skeletal model employed in [11] is considered sufficient. This skeletal model contains 17 joints and 17 segments. We name the 5 leaf joints *left wrist, right wrist, left ankle, right ankle* and *head,* all the other joints are categorized as intermediate joints, among which *pelvis* is set as the root in the skeletal tree structure.

For posture reconstruction, the movements of each segment need to be recovered. At the current moment, our attention is focused on the 12 more important segments which are hip, waist, chest, neck, upper arms, forearms, thighs, and shins, whose movement are resulted from proper rotations about their individual starting joints. To apply the rotations, 1 to 3 DOF(s) is assigned to each intermediate joint in the world coordinate system (WCS), and each of these joint is associated with a local coordinate system (LCS) [11]. The only exception is the joint *pelvis,* which has 6 DOFs (3 for translations and the other 3 for rotations), since the translation of the whole body is represented by the movement of *pelvis*.

According to biomechanical constraints [12] & [13], the rotational constraints of each intermediate joint in its associated LCS can be derived. In our system we choose to update the constraints employed in [8]. Details can be found in [11].

With above definitions, it is assumed that through proper translation of the *pelvis* and rotations of the 12 segments about each intermediate joint, any human posture could be obtained with the skeletal model from its initial pose.

3 Motion Reconstruction

In our reconstruction system, the accurate 2D posture correspondence in every frame is the only input, and manual adjustment for the 1st frame is always required, as described in our prior work [11]. However, such manual adjustment is only allowed for the 1st frame. The reconstruction process of all other frames is completely automatic and user interference is not allowed and totally unnecessary.

3.1 The Motion Trend Prediction Method

Human motion reconstruction is actually a process to reconstruct human posture at every frame, which should resemble the original postures in the source video as much as possible. During the process two observations about human motion are found and analyzed. Based on them, the original Motion Trend Predication method is proposed [11].

3.2 Improvement of the MTP Method

Through the original MTP method, the recovered human postures will be guaranteed to resemble the original and be consistent in 3D space; however jumpy rotations about each intermediate joint may still occur. It is a common knowledge that a certain posture could be achieved through different rotational configurations. To achieve the real smoothness between recovered human postures, we must also ensure the rotational smoothness of each segment. Three considerations are utilized for this target.

Firstly, the rotational orders are fixed for rotations about each intermediate joint. Secondly, before recovering the posture at the Kth frame, the searching space of rotational angles of each intermediate joint is re-adjusted according to rotational configurations obtained from reconstruction at the $(K\text{-}1)^{th}$ frame *(K•2)*. As human motion is generally smooth, the rotational angels of each joint should not change sharply between neighboring frames. The above considerations improve efficiency of the original MTP method significantly. They also help to ensure the rotational continuity of each segment.

The last consideration is, if the human motions in the input sequences are truly smooth, it can be assumed that for any intermediate joint its rotational accelerations in three axes of its LCS are always continuous. For such input sequences, a parametric formula to strengthen control on rotations of segments about the ith intermediate joint can be derived as Rotation Function (RF) shown in Eq.(1):

$$RF_i = abs\left|\alpha_i^K - \alpha_i^{K-1}\right| + abs\left|\beta_i^K - \beta_i^{K-1}\right| + abs\left|\gamma_i^K - \gamma_i^{K-1}\right| \left(K \geq 4\right) . \quad (1)$$

where ($\alpha_i^K, \beta_i^K, \gamma_i^K$) and ($\alpha_i^{K-1}, \beta_i^{K-1}, \gamma_i^{K-1}$) stand for the ith intermediate joint's rotational accelerations in three axes of LCS at the Kth and $(K\text{-}1)^{th}$ frame respectively. These accelerations can be computed through rotational angles obtained from posture reconstruction. If the original human motion is sufficiently smooth, value of such RF should approach 0 as much as possible, which means the rotational acceleration changes slightly with frames. Therefore RFs can function to ensure smoothness of each intermediate joint's rotations, when the input motions are truly smooth.

As discussed in [11], the minimum values of AFs guarantee that the recovered postures resemble the original from the same viewing direction, and each joint's positions are continuous during frames. Once a proper balance between the minimization of each RF_i and its corresponding AF_i is built up, sound 3D human postures can be recovered based on the 2D correspondence input, and thus smooth human animation resembling the original in all directions is considered as having been obtained.

3.3 The Balance Between RF and AF

To generate the best motion reconstruction from 2D monocular correspondence with the proposed MTP method, one of the most important considerations is to find the balance between the minimization of each RF_i and its corresponding AF_i. Currently the initial balance between the RF_i and the AF_i for rotation about each intermediate joint is set as 100:1 based on experimental data obtained from "synthesized" sequences as discussed in section 4, which means that when the minimization of $100*RF_i + AF_i$ is achieved for rotations about each ith intermediate joint the recovered posture is deemed the most optimised. However this balance is only applicable when the original motion is truly smooth. If any segment's movement accelerates or decelerates sharply during the original motion sequence, feedback routine has to be introduced to locate a new balance between the RF_i and AF_i. The feedback routine is based on the following idea: once the unsatisfactory prediction about motion trend of a certain segment is made in the current frame it will affect the segment's posture recovery in the subsequent frames; as a result the 2D residuals related to this certain segment will not be able to approach 0 when the unsatisfactory motion trend accumulates to a certain extend. Therefore a new balance between the RF_i and AF_i need to be established.

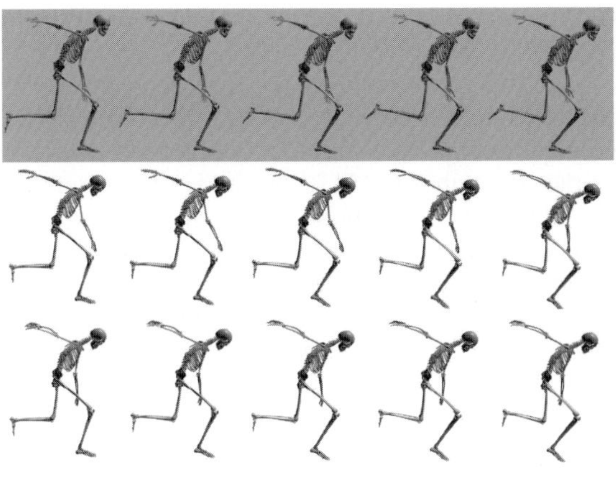

Fig. 1. Top: Original postures viewed from the side; Middle: Recovered postures from the same view angle (without feedback); Bottom: Recovered postures (with feedback)

In Fig. 1 a computer synthesized bowling sequence (100 frames) is presented to demonstrate the function of the feedback routine. This sequence is quite long but only 5 frames (41st – 45th frame) are shown here. The top figure presents original postures from the input sequence with a side view, while the middle and bottom are recovered postures without and with feedback routine applied. Clearly the results obtained with feedback resemble the original motion better.

Without feedback the motion trend of upper body can not be satisfactory for the above sequence. It is found that the wrong motion trend information of upper body is actually collected in the 34th frame; it does not show until the 57th frame, as the projections of the recovered human postures match their 2D correspondences in original quite well between the 34th and the 57th frame.

With the help of the feedback routine, the contribution of the rotational acceleration can be automatically strengthened or weakened during the run time. This way the balance between each RF_i and AF_i can be determined more accurately.

4 Experiments and Discussions

In order to generate reliable motion reconstruction, 2D feature information (2D correspondence) extracted from the source video must be highly accurate. Any error in feature extraction could lead to incorrect 2D configuration of human body geometry and 3D recovered human posture. There have been a large number of approaches to feature extraction in the image processing and computer vision area [14, 15, 16]. However up to date, no technique is able to guarantee the sufficient accuracy in feature extraction. Extraction error remains an unavoidable issue. As a matter of fact, such inaccuracy is one of the main factors preventing the progress of reconstruction technology. Besides, the lack of depth information in monocular image source makes it extremely difficult to evaluate the performance of any 3D reconstruction algorithm.

To enable accurate evaluation and assessment of the proposed MTP method, we use computer synthesized videos as input to test the MTP before applying it to real video data. Currently only monocular sequences with resolution of 640x480 pixels and frame rate of 20fps are used. All reconstructions are performed on a Standard Desktop (Pentium 4 CPU 3GHz + 3.01GHz, 1G RAM, GeForce FX 5200). According to statistics, the average time consumed in posture recovery at every single frame is approximately 74.611s without feedback and 103.634s with it. Detailed description and statistics of the experiments on computer synthesized data are available in [11], from which the accuracy of proposed MTP method is illustrated.

After the visual and numerical comparison based on synthesized input data, the MTP method is applied on real monocular videos to further test its accuracy. Since the depth information is not available in such cases, the algorithm can only be evaluated through the visual resemblance in the same viewpoint with the original, but the smoothness and reasonableness of the reconstructed motion are demonstrated also from other viewing directions.

Due to the page limitation only one real video motion sequence composed of walking and squatting (49frames) is presented here in Fig. 2, which is a general human motion including body translation. To ensure accurate image feature extraction and to reduce unnecessary noises, color labels are stuck to the human object at each joint's position. Image processing techniques such as those mentioned in [17] & [18]

are used to extract the 2D joint features from each frame of the video sequences. There bound to be errors in the feature extraction due to many factors such as noises, which will affect the accuracy of the final 3D reconstructed motion.

Fig. 2 clearly shows that the recovered postures resemble the original with the same view. When viewed from other viewpoints, these postures still appear continuous and natural.

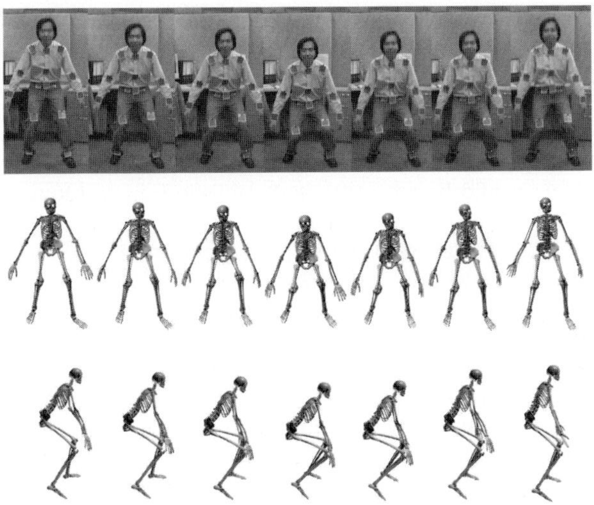

Fig. 2. Top: Two frames from the input video. Middle: Reconstructed motion - front view. Bottom: Reconstructed motion - side view (Walking and Squatting).

Statistics of 2D residuals at each frame are presented in Fig. 3 as well. The maximum value is 6.212234at the 35th frame. This peak residual is very low considering the 640*480 image size. Hence the reconstruction output from real video sequence can be considered as sufficiently accurate.

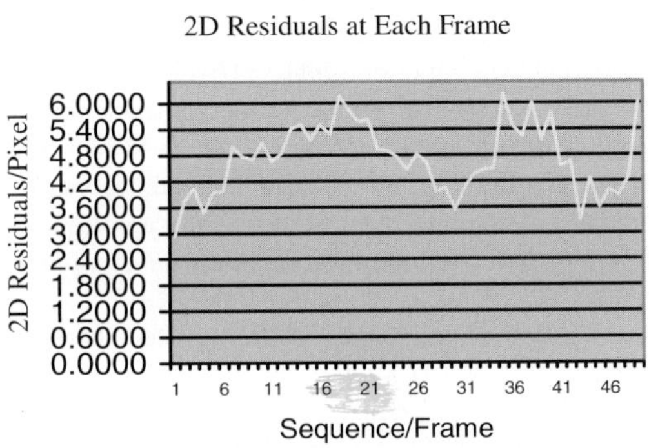

Fig. 3. 2D Residuals at each frame (Walking and squatting)

5 Conclusion

A model-based technique is proposed in this paper for motion reconstruction from un-calibrated monocular video sequences containing unrestricted human motion. The technique is named Motion Trend Prediction (MTP). It is based on the ideas that human motion in neighbouring frames are generally smooth, therefore 3D human body information gathered through posture reconstruction in previous frames could be utilized to recover human posture at current frame. To ensure proper evaluation of the suggested MTP method, "synthesized" data has been employed for visual and numerical comparison between the original and the reconstructed motion. After that real monocular video sequences containing unrestricted human motions are used as input to test the applicability of MTP.

The main advantage of the MTP method is that through it a truly wide range of monocular sequences could be reconstructed, and there is no requirement for camera calibration. All experiment outcomes demonstrate three properties: 1. the recovered motion resembles the original from the same direction the video was taken; 2. when viewed from any other viewpoint, the recovered motion appears smooth, natural, and believable; 3. movements of each and every individual body segments are continuous. In fact, experiments on synthesized input (where depth information is available for comparison only) show that the MTP is able to generate reconstructions which resemble the original motion in 3D. Therefore the proposed MTP method demonstrates great advantages over most of the previous methods, when 2D monocular data is the only available input.

As a future work we are planning to introduce control on the leaf joint. Plausible motions about hands, feet and head are expected to be simulated.

References

1. Hodgins J. K., O'Brien J. F., Bodenheimer R. E.: *Computer Animation*. In *Wiley Encyclopedia of Electrical and Electronics Engineering*, John G. Webster, ed., v. 3, 686-690, 1999
2. Taylor C. J.: Reconstruction of articulated objects from point correspondences in a single image. *Computer Vision and Image Understanding, Vol. 80, No. 3* (Dec. 2000), 349-363
3. Remondina F., Roditakis A.: Human figure reconstruction and modeling from single Image or monocular video sequence. In *Proceeding of the 4th International Conference on 3D Digital Imaging and Modeling* (Oct. 2003), 116-123
4. Liu Xiaoming, Zhuang Yueting, Pan Yunhe.: Video based Human animation technique. In *Proceeding of the 7th ACM International Conference on Multimedia* (Oct. 1999), 353-362
5. Park M. J., Choi M. G., Shin S. Y.: Human Motion Reconstruction from inter-frame feature correspondences of a single video stream using a notion library. In *Proceedings of the 2002 ACM SIGGRAPH/Eurographics symposium on Computer animation* (July 2002), 113-120
6. David E. DiFranco, Tat-Jen Cham, James M. Rehg.: Reconstruction of 3D figure motion from 2D correspondences. In *Proceeding of IEEE Computer Society Conference on Computer Vision and Pattern Recognition*, IEEE Computer Society, 2001
7. Fdor M.: Application of inverse kinenatics for skeleton manipulation in real-time. In *Proceedings of the 19th spring conference on Computer graphics* (Apr. 2003), 203-212

8. Zhao Jianhui, Li Ling.: Human motion reconstruction from monocular images using genetic algorithms. *Computer Animation and Virtual World, Vol. 15, No. 3-4* (July 2004), 407-414
9. Holt R. J., Netravali A. N., Huang T. S., Qian R. J.: Determining Articulated Motion from Perspective Views: A Decomposition Approach. *Pattern Recognition, Vol. 30* (1997), 1435-1449
10. Welch G., Bishop G..: An introduction for kalman filter. Technical report TR 95-041, Department of Computer Science, University of North Carolina at Chapel Hill, 1995
11. Zhang Li, Li Ling: 3D Human Animation from 2D Monocular Data Based on Motion Trend Prediction. In the *Proceedings of the 14th International Conference in Central Europe on Computer Graphics, Visualization and Computer Vision'* (Feb. 2006), 117-124
12. Rose C., Guenter B., Bodenheimer B., Cohen M. F.: Efficient generation of motion transitions using spacetime constraints. In *Proceedings of the 23rd annual conference on Computer graphics and interactive techniques* (Aug. 1996), 147-154
13. Popovic Z., Witkin A.: Physically based motion transformation. In *Proceedings of the 26th annual conference on Computer graphics and interactive techniques* (July 1999), 11-20
14. Agarwal A., Triggs B.: Learning to track 3D human motion from silhouettes. In *Proceedings of the 21st International Conference on Machine Learning* (July 2004), 9-16
15. Gibson D. J., Oziem D. J., Daltion C. J., Campbell N. W.: Capture and synthesis of insect motion. In *Proceedings of the 2005 ACM SIGGRAPH/Eurographics symposium on Computer animation* (Aug. 2005), 39-48
16. Sminchisescu C., Jepson A.: Generative modeling for continuous non-linearly embedded visual inference. In *Proceedings of the 21st International Conference on Machine Learning* (July 2004), 9-16
17. Juan C.D, Bodenheimer B.: Cartoon texture. In *Proceedings of the 2004 ACM SIGGRAPH/Eurographics symposium on Computer animation* (Aug. 2004), pp. 267-276
18. Müller M., Röder T., Clausen M.: Efficient content-based retrieval of motion capture data. *ACM Transactions on Graphics 24*, 3 (July 2005), 677-685

A Straightforward and Intuitive Approach on Generation and Display of Crack-Like Patterns on 3D Objects

Hsien-Hsi Hsieh and Wen-Kai Tai

Department of Computer Science and Information Engineering,
National Dong Hwa University, Taiwan, China
hsi@game.csie.ndhu.edu.tw, wktai@mail.ndhu.edu.tw

Abstract. In this paper a simple approach is proposed to render crack-like patterns and animate cracking propagations on surfaces of 3D objects. With some controllable parameters, generating cracks on an object with variant visual effects such as bumping or carving is flexible. Besides, a proposed script system could generate various cracking animation on 3D objects.

Keywords: Crack-like pattern, Rendering, Cracking propagation.

1 Introduction

Many researches on synthesizing the crack pattern focus on simulation of crack patterns which look like natural ones. However, what and how actually drive cracking are various and complex. Approximate simulation demonstrated good visual results but at the expense of huge amount of computation time. Alternatively, texturing is used to map a crack pattern on a given 3D object. Some inherent problems associated with texturing such as memory space requirement for texture libraries, orientation and scale consistency, the demands of seamless texturing, and animation of cracking propagation make this approach not be a straight and easy solution. A simple approach for crack-like pattern generation, rendering and animating cracking propagation is proposed in this paper.

Our approach is a non-physical approach, namely neither a physical approach nor a semi-physical solution. A feature pattern is extracted by basic image process operations from a crack-like pattern ranging from natural patterns, manual drawing patterns, procedural patterns, and so for forth. By tracking the pixel connectivity in a pattern image, the image could be vectorized and simplified as a planar graph, called a feature pattern. To generate a crack pattern on an object's surface, the planar graph is transformed onto the surface of the paraboloid bounding volume of the target object first. Then the intersections between the 3D object and the perspective polygons, formed by the edges of the transformed graph on the paraboloid bounding volume and corresponding reference points, construct the crack pattern on the object's surface. While rendering a crack pattern on a 3D object, a concept similar to bump mapping [1] is used to make

H.-P. Seidel, T. Nishita, and Q. Peng (Eds.): CGI 2006, LNCS 4035, pp. 554–561, 2006.

bumping or carving visual effect flexible. Finally, various animations of cracking propagation could be produced by proposed script-based traversal schemes.

The rest of paper is organized as follows. Some related works are surveyed in the section 2. In the section 3, we present the framework and describe each stage in the framework specifically. The experimental results are illustrated in section 4. Finally, we conclude the proposed approach and point out some future works.

2 Related Works

Roughly researches in computer graphics for generating cracks and animating fractures can be classified into classes: physical approaches and semi/non-physical approaches. Physical approaches propose a model to represent the structure of object and to simulate the reaction to internal/external forces, such as finite element method (FEM) [2, 3, 4, 5], an experimental system [6, 7], or spring networks [8, 9, 10].

Semi/non-physical approaches dedicated on demonstrating realistic results in visual rather than physical phenomenon, for example, by observation [11], geometrical rules [12], hybrid schemes [13, 14], projecting [15], or texturing [16, 17]. Some approaches can even have visual effects, such as loss of adhesion and curling effects of paint peeling [18] and the cracks found on batik wax paintings and dyeing technique on clothes [19].

3 Proposed Techniques

The framework of crack-like pattern generation and display on 3D objects consists of following stages:

- Applying image processing operations to a given crack-like pattern for obtaining a vectorized feature pattern, regarded as a planar graph
- Transforming the planar graph onto the surface of paraboloid bounding volume of a 3D object.
- Projecting and rendering the crack-like pattern on the surface of the 3D object.
- Animating cracking propagations using proposed traversal schemes.

3.1 Vectorizing Crack-Like Pattern

Various crack-like patterns can be input images. Basic image processing operations [20], like bi-leveling, segmentation, and thinning mechanism [21], are applied to identify a raw feature pattern, which consists of discrete pixels. Then a greedy algorithm is used [15] to construct planar graphs (feature pattern) from the raw feature pattern (thinned input pattern). After the vectorization, some attributes, like edge width, vertex degree, user-specified, etc., can be associated to vertices and edges of the graph to facilitate animation of cracking propagation.

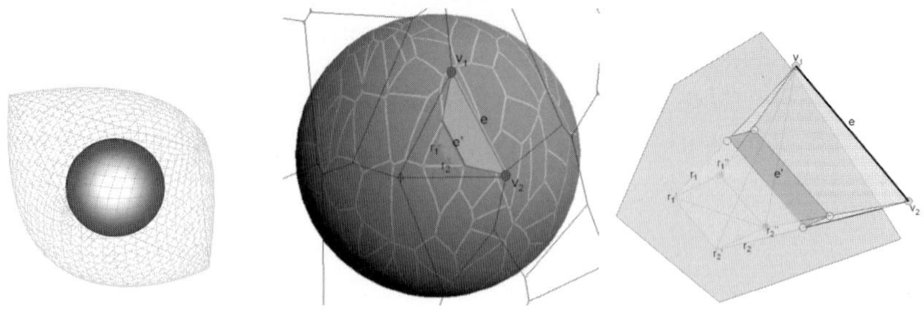

(a) (b) (c)

Fig. 1. Graph transformation and edge projection. (a) A paraboloid bounding volume and an object. (b) Projecting edges with multiple reference points: a quad is formed by an edge $e(v_1, v_2)$ and corresponding reference points r_1 and r_2. Edge e' is the intersection between the object and the quad. (c) Edge projection in quick preview: an octahedron is constructed by an edge $e(v_1, v_2)$ and four jittered vertices $\{r_1^{'}, r_1^{''}, r_2^{'}, r_2^{''}\}$ of the reference points r_1 and r_2. Edge e' is the area in green that will be rendered by graphics hardware.

3.2 Graph Transformation

To generate a planar graph, $G = < V, E >$, on a 3D object, corresponding relationship needs to be set up between vertices in G and the surface. This idea is similar to paraboloid mapping [22]. But instead of generating corresponding texture coordinates for vertices of the 3D object, vertices in G are transformed onto the surface of paraboloid bounding volume of the target object first. Then, all $v_i(x, y) \in V$ are normalized and translated into $v_i'(s, t)$ so that the new origin locates at the center of planar graph. At last, with a rotation factor $U(u, v, w)$, where $u, v, w \in [-4, 4]$, each $v_i'(s, t) \in V$ is transformed into a 3D vertex $v_i'(x, y, z)$ by

$$\begin{bmatrix} x \\ y \\ z \\ 1 \end{bmatrix} = R \begin{bmatrix} r\sin(\frac{s\pi}{2}) \\ -r\sin(\frac{t\pi}{2}) \\ r\cos(\frac{s\pi}{2})\cos(\frac{t\pi}{2}) \\ 1 \end{bmatrix}, \; R = \begin{bmatrix} \cos(\frac{u\pi}{2}) & -\sin(\frac{u\pi}{2})\sin(\frac{v\pi}{2}) & \sin(\frac{u\pi}{2})\cos(\frac{v\pi}{2}) & 0 \\ 0 & \cos(\frac{v\pi}{2}) & \sin(\frac{v\pi}{2}) & 0 \\ -\sin(\frac{u\pi}{2}) & -\cos(\frac{u\pi}{2})\sin(\frac{v\pi}{2}) & \cos(\frac{u\pi}{2})\cos(\frac{v\pi}{2}) & 0 \\ 0 & 0 & 0 & 1 \end{bmatrix},$$

where r is the radius of bounding sphere of the target object; R is the matrix formed by u, v, and w that is used to rotate the paraboloid volume against axis X, Y, and Z respectively. Therefore an object could be bounded by a paraboloid volumes and its mirrored one, as shown in Figure 1a.

3.3 Projecting Crack-Like Pattern

After the graph transformation, all vertices and edges of the planar graph are transformed on the surface of paraboloid bounding volume. All transformed vertices are pinch points if users need to directly edit the transformed graph. These edges are then mapped onto the target object by projecting them to the surface of the object with respect to corresponding reference points. As shown in Figure 1b, projected edges are obtained from the intersections of the object's facets and the polygons formed by endpoints of projecting edges and their corresponding reference points.

Generally a reference point is a point inside the object close to the geometric center of the object. For isotropic-like and convex-like objects like sphere whose shape does not much differ from paraboloid may have good results to one reference point at center, because the projecting edges will be uniformly projected on the surface of object. For other irregular and complex objects, more than one reference points are necessary. However, it is not so easy to select reference points appropriately. A simple and automatic reference points generation is proposed to make edges uniformly projected on the object according to the shape distribution of object.

3.4 Multiple Reference Points Generation

To conduct nonuniform projection, a set of reference points is used. For uniform distributed projection, reference points are generated according to the shape distribution of the target object: we use the vertex mean of the target object, $M(m_x, m_y, m_z)$, vertex variances in three main axises ,$\{\sigma_x, \sigma_y, \sigma_z\}$, and an user-controlled weight $W(w_x, w_y, w_z)$ to generate reference points for approximation of proper shape distribution. Each normalized vertex $v_i(s,t) \in V$ of a planar graph generates a reference point $p_i(x, y, z)$ with the same rotation factor U in graph transformation by

$$\begin{bmatrix} x \\ y \\ z \\ 1 \end{bmatrix} = \begin{bmatrix} \sigma_x w_x & 0 & 0 & m_x \\ 0 & \sigma_y w_y & 0 & -m_y \\ 0 & 0 & \sigma_z w_z & m_z \\ 0 & 0 & 0 & 1 \end{bmatrix} R \begin{bmatrix} \sin(\frac{s\pi}{2}) \\ -\sin(\frac{t\pi}{2}) \\ \cos(\frac{s\pi}{2})\cos(\frac{t\pi}{2}) \\ 1 \end{bmatrix},$$

where R is the rotation matrix as the same in graph transformation. Therefore the projection is more controllable and specific by modifying reference points.

The user-controlled weight W dominates the result of intersection: if W is $(0, 0, 0)$, then all edges in E are projected toward M, the center of target object; if W is anisotropic, the projected pattern will be deformed. If all reference points are inside the target object, the projected pattern will have the same topology as the feature pattern; otherwise, some edges or some parts of the feature pattern will not appear on the surface of the target object. Good reference points could approximately scatter crack projected on an object with equal distribution.

To provide an interactive environment for users to edit parameters of projection is a challenge. Projecting transformed 2D crack pattern on an object involves computation of intersections between perspective polygons and the target object which hardly be completed in realtime . Therefore, we use a stencil technique similar to the one used in the shadow volume [23] with hardware acceleration to have a quick preview and make the interactive control feasible.

3.5 Rendering

Rendering crack patterns on the surface of a 3D object to illustrate realistic visual effect is not a simple work. However, while taking a look at real crack patterns, the luminance of surface changes dramatically around the fracture, i.e., one side of the crack edge is lighter, and the other side is darker. This dramatic change of luminance makes the crack pattern more noticeable. A concept similar to the bump mapping [1] is used to approximate the visual perception of crack patterns. Let N_p be the normal vector at position p on the surface of an object, B_p be the bumping vector at p on a given bump map, and N' be the perturbed normal vector, then we can simply have $N'_p = N_p + B_p$. Considering the Phong lighting model, we have:

$$\begin{aligned} I_p &= I_a K_a + I_i[(N'_p \cdot L)K_d + K_s(N'_p \cdot H)^n] \\ &= I_a K_a + I_i\{[(N_p + B_p) \cdot L]K_d + K_s[(N_p + B_p) \cdot H]^n\} \\ &\approx I_a K_a + I_i[(N_p \cdot L)K_d + K_s(N_p \cdot H)^n] + I_i[(B_p \cdot L)K_d + K_s(B_p \cdot H)^n] \end{aligned} \tag{1}$$

In this approximation, we can divide lighting into two passes, say $I_{i,N}$ and $I_{i,B}$, as follow:

$$I_p \approx I_a K_a + I_i[(N_p \cdot L)K_d + K_s(N_p \cdot H)^n] + I_i[(B_p \cdot L)K_d + K_s(B_p \cdot H)^n] = I_{i,N} + I_{i,B} \tag{2}$$

Furthermore, we can have more flexible rendering results, $I_{i,N} \oplus I_{i,B}$, by blending these two passes, namely

$$I_{i,N} \oplus I_{i,B} = \alpha(p)I_{i,N} + (1 - \alpha(p))I_{i,B}, \text{ where } \alpha(p) \in [0, 1]. \tag{3}$$

Each crack edge is represented by two adjacent quads on the surface of 3D objects, as shown in Figure 1c. The normal at p on the quad, B_p, will be perturbed more when position p is closer the crack by the following equation:

$$B_p = f D_c(p)N_p + (1 - D_c(p))N_q, \tag{4}$$

$$D_c(p) = \begin{cases} \frac{d(C,p)}{dMax} & \text{if } 0 \le d(C,p) < dMax \\ 1 & \text{if } d(C,p) \ge dMax \end{cases}$$

$$d(C,p) = \frac{|(c_2 - c_1) \times (c_1 - x)|}{|c_2 - c_1|}, C = \overline{c_1, c_2}$$

Where $D_c(p)$ is a weight function defined in the interval $[0, dMax]$, $d(C,p)$ determines the distance between the crack C and position p, and $N_q = N_p \times \overrightarrow{c_1 c_2}$. The width of quad, $dMax$, determines how large the cracking effect will be on the surface of an object.

In equation 4, parameter f is a scaling factor to the vector N_p. This makes the representation of bumping effect more flexible, i.e., having smoother or sharper visual effect. Opacity parameter, α, in equation 3, can be a constant or a function of p.

3.6 Animating Cracking Propagation

Animation of cracking propagation can be produced by a sequence of edge traversal on a graph $G = < V, E >$. Different traversal schemes lead to different

Table 1. Commands of the proposed script system

Cmd	Description
B[n]	Propagate with edge connectivity based traversal scheme for n steps.
D[n]	Select a path to propagate for n steps.
P[n]	Edges in higher priority than n keep propagating.
R[n]	Randomly select n vertices as seeds for propagation.
F[n]	Spread a force of n within an iteration.
T[n]	Continuously enforce a force for n seconds.

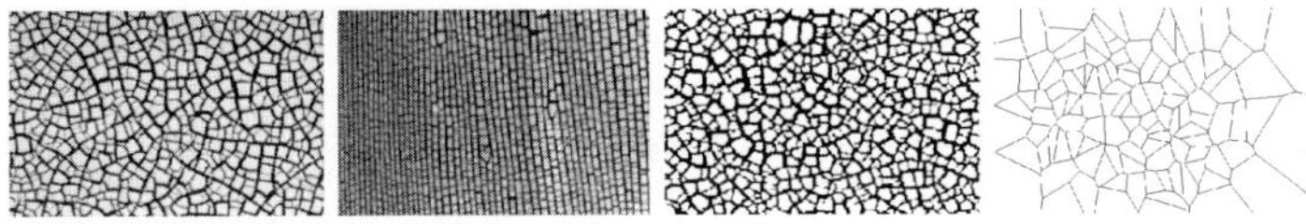

(a) (b) (c) (d)

Fig. 2. Some crack-like patterns: (a) a natural Aluminum Oxide crack pattern, (b) another natural Aluminum Oxide crack pattern, (c) a natural mud crack pattern, and (d) a Voronoi diagram pattern. Pattern a and b are obtained from website http://www.physics.utoronto.ca/nonlinear/gallery.html

cracking propagation. We proposed a script-based traversal system to animate cracking propagation. The scripting system is devised to provide the flexibility of producing variant combinations of cracking propagation. A script is a sequence of traversal schemes to iterate, and edge traversal is the consequence of script iterations. It exploits both the connectivity of graphs and priorities of edges on the object. External forces are given in script to drive the speed of cracking propagation. The scripts are applied to the propagation repeatedly until a stable state. Available schemes in a script are listed in Table 1.

The timing of animation is influenced by given force in iterations of cracking propagation. The propagation of an cracking edge at time t is

$$L(t) = (v' + \frac{F_c \times t_f}{m} - a_n \times t_f)t - \frac{a_n}{2}t^2, \tag{5}$$

where v' is the incoming cracking speed from adjacent edges, F_c is the cracking force, t_f is the forcing period, and a_n is an assumed negative acceleration of cracking propagation due to the resistance. Cracking propagation is progressively estimated frame by frame. For a cracking edge at frame i, the length of propagation will be $L(t_i) - L(t_{i-1})$.

4 Experimental Results

Four crack-like patterns are used in the experiment, as shown in Figure 2. Two visual effects are feasible: bumping and carving effects. Figure 3 shows the rendering results of cracks on 3D objects. As experimental results shown a generated pattern is similar to the original crack-like pattern, and visual effects are obvious and good for 3D objects.

An animation of cracking propagations using script based traversal schemes is shown in Figure 4. It shows six representative snapshots from a novel animation

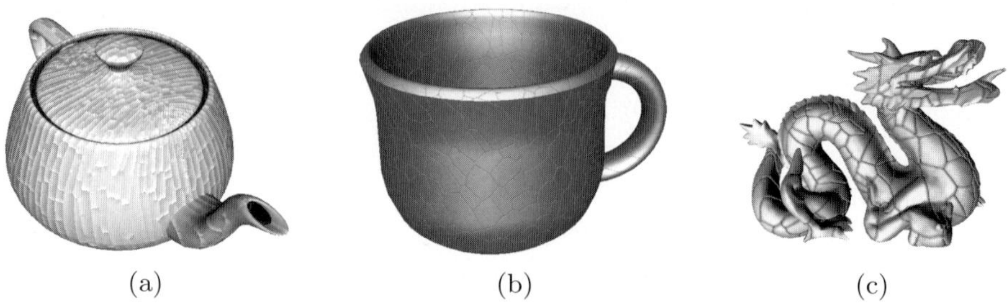

Fig. 3. Rendering crack-like patterns on 3D objects: (a) 2b bumped on a teapot, (b) 2c carved on a teacup, and (c) 2d carved on a dragon

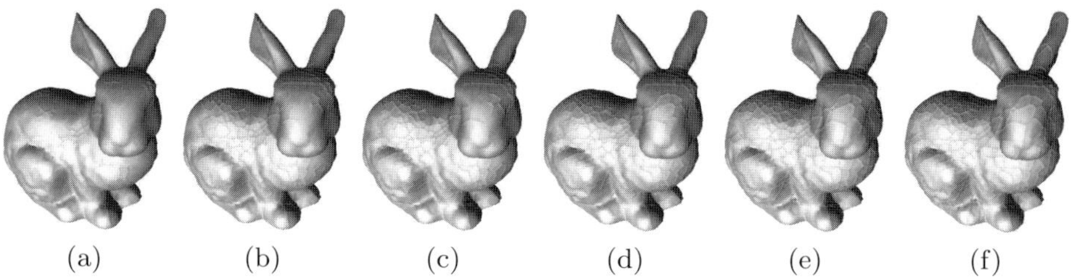

Fig. 4. Six representative snapshots selected from an animation of script based traversal scheme with pattern 2a

generated by a script. A complex script mixed by many traversal schemes could animate a novel propagation and could be used on different graphs or 3D objects to have variety.

5 Conclusion

In this paper, we introduce an approach for crack-like pattern generating, rendering and animation on the surface of a 3D object.

However, there are some limitations in our approach. The projection is not distortionless. Although multiple reference points balance the distortion of each reference point, projection is still not suitable for all objects. Due to the lack of physical material information and detail geometry of cracks, rendering of cracks depends only on the light position is not enough for realistic real cracks. Therefore, in the future, the projection model will be improved, and also will be the illumination model of the crack.

References

1. Blinn, J.F.: Simulation of wrinkled surfaces. In: Proceedings of ACM SIGGRAPH '78. (1978) 286–292
2. Terzopoulos, D., Fleischer, K.: Deformable models. The Visual Computer **4** (1988) 306–331

3. Terzopoulos, D., Fleischer, K.: Modeling inelastic deformation: viscolelasticity, plasticity, fracture. In: Proceedings of ACM SIGGRAPH '88. (1988) 269–278
4. O'Brien, J.F., Hodgins, J.K.: Graphical modeling and animation of brittle fracture. In: Proceedings of ACM SIGGRAPH '99. (1999) 137–146
5. O'Brien, J.F., Bargteil, A.W., Hodgins, J.K.: Graphical modeling and animation of ductile fracture. In: Proceedings of ACM SIGGRAPH 2002. (2002) 291–294
6. Bohn, S., Pauchard, L., Couder, Y.: Hierarchical crack pattern as formed by successive domain divisions. part i: Temporal and geometrical hierarchy. Physical Review E **71**(046214) (2005)
7. Bohn, S., Platkiewicz, J., Andreotti, B., Bedia, M.A., Couder, Y.: Hierarchical crack pattern as formed by successive domain divisions. part ii: Intrinsic transition from determinism to disorder. Physical Review E **71**(046215) (2005)
8. Norton, A., Turk, G., Bacon, B., Gerth, J., Sweeney, P.: Animation of fracture by physical modeling. The Visual Computer **7**(4) (1991) 210–219
9. Hirota, K., Tanoue, Y., Kaneko, T.: Generation of crack patterns with a physical model. The Visual Computer **14**(3) (1998) 126–137
10. Hirota, K., Tanoue, Y., Kaneko, T.: Simulation of three-dimensional cracks. The Visual Computer **16**(7) (2000) 371–378
11. Chiba, N., Wada, S., Kaino, K., Muraoka, K.: A behavioral model of cracks and its applications to CG. Systems and Computers in Japan **22** (1991) 82–91
12. Gobron, S., Chiba, N.: Crack pattern simulation based on 3D surface cellular automata. The Visual Computer **17**(5) (2001) 287–309
13. Müller, M., McMillan, L., Dorsey, J., Jagnow, R.: Real-time simulation of deformation and fracture of stiff materials. In: Proceedings of the Eurographic workshop on Computer animation and simulation. (2001) 113–124
14. Martinet, A., Galin, E., Desbenoit, B., Akkouche, S.: Procedural modeling of cracks and fractures. In: Proceedings of the Shape Modeling International 2004 (SMI'04). (2004) 346–349
15. Hsieh, H.H., Tai, W.K., Chiang, C.C., Yang, M.T.: Flexible and interactive crack-like patterns presentation on 3D objects. Lecture Notes in Computer Science **3280** (2004) 90–99
16. Neyret, F., Cani, M.P.: Pattern-based texturing revisited. In: Proceedings of ACM SIGGRAPH '99. (1999) 235–242
17. Soler, C., Cani, M.P., Angelidis, A.: Hierarchical pattern mapping. In: Proceedings of ACM SIGGRAPH 2002. (2002) 673–680
18. Paquette, E., Poulin, P., Drettakis, G.: The simulation of paint cracking and peeling. In: Graphics Interface 2002. (2002) 59–68
19. Wyvill, B., van Overveld, K., Carpendale, S.: Rendering cracks in batik. In: Proceedings of NPAR 04. (2004) 61–149
20. Gonzalez, R.C., Woods, R.E.: Digital Image Processing, 2nd. Addison-Wesley (2002)
21. Cychosz, J.M.: Efficient binary image thinning using neighborhood maps. Graphics gems IV (1994) 465–473
22. Heidrich, W., Seidel, H.P.: View-independent environment maps. In: Proceedings of the ACM SIGGRAPH/EUROGRAPHICS workshop on Graphics hardware. (1998) 39–ff.
23. Heidmann, T.: Real shadows, real time. Iris Universe **18** (1991) 23–31 Silicon Graphics, Inc.

Near-Optimum Adaptive Tessellation of General Catmull-Clark Subdivision Surfaces

Shuhua Lai and Fuhua (Frank) Cheng

Graphics & Geometric Modeling Lab, Department of Computer Science,
University of Kentucky, Lexington, Kentucky 40506-0046
{slai2, cheng}@cs.uky.edu

Abstract. A new adaptive tessellation method for general Catmull-Clark subdivision surfaces is presented. Development of the new method is based on the observation that *optimum adaptive tessellation* for rendering purpose is a *recursive error evaluation* and *globalization* process. The adaptive tessellation process is done by generating an inscribing polyhedron to approximate the limit surface for each individual patch. The inscribing polyhedron is generated through an adaptive subdivision on the patch's parameter space driven by a recursive error evaluation process. This approach generates less faces in the resulting approximating mesh while meeting the given precision requirement. The crack problem is avoided through globalization of new vertices generated in the adaptive subdivision process of the parameter space. No crack-detection or crack-elimination is needed in the adaptive tessellation process. Therefore, no mesh element splitting to eliminate cracks is necessary. The new adaptive tessellation method can precisely measure the error for every point of the limit surface. Hence, it has complete control of the accuracy of the tessellation result.

1 Introduction

Catmull-Clark subdivision scheme provides a powerful method for building smooth and complex surfaces. Given a control mesh, a *Catmull-Clark subdivision surface* (CCSS) is generated by iteratively refining (subdividing) the control mesh to form new and finer control meshes [3]. Subdivision surfaces can model/represent complex shape of arbitrary topology because there is no limit on the shape and topology of the control mesh of a subdivision surface [3]. But the number of faces in the uniformly refined meshes increases exponentially with respect to subdivision depth. Adaptive tessellation reduces the number of faces needed to yield a smooth approximation to the limit surface and, consequently, makes the rendering process more efficient.

2 Previous Work

A number of adaptive tessellation methods for subdivision surfaces have been proposed [9, 1, 13, 10, 4, 14]. Most of them are *mesh refinement based*, i.e., approximating the limit surface by adaptively refining the control mesh. This approach

H.-P. Seidel, T. Nishita, and Q. Peng (Eds.): CGI 2006, LNCS 4035, pp. 562–569, 2006.

requires the assignment of a subdivision depth to each region of the surface first. Several other adaptive tessellation schemes have been presented as well [1, 10, 4]. A common problem of these schemes is that they all have to develop complicated process to prevent the occurance of cracks.

In addition to various adaptive tessellation schemes, there are also applications of these techniques. In [8] adaptive tessellation method is used to render terrain and in [7] adaptive tessellation is combined with ray tracing techniques to generate some realistic scenes. Adaptive tessellation is so useful that an API has been designed for its general usage [11]. Actually hardware implementation of this technique has been reported recently as well [2].

A problem with mesh-refinement-based, adaptive tessellation techniques is the possible *over-tessellation problem.* Each region, such as a patch, where a subdivision depth is assigned is uniformly subdivided to the level specified by the subdivision depth. Since the subdivision depth is computed based on the largest possible curvature of the region, parts of the region which do not carry such a large curvature will be unnecessarily subdivided.

Another problem is the so called *crack-prevention requirement.* Because the number of new vertices generated on the boundary of a region depends on the subdivision depth, *cracks* would occur between adjacent regions if these regions are assigned different subdivision depths. Hence, such an adaptive tessellation method needs special mechanism to eliminate cracks. This is usually done by performing additional subdivision or splitting steps on the region with lower subdivision depth. As a result, many unnecessary mesh elements are generated.

3 Basic Idea

Given the control mesh of a CCSS and an error tolerance, ϵ, the goal is to generate an approximating polyhedron mesh close enough to the limit surface $\mathbf{S}(u, v)$, i.e., within the error tolerance of $\mathbf{S}(u, v)$, but with as few mesh faces as possible, so that the rendering process of $\mathbf{S}(u, v)$ can be performed efficiently. An approximating polyhedron mesh with the least number of mesh faces is called an *optimum approximating polyhedron mesh.*

Our first goal is to avoid the possible *over-tessellation problem.* It is easy to see that, to achieve such a goal, tessellation process within each patch should also be performed based on the flatness of each local region. This can be accomplished by doing *adaptive subdivision* on the parameter space of each patch that is driven by a *recursive error evaluation process.* Contrary to the *mesh refinement based approaches* which generate approximating polyhedra from 'outside' the limit surface that usually do not interpolate the limit surface, the approximating polyhedron generated by this approach is an *inscribing polyhedron* whose vertices interpolate the limit surface.

For a patch of $\mathbf{S}(u, v)$ defined on $[u_1, u_2] \times [v_1, v_2]$, we approximate it with the *base quadrilateral* formed by its four vertices $\mathbf{V}_1 = \mathbf{S}(u_1, v_1)$, $\mathbf{V}_2 = \mathbf{S}(u_2, v_1)$, $\mathbf{V}_3 = \mathbf{S}(u_2, v_2)$ and $\mathbf{V}_4 = \mathbf{S}(u_1, v_2)$. If the *distance* (error) (to be defined below) between the patch and its base quadrilateral is small than ϵ, the patch is considered *flat* enough and is replaced with the base quadrilateral in the tessellation process. Otherwise, we perform a *midpoint subdivision* on the parameter space by setting $u_{12} = (u_1 + u_2)/2$ and $v_{12} = (v_1 + v_2)/2$ to get four subpatches: $[u_1, u_{12}] \times [v_1, v_{12}]$, $[u_{12}, u_2] \times [v_1, v_{12}]$, $[u_{12}, u_2] \times [v_{12}, v_2]$, $[u_1, u_{12}] \times [v_{12}, v_2]$, and repeat the *flatness testing* (error evaluation) process on each of the subpatches. The process is recursively repeated until the distances (errors) between all the subpatches and their corresponding base quadrilaterals are smaller than ϵ. The vertices of the resulting subpatches are then used as vertices of the inscribing polyhedron that approximates the limit surface. For example, if the four rectangles in Figure 1(a) are the parameter spaces of four adjacent patches of $\mathbf{S}(u, v)$, and if the rectangles shown in Figure 1(b) are the parameter spaces of the resulting subpatches when the above *recursive flatness testing (error evaluation) process* stops, then the limit surface will be *evaluated* at the points marked with small solid circles to form vertices of an inscribing approximating polyhedron of the limit surface.

This is a simple and straightforward process, but the result could be very significant. Note that each face in the inscribed approximating polyhedron for a patch is built with the expectation that it is just close enough to the limit surface but with the maximum possible size. Therefore, if the recursive error evaluation process can indeed provide precise error estimate, then the approximating polyhedron mesh generated by this process is *optimum* or *near-optimum* (in case some faces from different sides of a common boundary of two patches can be merged into a bigger face with the same error size). To ensure that the approximating polyhedron mesh is precisely constructed, we must also be able to precisely evaluate a CCSS at any given parameter point. With parametrization of CCSS becoming available [12, 5], this is always possible now.

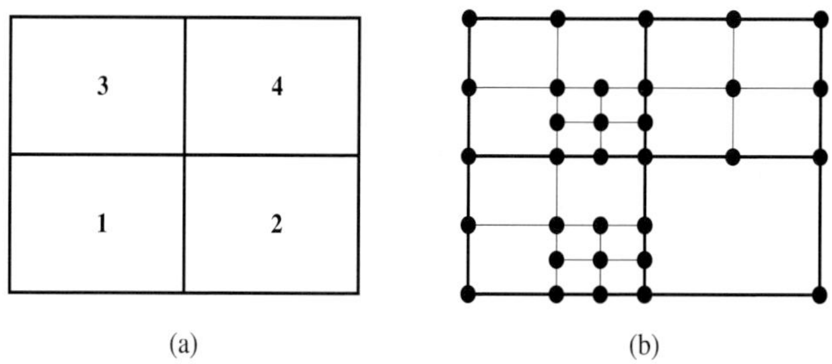

Fig. 1. Adaptive subdivision on parameter spaces of patches

Our second goal is to avoid the *crack prevention requirement.* Due to the fact that adjacent patches are usually approximated by base quadrilaterals from different levels of the midpoint subdivision process, cracks could occur between adjacent patches. For instance, in Figure 2, the left patch is approximated by one base quadrilateral but the right patch is approximated by 7 base quadrilaterals. Consider the boundary shared by the left patch and the right patch. On the left side, that boundary is approximated by a line segment defined by two vertices,

$\mathbf{A}_2$ and $\mathbf{A}_5$. But on the right side, the boundary is approximated by a polyline defined by four vertices, $\mathbf{A}_2$, $\mathbf{C}_4$, $\mathbf{B}_4$, and $\mathbf{A}_5$. They do not coincide unless $\mathbf{C}_4$ and $\mathbf{B}_4$ lie on the line segment defined by $\mathbf{A}_2$ and $\mathbf{A}_5$. But this usually is not the case. Hence, a crack would appear between the left patch and the right patch.

Fortunately Cracks can be removed simply by replacing edges of the base quadrilaterals with appropriate polylines in the tessellation process. Namely, each edge of a base quadrilateral should be replaced with a polyline defined with all the new vertices computed for that edge of the corresponding patch or subpatch. For example, in Figure 2, all the dashed lines should be replaced with the corresponding polylines. In particular, edge $\mathbf{A}_2\mathbf{A}_5$ of the base quadrilateral $\mathbf{A}_1\mathbf{A}_2\mathbf{A}_5\mathbf{A}_6$ should be replaced with the polyline $\mathbf{A}_2\mathbf{C}_4\mathbf{B}_4\mathbf{A}_5$. As a result, the left patch is approximated by the polygon $\mathbf{A}_1\mathbf{A}_2\mathbf{C}_4\mathbf{B}_4\mathbf{A}_5\mathbf{A}_6$, instead of the base quadrilateral $\mathbf{A}_1\mathbf{A}_2\mathbf{A}_5\mathbf{A}_6$, in the tessellation process. For rendering purpose this is fine because graphics systems like OpenGL can handle polygons with any number of vertices and the vertices do not have to be co-planar. Note that, with the above approach, there is no need to perform *crack detection* at all because the resulting approximating polyhedron contains no cracks. Besides, since this process does not increase the number of faces in an approximating polyhedron, the resulting approximating polyhedron is *optimum* or *near-optimum* for the entire CCSS. For convenience of subsequent reference, the process of replacing edges of base quadrilaterals with new polylines is called a *base quadrilateral replacement process.*

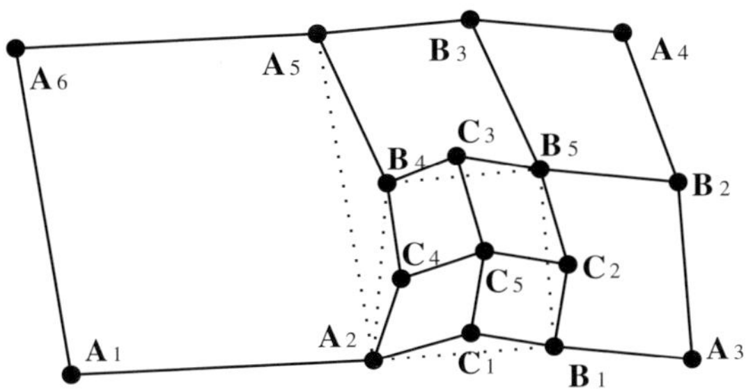

Fig. 2. Cracks between adjacent patches (subpatches)

Note that in previous methods for adaptive tessellation of subdivision surfaces [14, 9, 1, 10], the most difficult part is crack prevention. With the above approach, this part becomes the simplest part to handle and implement.

4 Flatness Testing (Error Evaluation)

In the *flatness testing process*, to measure the difference between a patch (or subpatch) and its *base quadrilateral*, we need to parametrize the base quadrilateral as well. The base quadrilateral can be parametrized with a simple bilinear interpolation:

$$\mathbf{Q}(u,v) = \tfrac{v_2-v}{v_2-v_1}\left(\tfrac{u_2-u}{u_2-u_1}\mathbf{V}_1 + \tfrac{u-u_1}{u_2-u_1}\mathbf{V}_2\right) + \tfrac{v-v_1}{v_2-v_1}\left(\tfrac{u_2-u}{u_2-u_1}\mathbf{V}_4 + \tfrac{u-u_1}{u_2-u_1}\mathbf{V}_3\right) \tag{1}$$

where $u_1 \le u \le u_2$, $v_1 \le v \le v_2$. The *difference* between the patch (or subpatch) and the base quadrilateral at (u, v) is defined as

$$d(u,v) = (\mathbf{Q}(u,v) - \mathbf{S}(u,v)) \cdot (\mathbf{Q}(u,v) - \mathbf{S}(u,v))^T \tag{2}$$

The *distance* between the patch (or subpatch) and the base quadrilateral is the maximum of all the differences:

$$D = \max\{ \sqrt{d(u,v)} \mid (u,v) \in [u_1,u_2] \times [v_1,v_2] \}.$$

To measure the distance between a patch (or subpatch) and the corresponding base quadrilateral, we only need to measure the norms of all local minima and maxima of $d(u, v)$. Note that $\mathbf{Q}(u, v)$ and $\mathbf{S}(u, v)$ are both C^1-continuous, and $d(\mathbf{V}_1)$, $d(\mathbf{V}_2)$, $d(\mathbf{V}_3)$ and $d(\mathbf{V}_4)$ are equal to 0. Therefore, by Mean Value Theorem, the local minima and maxima must lie either inside $[u_1, u_2] \times [v_1, v_2]$ or on the four boundary curves. In other words, they must satisfy at least one of the following three conditions:

$$\begin{cases} \frac{\partial d(u,v)}{\partial u} = 0 \\ v = v_1 \text{ or } v = v_2 \\ u_1 \le u \le u_2 \end{cases} \quad \begin{cases} \frac{\partial d(u,v)}{\partial v} = 0 \\ u = u_1 \text{ or } u = u_2 \\ v_1 \le v \le v_2 \end{cases} \quad \begin{cases} \frac{\partial d(u,v)}{\partial u} = 0 \\ \frac{\partial d(u,v)}{\partial v} = 0 \\ (u,v) \in (u_1,u_2) \times (v_1,v_2) \end{cases} \tag{3}$$

For a patch (or subpatch) that is not adjacent to an extraordinary point (i.e., $(u_1, v_1) \neq (0, 0)$), m is fixed and known $(m(u, v) = min\{\lceil log_{\frac{1}{2}} u\rceil, \lceil log_{\frac{1}{2}} v\rceil\})$. Hence Eq. (3) can be solved explicitly. With the valid solutions, we can find the difference for each of them using Eq. (2). Suppose the one with the biggest difference is $(\hat{u}, \hat{v})$. Then $(\hat{u}, \hat{v})$ is also the point with the biggest distance between the patch (or subpatch) and the corresponding base quadrilateral. The patch (or subpatch) is considered *flat* enough if

$$\sqrt{d(\hat{u}, \hat{v})} \le \epsilon \tag{4}$$

where ϵ is a given error tolerance. In such a case, the patch (or subpatch) is replaced with the corresponding base quadrilateral in the tessellation process.

For a patch that is adjacent to an extraordinary point (i.e. $(u_1, v_1) = (0, 0)$ in Eq. (3)), m is not fixed and m tends to ∞. As a result, Eq. (3) can not be solved explicitly. One way to resolve this problem is to use nonlinear numerical method to solve these equations. But numerical approach cannot guarantee the error is less than ϵ everywhere. For precise error control, a better choice is needed. In the following, an alternative method is given for that purpose.

$\mathbf{S}(u, v)$ and $\mathbf{Q}(u, v)$ both converge to $\mathbf{S}(0, 0)$ when $(u, v) \to (0, 0)$. Hence, for any given error tolerance ϵ, there exists an integer m_ϵ such that if $m \ge m_\epsilon$, then the distance between $\mathbf{S}(u, v)$ and $\mathbf{S}(0, 0)$ is smaller than $\epsilon/2$ for any $(u, v) \in [0, 1/2^m] \times [0, 1/2^m]$, and so is the distance between $\mathbf{Q}(u, v)$ and $\mathbf{S}(0, 0)$. Consequently, when $(u, v) \in [0, 1/2^m] \times [0, 1/2^m]$, the distance between $\mathbf{S}(u, v)$ and $\mathbf{Q}(u, v)$ is smaller than ϵ. The value of m_ϵ, in most of the cases, is a relatively small number and can be explicitly calculated [6].

For other regions of the unit square with $\lceil \log_{\frac{1}{2}} u_2\rceil \le m < m_\epsilon$, eq. (3) can be used directly to find the difference between $\mathbf{S}(u, v)$ and $\mathbf{Q}(u, v)$ for any fixed

$m \in (\lceil \log_{\frac{1}{2}} u_2 \rceil, m_\epsilon)$. Therefore, by combining all these differences, we have the distance between the given extra-ordinary patch (or subpatch) and the corresponding base quadrilateral. If this distance is smaller than ϵ, we consider the given extra-ordinary patch (or subpatch) to be flat, and use the base quadrilateral to replace the extra-ordinary patch (or subpatch) in the tessellation process. Otherwise, repeatedly subdivide the patch (or subpatch) and perform flatness testing on the resulting subpatches until all the subpatches satisfy Eq. (4).

5 Making Patches Visible to Each Other

Currently, all the subdivision surface parametrization and evaluation techniques are patch based [12, 5]. Hence, no matter which method is used in the tessellation process, a patch cannot see vertices evaluated by other patches from its own (local) structure even though the vertices are on its own boundary. For example, in Figure 2, vertices $\mathbf{C}_4$ and $\mathbf{B}_4$ are on the shared boundary of the left and the right patches. But the left patch can not see these vertices from its own structure because these vertices are not evaluated by this patch. So, the key here is to make adjacent patches visible to each other so that new vertices computed by one patch for the shared boundary can be accessed by the other patch. We call this process a *globalization process.*

To make adjacent patches visible to each other and to make subsequent *base quadrilateral replacement process* easier, one should assign a *global index ID* to each evaluated vertex so that all the evaluated vertices with the same 3D position have the same index *ID*. Global indexing allows subsequent processing to be performed on individual patches but still with a global visibility. We also need a step called *adaptive marking* to facilitate the *base quadrilateral replacement process.* The purpose of *adaptive marking* is to mark those points in *uv* space where the limit surface should be evaluated. With the help of the global index *ID*, this step can be done on an individual patch basis. Initially, all (u, v) points are marked 'white'. If surface evaluation should be performed at a point and the resulting vertex is needed in the tessellation process, then that point is marked in 'black'. This process can be easily implemented as a recursive function. A pseudo code for this step is given below.

```
AdaptiveMarking(P, u1, u2, v1, v2)
    Evaluate(P, u1, u2, v1, v2) and AssignGlobalID(P, u1, u2, v1, v2);
    if (FlatEnough(P, u1, u2, v1, v2)) then MarkBlack(P, u1, u2, v1, v2);
    else
        Set u12 = (u1 + u2)/2;   v12 = (v1 + v2)/2;
        AdaptiveMarking(P, u1, u12, v1, v12);
        AdaptiveMarking(P, u12, u2, v1, v12);
        AdaptiveMarking(P, u12, u2, v12, v2);
        AdaptiveMarking(P, u1, u12, v12, v2);
```

This routine adaptively marks points in the parameter space of patch **P**. Function 'Evaluate' evaluates limit surface at the four corners of patch or subpatch **P**

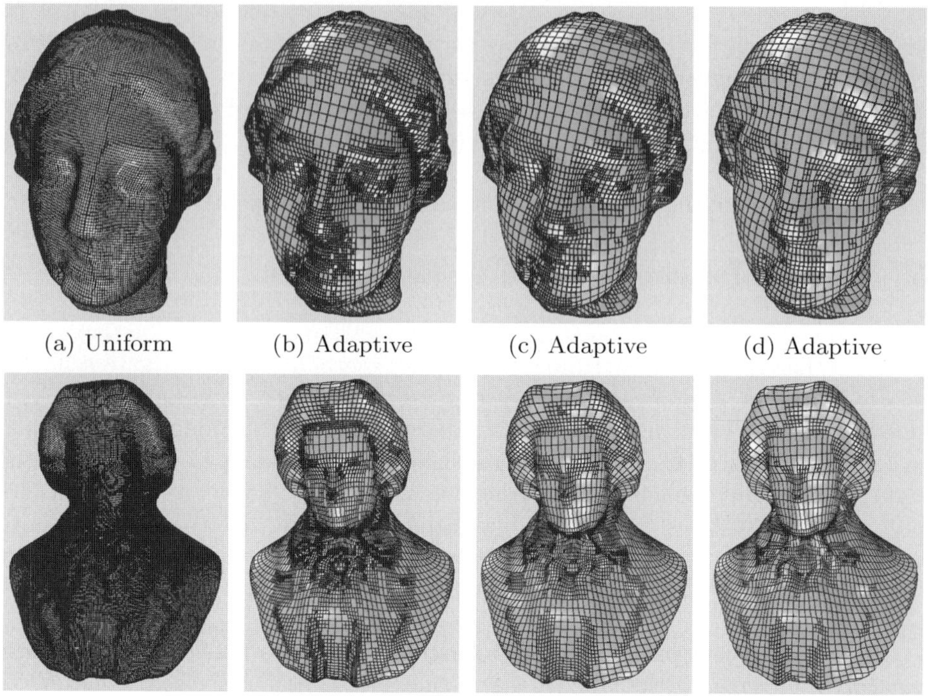

(a) Uniform (b) Adaptive (c) Adaptive (d) Adaptive

(e) Uniform (f) Adaptive (g) Adaptive (h) Adaptive

Fig. 3. Adaptive tessellation of surfaces with arbitrary topology

defined on $[u_1, u_2] \times [v_1, v_2]$. Function 'AssignGlobeID' assignes global index ID to the four corners of **P**. Function 'FlatEnough' uses the method given in Section 4 and Eq. (4) to tell if a patch or subpatch is flat enough. Function 'MarkBlack' marks the four corners of patch or subpatch **P** defined on $[u_1, u_2] \times [v_1, v_2]$ in black. All the marked corner points will be used in the tessellation process.

6 Implementation and Test Results

The proposed approach has been implemented in *C++* using *OpenGL* as the supporting graphics system on the Windows platform. Some of the tested results are shown in Fig. 3. All these testing models have some extra-ordinary points in the input meshes. For the Venus model, uniform subdivision (Fig. 3(a)) generates 65536 polygons, while with a similar or higher accuracy, adaptive tessellation only requires 29830, 21841, and 9763 polygons for Fig. 3(b), 3(c) and 3(d) respectively. For the Beethoven model, uniform subdivision (Fig. 3(e)) generates 65536 polygons, while with a similar or higher accuracy, adaptive tessellation only requires 20893, 15622, and 7741 polygons for Fig. 3(f), 3(g) and 3(h), respectively. Hence the proposed method indeed significantly reduces the number of faces in the resulting tessellation while satisfying the given error requirement.

7 Summary

A new adaptive tessellation method for general CCSSs is presented. The method is developed for rendering purpose and is based on the observation that *optimum adaptive tessellation* for rendering purpose is a *recursive error evaluation* and *globalization* process for indivisual patches. For a CCSS with multi-patches, the result of our work can be improved by running a post-processor to see if some faces from different sides of a patch boundary can be merged into a bigger face with the same error size. However, since the improvement is not significant and the computation is costly, it might not be worth the effort to do so.

Acknowledgement. Research work of the authors is supported by NSF under grants DMS-0310645 and DMI-0422126. Data sets for Fig. 3 are downloaded from the web site: http://research.microsoft.com/~hoppe .

References

1. Amresh A, Farin G, Razdan A, Adaptive Subdivision Schemes for Triangular Meshes, *Hierarchical and Geometric Methods in Scientific Visualization*, 2002.
2. M. Boo, M. Amor, M. Doggett, et.al., Hardware Support for Adaptive Subdivision Surface Rendering, *SIGGRAPH workshop on Graphics hardware* 2001, pp:33-40.
3. Catmull E, Clark J. Recursively generated B-spline surfaces on arbitrary topological meshes, *Computer-Aided Design*, 1978, 10(6):350-355.
4. Isenberg T, Hartmann K, König H, Interest Value Driven Adaptive Subdivision, In *Simulation und Visualisierung*, March 6-7, 2003, Magdeburg, Germany.
5. Lai S, Cheng F, Parametrization of General Catmull Clark Subdivision Surfaces and its Application, *Computer Aided Design & Applications 3*, 1-4, 2006.
6. Lai S, Cheng F, Near-Optimum Adaptive Tessellation of General Catmull-Clark Subdivision Surfaces (complete version), www.cs.uky.edu/~cheng/PUBL/adaptive.pdf.
7. Müller K, Techmann T, Fellner D, Adaptive Ray Tracing of Subdivision Surfaces *Computer Graphics Forum* Vol 22, Issue 3 (Sept 2003).
8. Rose D, Kada M, Ertl T, On-the-Fly Adaptive Subdivision Terrain. In *Proceedings of the Vision Modeling and Visualization Conference*, pp: 87-92, Nov. 2001.
9. Settgast V, Müller K, Fünfzig C, et.al., Adaptive Tesselation of Subdivision Surfaces, In *Computers & Graphics*, 2004, pp:73-78.
10. Smith J, Séquin C, Vertex-Centered Adaptive Subdivision, www.cs.berkeley.edu/~jordans/pubs/vertexcentered.pdf.
11. Sovakar A, Kobbelt L, API Design for adaptive subdivision schemes. 67-72, *Computers & Graphics*, 28, 1, Feb. 2004.
12. Stam J, Exact Evaluation of Catmull-Clark Subdivision Surfaces at Arbitrary Parameter Values, *Proceedings of SIGGRAPH* 1998:395-404.
13. Wu X, Peters J, An Accurate Error Measure for Adaptive Subdivision Surfaces, In *Shape Modeling International*, 2005.
14. Yong J, Cheng F, Adaptive Subdivision of Catmull-Clark Subdivision Surfaces, *Computer-Aided Design & Applications* 2(1-4):253-261, 2005.

Spline Thin-Shell Simulation of Manifold Surfaces

Kexiang Wang, Ying He, Xiaohu Guo, and Hong Qin

Department of Computer Science
Stony Brook University
Stony Brook, NY 11790-4400, USA
{kwang, yhe, xguo, qin}@cs.sunysb.edu

Abstract. It has been technically challenging to effectively model and simulate elastic deformation of spline-based, thin-shell objects of complicated topology. This is primarily because traditional FEM are typically defined upon planar domain, therefore incapable of constructing complicated, smooth spline surfaces without patching/trimming. Moreover, at least C^1 continuity is required for the convergence of FEM solutions in thin-shell simulation. In this paper, we develop a new paradigm which elegantly integrates the thin-shell FEM simulation with geometric design of arbitrary manifold spline surfaces. In particular, we systematically extend the triangular B-spline FEM from planar domains to manifold domains. The deformation is represented as a linear combination of triangular B-splines over shell surfaces, then the dynamics of thin-shell simulation is computed through the minimization of Kirchhoff-Love energy. The advantages given by our paradigm are: FEM simulation of arbitrary manifold without meshing and data conversion, and the integrated approach for geometric design and dynamic simulation/analysis. Our system also provides a level-of-detail sculpting tool to manipulate the overall shapes of thin-shell surfaces for effective design. The proposed framework has been evaluated on a set of spline models of various topologies, and the results demonstrate its efficacy in physics-based modeling, interactive shape design and finite-element simulation.

1 Introduction

Flexible plates and shells are the fundamental geometric structures found in many fields of applied engineering nowadays. Since physics-based method is of great popularity for geometric modeling and simulation in CAD/CAM, the simulation of thin-shell objects is frequently required in modern engineering design practice. However, the modeling and simulation of thin-shells have traditionally been treated as two different stages due to the lack of a common representation scheme. An intermediate data conversion process is often employed to couple the modeling and simulation, but it may deteriorate both accuracy and robustness of the whole system. Therefore, an unified representation would be ideal to overcome such difficulties.

In theory, FEM can provide an approximate solution to the problem of thin-shell deformation, but it still remains as a challenging problem due to two obstacles: Traditional finite-element is exclusively defined on planar domain, thus incapable of describe smooth surfaces and accompanying vector fields of complex manifolds and topologies without patching/trimming; Thin-shell finite-element must be at least C^1 continuous to

H.-P. Seidel, T. Nishita, and Q. Peng (Eds.): CGI 2006, LNCS 4035, pp. 570–577, 2006.

ensure the convergence of the solution according to Kirchhoff-Love theory. However, traditional finite-elements, endowed with purely local polynomial shape functions, usually suffer from the difficulties in enforcing the desired C^1 continuity across the element boundaries.

A number of different approaches have been attempted to combat the aforementioned obstacles in thin-shell simulation. Due to the inherent difficulties in C^1 interpolation, alternative methods have been proposed to compromise the C^1 continuity requirement, such as degenerated solid elements, reduced-integration penalty methods, and many others[1, 2]. Most recently, Cirak *et al.* [3] used the shape functions induced by subdivision rules for thin-shell finite-element simulation. Despite their modeling advantages, the subdivision surfaces do not allow close-form analytic for their basis functions, and have more unnecessary extraordinary points depending on the connectivity of the control mesh (instead of the intrinsic topology of the manifold). Another noteworthy FEM presented in [4] uses Element-Free Galerkin (EFG) method to simulate and analyze Kirchhoff shells and plates. However, it requires extra efforts to combine the model geometry with the simulation process via data conversion. In general, all these approaches fail to provide an effective way to handle thin-shell surfaces with sophisticated topology.

In this paper we articulate a novel framework that naturally couples the modeling and simulation processes for aribitrary thin-shell surfaces. Spline surfaces are prevalent in commercial modeling systems because of their unique advantages in shape modeling, manufacturing and visualization. With the recent development of manifold spline theory [5], which enables the flexible construction of splines over any manifold of arbitrary topologies, we particularly introduce a novel thin-shell finite-element based on triangular B-spline [6] defined over manifold domain. The advantages of our method over the previous state-of-the-art thin-shell simulation include: First, the shell objects of arbitrary topology can be easily modeled by manifold triangular B-splines, with a minimum number of singular points intrinsic to the topological structures of the manifolds; Second, the C^1 continuity requirement can be easily achieved for triangular B-splines; Finally, our spline-based primitive naturally integrates geometric modeling with physical simulation by avoiding unnecessary data conversion and meshing procedure, which can lead to faster product design and development cycle.

2 Spline Representation of Manifold Surfaces

In [5], Gu, He and Qin systematically build the theoretic framework of manifold spline, which locally is a traditional spline, but globally defined on the manifold. First, the manifold is covered by a special atlas, such that the transition functions are affine. Then, the knots are defined on the manifold and the evaluation of polar form is carried out on the charts. Although on different charts, the knots are different, the evaluation value is consistent and independent of the choice of charts. Furthermore, the existence of such atlas depends on the domain topology. This new paradigm unifies traditional subdivision surfaces and splines.

The geometric intuition of the definition of manifold spline is that first we replace a planar domain by the atlas of the domain manifold, and then all the constituent spline patches naturally span across each other without any gap. The central issue of

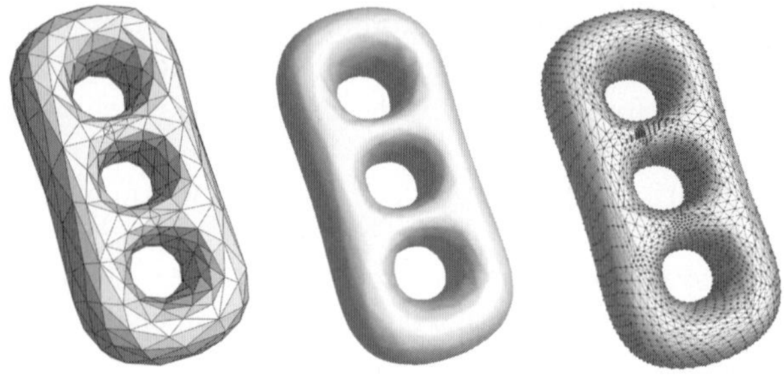

(a) domain (b) spline (c) control points

Fig. 1. A genus-3 manifold triangular B-spline. (a) domain manifold with 742 triangles. (b) cubic manifold triangular B-spline surface. (c) spline overlaid with control points.

constructing manifold splines is that the atlas must satisfy some special properties in order to meet all the requirements for the evaluation independence of chart selection.

In [5], Gu et al. show that for a local spline patch, the only admissible parameterizations differ by an affine transformation. This requires that all the chart transition functions are affine. Furthermore, they show that given a domain manifold M of genus g, a manifold triangular B-spline can be constructed with no more than $|2g-2|$ extraordinary points.

The manifold triangular B-spline can be written as follows:

$$\mathbf{F}(\mathbf{u}) = \sum_{I} \sum_{|\beta|=n} \mathbf{c}_{I,\beta} N(\phi(\mathbf{u})|V_{\beta}^{I}), \quad \mathbf{u} \in M \tag{1}$$

where $\mathbf{c}_{I,\beta} \in \mathbb{R}^3$ are the control points. Given a parameter $\mathbf{u} \in M$, the evaluation can be carried out on arbitrary charts covering $\mathbf{u}$.

Manifold triangular B-splines have many valuable properties which are critical for geometric and solid modeling. For examples, manifold triangular B-splines are piecewise polynomial defined on the manifold domain of arbitrary triangulation. Therefore, the computation of various differential properties, such as normals, curvatures, principal directions, are robust and efficient. The splines have local support, i.e., the movement of a single control point $\mathbf{c}_{I,\beta}$ only influences the surface on the triangle I and on the triangles directly surrounding I. The manifold triangular B-splines are completely inside the convex hull of the control points. The degree n manifold triangular B-splines are of C^{n-1}-continuous if there are no degenerate knots. Furthermore, by intentionally placing knots along the edges of the domain triangulation, we can model sharp features easily. The manifold spline of genus $g(\geq 1)$ has $2g-2$ singular points. See Figure 1 for an example of genus-3 manifold triangular B-spline.

3 Spline Thin-Shell Simulation

3.1 Elastic Thin-Shell Mechanics

The mechanical response of a spline surface with an attached thickness property can be computed with the classical Kirchhoff-Love shell theory. In the interest of smooth technical flow, let us briefly review the derivation of thin-shell equations. Detailed presentation of classical shell theories can be found elsewhere in mechanical engineering literatures.

Thin-shell is a particular form of three-dimensional solid whose thickness is significantly small as compared with the other two dimensions. Let $\mathbf{X}(\theta_1, \theta_2)$ denote the middle surface of the thin shell, where θ_1 and θ_2 are the parametric coordinates of the surface. The generic configuration of the shell can be described as

$$S = \{\mathbf{x} \in R^3 | \mathbf{x} = \mathbf{X}(\theta_1, \theta_2) + \theta_3 \mathbf{X}_{,3}(\theta_1, \theta_2), \quad -\frac{h}{2} \leq \theta_3 \leq \frac{h}{2}\},$$

where $\mathbf{X}_{,3}$ is a unit director vector normal to the middle surface of the shell both in the reference and deformed configuration under the Kirchhoff-Love hypothesis. The internal energy of the shell depends on the differential quantities of the middle surface, such as the metric and curvature tensor. Assuming linearized kinematics, the displacement field of the middle surface is introduced as $\mathbf{u}(\theta_1, \theta_2) = \mathbf{X}(\theta_1, \theta_2) - \mathbf{X}^0(\theta_1, \theta_2)$, where the superscript "0" is used to denote the measurement in the reference configuration. Thus, the linearized membrane and bending strain tensor can be expressed as:

$$\varepsilon_{ij} = \frac{1}{2}(\mathbf{X}^0_{,i} \cdot \mathbf{u}_{,j} + \mathbf{X}^0_{,j} \cdot \mathbf{u}_{,i}), \tag{2}$$

$$\rho_{ij} = -\mathbf{u}_{,ij} \cdot \mathbf{X}^0_{,3} + (\mathbf{J}^0)^{-1}[\mathbf{u}_{,1} \cdot (\mathbf{X}^0_{,ij} \times \mathbf{X}^0_{,2}) + \mathbf{u}_{,2} \cdot (\mathbf{X}^0_{,1} \times \mathbf{X}^0_{,ij})]. \tag{3}$$

where $\mathbf{J} = |\mathbf{X}_{,1} \times \mathbf{X}_{,2}|$, $\mathbf{X}_{,3} = \mathbf{J}^{-1}(\mathbf{X}_{,1} \times \mathbf{X}_{,2})$, and $|\mathbf{X}_{,3}| = 1$. Here, the subscripts take the values of 1 and 2, and a comma denotes partial differentiation. Note that, the derivation of the membrane and strain is independent of the introduction of the kirchhoff-Love hypothesis.

Under the assumption of linearity of elasticity, the strain energy density is defined as follows:

$$W(\mathbf{u}) = \frac{1}{2}\frac{Eh}{1-\nu^2} H^{\alpha\beta\gamma\delta} \varepsilon_{\alpha\beta}\varepsilon_{\gamma\delta} + \frac{1}{2}\frac{Eh^3}{12(1-\nu^2)} H^{\alpha\beta\gamma\delta} \rho_{\alpha\beta}\rho_{\gamma\delta}, \tag{4}$$

in which, the first term is the membrane strain energy density and the second one is the bending strain energy density. Thus, the overall potential energy is as follow:

$$E(\mathbf{u}) = \int_\Omega W(\mathbf{u}) d\Omega + E_{ext} = E_{int} + E_{ext},$$

where E_{int} is the internal elastic energy and E_{ext} is the potential of the applied forces. Following the principle of minimum potential energy, we can get the stable equilibrium configurations of the thin-shell. The Euler-Lagrange equations corresponding to the minimum principle may be expressed in the weak form as:

$$\langle DE_{int}(\mathbf{u}), \mathbf{v}\rangle + \langle DE_{ext}(\mathbf{u}), \mathbf{v}\rangle = 0 \tag{5}$$

where $\mathbf{v}$ is the trial displacement field.

3.2 Spline Element Discretization

Following the construction of manifold triangular B-splines given in (1), we can extract the basis functions and write them by:

$$\varphi^I(\phi(\mathbf{v})) = \sum_{\xi(I,\beta)=I} N(\phi(\mathbf{v})|V^I_\beta) \quad \mathbf{v} \in M \tag{6}$$

in which $\xi : \mathbb{N} \times \mathbb{N}^3 \rightarrow \mathbb{N}$ associates each local simplex-spline with an unique global shape functions it contributes to, ϕ is the conformal mapping, and $\phi(\mathbf{v})$ denotes the point in the planar domain, mapped from a manifold point $\mathbf{v}$. We will use these expression in the following discussion, and represent $\phi(\mathbf{v})$ by $\mathbf{x}$ if necessary.

Thus, we can easily extend the membrane and bending strain tensors from planar parametric domain to manifold domain and write them in the form:

$$\varepsilon(\phi(\mathbf{v})) = \sum_{l=1}^{L} \mathbf{M}^l(\phi(\mathbf{v}))\mathbf{u}_l, \tag{7}$$

$$\rho(\phi(\mathbf{v})) = \sum_{l=1}^{L} \mathbf{B}^l(\phi(\mathbf{v}))\mathbf{u}_l \tag{8}$$

where $\mathbf{B}^l$ are the membrane and bending strain matrices, and $\{\mathbf{u}_l, l = 1, \ldots, L\}$ are the nodal displacement vectors.

Substituting equations (7) and (8) into (5) yields the linear equations developed from the manifold domain as:

$$\mathbf{KU} = \mathbf{F} \tag{9}$$

where $\mathbf{K}$ is the stiffness matrix, $\mathbf{U}$ is the collection of nodal displacement $[\mathbf{u}_1^T \cdots \mathbf{u}_L^T]^T$, and $\mathbf{F}$ is the nodal force vector. $\mathbf{K}$ is a block matrix which can be conveniently assembled by filling in the following 3×3 matrices:

$$\mathbf{K}^{IJ} = \int_M \left[\frac{Eh}{1-\nu^2}(\mathbf{M}^I)^T\mathbf{H}\mathbf{M}^J + \frac{Eh^3}{12(1-\nu^2)}(\mathbf{M}^I)^T\mathbf{H}\mathbf{M}^J \right] dM$$

with the constitutive matrix $\mathbf{H}$ made of contravariant metric tensors, the definition of which is available in [3]. The construction of $\mathbf{F}$ will be discussed later.

3.3 Implementation Details

Numerical Integration: The thin-shell FEM simulation needs to compute the Kirchhoff energy of the deformed shell surfaces. However, the evaluation of the integrations over arbitrary manifold surfaces has been a challenging problem, which is usually awkwardly handled by piecewise parameterizations. With the global conformal mapping coupled with triangular B-splines theory, we can conduct the integration on an equivalent planar domain instead, and use any established numerical integration techniques. In our system, the shell elements are selected as the triangles of the tessellation, from which the triangular spline is constructed. Then we regularly subdivide each element into small congruent triangles, and compute the integration using triangle Gaussian quadratures.

Boundary Condition Handling: To facilitate the process of intuitive geometric design, we include point-based constraints as the input for our thin-shell simulation system. The users are allowed to pick up a group of points on the spline surfaces, i.e. $\mathbf{P}^0 = \{p_1^0, p_2^0, \ldots, p_n^0\}$, and assign them with desired positions after the deformation, i.e. $\mathbf{P} = \{p_1, p_2, \ldots, p_n\}$, where n denotes the total number of the point constraints. This linear constraints thus defined can be grouped in a matrix format as:

$$\mathbf{P}^0 + \mathbf{Cu} = \mathbf{P}$$

where $\mathbf{C}$ is an extremely sparse matrix that stores the basis function values at corresponding constraint points $\mathbf{P}^0$. To combine the constraints with the Equation (9), we solve for $\mathbf{u}$ in the Null-space of $\mathbf{C}$, such that:

$$\mathbf{u} = \mathbf{Nu}' + \mathbf{u}^0$$

where $\mathbf{CN} = 0$ and $\mathbf{Cu}^0 = \mathbf{P} - \mathbf{P}^0$. We use gaussian-jordan-elimination-like approach[7] to construct $\mathbf{N}$, and solve for $\mathbf{u}^0$ by either singular value decomposition (SVD) or QR decomposition method. Due to the extreme sparsity and rank-deficiency of $\mathbf{C}$, such method is computationally viable to handle point-based geometric constraints.

Level-of-Detail (LOD) Simulation: The shell objects with affluent surface details requires massive number of degrees of freedom (DOF) for accurate geometric modeling. However, the triangular B-splines models having large number of control points are not suitable for interactive geometric design. Thus, we incorporate a level-of-detail (LOD) strategy to accommodate thin-shell deformation of sophisticated models. Any thin-shell surfaces $\mathscr{S}$ can be decomposed to a smooth spline-based surface $\mathbf{S}_0$ and a scalar function d describing the additional displacements, i.e.:

$$\mathbf{S}(\mathbf{x}) = \mathbf{S}_0(\mathbf{x}) + d(\mathbf{x}) \cdot \mathbf{n}(\mathbf{x})$$

where $\mathbf{n}$ is the normal vector of $\mathbf{S}_0$. Practically, $\mathbf{S}_0$ can be estimated by fitting the original surface using manifold triangular B-spline with relatively small number of control points [8]. Then the magnitudes of the fitting errors along the normal directions will be further modeled as a spline-based function d with more degree of freedoms. For the LOD simulation of a complicated thin-shell model, our system allows users to sculpt on the base surfaces $\mathbf{S}_0$, then the previously recorded details will be automatically applied to give the final design results. Figure.2 gives two examples of geometric design with LOD thin-shell simulation.

4 Results

Our system is implemented on a Microsoft Windows XP PC with Intel Pentium IV 3.0GHz CPU, 1.0GB RAM, and an nVidia GeForce Fx 5600 Ultra GPU. We have run a variety of examples to verify and test the efficacy and performance of our method. These examples includes a female face, the stanford bunny, a torus and a kitty. Both the face and the bunny are LOD-modeled. And both the torus and the kitty models have non-trivial genus.

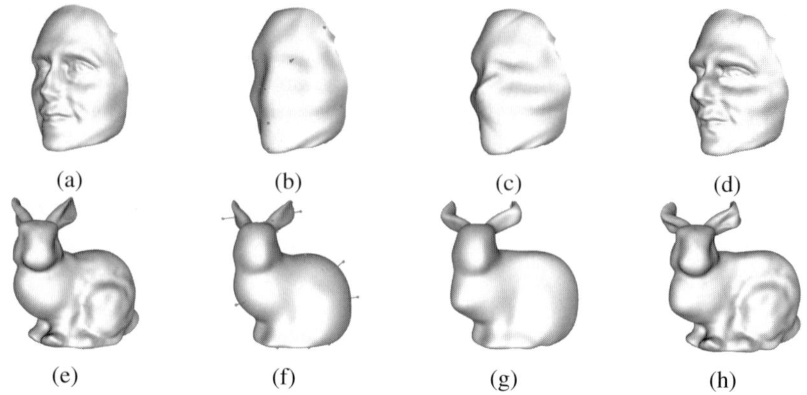

Fig. 2. LOD thin-shell simulation (a)(e) the original surfaces with feature details. (b)(f) the base surfaces with geometric constraints. (c)(g) the base surfaces after thin-shell deformation. (d)(h) the original surface after LOD thin-shell deformation.

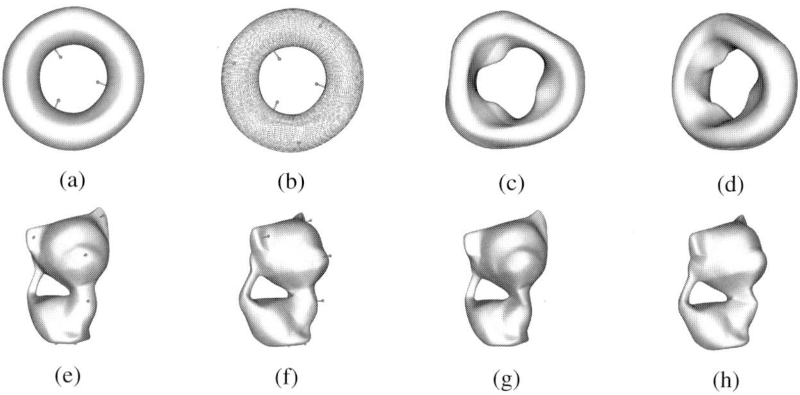

Fig. 3. (a)(b) 6 points constraints applied on the torus surface. (c)(d) torus shell after deformation. (e)(f) the front and side view of the kitty with points constraints. (g)(h) the front and side view of the deformed kitty shell.

5 Conclusion

In this paper, we propose a novel paradigm that successfully simulates the elastic deformation of thin-shell objects. We also provide users with a LOD sculpting tool for esthetical geometric design. The experiment results show demonstrate that the proposed thin-shell FEM method has the following advantages over the traditional ones. It can easily achieve the C^1 continuity requirement, and represent arbitrary thin-shell surfaces using splines with minimum number of singular points. Our spline-based primitive naturally integrates geometric modeling with physical simulation in the entire CAD/CAM process, thus unnecessary data conversion and meshing procedure is total avoided. For future work, we will extend current framework to handling large thin-shell deformation by considering non-linear elastic energy, and solve the simulation problem in temporal dimension for animation applications.

Acknowledgements

This research was partially supported by the NSF grant ACI-0328930, the ITR grant IIS-0326388, and the Alfred P. Sloan Fellowship.

References

1. Bucalem, M., Bathe, K.: Finite element analysis of shell structures. Arch. Comput. Method Eng. **4** (1997) 3–61
2. MacNeal, R.: Perspective on finite elements for shell analysis. Finite Elem. Anal. Des. **30** (1998) 175–186
3. Cirak, F., Ortiz, M., Schröder, P.: Subdivision surfaces: a new paradigm for thin-shell finite element analysis. Int. J. Numer. Methods Eng. **47** (2000) 2039–2072
4. Krysl, P., Belytschko, T.: Analysis of thin plates by the element-free galerkin method. Comput. Mech. **17** (1996) 26–35
5. Gu, X., He, Y., Qin, H.: Manifold splines. In: Proc. ACM Symp. Solid and Physical Modeling. (2005) 27–38
6. Dahmen, W., Micchelli, C.A., Seidel, H.P.: Blossoming begets b-spline built better by b-patches. Math. Comput. **59**(199) (1992) 97–115
7. Celniker, G., Welch, W.: Linear constraints for deformable non-uniform b-spline surfaces. In: Proc. ACM Symp. Interactive 3D Graphics. (1992) 165–170
8. He, Y., Qin, H.: Surface reconstruction with triangular b-splines. In: Proc. Geometric Modeling and Processing. (2004) 279–290

Target Shape Controlled Cloud Animation

Shengjun Liu[1], Xiaogang Jin[1], and Charlie C.L. Wang[2]

[1] State Key Lab of CAD&CG, Zhejiang University,
Hangzhou, 310027, P.R. China
{liushengjun, jin}@cad.zju.edu.cn
[2] Department of Automation and Computer-Aided Engineering,
The Chinese University of Hong Kong
cwang@acae.cuhk.edu.hk

Abstract. This paper proposes a geometry-based technique to control the target shape and the motion of clouds in computer animation so that the synthetic appearance of the clouds resembles a specified three-dimensional shape. The technology for automatically generating this special effect has been desired by the movie industry for many years. Our method is based on ellipsoid decomposition. Firstly, ellipsoids are employed to approximate a given mesh model which indicates the target shape of cloud animation. After that, the target object is represented in a blobby implicit surface using ellipsoidal blobs. Finally, two geometry-based schemes are introduced to generate the cloud animations with target shape controlled in two different ways: aggregated from several pieces of clouds or diffused from one piece of cloud.

1 Introduction

Cloud is an important element of natural scene with their various fascinating appearances. Moving clouds usually give plenty of space for imagination. We feel exciting when a cloud in the sunshiny sky resembles the shape of an animal or some other real objects. The purpose of this paper is to introduce an approach that can automatically generate the plausible motion for clouds, which resembles a user-specified 3D shape in the end.

An effective solution will be presented here. Our method involves using blobby models to approximate the given model and to simulate the metamorphosis between objects with cloudy appearances. The basic idea lies in the use of an ellipsoidal blobby model to approximate the shape of a given object. By the ellipsoidal blobs of a blobby model, it is very easy to control the shape of clouds during the motion which finally matches the target shape.

Major contributions of this paper include a geometric framework for the 3D animation of clouds with target shape controlled, an automatic scheme for approximating a given model by ellipsoidal blobby objects, and two novel geometry-based schemes for cloud animations — one simulates the motion of clouds in an aggregation manner while the other in a diffusion way.

H.-P. Seidel, T. Nishita, and Q. Peng (Eds.): CGI 2006, LNCS 4035, pp. 578–585, 2006.

2 Previous Work

Implicit surfaces are widely used in computer graphics applications. An implicit surface S is usually defined by a continuous scalar function $f(\mathbf{x})$ with $\mathbf{x} \in \Re^3$. The geometry of S is given by the locus of points at which the function $f(\mathbf{x}) = 0$. An important class of implicit surfaces is the so-called blobby model [1]. The implicit functions of these surfaces are the sum of radial symmetric functions that have a Gaussian profile, which are generally in the form of

$$f(\mathbf{x}) = -t + \sum_{i=1}^{n} \omega_i f_i(\mathbf{x}). \tag{1}$$

In this formula, the parameter t is the threshold of isosurface S, n is the number of blobby primitives, ω_i is the weight for the ith primitive with default value 1.0, and the function f_i describes the profile of a blobby sphere with a particular center and radius. For a model with complex shape such as a human body, it is a hard and tedious task to construct blobs for the model manually. Therefore, some automatic approaches [2, 3, 4] were developed — they all employed spheres as primitives. As spheres are isotropic, the aliasing errors on sharp or thin features are relative great when using spherical blobby objects to express the shape of given models. Thus, we will conduct an ellipsoidal blobby implicit surface to fit a given model so that the quality of approximation can be improved.

A novel practical method is proposed for automatically approximating polygonal meshes with ellipsoidal blobby models. First of all, the given object M is decomposed into a set of ellipsoids. The ellipsoids are then employed as initial primitives in the blobby model. In the following, the isosurface defined by these ellipsoidal blobs is refined to improve the approximation through a numerical optimization. Compared with other earlier techniques [2, 3, 4], the approach presented here is more robust and efficient. Objects with complex topology and geometry can be automatically approximated by ellipsoidal blobs in our scheme. This greatly benefits the animation applications.

In computer graphics, there are two categories of works to simulate the gaseous motion of clouds or smokes. The approaches in one category simulate the physical process of fluid dynamics [5, 6, 7, 8], and the ones in another category are heuristic [9, 10, 11, 12, 13, 14]. But none of aforementioned methods are sufficient for our purpose — to efficiently generate a target shape controlled cloud animation.

Based on the ellipsoidal blobby representation of target shapes, we proposed two schemes to realize cloud animations, by which controlling the shape and the motion of clouds becomes an easy task. The first scheme is to simulate the motion of clouds in an aggregation way by keeping the correspondences between the ellipsoidal blobs and interpolating the positions and shapes of blobs using key-frame technique. In the second scheme, we use the results of ellipsoid decomposition to generate a showing sequence of blobs and then produce the animation of cloud diffusion which matches the target object.

The rest of the paper is organized as follows. We present the process of ellipsoid decomposition for a given polygonal model in section 3. Next, the technology of using an ellipsoidal blobby model to approximate given objects is detailed in section 4. After that, we introduce the aggregation and the diffusion based cloud animation schemes followed by several results of ellipsoidal blobby model approximation and cloud animation. Lastly, the paper ends with the conclusion section.

3 Ellipsoid Decomposition

For a given polygonal mesh, obviously there are many different possible ellipsoid decompositions. In [15], Stephan and Kobbelt designed an algorithm to find one candidate among this multitude of decompositions that is locally optimal with respect to the shape, the orientation and the distribution of ellipsoids. Here, we follow their method with some necessary modifications to generate the initial ellipsoidal primitives of a blobby model.

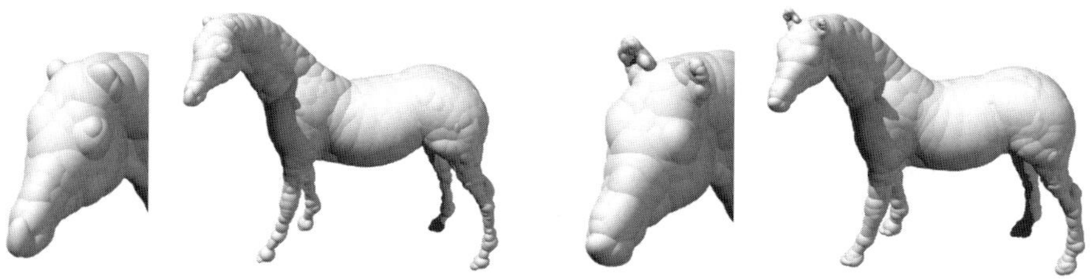

(a) The decomposition by using [15]. (b) The decomposition of our approach.

Fig. 1. Results of ellipsoid decomposition

- To grow the ellipsoid as big as possible, instead of using the exact touching points **p**, **q**, **r**, **s**, the authors in [15] employed points **p**′, **q**′, **r**′, **s**′ which are obtained by shifting the original points by some small offset ε along normal direction into the interior of the mesh. However, during our investigation, we found that processing the points in this manner will make some small features neglected during the ellipsoid selection because of their small volume contribution. Therefore, we generate the points **p**′, **q**′, **r**′, **s**′ by shifting the original points along normal direction outwards the mesh instead. The approximation error introduced by this point shifting will be compensated during the blobby fitting later.
- Furthermore, in the procedure of ellipsoid selection, the geometry significance is considered together with the volume contribution. We use the curvature at each seed point as the volume contribution weight so that the ellipsoids whose volume contributions are small but are important to the surface features can be selected. It is greatly helpful for preserving small features on the given model.
- Lastly, for the given model with a very dense mesh, we adopt the vertices of simplified model (with quadratic error controlled) as the seeds for generating ellipsoids, instead of randomly selected seed vertices. It is because

that random selection may result in losing some important features of the model, but using a good mesh simplification algorithm can preserve them on original models. In this paper, we adopt the algorithm of [16].

With above modifications, the ellipsoid decomposition result is significantly improved. For instance, two decomposition results shown in Fig. 1 are from the original approach [15] and our modification. It is easy to find that ours preserves the details much better, which provides a good start for the following ellipsoidal blobby model reconstruction.

4 Reconstruction of Ellipsoidal Blobby Models

With the ellipsoids decomposed from the given mesh model M as input, an ellipsoidal blobby model Ω approximating M is reconstructed from the ellipsoids by taking their centres as the skeletons with associated field functions. The isosurface of Ω approximates the surface of M. After that, the parameters of blobs in Ω are optimized to improve the approximation.

4.1 Mathematical Representation

Field functions employed in a blobby model can be classified into global and local ones. In this paper, we choose the following local field function

$$f_i(\mathbf{p}) = \begin{cases} B_i^2(1 - \frac{r_i^2}{R_i^2})^2, \text{ if } r_i \in [0, R_i] \\ 0, \qquad\qquad\qquad \text{elsewhere} \end{cases} \tag{2}$$

which is originally employed for a spherical blobby model, where i represents the index of a primitive, $r_i = d(\mathbf{p}, \mathbf{c}_i)$ returns the Euclidean distance from a given point $\mathbf{p}$ to the center of blob $\mathbf{c}_i$, $R_i = \sqrt{e_i^2(1 + A_i)}$ defines the influence region, e_i is the radius of ith sphere. A_i and B_i are two parameters that can be adjusted in a field function — A_i is used to adjust the influence radius and B_i is conducted to change the shape of f_i. Substituting the field functions into Eq.(1) defines an implicit surface using points as skeletons which is similar to the function in [4], but provides two more parameters on each field function to adjust the implicit surface.

When using the field function defined in Eq.(2), all primitives are spheres. We modified it in the following way to introduce ellipsoidal blobs

$$f_i^{new}(\mathbf{q}) = f_i(\mathbf{Tq}) = f_i(\mathbf{p}) \tag{3}$$

where $\mathbf{T}$ is a transformation matrix to map a point $\mathbf{q}$ on an ellipsoid E onto a point $\mathbf{p}$ on its largest inscribed sphere S. In general, an ellipsoid can be represented implicitly by a matrix $\mathbf{Q}$ as $[x\ y\ z\ 1]\mathbf{Q}[x\ y\ z\ 1]^T = 0$, and a sphere can be expressed as $[x\ y\ z\ 1]\mathbf{P}[x\ y\ z\ 1]^T = 0$, where $\mathbf{P}$ is a matrix. Relating them by $\mathbf{P} = \mathbf{TQT}^T$, we can determine the transformation matrix $\mathbf{T}$. The mathematical representation of an ellipsoidal blobby model is then obtained by substituting Eq.(3) into Eq.(1).

4.2 Model Reconstruction

The ellipsoidal blobby model Ω approximating a given polygonal object can then be reconstructed through an automatic procedure. First of all, we take the ellipsoids generated by the decomposition presented in section 3 as the initial blobs — the transformation matrix of each ellipsoid and its largest inscribed sphere are computed at the meanwhile. After that, a numerical optimization is conducted to reduce the difference between the isosurface of Ω and the given model. To accelerate the optimization procedure, the centers of blobs are fixed, so we have only two parameters to be optimized for each blob. For all the examples shown in this paper, the isosurfaces are computed on $f(\mathbf{x}) = 0$ with the threshold parameter $t = 1.0$. The approximation error on the isosurface of an ellipsoidal blobby model is improved through a numerical optimization, where the parameters A_i and B_i of each blob are computed.

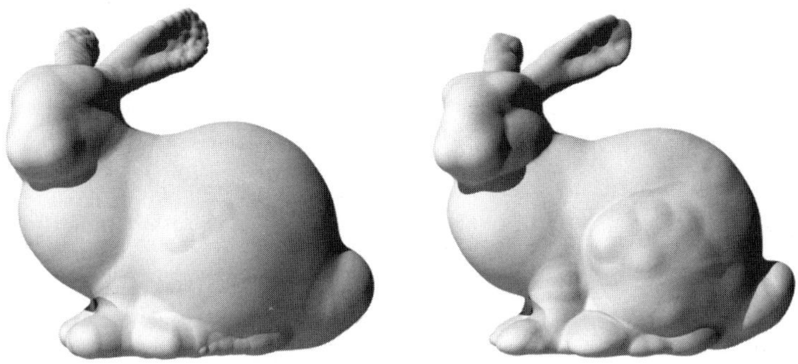

Fig. 2. The reconstructed implicit surfaces using spherical (left: with 422 blobs) and ellipsoidal (right: with 300 blobs) blobby objects respectively

Fig. 2 shows a comparison of the reconstructed blobby models using spherical blobs vs. ellipsoidal blobs, where the left is the result using a spherical blobby model defined by 422 blobs and the right one is an ellipsoidal blobby model with only 300 blobs. From the results, we can easily find that the ellipsoidal blobby model gives a better result with even less primitives.

5 Cloud Animation

In this section, two schemes are proposed for generating cloud animations with target shape controlled. The first one simulates a large scale cloud animation where several pieces of clouds are aggregated into the target shape progressively; in the second scheme, the cloud with a specified target shape is morphed starting from one piece of cloud in a diffusion manner. Both schemes are geometry-based and can generate cloud animations either automatically or semi-automatically.

5.1 Aggregation Scheme

The motion of clouds in an aggregation manner is produced backwards. To simulate the aggregation, the blobs approximating the target shape are firstly subdivided into several subsets. Then, the shape of clouds corresponding to each subset of blobs is modelled at several key-frames during the animation. Finally, the cloud animation is generated by interpolating the positions and shapes of blobs between key-frames. An example animation produced by this scheme will be shown in the following section.

5.2 Diffusion Scheme

Different from the aggregation scheme, in this scheme, the cloud animation is produced in a forward manner. When we progressively display the ellipsoidal blobs of a blobby model in some sequence, we can simulate the diffusion effect of fluid dynamics similar to [8].

To generate a diffusion-like animation, we classify the blobs into three categories:

- Category I: The initial cloud blob;
- Category II: The cloud blobs represent the target shape roughly;
- Category III: The blobs refine the target shape of clouds.

As the greedy optimization is conducted in the ellipsoid selection (section 3), the first selected ellipsoid is always with the largest volume (which is classified to the blob in category I) followed by the ellipsoids adding which leads to the most significant change of the volume among the rest ones. Thus, except the very beginning one, the first 10% blobs in the decomposition sequence are classified into category II while the rest 90% fall into the last category. The blobs of three categories are consecutively added into the implicit model (defined in Eq.(1)) to generate the diffusion-like cloud animation.

6 Results

We have implemented the methods proposed in this paper on a PC with standard configuration (Inter PIV 2.4GHz CPU + 512MB RAM). Our algorithm has been tested on a variety of polygonal models. Satisfactory results can be robustly obtained by our implementation. In the following, several examples will be given, where all the images are rendered by ray tracing.

Figures 3-4 show the experimental results of approximating polygonal meshes by ellipsoidal blobs. Each figure is arranged in pair, with a polygonal mesh and its corresponding ellipsoidal blobby model. Fig. 3 gives the bunny implicit surface defined by 300 ellipsoidal blobs whose mesh consists of 2557 vertices. In Fig. 4, the polygonal model which has 48486 vertices and the ellipsoidal blobby model of a horse with 400 blobs are shown.

An example of clouds animated by the aggregation scheme in section 5.1 is shown in Fig. 5. Eight frames from the animation sequence are selected. The

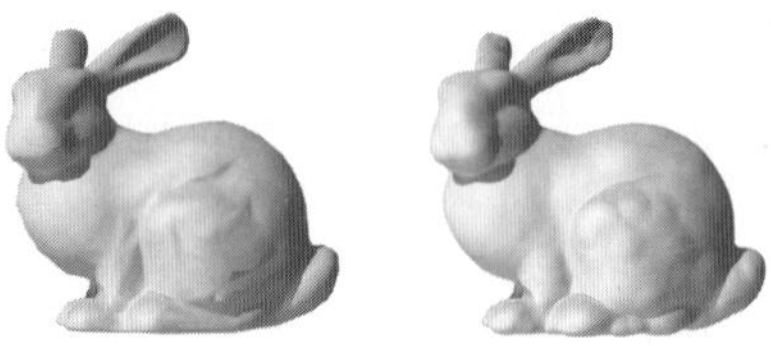

Fig. 3. Bunny: a polygonal model (left) and the implicit surface using ellipsoidal blobby fitting (right) with 300 blobs

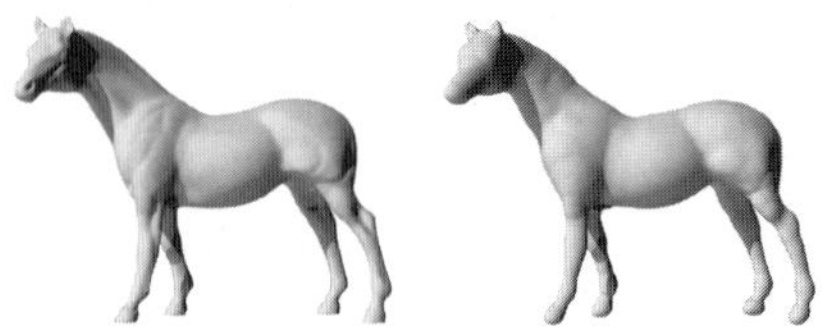

Fig. 4. Horse: a polygon model (left) and its ellipsoidal blobby representation (right) with 400 blobs

Fig. 5. The cloud animation forming a dragon shape produced by the aggregation scheme

animation simulates the special effect with several pieces of clouds morphing into a cloudy dragon.

7 Conclusion

This paper developed a technique for producing cloud animations with target shape controlled. Our approach is geometry-based. Therefore, compared with those physically-based modeling methods, the method presented in this paper is much faster. For a user specified target shape (representing in a polygonal mesh), we conduct an ellipsoidal blobby model to approximate it. Based on this blobby fitting, two schemes are introduced to produce the cloud animation. One scheme simulates the phenomenon that several pieces of clouds aggregate together to resemble the target cloudy shape, and the other scheme diffuses one piece of cloud into a cloud with the user specified target shape. Both of these schemes can efficiently generate realistic cloud animations that mimic the results produced by the time-consuming physics-based modeling approaches.

The limitation of the proposed approach is that aliasing exists on sharp features when using a blobby implicit surface to approximate the shape of a given polygonal model. Although the ellipsoidal blobs can improve the result in some degree comparing with the spherical blobs, the approximation does not converge to the discontinuous features even if the sampling rate is increased. This is because that the primitives in a blobby model are all continuous. To solve this convergence problem, some other quadratic primitives with sharp edges/corners will be considered in our future research.

Acknowledgements

This project is supported by the National Natural Science Foundation of China (Grant No. 60573153), Natural Science Foundation of Zhejiang Province (Grant No. R105431), Huo Ying-Dong Education Foundation (Grant No. 91069) and Program for New Century Excellent Talents in University (Grant No. NCET-05-0519). The author from the Chinese University of Hong Kong would like to thank the support from the projects CUHK/2050341.

References

1. J. F. Blinn. A generalization of algebraic surface drawing. *ACM Transactions on Graphics*, 1(3):235–256, 1982.
2. S. Muraki. Volumetric shape description of range data using blobby model. *Computer Graphics*, 25(4):227–235, July 1991.
3. E. Bittar, N. Tsingos, and M. P. Gascuel. Automatic reconstruction of unstructured 3D data: combining a medial axis and implicit surfaces. *Computer Graphics Forum*, 14:457–468, 1995.
4. X. G. Jin, S. J. Liu, C. C. L. Wang, J. Q. Feng, and H. Q. Sun. Blob-based liquid morphing. *Computer Animation and Virtual Worlds*, 16:391–403, 2005.
5. J. T. Kajiya and B. P. V. Herzen. Ray tracing volume densities. *Computer Graphics*, 18(3):165–174, 1984.
6. A. Treuille, A. McNamara, Z. Popovic, and J. Stam. Keyframe control of smoke simulations. *ACM Transactions on Graphics*, 22(3):716–723, 2003.
7. R. Fattal and D. Lischinski. Target-driven smoke animation. *ACM Transactions on Graphics*, 23(3):439–446, 2004.
8. L. Shi and Y. Z. Yu. Controllable smoke animation with guiding objects. *ACM Transactions on Graphics*, 24(1):1–25, Jan 2005.
9. D. S. Ebert. Volumetric modeling with implicit functions: a cloud is born. In *Visual Proc. of ACM SIGGRAPH'97*, page 147, 1997.
10. Y. Dobashi, T. Nishita, H. Yamashita, and T. Okita. Using metaballs to modeling and animate clouds from satellite images. *The Visual Computer*, 15(9):471–482, 1998.
11. T. Nishita and Y. Dobashi. Modeling and rendering methods of clouds. In *Pacific Graphics 99*, pages 218–219, 1999.
12. J. Schpok, J. Simons, D. S. Ebert, and C. Hansen. A real-time cloud modeling, rendering, and animation system. In *Symposium on Computer Animation'03*, pages 160–166, July 2003.
13. A. Bouthors and F. Neyret. Modeling clouds shape. In *Eurograhics'04 (short papers)*, 2004.
14. Y. Dobashi, K. Kaneda, H. Yamashita, T. Okita, and T. Nishita. A simple, efficient method for realistic animation of clouds. In *Proc. SIGGRAPH'00*, pages 19–28, 2000.
15. S. Bischoff and L. Kobbelt. Ellipsoid decomposition of 3D-models. In *Proc. 3DPVT'02*, pages 480–488, 2002.
16. M. Garland and P. S. Heckbert. Surface simplification using quadric error metrics. In *Proc. SIGGRAPH'97*, pages 209–216, 1997.

Plausible Locomotion for Bipedal Creatures Using Motion Warping and Inverse Kinematics

Guillaume Nicolas[1], Franck Multon[1,2], Gilles Berillon[3], and Francois Marchal[4]

[1] LPBEM, University Rennes 2, av. Charles Tillon, 35044 Rennes, France
[2] IRISA, Campus de Beaulieu, 35042 Rennes, France
[3] UPR 2147 CNRS, 44 rue de l'Amiral Mouchez, 75014 Paris, France
[4] UMR 6578 CNRS, Faculte de Medecine, 27 Bd Moulin, 13385 Marseille, France

Abstract. One of the main question addressed by paleoanthropologists is the recovery of plausible motions for extinct species whose knowledge is generally limited to incomplete bones and skeletons. Calculating locomotion for extinct species is mainly based on the direct application of captured trajectories to numerically reconstructed skeletons. The gait is judged realistic compared to another if it minimizes energy and preserves balance. In computer animation, adapting a motion to a skeleton is addressed by so-called motion retargeting techniques. The goal is then to ensure that the resulting motion is close to the initial one while dealing with new bones' dimensions. In this paper, we adapt methods used in computer animation in order to solve such a problem. This approach is based on a two-steps framework: first, a reference motion of the feet is warped in order to optimize a set of biomechanical general laws, such as energy and Jerk minimization. Second, the remaining degrees of freedom (denoted DOF) are calculated thanks to inverse kinematics (denoted IK). This method is applied on a small woman, a tall man, a chimpanzee and Lucy (*Australopithecus afarensis*).

1 Introduction

In computer graphics, retrieving plausible gestures for virtual creatures is generally performed manually by animators. If this creature is inspired from real ones, motion capture and films can help the animator to answer this question. For some other unreal creatures, the animator can also use a comparative approach assuming its motions may look like those of a real creature. However, we can assume that the way creatures move is mainly imposed by morphological parameters and general laws of motion. This question is also available in paleoanthropology where researchers have to deal with incomplete fossilized data.

In paleoanthropology, as it is impossible to examine and quantify the locomotion of extinct species experimentally, simulation is a promising issue. However, previous studies generally used pre-assigned kinematics derived from extant species (human and chimpanzee), but very few individual anatomical data [1][2]. Simulating bipedal locomotion has mainly been investigated in robotics and computer animation. In the former, the goal is mainly to make a robot walk without

H.-P. Seidel, T. Nishita, and Q. Peng (Eds.): CGI 2006, LNCS 4035, pp. 586–593, 2006.

falling without dealing with the naturalness of motion. On the opposite, computer animation has proposed methods to mimic motions of real creatures.To do so, the methods generally require knowledge on how the creatures walk to ensure calculating visually realistic motions. As we do not have examples for such a motion, we cannot use procedural approaches [3] or any approach requiring a database of motion, such as adapting a motion to geometric constraints [4], motion graphs [5], motion blending [6] or statistics-based methods [7].

Although it requires an initial motion, motion retargeting [8]addresses a quite similar problem. Indeed, this technique is generally used to adapt a motion to a new skeleton by considering bones dimensions and a set of spacetime constraints (such as ensuring foot contact without sliding with the ground). Those techniques generally use inverse kinematics to solve the spacetime constraints independently. The IK module is generally embedded in an iterative process that solves the constraints at some times only and that filters the results until continuous trajectories are obtained. Other authors [9] have proposed to interpolate various trajectories of the feet in a database which keys are anatomical parameters. However, all the techniques used to solve motion retargeting generally require knowing a complete reference motion which is subject to discussion for fossilized skeletons. Moreover, the duration of the support phase can change from one creature to another and consequently influences the spacetime constraints.

Methods based on motion warping [10] and spacetime optimization [11] could be considered if the constraints themselves are optimized together with the state vectors. Recently, approaches based on probabilistic roadmaps were proposed to animate human-like figures in constrained environments [12][13]. In those approaches trajectories of selected points of the skeleton are obtained by a motion planning algorithm while the remaining DOF are calculated by IK. The main advantage of such an approach is to solve separately external constraints and joint kinematics. However, probabilistic roadmaps do not take time into account during the planning process.

In this paper, we propose a new technique based on motion warping for external constraints and IK for the remaining DOF. Motion warping is used to optimize a reference trajectory of the feet until the resulting motion verifies general biomechanical laws.

2 Overview

The first step consists in collecting information on bones and the way they are connected one to each other. This kind of data is generally available whatever the application. In this paper, we only focus on the lower-part of the body including pelvis (3 rotations), thighs (3 rotations) and forelegs (1 rotation) leading to a vector of dimension 11.In addition to those topological data, joint limits, footprints and a rest posture are required. For living creatures, all those data could be retrieved thanks to specific experiments or previous publications. For fossil species, joint limits can be approximated according to the shape of the articulations [14].

Given topological data, an infinity of motions allows displacing the feet from one footprint to the next one. Among all the possible motions, the system has to select the one that looks natural. Many biomechanical and physiological studies [15] state that the internal work W_{int} evaluated indirectly thanks to the kinetic energy theorem reflects the amount of physiological energy expended during motion. It is currently assumed [16] that the work of the ground reaction force is negligible. Thus applying the kinetic energy theorem leads to:

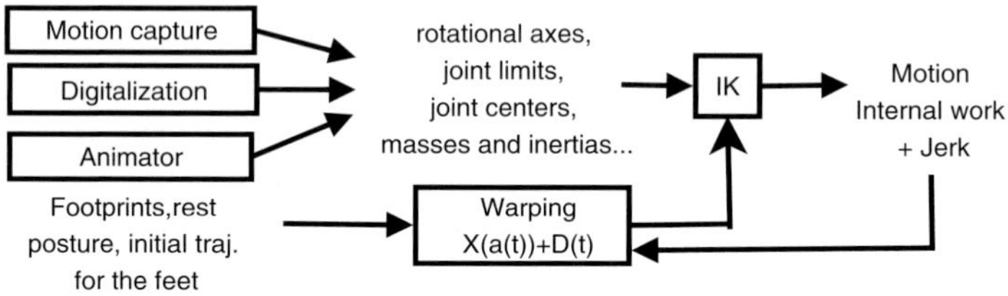

Fig. 1. Overview of the overall process

$W_{int} = \Delta E_k - mg\Delta z$ where E_k is the kinetic energy of the multi-body system, m is the total body mass and g is gravity. Then, we assumed that a plausible solution leads to a minimum value of W_{int}, assuming negative and positive works require the same amount of metabolic energy [15]:

$$min_\theta \frac{1}{t_f - t_0} \sum_{t=t_0}^{t_f} |W_{int}(\theta, t)| \tag{1}$$

where θ is the set of angles applied to the skeleton, t_0 and t_f are the initial and final sample of the sequence, and $W_{int}(\theta, t)$ is a function that returns the instantaneous internal work at time t depending on θ. Minimizing the internal work may not prevent from peaks of accelerations that do not appear generally in natural motions. We thus minimize the derivative of the acceleration, called Jerk:

$$min_\theta \sum_{t=t_0}^{t_f} \left(\frac{d^3\theta(t)}{dt^3} \right)^2 \tag{2}$$

Optimizing such a 11-DOF system is very complex. We propose to decompose the problem into two sub-problems. First, we search a trajectory for both feet (X_{left}, X_{right}), assuming symmetry. Hence, the problem only consists in finding the relative trajectory of one feet in the pelvis reference frame (for example, only X_{left}).

Second, an IK module [17] is used to calculate a plausible motion according to an imposed trajectory of the feet. It deals with joint limits avoidance, minimization of a distance to a rest posture, and energy minimization. The overall process is depicted in figure 1. In the remaining of the paper, we focus on the selection of a plausible trajectory for the feet, assuming that IK provides plausible motions.

3 Selecting an Ankle Trajectory

In order to calculate ankle trajectories, we chose to apply motion warping to an average captured trajectory called reference trajectory $X_a(t)$. We modify this trajectory thanks to a three-steps process. First, the whole trajectory is uniformly time-scaled in order to fit the step frequency imposed by the user. Second, we set control points at the beginning and the end of the trajectories. Additional control points are added for each axis, for each null-derivative point. Let PC be the set of control points for each axis. In a classical human-like trajectory of the ankle relatively to the pelvis, 5 intermediate control points can be determined (as depicted in figure 2 for the vertical and longitudinal axes): 2 for the lateral axis, 1 for the longitudinal axis and 2 for the vertical axis. Third, a global optimization process produces a sequence of offsets for each control point. The final trajectory of the ankle is then given by: $X(t) = X_a(a(t)) + \Delta(t)$ where $a(t)$ is a function that performs dynamic time warping and $\Delta(t)$ is a displacement map added to the resulting trajectory. Both $a(t)$ and $\Delta(t)$ depends on the modification applied to the control points.

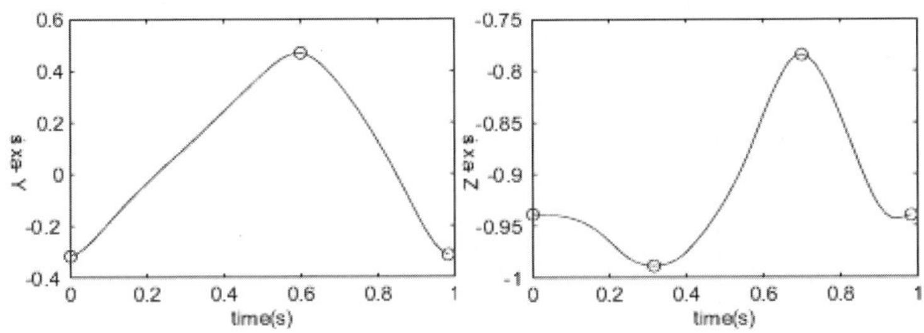

Fig. 2. Longitudinal and vertical displacement of the ankle relatively to the pelvis

The main problem is to select a motion for the ankles that ensures going through the footprints imposed by the user. As $X(t)$ is expressed in the pelvis reference frame, this constraint could be modeled as follows for the left leg: $-X_l(CP, t_{rFS}) + X_r(CP, t_{rFS}) = F_r - F_l$, where t_{rFS} is the time when a right foot-strike occurs, CP are the control points, F_r and F_l are respectively the next right and left footprints. This equation states that, when a foot-strike occurs, the vector between the two ankles must be equal to the one between the two successive footprints. As the first and last control points correspond to a left foot-strike, they are directly set to a compatible value. Only the right foot-strike must be controlled by minimizing the difference between the original and the new imposed footprints: $\Delta F = (F_r - F_l)_{new} - (F_r - F_l)_{old}$. The system has to search ΔCP and Δt_{rFS}:

$$\Delta(CP, t_{rFS}) = J(CP, t_{rFS})^{+}\Delta F + P_F(J)\delta_{CP} \quad (3)$$

where J is the Jacobian of function $h(CP, t_{rFS}) = (-X_l(CP, t_{rFS}) + X_r(CP, t_{rFS}))$. h returns the 3D vector joining the two ankles (depending on the control points

CP modeling the trajectory) when the right footstrike occurred t_{rFS}. J is composed of three raws and n columns if n is the number of parameters tuned by the system (time and value of each controlled DOF):

$$J(CP, t_{rFS}) = \begin{pmatrix} \frac{\partial h_x}{\partial CP_1} & \cdots & \frac{\partial h_x}{\partial CP_n} \\ \frac{\partial h_y}{\partial CP_1} & \cdots & \frac{\partial h_y}{\partial CP_n} \\ \frac{\partial h_z}{\partial CP_1} & \cdots & \frac{\partial h_z}{\partial CP_n} \end{pmatrix} \tag{4}$$

In equation 3, $P_F(J)$ is the projector operator into the kernel of this function $(I - J^+J)$ and δ_{CP} is an additional displacement. This displacement is provided by the iterative optimization process that tries to modify the control points until a minimum value of the cost function is found. This optimization process could be described as follows:

$finished = false$
$while\ not\ finished$
  $select\ next\ \delta_{CP}$
  $X_l = X_a + \Delta(CP,\ t_{rFS})$
  $X_r = symmetry(X_l)$
  $E_r = IK(X_l,\ X_r)$
  $finished = (\Delta Err < \epsilon)$

Function *select next* δ_{CP} is linked to the MultiDirectionalSearch (MDS) optimization method proposed in [18] that consists in displacing and scaling a simplex into the search space. $\Delta(CP,\ t_{rFS})$ is obtained using equation 3. *symmetry* is a function that returns the right symmetric trajectory of the ankle knowing the left one. IK is the inverse kinematics solver used to calculate a plausible motion according to the resulting trajectories of the ankles. This last function also returns the corresponding cost, considering both internal work and Jerk.

4 Results

We applied this method to humans, chimpanzee and fossil hominids. We obtained anatomical descriptions of both extant individuals (*Homo sapiens* and *Pan troglodytes*) and the fossil hominid specimen (A.L. 288-1, *Australopithecus afarensis*, known as "Lucy") by virtually building articular chains. To do so, we developed a procedure that couples a digitalizing process using a Microscribe 3D (Product of Immersion) and a rearticulating process using the 3DShop software (Produce of C4W). We use a unique and homologous procedure for both living and fossil species. From this virtual reconstruction, we extract the joint centers and the length of each segment.We then apply a frame reconstruction procedure of each bone, using Bezier curves and obtained a 3D geometric reconstruction of the chain and a VRML file.

To experiment our approach, we have chosen motion capture data of two subjects: 121Kg and 1.98m for subject S_1, 55Kg and 1.63m for subject S_2.

Figure 3 depicts the trajectory of the left ankle in the root reference frame before (in solid line) and after optimization, for the two subjects. This figure

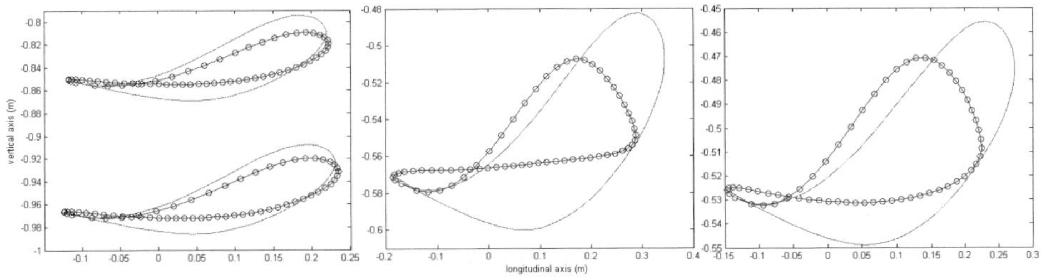

Fig. 3. Trajectory of the ankle (lateral view) in the pelvis reference frame for a small woman and tall man(left view), for a chimpanzee (middle view) and for Lucy (right view). The reference trajectory is depicted with solid lines.

clearly shows that the shape of the trajectories (in the sagital plane) before and after optimization are similar. The internal power is also similar for the reference ($22 J.Kg^{-1}.min^{-1}$) and optimized ($20\ J.Kg^{-1}.min^{-1}$) trajectory. For both subjects, this trajectory is compressed along the vertical axis, avoiding expending unnecessary energy for translating up and down the feet during the flying phase.

Figure 4 is a collection of screen shots obtained for the tall man, the chimpanzee and Lucy.

In figure 3, the same kind of results is depicted for the chimpanzee. Applying the reference trajectory leads to $50 J.Kg^{-1}.min^{-1}$ internal power whereas optimized trajectory leads to $30\ J.Kg^{-1}.min^{-1}$. This time, the shape of the trajectory is different. For the chimpanzee, the gain of internal work is high which demonstrates that the original trajectory was badly adapted to skeleton compared to the optimized one. To sum-up, whereas the optimization leads to few differences for the two human subjects, this difference increases for the chimpanzee. Although this is not a formal validation of the method, it shows that it produces coherent results for those two creatures.

Finally, we experimented our method with the anatomical data of the reconstructed Lucy (see figure 3). The shape of the resulting trajectory is different from those obtained for the two humans but is quite similar to the chimpanzee's one. The gain of energy is again very high: it decreases from $51 J.Kg^{-1}.min^{-1}$ to $19\ J.Kg^{-1}.min^{-1}$. This last value is similar to those calculated for the two humans. Contrary to humans and the chimpanzee, the optimized trajectory of the feet increased displacement in the horizontal plane leading to lateral displacements of the feet during the aerial phase.

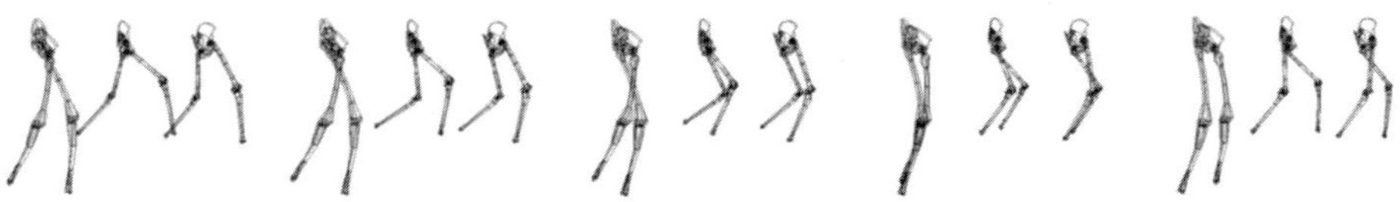

Fig. 4. Screenshots of walks calculated with our method for two humans, a chimpanzee and Lucy (from left to right)

5 Discussion

The work proposed in this paper is preliminary and has obviously some limitations. For example, in this paper, we performed a weighted sum of two cost functions in order to optimize the trajectory of the feet. But, what is exactly the influence of the weights on the resulting sequence and what is the adequate set of weights leading to realistic motions? In future works this question should be investigated more precisely. Moreover the feet and the upper-body were not used in our approach. However, in paleoanthropology, it is quite difficult to have a complete knowledge on the skeleton. In computer graphics where all this knowledge is available, the method should be extended in order to optimize, for example, relative trajectories of the wrists while walking.

Despite those limitations, this work is promising and is an interesting alternative to simply applying joint angles of living creatures to fossil bones without taking accurate anatomical knowledge and biomechanical laws into account. Our approach was first designed for paleoanthropologists where partial knowledge is available for the creatures. This application has guided the choices presented in this paper. We are currently validating this tool by comparing the motions calculated with our method to captured or published data for many various bipedal creatures. In computer graphics, this approach could be used to calculate plausible movements for imaginary creatures. However, the method should be first validated on a wider set of subjects and species. It should also consider multi-legged creatures.

Acknowledgments

The authors thank Dr. M. Mamitu of the National Museum of Addis Abeba (Ethiopia); Dr. B. Latimer and L. Jellema of The Cleveland Museum of Natural History (USA). Fundings: CNRS “Young Researcher” program (“ATIP Jeune Chercheur”) entitled “Evaluating locomotor abilities in early hominids”.

References

1. Crompton, R., Li, Y., Weijie, W., Gunther, M., Savage, R.: The mechanical effectiveness of erect and "bent-hip, bent-knee" bipedal walking in australopithecus afarensis. Journal of Human Evolution **35** (1998) 55–74
2. Kramer, P., Eck, G.: Locomotor energetics and leg length in hominid bipedality. Journal of Human Evolution **38** (2000) 651–666
3. Boulic, R., Magnenat-Thalmann, N., Thalmann, D.: A global human walking model with real-time kinematic personification. Visual Computer **6**(6) (1990) 344–358
4. Sun, H., Metaxas, D.: Automating gait generation. Proceedings of Siggraph'01 (2001) 261–269
5. Kovar, L., Gleicher, M., Pighin, F.: Motion graphs. In: Proceedings of the 29th annual conference on Computer graphics and interactive techniques, ACM Press (2002) 473–482

6. Ashraf, G., Wong, K.: Constrained framespace interpolation. Computer Animation 2001 (2001) 61–72
7. Safonova, A., Hodgins, J., Pollard, N.: Synthesizing physically realistic human motion in low-dimensional, behavior-specific spaces. In: Proceedings of ACM SIGGRAPH. (2004)
8. Gleicher, M.: Retargetting motion to new characters. In: Proc. of ACM SIGGRAPH. (1998) 33–42
9. Pronost, N., Dumont, G., Berillon, G., Nicolas, G.: Morphological and stance interpolations in database for simulating bipedalism of virtual humans. Visual Computer **22** (2006) 4–13
10. Witkin, A., Popović, Z.: Motion warping. In: Proceedings of the 22nd annual conference on Computer graphics and interactive techniques, ACM Press (1995) 105–108
11. Cohen, M.: Interactive spacetime control for animation. Proceedings of ACM SIGGRAPH '92 **.26** (1992) 293–302 Chicago, Illinois.
12. Choi, M., Lee, J., Shin, S.: Planning biped locomotion using motion capture data and probabilistic roadmaps. ACM Transactions on Graphics **22**(2) (2003) 182–203
13. Esteves, C., Arechavaleta, G., Pettre, J., Laumond, J.: Animation planning for virtual characters cooperation. ACM Trans. on graphics **(In Press)** (2006)
14. Berillon, G., Nicolas, G., Multon, F., Marchal, F., Dumont, G., Deloison, Y., Gommery, D.: Testing locomotor hypothesis in early hominids: 3d modeling and simulation of bipedalisms using anatomical data. American Journal of Physical Anthropology **106**(S 40) (2005) 73
15. Burdett, R., Skrinar, G., Simon, S.: Comparison of mechanical work and metabolic energy consumption during normal gait. Journal of orthopaedic research **1** (1983) 63–72
16. Winter, D.: A new definition of mechanical work done in human movement. Journal of Applied Physiology: Respirat. Environ.Exercise Physiol **46**(1) (1979) 79–83
17. Nicolas, G., Multon, F., Berillon, G.: Inverse kinematics for the calculation of plausible bipedal locomotion using anthropological knowledge. In: Proceedings of CASA, Geneva, Switzerland (2004) 103–110
18. Torczon, V.: Multi-directional Search: A Direct Search Algorithm for Parallel Machines. PhD thesis, Rice University, Houston, Texas, USA (1989)

Aerial Image Relighting: Simulating Time of Day Variations

Kartik Chandra, Neeharika Adabala, and Kentaro Toyama

Microsoft Research India,
Scientia, 196/36, 2nd Main, Sadashivanagar,
Bangalore 560080, India
kmuktinu@uci.edu,
{neeha, kentoy}@microsoft.com

Abstract. We present a technique for simulating variations in appearance of aerial images at different sun angles. The input to the algorithm is a single aerial image with information on the orientation of surfaces in the image. The location, date, and time at which the photograph was taken are also needed by the algorithm. The appearance of the aerial image at a new sun angle is synthesized by compensating for the direct sunlight component in the original image, and then relighting the image with sunlight from the new sun position. Techniques to remove cast shadows are also described. We demonstrate our results with images, and animations of changing lighting in aerial photographs as the sun follows a trajectory across the sky.

1 Introduction

Aerial images are being used increasingly with maps to give people an idea of the ground truths of a region. Acquiring aerial images is expensive, and is constrained by time and weather conditions. When people use aerial images to get an idea of a neighborhood, they may be interested in viewing the region at various times of the day. For example, if one is trying to purchase a building or a plot of land in a region, they would like to know the sunshine it receives at various times of the day and year. The ability to relight aerial images is an economical alternative to acquiring aerial images under various conditions.

Recently, aerial images are being stitched together and used to augment the information presented in a map [1, 2]. In these cases regions that change are regularly updated. This leads to scenarios in which images taken at various times of day and year have to be stitched together. Seamless stitching of aerial images is possible if one can relight the aerial images under similar sunlight. Ability to re-render an aerial image under various illumination conditions can also find applications in weather simulations and visualization.

In this work we investigate an approach to relight aerial images to capture the effects of different appearance with times of the day. The specific problem of relighting aerial images has not been addressed before, however there are some closely related works. Techniques for relighting of indoor scenes include the works

H.-P. Seidel, T. Nishita, and Q. Peng (Eds.): CGI 2006, LNCS 4035, pp. 594–605, 2006.

of Marschner [3, 4], and Beauchesne and Roy [5]. Some approaches have been developed for relighting of outdoor scenes, most of them require multiple images from which they recover the reflectance properties for each surface [6, 7] and then apply the relighting approaches. Most of the techniques assume complete knowledge of geometry of objects in the scene. Recent work Troccoli and Allen [8] explores relighting outdoor images. However, their technique uses range scan data along with overlapping pictures. Preetham et al. [9] have rendered outdoor scenes using physics based models for the sun and atmospheric phenomena. These scenes are generated using a path tracer that assumes complete geometric information of the scene. We develop an approach that is specifically applicable to aerial images where the position of the sun in the sky and the atmospheric absorption are the predominant factors that determine the appearance of the image. We use the image along with with some meta-data (including time stamp information, location, and elevation) to simulate an aerial scene from different sun positions. We demonstrate the effectiveness of our approach by generating videos of aerial views as the sun position changes during of the day.

Our approach makes use of a single image to compute the relighting. We formulate our knowledge about image formation into a model that will enable interpretation and manipulation of the image. Section 2 presents the physics-based image formation model that forms the basis of our approach. Section 3 describes the algorithm we propose to relight aerial images. Aerial images of urban areas contain buildings that cast shadows. Our relighting algorithm addresses the problem of simulating lighting due to the new sun position but does not address the shadow generation problem. However, a fixed cast shadow can have a disturbing effect on relighting simulations, therefore we propose methods to remove cast shadows. Two cast shadow removal techniques are described in section 4. Section summarizes the algorithm. Results are discussed in section 6, and conclusions are given in the final section.

2 Image Formation Model

In this section we describe the light interaction model we consider for the formation of aerial images. This model is applicable to natural and artificial diffuse surfaces. The radiance $I(\lambda)$ corresponding to an image pixel is given by

$$I(\lambda) = (E^d(\lambda) + Sky(\lambda))S(\lambda) + P(\lambda) \tag{1}$$

where λ is the wavelength. $E^d(\lambda)$ and $Sky(\lambda)$ are the sun and sky components of the illumination incident on the surface. $S(\lambda)$ and $P(\lambda)$ are the object surface reflectance and the path-scattered radiance respectively. $P(\lambda)$ depends on the depth of the object with respect to the camera and can be neglected for low depth scenes. Figure 1 illustrates the three components of light involved in aerial image formation.

The appearance of aerial image changes with the time of the day. This variation is both in color and intensity. It is primarily due to the variation of sun illumination $E^d(\lambda)$ with the sun angle. The sun illumination is modeled as

$$E^d(\lambda) = E^o(\lambda).T(\lambda, \theta_z)cos(\theta) \tag{2}$$

where θ_z is the sun zenith angle. $E^o(\lambda)$ is the extraterrestrial sun radiance for a given Julian day. θ is the angle of the sun with the surface normal. $T(\lambda, \theta_z)$ is the downward atmospheric transmittance and is dependent on the sun zenith angle. The Raleigh scattering of the air molecules, Mie scattering of aerosol particles, ozone and water vapor absorption primarily constitute atmospheric transmittance [10]. The downward atmospheric transmittance $T(\lambda, \theta_z)$ contributes to the color variation of the incident sun component. Preetham et. al [9] and Iqbal [10] describe this phenomenon in a more detailed manner. The $cos(\theta)$ component causes the intensity variation of a surface with the time of the day.

The aerial images we consider are taken in the Red-Green-Blue (RGB) bands. The spectral information of the illumination is initially converted to CIE [11] tristimulus values XYZ followed by conversion to RGB space. After the conversion the equation (1) is re-written as:

$$I_k = (E_k^d + Sky_k)S_k; \tag{3}$$

where k is one of the three RGB bands. The path-scattered radiance $P(\lambda)$ is neglected. Similarly equation (2) is written as

$$E_k^d = E_k^t(\theta_z)cos(\theta) \tag{4}$$

where $E^o(\lambda)$ and $T(\lambda, \theta_z)$ are coupled into terrestrial sun radiance $E_k^t(\theta_z)$.

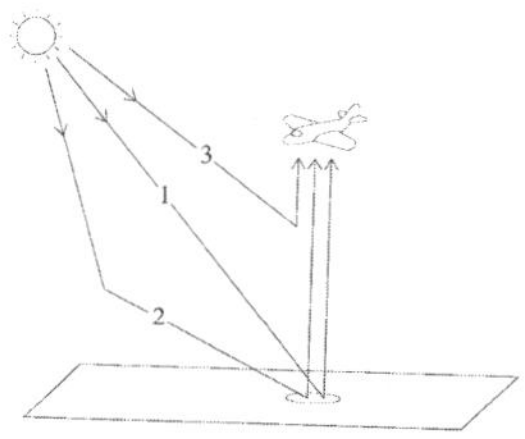

Fig. 1. Sun, Sky and path-scattered radiance contributions in image formation

3 Relighting at Different Sun Angles

The task of illuminating the image at different sun angles is broken up into three constituent sub-tasks:

- determination of orientation for each pixel,
- subtraction/compensation for initial sunlight, and
- relighting the image at a different sun angle.

We describe each of these subtasks in detail in the following subsections.

3.1 Orientation Determination

The value of sun illumination E_k^d is dependent on the the sun angle and the orientation of the object surface as shown in (4). The sun angle is obtained from the time stamp information (meta data) of the image. For orientation determination of the surface we adopt two different solutions for the landscape and urban scenes. The details are described in the following sections.

Landscape Images. The aerial images of landscapes used by us were taken by Pictometry [12]. These images have location and elevation information corresponding to all the pixels in the image. The elevation information was obtained using the digital elevation model (DEM) data from the USGS [13]. Figures 2(a) and 2(b) show a landscape image and the corresponding elevation map respectively. We use the elevation map to estimate the orientation for each pixel in the image. The orientation of a pixel is given by

$$(\partial z/\partial x, \partial z/\partial y, -1)$$

where z is the elevation of the pixel. We estimate the partial derivatives at the pixel (x, y) as

$$\partial z/\partial x(x,y) \approx (z(x+1,y) - z(x-1,y))/(2r) \tag{5}$$
$$\partial z/\partial y(x,y) \approx (z(x,y+1) - z(x,y-1))/(2r) \tag{6}$$

where r is the pixel resolution of the image. We smooth the normals $(\partial z/\partial x, \partial z/\partial y)$ with a Gaussian disk filter to remove sharp edges.

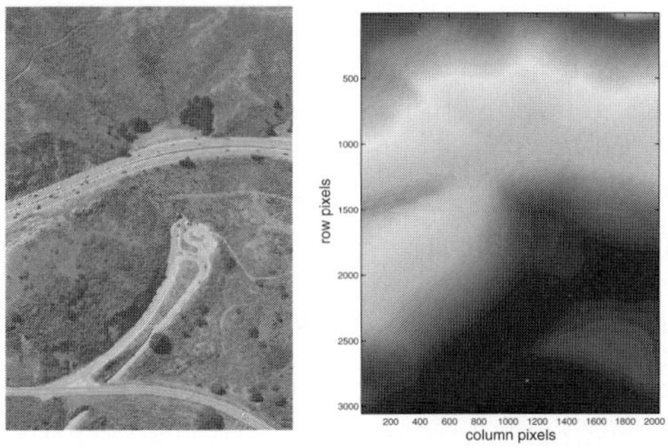

(a) (b)

Fig. 2. Elevation information for a landscape image (a)Landscape image (b) Elevation map of the landscape image. Red corresponds to high elevation and blue corresponds to low elevation.

City Images with Buildings. In case of cities with urban areas containing buildings the orientation of the faces of the building with respect to the incident light is required. This information is not available with pictometry images. Therefore, we manually segmented the building walls into parallelograms

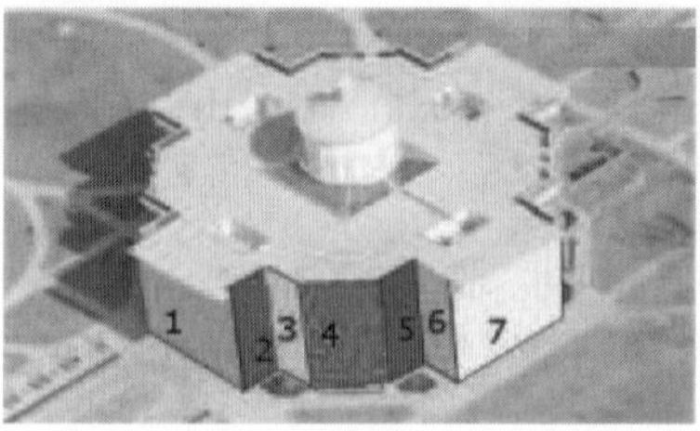

Fig. 3. A Pictometry image with segmented walls

as shown in the figure 3. We assume that all the walls are vertically built which fixes the zenith angle to $pi/2$. The azimuthal direction was determined based on the angle between the adjacent sides of the segmented walls.

We plan to investigate computer vision based approaches to automatically recognize the orientation of a building face by assuming a Lambertian reflectance model for the walls.

3.2 Subtraction/Compensation for Initial Sunlight

The original image has to be compensated for the initial sun light and direction. The initial sun conditions in most photographs can be computed based on its time stamp and location. The sun facing surfaces can be compensated using this information. However, we also need to compensate the illumination of the self-occluded surfaces. This is done by employing the sun-sky ratio as described in the following subsection.

Calculating the Sun-Sky Ratio. We consider the regions immediately inside and outside the shadow to compute the sun-sky ratio. We assume that this region will have the same material. Figure 4 shows the region considered for computing the sun-sky ratio. Using equation (3) the ratios of pixel intensities for the RGB bands inside and outside the shadow ρ_k is given by

$$\rho_k = (E_k^d + Sky_k)/Sky_k = E_k^d/Sky_k + 1 \tag{7}$$

for all the RGB bands. We are interested in the values $K_k = E_k^t(\theta_z)/Sky_k$ which is given by

$$K_k = (\rho_k - 1)sec(\theta_s) \tag{8}$$

where θ_s is the angle between the sun and the surface normal on which the shadow is incident. In figure 4 the shadow is incident on a horizontal surface. We take the average value of all the intensity ratios along the edge of the shadow to get an unbiased estimate of K_k..

The Compensation Equation. The compensated intensity I_k^{comp}, for the sun and sky illuminated surfaces is given by

$$I_k^{comp} = I_k/(E_k^t(\theta_{zi})(cos(\theta_i) + 1/K_k)) \approx S_k \tag{9}$$

Fig. 4. Sun-sky ratio is calculated using the pixels in the white bounding box

where θ_{zi} is sun zenith angle in the original image. θ_i is the angle between the sun and the surface normal in the original image. Similarly, for the self shadowed surfaces we have

$$I_k^{comp} = I_k.K_k/(E_k^t(\theta_{zi})) \approx S_k \tag{10}$$

3.3 Relighting the Image at Different Sun Angles

The final step in synthesizing the image at new sun angles is to recompute the illumination at each pixel. For this subtask we begin with the compensated image and compute the pixel values for the new sun angle. The equation for the pixels on surfaces that are illuminated both by the sun and sky is given by

$$I_k^{new} = I_k^{comp}(E_k^t(\theta_{znew})cos(\theta_{inew}) + E_k^t(\theta_{zi})/K_k) \tag{11}$$

where θ_{znew} is the new sun angle. θ_{inew} is the new angle between the sun and the surface normal in the original image. Similarly, the illumination on self shadowed surfaces is given by the equation

$$I_k^{new} = I_k^{comp}E_k^t(\theta_{zi})/K_k \tag{12}$$

4 Cast Shadow Removal

We can relight the self occluded objects using the techniques described in Section 3. However, the issue of cast shadows needs to be addressed. Simulating the motion of a cast shadow with the sun angle is a difficult task in the absence of complete geometric information of the aerial scene. However the presence of a wrong static cast shadow in an aerial image can be disturbing. Therefore, we need to remove the cast shadows from the original image.

A complete literature survey of all the shadow detection algorithms is presented in Prati et. al.' s [14]. An interesting geometry based shadow detection algorithm is described by Jacobs et al. [15]. We investigate applying a clustering based technique [16] and also propose a simple sun-sky ratio based technique for cast shadow removal.

The clustering based algorithm works on the assumption that the same material is present on both sides of a cast shadow. The pixels are divided into clusters

(a) (b) (c)

Fig. 5. Performance of clustering based shadow removal algorithm (a)Original image (b)Regions selected for the algorithm are shown in blue (c)Clustering based shadow removal algorithm output

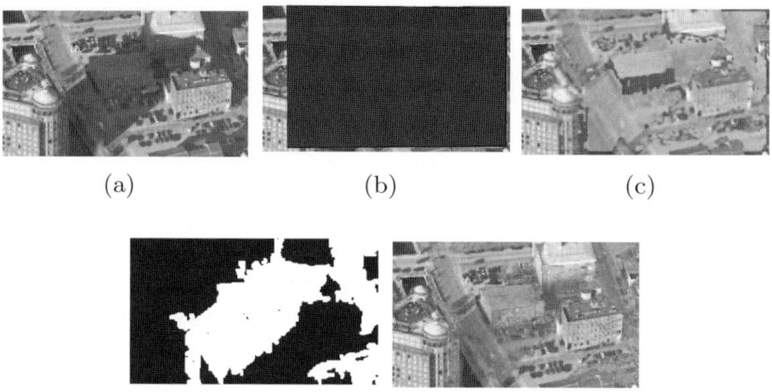

(a) (b) (c)

(d) (e)

Fig. 6. Performance of clustering based and sun-sky ratio based shadow removal algorithm (a)Original image (b) Regions selected for the algorithm are shown in blue (c) Clustering based shadow removal algorithm output.(d)Regions selected for the algorithm are shown in white (e)Sun-sky ratio based shadow removal algorithm output.

in the RGB space using the K-means clustering algorithm [17]. We identify the sun pixel clusters and shadow pixel clusters corresponding to each material assuming that their centroids are lined up in the color space. We then map the shadow pixel clusters to sun pixel clusters by shifting the mean and changing the variance followed by median filtering to reduce the fuzzy boundary artifacts.

We avoid choosing large portions of the image for the algorithm as the clustering of the pixels gets more difficult with increasing number of materials. We design a system where the user is required to input the region of the image on which the clustering algorithm will work. Figure 5 shows the original image, regions selected and the output of the shadow removal algorithm.

Figure 6 shows that the clustering based algorithm gets confused when new materials are present in the shadow. We propose a sun-sky ratio based technique as an alternative approach to the clustering based method. We employ the sun-sky ratio to compensate for the lack of sunlight in the pixels within the cast shadow.

We isolate the shadowed regions by thresholding the pixels of the image in the Hue-saturation-value (HSV) space. Recent work [18, 19] has showed that HSV color space is more accurate in distinguishing the shadowed regions. We mark a pixel as shadowed if

$$I_h < T_h \wedge I_s < T_s \wedge I_v < T_v$$

where I_h, I_s and I_v are the hue, saturation and value components of the pixel. T_h, T_s and T_v are the thresholds used in the HSV space. However, the choice of thresholds is manual and is based on the inspection of the image histograms in hue, saturation and value components.

The sun-sky ratio is computed using the technique described in Section 3.2. We then compensate the pixels in the shadowed region using the sun-sky ratio. The compensation equation is given by

$$I_k^c = I_k^s K cos(\theta_s) + I_k^s \tag{13}$$

where I_k^s is the intensity of the pixel in the cast shadow. I_k^c is the compensated pixel intensity and θ_s is the angle between the pixel surface and the sun. Figure 6 illustrates the result of this algorithm.

Note that there is a intensity mismatch for pixels within the shadow and outside the shadow. This problem can be alleviated if the mapping between the actual radiometric value and the intensity of the pixels is considered. Thus, knowledge of the camera response function can fix the intensity mismatch.

5 Summary of the Algorithm

The algorithm for relighting an aerial image is given by the following sequence of steps:

1. Determine orientation for each pixel in the image. In case of urban images containing buildings create manual annotations as shown in section 3.1 to define the orientation. In case of landscape images use the elevation information to determine orientation as described in section 3.1.
2. Compensate for the existing sunlight in the original aerial image by computing sun-sky ratio using pixels near shadow boundaries. The method is described in section 3.2. Compensation for the initial sun light and angle is done using equations (9) and (10).
3. Remove cast shadow using one of the algorithms described in section 4.
4. Relight the image for a given sun angle using equations (11) and (12).

6 Results and Discussion

The algorithm proposed in this paper has been implemented in MATLAB. We relight the image in figure 5(a) for various sun angles at different times of the day. The cast shadows are removed using the clustering based algorithm presented

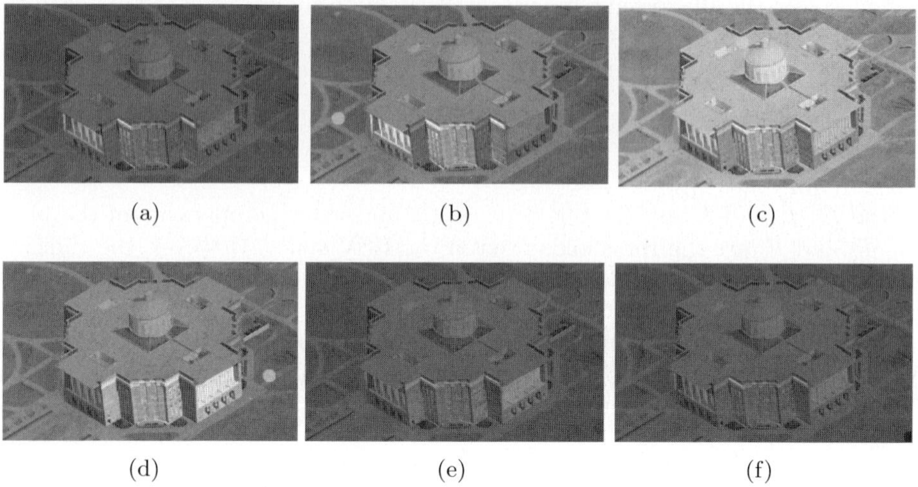

Fig. 7. Image relighted for various sun angles. The circular object shown in the pictures represents the sun $(a) Azimuth = 76^o, Zenith = 84^o (b) Azimuth = 54^o, Zenith = 69^o$ $(c) Azimuth = 9^o, Zenith = 36^o (d) Azimuth = -54^o, Zenith = 36^o (e) Azimuth = -77^o,$ $Zenith = 85^o (f) Azimuth = -88^o, Zenith = 88^o.$

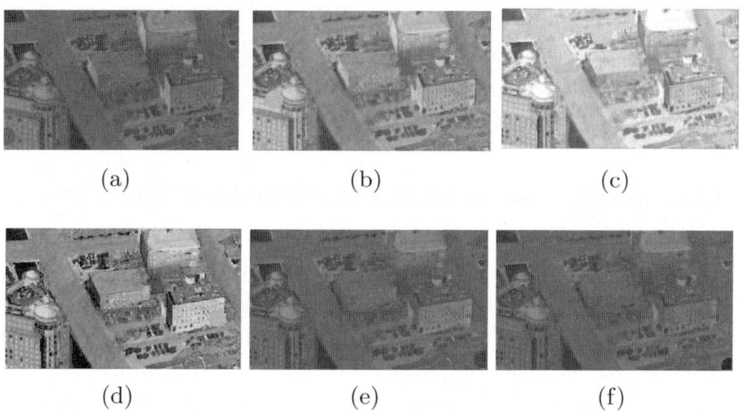

Fig. 8. A city image relighted for various sun angles. The circular object shown in the pictures represents the sun position $(a) Azimuth = 76^o, Zenith = 84^o$ $(b) Azimuth = 54^o, Zenith = 69^o (c) Azimuth = 9^o, Zenith = 36^o (d) Azimuth = -54^o,$ $Zenith = 36^o (e) Azimuth = -77^o, Zenith = 85^o (f) Azimuth = -88^o, Zenith = 88^o.$

in Section 3. Manual annotations shown in figure 3 are used for determining the orientation information. A video of the scene is generated depicting the variation in illumination for a sun path across the sky.

Figure 7 shows six frames from the video. East is toward the left of the image. The sun rises at the bottom left of the image, moves toward the top middle portion during mid-day and sets at the bottom right of the image. The sun

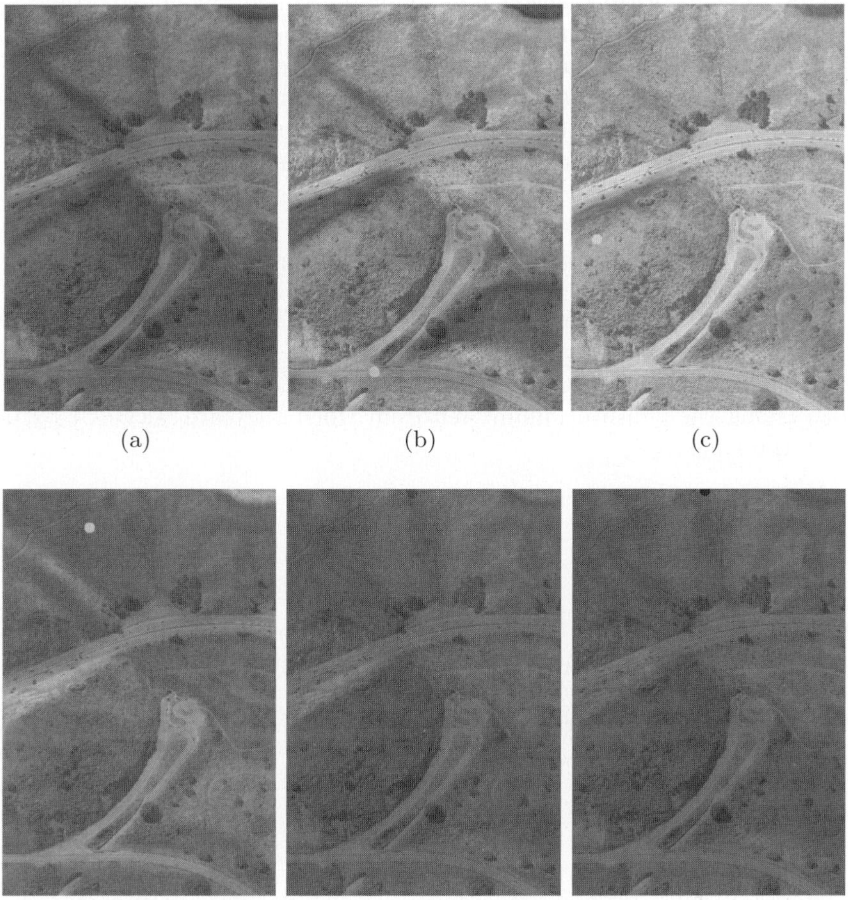

(a) (b) (c)

(d) (e) (f)

Fig. 9. A landscape image relighted for various sun angles. The circular object shown in the pictures represents the sun position $(a) Azimuth = 76^o, Zenith = 84^o$ $(b) Azimuth = 54^o, Zenith = 69^o (c) Azimuth = 9^o, Zenith = 36^o (d) Azimuth = -54^o,$ $Zenith = 36^o (e) Azimuth = -77^o, Zenith = 85^o (f) Azimuth = -88^o, Zenith = 88^o$.

is shown as a circular object with the color corresponding to the sun color at different times of the day. The orientation of the surfaces is observable for the annotated surfaces. All the other surfaces are assumed to be flat. We see that faces 1, 3 and 6 as marked in figure 3 are bright in figures 7(b) and 7(c) when the sun is at the left of the image. These faces get dark in figures 7(d) and 7(e) when they are in the sun shadow region. The Sun is towards the right of the image in this case. Faces 2, 5 and 7 are in the shadow region and are dark in figures 7(b) and 7(c). These faces get brighter in figures 7(d) and 7(e) when they face the sun. We also see that the figures 7(a) and 7(f) have a hue shifted towards red. This is due to the color change of the sun during the initial and final stages of the day. The algorithm successfully simulates changes in sun color and angle with the time of the day and relighting of self occluded surfaces. However it does not make use of complete three dimensional information, and therefore does not incorporate change in the cast shadows with the sun angle.

We also relight the image 6(a) for a hypothetical sun path. A video is generated for the sun trajectory and snapshots from the video are shown in figure 8.

Similarly we relight a landscape image in figure 2 for a hypothetical sun path. The elevation data corresponding to pixels in the image is used to determine the orientation. In this image East is towards the bottom. The sun rises at the bottom center of the image, moves toward the center left of the image during mid-day, and sets at the top center of the image. The change in the shading of the landscape with the sun angle can be observed in figure 9. The pixels are shaded based on their orientation. Occlusion is not considered, therefore some regions facing the sun are illuminated even when they are occluded by other parts of the landscape.

7 Conclusions

We presented a simple and approximate technique for relighting aerial images to simulate different times of day. This was achieved by modifying the main component of lighting in the scene, namely the direct sunlight component. We also described two cast shadow removal algorithms. Our algorithms need some manual intervention. We demonstrated our research by simulating a trajectory of the sun across the sky for aerial images of urban regions and landscapes.

Acknowledgments

The images of buildings and landscapes used in this paper have been provided by Pictometry. We thank Dr. Drew Steedly for providing us useful information on Pictometry data.

References

1. Msn local live. http://local.live.com/.
2. The google map http://maps.google.com/. http://maps.google.com/.
3. S. R. Marschner and D. P. Greenberg. Inverse lighting for photography. Fifth Color Imaging Conference: Color Science, Systems and Applications, pages 262–265, 1997.
4. S. R. Marschner. *Inverse Rendering for Computer Graphics*. PhD thesis, 1998.
5. E. Beauchesne and R. Roy. Automatic relighting of overlapping textures of a 3d model. IEEE Computer Society Conference on Computer Vision and Pattern Recognition, page 166, 2003.
6. Yizhou Yu and Jitendra Malik. Recovering photometric properties of architectural scenes from photograph. Proc. of SIGGRAPH 98, pages 207–217, 1998.

7. C. B. Madsen and R. Laursen. Image relighting: Getting the sun to set in an image taken at noon. Proceedings: Danish Conference on Pattern Recognition and Image Analysis, page 8 pages, 2004.
8. A. Troccoli and P. K. Allen. Relighting acquired models of outdoor scenes. 3 DIM, pages 245–252, 2005.
9. A. J. Preetham, P. Shirley, and B. Smits. A practical analytic model for daylight. Proc. of the 26th annual conference on Computer Graphics and interactive techniques, pages 91–100, 1999.
10. M. Iqbal. *An Introduction to Solar Radiation.* Academic Press, 1983.
11. International commission on illumination. http://www.cie.co.at/.
12. Pictometry. http://www.pictometry.com/.
13. The US Geological Survey website. http://www.usgs.gov/.
14. A. Prati, I. Mikic, M. M. Trivedi, and R. Cucchiara. Detecting moving shadows: Algorithms and evaluation. *IEEE Trans. Pattern Rec. Machine Intell.*, 25:918–923, 2003.
15. Katrien Jacobs, Cameron Angus, Celine Loscos, Jean-Daniel Nahmias, Alex Reche, and Anthony Steed. Automatic shadow detection and shadow generation for augmented reality. In *Proceedings of Graphics Interface 2005*, Vancouver, Canada, May 2005.
16. M. Baba and N. Asada. Shadow removal from a real picture. Proc. of the SIGGRAPH 2003 conference on Sketches and applications: in conjunction with the 30th annual conference on Computer graphics and interactive techniques, pages 1–1, 2003.
17. J.B. MacQueen. Some method for classication and analysis of multivariate observations. Proc. of the 5th Berkeley Symposium on Mathematical Statistics and Probability, 1967.
18. N. Heredotou, K. N. Plataniotis, and A. N. Venetasanopoulos. A color segmentation scheme for object-based video coding. IEEE symposium on Advances in Digital Filtering and Signal Processing, pages 25–29, 1998.
19. R. Cucchiara, C. Grana, M. Piccardi, A. Prati, and S. Sirotti. Improving shadow supression in moving object detection with hsv color information. IEEE intelligent transportation systems conference proceedings Oakland(CA), pages 334–339, 2001.

Compression of Complex Animated Meshes

Rachida Amjoun, Ralf Sondershaus, and Wolfgang Straßer

WSI-GRIS, University of Tübingen, Sand 14,
72076 Tübingen, Germany
{amjoun, sondershaus, strasser}@gris.uni-tuebingen.de

Abstract. We introduce a new compression algorithm for complex animated meshes of constant connectivity based on the local principal component analysis. The algorithm segments the animated mesh into segments using a region growing algorithm and transforms the original vertex coordinates into the local coordinate frame of their segment. This transformation leads to a strong clustering behavior of vertices and makes each region invariant to any deformation over time. Then each segment is efficiently encoded using the principal component analysis. The set of basis vectors and coefficients corresponding to each segment are quantized and entropy encoded. Experimental results show that our algorithm yields a significant improvement upon some current coders.

1 Introduction

Computer graphics is producing increasingly sophisticated tools (like Maya, 3D Studio Max, or Cinema 4D) which can build models with extremely complex geometric data and create highly realistic animations for different purposes such as computer games, movies, or scientific applications.

The animations often consist of frames each of which stores an own mesh. Even if key frame animations are used, the number of meshes that need to be stored can become large. But often the meshes differ only slightly between neighboring frames. The meshes contain a large redundancy between frames and between neighboring vertices in the same frame. With growing scene complexity it becomes more and more problematic to manipulate such animated meshes in real-time or to transmit and exchange them over networks. Therefore, efficient compression algorithms are needed that significantly reduce the storage space of animated models. A number of techniques have been developed for animated meshes with fixed connectivity. Lengyel [1] partitioned the mesh into submeshes and described the motion of the submeshes by rigid body transformations which are estimated to best match the trajectories of their vertices. Alexa et al. [2] used principal Component analysis (PCA) to achieve a compact representation of animation sequences. Karni and Gotsman [3] introduced linear prediction coding (LPC) to the PCA coefficients to further exploit the temporal coherence. Sattler et al. [4] proposed a compression scheme that is based on clustered PCA (CPCA). The mesh is segmented into meaningful clusters which are then compressed independently using PCA. Prediction and wavelet schemes [5] [6] [7] are also used to efficiently compress animated meshes.

H.-P. Seidel, T. Nishita, and Q. Peng (Eds.): CGI 2006, LNCS 4035, pp. 606–613, 2006.

The animated meshes often exhibit highly nonlinear behavior which is globally difficult to capture. Locally, the neighboring vertices have a strong tendency to behave and to move in a similar way. The nonlinear behavior can therefore be described in a linear fashion by segmenting the vertices of the mesh and by introducing a local coordinate frame for each segment. Figure 2(b) shows the path of six points of the dance model in the world coordinate system. Note the highly nonlinear behavior of the trajectories. Figure 2(c) shows the path of the points using a local coordinate system (LCS). Note the relative small changes and the tendency of the trajectory of a single point to cluster.

Contribution. We propose a new compression algorithm for animated meshes which segments the mesh into segments with a region growing algorithm and transforms the original positions of the vertices into the local coordinate frame of their segment. This automatically "transforms" the nonlinear behavior of the original vertices into the clustering behaviour which is very well compressable. The vertex positions will tend to cluster around the same position over time (see Fig. 2(c)). Thus, the segments themselves are almost invariant to any deformation. A PCA is then performed on each segment such that the (local) vertex coordinates are transformed into another basis which allows for very efficient compression. An error accumulation scheme ensures that the decompression does not introduce severe artifacts. To our knowledge the *combination of local coordinates and PCA* has never been performed before. We call our approach Relative Local Principal Component Analysis (RLPCA) compression. Our algorithm (1) achieves an increased compression performance, (2) reduces prediction errors to increase accuracy, (3) is computational inexpensive (compared to a PCA for the full mesh), and (4) is well suited for progressive transmission.

2 Animation Compression

Figure 1 illustrates an overview of the compression and decompression pipeline. Given a sequence of triangle meshes $M_i, i = 1, ..., F$ of constant connectivity with V vertices and F frames (meshes), we first segment the mesh into N segments where each contains $V_i, i = 1, ..., N$, vertices.

2.1 Segmentation

Our segmentation algorithm grows regions starting from several seed points. The regions grow uniformly around the set of selected seed points by first traversing the closest neighboring vertices until all vertices of the mesh are visited. The segmentation algorithm consists of three steps:

Step 1 ***(Initialization)*** initializes the N pieces S_i, $i = 1, ..., N$, to be empty.
Step 2 ***(Seed Selection)*** selects N seeds using the far distance approach [8] and we associate with each seed one of its incident triangles called *seed triangle*.
Step 3 ***(Region Growing)*** grows the regions starting from the seed triangles. Every region has a queue associated with it which consists of edges who

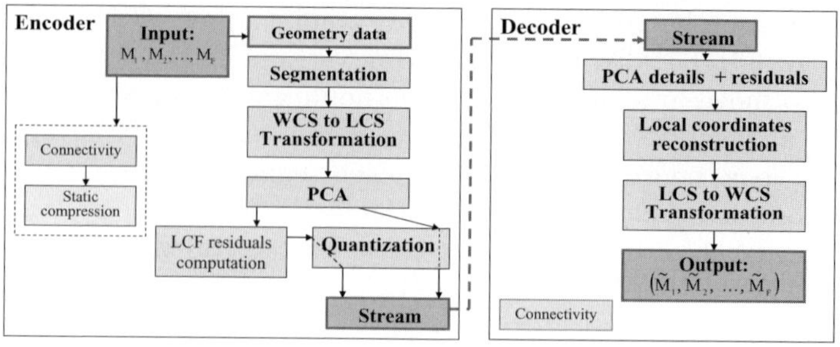

Fig. 1. Overview of the compression / decompression pipeline

separate between the interior of the region and the exterior. The queues drive the growing process. Every edge connects two triangles, one inside the region and one outside the region called *candidate triangle*. The vertex of the outside triangle that does not lie on the edge is called a *candidate vertex*. The queue of every region is initialized to the (three) edges of its seed triangle. The edges of the queues are sorted by the distance of their candidate vertices to the seed vertex; we use the average of all position of a vertex in all frames as vertex position. We iterate over all regions and for every region we add the candidate triangle whose candidate vertex has the lowest distance to the region. We update the queue by removing the edge and by adding the two remaining edges of the candidate triangle. The iteration stops if no more edges are in the queues. We end up with N segments that have V_i vertices each.

2.2 Local Coordinate System

Expressing the vertex locations in a LCF is an optimal way to exhibit the clustering behavior. It makes the local segment quite invariant over time. We consider that each region has its own LCF, defined on the seed triangle as depicted in Fig. 2(a) . The origin $\mathbf{o}$ is the center of one of its three edges (typically $(\mathbf{p_1}, \mathbf{p_2})$), the x-axis (red arrow) points down the edge $(\mathbf{p_1}, \mathbf{p_2})$, the y-axis (green arrow) is orthogonal to the x-axis in the plane of the seed triangle and the z-axis is orthogonal to the x- and y-axis. In contrast to the world coordinate system, moving the LCF moves the set of vertices relative to the local frame only and the coordinates of a vertices tend to cluster around one point. The transformation of a point $\mathbf{p}$ to its local coordinates $\mathbf{q}$ can be accomplished by an affine transformation with a translation $\mathbf{o}$ and a linear transformation $\mathbf{T}$ (orthonormal matrix): $\mathbf{q} = \mathbf{T}(\mathbf{p} - \mathbf{o})$.

2.3 Principal Component Analysis

Principal component analysis is a statistical technique that can reduce the dimensionality of a data set. It determines linear combinations of the original data which contain maximal variation and represents them in an orthogonal basis.

(a) (b) (c)

Fig. 2. Illustration of the local coordinate frame in each segment (a). The position of six different vertices over time (illustrated with different colors) are represented with global coordinates (b) and local coordinates (c).

If we have F frames of $3V$ dimension each, PCA produces a reduced number $L \ll F$ of principal components that represent the original data.

Let S_i^f be the i-th mesh segment in the f-th frame, $i = 1, ..., N$ and $f = 1, ..., F$. A single mesh segment S_i thus consists of F mesh segments (one for each frame) $S_i = \{\mathbf{S}_i^1, \mathbf{S}_i^2, ..., \mathbf{S}_i^F\}$ where $\mathbf{S}_i^f$ represents the vector with the geometry of the mesh segment i in frame f: $\mathbf{S}_i^f = (\mathbf{p}_1^{i,f}, \mathbf{p}_2^{i,f}, \mathbf{p}_3^{i,f}, \mathbf{q}_4^{i,f}, \mathbf{q}_5^{i,f}, .., \mathbf{q}_{V_i}^{i,f})^t$ whose elements are the world coordinates of the three vertices of the seed triangle used to construct its own LCF, and the local coordinates of the segmented points. All $\mathbf{S}_i^f$ have the same length $3V_i$, and construct a $3V_i \times F$ geometric matrix $\mathbf{A}_i = \left[\mathbf{S}_i^1 \mathbf{S}_i^2 ... \mathbf{S}_i^F\right]$. A singular value decomposition on $\mathbf{A}_i$ is computed to find $\mathbf{A}_i = \mathbf{U}_i \mathbf{D}_i \mathbf{V}_i^t$ where $\mathbf{U}_i$ is a $3V_i \times F$ column-orthogonal matrix that forms an orthogonal basis and contains the eigenvectors of the $\mathbf{A}_i \mathbf{A}_i^t$. $\mathbf{D}_i$ is a diagonal matrix whose nonzero elements represent the singular values which are sorted in decreasing order. To reduce the data set, we pick only the first L eigenvectors (L can be defined by the user). So, $\mathbf{U}_i^{'} = \{\mathbf{u}_{i,l}, l = 1, ..., L\}$ contains the most important principal components $\mathbf{u_i}$ that correspond to the largest eigenvalues. Then each segment $\mathbf{S}_i^f$ is projected into the new basis $\mathbf{U}_i^{'}$ to get a new matrix of coefficients $\mathbf{C}_i^{'} = \mathbf{U}_i^{'t} \mathbf{A}_i$ of size $L \times F$. After performing the PCA for all N segments S_i, we get N new sets of component and coefficient matrices with different sizes. $\{\mathbf{U}_1^{'}, \mathbf{U}_2^{'}, ..., \mathbf{U}_N^{'}\}$ and $\{\mathbf{C}_1^{'}, \mathbf{C}_2^{'}, ..., \mathbf{C}_N^{'}\}$ respectively.

2.4 Quantization and Arithmetic Coder

For further compression, the floating-point values (32 or 64 bits) are always quantized to a user specified number of bits per coordinate relative either to the tight axis-aligned bounding box for each frame or to the largest bounding box for all frames. In our algorithm, since we have to encode the basis vector values and the coefficients rather than the vertex coordinates, we use two different encoding contexts. The first concerns the matrices and the second the correction vectors (see sect 2.5). The basis matrix $\mathbf{U}_i^{'}$ and the coefficient matrix $\mathbf{C}_i^{'}$ of each segment S_i are truncated using a fixed number of bits q_u and q_c (typically $q_u =$

q_c). We first compute the minimums and the maximums values $(c_{min,i}, c_{max,i})$, $(u_{min,i}, u_{max,i})$ of $\mathbf{U}_i^{'}$ and $\mathbf{C}_i^{'}$ respectively. Then integer values are straightforwardly derived according to $u_{i_q}(m,j) = \lfloor u_i(m,j)/(u_{max,i} - u_{min,i}) \cdot 2^{q_u} + 1/2 \rfloor$ and $c_{i_q}(j,f) = \lfloor c_i(m,j)/(c_{max,i} - c_{min,i}) \cdot 2^{q_c} + 1/2 \rfloor$, where $m = 1,..,3V_i$, $j = 1,..,L$ and $f = 1,..,F$. The resulting integer values of the matrices are encoded with an adaptive arithmetic coder [9] and sent with the extreme numbers.

2.5 Local Coordinate Frame Correction

During the decoding, the LCFs should be correctly reconstructed. Currently, the three vertices $\mathbf{p}_1$, $\mathbf{p}_2$ and $\mathbf{p}_3$ are decoded and the transformation from world coordinates into the LCF is constructed from them (see sec. 2.2). This reconstructed transformation can contain error which can be significant if a small number of components is used or a coarse quantization is done. In order to diminish this error, we simply compute the correction vectors between the original and the reconstructed three points and quantize them to a user specified number of bits q_Δ relative to the minima extend of the bounding box defined by the maxima and the minima of all world coordinates. The integers are then encoded and sent with the PCA details. The errors of the LCFs are then due to quantization only and are negligible at up to 12 bits quantization. The total number of bits needed for storing correction vectors is very small. It ranges between 0.01 and 0.5 bits per vertex per frame when the quantization ranges between 12 and 18 bits depending of the number of components and quantization level.

2.6 Decompression

Figure 1 illustrates the decoding process. After receiving PCA details and correction vectors, we reconstruct the local coordinates of all vertices in each segment. In the second stage, we decode and undo quantization of correction vectors, build back the LCFs, and transform the local coordinates back to world coordinates. Finally, we collect all segments to reconstruct the sequence of meshes.

3 Results

To see the compression skill and the quality of the RLPCA scheme, we measured the number of bits per vertex per frame (bpvf), and we used the metric d_{KG} introduced by [3] to measure the distortion in the reconstructed animation with regard to the original animation. Furthermore, we used the $L2$ norm to compute the distortion per frame. We compare the performance of our algorithm against standard PCA, KG (PCA+LPC) [3], CPCA [4] and the wavelet (AWC) [6].

RLPCA vs. LPCA vs. PCA. To find out the influence of the segmentation and the local coordinates on the rate and on the reconstruction of animation, we performed local PCA (LPCA) in the world coordinates as well as in the local coordinates for a given number of segments and components. The quantization

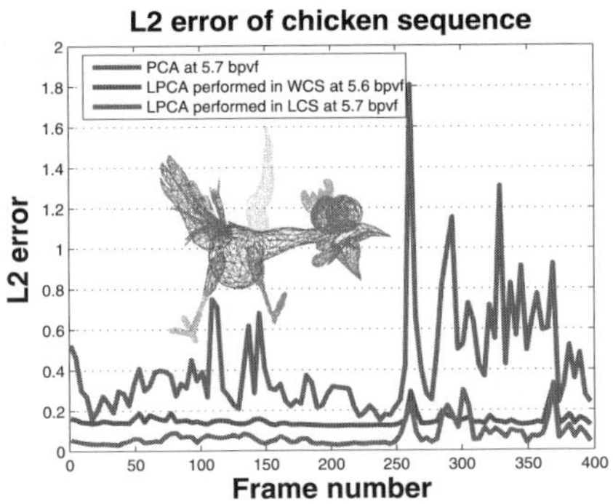

Fig. 3. Left: Results of error measurement (using L2 norm) of the chicken sequence using standard PCA and HPCA in the world and the local coordinates (using 15 segments). Right:Reconstructed chicken (frame 220): (a) original, (b) with 25 segments, (c) with 2 segments, using 20, 15, and 1 component(s) respectively and $q_u = q_c = 16$.

level was set to 16 bits. We also compared LPCA with standard PCA. Figure 4(d) shows that RLPCA has an excellent rate-distortion performance. The improvement in the dashed red curve is due to the segmentation process and to LPCA which extracts well the local linear behavior. This improvement increases when the vertex coordinates were transformed into LCS which forces the coordinates of a vertex to cluster around one point which is well compressable by PCA. The coding performance improvement over each frame can also be seen in Fig. 3 (left). Figure 3 (right) shows the reconstruction frame in the chicken sequence at different numbers of segments and components.

Comparison to other coders. Figure 4 illustrates the comparison to other methods as rate-distortion curves for the chicken, cow and dolphin animations. On the first sight, we can see that our approach achieves a better rate distortion performance than the standard PCA, LPC and TG. This result is obvious since the coding of animation using static mesh compression techniques exploits spatial coherence only and LPC uses temporal coherence only. On the other hand the standard PCA approximates the global linearity only and is less effective for nonlinear animation. Compared to the CPCA and AWC algorithms, we achieve better or similar results. Figure 4(a) shows that for the cow animation our method is significantly better than KG and than CPCA depending on the level of quantization used (32 or 18 bits) and it comes close to AWC. For the dolphin and the chicken sequences, our method performs better than the all above methods. This improvement is due to the segmentation of the model into meaningful parts as well as to the use of local coordinates rather than world coordinates. On the other side, the RLPCA performs well for the models with a large number of vertices in contrast to KG. Therefore, by combining RLPCA with LPC, we might achieve a better compression ratio. From the computational viewpoint, PCA is computational expensive but in combination with LPC, it gives a better compression ratio, particularly for a long sequence

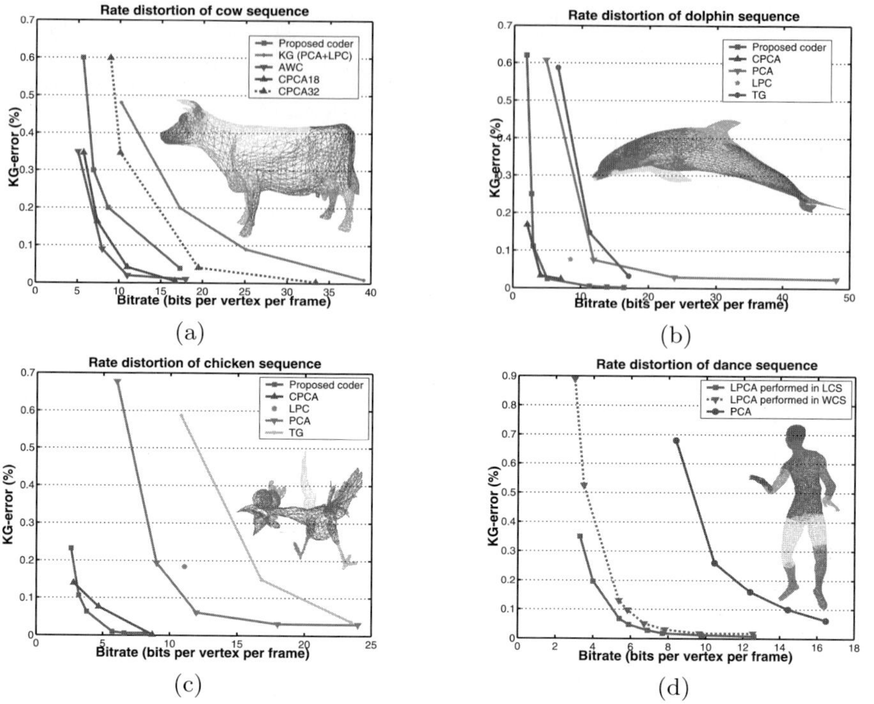

Fig. 4. Rate distortion curves for the cow, dolphin, chicken and dance sequences

Table 1. Comparison compression and decompression timings with CPCA

				CPCA				RLPCA					
Models	vertices	triangles	frames	bpvf	d_{KG}	$t^{enc}_{(sec)}$	$t^{FPS}_{(sec)}$	bpvf	d_{KG}	N	L	$t^{enc}_{(sec)}$	$t^{dec}_{(sec)}$
chicken	3030	5664	400	4.7	0.076	206	214	4.8	0.043	25	20	95	15
				2.8	0.139	395	215	3.0	0.107	10	20	88	10
cow	2904	5804	204	7.4	0.16	75	145	6.9	0.39	10	20	41	8
				3.8	0.5	59	218	5.2	1.2	6	20	39	7
dolphin	6179	12337	101	-	-	-	-	6.7	0.009	40	10	50	10
				-	-	-	-	5.1	0.024	20	10	43	8
				-	-	-	-	3.1	0.11	40	5	42	8
dance	7061	14118	201	-	-	-	-	6.9	0.028	50	20	175	23
				-	-	-	-	4.0	0.196	50	10	150	15
				-	-	-	-	3.3	0.35	30	10	103	12

of a small number of vertices. CPCA outperforms both methods by using robust segmentation (clustered PCA) but remains expensive. In contrast to that, our RLPCA uses a simple segmentation and transformation and achieves a similar or even better compression ratio.

Timings. Table 1 shows the timings in seconds of the coding (t^{enc}) and decoding (t^{dec}) processes for the four animations with a comparison to CPCA (t^{FPS} for display while decoding). We observe that for the chicken model our coder is much faster and performs better than CPCA. For the cow model, RLPCA is faster but CPCA gives a better compression ratio. Our timing results are measured on Pentium 4 with 2.53 GHz and CPCA on AMD Athlon64 XP 3200+.

4 Conclusions and Future Works

We have presented a new animated mesh compression scheme based on PCA and the use of local coordinates. To exploit the large space-time coherence, the mesh is segmented into segments and then, the world coordinates of each segment are transformed into LCS. This step is the key feature and enables the algorithm to compress an animated mesh efficiently. It exploits the "local" behavior of the local coordinates. Finally, a LPCA is performed. Our approach is simple, fast and achieves a better performance than some current coders. For very long sequences, we think that the motion of local coordinates becomes complex and nonlinear too. Therefore, we plan to develop an adaptive segmentation and encode the segments with different numbers of components and quantization levels.

Acknowledgements. We would like to thank Zachi Karni and Hector Briceño for providing us the animated mesh and Mirko Sattler and Igor Guskov for the results of their methods. The Chicken sequence is property of Microsoft Inc.

References

1. Lengyel, J.E.: Compression of time-dependent geometry. In: Proceedings of the 1999 symposium on Interactive 3D graphics, ACM Press (1999) 89–95
2. Alexa, M., Müller, W.: Representing animations by principal components. Comput. Graph. Forum **19**(3) (2000)
3. Karni, Z., Gotsman, C.: Compression of soft-body animation sequences. Computer and Graphics **28** (2004) 25–34
4. Sattler, M., Sarlette, R., Klein, R.: Simple and efficient compression of animation sequences. In: Proceedings of the 2005 ACM SIGGRAPH/Eurographics symposium on Computer animation, New York, NY, USA, ACM Press (2005) 209–217
5. Ibarria, L., Rossignac, J.: Dynapack: space-time compression of the 3d animations of triangle meshes with fixed connectivity. In: Proceedings of the 2003 ACM SIGGRAPH/Eurographics Symposium on Computer Animation. (2003)
6. Guskov, I., Khodakovsky, A.: Wavelet compression of parametrically coherent mesh sequences. In: SCA '04: Proceedings of the 2004 ACM SIGGRAPH/Eurographics symposium on Computer animation, ACM Press (2004) 183–192
7. Payan, F., Antonini, M.: Wavelet-based compression of 3d mesh sequences. In: Proceedings of IEEE ACIDCA-ICMI'2005, Tozeur, Tunisia (2005)
8. Yan, Z., Kumar, S., Kuo, C.C.J.: Error-resilient coding of 3-d graphic models via adaptive mesh segmentation. IEEE Trans. Circuits Syst. Video Techn. **11**(7) (2001) 860–873
9. Witten, I.H., Neal, R.M., Cleary, J.G.: Arithmetic coding for data compression. Communications of the ACM **30**(6) (1987) 520–540

A Video-Driven Approach to Continuous Human Motion Synthesis

Rongrong Wang[1,2], Xianjie Qiu[1], Zhaoqi Wang[1], and Shihong Xia[1]

[1] Institute of Computing Technology, Chinese Academy of Sciences,
Beijing, 100080, P.R. China
{wr, qxj, zqwang, xsh}@ict.ac.cn
[2] Graduate University, Chinese Academy of Sciences,
Beijing, 100039, P.R. China

Abstract. We propose a framework to reconstruct human motion based on monocular camera video and motion database. In this framework, we use silhouettes for rough motion estimation based on a set of discriminative features and search motion database to find out the exact motion clips that meet with the video content. We model motion as a first-order Markov process. The transition probabilities between motion clips are preprocessed with consideration of the continuousness and smoothness of human motion. To eliminate the discontinuities between motion clips, we also adopt a seamless motion stitch method using multiresolution analysis technique. We verify the effectiveness of our method by reconstructing trampoline sports video as an example. The reconstruction results are visually comparable to those motions obtained by a commercial motion capture system in the premise that similar motions are included in the motion database.

1 Introduction

The popularities of three-dimensional sports simulation and assistant training systems have demonstrated that generating natural human motion is an important problem. This problem has been solved by motion capture equipments. Motion capture data provides all the detail and nuance of live motion for all degrees of freedom of a simulated athlete. However, this solution is far too expensive for commercial use. It is also cumbersome, requiring the user to wear over 40 carefully positioned retro-reflective makers and skin-tight clothing. Moreover, motion capture, as an intrusive method, will turn out to be a hindrance to the performance of athletes to some extend. On the other hand, video, especially from monocular camera, is the main medium to record sport motions. Compared to motion capture data, sports video is easier to obtain and non-intrusive.

In this paper we propose a framework of motion synthesis from monocular camera. (Fig.1). In this framework, a motion database is set up with motion capture system previously. Given a video, the silhouettes and camera viewpoint are extracted. Synthetic silhouettes will be extracted by rendering a three dimensional human model at a plane using each frame motion data at the same viewpoint with video. We match the real silhouettes with synthetic ones, and corresponding motion clips will be retrieved. We keep K-closest matched motion clips and try to find the most probable

H.-P. Seidel, T. Nishita, and Q. Peng (Eds.): CGI 2006, LNCS 4035, pp. 614 – 621, 2006.

motion sequence. To ensure the naturalness of results, a motion stitch algorithm is applied to stitch the matched clips. Vision processing supplies partial information about the user's movement, and domain knowledge from the motion database supplements the necessary information to allow user's movement to be inferred.

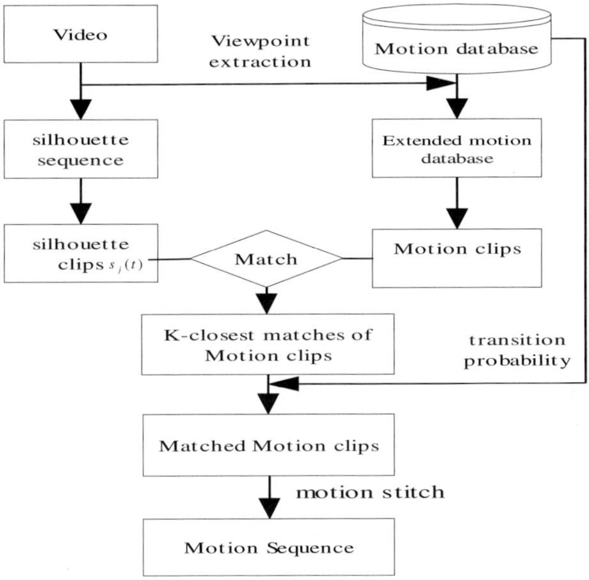

Fig. 1. System Overview

2 Research Background

2.1 Human Motion Database

The database must be large enough that good mappings can be found as needed. We construct a large and complete trampoline motion database using a Vicon optical motion capture system with twelve 120Hz Mx-40 cameras. And we use a standard biomechanical marker set with 42 markers. The motion database contains 62 motions of trampoline sports, which are 40383 frames in total. Each motion frame contains the position and orientation of root node (pelvis) and relative joint angles of 19 joints, omitting the finger joints. These joints are head, neck, thorax, waist, pelvis, and left and right clavicle, shoulder, elbow, wrist, hip, knee and ankle.

A motion is a time-varying function which provides a pose of an articulated figure at a time. We denote the position of root by a three-dimensional vector and the orientations by unit quaternion. We denote a motion by

$$m(t) = (p(t), q^1(t), \ldots q^i(t), \ldots q^n(t)) \tag{1}$$

where $p(t) \in R^3$ and $q^1(t) \in S^3$ represent the position and orientation of root node, and $q^i(t) \in S^3$ represent the orientation of the i th joints, and n is the number of joints plus 1(root orientation).

2.2 Silhouettes Matching

The silhouettes from video must be compared to the synthetic ones from three-dimensional motion database. So the first thing we need to do is extracting camera viewpoint from video. Utilizing virtual-true comparison technique of Qiu[8], the extrinsic parameters of camera are calculated by using feature 3D reconstruction, by which the viewpoint of the virtual scene is adjusted automatically to be the same as the video's.

How to describe the similarity between silhouettes is key to silhouette matching. Our previous work (Qiu [10]) selected one Hu moment and four affine moments as global statistical features of silhouette images: $(\phi_7, I_1, I_2, I_3, I_4)$. We denote the sequence of silhouettes from the video as a time-varying signal:

$$s(t) = (\phi_7(t), I_1(t), I_2(t), I_3(t), I_4(t)) \tag{2}$$

Given two silhouettes $s_i = (\phi_{i7}, I_{i1}, I_{i2}, I_{i3}, I_{i4})$, $s_j = (\phi_{j7}, I_{j1}, I_{j2}, I_{j3}, I_{j4})$ the difference is defined as eulidean distance between silhouette vectors

$$d(s_i, s_j) = \| s_i - s_j \| \tag{3}$$

Accordingly, the difference between two silhouette signals of equal length L is :

$$d(s_1(t), s_2(t)) = \sum_{i=0}^{L} d(s_{1i}, s_{2i}) \tag{4}$$

We use every frame in motion database to drive the virtue athlete and then synthetic silhouettes corresponding with those 3D frames will be gotten. One synthetic silhouette corresponds to one frame of motion. Then the feature vector of synthetic silhouettes, as defined above, can be computed. We extend the motion database by adding the silhouette vectors to the corresponding motion frames. Extended motion database is denoted as: $m_E(t) = (p(t), q^1(t), \ldots q^n(t), s_{syn}(t))$.

By matching synthetic silhouettes with real ones, the corresponding motion data will be found. Since at present we use video with fixed camera, the extension of motion database needs to be processed only once.

In our system, we divide silhouette signals both from video and from motion database into clips of equal length and then compare the video clips with synthetic ones. We find difference between the video clip being matched and each synthetic clips using Equation (4), and keep the K closest matches. The length of clips should be carefully chosen. Too short clips will turn out to be a heavy burden to path finding and motion stitch while too long clips might lead to unsatisfactory matching results.

Moreover, in real time application, too long clips will introduce a long delay. In our application, the length we choose is 25 frames.

We save more matching results than the closest match because more consideration should be taken than just how close the silhouette clips is to the synthetic ones. We must take into consideration which clips come first and next and how smoothness between them.

3 Motion Synthesis

3.1 Path Finding

Now we need to find a path to pass through the possible matches and form a continuous motion. Our criteria is to choose the path with largest probability. We model the motion data as a first-order Markov process, so the transition from one clip to the next depends only on the current clip. To measure the transition probability between motion clips, we create a probability matrix, the ijth component of which gives the probability for clip i to transfer to clip j.

For the two clips which are consecutive originally, the transition between them is likely to be pleasing. So, we set one to the probability between this kind of clips. For the clips which are not consecutive, we estimate the probability by measuring the difference at the stitching point, that is, the last frame of clip i and the first frame of clip j. Inspired by the work presented in Lee[5], we define the ij th component as:

$$P_{ij} = \begin{cases} 1 & \text{if Clip } i,j \text{ are consecutive} \\ \exp(-D_{ij}/\sigma) & \text{otherwise} \end{cases} \tag{5}$$

$$D_{ij} = d(m_{i,l_i-1}, m_{j,0}) + d(v_{i,l_i-1}, v_{j,0}) \tag{6}$$

The first term describes the difference between the last frame of clip i and the first frame of clip j. $m_{i,k}$ indicates the pose from clip i frame k, $0 \le k < l_i$, l_i is the length of clip i. The second term describes the difference between the velocities at the stitch point. $v_{i,k}$ indicates the velocity of frame k from clip i, $0 \le k < l_i$. l_i is the length of Clip i .The second term can help us to differ the similar pose from different motions, such as jumping upward and falling downward.

The difference between pose is defined as:

$$d(m_{i,l_i-1}, m_{j,0}) = \| p_{i,l_i-1} - p_{j,0} \|^2 + \sum_{k=1}^{N} w_k \| \log((q_{j,0}^{(k)})^{-1} q_{i,l_i-1}^{(k)}) \|^2 \tag{7}$$

The difference between velocities at the stitch point is defined as:

$$d(v_{i,l_i-1}, v_{j,0}) = \| (p_{i,l_i-1} - p_{i,l_i-2}) - (p_{j,1} - p_{j,0}) \|^2 \tag{8}$$

Here, the first subscript is for Clip, the second for Frame, and superscript is for joint. For example, $q^{(k)}_{i,l_i-1}$ is the unit quaternion for Clip i Frame $l_i - 1$ Joint k. Weights w_k are set to one for important joints such as head, shoulder, elbow, hip, knee and root; weights for other joints are set to zero.

3.2 Motion Stitch

Now that we have the most probable path, the ends of clips may still have discontinuities. A transition might be noticeable if the motion clips simply jumped from one to another, so we need to stitch them seamlessly. In this section, we adopted a motion stitch algorithm under the framework of multiresolution motion analysis proposed by Lee[12].

As we know the motion data captured by motion capture system are realistic and highly detailed. We decompose the original data into an overall motion signal and a sequence of different level of details. Then we respectively stitch the base signals, and levels of details. Finally, we compose the stitched base signal and stitched levels of details into a stitched highly detailed motion.

Let M_A and M_B are two motion signals, their multiresolution representations are constructed as:

$$M_A = (m_A^{(0)}, d_A^{(0)}, ..., d_A^{(1)}, d_A^{(N-1)}) \tag{9}$$

$$M_B = (m_B^{(0)}, d_B^{(0)}, ..., d_B^{(1)}, d_B^{(N-1)}) \tag{10}$$

The stitching result is denoted as M_C. Joints coefficients of M_C at the boundary of M_A and M_B are set to the average of the last joint coefficients of M_A and the first joint coefficients of M_B. Changes made in the boundary will be smoothly propagated to the neighboring frames as coefficients of M_C is recovered to highly detailed motion data from multiresolution representation.

4 Experiments

We implement our method on an Intel Pentium IV 2.8GHz 512MB PC. Experiments of our method are done with a trampoline sport video. The reconstructed three-dimensional motion sequence is shown in Fig. 3. The first column is video sequence, the second is the silhouettes extracted from video. The third, the forth and the fifth columns are the reconstruction results. The third is the final matched synthetic silhouettes, the forth is the corresponding three dimensional motion poses at the same viewpoint with the video, the fifth is the same motion poses viewed at a different viewpoint. Experiments are also done to demonstrate the effectiveness of motion stitch method. (Fig. 2) At the boundary of two clips, they are smoothly stitched and the angular (linearly) velocities are also quite fair.

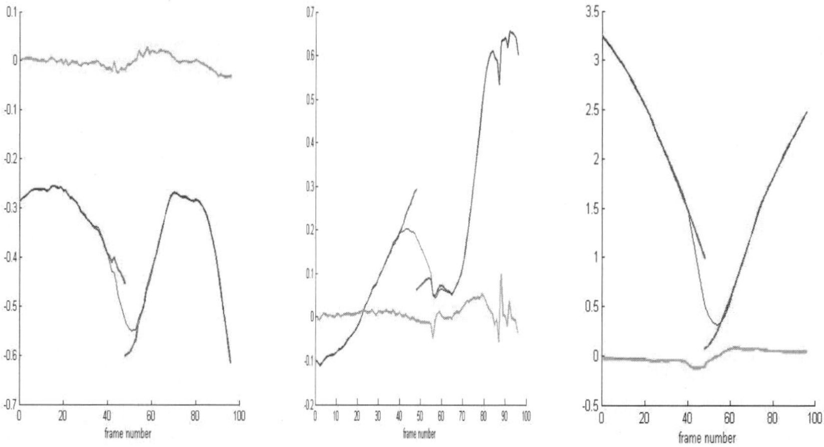

(a) left elbow **(b) left knee** **(c) root position**

Fig. 2. Stitch motion clips. The purple curves are matched motion clips from database. The blue are stitched clips. The green are the angular (linear) velocity curves. (a)(b)(c) visualize the motion signals corresponding to the y of left elbow, the x of right elbow and the y of root position.

5 Conclusion and Future Work

We have presented a method of motion synthesis in motion reconstruction based on video and verified the effectiveness of our method by trampoline video reconstruction. The results are visually comparable with motion capture data recorded by motion capture system. The major limitation of this method is that it requires a large and high quality motion database that similar motions in video are included. We believe that it is not a serious problem because in many applications the types of human behavior are limited. Another drawback of our method as it currently stands is the method for breaking the silhouette signal into clips. Now we divide the signal into clips of equal length. Though we have made the video frame rate be the same with motion data, this strategy is somewhat arbitrary. What is important is that both the real silhouette signal and synthetic one are broken at analogous locations. We are working to remedy this deficiency.

Acknowledgement

This work is supported by National973 project (2002CB312104); Key project of international technology cooperation (2005DFA11060); Key Project of NSF (60533070); NSF of China (60573162, 60403042, 60473002); 863 Plan of China (2005AA114010); National Special Item for Olympics (Z0004024040231, Z0004027040331); Beijing Natural Science Foundation (4051004,4062032); and Knowledge Innovation Project (20056380) of Institute of Computing Technology, Chinese Academy of Sciences.

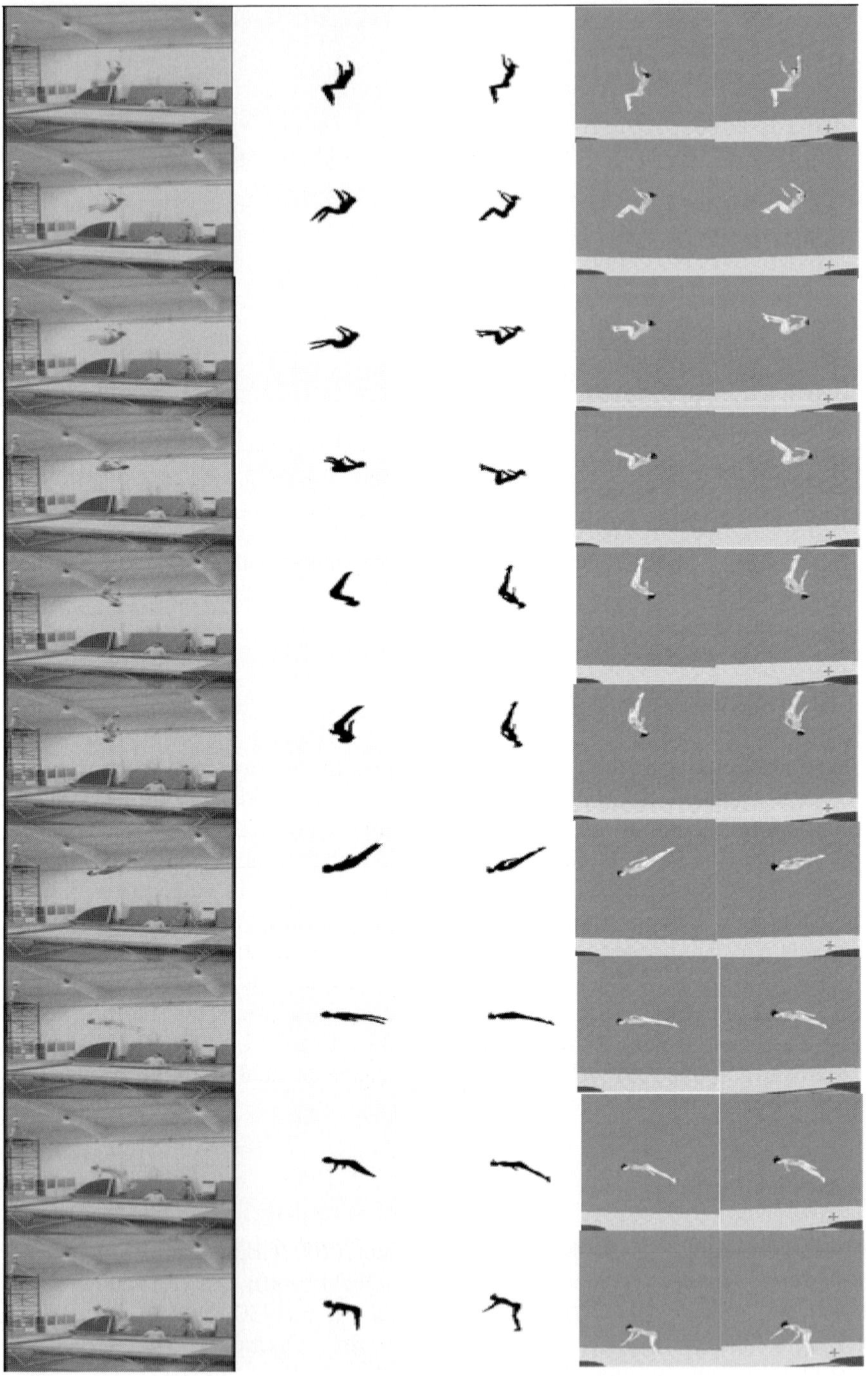

Fig. 3. Reconstruction of a trampoline video

References

1. Delamarre, Q., Faugeras, O.D.: 3D Articulated Models and Multi-view Tracking with Silhouettes, Proceedings of the International Conference on Computer Vision (1999), 716–721.
2. Shakhnarovich, G., Viola, P., Darrellj, T.: Fast Pose Estimation with Parameter-sensitive Hashing, IEEE International Conference on Computer Vision(2003),750–757.
3. Mori, G., Malik, J.: Estimating Human Body Configurations using Shape Context Matching, Proceedings of European Conference on Computer Vision(2002), Vol. 3. 666–680.
4. Pullen, K., Bregler, C.: Motion Capture assisted Animation: Texturingand Synthesis, Proceedings of SIGGRAPH (2002).
5. Lee, J., Chai, J., REITSMA, P. S. A., Hodgins, J. K., Pollard, N.S.: Interactive Control of Avatars Animated with Human Motion Data, Proc. SIGGRAPH (2002).
6. Ren, L., Shakhnarovich, G., Hodgins, J. K., Pfister, H., Viola, P.l.: Learning Silhouette Features for Control of Human Motion, Proceedings of the SIGGRAPH (2004)
7. Chai, J., Hodgins, J. K., Performance Animation from Low-dimensional Control Signals, ACM Transactions on Graphics (SIGGRAPH 2005) (2005),24(3).
8. Qiu, X., Wang,Z., Xia S.: A Novel Computer Vision Technique Used on Sport Video, Journal of WSCG (2004), 545-55.
9. Qiu, X. Wang, Z., Xia,S: Inferring 3D Pose from Uncalibrated Video by Contour Matching, Proceeding of International Conference on Computer Animation and Social gents (2005).
10. Qiu, X. Wang, Z., Xia,S, Sun, Y.: Inferring 3D Body Pose from Uncalibrated Video, Proceeding of RoboCup(2005).
11. Unuma, M., Anjyo, K., Tekeuchi, R.: Fourier Principles for Emotion-based Human Figure Animation, proc. SIGGRAPH (1995), 91–96.
12. Lee, J., Shin, S. Y.: A Coordinate-invariant Approachto Multiresolution MotionAnalysis, Graphical Models(2001),63, 2, 87–105.
13. Bruderlin,A., Williams, L.: Motion Signal Processing, proc. SIGGRAPH(1995), 97–104.
14. Hu, M.K: Visual Pattern Recognition by Moment Invariants, IRE Trans. on Inf. Theory(1962), 8,179~182.
15. Shoemake, K.: Animating Rotation with Quaternion Curves. Computer Graphics: Proceedings of SIGGRAPH(1985),19:245–254.

Spatio-temporal Visualization of Battlefield Entities and Events

Qiyue Fong[1], Foo Meng Ng[2], and Zhiyong Huang[1]

[1] School of Computer Science,
National University of Singapore
fongqiyue@gmail.com,
huangzy@comp.nus.edu.sg
[2] Human Factors Laboratory,
DSO National Labs, Singapore
nfoomeng@dso.org.sg

Abstract. In this work, we address visualization of spatio-temporal data for military application. Four different visualization prototypes have been developed to track the movement of military entities across a land surface over time; three more have been developed to track the occurrences of numerous war events. We have implemented the prototypes in a software system with a novel clock face GUI. Usability tests have been carried out and confirmed the effectiveness of the solution.

1 Introduction

As time progresses during warfare, it becomes increasingly difficult for commanders to manually analyze and spot patterns inherent in large, complicated sets of battlefield data. Limitations of human memory and our inability to compute complex calculations simply prevent us from performing such complex tasks. It may, perhaps, be wise to make use of the powerful computing capabilities of a computer and visual computer graphics to circumvent the problems stated above. The goal of this work is thus to research and explore existing solutions which capture and visualize the spatial relationships of battlefield entities over time within a single interactive picture. Four different visualization prototypes have been developed to track the movement of military entities across a land surface over time; three more have been developed to track the occurrences of numerous war events (one snapshot in Figure 1(a)). A novel clock face GUI has also been designed and implemented to help users of the software query the system with time constraints (Figure 1(b)). Usability tests have also been carried out on all the visualization prototypes as well as the Time Query GUI to determine their applicability and usefulness and to uncover any potential human factors problems.

H.-P. Seidel, T. Nishita, and Q. Peng (Eds.): CGI 2006, LNCS 4035, pp. 622–629, 2006.

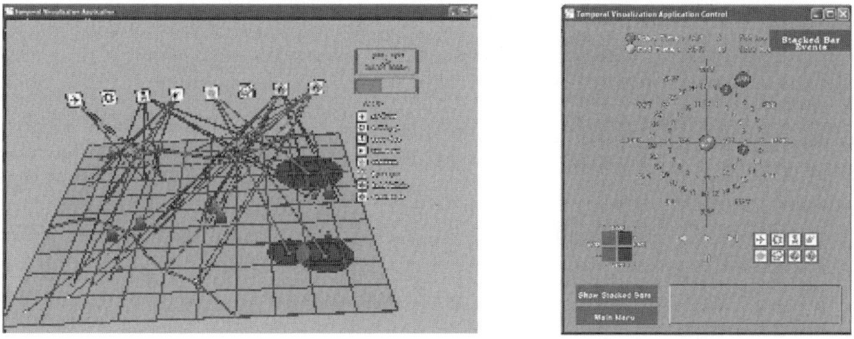

(a) (b)

Fig. 1. Illustration of the graphics display (a) and clock face GUI (b)

2 Related Work and Our Contributions

Different existing techniques which visualize spatio-temporal data are found in [1], [2], and [4]. In [5], a common thematic map known as the choropleth map, can represent different magnitudes of an attribute which changes over time using shaded units. Also, the Z-Axis in 3D space can be used to represent time, a technique used in [3]. Space represented by the first and second dimensions combined, while time by the third dimension in a 3D space is an innovative idea.

Our work adopts and improves on the techniques described above to serve our purposes. In general, it extends all existing ideas in 2D into 3D; and conducts experiments with all the aforementioned advanced techniques. It results in a plethora of spatio-temporal visualization prototypes.

Unlike most existing work, this work attempts not only to explore and describe the various ways of visualization, but also allows potential users to compare and contrast these various techniques through a single application and then determine empirically how preferred each technique is (or if there was simply no preference) over the others.

3 Our Work

3.1 The Clock Face GUI

To the best of our knowledge, most time query user interfaces make use of widgets or visual metaphors such as the timeline/time slider, time dials and calendar controls to form a time query. Each of these has limitation(s) that fail to serve the purposes of the temporal data being dealt with here. Temporal data in the military context is precise and accurate. Timelines and time dials do not allow selection of such precise values. A full calendar is space-wasting. Although a dynamic calendar (such as Microsoft's calendar) is space-saving, it only allows selection of a date but not time. Time can only be selected by clicking the "increase" or "decrease" button multiple times which is inefficient. This motivated us to design a novel time query interface, the clock face GUI (Figure 1(b)), that can overcome these limitations to serve our purposes.

The clock face GUI combines circular structures with the conventional calendar resulting in a compact, space-saving UI. It consists of three concentric circles each representing a particular time unit (Month/Day/Hour). Each circle is color coded to guide the user. Two grid lines intersecting at the center of the clock interface divides it into four quadrants to reduce search times for a value.

The clock face GUI together with other controls, form the complete interface to interact with the main display. It allows selection of 1) time moment, 2) time interval, 3) time range within a day, 4) battlefield events; and also animation playback functions.

3.2 The Spatio-temporal Visualization Prototypes

We describe the seven spatio-temporal visualization prototypes here. Four track locations (movement) of enemy battlefield entities that change over time while three track occurrences of battlefield events over time. The term "battlefield entities" refer to army units. Without loss of generality, we present the enemy data only.

Dot graph: It provides a snapshot of the distribution and strength of each enemy unit across the terrain at a particular time moment (Figure 2).

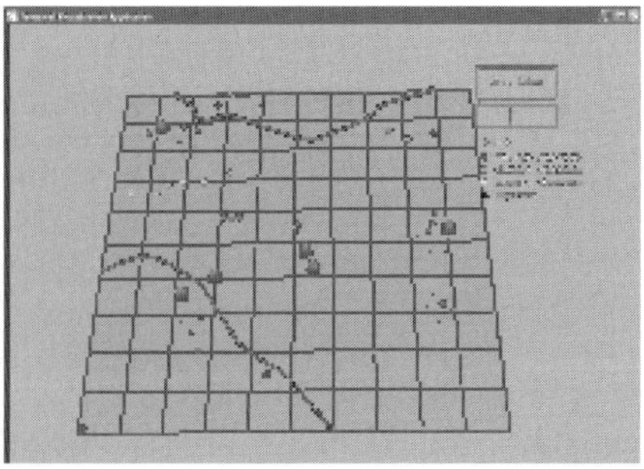

Fig. 2. The dot graph

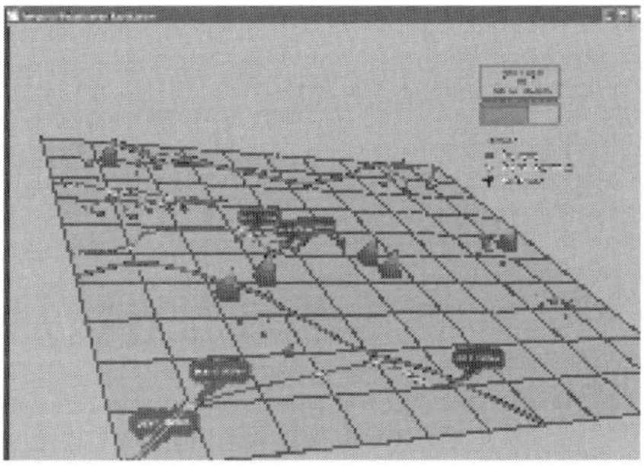

Fig. 3. The trail graph (with time tags)

Dots represent enemy units marking their locations on the terrain at some time moment, t. Each dot is colored which describes the strength of each unit. Dots on the map change color and increase in number over time due to the splitting of a unit. Such colored dot maps, hence, are an instance of a choropleth map.

Trail graph: It gives a snapshot of both the current as well as historical locations of each enemy unit in a given time interval. Dots mark a unit's location on the terrain. Curved lines (trails) connect a unit's historical and current locations together, showing movement. Trails approximate the path that a unit moves along. It solves a limitation posed by Dot Graph (ie. inability to show historical information).

This prototype, hence, is an instance of the 2D line plot graph extended into 3D. Users may click on the dots to display time tags to reveal time associated with each dot. Plotting these time tags on the terrain is analogous to the scatter plot graph. With these time tags, it is possible for user to estimate the speed at which a unit is moving.

Spoke graph: It functions like the trail graph with some enhancements. A spoke is a rod-like structure that extends along the y-axis in 3D space. Spokes were initially used to solve a drawback posed by the Trail Graph – inability to distinguish between two units that traveled along the same path at different times.

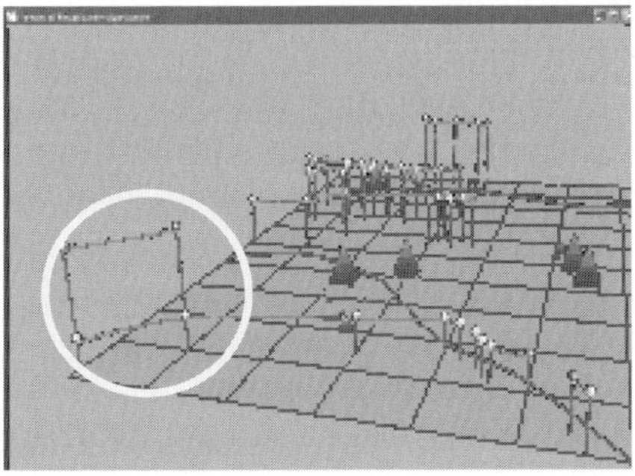

Fig. 4. Spokes to differentiate the enemy units

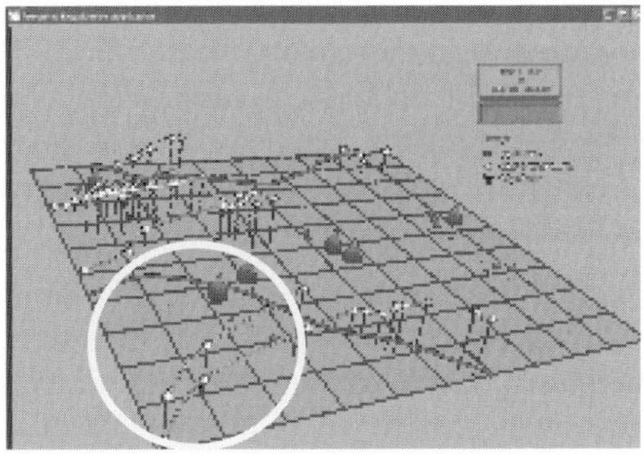

Fig. 5. Spokes to depict time value

Figure 4 shows how each dot along any trail is elevated by a spoke at a fixed height. The height of each spoke was used to identify one enemy unit (moving along a trail) from another (moving along another trail). As such, two different units (circled) moving along the same path can be distinguished.

However, it may not seem obvious that height is used to differentiate units. Hence, the spokes idiom was modified to depict the time value that an enemy unit was found located at some position on the terrain (Figure 5).

From Figure 5, each spoke drawn along a unique trail now take on different height values. User can have an intuitive feel of how much time has elapsed before a particular unit has moved on to a new location and to predict its speed. The spokes still preserve its ability to differentiate among units moving along the same path (circled).

Raster graph: Multiple snapshots of locations of enemy units at successive time moments (Figure 6) is shown. Raster is a horizontal translucent plane in 3D space. This idea came from 2D chess maps.

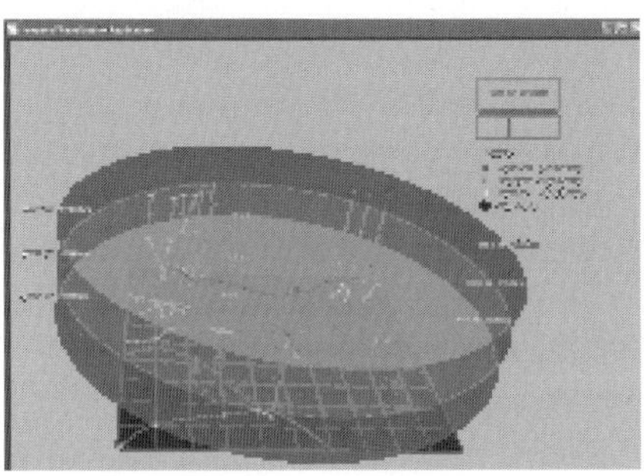

Fig. 6. The raster graph

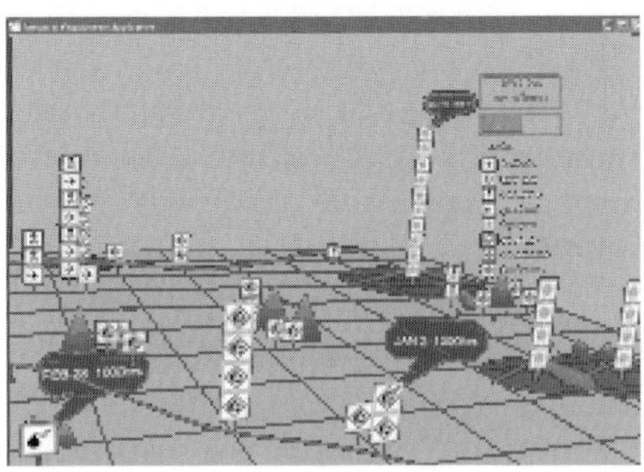

Fig. 7. The stacked bar graph

Each raster offers a snapshot of the locations of each enemy unit at a particular time. Vertical grey lines drawn through the rasters connect units representing the same army unit on each raster. Cyan colored lines depict splitting behavior. Rasters are displayed in successive times, allowing comparison of the movement and/or splitting behavior of the enemy units between two or more successive times. Such comparison is useful in seeing if any unit has remained in its position for a long time by looking down at the line projected from the unit in space to the unit on the map. If the unit is found on each n raster along this projected line, it means that it has not moved/split for the past n successive times.

The following three graphs are designed to track the occurrences of battlefield events.

Stacked bar graph: Stacked Bar Graph retrieves battlefield events found to be associated with a time moment or interval. Then, they are stacked in a vertical bar (Figure 7). Each vertical bar "holds" all the events that occurred at the same spatial location at a particular time moment or interval. In other words, it is able to convey what events occurred and where they occurred at some time moment or interval. To some extent, this prototype was inspired by the 2D bar graphs

Such a simple representation is capable of conveying lots of useful information. First, it can depict event recurrence at a location by observing the number of icons found in a stacked bar. Second, the events found in a stacked bar are sorted according to time, thus, the order of events occurring at a location can be inferred. Third, by clicking on an event icon in stacked bar, time tags are displayed. Time tags allow the inference of causality relationships between events.

Grouped links graph: Grouped Links Graph is capable of showing the distribution of events across a land surface effectively. It does so by grouping links that link to the same type of events on the terrain together (Figure 8). Links are lines joining an event icon to a particular location on the map. These links have the same color as that associated with the event icon it is joined to and are thus associated with the event that the event icon refers to. A link represents an occurrence of the event it is associated with. A thicker link means there are more than one occurrence of an event.

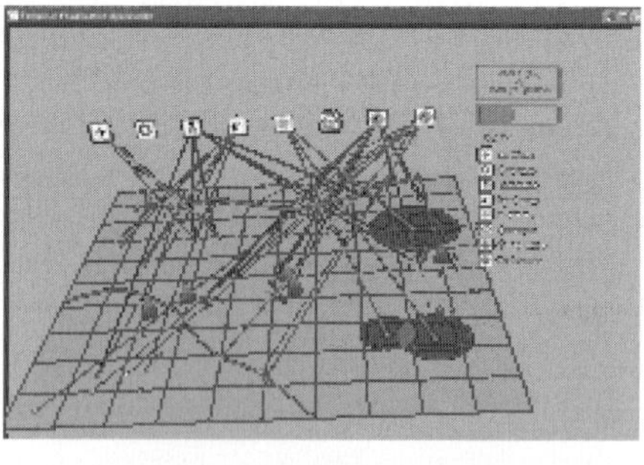

Fig. 8. Grouped links graph

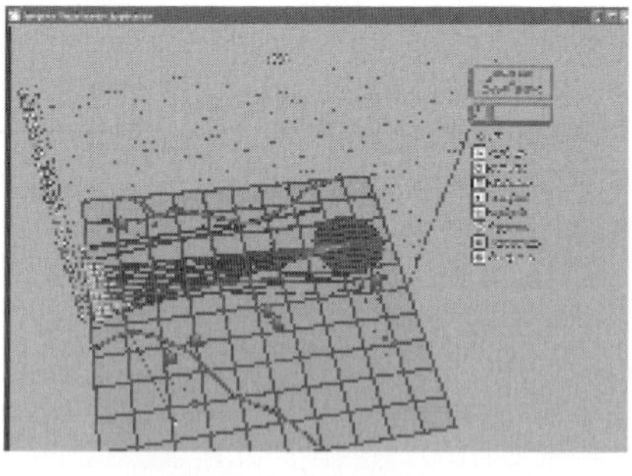

Fig. 9. The calendar graph

One useful feature of this visualization technique is that comparison of the number of occurrences of an event with another can be made intuitively (from the degree of the "meshing" of links) without having to count the exact numbers.

Calendar graph: It retrieves data about battlefield events found to be associated with a given time moment or a month and plots them onto a calendar drawn perpendicular to the map (Figure 9).

The calendar displays all the days of a month in rows. All event icons found in a row on the calendar are sorted according to time. This graph was inspired by GeoTime[3]. Some modifications were made to GeoTime to adapt to the type of data this project deals with.

In GeoTime, event icons are drawn directly above the location at which they occurred on the map. The height of the event icons corresponds to the date on the calendar. Two drawbacks can be observed in GeoTime. First, when the main display is rotated, it becomes hard to determine which date each event icon corresponds to because no link is drawn to connect the icon to the calendar. Second, GeoTime is unable to represent the scenario where two different types of events are occurring at the same location and at the same time. This is because only one event icon can be drawn above a location and mapped to a date on the calendar at any one time. The Calendar Graph attempts to improve on these drawbacks to serve its own purposes.

To solve the first drawback, event icons are directly plotted onto the calendar. To solve the second drawback, different types of events that occur concurrently at the same locations are represented by their respective icons plotted side by side on the same row in the calendar. Each of these icons is connected by a colored line to the location where it occurred. With a calendar, time information becomes obvious. It is like a neat report showing which events have occurred and at what date/time.

4 Usability Study

Our usability tests aim to determine 1) ease-of-use of the clock face GUI, 2) effectiveness of each prototype in conveying spatio-temporal information and 3) to uncover any potential human factors problems inherent in the system. A test methodology described by [6] was adopted for the tests.

Medium: Low-interaction method was used in tests on the clock face GUI to determine if the participants were able to complete certain tasks without any help or prior training. A mixture of low- and high-interaction methods was used in the tests on the prototypes to collect as many different interpretations of the visualizations as possible to determine if they are interpreted according to the original intentions.

Test specifications: A test has two participants: the test participant and the tester. Each test participant has to complete 10 test cases followed by a mini questionnaire. The test cases are briefly described as follows:

Test Cases 1 - 2 on the clock face GUI: They aim to determine the ease of use of the clock face GUI. For each task in a test case, the participant selects a given time query. Time taken for the participant to do a correct selection is measured using a stopwatch and recorded.

Test Case 3 on the complete clock face GUI: This aims to determine how easily the complete clock face GUI can be manipulated to do a given list of tasks.

Test Cases 4 -10 on the 7 spatio-temporal visualization prototypes: These require the participant to carry out a given task related to the prototype. The participant was then asked to describe what the visual graphics is that appear on the main display.

Choice of participants: Due to the classified nature of the project, only fellow colleagues and HYP students within the DSO organization were asked to participate. More information about the 8 participants is shown in Figure 10.

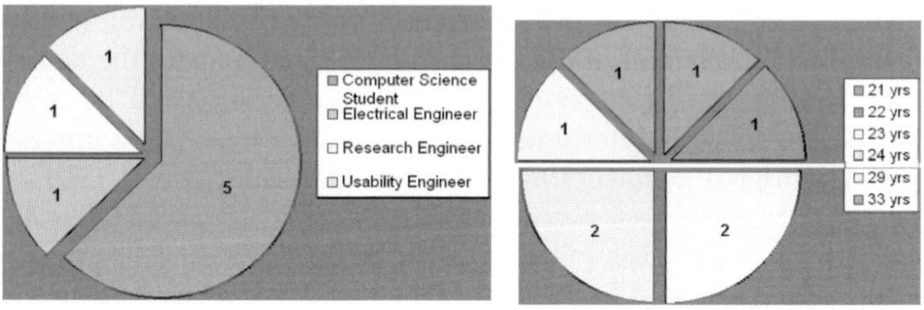

(a) (b)

Fig. 10. Participant information: (a) occupation and (b) age distribution

Test environment: Human Factors Engineering Lab at DSO@Kent Ridge. No audio or video recording was used.

Test data obtained are collated and analyzed empirically. To make these conclusions apply for a general population, a statistical method called the Student's T-Test for two independent samples was used. In Student's T-Test, a value known as the test statistic, t, is calculated and compared with a value, c, in the T-Table. For any two independent samples A and B, if $t < c$, then the null hypothesis (i.e. meanA = meanB) is accepted at some level of confidence. Otherwise, the null hypothesis is rejected (i.e. meanA < meanB or meanA > meanB, depending on the values of meanA and meanB from the data). From these results, we can make conclusions, at some level of confidence, about some observation that we are investigating over a general population.

Summary of test results

Test Cases 1-2: Time taken to select time units across 1, 2 or 3 quadrants in the clock face GUI appears to be the same. When a time interval was to be selected, time taken to do so generally increases by two to three times. Participants who managed to figure out certain shortcuts in selection took less time – at least by half of the time taken by non-shortcuts.

Test Case 3: Participants did not experience any difficulties using the complete clock face GUI. Positive responses were given to the clock face GUI in terms of aesthetics, ease-of-use, intuitiveness, effective feedback and usefulness.

Test Cases 4-10: Generally, all test participants gave interpretations for each of the 7 prototypes similar to the original intentions of the visualization design. Participants felt that all prototypes were useful and informative, but not necessarily communicative or intuitive. This concurs with the observation that participants usually take some time to study the visualization before giving their interpretations. However, once the "studying" stage was over, comments came flowing in. ${}^4C_2$ binary comparisons were made between 2 prototypes from the set: Dots, Trails, Spokes and Rasters. At 95% confidence level, users across a population found Trail Graph more informative and useful than Dot Graph but expressed no preference over any prototype in the other binary comparisons. ${}^{3}C_{2}$ binary comparisons were made between 2 prototypes from the set: Stacked Bar, Grouped Links and Calendar. At 95% confidence level, users across a population found Calendar more informative and useful than Grouped Links but expressed no preference over any prototype in the other binary comparisons.

5 Conclusion

In this paper, we have proposed and implemented a software system to visualize spatio-temporal data of a battlefield. Four different visualization prototypes have been developed to track the movement of military entities across a land surface over time; while three more have been developed to track the occurrences of numerous war events over time. A novel clock face GUI has also been designed and implemented. Usability tests have also been carried out to determine the applicability and usefulness as well as to uncover any potential human factors problems.

References

1. Andrienko, N., Andrienko, G., Gatalsky, P. (2000). Visualization of Spatio-Temporal Information in the Internet. In Proceedings of the 11th International Workshop on Database and Expert Systems Applications, IEEE Computer Society, Washington, DC, USA, 2000, pp 577-585.
2. Elvins, T.T. (1997). VisFiles: Presentation Techniques for Time-Series Data, ACM SIGGRAPH Computer Graphics, New York, USA, Volume 31, Issue 2, May 1997, pp 14-16.
3. Kapler, T., Wright, W. (2004).Visualization for Tracking Battlefield Events in Time and Space for C2. 2004 Command and Control Research and Technology Symposium, 2004, pp 1-11.
4. Müller, W., Schumann, H. (2003) Visualization Methods for Time-Dependent Data – An Overview. In Proceedings of the 2003 Winter Simulation Conference, New Orleans, Louisiana, 2003, pp 737-745.
5. Slocum, T.A., McMaster, R.B., Kessler, F.C., Howard, H.H. (2004). In Thematic Cartography and Geographic Visualization. Prentice Hall Series, Upper Saddle River, NJ07458, 2nd Edition, 2004.
6. Weinschenk, S., Jamar, P., Yeo, S.C. (1997). In GUI Design Essentials. Wiley Computer Publishing, New York, USA.

3D City Model Generation from Ground Images

Kyung Ho Jang and Soon Ki Jung

Department of Computer Engineering, Kyungpook National University
1370 Sankyuk-dong, Buk-gu, Daegu, 702-701 South Korea
{khjang, skjung}@knu.ac.kr

Abstract. In this paper, a 3D city model generation method is described. At first, the ground images around the area of interest are acquired using a camera mounted on a GPS device and digital compass, which provide the initial inaccurate pose of each image. An adjacency graph that spatially represents the adjacency between images or buildings is built to handle efficiently a huge number of unordered image sequences. A set of images with views of the same building is automatically grouped, and an optimization algorithm based on SFM corrects their poses. Finally, a method of global pose estimation is outlined that can register 3D isolated building models in a global coordinate system. We validate our approach with a set of experiments on some urban sites.

1 Introduction

The reconstruction of large-scale 3D building models is important for a variety of applications, such as fly-through rendering and simulations for urban mission planning. Many researchers have used aerial images [12], which provide wide area coverage, but it often has lack of facade information. 3D range scanning devices have provided accurate geometric and photorealistic 3D models [7]. Hybrid approach uses ground images and a laser scanner for 3D modeling [5]. Most commercial 3D range scanning systems are expensive because of the actuators required for the precise control of the camera and light projector.

Modeling from ground view images is a cost-effective means of obtaining detailed large-scale urban models. While several practical systems by the user interaction have been proposed [2,16], many researchers have also developed Structure from Motion (SFM) based algorithms for automatic 3D reconstruction [11,1,8]. Most of the SFM based techniques; however, apply to only limited small scales and partial reconstruction of buildings. Their approach cannot handle multiple image sequences. Sainz *et al.* [3] presented a method that uses a divide and conquer strategy to split the video sequences into subsequences. The poses of subsequences are estimated by SFM and self-calibration technique, independently. But subsequences have the different of internal camera parameters. Sato *et al.* [4] developed a method that acquires a dense 3D model of the outdoor scene from multiple image sequences captured by a video camera with a wide-angle lens. They use a set of predefined markers and natural features to extract external parameters. However,, the acquisition of 3-D positions of the markers in real world is a difficult task without any specific device. Furthermore, a large number of predefined markers are required for large-scale building modeling.

H.-P. Seidel, T. Nishita, and Q. Peng (Eds.): CGI 2006, LNCS 4035, pp. 630 – 638, 2006.

2 System Overview

So far, we investigate the limitation of classical SFM based system for reconstructing large-scale 3D building models. To solve the problem, an efficient method should be devised to handle a large number of image features obtained from multiple image sequences. Some auxiliary devices will solve the problem. Coorg and Teller [13] used spherical mosaics produced from accurately calibrated ground view cameras with a GPS device. This system has a difficulty to capture spherical mosaics for a wide area. Hence, we propose a simple acquisition system in which a hand-held digital camera equipped with a GPS and digital compass is used. The device assists the SFM based algorithms, and so a system based on SFM for large-scale site modeling is feasible.

The system consists of four parts: feature extraction, adjacency graph generation, isolated geometry reconstruction, and global pose estimation (see Fig. 1.). We capture unordered image sequences with their camera pose information around the area of interest. The pose information of each image is roughly acquired from a GPS and digital compass. Camera pose estimation and 3D geometry reconstruction of buildings are achieved by a classical SFM technique. In this case, the accurate internal parameters of the camera and reliable features among image sequences are required. Therefore, we extract several reliable features such as lines, corners and vanishing points (VPs) by using an enhanced feature extraction scheme. To handle image features, we obtain an adjacency graph that spatially represents the adjacency between images with views of the same building. Finally, global pose estimation is outlined that can register 3D isolated building models in a global coordinate system using a panoramic image or a image sequence.

This paper is organized as follows: Section 3 explains image feature extraction and adjacency graph for 3D reconstruction. Section 4 describes a reconstruction of isolated building geometry, followed by global pose estimation in section 5. Some experimental results and conclusion are discussed in section 6 and section 7.

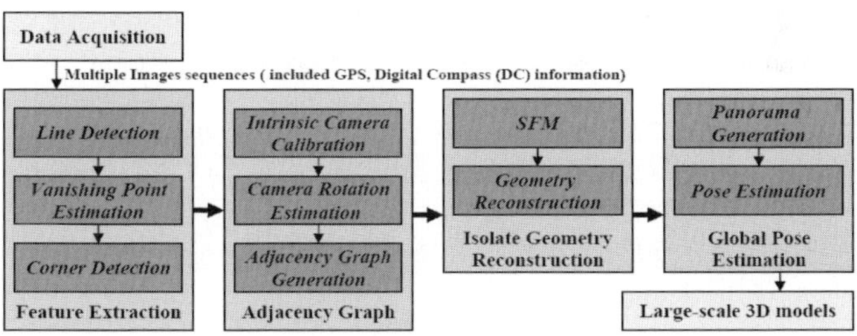

Fig. 1. System overview

3 Image Features and Adjacency Graph

3.1 Line Segments, Vanishing Point and Corner

Kesidis and Papamarkos proposed the inverse Hough transform (IHT) for straight-line detection and filtering [10]. However, the result is unsuitable for vanishing point computation and corner detection, because the algorithm is not designed to detect accurate line segments. Therefore, a modified IHT is proposed.

Firstly, a classical Hough transform with low resolution Hough cells is used to obtain a set of local maxima. Due to the resolution error, the true line exists within the range of $\rho_d-0.5\Delta_\rho\leq \rho \leq\rho_d+0.5\Delta_\rho$ and $\theta_d-0.5\Delta_\theta\leq \theta \leq\theta_d+0.5\Delta_\theta$, where (ρ,θ) is the parameter of the true line, (ρ_d,θ_d) is the local maxima, and $(\Delta_\rho,\Delta_\theta)$ is the size of each cell. We expand the cell (ρ_d, θ_d) into $n\times n$ sub-cells. The best-fit line L_{ij} is then estimated by performing IHT for each polar parameter (ρ_i, θ_i), where $\rho_i = \rho_d+ \Delta_\rho (i/n-0.5)$, $\theta_i =\theta_d + \Delta_\theta(i/n-0.5)$, and $0\leq i$, or $j\leq n$. For all edge points supporting the line L_{ij}, we cut the line into separate line segments if the distance between two adjacent edge points is greater than ε_d. To reduce the quantization effect of both the image and the parameter space and to eliminate the false line segments due to the low threshold in the Hough transform, we exploit solidity of line segments, which is the number of edge points supporting the line segment divided by its length. If the solidity of the line segment is less than ε_c, then the line segment is considered as noise. All the candidate line segments are sorted based on length to find the true local maxima. Finally the longest line segment is selected and subtracts one from the length of each line segments stored in the cells. Repeat this process until the next maximum length of the line segments is less than a predefined threshold. Prior to estimating the vanishing point, a group of line segments that is parallel in the 3D world needs to be identified. A global line clustering and vanishing points (VPs) diction algorithm are used based on uniform tessellations of a Gaussian sphere [12]. In order to eliminate superfluous corners in the area of uninteresting such as trees, the grouped lines of VPs used to eliminate corner features, except for the corner features of a building. This method can be easily executed by combining the grouped lines and corner features.

(a) (b)

(c) (d)

Fig. 2. Result of features extraction: (a) Results of line segments extraction ($\varepsilon_d=3$, $\varepsilon_c=0.6$) (b) Horizontal VP and Vertical VP (the accumulated cells in a Gaussian sphere.), (c) Result of Result of (b), and (d) Harris corners (left) and Corners on façade (right)

3.2 Adjacency Graph Generation

With respect to the camera calibration using the vanishing points, a recent study estimated the camera parameters using two orthogonal vanishing points (OVPs). Although Guillou *et al.* [6] presented a method using two OVPs, under assuming that the principal point is the image center. For a more accurate intrinsic calibration, we use a simple, geometrically intuitive method based on radical center estimation [14].

Three OVPs and the internal parameters give the camera rotation relative to a 3D model. Yet, many images only have two OVPs. Given two OVPs, another vanishing point can be easily computed using known intrinsic parameters. Let the vertical and horizontal vanishing points and the principal point be $U(x_u,y_u)$, $V(x_v,y_v)$ and $P(x_p,y_p)$. Third vector is $\vec{r}_w = \vec{r}_u \times \vec{r}_v$ where $\vec{r}_u = (x_u - x_c, y_u - y_c, f)^T$ and $\vec{r}_v = (x_v - x_c, y_v - y_c, f)^T$ in the camera coordinate system. The model-to-camera rotation R_{mc} is defined as follows:

$$R_{mc} = [\lambda_v \vec{r}_v \quad \lambda_u \vec{r}_u \quad \lambda_w \vec{r}_w], \text{ or } [\lambda_w \vec{r}_w \quad \lambda_u \vec{r}_u \quad \lambda_v \vec{r}_v]., \tag{1}$$

where λ_v, λ_u, λ_w are scaling factors. While λ_u is positive value because $\vec{r}_u$ is the view up vector, there exist ambiguities in the signs of λ_v, λ_w because there are four cases for the location of the model origin [12], which need to be resolved. We can determine the camera-to-world rotation matrix without the ambiguities by using digital compass information as depicted in Fig. 3, where (X_m, Y_m, Z_m), (X_w, Y_w, Z_w), and (X_c, Y_c, Z_c) denote the model, world, and camera coordinate systems. $Y_w=Y_m$ by assuming that the architectures are always vertical. The value θ of the digital compass represents the clockwise panning angle from Z_w(North) axis to the viewing direction , that is the projection of the vector $-Z_c$ onto the X_w,Z_w plane. The Z_w axis after panning motion $-\tilde{Z}_w$ is denoted by $\tilde{Z}_w = (-\sin\theta \quad 0 \quad \cos\theta)^T$ in the camera coordinates. The three world coordinate axes in the camera coordinates, X_{wc}, Y_{wc}, Z_{wc} are computed as

$$Y_{wc} = \lambda_u \vec{r}_u,\ X_{wc} = Y_{wc} \times \tilde{Z}_w, \text{ and } Z_{wc} = X_{wc} \times Y_{wc}. \tag{2}$$

From equation (2), the world-to-camera rotation matrix, $R_{wc} = [X_{wc}, Y_{wc}, Z_{wc}]^T$. Finally we choose any corner point in the building as the model origin. Then the signs of λ_v and λ_w are determined by comparing $\lambda_v \vec{r}_v$ with Z_{wc} and X_{wc} as illustrated in Fig. 5. After that, we will resolve the inconsistency during building the adjacency graph. An adjacency graph is built to efficiently handle multiple image sequences. A node in the graph includes image as well as feature information; such as VPs, and camera pose information from a GPS and digital compass. An edge in the graph then joins two nodes if the camera poses are adjacent. Fig. 4 shows an example of the capture configuration. The target architectures are indicated as I, II, III, and IV, plus each solid circle and its arrows denote the position and viewing direction of the camera, respectively. Firstly, we assign unique numbers to images by using accession-numbering scheme, in which numbers are assigned sequentially as new image is added to the image database. For each image, reliable image features are extracted as mentioned above section 3.1, and a node is added in the adjacency graph.

An edge is added for two nodes n_i and n_j if the following conditions are satisfied:

{1} Euclidean distance, nd_{ij}, is less than ε_{nd}. The node position is obtained from the GPS. Quadtree is useful for finding a set of candidate nodes { $n_j | nd_{ij} < \varepsilon_{nd}$ } for a node n_j.

{2} The difference between two camera panning angles, dc_{ij}, is less than ε_{dc}. The panning angle is obtained from the digital compass.

{3} Two nodes have two or more VPs, and the difference between a pair of horizontal VPs, dv_{ij}, is less than ε_{dv}, which is defined as $dv_{ij} = \cos^{-1}(\vec{r}_{ia} \cdot \vec{r}_{jb} / \|\vec{r}_{ia}\| \|\vec{r}_{jb}\|)$, where $\vec{r}_{ia}$ is the ath vanishing direction in the ith image.

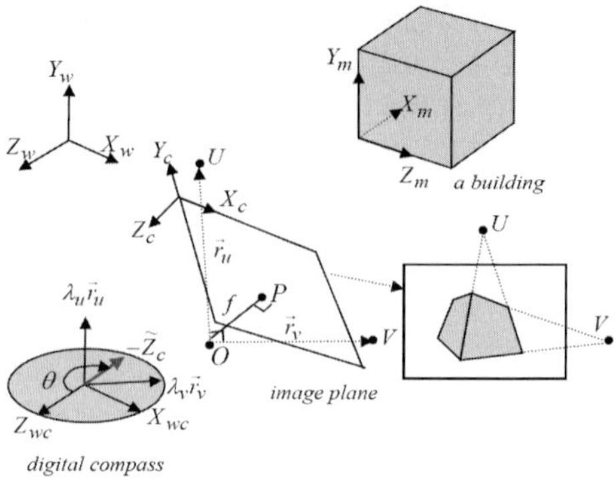

Fig. 3. Geometric relations between the two VPs and the three axes of the digital compass

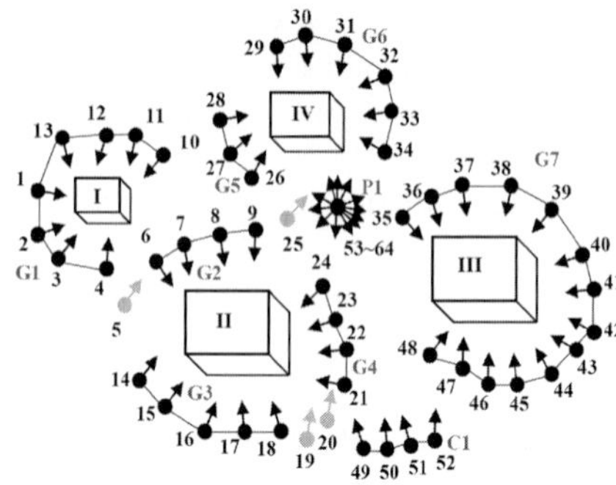

Fig. 4. Example of Adjacency Graph

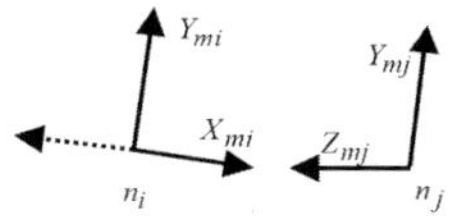

Fig. 5. Inconsistency of model coordinates

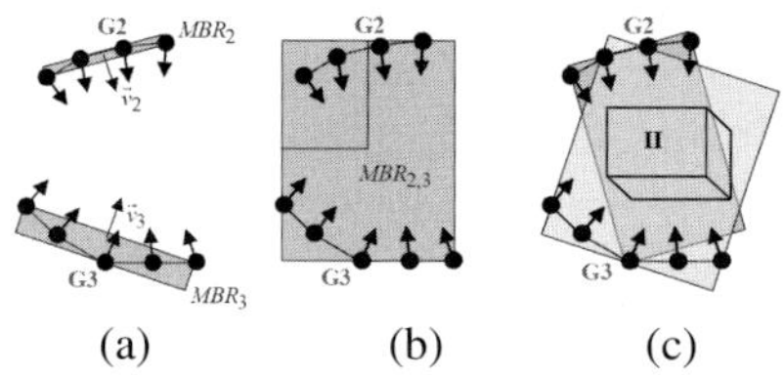

Fig. 6. Example of view overlapping geometry between two-isolated groups: (a) MBR_2 and MBR_3 (b) MBR_{23}, and (c) View overlapping.

In this case, the model coordinates inconsistency needs to be resolved. As illustrated in Fig. 5, two pairs of VPs for two nodes have a different relative direction. Yet, if X_{mi} and Z_{mi} have the opposite direction, the two pairs of VPs may actually correspond. The model coordinate system for the node n_j is updated and defined in equation (2). Given the adjacency graph, we extract a *panorama group P*, in which $\forall n_i, n_j \in nd_{ij} \cong 0$, and all nodes are connected with {2}. Next, a set of connected sub-graphs is extracted. Each connected sub-graph defines an isolated group, which can be utilized to reconstruct the isolated geometry by using SFM. For the remained nodes, {1} and {2} are tested. If both conditions are true, an edge between two nodes is inserted. Thereafter, a set of connected sub-graphs is extracted again from the graph. The connected sub-graph defines a connecting group. The panorama or connecting groups are used to estimate the global position. The nodes are classified into two types: an *intra-node* or *inter-node*, where an *intra-node* is in the isolated group, while an *inter-node* is in the panorama or connecting group. In Fig. 4, n_{53}~n_{64} form a panorama group P_1, G_1~G_7 are the isolated groups, and n_{49}~n_{52} are the connecting group C_1. Other nodes, n_5, n_{19}, n_{20}, and n_{26} are eliminated. Given the adjacency graph, a set of the isolated groups which views the same building is clustered for isolated building reconstruction. Firstly, the minimum-bounding rectangle, MBR_i of each isolated group G_i is created. Its one axis is the line between two end nodes of the isolated group. By summation of the viewing direction vectors for all nodes, the viewing direction, of the isolated group G_i is estimated as shown in Fig. 6(a). Secondly, a nearby MBR, MBR_j, of the MBR_i in the direction of $\vec{v}_i$ is found. Then the MBR of two isolated groups MBR_{ij} is computed. The length of its long axis is used to expand MBR_i and MBR_j with their normal directions, respectively, as shown in Fig. 6(b). The area of the overlapping region is then computed. If the area is above ε_{od}, two groups are merged.

4 Isolated Geometry Reconstruction

In isolated group, the first and second images of an isolated group are used to determine a reference frame. In order to consistent corresponding, we use RANSAC algorithm is used, and then the first and second projection matrices are determined using part of a multistage algorithm [8]. The structure is then refined using an Iterated Extended Kalman Filter for each point [11]. After we refine reconstructed structures through bundle adjustment [1]. To prevent error propagation, we use a divide and conquer strategy to split the image sequence of an isolated group into subsequences. As such, the poses of subsequences are independently estimated by SFM, and then the calibrated subsequences are integrated together. To unify the 3D results from subsequences, subsequences are mapped to the GPS position by using equation (3).

$$\min_{s,\theta,x_c,z_c} \sum_{i=1}^{N} D(m_{gi}, Tm_{si}), \tag{3}$$

where $D(m_{gi}, T_{msi})$ is Euclidean distance, $m_{gi}=(x_{gi}, z_{gi})$ and $m_{si}=(x_{si}, z_{si})$ are GPS position and camera position. s, θ , and (x_c, z_c) are scale, Z-axis rotation, translation, respectively. Transformation, T is defined by four parameters. The integration of two subsequences is performed in metric space based on the 3D-2D corresponding points. Meanwhile, GPS mapping is used to align two subsequences in the world position with about the same scaling. Therefore, the integration of subsequences can solve a linear equation. In order to apply space-carving algorithm [17], the universal voxel space is generated from reconstructed 3D points. The space resolution is $N_x \times N_y \times N_z = (X_{max}-X_{min}, Y_{max}-Y_{min}, Z_{max}-Z_{min})/S$, where $(X_{max}, Y_{max}, Z_{max})^T$ and $(X_{min}, Y_{min}, Z_{min})^T$ are 3D points, and S is the predefined scale.

5 Global Pose Estimation

We use the panorama or connecting nodes in the adjacency graph to compute the relative posture between two isolated building models. To capture a cylindrical panorama image of a real world scene, we use an image mosaic algorithm [18]. In this case, panning rotation only represents the relationship between two images.

Given the 3D-2D point correspondences between the inter-nodes in the panorama and intra-nodes in the isolated group, the relative posture can be estimated between two isolated buildings. To do this, a short image sequence between the panorama and isolated group is used. It helps us extract automatically the 3D-2D point correspondences. Let the projection matrix from each 3D model to an image of the intra-node n_j be denoted by $P_i = [R_{mci} | t_{mci}]$ and $P_j = [R_{mcj} | t_{mcj}]$, where R_{mcj} and t_{mcj} are the model-to-camera rotation and translation of the node n_i, respectively. When the six 3D to 2D point correspondences with respect to geometries are detected, the projection matrices can be estimated. The coordinate transformation from jth to ith model coordinates is defined by the following equation

$$E_{ij} = \begin{bmatrix} R_{mci} & t_{mci} \\ 0^T & 1 \end{bmatrix} \begin{bmatrix} R_{ji}(\phi) & 0 \\ 0^T & 1 \end{bmatrix} \begin{bmatrix} R_{mcj}^T & -R_{mcj}^T t_{mcj} \\ 0^T & 1 \end{bmatrix}, \tag{4}$$

where $R_{ij}(\phi)$ means the panning rotation from jth to ith model coordinates[18].

6 Implementation and Some Results

We have tested our method with some buildings in a University campus. The equipments used in the system are presented in Fig. 7. Fig. 8 shows the result of SFM after GPS mapping, where the blue-filled diamonds denote the GPS positions, and the yellow-filled diamonds denote the refined camera positions. Fig. 9 shows result of volumetric reconstruction. Fig. 10 shows the re-projection error for the three buildings, where the length estimated by the length of the camera paths. Fig. 11 shows the result of global pose estimation. For the global pose estimation, the building A in Fig. 11 was used as the reference building, where yellow circle, blue-sky circle and blue circle and are GPS position, camera position after GPS mapping and camera position after global pose estimation, respectively.

Equipments	Model	Error
GPS Receive	SIRF start II	0 < error < 5m
Digital compass	CMPS03	0 < error < 3°
Camera	Coolpix 5400	22 mm lens

Fig. 7. Used Equipments

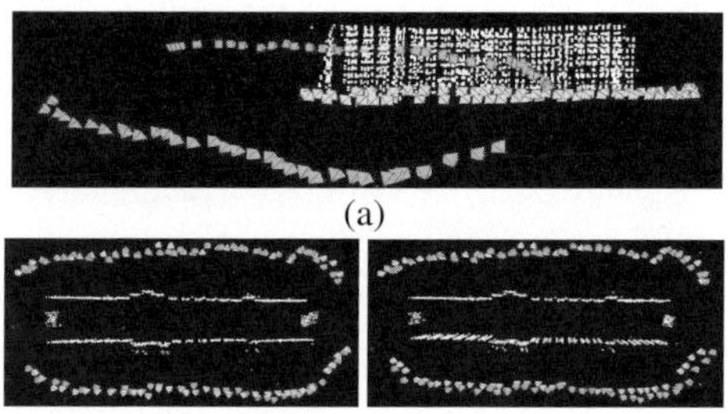

Fig. 8. Example of SFM: (a) Before GPS mapping, (b) After GPS mapping and (c) Integration

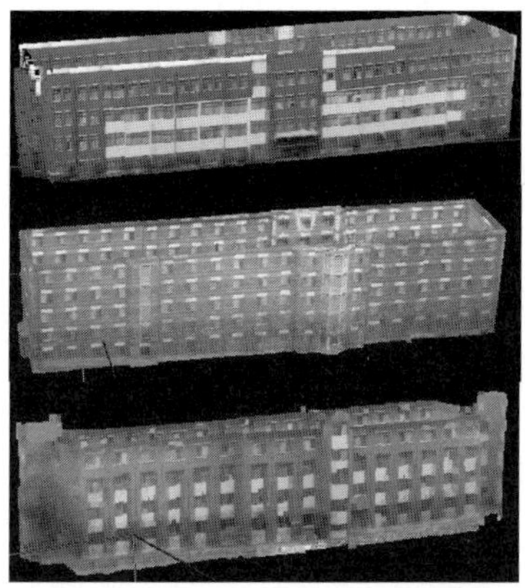

Fig. 9. Example of volumetric reconstruction

	#Intra node	Length	Reprojection error(pixel)
Fig. 9. top	65	280m	0.5214
Fig. 9 middle	76	300m	0.7742
Fig 9 bottom	53	310m	0.5932

Fig. 10. Results of error measurement

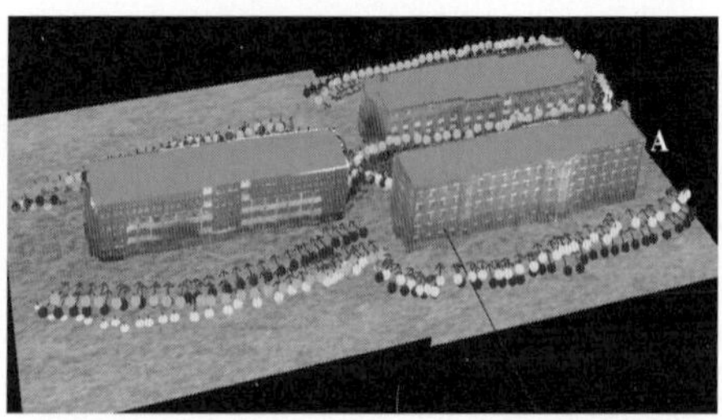

Fig. 11. Result of global pose estimation

7 Conclusion

In this paper, we presented a system for reconstructing large-scale 3D buildings using ground view images including a GPS and digital compass information. First, a modified inverse Hough Transform is proposed. By using this method, suitable line segments are extracted for estimating vanishing points and corresponding corners. In order to handle a huge number of images, an adjacency graph is devised. The adjacency graph represents the spatial adjacency between images or buildings and is automatically generated from a roughly known pose. Finally, a method of global pose estimation is outlined that can register 3D isolated building models in a global coordinate system, then a system based on SFM is presented for large-scale site modeling.

Acknowledgment

This work was supported by the Korea Research Foundation Grant funded by the Korean Government (MOEHRD) No. R05-2003-000-10741-0.

References

1. Pollefeys., M.: Self-Calibration and Metric 3D Reconstruction from Uncalibrated Image Sequence, PhD. Thesis, (1999).
2. Debevec., P. E., Taylor., C. J, Malik., J.: Modeling and Rendering Architecture from Photographs,. SIGGRAPH, (1996) 11-20.
3. Sainz, M., Susin, A., Bagherzadeh, N.: Camera Calibration of Long Image Sequences with the Presence of Occlusions, Int. Conf. on Image Processing, 1 (2003) 317-320.
4. Sato., T., Kanhara., M., Yokoya., N.: Outdoor Scene Reconstruction from Multiple Image Sequences Captured by a Hand-Held Video Camera, Proc. IEEE Int. Conf. on Multisensor Fusion and Integration for Intelligent System, (2003) 113-118.
5. El-Hakim., S. F *et al* Detailed 3D Reconstruction of Large-Scale Heritage Sites with Integrated Techniques, IEEE Computer Graphics and Application, 23(2) (2004) 21-29.
6. Guillou, E. *et al*,: Using Vanishing Points for Camera Calibration and Coarse 3D Reconstruction from A Single Image, The Visual Computer, (2000) 396-410.
7. Stamos., I., Allen., P.~K.: Automatic Registration of 2-D Width 3-D Imagery in Urban Environment, Int. Conf. on Compute Vision, 2 (2001) 731-736.
8. Zhang., Z.: A New Multistage Approach to Motion and Structure Estimation by Gradually Enforcing Geometric Constraints, Asian Conf. on Computer Vision, (1998) 567-574.
9. Cucchiara, R., Grana, C., Prati, A., Vezzani, R.: A Hough Transform-Based Methods for Radial Distortion Correction, Proc on Image Analysis and Processing, (2003) 182-187.
10. Kesidis., A. L., Papamarkos., N.: On the Inverse Hough Transform, IEEE Trans. on PAMI, 21(12) (1999) 1329-1343.
11. Beardseley ., P., Zisserman., A., Murry., D.: Sequential Updating of Projective and Affine Structure from Motion, International Journal of Computer Vision, 21(3), (1997) 235-259.
12. Lee., S. C. *et al*,: Automatic Integration of Facade Textures into 3D Building Models with a Projective Geometry Based Line Clustering, Computer Graphics Forum, 21 (2002) 511-519.
13. Coorg., S., Teller., S.: Extracting Textured Vertical Facades from Controlled Close-Range Imagery, Int. Conf. on Computer Vision and Pattern Recognition, (199) 625-632.

14. Jang., K. H., Lee., D. H., Jung., S. K.: A Moving Planar Mirror based Approach for Cultural Reconstruction, Computer Animation & Virtual Worlds, 15(3-4), (2004) 415-424.
15. Harris., C. J., Stephens., M.: A Combined Corner and Edge Detector, 4th Alvey Vision Conf., (1998) 147-151.
16. 3D PhotoModeler, http://www.photomodeler.com/, Eos Systems Inc.
17. Kutulakos., K., Seitz, S.: A theory of shape by space carving, In ICCV, (1999) 307-314.
18. Jang., K. H., Jung., S. K., Lee., MinHo.L Constructing cylindrical panoramic image using equidistance matching`, IEE Electronics Letters, 35(3), (1999) 1715-1716.

Anticipation Effect Generation for Character Animation*

Jong-Hyuk Kim[1], Jung-Ju Choi[1], Hyun Joon Shin[1], and In-Kwon Lee[2]

[1] Department of Digital Media, Ajou University, Rep. of Korea
{naidem, jungju, joony}@ajou.ac.kr
[2] Department of Computer Science, Yonsei University, Rep. of Korea
iklee@yonsei.ac.kr

Abstract. According to the principles of traditional 2D animation techniques, anticipation makes an animation convincing and expressive. In this paper, we present a method to generate anticipation effects for an existing animation. The proposed method is based on the visual characteristics of anticipation, that is, "Before we go one way, first we go the other way [1]." We first analyze the rotation of each joint and the movement of the center of mass during a given action, where the anticipation effects are added. Reversing the directions of rotation and translation, we can obtain an initially guessed anticipatory pose. By means of a nonlinear optimization technique, we can obtain a consequent anticipatory pose to place the center of mass at a proper location. Finally, we can generate the anticipation effects by compositing the anticipatory pose with a given action, while considering the continuity at junction and preserving the high frequency components of the given action. Experimental results show that the proposed method can produce the anticipatory pose successfully and quickly, and generate convincing and expressive anticipation effects.

1 Introduction

Recent progress in computer animation has been mainly focused on synthesizing realistic motions. Many approaches based on kinematics and dynamics, and especially recent techniques incorporating live motion capture data, allow us to synthesize lively animation efficiently. However, realistic motion from those approaches would not always conclude to success in animation. We can observe that publicly successful animations adopt the traditional 2D animation techniques even though they are neither physically correct nor realistic. Traditional 2D animation techniques describe and convey the situation to the audiences more efficiently than physical realism, by the means of exaggeration, anticipation, reaction, and so on [1].

According to the principles of 2D animation techniques, anticipation makes an animation more convincing and expressive [2]. Most animators consider an action as a sequence of the anticipation of the action, the action itself, and

* This research was supported by University IT Research Center Project.

H.-P. Seidel, T. Nishita, and Q. Peng (Eds.): CGI 2006, LNCS 4035, pp. 639–646, 2006.

the reaction [1]. Here, the anticipation is the preparation for the action, and the reaction is the result of the action. In general, most audiences expect an anticipatory action before a certain action itself, since the anticipatory action provides the audiences with visual cues for what are going to happen. Applying anticipation effects is one of the effective ways for successful animations; however, it is quite difficult for most animators to achieve. Even for experienced animators, it is time-consuming process.

To add anticipation effects, we first analyze the given short motion clip and find the directions of the joint rotations and the movement of the center of mass for the action to deal with. We then generate an anticipatory pose by reversing the directions of the given action. The final result is composed of two motions: one from the initial pose to the anticipatory pose and the other from the anticipatory pose to the original action. The proposed method in this paper can be used as a tool for less experienced animators to generate anticipation effects for producing expressive and convincing animations.

2 Related Work

Since J. Lasseter suggested that the principles of traditional 2D animation techniques can be effectively applicable to 3D animations [2], there have been a few research results presented. For instance, Opalach and Maddoc used multi-layer implicit surfaces to incorporate Disney effects such as squash-and-stretch, follow-through, anticipation, and exaggeration [3]. Rademacher simulated the irregular deformation observed in 2D animation for a 3D character animation [4]. Li et al. proposed a technique to deform models together with motion based on artistic drawings [5]. Bregler et. al tried to track the motion from traditional cartoon animations, and to retarget the motion onto 3D models [6]. Agarwala suggested a semi-automatic method to convert a video of a real scene into a cartoon animation [7]. Chenney et. al applied a squash-and-stretch technique to represent the rigidity of an object in a physical simulation [8]. Choi et. al proposed a method to produce anticipation effects for an existing facial animation based on principal component analysis [9].

There are also some related works to add effects to the pre-existing animation. Unuma et al. [10] and Bruderlin and Williams [11] independently introduced their approaches to modify animation in the frequency domain to variate the styles of the animations. Brand and Hertzmann suggested "Style Machine," which produces an animation with a variety of styles using hidden Markov models [12]. Liu et al. used nonlinear inverse optimization to stylize animation in a physically realistic manner [13]. Hsu et al. developed a mathematical model to analyze animations with different styles and apply the model to novel animations for stylizing them [14]. Chi et al. proposed "EMOTE" models which modify the visual styles of input motion clips based on Labanotation [15, 16]. More drastic effects, especially passive actions caused by interaction from the world, can be generated by the method proposed by Zordan and Hodgins [17]. Victor et al. further improved the technique [18].

Unfortunately, within the current knowledge of the authors, there is no known proposed technique to produce anticipation effects for multi-linked character animation. This paper presents a method of applying anticipation effects for character animation based on the visual characteristics of anticipation.

3 Anticipation Effect Generation

The primary visual characteristic of anticipation is that almost every anticipatory action occurs along the direction opposite to the main action. In the physical sense, we observe that the anticipation can be regarded as the action to make the motion trajectory longer than that of the main action so that the character can reach the same energy state at the extreme pose with smaller maximum force. Therefore, anticipation effects can be obtained by moving the character's body, especially its center of mass backward.

Our basic idea to add or exaggerate anticipation effects is to compose an anticipatory pose and to add the part of motion that passes through the pose. Here, the anticipatory pose has the joint angles rotated in the direction opposite to the original action and the center of mass of the character is also dragged backward. The anticipatory motion starts from the first pose of the action of interest and reaches the extreme pose of the action, passing through the anticipatory pose while maintaining the motion continuity and geometric constraints.

3.1 Anticipatory Pose

Anticipatory pose of an action can be defined as the pose in which basically every joint is dragged backward. Moreover, in order to maximize the effect of anticipation visually and dynamically, we also need to drag the center of mass of the character backward while maintaining important characteristics of the given motion by enforcing the geometric constraints, if any. The joint angles can be dragged backward kinematically in a simple way, but the center of mass cannot be dragged as easily as the joint angles. Moreover, enforcing the constraints sometimes prevents us from altering joint angles as we want. Therefore, we divide this problem into two steps: producing an initial guess with dragged joint angles and solving the pose with the given center of mass subject to the constraints.

Let t_0 and t_e be the user-specified time instances where the action of interest starts and reaches the extreme. The pose of a character is represented by the global position $\mathbf{p}$ and orientation $\mathbf{q}_0$, and the joint angles $\mathbf{q}_i$, $1 \leq i \leq n$, where n is the number of its joints. Given the poses at time t_0 and t_e, we compute an initial guess of the anticipatory pose, $\mathbf{p}_g$ and $\mathbf{q}_{i,g}$, by extrapolating them:

$$\begin{aligned} \mathbf{q}_{j,g} &= \text{slerp}(\mathbf{q}_{j,e},\ \mathbf{q}_{j,0}, -\alpha), \ \text{ where } 0 \leq j \leq n \\ \mathbf{p}_g &= (1+\alpha)\mathbf{p}_0 - \alpha \mathbf{p}_e, \end{aligned} \tag{1}$$

where α is an arbitrarily given constant such that $0 < \alpha \leq 1$. The user can control the amount of anticipation with this control parameter α. With a larger α, one can exaggerate anticipation more and he/she can keep the original motion better by specifying a smaller α. In our experiments, where we want to maximize anticipation effects, we set α to one.

Since the initial guess of the anticipatory pose is edited kinematically, it does not guarantee the translation of the center of mass along the opposite direction. Moreover, it may not meet the geometric constraints. Therefore, we refine the initially guessed pose using a nonlinear numerical optimization technique. The desirable location of the center of mass is defined similarly to the initial guess of the global position:

$$\mathbf{c}_a = (1+\alpha)\mathbf{c}_0 - \alpha\mathbf{c}_e, \tag{2}$$

where $\mathbf{c}_0$ and $\mathbf{c}_e$ are the centers of mass at time t_0 and t_e, and $\mathbf{c}_a$ is the center of mass of the desirable anticipatory pose. Given the center of each link $\mathbf{p}_i$ and its mass m_i, the center of mass of a character is defined as $\mathbf{c} = \sum \mathbf{p}_i m_i / \sum m_i$. We use average human mass distribution for m_i [19].

The energy function for our optimization problem is defined as:

$$E(\mathbf{p}, \mathbf{q}_i) = w_p \left\|\mathbf{p} - \mathbf{p}_a\right\|^2 + \sum_i w_i \left\|\log(\mathbf{q}_{i,a}^{-1}\mathbf{q}_i)\right\|^2 + \left\|\mathbf{c}_a - \mathbf{c}(\mathbf{p}, \mathbf{q}_i)\right\|^2. \tag{3}$$

Here, notice that the first two terms are for preserving the initial guess and the last term for placing the center of mass at the desired location. The weights w_i and w_p are set to specify human preference for the corresponding joint motion. For example, a joint on the spine is not likely rotated as freely as joints on the shoulder, so we assign larger w_i's for spine joints. In order to incorporate the geometric constraints specified explicitly, we minimize the energy function with respect to the constraints:

$$\underset{\mathbf{p}, \mathbf{q}_i}{\arg\min} \quad E(\mathbf{p}, \mathbf{q}_i) \qquad \text{subject to } f_k(\mathbf{p}, \mathbf{q}_i) = c_k, \tag{4}$$

where $f_k(\cdot) = c_k$ is the given geometric constraints. In our implementation, we reformulate the constraints with penalty functions and minimize the sum of the energy and the penalty functions together with the conjugate gradient method, instead of employing time-consuming constrained optimization techniques.

Since the initially guessed anticipatory pose of the Equation (4) is, in general, quite similar to the consequent anticipatory pose, the optimization can be solved very quickly. According to experimental results, solving the optimization problem without an initial guess does not produce a proper anticipatory pose (See Figure 1(d) and (h)).

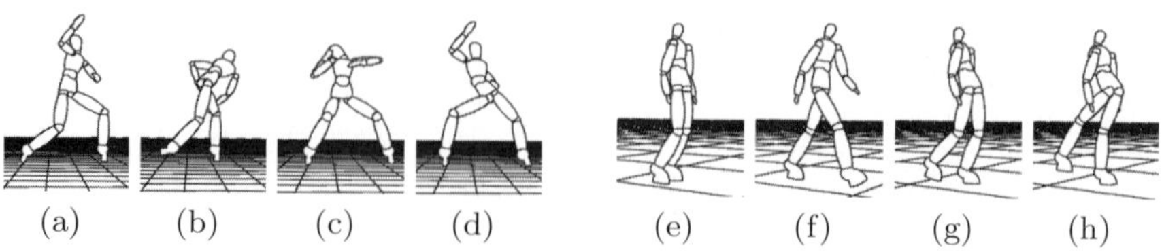

(a) (b) (c) (d) (e) (f) (g) (h)

Fig. 1. For given poses in (a)(e) and (b)(f) at time t_0 and t_e, anticipatory poses with and without an initial guess are shown in (c)(g) and (d)(h), respectively

3.2 Anticipatory Motion

The anticipation motion is generated based on the anticipatory pose and is plugged into the given motion. By adding anticipation effects, the character first moves backward to the action so it poses as the anticipatory pose, and then moves forward to the center of the action. Therefore, we divide the anticipatory motion into backward motion and forward motion, and generate them separately while maintaining continuity among them and the following motion.

To synthesize an anticipatory motion, we first need to determine the length of those two parts. Broadly speaking, the bigger a motion is, the longer time it takes. Therefore, the length of backward motion must be roughly proportional to the amount of anticipation effect, which is controlled by α in Equation (1).

Let L_e be the length of the time interval $[t_0 : t_e]$ in the given original animation (See Figure 2(a)). The time instance of anticipation t_a is determined by:

$$t_a = w_t \alpha L_e + t_0, \tag{5}$$

where w_t is the user-specified constant to control the length of backward motion more precisely. In our experiment, we obtained reasonable quality motion by setting w_t with one, that is, the length of backward motion is the same as that of the action. In terms of the forward motion, we preserve the length of time interval $[t_a, t_e]$: $t'_e = L_e + t_a$. By the backward motion, the amount of rotation angle of any joint enlarged. Therefore, preserving the length of the forward action makes the action itself look much faster and more dynamic, which also satisfies the visual characteristics of anticipation (See Figure 2(b)).

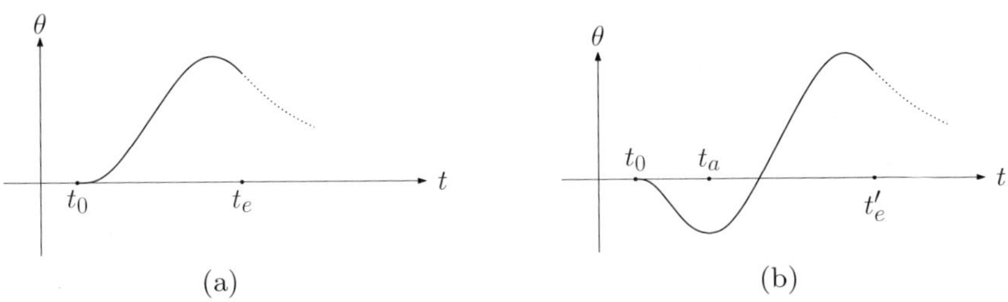

Fig. 2. (a) A typical animation curve without anticipation; (b) that with anticipation

Once the temporal length of the motion is determined, we generate motion segments interpolating the corresponding start and end poses while maintaining the continuity at the junction. Since the length of animation is pretty short, we model the animation curve of both parts as bundles of Hermite curve segments, which is defined by start and end points and their tangents, due to their simplicity and control for enforcing continuity.

The first motion segment needs to start with the pose $\mathbf{P}_0$ at t_0 and end with $\mathbf{P}_a$ at t_a. The tangents at the both ends are set to maintain the continuity. In detail, the tangents at t_0 must be the tangents $\mathbf{v}_{i,0}$ at t_0 in the original motion for i-th joint. The velocity at t_a is also set to maintain the continuity between the curve and the following curve. We set the velocity at t_a as $\mathbf{v}_{i,a} = \mathbf{v}_{i,0}$, which we will derive later.

In the forward motion part, we alter only low-frequency components of the original motion to conserve the motion quality. The high frequency terms of an individual joint in the given animation are the residuals between the original motion and the motion curve approximated by a Hermit segment (See Figure 3(a)). The fitting curve for i-th joint is defined with the poses at t_0 and t_e of the original motion and their tangents. The residuals are computed as the rotational differences between the joint angles from the original motion and those from the Hermite curve. The deformed curve segment is defined similarly. The Hermite segment for the deformed curve is defined with $\mathbf{P}_a$ and $\mathbf{P}_e$. In order to reduce the change from the original motion and maintain the continuity, the tangent at the starting end $\mathbf{v}_{i,a}$ needs to be $\mathbf{v}_{i,0}$, and that at the opposite end is $\mathbf{v}_{i,e}$. Adding the residuals to the deformed curve yields the final animation (See Figure 3(b)).

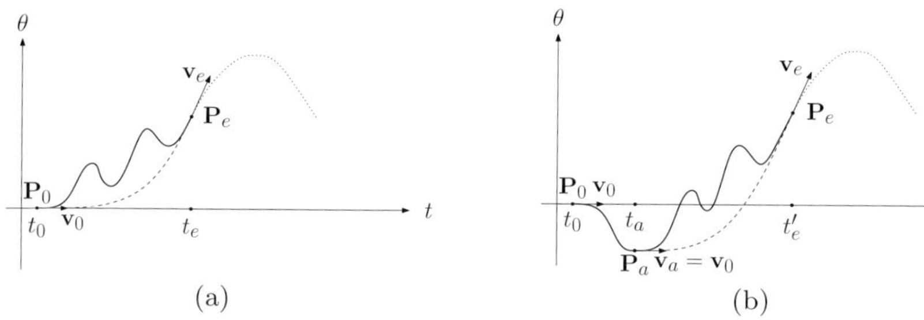

Fig. 3. Anticipatory motion composition: (a) from a given motion, high frequency terms are obtained between $\mathbf{P}_0$ and $\mathbf{P}_e$; (b) the terms are add to the Hermite interpolation curve of $\mathbf{P}_a$ and $\mathbf{P}_e$

3.3 Experimental Results

Figures 4, 5, and 6 show some examples of anticipation effects for given human motions. During the optimization, some geometric constraints are considered that the ends of the two hands or feet are constrained to contact on the ground. We can apply the same process repeatedly to the animation with anticipation, which can make the animation look more dynamic (See Figure 6(c)).

Fig. 4. (a) Running without anticipation; (b) that with anticipation

(a)

(b)

Fig. 5. (a) Throwing a ball without anticipation; (b) that with anticipation

(a)

(b)

(c)

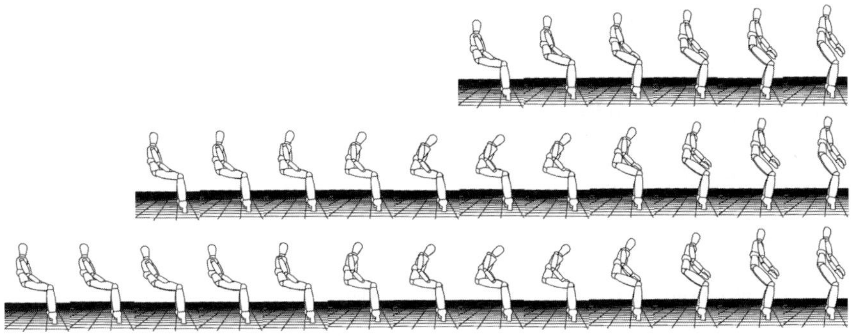

Fig. 6. (a) Standing up from a chair without anticipation; (b) that with anticipation; (c) that with double anticipation

4 Conclusions and Discussion

In this paper, we proposed a method of producing anticipation effects for a given animation. The proposed method is motivated from the visual characteristics of anticipation frequently shown in traditional animations. Our experimental results show that the animation with anticipation by the proposed method is more expressive and convincing. The proposed method can be used as a tool for less experienced animators to efficiently produce anticipation effects.

The major limitation of the proposed method is that our method relies on the user interaction to determine the durations of actions. In our experiment, we found that some users have to spend time to specify the center of action. It is well known that it is hard to develop a general algorithm to find a unit action from the given sequence of motion. We believe it will be possible to design a specialized method to determine the action duration since, in our case, the action duration is very short and does not need to be accurate. The other problem is that it is not always easy to control the length of backward motion. If the length is too short, either the anticipation effect is small, or the backward motion is too quick. On the other hand, if the length is too long, our method may cause unnatural motion, since the motion is synthesized with simple mathematical equations. However, as mentioned earlier, we found that a reasonable length of the backward action is highly dependent on an original motion.

References

1. Williams, R.: The Animator's Survival Kit. Faber and Faber (2001)
2. Lasseter, J.: Principles of traditional animation applied to 3D computer graphics. In: Proceedings of SIGGRAPH 87. (1987) 35–44
3. Opalach, A., Maddoc, S.: Disney effects using implicit surfaces. In: Proceedings of 5th Eurographics Workshop on Animation and Simulation. (1994)
4. Rademacher, P.: View-dependent geometry. In: Proceedings of SIGGRAPH 99. (1999) 439–446
5. Li, Y., Gleicher, M., Xu, Y.Q., Shum, H.Y.: Stylizing motion with drawings. In: Proceedings of the 2003 ACM SIGGRAPH/Eurographics Symposium on Computer Animation. (2003) 309–319
6. Bregler, C., Loeb, L., Chuang, E., Deshpande, H.: Turning to the masters: Motion capturing cartoons. ACM Transactions on Graphics **21**(3) (2002) 399–407
7. Agarwala, A.: SnakeToonz: a semi-automatic approach to creating cel animation from video. In: Proceedings of Non-Photorealistic Animation and Rendering. (2002) 139–148
8. Chenney, S., Pingel, M., Iverson, R., Szymanski, M.: Simulating cartoon style animation. In: Proceedings of Non-Photorealistic Animation and Rendering. (2002) 133–138
9. Choi, J.J., Kim, D.S., Lee, I.K.: Anticipation for facial animation. In: Proceedings of 17th International Conference on Computer Animation and Social Agents. (2004) 1–8
10. Unuma, M., Anjyo, K., Takeuchi, R.: Fourier principles for emotion-based human figure animation. In: Proceedings of SIGGRAPH 95. (1995) 91–96
11. Bruderlin, A., Williams, L.: Motion signal processing. In: Proceedings of SIGGRAPH 95. (1995) 97–104
12. Brand, M., Hertzmann, A.: Style machines. In: Proceedings of SIGGRAPH 2000. (2000) 183–192
13. Liu, C.K., Hertzmann, A., Popović, Z.: Learning physics-based motion style with nonlinear inverse optimization. ACM Transactions on Graphics **24**(3) (2005) 1071–1081
14. Hsu, E., Pulli, K., Popović, J.: Style translation for human motion. ACM Transactions on Graphics **24**(3) (2005) 1082–1089
15. Chi, D.M., Costa, M., Zhao, L., Badler, N.I.: The EMOTE model for effort and shape. In: Proceedings of SIGGRAPH 2000. (2000) 173–182
16. Zhao, L., Costa, M., Badler, N.I.: Interpreting movement manner. In: Proceedings of Computer Animation 2000. (2000) 98–103
17. Zordan, V.B., Hodgins, J.K.: Motion capture-driven simulations that hit and react. In: Proceedings of ACM SIGGRAPH Symposium on Computer Animation. (2002) 89–96
18. Zordan, V.B., Majkowska, A., Chiu, B., Fast, M.: Dynamic response for motion capture animation. ACM Transactions on Graphics **24**(3) (2005) 697–701
19. Winter, D.A.: Biomechanics and Motor Control of Human Movement. Wiley (1990)

Real-Time Simulation of Dynamic Mirage Scenes

Changbo Wang[1,2], Zhangye Wang[1], Qi Zhou[1],
Zhidong Jin[1], and Qunsheng Peng[1]

[1] State Key Lab. of CAD&CG, Zhejiang University, Hangzhou 310027, China
[2] Software Engineering Institute, East China Normal University,
Shanghai 200062, P.R. China
{cbwang, zywang, peng}@cad.zju.edu.cn

Abstract. Mirage is a peculiar nature phenomenon which is caused by the atmospheric refraction and total internal reflection under special weather conditions. In this paper, we propose a novel method to model and render this phenomenon. We first establish their corresponding atmospheric temperature models. Then adhering to the physical law, we calculate the light path and intensity attenuation during its propagation. To simulate the dynamic effect of mirages, we introduce a dynamic model based on atmospheric gravity waves. By incorporating GPU acceleration into the rendering process, different types of dynamic mirages under different conditions can be realistically rendered in real time, demonstrating the formation, change, and disappear of mirages.

1 Introduction

Mirage is an peculiar natural phenomenon which happens on sea, desert and road. Mirages are so charming that one had the chance to see them, especially in desert or at sea, always likes to talk with other people to share his unique experience and happiness. So realistic simulation of mirages will have much significance in science and will be found applications in many areas, such as meteorology, scientific visualization, virtual reality, special effects in film, TV and digital entertainment, etc.

Up to date, relatively few research works have been reported on the realistic simulation of mirages. In 1977, Khular [1] and Fabri [2] et al. put forward their explanation to mirage effect based on physics theories. In 1985, Tape et al. [3] studied the geometrical topological model of light when superior mirages are formed. In 1990, Berger [4] and Musgrave [5] et al. proposed a ray tracing method for simulating superior mirages, but they only provided a simple example and the approach is time-consuming. In 1996, Stam et al. [6] studied the non-constant atmospheric media and simulated continuous variation of refraction indices. In 1998, Tr̈nkle et al. [7] simulated the mirage at Aegean Sea, but the result is less convincing. In 2000, Kosa et al. [8] studied the causes of mirages theoretically, and carried out experiments that simulated mirages on walls. In 2001, Wang [9] derived the trajectory of light in the atmosphere of linear variation of refractive index. However, this model is yet a theoretical model of single mirages. In 2004, Shi [10] simulated the sunset mirage in a simple way. In 2005, Lintus et al. [11]

H.-P. Seidel, T. Nishita, and Q. Peng (Eds.): CGI 2006, LNCS 4035, pp. 647–654, 2006.

rendered the mirage effect during sunrise and provided a primary result of their simulation.

Above works either focus on the theoretically modeling of mirages or simulates one kind of mirage, fail to show the dynamic process of mirages changing with time and atmospheric conditions, which makes mirages magnificent and mythical.

Based on the physical theory of mirages, in this paper we propose a novel method to model and render this phenomenon. We investigate the atmospheric temperature models of different types of mirages, then calculate the light path and intensity attenuation during its propagation adhering to the physical rules. To simulate the dynamic effect of mirages, we present a dynamic model based on atmospheric gravity waves, and adapting GPU to accelerate the rendering. With the proposed method, we implement real-time rendering of various realistic mirages under diversified conditions, such as above the ocean, in deserts and on concrete roads. The formation, change and disappear of mirages are demonstrated clearly.

2 Modeling Mirages

Mirages happens when the temperature near the surface or sea surface is increasing dramatically by heating or decreasing due to the radiation cooling, and the refraction and total internal reflection of light rays occurs, just as shown in Fig.1. According to the imaging shape, formation conditions and other factors, mirages can be mainly classified into four kinds, i.e. superior mirage, inferior mirage, double mirage and complex mirages(fata morgana).

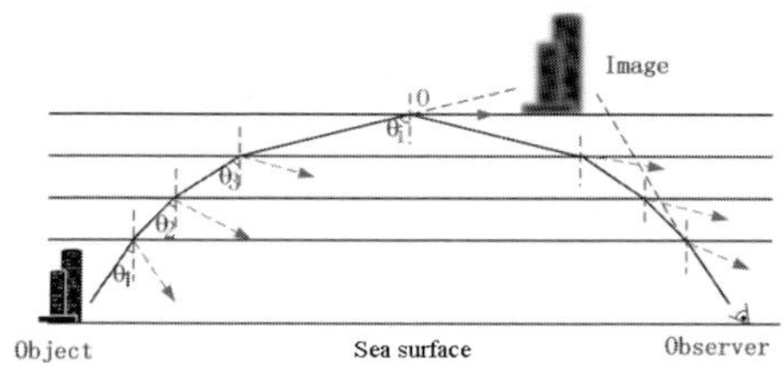

Fig. 1. The trajectory of a light ray of a mirage at sea surface

So we can establish a physical model for mirages which includes three aspects: (1)Determining the light path of mirages, which describes the imaging place and shape of mirage; (2)Computing the light energy attenuation, which is responsible for the imaging color and intensity of mirages; (3) Developing a dynamic model of mirages, which simulates its dynamic behave.

2.1 Ray Path of Mirages

Single mirages are the most simple type of mirages. In previous works, the atmosphere is divided into many layers, and the variation of atmospheric temperature is simplified as linear, the derived models are not very rational [9]. Here we build the continuous model of temperature gradient, which is more fit for the physical theory.

We take the inferior mirage as an example. According the experiment data of Khular [1], the variation of refractive index of the air near ground with the attribute height y can be expressed approximately as: $n^2(y) = n_0^2 + n_p^2(1 - e^{-\alpha y})$ where y represents the height above the ground, n_0 is the refractive index at surface, α is a constant, and n_p is related to the atmospheric temperature gradient, that is: $n_p = 1 + \frac{131.5}{(273.15+T(y))}$. Where T_y is the temperature profile. For the typical inferior mirage, the temperature profile, $T(y)$ can be expressed as[12]:

$$T(y) = a\exp(-\frac{y}{b}) - cy + d \tag{1}$$

where the first term in the right of the above equation represents the rapid increase of temperature near the ground. The second term represents the linear decrease of temperature with the increase of altitude. The parameter d is determined by the temperature of the ground surface, $T_1(0)$, and their relation can be expressed as: $d = T_1(0) - a$. Under different climatic and terrain conditions, parameters a, b, c and d can have different values according to different weather condition and different types of ground.

For one random point in the ray trace, we do its differential coefficient in the coordinate plane yoz, and can deduce the equation of ray travelling. And then we can calculate the intersection point between each ray emitted from the object and z axes, and gain the imaging place of objects.

For the superior mirage which appears on sea scene, the appropriate refractive index profile would be $n^2(y) = n_0^2 + n_p^2(1 - e^{-\alpha y})$. By similar method, we can gain the ray trajectory of the single mirage on the sea.

For the double mirage and triple mirage, the air temperature is not a monotonic function of the altitude. We also can build the corresponding model of temperature changing.

2.2 Ray Energy Attenuation

Usually the images of objects in mirages scene are not very clear due to the attenuation of atmosphere.

According to the principle of conservation of energy, and we can easily get: $S_1 = S_1' + S_2$. Here S_1, S_1', S_2 are energy of incidence light, reflection light and refraction light, respectively.

Based on the Fresnel Formula, the energy of refracted light can be expressed as:

$$S_2 = \frac{S_1}{2}[2 - (\frac{\sin(i_1 - i_2)}{\sin(i_1 + i_2)})^2 - (\frac{\tan(i_1 - i_2)}{\tan(i_1 + i_2)})^2] \tag{2}$$

The above equation is the energy attenuation between two adjacent layers. We can further divide the ray path of mirage into many layer according to the atmospheric refraction index, i.e., only if the difference of the refraction index of the atmosphere within a certain height is smaller than a threshold, we keep it as one layer. This method of adaptive layer partition is more precise than the approach of subdivision by height. Then by applying the above algorithm iteratively, we can easily get the last energy of light from the object after refraction and reflection.

2.3 Atmospheric Scattering Effects

To calculate the total incident energy received by an observer, the effect of atmospheric scattering should also be considered. That is why the mirages are always blurred. Rayleigh scattering should be considered here.

The total energy of mirage incident to the eyes of an observer is the sum of the atmospheric scattering energy (I_0) and the attenuated energy from the objects appearing (S_2). S_2 can be evaluated with Eq.(9), the intensity of exact atmospheric scattering can be evaluated by scattering theory[13].

So the total received energy by the eyes of observers is: $I = I_0 + S_2$.

2.4 Dynamic Model of Mirages Based on Atmospheric Gravity Waves

In general, the atmosphere conditions are not stable during the appearance period of mirages. That is why mirages are changing and slightly flickering all the time. Gossard et. al [12] owe this phenomenon to the atmospheric gravity wave. We use the kinematic equation of gravity wave here. Gravity wave usually travels in plane $y - z$ (y is the vertical direction, and z is the direction of sight). The equation sets are [14]:

$$\begin{cases} \frac{\partial u}{\partial t} = -\frac{1}{\rho_0}\frac{\partial \rho}{\partial z} \\ \frac{\partial w}{\partial t} = -\frac{1}{\rho_0}\frac{\partial \rho}{\partial y} - g\frac{\rho}{\rho_0} \\ \frac{\partial \rho}{\partial t} + w\frac{\partial \rho_0}{\partial y} = 0, \frac{\partial u}{\partial z} + \frac{\partial \omega}{\partial y} = 0 \end{cases} \tag{3}$$

where u, w represents the wave velocities in z and y directions, respectively. ρ and p are the waves of density and pressure, respectively. ρ_0 is the reference density, and is the acceleration of gravity.

According to the value of the perpendicularly varying temperature profiles, we can solve this equations set, and adjust the imaging position to simulate the dynamic change of mirages.

Here the influences to mirage induced by atmospheric gravity waves include two aspects: one is jagged-edge effect by artificial application of a gravity wave to a static mirage, in which the period is very short; the other one is periodic transformation effect, which corresponds the long periodic atmospheric waves.

3 Real-Time Rendering of Dynamic Mirages

3.1 Forming the Image of Mirages

In order to simulate mirages in real time, we introduce an improved fast ray tracing algorithm.

The classic ray tracing algorithm requests to trace each ray of slight and find its intersection with the 3D object it first hit in the scene. Nevertheless, in the picture of a mirage, the background is usually very vague and only the objects appearing dynamically, in the mirage attract the attention of the observers. Moreover, these objects are located far away from the observers. Thus, in our new ray tracing algorithm, we omit all the less important objects and project the remaining objects onto a plane which is perpendicular to the ground. During ray tracing, after passing through the atmosphere along the curved path, each ray of slight intersects with the vertical plane its intersection is regarded as that with the real 3D object. Finally we render the image, i.e. the virtual image of the mirage.

3.2 GPU Acceleration

We optimize these formulae of mirage models, including refraction path, atmospheric gravity waves, and energy attenuation to fit GPU acceleration.

Specifically, during calculating the refraction trace, we get the vertex position of the actual object through the refraction mode calculation in vertex shader, the GPU map the vertex position to the imaging position. When performing the gravity waves calculation step, we get the imaging position of every vertex from the first step after calculating the effect on the ray of atmospheric gravity waves and then the vertex position changes to a new one. During the energy attenuation calculation, we get the imaging position of every pixel, and process the energy model calculation after finishing that in pixel shader. Having getting the present of energy of the ray from the second step we store it into the alpha channel to blend. After that, CPU send an instruction to draw the real objects in the view frustum after accomplishing the three steps in GPU, and show the image of mirage scene.

We can also adopt GPU techniques to render the special effects on road, such as highlight on the car, heat shimmer and depth blur effect. These are all processed in pixel shader.

4 Results

We built various physical models for different types of mirages, and generated different mirage scenes on a PC with CPU of PIV 2.4GHz, Nvidia GeForce FX 6600GT graphics card and memory of 1.0GB. The average rendering speed is 60 frames per second. So it meets the requirements of real-time rendering.

Fig.2 shows the comparisons between our simulated results and the photos of real mirages for the scene of sea, desert and road, respectively. From those figures, we can see that the simulated results are quite satisfactory. Fig.3 is a simulated result of dynamic mirage on the sea scene. We can see that when the temperature gradient distribution is steady, the mirage scene is quite clear (see the left image of Fig. 3(a)), as the temperature gradient decrease, the mirage will moves farther and disappear at last(see the left image of Fig. 3(a)). Fig.3(b)(c) are double mirage and triple mirage. Fig.4 shows the dynamic effects of mirages in desert and on road, respectively. The "lake" or "wet" road in these frames

(a)Mirages at sea(left is the simulated result and right is real picture)

(b)Mirages in desert(left is the simulated result and right is real picture)

(c)Mirages on road(left is the simulated result and right is real picture)

Fig. 2. Comparisons between real mirage picture and simulated result

(a) single mirage at sea(left is appearing and right is disappearing)

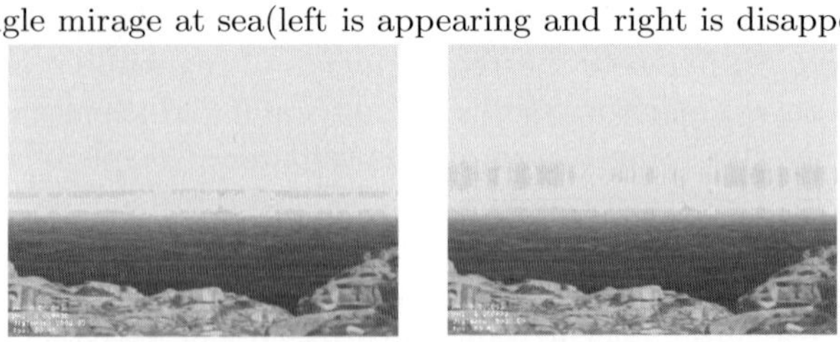

(b)double mirage and triple mirage at sea

Fig. 3. Simulated dynamic scenes of mirage at sea

Fig. 4. Simulated dynamic scenes of mirage in desert and on road(when moving near, the mirages are becoming smaller and disappear at last)

is in fact the imaging result of blue sky in the sunny day. When the viewpoint of an observer moves nearer and nearer, the area of "lake" or "wet road" will become smaller and smaller and disappear completely at last.

5 Conclusions

In this paper, we propose a novel method to model and render the dynamic scenes of mirage. We first analyze the physical causes of different types of mirages, and establish the intrinsic atmospheric temperature models. We then calculate light path and intensity attenuation during its propagation. To simulate the dynamic effect of mirages, we present a dynamic model based on atmospheric gravity waves. The GPU acceleration is also adopted to speed up the rendering process. Finally, we demonstrate the virtual images of different types of dynamic mirages, such as the mirages at sea, in desert and on road as well as the formation, change, and disappear of mirages. The average rendering speed reaches to 60 frames per second.

Future works include: building more detailed imaging model of mirage, considering the multi-scattering and refraction of atmosphere to realistically render other nature phenomenon, etc.

Acknowledgement

This paper was supported by 973 program of China under Grant No. 2002CB31201, Natural Science Foundation of China under Grant No. 60475013 and Wenyuan Foundation of Tongji University.

References

1. K. Thyagarajan E. Khular and A. Ghatak. A note on mirage formation. *American Journal of Physics*, 45:90–92, No. 1, Jan. 1977.
2. L. Lazzeri E. Fabri, G. Fiorio and P. Violino. Mirage in the laboratory. *American Journal of Physics*, 50:517–528, No. 6, June 1982.

3. W. Tape. The topology of mirages. *Scientific American*, pages 125–130, June 1985.
4. N. Levit M. Berger, T. Trout. Raytracing mirages. *IEEE Computer Graphics and Applications*, 10:36–41, May 1990.
5. M. Berger F. K. Musgrave. A note on ray tracing mirages. *IEEE Computer Graphics and Applications*, 10:10–12, Nov. 1990.
6. E. Languenou J. Stam. Ray tracing in non-constant media. *Rendering Techniques '96, Proceedings of the 7th Eurographics Workshop on Rendering, Porto, Portugal*, June 17-19, 1996.
7. E. Tr̈inkle. Simulation of inferior mirages observed at the halligen sea. *Applied Optics*, 37(9):1495C1505, 1998.
8. T. Kosa and P. Palffy-Muhoray. Mirage mirror on the wall. *American Journal of Physics*, 68(12):1120–1122, 2000.
9. Z. C. Wang. explain mirages by the model of linearly-varying refractive index. *College Physics*, 20(9):25–28, 2001.
10. K. Y. Shi. Ray tracing mirage. *Seminar of Light and Color in the nature*, pages 1–7, 2004.
11. M. Magnor A. Lintu, J. Haber. Realistic solar disc rendering. *Proceedings of WSCG 2005*, pages 79–86, February 2005.
12. E. E. Gossard and W. H. Hooke. Waves in the atmosphere. *Elsevier, New York*, Chap. 2:75–77, 1975.
13. Tadamura K. et. al Nishita T., Takao S. Display of the earth taking into account atmospheric scattering. *Computer Graphics*, 27(4):175–182, 1993.
14. W. K. Silvester W. H. Lehn and D. M. Fraser. Mirages with atmospheric gravity waves. *Applied Optics*, 33:4639C4643, 1994.

Improving the Interval Ray Tracing of Implicit Surfaces

Jorge Flórez, Mateu Sbert, Miguel A. Sainz, and Josep Vehí

Institut d'Informática i Aplicacions, Universitat de Girona, Campus Montilivi
17071 Girona, Spain
{jeflorez, vehi}@eia.udg.es,
{mateu, sainz}@ima.udg.es

Abstract. This paper presents a fast and reliable method to trim non-solution regions in an interval ray tracing process. The "trimming algorithm" uses interval analysis to perform rejection tests in a set of pixels simultaneously, instead of individual pixels at each time. With this approach, the presented algorithm runs faster than the traditional interval ray tracing algorithm. Also, an interval algorithm to remove aliasing in the rendering of implicit surfaces is introduced. This algorithm obtains better visualizations than the traditional point sampling. This algorithm can render thin features that would be impossible to obtain with point sampling algorithms.

1 Introduction

Interval Arithmetic is a mathematical theory developed by Ramon Moore [1] that has been used to solve problems of reliability caused by the floating-point arithmetic of computers. Floating-point calculation causes problems of numerical imprecision in geometric modeling and computer graphics [2, 3]. A particular application in which there are problems of reliability is ray tracing of implicit surfaces. These problems arise in the rendering of very special implicit functions with thin features that could be missed in the point sampling process. This paper proposes two improvements for the interval ray tracing algorithm. First, interval analysis is used to evaluate screen regions to perform rejection test over many pixels simultaneously. This implies a reduction of the number of intersection test performed in a traditional ray tracing algorithm. Secondly, interval analysis can also be used as an alternative for point sampling inside a pixel. A ray is infinitely thin, and a pixel covers a finite area. When rays are cast through a pixel, there is the possibility that some rays miss parts of the surface inside the pixel. With the approach presented in this paper, it is possible to evaluate all the area of the surface covered by the pixel instead of considering hits. This principle is used to implement an antialiasing algorithm that improves the traditional interval point sampling.

1.1 Interval Ray Tracing

Ray tracing is a process in which rays starting at a point (the camera or eye point) are sent through every pixel of a screen. These rays can intersect objects behind the screen. In that case, the first intersection point is recorded. In the intersection point, the normal of the surface is calculated and used to determine a shade value for the pixel. The ray is represented in a parametric way as:

H.-P. Seidel, T. Nishita, and Q. Peng (Eds.): CGI 2006, LNCS 4035, pp. 655 – 664, 2006.

$$\boldsymbol{p}(t) = c + t\,(s - c), \quad t \geq 0\,. \tag{1}$$

The point c is the camera or eye position. The magnitude s – c indicates the direction of the ray and the parameter t represents a fractional distance from c in the direction of s - c.

An intersection test must be performed between the rays and the implicit surfaces. Given an implicit function defined by:

$$f(x,y,z) = 0\,. \tag{2}$$

or in vector form:

$$f(p) = 0 \quad where \;\; p = (x,y,z)\,. \tag{3}$$

The intersection of the ray with the implicit surface is defined as:

$$f(\boldsymbol{p}(t)) = 0, \;\; \text{or,} \;\; f(c + t(s - c)) = 0\,. \tag{4}$$

To develop a reliable intersection test using interval analysis, the ray parameter is replaced with an interval T that represents a set of values of t. The equation used to find the intersections looks in an interval version as:

$$\mathrm{F(T)} = \mathrm{F}(c + \mathrm{T}(s - c))\,. \tag{5}$$

F(T) is known as the inclusion function of the intersection between the implicit surface and the ray. The result of the evaluation of the inclusion function is an interval. If this interval contains zero, a root could exist in the equation for the values of T. In the other case, the interval T can be rejected. This means that F(T) gives a reliable tool to perform rejection tests.

1.2 Previous Work

The requirement of a guaranteed ray tracing process to prevent that the intersection test miss thin features of the surface, has been pointed out by authors like Kalra [4], Capriani [5] and Mitchell [6]. They argue that point sampling is not a feasible algorithm to perform intersection test with surfaces that have thin features.

A few authors have proposed interval arithmetic as a solution to this problem, using different strategies to create reliable intersection test based on interval analysis [5, 6, 7, 8].

Mitchell [6] was the first author to propose an interval algorithm for the ray intersection test. He proposed two steps: root isolation and root refinement. Mitchell does not use interval arithmetic in the second step because he considered that an interval approach for root refinement was inefficient. Capriani et al [5] demonstrated that interval arithmetic could be used in both steps of Mitchell algorithm without loss of efficiency. They also propose other algorithms as the Newton interval method or Alefeld-Hansen method in the ray tracing process.

Sanjuan-Estrada [7] used a branch-and-bound strategy to make the intersection test without root isolation. They applied a rejection test using an interval inclusion function based on interval arithmetic. De Cusatis [8] suggest the use of affine arithmetic instead of interval arithmetic to solve the intersection test.

The algorithms previously mentioned consider only one interval variable (the ray parameter T). Those algorithms work sending one or more rays through every pixel in the screen.

Kalra and Barr [4] proposed a method for the intersection test based on Lipschitz constants. This method is used to prevent that the rays sampled in a pixel miss thin features of the surfaces.

2 Elimination of Screen Space Non-solution Regions

In this section, an algorithm for a fast trimming of screen regions that do not contain intersections with the implicit surface is presented. That is, the algorithm has to identify regions with pixels that should be shaded with the background color.

The rays are traced pixel by pixel, which makes ray tracing a slow algorithm. Interval arithmetic provides a way to evaluate many pixels simultaneously to accelerate the ray intersection process. Instead of a point in the screen, it is possible to take intervals for x and y coordinates to cover a set of pixels. Because the origin is still a point, the figure obtained looks like a pyramid instead of a ray (see figure 1). This process is similar to the beam tracing process introduced by Heckbert and Hanrahan [9] for polygonal objects.

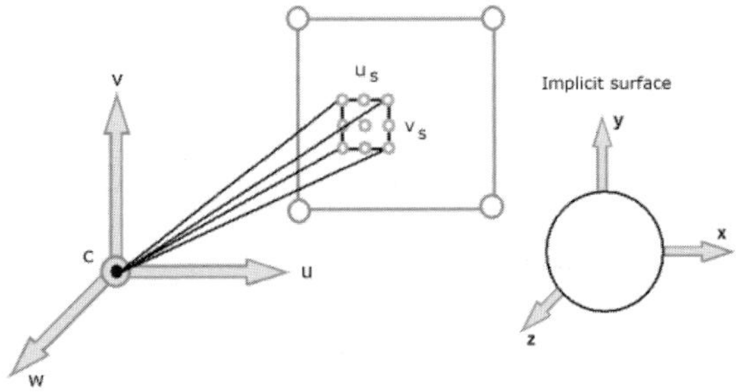

Fig. 1. A pyramid could be traced instead of a single ray to cover many pixels

The screen regions not trimmed must be ray traced pixel by pixel, because it is necessary to know the color for every single pixel. The objective of the trimming algorithm is to save time, that is, the algorithm presented is faster than an algorithm in which one or more rays are sent for all the pixels in the screen.

2.1 Mathematical Preliminaries

Equation (5) shows the inclusion function used to determine if the interval T contains roots. Figure 1 shows the new approach, in which s is a box instead of a point. The camera position can be in any place in the scene, for that reason, the rays are given in an arbitrary coordinate system uvw. The transformation of uvw coordinates to xyz coordinates must be an interval arithmetic operation.

Let $\mathrm{U_s}$ and $\mathrm{V_s}$ be intervals representing a set of pixels of the screen in uvw coordinates. Let w_s be the distance from the screen to the origin point c. The result of the transformation from uvw coordinates to xyz coordinates is represented as

$$\mathrm{S} = c + \mathrm{U_s}\mathbf{u} + \mathrm{V_s}\mathbf{v} + \mathrm{W_s}\mathbf{v} \,. \tag{6}$$

where S is an interval. A more detailed explanation of the transformation process (without intervals) is given by Shirley [10].

The inclusion function in our case is presented in the following equation:

$$F(\mathrm{T},\mathrm{S}) = F(c + \mathrm{T}(\mathrm{S} - c))\,. \tag{7}$$

If this condition is not accomplished, the evaluated interval S is rejected. This is used to reject a set of pixels that do not have intersections with the implicit function. This case occurs when $0 \notin F(\mathrm{T},\mathrm{S})$, which means there are no roots for the current values of T and S.

2.2 Algorithm Specification

With the equation (7), a set of pixels can be evaluated simultaneously with a unique intersection test, to determine if they intersect the implicit function. The algorithm explained in this section can reject regions without intersections in screen space. In other words, the algorithm offers a fast trimming of non-solution zones. The complete algorithm is presented in figure 2.

```
box.size = screen.size
add box to List_Box
for every box in List_Box
   if width(box)< miminum_box_size
      add box to Final_List
      exit for
   endif
   S = transform (box)
   T = (0, ∞)
   add T to List_T
   for every T in List_T
      if  width(T) < ∈_T exit for
      if (0 ∈ F(T,S))
         bisect T into T1,T2
         add T1,T2 to List_T
      endif
      drop T from List_T
   endfor
   if empty List_T
      bisect box into box1, box2
      add box1, box2 to List_Box
   endif
   drop box from List_box
endfor
for every box in Final_List
  for every pixel in box
   ray tracing pixel and shading
  endfor
endfor
```

Fig. 2. Algorithm for trimming non-solution boxes in screen space

The algorithm is based in a branch-and-bound strategy. The bisections are performed in both the screen space and in the interval parameter T. The algorithm starts making subdivisions of screen space in U_s and V_s coordinates to generate boxes. For every box, a new branch-and-bound algorithm is started in the interval parameter T. Every section of T is evaluated using the inclusion function (7) and the current value of S. The sections for which $0 \notin F(T,S)$ are rejected. Otherwise, the current interval T is subdivided and the evaluation performed in the new intervals.

The criterion used to stop the subdivision process over the parameter T is:

$$(T.Upper\_bound - T.Lower\_bound) < \in_T . \quad (8)$$

where $\in_T$ is the precision selected to stop the process.

Using a precision of 10^{-6}, the obtained results are feasible for the example surfaces (section 2.3).

The bisection over the boxes is terminated when a minimum size for the box is achieved. This precision represents the minimum accepted size of the box relative to the size of the screen, that is:

$$(screen\ size) * \in_{box} = minimum\ box\ size . \quad (9)$$

The boxes that achieve this precision are stored to be further ray traced. That is, the ray tracing will be performed only over the non- rejected boxes that achieve the minimum size box. The ray tracing algorithm used in this paper is called MRF, and it was introduced by Sanjuan-Estrada et al [4].

The algorithm presented uses a precision of 0.05 over the size of the screen in pixels. This precision has proved to be enough to obtain efficient results for the tested surfaces (section 2.3).

2.3 Experimental Results

The algorithm was tested using four surfaces (see table1 and Figure 5). The surfaces were rendered using an Intel Pentium 4, 2.4 GHz. The resolution used to render the images was 300 x 300 pixels. In the ray tracing process one ray is cast for every pixel and the precision used in the intersection test is 10^{-6}.

Table 1. Tested implicit surfaces

Surface	Equation
Sphere	$x^2 + y^2 + z^2 - 4 = 0$
Blobby	$x^2 + y^2 + z^2 + \sin(4*x) + \sin(4*y) + \sin(4*z) - 1 = 0$
Steiner	$(x^2*y^2 + y^2*z^2 + z^2*x^2)^2 + x*y*z = 0$
Mitchell	$4(x^4 + (y^2 + z^2)^2) + 17x^2(y^2 + z^2) - 20(x^2 + y^2 + z^2) + 17 = 0$

The results of the test are presented in table 2. Trimming time column represents the time of the trimming process to reject boxes in which there are no rays intersecting the implicit surface. Next column gives the time of a pixel-by-pixel ray tracing over the non-rejected boxes. The sum of both times is represented in total time column. Finally, the column "only ray tracing" shows the time of a traditional interval ray tracing over all the pixels in the screen for every surface.

Table 2. Results for the trimming algorithm (time in seconds)

Surface	Using trimming strategy			Only ray tracing	% Time saved
	Trimming time	Ray tracing	Total Time		
Sphere	0.791	40.678	41.469	53.226	22.08%
Blobby	1.33	62.842	64.172	107.59	40.35%
Steiner	1.59	92.84	94.43	152.63	38.13%
Mitchell	3.6	378.02	381.62	544.953	29.97%

The precision used in the pixel-by-pixel ray tracing process was $\in_T = 10^{-6}$ because the results obtained are feasible with that precision. Figure 3 shows the blobby surface visualized using different precisions.

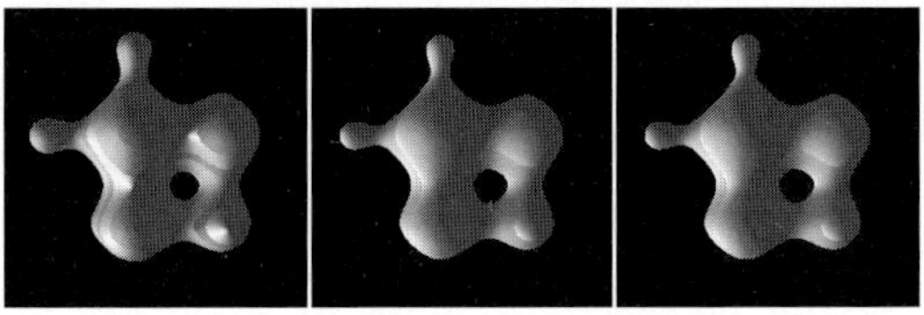

Fig. 3. Results for the Blobby surface for different precisions. In the first (*left image*) $\in_T = 10^{-2}$, in the next (*center image*) $\in_T = 10^{-6}$, finally (*right image*) $\in_T = 10^{-10}$. With a precision of 10^{-6}, the result obtained looks the same as using a higher precision. For a precision of 10^{-2} (figure 6a) the result is not acceptable.

In table 2, the total time of the algorithm using a trimming strategy summarizes the time of the interval ray tracing in the non-rejected boxes and the trimming process itself. In all the tested cases, the algorithm using a trimming strategy takes less time than an interval strategy based on a ray casting for all the pixels of the screen.

The intersection test takes more time in pixels corresponding to non-rejected boxes than rejected boxes. This is because the intersection test of rays that intersect the implicit surface must reach a smaller precision to obtain the value for the intersection. Rays that do not intersect the implicit function are rejected before this small precision is reached. Figure 4 shows a color map of the time that the intersection test takes in

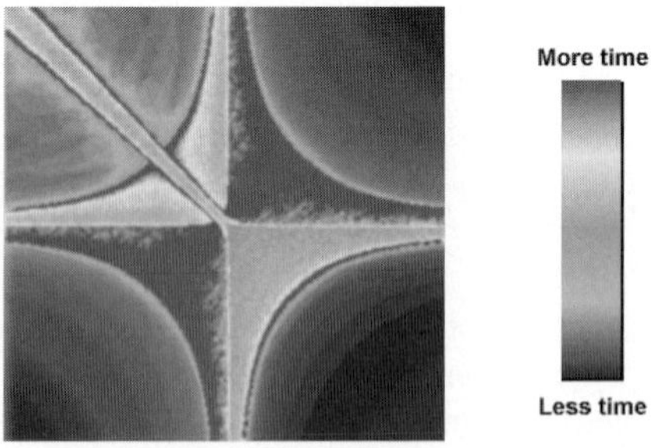

Fig. 4. Color map to represent the time that intersection test takes in different regions of the Steiner surface

every pixel in the Steiner surface. The pixels in which the intersection test fails take less time than pixels inside the implicit surface. Also note that in all the borders of the surface, the algorithm takes the maximum time.

Summarizing, the trimming algorithm is faster than the traditional interval ray tracing algorithm in the areas without intersections (the blue zones in figure 4). Table 3 compares the time spent by the trimming algorithm to reject non-solution boxes and the time that a pixel-by-pixel algorithm spends (one ray per pixel) in the same non-solutions boxes. Figure 9 shows the final results of the trimming and ray tracing algorithm for the tested surfaces.

Table 3. Comparison of the trimming algorithm and the classical interval ray tracing algorithm over the rejected boxes (time in seconds)

Surface	Trimming time	Pixel by pixel Time	% Time Saved
Sphere	0.791	12.548	93.69
Blobby	1.33	44.748	97.027
Steiner	1.59	59.79	97.34
Mitchell	3.6	166.933	97.84

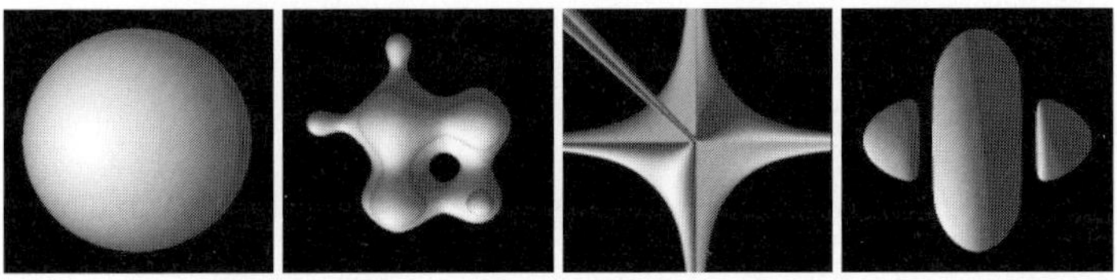

Fig. 5. Final result of the algorithm for the tested surfaces. From left to right and top to bottom, Sphere, Blobby, Steiner, Mitchell surfaces.

3 Antialiasing Using Interval Analysis

As was mentioned in section 2, some parts of the surfaces could be missed when methods based on point sampling are used. Figure 6 illustrates this situation.

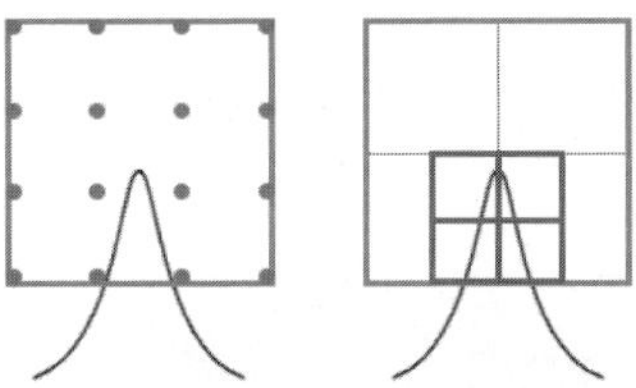

Fig. 6. Point sampling (*left*) and Sampled pixel using intervals (*right*). The evaluation in the sample points does not indicate the presence of the surface inside the pixel. No matter how many regularly distributed rays are sent through the pixel, there will be zones without rays traced and some rays could miss the surface. Using intervals, the pixel is subsampled and every region is considered in the evaluation of the function. There is no part of the surface missed in the evaluation.

3.1 Evaluation of the Pixel Area

Interval analysis can be used to develop an algorithm to "detect" if an implicit surface crosses any part of the pixel.

```
function detect_surface(area)
   S = transform(area)
   T = (0,∞)
   add T to List_T
   for every T in List_T
      if  width(T) < ∈T exit for
      if (0 ∈ F(T,S))
         bisect T into T1,T2
         add T1,T2 to List_T
      endif
      drop T from List_T
   endfor
   if empty List_T
      return false
   else
      return T
   endif
endfunction
```

Fig. 7. Algorithm to detect when a surface crosses a region of the pixel

The technique used is this algorithm is similar to the presented in section 2. The process is based in a branch and bound strategy, in which the pixel area is subdivided and every new area is further evaluated to find out whether it contains part of the surface. In this case, the same inclusion function (7) is used to evaluate a region of the pixel.

When only a ray is considered, the "detection algorithm" will return an intersection value. Using point sampling, if the ray misses the surface, there is no way to know if the surface crosses the pixel.

This algorithm is useful to visualize special cases, for example, the intersection of implicit surfaces. When two implicit surfaces intersect, the result is a curved line without thickness. This line cannot be visualized using point sampling because the rays will always miss the line. Using the presented algorithm, only an intersection test over the pixel is needed (see figure 8).

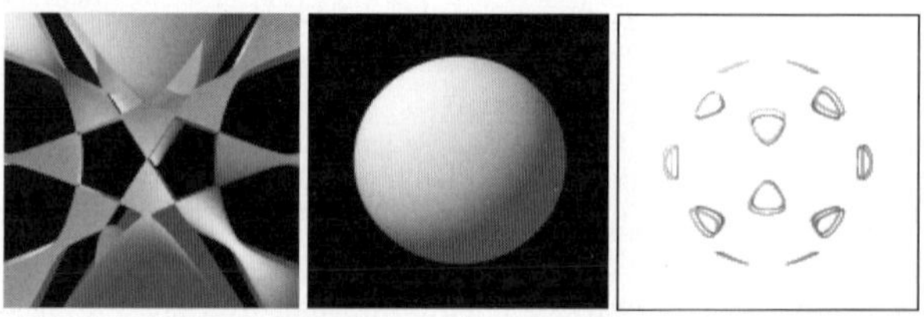

Fig. 8. Intersection between implicit surfaces

3.2 Antialiasing Strategy

In this section, the detection algorithm is used to "inform" when a pixel must be shaded, that is, if the pixel contains any part of the surface.

If the detection algorithm finds a part of the surface inside a pixel, a branch-and-bound process is started over the pixel to generate subpixels. Every subpixel region is evaluated to determine if it contains part of the surface. The subdivision process continues until a subpixel subdivision level is achieved. In that case, the normal at the surface is calculated and used to determine the shading color. If the evaluated region does not contain any part of the surface, the background color is assigned to the region. At the end, the shading value for every pixel is calculated according to the color and area of every subpixel.

3.3 Experimental Results

The described antialiasing algorithm was used to generate a visualization of the Steiner surface. This visualization is compared with the traditional interval ray tracing. The resulting images are shown in figure 9. In the sampling algorithm, 16 rays are sent for every pixel. In the interval antialiasing, the algorithm is stopped when the subdivision takes a size equivalent to 1/16 of the pixel area. The time spent by the interval antialiasing is 765.18 seconds, and the sampling algorithm takes 1504.31 seconds. The time difference is because the interval antialiasing algorithm verifies if a part of the surface is contained in every pixel before the algorithm starts to make subdivisions. In the sampling algorithm, 16 rays are sending for every pixel in the screen.

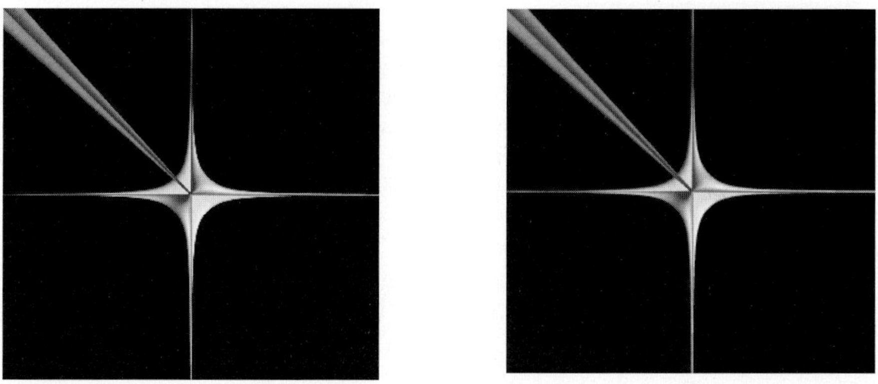

Fig. 8. Comparison of a point sampling algorithm and the interval antialiasing algorithm introduced in this paper. Using only point sampling (left) and using the interval antialiasing algorithm (right).

4 Conclusions

In this paper we have introduced several improvements to the ray tracing of implicit surfaces, using interval analysis. The first presented algorithm offers an important improvement in efficiency. Using intervals to perform intersection tests over regions of the screen is faster than an evaluation of individual pixels. The second algorithm improves the quality of the visualization of the surfaces. This is obtained using an interval evaluation of all the area of the pixel instead of sampled points. It is not possible to obtain that kind of improvement using algorithms based on the floating-point arithmetic of the computer.

As future work, we plan to add reflections and refractions to the presented algorithms. The idea is to create a more complete shader, applicable to visualize more realistic images.

Acknowledgements

This work has been partially funded by the European Union (European Regional Development Fund) and the Spanish Government (Plan Nacional de Investigación Científica, Desarrollo e Innovación Tecnológica, Ministerio de Ciencia y Tecnología) through the co-ordinated research projects DPI2002-04018-C02-02, DPI2003-07146-C02-02, DPI2004-07167-C02-02 and TIN2004-07451-C03-01 and by the government of Catalonia through SGR00296.

References

1. Ramon Moore. Interval analysis. Prentice-Hall, Englewood, 1966
2. Amitabh Agrawal and Aristides A. G. Requicha. A paradigm for the robust design of algorithms for geometric models. Eurographics'94, Computer Graphics Forum, Vol.13, No.3, pp.33-44, 1994
3. Helmut Ratschek and Jon Rokne. Geometric computations with interval and new robust methods. Horwood Publishing, 2003
4. D. Kalra and A. Barr. Guaranteed ray intersection with implicit surfaces. In Computer Graphics (Siggraph proceedings), volume 23, pages 297-- 306, 1989
5. O. Capriani, L. Hvidegaard, M. Mortensen and T. Schneider. Robust and efficient ray intersection of implicit surfaces. Reliable Computing, volume 6, p. 9 – 21, 2000
6. Don Mitchell. Robust ray intersection with interval analysis. Proceedings on graphics interface, pages 68-74. 1990
7. J.F. Sanjuan-Estrada, L.G. Casado and I. García. Reliable algorithms for ray intersection in computer graphics based on interval arithmetic. XVI Brazilian symposium on computer graphics and Image processing, pages 35-44, 2003
8. A. de Cusatis, L. de Figueiredo and M. Gatas. Interval methods for ray casting implicit surfaces with affine arithmetic. In Proceedings of SIBGRAPI'99, pages 65--71. IEEE Press, October 1999
9. Heckbert and Hanrahan, Beam Tracing Polygonal Objects. Proceedings of the 11th annual conference on computer graphics and interactive techniques, pages 119-127, 1984
10. Fundamentals of computer graphics. Peter Shirley. A K Peters Ltd., 2002

Algorithms for Vector Graphic Optimization and Compression

Mingkui Song[1], Richard R. Eckert[1], and David A. Goldman[2]

[1] Computer Science Department,
State University of New York at Binghamton, NY 13902, USA
{msong, reckert}@binghatmon.edu
http://cs.binghamton.edu/Faculty/reckert.html
[2] Soft Sight, Inc. 216 Main street, Vestal,
New York, 13850 USA
dgoldman@softsightinc.com
http://www.softsightinc.com

Abstract. The objective of metafile compositing is to retrieve multi-layered Windows Metafile command records from a picture file and translate them into a set of closed contours in a single layer that delineates a set of contiguous non-overlapping regions. Such processing is useful for a variety of engineering applications including vector graphic compression and optimization which is discussed here. Primary concerns here are the multitude of degeneracies that exist when implementing a geometric algorithm of this nature. These issues are left largely unaddressed in previous literature but can be of substantial importance when attempting to develop a robust implementation.

1 Introduction

Computer Graphics Metafiles (CGM) have been in use at the Los Alamos National Laboratory since early 1977 where these files were later formally designated as an international standard by ISO/IEC 8632/I-1:1992[2]. Vector graphics are composed of lines and curves defined by vectors, which describe such graphics according to their geometric characteristics. Most CGMs created by illustration packages, etc. contain three common phenomena that prevent or make difficult their direct use in many common engineering applications. First, they often contain redundant data where portions of some commands overlap areas of previously specified commands or even within a single command there may exist duplicate points or self-overlap within areas specified by that single command. Second, because most CGMs result from user input there are many instances where combinations of simple commands are placed adjacent to one another to effectively create more sophisticated commands. Thus, even a simple rendering of a circle may contain thousands of metafile command records. Third, because often the primary goal of a CGM is to produce a raster device rendering there is little consistency among how commands are specified (e.g. some may use counter-clockwise boundary specifications using winding fill rules while others may simply specify a pseudo-medial axis of lines or curves of a particular thickness to be created). Unfortunately, for many image understanding tasks consistency is typically quite important. For example, it may be useful to specify regions bounded by closed contours where the interior of such regions always lie to

H.-P. Seidel, T. Nishita, and Q. Peng (Eds.): CGI 2006, LNCS 4035, pp. 665 – 672, 2006.

the left of the contour. Thus, to avoid the pitfalls of rasterization and maintain a lossless and useful representation of picture data stored within a metafile it may be desirable to eliminate redundancies within vector data.

2 Vector Graphic Compression and Optimization with Compositing Algorithm

Many existing graphic compression methods such as ABO (Adaptive Binary Optimization), GIF (Graphics Interchange Format), PNG (Portable Network Graphics) and JPEG etc. do not work well for the compression of vector graphic files because these compression methods are based on compressing bitmap graphics with either statistical modeling algorithms or encoding algorithms. After compression, the file format is changed and the resolution-independent nature is also lost. A CGM compositing algorithm is proposed here for vector graphic file compression and optimization. In this algorithm there is no loss in the quality of the resulting image. Furthermore, the file format is not changed, which means that it is resolution independent. This method has two major advantages: First, applications do not have to call other software that supports a new file format as they do with most graphics compression applications. For example, if an application wants to open a JPEG file, it has to use extra JPEG related DLLs (Dynamic Link Libraries) to support this. Second, after compositing, the file is saved back to its original vector file format, thus maintaining its vector features so that geometric transformations such as rotation and scaling may be applied subsequently. Other compression software changes the format of the image file.

The strategy for vector graphic compression using a compositing algorithm is to eliminate the substantial redundancies contained within edge data in order to provide consistently ordered non-degenerate polygonal data. This is often an issue when metafile data is created by graphics artists using illustration packages where human factors or error can often introduce such redundancies and degeneracies.

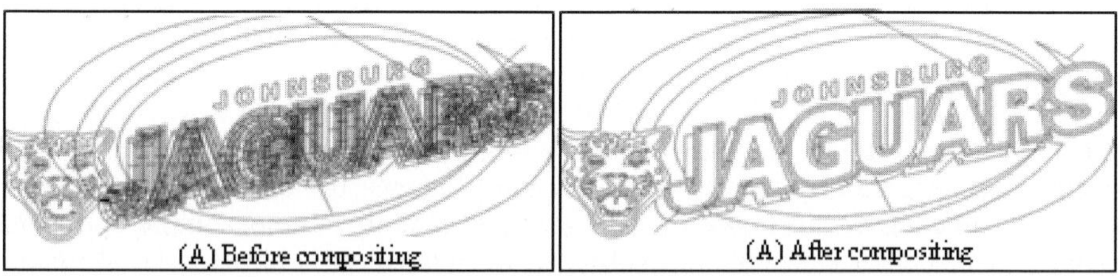

Fig. 1. Part A shows a metafile containing more than 10,000 polygonal objects (237k in physical size). Part B shows the same metafile after compositing in which there are now fewer than 100 polygon objects (165k in physical size). The images are identical after polygon fill; however, the number of records and physical disk size are reduced by 99% and 30% respectively.

The composting algorithm sequentially takes polygons with filling mode and color attributes as input and then outputs a set of consistently formed non-overlapping polygons. The input polygons need not necessarily be regular polygons, i.e. polygon vertices may be specified in any order (clockwise or counter-clockwise) and the polygon itself might be self-overlapped. The output is order-specified, i.e. the outline polygons are in counter clockwise order and any contours indicating holes are specified in a clockwise order. After compression with our CGM compositing algorithm, redundant records are removed and the output records are recreated in a consistent order. Therefore the vector graphic is optimized as a byproduct. Figure 1 illustrates the wire-frames of a vector file before and after compositing and they are visually identical after filling occurs during rasterization.

3 CGM Compositing Algorithm

Presented here is a brief overview of the compositing algorithm developed with particular emphasis on various degeneracies that may arise. More detailed information may also be found in [1][4]. The basic approach is to assume that a scan-line traverses the data from top to bottom and then left to right, halting at event points indicated by vertices or intersections within the polygonal input data. This process may be further broken down into three main steps as described next.

3.1 Finding Segment Pairs

A segment pair is comprised of two segments from the same polygonal region which intersect the sweep line and lie on opposite edges of the region which is bounded by them (i.e. indicating an area between the two segments that is part of a GDI fill area for a particular metafile record or polygonal region based on the CGM filling rules). Each segment pair is labeled at each event-point. It is very easy to find the segment pair if the original record uses an alternate edge fill mode. It can be done by just selecting the odd and even segments on the scan-line and pairing them up respectively. If a record uses a winding-rule fill mode, the original drawing direction must be stored and the fill depth must also be tracked. The segment pair has to be recalculated at any new event point.

3.2 Segment Selection, Removal, and Duplication

Separate segment pools are created for holding segments with different attributes (note: a segment's attributes are inherited from the attributes of its related polygonal object). Thus, segments having the same related attributes are grouped into a single pool. A polygonal object is said to be younger if it appeared sequentially later within the list of metafile records. If a polygonal object is seen earlier within the sequence, it is considered older. Segment selection and duplication are based on two factors: attribute values and the age of the related polygonal object. For example, for differently colored objects, segments that are from younger objects will be selected and duplicated for those older objects that are overlapped by them. Polygonal objects that are fully covered by other younger objects do not have their segments selected and placed within a segment pool. If an object is partially covered by other younger polygonal objects, the overlapping segments from the youngest object are copied to its associated segment pool and any segments that are overlapped by the region covered by this youngest object are removed. Thus, the sweep invariant for each segment pool is that each segment is unique (i.e. no two segments have the same end points).

3.3 Generating Objects from Each Segment Pool

The newly generated output polygons have simple polygon properties (Jordan curve properties)[7][8]. According the Jordan Curve Theorem[8], a method termed as an even-odd test is used for segment traversal; if a scan ray that starts at a left-most boundary is projected horizontally to the right, the resulting intersections with segments within a segment pool may be numbered. Specifically, the odd intersections (e.g. 1st , 3rd , 5th , etc) are referred to as **odd-segments** while the even intersections (e.g. 2nd , 4th, 6th, etc.) are called **even-segments**. Based on the odd-even segment test, the traversal methods are applied for each segment pool for final polygonal object construction.

3.4 Handling Degeneracies

The compositing algorithm must handle a variety of degenerate cases present within the original input as well as cases that arise at intermediate steps during processing. One of the fundamental problems addressed within this work is that of implementing theoretically correct algorithms within a computer system that is not inherently capable of exact computation. Specifically, inexact floating point number representations that are commonly used during mathematical computation within a microprocessor can easily cause such algorithms to fail or be completely unreliable.

Polygonal Object Boundary Intersection: The polygonal object boundary intersection algorithm used within the Metafile compositing algorithm is a variation of the sweep line intersection algorithm. In addition to the details presented within these algorithms [5][6][9][17], such cases as parallel overlapped segments intersection and segments shared end points must be handled specially. For overlapped segments, all interior endpoints are counted as intersections. Before an intersection is tested for using algebraic predicates[5][6], the end-points of the segments are checked to see whether they are identical. The end-points are reported as an intersection without further calculation if they are identical. This reduces the computation cost, but more importantly it eliminates a potential discrepancy due to floating point calculation errors if multiple segments share a common end-point.

Segment Selection and Duplication: Let $S_{face}(i)$ denote the face that is associated with segment S belonging to polygonal object i, where polygonal objects are ordered by their age. $\{SL_i, SR_i\}$ denotes a segment pair where SL_i denotes the left segment (of the pair) of the ith polygonal object at a specific event point and SR_i denotes the right segment. According to the CGM filling method, the following selection and duplication rules are defined:

Hidden Rule: if S_j is between any segment pair $\{SL_i,SR_i\}$, S_j will be hidden in either of the following two cases: Case 1: $j<i$ or Case 2: Attributes($S_{face}(i)$) = Attributes($S_{face}(j)$). If S_j is hidden, it will not be placed or duplicated into a segment pool.

Selection Rule: S_j will be moved to a segment pool in either of the following two cases: Case 1: S_j is not inside or between any segment pair $\{SL_i, SR_i\}$, or Case 2: Of all segment pairs that S_j lies between, let $\{SL_i, SR_i\}$ denote the youngest pair. If j>i and Attributes(S_{face}(i)) • Attributes(S_{face}(j)) S_j will be moved.

Duplication Rule: Of all segment pairs that Sj lies between, let {SLi,SRi} denote the youngest pair. If j>i and Attributes(S_{face}(i)) • Attributes(S_{face}(j)), let S_j' be the duplication of S_j where Attributes(S'$_{face}$(i)) are assigned Attributes(S_{face}(i)) and S_j' is placed into the associated segment pool.

When several segments overlap, it is difficult to decide the sequence of pop offs and push downs. Because when segments overlap, either of the overlapping segments could be the first *hit* by the scan ray. In such cases, segments need to be reordered. Let {S} be the overlap segments which intersect with the scan ray. Let $\{S_{left}\}$ be the segments in S that belong to the left group (i.e. segments that are marked as the left segment within their corresponding segment pairs) and similarly, let $\{S_{right}\}$ be the segments in S that are marked as right segments. $\{S_{left}\}$ and $\{S_{right}\}$ are then sorted by their related polygonal object's age (ascending order, youngest first). Let S_m and S_n denote the youngest segments within $\{S_{left}\}$ and $\{S_{right}\}$ respectively. denotes an empty segment set. Thus, the previously described selection and duplication rules may be improved as follows:

Overlapped Segment Selection Rules

(1) $\{\{S_{left}\} - S_m\}$ and $\{\{S_{right}\} - S_n\}$ shall not be selected/moved to any segment pool.

(2) S_m is NOT selected if any of the following conditions are true:

(i) if $\{S_{right}\} \neq \Phi$ and Attributes(S_{face}(m)) = Attributes(S_{face}(n)) ;

(ii) S_m is between youngest $\{SL_j, SR_j\}$, if m < j , or Attributes(S_{face}(m)) = Attributes(S_{face}(j)) .

(3) S_n is NOT selected if any of the following conditions are true:

(i) if $\{S_{left}\}$ • and Attributes(S_{face}(n)) = Attributes(S_{face}(m)) ;

(ii) S_n is between youngest $\{SL_j, SR_j\}$, if n < j or Attributes(S_{face}(n)) = Attributes(S_{face}(j)) .

Overlapped Segment Duplication Rules

(1)$\{\{S_{left}\} - S_m\}$ and $\{\{S_{right}\} - S_n\}$ shall not be duplicated/copied to any segment pool.

(2) S_m should be duplicated only if

(i) S_m is not between any segment pair. Or

(ii) S_m is between a youngest pair $\{SL_j, SR_j\}$ such that m > j and Attributes(S_{face}(m)) ≠ Attributes(S_{face}(j)) and $\{S_{right}\} = \Phi$.

(3) S_n can be duplicated only if

(i) S_n is not between any segment pair. Or

(ii) S_n is between a youngest pair $\{SL_j, SR_j\}$, such that n > j and Attributes(S_{face}(n)) ≠ Attributes(S_{face}(j)) and $\{S_{left}\} = \Phi$;

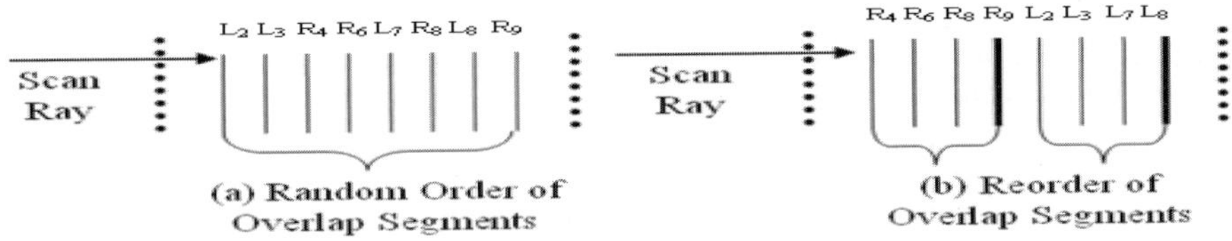

Fig. 2. Recorder of Overlap Segments hit by scan ray (i.e. segments have identical end points)

Additionally, according to these new overlapped segment selection and duplication rules, $\{S_{right}\}$ will be processed first then $\{S_{left}\}$. In the case of duplication, if there is at least one left segment and one right segment overlapping, even if they are not a filling pair, they will not be used for duplication. For selection, only the youngest left segment and youngest right segment will be selected. Let $SL_2 SL_3 SR_4 SR_6 SL_7 SR_8 SL_8 SR_9$ in Figure 2 (a) be overlapping segments where their order represents their intersection sequence with the scan ray. In this case, only SR_9 and SL_8 will be selected if the related face attributes of SR_9 and SL_8 are different. However, if the attributes of SR_9 and SL_8 are identical, neither SR_9 nor SL_8 will be selected or copied.

4 Experiments and Performance Analysis

Our CGM compositing application was developed in C++ and tested on Intel Pentium® IVPCs. An online tool was also developed and is at www.geolibs.com. The tool allows users to upload individual metafiles and then view the intermediate and output results of composting operations on metafiles uploaded.

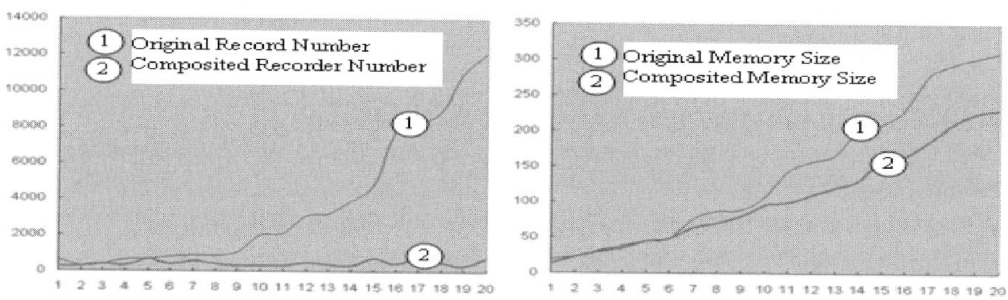

Fig. 3. Left chart illustrates the different number of records before and after Compositing. The right chart illustrates the physical memory size before and after compositing.

The experimental image set used here was composed of over 10,000 CGMs from various sources, including some that were created with commercial illustrator software such as Corel Draw®. Figure 3 show the results of tests made using our metafile compositing algorithm. In each case the numbers on the horizontal axis represent group numbers, in which each group contains 30-50 files containing similar record counts. The group numbers are ordered from groups containing small numbers of record counts to those containing large numbers of record counts. Figure 3 demonstrates how the size of the composited image is reduced after running the algorithm. The average reduction in physical memory size of all the CGM image files tested with the algorithm was 23.1%. However, a maximum record size reduction of 99% was obtained for one of the files, indicating that in some cases a truly dramatic degree of image compression can be achieved with the algorithm (Figure 1). The compositing algorithm has a huge impact on the number of records. That is because the records have been optimized in the output file. In an extreme case, for example, a 1000 polygon input record might become a one poly-polygon output record.

There are two primary factors affecting the performance of the CGM compositing algorithm: one is the number of unique object attributes (e.g. colors) within the file and the other is the number segments that intersect. An important feature is that performance is not largely dependent on the geometric size or physical memory size of the file being processed. More specifically, the computational complexity of the compositing algorithm may be described as follows: Let N be the number of polygonal object edges (i.e. number of segments) and k be the number of intersections among those edges. The number of iterations required for the compositing algorithm is N+k. The worst case cost of each operation (edge selection and copy) is O(logN). Therefore the total running time is O((N+k)logN) for segment placement. Because each edge can be copied at most only once, the traversal cost is less than 2*N. As in the original Bentley and Ottmann sweep-line algorithm [5], the cost of finding intersections is O((N+k)logN).

The cost of re-establishing segments in pools is described as follows: Let n denote the sum of segments in all segment pools and assume there are k segment pools; let n_i be a random variable denoting the number of elements placed in segment pool A[i]. The worse run time of re-establishing all segments in pools is:

$$\mathrm{T(n)} = \theta(\mathrm{n} * \mathrm{lgn}) + \sum_{i=1}^{k} O(n_i^2) \tag{1}$$

Since the probability of a segment being selected into A[i] is 1/k, by taking expectations of both sides, (1) can be reduced to:

$$T(n) = \theta(\mathrm{n} * \mathrm{lgn}) + \mathrm{n} - \mathrm{n/k} + \mathrm{n}^2 / k = \theta(\mathrm{n}^2) \tag{2}$$

Therefore, the total cost of the compositing algorithm is (n^2). Practical runtime performance cost can be further reduced by using advanced data structures such as priority queues and Fibonacci heaps for segment search within pools.

5 Conclusions

Vector graphics are becoming ever more prevalent, especially in web-based applications (such as scalable vector graphics), where sending large images across a network can significantly degrade performance. An efficient, robust algorithm is presented in this paper that compresses and optimizes Vector Graphic images fairly economically. Experimentation has shown that the tens of thousands of CGMs tested, even those metafiles with hundreds of thousands of records and hundreds of thousands of intersections, are typically processed in less than 1 second on modern PCs. Future work may include combining optimized record structures to achieve even higher compression ratio.

References

1. Song, M.: Robust Graphics Metafile Compositing: A Variation of the Map Overlay Problem Within Computational Geometry. Master's thesis, Binghamton University, 2003
2. Reed, T.: A Metafile for Efficient Sequential And Random Display of Graphics, Proceedings of the 9th annual conference on Computer graphics and interactive techniques, ACM 16 (1982), pp. 39-43

3. Carson, S., Dam, A.V., Puk, D., Henderson, L.R.: The history of Computer Graphics Standards Development, SIGGRAPH Computer Graphics, ACM 32(1998), pp. 34-38
4. Goldman, D., Song, M., Eckert, R.R.: Metafile Compositing for Automated Embroidery Design Generation, International Conference on Graphics, Vision and Image Processing (GVIP-05), Cairo, Egypt, December 2005
5. Bentley, J.L., Ottamann, T.A.: Algorithms for reporting and counting geometric intersections, IEEE Trans. Comput., C-28 (1979), pp. 643-647
6. Boissonnat, J., Preparata, F.P.: Robust Plane Sweep for Intersecting Segments, SIAM Journal on Computing, Volume 29(2000), Number 5 pp. 1401-1421
7. Wylie, C., Romney, G.W., Evans, D.C., Erdahl, A.C.: Halftone Perspective Drawings by Computer, In Proceedings of the Fall Joint Computer Conference(1967), Thomson Books, pp.49-58
8. Courant, R., Robbins, H.: What is Mathematics?, Oxford University Press, 1941
9. Balaban, I.J.: An optimal algorithm for finding segments intersections, Proceedings of the 11th Annual ACM Symposium on Computational Geometry, Vancouver, Canada (1995), pp. 211 C219
10. Mantyla, M.: Boolean Operations of 2-Manifolds through Vertex Neighborhood classification, ACM Transactions on Graphics, Vol 5, No. 1 January (1986), pp. 1-29
11. Sutherland, E.E., Hodgeman, G.W.: Reentrant polygon clipping, Commun. ACM 17 (1974), pp. 32-42
12. Liang, Y., Barskey, B.A.: An analysis and algorithm for polygon clipping, Commun. ACM 11 (1983), pp. 868-977
13. Weiler, K., Atherton, P.: Hidden Surface Removal Using Polygon Area Sorting, ACM SIGGRAPH (1977), pp. 214-222
14. Greiner, G., Hormann, K.: Efficient Clipping of Arbitrary Polygons, Trans. On Graphics, ACM 17 (1998), pp. 71-83
15. Vatti, B. R.: A generic solution to polygon clipping, commun. ACM 35 (1992), pp. 56-63.
16. Frank, A.U.: Overlay processing in spatial information systems, in AutoCarto 8, (1987), pp. 12-31
17. Badawy, W.M., Aref, W.G.: On Local Heuristics to Speed Up Polygon-Polygon Intersection Tests, ACM GIS 11 (1999), Kansas City, MO USA
18. Brown, W.S.: A simple but realistic model of floating-point computation, ACM Trans. Math. Softw. (1981), pp. 445-480
19. Burnikel, C., Mehlhorn, K., Schirra, S.: On degeneracy in geometric computations, Proceedings of the 5th ACM-SIAM Symposium on Discrete Algorithms, Arlington, VA (1994), pp. 16-23
20. Chazelle, B., Edelsbrunner, H.: An optimal algorithm for intersecting line segments in the plane, Journal of ACM, Vol. 39 (1992), pp. 1 C54
21. DeBerg, M.: Computing half-plane and strip discrepancy of planar point sets, Comput. Geom. Theory Appl., 6 (1996). pp. 69-83
22. Goldberg, D.: What Every computer Scientist Should Know About Floating-Point Arithmetic, ACM Computer Surveys, Vol 23 (1991), No 1, pp.5-48
23. Mount, D.M.: Intersection Detection and Separators for Simple Polygons, Proc. of the Eighth Annual ACM Symp. on Computational Geometry (1992), pp. 303 C311

Detail-Preserving Local Editing for Point-Sampled Geometry*

Yongwei Miao[1,2,**], Jieqing Feng[1], Chunxia Xiao[1], Hui Li[1], and Qunsheng Peng[1]

[1] State Key Lab. of CAD&CG, Zhejiang University, Hangzhou 310027, P.R. China
{miaoyw, jqfeng, cxxiao, lihui, peng}@cad.zju.edu.cn
[2] College of Science, Zhejiang University of Technology, Hangzhou 310032, P.R. China
Tel.: +86-571-883-60243
mywfjy@hzcnc.com

Abstract. In digital geometry processing, it is important to preserve the intrinsic properties of 3D models in geometry editing operations. One of such intrinsic properties can be described as geometric details. For point-sampled geometry, combining the Normal Geometric Details (NGDs) and the Position Geometric Details (PGDs), a useful interactive geometry local editing method is developed. The method deforms the sample points in a region of interest by manipulating handle points. In the preprocessing step, a non-local denoising algorithm is applied to smooth the input noisy point-sampled model and as a postprocessing step, a new up-sampling and relaxation procedure is proposed to refine the deformed model. The effectiveness of the proposed method is demonstrated by examples, i.e., the editing operation can deform the model while respecting the intrinsic geometric details.

1 Introduction

Efficient 3D geometry editing for mesh surfaces or point-sampled geometry is an active research topic in digital geometry processing [1, 3, 4, 5, 6, 8, 9, 10, 12, 14, 15, 17, 18, 20]. It is important to manipulate and modify 3D shapes while preserving their intrinsic geometric details. In the recent years several detail-preserving geometry editing techniques are proposed for meshes and point-sampled geometry, which are multi-resolution approach, differential domain approach, and discrete forms approach, etc.

Multi-resolution Approach. In the multi-resolution editing approach, a 3D model is decomposed into a base shape and a set of geometric details [5, 6, 19]. The geometric details are defined as differences between successive levels in the multi-resolution hierarchy, and are encoded in the local frames of their lower level geometry. The base shape can be modified interactively by using various transformation and deformation. The details are then coated on the base surface

* For Proceedings of the Computer Graphics International Conference 2006.

** Correspondence author.

H.-P. Seidel, T. Nishita, and Q. Peng (Eds.): CGI 2006, LNCS 4035, pp. 673–681, 2006.

of different levels. The problem with these methods is that the displacement vectors are manipulated independently at each vertex. Some artifacts may appear in highly deformed regions because details are not coupled and can not preserved uniformly over the whole model.

Differential Domain Approach. The Laplacian coordinates are now widely used in surface detail-preserving editing [1, 8, 10, 18], which are defined as the difference of a vertex position from the centroid of its local neighbors. They are invariant under translation, but not invariant under scaling and rotation. Lipman et al. [8] and Sorkine et al. [15] compensated these limitations by transforming the local coordinate frame. By extending surface Laplacian coordinates, Zhou et al. [18] presented a novel technique to process large deformations of mesh object by using the volumetric graph Laplacian, which provided the encoding of volumetric details.

Based on discretizing the Poisson equation with proper Dirichlet boundary condition, Yu et al. [17] manipulate the gradients of the coordinate functions defined on the mesh, and then propagate the rotation of handle to all the vertices in the region of interest. Sheffer and Kraevoy [14] represent the mesh by using rotation-invariant pyramid coordinates. However, the reconstruction from pyramid coordinates to vertex coordinates requires solving a nonlinear system, which is a time-consuming procedure.

Discrete Forms Approach. Recently, inspired by discrete differential geometry and surface fundamental theorem, Lipman et al. [9] introduce a rigid motion invariant mesh representation based on discrete forms defined on the mesh. This mesh representation implicitly defines a local frame at each vertex, and the two discrete forms encode the changes between adjacent frames. It can edit a mesh with the preservation of its local appearance under some global constraints.

Our Main Contributions. For point-sampled geometry, a useful interactive geometry local editing method is developed.

- A new normal geometric detail and a new framework of surface editing are proposed. Our editing approach can preserve both normal geometric details and position geometric details.
- As a preprocessing step, a non-local denoising algorithm is applied to smooth the input noisy sampled-point model.
- As a postprocessing step, a new up-sampling and relaxation procedure is proposed to fine tone the deformed geometry.

2 Define Normal Geometric Details (NGDs) by Implicit Surface Fitting

The normal geometric detail is based on the Laplacian operator over implicit surface. The later one interpolates the scattered point clouds and the associated normal vectors [11].

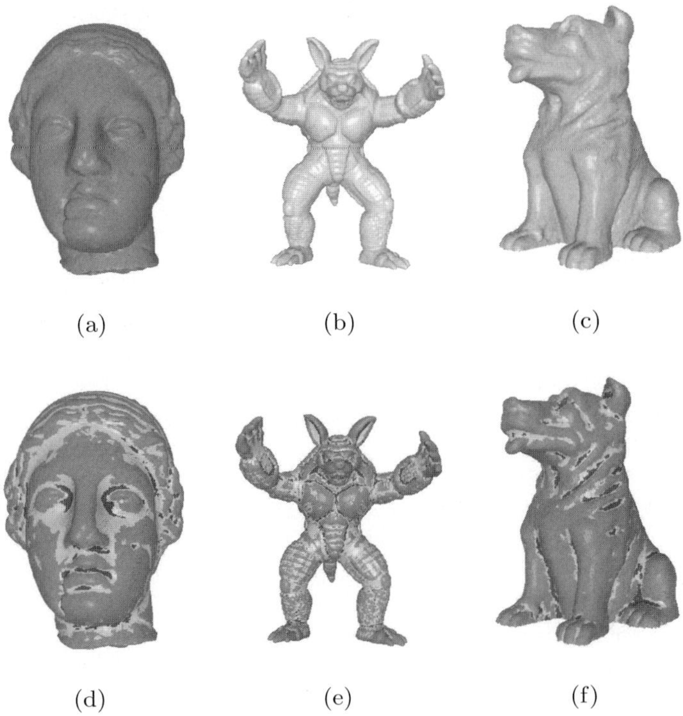

Fig. 1. The NGDs color map: (a),(d) fandisk model and color map of NGDs; (b),(e) Stanford Armadillo model and color map of NGDs; (c),(f) dog model and color map of NGDs

Given a scattered point cloud $\boldsymbol{P} = \{\mathbf{p}_i = (x_i, y_i, z_i), i = 1, 2, \cdots, N\}$, and the associated normal vectors $\boldsymbol{N} = \{\mathbf{n}_i = (n_{xi}, n_{yi}, n_{zi}), i = 1, 2, \cdots, N\}$. An implicit surface $S = \{\mathbf{p} | \rho(\mathbf{p}) = 0\}$ can be constructed to interpolate the points $\boldsymbol{P}$ and the associated normal vectors $\boldsymbol{N}$, which is:

$$\rho(\mathbf{p}) = \sum_{i=1}^{N} \omega_i(\mathbf{p}) \langle \mathbf{p} - \mathbf{p}_i, \mathbf{n}_i \rangle$$

where the weight function $\omega_i(\mathbf{p})$ is:

$$\omega_i(\mathbf{p}) = \frac{\frac{1}{\|\mathbf{p}-\mathbf{p}_i\|^2}}{\sum_{i=1}^{N} \frac{1}{\|\mathbf{p}-\mathbf{p}_i\|^2}} = \frac{\prod_{j \neq i} \|\mathbf{p} - \mathbf{p}_j\|^2}{\sum_{j=1}^{N} \prod_{k \neq j} \|\mathbf{p} - \mathbf{p}_k\|^2}$$

The gradient and Laplacian operators of weight function $\omega_i(\mathbf{p})$ can be derived as follows:

$$\nabla \omega_i(\mathbf{p}_i) = 0, \quad \nabla \omega_i(\mathbf{p}_j) = 0$$

and

$$\nabla^2 \omega_i(\mathbf{p}_i) = -2 \cdot \sum_{k \neq i} \frac{1}{\|\mathbf{p}_i - \mathbf{p}_k\|^2}$$

$$\nabla^2 \omega_i(\mathbf{p}_j) = \frac{2}{\|\mathbf{p}_i - \mathbf{p}_j\|^2}$$

By using the gradient and Laplacian properties of weight function $\omega_i(\mathbf{p})$, the second order Laplacian at sample point $\mathbf{p}_i$ is:

$$\Delta\rho(\mathbf{p}_i) = \sum_{j \neq i} \frac{2}{\|\mathbf{p}_i - \mathbf{p}_j\|^2} \langle \mathbf{p}_i - \mathbf{p}_j, \mathbf{n}_j \rangle$$

The above second order Laplacian is adopted to define the normal geometric details, abbreviated as NGDs:

$$\delta(\mathbf{p}_i) = \sum_{j \in N_i \backslash \{i\}} \frac{2}{\|\mathbf{p}_i - \mathbf{p}_j\|^2} \langle \mathbf{p}_i - \mathbf{p}_j, \mathbf{n}_j \rangle$$

where N_i denote the adaptive neighborhood of a regular point $\mathbf{p}_i$.

The NGDs record the surface curving degree at each sample point, which is invariant under rigid transformations, such as translation, rotation, etc. The color maps for different NGDs are shown in Fig. 1, where different color is corresponding to different value of NGDs.

3 Detail-Preserving Local Editing for Point-Sampled Geometry

3.1 Preprocessing: Non-local Denoising Algorithm

Generally, the input point-sampled models are prone to various kinds of undesirable noise due to a variety of physical factors and limitations of the data acquisition procedure. On the other hand, based on the Hermite interpolation for the scattered point clouds and the associated normal vectors, the normal geometric details are more sensitive to data with noise. It will be preferable to denoise the underlying geometry before carrying on further local geometry editing operation [7, 13, 16].

Based on non-local image denoising algorithm proposed by Buades et al. [2], a global denoising algorithm for 3D point-sampled geometry is proposed.

For each sample point, a fitting tangent plane is obtained through covariant method, and a local frame can be constructed based on the tangent plane and normal. The distance from the sample point to the local tangent plane can be computed, which is called geometry gray-level value or offset. The main idea of non-local denoising algorithm is a global weight average scheme, i.e., the geometry gray-level of each sample point is computed as a weighted average of all sample points on the whole model. According to the offset of each sample point, the underlying geometry can be reconstructed easily by moving each sample point along its normal direction. Generally, a satisfied model can be obtained after two or three iterative non-local averaging procedures.

The example with non-local denoising our scanned model is shown in Fig. 2(a) and 2(b).

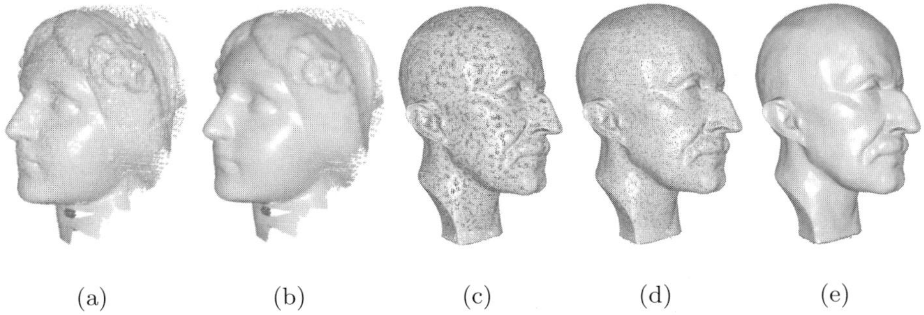

Fig. 2. Preprocessing and postprocessing: (a) original scanned model; (b) denoised model by non-local denoising scheme; (c) poor point-sampled model; (d) refined model after up-sampling scheme; (e) render refined model

3.2 Detail-Preserving Local Editing

For detail-preserving editing of point-sampled geometry, it is important to modify large scale features of the underlying object, while keeping its local geometric details unchanged. In our proposed method, the intrinsic geometric details are encoded by normal geometric details (NGDs) and position geometric details (PGDs).

In general, a point-sampled geometry consists of an unstructured point cloud $S = \{\mathbf{p}_i = (x_i, y_i, z_i), i = 1, 2, \cdots, N\}$ sampled from a surface S. Each sample point $\mathbf{p}_i$ is equipped with the associated normal vectors $\mathbf{n}_i = (n_{xi}, n_{yi}, n_{zi}), i = 1, 2, \cdots, N$.

During intrinsic editing of point-sampled geometry, it should consider both normal details and position details. So, the intrinsic geometry is described by two terms, one is normal geometric details (NGDs), i.e.,

$$\delta(\mathbf{p}_i) = \sum_{j \in N_i \setminus \{i\}} \frac{2}{\|\mathbf{p}_i - \mathbf{p}_j\|^2} \langle \mathbf{p}_i - \mathbf{p}_j, \mathbf{n}_j \rangle$$

where N_i denote the adaptive neighborhood of a regular point $\mathbf{p}_i$.

The other one is position geometric details (PGDs) or position Laplacian, i.e.,

$$L(\mathbf{p}_i) = \mathbf{p}_i - \sum_{j \in N_i} \omega_{ij}^P \mathbf{p}_j, \sum_{j \in N_i} \omega_{ij}^P = 1$$

for each sample point $\mathbf{p}_i$, where ω_{ij}^P is the positive weight for point $\mathbf{p}_j$.

To perform detail-preserving editing by using the NGDs and PGDs, user specify the deformed absolute positions $\mathbf{q}_i, i \in \{1, 2, \cdots, m\}$ for a subset of point clouds, i.e.,

$$\mathbf{p}'_i = \mathbf{q}_i, i \in \{1, 2, \cdots, m\}$$

and the system will solve the deformed position of remaining sampled points $\{\mathbf{p}'_i\}, i \in \{m, m+1, \cdots, K\}$ in a region of interest (ROI) through fitting the NGDs and PGDs of the geometry $S' = \{\mathbf{p}'_i, i = 1, 2, 3, \cdots, K\}$ to the given geometric details of input surface S.

The deformed positions of the sample points in ROI $\{\mathbf{p}'_i\}, i \in \{1, 2, \cdots, K\}$ can be obtained by solving the following quadratic minimization problem:

$$\min_{\mathbf{p}'} \alpha \sum_{i=1}^{K} \|\delta(\mathbf{p}'_i) - \delta_i\|^2 + \beta \sum_{i=1}^{K} \|L(\mathbf{p}'_i) - L_i\|^2 + \sum_{i=1}^{m} \|\mathbf{p}'_i - \mathbf{q}_i\|^2$$

The first term represents preservation of normal geometric details of deformed sample points, the second one represents preservation of position geometric details of deformed sample points, and the third term represents position constraints specified by the user. The parameter α and β balance between two kinds of geometric details, for NGDs and PGDs respectively. They also balance between the detail-preserving requirement and the position constraints.

After the deformed positions of handle sample points are specified by user, the deformed positions of sample points in the ROI can be computed by minimizing the quadratic energy. It can be converted into a quasi-linear system $\mathbf{Ax} = \mathbf{b}$, and can be solved by iterative scheme using the conjugate gradient method to the associated normal equations $(\mathbf{A}^T\mathbf{A})\mathbf{x} = \mathbf{A}^T\mathbf{b}$.

3.3 Postprocessing: Up-Sampling Algorithm

After local geometry editing, e.g., stretching or twisting, it may cause some distortions in the distribution of sample points in the ROI, and can lead to an insufficient local sampling density. To refine the deformed results, it is necessary to up-sample the model.

The up-sampling procedure for deformed sampled-point geometry can be decomposed into three steps:

The first step is to detect hole on the model. For sample point $\mathbf{p}_i$, all of neighbors are projected onto the fitting tangent plane on $\mathbf{p}_i$, which are denoted as $\{\mathbf{q}^*_{ij}\}$. The corresponding covariance matrix can be constructed for $\{\mathbf{q}^*_{ij}\}$, and two eigenvectors $\mathbf{e}^1_i$ and $\mathbf{e}^2_i$ are computed which corresponds to the two nonzero eigenvalues. The sampling densities along directions $\mathbf{e}^1_i, -\mathbf{e}^1_i, \mathbf{e}^2_i, -\mathbf{e}^2_i$ are computed. If the density along one direction is approximate zero, it shows that $\mathbf{p}_i$ is on the boundary of the hole, and the geometry should be up-sampled along the sparse direction. The second step is up-sampling along the sparse direction near the hole according to pre-defined density threshold. Finally, to obtain a more uniform sampling geometry, a relaxation operator will be applied to the up-sampled object, which re-arranges the sample points on the surface similar to the relaxation approach proposed by Pauly et al. [12].

The example with up-sampling Max-Planck model is shown in Fig. 2(c) and 2(d,e).

(a) (b) (c) (d) (e)

Fig. 3. Local editing of dog model: (a) dog model; (b) ROI on dog jaw; (c) local editing result for dog jaw; (d) ROI on dog left ear; (e) local editing result for dog left ear

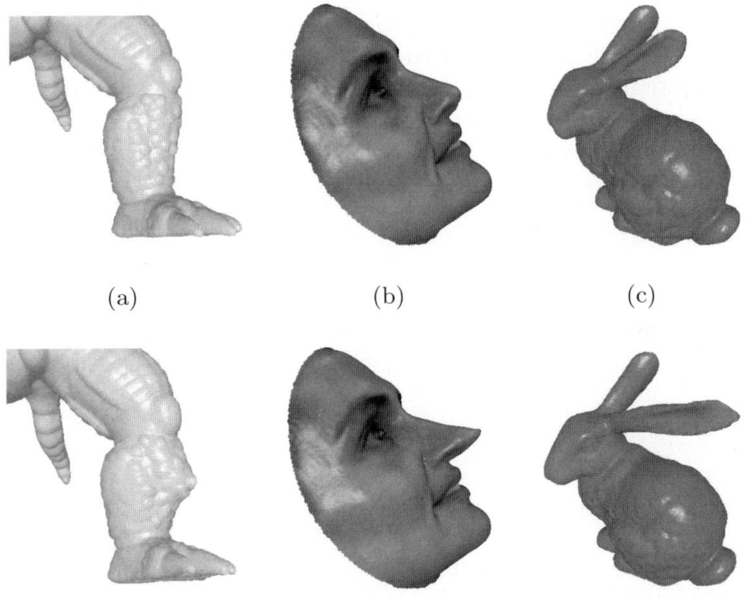

(a) (b) (c)

(d) (e) (f)

Fig. 4. Local editing of different models: (a) bumpy leg of Stanford Armadillo; (b) face model; (c) Stanford bunny model; (d) local editing result for Armadillo leg; (e) local editing result for face model; (f) local editing result for bunny model

4 Experimental Results

Experimental examples with local editing on dog model is given. The local editing for dog model contains two steps, the first one is to edit dog jaw (see Fig. 3(c)) and the second one is to edit dog left ear (see Fig. 3(e)). The local editing results for bumpy leg of Stanford Armadillo, face model, and Stanford bunny with elongated nose and unfolded ear are shown in Fig. 4.

5 Conclusions and Future Works

In this paper, a new intrinsic geometric representation is proposed —normal geometric details (NGDs) for point-sampled geometry. Combining the normal geometric details and the existing position geometric details, a useful interactive editing approach is developed, which is controlled by handle points and user specified ROI. The deformation of handle point will be spread to the points in the ROI by solving a quadratic minimization problem.

A non-local denoising algorithm is also proposed for preprocessing the input noisy point-sampled geometry based on a non-local averaging of all sample points, and a new up-sampling and relaxation procedure is proposed for post-processing the deformed model for sake of uniform sampling density.

In the future, more interactive editing and deformation operations based on geometric details will be investigated, for example, large deformation of point-sampled geometry, shape interpolation, and morphing, etc. Another future work may be the investigation of other rigid motion invariant intrinsic representation of point-sampled geometry.

Acknowledgements

The research is jointly supported by the National Natural Science Foundation of China under Grant Nos.60373036,60333010,60503056, the National Grand Fundamental Research 973 Program of China under Grant No.2002CB312101, the Doctoral Program of Higher Education (Specialized Research Fund) under grant No.20050335069.

References

1. Alexa, M.: Differential coordinates for local mesh morphing and deformation. The Visual Computer 19(2) (2003) 105-114
2. Buades, A., Coll, B., Morel, J.-M.: A non-local algorithm for image denoising. IEEE International Conference on Computer Vision and Pattern Recognition (2005) 60-65
3. Guo, X., Hua, J., Qin, H.: Point set surface editing techniques based on level-sets. Proceedings of the Computer Graphics International Conference (2004) 52-59
4. Guo, X., Hua, J., Qin, H.: Scalar-function-driven editing on point set surfaces. IEEE Computer Graphics and Application 24(4) (2004) 43-52

5. Guskov, I., Sweldens, W., Schroder, P.: Multiresolution signal processing for meshes. ACM SIGGRAPH'99 (1999) 325-334
6. Kobbelt, L., Campagna, S., Vorsatz, J., Seidel, H.-P.: Interactive multi-resolution modeling on arbitrary meshes. ACM SIGGRAPH'98 (1998) 105-114
7. Lange, C., and Polthier, K.: Anisotropic smoothing of point sets. Computer Aided Geometric Design 22 (2005) 680-692
8. Lipman, Y., Sorkine, O., Cohen-Or, D., Levin, D., Rossl, C., Seidel, H.-P.: Differential coordinates for interactive mesh editing. Proceedings of Shape Modeling International (2004) 181-190
9. Lipman, Y., Sorkine, O., Levin, D., Cohen-Or, D.: Linear rotation-invariant coordinates for meshes. ACM Transactions on Graphics 24(3) (2005) 479-487
10. Nealen, A., Sorkine, O., Alexa, M., Cohen-Or, D.: A sketch-based interface for detail-preserving mesh editing. ACM Transactions on Graphics 24(3) (2005) 1142-1147
11. Nielson, G.M.: Radial Hermite operators for scattered point cloud data with normal vectors and applications to implicitizing polygon mesh surfaces for generalized CSG operations and smoothing. Proceedings of IEEE Visualization (2004) 203-210
12. Pauly, M., Keiser, R., Kobbelt, L., Gross, M.: Shape modeling with point-sampled geometry. ACM Transactions on Graphics 22(3) (2003) 641-650
13. Schall, O., Belyaev, A., Seidel, H.-P.: Robust filtering of noisy scattered point data. Eurographics Symposium on Point-Based Graphics (2005) 71-77
14. Sheffer, A., and Kraevoy, V.: Pyramid coordinates for morphing and deformation. Second International Symposium on 3D Data Processing, Visualization and Transmission (2004) 68-75
15. Sorkine, O., Lipman, Y., Cohen-Or, D., Alexa, M., Rossl, C., Seidel, H.-P.: Laplacian surface editing. Proceedings of the ACM SIGGRAPH Symposium on Geometry Processing (2004) 179-188
16. Xie, H., McDonnell, K.T., Qin, H.: Surface reconstruction of noisy and defective data-sets. Proceedings of IEEE Visualization (2004) 259-266
17. Yu, Y., Zhou, K., Xu, D., Shi, X., Bao, H., Guo, B., Shum, H.-Y.: Mesh editing with poisson-based gradient field manipulation. ACM Transactions on Graphics 23(3) (2004) 641-648
18. Zhou, K., Huang, J., Snyder, J., Liu, X., Bao, H., Guo, B., Shum, H.-Y.: Large mesh deformation using the volumetric graph laplacian. ACM Transactions on Graphics 24(3) (2005) 496-503
19. Zorin, D., Schroder, P., Sweldens, W.: Interactive multiresolution mesh editing. ACM SIGGRAPH'97 (1997) 259-268
20. Zwicker, M., Pauly, M., Knoll, O., Gross, M.: Pointshop 3d: An interactive system for point-based surface editing. ACM Transactions on Graphics 21(3) (2002) 322-329

Automatic Stained Glass Rendering

Vidya Setlur and Stephen Wilkinson

Nokia Research Center

Abstract. Based on artistic techniques for the creation of stained glass, we introduce a method to automatically create images in stained glass stylization of images. Our algorithm first applies segmentation, and performs region simplification to merge and simplify the segments. The system then queries a database of glass swatch images and computes an optimal matching subset based on color and texture metrics. These swatches are then mapped onto the original image and 3D rendering effects including normal mapping, translucency, lead came and refraction are applied to generate the stained glass output.

1 Introduction

Stained glass is an extraordinary and vibrant medium for creating significant art and expression using a balance of light source, color and visual perception. This ancient art essentially includes tracing a pattern onto the glass and the glass is scored and cut. The artist then grinds the pieces to fit, foils each piece and reassembles, soldering the units together with lead came (Lead came is made from lead with small amounts of other metals such as copper, tin, antimony and bismuth) [1].

Gothic or medieval form of stained glass art involves the assembly of a complex mosaic of bits of colored glass joined with lead into an intricate pattern. Medieval craftmen were more interested in illustrating and idea rather than creating more natural looking art. Hence, when medieval stained glass is viewed, it appears not as a picture, but often as a network of black lines and colored light [2].

Modern or Tiffany stained glass on the other hand, involves a controlled level of artistic abstraction. Large homogenous regions comprise each glass segment while minute details are ignored in the final creation of the art piece. The effect of such abstraction allows one to appreciate the gross form and shape of the object without being distracted by superfluous features [3]. Our algorithm is largely motivated by modern stained glass as a tool for artistic abstraction.

Abstraction is often used by artists in visual art for representing objects to be more identifiable, that is, to some degree, stress the essential rather than the particular [4]. Artists rarely try to faithfully reproduce images, but even when this is the goal, it is impossible for them to achieve it, because of the intrinsic reproductive limits of the medium. However, visual abstraction is not always imposed by the medium. It may be a deliberate choice of the artist. Stained glass artists typically use one glass sample for each large homogenous region to minimize labor involved in glass cutting and applying lead came, but also to make the art piece more distinctive and identifiable.

The contribution of this paper is the automatic creation of modern stained glass stylization effects for images (Figure 1). This includes optimizing the segmentation to minimize the number of fragmented segments, mapping glass image swatches onto each

H.-P. Seidel, T. Nishita, and Q. Peng (Eds.): CGI 2006, LNCS 4035, pp. 682–691, 2006.

Fig. 1. Automatic stained glass rendering of an image. From left to right: The source image. The stained glass result generated by our system. An actual stained glass artpiece.

segment based on color and texture properties, applying 3*D* surface properties such as normal maps and lead came and using hardware accelerated graphics techniques for real time rendering of the stained glass results.

2 Related Work

Like many non-photorealistic techniques, our work also draws inspiration from the concept of stylized abstraction of images, preserving the form and shape and minimizing high level detail [5, 6, 7, 8, 9, 10]. Our algorithm represents another flavor of stylized image abstraction by applying stained glass techniques as a form of expressive rendering.

Though there exist commercial software like Adobe Photoshop [11], Corel Paint [12], Glass Eye 2000 [13] that allow users to apply stained glass filters to images, the process often requires the user to manually split the image into segments and select the degree of translucency/color and texture for each region and apply leading. This is typically manually intensive for large sets of images.

On a similar tangent, there has been some work on creating mosaic patterns in images. While mosaic and stained glass do share some similarities based on segmentation of the picture, the biggest difference between stained glass and mosaics has to do with how they use light, and how they are assembled. Stained glass is designed so that light passes through it, while mosaics are generally used to adorn a surface such as a floor or wall. Also, mosaics are created by placing small segments or tiles rather than larger homogenous regions in the case of stained glass [14]. Kim and Pellacini introduce a new kind of mosaic, called Jigsaw Image Mosaic (JIM), where image tiles of arbitrary shapes are used to compose the final picture as compactly as possible [15]. Hausner presents a method for simulating decorative tile mosaics by using centroidal Voronoi diagrams to arrange points in regular hexagonal grids [16].

Our paper is motivated by the modern looking Tiffany glass style, while previous non-photorealistic work on stained glass [17], tends to emphasize a more medieval-style . The novelty in our approach is a glass swatch selection process, based on color texture matching rather than cartoonization. Glass image swatches enhance the amount of interesting variations in color and texture features in the result.

3 The Stained Glass Rendering Process

Figure 2 summarizes the algorithm. We first segment the source image into regions. In Section 3.1 we discuss the techniques involved in segmenting the image, and combining adjacent regions based on their spatial distribution of color/intensity. We then retrieve glass image swatches from a database for each segment in the image based on color and texture features. These swatches are then enlarged using texture synthesis and replace the original image segments. These steps are described in Section 3.2. The next step involves creating normal maps to highlight the textural variations in the image segments and leading came between segments (Section 3.3). Finally, this image is rendered in real time with effects such as lighting, refraction, translucency as described in Section 3.4.

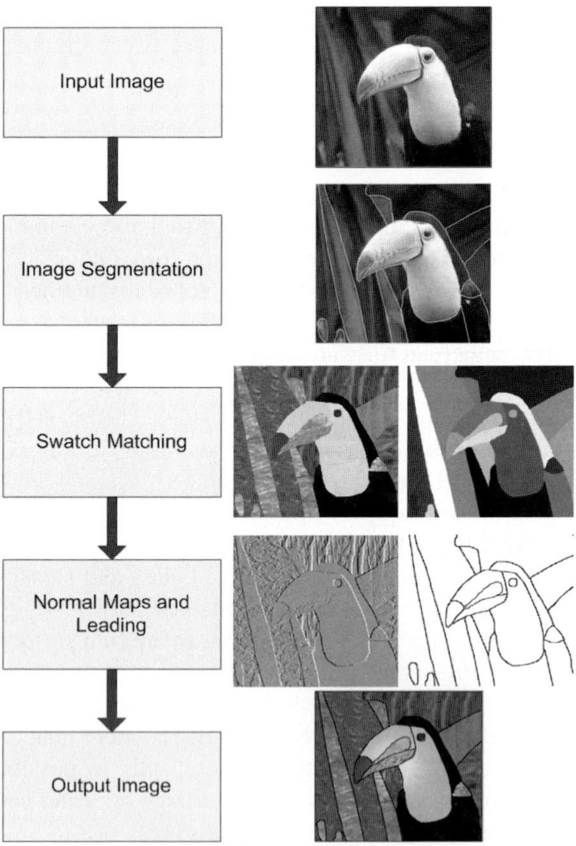

Fig. 2. Flowchart of the stained glass rendering process. The algorithm minimizes fragmented and small segments, matches glass swatches to each segment to create different stained glass patterns.

3.1 Image Segmentation

In order to create glass fragments in the stained glass rendering of the image, we must first segment the image. We apply mean-shift image segmentation [18] to decompose the given image into homogeneous regions. The advantages of this approach include flexible modeling of the image and noise processes, consequent robustness in segmentation and simplicity of the algorithm.

The segmentation routine takes as input, the parameters: spatial radius h_s, color radius h_r, and the minimum number of pixels M that constitute a region. As with other segmentation methods, choosing optimal parameter values is often difficult. Therefore we over-segment the image using lower values of h_r and M and merge adjacent regions based on color and intensity distributions in a perceptually uniform color space, CIE-Luv. In practice, values of $h_s = 7, h_r = 6$, and $M = 150$, tend to work well for over-segmentation for most images.

Our system then performs region simplification by merging similarly colored adjacent regions of the segmented image and then smoothening the outlines of the regions. We first apply a color distance measure called histogram intersection [20] to determine color similarity between regions. Often the segment boundaries are too noisy, resulting in a high degree of jagginess that is not typical of modern stained glass. If the segment outlines are considered to be Bezier curves, reducing the number of control points in the outlines creates a more optimal collection of smoother curves. The second part of the region simplification involves the use a vertex reduction technique, which is a simple and fast O(n) algorithm [21]. Control points with minimum separation are simplified iteratively until a given tolerance value is met. In practice, we have found that a tolerance value of 0.25 tends to work well with most images used in our system. Figure 3 illustrates an example of this technique.

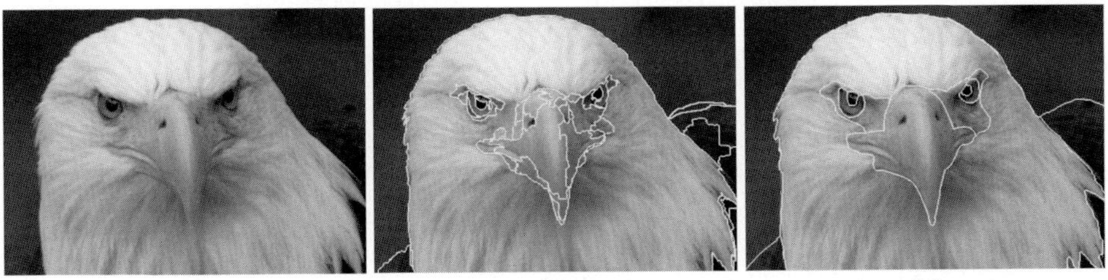

(a) (b) (c)

Fig. 3. Image segmentation. a) The original image b) Applying mean-shift with parameters $h_s = 7$, $h_r = 6$, and $M = 150$. d) Performing region simplification on (b).

3.2 Swatch Selection

After applying segmentation, we query an image database of glass swatches to map a subset of swatches to each segment of the image. The collection of swatches comprise of 2489 color images from an online image stock database [22]. As the swatches are 64×64 in dimension, and the image segments onto which they are composited are often larger (target images are typically 640×480), we apply texture synthesis using graphcuts to enlarge these swatches [23]. Most of the swatches tend to be homogenous, and hence the resulting larger texture synthesized swatches have minimal visual artifacts.

The method of query we use is a combination of the image segments' color and texture information. The color property indicates the significant colors that contribute to the appearance of an image segment, while the texture property refers to the spatial property of the segment. Swatch selections using only color features often do not match high frequency information in the segments. For example, texture features extracted from a scene of a field of grass can be distinguished from that of trees, whereby color alone may not provide sufficient determination. Combining both color and texture creates a more effective characterization of the image content, and is commonly used in image retrieval [24]. The goal of our work is to also utilize existing colored glass swatch images, attempting to generate results consistent with stained glass imagery. Figure 4b illustrates an example when our system applies only color based swatch selection. Although the dominant colors of the swatches chosen are consistent with the colors in the respective image segment, high frequency details may not be accurately represented. However, using a combination of color and texture tends to retain this high frequency information, thus serving a dual purpose of a more accurate abstraction, and interesting aesthetics.

The swatch retrieval process utilizes histogram techniques to compute color distances and employs Gabor filters as a channel energy model to compute image texture. Color matching is done again using histogram intersection. Although there are several algorithms to compute Gabor filters, our method is based on that of Manjunath et al [25].

Filtering an image $I(x,y)$ with Gabor filters g_{mn} results in its Gabor wavelet transform W_{mn} to be:

$$W_{mn}(x,y) = \int I(x_1,y_1)g^*{}_{mn}(x-x_1,y-y_1)dx_1dy_1$$

The mean and standard deviation of the magnitude $|W_{mn}|$ are used for the feature vector. Given an input query of color and textural features of a segment in the image, the swatches in the database are firstly ranked using color features. Then the top ranked images are re-ranked according to their texture features. We first select the top 5 best matched swatches based on histogram intersection and then further refine the retrieved set by applying Gabor feature vectors to select the top 3 best matched swatches. A random swatch is then picked from the 3 and mapped onto the input image segment. Figure 5 illustrates the process.

3.3 Computing Normal Maps and Leading

The results of the segmentation process are then prepared for real-time rendering. The goal was to demonstrate a realistic representation of a pane of stained glass using programmable 3D hardware on a typical PC. The examples provided in this paper use an Nvidia 6600*GT* and an ATI 9700. The shaders include approximations of the physical properties of a thin sheet of non-uniform glass including specular bump-mapped surface, reflection and refraction as well as appropriate appearance of the lead came.

(a) (b) (c) (d)

Fig. 4. Comparison of swatch selection based on only color and a combination of color and texture. a) Original image. b) Color based swatch selection. c) One example of color + texture based swatch selection. d) Another example of color + texture based swatch selection.

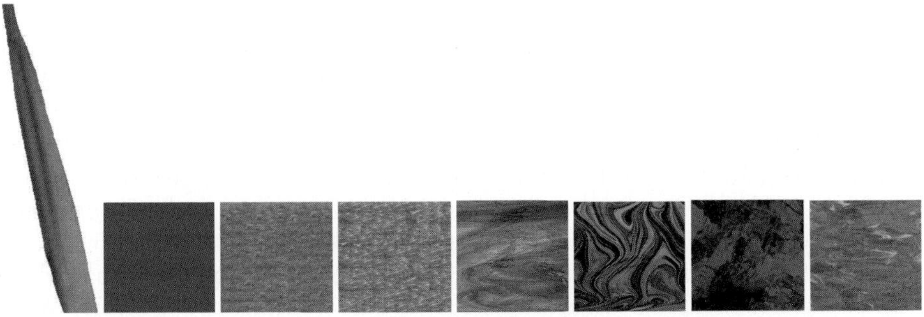

Histogram distances d_{hist} from left to right: 0.3224, 0.3775, 0.4224, 0.6893, 0.7013, 0.8633, 0.9422

Gabor feature vectors from left to right: 0.0138, 0.0156, 0.1329, 0.2003, 0.3852

Fig. 5. Using color and texture features to retrieve swatches from an image database given an input image segment. We first select the top 5 best matched swatches based on histogram intersection and then further refine the retrieved set by applying Gabor feature vectors to select the top 3 best matched swatches. A random swatch is then picked from the 3 and mapped onto the input image segment.

As a preprocessing step, normal maps are constructed for the sample glass swatches used in the output color image. Since no actual surface texture information is available for these samples, an approximation is used: each swatch is converted to a greyscale image and the image gradient intensity was mapped to height and run through a normal-map generation process. Then, a second pass over the output of the segmentation algorithms copies the texels from the normal maps rather than the glass color images to create an image representing the approximate texture of the glass surface for all texels in the segmented image.

Next, information about the lead came is generated in a separate preprocessing step. This information is generated from the image containing the segment IDs (where each segment is represented with a unique color). To locate where the lead came should be placed, an edge detection filter is run on the ID image to locate the boundaries between each segment. These edges are dilated slightly to provide a thicker border appropriate to stained glass. The result of the dilation filter is then again interpreted as a height field by mapping the image gradient intensity to height and passed through a normal-map generation process. The grayscale edge image is copied to the alpha channel of the lead came texture to allow us to blend the segment interiors from the opaque lead border. The edge detection, dilation, and conversion to a normal map could all be performed within shaders on the GPU. However in this example, these masks are not dynamic and therefore results were simply precomputed and stored as textures.

3.4 Real Time Rendering and Shading

These examples provide an approximation of a realistic piece of stained glass suitable for real-time rendering. This effect uses two shaders and three passes. The first shader builds the glass effect from several intermediate terms which are illustrated in Figure 6. Then the preprocessed per-pixel normal-map generated earlier is used to calculate per-pixel diffuse lighting contributions. The contributions of both reflected light and refracted light relative to the viewer are also calculated with these surface normals. These reflection and refraction vectors are used to lookup into a dynamic cube-map of the environment to provide realistic appearance of the environment. Next, the reflection contribution is modulated by an approximation to the Fresnel term [26]. Finally for this pass, the specular contributions are calculated and combined separately using the per-pixel normals. The alpha component used for compositing to the frame buffer is set to the specular intensity to prevent the specular highlights being blended with the scene.

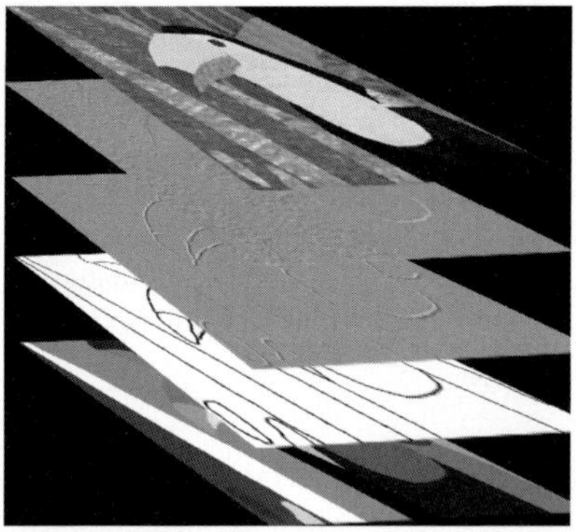

Fig. 6. Precalculated inputs (normals, color and alpha mask) for the shader lighting calculations

The final step is to provide the appearance of the lead came between the pieces of glass. The dilated edge mask is used in a shader program with an additional pass over the geometry. Any texels within the dilated edges are shaded using lights in the scene. However, only diffuse lighting with a constant dark blue-grey color is used to simulate the dull, fully diffuse appearance of real lead. The normal-map calculated from the dilated edge map is used to give the appearance that the leading is rounded. The

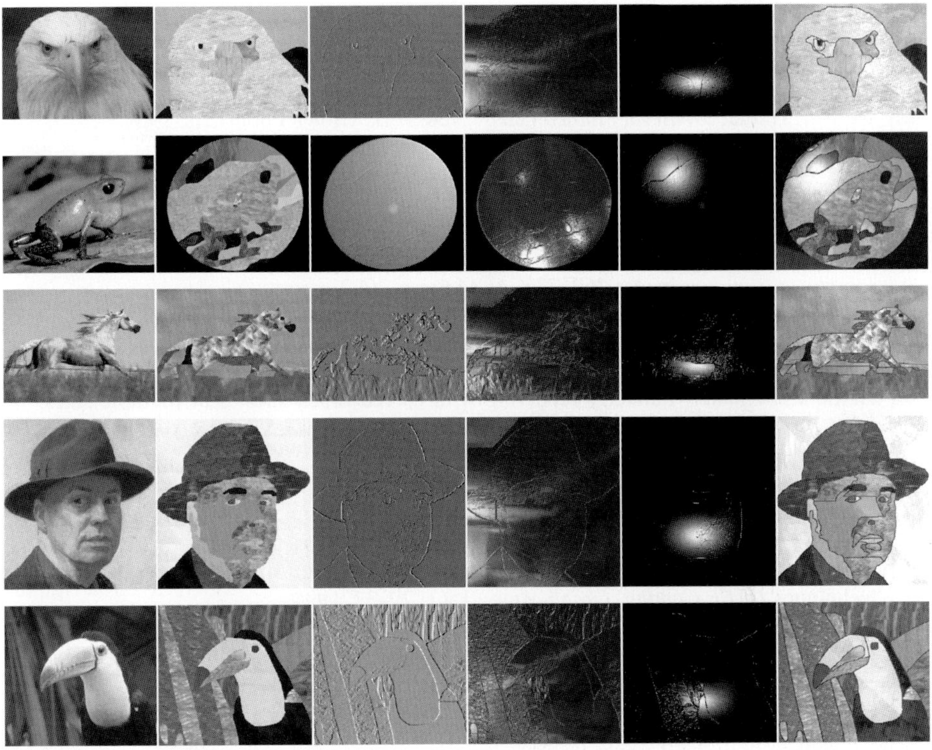

Original image | **Swatch mapped** | **Normal maps** | **Reflection and refraction parameters** | **Specular parameter** | **Final stained glass image**

Fig. 7. An example set of input images, their intermediate results and the final rendered stained glass output

results of this pass are composited with the previous pass using the information in the alpha channel of the edge mask texture where texels within the lead came are the only fragments blended into the scene.

4 Conclusion

This paper documents an automated technique that filters an image to create results stylistically similar to modern stained glass artwork. Our contributions include the use of image segmentation, selective merging of adjacent segments and the matching of swatch images to the image segments based on color and texture features. We also provide several examples of this technique rendered in real time on readily available programmable PC 3*D* hardware. We have shown that this technique can be used to automatically create realistic representations of stained glass as well as capturing some of the style, vibrancy and expression of the art form.

References

[1] Robert Metcalf. *Making Stained Glass: a Handbook for the Amateur and the Professional*. New York: McGraw-Hill, 1972.
[2] Heribert Hutter. *Medieval Stained Glass*. New York: Crown Publishers, 1964.
[3] Mario Amaya. *Tiffany Glass*. New York: Walker, 1967.
[4] San Hunter and John Jocobis. *Modern Art: Painting/ Sculpture/ Architecture*. Prentice-Hall, Inc., 1976.
[5] Doug DeCarlo and Anthony Santella. Stylization and abstraction of photographs. In *SIGGRAPH 2002: Proceedings of the 29th annual conference on Computer graphics and interactive techniques*, pages 769–776. ACM Press, 2002.
[6] Paul Haeberli. Paint by numbers: abstract image representations. In *SIGGRAPH '90: Proceedings of the 17th annual conference on Computer graphics and interactive techniques*, pages 207–214. ACM Press, 1990.
[7] Aaron Hertzmann. Painterly rendering with curved brush strokes of multiple sizes. In *SIGGRAPH '98: Proceedings of the 25th annual conference on Computer graphics and interactive techniques*, pages 453–460. ACM Press, 1998.
[8] Bruce Gooch, Greg Coombe, and Peter Shirley. Artistic vision: painterly rendering using computer vision techniques. In *NPAR '02: Proceedings of the 2nd international symposium on Non-photorealistic animation and rendering*. ACM Press, 2002.
[9] John Lansdown and Simon Schofield. Expressive rendering: A review of nonphotorealistic techniques. *IEEE Comput. Graph. Appl.*, 15(3):29–37, 1995.
[10] Georges Winkenbach and David H. Salesin. Computer-generated pen-and-ink illustration. In *SIGGRAPH 1994: Proceedings of the 21st annual conference on Computer graphics and interactive techniques*, pages 91–100. ACM Press, 1994.
[11] http://www.adobe.com. Adobe Photoshop.
[12] http://www.corel.com. CorelPaint.
[13] http://www.dfly.com/glasseye.html. Glass Eye 2000.
[14] Emma Biggs. *Encyclopedia of Mosaic Techniques*. Running Press Book Publishers, 1999.
[15] Junhwan Kim and Fabio Pellacini. Jigsaw image mosaics. In *SIGGRAPH '02: Proceedings of the 29th annual conference on Computer graphics and interactive techniques*, pages 657–664, New York, NY, USA, 2002. ACM Press.
[16] Alejo Hausner. Simulating decorative mosaics. In *SIGGRAPH '01: Proceedings of the 28th annual conference on Computer graphics and interactive techniques*, pages 573–580. ACM Press, 2001.
[17] David Mould. A stained glass image filter. In *EGRW '03: Proceedings of the 14th Eurographics workshop on Rendering*, pages 20–25. Eurographics Association, 2003.
[18] Peter Meer and Bogdan Georgescu. Edge detection with embedded confidence. *IEEE Transactions on Pattern Analysis and Machine Intelligence*, 23(12), 2001.
[19] Yining Deng and b. s. Manjunath. Unsupervised segmentation of color-texture regions in images and video. volume 23, pages 800–810, Washington, DC, USA, 2001. IEEE Computer Society.
[20] M Swain and D Ballard. Color indexing. *International Journal on Computer Vision*, 7(1):11–32, 1991.
[21] David Douglas and Thomas Peucker. Algorithms for the reduction of the number of points required to represent a digitized line or its caricature. volume 10, pages 112–122, 1973.
[22] http://www.indexstock.com. IndexStock Photo Database.
[23] Vivek Kwatra, Arno Schodl, Irfan Essa, Greg Turk, and Aaron Bobick. Graphcut textures: image and video synthesis using graph cuts. volume 22, pages 277–286, New York, NY, USA, 2003. ACM Press.

[24] BJohn R. Smith and Shih-Fu Chang. Automatic image retrieval using color and texture. In *IEEE Transactions on Pattern Analysis and Machine Intelligence*, volume 18, pages 837–842. IEEE Press, 1996.

[25] B.S. Manjunath and W.Y. Ma. Texture features for browsing and retrieval of image data. In *IEEE Transactions on Pattern Analysis and Machine Intelligence*, volume 18, pages 837–842. IEEE Press, 1996.

[26] Chris Brennan. *Accurate Environment Mapped Reflections and Refractions by Adjusting for Object Distance*. Wordware Publishing, Inc., 2002.

Vision-Based Augmented Reality Visual Guidance with Keyframes

Timothy S.Y. Gan and Tom W. Drummond

Cambridge University, Engineering Department,
Trumpington Street, Cambridge CB2 1PZ, UK
syg21@cam.ac.uk, twd20@eng.cam.ac.uk

Abstract. A vision-based augmented reality visual guidance system is presented. It utilises naturally occurring point features and does not require a global reference frame. Keyframes extracted from a training sequence are used to provide multiple local reference frames. These keyframes are selected by minimising the uncertainties in structure recovery to find an optimal tradeoff between narrow and wide baselines.

1 Introduction

Augmented Reality (AR) describes the composition of real and virtual scenes to add value for a user when performing tasks. Usually, this involves overlaying computer graphics onto a display which shows real scenes via a visual input.

This paper addresses a navigation task with a tablet computer as the AR platform. The classic navigation method is with a map and compass. Although this has served us well, it is nevertheless a cumbersome solution: it is not intuitive and requires certain skills. Overlaying computer graphics on to a video display device is ideal for such tasks. It removes the need to learn map reading and other topographical skills and can be made intuitive where the user just has to follow directional cues (e.g. arrows, compass, bird's eye view) which are overlaid onto the screen. The task of navigation has now become one of follow-the-arrow.

There are several systems in the literature which aim to provide AR technology to such tasks. Some of these systems use GPS [1], together with inertial sensors [2] or ultrasound, like the BAT [3] to provide localisation. A vision-based system has been developed in [4] which utilises ARToolkit. Both the BAT and ARToolkit systems require the environment to be instrumented. This paper presents a vision-based system where the only sensor is an inexpensive Firewire camera which uses natural features found in the environment, thereby eliminating the need for instrumentation.

In contrast to systems like GPS where the user is localised in a global reference frame, we show that navigation can still be performed by using only models of small parts of the world. These models are constructed from keyframes taken from a training sequence.

Keyframes can be thought of as reference frames scattered in a sequence. We present a keyframe extraction algorithm based on the geometry of the scene and by minimising uncertainties in recovered scene structure.

H.-P. Seidel, T. Nishita, and Q. Peng (Eds.): CGI 2006, LNCS 4035, pp. 692–701, 2006.

Applications which extract keyframes can be broadly split into two types: *video analysis/retrieval* and *motion related tasks* (such as tracking and structure from motion). We focus on the latter. Some approaches for keyframe extraction are based on heuristic rules [5], inter-frame feature similarities [6, 7, 8], or a combination of both [9]. The Geometric Robust Information Criterion (GRIC) [10] model selection is somewhat similar to our technique as it is also based on the geometry of the scene. The GRIC was applied in [11] to compare between using a fundamental matrix model or a homography model for the tasks of recovering structure and matching features. In [12], the GRIC was combined with setting a threshold of similar inter-frame features for the task of reconstructing 3D models. In [13], keyframe selection was catered towards a final bundle adjustment step so that the estimation error of the adjustment was minimised.

1.1 Alternative Techniques

Select Every N Frames: This is the simplest technique to implement, but is unlikely to produce good results. The obvious pitfall is the assumption of constant speed. If the camera stops moving, this technique will continue to select keyframes every N frames. This will lead to frames which have virtually no translation to be selected and it will lead to an ill-conditioned $\mathbf{T}$. In a scenario of an accelerating camera, the keyframes selected could have no common or very little common features. This scenario does not occur only for sequences with high acceleration; it will occur when the acceleration is greater than the implicit bound express by N.

Select Frames When Matches Fall Below a Threshold: A threshold of features is a simple and at times sufficient method of keyframe selection [6, 7]. Firstly, there is the key question of what the threshold should be. Many times, it may be sufficient to err on the side of caution and set a relatively high threshold but this selection is quite arbitrary and most times, not well motivated. Secondly, the threshold largely depends on the environment which the camera is looking at. If the environment has sections which are not as densely populated with features as some other sections, then it will be much more difficult to set a global threshold. One could use a proportional measure rather than an absolute number which will make it slightly more robust but still unsatisfactory. Using features as a criteria only hints at the notion of uncertainties in pose estimation.

2 Overview

The task is visual guidance of a user from point A to point B by providing directional cues with computer graphics overlaid on the user's tablet computer. The entire visual guidance system consists of a training and runtime phase.

Training (described in Section 3): The system is brought for a walk from point A to point B and the camera records this training sequence. Keyframes are extracted from this sequence together with the pose displacement between consecutive keyframes. The use of keyframes reduces both the amount of training data and the amount of data to be processed during runtime.

Runtime (described in Section 4): When the system is switched on, it enters an initialisation phase to localise itself to a keyframe. It then provides directional cues to guide the user to point B. It is assumed that the initialisation location is close to point A.

3 Training

The classic dilemma involved in choosing frame pairs is the narrow *vs* wide baseline problem. Adjacent frames tend to have a high number of matches but poor motion estimates, i.e. the translation between them is ill-conditioned. As the baseline gets wider, correspondences tend to be poorer. Therefore, there is a trade-off involved and an optimal baseline can be found. This is depicted in Figure 1 where the task is to find the optimal partner for Frame 0. Note how the number of matches tail off towards the end. A further explanation of the figure is given in Subsection 3.3.

3.1 Choosing Frame Pairs

Given a calibrated pinhole camera with a stereo pair taken from a scene, the relationship between corresponding points is expressed by the epipolar constraint [14]: $\mathbf{p'}^{\top}\mathbf{E}\,\mathbf{p} = 0$, where $\mathbf{E}$ is the 3×3 essential matrix, $\mathbf{p}$ is the normalised homogenous coordinate of a point in one image, $(u, v, 1)^{\top}$ and $\mathbf{p'}$ is its associated point, $(u', v', 1)^{\top}$ in the other image. With $\mathbf{E}$, the pose $\mathbf{R}$, $\mathbf{T}$ between the two frames can be recovered and has the form $\mathbf{E} = [\mathbf{T}]_{\times}\mathbf{R} = \mathbf{R}[\mathbf{R}^{\top}\mathbf{T}]_{\times}$, where $[\cdot]_{\times}$ is the anti-symmetric matrix operation. $\mathbf{R}$ is a 3×3 matrix which describes all rotations in three-dimensional space and is parameterised by three parameters. $\mathbf{T}$ is the translation vector in x, y, z directions. The essential matrix has only five degrees of freedom: both $\mathbf{R}$ and $\mathbf{T}$ have three degrees of freedom but there is an overall scale ambiguity in $\mathbf{T}$.

3.2 Point Features

FAST features [15] with non-maximal suppression are used as feature points and local image patches centred on the features are used as feature vectors. Normalised cross correlation (NCC) is used as the similarity measure to match features. Three further criterions are used to achieve better matches: Firstly, matches which do not satisfy the epipolar constraint are discarded. Secondly, bi-directional married matches are used. These are features which have complimentary matches such that a feature, p_i matches best to p'_i and p'_i also matches best to p_i. Finally, an NCC threshold is also used to further cull matches.

3.3 Analysis of Covariances

Pose which is defined as **R** and **T** can be written as a transformation matrix:

$$\mathbf{P} = \begin{bmatrix} \mathbf{R} & \mathbf{T} \\ 0\ 0\ 0 & 1 \end{bmatrix} . \tag{1}$$

P belongs to the special Euclidean Lie group, SE(3). A point **p** in one image will cast a line in the other image and this line is called the epipolar line. This line is given by **Ep** such that for any point **x** on this line: $\mathbf{xEp} = 0$. For the epipolar constraint to hold, the match of **p** which is $\mathbf{p}'$ must lie on this line. An error function relating the homogenous image coordinates of a match $(\mathbf{p}, \mathbf{p}')$ is defined as the Euclidean distance between $\mathbf{p}'$ and the epipolar line cast by **p**. The relationship between the changes of this error and the changes of the six parameters of the pose is examined. This results in a Jacobian matrix with each term being

$$J = \frac{\partial d(l(\mathbf{p}), \mathbf{p}')}{\partial \alpha_i} , \tag{2}$$

where $d(\cdot)$ is the Euclidean distance function, $l(\mathbf{p})$ is the epipolar line cast by **p** and α_i, $i \in \{1, ..., 6\}$ is the six parameters of the SE(3) pose. Therefore, **J** is a $N \times 6$ matrix where N is the number of measurements and $\mathbf{J}^\top\mathbf{J}$ is a 6×6 matrix, which is the first order approximation of the Information Matrix. Strictly speaking, $\mathbf{J}^\top\mathbf{J}$ should be $\mathbf{J}^\top\mathbf{U}^{-1}\mathbf{J}$ where **U** is the measurement noise, but for the purpose of comparing different pose estimates where measurement noise is the same throughout, **U** can be discarded and just $\mathbf{J}^\top\mathbf{J}$ considered.

The Information Matrix is a positive semidefinite matrix and describes a six-dimensional ellipsoid. The eigenvectors of the Information Matrix are the principal axes and the eigenvalues $\lambda_i = \frac{1}{\sqrt{r_i}}$, where $i \in \{1, ..., 6\}$ and r is the radius. Therefore, $\lambda \propto \frac{1}{r}$ and since the radius is a measure of the uncertainty which yields $\lambda \propto$ *certainty*.

The amount of certainty in the pose parameters is present in the diagonal of the Information Matrix. One of the elements in the diagonal will be small because of the scale ambiguity, meaning little (highly uncertain) is known. Therefore, the eigenvalues of the Information Matrix will indicate the amount of certainty (information) there is in the corresponding eigenvector. One of the eigenvalues is zero because of the scale ambiguity. With these eigenvalues, it is now possible to compare the pose estimation between frames pairs.

3.4 Comparing Pose Estimations

Given one frame, F_1 and two candidate frames, F_2, F_3, which candidate will result in a pose estimation with less uncertainties? The comparison can be done by analysing the eigenvalues of the Information Matrix for each frame pair. Note, there are six eigenvalues since pose has six DOF but only five should be considered because of the scale ambiguity.

Given pose estimations from frames, denoted by (F_1, F_2) and (F_1, F_3), their respective Information Matrices and eigenvalues, there are several ways of comparing them to decide on a better pose estimate:

$$\begin{aligned}\textbf{Min} &: arg\ max(min(EV(F_1,F_2)),\ \ min(EV(F_1,F_3)))\ ,\\ \textbf{Max} &: arg\ max(max(EV(F_1,F_2)),\ \ max(EV(F_1,F_3)))\ ,\\ \textbf{L}_\textbf{2}\textbf{Norm} &: arg\ max(L_2(F_1,F_2),\ \ L_2(F_1,F_3))\ ,\end{aligned}$$

where $EV(\cdot)$ is the vector of five eigenvalues and L_2 is the L_2 Norm. We argue that the Min comparison is most useful because this will select the highest least uncertain pose estimate. In other words, if two pose estimates are uncertain, we want the least uncertain one. Max will most likely only consider the eigenvalues associated with rotation because rotation is well conditioned by the essential matrix. It is **T** which can ill-conditioned. The alternative is to only consider translation associated eigenvalues in Max. This will give an upper bound of the certainty on the pose estimation but will neglect the uncertainties present in the pose estimation. L_2 *Norm* is a compromise between Min and Max. It gives a general description of the size of the ellipsoid and does not yield useful insights to the uncertainties. Besides, the L_2 Norm value could be dominated by the largest eigenvalue if the range of eigenvalues is large.

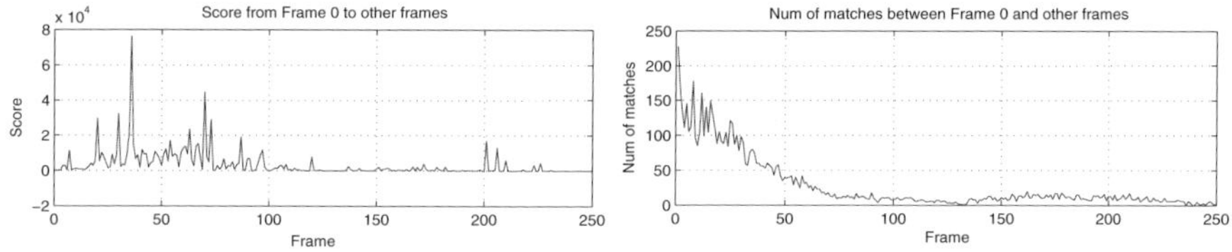

Fig. 1. Looking for best partner. Left: Partner of Frame 0 is at Frame 36 which is a distinct peak. Right: Number of matches between Frame 0 and other frames which pass the epipolar geometry test.

Figure 1 shows the search for the optimal partner frame of Frame 0. Notice that the close neighbours of Frame 0 yields a high number of matches but their associated scores are low. This shows the narrow baseline scenario. The number of matches drop off as the search proceeds further along the sequence. But the score rises till an optimal point depicted by the peak. The associated frame is then viewed as the optimal partner frame of Frame 0. In frames where the score is zero, it means that the number of matches falls below the number of matches required for essential matrix computation.

A summary of the scheme is as follows: Start at Frame 0, find its optimal partner. Now, find the optimal partner of Frame 0's partner. This is done recursively till the end of the sequence.

4 Runtime

4.1 Initialisation

The initial frame is compared to all key-frames and the number of matches recorded. The key-frame which yields the highest number of matches is taken to the closest training frame and the runtime frame is localised to that. Let this frame be denoted F_L. Two other frames, F_{L-1} and F_{L+1} are considered and by comparing the triplet matches between the initial frame, F_L and F_{L-1} and the triplet matches between the initial frame, F_L and F_{L+1}, a frame pair is chosen as the initial frame pair. At the end of this stage, we have a runtime frame, F_r localised to a frame pair from training.

4.2 Movement

Let the frames from the localised frame pair be denoted by F_a and F_b where F_a is towards point A and F_b is towards point B. From training data, Frames F_a and F_b have a set of matches, M_{ab} and the pose displacement, $\mathbf{P}_{ab}$ between them are known. Note that the magnitude of the translation vector is set to one.

With M_{ab}, $\mathbf{P}_{ab}$ and the features of the runtime frame f_r, the runtime frame can be localised with respect to F_a and F_b. It is essential first to find the set of matches across all of the three frames, F_a, F_b and F_r. Let this set of triplet matches be denoted by M_{abr}. There are two ways of viewing this set of triplet matches. The first is: $M_{abr} = M_{ar} \cap M_{rb}$, and the second is: $M_{abr} = M_{ab} \cap f_r$. The intuition behind the first view is that all three frames are independent of each other and therefore the set of triplet matches should be the intersection of two sets of matches, namely M_{ar} and M_{rb}. This requires three matching functions. The reasoning behind the other view is that since F_a, F_b and F_r are local to each other, it is safe to assume that they are not truly independent. The advantage of the second option is that it yields a considerable increase in speed: Since M_{ab} is already known from training data, only one matching function where f_r is intersected with M_{ab} is required.

The triplet matches have associated 3D coordinates in the coordinate frame defined by F_a, F_b. These 3D coordinates are triangulated during the training phase as well. With M_{abr} and their associated 3D coordinates, an optimisation step is required to localise F_r with respect to F_a, F_b. The Levenberg-Marquardt method is used on each runtime frame to provide the localisation.

4.3 Reweighted Levenberg-Marquardt

The inputs are triplet matches, M_{abr} and their associated 3D coordinates, X. The output will be the pose, $\mathbf{P}_r$ of the runtime frame with respect to F_a and F_b. Let $\boldsymbol{\mu}$ denote the vector of parameters. The error to be minimised is the difference between measured image coordinates and predicted image coordinates. Therefore the error function is the sum of errors of each triplet match. Predicted image coordinates are obtained by projecting X_i with $\mathbf{P}_r$. For the first frame at initialisation, $\mathbf{P}_r$ is the Identity matrix. For subsequent frames, $\mathbf{P}_r$ is initialised with the pose estimate from the previous frame.

At each time step (i.e. at each frame), the aim is to compute a $\Delta\boldsymbol{\mu}$ which when applied to $\boldsymbol{\mu}$ will result in a decrease of the error function. $\Delta\boldsymbol{\mu}$ is expressed as

$$\Delta\boldsymbol{\mu} = [\mathbf{J}^\top\mathbf{J} + \lambda\mathbf{I}]^{-1}(\mathbf{J}^\top\mathbf{e}) \ , \tag{3}$$

where $\mathbf{J}$ is the Jacobian Matrix of predicted image coordinates with respect to the six pose parameters, $\mathbf{e}$ is a vector of errors and λ is the Levenberg-Marquardt variable which varies depending on the result of the time step. Using Equation 3 means that each match and its error is treated the same and given the same weighting. This is fine provided that there are no erroneous matches which result in large errors. If there are such matches and since the Levenberg-Marquardt algorithm gives a least-squares solution, the large erroneous errors will skew the result drastically.

Therefore, a reweighted Levenberg-Marquardt algorithm is used instead. With the addition of weights, Equation 3 becomes

$$\Delta\boldsymbol{\mu} = [\mathbf{J}^\top\mathbf{w}^2\mathbf{J} + \lambda\mathbf{I}]^{-1}(\mathbf{J}^\top\mathbf{w}^2\mathbf{e}) \ , \tag{4}$$

where $\mathbf{w}$ is the weight and is a function of $\mathbf{e}$. The idea is that points with large errors are weighted down and contribute less overall. The weighting function used was $w(e) = \frac{1}{\sigma+|e|}$ where σ is the inlier standard deviation. This yields an objective function of $o(e) = \int ew(e)de = |e| + \sigma\log(\sigma + w(e))$, and the sum across all triplet matches of this function is to be minimised.

4.4 Example

It is best to illustrate the workings of the system with an example in Figure 2. Let the origin be at F_a, the Euclidean distance between F_a and F_b be one unit and $\mathbf{P}_b$ is known from training. With the Levenberg-Marquardt algorithm above, the pose $\mathbf{P}_r$ can be localised with respect to F_a and F_b. Thus, the distance from F_a to F_r and F_b to F_r can be easily computed. The translation from F_a to F_r is merely the translation vector of $\mathbf{P}_r$ and the distance is the magnitude of vector $\mathbf{T}_r$. The displacement from F_r to F_b is given as $\mathbf{P}_{rb} = \mathbf{P}_b\,\mathbf{P}_r^{-1}$. Therefore, the

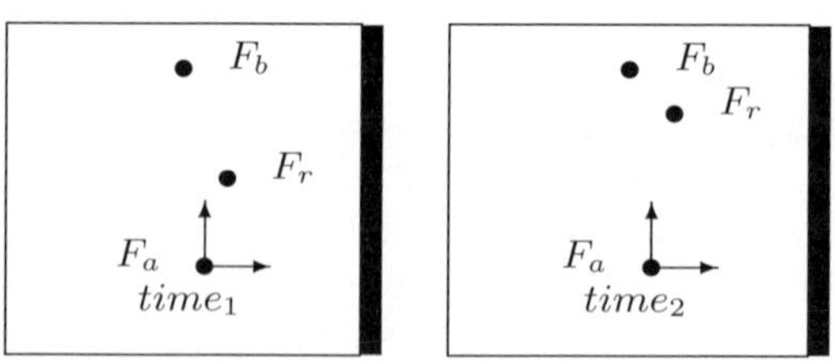

Fig. 2. Example of runtime frame movement over two time steps. A top-down view with origin at F_a, horizontal axis represents x-axis, vertical axis represents z-depth.

distance from F_r to F_b is the magnitude of $\mathbf{T}_{rb}$. When the distance from F_r to F_b is small enough, we conclude that F_r has "reached" F_b. If F_b is not the destination frame (i.e. point B), we increment the frame pair, so that the new F_a is F_b and the new F_b is the following frame.

5 Experiments

The task is to provide visual guidance to a user to aid navigation. This is achieved by overlaying graphics of directional cues onto a tablet setup.

Each frame pair extracted at training forms a local reference coordinate frame. The runtime frame moves from one local reference frame to the next. It is by following this chain of keyframes that the user is guided from points A to B. This strategy removes the need for a global reference coordinate frame. The hardware platform used is describes below.

5.1 Hardware

A HP Compaq tablet computer (Figure 3) and a Fire-i Firewire camera was used. The camera was mounted on an angled bracket so that it would still be forward facing when the tablet was tilted to a more comfortable viewing angle.

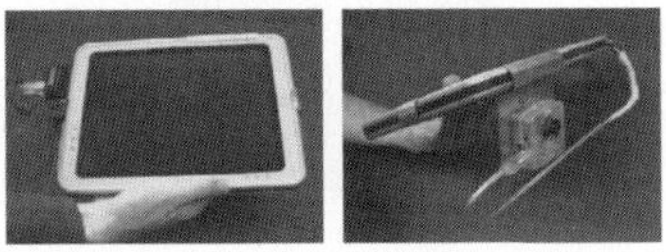

Fig. 3. Tablet with attached camera

5.2 Directional Cues

Two visual cues are presented to the user: A compass which points from F_r to F_b and a top-down bird's eye view which illustrates the relative position of F_r with respect to F_a and F_b (which form the local reference frame). Since F_r is localised to the reference frame of F_a and F_b, an imaginary tunnel from F_a to F_b can be projected into the view of F_r. This projected "tunnel" is illustrated by rendering concentric squares. As the user moves forward, the squares increase in size, creating the impression that the user is walking in it and Figure 4 illustrates this. Figure 4 shows left and right translations followed by forward movement. In addition, it also illustrates the change of local reference frames. The compass is illustrated as a triangle and it points in the direction of F_b from F_r. The illustration above the compass is the top-down view of the current position of all three frames. It depicts the x axis as horizontal and z depth as vertical. The frames are marked by: $F_a(\top)$, $F_b(\bot)$ and $F_r(\bullet)$. This test sequence starts off in the middle where the user is in the tunnel. This can be seen by the three markers lining up close to a line. The user then makes a left translation while still having the camera forward facing. The left side of the tunnel can now be seen as it is projected into the view of F_r. As the user moves further to the left, the compass points further to the right showing the direction of F_b. The respective opposites can be said when the user moves to the right. The long erroneous match in the rightmost frame is weighted down significantly and contributes very little to the pose estimation. After the left and right translation, the user moves forward. This is illustrated by $F_r(\bullet)$ which was once closer to $F_a(\top)$, moving upwards towards F_b. A transition between one local reference coordinate and the next occurs at the top two frames. When the transition happens, F_b becomes the new F_a and the new F_b is its partner from training. Notice that the position of F_r is topological correct: Behind F_b before the transition, and still before the new F_a after the transition.

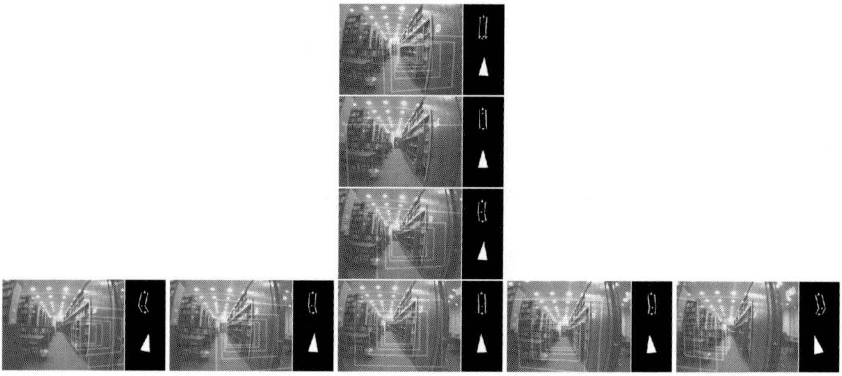

Fig. 4. Left, right and forward movement. The compass points in the direction of F_b from F_r. The illustration above the compass is the top-down view of the current position of all three frames illustrating the x and z axes. x axis being horizontal and z depth being vertical. The sequence starts in the middle frame of the bottom row, moves left and right and then forwards (towards the top). The markers are $F_a(\top)$, $F_b(\bot)$ and $F_r(\bullet)$. In the starting frame, F_a is at the bottom closest to the compass, F_r is further up and F_b is at the top.

6 Summary and Future Work

We have demonstrated a vision-based AR visual guidance system with a camera as its only sensor. It relies on natural features for localisation and does not require a global reference frame.

A new keyframe extraction algorithm based on the uncertainties of pose recovery was introduced. It utilises epipolar geometry to recover pose and computes the optimal location on the narrow and wide baseline spectrum when selecting frame pairs.

Avenues for future work include an in-depth usability study of directional cues, and other techniques and optimisation to improve robustness of the system.

Acknowledgements

Many thanks to The Boeing Company for providing funding for this research.

References

1. Thomas, B., Demczuk, V., Piekarski, W., Hepworth, D., Gunther, B.: A wearable computer system with augmented reality to support terrestrial navigation. In: International Symposium on Wearable Computers. (1998)
2. Höllerer, T., Feiner, S., Terauchi, T., Rashid, G., Hallaway, D.: Exploring MARS: developing indoor and outdoor user interfaces to a mobile augmented reality system. Computer & Graphics (1999)
3. Newman, J., Ingram, D., Hopper, A.: Augmented reality in a wide area sentient environment. In: International Symposium on Augmented Reality. (2001)
4. Reitmayr, G., Schmalstieg, D.: Location based applications for mobile augmented reality. In: Australasian User Interface Conference. (2003)
5. Calic, J., Thomas, B.: Spatial analysis in key-frame extraction using video segmentation. In: Image Analysis for Multimedia Interactive Services. (2004)
6. Vacchetti, L., Lepetit, V., Fua, P.: Stable real-time 3d tracking using online and offline information. Pattern Analysis and Machine Intelligence (2004)
7. Royer, E., Lhuillier, M., Dhome, M., Chateau, T.: Localization in urban environments: monocular vision compared to a differential gps sensor. In: Computer Vision and Pattern Recognition. (2005)
8. Zhao, L., Qi, W., Li, S., Yang, S., Zhang, H.: Key-frame extraction and shot retrieval using nearest feature line. In: Multimedia Information Retrieval, ACM Multimedia Conference. (2000)
9. Royer, E., Lhuillier, M., Dhome, M., Chateau, T.: Towards an alternative gps sensor in dense urban environment from visual memory. In: British Machine Vision Conference. (2004)
10. Torr, P.: An assessment of information creiteria for motion model selection. In: Computer Vision and Pattern Recognition. (1997)
11. Torr, P., Fitzgibbon, A., Zisserman, A.: Maintaining multiple motion model hypotheses through many views to recover matching and structure. In: International Conference on Computer Vision. (1998)
12. Repko, J., Pollefeys, M.: 3d models from extended uncalibrated video sequences: Addressing key-frame selection and projective drift. In: 3-D Digital Imaging and Modeling. (2005)
13. Thormählen, T., Broszio, H., Weissenfeld, A.: Keyframe selection for camera motion and structure estimation from multiple views. In: European Computer Vision Conference. (2004)
14. Hartley, R., Zisserman, A.: Multiple View Geometry in Computer Vision. Cambridge University Press (2004)
15. Rosten, E., Drummond, T.: Machine learning for high-speed corner detection. In: European Conference on Computer Vision. (2006)

Optimized Framework for Real Time Hair Simulation

Rajeev Gupta, Melanie Montagnol, Pascal Volino,
and Nadia Magnenat-Thalmann

MIRALab, University of Geneva, Battelle, 7, route de Drize,
CH-1227 Carouge, Geneva, Switzerland
{gupta, montagnol, volino, thalmann}@miralab.unige.ch
http://www.miralab.ch

Abstract. Despite tremendous work in hair simulation a unified framework for creating realistically simulated hairstyles at interactive rates is yet not available; the main reason is that complex dynamic and optical behavior of hair are computationally expensive to simulate. To have such a framework, it is essential to find optimized solutions, especially for the various physics-based tasks, which is the main bottleneck in the simulation. In this paper, we discuss various technical advancements and achievements that have been made in formulating key techniques to handle the different challenging issues involved in simulation of hair at interactive rates. Effort has been put in all the three modules of the hair simulation - hair shape modeling, hair dynamics and hair rendering.

Keywords: Hair Simulation, Hair Modeling, Real Time Animation, Volume Deformation, Interactive Rendering.

1 Introduction

Hair forms an important part of human appearance and is thus essential to be simulated realistically for creating believable Virtual Humans. Besides believability, applications require hair simulation to accommodate varying hairstyles and visualization processes for which interactivity and real-time rendering are the key features. To handle the time-constrained situation, usually the techniques developed have to compromise between interactivity and realistic appearance. The difficulties in human hair simulation arise due to the number. These issues make it a challenge for both animating and rendering them with performances compatible with real-time. Optically, hair has many interesting phenomena such as anisotropic reflection, strong forward scattering, and translucency. A correct reflectance model is thus needed to compute reflectance off the individual hair geometry. To have a unified interactive framework, it is desirable to consider relations between various hair simulation components and to simulate the collective effect. Further-more, the increasing of the sense of immersion, requires integrating a haptic interface that provides user with increased degree of freedom as compared to a mouse and considerably increases the comfort, performance and productivity. The specific contributions of this paper are:

H.-P. Seidel, T. Nishita, and Q. Peng (Eds.): CGI 2006, LNCS 4035, pp. 702–710, 2006.

– Simplified mechanical model effectively adapted to real time.
– Optimized scattering based rendering algorithm.
– An interactive application, efficiently utilizing animation and rendering.

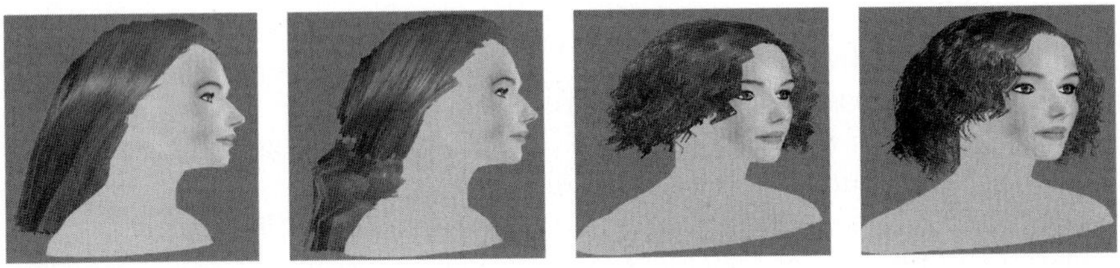

Fig. 1. Sequence of images demonstrating the potentiality of our optimized framework

The rest of this paper is organized as follows: in the following section, we give a brief overview of various works done in hair simulation. In Section 3, we give an overview of our framework methodology. Section 4 is dedicated to our lattice based mechanical model. Section 5 gives the description of our scattering based illumination model for rendering at interactive rates. We demonstrate utilities of our optimized framework for performing hairstyling operation in Section 6 followed by the results and discussion on the performance for this unified hairstyling application in Section 7. We conclude with a survey of avenues of future work in Section 8.

2 Related Work

Specific advancements have been made in each of these tasks (Hair: modeling, rendering, animation), an overview of which can be found in [21]. Here we discuss the recent developments in all the related tasks.

The developed tool, in [20], allows user to choose number of patches, position them and then individually or collectively modify parameters such as length, stiffness, blending for the patches. The system in [8] is based on a 2D paint program interface and color scale images to specify hair characteristics. Some of the researchers have also presented systems exploiting fluid flow [6] and vector fields [27] for explicit hair modeling. Other techniques [12][24] use hybrid models combining benefits of wisp model and strand model. In general, all these systems result in creating nice static hairstyles, but are too slow to be able to interact with hairstyles when dynamic behavior is added.

A Wisp technique was defined by Watanabe et al [25], and has been frequently used since with many variations in [3][4][19][26]. Another evolution is to replace the hairs by approximate surfaces (strips or patches), as done by Koh et al [13][14], or even volumes that can easily be modeled as polygonal meshes, such as the thin shell approach of Kim et al [10]. A good example of combining various approaches developed by Bertails et al [1] is based on wisps tree, and a similar approach from Kim et al [12] is based on multiresolution clusters. Advanced Level-of-Detail methods also include combination of strands, clusters and strips modeled with subdivision schemes and animated using advanced collision techniques, as developed by Ward et al. [23]. In the context of fast real-time applications, cluster and strip models are good candidates.

Kajiya et al. [9], were the first to derive a local anisotropic lighting model for hair which has been widely adopted for real-time hair rendering. Simulating self-shadows in hair has been an important contribution of [11] and [16], though these techniques are not suitable for real-time. Koster et al. [15] intensively utilize the GPU for fast shadow map computation, though it does not take animation of the hair into consideration. Mertens et al. [18], efficiently deal with the issue of shadow in dynamic hair by computing a 3D density field and storing the samples of the hair density function in a compact way, resulting in better rendering speed and quality. More recently, Bertails et al [2] presented an animated hair self-shadowing model based on a 3D light oriented density map, with computations performed on a standard CPU independent of any GPU, at interactive rates.

3 Framework Methodology

Hair styling scheme can be divided in two parts: firstly, defining a set of general characteristics of a hair style, and secondly, varying set of characteristics of an individual hair. We choose to model hair utilizing the data representation of animation model [22]. This hair modeling technique is divided in two phases. First, we propose a set of static parameters for hair styling (geometric modifications), and then we animate using these parameters (update simulation).

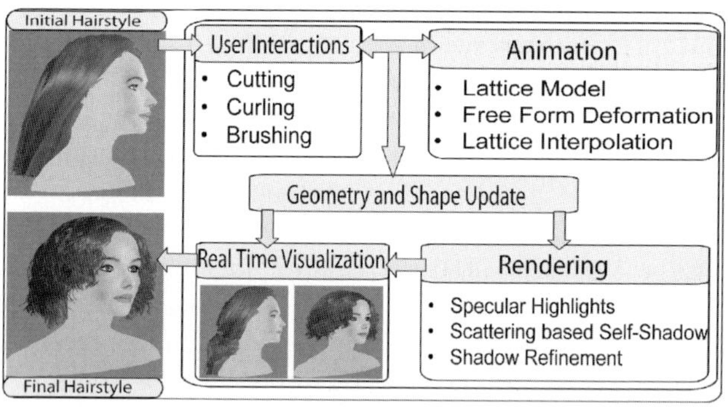

Fig. 2. Hair Simulation Framework

In order to increase the user interactivity, we chose to use a haptic interface. We present a system that provides the user with interactive and easy-to-use tools for hairstyling. Even though we have used a mechanical model in our simulation, the system is fast and the user can make modifications at interactive rates. In addition, the dynamic behavior results in more accurate and realistic simulation, as it includes influence on the styles due to gravity and other external forces.

For animation, the system should be compatible with most approaches used for hairstyle representation and real-time rendering, and offer the designer the possibility of creating any kind of hairstyle that can robustly be simulated in any animation con-text. We construct an efficient lattice mechanical deformation model which represents the volume behavior of the hair strands.

We also aim to have an optimized technique that decreases the complexities involved in hair rendering and simulates optical effects while incorporating hair animations at interactive rates. The local illumination of hair is defined by a Gaussian function adapted to our strip representation of hair. Our method's efficiency towards achieving fast shadow updates for animated hair is highly credited to the division of the pre-processing and the run-time tasks of the simulation. This contributes to the speedy performance of our illumination model without any significant degradation in quality.

4 Simplified Mechanical Model for Animating Hair

The challenge in realistic animation of hair is to build a mechanical model of the hairstyle which is sufficiently fast for real-time performance while preserving the particular behavior of the hair medium and maintaining sufficient versatility for simulating any kind of complex hairstyles. The difficulties are overcome through the design of a hair animation model based on volume deformations, with the aim of animating any complex hairstyle design in real-time.

4.1 The Lattice Model

We construct a 3D lattice around the head that includes all the hair. During animation, the lattice is moved according to the head motion. The lattice is furthermore deformed by mechanical computation.

4.2 The Mechanical Model

A spring-mass approach is used for designing this mechanical lattice deformation model. A particular kind of interaction force is created that uses as attachment points any arbitrary point of the lattice, defined by its lattice coordinates. The attachments of the hair extremities to the skull are modeled by stiff viscoelastic lattice attachments, which are positioned exactly at the end of each hair. Additionally, some "ether forces" are defined between the lattice nodes and their rest positions defined by the rigid motion of the head. They are mainly aimed at pulling back the hairstyle to its initial position, ensuring stability of the simulation, as well as modeling some additional stiffness in the hairstyle. Aerodynamic drag forces are also added in this way.

4.3 Lattice Interpolation

As the lattice is deformed during animation, another issue is to recompute the cur-rent position of each hair features for each frame. For the best compromise between continuity and computation speed, we have selected quadratic B-Spline curves as interpolating shape functions, which offer second-order interpolation continuity. In our adaptation, we use linear extrapolation to handle border nodes so as to decrease deformations for points located outside the lattice. We can take advantage of the interpolation to enhance the attachment of the hair on the skull through rigid motion. For each interpolated feature, a deformation coefficient is defined which is a blending coefficient between the motion defined by the rigid head motion and the motion defined by the interpolated lattice position.

5 Optimized Hair Rendering Model

Two main optical effects that contribute the most to realistic hair are the anisotropic reflection and self-shadows. We have used a scattering-based fast and efficient algorithm that handles both the local specular highlights and global self-shadow in animated hair at interactive rates as presented by Gupta et al [5].

5.1 Scattering-Based Local Illumination

One of the features of our local illumination model is that it takes into the Fresnel reflection and orientation of the cuticles on the hair which gives a control on defining the anisotropy of the hair. We consider the Gaussian function taking into account slope variations both along the tangent and the bi-normal of the strip vertices. The model takes care of both the diffuse and the specular reflectance. Various parameters control the width and the shift of the specular highlights as well as the sharpness and the anisotropy displayed by the strips.

5.2 Scattering-Based Self-shadow in Hair

Our scattering-based approach considers two functions for shadow contribution as shown in Figure 4. One function gives a measure of the absorption of light reaching a hair vertex and the other function considers the scattering from the hair. Since our shadowing model considers hair densities within the cells rather than explicit hair geometry, both the functions result in an overall reduced intensity of the hair vertex as visible to the viewer, which gives the shadowing effect within the hair. Analytically, the absorption term generates self shadows due to its geometric and translucent nature while the scattering term is an additional component contributing to hair shading due to its material property. It is the collective effect of the two components computed for hair that gives light's intensity as perceived by the viewer and is correlated to the hair's shadow color, giving it a natural look.

5.3 Shadow Refinement in Animated Hair

The approach for incorporating variations in shadow in animated hair assumes that the hair vertices within a cell at initialization always stay within one cell after displacement. This assumption is valid not only from the physical aspect of the FFD-based animation model but also from real hair animation considerations where there is coherence among neighboring strands when hair is moving. We encode the displacement of the particle during animation to give a measure of variation in hair density in the cells of the rendering lattice.

6 Application and User Interactions

Our main motivation for developing the animation and rendering model is to provide the user with an easy-to-use set of tools for styling hair with visualization of variations in dynamic and optical behavior at interactive rates. The system gives the user freedom to choose tools to modify hair collectively (using guide hairs) or individually. Using the buttons provided with the PHANToM, the user can also choose the tool to apply on the selection. For the animation of the parameters we have proposed different methods:

6.1 Hair Selection

The first step in designing a hairstyle is to select a set of hair. The user can choose hair via a 2D scalp map or make a more precise selection directly in 3D using a PHANToM. The selection, via the PHANToM, is done by the position of the stylus. If the stylus intersects a cell in the lattice, all the hair in that box are selected. This selection mode is linked to the discretization of the lattice, and does not allow selecting a set of hair between two cells. But generally, the hairdresser doesn't cut hair under long hair. After this selection step the user can "add" a set of hair using "copy and paste" tool and shift (via haptic) the duplicate set of hair.

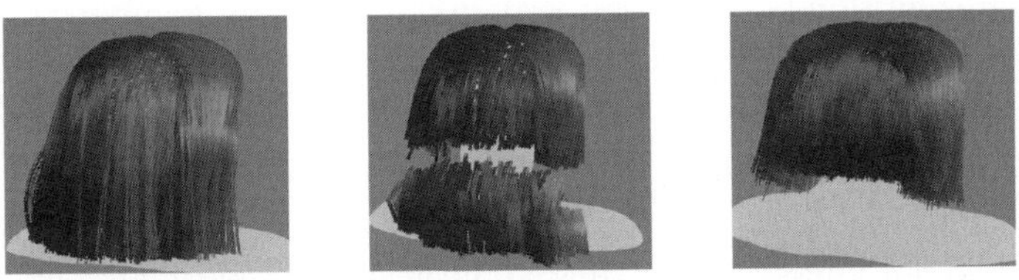

Fig. 3. Cut Hair Sequence

Fig. 4. Hairstyle created using Brushing Tool

For hairstyling operators, we have limited the animation to only parts where modifications are applied. Thus, we create a lattice just for the selected set of hair and only this set is later animated. Limiting the lattice to a specific section of hair decreases the computational time and allows efficiently using the geometrics methods. These geometrics modifications don't change the form of the lattice. This technique also avoids a computation of self-collision detection between strips and provides good result in simulation.

6.2 Virtual Scissor

The most important tools for a hairdresser are probably the scissors. In our technique, we first choose a cut plane for modifying the hair. Several inclided or curves (like sines functions) planes are proposed. The variety of these cut planes afford realization of numbers cut types. After, this selection, it is possible to change the position, orientation via a the 6DOF of the haptic. A mass-spring system representation is used for all strands in order to simulate drop-ping the hair cut during the cutting process. The implementation of this modeling is easy, and allows obtaining good results in short time.

6.3 Virtual Brush

The virtual brushing/waviness tool involves a function of some parameters (radius, length of curve, direction of the brushing, degree of curl) of strands. Based on these parameters, a mathematical function is applied on the last node of all the selected hair resulting in curve hair to obtain visual movement. When simulating waviness, the visual effect is similar to a compressed spring movement from top to bottom. When brushing, the movement of lattice node is away from the head and following the direction of the brush. The use of these techniques avoids us to compute collision between hair and an object (tools, comb for example)and visual realism is maintained because the simulation seems to be real.

7 Results and Discussion

We have tested our unified hair styling application for creating various hairstyles. The implementations are done on a workstation with Intel Pentium4 and 3.4 GHz processor with a 1 GB main memory and a GeForce 6800 graphics card. Our computation algorithm is written in standard C++ and rendering is done using the OpenGL API. The initial hairstyle has been created using our in-house home hairstyler based on fluid dynamics [8].

We ran our algorithm to create short, curly and brushed hairstyles using our unified framework. We have tested the hairstyles with various complexities of the mechanical representation and have found that a mechanical model containing 100 attachments and 400 springs built on 343 lattice nodes is fairly accurate and with fast simulation. The model reacts to collisions with the head and the shoulder using 7 metaballs. For shadow computation we found that for all the hairstyles a lattice size of 128 × 128 × 32 was optimal enough to provide an interactive frame rate. While performing the user interactions, as the simulation is limited to only section of the hair to be modified, the average performance is better.

8 Conclusion and Future Work

We have presented an easily usable framework for animating, rendering with optimized features for interactive hairstyling. With initial results of our unified framework being quite promising, we look forward to adding more features for more interactivity and enhanced visualization. We plan to add more interactivity as well as "sense of touch" during hair styling.

Acknowledgement. This project is funded by the Swiss National Research Foundation (FNRS).

References

1. Bertails F., Kim T.-Y., Cani M.-P., Neumann U.: Adaptive wisp tree-a multiresolution control structure for simulating dynamic clustering in hair motion. Proc. Symposium on Computer Animation (2003) 207–377
2. Bertails F., Menier C., Cani M.-P.: A practical self-shadowing algorithm for interactive hair animation. Graphics Interface (2005) 71–78
3. Chang J., Jin J., Yu Y.: A practical model for mutual hair interactions. Proc. Symposium on Computer Animation 2002 (2002) 51–58
4. Chen L., Saeyor S., Dohi H., Ishizuka M.: A system of 3d hairstyle synthesis based on the wisp model. The Visual Computer (1999) 159–170
5. Gupta R., Magnenat-Thalmann N.: Scattering-Based Interactive Hair Rendering IEEE CAD and Graphics'05 (2005) 489–494
6. Hadap S., Magnenat-Thalmann N.: Interactive hair styler based on fluid flow Proc. Eurographics Workshop on CAS (2000) 87–99
7. Hadap S., Magnenat-Thalmann N.: Modeling dynamic hair as a continuum Proc. EuroGraphics, Computer Graphics Forum **20** 3 (2001) 329–338
8. Heranandez B., Rudomin I.: Hair Paint IEEE Proc. Computer Graphics International, Creta, Grecia, Junio 16 - 19 (2004) 578–581
9. Kajiya J. T., Kay T. L.: Rendering fur with three dimensional textures Proc. SIGGRAPH '89 (1989) **23** 271–280
10. Kim T., Neumann U.: A thin shell volume for modelling human hair IEEE Proc. Computer Animation (2000) 104–111
11. Kim T., Neumann U.: Opacity shadow maps Proc. Eurographics Rendering Workshop (2001) 177–182
12. Kim T.-Y., Neumann U.: Interactive multiresolution hair modeling and editing Proc. SIGGRAPH '02 (2002) 287–294
13. Koh C., Huang Z.: Real-time animation of human hair modeled in strips Computer Animation and Simulation, Springer-Verlag, (2000) 101–110
14. Koh C., Huang Z.: A simple physics model to animate human hair modeled in 2d strips in real time Proc. Eurographics workshop on CAS (2001) 127–138

15. Koster M., Haber J., Seidel H. P.: Real-time rendering of human hair using programmable graphics hardware IEEE Proc. Computer Graphics International (2004) 248–256
16. Lokovic T., Veach E.: Deep shadow maps Proc. SIGGRAPH '00 (2000) 385–392
17. Marschner S. R., Jensen H. W., Cammarano M., Worley S., Hanrahan P.: Light scattering from human hair fibers Proc. SIGGRAPH '03 **22** (2003) 780–791
18. Mertens T., Kautz J., Bekaert P., Reeth F. V.: A self-shadow algorithm for dynamic hair using clustered densities Proc. Eurographics Symposium on Rendering (2004) 173–178
19. Plante E., Cani M.-P., Poulin P.: A layered wisp model for simulating interactions inside long hair Proc. Eurographic workshop on CAS (2001) 139–148
20. Schmith C., Koster M., Haber J., Seidel H-P.: Modeling Hair using a Wisp Hair Model Research Report MPI-I-2004-4-001 (2004)
21. Magnenat-Thalmann N., Hadap S., Kalra P.: State of the art in hair simulation International Workshop on Human Modeling and Animation (2000) 3–9
22. Volino P., Magnenat-Thalmann N.: Animating complex hairstyles in realtime ACM Symposium on Virtual Reality Software and Technology (VRST) (2004) 41–48
23. Ward K., Lin M. C.: Adaptive grouping and subdivision for simulating hair dynamics Pacific Graphics Conference on Computer Graphics and Applications (2003) 234–243
24. Ward K., Lin M. C., Lee J., Fisher S., Macri D.: Modeling hair using level-of-detail representations IEEE Proc. Computer Animation and Social Agents (2003) 41–47
25. Watanabe Y., Suenaga Y.: Drawing human hair using the wisp model Special issue on computer graphics international **7** (1989) 97–103
26. Yang X.D., Xu Z., Yang J., Wang T.: The Cluster Hair Model Graphical Models, Elsevier **65**(2)(2000) 85–103
27. Yu Y.: Modeling realistic virtual hairstyles Proc. Pacific Graphics (2001) 295–304

Optimizing Mesh Construction for Quad/Triangle Schemes

Koen Beets, Johan Claes, and Frank Van Reeth

Expertise Center for Digital Media
Hasselt University
Transnationale Universiteit Limburg
Universitaire Campus
B-3590 Diepenbeek, Belgium
{koen.beets, johan.claes, frank.vanreeth}@uhasselt.be
http://edm.uhasselt.be

Abstract. Modelling high-quality free-form 3D objects is a very time-consuming task. Recently, hybrid subdivision surface schemes have been proposed, allowing quads to be used in surface areas with two-directional symmetry and triangles for the more free-form regions. Until now, this kind of scheme was rather theoretical, as it was not obvious how to create optimal objects with it for e.g. practical animation purposes. We describe a sketching system for quick 3D modelling using such hybrid subdivision, starting from user-drawn 2D curves. These curves are triangularized, and a skeleton is calculated, along with the 3D object. This skeleton can be used to deform the object later on. At the same time, we try to maximize surface quality, and limit the number of faces and vertices. In cases where only little detail is desired, the resulting objects can be used directly, while the object's structure also makes them suitable for subsequent editing and adding detail, using commercially available subdivision modellers.

Keywords: subdivision, modelling, sketching, quad/triangle, mesh construction.

1 Introduction and Related Work

Subdivision surfaces have become a common technique for representing surfaces. They define a surface as the limit of a series of refinements, starting from a coarse control mesh. A good introduction can be found in [1]. Until recently, subdivision schemes were optimized for meshes consisting of either triangles or quadrilaterals exclusively. In the last years, however, schemes have appeared which generate good results when applied to meshes which contain both triangular and quadrilateral regions [2], [3]. These kinds of schemes turn out to be very useful for modelling animations, because there, in symmetric (e.g. cylindrical) areas, quads and vertices with valence 4 are preferred, to support the symmetry. On the other hand, in freeform areas, triangles and vertices having valence 6 are preferred. Other advantages of the subdivision representation are,

H.-P. Seidel, T. Nishita, and Q. Peng (Eds.): CGI 2006, LNCS 4035, pp. 711–718, 2006.

among others: computational efficiency, support for arbitrary topology, precise control over the surface, and efficient representation of complex geometry because of its multiresolution properties. Special purpose editors using subdivision techniques have been described, e.g. Skaria et al. make use of a modified quadrilateral Catmull-Clark subdivision scheme to model specific cartoon faces [4]. Their system can generate a wide variety of cartoon faces.

One of the most well-known 3D sketching systems is Teddy [5]. Teddy is a sketching interface for designing 3D freeform objects, which creates polygonal mesh objects out of 2D silhouettes. Afterwards, the same authors extended this approach to overcome some of the artifacts introduced by Teddy by using a fairing technique [6]. Other approaches are using implicit surfaces: Karpenko et al. use variational implicit surfaces as a representation for a free-form modeller [7]. They take advantage of the implicit representation to support extrusion and blending.

2 Object Construction

Our approach starts with a closed 2D user-drawn cubic subdivision curve, lying in the XY plane. This curve is the only user input at the start of the algorithm. In the preprocessing step, we remove unwanted vertices, and at the same time we add vertices to facilitate later stages in the construction. The objects are constructed out of several construction layers, which are parallel to the plane containing the input curve. The thickness of the object at a particular vertex of the input curve, is determined as the distance of that vertex to its equivalent vertex on the chordal axis. In this section we first present some preprocessing steps on the input curve, along with some construction parameters which can be used to fine-tune the results. This is followed by the construction of the top layer, and of the intermediate layers. Finally, we close the object.

2.1 Preprocessing Steps

To start with the algorithm, we begin with triangulating the closed input curve I, using constrained Delaunay triangulation. Next, we calculate the chordal axis, by connecting the midpoints of the internal edges of the triangularized control polygon. Then the axis is smoothed, to limit influence of single vertices.

In the first preprocessing step, we remove the vertices in the control polygon which make an angle α with their neighbors, close to 180°. Experimental results suggest that a good threshold is $\alpha > 170^o$. Furthermore, the distance of these vertices to their corresponding vertices on the axis have to be more or less the same. A good criterion is that these distances should differ no more than 15 percent, which we determined empirically. In short, in this first step we remove vertices which do not make sharp angles in the input polygon, and which do not represent significant changes in thickness in the input polygon.

Secondly, we add extra vertices in regions where there is a large change in thickness between consecutive vertices. Consider the situation depicted in Figure 1, with the adjacent vertices a and b. a' is the vertex on the axis which

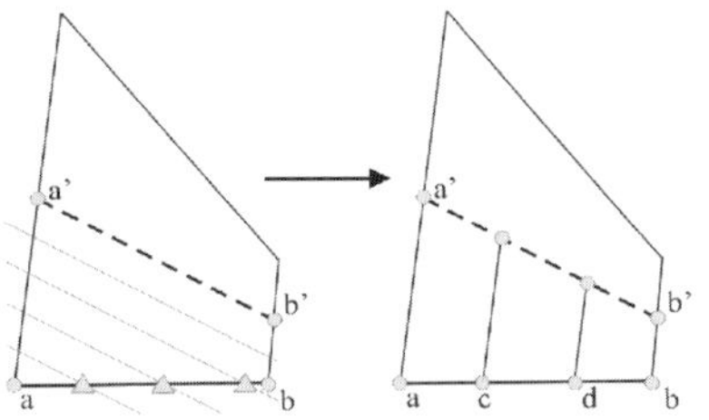

Fig. 1. Adding extra vertices in the input polygon

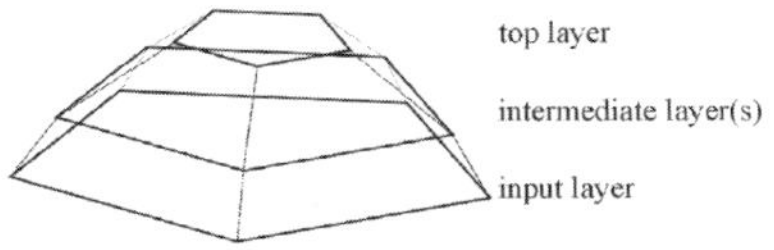

Fig. 2. Schematic overview of the layers

corresponds to a, and the same applies to b and b'. We denote the number of layers at a vertex v as l_v. Let $l_a = |aa'|/lt_{max}$ and $l_b = |bb'|/lt_{max}$, where we define lt_{min} as the smallest distance $|vv'|$ for all $v \in I$, and lt_{max} as $lt_{min} * 3$. Both l_a and l_b must be smaller than or equal to l_{max}. If this is not the case, they are set to be equal to l_{max}. Now, between every a and b, we add $(l_{diff} - 1)$ vertices equally distributed between a and b, with $l_{diff} = abs(l_a - l_b)$. This way, we avoid extraordinary vertices later on.

2.2 Construction of the Top Layer

The first real construction stage is the creation of the top layer. This top layer sits on top of all previous layers, which are created afterwards. A schematic view of the different layers is shown in Figures 2 and 4, where the input curve I is the lowest layer. Construction of the top layer goes as follows:

Adding Vertices of the Top Layer. For each vertex $b \in I$, we add a vertex b_h in the top layer L_h. We calculate a circular arc C_b with b' as origin, which goes through b, and which is orthogonal to the input plane. We obtain b_h by intersecting this circle with a plane $P_{h,b}$, which is defined as follows: $P_{h,b} \leftrightarrow Z = |bb'| * f$. Here f is a scaling factor, which we experimentally set to 0.85, but it can be adjusted by the user. Without this factor, intersections will always be found at b'. After doing this for all b, we have a polygon L_h. However, we do not merely add this polygon to the object. Instead, we divide it into several quadrangles and triangles, and add these to the final object.

Simplify. In the next stage we remove edges between adjacent vertices of L_h which have become too short. Very short edges are problematic for surface quality, and have to be removed. However, this has to be done carefully to prevent vertices of high valence to appear. For every pair of adjacent vertices a and b in L_h where $|ab| < el_{min}$, we remove that vertex which merges ab with the shortest adjacent edge. This el_{min}, which is the smallest allowed edge length, is defined as $\frac{1}{4}*$ the average edge length. However this value is arbitrary and can be adapted by the user.

Fill the Polygon with Faces. The next step is to fill the polygon at the highest layer with quadrangles and triangles, in a way which produces optimal

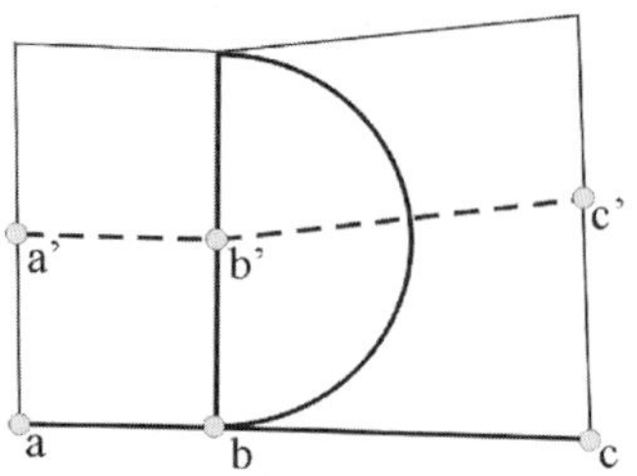

Fig. 3. Creating an arc C_b, with origin b' and going through b

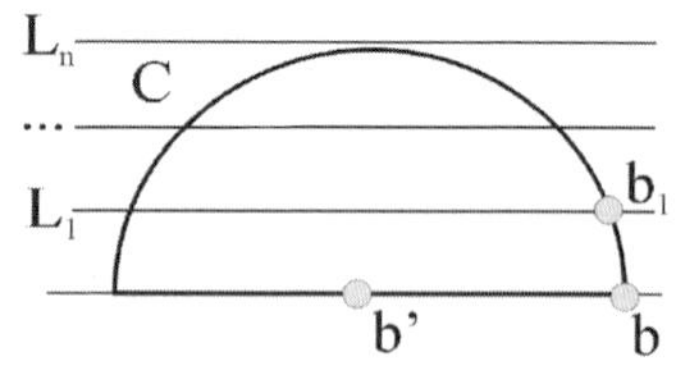

Fig. 4. Intersecting C_b with layers L_1 through L_h

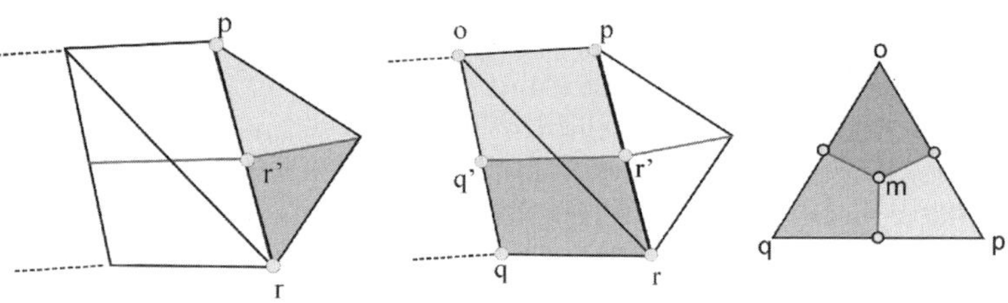

Fig. 5. Creation of 2 triangles at end vertices of the axis (left), of 2 quads along arms of the axis (centre), end at crossings (right).

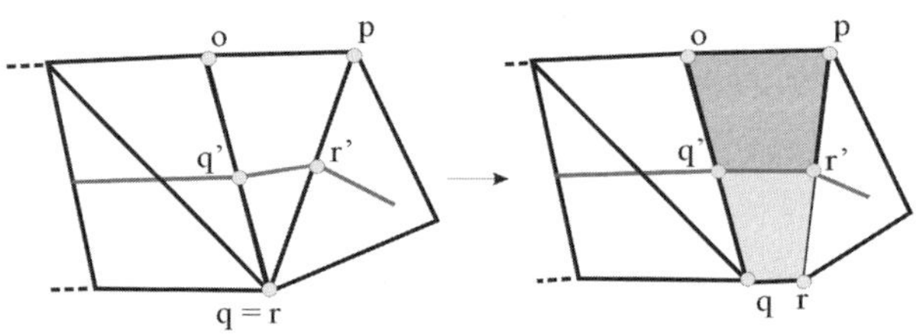

Fig. 6. Adding an extra vertex in the case of an odd number of triangles

surfaces. Here we discern 3 different cases: at the end of the axis, where axes cross, and along the legs of the axes. First, at the end vertices of the axis, we create 2 new triangles instead of the original single triangle. This is shown in Figure 5 (left).

Along the legs of the axis, we start at the end vertices, and for every pair of vertices q' and r' (shown in Figure 5 (centre)), we find the corresponding vertices o, p, q and r in the polygon, and connect them to form 2 new quads.

It is possible that we will end up with not enough vertices to complete the construction in this way. In this case, we add a new vertex in the polygon and resume. This is shown in Figure 6, where originally q was equal to r.

Finally, the last type of triangles we observe in the triangulated input polygon are intern triangles, where the axis has three branches, which emerge from a vertex placed in the center of the triangle. We replace this triangle by 3 quads which are constructed as shown in Figure 5 (right), and which are $(o, (o+p)/2, m, (o+q)/2)$, $(p, (o+p)/2, m, (p+q)/2)$ and $(q, (q+p)/2, m, (o+q)/2)$.

2.3 Creation of the Sides

The sides connect the lowest layer polygon I, with the top layer L_h. This is done by placing a number of layers in between, and connecting them, while taking care not to introduce vertices with very high or low valence.

Calculation of the Intermediate Layers. For every vertex $b \in I$, we calculate b_i, where i is the index of the layer where b_i belongs to. For every b, the number of layers at that vertex can differ widely. This number is derived from the distance $|bb'|$, and is calculated by: $l_b = |bb'|/lt_{max}$ Also, make sure this number falls between l_{min} and l_{max}. This way, we create a set of layers L_i, containing less and less vertices with increasing value for i. Also, for every layer, we apply the simplification step mentioned in section 2.2, to remove edges which have become very short in this step.

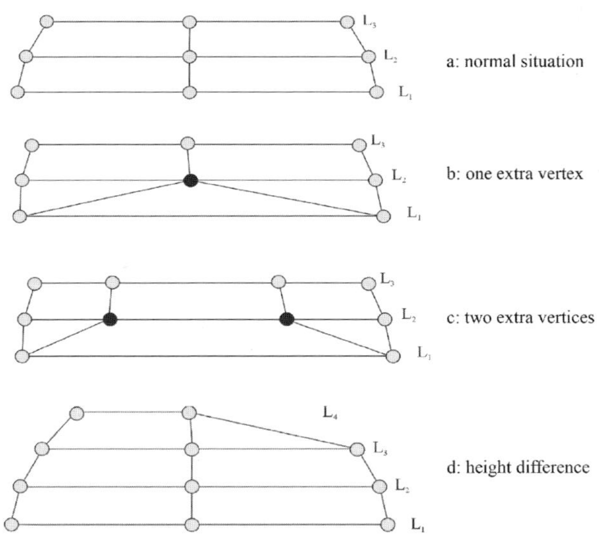

Fig. 7. Construction of the sides

Connecting the Layers. With all layers having the same number of vertices, connecting all layers together is simple: quadrangles can be formed everywhere, using vertices with regular connectivity, as shown in Figure 7(a). However, since the number of vertices can vary widely throughout layers, we have to pay attention not to create vertices with high valence. If for every pair of corresponding vertices ab and $a"b"$ in subsequent layers, there are never more than 2 new vertices in between, we can use triangles to fix the situation. If, however, there are more than 2 vertices between $a"b"$, an extra layer will be created between the two layers. These situations are shown in Figures 7(b) and 7(c).

There also can be differences in the number of layers between adjacent vertices. To fix those gaps, we introduce triangles, as illustrated in Figure 7(d). Note that, because of the first preprocessing step where vertices were selectively inserted into the input curve, we never have a difference in height larger than 1, since the height difference between consecutive vertices is now limited.

2.4 Closing the Object

Now we have constructed one half of a closed symmetric object. To close it, we duplicate the current object, mirror it along the XY plane which contains the input polygon I, and translate it so that the input polygon and its copy collide exactly.

3 Editing the Object

We allow the user to edit the generated object after construction, by deforming the 3D axis. This allows quick manipulation, which makes the system suitable for quick animations using a keyframing system. Also, our objects have a very limited number of control vertices (also depending on the number of input vertices), which makes them suitable for editing in commercial 3D modellers. This way, the user can e.g. easily paint on the objects, or execute advanced operations on them which might be difficult to obtain in our sketching system. After construction, the created object is symmetric in regard to the XY plane. However, the user can deform the object easily by moving axis vertices.

4 Surface Quality

As mentioned before, we employ the Quad/Triangle scheme by Stam and Loop [3]. Due to the construction method, our system generates objects which consist for the most part of regular quadrilateral regions, where vertices have valence 4. These can be found in the sides of the object, which are constructed by intersecting the planes with circles. Triangles are used to fill height differences, and at the end of an axis. By using several construction layers, we can avoid very high or low valence, and *n-gons* in the sides, where n is different from 3 and 4. Distances between layers depend on the thickness of the object locally. In thicker regions there are more layers, which are further apart.

5 Results

Figure 8 shows a *quadpod*, an imaginatory object, which was created starting from a simple curve. Afterwards, the user deformed the axis to obtain a bulge in the center, and to pull down some legs. Figures 9 and 10 show two other examples.

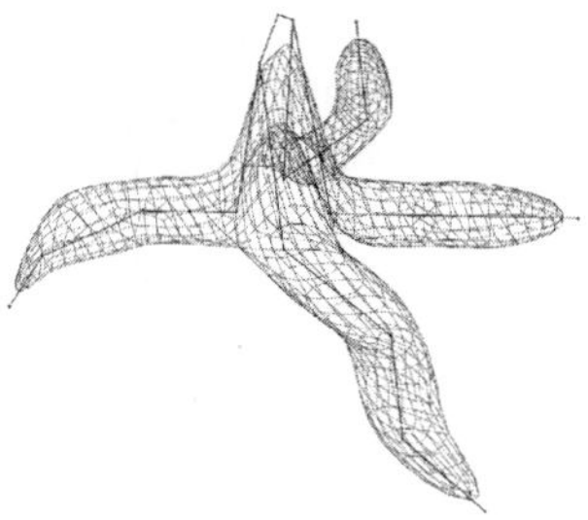

Fig. 8. A 'quadpod' with skeleton

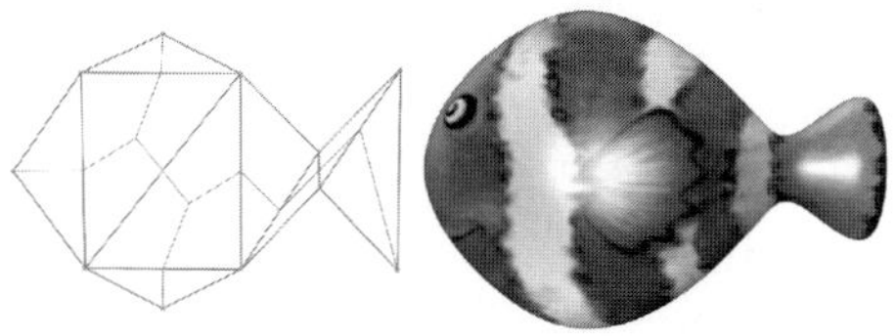

Fig. 9. A fish (textured by Xemi Morales)

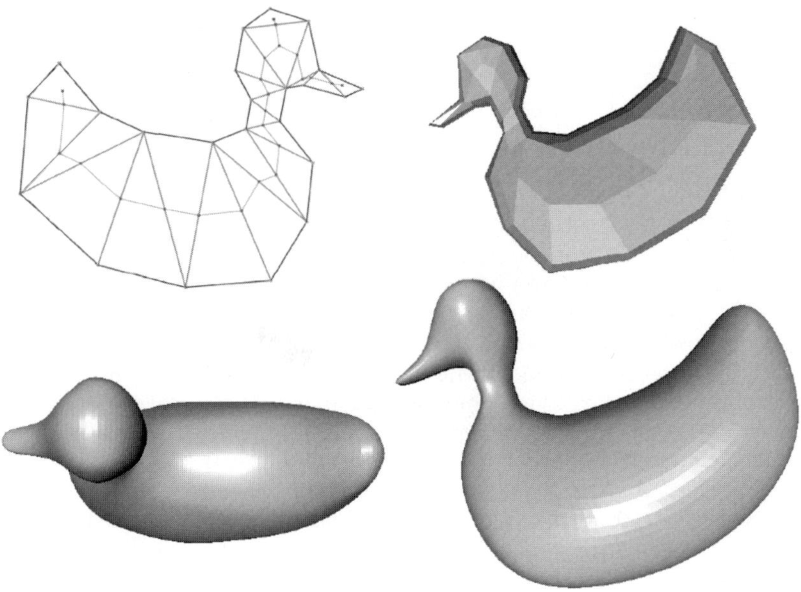

Fig. 10. A duck

6 Conclusions and Future Work

We presented a system for rapid sketching of free-form 3D objects. To our knowledge this is the first in literature to create meshes optimized for hybrid Quad/Triangle subdivision. As described in [3], we achieve surfaces which are C^1 everywhere, have bounded curvature at the quad/triangle border. Furthermore, they can be easily designed by the inexperienced user. At extraordinary vertices, which we cannot avoid in all situations, we still obtain C^1 continuity, but without curvature continuity. Since we construct an axis through the object, the technique is very suitable for quick and easy animation using keyframing. Finally, the coarse control meshes with limited number of vertices make it possible to edit the objects in commercially available modellers, in contrast to most other sketching systems in literature. With respect to future work we are looking into using subdivision schemes which tend to minimize curvature variations, such as [8].

Acknowledgements

The authors are pleased to acknowledge that this work has been partially funded by the European Fund for Regional Development and the Flemish Government.

References

1. Warren, J., Weimer, H.: Subdivision Methods for Geometric Design: A Constructive Approach. Morgan-Kaufmann (2002)
2. Beets, K., Claes, J., Van Reeth, F.: A combined quadrilateral-hexagonal subdivision scheme. In: SIAM Conference on Geometric Modelling and Computing. (2003) 53–68
3. Stam, J., Loop, C.: Quad/triangle subdivision. Computer Graphics Forum **22**(1) (2003) 79–85
4. Skaria, S., Akleman, E., Parke, F.I.: Modeling subdivision control meshes for creating cartoon faces. In: Proceedings of the International Conference on Shape Modeling and Applications. (2001) 216–225
5. Igarashi, T., Matsuoka, S., Tanaka, H.: Teddy: A sketching interface for 3d freeform design. Proceedings of SIGGRAPH 99 (August 1999) 409–416
6. Igarashi, T., Hughes, J.: Smooth meshes for sketch-based freeform modeling. In: Proceedings of the ACM Symposium on Interactive 3D Graphics. (2003) 139–142
7. Karpenko, O., Hughes, F.: Smooth free-form sketching with variational implicit surfaces. Computer Graphics Forum **21**(3) (2002) 585–594
8. Beets, K., Claes, J., Van Reeth, F.: A subdivision scheme to model surfaces with spherelike features. In Skala, V., ed.: Proceedings of WSCG. (2005) 103–108

Rendering Optical Effects Based on Spectra Representation in Complex Scenes

Weiming Dong*

Project ALICE, INRIA Lorraine/Loria, France
Weiming.Dong@loria.fr

Abstract. Rendering the structural color of natural objects or modern industrial products in the 3D environment is not possible with RGB-based graphics platforms and software and very time consuming, even with the most efficient spectra representation based methods previously proposed. Our framework allows computing full spectra light object interactions only when it is needed, i.e. for the part of the scene that requires simulating special spectra sensitive phenomena. Achieving the rendering of complex scenes with both the full spectra and RGB light and object interactions in a ray-tracer costs only some additional fractions of seconds. To prove the efficiency of our framework, we implemented a "Multilayer Film" in a simple ray-tracer. However, the framework is convenient for any complex lighting model, including diffraction or fluorescence.

1 Introduction

Many phenomena and materials, in nature or in industry, have complex optical effects, namely interference, diffraction, fluorescence, dispersion, phosphorescence, etc. These physical effects cannot be rendered with current RGB-based graphics platforms and software. However, as pointed in [1] and [2], color computations in a renderer have to be performed in spectral space if the output is to be used for predictive purpose.

To simulate these optical effects, some researches have been focused on the full spectra representation of light and objects [1]. These methods are not tractable when a complex scene has to be rendered. Recently in [3], for example, a multilayer films model is coded with their efficient spectra representation [4] and implemented in a popular RGB-based renderer. However, the optical effects of the object presented (insect) are computed independently of its 3D environment, although they are highly dependent on the lighting conditions of this environment and interactive with it. Our rendering process overcomes this problem.

Our idea is based on the observation that usually, only a part of a scene needs to be simulated with a full spectra representation. In Figure 1, only a part of the insect has a structural color. In Figure 2, the insects are even partly hidden. In the two figures, color of leaves and flowers, as well as some parts of the insect itself, are due to pigmentation. Moreover, the light transport needs

* This research was done when Weiming Dong was a visiting student in the Sino French Lab in Computer Science, Automation and Applied Mathematics (LIAMA).

H.-P. Seidel, T. Nishita, and Q. Peng (Eds.): CGI 2006, LNCS 4035, pp. 719–726, 2006.

to be simulated with full spectra representation, only when the optical effects of the material have a visual impact on other objects.

This paper presents the rendering process of complex scenes with both the full spectra and RGB light and object interactions. Unlike conventional systems that perform color calculations with tristimulus color values, our system allows to embed any kind of representation of the spectra to calculate colors of complex optical effects. Unlike spectral rendering systems previously proposed [1], our rendering process allows to use and compute spectra in complex scenes only when it is needed, i.e. when they have a significant impact in the transport process, and the final image.

Fig. 1. The *Edgar Poe Gold Bug* is rendered with a full spectral function representation while the main part of the 3D scene is computed with RGB models

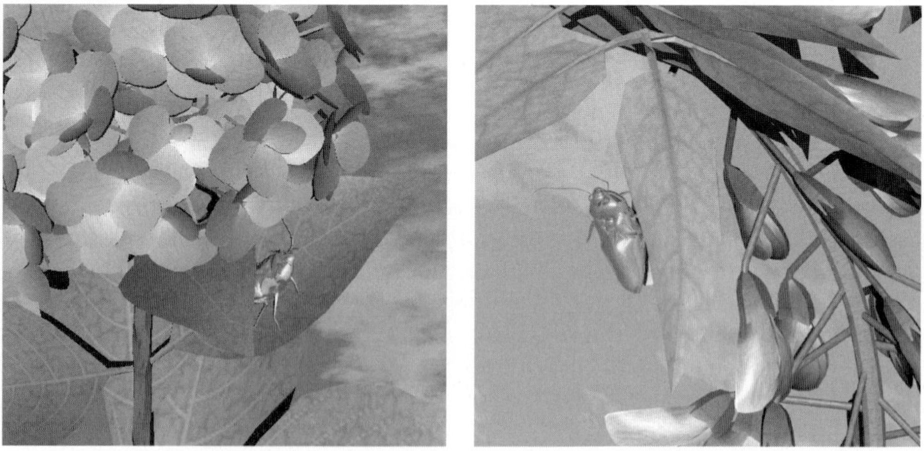

(a) (b)

Fig. 2. Two examples of our framework

In the following sections, we first discuss some related works. Then we describe the color representation models used in our system, and also give the whole work flow of the render. We show some images generated by our system and address the advantages comparing with the traditional methods in the fifth section. Finally we draw the conclusion and discuss about the future work.

2 Related Works

Many works have been focused on developing physically based lighting models and perceptually based rendering procedures for computer graphics that will produce synthetic images that are visually and measurably indistinguishable from real-world images [1][5][6][7]. Greenberg et al. [8] proposed a framework which subdivided the whole rendering process into three sub-sections: the local light reflection model, the energy transport simulation, and the visual display algorithms. Glassner provided a mathematical framework for phosphorescence and fluorescence [9][2]. Stam [10] developed a reflection models for metallic surfaces that handle the effects of diffraction. To accurately simulate the optical phenomena, Sun et al. [4] proposed a rendering framework which emphasized real spectra as input, retains full spectral light-object interactions, and generates spectral images (convertible to RGB images for display). This framework is capable of handling wavelength-related optical effects including dispersion, interference, diffraction, and fluorescence, but still very costly, especially when objects with complex spectrum based materials are present only in a part of the scene. Another problem is to render the scene users need to set all the object materials with spectrum, usually it is difficult to get all the spectral data of the materials in the scene.

An accurate and efficient spectral representation is required in our framework. Many methods have been proposed like sampling [11][12], linear model representation [13], and using polynomials [14]. Unfortunately these methods all have difficulties in balancing the accuracy and efficiency. To overcome the drawbacks of the previous methods, Sun et al. proposed a composite spectral model by decomposing all spectra into a smooth background and a list of spikes [15][4][3]. They represented the smooth part with Fourier coefficients and a spike is specified by its location and height. We also use this spectral representation model in our framework.

We use Hirayama et al.'s work [16] for rendering objects coated with multilayer thin films to test our framework. Their method is based on wave optics, and is able to accurately visualize the optical effects of multilayer films.

In [3], a multilayered films is also proposed. The model has several new nice properties. However, the complex optical effects of the *Morpho Rethenor* that is chosen as an illustration cannot be rendered with an approximated interference scheme. In fact, the irregularity in the ridge height of the *Morpho Rethenor* eliminates the interference among the ridges, which results in the diffuse and broad reflection of a uniform color [17]. So due to its complex microstructure, the structural color combines both diffraction and interference in a complex microstructure.

3 Efficient Renderer for Rendering Natural Scenes

We develop a new framework for realistic rendering. In this framework, we use RGB and spectrum together to represent the materials, light sources and the pixel colors of the synthesized image.

3.1 Materials and Light Sources

First, to simulate the natural phenomena which can not be accurately calculated with simple RGB models, and protect the efficiency if the objects also have some RGB oriented properties at the same time, we allow RGB and spectrum to work together to represent one material, different element of the material can have different type of representative model. This means that we set the "natural" part of the material with spectral model and let the other parts still be represented by RGB. For example, considering an object with both interference effect and simple diffuse appearance, we integrate the interference part with the related physical based model (like a spectrum based BRDF model) and define the diffuse value which is independent of wavelength with RGB.

To synthesize realistic images of natural phenomena, we use light sources described with spectral power distributions (SPDs) in the scenes which have spectral effects. Like Sun's spectrally based framework [4], we also recommend the using of real spectral data in order to ensure the accuracy of spectral effect simulation.

At the same time, we also allow RGB light sources in the same scene, this feature is to facilitate the use of monochromatic light sources and the approximation of the real light sources when there is no getatable spectral data. The user can simply choose the RGB color of the light source and convert it into spectrum in the rendering process. In our system, we use Sun's method to derive spectra from colors [15].

3.2 Color Representation

Based on Huygens' principle of independent propagating of light [18], we separately calculate the effect of the light sources, no matter it is an RGB or spectral light source. Then we integrate the effect together as the final results of the local illumination. In our system, we decompose the color of one point into two parts: the RGB part and the spectrum part. Formally the color is the sum of the two parts. We use it as the intermediate format during the rendering process. The color of one point $\boldsymbol{x}$ can be written as follows

$$Color_{inter}(\boldsymbol{x}) = Color_{RGB}(\boldsymbol{x}) + Color_{spectrum}(\boldsymbol{x})$$

where $Color_{RGB}(\boldsymbol{x})$ is the RGB value generated by the interaction between the RGB based material elements and the light sources (represented with RGB model), and $Color_{spectrum}(\boldsymbol{x})$ is the spectral effect caused by the spectral elements of the material.

In fact, for one light source, we first calculate the irradiance of it at the point. Then the radiance (color) of the point will be evaluated according to the type of the material element. If the element is RGB based, we convert the SPD of the spectral light source into RGB and add the value (radiance) to the RGB part of the point color. On the other hand, the RGB light source should be converted to spectrum if the material element is spectrum based. So the color of the point generated by one light source can be written as

$$Color_{inter}(\boldsymbol{x}) = \sum_{i=1}^{m} Color^{i}_{RGB}(\boldsymbol{x}) + \sum_{j=1}^{n} Color^{j}_{spectrum}(\boldsymbol{x})$$

where m is the number of the RGB based material elements, $Color^{i}_{RGB}(\boldsymbol{x})$ is the RGB radiance (represented with RGB model) generated by the light source, m is the number of the spectral material elements, and $Color^{j}_{spectrum}(\boldsymbol{x})$ is the spectral value which is computed (represented with spectrum) according to the spectral function. So we write the final equation of the color at one point generated by multiple light sources as follows

$$Color_{inter}(\boldsymbol{x}) = \sum_{k=1}^{N}(\sum_{i=1}^{m} Color^{i}_{RGB}(\boldsymbol{x}) + \sum_{j=1}^{n} Color^{j}_{spectrum}(\boldsymbol{x}))$$

where N is the number of light sources in the scene.

3.3 Acceleration

To accelerate the rendering process at run time, we save both the RGB value and the spectral value of all the light sources in the pre-processing step, so we need not do the spectrum-to-RGB or RGB-to-spectrum operation when the irradiance of one point is being calculated. The only work we need to do is to choose the proper value corresponding to the type of the material element.

4 Rendering Pipeline

The whole rendering pipeline comprises three stages: preprocessing, rendering and color transformation. In the first stage, the SPD of the spectral light sources and the spectral functions of the spectral material elements are represented through loading data from the spectral database. The intensity of the RGB light sources and the RGB parts of the materials are also set by the user (or from texture). Then we pre-compute the RGB value of the spectral light sources and the spectra of the RGB light sources. We save these values together with the original data. The second stage is most important: here an intermediate image is generated based on local and global illumination models with ray tracing. The intermediate image is similar to a color image except that for every pixel the information is the combination of a spectrum and a RGB value instead of a color. In the rendering process, when calculating the reflectance intensity, if the reflectance of the material is RGB based, we need to convert the spectral part of the reflectance intensity gathered by the reflected ray into RGB. Contrarily, if the reflectance of the material is spectrum based, we need to convert the RGB part of the reflectance intensity gathered by the reflected ray into spectrum. The same for the transmittance calculation. Finally we transform the spectral part of the intermediate image into RGB [15] and plus the previous RGB part. This will generate an RGB image for displaying on the screen.

Compared to previous frameworks [8][4], the intermediate color format, the separate light-material element interaction and the intermediate image in our pipeline are new elements. Note that we can also store the spectral part of the intermediate image as a spectral image like [4] to identify errors for particular wavelengths and finding effective improvements. On the other hand, compared with Sun et al.'s [4] framework, we only add a RGB data which can be stored by three "double" variables for each pixel in the rendering process, the memory increase will not be a problem.

Table 1. The information of result images

Items	Figure 1	Figure 2(a)	Figure 2(b)
Triangle Number of Plant	18086	32848	60894
Triangle Number of Insect	49832	49832	49832
Resolution (Pixels)	680 × 680	600 × 600	600 × 600
Our Rendering Time (Seconds)	7.63	12.84	15.97
Sun's Rendering Time (Seconds)	80.23	188.49	234.13
Our Rendering Time without the Insect (Seconds)	3.12	11.02	13.08
Sun's Rendering Time without the Insect (Seconds)	45.66	173.38	198.52

5 Results and Discussion

Figure 1 shows a natural scene with an Edgar Poe Golden Bug rendered by our system, the material is constructed by coating cooper with a 500 nm gold film [16], and the specular value for the high light is an RGB value [1]. The plant and the background are both constructed with RGB models. A parallel light source with the spectral distribution of the CIE standard illumination D_{65} [2] is set above the plant. It will cause wavelength computation only when the traced ray intersects with the bug. Figure 2(a) shows one bug on a plant with many flowers. In this scene, only the the bug is integrated with spectrum based material. The material is the same as the bug in Figure 1, but the position of the camera and the light source (also D_{65}) is different. We can see the different appearance of the iridescence caused by the thin film. Figure 2(b) is another example, we change the thickness of the gold film to 300nm, one can see the appearance is different with the previous two images. We can also notice that in the two images of Figure 2, the insects only occupy a very small part of the scene. Here our system

[1] The original insect model was downloaded from http://www.turbosquid.com. All the plant models used in this paper were downloaded from http://www.toucan.co.jp/indexE.html

is much more efficient than the full spectra rendering framework [4] while the image quality is almost the same. The rendering information of the results is shown in Table 1. All the images are generated on a PC of P4 3.2GHz and 1GB RAM. One can see that our system is nearly 15 times faster than the system of [4]. And we can also see that adding the insect to the scene will only cost a very few additional time comparing with the whole rendering time if the insect will only occupy a small part of the rendering window (for Figure 2(a) 1.82 seconds and for Figure 2(b) 2.89 seconds).

6 Conclusion and Future Work

This paper proposed an efficient framework for realistic image synthesis which can use real spectral data and RGB value together as input, retains full spectral interactions between lights and the spectral parts of the material of the objects, and generate images described with a format combining of both RGB and spectrum. We have shown that this framework suffices to describe the natural optical effects in realistic image synthesis, and have facilitated its practical application through a new color representation model - the combination model. Unifying previous research on traditional and spectral modeling and rendering, this new framework provides a useful and efficient basis for simulating general complicated phenomena.

A lot of work is needed to demonstrate the efficiency of the method and to control the visual impact of the rendering in complex global illuminated environments. We plan to implement and test our rendering process in a Photon Mapping Renderer [19] in complex geometric and physical scenes. Our tests use the the *Thin Film Model* for iridescence [16] and the Sun et al.'s dual method for spectra functions coding [4]. Improvements can be done in theses two areas. In particular, design a complex biology based micro structure model that can combines interference and diffraction is still an open problem as well as in Computer Graphics than in Optical Engineering.

References

1. Devlin, K., Chalmers, A., Wilkie, A., Purgathofer, W.: State of the art report: Tone reproduction and physically based spectral rendering. In: Proceedings of Eurographics 2002. (2002) 101–123
2. Glassner, A.S.: Principles of Digital Image Synthesis. Morgan Kaufmann Publishers Inc., San Francisco, CA, USA (1995)
3. Sun, Y.: Rendering biological iridescences with rgb-based renderers. ACM Trans. Graph. (2006)
4. Sun, Y., Fracchia, F.D., Drew, M.S., Calvert, T.W.: A spectrally based framework for realistic image synthesis. The Visual Computer **17**(7) (2001) 429–444
5. Hall, R.A., Greenberg, D.P.: A testbed for realistic image synthesis. **3**(8) (1983) 10–20
6. Rougeron, G., Péroche, B.: An adaptive representation of spectral data for reflectance computations. In: Proceedings of the Eurographics Workshop on Rendering Techniques '97, London, UK, Springer-Verlag (1997) 127–138

7. Iehl, J.C., Péroche, B.: An adaptive spectral rendering with a perceptual control. Comput. Graph. Forum **19**(3) (2000)
8. Greenberg, D.P., Torrance, K.E., Shirley, P., Arvo, J., Lafortune, E., Ferwerda, J.A., Walter, B., Trumbore, B., Pattanaik, S., Foo, S.C.: A framework for realistic image synthesis. In: SIGGRAPH '97: Proceedings of the 24th annual conference on Computer graphics and interactive techniques, New York, NY, USA, ACM Press/Addison-Wesley Publishing Co. (1997) 477–494
9. Glassner, A.S.: A model of fluorescence and phosphorescence. In: Proceedings of the 5th Eurographics Workshop on Rendering., Berlin Heidelberg New York, Springer (1994) 57–68
10. Stam, J.: Diffraction shaders. In: SIGGRAPH '99: Proceedings of the 26th annual conference on Computer graphics and interactive techniques, New York, NY, USA, ACM Press/Addison-Wesley Publishing Co. (1999) 101–110
11. Cook, R.L., Torrance, K.E.: A reflectance model for computer graphics. ACM Trans. Graph. **1**(1) (1982) 7–24
12. Meyer, G.W.: Wavelength selection for synthetic image generation. Comput. Vision Graph. Image Process. **41**(1) (1988) 57–79
13. Peercy, M.S.: Linear color representations for full speed spectral rendering. In: SIGGRAPH '93: Proceedings of the 20th annual conference on Computer graphics and interactive techniques, New York, NY, USA, ACM Press (1993) 191–198
14. Raso, M.G., Fournier, A.: A piecewise polynomial approach to shading using spectral distributions. In: Graphics Interface 91, Toronto, Canada, Canadian Information Processing Society (1991) 40–46
15. Sun, Y., Fracchia, F.D., Calvert, T.W., Drew, M.S.: Deriving spectra from colors and rendering light interference. IEEE Comput. Graph. Appl. **19**(4) (1999) 61–67
16. Hirayama, H., Kaneda, K., Yamashita, H., Yamaji, Y., Monden, Y.: Visualization of optical phenomena caused by multilayer films with complex refractive indices. In: PG '99: Proceedings of the 7th Pacific Conference on Computer Graphics and Applications, Washington, DC, USA, IEEE Computer Society (1999) 128–137
17. Kinoshita, S., Yoshioka, S., Kawagoe, K.: Mechanisms of structural colour in the morpho butterfly: cooperation of regularity and irregularity in an iridescent scale. Proc. R. Soc. Lond. B 266 **269**(1499) (2002) 1417–1421
18. Baker, B.B., Copson, E.T.: The Mathematical Theory of Huygens' Principle. Second edn. Oxford University Press, Oxford, England (1950)
19. Jensen, H.W.: Realistic Image Synthesis Using Photon Mapping. A. K. Peters, Ltd., Natick, MA, USA (2001)

GVF-Based Transfer Functions for Volume Rendering

Shaorong Wang[1,2] and Hua Li[1]

[1] National Research Center for Intelligent Computing Systems, Institute of Computing Technology, Chinese Academy of Sciences, China, 100080
[2] Graduate School of the Chinese Academy of Sciences, Beijing, China, 100039
{shrwang, lihua}@ict.ac.cn
www.ict.ac.cn

Abstract. Transfer function is very important for volume rendering. One common approach is to map the gradient magnitude to opacity transfer functions. However, it catches too many small details. Gradient vector flow (GVF) vectors have large magnitudes in the immediate vicinity of the edges, where the GVF vectors keep coordinate with the vectors of the gradient of the edge map. While in homogeneous regions where the intensity is nearly constant, the magnitudes of gradient vectors are nearly zero and GVF diffuses the edge gradient. Because of these aspects, we extend GVF to color space and apply it for opacity transfer functions. Experiments show that our method enhances edge features and makes a visual effect of diffusing along the edges.

1 Introduction

Several data sets become available from projects such as the "Visible Human Project" at the National Library of Medicine, the "Whole Frog Project" at Lawrence Berkeley, and the "Chinese Digital Human Project" at the Institute of Computing Technology of Chinese Academy of Sciences. It's a big challenge to get realistic volume visualization of these photographic volume data sets.

The currently dominant techniques for volume visualization consist of surface-based rendering and direct volume rendering [1]. Generally, the first step of surface-based rendering technique is to reconstruct the surface by 2D contour reconstructing method [2] or iso-surface extraction method such as the Marching Cubes algorithm [3] or Morse theory [4]. And then surface is rendered after being reconstructed. Usually the reconstruction step needs a segmentation performance, which can be very difficult. On the contrary, direct volume rendering method maps voxel directly into screen space without using geometric primitives as an intermediate representation. Ray-Casting method [5], Splatting method [6] and Shear-Warp method [7] are the most common direct volume rendering methods. All these algorithms perform the following processes. First, assign color value and opacity value to each voxel. Then project the voxel into the image plane. Finally compose the projected samples.

Transfer functions are used to map image properties to visualization characteristics, such as color, opacity, and texture. A review of transfer function techniques is given in [8]. Many previous studies on transfer function brought out approach by mapping gradient magnitude to opacity value. For color image processing is nonlinear, it is important to choose an appropriate color space [9]. In [10], Ebert and etc study color

H.-P. Seidel, T. Nishita, and Q. Peng (Eds.): CGI 2006, LNCS 4035, pp. 727 – 734, 2006.

spaces for volume rendering, and give some transfer functions by mapping the voxel's color gradient magnitude to opacity value according to the color distance defined in RGB color space and CIE LUV color space. The results show that this method can generate high quality image which display multi-organs such as fattiness, muscles and bones.

Our work of deriving opacity values is different from traditional transfer function approaches in the following ways:

We map gradient vector flow magnitude to opacity transfer function instead of gradient magnitude. Compared with other transfer function, GVF transfer function has two main advantages: First, it captures the strong edges information and gets rid of the weak edges which may be noise and disturb the whole visual effect. Second, GVF transfer function also catches the details in homogeneous regions. Finally, the opacity of the voxel is small when the voxel is near away from the edges, which makes a special visual effect.

We extend GVF model to vector data. Tradition GVF model only deal with scalar data and the edge map must be gradient magnitude if it is applied to vector data. We extend GVF model using an auxiliary image, which is usually a component standing for image luminance in the color space.

2 Extended GVF

Gradient vector flow is firstly used to describe external force of snake model [11]. Snake model or active contour model [12] is dynamic force model, which draw the closed curve or surface to the object edge or surface. The driving forces consist of internal forces and extern forces: $E=\int_0^1 E_{\mathrm{int}}+E_{ext}ds$, where E_{int} are internal forces that hold the curve together and keep the curve from bending too much. And E_{ext} are external forces that attract the curve toward the object boundaries. There are several kinds of external forces, in which the most common are:

$$\mathrm{E}_{\mathrm{ext}}=-I(x,y), \mathrm{E}_{\mathrm{ext}}=-|\nabla I(x,y)|, \mathrm{E}_{\mathrm{ext}}=-G_{\sigma}(x,y)*\nabla I(x,y).$$

The basic idea of snake model is to design the external forces to move the active contour toward the edges by difference of intensity or intensity gradient. Gradient fields have some important properties listed below: First, gradient vectors are normal to the edge; Second the magnitudes get the large value in the immediate vicinity of the edges. Third, the intensity is nearly constant and the gradient magnitude is nearly zero in homogeneous regions. The last two properties result in that capture range of the gradient is small and the active contour can not converge to the concave boundary such as U-shaped object.

GVF field is an extern force field that has much larger capture range than any other field based gradient has. It diffuses the gradient vectors of an edge map computed from the image. For a 2D image, GVF vector $\mathrm{V(x,y)=(u(x,y),v(x,y))}$ is defined by minimizing the energy functional,

$$E=\iint \mu\nabla^2 V+|\nabla f|^2 |V-\nabla f|^2 \, dxdy \tag{1}$$

Where edge map *f(x, y)* derived from image and has the similar style as the common extern forces of active contour model.

To minimize the energy functional, *V* is set to be ∇f when $|\nabla f|$ is large for the second term dominates the functional. The functional is dominated by the first term when $|\nabla f|$ is small and V can be slowly-varying vector to get lower energy. GVF vector is nearly equal to the gradient of edge map when it is near the edge and then diffuses to the homogeneous regions away from the edges.

As shown in the definition of GVF, edge map *f(x, y)* is a scalar field. In order to calculate GVF vector of color data, the GVF vector can be solved by using the calculus of variations:

$$\begin{cases} u(X,t) = \mu\nabla^2 u(X,t) - (u(X,t) - f_x)(f_x^{\ 2} + f_y^{\ 2}) \\ v(X,t) = \mu\nabla^2 v(X,t) - (v(X,t) - f_y)(f_x^{\ 2} + f_y^{\ 2}) \end{cases} \tag{2}$$

In Equation(2), only the partial derivatives of the edge map *f* are used. So the GVF model can be extended to vector data field if the partial derivatives of the edge map are given.

Considering that most common color spaces have three components, we suppose the edge map is $f = (f_1, f_2, f_3)$. We define the distance of two vectors in the color space as in [10]: $f(X) - f(Y) = \sqrt{(f_1(X) - f_1(Y))^2 + (f_2(X) - f_2(Y))^2 + (f_3(X) - f_3(Y))^2}$, so

$$\begin{aligned} f_x &= \lim_{h\to 0}\left(\frac{f(x+h, y) - f(x, y)}{h}\right) = \pm\sqrt{\left(\frac{\partial}{\partial x} f_1\right)^2 + \left(\frac{\partial}{\partial x} f_2\right)^2 + \left(\frac{\partial}{\partial x} f_3\right)^2}\,, \\ f_y &= \lim_{h\to 0}\left(\frac{f(x, y+h) - f(x, y)}{h}\right) = \pm\sqrt{\left(\frac{\partial}{\partial y} f_1\right)^2 + \left(\frac{\partial}{\partial y} f_2\right)^2 + \left(\frac{\partial}{\partial y} f_3\right)^2} \end{aligned} \tag{3}$$

In equation (3), the sign of partial derivatives need to be confirmed. In this paper we introduce the partial derivatives of a reference scalar image *fa* as an auxiliary data, and assign the sign of *fa* to that of f_x and f_y. We take the gray component of RGB, I component of HSI and L component of CIELUV as the auxiliary image respectively. This approach is feasible because the auxiliary images stand for luminary in their respective color space.

3 GVF Transfer Function

The design of the transfer function is to classify each voxel into different types. For scalar data, the most common method to classify the voxel is to segment data according to the data intensity. But for vector data, especially color image data of human organize, there are no automatic and reliable approach to segment or classify the all the materials. One of the most useful classification methods is by human interaction, marking and editing the materials little by little according to the professional knowledge of the corresponding field. But in fact it is a time-consuming and tedious work. Design of transfer function which maps the image color or intensity to opacity value, is a substitute way and has been proofed to be efficient.

The choice of the color space is very important for transfer function. In [10], the color vector distance and gradient are defined to design transfer function in RGB and CIELUV color space. The general opacity in the rending process is as $opacity = (vo * s)^{exp}$, where s is a factor, exp is an exponent coefficient, and vo is gradient magnitude.

The basic idea of our approach is to take the magnitude of the GVF vector as the desired transfer function. We first choose a proper color space. And then produce an edge map. Finally we map the GVF vector derived from the edge map to opacity transfer function.

As discussed in section 3, GVF transfer function has the following properties. First, it captures boundary of the image where gets a small opacity value. The much stronger the boundary is (it means that the gradient magnitude is large), the bigger opacity value is. Second, GVF transfer function diffuses the edge gradient to the slow-varying region. From equation (1) we know that each GVF vector is dependent to the vectors in the region nearby, and GVF transfer function is a global function and robust to the noise. On the other hand, the gradient function is local function, and each gradient vector is calculated only by the data in its neighborhood.

4 Results and Discussion

We introduce RGB, CIELUV and HSI color space in this paper. As opacity is some dependent to luminance and the human's ocular system is more sensitive to luminance than color's thickness, L component of LUV and I component of HIS are fit for designing the transfer function.

We take some notations to denote the different kinds of transfer functions. *X-G* represents gradient magnitude of *X* component. For instant, *L-G* is gradient magnitude of L component. *X-GVF* stands for magnitude of GVF vector whose edge map is gradient magnitude of X component, and *X-GVF2* denotes magnitude of GVF vector whose edge map is X component. *X-GVF* and *X-GVF2* differ from their edge maps.

In HSI color space, $I \in [0,255]$ and $H, S \in [0,1]$. I component is the principal component and H and S component can be neglected. The transfer function pairs such as (*HSI-G, I-G*), (*HSI-GVF, I-GVF*) have the similar visual effects.

In the following experiments we firstly render some regular geometry volume objects. Then we apply our approach to human organ volume data.

4.1 Simple Object

Our first experimental materials are some regular volume objects. They are circle, rectangle and textured rectangle annulations, as shown in Fig. 1.

The gradient effect only exists in the region several voxels around the edge and gradient transfer function only captures the edge, as shown in Fig. 2a. On the contrary, GVF diffuses edge gradient to the homogeneous region away from the edges. The opacity is large in the immediate vicinity of edges, and the visual effect is much better, as shown in Fig. 2b.

a. circle b. rectangle c. textured

Fig. 1. Source images

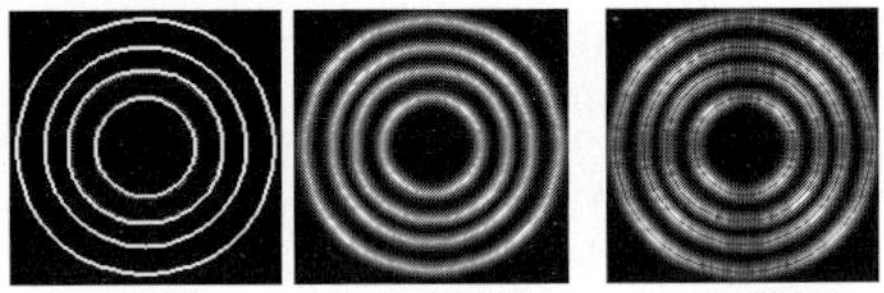

a. *I-G* b. *I-GVF2* c. *I-GVF*

Fig. 2. Circle

X-GVF transfer function is gradient magnitude is anisotropic. Gradient operator is anisotropic in numerical algorithm and calculating the gradient is an important step in the GVF. When the edge map is processed by gradient operator, the anisotropy is accumulated. The rendering results show the unhomogeneity of *X-GVF* transfer function, as in Fig. 2c, while X-GVF2 transfer is much better (Shown in Fig. 2b).

GVF weakens the edges whose gradient magnitude is small. As discussed in section 3, E is mainly dominated by the smooth term when $|\nabla f|$ is small. We apply a transform $f_{out} = (f_{in})^{coeff}$ to the edge map to enhance the weak edge. When $coeff < 1$, the weak edge is enhanced. Shown in Fig. 3, Fig. 3a is the map of I-GVF and Fig. 3b-d are the figures of I-GVF whose transform coefficients are 1, 1.5, 0.5 respectively. Shown in Fig. 3d, the weak edges in the bottom of the rectangle are enhanced and majority of texture details are maintained.

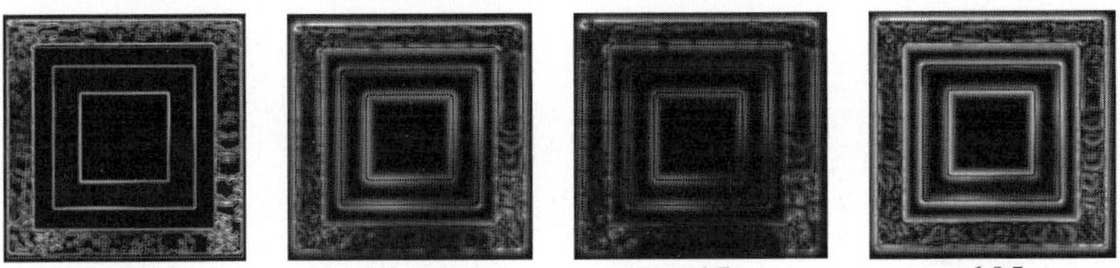

a. I-G b.0 c.1.5 d.0.5

Fig. 3. Enhance edges

The final rendering results are shown in Fig. 4.

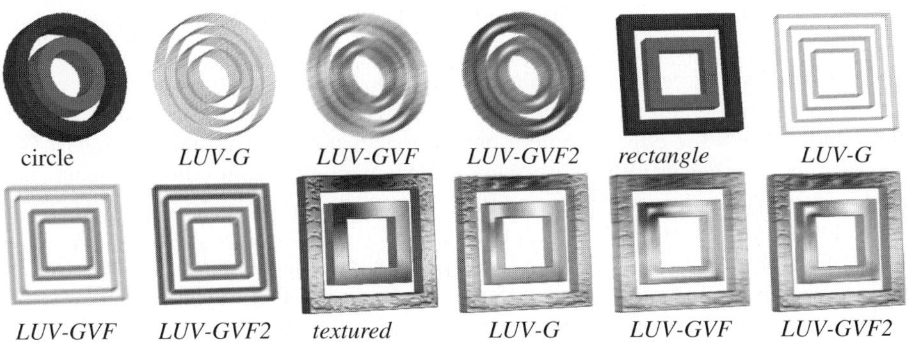

Fig. 4. Rendering results

4.2 Volume Data

We take takes 128 slices from the thorax section of the Male data set of VHP(slice 1300 to slice 1427) to form a volume data with size 587*341*128.

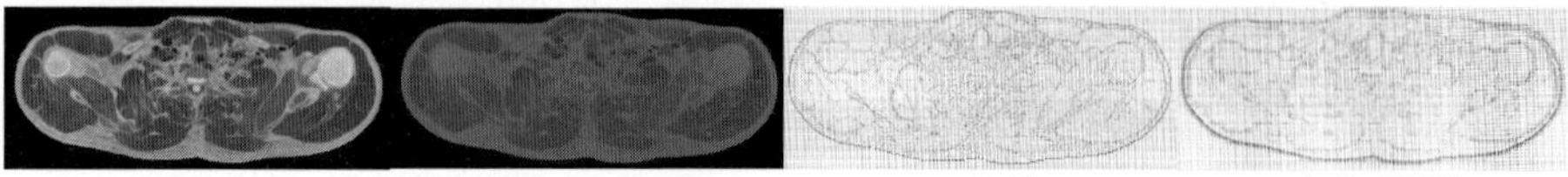

a. source b. L component c. *L-G* d. *L-GVF*

Fig. 5. VHP slice

To explore the effectiveness of our transfer functions, we choose a slice (slice 1300, shown in Fig 5-a) to test our approach. Fig. 5b is L component of the slice and Fig. 5c is the gradient of L component. Comparing gradient vector map with GVF vector map (Fig. 5d), gradient snaps more weak edges, while GVF catches the strong edges and diffuses the edges gradient. The edges of GVF vector map look much "thicker". Observing the close-up figures of *L-G* and *L-GVF* in Fig. 6, gradient vectors are much disordered while GVF vectors look more regular and uniform.

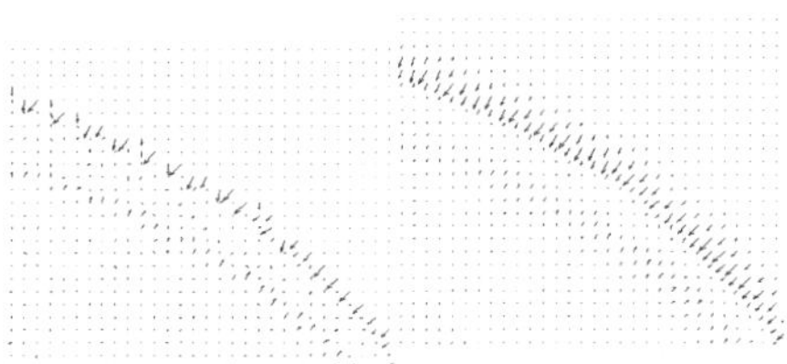

a. close-up of *L-G* b. close-up of *L-GVF*

Fig. 6. Close-up

We first give some volume rendering results without any special transfer function, as shown in Fig. 7a. And the rendering results with transfer function *L-G* are shown in Fig. 7b. The information in gradient transfer function includes the most of stronger edges and lots of weak edges, which makes the large edges inconspicuous and the little edges indistinct because of too many edges and little discrimination.

Compared with gradient transfer function, GVF transfer function captures the large edges and diffuses the edges gradient, which makes a special visual effect. The GVF transfer functions, especially those whose edge maps are from color intensity, have good uniformity because of diffusion effect.

As discussed in section 4.1, a transform can be taken to the input edge maps. In Fig. 7c-f, GVF transfer functions in the same row are the same types, but their edge maps have been transformed with different coefficients. The transform coefficient in the first column is less than that in the second column. Comparing the rendering results, we can find that *X-GVF2* with larger transform coefficient has better visual

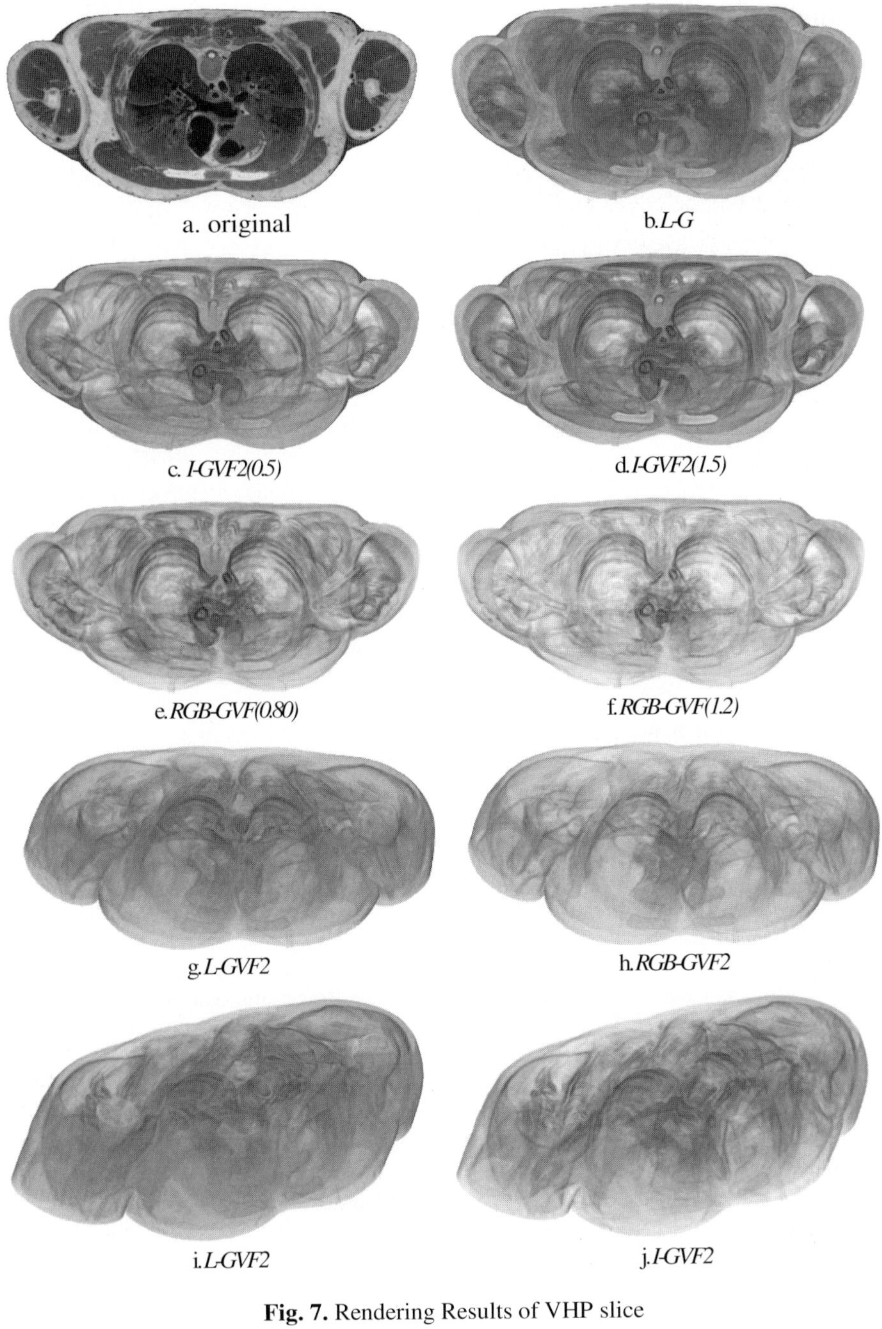

Fig. 7. Rendering Results of VHP slice

effect, while smaller pre-transform coefficient produces better *X-GVF* transfer function. From the results, we also know *X-GVF2* transfer function is better than *X-GVF*. Fig 7g-j shows other rendering results of our VHP data.

5 Conclusion

In this paper, we design opacity transfer function based on GVF vector magnitude. The experiment shows that choosing the approximate color space, component, and pre-transform coefficient, GVF transfer function is better than that based on gradient magnitude. GVF transfer function captures and enhances the large edges and diffuses them, which make the edges look "thick".

Acknowledgment. This work was funded by National Key Basic Research Plan (grant No: 2004CB318006) and National Natural Sciences Plan (grant No: 30471744, 60573154). All the research work is conducted on Dawn 4000A Server Platform of Institute of Computing Technology, Chinese Academy of Sciences. And Mrs. Jingcai Shi gives us a lot of useful help.

References

1. Peter Shirley and Allan Tuchman. Volume visualization methods for scientific computing.
2. Bernhard Geiger. Three-dimensional modeling of human organs and its application to diagnosis and surgical planning. PhD thesis, INRIA, France, 1993.
3. William E. Lorenson and Harvey Cline. Marching cubes: A high-resolution 3D surface construction algorithm. In Proceedings of SIGGRAPH 1987, pages 163--169, 1987.
4. Milnor, J. W. *Morse Theory*. Princeton, NJ: Princeton University Press, 1963
5. M. Levoy. Display of surfaces from volume data. IEEE Computer Graphics and Applications, vol. 8, no. 5, pp: 29--37, May 1988.
6. L. Westover, Footprint evaluation for volume rendering. Computer graphics, vol. 24, no. 4, 1990.
7. T. Todd Elvins. A Survey of Algorithms for Volume Visualization. Computer Graphics, Volume 26, Number 3, August 1992, pp. 194-201.
8. Pfister, H., Lorensen, B., Bajaj, C., Kindlmann, G., Schroeder, W., Avila, L. S., Martin, K., Machiraju, R., Lee, J.: The transfer function bake-off. IEEE Comput. Graphics Appl. 21,3 (2001), 16--22.
9. G.Sapiro and D.L.Ringach, "Anisotropic Diffusion of Multivalued Images with Applications to Color Filtering," IEEE Trans. Image Processing, vol. 5, no. 11, pp. 1582-1586, 1996.
10. D.S. Ebert, C.J. Morris, P. Rheingans, and T.S. Yoo. Designing effective transfer functions for volume rendering from photographic volumes. IEEE Transactions on Visualization and Computer Graphics, 8(2):183--197, June 2002.
11. C. Xu and J.L. Prince, "Snakes, Shapes, and Gradient Vector Flow," IEEE Trans. Pattern Analysis and Machine Intelligence, vol. 7, no. 3, pp. 359-369, Mar. 1998.
12. M. Kass, A. Witkin, and D. Terzopoulos, "Snakes: Active contour models," Int'l J. Computer Vision, vol. 1, pp. 321-331, 1987.

Quasi-physical Simulation of Large-Scale Dynamic Forest Scenes

Long Zhang, Chengfang Song, Qifeng Tan, Wei Chen*, and Qunsheng Peng

State Key Lab of CAD&CG, Zhejiang University, 310027, Hangzhou, China
{lzhang, songchengfang, tanqifeng, chenwei, peng}@cad.zju.edu.cn

Abstract. This paper presents a quasi-physically based approach for interactively simulating large-scale dynamic forest scenes under different wind conditions. We introduce theories from the *wind engineering*, and model the natural wind field as a stationary stochastic process. To reduce the geometry complexities without sacrificing much image quality, we adopt a hybrid geometry/image representation scheme to faithfully model the appearance of trees. Some simplified mechanical rules are employed to compute the movement of such tree models. Three kinds of level of details concerning the scene geometry, the movement of trees and the wind field, are exploited to accelerate the simulation. For forest scenes with tens of thousands of animated trees, our implementation with programable graphics hardware achieves visually plausible results at interactive frame rates on consumer PC platforms.

1 Introduction

Over the past decade, simulation of natural phenomena has become an indispensable requirement for a wide variety of applications including environment assessment, video games and virtual reality. One of the hot research topics is the modeling and rendering of large-scale forest scenes. Although lots of approaches have been extensively studied, the rapidly growing demands on the scene complexity, the physical fidelity and the visual realism, still overwhelm the capabilities of current solutions.

The major difficulty of the simulation of large-scale dynamic forest scenes is of course due to the high complexity in both geometry and appearance. Few previous approaches can simultaneously meet the requirements of both interactive rendering speed and high image quality. In time-critical applications such as video games, one common way is to represent trees with billboards. This technique provides extremely high rendering speed yet poor image quality, and apparently, cannot support animations of trees. On the other hand, if the image quality is of primary importance, one may rely on detailed geometric models of trees. However, as millions of triangles are required to faithfully represent the shape details of one tree, accurate simulation of physical behavior of a forest under the wind seems to be a formidable task on today's PC.

* Corresponding author.

H.-P. Seidel, T. Nishita, and Q. Peng (Eds.): CGI 2006, LNCS 4035, pp. 735–742, 2006.

In this paper, we propose a quasi-physically based approach for interactive animation of large-scale forest scenes under adjustable wind conditions. Our contributions lie in several aspects. Firstly, we introduce a physical fidelity model of the wind field for realistic tree animations. Secondly, we provide simplifications for both the geometric model and physical rules, which greatly reduces the simulation cost. Lastly, we exploit novel LOD techniques which efficiently simplifies the computation involved in tree animations.

2 Related Work

There are a variety of well-established approaches for modeling trees. Lindenmayer and Prusinkiewicz[1] introduced the L-system to construct the geometric models of plants. Thereafter, Aono and Kunii[2] improved this method for 3D cases. The fractal approach by Oppenheimer[3] provides another solution for plant modeling. All these methods are based on the common assumption that complex plant geometry may be approximated with simple rules plus stochastic variation. Emphasizing the overall geometrical structure of tree, Weber and Penn[4] presented a parameterized procedural model which provides a more direct and intuitive control interface over the shape of trees.

Image-based rendering techniques have demonstrated advantage that the resultant models are independent of the geometric complexity. Recently, the Billboard Clouds technique was introduced to simplify the plant models by Bromberg[5]. Though they achieve high image quality, they cannot support dynamic simulations of large-scale forest under different wind conditions.

Much work has been conducted well on the dynamic simulation of trees. Ono[6] proposed to adopt Perlin noise to generate the turbulence and calculate the motion of tree based on mass-spring model. Sakaguchi *et al*[7] assumed branch segments as rigid sticks, calculated the rotation of each branch independently and integrate all movements for the motion of a whole tree. By representing the wind forces as $1/f^{\beta}$ noise, Ota *et al*[8] modeled branches as cantilever flat-springs and computed the rotations of leaves by using $1/f^{\beta}$ noise function directly. Coupling stochastic approaches and dynamics equation, Shinya and Fournier[9] synthesized realistic motion of trees, grass and snow under the influence of the wind field. Likewise, Stam[10] synthesized turbulence by filtering a white noise in the Fourier domain and solve the displacements directly. Giacomo *et al* [11] combined procedural approach and physically based method to animate a moderate sized forest. Recently developed commercial software SpeedTree[12] provides appealing results for real-time walk-through of large-scale forest scenes.

3 Construction of the Wind Field

We derive a wind field model from the wind engineering. The key component of our model is a stochastic process that faithfully mimics the stochastic properties of the wind field. This contributes to the visual and physical realism of the trees swaying in the wind.

Wind Velocity Vector: From the viewpoint of the mechanics, the velocity vector of a three-dimensional air flow is composed of three orthogonal components [13], namely, the longitudinal component $U(t)$ along the mean wind direction, the lateral component $V(t)$, and the vertical component $W(t)$. $U(t)$ is the sum of the mean component, denoted by $\bar{U}(z)$ and fluctuating component, while $V(t)$ and $W(t)$ have only fluctuating components. The wind velocity at point $\mathbf{Q}(x, y, z)$ can be represented as:

$$U(\mathbf{Q};t)=\bar{U}(z)+u(\mathbf{Q};t), \quad V(\mathbf{Q};t)=v(\mathbf{Q};t), \quad W(\mathbf{Q};t)=w(\mathbf{Q};t) \tag{1}$$

Cross-Power Spectrum Density Matrix: We model each fluctuating component of the velocity vector by a stationary Gaussian stochastic process. Their spatial-temporal properties in the frequency domain are represented by Cross-Power Spectral Density Matrix($CPSDM$):

$$\mathbf{S}_\epsilon(\omega) = \begin{bmatrix} s_{\epsilon_1\epsilon_1}(\omega) & s_{\epsilon_1\epsilon_2}(\omega) & \dots & s_{\epsilon_1\epsilon_n}(\omega) \\ s_{\epsilon_2\epsilon_1}(\omega) & s_{\epsilon_2\epsilon_2}(\omega) & \dots & s_{\epsilon_2\epsilon_n}(\omega) \\ \vdots & \vdots & \ddots & \vdots \\ s_{\epsilon_n\epsilon_1}(\omega) & s_{\epsilon_n\epsilon_2}(\omega) & \dots & s_{\epsilon_n\epsilon_n}(\omega) \end{bmatrix} \qquad (\epsilon = u, v, w) \tag{2}$$

where ω is the angular frequency, and $s_{\epsilon_j\epsilon_k}$ is the cross-power spectrum density:

$$s_{\epsilon_j\epsilon_k}(\omega)=\sqrt{s_{\epsilon_j\epsilon_j}(\omega)s_{\epsilon_k\epsilon_k}(\omega)}\, Coh(\mathbf{Q}_j, \mathbf{Q}_k; \omega) \tag{3}$$

Each $s_{\epsilon_j\epsilon_j}$ is normally represented by various formula which serve different applications[14]. After investigating all representations collected by Solari *et al*[15], we derive a new unified form: which serves for assessing and choosing the coefficients suitable to our case.

$$s_{\epsilon_j\epsilon_k}(\omega) = \frac{U_*^2 A_\epsilon \nu^\gamma}{(\omega/2\pi)[1 + B_\epsilon \nu^\alpha]^\beta} \tag{4}$$

where $\nu=\omega z/2\pi\bar{U}(z)$ is the Monin coordinate, U_* is the shear velocity, and A_ϵ, B_ϵ, α, β, γ are adjustable coefficients.

The coherence function (Coh) in Equation 3 is expressed as follows:

$$Coh(\mathbf{Q}_j, \mathbf{Q}_k; \omega)=\exp\left\{-\frac{\omega \sum_r C_{r\epsilon} \mid r_j - r_k \mid}{\pi\left[\bar{U}_j + \bar{U}_k\right]}\right\} \qquad (r=x, y, z) \tag{5}$$

Here, $C_{r\epsilon}$ is the exponential decay coefficient.

Evaluation of Wind Velocity: In most cases, $CPSDM$ is real symmetric and positive definite. Thus we decompose it using the Choleski method:

$$\mathbf{S}_\epsilon(\omega)=\mathbf{H}(\omega)\,\mathbf{H}^*(\omega)^T \tag{6}$$

where $\mathbf{H}(\omega)$ is a lower triangular matrix. Then the fluctuating component at time t can be expressed as:

$$\epsilon_i(\mathbf{Q}_i;t) = 2\sum_{j=1}^{N}\sum_{k=1}^{i}\left[h_{ik}(\omega_j)G_j^{(k)}(t)\right]\sqrt{\Delta\omega} \qquad (\epsilon = u,v,w)\ (i = 1,2,...,n) \quad (7)$$

where $\omega_j{=}j\Delta\omega$, $N\Delta\omega{=}\omega_u$ is the upper cut-off frequency. $G_j^{(k)}$ is a random value.

Finally, the wind force at $\mathbf{Q}(x,y,z)$ can be calculated as:

$$\mathbf{F}(\mathbf{Q};t) = \tfrac{1}{2}\rho \left\|\mathbf{T}\right\| \cdot \mathbf{T}, \quad \mathbf{T} = (U,V,W) \quad (8)$$

where ρ is the air density.

4 Quasi-physically Based Animation of Trees

Our quasi-physically based animation scheme is based on a hybrid geometry/image representation of trees.

4.1 The Hybrid Representation of Trees

Conceptually a tree consists of branches and leaves. Branches are represented by geometry primitives with associated textures. Leaves are clustered and represented as a list of billboards. Compared with traditional pure geometry based or pure image based representations, our hybrid tree representation is a good balance in terms of rendering quality and efficiency. Figure 1(a) illustrates an example with the proposed hybrid representation.

Models with the hybrid representation can be derived from existing tree models conveniently. In practice, we build a parametric modeling system to generate various tree models. The adopted parameters that control the shape of the branches are similar to those introduced by Weber and Penn[4]. Leaf clusters are generated around the branches. Each leaf cluster is tied to a branch at a hanging point. The distribution of leaf clusters are determined by global parameters. The textures for the leaf billboards can be taken from real captured images or created by artists.

4.2 Quasi-physically Based Animation

We approximate the movement of branches with a set of rigid transformations. Each branch is split into several *segments*. Each segment is assumed to be rigid and can only rotate around the *joint* which links itself either to its parent branch or to its predecessor. Each joint defines a local frame in which the z axis directs to its child segment. We animate the branches by manipulating the local frames of each joint. The damping angular spring model is adopted to compute the transformation matrices. Figure 1(b) shows the distortion of a branch with three segments during the animation.

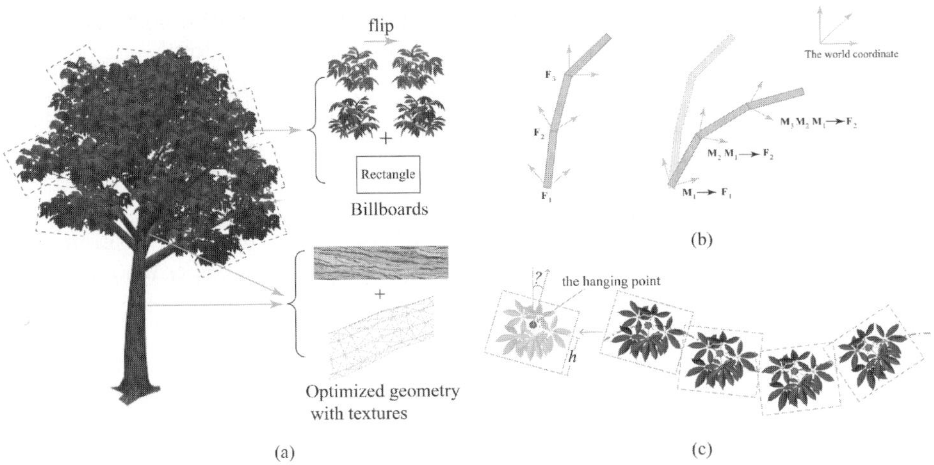

Fig. 1. Quasi-physically based animation of trees: (a) the hybrid representation of trees; (b) branch animation; (c) animation of leaf clusters

The movement of the leaves are primarily driven by that of the host branches. Furthermore, the leaves may vibrate due to the blowing of the wind. We simply model this type of motion as a periodically clockwise swaying, i.e., each leaf swings around its hanging point. Both the frequency and the swing are dependent on the wind strength, which are estimated with simple empirical formulas. The animation scheme is demonstrated in Fig.1(c).

4.3 Level of Details

We introduce three kinds of level of detail representations for the scene geometry, the movement of trees and the wind field. The appropriate level regarding each aspect is determined by multiple criteria, including the distance to the viewpoint, the visual importance and the priority of the image quality.

Geometry LOD. We build the LODs for branches and leaf clusters in a separate way. Geometry simplification of branches is accomplished by dropping relatively smaller branches. The resultant variance of the overall shapes can hardly be noticed in practice since small branches are usually covered by the leaves and hence attract little attentions.

Geometry simplification for leaf clusters are performed by consolidating neighboring leaves, which yields a set of reduced leaves. In order to keep the fullness of the tree, we enlarge the remaining leaf clusters by an adjustable ratio. For the sake of performance we use the same leaf textures for lower level models. Smooth transition of consecutive LODs is obtained using an image-space blending technique.

Animation LOD. Since the main cost to compute the tree movement lies in updating the local frames, we simplify the computation by deactivating related joints, whose local frames are not recomputed during the animation. Deactivating a joint means to omit the local distortions caused by its rotation.

We assign a priority to each joint, which is estimated by the total mass of the branches it controls. When an active joint is to be deactivated or vice versa, smooth transitions are performed by blending its transformation matrix with identity matrix.

Wind-Field LOD. We generate the wind fields in a mipmap fashion. For trees far from the view point, we adopt the coarse version, with which lots of trees suffer from the same average wind force. This is amenable for instance-based simulation, which is popular in vegetation rendering. For all instances of one tree suffering from a same wind force, they share a same distortion. When zooming in or zooming out, smooth transitions are accomplished by interpolating corresponding transformation matrices.

5 Experimental Results

We have implemented our approach with OpenGL 1.5. All experiments were performed on a PC with AMD AthlonXP 3000+ CPU (1.8 GHZ), 512 MB RAM and NVidia 6600 GT video card.

5.1 Calculation of the Wind Velocity

In our experiments, we employed the *Blunt models* proposed in[14] to calculate the wind velocity. The coefficients for the wind power spectrum density are set to: $\alpha=1, \beta=5/3, \gamma=1$, the other three coefficients for different fluctuating components are shown in Table 1. The values of exponential decay coefficients in coherency functions are listed in Table 2.

Table 1. Coefficients for power spectrum density of three components

A_u	B_u	A_v	B_v	A_w	B_w
252.625	60.62	53.76	20.16	5.125	4.92

Table 2. Exponential decay coefficients for coherency functions

C_{xu}	C_{yu}	C_{zu}	C_{xv}	C_{yv}	C_{zv}	C_{xw}	C_{yw}	C_{zw}
3.0	19.7	9.5	6.0	12.0	7.0	0.5	7.5	3.7

We divide the scenes into 100×100 cells and compute the wind velocity vector at each cell. The time for calculating the array of velocity vectors for one frame is $50ms$. It costs 144 MB memory space to store the data of one wind velocity field for 1000 frames. Normally, we need pre-compute the wind velocity fields for 1000∼2000 frames and save them as three dimensional arrays.

5.2 Rendering of Forest Scenes

We have tested four forest scenes (denoted by A, B, C and D)with different scene complexities. The snapshots for C and D are shown in Fig.2. Under given wind condition, these scenes can be displayed interactively with physically plausible behaviors. Table 3 lists the performance statistics for the four scenes. The second row reports the number of trees. The frame rates achieved by disabling one of the three LOD techniques are reported in the third, fourth and fifth rows. By integrating all these techniques, our adaptive rendering scheme achieves up to 1000% performance improvement, as shown in the last row.

Fig. 2. The snapshots of one forest scene at the image resolution of 1024 × 768

Table 3. The rendering performance in FPS. The image resolution is 1024 × 768.

Scene	A	B	C	D
#Tree	1000	3000	10000	50000
Without Geometry LOD	15.3	9.5	3.9	1.0
Without Animation LOD	14.9	11.6	7.4	2.1
Without Wind-Field LOD	7.8	3.4	1.1	0.2
With all LODs	20.0	14.5	8.3	2.2

6 Conclusions and Future Work

In this paper we present a quasi-physically based approach for animating large-scale forest scenes under various wind conditions. Our approach achieves interactive frame rates when simulating dynamic forest scenes with tens of thousands of trees.

In the future, we would like to take the mutual influence of trees into consideration, such as attenuation and reduction of wind forces. In addition, we want to study more accurate (efficient) animation schemes for close (distant) trees.

Acknowledgments

This work is partially supported by 973 program of China (No.2002CB312100), NSF of China for Innovative Research Groups (No.60021201), Zhejiang Provincial Natural Science Fund (No.Y105269), National Natural Science Fund of China (No.60303028) and Zhejiang Provincial Natural Science Special Fund for Youth Scientists' Cultivation (No.R603046).

References

1. P.Prusinkiewicz, A.Lindenmayer: The Algorithmic Beauty of Plants. Springer-Verlag, New York (1990)
2. M.Aono, T.Kunii: Botanical tree image generation. IEEE Computer Graphics and Application **4**(5) (1984) 10–34
3. P.E.Oppenheimer: Real time design and animation of fractal plants and tree. Computer Graphics (Proc. of ACM SIGGRAPH'1986) **20**(4) (1986) 55–64
4. J.Weber, J.Penn: Creation and rendering of realistic tree. In: Proceedings of ACM SIGGRAPH 1995, Los Angeles, CA (1995) 119–128
5. Behrendt, S., Colditz, C., Franzke, O., Kopf, J., Deussen, O.: Realistic real-time rendering of landscapes using billboard clouds. In: Proceedings of Eurographics 2005, Ireland (2005) 507–516
6. H.Ono: Practical experience in the physical animation and destruction of trees. In: Eurographics Workshop on Animation and Simulation 1997, Budapest, Hungary (1997) 149–159
7. T.Sakaguchi, J.Ohya: Modeling and animation of botanical tree for interactive virtual environment. In: Proceedings of ACM Symposium on Virtual Reality Software and Technology (ACM/VRST99). (1999) 139–146
8. Ota, S., Tamura, M., Fujimoto, T., Muraoka, K., Chiba, N.: A hybrid method for real-time animation of trees swaying in wind fields. The Visual Computer **20**(10) (2004) 613–623
9. M.Shinya, A.Fournier: Stochastic motion-motion under the influence of wind. In: Proceedings of Eurographics 1992. (1992) 119–128
10. J.Stam: Simulating the effects of turbulence on flexible structures. In: Proceedings of Eurographics 1997. (1997) 159–164
11. T.D.Giacomo, S.Capo, F.Faure: An interactive forest. In: Eurographics Workshop on Animation and Simulation 2001. (2001) 65–74
12. Interactive Data Visualization Inc.: SpeedTree product homepage. (2004)
13. E.Simiu, R.H.Scanlan: Wind Effects on Structures(2nd Edition). Wiley, New York (1985)
14. H.W.Tieleman: Universality of velocity spectra. Journal of Wind Engineering and Industrial Aerodynamics **56** (1995) 55–69
15. G.Solari, G.Piccardo: Probabilistic 3-d turbulence modeling for gust buffeting of structures. Probabilistic Engineering Mechanics **16** (2001) 73–86

Properties of G1 Continuity Conditions Between Two B-Spline Surfaces

Nailiang Zhao[1] and Weiyin Ma[2]

[1] Hangzhou Dianzi University, Hangzhou, Zhejiang, 310018, P.R. China
znl@hziee.edu.cn
[2] City University of Hong Kong, Kowloon, Hong Kong SAR, China
mewma@cityu.edu.hk

Abstract. This paper addresses some properties of G^1 continuity conditions between two B-spline surfaces with arbitrary degrees and generally structured knots. Key issues addressed in the paper include necessary G^1 continuity conditions between two B-spline surfaces, general connecting functions, continuities of the general connecting functions, and intrinsic conditions of the general connecting functions along the common boundary. In general, one may use piecewise polynomial functions, i.e. B-spline functions, as connecting functions for G^1 connection of two B-spline surfaces. Based on the work reported in this paper, some recent results in literature using linear connecting functions are special cases of the general connecting functions reported in this paper. In case that the connecting functions are global linear functions along the common boundary commonly used in literature, the common boundary degenerates as a Bézier curve for proper G^1 connection. Several examples for connecting two uniform biquadratic B-spline surfaces with G^1 continuity are also presented to demonstrate the results.

1 Introduction

Non-uniform rational B-splines (NURBS) are by far the most popular representation and the de-facto standard for computer aided design and manufacturing (CAD/CAM). Nevertheless, it is still awkward for practical modelling using multiple B-spline surfaces with continuity requirement. To our knowledge, most of the published work on continuity conditions focuses on Bézier surfaces [1] and only a few directly address the continuity connection of adjacent B-spline surfaces.

Among the publications in connection of B-spline surfaces, Milroy et al proposed a procedure for achieving approximate global G^1 continuity [2]. Ma et al improved this method in [3] and produced exact and high-order continuity conditions, except near extraordinary corner positions where approximate G^1 continuity condition is achieved. Another approach was developed by Eck and Hoppe for automatic construction of a special kind of B-spline surfaces from unorganized points with exact G^1 continuity [4]. Piegl and Tiller also presented an algorithm for generating a collection of G^ε continuous NURBS surfaces that fill

H.-P. Seidel, T. Nishita, and Q. Peng (Eds.): CGI 2006, LNCS 4035, pp. 743–752, 2006.

an arbitrary n-sided region [5]. More recently, Shi et al discussed the geometric continuity conditions of biquartic, biquintic and bicubic B-spline surfaces respectively with single interior knots and linear connecting functions [6, 7, 8]. Che et al also provided the necessary and sufficient conditions of G^1 continuity for connecting two adjacent NURBS surfaces with arbitrary degrees, and presented two kinds of sufficient conditions with special connecting functions [9].

In this paper, we further study the properties of G^1 continuity conditions of two B-spline surfaces with arbitrary degrees, generally structured knots and general connecting functions. We also analyze the continuity of general connecting functions and the intrinsic conditions imposed to general connecting functions along the common boundary. The study leads to better understanding of G^1 continuity conditions for B-spline surfaces and the results are also easy to implement.

2 Definitions and Preliminaries

We first define two B-spline surfaces $B(u, v)$ and $C(u, s)$ for later discussions on G^1 continuity conditions. Without the lost of generality, we assume that the parametric directions of the two surfaces are shown in Fig. 1. We assume that the two surfaces share the same degree and the same set of knots for the common u-boundary, $B(u, 0)$ or $C(u, 0)$. In case of incompatible knots for the u-direction, one may apply degree elevation and knots refinement algorithms before further processing.

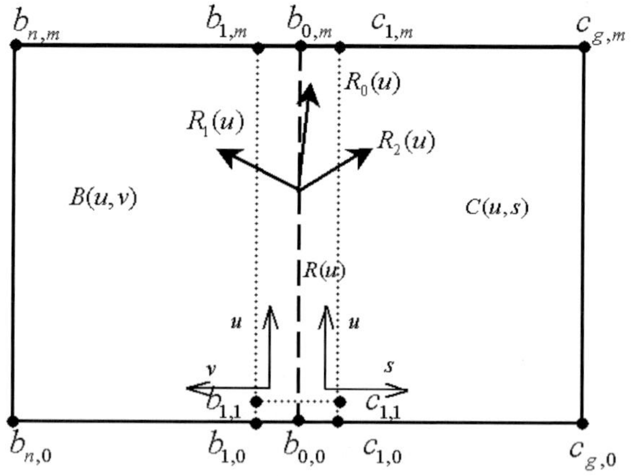

Fig. 1. The layout of two adjacent B-spline surfaces

One of the B-spline surfaces $B(u, v)$ can be defined by the following equation

$$B(u, v) = \sum_{i=0}^{m} \sum_{j=0}^{n} b_{i,j} N_{i,p}(u) N_{j,q}(v) \tag{1}$$

where $(u, v) \in [0, 1] \times [0, 1]$. It can be uniquely defined by its degrees p and q, a set of bidirectional control points $\{b_{i,j} \in R^3\}_{i=0,j=0}^{m,n}$, and two sets of normalized

B-spline basis functions $N_{i,p}(u), i = 0, 1, ..., m$ and $N_{j,q}(v), j = 0, 1, ..., n$ based on the following non-periodic knot sequences

$$U = \{\underbrace{u_0 = 0, .., 0}_{p+1}, \underbrace{u_1, .., u_1}_{k_1}, .., \underbrace{u_{\tilde{m}}, .., u_{\tilde{m}}}_{k_{\tilde{m}}}, \underbrace{u_{\tilde{m}+1} = 1, .., 1}_{p+1}\}$$

$$V = \{\underbrace{v_0 = 0, .., 0}_{q+1}, \underbrace{v_1, .., v_1}_{\tilde{k}_1}, .., \underbrace{v_{\tilde{n}}, .., v_{\tilde{n}}}_{\tilde{k}_{\tilde{n}}}, \underbrace{v_{\tilde{n}+1} = 1, .., 1}_{q+1}\}$$

In the above equation, the symbol $k_l(1 \le k_l < p)$ for $l = 1, 2, ..., \tilde{m}$ is the multiplicity of the interior knot u_l with $0 < u_l < 1, u_{l-1} < u_l < u_{l+1}$ and $m = \sum_{l=1}^{\tilde{m}} k_l + p$. The symbol $\tilde{k}_l(1 \le \tilde{k}_l < q)$ for $l = 1, 2, ..., \tilde{n}$ is the multiplicity of interior knot v_l with $0 < v_l < 1, v_{l-1} < v_l < v_{l+1}$ and $n = \sum_{l=1}^{\tilde{n}} \tilde{k}_l + q$.

In a similar way, one may also define the other B-spline surface $C(u, s)$ for $(u, s) \in [0, 1] \times [0, 1]$ as

$$C(u, s) = \sum_{i=0}^{m} \sum_{j=0}^{g} c_{i,j} N_{i,p}(u) N_{j,r}(s) \tag{2}$$

where $N_{j,r}(s), j = 0, 1, ..., g$ are the basis functions defined on knot sequences

$$S = \{\underbrace{s_0 = 0, .., 0}_{r+1}, \underbrace{s_1, .., s_1}_{\bar{k}_1}, .., \underbrace{s_{\tilde{g}}, .., s_{\tilde{g}}}_{\bar{k}_{\tilde{g}}}, \underbrace{s_{\tilde{g}+1} = 1, .., 1}_{r+1}\}$$

The symbol $\bar{k}_l(1 \le \bar{k}_l < r)$ for $l = 1, 2, ..., \tilde{g}$ is the multiplicity of the interior knot s_l with $0 < s_l < 1, s_{l-1} < s_l < s_{l+1}$ and $g = \sum_{l=1}^{\tilde{g}} \bar{k}_l + r$. From [10], we have

Theorem 1. *Let $B(u, v)$ and $C(u, s)$ be two B-spline surfaces defined by equations (1) and (2) respectively, the sufficient and necessary conditions of G^0 continuity between $B(u, v)$ and $C(u, s)$ is:*

$$b_{i,0} = c_{i,0} \quad i = 0, 1, 2, ..., m \tag{3}$$

Denote $R(u) = B(u, 0) = C(u, 0)$ the common boundary curve of the two connected B-spline surfaces, see Fig. 1. $R(u)$ is a B-spline curve defined on knot sequence U

$$R(u) = \sum_{i=0}^{m} b_{i,0} N_{i,p}(u) \quad u \in [0, 1] \tag{4}$$

Now we define three tangent vector functions on curve $R(u)$ as shown in Fig. 1.

$$\begin{aligned}
R_2(u) &= \left.\frac{\partial C(u,s)}{\partial s}\right|_{s=0} = \frac{r}{s_1} \sum_{i=0}^{m} c_i N_{i,p}(u) = \frac{r}{s_1} \sum_{i=0}^{m} (c_{i,1} - c_{i,0}) N_{i,p}(u) \\
R_1(u) &= \left.\frac{\partial B(u,v)}{\partial v}\right|_{v=0} = \frac{q}{v_1} \sum_{i=0}^{m} b_i N_{i,p}(u) = \frac{q}{v_1} \sum_{i=0}^{m} (b_{i,1} - b_{i,0}) N_{i,p}(u) \\
R_0(u) &= \left.\frac{\partial B(u,v)}{\partial u}\right|_{v=0} = p \sum_{i=0}^{m-1} \frac{d_i}{\bar{u}_{i+p+1} - \bar{u}_{i+1}} N_{i,p-1}(u) = p \sum_{i=0}^{m-1} \frac{(b_{i+1,0} - b_{i,0})}{\bar{u}_{i+p+1} - \bar{u}_{i+1}} N_{i,p-1}(u)
\end{aligned} \tag{5}$$

where $b_i = b_{i,1} - b_{i,0}$, $c_i = c_{i,1} - c_{i,0}$ and $d_i = b_{i+1,0} - b_{i,0}$. $N_{i,p-1}(u), i = 0, 1, ..., m - 1$ are the basis functions defined on nonperiodic knot sequences

$$\bar{U} = \{\underbrace{0, .., 0}_{p}, \underbrace{u_1, .., u_1}_{k_1}, .., \underbrace{u_{\tilde{m}}, .., u_{\tilde{m}}}_{k_{\tilde{m}}}, \underbrace{1, .., 1}_{p}\}$$

Following [9-10], we have the following theorem for B-spline surfaces.

Theorem 2. *Let $B(u, v)$ and $C(u, s)$ be two B-spline surfaces defined by equations (1) and (2) respectively, and satisfy the G^0 continuity conditions (3) of theorem 1. We have then the following sufficient and necessary condition of G^1 continuity between the two surfaces, i.e. there exist three piecewise polynomial functions $\alpha(u)$,$\beta(u)$ and $\gamma(u)$,$u \in [0, 1]$ such that the following equation holds along $R(u)$:*

$$\alpha(u)R_2(u) + \beta(u)R_1(u) + \gamma(u)R_0(u) = 0 \quad u \in [0, 1] \tag{6}$$

where $\alpha(u)\beta(u) < 0$. The knots of the piecewise polynomial functions coincide with the interior knot sequence of U. The degree of $\alpha(u)$,$\beta(u)$ and $\gamma(u)$ are respectively $deg(\alpha(u)) \le 2p - 1$, $deg(\beta(u)) \le 2p - 1$ and $deg(\gamma(u)) \le 2p$.

For convenience, we rewrite equation (6) as follow

$$R_2(u) = f(u)R_1(u) + g(u)R_0(u) \quad u \in [0, 1] \tag{7}$$

where we denote $f(u) = \beta(u)/\alpha(u) > 0$, $g(u) = \gamma(u)/\alpha(u) \neq 0$, and call $f(u)$ and $g(u)$ as connecting functions of two adjacent B-spline surfaces, that is, the tangent vectors $R_0(u)$, $R_1(u)$ and $R_2(u)$ should be on the same tangent plane at any point of the common boundary $R(u)$ to ensure G^1 continuity. For general applications, we always select $f(u)$ and $g(u)$ within each knot interval $U_l = [u_{l-1}, u_l], l = 1, 2, ..., \tilde{m} + 1$ as follows

$$f(u) = \alpha^l > 0, g(u) = \beta^l u + \gamma^l \quad u \in [u_{l-1}, u_l] \tag{8}$$

We call $f(u)$ and $g(u)$ of (8) as piecewise linear connecting functions.

3 Properties of G1 Connected Two B-Spline Surfaces

3.1 Constraints of the Connecting Functions

Following the properties of B-spline surfaces, $R_1(u)$ and $R_2(u)$ are continuous at $u = u_l$ up to C^{p-k_l}, and $R_0(u)$ is continuous at $u = u_l$ up to C^{p-k_l-1}.

Let us assume that $k_l \le p - 1$. If the G^1 continuity has been achieved using equations (3) and (7) along the entire common boundary curve $0 < u < 1$, as a result of the C^0 continuity of the three tangent vectors $\forall u \in [0, 1]$, we have

$$\begin{cases} R_2(u) = f(u^+)R_1(u) + g(u^+)R_0(u) \\ R_2(u) = f(u^-)R_1(u) + g(u^-)R_0(u) \end{cases} \tag{9}$$

Further subtracting the two equations leads to the following equation

$$[f(u^+) - f(u^-)]R_1(u) + [g(u^+) - g(u^-)]R_0(u) = 0 \tag{10}$$

As $R_1(u)$ and $R_0(u)$ are two linearly independent vectors along the common boundary, we can conclude that the connecting functions $f(u)$ and $g(u)$ are also C^0 continuous functions along the entire common boundary, including at all interior knots $u = u_l$, for $l = 1, 2, ..., \tilde{m}$, i.e.

$$f(u_l^-) = f(u_l^+), g(u_l^-) = g(u_l^+) \quad l = 1, 2, ..., \tilde{m} \tag{11}$$

For $j = 1, 2, ..., p - k_l - 1$, we can further evaluate the derivatives of $R_2(u)$ versus u of (9), which yields

$$\frac{\partial^j R_2(u)}{\partial u^j} = \sum_{i=0}^{j} C_j^i \frac{\partial^{(j-i)} f(u)}{\partial u^{(j-i)}} \frac{\partial^i R_1(u)}{\partial u^i} + \sum_{i=0}^{j} C_j^i \frac{\partial^{(j-i)} g(u)}{\partial u^{(j-i)}} \frac{\partial^i R_0(u)}{\partial u^i} \tag{12}$$

where $C_j^i = j!/(i!(j-i!))$.

As a result of the C^{p-k_l} continuity of $R_1(u)$ and $R_2(u)$ and C^{p-k_l-1} continuity of $R_0(u)$ along the entire common boundary $0 < u < 1$, and observing (11) and (12), the connecting functions $f(u)$ and $g(u)$ are C^1 continuous functions following a similar reasoning to obtain (11). With the results of C^0 and C^1 continuities of $f(u)$ and $g(u)$, and observing (11), we further know in a similar way that $f(u)$ and $g(u)$ are also C^2 continuous functions along the entire common boundary. Continue the reasoning further, we can finally conclude that the connecting functions $f(u)$ and $g(u)$ are C^j continuous functions, for $j = 1, 2, ..., p - k_l - 1$, along the entire common boundary including at all interior knots $u = u_l$, for $l = 1, 2, ..., \tilde{m}$, i.e.

$$\left.\frac{\partial^j f(u)}{\partial u^j}\right|_{u=u_l-} = \left.\frac{\partial^j f(u)}{\partial u^j}\right|_{u=u_l+}, \left.\frac{\partial^j g(u)}{\partial u^j}\right|_{u=u_l-} = \left.\frac{\partial^j g(u)}{\partial u^j}\right|_{u=u_l+} \tag{13}$$

Therefore, we have following necessary conditions of G^1 continuity.

Theorem 3. *Let $B(u, v)$ and $C(u, s)$ be two B-spline surfaces defined by equations (1) and (2) respectively, and satisfy the G^1 continuity conditions (3) and (7). The connecting functions $f(u)$ and $g(u)$ should also be C^{p-k_l-1} continuous along the entire common boundary* $[0, 1]$.

As a special case, if $k_l < p - 1$ for $l = 1, 2, ..., \tilde{m}$, the piecewise linear connecting functions of (8) should be the same across all interior knots as follows.

$$R_2(u) = \alpha R_1(u) + (\beta u + \gamma) R_0(u) \quad u \in [0, 1] \tag{14}$$

where $\alpha > 0$ and $\beta^2 + \gamma^2 \neq 0$. We call $f(u) = \alpha$ and $g(u) = \beta u + \gamma$ of (14) linear connecting functions. For example, equation (14) is always true if we adopt single/unique interior knots, $k_l = 1$ for $l = 1, 2, ..., \tilde{m}$, and at least cubic B-spline at u direction, i.e., $p \geq 3$.

3.2 Intrinsic Conditions of the Common Boundary

By setting $j = d = p - k_l$ at an interior knot $u = u_l$ in (12), together with the continuity of functions $R_1(u)$, $R_2(u)$ and $R_0(u)$, and the C^{p-k_l-1} continuity of connecting functions $f(u)$ and $g(u)$ in theorem 3, we have

$$\left(\frac{\partial^{(d)} f(u)}{\partial u^{(d)}}\bigg|_{u=u_l+} - \frac{\partial^{(d)} f(u)}{\partial u^{(d)}}\bigg|_{u=u_l-} \right) R_1(u_l) + \left(\frac{\partial^{(d)} g(u)}{\partial u^{(d)}}\bigg|_{u=u_l+} - \frac{\partial^{(d)} g(u)}{\partial u^{(d)}}\bigg|_{u=u_l-} \right) R_0(u_l) + \left(\frac{\partial^{(d)} R_0(u)}{\partial u^{(d)}}\bigg|_{u=u_l+} - \frac{\partial^{(d)} R_0(u)}{\partial u^{(d)}}\bigg|_{u=u_l-} \right) g(u_l) = 0 \tag{15}$$

It is clear that if the following conditions hold

$$\frac{\partial^{(d)} f(u)}{\partial u^{(d)}}\bigg|_{u=u_l-} = \frac{\partial^{(d)} f(u)}{\partial u^{(d)}}\bigg|_{u=u_l+}, \quad \frac{\partial^{(d)} g(u)}{\partial u^{(d)}}\bigg|_{u=u_l-} = \frac{\partial^{(d)} g(u)}{\partial u^{(d)}}\bigg|_{u=u_l+} \tag{16}$$

then we have

$$\frac{\partial^{(d)} R_0(u)}{\partial u^{(d)}}\bigg|_{u=u_l-} = \frac{\partial^{(d)} R_0(u)}{\partial u^{(d)}}\bigg|_{u=u_l+} \tag{17}$$

Based on above discussion, we can obtain the so-called intrinsic conditions of the common boundary $R(u)$.

Theorem 4. *Let $B(u, v)$ and $C(u, s)$ be two B-spline surfaces defined by equations (1) and (2) respectively, and satisfy the G^1 continuity conditions (3) and (7). If single interior knots are adopted, i.e., $k_1 = k_1 = ... = k_{\tilde{m}} = 1$, and the connecting functions $f(u)$ and $g(u)$ are C^{p-1} continuous, then the common boundary $R(u)$ is a polynomial function with degree p.*

Proof. Let $k_1 = k_1 = ... = k_{\tilde{m}} = 1$ in equations (15), (16) and (17), we have then

$$\frac{\partial^{(p-1)} R_0(u)}{\partial u^{(p-1)}}\bigg|_{u=u_l-} = \frac{\partial^{(p-1)} R_0(u)}{\partial u^{(p-1)}}\bigg|_{u=u_l+} \tag{18}$$

for $l = 1, 2, ..., \tilde{m}$. Following (5), we also have

$$\frac{\partial^{(p)} R(u)}{\partial u^{(p)}}\bigg|_{u=u_l-} = \frac{\partial^{(p)} R(u)}{\partial u^{(p)}}\bigg|_{u=u_l+} \tag{19}$$

□

That is, the common boundary $R(u)$ $u \in [0, 1]$ is a Bézier curve of degree p as follows under the condition (18).

$$R(u) = \sum_{i=0}^{p} \bar{b}_i B_{i,p}(u) \quad u \in [0, 1] \tag{20}$$

where $\{B_{i,p}(u)\}_{i=0}^{p}$ are the Bernstein basis functions with $p-th$ degree. For knot interval $U_l = [u_{l-1}, u_l]$, $l = 1, 2, ..., \tilde{m} + 1$, we denote them as follows

$$R^l(t) = \sum_{i=0}^{p} \bar{b}_i^l B_{i,p}(t) \quad t \in [0, 1] \tag{21}$$

Then the intrinsic conditions (19) of the common boundary $R(u)$ can also be expressed as

$$\Delta^{(p)}\bar{b}_0^{l+1}(u_l - u_{l-1})^{(p)} = \Delta^{(p)}\bar{b}_0^l(u_{l+1} - u_l)^{(p)} \quad l = 1, 2..., \tilde{m} \tag{22}$$

where $\Delta\bar{b}_i^l = \bar{b}_{i+1}^l - \bar{b}_i^l$, $\Delta^{(j)}\bar{b}_i^l = \Delta^{(j-1)}\bar{b}_{i+1}^l - \Delta^{(j-1)}\bar{b}_i^l$ for $j = 1, 2, ..., p$.

4 Case Study for Two Biquadratic B-Spline Surfaces

In this section, we study the case of two uniform biquadratic G^1 connected B-spline surfaces, that is $p = q = 2$, with $n = m = g \geq 4$. For other cases, one can obtain similar results using the method of this paper.

In this case, equations (1) and (2) can be written as follows

$$\begin{cases} B(u,v) = \sum\limits_{i=0}^{n}\sum\limits_{j=0}^{n} b_{i,j}N_{i,2}(u)N_{j,2}(v) \\ C(u,s) = \sum\limits_{i=0}^{n}\sum\limits_{j=0}^{n} c_{i,j}N_{i,2}(u)N_{j,2}(s) \end{cases} \tag{23}$$

where $U = V = S = \{0, 0, 0, t_3, t_4, ..., t_n, 1, 1, 1\}$, $h = t_{l+3} - t_{l+2} = 1/(n-1)$, $l = 0, 1, 2, ..., n-2$.

Suppose $R(u) = B(u, 0) = C(u, 0)$ is the common boundary of two adjacent B-spline surfaces, then $b_{i,0} = c_{i,0}$ for $i = 0, 1, ..., n$ must be hold for G^0 continuity.

First, we consider the linear connecting functions, that is

$$R_2(u) = \alpha R_1(u) + (\beta u + \gamma)R_0(u) \quad u \in [0, 1] \tag{24}$$

then equation (5) becomes

$$\begin{cases} R_1(u) = \frac{2}{h}\sum\limits_{i=0}^{n} b_i N_{i,2}(u) \\ R_2(u) = \frac{2}{h}\sum\limits_{i=0}^{n} c_i N_{i,2}(u) \quad u \in [0, 1] \\ R_0(u) = 2\sum\limits_{i=0}^{n-1} N_{i,1}(u)\frac{d_i}{t_{i+3}-t_{i+1}} \end{cases} \tag{25}$$

Following Theorem 3 and a similar method described in [6, 7, 8], the constraints for G^1 continuity become the following intrinsic conditions that make the common boundary $R(u)$ to be a Bézier curve of degree 2

$$\begin{cases} 2d_1 = 2d_0 + d_2 \\ 2d_l = d_{l+1} + d_{l-1} \quad\quad l = 2, ..., n-3 \\ 2d_{n-2} = d_{n-3} + 2d_{n-1} \end{cases} \tag{26}$$

together with (27)

$$\begin{cases} c_0 = \alpha b_0 + \lambda_0 d_0, c_1 = \alpha b_1 + (2\lambda_1 d_0 + \lambda_0 d_1)/4 \\ c_l = \alpha b_l + ((l^2 - 3l + 2)\lambda_0 - (l^2 - 2l + 1/2)\lambda_1)d_0 + \\ ((l^2 - l)\lambda_1 - (l^2 - 2l + 1/2)\lambda_0)d_1/2 \quad\quad l = 2, 3, ...n-2 \\ c_{n-1} = \alpha b_{n-1} + (\lambda_{n-1}d_{n-2} + 2\lambda_{n-2}d_{n-1})/4, c_n = \alpha b_n + \lambda_{n-1}d_{n-1} \end{cases} \tag{27}$$

where $\lambda_i = i\beta h + \gamma, i = 0, 1, ..., n-1$.

Therefore, we must first define a quadratic Bézier curve as the common boundary

$$R(u) = \sum_{i=0}^{2} \bar{b}_i B_{i,2}(u) \qquad u \in [0,1] \tag{28}$$

where

$$\begin{cases} b_{0,0} = \bar{b}_0, b_{n,0} = \bar{b}_2, d_0 = b_{1,0} - b_{0,0} = (\bar{b}_1 - \bar{b}_0)/(n-1) \\ d_{n-1} = b_{n,0} - b_{n-1,0} = (\bar{b}_2 - \bar{b}_1)/(n-1) \end{cases} \tag{29}$$

It is clear that if we predefine $\{b_{0,0}, b_{1,0}, b_{n,0}\}$, from the first three equations of (29), we can obtain $\bar{b}_1$, and then obtain d_{n-1}. By substituting $\{d_0, d_{n-1}\}$ into intrinsic conditions (26), we can obtain $\{d_i, i = 0, 1, ..., n-1\}$.

According to (26), we obtain the control points of the common boundary $R(u)$ (a Bézier curve in B-spline format)

$$\begin{cases} b_{0,0} = \bar{b}_0, b_{1,0} = b_{0,0} + (\bar{b}_1 - \bar{b}_0)/(n-1), b_{n,0} = \bar{b}_2 \\ b_{l+1,0} = b_{l,0} + 2((\bar{b}_0 - 2\bar{b}_1 + \bar{b}_2)l/(n-1) + (\bar{b}_1 - \bar{b}_0))/(n-1) \;\; l = 1, ..., n-2 \end{cases} \tag{30}$$

Then, we can only consider (27) with $\{\alpha, \beta, \gamma\}$ for the G^1 continuity of two biquadratic B-spline surfaces.

Fig. 2(a) and Fig. 2(b) demonstrate how to combine two uniform biquadratic B-spline surfaces with G^1 continuity under linear connecting functions (24). We set $n = m = g = 4$, and $U = V = S = \{0, 0, 0, 1/3, 2/3, 1, 1, 1\}$. Fig. 2(a) shows two separated B-spline surfaces and the mesh of control points. We obtain G^0 connection just by replacing the control points of the left column of the right surface with the adjacent control point of left surface to achieve (3). Then, we use

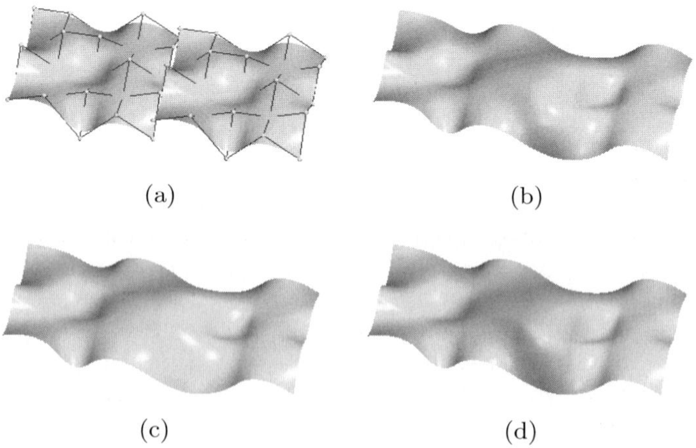

Fig. 2. G1 connection of two B-spline surfaces: (a) Two separate B-spline surfaces; (b) G1 with linear connecting functions; (c) G1 with piecewise linear functions I; and (d) G1 with piecewise linear functions II

the method discussed above to construct the common Bézier curve $R(u)$ in (28), where we keep the three control points $\{b_{0,0}, b_{1,0}, b_{n,0}\}$ unchanged. Fig. 2(b) shows the final obtained two G^1 connected B-spline surfaces with constraints (30) and (27).

For the piecewise linear connecting functions, the discussion is similar, however, according to Theorem 3 and Theorem 4, we can adopt piecewise linear connecting functions as follow

$$R_2(t) = \alpha R_1(t) + (\lambda_l(1-t) + \lambda_{l+1}t)R_0(t) \quad t = (u - t_{l+2})/h \tag{31}$$

for $u \in [t_{l+3}, t_{l+2}]$, $l = 0, 1, 2, ..., (n-2)$, where $\lambda_i, i = 0, 1, ..., n-1$ are independent.

The G^1 constraints for the whole common boundary can be expressed as follow.

$$\begin{cases} c_0 = \alpha b_0 + \lambda_0 d_0, c_1 = \alpha b_1 + (2\lambda_1 d_0 + \lambda_0 d_1)/4 \\ c_l = \alpha b_l + (\lambda_l d_{l-1} + \lambda_{l-1} d_l)/4 \qquad l = 2, 3..., n-2 \\ c_{n-1} = \alpha b_{n-1} + (\lambda_{n-1} d_{n-2} + 2\lambda_{n-2} d_{n-1})/4, c_n = \alpha b_n + \lambda_{n-1} d_{n-1} \end{cases} \tag{32}$$

and

$$\begin{cases} 2\lambda_1 d_0 + (\lambda_0 + \lambda_2 - 4\lambda_1) d_1 + \lambda_1 d_2 = 0 \\ \lambda_l d_{l-1} + (\lambda_{l-1} + \lambda_{l+1} - 4\lambda_l) d_l + \lambda_l d_{l+1} = 0 \qquad l = 2, ..., n-3 \\ \lambda_{n-2} d_{n-3} + (\lambda_{n-3} + \lambda_{n-1} - 4\lambda_{n-2}) d_{n-2} + 2\lambda_{n-2} d_{n-1} = 0 \end{cases} \tag{33}$$

To construct two biquadratic B-spline surfaces with G^1 continuity using piecewise linear connecting functions, we must first define piecewise linear connecting functions and three control points of the B-spline surface along the common boundary, e. g.

$$\{\lambda_i, i = 0, 1, ..., n-1, b_{0,0}, b_{1,0}, b_{n,0}\} \tag{34}$$

With intrinsic conditions (33), we then obtain the control points of boundary B-spline curve $\{b_{i,0}, i = 0, 1, ..., n\}$.

We then just adopt (32) with $\{\alpha, \lambda_i, i = 0, 1, ..., n-1\}$ for the G^1 continuity of two biquadratic B-spline surfaces.

In comparison with linear connecting functions, we have more freedoms with $\{b_i, i = 1, 2..., n-2\}$ to construct the two G^1 connected biquadratic B-spline surfaces, and the common boundary $R(u)$ is a B-spline curve, not just a Bézier curve.

Fig. 2(c) and Fig. 2(d) demonstrate two uniform biquadratic B-spline surfaces with G^1 continuity under piecewise linear connecting functions (31). The two original B-spline surfaces are the same as that in Fig. 2(a). By setting $\lambda_i, i = 0, 1, ..., n-1$ freely, we obtain G^0 connected B-spline surfaces with (33), which is a B-spline curve constrained by $\lambda_i, i = 0, 1, ..., n-1$. Fig. 2(c) shows the final obtained two G^1 connected B-spline surfaces with constraints (33) and (32). Fig. 2(d) is similar to Fig. 2(c). We just choose another set of connecting functions as (34) to get a different common boundary.

5 Conclusions

This paper presents some original results on the continuity conditions for smoothly connecting two B-spline surfaces with arbitrary degrees, generally structured knots and general connecting functions. That is, if two adjacent B-spline surfaces are connected with G^1 continuity under general connecting functions $f(u)$ and $g(u)$, at each interior knot u_l with multiplicity k_l, $l = 1, 2, ..., \tilde{m}$, the connecting functions$f(u)$ and $g(u)$ have at least C^{p-k_l-1} continuity, and the common boundary will be C^{p-k_l} continuous if $f(u)$ and $g(u)$ reach C^{p-k_l} continuity. According to these conclusions, we provide several construction examples of two uniform biquadratic B-spline surfaces with G^1 continuity. The presented conclusions of this paper can be applied to, e.g., multiple B-spline surface fitting, B-spline surface blending and multi-sided region filling. It can also be extended to support NURBS representation.

Acknowledgements

The work described in this paper was supported by a Strategic Research Grant No. 7001296 from City University of Hong Kong and Zhejiang Provincial Natural Science Foundation of China under Grant No. Y105213.

References

1. Piegl, L. and Tiller, W.: The NURBS Book. Springer Press, New York, , 1997
2. Milroy, M.J., Bradley, C., Vickers, G.W. and Weir, D.J.: G1 continuity of B-spline surface patches in reverse engineering. Computer Aided Design **27(6)** (1995) 471–478
3. Ma, W., Leung, P.C., Cheung, E.H.M., Lang, S.Y.T. and Cui, H.: Smooth multiple surface fitting for reverse engineering. Proceedings of the 32nd CIRP International Seminar on Manufacturing Systems, Katholieke Universteit Leuven, Belgium (1999) 53–62
4. Eck, M. and Hoppe, H.: Automatic reconstruction of B-spline surfaces of arbitrary topology type. Computer Graphics **30(8)** (1996) 325–334
5. Piegl, L.A., and Tiller, W.: Filling n-sided regions with NURBS patches. The Visual Computer **15(2)** (1999), 77–89
6. Shi, X., Yu, P. and Wang, T.: G1 continuous conditions of biquartic B-spline surfaces. Journal of Computational and Applied Mathematics **144(1-2)** (2002), 251–262
7. Shi, X., Wang, T. and Yu, P.: A practical construction of G1 smooth biquintic B-spline surfaces over arbitrary topology. Computer Aided Design **36(5)** (2004), 413–424
8. Shi, X., Wang, T., Wu, P. and Liu, F.: Reconstruction of convergent G1 smooth B-spline surfaces. Computer Aided Geometric Design **21(9)** (2004), 893–913
9. Che, X., Liang, X. and Li, Q.: G1 continuity conditions of adjacent NURBS surfaces. Computer Aided Geometric Design **22(4)** (2005), 285–298
10. Che, X. and Liang, X.: G1 continuity conditions of B-spline surfaces. Northeastern Math. J. **18** (2002), 343–352

Automated Face Identification Using Volume-Based Facial Models

Jeffrey Huang, Neha Maheshwari, and Shiaofen Fang

Department of Computer and Information Science,
Indiana University Purdue University, Indianapolis, IN 46202
{huang, nmaheshw, sfang}@cs.iupui.edu
http://www.cs.iupui.edu

Abstract. Face represents complex, multi dimensional, meaningful visual stimuli. Computational models for face recognition represent the problem as a high dimensional pattern recognition problem. This paper introduces an innovative facial identification method using eigenface approach on volume-based graphics rather than 2D photo-images. We propose to convert polygon mesh surface to a volumetric representation by regular sampling in a volumetric space. Our motivation is to extend existing 2D facial analysis techniques to a 3D image space by taking advantage of use of the volumetric representation. We apply principle component analysis (PCA) for dimensionality reduction. Face feature patterns are projected onto a lower dimensional PCA sub-space that spans the known facial patterns. 3D eigenface feature space is constructed for face identification.

1 Introduction

Face authentication techniques, including both face recognition and discrimination of facial expressions, is a typical signal processing and pattern recognition problem with many potential applications in fields like human computer interaction, medicine, and biometrics. It has the benefit of being a passive, non-intrusive system for verifying personal identity. Building automated systems that accomplish this task is, however, very difficult because of the inherent variability of the image formation process in terms of image quality and photometry, geometry, and occlusion, change and disguise. Recent surveys on face recognition by Bruce [1], Samal [2], and Chellappa [3], discuss these challenges and possible solutions in some detail from both psychological and computational perspective. The variety of methods published in the literature show that there is not a unique or generic solution to the face recognition problem.

There have been many attempts at facial recognition systems, and none has shown a consistently high rate of accurate identification. These are all based on 2D video photography using fixed cameras. They suffer from the image content limitations of typical video photography and the information content limitation inherent in 2-D photography. These limitations are exacerbated by differences in both the lighting and the pose of the subject between the original enrollment photo and the subsequent recognition photography. Studies show, the performance of an individual 3D face is better than a 2D face based on basic algorithm such as eigenface [4]. To deal with the shortcomings of 3D facial recognition, a 3D range sensor is utilized to increase the

H.-P. Seidel, T. Nishita, and Q. Peng (Eds.): CGI 2006, LNCS 4035, pp. 753 – 760, 2006.

amount of information and minimize facial angle and lighting-imposed differences to make more robust identification.

3D face datasets often come from range scanning devices such as laser scanners that can capture the 3D geometry and texture information of a facial surface. Most of 3D face recognition methods were based on three-dimensional geometric models, such as polygon meshes, so that curvature and texture features on 3D surface can be extracted for matching [5]. As early as a decade ago, Gordon [6] proposed a 3D face recognition method using a curvature calculation based on range image data obtained from a rotating laser scanner. The image was first mapped on a cylindrical coordinate system. The magnitude and angle of the minimum and maximum normal curvatures for each point were computed as input feature vectors for recognition. Tanaka *et al.* [7] extended the concept of the free-form curved surface in 3D shape recognition problem to 3D face recognition application. Based on Extended Gaussian Image (EGI) representation, they extracted face signatures using principal curvatures and their directions. Beumier and Acheroy [8] used central and lateral facial profiles to generate curvature values as feature vectors for face authentication. Some studies suggested fusion of a 2D texture map (intensity image) with Gabor kernel filtering and 3D shape information as features, called point signature-based features to improve recognition performance. Recently, Blanz and Vetter [9] presented a morphable 3D model that automatically estimates 3D shape, texture, and parameters from a given facial image. The coefficients, which represent intrinsic shape and texture, fit the 3D model with a linear combination and are used for recognition. Based on morphable modeling, Blanz's group [10] proposed component-based recognition methods for face recognition. Their idea was to apply 3D morphable models for creating many synthetic images with various poses and illumination conditions based on only two input images. These synthetic images were used to train a component-based face recognition system. Components were extracted based on the correspondence information given by the morphable model.

Due to the irregular sampling patterns and complex topological structures, many of the standard facial analysis techniques called base-line algorithms are difficult to be applied to the polygon mesh surfaces. On the other hand, any polygon mesh surface can be converted to a volumetric representation by regular sampling in a volumetric space [11]. The resulting volume contains complete 3D geometric information embedded within a 3D image space. In this paper, we propose a strategy of uniform sampling over the surface area of the original model and convert polygon mesh surface into a volumetric representation [12]. A clear advantage of such representation is that it allows most of the existing 2D facial analysis techniques to be directly generalized to a 3D image space. Standard image processing and signal processing operations can also be directly applied with a straightforward 3D extension. An automatic processing algorithm was developed for facial alignment, cropping, and normalization process. The identification method is based on eigenface approach on volume-based graphics rather than 2D photo-images. Principle component analysis (PCA) is used for dimensionality reduction and the construction of 3D eigenface feature space [13]. A standard nearest neighbor classifier using cosine distance serves for face matching.

2 Automatic 3D Facemask Cropping and Alignment

The 3D range scanners utilized for scanning human faces produce dense triangle mesh surfaces called 'raw' triangle meshes. These raw mesh surfaces need to be processed to retrieve a clean 3D front central part of the facial mesh that can be used in classification algorithms. This processing of the raw meshes involves excluding outliers, irregular boundaries and other parts such as hair, neck or shoulders. Our automatic face cropping processing is mainly based on the method of Zhang *et al.* [14].

The algorithm relies on the intrinsic geometry of each individual facial raw mesh and output a clean mesh of the central part of the 3D face. The first step in the algorithm is to separate the head from the shoulders and discard the mesh corresponding to the shoulders, which can be accomplished by performing Principal Components Analysis (PCA).

The raw mesh is intersected with planes parallel to the largest eigen vector and an integral is calculated for each point on the intersected curves. The point S^* corresponding to the largest value after the integral is taken to be the point lying roughly on the nose. We find *n*-rings of neighboring vertices around S^* based on the adjacency information of vertices in raw mesh. The Iterative Closest Point (ICP) algorithm [15] is used to refine the position of symmetry plane. The first feature point S_{NT} is the point corresponding to the largest value of an integral as the nose tip. $S_{NB,}$ the nose bridge and $S_{NL,}$ the lowest nose point are found by calculating the local extreme curvature values of the symmetry curve. S_N is the midpoint of S_{NB} and S_{NT}. The top point S_T and bottom point S_B are found by doing curvature analysis of the symmetry curve at the extreme local locations within predefined distances above and below the nose tip. The transverse curve is the intersection of raw facial mesh and the plane with S_N as a point on the plane and the normal vector given by $(S_{NB} - S_{NT})/\|S_{NB}-S_{NT}\|$. Three feature points S_{SL}, S_{SR}, and S_C identified on this transverse curve represent the left nose side point, the right nose side point, and the start point, respectively. Figure 1a illustrates the symmetry plane while Figure 1b illustrates these feature points on a raw facial mesh.

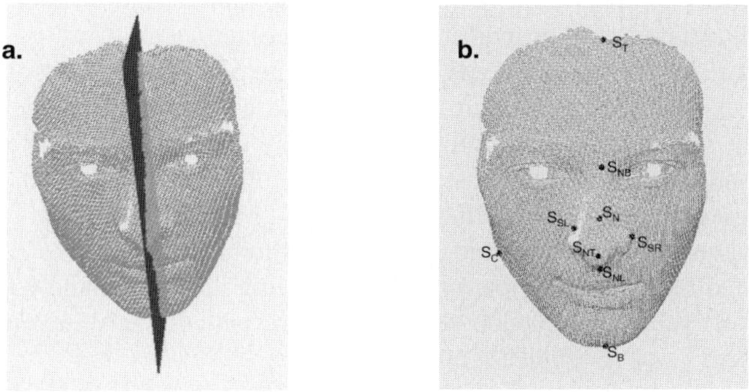

Fig. 1. (a) symmetry plane and (b) the various feature points defined on the symmetry curve and the transverse curve

Different facial meshes of an individual obtained by the same scanner are not aligned with respect to each other. In order to compare the faces and match them, we use the feature points S_{NB}, S_{NT} and S_{NL} to form a new 3D coordinate system. The mesh is cut by a 3D ellipse with S_N as the center to generate a final clean facial mask. Figure 2 shows examples of clean masks located at the front central part of the face.

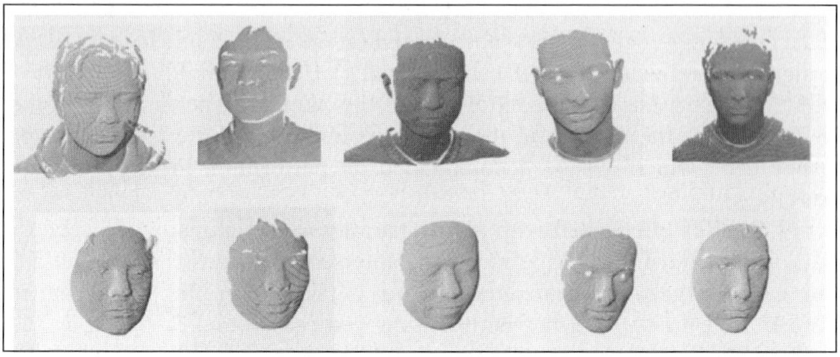

Fig. 2. Example of clean facial masks cut from the original raw mesh

3 Voxelization

Voxelization is a process of converting a geometric model, in this case a polygon mesh face surface, into a volumetric representation. It is a fundamental operation for volume graphics [16]. It is also the first step in our human identification method. A large number of voxelization algorithms have been developed for polygonal surfaces [17]. Broadly speaking, these algorithms aim to provide extensions of 2D scan conversion methods to a volumetric domain, but are generally too slow for real-time or interactive applications. This is particularly true for 3D scanning data since the number of polygons in a dense polygon mesh can be very large. However, in our application, fast voxelization is essential as human identification often requires on-site scanning and decision making within a matter seconds.

In the past few years, we have developed a suite of fast voxelization algorithms for various types of geometric models using hardware features in modern graphics engines [18][19]. These algorithms attempt to display the geometric surface in a slice by slice order, and then collect the resulting framebuffer images to form a volume dataset. Using hardware assisted voxelization, we will be able to provide fast voxelization for each polygon mesh surface, and generate a volumetric image for each face dataset for analysis and human identification. The resulting volume image contains an intensity (gray-level) value within each voxel that represents the existence of surface inside the voxel space.

4 Principle Component Analysis (PCA) for 3D Eigenfaces

A fundamental problem in digital signal processing is to find a suitable representation for a signal. Usually different signal representations are based on linear transformations of the signals onto different bases. Several principles have been developed in statistics, neural computing and signal processing to find a suitable linear representation of a random signal. For a volume-based facial recognition, the vulnerability of direct matching methods using voxel-based 3D images lies in their attempt to carry out the required classification in a space of extremely high dimensionality. To overcome the curse of dimensionality, the connectionist equivalent of data compression methods is employed first. Principal Component Analysis (PCA) is a popular technique used to derive a starting set of features. Turk and Pentland [20] popularized the use of PCA for 2D pixel-based face recognition and defined a subspace whose basis vectors, called eigenfaces, are principal components of face database. Baback and Pentland [21] propose a probabilistic method for face recognition based on eigenfaces.

Principal Component Analysis is based on Karhunen-Loève transformation (KLT) which was originally introduced as a series expansion for continuous random processes by Karhunen. Karhunen-Loève transformation is an information theory approach of coding and decoding face images. In mathematical terms, the principal components of the distribution of faces are extracted and are viewed as a set of features that together characterize the variation between face images. Hence it is also known as Principal Component Analysis (PCA). The principal components are the eigenvectors of the covariance matrix of the set of face images, treating an image as a point or vector in a very high dimensional space. These eigenvectors are called eigenfaces and each individual face image can be represented exactly in terms of linear combination of the eigenfaces. Hence, principal components (PCs) are a set of orthonormal basis vectors that maximize the scatter of all training samples. It is a standard decorrelation technique that derives orthonormal projections basis, which lead to dimensionality reduction and feature selection. An important property of PCA is decorrelation, i.e., the components of the transformation are decorrelated since the covariance matrix of transformed data is diagonal and the diagonal elements are the variances of the corresponding components. Another property of PCA is its optimal signal reconstruction in the sense of minimum Mean Square Error (MSE) when only a subset of principal components is used.

In mathematical terms, a set of m training 3D models $\mathbf{T}$, $\mathbf{T}=[T_1, T_2,\ldots,T_m]$ is normalized and the grand mean is subtracted to form a new data set $\mathbf{Y}=[\mathrm{Y}_1, \mathrm{Y}_2,\ldots,\mathrm{Y}_m]$ where $\mathrm{Y}_i=(y_{i1}\ y_{i2,\ldots}y_{iN})^T$, where N is the number of features, i.e., the number of total voxels in our case. Thus the models are viewed as points in $\Re^N$ space. The covariance matrix $\mathbf{\Omega}$ is defined as

$$\mathbf{\Omega} = E\{\mathbf{YY}^{\mathrm{T}}\} \text{ and } \mathbf{Y} = \mathbf{T} - E\{\mathbf{T}\} \tag{1}$$

where $E\{\cdot\}$ is the expectation operator.

The size of matrix $\mathbf{\Omega}$, however, is the square of total number of voxels. It is an intractable task to compute such a large size of square matrix and determine the eigenvectors and eigenvalues. The alternative way to solve for this high dimensional eigenvectors in this case by solving for the eigenvectors of an m-by-m matrix $\mathbf{\Phi}$ instead of N-by-N matrix $\mathbf{\Omega}$, because of $m<<N$. We then compute a m-by-m eigenvector matrix v and estimate for N-by-m eigenvectors Ξ for the original N-by-N covariance matrix

$$\Xi = Y^T v \tag{2}$$

The principal components are the approximated eigenvectors of $\mathbf{\Omega}$. The eigenvectors Ξ are sorted by order of decreasing eigenvalue ($\mathbf{\Lambda}$) and to then truncate Ξ, keeping only the most d significant principal components. The result is an N-by-d orthogonal projection matrix Ξ_d. These basis vectors are also known as *eigenfaces* for face recognition. The new feature set **Z** with lower dimensionality d ($d<<N$) is computed as

$$\mathbf{Z}=\Xi_d{}^{\mathrm{T}}\,\mathbf{Y} \tag{3}$$

The features generated by KL projection are also *Most Expressive Features* (MEFs). When a query image is presented to the system, it is mapped to the same PCA space and a nearest neighbor classifier operating in PCA subspace is used for verification of face images.

There are three related arguments for matching images in the subspace of d eigenvectors. The first is compression. It is computationally more efficient to compare images in subspaces with significantly reduced dimensions. The second argument is that some axes in the space encode noise. Hence, proper choice of features in the reduced space removes noise. The third argument is that since all images are pre-processed by subtracting the mean value from each image and scaling them to form unit vectors. This projects the images into a subspace where cosine distance is inversely proportional to correlation between the source images. This justifies a nearest neighbor classifier using cosine distance as an efficient estimation of image correlation.

5 Face Identification Based on Volume Graphic

Our face identification procedure consists of several steps for both enrollment (Figure 3a) and identification (or matching) (Figure 3b) scenarios. First, range images are captured by 3D laser sensor. The 3D shape of facial surface represents the facial structure invariant to environmental condition, such as lighting or shadow. Totally 39 images were scanned, which are corresponding to 10 different subjects and each individual contains multiple faces.

In order to properly compare 3D facial datasets, all face scans need to be precisely aligned in a common coordinate system. This can be done by the automated face mask trimming procedure discussed previously. After face alignment, the models are normalized using the location of eye with constant binocular distance and voxelized into 87x128x66 (x-by-y-by-z) volume images. The resulting volume image contains an intensity value within each voxel that represents the existence of surface inside the voxel space. The facial data set of 39 examples for 10 individuals (10 classes) are randomly partitioned into 26 samples for training and 13 for testing. The set of the eigenfaces is generated based on the training set. The projections of training data on the eigenspace are stored in the database for identification phase. As a result, the 26 largest components (eigenvector) are selected. Figure 4a shows a sample volumetric image in the voxel space and figure 4b shows the first reconstructed 3D eigenface that retains the most expressive features among those training images. We use the cos distance metrics by computing angle between the projections as a measure of the similarity to find the exemplar 3D image nearest to the query.

The cosine distance $\theta = \cos^{-1}(-X^T Y / \|X\| \|Y\|)$ indicates a measure of the similarity between the projection of the testing sample X and the projection of the training sample Y in the eigenspace. The overall performance of our PCA with volumetric 3D facial representation ordering in a 26 dimensional space is 76.92%. 3 out of 13 faces are misclassified.

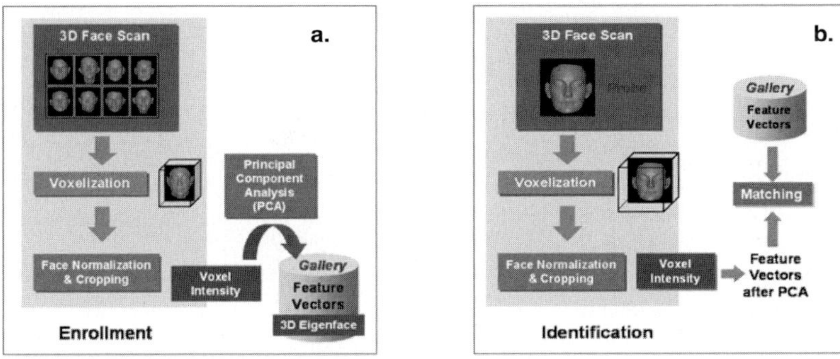

Fig. 3. 3D face identification procedures: (a) subject enrollment (training) phase and (b) identification (testing) phase

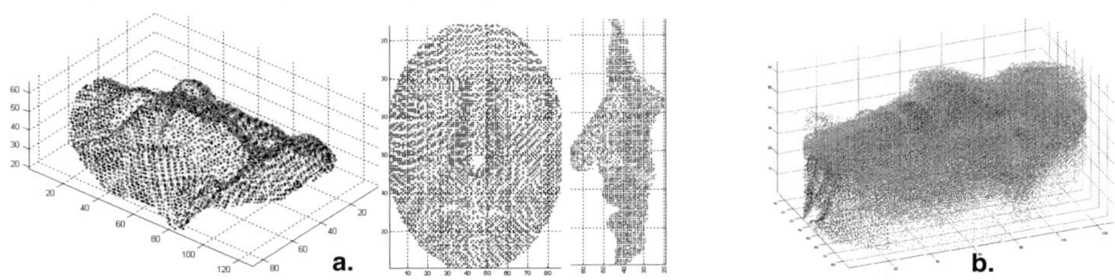

Fig. 4. (a) Voxelized image sample, and (b) The first eigenface calculated from the voxelized training face models

6 Conclusions

We have introduced in this paper a methodology that integrates signal representation and volume-based facial data for 3D facial identification. PCA reduces the dimensionality from original high dimensional feature spaces to 26 principle components (PCs). The experimental results reported indicate that voxelized images generate good classification performance. The resulting feature sets also appear to be robust in the sense that they can be used as the basis for building effective classifiers using approaches other than simple nearest neighbor classifier based on cosine distance measurement. The volumetric representation allows most of the existing 2D facial analysis techniques to be generalized to a 3D image space, therefore the standard image processing and signal processing operations can directly applied with a 3D extension.

References

1. Bruce, V. and M. Burton (1989), Computer recognition of faces, in A. W. Young and H. D. Ellis (editors) *Handbook of Research on Face Processing*, , Elsevier Science Publishers B.V. (Noth Holland), pp.487-506
2. Samal A. and P. Iyengar (1992), Automatic Recognition and Analysis of Human Faces and Facial Expressions: A Survey, *Pattern Recognition*, 25, pp.65-77
3. Chellappa R., C. L. Wilson, and C. Sirohey (1995), Human and Machine Recognition of Faces: A Survey, *IEEE Trans. on PAMI*, 83, pp.705-740.
4. Chang, K, K. Bowyer, and P.J. Flynn (2003), Face Recognition Using 2D and 3D Facial Data, *Workshop in Multimodal User Authentication*, Santa Barbara, California, pp.25-32
5. Lu, X. and A. Jain (2005), Integrating Range and Texture Information for 3D Face Recognition, *IEEE Workshop on Applications of Computer Vision*, Colorado, pp.156-163
6. Gordon, G. (1991), Face recognition based on depth maps and surface curvature, *SPIE proc. on Geometric Method in Computer Vision*, 1570, pp.234-247
7. Tanaka, H. T., M. Ikeda, H. Chiaki (1998), Curvature-Based Face Surface Recognition Using Spherical Correlation - Principal Directions for Curved Object Recognition. *3rd IEEE International Conference on Face & Gesture Recognition*, Nara, Japan, pp. 372-377
8. Beumier, C., M. P. Acheroy (1998), Automatic Face Authentication from 3D Surface, *British Machine Vision Conference* (*BMVC'98*), University of Southampton UK, pp 449-458
9. Blanz, V. and T. Vetter (2003), Face Recognition Based on Fitting a 3D Morphable Model, *IEEE Trans. on Pattern Analysis and Machine Intelligence,* 25(9), pp.1063-1073
10. Kaufman, A. (1998), Efficient Algorithms for Scan-converting 3D Polygons. *Computers and Graphics*, 12(2), pp.213-219
11. Huang, J., V. Blanz, B. Heisele (2002), Face Recognition Using Component-Based SVM Classification and Morphable Models, in *SVM 2002,* S.-W. Lee and A. Verri (Eds.), LNCS 2388, Springer-Verlag, Berlin Heidelberg, pp.334-341
12. Nehab, D. and P. Shilane (2004), Stratified Point Sampling of 3D Models, *Eurographics Symposium on Point-Based Graphics,* M. Alexa, and S. Rusinkiewicz (Editors).
13. Jain, A and J. Huang, (2004). Integrating Independent Components and Support Vector Machines for Gender Classification, *IEEE International Conference on Pattern Recognition, (ICPR'2004)*, pp. 558-561
14. Zhang, L., A. Razdan, G. Farin, M.S. Bae, J. Femiani, 3D Face Authentication and Recognition Based in Bilateral Symmetry Analysis, *IEEE Trans. on PAMI* (under revision)
15. Besl, P. and N. McKay (1992), A Method for Registration of 3D Shapes, *IEEE Trans. on PAMI,* 14 (2), pp. 239-256.
16. Kaufman, A., D. Cohen, and R. Yagel (1993). Volume graphics. *IEEE Computer Graphics and Applications*, 13, pp.51-64
17. Cohen, D. and A. Kaufman (1991). Scan-conversion algorithms for linear and quadratic objects, in A. Kaufman (editor), *Volume Visualization*, pp.280-301.
18. Fang, S. and H. Chen (2000), Hardware accelerated voxelization, *Volume Graphics,* Springer-Verlag, pp.301-315
19. Fang, S. and D. Liao (2000), Fast CSG voxelization by Frame Buffer Pixel Mapping, *Porc. IEEE/ACM Symposium on Volume Visualization*, pp. 43-48
20. Turk, M. and A. Pentland (1991), Eigenfaces for recognition, *J. of Cognitive Neuroscience*, 3(1), pp. 71-86
21. Moghaddam, B., W. Wahid and A. Pentland (1998), Beyond eigenfaces: probabilistic matching for face recognition, *3rd IEEE International Conference on Face & Gesture Recognition*, Nara, Japan, pp. 30-35

Feature Curves with Cross Curvature Control on Catmull-Clark Subdivision Surfaces*

A. Nasri[1,**], M. Sabin[2], R. Abu Zaki[1], N. Nassiri[3], and R. Santina[1]

[1] Department of Computer Science, American University of Beirut,
P.O.Box 11-236, Beirut, Lebanon
{anasri, rna15, rrs20}@aub.edu.lb
[2] Numerical Geometry Ltd.
malcolm@geometry.demon.co.uk
[3] Higher College of Technology
nasser.nassiri@hct.ac.ae

Abstract. This paper presents an algorithm for interpolating curves with predefined cross curvature on subdivision surfaces using polygonal complexes. The cross curvature is defined by a separate 2-D polygon which can be used to generate a complex along the control path. A straightforward application is the generation of Catmull-Clark subdivision surfaces that flow nicely along feature curves. Interactive manipulation of the 2-D polygon will correspond to a variety of features along the interpolated curves such as ribs, bumps, cavities, or even sharp creases.

1 Introduction

One of the reasons behind the popularity of subdivision surfaces is the ability to handle various interpolation constrains. A taxonomy of these constraints has been outlined by Nasri and Sabin, see [2, 3] and the cited references therein. Of the remaining constraints was the interpolation of curves with a predefined cross curvature.

Given a tagged control path on a polyhedron and a value of cross curvature K we need to generate a Catmull-Clark subdivision surface [1] that interpolates the curve (called *feature*) defined by that path with a cross curvature K, see Fig. 1. Along the feature curve, the mesh topology should be rectangular, giving tensor product structure. Extraordinary vertices may however fall around the feature, thus not causing any lateral artifact and leaving the shape to flow nicely along the feature's path. Catmull-Clark will be the main subdivision scheme used, thus the regular region are simply cubic B-splines. For purposes of exposition we also assume uniform B-splines.

A straightforward application of this problem is in the generation of subdivision surfaces interpolating feature curves with various shapes along these

* Supported by URB grant #DDF111130-688129.

** Corresponding author.

H.-P. Seidel, T. Nishita, and Q. Peng (Eds.): CGI 2006, LNCS 4035, pp. 761–768, 2006.

features such as boss/pocket, rib/groove, and bump/cavity. Recent approaches were devised to add features to surfaces with fewer control parameters, more flexibility, and closer to the designer's need. We mention two of them. Cheutet et al. [7] proposed an approach based on the mechanical force density method applied to a bar network. They defined two types of constraint lines: A *target* line, which is a 3D curve (not on the surface) giving the global direction of the deformation, and a *limiting* line which specifies the extent of deformation and helps define the shape of the feature. Catalano et al.'s approach focused on the insertion of features by means of generalized sweep operations applied on subdivision surfaces [6]. The approach is based on the feature taxonomy proposed by Fontana et al. [8]. The deformation consists of propagating a profile s called *section* along a specified curve called *directrix*. Our proposed approach can also be used to address these features with the capability of cross curvature control.

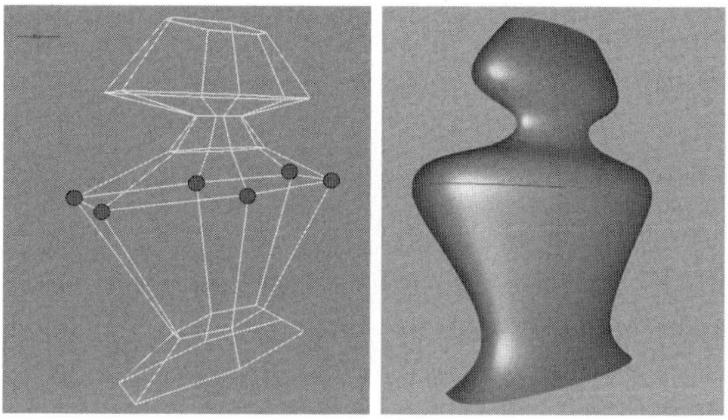

Fig. 1. One curve interpolated with predefined cross curvature

The paper is structured as follows. Section 2 gives the formula for controlling the curvature, and Section 3 gives a brief outlines of the notion of polygonal complexes. Section 4 describes the main algorithm and the details of the steps to be followed in constructing a polygonal complex for interpolating the feature curve. Finally, Section 6 gives conclusions and future work.

2 Controlling the Curvature

The curvature at a point of a uniform cubic B-spline curve can be determined as shown in Fig. 2 by:

$$c = \frac{8h}{a^2} \tag{1}$$

Expressing h and a in terms of B-spline control point indicates that the curvature of a cubic B-spline curve at the junction point, P_i, corresponding to V_i can be actually controlled by the three vertices V_{i-1}, V_i, and V_{i+1}.

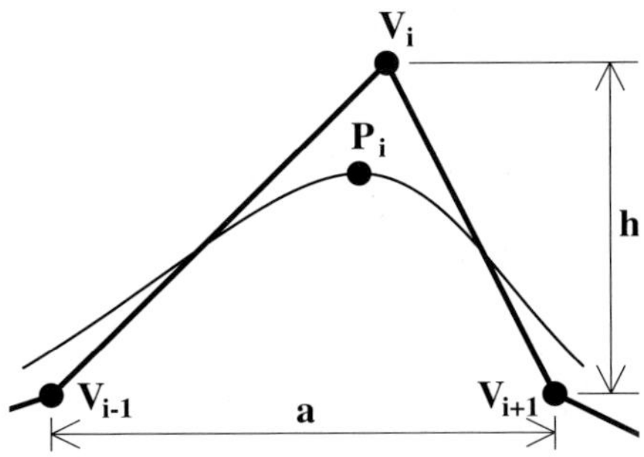

Fig. 2. The curvature of a B-spline curve

3 Curve Interpolation by Polygonal Complexes

One major approach for interpolating curves by subdivision surfaces is the polygonal complex approach [4]. Typically, the topology of a polygonal complex depends on the subdivision scheme to be used. A polygonal complex is typically a control mesh that under subdivision converges to a curve rather than a surface. If such a complex is embodied in the polyhedron defining a subdivision surface then the limit curve of the complex is automatically interpolated by the corresponding limit surface.

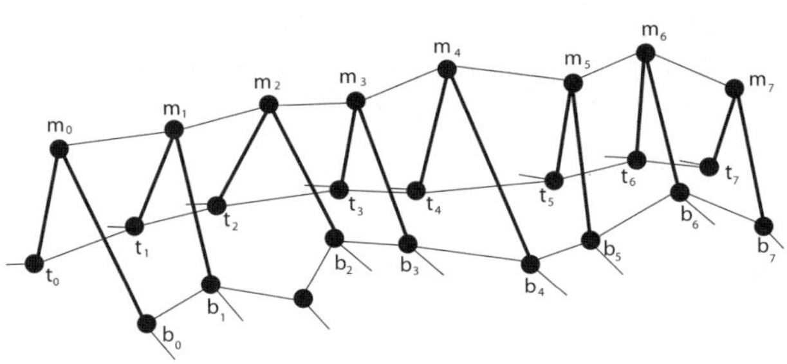

Fig. 3. An example of a Catmull-Clark polygonal complex

To be useful, the limit curve of a complex should be identified. In the Catmull-Clark setting [5], a polygonal complex can be defined by a sequence of triples (t_i, m_i, b_i) sharing two strips of faces (not necessarily 4-sided), see Fig. 3. If all shared faces are 4-sided (otherwise one step of Catmull-Clark will guarantee this), the limit of this complex is simply the uniform cubic B-spline whose control polygon is given by a set of vertices defined by:

$$\frac{1}{6}\begin{pmatrix}1 & 4 & 1\end{pmatrix} \times \begin{pmatrix} t_0 & t_1 & .. & t_{n-1} \\ m_0 & m_1 & .. & m_{n-1} \\ b_0 & b_1 & .. & b_{n-1} \end{pmatrix} \qquad (2)$$

A straightforward application of this property is to constrain a subdivision surface to interpolate the uniform B-spline curve defined by a tagged control polygon (m_i) on its polyhedron. This can be achieved by repositioning the triples (t_i, m_i, b_i) to another (t'_i, m'_i, b'_i) such that $6m_i = 4m'_i + t'_i + b'_i$. Certainly one can reposition m_i only but this will change the embodied curvature.

4 Feature Curves with Cross Curvature

The scenario that we consider here is a tagged control path on a polyhedron and an initial triple (called *curvature triple*) defining the cross curvature. Let the curvature triple be (M, O, N), $a = |MN|$ and $h = \texttt{distance}(O, MN)$, the corresponding curvature K can then be given by a formula similar to the one stated in 1.

Our assumption is that along the path the mesh topology should be rectangular. This is in order to avoid lateral artifacts that may spoil the shape of the surface which ought to flow nicely along the feature's path. As such, each vertex E_i on this path is adjacent to two vertices B_i and H_i from either side of the path, thus forming a triple (B_i, E_i, H_i). These triples need to be repositioned to form a polygonal complex that can be manipulated to interpolate the curve defined by the control path (E_i) with a cross curvature K, see Fig. 4. The following gives a general overview of the proposed approach, followed by a detailed algorithm.

There are two planes of importance in the process of controlling the cross curvature. The plane formed by the triple itself (B_i, E_i, H_i), and the plane perpendicular to the limit curve at the limit point corresponding to E_i. Our approach is to control the curvature of the cross-section of the limit surface by the second plane. This is not the same as the curvature of the other isoparametric line, which can be either smaller (if it crosses the controlled path at other than right angle), or larger (if its osculating plane does not contain the surface normal.) As such our goal is to construct a triple in this plane so that the cross curvature value stemming out is indeed K.

In order to construct a triple of a given curvature K in this plane, we need to control the rotation of the triple about that tangent. The natural thing to do is to try to perturb the surface normal as little as possible, which can be achieved by first projecting the triple into the perpendicular plane giving B'_i, E_i, H'_i. We

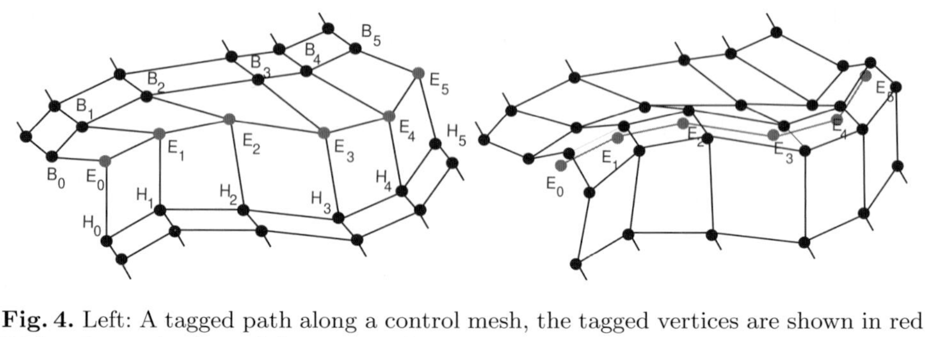

Fig. 4. Left: A tagged path along a control mesh, the tagged vertices are shown in red. Right: the mesh after triple construction.

then shear this triple to get another B''_i, E_i, H''_i to achieve the curvature K, keeping its base parallel to $B'_iH'_i$. After that, B''_i, E_i, H''_i is un-projected back into the initial plane $B_iE_iH_i$ giving a triple (B'''_i, E_i, H'''_i).

The process above is repeated *recursively*, where all vertices generated from the feature control path are also tagged for triple construction. At the limit the given curvature K will cover the entire curve and not only isolated points.

The following section explains the various steps in more details, see Figs. 5- 6.

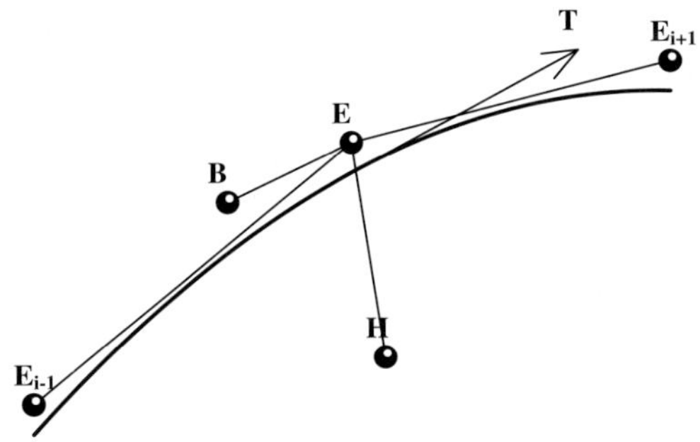

Fig. 5. The limit curve to be interpolated by the surface is defined by the control polygon of tagged vertices, (E_i). The tangent direction T at the limit point corresponding to E_i is parallel to $E_{i+1} - E_{i-1}$.

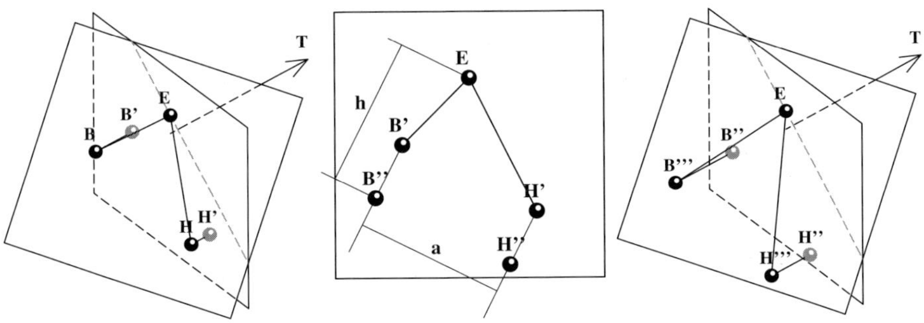

Fig. 6. Left: Projection of B and H along the direction T on the perpendicular plane. Middle: Fixing the curvature ratio. Right: Un-projection back in the plane BEH.

4.1 The Algorithm

The input is a polyhedron P_0, a feature path, and a curvature triple whose corresponding value is K.

1. Apply one Catmull-Clark refinement to P_0. This ensures that the path has adjacent quad facets all the way along.
2. For each tagged vertex E_i on the feature path Do

(a) Let T_i be the tangent to the surface along the path at the limit point corresponding to E_i.
(b) Let Q_i be the plane perpendicular to the path at the limit point corresponding to E_i.
(c) Let (B_i', E_i, H_i') be the projection of the triple (B_i, E_i, H_i) into Q_i along the tangent T_i.
(d) Shear (B_i', E_i, H_i') into (B_i'', E_i, H_i'') to adjust the curvature to K.
(e) Un-project the triple (B_i'', E_i, H_i'') back into the original plane (B_i, E_i, H_i) and along T_i giving (B_i''', E_i, H_i''').

3. Make a polygonal complex out of the triples (B_i''', E_i, H_i''').
4. Replace the original triples by the triples (B_i''', E_i, H_i''').
5. Perform one Catmull-Clark refinement, except that the new V-vertices corresponding to the E_i and the new E-vertices corresponding to the edges of the control path should be constructed by polygon refinement rather than the Catmull-Clark construction.
6. Tag all V- and E-vertices corresponding to edges and vertices of the path.
7. Apply the steps from 2 to 6 as many times as needed.

It should be noted that the iteration process can be stopped at any level, after which normal Catmull-Clark subdivision can be used. This is done after modifying the polygonal complex as suggested in Section 3.

The essential step is then how to construct the final triple from an original one which will be discussed in the following section.

4.2 Mapping the Initial Triplet

Let us take a triple[1] (B, E, H) on the path as shown in Fig. 5. We need to map the curvature K at each point of the control path by modifying the triple at this point as follows (the steps are numbered according to the second item in Sect. 4.1):

2(a) Let T be the tangent at the limit point of the curve corresponding to E. This is given by:

$$T = \frac{E_{i+1} - E_{i-1}}{2}$$

2(b) Let Q be the plane perpendicular to T at the limit point.

2(c) Project the triplet (B, E, H) into the plane Q along the direction of T. This gives a new triplet (B', E, H').

2(d) Typically the triplet (B', E, H') does not have the ratio h to a^2 which is defined by the curvature triple (M, O, N). As such, we need to scale $B'H'$ by a factor of $|B'H'|/a$ and then move the scaled points within the perpendicular plane so that it becomes right. The base points of the triple B' and H' are repositioned to B'' and H'', respectively, as given by:

$$B'' = B' + \epsilon_1 V \text{ and } H'' = H' + \epsilon_2 V$$

[1] We drop the indices for simplicity.

where V is a unit vector in the direction of of

$$[H' - B'] \times T$$

with

$$\epsilon_1 = \epsilon_2 = [E - B].V - \frac{2h}{3}$$

2(e) Since we really want the control points to be as far as possible compatible with the flow of the original mesh, we un-project B'' and H'' along the direction of T back in the plane (B, E, H). We get B''' and H'''. Accordingly, B''' and H''' are then given by:

$$B''' = B'' + \alpha T \ \texttt{and} \ H''' = H'' + \gamma T$$

where α and γ are given:

$$\alpha = \frac{-[B'' - E].N_o}{T.N_o} \ \texttt{and} \ \gamma = \frac{-[H'' - E].N_o}{T.N_o}$$

Note that neither T nor N_o need to be normalized for this purpose.

Fig. 7. Example of curve interpolation with various features

5 Conclusions and Future Work

It is possible to control a subdivision surface by forcing it to interpolate given curves, with Hermite conditions (slope, curvature) across the given curve, thus expanding the taxonomy of interpolation constraints on such surfaces.

A frequent requirement is for the feature to have a constant curvature across the tagged curve. When this is the case, the design user interface can be significantly simplified by having a single 2D polygon (triple curvature) by which the user controls the desired curvature. The feature curves can be easily turned into cavities, bumps, or even sharp creases as seen in Fig. 7.

For space reasons we have elaborated the theory in the uniform context. The extension to the non-uniform case is largely straightforward, though tedious.

References

1. E. Catmull and J. Clark, Recursively Generated B-spline Surfaces on Arbitrary Topological Meshes, Computer Aided Design, 1978, 10:6, 350-355. Also published in Seminal Graphics, Ed. Rosalee Wolfe, p. 183-188, Acm Press, 1988, Isbn 1-58113-052-X.
2. A. Nasri and M. Sabin, Taxonomy of Interpolation Conditions in Recursive Subdivision Curves, Journal Visual Computer, 2002, 18:4, 259-272.
3. A. Nasri and M. Sabin, Taxonomy of Interpolation Conditions in Recursive Subdivision Surfaces, Journal Visual Computer, 2002, 18:6, 382-403
4. A. Nasri, Recursive subdivision of polygonal complexes and its applications in CAGD, Computer Aided Geometric Design, 2000, 17, 595–619. Presented also at The $5th$ SIAM Conferenc On Geometric Design, Nashville, 1997.
5. A. Nasri and A. Abbas, Designing Catmull-Clark subdivision surfaces with curve interpolation constraints, Computer & Graphics, 2002, 26:3, 393-400.
6. C. E. Catalano, and F. Giannini, and B. Falcidieno., Introducing Sweep Features in Modeling with Subdivision Surfaces, Journal of WSCG, 2004, 12:1, 81–88
7. V. Cheulet, and C. E. Catalano, and J. P. Pernot, and B. Falcidieni, and F. Giannini, and J. C. Leon., 3D Sketching with Fully Free Form Deformation Features for Aesthetic Design, Workshop on Sketch Based Interfaces and Modeling, 2004,
8. M. Fontana, and F. Giannini, and M. Meirana., Free Form Features for Aesthetic Design., International Journal on Shape Modeling, 2000.

Author Index

Lecture Notes in Computer Science

For information about Vols. 1–3965

please contact your bookseller or Springer

Vol. 4063: I. Gorton, G.T. Heineman, I. Crnkovic, H.W. Schmidt, J.A. Stafford, C.A. Szyperski, K. Wallnau (Eds.), Component-Based Software Engineering. XI, 394 pages. 2006.

Vol. 4060: K. Futatsugi, J.-P. Jouannaud, J. Meseguer (Eds.), Algebra, Meaning and Computation. XXXVIII, 643 pages. 2006.

Vol. 4059: L. Arge, R. Freivalds (Eds.), Algorithm Theory – SWAT 2006. XII, 436 pages. 2006.

Vol. 4058: L.M. Batten, R. Safavi-Naini (Eds.), Information Security and Privacy. XII, 446 pages. 2006.

Vol. 4057: J.P. W. Pluim, B. Likar, F.A. Gerritsen (Eds.), Biomedical Image Registration. XII, 324 pages. 2006.

Vol. 4056: P. Flocchini, L. Gąsieniec (Eds.), Structural Information and Communication Complexity. X, 357 pages. 2006.

Vol. 4055: J. Lee, J. Shim, S.-g. Lee, C. Bussler, S. Shim (Eds.), Data Engineering Issues in E-Commerce and Services. IX, 290 pages. 2006.

Vol. 4054: A. Horváth, M. Telek (Eds.), Formal Methods and Stochastic Models for Performance Evaluation. VIII, 239 pages. 2006.

Vol. 4053: M. Ikeda, K.D. Ashley, T.-W. Chan (Eds.), Intelligent Tutoring Systems. XXVI, 821 pages. 2006.

Vol. 4046: S.M. Astley, M. Brady, C. Rose, R. Zwiggelaar (Eds.), Digital Mammography. XVI, 654 pages. 2006.

Vol. 4045: D. Barker-Plummer, R. Cox, N. Swoboda (Eds.), Diagrammatic Representation and Inference. XII, 301 pages. 2006. (Sublibrary LNAI).

Vol. 4044: P. Abrahamsson, M. Marchesi, G. Succi (Eds.), Extreme Programming and Agile Processes in Software Engineering. XII, 230 pages. 2006.

Vol. 4043: A.S. Atzeni, A. Lioy (Eds.), Public Key Infrastructure. XI, 261 pages. 2006.

Vol. 4041: S.-W. Cheng, C.K. Poon (Eds.), Algorithmic Aspects in Information and Management. XI, 395 pages. 2006.

Vol. 4040: R. Reulke, U. Eckardt, B. Flach, U. Knauer, K. Polthier (Eds.), Combinatorial Image Analysis. XII, 482 pages. 2006.

Vol. 4039: M. Morisio (Ed.), Reuse of Off-the-Shelf Components. XIII, 444 pages. 2006.

Vol. 4038: P. Ciancarini, H. Wiklicky (Eds.), Coordination Models and Languages. VIII, 299 pages. 2006.

Vol. 4037: R. Gorrieri, H. Wehrheim (Eds.), Formal Methods for Open Object-Based Distributed Systems. XVII, 474 pages. 2006.

Vol. 4036: O. H. Ibarra, Z. Dang (Eds.), Developments in Language Theory. XII, 456 pages. 2006.

Vol. 4035: T. Nishita, Q. Peng, H.-P. Seidel (Eds.), Advances in Computer Graphics. XIX, 771 pages. 2006.

Vol. 4034: J. Münch, M. Vierimaa (Eds.), Product-Focused Software Process Improvement. XVII, 474 pages. 2006.

Vol. 4033: B. Stiller, P. Reichl, B. Tuffin (Eds.), Performability Has its Price. X, 103 pages. 2006.

Vol. 4031: M. Ali, R. Dapoigny (Eds.), Innovations in Applied Artificial Intelligence. XXIII, 1353 pages. 2006. (Sublibrary LNAI).

Vol. 4027: H.L. Larsen, G. Pasi, D. Ortiz-Arroyo, T. Andreasen, H. Christiansen (Eds.), Flexible Query Answering Systems. XVIII, 714 pages. 2006. (Sublibrary LNAI).

Vol. 4026: P.B. Gibbons, T. Abdelzaher, J. Aspnes, R. Rao (Eds.), Distributed Computing in Sensor Systems. XIV, 566 pages. 2006.

Vol. 4025: F. Eliassen, A. Montresor (Eds.), Distributed Applications and Interoperable Systems. XI, 355 pages. 2006.

Vol. 4024: S. Donatelli, P. S. Thiagarajan (Eds.), Petri Nets and Other Models of Concurrency - ICATPN 2006. XI, 441 pages. 2006.

Vol. 4021: E. André, L. Dybkjær, W. Minker, H. Neumann, M. Weber (Eds.), Perception and Interactive Technologies. XI, 217 pages. 2006. (Sublibrary LNAI).

Vol. 4020: A. Bredenfeld, A. Jacoff, I. Noda, Y. Takahashi (Eds.), RoboCup 2005: Robot Soccer World Cup IX. XVII, 727 pages. 2006. (Sublibrary LNAI).

Vol. 4018: V. Wade, H. Ashman, B. Smyth (Eds.), Adaptive Hypermedia and Adaptive Web-Based Systems. XVI, 474 pages. 2006.

Vol. 4016: J.X. Yu, M. Kitsuregawa, H.V. Leong (Eds.), Advances in Web-Age Information Management. XVII, 606 pages. 2006.

Vol. 4014: T. Uustalu (Ed.), Mathematics of Program Construction. X, 455 pages. 2006.

Vol. 4013: L. Lamontagne, M. Marchand (Eds.), Advances in Artificial Intelligence. XIII, 564 pages. 2006. (Sublibrary LNAI).

Vol. 4012: T. Washio, A. Sakurai, K. Nakajima, H. Takeda, S. Tojo, M. Yokoo (Eds.), New Frontiers in Artificial Intelligence. XIII, 484 pages. 2006. (Sublibrary LNAI).

Vol. 4011: Y. Sure, J. Domingue (Eds.), The Semantic Web: Research and Applications. XIX, 726 pages. 2006.

Vol. 4010: S. Dunne, B. Stoddart (Eds.), Unifying Theories of Programming. VIII, 257 pages. 2006.

Vol. 4009: M. Lewenstein, G. Valiente (Eds.), Combinatorial Pattern Matching. XII, 414 pages. 2006.

Vol. 4007: C. Àlvarez, M. Serna (Eds.), Experimental Algorithms. XI, 329 pages. 2006.

Vol. 4006: L.M. Pinho, M. González Harbour (Eds.), Reliable Software Technologies – Ada-Europe 2006. XII, 241 pages. 2006.

Vol. 4005: G. Lugosi, H.U. Simon (Eds.), Learning Theory. XI, 656 pages. 2006. (Sublibrary LNAI).

Vol. 4004: S. Vaudenay (Ed.), Advances in Cryptology - EUROCRYPT 2006. XIV, 613 pages. 2006.

Vol. 4003: Y. Koucheryavy, J. Harju, V.B. Iversen (Eds.), Next Generation Teletraffic and Wired/Wireless Advanced Networking. XVI, 582 pages. 2006.

Vol. 4001: E. Dubois, K. Pohl (Eds.), Advanced Information Systems Engineering. XVI, 560 pages. 2006.

Vol. 3999: C. Kop, G. Fliedl, H.C. Mayr, E. Métais (Eds.), Natural Language Processing and Information Systems. XIII, 227 pages. 2006.

Vol. 3998: T. Calamoneri, I. Finocchi, G.F. Italiano (Eds.), Algorithms and Complexity. XII, 394 pages. 2006.

Vol. 3997: W. Grieskamp, C. Weise (Eds.), Formal Approaches to Software Testing. XII, 219 pages. 2006.

Vol. 3996: A. Keller, J.-P. Martin-Flatin (Eds.), Self-Managed Networks, Systems, and Services. X, 185 pages. 2006.

Vol. 3995: G. Müller (Ed.), Emerging Trends in Information and Communication Security. XX, 524 pages. 2006.

Vol. 3994: V.N. Alexandrov, G.D. van Albada, P.M.A. Sloot, J. Dongarra (Eds.), Computational Science – ICCS 2006, Part IV. XXXV, 1096 pages. 2006.

Vol. 3993: V.N. Alexandrov, G.D. van Albada, P.M.A. Sloot, J. Dongarra (Eds.), Computational Science – ICCS 2006, Part III. XXXVI, 1136 pages. 2006.

Vol. 3992: V.N. Alexandrov, G.D. van Albada, P.M.A. Sloot, J. Dongarra (Eds.), Computational Science – ICCS 2006, Part II. XXXV, 1122 pages. 2006.

Vol. 3991: V.N. Alexandrov, G.D. van Albada, P.M.A. Sloot, J. Dongarra (Eds.), Computational Science – ICCS 2006, Part I. LXXXI, 1096 pages. 2006.

Vol. 3990: J. C. Beck, B.M. Smith (Eds.), Integration of AI and OR Techniques in Constraint Programming for Combinatorial Optimization Problems. X, 301 pages. 2006.

Vol. 3989: J. Zhou, M. Yung, F. Bao, Applied Cryptography and Network Security. XIV, 488 pages. 2006.

Vol. 3988: A. Beckmann, U. Berger, B. Löwe, J.V. Tucker (Eds.), Logical Apporaches to Computational Barriers. XV, 608 pages. 2006.

Vol. 3987: M. Hazas, J. Krumm, T. Strang (Eds.), Location- and Context-Awareness. X, 289 pages. 2006.

Vol. 3986: K. Stølen, W.H. Winsborough, F. Martinelli, F. Massacci (Eds.), Trust Management. XIV, 474 pages. 2006.

Vol. 3984: M. Gavrilova, O. Gervasi, V. Kumar, C.J. K. Tan, D. Taniar, A. Laganà, Y. Mun, H. Choo (Eds.), Computational Science and Its Applications - ICCSA 2006, Part V. XXV, 1045 pages. 2006.

Vol. 3983: M. Gavrilova, O. Gervasi, V. Kumar, C.J. K. Tan, D. Taniar, A. Laganà, Y. Mun, H. Choo (Eds.), Computational Science and Its Applications - ICCSA 2006, Part IV. XXVI, 1191 pages. 2006.

Vol. 3982: M. Gavrilova, O. Gervasi, V. Kumar, C.J. K. Tan, D. Taniar, A. Laganà, Y. Mun, H. Choo (Eds.), Computational Science and Its Applications - ICCSA 2006, Part III. XXV, 1243 pages. 2006.

Vol. 3981: M. Gavrilova, O. Gervasi, V. Kumar, C.J. K. Tan, D. Taniar, A. Laganà, Y. Mun, H. Choo (Eds.), Computational Science and Its Applications - ICCSA 2006, Part II. XXVI, 1255 pages. 2006.

Vol. 3980: M. Gavrilova, O. Gervasi, V. Kumar, C.J. K. Tan, D. Taniar, A. Laganà, Y. Mun, H. Choo (Eds.), Computational Science and Its Applications - ICCSA 2006, Part I. LXXV, 1199 pages. 2006.

Vol. 3979: T.S. Huang, N. Sebe, M.S. Lew, V. Pavlović, M. Kölsch, A. Galata, B. Kisačanin (Eds.), Computer Vision in Human-Computer Interaction. XII, 121 pages. 2006.

Vol. 3978: B. Hnich, M. Carlsson, F. Fages, F. Rossi (Eds.), Recent Advances in Constraints. VIII, 179 pages. 2006. (Sublibrary LNAI).

Vol. 3977: N. Fuhr, M. Lalmas, S. Malik, G. Kazai (Eds.), Advances in XML Information Retrieval and Evaluation. XII, 556 pages. 2006.

Vol. 3976: F. Boavida, T. Plagemann, B. Stiller, C. Westphal, E. Monteiro (Eds.), NETWORKING 2006. Networking Technologies, Services, and Protocols; Performance of Computer and Communication Networks; Mobile and Wireless Communications Systems. XXVI, 1276 pages. 2006.

Vol. 3975: S. Mehrotra, D.D. Zeng, H. Chen, B. Thuraisingham, F.-Y. Wang (Eds.), Intelligence and Security Informatics. XXII, 772 pages. 2006.

Vol. 3973: J. Wang, Z. Yi, J.M. Zurada, B.-L. Lu, H. Yin (Eds.), Advances in Neural Networks - ISNN 2006, Part III. XXIX, 1402 pages. 2006.

Vol. 3972: J. Wang, Z. Yi, J.M. Zurada, B.-L. Lu, H. Yin (Eds.), Advances in Neural Networks - ISNN 2006, Part II. XXVII, 1444 pages. 2006.

Vol. 3971: J. Wang, Z. Yi, J.M. Zurada, B.-L. Lu, H. Yin (Eds.), Advances in Neural Networks - ISNN 2006, Part I. LXVII, 1442 pages. 2006.

Vol. 3970: T. Braun, G. Carle, S. Fahmy, Y. Koucheryavy (Eds.), Wired/Wireless Internet Communications. XIV, 350 pages. 2006.

Vol. 3969: Ø. Ytrehus (Ed.), Coding and Cryptography. XI, 443 pages. 2006.

Vol. 3968: K.P. Fishkin, B. Schiele, P. Nixon, A. Quigley (Eds.), Pervasive Computing. XV, 402 pages. 2006.

Vol. 3967: D. Grigoriev, J. Harrison, E.A. Hirsch (Eds.), Computer Science – Theory and Applications. XVI, 684 pages. 2006.

Vol. 3966: Q. Wang, D. Pfahl, D.M. Raffo, P. Wernick (Eds.), Software Process Change. XIV, 356 pages. 2006.